YEARBOOK OF AMERICAN & CANADIAN CHURCHES 2008

Edited by Eileen W. Lindner

Prepared and edited for the
National Council of the Churches of Christ in the U.S.A.
475 Riverside Drive, New York, NY 10115-0050

Published and distributed
by Abingdon Press
Nashville

YEARBOOK OF AMERICAN & CANADIAN CHURCHES 2008

Previous Issues & Editors

1916, 1917
Federal Council Year Book, H. K. Carroll

1918, 1919
Yearbook of the Churches, C. F. Armitage

1920
Yearbook of the Churches, S. R. Warburton

1922, 1923, 1925
Yearbook of the Churches, E. O. Watson

1927
The Handbook of the Churches, B. S. Winchester

1931
The New Handbook of the Churches, Charles Steizle

1933, 1935, 1937, 1939
Yearbook of American Churches, H. C. Weber

1941, 1943, 1945
Yearbook of American Churches, B. Y. Landis

1947
Yearbook of American Churches, B. Y. Landis and G. F. Ketcham

1949, 1951
Yearbook of American Churches, G. F. Ketcham

1952–1965
Yearbook of American Churches, B. Y. Landis

1966
Yearbook of American Churches, C. H. Jacquet

1967, 1968
Yearbook of American Churches, L. B. Whitman

1969–1972
Yearbook of American Churches, C. H. Jacquet

1973–1990
Yearbook of American & Canadian Churches, C. H. Jacquet

1991
Yearbook of American & Canadian Churches, C. H. Jacquet and Alice M. Jones

1992
Yearbook of American & Canadian Churches, Kenneth B. Bedell and Alice M. Jones

1993–1997
Yearbook of American & Canadian Churches, Kenneth B. Bedell

1998–2007
Yearbook of American & Canadian Churches, Eileen W. Lindner

YEARBOOK OF AMERICAN & CANADIAN CHURCHES 2008
Copyright © 2008
All rights reserved
by the National Council of the Churches of Christ
in the United States of America

For permission to duplicate any of the material found in the *Yearbook,* contact the Office of the Yearbook of American & Canadian Churches, 475 Riverside Drive, Room 880, New York, NY 10115-0050.
Telephone: (212) 870-2031
Fax: (212) 870-2817
E-mail: yearbook@ncccusa.org

Printed in the United States of America
ISBN 978-0-687-65149-8
ISBN 0195-9034

Preparation of this Yearbook is an annual project of the National Council of the Churches of Christ in the United States of America.

This is the seventy-sixth edition of a yearbook that was first published in 1916. Previous editions have been entitled: *Federal Council Yearbook* (1916–1917), *Yearbook of the Churches* (1918–1925), *The Hand-book of the Churches* (1927), *The New Handbook of the Churches* (1928), *Yearbook of American Churches* (1933–1972), and *Yearbook of American & Canadian Churches* (1973–2007).

Eileen W. Lindner	*Editor*
Marcel A. Welty	*Associate Editor*
Tenny Thomas	*Assistant Editor*

Contents

Editor's Preface 7

I
PERSPECTIVES ON AMERICA'S RELIGIOUS LANDSCAPE

Trends & Developments, 2007 9
   Table 1. Longitudinal Inclusive Membership 1890–2006 10
   Table 2. U.S. Membership Church Ranking: Largest 25 Churches . . 11
   Table 3. Patterns of U.S. Membership Change of Selected Large
           Churches 2003–2006 12
   Table 4. U.S. Financial Summaries 1999–2006 12
When Did We See Thee Sick? Congregations Respond 16

II
DIRECTORIES

1. United States Cooperative Organizations, National 21
2. Canadian Cooperative Organizations, National 50
3. Religious Bodies in the United States 58
   Religious Bodies in the United States Arranged by Family 177
4. Religious Bodies in Canada 180
   Religious Bodies in the Canada Arranged by Family. 210
5. Sources of Religion-Related Research 212
    I. Directory of Selected Research Organizations. 212
    II. Directory of Selected Faith Communities in America 221
6. United States Regional and Local Ecumenical Bodies 233
   Index of Select Programs for U.S. Regional and
   Local Ecumenical Bodies. 269
7. Canadian Regional and Local Ecumenical Bodies 292
8. Theological Seminaries and Bible Colleges in the United States 295
9. Theological Seminaries and Bible Colleges in Canada 317
10. Religious Periodicals in the United States 323
11. Religious Periodicals in Canada 345
12. Church Archives and Historical Records Collections 352

III
STATISTICAL SECTION

Guide to Statistical Tables 361
1. Membership Statistics in Canada 362
2. Membership Statistics in the United States 369
3. Membership Statistics for the National Council of Churches USA . . 382
4. Selected Statistics of Church Finances—Canadian Churches 384
5. Selected Statistics of Church Finances—United States Churches 386
Trends in Seminary Enrollment 392

IV
A CALENDAR FOR CHURCH USE

A Calendar for Church Use, 2008–2011 395

V
INDEXES

Organizations 399
Individuals 411

Editor's Preface

This seventy-sixth edition of the *Yearbook of American & Canadian Churches* marks anniversary that affirms the remarkable service this resource has played in preserving a fascinating record of our ever-changing religious institutions. We are especially conscious of the intense labors of previous editors and contributors who shaped this annual compilation of data in earlier years, and we are grateful to maintain their legacy. This 2008 edition is accessible in both hardcopy and electronically over the Internet using the unique pass code printed on the inside back cover of this volume. Updated information is reflected in the electronic edition twice during the year. In addition, a compact disc exists of data dating from 1916 through 2000, and brings these longitudinal data into ready availability.

Recognizing the Contributions of Many

The field of church statistics is complex and, of necessity, filled with inconsistencies. In recent years, electronic reporting has enabled greater amounts of time at each data collection level to raise questions and to recalculate and refine reports. We at the *Yearbook* are pleased to take our place in this important task of annually capturing a snapshot of American religious life. Reflection upon such findings tells us much about ourselves as well as the institutional religious life in a country that has been referred to as a "nation with the soul of a church."

Our colleagues in the compilation of each edition of the *Yearbook* are the thousands, perhaps tens of thousands, of individuals who keep church records. We rely and build upon the efforts of church pastors, deacons, secretaries and vestrymen and women who carefully review and report church membership statistics and financial giving. We acknowledge the contributions of those at congregational, regional and especially denominational levels who respond with good cheer (most of the time!) and expeditiously (at least at our second request!) in furnishing us with the detailed data we require in the format that we request. We hope that being a part of the record and analysis offered by the *Yearbook* contributes to their sense of satisfaction for a job well done.

For various chapters of the *Yearbook* we are indebted to specific individuals for their assistance in gathering, analyzing and corroborating the information we publish. As she has for the last several years, Nancy Merrill of the Association of Theological Schools in the United States and Canada has furnished us with the data and analysis concerning seminary enrollments. Mark Duffy has povided updated information regarding church archives and historical records collections. Our colleague, Sarosh Koshy of the National Council of Churches USA, keeps stewardship over our evolving and improving Directory of Selected Faith Traditions in America. Our colleague Tracy DeLuca, Librarian of the Interchurch Center in New York, is a regular and reliable consultant to us. Likewise, Seth Kasten, Librarian at the Burke Library of Union Theological Seminary in New York, is ever ready to offer able assistance and counsel. Cathy Lavendar of the United States Census Bureau assured that the Statistical Abstract remains current with *Yearbook* data.

Annual production of the *Yearbook* requires a variety of skills and commitments within our own editorial offices. Associate Editor, Marcel A. Welty, gives leadership and prodigious effort to the logistics of researching, requesting, compiling, confirming, correcting, formatting and preparing data for analysis. Earl Davis is invaluable as the Editor's Assistant, aiding in confirming data and preparing the theme chapter text for publication. Assistant Editor, Tenny Thomas, is creative and efficient in organizing a virtual mountain of information quickly and accurately, and helping to review the text before publication. Almost as closely associated with us as those we see each day are our colleagues and friends of long standing, John and Sylvia Ronsvalle, of the *empty tomb, inc*. Nationally recognized for their steadfast attention to the patterns of church giving, the Ronsvalles are unfailingly gracious in providing expert assistance and in enabling our own analysis. As we went to press, their excellent analysis of church giving, *The State of Church Giving Through 2005* (17th edition, Oct. 2007), was just becoming available, and comes highly recommended to those inerested in church benevolence.

7

On behalf of those readers, we extend our gratitude for the wisdom, skill, patience and generosity of those we acknowledge here. No small group of individuals could hope to have the knowledge needed to compile a text as far ranging as the *Yearbook*. Our efforts strengthened by the contributions of all those named above have led to the seventy-sixth edition of the *Yearbook of American & Canadian Churches*; we wish to express our deepest thanks to each of them.

The 2008 Edition *Features*

- Reports on 224 national church bodies, which itself is reflective of a remarkably robust immigrant history and the cultural and constitutional freedom of religion so characteristic of the United States.
- Signals that churches reporting in *Yearbook* statistics reflect continued high overall church participation and account for the religious affiliation of almost 164 million Americans.
- Reports on 224 national church bodies include brief histories, leadership, and headquarter information and are broadly inclusive of the varieties of American Christianity.
- In this day of increasing awareness of religious pluralism the *Yearbook* offers an updated Directory of Selected Faith Traditions in America.
- Continues to offer the only accurate and inclusive directory of U.S. local and regional ecumenical bodies with program and contact information.
- Provides listings of theological seminaries and Bible schools, religious periodicals and guides to religious research including church archive listings.
- Accurate and timely information through the *Yearbook*'s Internet edition, in its sixth year. As personnel changes, area codes and old email addresses are replaced with new ones, and any new information is submitted to the *Yearbook*, our readers are kept current with those changes through two regular electronic updates throughout the year. Access is provided through a unique passcode printed inside the back cover of the *Yearbook*.

The 2008 Edition *Updates*

- Ranks the 25 largest churches by membership. Only three of the top ten are "mainline" protestant churches. Reports the fastest growing churches in this group as: the Church of Jesus Christ of Latter-day Saints, the Catholic Church, and the Assemblies of God.
- Analyzes the financial data from 65 churches representing 46 million members and more than $34 billion dollars.

The 2008 Edition *Trends*

- Reports the summary findings of the nation's largest study of health ministries in local congregations under the theme *"When Did We See Thee Sick? Congregations Respond"* (p. 16).
- After a decade of steady growth, records a downturn in Canadian enrollment in theological schools and a continuing upward trend in part time enrollment in both U.S. and Canadian theological seminaries (p. 392).
- Reports on the largest decline (-6.75%) in a decade of African Americans enrolled in theological seminaries (p. 394).
- Notes a slowing of church membership growth rates and raises new questions about patterns of affiliation (p. 12).
- Records a $29.21 increase in per capita financial contributions (p. 15).

Eileen W. Lindner
Editor
New York, 2007

I

PERSPECTIVES ON AMERICA'S RELIGIOUS LANDSCAPE

Trends & Developments, 2007

Methodological Considerations

The *Yearbook of American & Canadian Churches* reports annually on data gathered from national religious bodies that reflect the religious affiliations and financial giving patterns of hundreds of millions of Americans. However, these data generally represent information gathered two calendar years prior to the year of publication. For instance, data reported in this 2008 edition of the *Yearbook* reflects information for 2006 that was collected by national church structures in 2007 and reported to the *Yearbook* at the end of 2007 for publication in the 2008 *Yearbook*. This "lag time" often leads our readers to ask if such data is out of date by the time it is printed. In response we would give a qualified "no." Massive national agencies such as the churches reporting through the *Yearbook* move in their institutional lives at nearly imperceptible rates of speed. Moreover, given the vast size and complexity of such diverse organizations, partial data reported more frequently might well have the unintended effect of conveying a sense of "trend" to momentary or regionally isolated patterns of reporting, affiliation and/or financial giving. Now in the 76th edition, the *Yearbook* believes that an annual review of data continues to provide an appropriate interval for tracking the changes in institutional patterns.

No single standard for data collection exists across the variety of ecclesiastical structures reported in the *Yearbook*. Moreover, the definitions of membership and related terms differ widely from one church structure to another. This lack of universal definition and collection methodology has frequently led to questions about the validity and reliability of self-reported data. Recognizing the limitations of the data reported herein, we continue to have confidence in the overall value of trends and other findings based on these figures and this methodology. While church data collection and analytical practices differ across various institutional and organizational margins, they tend to be remarkably consistent *within* specific organizations over time. (Where we are made aware of changes in a particular church's reporting methods, we will note them for the reader.) This consistency within organizations brings a greater degree of confidence to the relative data of a given church over time. For the same reason the *relative* size of one church to another as reported here, we believe, provides an accurate picture even while lacking a degree of absolute precision of membership statistics, particularly over time. Thus, we believe that the Southern Baptist Convention is roughly twice the size of The United Methodist Church, for example, and that changes relative to each other over several years are probably an accurate reflection of actual membership trends. Moreover, these data are the most exacting figures presently available, and thus serve as the national standard.

The first eight decades of record keeping represented by the *Yearbook of American & Canadian Churches* is contained on a comprehensive Historic Archive on CD-ROM (which contains membership and financial data from 1916–1999). This CD provides a longitudinal backdrop for the analysis that follows. Only through such a longitudinal

9

Table 1
LONGITUDINAL INCLUSIVE MEMBERSHIP 1890–2006

Year	Membership	Source	Year	Membership	Source
1890	41,699,342	CRB	1968	128,469,636	YBAC
1906	35,068,058	CRB	1969	128,505,084	YBAC
1916	41,926,852	CRB	1970	131,045,053	YBAC
1926	54,576,346	CRB	1971	131,389,642	YBAC
1931	59,268,764	CH	1972	131,424,564	YBAC
1932	60,157,392	CH	1973	131,245,139	YBAC
1933	60,812,624	CH	1974	131,871,743	YBAC
1934	62,007,376	CH	1975	131,012,953	YBACC
1935	62,678,177	CH	1976	131,897,539	YBACC
1936	55,807,366	CRB	1977	131,812,470	YBACC
1936	63,221,996	CH	1978	133,388,776	YBACC
1937	63,848,094	CH	1979	133,469,690	YBACC
1938	64,156,895	YBAC	1980	134,816,943	YBACC
1940	64,501,594	YBAC	1981	138,452,614	YBACC
1942	68,501,186	YBAC	1982	139,603,059	YBACC
1944	72,492,699	YBAC	1983	140,816,385	YBACC
1945	71,700,142	CH	1984	142,172,138	YBACC
1946	73,673,182	CH	1985	142,926,363	YBACC
1947	77,386,188	CH	1986	142,799,662	YBACC
1948	79,435,605	CH	1987	143,830,806	YBACC
1949	81,862,328	CH	1988	145,383,739	YBACC
1950	86,830,490	YBAC	1989	147,607,394	YBACC
1951	88,673,005	YBAC	1990	156,331,704	YBACC
1952	92,277,129	YBAC	1991	156,629,918	YBACC
1953	94,842,845	YBAC	1992	156,557,746	YBACC
1954	97,482,611	YBAC	1993	153,127,045	YBACC
1955	100,162,529	YBAC	1994	158,218,427	YBACC
1956	103,224,954	YBAC	1995	157,984,194	YBACC
1957	104,189,678	YBAC	1996	159,471,758	YBACC
1958	109,557,741	YBAC	1997	157,503,033	YBACC
1959	112,226,905	YBAC	1998[1]	150,105,525	YBACC
1960	114,449,217	YBAC	1999[1]	151,161,906	YBACC
1961	116,109,929	YBAC	2000[1]	152,134,407	YBACC
1962	117,946,002	YBAC	2001	158,952,292	YBACC
1963	120,965,238	YBAC	2002	161,202,780	YBACC
1964	123,307,449	YBAC	2003	163,128,935	YBACC
1965	124,682,422	YBAC	2004	163,432,280	YBACC
1966	125,778,656	YBAC	2005[2]	163,677,894	YBACC
1967	126,445,110	YBAC	2006	163,774,246	YBACC

1. The total membership figure for this year excludes the membership of the National Baptist Convention, U.S.A., Inc., which was included in the total membership figure of other years.
2. This figure reflects a 2,200,429 downward revision in total church membership, reflecting a change requested by the Catholic Church after publication of the 2007 ed.

Source Key:
CRB—Census of Religious Bodies, Bureau of the Census, Washington
CH—*The Christian Herald*, New York
YBAC—*Yearbook of American Churches*, New York
YBACC—*Yearbook of American and Canadian Churches*, New York

study of growth and decline in membership are we able to capture and analyze the emerging patterns. Our annual trends analysis should be regarded as a snapshot taken at a discrete moment in history. The meaning of the figures within that snapshot will best be given definition by the larger and longer context of which they are a part.

The reader is invited to utilize both the current edition and the *Yearbook of American & Canadian Churches'* historic CD to test and amplify the analysis that follows. To obtain the Historic Archive on CD-ROM call 1-888-870-3325 or visit www.electronicchurch.org.

Table 1   Longitudinal Inclusive Membership

This Table represents a longitudinal view of aggregated membership totals for all churches reporting to the *Yearbook*. These data do not reflect the entirety of national

Table 2 US MEMBERSHIP CHURCH RANKING: Largest 25 Churches			
Denomination Name	**Current Ranking (2007 Edition)**	**Inclusive Membership**	**Percentage Increase/ Decrease**
The Catholic Church	1(1)	67,515,016	0.87%
Southern Baptist Convention	2(2)	16,306,246	0.22%
The United Methodist Church	3(3)	7,995,456	-0.99%
The Church of Jesus Christ of Latter-day Saints	4(4)	5,779,316	1.56%
The Church of God in Christ	5(5)	5,499,875	*0.00%*
National Baptist Convention, U.S.A., Inc.	6(6)	5,000,000	*0.00%*
Evangelical Lutheran Church in America	7(7)	4,774,203	-1.58%
National Baptist Convention of America, Inc.	8(8)	3,500,000	*0.00%*
Presbyterian Church (U.S.A.)	9(9)	3,025,740	-2.36%
Assemblies of God	10(10)	2,836,174	0.19%
African Methodist Episcopal Church	11(11)	2,500,000	*0.00%*
National Missionary Baptist Convention of America	11(11)	2,500,000	*0.00%*
Progressive National Baptist Convention, Inc.	11(11)	2,500,000	*0.00%*
The Lutheran Church—Missouri Synod (LCMS)	14(14)	2,417,997	*-0.94%*
Episcopal Church	15(15)	2,154,572	-4.15%
Churches of Christ	16(16)	1,639,495	*0.00%*
Greek Orthodox Archdiocese of America	17(17)	1,500,000	*0.00%*
Pentecostal Assemblies of the World, Inc.	17(17)	1,500,000	*0.00%*
The African Methodist Episcopal Zion Church	19(19)	1,443,405	0.21%
American Baptist Churches in the U.S.A.	20(20)	1,371,278	-1.82%
United Church of Christ	21(21)	1,218,541	-0.47%
Baptist Bible Fellowship International	22(22)	1,200,000	*0.00%*
Christian Churches and Churches of Christ	23(23)	1,071,616	*0.00%*
The Orthodox Church in America	24(24)	1,064,000	*0.00%*
Jehovah's Witnesses	25(25)	1,069,530	2.25%
TOTAL		**147,382,460**	**0.24%**

Last Year's Ranking	
Denomination Name	**Inclusive Membership Figures Reported in Last Year's *Yearbook***
The Catholic Church[1]	66,934,825
Southern Baptist Convention	16,270,315
The United Methodist Church	8,075,010
The Church of Jesus Christ of Latter-day Saints	5,690,672
The Church of God in Christ	5,499,875
National Baptist Convention, U.S.A., Inc.	5,000,000
Evangelical Lutheran Church in America	4,850,776
National Baptist Convention of America, Inc.	3,500,000
Presbyterian Church (U.S.A.)	3,098,842
Assemblies of God	2,830,861
African Methodist Episcopal Church	2,500,000
National Missionary Baptist Convention of America	2,500,000
Progressive National Baptist Convention, Inc.	2,500,000
The Lutheran Church—Missouri Synod (LCMS)	2,440,864
Episcopal Church	2,247,819
Churches of Christ[2]	1,639,495
Greek Orthodox Archdiocese of America	1,500,000
Pentecostal Assemblies of the World, Inc.	1,500,000
The African Methodist Episcopal Zion Church	1,440,405
American Baptist Churches in the U.S.A.	1,396,700
United Church of Christ	1,224,297
Baptist Bible Fellowship International	1,200,000
Christian Churches and Churches of Christ	1,071,616
The Orthodox Church in America	1,064,000
Jehovah's Witnesses	1,046,000
TOTAL	**147,022,378**

NOTE: Percentage changes in ***italic/bold*** signify that membership was not updated for this edition
1. This figure reflects a revision by the Catholic Church of the previously submitted (2007 ed.) membership figure of 69,135,254
2. This membership figure represents a change in estimation methods

Table 3
PATTERNS OF U.S. MEMBERSHIP CHANGE OF SELECTED LARGE CHURCHES 2003–2006

Denomination	2003 Membership Change	Percentage Change	2004 Membership Change	Percentage Change	2005 Membership Change	Percentage Change	2006 Membership Change	Percentage Change
The Catholic Church	852,663[1]	1.28	561,065	0.83	-886,008[2]	-1.31	580,191	0.87
Southern Baptist Convention	67,314[1]	0.42[1]	62,444[1]	0.39[1]	2,821	0.02	35,931	0.22
The United Methodist Church	133	0.002	-64,921	-0.79	-111,244	-1.36	-79,554	-0.99
Evangelical Lutheran Church in America	-53,081	-1.05	-54,496	-1.09	-79,653	-1.62	-76,573	-1.58
The Church of Jesus Christ of Latter-day Saints	92,648	1.71	95,985	1.74	91,495	1.63	88,644	1.56
Presbyterian Church (U.S.A.)	-166,020	-4.87	-51,736	-1.60	-90,731	-2.84	-73,102	-2.36
The Lutheran Church—Missouri Synod	-23,778	-0.95	-25,189	-1.01	-22,883	-0.93	-22,867	-0.94
Assemblies of God	42,196	1.57	49,533	1.81	51,766	1.86	5,313	0.19
American Baptist Churches in the U.S.A.	-51,216	-3.45	-8,235	-0.57	-28,140	-1.97	-25,422	-1.82

1. These figures reflect corrections discussed in the 2006 edition.
2. This figure reflects a revision by the Catholic Church requested after publication of the 2007 edition.

Table 4
U.S. FINANCIAL SUMMARIES 1999–2006

Year	Number Reporting	Full or Confirmed Members	Inclusive Members	Total Contributions	Per Capita Full or Confirmed Members	Per Capita Inclusive Members	Total Congregational Contributions
1999	62	44,288,906	49,196,965	$26,997,610,588	$609.58	$548.77	$22,801,548,715
2000	65	44,401,451	49,178,675	$29,464,889,024	$663.60	$599.14	$24,475,897,453
2001	62	45,359,589	49,828,003	$31,041,852,581	$684.35	$622.98	$26,587,142,109
2002	59	43,694,611	47,773,814	$31,465,090,286	$720.11	$658.63	$26,908,804,274
2003	63	44,211,342	48,266,164	$32,269,713,588	$725.78	$667.34	$27,723,558,838
2004	63	43,823,753	47,850,712	$33,214,186,254	$757.90	$694.12	$28,294,047,495
2005	65	43,565,587	47,922,181	$34,170,801,942	$784.35	$713.05	$29,002,718,319
2006	65	42,224,304	46,101,429	$34,219,114,885	$810.41	$742.26	$28,773,748,252

Year	Per Capita Full or Confirmed Members	Per Capita Inclusive Members	Total Benevolences	Per Capita Full or Confirmed Members	Per Capita Inclusive Members	Benevolences as a Percentage of Total Contributions
1999	$514.84	$463.47	$4,197,087,981	$94.77	$85.31	16%
2000	$551.24	$497.69	$4,988,352,266	$112.35	$101.43	17%
2001	$586.14	$533.58	$4,510,947,817	$99.45	$90.53	15%
2002	$615.84	$563.25	$4,555,191,495	$104.25	$95.35	14%
2003	$627.07	$574.39	$4,748,202,343	$107.40	$98.38	15%
2004	$645.63	$591.30	$4,921,921,435	$112.31	$102.86	15%
2005	$665.73	$605.20	$5,168,083,623	$118.63	$107.84	15%
2006	$681.45	$624.14	$5,389,573,754	$127.64	$116.91	16%

church membership since some churches either do not gather such data, or do not report them to the *Yearbook*. These figures moreover do not include membership of independent congregations including megachurches. Substantial numbers of church members, therefore, are not accounted for in nationally-gathered membership data. With nearly 164 million adherents, the churches collectively continue to maintain a substantial organizational and institutional presence within the United States.

Table 2   U.S. Membership Church Ranking

This table allows comparison in size as determined by membership of the largest twenty-five churches in the nation. Dwarfing any single other church is the Catholic Church, reporting over 67 million adherents. The remainder of the top twenty five are Protestant churches with three exceptions; the Greek Orthodox Archdiocese, which is ranked 17th; The Orthodox Church in America, which is ranked 24th; and the Jehovah's Witnesses, which is ranked 25th.

The patterns of affiliation reflected in this table offer a numerical view and summary of American church history. Protestantism has, since the founding of the republic and until the present moment, enjoyed cultural hegemony accompanied throughout by a consistent substantial Catholic presence.

Three of the twenty-five largest churches are Pentecostal in belief and practice. Strong figures from the Assemblies of God might suggest a continuing increase in numbers of adherents to Pentecostal groups, though it is impossible to state unequivocally from this table since the other two charismatic churches in this ranking have not reported in some years. The three largest Pentecostal churches are: The Church of God in Christ, Assemblies of God, and the Pentecostal Assemblies of the World, Inc.

The ranking of churches on the basis of membership remains stable as indicated by the first column of numbers in Table 2. The last column presents increases (decreases) as a percentage change from last reported membership figures. With the exception of The Episcopal Church the largest twenty-five churches are maintaining their respective rates of growth (or decline) in membership and therefore their ranking relative to each other. The Episcopal Church reports a -4.15% decrease in membership, more than doubling the rate of decline reported in the 2007 edition of the *Yearbook*, -1.59%, or that of the report in 2006 of -1.55%.

The top fifteen churches, those with membership exceeding 2 million members, reflect the constancy of the Historic Black Churches. Six of the fifteen largest churches (The Church of God in Christ, National Baptist Convention, U.S.A., Inc., National Baptist Convention of America, Inc., National Missionary Baptist Convention of America, Progressive National Baptist Convention, Inc., and African Methodist Episcopal Church) are predominately African American churches. This of course is reflective of the historic strength of the church within the African American community.

In the last quarter century there has been much analysis and debate concerning the decline of "mainline" Protestantism. Whatever the specific rates of growth or decline may be for individual mainline denominations, this ranking illustrates a significant aggregate presence in the American religious landscape. Of the top ten largest churches, three are mainline Protestant (United Methodist, Evangelical Lutheran, and Presbyterian Church USA). In the top twenty five churches, six are mainline Protestant, though all of them report an overall loss of membership for the latest reporting year. In addition to the three noted above, the mainline churches ranked in the top twenty five include: the Episcopal Church, the American Baptist Churches and the United Church of Christ.

Table 3   Patterns of Membership Gains and Losses

Table 3 offers longitudinal data on rate of growth or loss of church membership of a selected group of large churches for four years, 2003–2006.

The three large churches with the biggest growth measured by percentage of membership are: the Church of Jesus Christ of Latter-day Saints (1.56%), the Catholic Church (0.87%), the Southern Baptist Convention (0.22%), and the Assemblies of God (0.19%). It may be observed that while each of these churches is growing, none are achieving the *rate* of growth represented in the earliest period reported in this table when respectively they experienced growth rates of 1.71%, 1.28%, 0.42% and 1.57%. This slowing of the *rate* of growth ought to be the focus of further research and thoughtful inquiry. None of the four churches listed above would ordinarily be considered "liberal" churches, hence, any appeal to explanations that revolve around theological orientation are unlikely to account for such overall slowing of the rate of growth. Some will wish to argue that the slowing growth rate is evidence of an increasing secularization of American postmodern society. While such an explanation will satisfy some, caution in drawing such a conclusion is warranted. American society has not experienced the kind and rate of secularization so clearly demonstrated during the last quarter century in Western Europe. Indeed, American church membership trends have defied gravity, particularly when the Pentecostal experience is included. Alternative explanations for slowed membership growth must be carefully drawn during the next few years if we are to make sense of the patterns that are now emerging. Several factors will need to be weighed afresh including the very centrality of the concept of church membership itself. For the age cohorts known as Gen X'ers and Millennials (people now in their 30s and 20s, respectively) formal membership may lie outside of their hopes and expectations for their church relationships. For both of these age cohorts membership and commitment to institutions is no longer perceived as a mark of maturity or assumption of generational responsibility. Membership is sometimes perceived as an unnecessary and even undesirable exercise in over-institutionalization. Hence, for some young adults, church attendance, participation in fellowship or mission activities, and even financial support of a local congregation do not translate into a desire to formally "join" and be listed among those in membership. The growing prevalence of this practice is reported anecdotally and can often be noted in leafing through local church directories. At the conclusion of the membership directory there typically follows a section labeled as "Friends of the Congregation." If indeed this proves to be a growing tendency among successive generations, church *membership* as opposed to "affiliation data" may itself need to be reconsidered. Several other factors, emerging patterns of affiliation, and organizational considerations make this demographic inquiry a rich field for further inquiry.

Churches listed here experiencing the highest rate of loss of membership are: the Presbyterian Church USA (-2.36%), the American Baptist Churches (-1.82%), and the Evangelical Lutheran Church in America (-1.58%). For each of these churches, these latest figures represent a relatively consistent rate of membership decline.

Table 4   Financial Trends

Second only to the interest in membership trends is the interest of media and the church world alike in the financial trends reported in the *Yearbook*. While not all churches report their financial information to the *Yearbook*, 65 churches have provided full data for the 2008 edition providing an important glimpse into United States church giving. More than $34 billion dollars are accounted for in the reports of these churches and this is, of course, but a portion of the whole of church giving.

The financial reporting for this 2008 *Yearbook* is based on the financial income reports of the 65 churches reporting complete figures. The records of those 65 reporting churches are detailed in Table 4. The 46 million inclusive members contributed a total of over $34 billion, marking an increase in the total amount of income to the churches of more than $48 million. It is particularly useful to view this increase in its *per capita*

14

terms. The $742 contributed per person is an increase of $29.21 per person from the previous year. The 4.1 % increase in *per capita* giving exceeds the official inflation figure for 2006. It must be remembered that many individuals are contributing to parishes with a declining number of members. In such settings the increase in giving will offset some of the financial loss associated with membership decline and rising prices. This increase in *per capita* giving will be a source of encouragement particularly when it is remembered that this increase occurred during the same period that giving continued to church-related aid and relief agencies that were active in rebuilding the Gulf Coast following hur-ricanes Katrina and Rita.

Benevolence giving for 2006, in our sample of United States churches reporting, increased from last report to 16%. This ratio of benevolence to total giving reflects a modest gain over the previous three years. An interesting comparison can be made with benevolence reported by Canadian churches. While admittedly reporting on a far smaller sample and reflecting a much lower level of total giving, the *percentage* of benevolence giving for Canadian churches is consistently in the 18% to 20% range compared to the U.S. figure of 16%.

This year's 16% percent U.S. benevolence giving is a slight increase over last year, but remains at the low end in the range of benevolent giving over the period of the last decade. This level of giving for benevolence will be the source of sober reflection for some. The overall increase in giving to the churches, at this reporting, is occurring simultaneously with a nearly stagnant posture in benevolence as a percentage. The churches that seek generosity from their supporters have not, at least in this sample, matched that generosity with an increase in their own benevolence giving. The practical consequences of such a decline continues to translate in local settings to less support for church-sponsored day care, fewer soup kitchens meals, less emergency help to persons with medical problems, or reduced transportation to the elderly.

No one has given greater attention to church giving patterns than John and Sylvia Ronsvalle. For a fulsome discussion of the giving patterns of churches, see their *The State of Church Giving* series of publications, by writing to: empty tomb, inc. P.O. Box 2404, Champaign, IL 61825; or through their Website: www.emptytomb.org.

When Did We See Thee Sick?
Congregations Respond

Rev. Eileen W. Lindner, Ph.D.
Principal Investigator

The ancient Hebrew prophet Jeremiah asks, "Is there no balm in Gilead?" For Christians, health—physical, mental, and spiritual—has historically been a focus of ministry and mission following the example of Jesus. Within the United States much of what we know as the complex infrastructure of health care has its origins in the religious communities. Today the landscape is still dotted with voluntary hospitals whose titles reflect their origins: Augustana Hospital, Presbyterian St. Luke's, Baptist Hospital. Many Christians are highly conscious of the central role of healing within the ministry of Jesus. Indeed, there are some forty-two accounts of Jesus providing healing contained within the Gospels—a larger number of accounts than those of Jesus preaching or teaching. The expression of faith through the provision of health services is not limited to specialized church-related health institutions but is an intrinsic part of the witness and mission of local congregations as well. The Congregational Health Ministry Survey (or CHMS), conducted by the National Council of Churches USA in 2006–07, represents a modest attempt to understand more fully the nature of congregational involvement in the provision of health education, provision of direct health services, and advocacy activities related to health care policies. This summary of that study suggests some implications from its findings, which may be of interest to pastors, denominational leaders, health care advocates, and the public at large concerned with the state of health care policies in the United States today.

Why Study the Congregations' Health Ministries? Why Now?

The National Council of the Churches of Christ USA is the nation's preeminent ecumenical agency comprised of thirty-five member churches with a constituent membership approaching 44 million believers. Throughout its long history the NCC has been a venue for the member churches to work together on a wide variety of issues related to health and health care policy. In recent years the NCC and its member churches have shared with the American public a growing concern for the issues of the cost and fairness of access to quality health care for all within the society. Moreover, within the national dialogue, which has increasingly addressed concerns about the American health care system, various observers have suggested an expanded role for the "faith-based" sector in meeting the health care needs of our society. No research is available to judge the extent to which the faith-based community plays a role in health care, how it works with others in providing health care, or whether such service delivery leads local congregations to advocacy for policy reform.

The Sample

The Congregational Health Ministry Survey consisted of fifteen questions, including identifier and demographic questions, and questions pertaining to congregations' involvement in an array of health activities over "the past 12 months." *Health ministry* is understood as compassionate care activities related to health needs conducted as a part of a church's overall mission. A listing of health activities was presented in areas of education, provision, voluntarism, events, and advocacy. Open-ended questions permitted reporting of alternative or specific health-related activities. The six-page survey was mailed in stages to an available sample of 88,400 congregations between December 2006 and April 2007.

Who Responded to the Survey?

By the close of the data collection phase of the project 6,037 usable surveys (7%) had been returned electronically, via fax, or by return mail. While the largest number of responses were provided by the larger mainline Protestant denominations, notably United Methodists and Presbyterians, the total sample is drawn primarily from eleven national church bodies and ecumenical agencies.

Racial composition of the respondents was overwhelmingly identified as Caucasian (90%). African American congregations represented 16% of the surveyed sample and 4.7% (282 individual cases) of respondents. Additional means will need to be pursued in order to gain a fuller picture of the health care ministries within minority communities.

Congregational size was thought to be an important consideration in a congregation's capacity to initiate and sustain health care ministries given the labor-intensive nature of the tasks to be undertaken. It was not surprising therefore to discover that responding congregations represented congregations that are, on the average, larger (397 members) than all US congregations as reported in the highly respected National Congregations Study (307 members).

More than one quarter of all the responding congregations are located in suburban settings, with an additional 20% reporting their community type as "rural non-farming." Rural farming and small city communities accounted for 15% each in terms of the community type reported by responding congregations. Ten percent reported their location as within a small town with only 9% reporting their location in the inner city.

What Can We Learn from This Survey?

The Congregational Health Ministry Survey constitutes a pioneering study in the field of health activities and congregations. The results of this study:

- Document the very large amount of congregational activity addressing health issues;
- Portray the range and distribution of the health-related activities in congregations;
- Suggest the characteristics of congregations that are most involved in the provision of health services.

The 6,037 congregations who responded to the survey and their collective 2.5 million members have responded to the needs of their communities through programs of education, direct services, and advocacy. While this initial survey leaves undocumented much of the congregational landscape of the United States, it does provide an important basis upon which future studies might build. Used within appropriate constraints the findings of this study do much to advance our knowledge of congregational responses to health care needs within the reporting communities and their capacity to address those needs.

What Patterns of Health Care Ministries Were Reported?

Only 6.4% of the respondents reported that their congregations offered no programs of any kind in health care ministries. It should be noted that this figure is probably lower in all churches as some recipients of this survey may have chosen not to complete it since, in their perception, the survey was "not for them" because they provide no such services. The sample of the 6,037 responding congregations report a staggering total of 78,907 programs of health ministries or an average of 13.07 health-related activities per congregation.

The three program areas that served as the foci of this survey were:

1) health education,
2) direct provision of health services, and
3) advocacy of public policies related to health care.

In order to isolate these three types of health care ministries from more typical volunteer services routinely offered by congregations and from one time "health events," which are not necessarily sustained programs, separate responses were also recorded for volunteer services and health events. Table 1 reports the frequency of report in each of the five areas of programming.

Table 1—Frequency of Reporting in Health Care Program Areas

Program Frequency	Percent	Total
Volunteer Services	87%	18,754
Direct Service	70%	13,033
Health Education	65%	24,072
Health Events	57%	17,988
Advocacy	35%	5,052

NOTE: Programs reported by percent of congregations and number of programs.

Within the congregations, provision of *volunteer services* routinely takes place independent of other health care ministries. Fully 87% of the congregations reported their participation in such activities.

Health-related events, such as use of the church facilities for blood donor drives or health fairs, are by definition limited-time events rather than ongoing programs and therefore require less structure, staffing, and budget to accomplish. The impetus for health events, such as a blood drive, may originate outside of the congregation. Indeed congregations may simply permit the use of their facilities for such events that are actually planned, initiated, and conducted by community health agencies. Such events may serve to sensitize congregations to largely unspoken health concerns that are not adequately addressed by existing systems. A full 57% of the respondents reported hosting health events within their congregations.

More than 65% of the respondents report offering *health education* programs within their community. With a median of four programs per congregation more than 24,000 health education programs were offered by the sample as a whole. Table 2 lists the kinds and frequency of the content of these educational programs.

Table 2—Respondents Reporting Health Education Activities

Health Education Program	Percent	Health Education Program	Percent
Prevention	28%	Dementia	12%
Older Adults	28%	Drugs	12%
Explain Programs	24%	Organ Donation	12%
Members' Health	24%	State or Regional Health	11%
Exercise	24%	Diabetes	11%
End of Life	23%	Obesity	10%
Spiritual/Alternative	21%	Teenagers	10%
Nutrition	21%	Child	10%
High Blood Pressure	20%	Uninsured	9%
Additions	20%	Needed Resources	8%
Handicap Accessibility	17%	AIDS	8%
Alcohol	16%	Smoking	7%
Mental Health	15%	State Child Health Insurance Program (SCHIP)	4%
Government Policies	14%	Family Planning	3%

NOTE: Responding congregations reporting engagement in health-related education, by highest reported.

Surprisingly, more congregations in the sample engage in the *provision of direct health services* (70%), than provide educational health programs (65%). Direct services are understood to mean provision of medical care provided directly to individuals, usually by someone specifically trained to do so. However, a lower total number of direct service programs (13,033) are offered than total educational programs (24,072). This is probably explained by the greater need for organization, financial resources, and personnel required to sustain direct service programs. The array and frequency of direct service programs offered is reported in Table 3. Health screenings were by far the most common form of direct service activity that has an exclusively health related focus, and that is provided by with high degree of congregational involvement. Approximately 27% of all responding congregations providing some form of screening.

Table 3—Direct Services

Type of health-related service	Percent
Counseling (Referrals)	32%
12-Step Program	32%
Screening	27%
Emergency Medical Funding	25%
Exercise	23%
Counseling (mental health)	22%
Clinic	20%
Counseling (provide service)	20%
Support Group	20%
Parish Nurse	18%
Referrals	16%
Daycare Health	8%
Health Minister	5%

NOTE: Percent of responding congregations reporting provision of specific health-related services, by highest reported

18

Larger congregations (higher average attendance) were more likely to provide greater numbers of direct service programs. Suburban and urban downtown congregations provided significantly more direct service programs than congregations in other community types. Neither denominational affiliation nor the predominant race of the congregation had a significant effect.

Who Receives the Direct Services?

The survey explored the balance between the provision of direct service to "congregation only" or to the community. Larger congregations were less likely to emphasize "congregation only" services. Downtown urban congregations were also significantly less likely to emphasize "congregation only" services as they were to offer programs for the wider community. Rural congregations had more direct services for the "congregation only" as opposed to services provided to the wider community. No significant effects of race, denomination, or region were observed.

The most significant finding is that services offered to both the broader community as well as congregation members is the most common practice of congregations offering direct services.

Taken as a whole, the patterns of service to congregation and community underscore the extent to which congregational involvement in health services is viewed by congregations as a ministry within the broader community rather than an intramural benefit of church membership.

As might have been expected, public policy advocacy was a far less common practice. Advocacy can be understood as efforts to inform and/or urge action on health policies and practices on a systemic level, usually involving public officials. About a quarter of all congre- gations engaged in any form of advocacy. Of these, 60% of congregations (15% of all congregations) participated in two or more forms of advocacy.

Why Do Some Congregations Engage in Health Care Ministries and Others Do Not?

As has been suggested by several of the findings above, size of congregation has

> ### Casting a Broad Net
> The 6,037 congregations reporting through the Congregational Health Ministry Survey do indeed cast a broad net in providing programs that meet local need. They include a tiny parish in upstate New York with two retired lawyers who volunteer to assist the elderly and migrant workers in completing health insurance and Medicaid forms to three Alabama congregations that sponsor a free health clinic. Thousands of churches offer screening for diabetes, hypertension, vision, hearing, and referrals to appropriate health facilities for follow-up care. Robust education programs assist homeowners in retrofitting homes to accommodate new physical restrictions, inform participants about blood and organ donation provisions, and a host of topics geared to meet the needs of parents of young children in safety-proofing homes, counseling teens regarding drug and alcohol use, and providing nutrition and exercise classes for senior citizens. Working with community agencies, churches recruit, train, and sponsor volunteers for hospitals, nursing homes and in-home respite care. Large congregations in Chicago, Cleveland, and Atlanta provide health care screenings, dental clinics, and referrals for clients at soup kitchens, homeless shelters, and in drop in centers. Parish nurses educate, coordinate, and enable congregational members and community residents in making lifestyle changes and in securing the medical and mental health services they need. In California and elsewhere church committees organize, petition, and invite governmental officials to public meetings to discuss gaps in the health care system and to explore ways to close such gaps through policy reform. Churches reach out to hospitals, build their own clinics, and offer financial assistance to the uninsured facing medical calamity. In local communities large and small congregations are engaged in vibrant, innovative approaches to health care education, direct service provision and public policy advocacy. Drawing on congregational, community, and denominational resources, congregations in service to the wider community continue to cast a broad net in ministry to those in need.

been a significant factor in predicting congregational engagement in education, direct service, or advocacy activities related to health care. But size alone is not sufficient to predict broad and multifaceted embrace of health care as a field of ministry activity. Our reflection on both the statistical analysis and the substantial anecdotal information that was received with the returned surveys suggests a more complex confluence of factors. These factors, taken together might be described as capacity, leadership, and opportunity.

Capacity often comes with size especially as relates to organizational coherence, financial and human resources, and a congregational orientation toward active programming in addition to the worship activities of the congregation. Capacity is also measured in terms of the stature of the congregation

19

within the community and whether it is looked to within the community as a source of community service and programming in relation to issues such as child care, feeding programs, or homeless shelter.

Leadership appears to be a critical element in congregational provision of education, direct service, and policy advocacy activities. The study strongly suggests the importance of pastoral leadership in enabling congregational participation in policy advocacy. With regard to health education and direct service provision as well as advocacy activities, a number of other sources of leadership were noted in the anecdotal material. Parish nurses and, far less commonly, health ministers provide crucial leadership in forming and maintaining health initiatives within congregations.

Opportunity might express a final critical element in relation to congregational provision of health care programs of education, direct service, and advocacy. This matter of opportunity is related to leadership but is also closely related to awareness of health needs in the specific community surrounding the congregation. Opportunity seems to present itself through a variety of means judging from the anecdotal responses from the sample. Health events initiated by a municipal office or neighboring hospital may serve to quicken a congregation's awareness of the need for greater education about diabetes or hypertension, for example. Sponsoring or serving as volunteers at homeless shelters often awakens congregational awareness of chronic physical and mental health needs among that population. This awareness, in fact, becomes opportunity for service as congregational members seek ways to address unmet needs. It is not uncommon for congregations to discover holes in the fabric of the health care system and seek to address such needs directly through preventative education, medical services, or advocacy.

Within congregational life then, capacity, leadership, and opportunity, it seems form a kind of "fire triangle" that best explains the combustion that results in congregational initiation of health care ministries of education, direct service, and advocacy. The form that initiative takes is unique to the community and to the congregation.

To review the whole report of the CHMS see www.health-ministries.org.

20

II

DIRECTORIES

1. United States Cooperative Organizations, National

The organizations listed in this section are cooperative religious organizations that are national in scope. Regional cooperative organizations in the United States are listed in Directory 7, "United States Regional and Local Ecumenical Bodies."

The Alban Institute, Inc.

The Alban Institute is an independent, not-for-profit cradle of learning, grounded in faith and devoted to helping American congregations become greater communities of faithfulness, health, creativity, hospitality and leadership. Alban is the largest congregational resource and advocacy membership organization in the United States, reaching hundreds of thousands of congregants across all faith traditions with our signature of congregation building known as The Alban Way. From Alban's groundbreaking consulting practice, to original research, publications and seminars on leadership, conflict, planning and transitions, The Alban Institute knows what it takes to build vital, enduring communities of faith. Alban draws on a vast reservoir of congregational know-how and wisdom born on the firing line. Clergy and lay leaders seek guidance from the most respected problem solvers, strategists and teachers in the business.

Headquarters

2121 Cooperative Way, Suite 100, Herndon, VA 20171 Tel. (800)486-1318
Media Contact, Director of Research, Dr. Ian Evison

Officers

Pres., The Rev. James P. Wind, Ph.D.

The Alliance for Christian Media

The Alliance for Christian Media is an ecumenical organization dedicated to producing media resources from a mainline Protestant point of view. The flagship production is the weekly radio show, "Day 1," formerly "The Protestant Hour." The Web site www.day1.net provides sermon transcripts and audio resources. Day 1 features preachers from the Cooperative Baptist Fellowship, Episcopal Media Center, Evangelical Lutheran Church in America, Presbyterian Church (U.S.A.), United Church of Christ, and the United Methodist Church. The Web site www.Day1.net provides sermon transcripts and audio resources, and www.episcopalmedia.org offers audio and video resources for churches and individuals.

Headquarters

644 West Peachtree St, Suite 300, Atlanta, GA 30308-1925 Tel. (404)815-9110 Fax (404) 815-0258
Media Contact, Nan Ross

Officers

Bd. Chpsn., The Rev. Dr. Mary Miller Brueggemann
Vice-Chpsn., Laurin M. McSwain
Pres., The Rev. Canon Louis C. Schueddig
V.P., The Rev. Peter M. Wallace
Treas., Jim O. Llewellyn
Sec., Frank Troutman, Jr.

American Bible Society

In 1816, pastors and laymen representing a variety of Christian denominations gathered in New York City to establish an organization "to disseminate the Gospel of Christ throughout the habitable world." Since that time the American Bible Society (ABS) has continued to provide God's Word, without doctrinal note or comment, wherever it is needed and in the language and format the reader can most easily use and understand. The American Bible Society is the servant of the denominations and local churches.

The American Bible Society is committed to promoting personal engagement with the Holy Scriptures with the goal of changed lives. A special emphasis is placed upon advocacy for the Bible cause, partnerships with like-minded churches and para-church organizations, and with provision of Scripture. Today the ABS serves more than 100 denominations and agencies, and its board of trustees is composed of distinguished laity and clergy drawn from these Christian groups.

21

The American Bible Society played a leading role in the founding of the United Bible Societies, a federation of 140 national Bible Societies around the world that enables global cooperation in Scripture translation, publication and distribution in more than 200 countries and territories. The Bible Society contributes generously to the support provided by the United Bible Societies to those national Bible Societies that request support to meet the total Scripture needs of people in their countries.

The work of the American Bible Society is supported through gifts from individuals, local churches, denominations and cooperating agencies.

Headquarters

National Service Center, 1865 Broadway, New York, NY 10023 Tel. (212)408-1200

Media Contact, Senior Manager, Media Relations, Roy Lloyd, Tel. (212)408-8731 Fax (212)408-1456, Email: rlloyd@americanbible.org

Officers

Chpsn., Rev. R. Lamar Vest

Vice Chpsn., Dennis Dickerson

Pres., Rev. Dr. Paul G. Irwin

Vice President for Development, Robert L. Briggs

Vice President and Executive Director for Bibles.com, John Cruz

Senior Vice President for Domestic Ministries, Rev. Emilio Reyes

Vice President and General Counsel, Peter Rathbun

Vice President for Corporate Services and CFO, Richard Stewart

Dean, Nida Institute for Biblical Scholarship, Dr. Robert Hodgson

Director of Internal Audit, Donald Cavanaugh

Director for Publishing Services, Bibles.com, Thomas Durakis

Director for Finance and Production Services, Bibles.com., Gary Ruth

DEPARTMENT HEADS

Chief Communications Officer, Denise London

Assistant to Vice President of Finance, Stephen King

Director of Operations, Cheryl Berlamino

Director of Building Management Services, John Colligan

Director of Research, Dr. Joseph Crockett

Chief Technology Officer, Nicholas Garbidakis

Director of Operations, Bibles.com, Dr. John Greco

Editorial and Publications Manager, Charles Houser

Director of Direct Response Programs, H. Lee Manis

Controller, Stephen Sharp

Director of Investments, Nicholas Pagano

Director of Human Resources, Sharon Roberts

Director of Church Relations, David Ramos

Director of Programs, Karina Lucero

Director of Sales and Marketing, Bibles.com, Brian Sherry

Director of Development, Melinda Trine

Director of Relationship Development, Karmen Wynick

American Council of Christian Churches

The American Council of Christian Churches is a Fundamentalist multidenominational organization whose purposes are to provide information, encouragement, and assistance to Bible-believing churches, fellowships, and individuals; to preserve our Christian heritage through exposure of, opposition to, and separation from doctrinal impurity and compromise in current religious trends and movements; to protect churches from religious and political restrictions, subtle or obvious, that would hinder their ministries for Christ; and to promote obedience to the inerrant Word of God.

Founded in 1941, The American Council of Christian Churches (ACCC) is a multi-denominational agency for fellowship and cooperation among Bible-believing churches in various denominations—fellowships, Bible Presbyterian Church, Evangelical Methodist Church, Fellowship of Fundamental Bible Churches (formerly Bible Protestant), Free Presbyterian Church of North America, Fundamental Methodist Church, Independent Baptist Fellowship of North America, Independent Churches Affiliated, along with hundreds of independent churches. The total membership nears 2 million. Each denomination retains its identity and full autonomy, but cannot be associated with the World Council of Churches, National Council of Churches or National Association of Evangelicals.

Headquarters

P.O. Box 5455, Bethlehem, PA 18015 Tel. (610)865-3009 Fax (610)865-3033

Media Contact, Exec. Dir., Dr. Ralph Colas

Officers

Pres., Dr. John McKnight

Vice Pres., Rev. Randy Ardis

Exec. Sec., Dr. Ralph Colas

Sec., Rev. Craig Griffith

Treas., Rev. John Yessa

Commissions, Chaplaincy; Education; Laymen; Literature; Missions; Radio & Audio Visual; Relief; Youth

American Friends Service Committee

Founded, 1917, Regional offices, 9. Founded by and related to the Religious Society of Friends (Quakers) but supported and staffed by individuals sharing basic values regardless of religious affiliation. Attempts to relieve human suffering and find new approaches to world peace and social justice through nonviolence. Work in 20 countries includes development and refugee relief, peace education, and community organizing. Sponsors off-the-record seminars around the world to build better international understanding. Conducts programs with U.S. communities on the problems of minority groups such as housing, employment, and denial of legal rights. Maintains Washington, D.C. office to present AFSC experience and perspectives to policymakers. The Quaker United Nations offices in New York City and Geneva, Switzerland arrange seminars, testimony before UN committees and behind-the-scence discussions with UN delegates. Seeks to build informed public resistance to militarism. A co-recipient of the Noble Peace Prize. Programs are multiracial, non-denominational, and international. Divisions, Community Relations Unit, International Programs, Peacebuilding Unit

Headquarters

1501 Cherry St., Philadelphia, PA 19102 Tel. (215)241-7000 Fax (215)241-7275
Dir. of Media Relations, Janis Shields

Officers

Presiding Clerk., Paul Lacey
Treas., James Fletcher
General Secretary, Mary Ellen McNish

The American Theological Library Association

The American Theological Library Association (ATLA) is a library association that works to improve theological and religious libraries and librarianship by providing continuing education, developing standards, promoting research and experimental projects, encouraging cooperative programs and publishing and disseminating research tools and aids. Founded in 1946, ATLA currently has a membership of over 245 institutions and 550 individuals.

Headquarters

250 S. Wacker Dr., Suite 1600, Chicago, IL 60606-5889 Tel. (312)454-5100 Fax (312) 454-5505
Media Contact, Jonathan West, Web Editor

Officers

Pres., Paul Schrodt, Methodist Theological School in Ohio, 3081 Columbus Pike, P.O.Box 8004, Delaware, OH 43015-8004
Vice Pres., Paul F. Stuehrenberg, Yale University Divinity School Library, 409 Prospect St., New Haven, CT 06511
Sec., Anne Womack, Vanderbilt University Divinity Library, 419 21st Ave. South, Nashville, TN 37240-0007
Exec. Dir., Dennis A. Norlin, ATLA, 250 S. Wacker Dr., Suite 1600, Chicago, IL 60606-5889

American Tract Society

The American Tract Society is a nonprofit, interdenominational organization, instituted in 1825 through the merger of most of the then-existing tract societies. As one of the earliest religious publishing bodies in the United States, ATS has pioneered in the publishing of Christian books, booklets and leaflets. The volume of distribution has risen to over 35 million pieces of literature annually. For free samples or a free catalog contact 1-800-54-TRACT.

Headquarters

P.O. Box 462008, Garland, TX 75046 Tel. (972)276-9408 Fax (972)272-9642
Media Contact, V.P. Evangelism/Outreach, David Leflore

The American Waldensian Society

The American Waldensian Society (AWS) promotes ministry linkages, broadly ecumenical, between U.S. churches and Waldensian (Reformed)-Methodist constituencies in Italy and Waldensian constituencies in Argentina-Uruguay. Founded in 1906, AWS aims to enlarge mission discovery and partnership among overseas Waldensian-Methodist forces and denominational forces in the U.S.

AWS is governed by a national ecumenical board, although it consults and collaborates closely with the three overseas Waldensian and Waldensian-Methodist boards.

The Waldensian experience is the earliest continuing Protestant experience.

Headquarters

American Waldensian Society, VistaCom, Ste. #1, 1902 Vultee St., Allentown, PA 18103-2958 Tel. (866)825-3373 Fax (610)797-9723, Email: info@waldensian.org, Web: www.waldensian.org
Media Contact, Jack Ferlino

Officers

Pres., The Rev. Francis Rivers '05 PC (*USA)
Vice Pres., The Rev. Gabriella Lettini '05 WC
Sec., Ms. June Rostan '06

Appalachian Ministries Educational Resource Center (AMERC)

The mission of AMERC is to promote contextual, cross-cultural education for theological students, faculties, ministers, and other Christian leaders. Working through an ecumenical consortium of theological schools and denominational judicatories, AMERC supports experiential learning about the theological, spiritual, social, economic and environmental aspects of Appalachian culture, especially for rural and small town settings for ministry.

Since 1985 AMERC has provided quality educational programs and learning experiences for seminaries and other religious leaders inter-

23

ested in ministry in Appalachia and other rural areas. The centerpiece of these programs has been and continues to be in-depth, contextually based dialogue with local people engaged in creative ministries, exploring with them social, economic, political, ecological, cultural, and religious issues. Intense theological reflection is used to understand these issues through the eyes of faith, equipping students and other leaders for ministry in the Appalachian context.

In the new millennium AMERC's form of ministry has changed. AMERC is now supporting its consortium of members by providing program grants, technical and library support, and leadership consultation. The consortium seminaries and other groups, in turn, design and offer an even wider variety of experiential programs in rural and small town ministry in the context of Appalachia. Both seminary, for credit, and continuing education courses are offered. In 2000 AMERC launched its Grants Program for members of the consortium. Since that time AMERC has funded twenty-four winter and summer Travel Seminars, a spring course with an immersion component, a Seminary Faculty Immersion experience and a summer intern program. A consultation and six continuing education events with grants of up to $15,000.

Headquarters
298 Harrison Rd., Berea, KY 40403 Tel. (859) 986-8789 Fax (859)986-2576, Email: loliver@amerc.org, Web: www.amerc.org
Media Contact, Rev. Dr. Lon D. Oliver, Executive Director
Executive Assistant, Marsha Baker

Officers
Chair, Rev. Dr. Barbara Blodgett, Yale Divinity School
Vice Chair, Rev. Dr. Jackie Johns, Church of God Theological Seminary
Secretary, Ms. Tena Willemsma, Commission on Religion in Appalachia
Treasurer, Mr. Jim Strand, Berea College

The Associated Church Press
The Associated Church Press was organized in 1916. Its membership includes periodicals and Web sites of major Protestant, Catholic, and Orthodox, and ecumenical groups in the United States and Canada and abroad; individual members who supply publishing services on a freelance or student basis; and affiliate members who supply the Christian press with news, information, and vendor services. It is a professional Christian journalistic association seeking to promote excellence among editors and writers, recognize achievements, and represent the interests of the religious press. It sponsors seminars, conventions, awards programs, and workshops for editors, staff people, and business managers. It is active in postal rates and regulations on behalf of the religious press.

Headquarters
Media Contact, Exec. Dir., Mary Lynn Hendrickson, 1410 Vernon St. Stoughton , WI 53589-2248 Tel.(608)877-0011 Fax (608)877-0062

Officers
Exec. Dir., Mary Lynn Hendrickson,1410 Vernon St. Stoughton, WI 53589-2248, Tel.(608)877-0011 Fax (608)877-0062, Email: acpoffice@earthlink.net
Pres., Jerry Van Marter, Presbyterian News Service, 100 Witherspoon St., Louisville, KY 40202-1396, Tel. (502)569-5493 Fax (502) 569-8073, Email: jvanmart@ctr.pcusa.org
Vice Pres., Terry DeYoung, The Church Herald, 4500-60th St. SE, Grand Rapids, MI 49512-9642 Tel. (616)698-7071 Fax (616)698-6606, Email: tdeyoung@rca.org
Past Pres., Victoria A. Rebeck, The Minnesota Connect, 122 W. Franklin, Ste. 400, Minneapolis, MN 55404-2472 Tel. (612)870-0058 x 232 Fax (612)870-1260, Email: victoria.rebeck@mnumc.org
Treas., Silvia Chavez, The Lutheran, 8765 W. Higgins Rd., Chicago, IL 60631-4189 Tel. (773)380-2543 Fax (773)380-2751, Email: schavez@elca.org

The Associated Gospel Churches
Organized in 1939, The Associated Gospel Churches (AGC) endorses chaplains primarily for strong evangelical Independent Baptist and Bible Churches to the U.S. Armed Forces. The AGC has been recognized by the U.S. Department of Defense for 65 years as an Endorsing Agency, and it supports a strong national defense. The AGC also endorses VA chaplains, police, correctional system and civil air patrol chaplains.

The AGC provides support for its constituent churches, seminaries, Bible colleges and missionaries.

The AGC believes in the sovereignty of the local church, the historic doctrines of the Christian faith and the infallibility of the Bible.

The AGC is a member of the National Conference on Ministry to the Armed Forces (NCMAF) and the Endorsers Conference for Veterans Affairs Chaplaincy (ECVAC).

Headquarters
Media Contact, Pres., Billy Baugham, D.D., National Hdqt., P.O. Box 733, Taylors, SC 29687 Tel. (864)268-9617 Fax (864)268-0166

Officers
Commission on Chaplains, Pres. and Chmn., Billy Baugham, D.D.
Vice Pres., Rev. Chuck Flesher
Sec.-Treas., Eva Baugham
Executive Committee, Chaplain (Captain) James Poe, USN Member

Association of Catholic Diocesan Archivists

The Association of Catholic Diocesan Archivists, which began in 1979, has been committed to the active promotion of professionalism in the management of diocesan archives. The Association meets annually, in the even years it has its own summer conference, in the odd years it meets in conjunction with the Society of American Archivists. Publications include Standards for Diocesan Archives, Access Policy for Diocesan Archives and the quarterly Bulletin.

Headquarters
Archives & Records Center, 711 West Monroe, Chicago, IL 60661 Tel. (312)831-0711 Fax (312)736-0488
Media Contact, Brian P. Fahey

Officers
Episcopal Mod., Most Rev. Thomas J. Paprocki, Auxiliary Bishop, Archdiocese of Chicago
Pres., Joseph w. Coen, Diocese of Brooklyn, 310 Propspect Park West, Brooklyn, NY 11215
Vice Pres., Audrey Newcomer, Diocese of St. Louis, 20 Archbishop May, St. Louis, MO 63119
Treas., John J. Treanor, Archdiocese of Chicago, 711 West Monroe St., Chicago IL 60661
Sec., Lori Vodden, Diocese of Peoria, 417 NR Monroe Avenue, Peoria IL 601603.
Newsletter Editor, Brian P. Fahey, Diocese of Charleston, 114 Broad Street Rear Building, Charleston, SC 29402

ADRIS-Association for the Development of Religious Information Services

The Association for the Development of Religious Information Services was established in 1971 to facilitate coordination and cooperation among information services that pertain to religion. Its goal is a worldwide network that is interdisciplinary, inter-faith and interdenominational to serve both administrative and research applications. ADRIS publishes a blog and provides internet consulting services.

Headquarters
ADRIS Newsletter Office, P.O. Box 210735, Nashville, TN 37221-0735 Tel. (615)429-8744
Media Contact, Editor., Ed Dodds, P.O. Box 210735, Nashville, TN 37221-0735 Tel. (615) 429-8744
Web: www.adris.org
ICQ: 49457096
AIM: ed1dodds
SKYPE: ed_dodds_skype
JABBER: Ed_Dodds@jabber.org
GoogleTalk: ed.dodds@gmail.com
Yahoo: ed_dodds
MSN: ed_dodds@hotmail.com

Association of Gospel Rescue Missions

The Association of Gospel Rescue Missions (AGRM), formerly the International Union of Gospel Missions, is an association of 300 rescue missions and other ministries that serve more than 7 million homeless and needy people in the inner cities of the United States, Canada, and overseas each year. Since 1913, AGRM member ministries have offered emergency food and shelter, evangelical outreach, Christian counsel, youth and family services, prison and jail outreach, rehabilitation and specialized programs for the mentally ill, the elderly, the urban poor and street youth. The AGRM operates RESCUE College, an Internet-based distance education program to prepare and train rescue mission workers. The AGRM sponsors Alcoholics Victorious, a network of Christian support groups. AGRM is affiliated with the City Mission World Association, representing over 500 City Mission around the world.

Headquarters
1045 Swif Ave., Kansas City, MO 64116-4127 Tel. (816)471-8020 Fax (816)471-3718
Media Contact, Exec. Dir., Rev. John Ashmen or Phil Rydman

Officers
Exec. Dir., Rev. John Ashmen
Pres., Mr. Rick Alvis, Box 817, Indianapolis, IN 46206 Tel. (317) 635-3575
Fax (317) 687-3629
Sec., Mr. David Traedwell, 1350 R St NW, Washington DC 20009-4323 Tel. (202)745-7118 Fax (202)232-7072
Vice Pres., Mr. Perry Jones, IIIl, 259 s Pearl St., Albany, NY 12202 Tel.(518)462-0459, Fax (518)462-0489

Association of Statisticians of American Religious Bodies

This Association was organized in 1934 and grew out of personal consultations held by representatives from The Yearbook of American Churches, The National (now Official) Catholic Directory, The Jewish Statistical Bureau, The Methodist (now The United Methodist), the Lutheran and the Presbyterian churches.

ASARB has a variety of purposes: to bring together those officially and professionally responsible for gathering, compiling, and publishing denominational statistics; to provide a forum for the exchange of ideas and sharing of problems in statistical methods and procedure; and to seek such standardization as may be possible in religious statistical data.

Headquarters
Dale Johnson, Church of the Nazarene, 6402 The Paseo, Kansas City, MO 64131 Tel. (800)306-9928
Media Contact, Sec.-Treas., Dale Johnson

Officers

Pres., Mary Gautier, Center for Applied Research in the Apostolate, Georgetown University, Washington, DC 20057 Tel. (202)687-8086 Fax (202)687-8083, Email: gautierm@georgetown.edu

Immediate Past Pres., Rich Houseal, Church of the Nazarene, 6401 The Paseo, Kansas City, MO 64131 Tel. (816)333-7000 x 2473 Fax (816)361-5202, Email: rhouseal@nazarene.org

1st Vice Pres., Major Diana E. Smith, The Salvation Army, 440 West Nyack Road, Box C-635, West Nyack, NY 10994-1739 Tel. (845)620-7382 Fax (845)620-7777 Email: Diana_Smith@use.salvationarmy.org

2nd Vice Pres., John O'Hara, Lutheran Church-Missouri Synod, 1333 S. Kirkwood Road, St. Louis, MO 63122 Tel. (314)965-9917 Fax (314)996-1133 Email: john.ohara@lcms.org

MEMBERS-AT-LARGE

Carl Royster, 21st Century Christian, 2809 12th Ave. S, P.O. Box 40526, Nashville, TN 37204 Tel. (615)383-3842 Fax (615)292-5983, Email: royster@21stcc.com

Destiny Shellhammer, United Church of Christ, 700 Prospect Ave, Cleveland, OH 44111 Tel. (216)736-2149 Fax (216)736-2276, Email: shellhad@ucc.org

The Association of Theological Schools in the United States and Canada

The Association of Theological Schools in the United States and Canada (ATS) is a membership organization of more than 250 graduate schools that conduct post-baccalaureate professional and academic degree programs to educate persons for the practice of ministry and for teaching and research in the theological disciplines. The ATS Commission on Accrediting accredits schools and approves the degree programs they offer.

Headquarters

10 Summit Park Drive, Pittsburgh, PA 15275-1110 Tel. (412)788-6505 Fax (412)788-6510
Media Contact, Dir. Of Comm., Nancy Merrill, Tel. (412)788-6505 x 234
Officers
Pres., Donald Senior, Catholic Theological Union, Chicago, IL
Vice Pres., John Kinney, Samuel DeWitt - Proctor - School of Theology of Virginia Union University, Richmond, VA
Secretary, Leland V. Eliason, Bethel Seminary of Bethel University, St. Paul, MN
Treasurer, Thomas R. Johnson, Kirkpatrick & Lockhart Nicholson Graham, Pittsburgh, PA

Blanton-Peale Institute

Blanton-Peale Institute is dedicated to helping people overcome emotional obstacles by joining mental health expertise with religious faith and values. The Blanton-Peale Graduate Institute provides advanced training in marriage and family therapy, psychotherapy and pastoral care for ministers, rabbis, sisters, priests and other counselors. The Blanton-Peale Counseling Centers provide counseling for individuals, couples, families and groups. Blanton-Peale also offers a nationwide telephone support service for clergy, social service agencies, and other employers and promotes interdisciplinary communication among theology, medicine and the behavioral sciences. Blanton-Peale was founded in 1937 by Dr. Norman Vincent Peale and psychiatrist Smiley Blanton, M.D.

Headquarters

3 W. 29th St., New York, NY 10001 Tel. (212)725-7850 Fax (212)689-3212

Officers

Chpsn., John Allen
Vice Chpsn., Arthur Caliandro
Sec., Janet E. Hunt
Treas., Mary McNamara
Pres. & CEO, Dr. Holly Johnson

Bread For The World

Bread for the World is a non-profit, nondenominational Christian citizen's movement of 55,000 members, including 2,500 local churches, that advocates specific hunger policy changes and seeks justice for hungry people at home and abroad. Founded in 1974, Bread for the World is supported by more than 45 Protestant, Catholic and Evangelical denominations and church agencies. Rooted in the gospel of God's love in Jesus Christ, its 55,000 members write, call and visit their members of Congress to win specific legislative changes that help hungry people, and place the issue of hunger on the nation's policy agenda.

Bread for the World works closely with Bread for the World Institute. The Institute seeks to inform, educate, nurture and motivate concerned citizens for action on policies that affect hungry people.

Headquarters

50 F St., NW, Ste. 500, Washington, DC 20001 Tel. (202)639-9400 Fax (202)639-9401
Media Contact, Shawnda Eibl

Officers

Pres., Rev. David Beckmann
Bd. Chpsn., Matthew McHugh.
Bd. Vice-Chpsn., Eleanor Butt Crook

Campus Crusade for Christ International

Campus Crusade for Christ International is an interdenominational, evangelistic and discipleship ministry dedicated to helping fulfill the Great Commission through the multiplication strategy of "win-build-send." Founded in 1951 on the campus of UCLA, the organization now includes 60 plus ministries and special projects reaching out to almost every segment of society. There are more than 27,000 staff members and 226,000 trained volunteers in 190 countries.

Headquarters
100 Lake Hart Dr., Orlando, FL 32832 Tel. (407)826-2000 Fax (407)826-2120
Media Contact, James Woelbern

Officers
Chmn. & Pres., Steve Douglass
Chief Operating Officer, J. Roger Bruehl
Chief Financial Officer, Roger L. Craft

Center on Conscience & War

CCW(formerly NISBCO), formed in 1940, is a nonprofit organization supported by individual contributions and related to more than thirty religious organizations. Its purpose is to defend and extend the rights of conscientious objectors to war. CCW provides information on how to register for the draft while documenting one's convictions as a conscientious objector, how to cope with penalties if one does not cooperate, and how to qualify as a conscientious objector while in the Armed Forces. It also provides information for counselors and the public about conscientious objection, military service and the operation of the draft. It provides information to and support for conscientious objectors in other countries.

As a national resource center it assists research in its area of interest including the peace witness of religious bodies. Its staff provides referral to local counselors and attorneys and professional support for them. Through publications and speaking, CCW encourages people to decide for themselves what they believe about participation in war and to act on the basis of the dictates of their own informed consciences.

Headquarters
1830 Connecticut Ave. NW, Washington, DC 20009-5732 Tel. (202)483-2220 Fax (202) 483-1246
Media Contact, Exec. Dir., J.E. McNeil

Officers
Exec. Dir., J.E. McNeil
Chpsn., David Miller
Sec., James Feldman
Treas., Jean Martensen

Center for Parish Development

The Center for Parish Development is an ecumenical, non-profit research and development agency whose mission is to help church bodies learn to become faithful expressions of God's mission in today's post-modern, post-Christendom world. Founded in 1968, the Center brings to its client-partners a strong theological orientation, a missional ecclesial paradigm with a focus on faithful Christian communities as the locus of mission, research-based theory and practice of major change, a systems approach, and years of experience working with national, regional, and local church bodies.

The Center staff provides research, consulting and training support for church organizations engaging in major change. The Center is governed by a 12-member Board of Directors.

Headquarters
1448 East 53rd St., Chicago, IL 60615 Tel. (773)752-1596 Fax (773)752-5093
Media Contact, Office Manager, Beatrice Vansen

Officers
Chpsn., John Rottenberg, 2047 Fawnwood Drive SE, Kentwood, MI 49508
Vice-Chpsn., Stephen B. Bevens, 5401 S. Cornell Avenue, Chicago, IL 60615
Sec., Delton Krueger, 10616 Penn Ave. South, Bloomington, MN 55431
Managing Directors, Raymond Schulte and Dale Ziemer

Chaplaincy of Full Gospel Churches

The Chaplaincy of Full Gospel Churches (CFGC) is a unique coalition of 1500 nondenominational churches and networks of churches united for the purpose of being represented in military and civilian chaplaincies. Since its inception in 1984, CFGC has grown rapidly. Today CFGC represents over 7.5 million American Christians. Additionally, we are connected with another 144 fellowship groups consisting of another 7.5 million members, which gives CFGC the potential of representing a total 15 million.

Churches, fellowships and networks of churches which affirm the CFGC statement of faith that "Jesus is Savior, Lord and Baptizer in the Holy Spirit today, with signs, wonders and gifts following" may join the endorsing agency. CFGC represents its member-networks of churches (consisting of over 90,000 churches nation wide) before the Pentagon's Armed Forces Chaplains Board, the National Conference of Ministry to the Armed Forces, Endorsers Conference for Veterans Affairs Chaplaincy, Federal Bureau of Prisons, Association of Professional Chaplains, and other groups requiring professional chaplaincy endorsement (State/County/City Correctional, Healthcare, Law Enforcement, Workplace). The organization also ecclesiastically credentials professional counselors.

Headquarters
2715 Whitewood Dr., Dallas, TX 75233-2713 Tel. (214)331-4373 Fax (214)333-4401
Media Contact, Rev. Dr. E. H. Jim Ammerman

Officers
Pres., Rev. Dr. E. H. Jim Ammerman

27

Christian Council on Persons with Disabilities

Created in 1988, the Christian Council on Persons with Disabilities (CCPD) is a coalition of churches, non-profit organizations and individuals advocating an evangelical perspective concerning people with disabilities and their place in God's world. The coalition provides a national voice for Christians involved in disability ministry, framing the Christian community's response to issues relating to disability.

CCPD provides information and responses on issues specifically relating to the church such as accessibility, disability theology and outreach; as well as disability-related issues of concern to the general public such as genetic research, end-of-life care and cloning.

Advocacy, professional development, networking and education are all part of the coalition's activities. Annual conferences (both national & regional), chapter groups and mentoring programs are part of the coalition's strategy in strengthening the network of disability ministry.

Headquarters
301 E. Pine St. Suite 150, Orlando, FL 32801 Tel. (407)210-3917, Email: ccpd@ccpd.org, Web: www.ccpd.org

Officers
Exec. Dir., Jim Hukill
Pres., Gary Wagner, Of Camp Verde, AZ
Treas., Stan Higgins, of Rohnert Park, CA

Christian Endeavor International

Christian Endeavor International is a Christ-centered, youth-oriented ministry which assists local churches in reaching young people with the gospel of Jesus Christ, discipling them in the Christian faith, and equipping them for Christian ministry and service in their local church, community and world. It trains youth leaders for effective ministry and provides opportunities for Christian inspiration, spiritual growth, fellowship, and service. Christian Endevor International reaches across denominational, cultural, racial and geographical boundaries. All materials are on the internet at www.teamce.com

Headquarters
424 E. Main St., P.O..Box 377, Edmore, MI 48829 Tel. (989)427-3737 Fax (989)427-5530, Email: contact@teamce.com, Media Contact, Luke Sawyer

Officers
Chief Executive Officer, Timothy Eldred

Christian Management Association

Christian Management Association (CMA) provides leadership training, management resources and strategic networking relationships for leaders and managers of Christian organizations and growing churches. Its membership represents leaders and managers from more than 1,500 Christian organizations and larger churches in the United States. CMA publishes Christian Management Report magazine, CMA Management Monthly e-newsletter, Total Compensation Survey Report for Christian Ministries, www.CMAonline.org website, CMA Management Tape Library and many other resources. CMA provides management training, resourcing and networking opportunities through its annual conference for Christian organizations and churches, CEO Dialogues one-day roundtables, chapters in selected cities, online Job Market, and many other programs. It also features annually the Best Christian Places to Work finalists and the CMA Management Award. Membership is open to Christian organizations, ministries and churches. Businesses that provide products or services for Christian organizations and churches may apply for a business membership. For complete membership information, go to www.CMA online.org and click on "Membership."

Headquarters
P.O. Box 4090, San Clemente, CA 92674
Tel. (800) 727-4262 Fax (949) 487-0927
CEO, John Pearson, Email: John@CMAonline. org
Director of Management Resources, DeWayne Herbrandson, Email: DeWayne@CMAonline. org
Senior Consultant, Marketing, Dick Bahruth, Email: Dick@CMAonline, org
Director of Conferences & Meetings, Marsha Lyons, Email: Marsha@CMAonline.org
Director of Administration/COO, Suzy West, Email: Suzy@CMAonline.org

Officers
Chairman, Pres./CEO, ECCU, Mark G. Holbrook
Vice Chairman, C.E. Crouse, Managing Partner, Capin Crouse, LLP
Treas., Robert T. Lipps, Lockton Insurance Brokers of San Francisco
Sec., Mark A. Bankord, Managing Principal/Chairman, Cap Trust Asset Management

A Christian Ministry in the National Parks

This ministry is recognized by over 40 Christian denominations and extends the ministry of Christ to the millions of people who live, work and vacation in our National Parks. Ministry Staff Members conduct services of worship in the parks on Sundays. The staff are employed by park concessionaires and have full-time jobs in which their actions, attitudes, and commitment to Christ serve as witness. Room and board are provided at a minimal cost; minimum commitment of 90 days needed.

Officers
Dir., The Rev. Richard P. Camp, Jr.
Deputy Director, Gordon Compton

Church Growth Center—Home of Church Doctor Ministries

The Church Growth Center is an interfaith, nonprofit, professional organization which exists to bring transformational change of the Christian church toward the effective implementation of the Lord's Great Commission, to make disciples of all people. This effort is done through consultations, resources, and educational events.

Founded in 1978 by leader Kent R. Hunter, the Church Growth Center offers over 17 different consultation services, including church consultations by experienced consultants, cutting edge resources through The Church Doctor™ Resource Center, and by providing educational events at churches and organizations in the way of providing speakers and resources at seminars, workshops, and conferences. The bi-monthly e-newsletter is the Church Doctor Report.

Headquarters
P.O.Box 145, 1230 U. S. Highway Six, Corunna, IN 46730 Tel. (800)626-8515 Fax (260)281-2167, Web: www.churchdoctor.org, Media Contact, Assistant to President, Cindy Warren

Officers
President, Dr. Kent R. Hunter, D.Min, Ph.D.
Vice Pres., Greg Ulmer
Treas., Rob Olsen

Church Women United in the U.S.A.

Church Women United in the U.S.A. is a racially, culturally, theologically inclusive Christian women's movement, celebrating unity in diversity and working for a world of peace and justice. Founded in 1941, Church Women United is a movement representing Protestant, Roman Catholic, Orthodox and other Christian women; biblically based, shared Christian faith; organized into more than 1200 state and local units working for peace and justice in the United States and Puerto Rico; supported by constituents in state and local units and denominational women's organizations; impassioned by the Holy Spirit to act on behalf of women and children throughout the world; and recognized as a non-governmental organization by the United Nations.

Headquarters
475 Riverside Dr., Ste. 1626, New York, NY 10115 Tel. (800) CWU-5551 or (212)870-2347 Fax (212)870-2338, Office manager, Julie Drews, Email: juliedrews@churchwomen. org

CWU Washington Office, 100 Maryland Ave. NE, Rm. 100, Washington, DC 20002 Tel. (202)544-8747 Fax (202)544-9133

Legislative Dir., Wash. Office, Patricia Burkhardt, Email: pburkhardt@churchwomen. org

Officers
Pres., Gail Mengel, Independence, MO
Vice Pres., Vera Zander, Tucson, AZ

Secretary, Carol Kolsti, Austin, TX
Treasurer, Ann Kohler, Baldwinsville, NY
Regional Coordinators, Central, Susan Becker, Madison, WI; East Central, Margaret Tweet, Rock Island, IL; Mid-Atlantic, Blanche Simmons, Landover, MD; Northeast, Vivian Love-Jones, Newburg, NY; Northwest, Betty Luginbill, Boise, ID; South Central, Martha Moody Boone, Keithville, LA; Southeast, Pat Zangmeister, Tamarac, FL; Southwest, Jenny Ladefaged, Alisa Viego, CA

Churches Uniting in Christ

Churches Uniting in Christ (CUIC) was inaugurated on January 20, 2002, in Memphis Tennessee as a new relationship among nine communions which agreed to start living more fully into their unity in Christ. CUIC is the successor to the Consultation on Church Union (COCU) which was, in 1962 organized to explore the formation of a uniting church. At the 1999 COCU Plenary the nine member communions affirmed eight "Marks" of Churches Uniting in Christ and agreed to move into the new relationship of covenanted communion to be called Churches Uniting in Christ. Following confirmation actions by each of the communions, all nine communions officially constituted Churches Uniting in Christ. The nine member communions are: The African Methodist Episcopal Church, the African Methodist Episcopal Zion Church, the Christian Church (Disciples of Christ), the Christian Methodist Episcopal Church, The Episcopal Church, the International Council of Community Churches, the Presbyterian Church (USA), the United Church of Christ, and the United Methodist Church. Also participating at present are two Partners in Mission and Dialogue, the Evangelical Lutheran Church in America and the Moravian Church (Northern Province). The Catholic Church participates as an observer. Other communions are exploring various possibilities for relating to CUIC.

CUIC is a bold venture, expressed through the participating communions' covenant to seek to live a new relationship that bears witness to a church that is truly catholic, truly evangelical, and truly reformed. Among the goals for bearing witness to that unity are two very challenging endeavors: to heed the "emphatic call to 'erase racism' by challenging the system of white privilege that has so distorted life in this society and in the churches themselves;" and to "provide a foundation for the mutual recognition and reconciliation of ordained ministry by the members of Churches Uniting in Christ by the year 2007. Notably, the commitment to address racism is named as a hallmark of the new relationship and, following the Inaugural ceremony,on Dr. Martin Luther King, Jr. Day, January 21, 2002, the Heads of Communion signed an Appeal to the Churches to work together for the eradication of racism.

The Ecumenical Officers of each of the communions will carry major responsibility for the engagement of their congregations and members in the CUIC relationship. Neighboring congregations are encouraged to celebrate the Eucharist together; invite the participation of each in services of baptism, ordinations and installation as well as other special events in the congregations' lives; and to discover ways in which they might witness together in combating social injustices, especially racism. In addition to the representational Coordinating Council, three task forces will work to enhance the collaborative endeavors of CUIC: Ministry, Racism, and Local and Regional Ecumenism.

The Rev. Dr. Bertrice Y. Wood serves as the Director of CUIC with the office located at 700 Prospect Avenue, Cleveland, OH 44115-1100 Tel. (216)736-3294. The Rev. C. Dana Krutz is President of the Coordinating Council.

Headquarters
700 Prospect Ave., Cleveland, OH 44115-1100 Tel.(216)736-3294 Fax (216)736-3296 Email: cuicwood@ucc.org or cuic@ucc.org
Media Contact: The Rev. Dr. Bertrice Y. Wood

Officers
Dir., The Rev. Dr. Bertrice Y. Wood, 700 Prospect Ave., Cleveland, OH 44115-1100
President of the Coordinating Council, The Rev. C. Dana Krutz (The Episcopal Church), 660 N. Foster Dr. Ste. A-225, Baton Rouge, LA 70806
Vice Pres., Bishop E. Earl McCloud, Jr. (African Methodist Episcopal Church)
Sec., Mr. Abraham Wright, International Council of Community Churches
Trea., Elder James N. Tse (Presbyterian Church USA)

COORDINATING COUNCIL REPRESENTATIVES FROM MEMBER COMMUNIONS
African Methodist Episcopal Church, Bishop E. Earl McCloud, Jr.
African Methodist Episcopal Zion Church, The Rev. Dr. Harrison Bonner
Christian Church (DISCIPLES OF CHRIST), The Rev. Dr. Suzanne Webb
Christian Methodist Episcopal Church, Bishop Ronald Cunningham
The Episcopal Church (USA), The Rev. C. Dana Krutz
International Council of Community Churches, Mr. Abraham Wright
Presbyterian Church (USA), Elder James N. Tse
United Church of Christ, The Rev. Lydia Veliko
The United Methodist Church, Bishop Albert F. Mutti

Evangelical Council for Financial Accountability
Founded in 1979, the Evangelical Council for Financial Accountability has the purpose of helping Christ-centered, evangelical, nonprofit organizations earn the public's trust through their ethical practices and financial accountability. ECFA assists its over 1,200 member organizations in making appropriate public disclosure of their financial practices and accomplishments, thus materially enhancing their credibility and support potential among present and prospective donors.

Headquarters
440 W. Jubal Early Drive Ste. 130, Winchester, VA 22601-6319 Tel. (540)535-0103 Fax (540)535-0533
Media Contact, Pres., Ken Behr

Officers
Pres., Ken Behr
Vice Pres., Dan Busby

Evangelical Press Association
The Evangelical Press Association is an organization of editors and publishers of Christian periodicals which seeks to promote the cause of Evangelical Christianity and enhance the influence of Christian journalism.

Headquarters
P.O. Box 28129, Crystal, MN 55428 Tel. (763) 535-4793 Fax (763) 535-4794
Media Contact, Exec. Dir., Ronald Wilson

Officers
Pres., David Neff, Christianity Today, 465 Gundersen Dr., Carol Stream, IL, 60188
Pres-Elect, Terry White, Inside Journal, P.O. Box 17429, Washington, DC 20041-0429
Treas., Lamar Keener, Christian Times, P.O. Box 2606, El Cajon, CA 92021
Sec., Jeanette Thomason, Aspire, 107 Kenner Ave., Nashville, TN 37205
Advisor, Dean Ridings, Christian Camp & Conference Journal, P.O. Box 62189, Colorado Springs, CO 80962-2189
Advisor, Brian Peterson, New Man, 600 Rinehart Rd., Lake Mary, FL 32746
Exec. Dir., Ronald Wilson

Faith & Values Media
(*See also National Interfaith Cable Coalition, Inc.*)
Faith & Values Media is a nation's largest coalition of Jewish and Christian faith groups dedicated to media production, distribution and promotion. It is a service of the National Interfaith Cable Coalition, Inc., established in 1987.

Faith & Values Media member association includes more than 40 faith groups and religious organizations representing 200,000 congregations and 120 million congregants. Its mission is to use television and other media to promote the vitality of religious experience in everyday life.

Award-winning programming from Faith & Values Media is available on Hallmark Channel and on www.faithstreams.com

74 Trinity Place, Suite 1550, New York, NY 10006 Tel. (212)406-4121 Fax (212)406-4105, Media Contact, Christine Luzano

Officers
Chair, Dr. Daniel Paul Matthews
Vice Chair, Elder Ralph Hardy Jr., Esq.
Secretary, Rabbi Daniel Freelander
Treasurer, Betty Elam

Staff
President and CEO, Edward J. Murray
Exec. Vice President, Beverly Judge

Federation of Christian Ministries

The Federation of Christian Ministries (FCM)is an ecumenical, faith community founded in 1968.FCM stresses inclusiveness, opening its membership to women and men of varying faith backgrounds who share its vision of an ecumenical, nondenominational community. Its ministers work in many ways: pastoring house churches or congregations/parishes; serving as chaplains in nursing homes, correctional facilities, hospitals; offering healing ministries; promoting groups dedicated to peace and justice. FCM is a member of the International Council of Community Churches and a faith group member of the Association for Clinical Pastoral Education. Its educational branch, Global Ministries University, offers online degree completion, both undergraduate and postgraduate, for adult learners in the field of ministry. Contact: GlobalMinistriesUniversity.com.

Headquarters
1905 Bugbee Rd., Ionia, MI 48846-9663 Tel. (800)538-8923 or (616)527-0419 Fax (616) 527-0419, Email: info@FederationofChristian Ministries.org
Media Contact, Co-president, Eileen Mackin, Tel.(303)740-7665, Email: cdewall@pcisys. net

Officers
Chairperson(s): Jan & Paul Reithmaier, 7415 K Triwoods Dr., Shrewsbury, MO 63119-4456 Tel. (314)962-6220, Email: p.reithmaier@ worldnet.att.net
President(s): Eileen Mackin & Clem DeWall, 11298 E. Maplewood Pl., Englewood, CO 80111-5808 Tel. (303)740-7665, Email: cdewall @pcisys.net.
Treasurer: Roger J. Fecher, 8330 Catamaran Dr., Indianapolis, IN 46236-9585 Tel. (317)826-8940, Email: rjfecher@aol.com.
Secretaries/Central Office: Edward & Judy Kalmanek, 1905 Bugbee Rd., Ionia, MI 48846-9663 Tel. (616)527-0419, Email: ejkalmanek@home.ionia.com.
Development Directors: Frederick A. Mason, 12830 Paulina St. Ste 2E, Calumet Park, IL 60827-5951 Tel. (708)589-3357, Email: Mcrincorg@sbcglobal.net.

Bonnie J. McCulley, 3818 Eagle Ridge Dr., Cape Giradeau, MO 63701-1703 Tel. (573) 332-1228, Email: bjmc27@aol.com
Member at Large: William Manseau, 12 Catherwood Rd., Tewksbury, MA 01876-2620 Tel. (978)851-5547

REGIONAL VICE PRESIDENTS:
Pacific Region: Peggy & Phil Ripp, 2869 Donizetti Ct., San Jose, CA 95132-2310 Tel. (408)272-8184, Email: philandpeg@sbcglobal.net
Mountains & Plains: Rebecca David, 624 E. Dover St., Davenport, IA 52803-2611 Tel. (563)323-5740, Email: irishblue03@earthlink. net
Great Lakes: Pamela Spence, P. O. Box 204, Ostrander, OH 43061-0204 Tel. (740)666-3204, Email: allespen@midohio.net
Southern: Eleonora V. Marinaro and David Gaboury, 10231 Oakhill Dr., Port Richey, FL 34668-3291 Tel (727)697-2763, Email: elly@ helpwithdreams.com
Northeast: Michaelita & Thomas Quinn, 93 Post Rd., Danbury, CT 06810-8367 Tel. (203)792-6968, Email: quinnems@aol.com

Foundation for a Conference on Faith and Order in North America

A Foundation for a Conference on Faith and Order is a not-for-profit organization dedicated to promoting the unity of the North America Churches by keeping before the Churches the gospel call to unity in Faith and Order. It engages in educational studies and programs that relate to issues affecting Faith and Order, and promotes, plans, and administers conferences on Faith and Order in North America. The purpose of these conferences is to encourage and promote the unity of the Churches in Faith and Order.

Headquarters
77 Park Ave., Suite 298-A, New York, NY 10016 Tel. (212)725-7435

MEMBERS OF THE BOARD
Bishop Vinton Anderson
Dr. Wallace M. Alston, Jr.
Dr. Susan E. Davies
Archbishop Demetrios
Dr. Robert M. Franklin
Dr. Donna Geernaert, SC
The Right Rev. Richard F. Grein
Dr. Robert W. Jenson
Dr. Cheryl Bridges Johns
William Cardinal Keeler
Dr. Kevin W. Mannoia
The Rt. Rev. Victoria Matthews
Bishop Donald J. McCoid
Dr. Richard Mouw
Dr. Willam G. Rusch
Dr. George Vandervelde
Dr. Eldin Villafane
The Rev. Portia Turner Williamson

Friends World Committee for Consultation (Section of the Americas)

The Friends World Committee for Consultation (FWCC) was formed in 1937. There has been an American Section as well as a European Section from the early days and an African Section was organized in 1971. In 1974 the name, Section of the Americas, was adopted by that part of the FWCC with constituency in North, Central, and South America and in the Caribbean area. In 1985 the Asia-West Pacific Section was organized. The purposes of FWCC are summarized as follows, To facilitate loving understanding of diversities among Friends while discovering together, with God's help, a common spiritual ground; and to facilitate full expression of Friends' testimonies in the world.

Headquarters
1506 Race St., Philadelphia, PA 19102 Tel. (215)241-7250 Fax (215)241-7285 Email: americas@fwcc.quaker.org www.quaker.org/fwcc/americas/americas.html
Media Contact, Exec. Sec., Margaret Fraser
Latin American Office, Guerrero 223 Pte., Zona Centro, Cd. Mante, TAM 89800 Mexico

The Fund for Theological Education, Inc.

Begun in 1954 with the goal of supporting excellence in the profession of ministry, the Fund for Theological Education has enjoyed a long and rich history, providing gifted women and men with nearly 5000 fellowships and generating innovative new programs for support of persons preparing for ministry and theological teaching. Supported by individuals and grants from a group of U.S. Foundations, FTE envisions new and imaginatve programs to encourage diversity and excellence in the churches and seminaries of North America.

Headquarters
825 Houston Mill Rd., Suite 250, Atlanta, GA 30329 Tel. (404)727-1450 Fax (404)727-1490 Email: fte@thefund.org, Website: www.thefund.org, www.exploreministry.org

Officers
President, Ann Svennungsen
Vice Pres. for Advancement, Jack Gilbert
Dir., Expanding Horizons Partnership, Dr. Sharon Watson Fluker
Dir., Partnership for Excellence, Melissa Wiginton

Glenmary Research Center

The Research Center is a department of the Glenmary Home Missioners, a Catholic society of priests and brothers. The Center was established in 1966 to serve the rural research needs of the Catholic Church in the United States. Its research has led it to serve ecumenically a wide variety of church bodies. Local case studies as well as quantitative research is done to understand better the diversity of contexts in the rural sections of the country. The Center's statistical profiles of the nation's counties cover both urban and rural counties.

Headquarters
1312 Fifth Ave. North, Nashville, TN 37208 Tel. (615)256-1905 Fax (615)251-1472

Officers
Pres., Rev. Daniel Dorsey, P.O. Box 465618, Cincinnati, OH 45246-5618
1st Vice Pres., Rev. Robert Poandl, P.O. Box 465618, Cincinnati, OH 45246-5618
2nd Vice Pres., Rev. Dominic Duggins, P.O. Box 465618, Cincinnati, OH 45246-5618
Treas., Ms. Saney Wissel, P.O. Box 465618, Cincinnati, OH 45246-5618
Dir., Kenneth M. Sanchagrin, Ph.D. Email: ksanchagrin@glenmary.org
Assoc. Dir., Fr. Wil Steinbacher, 1312 5th Ave.N., Nashville, TN 37208, Email: wjsteinba@aol.com

Graymoor Ecumenical & Interreligious Institute (GEII)

Graymoor Ecumenical & Interreligious Institute has its roots in the Graymoor Ecumenical Institute which was founded in 1967 by the Franciscan Friars of the Atonement, to respond to the Friars' historical concern for Christian Unity in light of the theological and ecumenical developments arising from the Second Vatican Council.

In 1991, in response to developments in both the Institute and the wider ecumenical scene, the Graymoor Ecumenical Institute was expanded into an information and service organization with a mission of Christian Unity and interreligious dialogue. Today, the Graymoor Ecumenical & Interreligious Institute employs several means to accomplish this goal. Among these is the annual Week of Prayer for Christian Unity, "a worldwide observance initiated in 1908 by the Rev. Paul Wattson, co-founder of the Society of the Atonement," the theme and text of which are now chosen and prepared by the Pontifical Council for Promoting Christian Unity and representatives of the World Council of Churches. The Institute publishes the monthly journal Ecumenical Trends-to keep clergy and laity abreast of developments in the ecumenical and interreligious movements; provides membership in, and collaboration with, national and local ecumenical and interreligious organizations and agencies; and cooperates with individuals engaged in ecumenical and interreligious work. A new website, www.geii.org has been launched and will continue to be developed as a resource for ecumenical and interreligious research.

Over the years, the Graymoor Ecumenical & Interreligious Institute has sponsored and cosponsored meetings, colloquia, and workshops in areas of ecumenical and interreligious dialogue.

Headquarters

475 Riverside Dr., Rm. 1960, New York, NY 10115-1999 Tel. (212)870-2330 Fax (212) 870-2001

Officers

Dir., Desk for Interreligious Affairs, Rev. James Loughran, SA, Tel. (212)870-2330, Email: jlgeii@aol.com

Assoc. Director, Rev. Dr. Timothy MacDonald, SA, Tel. (212)870-2331, Email: tmdgeii@aol.com

Assoc. Dir., Ecumenical Research Desk, Rev. Wilfred L. Tyrrell, SA, Tel.(212)870-2332, Email: wltgeii@aol.com

Assoc. Dir., Week of Prayer for Christian Unity, Rev. Thomas Orians, SA, Tel.

(212)870-2330, Email: togeii@aol.com Editor, Ecumenical Trends, Rev. James Loughran SA., Graymoor, Route 9, P.O. Box 300 Garrison, NY 10524-0300 Tel. (845)424-3671 x 3323, Email: jlgeii@aol.com

Business Manager, Week of Prayer for Christian Unity Office, Mrs. Veronica Sullivan, Graymoor, Rt. 9, P.O. Box 300, Garrison, NY 10524-0300 Tel. (800)338.2620 x 2109 or (845)424-2109 Fax (845)424-2163, Email: rsullivan@atonementfriars.org

InterVarsity Christian Fellowship of the U.S.A.

InterVarsity Christian Fellowship is a non-profit, interdenominational student movement that ministers to college and university students and faculty in the United States. InterVarsity began in the United States when students at the University of Michigan invited C. Stacey Woods, then General Secretary of the Canadian movement, to help establish an Inter-Varsity chapter on their campus. InterVarsity Christian Fellowship-USA was incorporated two years later, in 1941.

InterVarsity's uniqueness as a campus ministry lies in the fact that it is student-initiated and student-led. InterVarsity strives to build collegiate fellowships that engage their campus with the gospel of Jesus Christ and develop disciples who live out biblical values. InterVarsity students and faculty are encouraged in evangelism, spiritual discipleship, serving the church, multiethnicity, righteousness, vocational stewardship and world evangelization. The Urbana triennial missions convention has long been a launching point for missionary service. For more detials on urbana please visit www.urbana.org.

Headquarters

6400 Schroeder Rd., P.O. Box 7895, Madison, WI 53707 Tel. (608)274-9001 Fax (608)274-7882, Web: www.intervarsity.org, Email: info@intervarsity.org

Media Contact, Gordon Govier

Officers

Pres. & CEO, Alec Hill

Vice Pres., C. Barney Ford; Robert A. Fryling; Karon Morton, Jim Lundgren, Paula Fuller, Jim Tebbe

Bd. Chpsn., Donald Kolowsky

Bd. Vice Chpsn., E. Kenneth Nielson

Interfaith Impact for Justice and Peace

Interfaith Impact for Justice and Peace is the religious community's united voice in Washington. It helps Protestant, Jewish, Muslim and Catholic national organizations have clout on Capitol Hill and brings grassroots groups and individual and congregational members to Washington and shows them how to turn their values into votes for justice and peace.

Interfaith Impact for Justice and Peace has established the following Advocacy Networks to advance the cause of justice and peace, Justice for Women; Health Care; Hunger and Poverty; International Justice and Peace; Civil and Human Rights. The Interfaith Impact Foundation provides an annual Legislative Briefing for members.

Members receive the periodic Action alerts on initiatives, voting records, etc., and a free subscription to the Advocacy Networks of their choice.

Headquarters

100 Maryland Ave. N.E., Ste. 200, Washington, DC 20002 Tel. (202)543-2800 Fax (202)547-8107

Media Contact, Jane Hull Harvey

Officers

Chpsn. of Bd., Jane Hull Harvey, United Methodist Church

MEMBERS

African Methodist Episcopal Church
African Methodist Episcopal Zion Church
Alliance of Baptists
American Baptist Churches, USA, Washington Office; World Relief Office
American Ethical Union
American Muslim Council
Center of Concern
Christian Methodist Episcopal (CME) Church
Christian Church (Disciples of Christ)
Church of the Brethren
Church Women United
Commission on Religion in Appalachia
Episcopal Church
Episcopal Urban Caucus
Evangelical Lutheran Church in America
Federation of Southern Cooperatives-LAF
Federation for Rural Empowerment
Graymoor Ecumenical and Interreligious Institute
Jesuit Social Ministries
Maryknoll Fathers and Brothers

33

Moravian Church in America
National Council of Churches USA, Church World Service; Washington Office
National Council of Jewish Women

NETWORK:
Peoria Citizens Committee
Presbyterian Church (USA)
Progressive National Baptist Convention
Presbyterian Hunger Fund
Reformed Church in America
Rural Advancement Fund
Society of African Missions
Southwest Organizing Project
Southwest Voter Registration-Education Project
Toledo Metropolitan Ministries
Union of American Hebrew Congregations
Unitarian Universalist Association
Unitarian Universalist Service Committee
United Church of Christ, Bd. for Homeland Ministries; Bd. for World Ministries; Hunger Action Ofc.; Ofc. of Church in Society
United Methodist Church, Gen. Bd. of Church & Society; Gen. Bd. of Global Ministries Natl. Div.; Gen. Bd. of Global Ministries Women's Div.; Gen. Bd. of Global Ministries World Div.
Virginia Council of Churches
Western Organization of Resource Councils

Interfaith Worker Justice

Interfaith Worker Justice is a network of sixty interfaith groups and people of faith who educate and mobilize the U.S. religious community on issues and campaigns to improve wages, benefits and working conditions for workers, especially low-wage workers. The organization rebuilds relationships between the religious community and organized labor.

The organization supports and organizes local interfaith worker justice groups around the country, publishes Faith Works six times a year providing congregations resources and updates on religion-labor work, coordinates the Poultry Justice project to improve conditions for poultry workers, and promotes healthy dialogue between management and unions in religious owned or sponsored health care facilities.

Headquarters

1020 West Bryn Mawr, 4th floor, Chicago, IL 60660-4627 Tel. (773)728-8400 Fax (773) 728-8409
Media Contact, Cynthia Brook, Email: cbrooke @iwj.org

Board of Directors

President: Rev. Nelson Johnson, Pulpit Forum of Greensboro and Faith Community Church
Vice President: Bishop Gabino Zavala, Archdiocese of Los Angeles
Finance Chair: Rev. Dr. Paul Sherry, National Council of Churches USA
Fundraising Chair: Rev. Jim Sessions, United Methodist Church

Action Committee Chair: Ms. Edith Rasell, UCC Minister for Labor Relations
Education Committee Chair: Ms. Evely Laser Shlensky,* Commission on Social Action of Reform Judaism (URJ & CCAR)
Board Development Chair: Imam Mahdi Bray, Muslim American Society Freedom Foundation
Dr. Charles Amjad-Ali, Luther Seminary
Mr. Hussam Ayloush, Council on American-Islamic Relations - Southern California
Mr. John Boonstra, Washington Association of Churches
Ms. Linda Chavez-Thompson, AFL-CIO
Ms. Marilyn Clement, Campaign for a National Health Program NOW
Rev. Darren Cushman-Wood, Speedway United Methodist Church
Mr. Robert DeRose, Barkan+Neff
Bishop William DeVeaux, African Methodist Episcopal Church
Dr. Mary Heidkamp, Dynamic Insights International
Ms. Karen Herrling, Catholic Legal Immigration Network, Inc
Ms. Karen McLean Hessel, Justice for Women, National Council of Churches
Rev. Clete Kiley, Bishop's Committee, U.S. Conference of Catholic Bishops
Mr. Jeffry Korgen, The Roundtable
Rabbi Mordechai Liebling, Shefa Fund
Rev. Christopher Lockard, Jesuit Refugee Service
Ms. Linda Lotz, American Friends Service Committee
Rabbi Robert Marx,** Congregation Hakafa
Ms. Cynthia Nance,* University of Arkansas
Rev. J. Herbert Nelson, Liberation Community Church/Mid-South Interfaith Committee for Worker Justice
Rev. Sinclair Oubre, Catholic Labor Network
Mr. Mark Pelavin, Religious Action Center of Reform Judaism
Ms. Rosalyn Pelles, Union Community Fund
Sister Mary Priniski, OP, Catholic Committee of the South
Rev. Meg Riley, Unitarian Universalist Association of Congregations
Rev. Michael Rouse,* St. Catherine AME Zion Church
Mr. Chris Sanders, Political Consultant, UFCW
Mr. Thomas Shellabarger, U.S. Conference of Catholic Bishops
Honorable Charles Steele, Southern Christian Leadership Conference
Rev. Ron Stief, UCC Justice and Witness Ministries Public Life and Social Policy
Mr. Monroe Sullivan, Retired Businessman / Social Activist
Rev. Phil Tom, Urban Ministry Office, Presbyterian Church USA
Rev. Mark Wendorf, McCormick Theological Seminary

Rev. Bennie Whiten, Jr., United Church of Christ Special Advisors
Bishop Jesse DeWitt,** Retired, United Methodist Church
Rev. Jim Lawson, Holman United Methodist Church
Rev. Joseph Echols Lowery, Southern Christian Leadership Conference
Rev. Addie Wyatt, Vernon Park Church of God
Executive Director, Kim Bobo
* Former Board Officer
** Former Board President

Interreligious Foundation for Community Organization (IFCO)

IFCO is a national ecumenical agency created in 1966 by several Protestant, Roman Catholic and Jewish organizations, to be an interreligious, interracial agency for support of community organization and education in pursuit of social justice. Through IFCO, national and regional religious bodies collaborate in development of social justice strategies and provide financial support and technical assistance to local, national and international social-justice projects.

IFCO serves as a bridge between the churches and communities and acts as a resource for ministers and congregations wishing to better understand and do more to advance the struggles of the poor and oppressed. IFCO conducts workshops for community organizers and uses its national and international network of organizers, clergy and other professionals to act in the interest of justice.

Churches, foundations and individual donors use IFCO services as a fiscal agent to make donations to community organizing projects.

IFCO's global outreach includes humanitarian aid shipments through its Pastors for Peace program to Cuba, Haiti, Nicaragua, Honduras, and Chiapas, Mexico.

Headquarters
402 W. 145th St., New York, NY 10031 Tel. (212)926-5757 Fax (212)926-5842
Media Contact, Dir. of Communications, Gail Walker

Officers
Pres., Rev. Schuyler Rhodes
Vice President & Treasurer, Marilyn Clement

The Kairos Institute, Inc.

The Kairos Institute provides quality support, consultation and in-depth educational opportunities to the professional, medical, mental health and religious communities and promotes assistance, consultation, education and care to families of exceptional children. Its clergy consultation service provides care to many denominations and clergy. "Career Path" offers candidate assessment for ordination and consultation for clergy in transition.

Headquarters
107 Green Ave., Madison, NJ 07940 Tel. (973) 966-9099 Fax (973)377-8509

Officers
Executive Director, Kathryn (Penny) Vennard Clark, MSW, LCSW
Clergy Services: The Rev. Dr. Dan Bottorff & The Rev. Dr. Richard Crocker

The Liturgical Conference

The Liturgical Conference works to renew liturgy within the churches for the reunion of the Body of Christ for the life of the world.

As an ongoing movement with the ecumenical church, founded in 1944, it seeks to provide an ecumenical forum for articulating standards of liturgical excellence and for supporting persons who have a common interest and concern for the liturgical life and the liturgical arts of the church. It is the publisher of the journals Liturgy and Homily Service.

Headquarters
P.O. Box 31, Evanston, IL 60201

Officers
Pres., E. Byron Anderson
Vice Pres., Todd Johnson
Sec., Craig Mueller
Treas., Victor Cinson

Lombard Mennonite Peace Center

The Lombard Mennonite Peace Center (LMPC) is a nonprofit organization with the mission "to proclaim Christ's good news, the gospel of peace and justice—and to be active in the sacred ministry of reconciliation." With an emphasis on equipping clergy and churches to function in healthy ways, LMPC offers training in conflict transformation and in a family systems approach to church leaders' management of themselves and their congregations.

One- and two-day educational workshops and a five-day "Mediation Skills Training Institute for Church Leaders" are offered throughout the United States. Ongoing clergy clinics provide church leaders with regular opportunities to reflect on their own functioning. LMPC also provides educational events, consultation and mediation services for congregations and judicatories of all denominations, as well as consultation for individual clergy.

Founded in 1983 as a ministry of a local congregation, LMPC became an independent, 501(c)3 corporation in 1997.

Headquarters
101 W. 22nd St., Suite 206, Lombard, IL 60148 Tel. (630)627-0507 Fax (630)627-0519, Email: admin@LMPeaceCenter.org, Web: www.LMPeaceCenter.org

Officers
Executive Director, Richard G. Blackburn

35

The Lord's Day Alliance of the United States

The Lord's Day Alliance of the United States, founded in 1888 in Washington, D.C., is the only national organization whose sole purpose is the preservation and cultivation of Sunday, the Lord's Day, as a day of rest and worship. The Alliance also seeks to safeguard a Day of Common Rest for all people regardless of their faith. Its Board of Managers is composed of representatives from 25 denominations. It serves as an information bureau, publishes a magazine, Sunday, and furnishes speakers and a variety of materials such as pamphlets, videos, posters, radio spot announcements, cassettes, news releases, articles for magazines and television programs.

Headquarters

2930 Flowers Rd. S., Atlanta, GA 30341-5532 Tel. (770)936-5376 or (800)746-4422 x 376 Fax (770)936-5385, Email: tnorton@1dausa. org, Web: www.sundayonline.org
Media Contact, Exec. Dir. & Ed., Rev. Timothy A. Norton

Officers

Pres., Dr. Roger A. Kvam
Pres. Emeritus, Paul J. Craven
Senior Vice Pres., Wendell J. Schaal
Vice Pres., Brian W. Hanse, David C. McNair, Eugene J. Nicodemus, W. David Sapp, William B. Shea
Sec., Donald R. Pepper
Asst. Sec., Betty Jo Craft
Trea., E. Larry Eidson

Lutheran World Relief

Lutheran World Relief (LWR) is an overseas development and relief agency based in Baltimore which responds quickly to natural and man-made disasters and supports more than 160 long-range development projects in countries throughout Africa, Asia, the Middle East and Latin America.

As its mission, Lutheran World Relief works with partners in 50 countries to help people grow food, improve health, strengthen communities, end conflict, build livelihoods, and recover from disasters.

Headquarters

700 Light Street, Baltimore, MD 21230-3850 Tel. (410)230-2700 Fax (410)230-2882

Officers

Pres., John A. Nunes

The Mennonite Central Committee

The Mennonite Central Committee is the relief and service agency of North American Mennonite and Brethren in Christ Churches. Representatives from Mennonite and Brethren in Christ groups make up the MCC, which meets annually in June to review its program and to approve policies and budget. Founded in 1920, MCC administers and participates in programs of agricultural and economic development, education, health, self-help, relief, peace and disaster service. MCC has about 1000 workers serving in 55 countries in Africa, Asia, Europe, Middle East and South, Central and North America.

MCC has service programs in North America that focus both on urban and rural poverty areas. There are also North American programs focusing on such diverse matters as community conciliation, employment creation and criminal justice issues. These programs are administered by two national bodies-MCC U.S. and MCC Canada.

Contributions from North American Mennonite and Brethren in Christ provide the largest part of MCC's support. Other sources of financial support include the contributed earnings of volunteers, grants from private and government agencies and contributions from Mennonite churches abroad. The total income in FYE2004, including material aid contributions, amounted to $69.4million (US dollars).

MCC tries to strengthen local communities by working in cooperation with local churches or other community groups. Many personnel are placed with other agencies, including missions. Programs are planned with sensitivity to locally felt needs.

Headquarters

21 S. 12th St., P.O. Box 500, Akron, PA 17501-0500 Tel. (717)859-1151 Fax (717)859-2171
Canadian Office, 134 Plaza Dr., Winnipeg, MB R3T 5K9 Tel. (204)261-6381 Fax (204)269-9875
Media Contact, Larry Guengerich, P.O. Box 500, Akron, PA 17501 Tel. (717)859-1151 Fax (717)859-2171

Officers

Exec. Directors., Intl., Ronald J.R. Mathies; Canada, Donald Peters; U.S.A., Rolando Santiago

National Association of Ecumenical and Interreligious Staff

NAEIS is an association of professional staff in ecumenical and interreligious work. Founded as the Association of Council Secretaries in 1940, the Association was widened to include program staff in 1971, and renamed the National Association of Ecumenical Staff. It has included staff of any faith engaged in interreligious work since 1994. NAEIS provides means for personal and professional growth, and for mutual support, through national and regional conferences, a newsletter and exchange among its membership.

NAEIS was established to provide creative relationships among them and to encourage mutual support and personal and professional growth. This is accomplished through training programs, through exchange and discussion of common concerns at conferences, and through the publication of the Corletter, in collaboration with NCCC Ecumenical Networks.

Headquarters

Best reached through Janet Leng, Membership Officer, P.O.Box 7093, Tacoma, WA 98406-0093 Tel. (253)759-0142, Email: naeisjan@aol.com

Officers

Pres., 2005-2007: The Rev. Samuel Muyskens, Interfaith Ministers–Wichita, 820 North Market Street, Wichita, KS 67214-1157 Tel. (512)451-2062, Email: smuyskens@ifmnet.org

Vice Pres., 2005-2007: Mr. Marcus White, Exec. Dir., Interfaith Conference of Greater Milwaukee, 1442 N. Farwell Ave., Ste 200, Milwaukee, WI 53202 Tel. (414)276-9050, Email: marcusifc@sbcglobal.com

Immediate Past Pres.: Barbara White, Social Services, Church of God in Christ, 3500 W. Mother Daniels' Way, Milwaukee, WI 53209 Tel. (414)466-1800, Email: uniquebarbara@hotmail.com

Sec., 2005-2007: The Rev. Dr. Clark Lobenstine, Exec. Dir., Interfaith Conference of Metropolitan Washington, 1426 Ninth St. NW, 2nd Floor, Washington, DC 20001-3330 Tel. (202) 234-6300, Email: clarkifc@aol.com

Treas., 2005-2007: Ms. Lisa H. Mitchell, Grand Rapids Center for Ecumenism, 207 Fulton St., Grand Rapids, MI 49503 Tel. (616)774-2042. Email: lmitchell@graceoffice.org

The National Association of Evangelicals

The National Association of Evangelicals (NAE) is a voluntary fellowship of evangelical denominations, churches, organizations and individuals demonstrating unity in the body of Christ by standing for biblical truth, speaking with a representative voice, and serving the evangelical community through united action, cooperative ministry and strategic planning.

The association is comprised of approximately 45,000 congregations nationwide from 52 member denominations and fellowships, as well as several hundred independent churches. The membership of the association includes over 250 parachurch ministries and educational institutions. Through the cooperative ministry of these members, NAE directly and indirectly benefits over 30 million people. These ministries represent a broad range of theological traditions, but all subscribe to the distinctly evangelical NAE Statement of Faith. The association is a nationally recognized entity by the public sector with a reputation for integrity and effective service.

The cooperative ministries of the National Association of Evangelicals demonstrate the association's intentional desire to promote cooperation without compromise.

Headquarters

NAE-Washington, 701 G. St., SW, Washington, DC 20024 Tel. (202)789-1011 Fax (202)842-0392

Media Contact, Rev. Rich Cizik, (202)789-1011

Officers

President, Rev. Leith Anderson

Vice President of Governmental Affairs, Rev. Rich Cizik

National Bible Association

The National Bible Association is an autonomous, interfaith organization of lay people who advocate regular Bible reading and sponsors National Bible Week (Thanksgiving week) each November. Program activities include public service advertising, distribution of nonsectarian literature and thousands of local Bible Week observances by secular and religious organizations. The Association also urges constitutionally acceptable use of the Bible in public school classrooms, i.e.the study of the Bible in literature. All support comes from individuals, corporations and foundations.

Founded in 1940 by a group of business and professional people, the Association offers daily Bible readings in several English and Spanish translations on its website and has the IRS nonprofit status of a 501(c)(3) educational association.

Headquarters

1865 Broadway, New York, NY 10023 Tel. (212)408-1390 Fax (212)408-1448

Media Contact, Pres., Thomas R. May

Officers

Cpsn., Philip J. Clements

Vice Cpsns.; Robert Cavalero; John W. Pugsley; John M. Templeton,Jr., M.D.

Pres., Thomas R. May

Treas., Paul Werner

Sec., J. Marshall Gage

The National Conference for Community and Justice

The National Conference for Community and Justice, founded in 1927 as the National Conference of Christians and Jews, is a human relations organization dedicated to fighting bias, bigotry and racism in America. The NCCJ promotes understanding and respect among all races, religions and cultures through advocacy, conflict resolution and education.

Programmatic strategies include interfaith and interracial dialogue, youth leadership workshops, workplace training, human relations research, and the building of community coalitions. NCCJ has 65 regional offices staffed by approximately 350 people. Nearly 200 members comprise the

37

National Board of Advisors and members from that group form the 27-member National Board of Directors. Each regional office has its own Regional Board of Directors with a total of about 2,800. The National Board of Advisors meets once annually, the National Board of Directors at least three times annually.

Headquarters
328 Flatbush Ave., Brooklyn, NY 11217 Tel. (718)783-0044 Fax (718)783-4143

Media Contact, Dir. of Communications, Diane Powers

Officers
Pres. & CEO, Sanford Cloud, Jr.

National Conference on Ministry to the Armed Forces

The Conference is an incorporated civilian agency. Representation in the Conference with all privileges of the same is open to all endorsing or certifying agencies or groups authorized to provide chaplains for any branch of the Armed Forces.

The purpose of this organization is to provide a means of dialogue to discuss concerns and objectives and, when agreed upon, to take action with the appropriate authority to support the spiritual ministry to and the moral welfare of Armed Forces personnel.

Headquarters
4141 N. Henderson Rd., Ste. 13, Arlington, VA 22203 Tel. (703)276-7905 Fax (703)276-7906

Media Contact, Jack Williamson

Officers
Chpsn., David Peterson
Chpsn.-elect, Robert Jemerson
Sec., Lemuel Boyles
Treas., John Murdoch

STAFF
Coord., Jack Williamson
Admn. Asst., Maureen Francis

National Council of the Churches of Christ in the U.S.A.

The National Council of the Churches of Christ in the U.S.A. is the preeminent expression in the United States of the movement toward Christian unity. The NCC's 35 member communions, including Protestant, Orthodox and Anglican church bodies, work together on a wide range of activities that further Christian unity, that witness to the faith, that promote peace and justice and that serve people throughout the world. Approximately 44 million U.S. Christians belong to churches that hold Council membership. The Council was formed in 1950 in Cleveland, Ohio, by the action of representatives of the member churches and by the merger of 12 previously existing ecumenical agencies, each of which had a different program focus. The roots of some of these agencies go back to the 19th century.

Headquarters
475 Riverside Dr., New York, NY 10115. Tel. (212)870-2141

Media Contact, Philip E. Jenks Media Relations Specialist, Tel. (212)870-2228 Fax (212)870-2030, Email: nccnews@nccusa.org Website: www.councilofchurches.org

General Officers
Pres., Archbishop Vicken Aykazian
Gen. Sec., The Rev. Dr. Michael Kinnamon
Pres.Elect, The Rev. Peg Chemberlin
Immediate Past Pres., The Rev. Michael E. Livingston
Sec., The Rev. José Luis Casal
Vice Pres., The Rev. Dr. Cheryl Wade
Vice Pres., The Right Rev. Johncy Itty
Vice Pres. at Large, Mr. Stan Noffsinger
Vice Pres. at Large, The Rev. Dr. Raymon E. Hunt

THE GENERAL SECRETARIAT
General Secretary, The Rev. Dr. Michael Kinnamon, Tel. (212)870-2141 Fax (212)870-2817

ADMINISTRATION AND FINANCE
Chief Operating Officer, Ms. Clare J. Chapman, Tel. (212)870-3366
Controller, Ms. Karen Wang, Tel. (212) 870-3351
Assistant Director of Administration and Human Resources, Ms. Joan Gardner, Tel. (212)870-3112
Database Administrator, The Rev. Marcel A. Welty, Tel. (212)870-2379

ORGANIZATIONAL DEVELOPMENT
Director of Organizational Development, The Rev. Dr. Eileen W. Lindner, Tel. (212)870-2333

YEARBOOK OF AMERICAN & CANADIAN CHURCHES
Editor, The Rev. Dr. Eileen W. Lindner, Tel. (212)870-2333
Assoc. Ed., The Rev. Marcel A. Welty, Tel. (212) 870-2379
Asst. Ed., Mr. Tenny Thomas, Tel. (212)870-2031 Fax (212)870-2817
Asst. to the Ed., Mr. Earl Davis, Tel. (212) 870-2333

WASHINGTON OFFICE
110 Maryland Ave. NE Washington, D.C. 20002 Tel. (202)544-2350 Fax (202)543-1297

EDUCATION AND LEADERSHIP MINISTRIES COMMISSION
Senior Program Director, The Rev. Garland Pierce, Tel. (212)870-2267

FAITH AND ORDER AND INTERFAITH RELATIONS COMMISSION
Senior Program Director, Dr. Antonios Kireopoulos, Tel. (212)870-3422

JUSTICE, ADVOCACY AND COMMUNICATION COMMISSION

Senior Program Director, Mr. Wesley M. Pattillo, Tel. (212)870-2227 Fax (212)870-2030

Media Relations Specialist, Mr. Philip E. Jenks, Tel. (212)870-2228

Coord. of Television Programming, Ms. Shirley W. Struchen, Tel. (212)870-2227

Eco-Justice Programs, Dir., Ms. Cassandra Carmichael, Tel. (202)544-2350 x 205

Eco-Justice Programs, Asst. Dir., Mr. Jordan Blevins. Tel. (202)481-6943

Progam for Women's Ministry, Dir., Rev. Ann Tiemeyer, Tel. (212)870-3407

RELATED ORGANIZATIONS

Agricultural Missions, Dr. Winston Carroo, Exec. Dir., Tel. (212)870-2554

Interfaith Center for Corporate Responsibility, Sr. Patricia Wolf, RSM Exec. Dir., Tel. (212)870-2295

Natl. Farm Worker Ministry, Executive Director, Ms. Virginia Nesmith, 438 N. Skinner Blvd., St. Louis, MO 63130 Tel. (314)726-6470

CHURCH WORLD SERVICE AND WITNESS

Chair, The Right Rev. Johncy Itty

First Vice Pres., Ms. Deborah Bass

Second Vice Pres., Rev. Canon Benjamin Musoke-Lubega

Treasurer, The Rev. Jimmie Hawkins

Secretary, The Rev. Jennifer Riggs

Immediate Past Chair, Ms. Betty Voskuil

CEO and Executive Director, The Rev. John L. McCullough, Tel. (212)870-2175

Senior Advisor to the Exec. Dir., The Rev. Dr. Cheryl Dudley, Tel. (212)870-2669

Senior Advisor to the Exec. Dir., Mr. David Weaver, Tel. (212)870-2818

Deputy Dir., Operations and CFO, Ms. Joanne Rendall, Tel. (574)264-3102

Deputy Dir., Programs, Mr. Maurice Bloem, Tel. (212)870-2798

Dir., Dev., The Rev. William Wildey, Tel. (574)264-3102

Chief Dev. Officer, Mr. Reginald Ingram, Tel. (626)798-4511

Dir., Human Resources, Mr. Bernard Kirchhoff, Tel. (574)264-3102

Interim Dir., Mission Relationships & Witness Program, The Rev. Dr. Cheryl Dudley, Tel. (212)870-2643

Dir., Education & Advocacy for International Justice & Human Rights Program, Ms. Rajyashri Waghray, Tel. (212)870-2497

Interim Dir., Social and Economic Development Program, Mr. Richard Williams, Tel. (212)870-2372

Dir., Emergency Response Program, Ms. Donna Derr, Tel. (212)870-3151/ (202)544-2350

Dir., Immigration & Refugee Program, The Rev. Joseph Roberson, Tel. (212)870-2178

Dir, Marketing and Communications, Ms. Ann Walle, Tel. (212)870-2654

CONSTITUENT BODIES
(with membership dates)

African Methodist Episcopal Church (1950)

African Methodist Episcopal Zion Church (1950)

The Alliance of Baptists in the U.S.A. (2000)

American Baptist Churches in the U.S.A. (1950)

Armenian Apostolic Church, Diocese of the (1957)

Christian Church (Disciples of Christ) (1950)

Christian Methodist Episcopal Church (1950)

Church of the Brethren (1950)

Coptic Orthodox Church (1978)

The Episcopal Church (1950)

Evangelical Lutheran Church in America (1950)

Friends United Meeting (1950)

Greek Orthodox Archdiocese of America (1952)

Hungarian Reformed Church in America (1957)

Intl. Council of Community Churches (1977)

Korean Presbyterian Church in America, Gen. Assembly of the (1986)

Malankara Orthodox Syrian Church, Diocese of America (1998)

Mar Thoma Church (1997)

Moravian Church in America, Northern Province, Southern Province (1950)

National Baptist Convention of America, Inc. (1950)

National Baptist Convention, U.S.A., Inc. (1950)

National Missionary Baptist Convention of America (1995)

Orthodox Church in America (1950)

Philadelphia Yearly Meeting of the Religious Society of Friends (1950)

Polish Natl. Catholic Church of America (1957)

Presbyterian Church (U.S.A.) (1950)

Progressive Natl. Baptist Convention, Inc. (1966)

Reformed Church in America (1950)

Russian Orthodox Church in the U.S.A., Patriarchal Parishes of the (1966)

Serbian Orthodox Church in the U.S.A. & Canada (1957)

The Swedenborgian Church (1966)

Syrian (Syriac) Orthodox Church of Antioch (Archdiocese of the U.S. and Canada) (1960)

Ukrainian Orthodox Church of the U.S.A.(1950)

United Church of Christ (1950)

The United Methodist Church (1950)

National Institute of Business and Industrial Chaplains

NIBIC is the professional organization for workplace chaplains, that includes members from a wide variety of faith groups and work settings, including corporations, manufacturing plants, air and sea ports, labor unions and pastoral counseling centers. NIBIC has six membership categories, including Certified, Clinical, Professional, Affiliates and Organizational.

NIBIC works to establish professional standards for education and practice; promotes and conducts training programs; provides mentoring,

39

networking and chaplaincy information; encourages research and public information dissemination; communicates with business leaders and conducts professional meetings. NIBIC publishes a quarterly newsletter and co-sponsors The Journal of Pastoral Care and Counseling. A public membership meeting and training conference is held annually. NIBIC provides certification for qualified clinical members.

Headquarters
1900 St. James Place, Suite 880, Houston, TX 77056 Tel. (713)266-2456 Fax (713)266-0845
Media Contact, Rev. Diana C. Dale, D.Min., 1900 St. James Place, Suite 880 Houston, TX 77056 Tel. (713)266-2456 Fax (713)266-0845

Officers
Executive Dir., Rev. Diana C. Dale, D.Min.
President, Rev. Robert L. Lewis, Jr., STM
Vice Pres., Rev. Dr. Juliette Jones
Treas., Rev. Gregory Edwards Board Member, Timothy Bancroft, D.Min.

National Interfaith Cable Coalition, Inc. (NICC)

The National Interfaith Cable Coalition, Inc. (NICC) was formed as a not-for-profit 501(c)3 corporation, in December 1987, and is currently comprised of more than 40 faith groups and organizations from the Jewish and Christian traditions. In September 1988, NICC launched a religious cable network called VISN (Vision Interfaith Satellite Network), later known as the Odyssey Network. Now known as the Hallmark Channel, it is owned and operated by Crown Media Holdings, Inc., in which NICC is a strategic investor. NICC provides regular and prime-time special programming on the network. In 2000, NICC adopted Faith & Values Media as its service mark and expanded its mission to include a significant Web presence, www.FaithStreams.com, which features streaming video and video-on-demand service.

Headquarters
74 Trinity Place, Ste. 1550, New York, NY 10006 Tel. (212)406-4121 Fax (212)406-4105
Media Contact, Christine Luzano

Officers
Chair, Dr. Daniel Paul Matthews
Vice Chair, Elder Ralph Hardy Jr., Esq.
Secretary, Rabbi Daniel Freelander
Treasurer, Betty Elam

Staff
President and CEO, Edward J. Murray
Exec. Vice President, Beverly Judge

National Interfaith Coalition on Aging

National Interfaith Coalition on Aging (NICA), a constituent unit of the National Council on Aging, is composed of Protestant, Roman Catholic, Jewish and Orthodox national and regional organizations and individuals concerned about the needs of older people and the religious community's response to problems facing the aging population in the United States. NICA was organized in 1972 to address spiritual concerns of older adults through religious sector action.

Mission Statement—The National Interfaith Coalition on Aging (NICA), affiliated with the National Council on the Aging (NCOA), is a diverse network of religious and other related organizations and individual members which promotes the spiritual well being of older adults and the preparation of persons of all ages for the spiritual tasks of aging. NICA serves as a catalyst for new and effective research, networking opportunities, resource development, service provision, and dissemination of information.

Headquarters
c/o NCOA, 1910 L Street, NW, 4th Floor, Washington, DC 20036 Tel. (202)479-6655 Fax (202)479-0735
Media Contact, Rita Chow, Ed.D.

Officers
Chpsn., Rev. Ronald Field
Chpsn.-Elect, Beth Schwartz
Past Chpsn., Jane Stenson
Sec., Donald R. Koepke
Dir., Dr. Rita K. Chow

National Religious Broadcasters

National Religious Broadcasters is an association of Christian communicators, 1,500 organizations which produce religious programs for radio and television and other forms of electronic mass media or operate stations carrying predominately religious programs. NRB member organizations are responsible for more than 75 percent of all religious radio and television in the United States, reaching an average weekly audience of millions by radio, television, and other broadcast media.

Dedicated to the communication of the Gospel, NRB was founded in 1944 to safeguard free and complete access to the broadcast media. By encouraging the development of Christian programs and stations, NRB helps make it possible for millions to hear the good news of Jesus Christ through the electronic media.

Headquarters
9510 Technology Drive, Manassas, VA 20110. Tel. (703)330-7000 Fax (703)330-7100
Media Contact, Pres., Dr. Frank Wright

Officers
Chmn., Ron. L. Harris
1st Vice Chmn., Janet Parshall
2nd Vice Chair: John Fuller
Sec.: Richard Bott
Treas.: Roger Kemp

National Woman's Christian Temperance Union

The National WCTU is a not-for-profit, non-partisan, interdenominational organization dedicated to the education of our nation's citizens, especially children and teens, on the harmful effects of alcoholic beverages, other drugs and tobacco on the human body and the society in which we live. The WCTU believes in a strong family unit and, through legislation, education and prayer, works to strengthen the home and family.

WCTU, which began in 1874 with the motto, "For God and Home and Every Land," is organized in 58 countries.

Headquarters

1730 Chicago Ave., Evanston, IL 60201 Tel. (708)864-1396
Media Contact, Sarah F. Ward Tel. 765-345-7600

Officers

Pres., Sarah F. Ward, 33 N. Franklin, Knightstown, IN 46148 Email: sarah@wctu.org
Vice Pres., Rita Wert, 2250 Creek Hill Rd., Lancaster, PA 17601
Promotion Dir., Nancy Zabel, 1730 Chicago Ave., Evanston, IL 60201-4585
Treas., Faye Pohl, P.O. Box 739, Meade, KS 67864
Rec. Sec., Dorothy Russell, 18900 Nestueca Dr., Cloverdale, OR 97112
MEMBER ORGANIZATIONS
Loyal Temperance Legion (LTL), for boys and girls ages 6-12
Youth Temperance Council (YTC), for teens through college age

North American Baptist Fellowship

Organized in 1964, the North American Baptist Fellowship is a voluntary organization of Baptist Conventions in Canada and the United States, functioning as a regional body within the Baptist World Alliance. Its objectives are, (a) to promote fellowship and cooperation among Baptists in North America and (b) to further the aims and objectives of the Baptist World Alliance so far as these affect the life of the Baptist churches in North America. Its membership, however, is not identical with the North American membership of the Baptist World Alliance.

Church membership of the Fellowship bodies is more than 28 million.

The NABF assembles representatives of the member bodies once a year for exchange of information and views in such fields as evangelism and education, missions, stewardship promotion, lay activities and theological education. It conducts occasional consultations for denominational leaders on such subjects as church extension. It encourages cooperation at the city and county level where churches of more than one member group are located.

Headquarters

P.O. Box 6412, Falls Church, VA 22040
Media Contact, Gen. Sec., Rev. Alan Stanford, Ph.D. Tel. (703)655-9696

Officers

Pres., Dr. David Emmanuel Goatley, 300 I Street, NE, Suite 104, Washington D.C. 20002
Vice Pres., Dr. Derrick Harkins, 4606 16th St. NW, Washington, DC 20011
Vice Pres., Mrs. Bertha Williams, 13520 Corby Rd., Cleveland, OH 44120
Vice Pres., Dr. Ken Belous, 414-195, The West Mall, Etobicoke, ON M9C5K1, Canada Vice Pres., Dr. Don Sewell, 333 N. Washington St., Dallas, TX 75246-1798

Oikocredit—Ecumenical Development Cooperative Society

Based in the Netherlands, EDCS is often called "the churches' bank for the poor." EDCS borrows funds from churches, religious communities and concerned individuals and re-lends the funds to enterprises operated by low-income communities. Launched in 1975 through an initiative of the World Council of Churches, EDCS is organized as a cooperative of religious institutions and is governed by annual membership meetings and an elected board of religious leaders and development and financial professionals.

An international network of 15 EDCS Regional Managers is responsible for lending funds to cooperative enterprises and microcredit institutions. At the present time over $400 million is at work in coffee shops, fishing enterprises, handicraft production, truck farming, and many other commercial ventures owned and operated by poor people.

EDCS is represented in the United States by the Ecumenical Development Corporation-USA (EDC-USA), a 501(c)3 non-profit corporation. American individuals and congregations can invest in EDCS by purchasing one, three, and five year notes paying 0-2% interest that are issued by EDC-USA.

U.S. HEADQUARTERS

P.O. Box 11000, Washington, D.C. 20008 Tel. (202)265-0607 Fax (202)265-7029, Email: office.us@oikocredit.org, Website: oikocredit.org
Media Contact, Regional Manager for North America, Rev. Terry Provance

OFFICERS, EDCS-USA

Exec. Dir., Rev. Terry Provance
Chair, John Paarlberg
Treas., Richard Gist

Parish Resource Center, Inc.

Parish Resource Center, Inc. promotes, establishes, nurtures and accredits local Affiliate Parish Resource Centers. Affiliate

41

centers educate, equip and strengthen subscribing congregations of all faiths by providing professional consultants, resource materials and workshops. The Parish Resource Center was founded in 1976. In 2006, there were four free-standing affiliates located in Lancaster, PA; Long Island, NY; Denver, CO.; and New York City. These centers serve congregations from 49 faith traditions.

Headquarters

633 Community Way, Lancaster, PA 17603 Tel. (717)299-2223 Fax (717)299-7229
Media Contact, Pres., Dr. D. Douglas Whiting

Officers

Chair, Dr. Robert D. Webber
Vice Chair, Rev. Sidney Lovett
Sec./Treas., David P. Harrison
Pres., Dr. D. Douglas Whiting

Pentecostal-Charismatic Churches of North America

The Pentecostal-Charismatic Churches of North America (PCCNA) was organized October 19, 1994, in Memphis TN. This organizational meeting came the day after the Pentecostal Fellowship of North America (PFNA) voted itself out of existence in order to make way for the new fellowship.

The PFNA had been formed in October 1948 in Des Moines, IA. It was composed of white-led Pentecostal denominations. The move to develop a multiracial fellowship began when the PFNA Board of Administration initiated a series of discussions with African-American Pentecostal leaders. The first meeting was held July 10-11, 1992, in Dallas, TX. A second meeting convened in Phoenix, AZ, January 4-5, 1993. On January 10-11, 1994, 20 representatives from each of the two groups met in Memphis to make final plans for a Dialogue which was held in Memphis, October 1994.

This racial reconciliation meeting has been called "The Memphis Miracle." During this meeting the PFNA was disbanded, and the PCCNA was organized. The new organization quickly adopted the "Racial Reconciliation Manifesto." Subsequent meetings were held in Memphis, TN (1996), Washington, DC (1997), Tulsa, OK (1998), and Hampton, VA (1999)

In an effort to further increase the spirit of reconciliation, the PCCNA meeting of 2000 was held during the North American Renewal Service committee (NARSC) Conference in St. Louis, Missouri. Furthermore, the PCCNA acted as host for the 19th Pentecostal World Conference held in Los Angeles, California, May 2001.

Headquarters

1445 N. Boonville Ave., Springfield, MO 65802 Tel. (417)862-2781 x 3010 Fax (417)683-6614, Email: PCCNA@ag.org
Media Contact, Dr. Charles Crabtree

PCCNA EXECUTIVE BOARD

Chairperson, Dr. Charles T. Crabtree, General Council of the Assemblies of God, 1445 N. Boonville Ave., Springfield, MO 65802 Tel. (417)862-2781 x 3010 Fax (417)683-6614, Email: PCCNA@ag.org
Co-Chairperson, Bishop Jerry Macklin, Church of God in Christ, 1027 W. Tennyson Rd, Hayward, CA 94544 Tel. (510)783-9377 Fax (510)783-8673, Email: PastorJWM@aol.com
Secretary, Dr. R. Lamar Vest, Church of God, P.O. Box 2430, Cleveland, TN 37320-2430 Tel. (423)478-7308 Fax (423)478-7334
Treasurer, Bishop Randy Howard, Church of God of Prophecy, P.O. Box 2910, Cleveland, TN 37320-2910 Tel. (423)559-5203 Fax (423)472-5037 Email: wmcogop@aol.com

EXECUTIVE COMMITTEE MEMBERS-AT-LARGE

Dr. Ron Carpenter, International Pentecostal Holiness Church, P.O. Box 12690, Oklahoma City, OK 73157
Rev. Daniel de Leon, Templo Calvario, 261 W. 5th St, Santa Ana, CA 92703
Rev. Jeff Farmer, Open Bible Churches, 2020 Bell Ave, Des Moines, IA 50315
Rev. Art Gray, International Church of the Foursquare Gospel, 1910 W. Sunset Blvd; Ste 200, Los Angeles, CA 90026
Bishop Clyde Hughes, International Pentecostal Church of Christ, P.O. Box 439, London, OH 43130
Dr. William Morrow, Pentecostal Assemblies of Canada, 2459 Milltower Ct., Mississauga, ON L5N 5Z6
Bishop Elijah Williams, The United Holy Church of America, 901 Briarwood St., Reidsville, NC 27320

Project Equality, Inc.

Project Equality is a national, non-profit, interfaith program for affirmative action and equal employment opportunity. Through a Buyer's Guide that is provided to sponsoring organizations and individuals, Project Equality serves as a registry for suppliers of goods and services who commit to equal employment practices. This allows members and friends to economically support those who practice equality and justice with their employees. Project Equality also provides consultation and training for workplace diversity, does EEO audits, and is a resource for Human Resource practices. Project Equality is a leader in creating inclusive and just communities.

Headquarters

7132 Main St., Kansas City, MO 64114-1406 Tel. (816) 361-9222 Fax (816) 361-8997

Officers

Board Chair, Salvador Mendoza
Interim Executive Director, Cathleen D. Cackler-Veazey, Ph.D.

The Religion Communicators Council, Inc.

RCC is an interfaith, interdisciplinary association of professional communicators who work for religious groups and causes. It was founded in 1929 and is the oldest non-profit professional public relations/communications organization in the world. RCC's more than 600 members include those who work in communications and related fields for church-related institutions, denominational agencies, non-and interdenominational organizations and communications firms who primarily serve religious organizations.

Members represent a wide range of faiths, including Presbyterian, Baptist, United Methodist, Lutheran, Episcopalian, Mennonite, Roman Catholic, Seventh-day Adventist, Jewish, Salvation Army, Brethren, Bahá'í, Disciples, Muslim, Latter-Day Saints and others.

On the national level, RCC sponsors an annual three-day convention, and has published seven editions of a Religious Public Relations Handbook for churches and church organizations, and a videostrip, The Church at Jackrabbit Junction. Members receive a quarterly newsletter (Counselor). There are 13 regional chapters.

RCC administers the annual Wilbur Awards competition to recognize high quality coverage of religious values and issues in the public media. Wilbur winners include producers, reporters, editors and broadcasters nationwide. To recognize communications excellence within church communities, RCC also sponsors the annual DeRose-Hinkhouse Awards for its own members.

In 1970, 1980, 1990, 2000, and in planning form April 7 - 10, 2010 (www.rccongres2010. org). RCC initiated a global Religious Communications Congress bringing together thousands of persons from western, eastern and third-world nations who are involved in communicating religious faith.

Headquarters

475 Riverside Dr., Rm. 1355, New York, NY 10115 Tel. (212)870-2985 Fax (212)870-2171 Exec. Dir., Shirley Whipple Struchen, Tel. (212) 870-2402, Email:sstruchen@rcn.com, Web: www.religiouncommunicators.org

Officers

President., Philip Poole, Exec. Dir., University Communications, Samford Univ., 800 Lakeshore Dr., Birmingham, AL 35229 Tel. (205) 726-2823 Fax: (205)726-4044 Email: ppoole @samford.edu

Vice Pres., Ellen W. Price, Asst. Dir., Communications, US. Bahai National Center, 1233 Central St., Evanston, IL 60201 Tel. (847)733-3559 Fax. (847)733-3430, Email: Eprice@usbwc.orgSec., Barry Creech, Coordinator, Information & Planning, Presbyterian Church (USA), 100 Witherspoon St., #5430,

Louisville, 40202-1396 Tel. (502) 569-5127 Fax (502) 569-8099, Email: barry.creech@ pcusa.org

Treas., Dan Gangler, Director of Communications, Indiana Area UMC, 1100 West 42nd St., #210 Indianapolis, IN 46208 Tel. (317)924-1321 x 18 Fax (317)924-4859 Email: dgangler@inareaumc.org

Religion In American Life, Inc.

Religion In American Life (RIAL) is a unique cooperative program of some 50 major national religious groups (Catholic, Eastern Orthodox, Jewish, Protestant, Muslim, etc.). It provides services for denominationally-supported, congregation-based outreach and growth projects such as the current Invite a Friend program. These projects are promoted through national advertising campaigns reaching the American public by the use of all media. The ad campaigns are produced by a volunteer agency with production-distribution and administration costs funded by denominations and business groups, as well as by individuals.

Since 1949, RIAL ad campaign projects have been among the much coveted major campaigns of The Advertising Council. This results in as much as $35 million worth of time and space in a single year, contributed by media as a public service. Through RIAL, religious groups demonstrate respect for other traditions and the value of religious freedom. The RIAL program also includes seminars and symposia, research and leadership awards and produces a weekly syndicated radio broadcast, "SpiriTalk."

Headquarters

250 E 87th St., Suite 12F, New York, NY 10128-3116 Tel. (203)355-1220 Fax (203)355-1221 Media Contact, Exec. Admin., Martha Mesiti Tel (203)355-1220

EXECUTIVE COMMITTEE

Natl. Chpsn., Thomas S. Johnson, Chairman & CEO, Greenpoint Bank, NY

Chpsn. of Bd., Rev. Dr. Gordon Sommers

Vice-Chpsns., Bishop Khajag Barsamian, Primate (Armenian Church of America); Most Rev. William Cardinal Keeler, (Archbishop, Catholic Church); Rabbi Ronald B. Sobel, (Cong. Emanu-El of the City of N.Y.)

Sec.,Timothy A. Hultquist (Morgan Stanley Dean Witter)

Treas., Robertson H. Bennett (Smith Barney)

STAFF

Pres. & CEO, Robert B. Lennick, Rabbi, D.Min.
Exec. Admin., Martha Mesiti

Religion News Service

Religion News Service (RNS) has provided news and information to the media for over 70 years. Owned by Newhouse News Service, it is staffed by veteran jounalists who cover stories on

43

all of the world religions as well as trends in ethics, morality and spirituality.

RNS provides a daily news service, a weekly news service, and photo and graphic services. The daily service is also available via the AP Data Features wire, or email. The weekly report is available by wire or email. RNS's Photos Service features stock images, news photography and related graphics. RNS also offers Religion Press Release Services, which distributes press releases and advisories to religion editors. RNS is syndicated in the United States by Universal Press Syndicate and in Canada by Canadian Press.

Headquarters
1101 Connecticut Ave. NW, Ste. 350, Washington, DC 20036 Tel. (202)463-8777 Fax (202)463-0033, Email: info@religionnews.com, Web: www.religionnews.com

Officers
Editor, Kevin Eckstrom

Religion Newswriters Association and Foundation

Founded in 1949, the RNA is a professional association of journalist who write and edit about religion in the general circulating news media. It sponsors annual contests, conferences, online tools and Religion links. It also offers the Lilly Scholarships in Religion to journalists in the US and Canada to take religion courses of their choice. Annual meetings are held in the fall.

Our Mission: To promote excellence in religion reporting in the news media.

Our Vision: RNA will achieve its mission by providing education and other resources for its members by raising awareness of the importance of religion coverage in the secular media.

Headquarters
P.O. Box 2037, Westerville, OH 43086 Tel. (614)891-9001 Fax (614)891-9774, Email: mason@RNA.com, Web: www.RNA.org or www.religionlink.org

Media Contact, Exec. Dir., Debra Mason

Religions for Peace-USA, Inc.

Religions for Peace-USA, formerly the United States Conference of Religions for Peace, began in the 1970s as a program area and chapter of the World Conference of Religions for Peace (now known simply as Religions for Peace), the world's largest representative interreligious organization. Today, the organization is separately incorporated and registered as an independent 501(c)(3) and focuses its mandate on U.S.-based issues, while retaining a strong link to the international work of the Religions for Peace. As the largest and most broadly based representative multi-religious forum in the United States, RFP-USA engages the religious leaders and experts in interreligious affairs and peace

and justice of more than 50 religious traditions. By building on the spiritual, human, and institutional resources of these communities, RFP-USA establishes cooperative efforts among them to address shared challenges. Primary areas of concern for the organization include building interreligious relationships, creating mutual understanding amidst the country's increasing diversity, and advocating for the responsibility of the United States as a citizen of the global community, with particular regard to peace, human rights, and development.

Headquarters
RFP-USA, 777 United Nations Plaza, 9th Floor, New York, NY 10017 Tel. (212)338-9140 Fax (212)983-0566

Officers
Sec. Gen./Executive Dir., Rev. Bud Heckman, Email: bheckman@rfpusa.org

Moderator, The Very Rev. Leonid Kishkovsky

Religious Conference Management Association, Inc.

The Religious Conference Management Association, Inc. (RCMA) is an interfaith, nonprofit, professional organization of men and women who have responsibility for planning and-or managing meetings, seminars, conferences, conventions, assemblies or other gatherings for religious organizations.

Founded in 1972, RCMA is dedicated to promoting the highest professional performance by its members and associate members through the mutual exchange of ideas, techniques and methods.

Today RCMA has nearly 3,400 members who plan over 17,000 conventions and meetings that annually attract 13.2 million attendees.

The association conducts an annual conference and exposition that provides a forum for its membership to gain increased knowledge in the arts and sciences of religious meeting planning and management.

RCMA publishes a bi-monthly magazine, Religious Conference Manager; a conference daily, RCMA Highlights; plus a monthly e-newsletter.

Headquarters
One RCA Dome, Ste. 120, Indianapolis, IN 46225 Tel. (317)632-1888 Fax (317)632-7909, Web: www.RCMAWEB.ORG

Media Contact, Exec. Dir., Dr. DeWayne S. Woodring

Officers
Pres., Rev. Thomas M. Jackson, United Pentecostal Church International, 8855 Dunn Rd., Hazelwood, MO 63042

Vice Pres., Ms. Marcia Bullock, Jamaica Tourist Board, 5201 Blue Lagoon Dr., Ste.670, Miami, FL 33126

Sec.-Treas., Dr. Melvin Worthington, Natl.

Assoc. of Free Will Baptists, 4878 Ayden Golf Club Rd., Ayden, NC 28513
Exec. Dir., Dr. DeWayne S. Woodring

The Seminary Consortium for Urban Pastoral Education (SCUPE)

Founded in 1976, SCUPE is an interdenominational agency committed to the development of individuals, congregations and organizations for leadership in urban ministry. For individuals, we offer four accredited graduate-level academic programs, the semester- and-or summer-term Graduate Theological Urban Studies program for seminary students; an M.A. in Community Development degree developed in partnership with North Park University; Nurturing the Call, a year-long sequence of graduate courses in theology and ministry for urban pastors who have not previously attended seminary; and Center for African American Theological Studies, an Africentric 3-year M.Div program.

SCUPE also consults to other ministries and urban institutions, providing specially-designed training programs around issues including diversity, strategic planning, leadership development , and human resource mobilization. We operate an urban ministry resource center and publish the Resource Review, as well as other occasional materials, as a service to the urban church. Every two years, SCUPE also organizes the Congress on Urban Ministry as a training and networking event for those in urban ministry.

Headquarters
200 N. Michigan Ave., Suite 502, Chicago, IL 60601 Tel. (312)726-1200 Fax (312)726-0425
Media Contact, President, Dr. David Frenchak; Director of Development, Nancy Renick

Officers
Chair, Rev. Donald Sharp
Vice Chair, Ms. Cheryl Hammock
Treasurer, Mr. Lamont Change
Secretary, Dr. Bill VanWyngaarden
Lead Program Staff
President, Dr. David Frenchak
Co-Directors, M.A. in Community Development, Rev. Carol Ann McGibbon & Dr. Arthur Lyons
Director, Graduate Theological Urban Studies (GTUS), Glenn Martin Klaassen
Director, Center for African American Theological Studies (CAATS), Sean McMillan Director, Nurturing the Call (NtC), Cynthia Milsap
Registrar, Dody Finch

Transnational Association of Christian Colleges and Schools

Transnational Association of Christian Colleges and Schools (TRACS). TRACS was established in 1979 to promote the welfare, interests, and development of postsecondary institutions, whose mission is characterized by a distinctly Christian purpose, as defined in our Foundational Standards. TRACS is a voluntary, non-profit, self-governing organization that provides accreditation to Christian postsecondary institutions offering certificates, diplomas, and/or degrees. TRACS is recognized by the United States Department of Education, the Council for Higher Education Accreditation, and the International Network for Quality Assurance Agencies in Higher Education as a national accrediting body for Christian institutions, colleges, universities, and seminaries. The geographic territory of TRACS currently consists of the United States and its territories.

Headquarters
P.O. Box 328, Forest, Virginia 24551 Tel. (434)525-9539 Fax (434)525-9538, Email: info@tracs.org, Web: www.tracs.org
Media Contact: Exec. Dir., Dr. Russell G. Fitzgerald

Officers
Accreditation Commission Chairman, Dr. Boyd C. Rist
Exec. Dir., Dr. Russell G. Fitzgerald
Assoc. Exec. Dir., Dr. Jeff McCann

United Ministries in Higher Education

United Ministries in Higher Education is a cooperative effort to provide religious programs and services to those engaged in higher education ministries.

Headquarters
7407 Steele Creek Rd., Charlotte, NC 28217 Tel. (704) 588-2182 Fax (704) 588-2182
Media Contact, Res. Sec., Linda Danby Freeman Email: linda_freeman@msn.com

Officers
Treas., Dennis Landon, 11477 Olde Cabin Rd., Suite 310, St. Louis, MO 63141-7130
Personnel Service, Kathy Carson, 117 Alicia Circle Ct., Ballwin, MO 63021
Resource Center, Linda Danby Freeman

United Religions Initiative

The purpose of the United Religions Initiative is to promote enduring, daily interfaith cooperation, to end religiously motivated violence and to create cultures of peace, justice, and healing for the Earth and all living beings.

The United Religions Initiative is a growing, global community of over 130 Cooperation Circles, involving thousands of people around the world. The URI is inspired by the leadership potential inherent in every individual, leadership that is discovered and deepened through dialogue with others when dreams are shared and cooperative destinies are realized. The individuals who

45

make up the URI network are committed to interfaith peacebuilding, recognizing that for peace to prevail on earth, "peace must begin with me." They believe that by talking with others who come from different faiths, cultures or spiritual traditions all involved can begin to better understand their own beliefs and recognize their common bonds.

The URI seeks to create safe spaces throughout the world where these interfaith partnerships can be seeded, and the ideas and initiatives that they spark can be practically applied. With the mandate in the URI Charter that each Cooperation Circle represents at least three different faith traditions, the very act of coming together builds peace by creating interfaith cooperation among neighbors and within communities where it may never before have been possible. The Charter "Guidelines for Action" affirms the "essentially self-organizing nature" of the Cooperation Circles and empowers CC participants to "choose what they want to do" while providing guidance for community building. The Guidelines assure that all URI activities and actions demonstrate the following heartfelt considerations, (a) sharing the wisdom and cultures of different faith traditions; (b) nurturing cultures of healing and peace; (c) upholding human rights; (d) supporting the health of the entire Earth; (e) integrating spirituality in issues of economic justice; and (f) providing grassroot support for all URI activities.

The initial vision for the United Religions Initiative began in 1993 with a dream by its founder, Bishop William Swing. He writes that it came with "a sudden realization that religions, together, have a vocation to be a force for good in the world." In just seven years, tens of thousands of people in more than sixty countries around the world have responded to this vision with a resounding, "Yes!" Their affirmations have taken on a myriad of forms. For example, during the 72 Hours Project at the turn of the Millennium, over a million people in 40 countries participated in 200 projects for peace. Highlights included a 12-day interfaith pilgrimage across Pakistan and the celebration of 1 million signatures on a petition to ban handguns in Rio de Janeiro.

Headquarters

P.O. Box 29242, San Francisco, CA 94129-0242
Tel. (415)561-2300 Fax (415)562-2313
Media Contact, Kristin Swenson

Staff

Executive Director, Rev. Cn Charles P. Gibbs
Peacebuilding, Barbara H. Hartford & Sarah Talcott
Global Fundraising, Philanthropy, Jennifer Kirk & LaTonya Trotter
Membership and Organizational Development, Sally Mahe & Cory Robertson
Visions for Peace Among Religions Project,

Nancy Nielsen
Annual Giving and Knowledge Management, Sarah Talcott
Financial Manager, Ray Signer

GLOBAL COUNCIL

President and Founding Trustee, Bishop William Swing

AFRICA

Malawi, Joyce N'goma
Uganda, Despina Namwembe
Mozambique, Sabapath Alagiah

ASIA

Pakistan, James Channan
Korea, Jinwol Lee
India, Mohinder Singh

EUROPE

Netherlands, Annie Imbens
United Kingdom, Deepak Naik
Germany, Karimah Stauch

LATIN AMERICA AND THE CARIBBEAN

Argentina, Rosalia Guiterrez
Mexico, Jonathan Rose
Chile, Gerardo Gonzalez

MIDDLE EAST

Isreal, George Khory
Isreal, Yehuda Stolov
Egypt, Mohamed Mosaad

MULTI-REGIONAL/NON-GEOGRAPHIC

Yoland Trevino
Jack Lundin
Munirah Shahidi

NORTH AMERICA

United States of America, Don Frew
United States of America, Kay Lindhal
United States of America, Heng Sure

THE PACIFIC

New Zealand, George Armstrong
Philippines, Bonifacio Quirog
Philippines, Shakuntala Moorjani-Vaswani

TRANSITION ADVISORY COMMITTEE

Iftekhar Hai
Rita Semel
Bob Walter

United States Conference for the World Council of Churches

The United States Conference of the World Council of Churches was formed in 1938 when the WCC itself was still in the "Process of Formation." Henry Smith Leiper, an American with many national and international connections, was given the title of "Associate General Secretary" of the WCC and asked to carry out

WCC work in the U.S. After the World Council of Churches was officially born in 1948 in Amsterdam, Netherlands, Leiper raised millions of dollars for WCC programs.

Today the U.S. Conference of the WCC is composed of representatives of U.S. member churches of the worldwide body. The U.S. Office of the WCC works to develop relationships among the churches, advance the work of WCC and interpret the council in the United States.

Headquarters

475 Riverside Dr., Rm. 1371, New York, NY 10115 Tel. (212)870-3260 Fax (212)870-2528

Officers

Moderator: The Rev. Dr. Bernice Powell Jackson
Vice Moderator: Rev. Tyrone Pitts
Vice Moderator and Secretary/Treasurer: Ms. Anne Glynn Mackoul

STAFF
Program Executive for the U.S: Deborah DeWinter, Tel. (212)870-2522
Program Assistant: Jim Stokes-Buckles, Tel. (212)870-3260

Vellore Christian Medical College Board (USA), Inc.

The Vellore Christian Medical College Board (USA) supports the wide range of programs at Christian Medical College (CMC), Vellore, Tamil Nadu, India, by securing contributions for its major capital equipment and construction goals; grants for program educational, research and health care programs; and funds to support scholarships for medical nursing and allied health students at Vellore and senior faculty study outside of India. The Board also facilitates opportunities for North Americans to volunteer at CMC and fosters working relationships between CMC and institutions in the United States. Print, DVD and electronic materials about CMC's 100+ years as a leading medical college and hospital are available as part of the Board's public education program. A capital campaign to raise one million dollars toward a new campus is now underway.

Headquarters

475 Riverside Dr., Rm. 243, New York, NY 10115 Tel. (212)870-2640 Fax (212)870-2173
Media Contact, President, Dr. Louis L. Knowles
Email: usaboard@vellorecmc.org

Officers

Pres., Dr. Louis L. Knowles
Chair, Mrs. Edwina Scudder-Youth, 211 Blue Ridge Dr., Levittown, PA 19057
Vice Chair, Mr. Anish Mathai, 475 Riverside Dr., Rm. 243, New York, NY 10115
Sec., Dr. Alexander Kuruvila, 2063 Gainsborough Dr., Riverside, CA 92606
Treas., Mr. Richard L. Vreeland, 182 Ameren Way, Ballwin, MO 63021

World Day of Prayer International Committee

World Day of Prayer is an ecumenical movement initiated and carried out by Christian women in 170 countries who conduct a common day of prayer on the first Friday of March to which all people are welcome. There is an annual theme for the worship service that has been prepared by women in a different country each year. For 2008 the WDP Committee of Guyana has prepared a worship service on the theme, God's Wisdom Brings New Understanding. The offering at the WDP is gathered by each WDP National or Regional Committee and given to help people who are in need.

Headquarters

World Day of Prayer International Comm., 475 Riverside Dr., Rm. 729, New York, NY 10115 Tel. (212)870-3049 Fax (212)864-8648, Email: wdpic@worlddayofprayer.net
Media Contact, Exec. Dir., Eileen King
World Day of Prayer USA, 475 Riverside Dr., Suite 300, New York, NY 10115 Tel. (212) 870-2466 Fax (212)870-2456, Toll-free 866 WDP USA, (866)937-8720, Email: ecalvin @wdpusa.org, Web: wdpusa.org, Media Contact, Executive Director, Elizabeth Calvin

Officers

Chairperson, S. Annette Poitier
Treasurer, Marcia L. Florkey
Africa, Suzie Bayiha II, Assah E. Mgonja
Asia, Zenaida Maturan, Sheree, Suk-Ling Wong
Caribbean and North America, Alison Carter, Marilyn Fortin
Europe, Jean Hackett, Corinna Harbig
Latin America, Elisabeth Delmonte,Ormara Nolla
Middle East, Laila Carmi, Lucy Ishak Guiriguis
Pacific, Vaieli Fuiono Piita, Pauline Smit
Member at Large for Orthodox Churches, Marija Ciceva-Aleksic

World Methodist Council-North American Section

The World Methodist Council, one of the 30 or so "Christian World Communions," shares a general tradition which is common to all Christians.

The world organization of Methodists and related United Churches is comprised of 76 churches with roots in the Methodist tradition. These churches found in 132 countries have a membership of more than 40 million.

The Council's North American Section, comprised of ten Methodist and United Church denominations, provides a regional focus for the Council in Canada, the United States and Mexico. The North American Section meets at the time of the quinquennial World Conference and Council, and separately as Section between world meetings. North American Churches related to the World Methodist Council have a

47

membership of approximately 16 million and a church community of more than 30 million.

Headquarters

P.O. Box 518, Lake Junaluska, NC 28745 Tel. (828)456-9432 Fax (828)456-9433
Media Contact, Gen. Sec., George H. Freeman

Officers

General Sec., Dr. George H. Freeman

World Vision

World Vision is a Christian relief and development organization dedicated to helping children and their communities worldwide reach their full potential by tackling the causes of poverty. Motivated by our faith in Jesus, we serve the poor as a demonstration of God's unconditional love for all people. World Vision works with communities in nearly 100 countries to develop long-term solutions that alleviate poverty, provides emergency assistance to children and families affected by natural disasters and civil conflict, and advocates for justice on behalf of the poor. World Vision U.S.—one of 52 national offices in the World Vision Partnership—serves in key United States metropolitan areas, providing intervention for challenged youth, tools that equip strong community leaders, and storehouses that provide essentials for living.

World Vision's Church Relations department facilitates chuch partnerships, connecting U.S. congregations with critical ministry among people in need locally and internationally. Church opportunities include partnerships with international projects, volunteer options through U.S. programs, and educational programs, including youth-oriented 30 Hour Famine and One Life Revolution, and child sponsorship.

Headquarters

P.O. Box 9716, Federal Way, WA 98063-9716 Tel. (253)815-1000
Church Relations Vice President, Steve Haas, Tel. (253)815-2698
Media Contact, Dean Owen, Tel. (253)815-2158

Officers

President, Richard Stearns
Senior Vice Presidents, Joan Mussa, Lawrence Probus, Julie Regnier, Atul Tandon, George Ward, Michael Veitenhans

YMCA of the U.S.A.

The YMCA is one of the largest private voluntary organizations in the world, serving about 30 million people in more than 100 countries. In the United States, more than 2,000 local branches, units, camps and centers annually serve more than 14 million people of all ages, races and abilities. About half of those served are female. No one is turned away because of an inability to pay.

The Y teaches youngsters to swim, organizes youth basketball games and offers adult aerobics. But the Y represents more than fitness—it works

to strengthen families and help people develop values and behavior that are consistent with Christian principles.

The Y offers hundreds of programs including day camp for children, child care, exercise for people with disabilities, teen clubs, environmental programs, substance abuse prevention, family nights, job training and many more programs from infant mortality prevention to overnight camping for seniors.

The kind of programs offered at a YMCA will vary; each is controlled by volunteer board members who make their own program, policy, and financial decisions based on the special needs of their community. In its own way, every Y works to build strong kids, strong families, and strong communities.

The YMCA was founded in London, England, in 1844 by George Williams and friends who lived and worked together as clerks. Their goal was to save other live-in clerks from the wicked life of the London streets. The first members were evangelical Protestants who prayed and studied the Bible as an alternative to vice. The Y has always been nonsectarian and today accepts those of all faiths at all levels of the organization.

Headquarters

101 N. Wacker Dr., Chicago, IL 60606 Tel. (312)977-0031 Fax (312)977-9063
Media Contact, Media Relations Manager, Arnie Collins

Officers

Board Chairman., Daniel E. Casey
Exec. Dir., Niel Nicoll
(Int.) Public Relations Assoc., Arnold Collins

YWCA of the U.S.A.

The YWCA of the U.S.A. is comprised of 313 affiliates in communities and on college campuses across the United States. It serves one million members and program participants. It seeks to empower women and girls to enable them, coming together across lines of age, race, religious belief, economic and occupational status to make a significant contribution to the elimination of racism and the achievement of peace, justice, freedom and dignity for all people.

Headquarters

1015 18th St. Suite 1100, Washington, DC 20036 Tel. (202) 467-0801 Fax. (202) 467-0802
Media Contact, Khristina Lew, Email: info @ywca.org

Officers

National Pres., Leticia Paez
Sec., Carol O. Markus
Chief Exec. Officer, Margaret Tyndall

Youth for Christ-USA

Founded in 1944, as part of the body of Christ, our vision is to see every young person in every people group in every nation have the opportunity to make an informed decision to be a follower of Jesus Christ and become a part of a local church.

There are 220 locally controlled YFC programs serving in cities and metropolitan areas of the United States.

YFC's Campus Life Club program involves teens who attend approximately 58,236 high schools in the United States. YFC's staff now numbers approximately 1,000. In addition, nearly 10,000 part-time and volunteer staff supplement the full-time staff. Youth Guidance, a ministry for nonschool-oriented youth includes group homes, court referrals, institutional services and neighborhood ministries. The year-round conference and camping program involves approximately 200,000 young people each year. Other ministries include DC Ministries, World Outreach, Project Serve, and Teen Moms. Independent, indigenous YFC organizations also work in 127 countries overseas.

Headquarters

U.S. Headquarters, P.O. Box 228822, Denver, CO 80222 Tel. (303)843-9000 Fax (303)843-9002

Canadian Organization, 2540 - 5th Ave, NW, Calgary, AB T2N 0T5

Media Contact, Pres., Roger Cross

Officers

United States, President, Roger Cross
Canada, Pres., vacant a/o 6/1/02
Intl. Organization, Pres., Jean-Jacques Weiler

49

2. Canadian Cooperative Organizations, National

In most cases, the organizations listed here work on a national level and cooperate across denominational lines. Regional cooperative organizations in Canada are listed in directory 8, "Canadian Regional and Local Ecumenical Bodies."

Alcohol and Drug Concerns Inc.

Alcohol and Drug Concerns is a registered, non-profit, charitable organization that has a long association with the Christian Church. The organization's mission is to empower youth to make positive lifestyle choices relating to alcohol, tobacco, and other drugs.

The organization was granted a national charter in 1987, moving from an Ontario charter dating back to 1934. Among its services are, Choices F.I.T. (Fostering Independent Thinking)- a substance abuse prevention resource for grade 4 to 8 teachers; an Institute on Addiction Studies; Making the Leap- a substance abuse prevention resource for grade 7 to 8 teachers created by high school students; Drug and Alcohol Game Show for grades 6 to 9- a classroom activity; education and awareness courses for clients of the Ontario Ministry of Corrections.

Headquarters
4500 Sheppard Ave. E, Ste. 112, Toronto, ON M1S 3R6 Tel. (416)293-3400 Fax (416) 293-1142
Media Contact, Robert Walsh, CEO

Officers
Pres., Jean Desgagne, Toronto
Treas., Peter Varley, Toronto
Vice Pres., Nanci Harris, Toronto
Vice Pres., Valerie Petroff, Oak Ridges
Vice Pres., Heidi Stanley, Orillia
Past Pres., Larry Gillians, Napanee
CEO, Robert Walsh

Canadian Bible Society

The Canadian Bible Society is a non-denominational and inter-confessional organization that exists to translate, publish, distribute and encourage the use of the Scriptures, without doctrinal note or comment. Bible Society work was begun in Canada in 1804 by the British and Foreign Bible Society. In 1906, the various auxiliaries of the British and Foreign Bible Society joined together to form the Canadian Bible Society. Today, the Canadian Bible Society has 16 district offices across Canada, a Scripture Translation Office in Kitchener, a French Services Office in Montreal, and a National Support Office in Toronto. Additionally, the Bermuda Bible Society is constituted as an Associate District of the Canadian Bible Society. The Society holds quarterly Board meetings involving one elected representative from each of the districts and from the francophone sector. About 90% of the Society's revenue comes through the generosity of Canadian supporters in the form of donations, bequests and annuity income. Through the Canadian Bible Society's membership in the United States Societies' fellowship, over 67.5 million Bibles, Testaments and Portions were distributed globally in 2004. The complete Bible has been published in over 420 languages, with at least one book of the Bible available in 2377 languages.

Headquarters
C.B.S. National Support Office, 10 Carnforth Rd., Toronto, ON M4A 2S4 Tel. (416)757-4171 Fax (416)757-3376

Officers
National Director, Ted Seres, 10 Carnforth Rd., Toronto, ON M4A 2S4 Tel. (416)757-4171 Fax (416)757-1292, Email: pnesbitt@bible society.ca
Director of Fonance, Mr. Nesa Gulasekharam, 10 Carnforth Rd., Toronto, ON M4A 2S4 Tel. (416)757-4171 Fax (416)757-3376, Email: ngulasekharam@biblesociety.ca
Director of Scripture Translation, Mr. Hart Wiens, Frederick Mall (2nd Floor), 385 Frederick Street, Kitchener, ON N2H 2P2 Tel. (519)741-8285 Fax (519)741-8357, Email: hwiens@biblesociety.ca
Directeur du Secteur francophone, M. Serge Rhéaume, 4050 avenue du Parc-Lafontaine, Montreal, QC H2L 3M8 Tel. (514)524-7873 Fax (514)524-6116, Email: srheaume@societe biblique.ca
Director of Donor Support & Development, Mr. Erwin van Laar, 10 Carnforth Rd., Toronto, ON M4A 2S4 Tel. (416)757-4171 Fax (416) 757-3376, Email: evanlaar@biblesociety.ca
Director of Scripture Resources, M. Serge Rheaume, 10 Carnforth Rd., Toronto, ON M4A 2S4 Tel. (416)757-4171, Fax (416)757-3376, Email: srheaume@biblesociety.ca
Human Resources Manager/Volunteer Program Coordinator, Ms. Meggy Kwok, 10 Carnforth Rd., Toronto, ON M4A 2S4 Tel. (416)757-4171 Fax (416)757-3376, Email: mkwok@ biblesociety.ca

Canadian Centre for Ecumenism

The Centre has facilitated understanding and cooperation among believers of various Christian traditions and world religions since 1963. An active interdenominational Board of Directors meets annually.

Outreach: ECUMENISM, a quarterly publication, develops central themes such as Rites of Passage, Sacred Space, Interfaith Marriages, Care of the Earth, etc. through contributions from writers of various churches and religions in addition to its regular ecumenical news summaries, book reviews and resources. A specialized library is open to the public for consultation in the areas of religion, dialogue, evangelism, ethics, spirituality, etc. Conferences and sessions are offered on themes such as Ecumenism and Pastoral Work, Pluralism, World Religions, Prayer and Unity.

Headquarters
2065 Sherbrooke St. W. Montreal, QC H3H 1G6 Tel. (514)937-9176 Fax (514)937-4986
Email: ccocce@oecumenisme.ca, Web: www. oecumenisme.ca

Officers
Media Contact, Bernice Baranowski
Exec. Dir., Dr. Stuart Brown
Assistant Director, Adèle Brodeur

The Canadian Council of Churches
The Canadian Council of Churches was organized in 1944. Its basic purpose is to provide the churches with an agency for conference and consultation and for such common planning and common action as they desire to undertake. It encourages ecumenical understanding and action throughout Canada through local councils of churches. It also relates to the World Council of Churches and other agencies serving the worldwide ecumenical movement.

The Council has a Governing Board which meets semiannually and an Executive Committee. Program is administered through two commissions—Faith and Witness, Justice and Peace.

Headquarters
47 Queen's Park Crescent East, Toronto, ON M5S 2C3 Tel. (416)972-9494 x 22 Fax (416) 927-0405, Email: Hamilton@ccc-cce.ca, Web: www.ccc-cce.ca
Media Contact, Rev. Dr. Karen Hamilton

Officers
President, Professor Richard Schneider, 47 Queen's Park Crescent East, Toronto ON M5S 2C3 Tel. (416)972-9494, Email: rschneid@ yorku.ca
Vice Presidents, The Rev. Dr. James Taylor Christie, 47 Queen's Park Crescent East, Toronto ON M5S 2C3 Tel. (416)972-9494, Email: sperocontraspem@rogers.com ; Ms. Sandra Demson, 47 Queen's Park Crescent East, Toronto ON M5S 2C3 Tel. (416)972-9494 Fax (416)922-9328, Email: srd@idirect. com ; The Rev. Dr. J. Daniel Gibson, 47

Queen's Park Crescent East, Toronto ON M5S 2C3 Tel. (416)972-9494, Email: gibsond @execulink.com
Treasurer, Mr. Don Taylor, 47 Queen's Park Crescent East, Toronto ON M5S 2C3 Tel: (416)972-9494, Email: maryanddontaylor @sympatico.ca
General Secretary, The Rev. Dr. Karen Hamilton, 47 Queen's Park Crescent East, Toronto ON M5S 2C3 Tel. (416)972-9494 x 22, Email: hamilton@ccc-cce.ca

MEMBER CHURCHES
Anglican Church Canada
Archdiocese of Canada of the Orthodox Church in America
Armenian Orthodox Church-Diocese of Canada
Baptist Convention of Ontario and Quebec
British Methodist Episcopal Church of Canada*
Canadian Conference of Catholic Bishops
Canadian Yearly Meeting of the Religious Society of Friends, Quakers
Christian Church (Disciples of Christ)
Christian Reformed Church in North America-Canadian Ministries
Coptic Orthodox Church of Canada
Ethiopian Orthodox Church in Canada
Evangelical Lutheran Church in Canada
Greek Orthodox Metropolis of Toronto(Canada)
Mennonite Church Canada
Old Catholic Church Union of Utrecht
Presbyterian Church in Canada
Regional Synod of Canada–Reformed Church in America
The Salvation Army - Canada and Bermuda
The United Church of Canada
Ukrainian Orthodox Church of Canada
*Associate Member

Canadian Evangelical Theological Association
In May 1990, about 60 scholars, pastors and other interested persons met together in Toronto to form a new theological society. Arising out of the Canadian chapter of the Evangelical Theological Society, the new association established itself as a distinctly Canadian group with a new name. It sponsored its first conference as CETA in Kingston, Ontario, in May 1991.

CETA provides a forum for scholarly contributions to the renewal of theology and church in Canada. CETA seeks to promote theological work which is loyal to Christ and his Gospel, faithful to the primacy and authority of Scripture and responsive to the guiding force of the historic creeds and Protestant confessions of the Christian Church. In its newsletters and conferences, CETA seeks presentations that will speak to a general theologically-educated audience, rather than to specialists.

CETA has special interest in evangelical points of view upon and contributions to the wider conversations regarding religious studies

51

and church life. Members therefore include pastors, students and other interested persons as well as professional academicians. CETA currently includes about 100 members, many of whom attend its annual conference in the early summer. It publishes the Canadian Evangelical Review and supports an active internet discussion group, which may be accessed by emailing ceta-l@egroups.com.

Headquarters
Prof. David Guretzki, Briercrest College, Caronport, Saskatchewan, S0H 0S0
Email: dguretzki@briercrest.ca
Media Contact, Prof. David Guretzki

Officers
President: Prof. David Guretzki
Secretary-Treasurer: Revd. Dr. Archie Pell
Editor, Canadian Evangelical Review: Dr. Archie Spencer
Executive Members-at-large: Nicholas Jesson, Dustin Resch

Canadian Tract Society
The Canadian Tract Society was organized in 1970 as an independent distributor of Gospel leaflets to provide Canadian churches and individual Christians with quality materials proclaiming the Gospel through the printed page. It is affiliated with the American Tract Society, which encouraged its formation and assisted in its founding, and for whom it serves as an exclusive Canadian distributor. The CTS is a nonprofit international service ministry.

Headquarters
P.O. Box 2156, LCD 1, Brampton, ON L6T 3S4
Tel. (905)457-4559 Fax (905)457-0529
Media Contact, Mgr., Donna Croft

Officers
Director-Sec., Robert J. Burns
Director, John Neufeld
Director, Patricia Burns

Canadian Society of Biblical Studies-Société Canadienne des Études Bibliques
The object of the Society shall be to stimulate the critical investigation of the classical biblical literatures, together with other related literature, by the exchange of scholarly research both in published form and in public forum.

Headquarters
Media Contact, Exec. Sec., Michele Murray, Dept. of Religion, Bishop's University, Lennoxville, PQ J1M 1Z7, Email mmurray@ubishops.ca, Website www.ccsr.ca/csbs

Officers
Pres., Mary Rose D'Angelo, Dept. of Theology, University of Notre Dame, Notre Dame, IN 46556 Tel. (219)631-7040 Fax (219)631-6842

Vice Pres., J. Glen Taylor, Wycliffe College, 5 Hoskin Ave., Toronto, ON M57 1H7 Tel. (416)946-3541 Fax 416-946-3541, Email: glen.Taylor@utoronto.ca
Exec. Sec., Michele Murray, Dept. of Religion, Bishop's University, Lennoxville, QC J1M 1Z7 Tel. (819)822-9600 Fax (819)822-9661, Email: mmurray@ubishops.ca
Treas., Robert A. Derrenbacker, Jr., Regent College, 5800 University Blvd, Vancouver, BC, V6T 2E4 Tel. (604)221-3349 Fax (604)224-3097, Email: rderrenbacker@regent-college.edu
Prog. Coord., Christine Mitchell, St. Andrews College, 1121 College Dr., Saskatoon, SK S7N 0W3, Email: ckm365@duke.usask.ca
Comm. Officer, Richard Ascough, Queens' Theological College, Kingston, ON K7L 3N6 Tel. (613)533-6000 Fax (613)533-6879, Email: rsa@post.queensu.ca
Student Liason Officer, Derek Suderman, Emmanuel College, 11739 McCowan Rd., Stouffville, ON L4A 7X5, Email: derek.suder-man@utoronto.ca

The Church Army in Canada
The Church Army in Canada has been involved in evangelism and Christian social service since 1929.

Headquarters
105 Mountain View Dr., Saint John, NB E2J 5B5 Tel. (888)316-8169 Fax (506)642-4005, Email: bsmith@churcharmy.com
Media Contact, National Dir., Capt. R. Bruce Smith

Officers
National Dir., Capt. R. Bruce Smith
Bd. Chmn., Mr. Peter Bloom

The Churches' Council on Theological Education in Canada, An Ecumenical Foundation
The Churches' Council (CCTE,EF) maintains an overview of theological education in Canada on behalf of its constituent churches and functions as a bridge between the schools of theology and the churches which they serve.

Founded in 1970 with a national and ecumenical mandate, the CCTE,EF provides resources for research into matters pertaining to theological education, opportunities for consultation and cooperation and a limited amount of funding in the form of grants for the furtherance of ecumenical iniatives in theological education.

Headquarters
47 Queen's Park Cres., E., Toronto, ON M5S 2C3 Tel. (416) 928-3223 Fax (416) 928-3563, Email: director@ccte.ca, Web: www.ccte.ca
Media Contact, Exec. Dir., Robert Faris

Officers

Bd. of Dir., Chpsn., Dr. Richard C. Crossman, Waterloo Lutheran Seminary, 75 University Ave. W., Waterloo, ON N2L 3C5

Bd. of Dir., Vice-Chpsn., Dr. Dorcas Gordon, Knox College

Treas., Mr. Brian Cox

Exec. Dir., Robert Faris

MEMBER ORGANIZATIONS

The General Synod of the Anglican Church of Canada

Canadian Baptist Ministries

The Evangelical Lutheran Church in Canada

The Presbyterian Church in Canada

The Canadian Conference of Catholic Bishops

The United Church of Canada

Evangelical Fellowship of Canada

The Fellowship was formed in 1964. There are 31 denominations, 124 organizations, 1,200 local churches and 11,000 individual members.

Its purposes are, "Fellowship in the gospel" (Phil. ch.1 vs.5), "the defence and confirmation of the gospel" (Phil. ch.1 vs.7) and "the furtherance of the gospel" (Phil. ch.1 vs.12). The Fellowship believes the Holy Scriptures, as originally given, are infallible and that salvation through the Lord Jesus Christ is by faith apart from works.

In national and regional conventions the Fellowship urges Christians to live exemplary lives and to openly challenge the evils and injustices of society. It encourages cooperation with various agencies in Canada and overseas that are sensitive to social and spiritual needs.

Headquarters

Office, 600 Alden Rd. Ste. 300, Markham, ON L3R 0E7 Tel. (905)479-5885 Fax (905)479-4742

Mailing Address, M.I.P. Box 3745, Markham, ON L3R 0Y4

Media Contact, Pres., Dr. Gary Walsh, 600 Alden Rd., Ste. 300, Markham, ON L3R 0E7 Tel. (905)479-5885 Fax (905)479-4742

Officers

Pres., Dr. Gary Walsh

Chair, Dr. Paul Magnus

Vice Chair, Dr. Rick Penner

Treas., Lt. Col. David Luginbuhl

Past Pres., Dr. Brian Stiller

EXECUTIVE COMMITTEE

Rev. Scott Campbell; Rev. Carson Pue; Ms. Ruth Andrews; Rev. Stewart Hunter; Ms. Jacqueline Dugas; Dr. Rick Penner; Lt. Col. David Luginbuhl; Dr. Ralph Richardson; Rev. Abe Funk; Rev. Gillis Killam; Dr. Paul Magnus; Rev. Winston Thurton

Task Force on Evangelism-(Vision Canada), Interim Chair, Gary Walsh

Social Action Commission, Chpsn., Dr. James Read

Education Commission, Chpsn., Dr. Glenn Smith

Women in Ministry Task Force, Chpsn., Rev. Eileen Stewart-Rhude

Aboriginal Task Force, Co-Chairs, Ray Aldred; Wendy Peterson

Religious Liberties Commission, Chpsn., Dr. Paul Marshall

Task Force on Global Mission, Chpsn., Dr. Geoff Tunnicliffe

Inter-Varsity Christian Fellowship of Canada

Inter-Varsity Christian Fellowship is a non-profit, interdenominational student movement centering on the witness to Jesus Christ in campus communities, universities, colleges and high schools and through a Canada-wide Pioneer Camping program. It also ministers to professionals and teachers through Nurses and Teacher Christian Fellowship.

IVCF was officially formed in 1928-29 by the late Dr. Howard Guinness, whose arrival from Britain challenged students to follow the example of the British Inter-Varsity Fellowship by organizing themselves into prayer and Bible study fellowship groups. Inter-Varsity has always been a student-initiated movement emphasizing and developing leadership in the campus to call Christians to outreach, challenging other students to a personal faith in Jesus Christ and studying the Bible as God's revealed truth within a fellowship of believers. A strong stress has been placed on missionary activity, and the triennial conference held at Urbana, IL. (jointly sponsored by U.S. and Canadian IVCF) has been a means of challenging many young people to service in Christian vocations. Inter-Varsity works closely with and is a strong believer in the work of local and national churches.

Headquarters

Unit 17, 40 Vogell Rd., Richmond Hill, ON L4B 3N6 Tel. (905)884-6880 Fax (905)884-6550

Media Contact, Gen. Dir., Rob Regier

Officers

Gen. Dir., Rob Regier

Interchurch Communications

Interchurch Communications is made up of the communication units of the Anglican Church of Canada, the Evangelical Lutheran Church in Canada, the Presbyterian Church in Canada, the Canadian Conference of Catholic Bishops (English Sector), and the United Church of Canada. ICC members collaborate on occasional video or print coproductions and on addressing public policy issues affecting religious communications.

Headquarters

3250 Bloor St. W., Etobicoke, ON M8X 2Y4

Mr. William Kokesch, Canadian Conference of Catholic Bishops, 90 Parent Ave., Ottawa, ON K1N 7B1 Tel. (613)241-9461 Fax (613)241-8117, Email: kokesch@cccb.ca

Religious Television Associates, 3250 Bloor St. W., Etobicoke, ON M8X 2Y4 Tel. (416)231-7680 Fax (416)232-6004

John Howard Society of Ontario

The John Howard Society of Ontario is a registered non-profit charitable organization providing services to individuals, families and groups at all stages in the youth and criminal justice system. The Society also provides community education on critical issues in the justice system and advocacy for reform of the justice system. The mandate of the Society is the prevention of crime through service, community education, advocacy and reform.

Founded in 1929, the Society has grown from a one-office service in Toronto to 17 local branches providing direct services in the major cities of Ontario and a provincial office providing justice policy analysis, advocacy for reform and support to branches.

Headquarters

6 Jackson Pl., Toronto, ON M6P 1T6 Tel. (416) 604-8412 Fax (416)604-8948

Media Contact, Exec. Dir., William Sparks

Officers

Pres., Susan Reid-MacNevin, Dept. of Sociology, Univ. Of Guelph, Guelph, ON N1G 2W1

Vice Pres., Richard Beaupe, 4165 Fernand St., Hamner, ON B3A 1X4

Treas., Jack Battler, Waterloo, ON

Sec., Peter Angeline, OISE, 252 Bloor St. W., Toronto, ON

Exec. Dir., William Sparks

LOCAL SOCIETIES

Collins Bay; Hamilton; Kingston; Lindsay; London; Niagara; Oshawa; Ottawa; Peel; Peterborough; Sarnia; Sault Ste. Marie; Sudbury; Thunder Bay; Toronto; Waterloo; Windsor

Lutheran Council in Canada

The Lutheran Council in Canada was organized in 1967 and is a cooperative agency of the Evangelical Lutheran Church in Canada and Lutheran Church-Canada.

The Council's activities include communications, coordinative service and national liaison in social ministry, chaplaincy and scout activity.

Headquarters

302-393 Portage Ave., Winnipeg, MB R3B 3H6 Tel. (204)984-9150 Fax (204)984-9185

Media Contact, Pres., Rev. Ralph Mayan, 3074 Portage Ave., Winnipeg, MB R3K 0Y2 Tel. (204)895-3433 Fax (204)897-4319

Officers

Pres., Bishop Raymond Schultz

Sec., Rev. Leon C. Gilbertson

Vice Pres., Rev. Ralph Mayan

Mennonite Central Committee Canada (MCCC)

Mennonite Central Committee Canada was organized in 1964 to continue the work which several regional Canadian inter-Mennonite agencies had been doing in relief, service, immigration and peace. All but a few of the smaller Mennonite groups in Canada belong to MCC Canada.

MCCC is part of the Mennonite Central Committee (MCC) International which has its headquarters in Akron, Pa. from where most of the overseas development and relief projects are administered. In 2000-2001 MCCC's income was $25 million, about 47 percent of the total MCC income. There were 408 Canadians out of a total of 867 MCC workers serving in North America and abroad during the same time period.

The MCC office in Winnipeg administers projects located in Canada. Domestic programs of Voluntary Service, Native Concerns, Peace and Social Concerns, Food Program, Employment Concerns, Ottawa Office, Victim-Offender Ministries, Mental Health and Immigration are all part of MCC's Canadian ministry. Whenever it undertakes a project, MCCC attempts to relate to the church or churches in the area.

Headquarters

134 Plaza Dr., Winnipeg, MB R3T 5K9 Tel. (204)261-6381 Fax (204)269-9875

Communications, Rick Fast, 134 Plaza Dr., Winnipeg, MT R3T 5K9 Tel. (204)261-6381 Fax (204)269-9875

Officers

Exec. Dir., Donald Peters

Project Ploughshares

Project Ploughshares is an ecumenical peace centre of the Canadian Council of Churches, established in 1976 to implement the churches' imperative to seek and pursue peace. Project Ploughshares works with churches, governments, and non-governmental organizations, in Canada and internationally, to identify, develop, and advance approaches that build peace and prevent war, and promote the peaceful resolution of political conflict. Project Ploughshares is sponsored by eight national Canadian churches and is affiliated with the Institute of Peace and Conflict Studies, Conrad Grebel University College, University of Waterloo. Publications include The Ploughshares Monitor (quarterly), The Armed Conflicts Report (annually), Briefings and Working Papers (occasional).

Headquarters

Project Ploughshares, 57 Erb Street West,

Waterloo, ON, Canada N2L 6C2 Tel. (519) 888-6541 Fax (519)888-0188, Email: plough @ploughshares.ca, Web: www.ploughshares.ca
Media Contact: Director, John Siebert, Tel. (519) 888 6541 x702, Email: jsiebert@ ploughshares. ca

Officers
Executive Director, John Siebert
Associate Director, Nancy Regehr
Chair, Moira Hutchinson
Treasurer, Philip Creighton
Secretary, Rev. Dr. Martin Rumscheidt

SPONSORING ORGANIZATIONS
Anglican Church of Canada
Canadian Catholic Organization for Development & Peace
Canadian Unitarian Council
Canadian Voice of Women for Peace
Canadian Yearly Meeting, Religious Society of Friends
Evangelical Lutheran Church in Canada
Mennonite Central Committee Canada
Presbyterian Church in Canada
United Church of Canada

Religious Television Associates
Religious Television Associates was formed in the early 1960s for the production units of the Anglican, Baptist, Presbyterian, Roman Catholic Churches and the United Church of Canada. In the intervening years, the Baptists have withdrawn and the Lutherans have come in. RTA provides an ecumenical umbrella for joint productions in broadcasting and development education. The directors are the heads of the Communications Departments participating in Interchurch Communications.

Headquarters
c/o The United Church of Canada, 3250 Bloor St. W., Etobicoke, ON M8X 2Y4 Tel. (416)231-7680 x 4076 Fax (416)231-3103
Media Contact, Shane Chadden

Officers
The Anglican Church of Canada
Canadian Conference of Catholic Bishops
The Canadian Council of Churches
The Evangelical Lutheran Church in Canada
The Presbyterian Church in Canada
The United Church of Canada

Scripture Union
Scripture Union is an international interdenominational missionary movement working in 130 countries.

Scripture Union aims to work with the churches to make God's Good News known to children, young people and families and to encourage people of all ages to meet God daily through the Bible and prayer.

In Canada, a range of daily Bible guides are offered to individuals, churches, and bookstores from age four through adult. Sunday School curriculum and various evangelism and discipling materials are also offered for sale.

Children's ministry is offered to churches through summer sports camps and training for sports outreach programs.

Headquarters
1885 Clements Rd., Unit 226, Pickering, ON L1W 3V4 Tel. (905)427-4947 Fax (905)427-0334,
Media Contact, President, John Irwin, Email: jirwinc617@rogers.com

Officers
Chair of the Board, Harold Murray, 216 McKinnon Pl. NE, Calgary, AB T2E 7B9 Tel. (403)276-4716, Email: hjmurray@home.com
President, Robert Szo, 1885 Clements Rd., Unit 226, Pickering, ON L1W 3V4 Email: robert @scriptureunion.ca

Student Christian Movement of Canada
The Student Christian Movement of Canada was formed in 1921 from the student arm of the YMCA. It has its roots in the Social Gospel movements of the late 19th and early 20th centuries. Throughout its intellectual history, the SCM in Canada has sought to relate the Christian faith to the living realities of the social and political context of each student generation.

The present priorities are built around the need to form more and stronger critical Christian communities on Canadian campuses within which individuals may develop their social and political analyses, experience spiritual growth and fellowship and bring Christian ecumenical witness to the university.

The Student Christian Movement of Canada is affiliated with the World Student Christian Federation.

Headquarters
310 Danforth Ave., Toronto, ON M4K 1N6 Tel. (416)463-4312 Fax (416)466-6854
Media Contact, Natl. Coord., Sheilagh McGlynn

Officers
Natl. Coord., Sheilagh McGlynn, Email: info@ scmcanada.org

Women's Inter-Church Council of Canada
Women's Inter-Church Council of Canada is a national Christian women's council that encourages women to grow in ecumenism, to strengthen ecumenical community, to share their spirituality and prayer, to engage in dialogue about women's concerns and to stand in solidarity with one another. The Council calls women to respond to national and international issues affecting women and to take action together for justice. WICC sponsors the World Day of Prayer and

55

Fellowship of the Least Coin in Canada. Human rights projects for women are supported and a quarterly magazine "Making Waves" distributed.

Headquarters
47 Queen's Park Cres. E, Toronto, ON M5S 2C3 Tel. (416)929-5184 Fax (416)929-4064
Media Contact, Communications Coordinator, Gillian Barfoot

Officers
Pres., Claire Heron
Exec. Dir., Pat Allinson

CHURCH MEMBER BODIES
African Methodist Episcopal, Anglican Church of Canada, Canadian Baptist Ministries, Christian Church (Disciples of Christ), Evangelical Lutheran Church in Canada, Mennonite Central Committee, Presbyterian Church in Canada, Religious Society of Friends, Roman Catholic Church, The Salvation Army in Canada, United Church of Canada

World Vision Canada
World Vision Canada is a Christian humanitarian relief and development organization. Although its main international commitment is to translate child sponsorship into holistic, sustainable community development, World Vision also allocates resources to help Canada's poor and complement the mission of the church.

World Vision's Reception Centre assists government-sponsored refugees entering Canada. The NeighbourLink program mobilizes church volunteers to respond locally to people's needs. A quarterly publication, Context, provides data on the Canadian family to help churches effectively reach their communities. The development education program provides resources on development issues. During the annual 30-Hour Famine, people fast for 30 hours while discussing poverty and raising funds to support aid programs.

Headquarters
1 World Dr., Mississauga, ON L5T 2Y4 Tel. (905)821-3030 Fax (905)821-1356
Media Contact, Philip Maher, Tel. (905)567-2726

Officers
Pres., Dave Toycen
Vice Pres., Intl. & Govt. Relations, Linda Tripp; Natl. Programs, Don Posterski; Fin. & Admin., Charlie Fluit; Donor Development Group, Brian Tizzard

Young Men's Christian Association in Canada
The YMCA began as a Christian association to help young men find healthy recreation and meditation, as well as opportunities for education, in the industrial slums of 19th century England. It came to Canada in 1851 with the same mission in mind for young men working in camps and on the railways.

Today, the YMCA maintains its original mission, helping individuals to grow and develop in spirit, mind and body, but attends to those needs for men and women of all ages and religious beliefs. The YMCA registers 1.5 million participants in 250 communities that are served by 64 autonomous associations across Canada.

The program of each association differs according to the needs of the community, but most offer one or more programs in each of the following categories, health and fitness, child care, employment councelling and training, recreation, camping, community support and outreach, international development and short-term accommodation.

The YMCA encourages people of all ages, races, abilities, income and beliefs to come together in an environment which promotes balance in life, breaking down barriers and helping to create healthier communities.

Headquarters
42 Charles St. E., 6th Floor., Toronto, ON M4Y 1T4 Tel. (416)967-9622 Fax (416)967-9618
Media Contact, Sol Kasimer

Officers
Chpsn., Ray Mantha
CEO, Sol Kasimer

Young Women's Christian Association of-du Canada
The YWCA of-du Canada is a national voluntary organization serving 44 YWCAs and YM-YWCAs across Canada. Dedicated to the development and improved status of women and their families, the YWCA is committed to service delivery and to being a source of public education on women's issues and an advocate of social change. Services provided by YWCAs and YM-YWCAs include adult education programs, residences and shelters, child care, fitness activities, wellness programs and international development education. As a member of the World YWCA, the YWCA of-du Canada is part of the largest women's organization in the world.

Headquarters
80 Gerrard St. E., Toronto, ON M5B 1G6 Tel. (416)593-9886 Fax (416)971-8084
Media Contact, Int. CEO, Margaret MacKenzie

Officers
Pres., Ann Mowatt

Youth for Christ-Canada
Youth For Christ is an interdenominational organization founded in 1944 by Torrey Johnson. Under the leadership of YFC's 11 national board of directors, Youth For Christ-Canada cooperates with churches and serves as a mission agency

reaching out to young people and their families through a variety of ministries.

YFC seeks to have maximum influence in a world of youth through high-interest activities and personal involvement. Individual attention is given to each teenager through small group involvement and counselling. These activities and relationships become vehicles for communicating the message of the Gospel.

Headquarters
822-167 Lombard Ave., Winnipeg, MB R3B 0V3
  Tel. (204)989-0056 Fax (204)989-0067

Officers
Natl. Dir., Randy L. Steinwand

3. Religious Bodies in the United States

The United States, with its staunch constitutional stance on religious freedom and successive waves of immigrants over the last three centuries, has proved to be a fertile soil for the development of varied Christian traditions. In the directory that follows, some 224 distinct church traditions are represented. Many of these groups represent the processes of dividing and re-uniting that are a hallmark of American religious life. Many churches listed here represent those with a long tradition in Europe, Africa, or Asia predating their American tenure. Others are American-born churches. The researcher may be helped by consulting the churches grouped by tradition at the end of this directory in the section entitled, "Religious Bodies in the United States Arranged by Families." In this section, all the Baptists bodies are listed together, all the Lutheran bodies, Methodists, etc.

The following directory information is supplied by the national headquarters of each church. Each listing contains a brief description of the church, followed by the national headquarters contact information, which includes a mailing address, telephone and fax numbers, email and website addresses (when available), and the name of the media contact. After the headquarters, there are data regarding the church officers or leaders, including names, titles, and contact information (when contact information differs from the headquarters). There is a staggering array of churches, each with its own form of organization; not all of them refer to their leaders as "officers." In some places, the reader will find the term "Bishops," "Board Members," or "Executives" in place of "Officers." Finally, when applicable, each entry contains a list of the names of church publications.

The churches are printed in alphabetical order by the official name of the organization. There are a few instances in which certain churches are more commonly known by another name. In such cases, the reader is referred incidentally within the text to the appropriate official name. Churches that are member communions of the National Council of the Churches of Christ in the U.S.A. are marked with an asterisk (*).

Other useful information about the churches listed here can be found in other chapters or directories within the book: Statistical information for these churches can be found in the tables toward the end of this book in chapter III. Further, more extensive information about the publications listed in this directory can be found in directory 10, "Religious Periodicals in the United States.

The organizations listed here represent the denominations to which the vast majority of church members in the United States belong. It does not include all religious bodies functioning in the United States. *The Encyclopedia of American Religions* (Gale, 27500 Drake Road, Farmington Hills, MI 48331, 800-877-4253) contains names and addresses of additional religious bodies.

Advent Christian Church

The Advent Christian Church is a conservative, evangelical denomination which grew out of the Millerite movement of the 1830s and 1840s. The members stress the authority of Scripture, justification by faith in Jesus Christ alone, the importance of evangelism, disciplemaking, and world missions and the soon visible return of Jesus Christ.

Organized in 1860, the Advent Christian Church maintains headquarters in Charlotte, N.C., with regional offices in Rochester, N. H., Princeton, N.C., Ellisville, MO., Sumas, WA, and Lenoir, N.C. Missions are maintained in India, Nigeria, Ghana, Japan, Liberia, Croatia, New Zealand, Malaysia, the Philippines, Mexico, South Africa, Namibia, Honduras, China, Kenya, Malawi, Mozambique, Congo, Romania, and Memphis, Tenn.

The Advent Christian Church maintains doctrinal distinctives in three areas—conditional immortality, the sleep of the dead until the return of Christ and belief that the kingdom of God will be established on earth made new by Jesus Christ.

Headquarters

P.O. Box 690848, Charlotte, NC 28227 Tel. (704)545-6161 x 202 Fax (704)573-0712

Media Contact, Exec. Director, Ronald P. Thomas, Jr.

Email: acpub@adventchristian.org

Web: www.adventchristian.org

Periodicals

Advent Christian News, *Maranatha*, *Advent Christian Witness*, *Prayer & Praise*, Weekly E-newsletter: www.ACGC.us

African Methodist Episcopal Church*

This church began in 1787 in Philadelphia when persons in St. George's Methodist Episcopal Church withdrew as a protest against color segregation. In 1816 the denomination was started, led by Rev. Richard Allen who had been ordained deacon by Bishop Francis Asbury and was subsequently ordained elder and elected and consecrated bishop.

Headquarters

3801 Market St., Suite 300, Philadelphia, PA 29204 Tel. (215)662-0506

Email: cio@ame-church.com

Web: www.AME-Church.com

Officers

Senior Bishop, Bishop Philip Robert Cousin,

58

Presiding Bishop, Fourth Episcopal District, African Methodist Episcopal Church, 404 East 41st Street, Suite 114, Chicago, IL 60653 Tel. (773)373-6587 Fax (773)373-8356

Chief Ecumenical & Urban Affairs Officer, Bishop E. Earl McCloud, African Methodist Episcopal Church, P.O. Box 310043, Atlanta, GA 31131-0043 Tel. (770)475-2966, Email: emccloudjr@aol.com

Pres., Gen. Bd., Bishop McKinley Young, 101 East Union Street, Jacksonville FL 32202 Tel. (904)355-8262 Fax (904)356-1617.

Pres. Council of Bishops 2005-2006, Bishop Preston Warren Williams II, 110 Pisgah Church Road, Columbia, SC 29203 Tel. (803)935-0500 Fax (803)935-0830.

GENERAL OFFICERS

Dr. Clement W. Fugh; Dr. Richard Allen Lewis; Dr. Daryl B. Ingram; Dr. Johnny Barbour; Jr., Dr. George F. Flowers; Dr. Dennis C. Dickerson; Dr. Jerome V. Harris; Dr. James Wade; Dr. Calvin H. Sydnor, III

Bishop E. Earl McCloud, Ecumenical Officer/Chaplains; Bishop Richard Franklin Norris (First Episcopal Dist.); Bishop Adam Jefferson Richardson, Jr. (Second Episcopal Dist.); Bishop Robert Vaughn Webster (Third Episcopal Dist.); Bishop Philip Robert Cousin, Sr. (Fourth Episcopal Dist.); Bishop John Richard Bryant (Fifth Episcopal Dist.); Bishop William Phillips DeVeaux (Sixth Episcopal Dist.); Bishop Preston Warren Williams, II (Seventh Episcopal Dist.); Bishop Cornal Garnett Henning, Sr. (Eighth Episcopal Dist.); Bishop Theodore Larry Kirkland (Ninth Episcopal Dist.); Bishop Gregory Gerald McKinley Ingram (Tenth Episcopal Dist.); Bishop McKinley Young (Eleventh Episcopal Dist.); Bishop Richard Allen Chappelle, Sr. (Twelfth Episcopal Dist.); Bishop Vashti Murphy McKenzie (Thirteenth Episcopal Dist.); Bishop David Rwhynica Daniels, Jr. (Fourteenth Episcopal Dist.); Bishop Samuel Lawrence Green, Sr. (Fifteenth Episcopal Dist.); Bishop Carolyn Tyler Guidry (Sixteenth Episcopal Dist.); Bishop Paul Jones Mulenga Kawimbe (Seventeenth Episcopal Dist.); Bishop Sarah Frances Davis (Eighteenth Episcopal Dist.); Bishop James Levert Davis (Nineteenth Episcopal Dist.); Bishop Wilfred Jacobus Messiah (Twentieth Episcopal District)

Periodicals

The A.M.E. Review, The Christian Recorder, Journal of Christian Education, Women's Missionary Magazine, Secret Chamber, Voice of Missions

The African Methodist Episcopal Zion Church*

The A.M.E. Zion Church is an independent body, having withdrawn from the John Street Methodist Church of New York City in 1796. The first bishop was James Varick.

Headquarters

Dept. of Records & Research, 3225 West Sugar Creek Rd., Charlotte, NC 28269 Tel.(704)599-4630 Fax (704)688-2549, Email: j1gsa@aol.com

Media Contact, Gen. Sec.-Aud., Dr. W. Robert Johnson, III

Email: rojohnson@amezhqtr.org; eljohnson@amezhqtr.org

Website: www.amez.org

Officers

Sr. Bishop, Bishop George W.C. Walker, Sr.

BOARD OF BISHOPS OFFICERS

*Pres., George Washington Carver Walker, Sr., 3225 West Sugar Creek Rd., Charlotte, NC 28269 Tel. (704)599-4630 Fax (704)688-2540, Mailing Address: P.O. Box 26770, Charlotte, NC 28221, Email: gwalker046@aol.com

Sec., Clarence Carr, 965 Charlton Trace, Marietta, GA 30064 Tel. (770)420-9332 Fax (770)590-4943, Email: bishopccarr@comcast.net

Asst. Sec., Kenneth Monroe, 4633 Old Lowery Road, Shannon, NC 28386, Mailing Address P.O. Box 26315, Fayettville, NC 28314 Tel. (910)843-8274; Office Phone (910)987-1991 Fax (910)843-8702, Email: zion95@earthlink.net

Treas., George Washington Carver Walker, Sr., 3225 W. Sugar Creek Rd., Charlotte, NC 28269 Tel. (704)599-4630 Fax (704-688-2540, Mailing Address: P.O. Box 26770, Charlotte, NC 28221, Email: gwalker046@aol.com

*Note: Presidency rotates every six (6) Months according to seniority.

ACTIVE MEMBERS

George Edward Battle Jr., 18403 Dembridge Lane, Davidson, NC 28036 Tel. (704)895-2236, Office: Two Wachovia Center, 301 South Tryon St., Ste. 1755, Charlotte, NC 28202 Tel. (704)332-7600 Fax (704)343-3745, Email: gebjneed@bellsouth.net

Warren Matthew Brown, 12904 Canoe Court, Ft. Washington, MD 20744 Tel. (301)203-1677, Office: 8700 Central Avenue, Suite 307, Landover, MD 20785 Tel. (301)499-6890 Fax (301)499-6893, Email: amezmidatlantic2@aol.com

Clarence Carr, 965 Charlton Trace, Marietta, GA 30064 Tel. (770)420-9332 Fax (770)590-4943, Email: bishopccarr@comcast.net

Samuel Chuka Ekemam, Sr., Office-Mail: A.M.E. Zion Church Area Headquarters, 1 Zion Hill Plaza, (Ugwu Orji), Okigwe Road, P.O. Box 8000, Owerri, Imo State, Nigeria West Africa; Home Phone from US: (1pm-5pm est) 011-234-803-301-8280, Office and

Fax from US: 011-234-83-232-271, Email: bishopamezng@yahoo.com

Roy A. Holmes, 22071 Sunset Dr., Richton Park, IL 60471 Tel. (708)679-1552 Fax (708)679-1562, Email: bishopraholmes92@sbcglobal.net

Louis Hunter, Sr., 4290 Bells Ferry Road, Suite 106, PMB#643, Kennesaw, GA 30144 Tel. (678)445-1453 Fax (678)445-1371, Email: bishoplouishunter@swdelta.com

Nathaniel Jarrett, Jr., 18031 S. Pheasant Lake Dr., Tinley Park, IL 60477 Tel. (708)802-9873 Fax (708)429-3911

James E. McCoy, 808 S. Lawrence St., Montgomery, AL 36104-5055 Tel. (334)269-6365 Fax (334)269-6369, Email: aflamez@bellsouth.net

Kenneth Monroe, 4633 Old Lowery Road, Shannon, NC 28386; Mailing Address P.O. Box 26315, Fayetteville, NC 28314 Tel. (910)843-8274, (910)987-1991 Fax (910)843-8702, Email: Zion95@earthlink.net

Richard Keith Thompson, 3050 Berks Way, Raleigh, NC 27614 Tel. (919)554-8994/ (919)556-4298 Fax (919)556-6049

George Washington Carver Walker, Sr., 3225 W. Sugar Creek Rd., Charlotte, NC 28269 Tel. (704)599-4630 Fax (704)688-2540, Mailing Address: P.O. Box 26770, Charlotte, NC 28221, Email: gwalker046@aol.com

Milton Alexander Williams (Deceased)

RETIRED MEMBERS

William Alexander Hilliard, 690 Chicago Blvd., Detroit, MI 48202

John Henry Miller, Sr., (Deceased)

Cecil Bishop, P.O. Box 73585, Charlotte, NC 28271 Tel. (704)996-7669 Fax (704)770-0348

Joseph Johnson, 320 Walnut Point Dr., Matthews, NC 28105 Tel. (704)849-0521; Mailing Address: P.O. Box 608, Matthews, NC 28106, Email: djjjj85@alltel.net

Enoch Benjamin Rochester, (Deceased)

Marshall H. Strickland, I, 2000 Cedar Circle Dr., Baltimore, MD 21228 Tel. (410)744-7330 Fax (410)788-5510

EPISCOPAL ASSIGNMENTS

Piedmont Episcopal District: Blue Ridge, West Central North Carolina, Western North Carolina, and Jamaica Conferences: Bishop George W. C. Walker, Sr.

Mid-West Episcopal District: Indiana, Kentucky, Michigan, Missouri, Tennessee, Central Africa (Malawi and Mozambique) and South Africa Conferences: Bishop Milton A. Williams, Sr. (Deceased)

Eastern West Africa Episcopal District: Central Nigeria, Lagos—West Nigeria, Nigeria, Northern Nigeria, Rivers, Mainland, Cross River, South Eastern, and Southern Conferences: Bishop Samuel Chuka Ekemam, Sr.

North Eastern Episcopal District: New England, New York, Western New York, and Bahamas Islands Conferences: Bishop George Edward Battle, Jr.

Eastern North Carolina Episcopal District: Albemarle, Cape Fear, Central North Carolina, North Carolina, Virgin Islands, and South Africa (Zimbabwe) Conferences: Bishop Richard Keith Thompson

South Atlantic Episcopal District: Georgia, Palmetto, Pee Dee, and South Carolina Conferences: Bishop Clarence Carr

Mid-Atlantic I Episcopal District: Allegheny, New Jersey, Ohio, Guyana, Trinidad-Tobago, and Barbados Conferences: Bishop Nathaniel Jarrett, Jr.

Mid-Atlantic II Episcopal District: East Tennessee-Virginia, India, London-Birmingham, Manchester-Midland, Philadelphia-Baltimore, Virginia and Angola Conferences: Bishop Warren M. Brown

Western Episcopal District: Alaska, Arizona, California, Oregon-Washington, Southwest Rocky Mountain, and Colorado Conferences: Bishop Roy A. Holmes

Southwestern Delta: Arkansas, Louisiana, Oklahoma, South Mississippi, West Tennessee-Mississippi and Texas Conferences: Bishop Louis Hunter, Sr.

Alabama/Florida Episcopal District: Alabama, Cahaba, Central Alabama, North Alabama, South Alabama, West Alabama, Florida, and South Florida Conferences: Bishop James E. McCoy

Western West Africa: Cote D'Ivoire, East Ghana, Liberia, Mid-Ghana, North Ghana, Togo and West Ghana Conferences: Bishop Kenneth Monroe

GENERAL OFFICERS AND DEPARTMENTS

Address and telephone number for all Departments (except where indicated) is 3225 West Sugar Creek Rd., Charlotte, NC 28269 Tel. (704)599-4630 and Mailing Address for all Departemnts (except where indicated) is P.O. Box 26670, Charlotte, NC 28221.

Department of Records and Research: W. Robert Johnson, III, Gen. Sec.-Aud. Fax (704)688-2549, Email: j1gsa@aol.com or wajohnson@amezhqtr.org

Department of Finance: Mrs. Shirley Welch, Chief Financial Officer Fax (704)688-2553, Email: shwelch@amezhqtr.org

Star of Zion: Michael Lisby, Editor Fax (704) 688-2546, Email: editor@starofzion.org.

A.M.E. Zion Quarterly Review and Secretary A.M.E. Zion Historical Society: James D. Armstrong, Sec.-Editor, P.O. Box 33247, Charlotte, NC 28233 Fax (704)688-2544, Email: jaarmstrong@amezhqtr.org

Heritage Hall, Livingstone College, 701 W. Monroe St., Salisbury, NC 28144 Tel. (704) 216-6094

Department of Overseas Missions and Missionary Seer: Kermit DeGraffenreidt, Sec.-Editor, 475 Riverside Drive, Room 1935, New York, NY 10115 Tel. (212)870-2952 Fax (212)870-2808

Department of Brotherhood Pensions and Ministerial Relief: David Miller, Sec.-Treas. Fax (704)599-4580; Mailing Address: P.O. Box 217114, Charlotte, NC 28221, Email: damiller@amezhqtr.org

Christian Education Department: Raymon Hunt, Sec. Fax (704)688-2550, Email: rehunt@ amezhqtr.org

Department of Church School Literature: Mary A. Love, Editor Fax (704)688-2548, Email: malove@amezhqtr.org

Department of Church Extension and Home Missions: Terrence J. Jones, Sec.-Treas. Fax (704)688-2552, Email: tejones@amezhqtr.org

Bureau of Evangelism: Darryl B. Starnes, Dir., P.O. Box 217258, Charlotte, NC 28221-7258 Fax (704)688-2547, Email: dbstarnesevangel@aol.com

Public Affairs and Convention Manager: George E. McKain, II, Dir., P.O. Box 1417, Summerville, SC 29484 Tel. (843)276-3411 Fax (843)821-1735, Email: zionpagem2@ aol.com; Hqtrs. Tel. (704)599-4630

Department of Health and Social Concerns: Bernard Sullivan, Dir.

A.M.E. Zion Publishing House: David Baker, General Manager Fax (704)688-2541, Email: dabaker@amezhqtr.org

JUDICIAL COUNCIL

Honorable Adele M. Riley, 625 Ellsworth Dr., Dayton, OH 45426

Rev. Dr. George L. Blackwell, 220 N. Elm St., Williamston, NC 27892

Rev. Dr. E. Alex Brower, Esq., 11510-115th Ave., Jamaica, NY 11434

Rev. Dr. Richard Chappelle, 4026 Huron Ct., Cheswick, PA 15024

Ms. Elmira Jackson, Esq., 194 Wood Hollow Lane, New Rochelle, NY 10804

Mr. Neville Tucker, Esq., 865 South Figueroa, Ste. 2640, Los Angeles, CA 90017

Rev. Dr. Jewett L. Walker, 910 Bridle Path Lane, Charlotte, NC 28211

Mr. Jerome Willingham, Esq.

Rev. Dr. Reid R. White, Jr., 6608 Cartwright Dr., Columbia, SC 29223

CONNECTIONAL LAY COUNCIL

Pres., David A. Aiken, Sr., 115-21 142nd St., South Ozone Park, NY 11436 Tel. (718)322-1893 Fax (718)529-6045, Email: laypresident @att.net

First Vice Pres., Yvonne A. Tracey, 130 Stanwyck Road, Salisbury, NC 28147 Tel. (704)637-8687, Email: ytracey@livingstone. edu

Second Vice Pres., Jessie M. Riddick, 305 Culpepper Street, Elizabeth City, NC 27909

Tel. (252)335-3450, Email: riddick-aka2hot mail.com

Sec., Mary J. Matthews, P.O. Box 3155, Sanford, NC 27331 Tel. (919)775-2056 Fax (919)499-1187

Treas., Connie B. Williams, 8518 Fansworth, Charlotte, NC 28215 Tel. (704)531-2931 Fax (704)688-2551

Financial Sec., Jerry L. McCombs, P.O. Box 1444, Newton, NC 28658 Tel. (828)464-9609 Fax (828)466-1496, Email: jlmcableman@ charter.net

Chaplain, Charles Montgomery, 11436 Studebaker Road, Norwalk, CA 90650 Tel. (562)868-6683, Email: cpmonty@aol.com

Editor, "The Laity Speaks/The Connection", Rhandi M. Stith, Carrington Arms, 33 Lincoln Ave., Apt. 10L, New Rochelle, NY 10801 Tel. (914)235-3596 Fax (914)637-2518, Email: Rhandim@aol.com

Pres. Emeritus, Betty V. Stith, Carrington Arms, 33 Lincoln Ave., Apt. 10L, New Rochelle, NY 10801 Tel. (914)235-3596 Fax (914)637-2518

GENERAL OFFICERS OF THE WOMEN'S HOME AND OVERSEAS MISSIONARY SOCIETY

Gen. Pres., Dr. Barbara L. Shaw, 4002 Maine Ave., Baltimore, MD 21207 Tel. (410)578-8239 Fax (410)578-0261, Email: bshaw-max@comcast.net

First Vice Pres., Dr. Gloria G. Williams, P.O. Box 23, Raeford, NC 28376 Tel. (910)875-2205

Second Vice Pres., Mrs. Joyce A. Reid, 5309 Dayan Dr., Charlotte, NC 28216 Tel (704)596-3842 Fax (704)921-8323

Exec. Sec., Mrs. Rosetta J. Dunham, P.O. Box 26846, Charlotte, NC 28221-6846, Email: rodunham@amezhqtr.org

Recording Sec., Ms. Dorothy McFarlane, 88 Fawcett Close, Wye Street, Batterea London SW 112LU England

Gen. Treas., Ms. Pamela R. Valentine, 692 N. Hawkins Ave., Akron, OH 44313 Tel./Fax (330)864-4890

General Coord. of YAMS, Mrs. Dawn L. Walker, 823 South Indiana Ave., Griffith, Indiana 46319 Tel. (219)922-1361

Sec. of Youth Missionaries, Mrs. Charlrean B. Mapson, P.O. Box 1267, Wilmington, NC 28402 Tel. (910)251-0682 Fax (910)362-9202, Email: ysec@chuckmapson.net

Superintendent of Buds of Promise, Ms. Barbara J. Epps, 3204 Reid Ave., Charlotte, NC 28208 Tel. (704)372-7580

Sec., Bureau of Supplies, Mrs. Henrietta Daniels, 7535 Apache Plume Dr., Houston, TX 77071 Tel. (713)729–3436 Fax (713)728-9486

Chair, Life Members Council, Mrs. Loveleen "Dee" Perkins, 5303 Brewer Road, Beltsville,

61

MD 20705 Tel. (301)937-0244 Fax (301)937-4041

Editor, Woman's Section, Missionary Seer, Mrs. Christina B. Penrose, 10811 Richmond Ave. Apt.#39, Houston, TX 77042

Periodicals

Star of Zion, Quarterly Review, Church School Herald, Missionary Seer, Vision Focus, Evangel

Albanian Orthodox Archdiocese in America

The Albanian Orthodox Church in America traces its origins to the groups of Albanian immigrants which first arrived in the United States in 1886, seeking religious, cultural and economic freedoms denied them in the homeland.

In 1908 in Boston, the Rev. Fan Stylian Noli (later Archbishop) served the first liturgy in the Albanian language in 500 years, to which Orthodox Albanians rallied, forming their own diocese in 1919. Parishes began to spring up throughout New England and the Mid-Atlantic and Great Lakes states. In 1922, clergy from the United States traveled to Albania to proclaim the self-governance of the Orthodox Church in the homeland at the Congress of Berat.

In 1971 the Albanian Archdiocese sought and gained union with the Orthodox Church in America, expressing the desire to expand the Orthodox witness to America at large, giving it an indigenous character. The Albanian Archdiocese remains vigilant for its brothers and sisters in the homeland and serves as an important resource for human rights issues and Albanian affairs, in addition to its programs for youth, theological education, vocational interest programs and retreats for young adults and women.

Headquarters

523 E. Broadway, S. Boston, MA 02127

Media Contact, Sec., Dorothy Adams, Tel. (617)268-1275 Fax (617)268-3184

Web: www.oca.org

Officers

Metropolitan Herman, Tel. (617)268-1275

Chancellor, V. Rev. Arthur E. Liolin, 60 Antwerp St., East Milton, MA 02186 Tel. (617)698-3366

Lay Chpsn., William Poist, 40 Forge Village Rd., Westford, MA 01885 Tel. (978)392-0759

Treas., Cynthia Vasil Brown, 471 Capt. Eames Circle, Ashland, MA 01721 (508)881-0072

Albanian Orthodox Diocese of America

This Diocese was organized in 1950 as a canonical body administering to the Albanian faithful. It is under the ecclesiastical jurisdiction of the Ecumenical Patriarchate of Constantinople (Istanbul).

Headquarters

6455 Silver Dawn Lane, Las Vegas, NV 89118 Tel. (702)365-1989 Fax (702)365-1989

Media Contact, His Grace Bishop Ilia

Officers

His Grace Bishop Ilia, 6455 Silver Dawn Lane, Las Vegas, NV 89118 Tel. (702)365-1989 Fax (702)365-1989

The Allegheny Wesleyan Methodist Connection (Original Allegheny Conference)

This body was formed in 1968 by members of the Allegheny Conference (located in eastern Ohio and western Pennsylvania) of the Wesleyan Methodist Church, which merged in 1966 with the Pilgrim Holiness Church to form The Wesleyan Church.

The Allegheny Wesleyan Methodist Connection is composed of persons "having the form and seeking the power of godliness, united in order to pray together, to receive the word of exhortation, and to watch over one another in love, that they may help each other to work out their salvation." There is a strong commitment to congregational government and to holiness of heart and life. There is a strong thrust in church extension within the United States and in missions worldwide.

Headquarters

P.O. Box 357, Salem, OH 44460 Tel. (330)337-9376 Fax (330)337-9700

Media Contact, Pres., Rev. William Cope

Email: awmc@juno.com

Officers

Pres., Rev. William Cope, P.O. Box 357, Salem, OH 44460

Vice Pres., Rev. David Blowers, 1865 Marion-Williamsport Road, E, Marion, OH 43302

Sec., Rev. Ray Satterfield, 31 S. 12th Street, Indiana, PA 15701

Treas., James Kunselman, 1022 Newgarden Ave., Salem, OH 44460

Periodicals

The Allegheny Wesleyan Methodist

The Alliance of Baptists*

The Alliance of Baptists is an association of individuals and churches dedicated to the preservation of historic Baptist principles, freedoms, and traditions, and to the expression of our ministry and mission through cooperative relationships with other Baptist bodies and the larger Christian community.

From its inception in early 1987, the Alliance has stood for those values that have distinguished the Baptist movement from its beginnings nearly four centuries ago — the freedom and accountability of every individual in matters of faith; the freedom of each congregation under the authority of Jesus Christ to determine its own ministry and mission; and religious freedom for all in relationship to the state.

Headquarters
1328 16th St. N.W., Washington, DC 20036 Tel. (202)745-7609 Fax (202)745-0023
Media Contact, Exec. Dir., Rev. Dr. Stan Hastey
Email: shastey@allianceofbaptists.org
Website: www.allianceofbaptists.org

Officers
Exec. Dir., Rev. Dr. Stan Hastey
Assoc. Dir., Jeanette Holt
Pres., Rev. Jim Hopkins, Oakland, CA
Vice Pres., Kristy Arneson Pullen, Ashburn, VA
Sec., Amy Jacks Dean, Charlotte, NC

Periodicals
Connections

The American Association of Lutheran Churches

This church body was constituted on November 7, 1987. The AALC was formed by laity and pastors of the former American Lutheran Church in America who held to a high view of Scripture (inerrancy and infallibility). This church body also emphasizes the primacy of evangelism and world missions and the authority and autonomy of the local congregation.

Congregations of the AALC are distributed throughout the continental United States from Long Island, N.Y., to Los Angeles. The primary decision-making body is the General Convention, to which each congregation has proportionate representation.

Headquarters
The AALC National Office, 6600 N. Clinton Street, Augustine Hall, #13, Fort Wayne, Indiana 46825, Tel. (260)452-3213 Fax (260) 452-3215 Mailing Address: The AALC, 921 East Dupont Rd., #920, Fort Wayne, IN 46825-1551
Media Contact, Admn. Asst. to the AALC, Rev. Richard Shields
Email: theaalc@taalc.org
Website: www.taalc.org

Officers
Rev. Franklin E. Hays, Presiding Pastor, The American Association of Lutheran Churches, Tel. (260)452-3213, Email: presidingpastor@taalc.org Rev. Richard Shields, ALTS President (pro tem); Nat'l Home Mission Director; Administrative Ass't. to the Presiding Pastor; Administrative Ass't. to The AALC, Tel. (260)452-3213, Email: theaalc@ taalc.org Rev. Fred Balke, Director of Communications, The AALC; Evangel Editor, Email: evangel@ taalc.org
American Lutheran Theological Seminary (ALTS), Pres., Rev. Richard Shields, 6600 N. Clinton Street, Fort Wayne, IN 46825, Tel. (260)452-3218, Email: president@alts.edu

Periodicals
The Evangel

The American Baptist Association

The American Baptist Association (ABA) is an international fellowship of independent Baptist churches voluntarily cooperating in missionary, evangelistic, benevolent and Christian education activities throughout the world. Its beginnings can be traced to the landmark movement of the 1850s. Led by James R. Graves and J.M. Pendleton, a significant number of Baptist churches in the South, claiming a New Testament heritage, rejected as extrascriptural the policies of the newly formed Southern Baptist Convention (SBC). Because they strongly advocated church equality, many of these churches continued doing mission and benevolent work apart from the SBC, electing to work through local associations. Meeting in Texarkana, TX, in 1924, messengers from the various churches effectively merged two of these major associations, the Baptist Missionary Association of Texas and the General Association, forming the American Baptist Association.

Since 1924, mission efforts have been supported in Australia, Africa, Asia, Canada, Central America, Europe, India, Israel, Japan, Korea, Mexico, New Zealand, South America and the South Pacific. An even more successful domestic mission effort has changed the ABA from a predominantly rural southern organization to one with churches in 48 states.

Through its publishing arm in Texarkana, the ABA publishes literature and books numbering into the thousands. Major seminaries include the Missionary Baptist Seminary, founded by Dr. Ben M. Bogard in Little Rock, AR; Texas Baptist Seminary, Henderson, TX; Oxford Baptist Institute, Oxford, MS; and Florida Baptist Schools in Lakeland, FL.

While no person may speak for the churches of the ABA, all accept the Bible as the inerrant Word of God. They believe Christ was the virgin-born Son of God, that God is a triune God, that the only church is the local congregation of scripturally baptized believers and that the work of the church is to spread the gospel.

Headquarters
4605 N State Line Ave. Texarkana, TX 75503 Tel. (903)792-2783
Media Contact, Steve Reeves, Public Relations Director
Email: bssc@abaptist.org
Website: www.abaptist.org

Officers
President, David Butimore, Sr., 197 W. Railto Ave., Clovis, CA 93612
Vice Presidents, Neal Clark, Rt. 1, Box 48A, Daingerfield, TX 75638; John Owen, P.O. Box 142, Bryant, AR 72089; Donald R. Price, 210 West Mill St., Malvern, 72104

Recording Clerks, Larry Clements, 270 Tracy Dr., Monticello, AR 71655; Lonnie Wiggins, 1114 Occidental St., Redlands, CA 92374

Publications, Editor in Chief, Bill Johnson; Bus. Mgr., Wayne Sewell, 4605 N. State Line Ave., Texarkana, TX 75503

Meeting Arrangements Director, Edgar N. Sutton, P.O. Box 240, Alexander, AR 72002

Sec.-Treas. of Missions, Randy Cloud, P.O. Box 1050 Texarkana, TX 75504

American Baptist Churches in the U.S.A.*

Originally known as the Northern Baptist Convention, this body of Baptist churches changed the name to American Baptist Convention in 1950 with a commitment to hold the name in trust for all Christians of like faith and mind who desire to bear witness to the historical Baptist convictions in a framework of cooperative Protestantism.

In 1972 American Baptist Churches in the U.S.A. was adopted as the new name. Although national missionary organizational developments began in 1814 with the establishment of the American Baptist Foreign Mission Society and continued with the organization of the American Baptist Publication Society in 1824 and the American Baptist Home Mission Society in 1832, the general denominational body was not formed until 1907. American Baptist work at the local level dates back to the organization by Roger Williams of the First Baptist Church in Providence, R. I. in 1638.

Headquarters

American Baptist Churches Mission Center

P.O. Box 851, Valley Forge, PA 19482-0851 Tel. (610)768-2000 Fax (610)768-2320

Media Contact, Assoc. Gen'l. Sec.ty. For Mission Resource Development, the Rev. Dr. Leo S. Thorne, Tel. (610)768-2318 Fax (610) 768-2320

Email: richard.schramm@abc-usa.org

Website: www.abc-usa.org

Officers

Pres., Arlee Griffin, Jr

Vice Pres., Mary Hulst

Budget Review Officer, James Ratliff

Gen. Sec., A. Roy Medley; Tel. (610)768-2273, Email: roy.medley@abc-usa.org

Assoc. Gen. Sec.-Treas., Llyod Hambin; Tel. (610)768-2280, Email: lloyd.hamblin@abc-usa.org

REGIONAL ORGANIZATIONS

Central Region, ABC of, Steve Van Ostran, 5833 SW 29th St. Ste. A, Topeka, KS 66614-5500

Chicago, ABC of Metro, Larry L. Greenfield, 8765 W. Higgins Road., Ste. 240, Chicago, IL 60631

Cleveland Baptist Assoc., Leonard Thompson, 6060 Rockside Woods Blvd., Ste. 317, Cleveland, OH 44131

Connecticut, ABC of, Judy G. Allbee, 100 Bloomfield Ave., Hartford, CT 06105-1097

Dakotas, ABC of, Riley H. Walker, 1101 W. 22nd St., Sioux Falls, SD 57105-1699

District of Columbia Bapt. Conv., Jeffrey Haggray, 1628 16th St., NW, Washington, DC 20009-3099

Evergreen Baptist Association, Marcia Patton, 409 Third Ave., South Ste. A, Kent, WA 98032

ABC of the Great Rivers Region, J. Dwight Stinnett, P.O. Box 3786, Springfield, IL 62708-3786

Indiana, ABC of, Larry D. Mason, 1350 N. Delaware St., Indianapolis, IN 46202-2493

Indianapolis, ABC of Greater, Sarah Hallstrand, P.O. Box 421487., Indianapolis, IN 46242-1487

Los Angeles, ABC of, Samuel S. Chetti, 3325 Wilshire Blvd., # 800, Los Angeles, CA 90010-1746

Maine, ABC of, Alfred Fletcher, P.O. Box 6149, China Village, ME 04926-6149

Massachusetts, ABC of, Anthony Pappas, 20 Milton St., Dedham, MA 02026-2967

Metropolitan New York, ABC of, James O. Stallings, 475 Riverside Dr., Rm. 432, New York, NY 10115-0432

Michigan, ABC of, Michael A. Williams, 4578 S. Hagadorn Rd., East Lansing, MI 48823-5396

Mid-American Baptist Churches, Marshall Peters, 2400 86th St. Ste. !5., Des Moines, IA 50322-4380

Nebraska, ABC of, Susan E. Gillies, 6404 Maple St., Omaha, NE 68104-4079

New Jersey, ABC of, Lee Spitzer, 3752 Nottingham Way, Ste. 101, Trenton, NJ 08690-3802

New York State, ABC of, William A. Carlsen, 5842 Heritage Landing Dr., East Syracuse, NY 13057-9359

Northwest, ABC of, Charles Revis, 601 S. Ross Point Road, Post Falls, ID 83854-7726

Ohio, ABC of, Lawrence Swain, 136 N. Galway Dr., Granville, OH 43023-0376

Oregon, ABC of, W. Wayne Brown, 0245 SW Bancroft St., Ste. G, Portland, OR 97201-4270

Pennsylvania & Delaware, ABC of, Frank T. Frisch Korn, 106 Revere Lane, Coatesville, PA 19320

Philadelphia Baptist Assoc., James E. McJunkin, Jr., 100 N. 17th St. 11th floor, Philadelphia, PA 19103-2736

Puerto Rico, Baptist Churches of, Cristino Diaz-Montanez, PMB 477, P.O.Box 6022, Carolina, PR 00984-6022

Rhode Island, ABC of, Liliana Da Valle, P.O. Box 330, Exeter, RI 02822

Rochester-Genesee Region, ABC of, Alan Newton, St .# 320, 1100 S. Goodman., Rochester, NY 14620

Rocky Mountains, ABC of, Lawrence Van Spriell, 6855 S. Havaba St. # 220, Centennial, CO 80112

South, ABC of the, Walter L. Parrish, II, 5124 Greenwich Ave., Baltimore, MD 21229-2393

Vermont-New Hampshire, ABC of, Rohn Peterson, One Oak Ridge Rd., Bldg. B 3, Suite 4A, West Lebanon, NH 03784-3121

West, Growing Healthy Churches, ABC of the, Paul D. Borden, 2420 Camino Ramon, Ste. 140, San Ramon, CA 94583-4207

West Virginia Baptist Convention, David L. Carrico, P.O. Box 1019, Parkersburg, WV 26102-1019

Wisconsin, ABC of, Arlo R. Reichter, 15330 Watertown Plank Rd., Elm Grove, WI 53122-2391

BOARDS

American Baptist Assembly, Green Lake, WI 54941; Pres., Kenneth P. Giacoletto

American Baptist Historical Society, 1106 S. Goodman St., Rochester, NY 14620; or P.O. Box 851, Valley Forge, PA 19482-0851, Admn. Archivist, Deborah B. VanBroekhoven; Pres., Trinette V. McCray

American Baptist Men, Pres., Manuel Luguin

American Baptist Women's Ministries, Exec. Dir., Virginia Holmstrom; Pres., Terri Simpkins

Bd. of Intl. Ministries, Exec. Dir., Reid Trulson; Pres., James Stinespring

Bd. of Natl. Ministries, Exec. Dir., Aidsand F. Wright-Riggins; Pres., Peter Wolf

Ministers & Missionaries Benefit Bd., Exec. Dir., Sumner M. Grant; Pres., George Tooze, 475 Riverside Dr., New York, NY 10115

Minister Council, Dir., Carole (Kate) H. Harvey; Pres., Alice B. Greene

Periodicals

Tomorrow Magazine, *The Secret Place*, *American Baptist Quarterly*

The American Carpatho-Russian Orthodox Greek Catholic Church

The American Carpatho-Russian Orthodox Greek Catholic Church is a self-governing diocese that is in communion with the Ecumenical Patriarchate of Constantinople. The late Patriarch Benjamin I, in an official Patriarchal Document dated Sept. 19, 1938, canonized the Diocese in the name of the Orthodox Church of Christ.

Headquarters

312 Garfield St., Johnstown, PA 15906 Tel. (814)539-4207 Fax (814)536-4699

Media Contact, Chancellor, V. Rev. Protopresbyter Frank P. Miloro, Tel. (814)539-8086 Fax (814)536-4699

Email: archdiocese@goarch.org

Website: www.goarch.org

Officers

Bishop, Metropolitan Nicholas Smisko, 312 Garfield St., Johnstown, PA 15906 Tel. (814)539-4207 Fax (814)536-4699

Chancellor, V. Rev. Protopresbyter Frank P.

Miloro, 249 Butler Ave., Johnstown, PA 15906 Tel. (814)539-9143 Fax (814)536-4699, acrod@helicon.net

Treas., V. Rev. Protopresbyter Ronald A. Hazuda, 115 East Ave., Erie, PA 16503 Tel. (814)453-4902

Periodicals

The Church Messenger

American Evangelical Christian Churches

Founded in 1944, the A.E.C.C is composed of individual ministers and churches who are united in accepting "Seven Articles of Faith." These seven articles are-the Bible as the written word of God; the Virgin birth; the deity of Jesus Christ; Salvation through the atonement; guidance of our life through prayer; the return of the Saviour; the establishment of the Millennial Kingdom.

The American Evangelical Christian Churches offers the following credentials-Certified Christian Worker, Commission to Preach, Licensed Minister and Ordained Minister to those who accept the Seven Articles of Faith, who put unity in Christ first and are approved by A.E.C.C.

A.E.C.C seeks to promote the gospel through its ministers, churches and missionary activities.

Churches operate independently with all decisions concerning local government left to the individual churches.

The organization also has ministers in Canada, England, Bolivia, Philippines Thailand, Brazil and South America.

Headquarters

P.O. Box 47312, Indianapolis, IN 46227 Tel. (317)788-9280 Fax (317)788-1410

Media Contact, Dr. Charles Wasielewski, Sr., 51 Wells Rd, Barton, NY 13734-1818

Email: aeccoffice@infoblvd.net

Website: www.aeccministries.com

INTERNATIONAL OFFICERS

Mod., Dr. Charles Wasielewski, Box 51, Wells Rd., Barton, NY 13734 Tel. (607)565-4074

Sec., Dr. Gene McClain, 520 Blooming Pike, Morgantown, IN 46160, Tel. (812)597-5021

Treas., Dr. Michael Ward, Sr., 4802 Chervil Ct., Indianapolis, IN 46237, Tel. (317)888-2095

Bd. Member, Dr. Allen Kent, 550 E. Shoeline Drive, Long Beach, CA 90802, Tel. (562)590-7294

Missions Coordinator, Dr. Douglas Schlemmer, P.O. Box 409, Twin Peaks, CA 92391, Tel. (909)338-6495

REGIONAL MODERATORS

Northwest Region, Rev. Alvin House, P.O. Box 393, Darby MT 59829 Tel.(406)821-3141

Central-West Region, Rev. Charles Clark, Box 314, Rockport, IL 62370 Tel.(217)437-2507

Far West Region, Pastor Richard Cuthbert, 1195 Via Serville, Cathedral City, CA 92234, Tel. (706)321-6682

65

Lowell Ford, 397 Shamrock Lane, Newark, OH, 43055, Tele. (614)309-3419

Northeast Region, Rev. John Merrill, P.O. Box 183, East Smithfield, PA 18817 Tel.(717)596-4598

East Region, James R. Brown, 17404 W. Washington, Hagerstown, MD 21740, Tel. (301)797812f1

Southeast Region, Rev. James Fullwood, 207 5th Avenue, N.E., Lutz, FL 33549

STATE MODERATORS

Rev. James Brown, Maryland
Rev. John W. Coats, Delaware
Brenda Osborne, New York
Dr. Berton G. Heleine, Illinois
Rev. R. Eugene Hill, New Jersey
Rev. Kenneth Pope, Washington
Rev. Art Mirek, Michigan
Rev. Charles Jennings, Pennsylvania
Rev. Jerry Myers, Indiana

FOREIGN OUTREACH MINISTRIES

American Evangelical Christian Churches-Canada

Regional Moderator, Dr. Stephen K. Massey, 730 Ontario Street, Suite 709, Toronto, Ontario M4X 1N3, Tel. (416)323-9076

Philippine Evangelical Christian Churches

Director, Rev. Alan A. Olubalang, P.O. Box 540, Cotabato City, Philippines 9600

American Evangelical Christian Churches-Philippines

Regional Moderator, Rev. Oseas Andres, P.O. Box 2695, Central Post Office, 1166 Q.C. Metro Manila, Philippines

Periodicals

The American Evangelical Christian Churches Newsletter "AECC Communique"

American Rescue Workers

Major Thomas E. Moore was National Commander of Booth's Salvation Army when a dispute flared between Booth and Moore. Moore resigned from Booth's Army and due to the fact that Booth's Army was not incorporated at the time, Moore was able to incorporate under said name. The name was changed in 1890 to American Salvation Army. In 1913 the current name American Rescue Workers was adopted.

It is a national religious social service agency which operates on a quasimilitary basis. Membership includes officers (clergy), soldiers-adherents (laity), members of various activity groups and volunteers who serve as advisors, associates and committed participants in ARW service functions.

The motivation of the organization is the love of God. Its message is based on the Bible. This is expressed by its spiritual Ministry, the purposes of which are to preach the gospel of Jesus Christ and to meet human needs in his name without discrimination. It is a branch of the Christian Church . . . A Church with a Mission.

Headquarters

Operational Headquarters, 25 Ross Street, Williamsport, PA 17701 Tel. (570)323-8693 Fax (570)323-8694

National Field Office, 11116 Gehr Road, Waynesboro, PA 17268-9101 Tel. (717)762-2965

Media Contact, Natl. Communication Sec./Natl Special Services Dir., Col. Robert N. Coles, Rev., Natl. Field Ofc. Fax (717)762-8109

Email: amerscwk@pcspower.net

Website: www.arwus.com

Officers

Commander-In-Chief & Pres. Of Corp., General Claude S. Astin, Jr. Rev

Natl. Bd. Pres., Col. Sam Astin (Claude S. Astin, III)

Ordination Committee, Chpsn., Gen. Paul E. Martin, (Emeritus) Rev.

Natl. Chief Sec., Col. Dawn R. Astin, NQ-643 Elmira St., Williamsport, PA 17701

Periodicals

The Rescue Herald

Amish—please see Old Order Amish Church.

The Anglican Orthodox Church—please see The Episcopal Orthodox Church.

The Antiochian Orthodox Christian Archdiocese of North America

The spiritual needs of Antiochian faithful in North America were first served through the Syro-Arabian Mission of the Russian Orthodox Church in 1895. In 1895, the Syrian Orthodox Benevolent Society was organized by Antiochian immigrants in New York City. Raphael Hawaweeny, a young Damascene clergyman serving as professor of Arabic language at the Orthodox theological academy in Kazan, Russia, came to New York to organize the first Arabic-language parish in North America in 1895, after being canonically received under the omophori-on of the head of the Russian Church in North America. Saint Nicholas Cathedral, now located at 355 State St. in Brooklyn, is considered the "mother parish" of the Archdiocese.

On March 12, 1904, Hawaweeny became the first Orthodox bishop to be consecrated in North America. He traveled throughout the continent and established new parishes. The unity of Orthodoxy in the New World, including the Syrian Greek Orthodox community, was rup-tured after the death of Bishop Raphael in 1915 and by the Bolshevik revolution in Russia and the First World War. Unity returned in 1975 when Metropolitan Philip Saliba, of the Antiochian Archdiocese of New York, and Metropolitan Michael Shaheen of the Antiochian Archdiocese of Toledo, Ohio, signed the Articles of Reunification, ratified by the Holy Synod of the Patriarchate. Saliba was recognized as the Metropolitan Primate and Shaheen as Auxiliary

Archbishop. A second auxiliary to the Metropolitan, Bishop Antoun Khouri, was consecrated at Brooklyn's Saint Nicholas Cathedral, in 1983. A third auxiliary, Bishop Basil Essey was consecrated at Wichita's St. George Cathedral in 1992. Two additional bishops were added in 1994, Bishop Joseph Zehlaoui and Bishop Demetri Khoury.

The Archdiocesan Board of Trustees (consisting of 60 elected and appointed clergy and lay members) and the Metropolitan's Advisory Council (consisting of clergy and lay representatives from each parish and mission) meet regularly to assist the Primate in the administration of the Archdiocese. Currently, there are 245 parishes and missions in the Archdiocese.

Headquarters
358 Mountain Rd., Englewood, NJ 07631 Tel. (201)871-1355 Fax (201)871-7954

Media Contact, Very Rev. Fr Thomas Zain, 52 78th St., Brooklyn, NY 11209 Tel. (718)748-7940 Fax (718)855-3608

Email: FrJoseph@antiochian.org

Website: www.antiochian.org

Officers
Primate, Archbishop Philip Saliba, 358 Mountain Road, Englewood, NJ 07631—Metropolitan of New York and all North America, Tel. (210) 871-1355

Bishop Antoun Khouri, 358 Mountain Road, Englewood, NJ 07631- Bishop of Miami and the Southeast, Tel. (201)871-1355

Bishop Joseph Zehlaoui, 454 S. Lorraine Blvd., Los Angeles, CA 90020—Bishop of Los Angeles and the West, Tel. (323)934-3131

Bishop Basil Essey, 1559 N. Woodlawn, Wichita, KS 67208—Bishop of Wichita and Mid-America, Tel. (316)687-3169

Bishop Thomas Joseph, P.O. Box 638, Ligionier, PA 15658—Bishop of Oakland, PA, Charleston, WV and the Mid Atlantic, Tel. (724)787-9832 Bishop Alexander Mufarrij, 10820 Rue La Verdue, Montreal, QC H3L2L9—Bishop of Ottawa, Eastern Canada and Upstate New York, Tel. (514)388-4344

Periodicals
The Word, Again Magazine

Apostolic Catholic Assyrian Church of the East, North American Dioceses
The Holy Apostolic Catholic Assyrian Church of the East is the ancient Christian church that developed within the Persian Empire from the day of Pentecost. The Apostolic traditions testify that the Church of the East was established by Sts. Peter, Thomas, Thaddaeus and Bartholomew from among the Twelve and by the labors of Mar Mari and Aggai of the Seventy. The Church grew and developed carrying the Christian gospel into the whole of Asia and islands of the Pacific. Prior to the Great Persecution at the hands of Tamer'leng the Mongol, it is said to have been the largest Christian church in the world.

The doctrinal identity of the church is that of the Apostles. The church stresses two natures and two Qnume in the One person, Perfect God-Perfect man. The church gives witness to the original Nicene Creed, the Ecumenical Councils of Nicea and Constantinople and the church fathers of that era. Since God is revealed as Trinity, the appellation "Mother of God" is rejected for the "Ever Virgin Blessed Mary Mother of Christ," we declare that she is Mother of Emmanuel, God with us!

The church has maintained a line of Catholicos Patriarchs from the time of the Holy Apostles until this present time. Today the present occupant of the Apostolic Throne is His Holiness Mar Dinkha IV, 120th successor to the See of Selucia Ctestiphon.

Headquarters
Catholicos Patriarch, His Holiness Mar Dinkha, IV, Metropolitanate Residence, The Assyrian Church of the East, Baghdad, Iraq

Media Contact, Father Sleiman Shequel, 7201 N. Ashland, Chicago, IL 60626 Tel. (773)465-4777 Fax (773)465-0776

Email: ABSoro@aol.com

Website: www.cired.org/ace

BISHOPS—NORTH AMERICA
Diocese Eastern USA, His Grace Bishop Mar Aprim Khamis, 8908 Birch Ave., Morton Grove, IL 60053 Tel. (847)966-0617 Fax (847)966-0012; Chancellor to the Bishop, Rev. Chancellor C. H. Klutz, 7201 N. Ashland, Chicago, IL 60626 Tel. (773)465-4777 Fax (773)465-0776

Diocese Western USA, St. Joseph Cathedral, 680 Minnesota Ave., San Jose, CA 95125 Tel. (408)286-7377 Fax (408)286-1236

Diocese of Canada, His Grace Bishop Mar Emmanuel Joseph, St. Mary Cathedral, 57 Apted Ave., Weston, ON M9L 2P2 Tel. (416) 744-9311

Comm. on Inter-Church & Religious Ed., His Grace Bishop Mar Bawai, Diocese of Seattle in WA, 165 NW 65th, Seattle, WA 98117 Tel. (206)789-1843

Apostolic Catholic Church
The Apostolic Catholic Church, rooted in the New Testament, affirms the empowerment and the dignity of the poor, the needy and the oppressed by adopting a preferential option for those who are disenfranchised and marginalized in this society. Apostolic Catholicism is radically committed to the unconditional acceptance of all who are in need.

The special mission of the Apostolic Catholic Church is to be Christ's arms and legs, reaching out to those who suffer and are ignored by the world. We choose to serve others, ever mindful of the example of Christ, who "did not cling to his equality with God, but emptied himself to assume the condition of a slave." (Philippians 2:6-7)

Member: The Council of North American Old Catholic Bishops, the Florida Council of Churches, and International Council of Community Churches.

Headquarters

Apostolic Catholic Church, 7813 N. Nebraska Avenue, Tampa, FL 33604

Media Contact: Bishop Charles Leigh (813)238-6060

Email: Bishop-Chuck@apostoliccatholicchurch. com

Website: www.apostoliccatholicchurch.com

Other Institutions

Family Counseling Center, Temeous Catholic Worker House, St James Catholic Worker House.

Periodicals

The Shofar

Apostolic Catholic Orthodox Church

The Apostolic Catholic Orthodox Church (ACOC) is a communion of persons gathered for worship and public ministry outreach within the Christian Apostolic tradition. The ACOC is creedal, renewal-oriented, and is a part of the autocephalous (self-ruling) Old Catholic Movement, which has its origins in the ancient Catholic Church of the Netherlands. The immediate history of the Old Catholic churches comes out of the reform movement that took place after the First Vatican Council (1869–70). The ACOC maintains a friendly relationship with the Old Catholic Church in the Netherlands.

The bishops of the newly forming churches received episcopal consecration in valid Apostolic lines from the church of the Netherlands, based in Utrecht, which had been a fully autonomous Catholic church. These churches became known as "Old Catholic" in reference to their insistence upon return to the basic tenets of Apostolic Christianity, and as defined by the seven Ecumenical Councils of the undivided Eastern and Western Christian churches.

The Old Catholic independent church movement came to the United States as early as the 1880s. Bishop DeLandes Berghes, an Austrian nobleman, ordained and consecrated a bishop with valid Old Catholic Apostolic lines, was sent to North America in 1914. Two of the bishops he consecrated in 1916, Carmel Henry Carfora and William Francis Brothers, are whom the ACOC derives its lines of Apostolic Succession.

The Apostolic Catholic Orthodox Church's governance is collegial and synodal, with clergy and lay persons sharing in its spiritual leadership and pastoral outreach, in the Spirit of Christ.

Clerical celibacy (which is a matter of discipline) is optional among Old Catholics. In the ACOC, Holy Orders are open to both women and men, single or married. Graduate, Seminary and Clinical Pastoral education are required for candidates for ordination. Decisions pertaining to family planning are left to the concience of married couples, through prayer and counseling.

Matters of faith in the Apostolic Catholic Orthodox Church are the same as in other liturgical churches as formulated in the apostles and Nicene Creeds. The Offices of bishop, priest, and deacon exist for the service of spiritual leadership in facilitating expressions of life with God—in the celebration of the sacraments, counseling and pastoral care, teaching, and public advocacy of Gospel values. The sacraments are never denied to any person on grounds of gender, race, or marital status. The Holy Eucharist is the center of worship for the ACOC and all who are baptized are welcomed at the Lord's Table.

The Apostolic Catholic Orthodox Church emphasizes the importance of the life of the church as community, that all may be one in Christ (John 17), through mutual helpfulness, ministering to one another and all creation in love, through the diversity of personal giftedness and sensitivity to the particular needs of those being served. The church values and promotes spiritually based, courageous, and compassionate ministry to both personal and global needs. Ongoing spiritual growth is to be nourished through sacred study and contemplative prayer. The ACOC values ecumenical dialogue as an expression of the life of the church.

Headquarters

1900 St. James Place, Suite 880, Houston, TX 77056-4129 Tel (713)266-2456 or (713)977-2855 Fax (713)266-0855

Website: www.apostoliccatholic.org

Officers

Presiding Bishop, Most Rev. Diana C. Dale, 1900 St. James Place, Suite 880, Houston, TX 77056-4129 Tel. (713)266-2456

Email: dcdale@apostoliccatholic.org

Tresurer, Elizabeth F. Burleigh, J.D., 1770 St. James Place, Suite 550, Houston, TX 77056 Tel. (713)334-0499

Ecumenical Officer, Very Rev. Robert L. Lewis Jr., P.O. Box 10483, Rockville, MD 20849 Tel. (240)401-0178

Register Agent, Rev. Lance Beizer, J.D., P.O. Box 1121, Campbell, CA 9009-1121

BOARD REGIONAL REPRESENTATIVES

West, Rev. Gale Bellinger, 2033 S.15th St., Centerville, IA 52544-3016

Mid-Continent, Rev. Robert M. Palmer, 871 Stone Blvd. Nolensville, TN 37135

Atlantic, Very Rev. Robert L. Lewis Jr. 2639 Ridge Rd.

Institute of Worklife Ministry, 1900 St. James Place, Suite 880, Houston, TX 77056-4129, Tel (713)266-2456 Fax(713)266-0805

Periodicals

ACOC Quarterly Bulletin, Worklife Quarterly Newsletter

Apostolic Christian Church (Nazarene)

This body was formed in America by an immigration from various European nations, from a movement begun by Rev. S. H. Froehlich, a Swiss pastor, whose followers are still found in Switzerland and Central Europe.

Headquarters

Apostolic Christian Church Foundation, 1135 Sholey Rd., Richmond, VA 23231 Tel. (804) 222-1943 Fax (804)236-0642
Media Contact, Exec. Dir., James Hodges
Email: accf@sprynet.com

Officers

Exec. Dir., James Hodges

Apostolic Christian Churches of America

The Apostolic Christian Churches of America was founded in the early 1830s in Switzerland by Samuel Froehlich, a young divinity student who had experienced a religious conversion based on the pattern found in the New Testament. The church, known then as Evangelical Baptist, spread to surrounding countries. A Froehlich associate, Elder Benedict Weyeneth, established the church's first American congregation in 1847 in upstate New York. In America, where the highest concentration today is in the Midwest farm belt, the church became known as Apostolic Christian.

Church doctrine is based on a literal interpretation of the Bible, the infallible Word of God. The church believes that a true faith in Christ's redemptive work at Calvary is manifested by a sincere repentance and conversion. Members strive for sanctification and separation from worldliness as a consequence of salvation, not as a means to obtain it. Security in Christ is believed to be conditional based on faithfulness. Uniform observance of scriptural standards of holiness are stressed. Holy Communion is confined to members of the church. Male members are willing to serve in the military, but do not bear arms. The holy kiss is practiced and women wear head coverings during prayer and worship.

Doctrinal authority rests with a council of elders, each of whom serves as a local elder (bishop). Both elders and ministers are chosen from local congregations, do not attend seminary and serve without compensation. Sermons are delivered extemporaneously as led by the Holy Spirit, using the Bible as a text.

Headquarters

3420 N. Sheridan Rd., Peoria, IL 61604
Media Contact, Secretary., William R. Schlatter, 14834 Campbell Rd., Defiance, OH 43512 Tel. (419)393-2621 Fax (419)393-2144
Email: Questions@ApostolicChristian.org or wrschlatter@juno
Website: www.apostolicchristian.org

Officers

Sec., Elder William R. Schlatter, 14834 Campbell Rd., Defiance, OH 43512 Tel. (419)393-2621 Fax (419)393-2144
Apostolic Christian World Relief—Humanitarian Aid to the World—www.acworldrelief.org

Periodicals

The Silver Lining

Apostolic Episcopal Church

The Apostolic Episcopal Church on Sept. 23-24, 2000 in New York City signed Concordats of Intercommunion with the following Christian Churches-The Anglican Independent Communion, The Ethiopian Orthodox Coptic Archdiocese of North and South America, The Uniate Western Orthodox Catholic Church, and the Byelorussian Orthodox National Church in Exile under the administration of His Beatitude Yury I.

In effect, the Apostolic Episcopal Church thus became a Uniate Western Rite of the Orthodox Church of the East, using the 1928 Book of Common Prayer. In 1905, under the guidance of Archbishop Tikhon Bellavin (later Patriarch of Moscow), the Holy Synod in St. Petersburg approved the use of the Anglican Liturgy for Western Rite Orthodox Christians. Today this usage is called the Rite of St. Tikhon and is in use among many Orthodox Western Rite Jurisdictions.

This Pilgrimage to Orthodoxy among Anglicans began in 1712 with the Non-Jurors Anglican Hierarchy and faithful. These Non-Jurors were Anglican Clergy who in 1689 refused allegiance to King William III and Queen Mary, the usurpers who had overthrown King James II. In 1712 Metropolitan-Bishop Arsenios of the Alexandrine Patriarchate visited England and received many of these "British Katholicks" into the Orthodox Church.

Headquarters

World Mission HQS: 80-46 234 St. Jamaica, NY 11427-2116, Attn.: the Rt. Rev. Francis C. Spataro DD, Tel. (917)529-0585
The Province of Guyana and the Caribbean, c/o The Rev. Lloyd U. Samuel OCR, P.O. Box 10844, Georgetown, Guyana, South America, 630875
Ohio Vicariate: the V. Rev. Michael B. Reed, St. Peter the Aleut Mission, 3423 Hunter Dr., N. Olmstead, OH 44070 Tel. (216)779-0272
Pennsylvania Vicariate: Rev. Dr. Sam Guido DD, OCR, St. Paul's Chapel, 620 Main St. Slatington, PA 18080

Shenouda Seminary Dir.: Rev. Dr. Paget Mack, OCR, OSBM, P.O. Box 673, New York, NY 10035

Belarus Home Mission, AWP, 19 Aqueduct St, Ossining, NY 10562 Tel. (914)762-7093

Media Contact,The.Rev. S.C. Douglas, MA, P.O. Box 5016 Athens, GA 30604

Email: apostolic.episcopal@gmail.com

Website: www.apostolic-episcopal.org

Officers

President, The Rt. Rev. Francis C. Spataro, DD, OCR Tel. (718)740 4134 (24 hour number) Email: vil11427@mycingular.blackberry.net

Archbishop of the Central & Western Province, USA, Dr. Wayne Ellis, PhD, OCR, Email: wayneellis@charter.net

OCR Primate: The Rt. Rev. Peter P. Brennan, OCR, DD, Email: ddamdg@aol.com

Vicar for Guyana & the Caribbean: Rev Lloyd U. Samuel, OCR

Vicar for Ohio: The V. Rev. Michael B. Reed, OCR

Emeritus Primate for the AEC, The M. Rev. Bertil Persson, ThD, OCR , Archbishop of Scandinavia & Baltic Republics, Illerstigen 22, S-170 71, Solna, Sweden

Pennsylvania Vicariate: Rev. Dr. Sam Guido, DD LOC, Email: samsamtheman@aol.com

Shenouda Seminary Dir.: Rev. Dr. Paget Mack, OSBM

Vicar for Belarus: M. Rev. Emigidiusz J. Ryzy, OCR, DD, Email: amworldpat@aol.com

The Order of Corporate Reunion; The Vilatte Guild/Society of St. Cassian

Periodicals

The Tower of St. Cassian

Apostolic Faith Mission Church of God

The Apostolic Faith Mission Church of God was founded and organized July 10, 1906, by Bishop F. W. Williams in Mobile, Alabama.

Bishop Williams was saved and filled with the Holy Ghost at a revival in Los Angeles under Elder W. J. Seymour of The Divine Apostolic Faith Movement. After being called into the ministry, Bishop Williams went out to preach the gospel in Mississippi, then moved on to Mobile.

On Oct. 9, 1915, the Apostolic Faith Mission Church of God was incorporated in Mobile under Bishop Williams, who was also the general overseer of this church.

Headquarters

Ward's Temple, 806 Muscogee Rd., Cantonment, FL 32533

Media Contact, Natl. Sunday School Supt., Bishop Thomas Brooks, 3298 Toney Dr., Decatur, GA 30032 Tel. (404)284-7596

BOARD OF BISHOPS

Presiding Bishop, Donice Brown, 2265 Welcome Cir., Cantonement, FL 32535 Tel. (904)968-5225

Bishop T.C. Tolbert Sr., 226 Elston Ave., Anniston, AL, 36201; Bishop John Crum, 4236 Jackson St., Birmingham, AL, 35217; Bishop Samuel Darden, 25 Taunton Ave., Hyde Park, MA 02136; Bishop James Truss, P.O. Box 495, Lincoln, AL, 35096; Bishop T.C. Tolbert, Jr., 768 Grayton Rd., Ohatchee, AL 36271; Bishop Thomas Brooks, 3298 Toney Drive, Decatur, GA. 30032 Tel. (404)284-7596 Fax (404)284-7173; Bishop Johnny Cunningham, P.O.Box 472 Century, FL 32535 Tel. (850)256-2443; Bishop Wayne Smiley, 228 Seville Circle, Mary Ester, FL 32569

NATIONAL DEPARTMENTS

Missionary Dept., Pres., Rosa Tolbert, Anniston, AL

Youth Dept., Pres., Johnny Kennedy, Birmingham, AL

Sunday School Dept., Supt., Thomas Brooks, Decatur, GA

Mother Dept., Pres., Mother Bessie Davis, 1003 Northeast St., Pensacola, FL 32501

INTERNATIONAL DEPARTMENTS

Morobia, Liberia, Bishop Beter T. Nelson, Box 3646, Bush Rhode Islane, Morobia, Liberia

Periodicals

The Three-Fold Vision

Apostolic Faith Mission of Portland, Oregon

The Apostolic Faith Mission of Portland, Oregon, was founded in 1907. It had its beginning in the Latter Rain outpouring on Azusa Street in Los Angeles in 1906.

Some of the main doctrines are justification by faith which is a spiritual new birth, as Jesus told Nicodemus and as Martin Luther proclaimed in the Great Reformation; sanctification, a second definite work of grace; the Wesleyan teaching of holiness; the baptism of the Holy Ghost as experienced on the Day of Pentecost and again poured out at the beginning of the Latter Rain revival in Los Angeles.

Mrs. Florence L. Crawford, who had received the baptism of the Holy Ghost in Los Angeles, brought this Latter Rain message to Portland on Christmas Day 1906. It has spread to the world by means of literature which is still published and mailed everywhere without a subscription price. Collections are never taken in the meetings and the public is not asked for money.

Camp meetings have been held annually in Portland, Oregon since 1907, with delegations coming from around the world.

Missionaries from the Portland headquarters have established churches in Korea, Japan, the Philippines, Romania and many countries in Africa.

Headquarters

6615 SE 52nd Ave., Portland, OR 97206 Tel. (503)777-1741 Fax (503)777-1743

Media Contact, Superintendent, Darrel D. Lee
Website: www.apostolicfaith.org

Officers

President, Rev. Darrel D. Lee

Periodicals

Higher Way

Apostolic Lutheran Church of America

Organized in 1872 as the Solomon Korteniemi Lutheran Society, this Finnish body was incorporated in 1929 as the Finnish Apostolic Lutheran Church in America and changed its name to Apostolic Lutheran Church of America in 1962.

This body stresses preaching the Word of God. There is an absence of liturgy and formalism in worship. A seminary education is not required of pastors. Being called by God to preach the Word is the chief requirement for clergy and laity. The church stresses personal absolution and forgiveness of sins, as practiced by Martin Luther, and the importance of bringing converts into God's kingdom.

Headquarters

P.O. Box 2948, Battle Ground, WA 98604-2948
Media Contact, Secretary, Ivan M. Seppala
Website: www.apostolic-lutheran.org

Officers

Chairman, Richard C. Juuti, RRI, Bentley, AB T0C 0J0, Canada
Treas., Ben Johnson, 98920 Keller Rd., Astoria, OR 97103
Secretary, Ivan M. Seppala, 332 Mt. Washington Way, Clayton, CA 94517

Periodicals

Christian Monthly

Apostolic Orthodox Catholic Church of North America—please see Holy Synod for the American Diaspora.

Armenian Apostolic Church of America

Widespread movement of the Armenian people over the centuries caused the development of two seats of religious jurisdiction of the Armenian Apostolic Church in the World-the See of Etchmiadzin, in Armenia, and the See of Cilicia, in Lebanon.

In America, the Armenian Church functioned under the jurisdiction of the Etchmiadzin See from 1887 to 1933, when a division occurred within the American diocese over the condition of the church in Soviet Armenia. One group chose to remain independent until 1957, when the Holy See of Cilicia agreed to accept them under its jurisdiction.

Despite the existence of two dioceses in North America, the Armenian Church has always functioned as one church in dogma and liturgy.

Headquarters

Eastern Prelacy, 138 E. 39th St., New York, NY 10016 Tel. (212)689-7810 Fax (212)689-7168, Email: email@armenianprelacy.org
Western Prelacy, 6252 Honolulu Ave., La Crecsenta, CA 91214 Tel. (818)248-7737 Fax (818)248-7745, Email: prelacy@aol.com
Media Contact, Vazken Ghougassian
Email: prelacy@gis.net
Website: www.armprelacy.org

Officers

Eastern Prelacy, Prelate, Archbishop Oshagan Choloyan
Eastern Prelacy, Chpsn., Jack Mardoian, Esq.
Western Prelacy, Prelate, Archbishop Moushegh Mardirossian
Western Prelacy, Chpsn., Dr. Garo Hagopian

DEPARTMENTS

Eastern Prelacy Offices, Executive Director, Vazken Ghougassian
AREC, Armenian Religious Educ. Council, Exec. Coord., Deacon Shant Kazanjian
ANEC, Armenian Natl. Educ. Council, Exec. Coord., Nayira Balanian

Periodicals

Outreach

Armenian Apostolic Church, Diocese of America*

The Armenian Apostolic Church was founded at the foot of the biblical mountain of Ararat in the ancient land of Armenia, where two of Christ's Holy Apostles, Saints Thaddeus and Bartholomew, preached Christianity. In A.D. 303 the historic Mother Church of Etchmiadzin was founded by Saint Gregory the Illuminator, the first Catholicos of All Armenians. This cathedral still stands and serves as the center of the Armenian Church. A branch of this Church was established in North America in 1889. The first church building was consecrated in 1891 in Worcester, MA. The first Armenian Diocese was set up in 1898 by the then-Catholicos of All Armenians, Mgrditch Khrimian. Armenian immigrants built the first Armenian church in the new world in Worcester, MA, under the jurisdiction of Holy Etchmiadzin.

In 1927, the churches and the parishes in California were formed into a Western Diocese and the parishes in Canada formed their own diocese in 1984. Other centers of major significance of the Armenian Apostolic Church are the Catholicate of Cilicia, now located in Lebanon, the Armenian Patriarchate of Jerusalem and the Armenian Patriarchate of Constantinople.

Headquarters

Eastern Diocese, 630 Second Ave., New York, NY 10016-4885 Tel. (212)686-0710 Fax (212) 779-3558
Western Diocese, 3325 North Glenoaks Blvd., Burbank, CA 91504 Tel. (818)558-7474 Fax

(818)558-6333, Email: mgizlechyan@armenian
churchwd.com
Canadian Diocese, 615 Stuart Ave., Outremont,
QC H2V 3H2 Tel. (514)276-9479 Fax
(514)276-9960
Media Contact, Dir., Public Relations, Chris
Zakian, Eastern Diocese
Diocesan Council Chpsn., Haig Dadourian, 415
Madison Ave., 7th Fl., New York, NY 10017
Wester Diocese, Pirmate, His Em. Archbishop
Vatche Hovsepian, Western Diocese Ofc.
Diocesan Council, Chpsn., Dn. Dr. Varouj
Alterbarmakian, 7290 North San Pedro,
Fresno, CA 93011
Diocesan Council, Sec., Mr. John Yaldezian,
23221 Aetna St., Woodland Hills, CA 91367
Tel. (B) (818)346-6163
Canadian Diocese, Primate, His Em. Archbishop
Hovnan Derderian
Diocesan Council, Chpsn., Mr. Takvor Hopyan,
20 Pineway, Blvd., Willowdale, ON M2H 1A1
Tel. (B) (416)222-2639
Diocesan Council, Secretary, Mr. Vahe Ketli, 750
Montpellier, #909, St. Laurens, QC H4L 5A7
Tel. (514)747-1347
Email: mgizlechyan@armenianchurchwd.com
Website: www.armenianchurch.org

Officers

Eastern Diocese:
Primate, Archbishop Khajag Barsamian, Eastern
Diocese Ofc.
Diocesan Council, Chpsn., Haig Dadourian, 415
Madison Ave., 7th Fl., New York, NY 10017
Western Diocese:
Primate, His Em. Archbishop Vatche Hovsepian,
Western Diocese Ofc.
Diocesan Council, Chpsn., Dn. Dr. Varouj
Altebarmakian, 7290 North San Pedro,
Fresno, CA 93011
Diocesan Council, Sec., Mr. John Yaldezian,
23221 Aetna St., Woodland Hills, CA 91367
Tel. (B) (818)346-6163
Canadian Diocese:
Primate, His Em. Archbishop Hovnan Derderian‑
Diocesan Council Chpsn, Mr. Takvor Hopyan,
20 Pineway,Blvd., Willowdale, ON M2H 1A1,
Canada Tel (B) (416)222-2639
Diocesan Council secretary., Mr. Vahe Ketli, 750
Montpellier, # 909, St. Laurens, QC H4L 5A7,
Canada Tel (R) (514)747-1347

Periodicals

The Armenian Church, The Mother Church

Assemblies of God

From a few hundred delegates at its founding
convention in 1914 at Hot Springs, Ark., the
Assemblies of God has become one of the largest
church groups in the modern Pentecostal movement with over 57 million adherents worldwide.
Throughout its existence it has emphasized the
power of the Holy Spirit to change lives and the
participation of all members in the work of the
church.

The revival that led to the formation of the
Assemblies of God and numerous other church
groups early in the 20th century began during
times of intense prayer and Bible study. Believers
in the United States and around the world received
spiritual experiences like those described in the
Book of Acts. Accompanied by baptism in the
Holy Spirit and its initial physical evidence of
"speaking in tongues," or a language unknown to
the person, their experiences were associated with
the coming of the Holy Spirit at Pentecost (Acts
2), so participants were called Pentecostals.

The church also believes that the Bible is
God's inspired infallible Word to man, that salvation is available only through Jesus Christ, that
divine healing is made possible through Christ's
suffering and that Christ will return again for
those who love Him. In recent years, this
Pentecostal revival has spilled over into almost
every denomination in a wave of revival sometimes called the charismatic renewal.

Assemblies of God leaders credit their
church's rapid and continuing growth to its
acceptance of the New Testament as a model for
the present-day church. Aggressive evangelism
and missionary zeal at home and abroad charac-
terize the denomination.

Assemblies of God believers observe two
ordinances-water baptism by immersion and the
Lord's Supper, or Holy Communion. The church
is Trinitarian, holding that God exists in three
persons-Father, Son and Holy Spirit.

Headquarters

Media Contact: Juleen Turnage, Dir. of Public
Relations, Assemblies of God 1445 N.
Boonville Ave., Springfield, MO 65802-1894
Tel. (417)862-2781 Fax (417)862-0133 Email:
info@ag.org
Email: Statistics@ag.org
Website: www.ag.org/top

Officers

Gen. Supt., George O. Wood
Asst. Supt., L. Alton Garrison
Gen. Sec., John M. Palmer
Gen. Treas., James K. Bridges
World Missions, Exec. Dir., L. John Bueno
AG U.S. Missions, Exec. Dir., Zollie L. Smith,
Jr.
Great Lakes: Douglas E. Clay, 8405 Pulsar Pl,
Columbus, OH Tel. (614)396-0700 Fax
(614)396-0701
Gulf: Douglas Fulenwider, P.O. Box 7388,
Alexandria, LA 71306 Tel. (318)445-6238
Fax (318)473-9344
North Central: Clarence W. St John, 1315
Portland Ave. S., Minneapolis, MN 55404,
Tel. (612)332-2409 Fax 612-332-2510
Northeast: H. Robert Rhoden, 3525 Corrotoman
Rd., Glen Allen, VA 23060 Tel. (804)755-6181
Northwest: Warren Bullock, 3535 Auburn Way
S, Auburn, WA 98092 Tel. (253)833-8252 Fax
(253)351-2943

South Central: J. Don George, 4401 N. Highway 161, Irving, TX 75038 Tel. (972)261-1919 Fax (972)261-1895

Southeast: Dan Betzer, 4701 Summerlin Rd., Ft. Myers, FL 33919 Tel. (239)936-6277 Fax 239-936-9365

Southwest: Richard Dresselhaus, 6126 Bernadette Ln., San Diego, CA Tel. (619)286-9361

Language Area Spanish: Jesse Miranda, 55 Fair Drive, Costa Mesa, CA 92626 Tel. (714)556-3610 Fax 714-966-5471

Language Area Other: Nam Soo Kim, 130-30 31st Ave., 4th Fl, Flushing, NY 11354 Tel. (718)321-7800 Fax (718)321-9394

Ethnic Fellowship: John E. Maracle, 2329 W. Bent Tree Dr., Phoenix, AZ 85085 Tel. (602)261-6001 Fax (602)261-6004

Division of the Treasury: Gen. Treas., James K. Bridges Division of Church Ministries, Executive Liaison, L. Alton Garrison

Division of World Missions: Exec Dir., L. John Bueno

Division of U.S. Missions: Exec. Dir., Zollie L. Smith, Jr.

Division of Publication: Gospel Publishing House, Natl. Dir., J. T. Wray

Division of Communications: Natl. Dir., Juleen Turnage

Periodicals
Enrichment—A Journal for Pentecostal Ministry High Adventure, Today's Pentecostal Evangel, Heritage, On Course

Assemblies of God International Fellowship (Independent/Not affiliated)

April 9, 1906 is the date commonly accepted by Pentecostals as the 20th-century outpouring of God's spirit in America, which began in a humble gospel mission at 312 Azusa Street in Los Angeles. This spirit movement spread across the United States and gave birth to the Independent Assemblies of God (Scandinavian). Early pioneers instrumental in guiding and shaping the fellowship of ministers and churches into a nucleus of independent churches included Pastor B. M. Johnson, founder of Lakeview Gospel Church in 1911; Rev. A. A. Holmgren, a Baptist minister who received his baptism of the Holy Spirit in the early Chicago outpourings, was publisher of Sanningens Vittne, a voice of the Scandinavian Independent Assemblies of God and also served as secretary of the fellowship for many years; Gunnar Wingren, missionary pioneer in Brazil; and Arthur F. Johnson, who served for many years as chairman of the Scandinavian Assemblies.

In 1935, the Scandinavian group dissolved its incorporation and united with the Independent Assemblies of God of the U.S. and Canada which by majority vote of members formed a new corporation in 1986, Assemblies of God

International Fellowship (Independent/Not Affiliated).

Headquarters
6325 Marindustry Dr. , San Diego, CA 92121 Tel. (858)677-9701 Fax (858)677-0038
Media Contact, Exec. Dir. & Ed., Rev. T. A. Lanes
Email: admin@agifellowship.org
Website: www.agifellowship.org

Officers
Exec. Dir., Rev. T. A. Lanes
Sec., Rev. George E. Ekeroth
Treas., M. J. Ekeroth
Canada, Sec., Harry Nunn, Sr., 15 White Crest Ct., St. Catherines, ON 62N 6Y1

Periodicals
Fellowship

Associate Reformed Presbyterian Church (General Synod)

The origin of the Associate Reformed Presbyterian Church began in Scotland with the Covenanters of the seventeenth century and Seceder movement of the eighteenth. The Covenanters broke from the established Church of Scotland to eventually form separate "praying societies," which led to the Reformed Presbyterian Church of Scotland. The Seceders, about a hundred years later, became the Associate Church of Scotland.

The Associate Reformed Presbyterian Church stems form the 1782 merger of these two groups in America. In 1822 the "Synod of the South" was granted independent status from the national body. It continued to hold to the 1799 Constitution of the church with no changes, and probably consisted of around 2,000 members. The present Associate Reformed Presbyterian Church, (General Synod), is the ongoing denomination resulting from that actions, the original "General Synod" of the denomination having become a part of the United Presbyterian Church.

The government is by a three-layered court system, the local "Session," the regional "Presbytery" and the national "General Synod," each of which is composed of both ruling and teaching elders. The Standards of the denomination include the Westminster Confession of Faith, the Catechisms and the Forms of Government, Worship and Discipline.

Headquarters
Associate Reformed Presbyterian Center, One Cleveland St., Greenville, SC 29601-3696 Tel. (864)232-8297 Fax (864)271-3729
Media Contact, Principal Clerk, The Rev. C. Ronald Beard, D.D., 3132 Grace Hill Rd., Columbia, SC 29204 Tel. (803)787-6370.
Moderator, The Rev. William B. Evans, Ph.D., P.O. Box 275, Due West, SC 29639 Tel. (864)379-2570 Email: wbevans@erskine.edu (to June 6, 2006)

Moderator-Elect, Mr. Tom Patterson, P.O. Box 1283, Mooresville, NC 28115-1283 Tel. (704) 663-2611 Email: tpatterson@arpsynod.org
Website: www.arpsynod.org

AGENCIES AND INSTITUTIONS (In the A.R. Presbyterian Center in Greenville)

Admn. Ser. Dir., Ed Hogan
Covenant Discipleship (Christian Education), Dir., Dr. David Vickery
Outreach North America (Church Extension), Dir., Rev. Alan Avera
Publications, Editor, Sabrina Cooper
Treasurer, Guy H. Smith, III
World Witness, Bd. of Foreign Missions, Exec. Sec., The Rev. P. Frank vanDalen Tel. (864)833-5226 Email: fvandalen@world witness.org

OTHER INSTITUTIONS
Bonclarken Conference Center, Dir., James T. Brice, 500 Pine St., Flat Rock, NC 28731 Tel. (704)692-2223
Erskine College, Two Washington Street, Due West, SC 29639 President Emeritus, The Rev. John L. Carson, Ph.D.,Tel. (864)379-8759
Erskine Theological Seminary, Two Washington Street, Due West, SC 29639 Vice President, The Rev. H. Neely Gaston, Tel. (964)379-2171, Dean, Ralph J. Gore, Jr., Ph.D., Due West, SC 26939 Tel. (864)379-8885

Periodicals
The Associate Reformed Presbyterian, *The Adult Quarterly*

The Association of Free Lutheran Congregations

The Association of Free Lutheran Congregations, rooted in the northern European revival movements, was organized in 1962 by a Lutheran Free Church remnant which rejected merger with The American Lutheran Church. The original 42 congregations were joined by other like-minded conservative Lutherans, and there has been more than a sixfold increase in the number of congregations. Members subscribe to the Apostles', Nicene and Athanasian creeds; Luther's Small Catechism; and the Unaltered Augsburg Confession. The Fundamental Principles and Rules for Work (1897) declare that the local congregation is the right form of the kingdom of God on earth, subject to no authority but the Word and the Spirit of God.

Distinctive emphases are, (1) the infallibility and inerrancy of Holy Scriptures as the Word of God; (2) congregational polity; (3) the spiritual unity of all believers, resulting in fellowship and cooperation transcending denominational lines; (4) evangelical outreach, calling all to enter a personal relationship with Jesus Christ; (5) a wholesome Lutheran pietism that proclaims the Lordship of Jesus Christ in all areas of life and results in believers becoming the salt and light in their communities; (6) a conservative stance on current social issues.

A two-year Bible school and a theological seminary are in suburban Minneapolis. The AFLC is in fellowship with sister churches in Canada, Brazil, Mexico, and India.

Headquarters
3110 E. Medicine Lake Blvd.,Minneapolis, MN 55441 Tel. (763)545-5631 Fax (763)545-0079
Media Contact, Pres., Rev. Elden K. Nelson
Email: webmaster@aflc.org
Website: www.aflc.org

Officers
Pres., Rev. Elden K. Nelson, 3110 E. Medicine Lake Blvd.,Minneapolis, MN 55441 Tel (763)545-5631 Fax (763)545-0079, Email: president@aflc.org
Vice Pres., Rev. Michael Brandt, 3110 E. Medicine Lake Blvd.,Minneapolis, MN 55441 Tel. (763)545-5631, Email: vpres@aflc.org
Sec., Rev. Brian Davidson, 3110 E. Medicine Lake Blvd., Minneapolis, MN 55441 Tel. (763) 545-5631 Fax (763)545-0079 Email: briand @aflc.org

Periodicals
The Lutheran Ambassador

Association of Independent Evangelical Lutheran Churches

The AIELC was established, as a response to the affiliation need of independent missions and churches originally of the Latino community in the USA and then worldwide, committed to the learning and teaching of Lutheran Doctrine and Theology. We are a Lutheran denomination that provide support and guidance to independent missions and churches to be better prepared for the work in the Kingdom of God at the light of Lutheran understanding of Confessing Christ. As part of our affiliation process we don't ask those independent missions and churches to surrender their buildings or administrative independency; and we don't require them to provide financial support to the main denomination itself.

Our current worlwide membership is estimated as approximately 35,000 members with Churches in Scotland, Channel Islands, India, Pakistan, South Africa, Argentina, Ecuador, Colombia, Puerto Rico, Haiti, Chile and the USA. We have active Concordat with religious bodies in the USA and abroad, among them the Evangelical Community Church-Lutheran, the Athanasian Catholic Church of the Augsburg Confession, and the Lutheran Orthodox Church. We hold active membership at the Queens Federation of Churches in New York.

Headquarters
Email: mainoffice@aielc.org
Website: www.associationofindependentevan-gelicallutheranchurches.org

Officers

The Rev. Dr. Pedro Bravo-Guzmán, Presiding Bishop, 14-22 27th Ave, Astoria, NY 11102 Tel. (718)932-1633, Email: pbravoguzman@aielc.org

The Rev. Dr. Francis C. Spataro, Bishop Emeritus, 14-22 27th Ave, Astoria, NY 11102 Tel. (718)932-1633, Email: vil11427@mycingular.blackberry.net

The Rev. Dr. Peter P. Brennan, Bishop Visitor, 14-22 27th Ave, Astoria, NY 11102 Tel. (718)932-1633, Email: Ddamdg@aol.com

The Rev. Bishop Louis Marcel Pierre, Bishop for the Caribbean, 14-22 27th Ave, Astoria, NY 11102 Tel. (718)932-1633, Email: louispierre_73@hotmail.com

The Rev. Bishop Louis Mphahlele, Bishop for Africa, 14-22 27th Ave, Astoria, NY 11102 Tel. (718)932-1633, Email: lutheranunited@webmail.co.za

The Rev. Bishop Adolfo Acuña, Bishop for South America, 14-22 27th Ave, Astoria, NY 11102 Tel. (718)932-1633, Email: iluterana@yahoo.com.ar

The Rev. Paul Lorentzen, Assistant to the Presiding Bishop, 14-22 27th Ave, Astoria, NY 11102 Tel. (718)932-1633, Email: pentateuco754@hotmail.com

Miss Christine Dobush, Public Relations Director, 14-22 27th Ave, Astoria, NY 11102, Tel. (718)932-1633, Email: cdobush@inch. com

Mr. Antonio Hunneus, Secretary, 14-22 27th Ave, Astoria, NY 11102 Tel. (718)932-1633, Email: aielcsecretariat@aielc.org

Dr. Jeannette Cano-Landivar, M.D., Treasurer, 14-22 27th Ave, Astoria, NY 11102, Tel. (718)932-1633, Email: jacala@inch.com

Other Organizations

Global Aid Foundation

Association of Vineyard Churches

The Association of Vineyard Churches is a worldwide community of 1400 churches committed to building the church and living under the reign of God. It officially started in Southern California in 1982 under the leadership of John Wimber. The Board of Directors is the governing Board for the Association. The form of government is free church and thus the local Vineyards are free to govern as they desire as long as they do not violate the faith or practices of the Vineyard community. The Association consists of eight regions under the direction of a Regional Overseer. Most regions also have Area Pastoral Care Leaders who give oversight to a small group of pastors in a geographic area. The National Director is the CEO of the National Office and works with the National Board to see that the Association achieves its purpose.

Headquarters

5115 Grove West Blvd., Stafford, TX 77477 Tel. (281)313-8463 Fax (281)313-8464

Email: info@vineyardusa.org
Website: vineyardusa.org

Officers

National Dir., Berten A. Waggoner, Email: christian@vineyardusa.org

Secretary, Jane Hardesty, Email: janehardesty@vineyardusa.org

Treasurer, Wendell Richardson

Vineyard Music USA

Periodicals

Cutting Edge

Baptist Bible Fellowship International

Organized on May 24, 1950 in Fort Worth, Tx., the Baptist Bible Fellowship was founded by about 100 pastors and lay people who had grown disenchanted with the policies and leadership of the World Fundamental Baptist Missionary Fellowship, an outgrowth of the Baptist Bible Union formed in Kansas City in 1923 by fundamentalist leaders from the Southern Baptist, Northern Baptist and Canadian Baptist Conventions. The BBF elected W. E. Dowell as its first president and established offices and a three-year (now four-year with a graduate school) Baptist Bible College.

The BBF statement of faith was essentially that of the Baptist Bible Union, adopted in 1923, a variation of the New Hampshire Confession of Faith. It presents an infallible Bible, belief in the substitutionary death of Christ, his physical resurrection and his premillennial return to earth. It advocates local church autonomy and strong pastoral leadership and maintains that the fundamental basis of fellowship is a missionary outreach. The BBF vigorously stresses evangelism and the international missions office reports 901 adult missionaries working on 110 fields throughout the world.

There are BBF-related churches in every state of the United States, with special strength in the upper South, the Great Lakes region, southern states west of the Mississippi, Kansas and California. There are seven related colleges and one graduate school or seminary.

A Committee of Forty-Five, elected by pastors and churches within the states, sits as a representative body, meeting in three subcommittees, each chaired by one of the principal officers-an administration committee chaired by the president, a missions committee chaired by a vice-president and an education committee chaired by a vice-president.

World Mission Service Center

Baptist Bible Fellowship Missions Bldg., 720 E. Kearney St., Springfield, MO 65803 Tel. (417)862-5001 Fax (417)865-0794

Mailing Address, P.O. Box 191, Springfield, MO 65801

75

Media Contact, Mission Dir., Dr. Bob Baird, P.O. Box 191, Springfield, MO 65801
Email: csbc@cherrystreet.org,
Website: www.bbfi.org

Officers

Pres., Rev. Bill Monroe, P.O.Box 12809, Florence, SC 29504 Tel. (843)662-0453, WK (417)-862-5001

First Vice Pres., Rev. Mike Peper, 4150 Market St., Aston, PA 19014 Tel. (610)497-0700, WK (417)862-5001

Second Vice Pres., Keith Gillming , 3025 N Lindbergh Blvd., St. Louis, MO 63074 Tel. (314)291-6919

Sec., Rev. Don Elmore, P.O.Box 7150, Springdale, AR 72766 Tel. (479)751-4255

Treas., Rev. Ken Armstrong, 2200 Prairin St., Emporia, KS Tel. (316)342-4142

Periodicals

The Baptist Bible Tribune, *The Preacher*

Baptist General Conference

The Baptist General Conference, rooted in the pietistic movement of Sweden during the 19th century, traces its history to Aug. 13, 1852. On that day a small group of believers at Rock Island, Illinois, under the leadership of Gustaf Palmquist, organized the first Swedish Baptist Church in America. Swedish Baptist churches flourished in the upper Midwest and Northeast, and by 1879, when the first annual meeting was held in Village Creek, Iowa, 65 churches had been organized, stretching from Maine to the Dakotas and south to Kansas and Missouri.

By 1871, John Alexis Edgren, an immigrant sea captain and pastor in Chicago, had begun the first publication and a theological seminary. The Conference grew to 324 churches and nearly 26,000 members by 1902. There were 40,000 members in 1945 and 135,000 in 1993.

Many churches began as Sunday schools. The seminary evolved into Bethel, a four-year liberal arts college with 1,800 students, and theological seminaries in Arden Hills, Minnesota. and San Diego, California. Missions and the planting of churches have been main objectives both in America and overseas. Today churches have been established in the United States, Canada and Mexico, as well as twenty countries overseas. In 1985 the churches of Canada founded an autonomous denomination, The Baptist General Conference of Canada.

The Baptist General Conference is a member of the Baptist World Alliance, the Baptist Joint Committee on Public Affairs and the National Association of Evangelicals. It is characterized by the balancing of a conservative doctrine with an irenic and cooperative spirit. Its basic objective is to seek the fulfillment of the Great Commission and the Great Commandment.

Headquarters

2002 S. Arlington Heights Rd., Arlington Heights, IL 60005 Tel. (847)228-0200 Fax (847)228-5376
Email: gmarsh@baptistgeneral.org
Website: www.bgcworld.org

Officers

Pres. & Chief Exec. Officer, Dr. Gerald Sheveland, 2002 S. Arlington Hts. Rd., Arlington Heights, IL 60005 Tel. (847)228-0200 Fax (847)228-5376, Email: jsheveland@baptistgeneral.org

Exec, Vice Pres., Ray Swatkowski, (address/ph/fax same as above), Email: rswatkowski@baptistgeneral.org

Director of Mission Advance, Dr. Lou Petrie, (address/ph/fax same as above), Email: lpetrie@baptistgeneral.org

Director of Finance, Stephen R. Schultz, (address/ph/fax same as above), Email: sschultz@baptistgeneral.org

Director of National Ministries, Rev. Paul Johnson, (address/ph/fax same as above), Email: pauljchp@aol.com

Director of International Ministries: Dr. Ronald Larson, (address/ph/fax same as above), Email: rlarson@aol.com

OTHER ORGANIZATIONS

Bd. of Trustees, Bethel College & Seminary, Pres., Dr. George K. Brushaber, 3900 Bethel Dr., St. Paul, MN 55112

Periodicals

BGC World

Baptist Missionary Association of America

A group of regular Baptist churches organized in associational capacity in May, 1950, in Little Rock, Ark., as the North American Baptist Association. The name changed in 1969 to Baptist Missionary Association of America. There are several state and numerous local associations of cooperating churches. In theology, these churches are evangelical, missionary, fundamental and for the most part premillennial.

Headquarters

9219 Sibly Hole Rd., Little Rock, AR Tel. (501)455-4977 Fax (501)455-3636

Mailing Address, P.O. Box 193920, Little Rock, AR 72219-3920

Media Contact, Dir. of Disciple Guide Information Services, P.O. Box 7270, Texarkana, TX 75505 Tel. (870)772-4550 Fax (903)586-0378
Email: bmaam@bmaam.com
Website: www.bmaam.com

Officers

Pres., David Watkins, 318 E. Main St., Magnolia, AR 71753-0456 Tel. (870)234-4292

Vice Pres., Dr. Philip Attebery, 3030 Meadowlark

Ln., Tylor, TX 75701-6042 Tel. (903)586-2500; Dr. Roy L. McLaughlin, 3114 Derby Ln., Swartz Creek, MI 48473-7984 Tel. (810)635-9568

Rec. Sec., Don J. Brown, P.O. Box 8181, Laurel, MS 39441-8000; Tel. (601)425-1258, Greg Medenwald, 310 Qualil Hollow Pl., Hattlesburg, MS 39402-8974; Tel. (601)264-8087; James Ray Raines, 5609 N. Locust, N. Little Rock, AR 72116 Tel. (501)945-2640

DEPARTMENTS

Missions, Gen. Sec., Rev. Grady L. Higgs, P.O. Box 193920, Little Rock, AR 72219-3920

Publications, Ed.-in-Chief, Rev. James L. Silvey, 311 Main St., P.O. Box 7270, Texarkana, TX 75505

Christian Education, Bapt. Missionary Assoc. Theological Sem., Pres., Dr. Charley Holmes, Seminary Heights, 1530 E. Pine St., Jacksonville, TX 75766

Baptist News Service, Dir., Bobby L. Hudgens, P.O.Box 7270, Texarkana, TX 75505-7270 Tel. (870)772-4550

Life Word Broadcast Ministries, Dir., Rev. George Reddin, P.O. Box 6, Conway, AR 72032

Armed Forces Chaplaincy, Exec. Dir., Bobby C. Thornton, P.O. Box 240, Flint, TX 75762

BMAA Dept. of Church Ministries, Donny Parish, P.O. Box 10356, Conway, AR 72033

Daniel Springs Encampment, James Speer, P.O. Box 310, Gary, TX 75643

Ministers Resource Services, Craig Branham, 4001 Jefferson St., Texarkana, TX 75501

OTHER ORGANIZATIONS

Baptist Missionary Assoc. Brotherhood, Pres., Matt Hudson, 264 Columbia 25, Magnolia, AR 71753-9141 Tel. (870)234-4893

National Women's Missionary Auxiliary, Pres., Mrs. Janet Widger, 7409 Rupert Ave., Richmond Height, MO 63117 Tel. (314)644-5009

Beachy Amish Mennonite Churches

The Beachy Amish Mennonite Church was established in 1927 in Somerset County, Pa. following a division in the Amish Mennonite Church in that area. As congregations in other locations joined the movement, they were identified by the same name. There are currently 97 churches in the United States, 9 in Canada and 34 in other countries. Membership in the United States is 7,059, according to the 1996 Mennonite Yearbook.

Beachy Churches believe in one God eternally existent in three persons (Father, Son and Holy Spirit); that Jesus Christ is the one and only way to salvation; that the Bible is God's infallible Word to us, by which all will be judged; that heaven is the eternal abode of the redeemed in Christ; and that the wicked and unbelieving will endure hell eternally.

Evangelical mission boards sponsor missions in Central and South America, Belgium, Ireland, and in Kenya, Africa.

The Mission Interests Committee, founded in 1953 for evangelism and other Christian services, sponsors homes for handicapped youth and elderly people, mission outreaches among the North American Indians in Canada and a mission outreach in Europe.

Headquarters

Media Contact, Paul L. Miller, 7809 S. Herren Rd. Partridge, KS 67566 Tel. (620)567-2286

Officers

Amish Mennonite Aid, Sec.-Treas., Ivan Beachy, 8916 Mission Home Rd., Free Union, VA 22940 Tel. (434)985-4954

Mission Interests Committee, Sec.-Treas., Melvin Gingerich, 42555 900W, Topeka, IN 46571 Tel. (219)593-9090

Choice Books of Northern Virginia, Supervisor, Simon Schrock, 4614 Holly Ave., FairFax, VA 22030 Tel. (703)830-2800

Calvary Bible School, HC 61, Box 202, Calico Rock, AR 72519 Tel. (501)297-8658; Sec.-Treas., Elmer Gingerich, HC 74, Box 282, Mountain View, AR 72560 Tel. (501)296-8764

Penn Valley Christian Retreat, Bd. Chmn., Wayne Schrock, RR 2, Box 165, McVeytown, PA 17015 Tel. (717)529-2935

Periodicals

The Calvary Messenger

Berean Fellowship of Churches

Founded 1932 in North Platte, Nebraska, this body emphasizes conservative Protestant doctrines.

Headquarters

5 Camelot Way, Box 1264, Kearney, NE 68845 Tel (308)234-5373 Fax (308)234-5373
Media Contact, Pres., Pastor Doug Shada
Email: BereanChurches@aol.com
Website: www.bereanfellowship.org

Officers

Pres., Doug Shada

Vice Pres., Richard Crocker, 419 Lafayette Blvd., Cheyenne, WY 82009 Tel. (307)635-5914

Sec., Frank Van Campen, 513 Education Dr., Malcolm, NE 68402

Treas., Virgil Wiebe, 125 Split Rock Cir., Hollister, MO 65672

The Bible Church of Christ, Inc.

The Bible Church of Christ was founded on March 1, 1961 by Bishop Roy Bryant, Sr. Since that time, the Church has grown to include congregations in the United States, Africa and India. The church is Trinitarian and accepts the Bible as the divinely inspired Word of God. Its doctrine includes miracles of healing, deliverance and the baptism of the Holy Ghost.

Headquarters

1358 Morris Ave., Bronx, NY 10456 Tel. (718)588-2284 Fax (718)992-5597
Media Contact, Pres., Bishop Roy Bryant, Sr
Email: bccbookstore@earthlink.net
Website: www.thebiblechurchofchrist.org

Officers

Pres., Bishop Roy Bryant, Sr.
Vice Pres., Bishop Darue Bryant
Sec., Mother Sissieretta Bryant
Treas., Elder Artie Burney

EXECUTIVE TRUSTEE BOARD

Chpsn., Bishop Christopher Powell, 1069 Morris Ave., Bronx, NY 10456 Tel. (718)992-4653

OTHER ORGANIZATIONS

Christian Bookstore, Mgr., Deacon Kenneth Anderson, Tel. (718)293-1928
Foreign Missions, Pres., Sr. Autholene Smith, Tel. (914)664-4602
Home Missions: Pres., Evangelist Mary Jackson, Tel. (718)992-4653
Minister of Education: Minister Abraham Jones, Tel. (718)588-2284
Ministers of Music, Ray Crenshaw, Tyrone Sumter, Ann Dunston
Prison Ministry Team, Evangelist Marvin Smith
Public Relations, Minister Abraham Jones
Sunday Schools, Gen. Supt., Elder A. M. Jones
Alan Bryant Memorial Institute, Principal, Moses Tolborh, Chocolate City, Monrobia, Liberia
Theological Institute, Pres., Dr. Roy Bryant, Sr.; Dean, Elder A. M. Jones
Vessels Unto Honor Deliverance Ministries, Pres., Elder Antoinette Cannaday
Youth, Pres., Deacon Tommy Robinson
Bishops: Bishop Roy Bryant, Sr., Bishop Eddie Citronnelli, Bishop Christopher Powell
Presiding Elders: Delaware: Elder Edward Cannon, R R Box 70-B5, Daimond Acre, Dagsboro, DE 19939, Tel. (302)732-3351; Mount Vernon: Elder Artie Burney, 100 W. 2nd St., Mount Vernon, NY 10550, Tel. (914)664-4602; Bronx, Elder Anita Robinson, 1358 Morris Ave., Bronx, NY 10456, Tel. (718)588-2284; Annex, Elder Reginald Gullette, 1069 Morris Ave., Bronx, NY 10456 Tel. (718)992-4653; Schenectady, New York: Elder Monica Hope, 1132 Congress St., Schenectady, New York 12303, Tel. (518)382-5625; North Carolina: Elder Darue Bryant, 512 W. Vernon Ave., Kingston, N.C. 28502, Tel. (252)527-7739; India, Dr. B. Veeraswamy, 46-7-34, Danavaya Peta, Rajahmunry, India, 533103

Periodicals

The Gospel Light, *The Challenge*

Bible Fellowship Church

The Bible Fellowship Church grew out of divisions in the Mennonite community in Pennsylvania in the 1850s. Traditional church leadership resisted the freedom of expression and prayer meetings initiated by several preachers and church leaders. These evangelical Mennonites formed the Evangelical Mennonite Society. Over the next two decades various like minded groups in Canada, Ohio and Pennsylvania joined the Society.

In 1959 the Conference became the Bible Fellowship Church and new articles of faith were ratified. They now hold a unique combination of Reformed doctrines with insistence on "Believer Baptism" and Premillennialism.

Headquarters

Bible Fellowship Church, 25 Lemon St., Lititz, PA 17543
Media Contact, David J. Watkins, 416 Cedar Crest Ct., Quakertown PA, PA 18950 Tel. (215)529-7453
Email: watkins58@verizon.net
Email: bfc@bfc.org
Website: www.bfc.org

Officers

Chmn., Randall A. Grossman, 23 Anglin Dr. Newark, Delaware 19713
Vice-Chmn., Clifford B. Booke, 1256 Clearview Cr, Allentown, PA
Sec., David A. Thomann, 745 Village Rd., Lancaster, PA 17602
Asst. Sec., Robert W. Smock, 38 W. Sunset Ave., Ephrata, PA 17522

BOARDS AND COMMITTEES

Bd. of Dir., Bible Fellowship Church
Bd. of Christian Education
Board of Extension
Bible Fellowship Church Homes, Inc.
Board of Pensions
Board of Pinebrook Bible Conference
Board of Missions Committee On Credentials
Board of Publication and Printing
Bd. of Victory Valley Camp
Board of Higher Education Board Of Youth & Adults Committee On Ministerial Candidates Strategic Planning Committee Ministerial Relations Committee Conference Judicatory

Periodicals

Fellowship News

Bible Holiness Church

This church came into being about 1890 as the result of definite preaching on the doctrine of holiness in some Methodist churches in southeastern Kansas. It became known as The Southeast Kansas Fire Baptized Holiness Association. The name was changed in 1945 to The Fire Baptized Holiness Church and in 1995 to Bible Holiness Church. It is entirely Wesleyan in doctrine, episcopal in church organization and intensive in evangelistic zeal.

Headquarters

304 Camp Dr., Independence, KS 67301 Tel. (620)331-3049
Media Contact, Gen. Supt., Leroy Newport

Officers

Gen. Supt., Leroy Newport

Gen. Sec., Michael Schaper, 944 Linns Mill Rd., Troy, MO 63379

Gen. Treas., Philip Davolt, 10624 Bluestem, Wichita, KS 67207

Periodicals

The Flaming Sword, John Three Sixteen

Bible Way Church of Our Lord Jesus Christ World Wide, Inc.

This body was organized in 1957 in the Pentecostal tradition for the purpose of accelerating evangelistic and foreign missionary commitment and to effect a greater degree of collective leadership than leaders found in the body in which they had previously participated.

The doctrine is the same as that of the Church of Our Lord Jesus Christ of the Apostolic Faith, Inc., of which some of the churches and clergy were formerly members.

This organization has churches and missions in Africa, England, Guyana, Trinidad and Jamaica, and churches in 25 states in America. The Bible Way Church is involved in humanitarian as well as evangelical outreach with concerns for urban housing, education and economic development.

Headquarters

4949 Two-Notch Rd., Columbia, SC 29204 Tel. (800)432-5612 Fax (803)691-0583

Media Contact, Chief Apostle, Presiding Bishop Huie Rogers

Email: mr.ed5strings@worldnet.att.net

Website: www.biblewaychurch.org

Officers

Presiding Bishop, Bishop Huie Rogers, 4949 Two Notch Rd., Columbia, SC 29204 Tel. (800)432-5612 Fax (803)691-0583

Brethren in Christ Church

The Brethren in Christ Church was founded in Lancaster County, Pa. in about the year 1778 and was an outgrowth of the religious awakening which occurred in that area during the latter part of the 18th century. This group became known as "River Brethren" because of their original location near the Susquehanna River. The name "Brethren in Christ" was officially adopted in 1863. In theology they have accents of the Pietist, Anabaptist, Wesleyan and Evangelical movements.

Headquarters

General Church Office, P.O. Box A, Grantham, PA 17027 Tel. (717)697-2634 Fax (717)697-7714

Media Contact, Dr. Warren L. Hoffman, Mod., Tel. (717)697-2634 Fax (717)697-7714

Email: dwinger@messiah.edu

Website: www.bic-church.org

Officers

Dr. Warren L. Hoffman, Mod. & Gen. Church Office Contact info.

Darrell S. Winger, Gen. Sec. & Gen. Church Office Contact info.

Elizabeth Brown, Treas. & Gen. Church Office Contact info.

OTHER ORGANIZATIONS

General Conference Board, Chpsn., Dr. Mark Garis, 504 Swartley Rd., Hatfield, PA 19440

Bd. for World Missions, Dr. Grace Holland, Chair, 21A Junction Rd., Dillsburg, PA. 17019-9469; Exec. Dir., Rev. John Brubaker, P.O. Box 390, Grantham, PA 17027-0390

Bd. for Stewardship Services, Terry Hoke; Chair; Box A, Grantham, PA 17027; Pension Fund Trustees, Eric Mann, Chair

Brethren in Christ Foundation, Elvin H. Peifer, CEO, P.O.Box 290, Grantham, PA, 17027-0290

Brethren Church (Ashland, Ohio)

The Brethren Church (Ashland, Ohio) was organized by progressive-minded German Baptist Brethren in 1883. They reaffirmed the teaching of the original founder of the Brethren movement, Alexander Mack, and returned to limited congregational government.

Headquarters

524 College Ave., Ashland, OH 44805 Tel. (419)289-1708 Fax (419)281-0450

Media Contact, Rev. Ken Hunn Official Position: Executive Director, Tel, (419)289-1708 Fax (419)281-0450 Email: Ken@brethrenchurch.org

Email: brethren@brethrenchurch.org

Website: www.brethrenchurch.org

Officers

Executive Dir., Rev. Ken Hunn

Dir. Of Administrative Services, Mr. Stanley Gentle

Periodicals

The Brethren Evangelist

Calvary Chapel

Calvary Chapel is a non-denominational Christian church which began in 1965 in Costa Mesa, California. Calvary Chapel's pastor, Chuck Smith became a leading figure in what has become known as the "Jesus Movement."

It has been estimated that in a two-year period in the mid '70s, Calvary Chapel of Costa Mesa had performed well over eight thousand baptisms. During that same period, we were instrumental in 20,000 conversions to the Christian faith. Our decadal growth rate had been calculated by church growth experts to be near the ten thousand percent level. Calvary Chapel also ministers over the airwaves, and this must account for many of those who travel long distances to fellowship here. A Nielsen survey indicated that

79

our Sunday morning Calvary Chapel service is the most listened-to program in the area during the entire week. As of 1987, Calvary's outreach has included numerous radio programs, television broadcasts, and the production and distribution of tapes and records. The missions outreach is considerable. Calvary Chapel not only supports Wycliffe Bible Translators, Campus Crusade, Missionary Aviation Fellowship, and other groups, but we donate to Third World needs. We then built a radio station in San Salvador and gave it to the local pastors there. We also gave money to Open Doors to purchase the ship that, in tandem with a barge, delivered one million Bibles to mainland China. Our financial commitment to missions exceeds the local expense budget by over 50%.

Today, Calvary Chapel of Costa Mesa, the church which only had twenty-five members has established more than five hundred affiliate Calvary Chapels across the world and is among the world's largest churches with more than thirty-five thousand calling it their home church. It is one of the ten largest Protestant churches in the United States.

Headquarters
Calvary Chapel of Costa Mesa (Main Office), 3800 S. Fairview Street, Santa Ana, CA 92704-7014 Tel. (714)979-4422

The Catholic Church
The largest single body of Christians in the United States, The Catholic Church is under the spiritual leadership of His Holiness the Pope. Its establishment in America dates back to the priests who accompanied Columbus on his second voyage to the New World. A settlement, later discontinued, was made in 1565 at St. Augustine, Florida. The continuous history of this Church in the Colonies began at St. Mary's in Maryland, in 1634.

INTERNATIONAL ORGANIZATION
His Holiness the Pope, Bishop of Rome, Vicar of Jesus Christ, Supreme Pontiff of the Catholic Church.
Pope Benedict XVI, Joseph Ratzinger (born April 16, 1927; installed April 24, 2005)

APOSTOLIC NUNCIO TO THE UNITED STATES
Archbishop Gabriel Montalvo, 3339 Massachusetts Ave., N.W., Washington, DC 20008 Tel. (202) 333-7121 Fax (202)337-4036

U.S. ORGANIZATION
United States Conference of Catholic Bishops, 3211 Fourth St NE, Washington, DC 20017-1194. Tel. (202)541-3000

The United States Conference of Catholic Bishops (USCCB) is an assembly of the hierarchy of the United States and the U.S. Virgin Islands who jointly exercise certain pastoral functions on behalf of the Christian faithful of the United States. The purpose of the Conference is to promote the greater good which the Church offers humankind, especially through forms and programs of the apostolate fittingly adapted to the circumstances of time and place. This purpose is drawn from the universal law of the Church and applies to the episcopal conferences which are established all over the world for the same purpose.

The bishops themselves constitute the membership of the Conference and are served by a staff of over 350 people, priests and religious located at the Conference headquarters in Washington, DC. There is also a small Office of Film and Broadcasting in New York City and a branch office of Migration and Refugee Services in Miami.

The Conference is organized as a corporation in the District of Columbia. Its purposes under civil law are, "To unify, coordiante, encourage, promote and carry on Catholic activities in the United States; to organize and conduct religious, charitable and social welfare work at home and abroad; to aid in education; to care for immigrants; and generally to enter into and promote by education, publication and direction the objects of its being."

On July 1, 2001 the NCCB and the USCC were combined to form the United States Confer-ence of Catholic Bishops (USCCB). The USCCB continues all of the work formerly done by the NCCB and the USCC with the same staff. The bishops themselves form approximately 50 committees, each with its own particular responsibility.
Email: commdept@usccb.org
Website: www.usccb.org

UNITED STATES CONFERENCE OF CATHOLIC BISHOPS (USCCB) GENERAL SECRETARIAT
General Sec., Msgr. David Malloy
Assoc. Gen. Sec., Mr. Bruce E. Egnew, two other associate positions vacant at time of printing

Officers
Pres., Bishop William S. Skylstad
Vice Pres., Cardinal Francis George, OMI
Treas., Bishop Dennis M. Schnurr
Sec., Archbishop Michael J. Sheehan

ADMINISTRATIVE COMMITTEE— USCCB
Administrative Committee, Chmn., Bishop William S. Skylstad
Executive Committee, Chmn., Bishop William S. Skylstad
Committee on Budget and Finance, Chmn., Bishop Dennis M. Schnurr
Committee on Personnel, Cardinal Francis George, OMI
Committee on Priorities and Plans, Chmn., Archbishop Michael J. Sheehan
African American Catholics, Chmn., Bishop Joseph N. Perry

Canonical Affairs, Chmn., Archbishop John J. Myers

Church in Latin America, Chmn., Bishop John R. Manz; Chmn.-elect Bishop Jaime Soto

Consecrated Life, Chmn., Archbishop Jerome G. Hanus, OSB; Chm.-elect, Bishop J. Terry Steib, SVD

Communications Chmn. Bishop Gerald F. Kicanas; Chmn.-elect, Bishop George H. Niederauer

Diaconate, Chmn., Bishop Frederick F. Campbell

Doctrine, Chmn.,Bishop Arthur J. Serratelli; Chmn.-elect, Bishop William E. Lori

Education, Chmn. Bishop Robert J. McManus

Ecumenical and Interreligious Affairs, Chmn., Bishop Richard J. Sklba

Evangelization, Chmn., Bishop Samuel G. Jacobs

Hispanic Affairs, Chmn., Bishop Placido Rodriguez, CMF

Home Missions, Chmn., Bishop J. Peter Sartain; Chmn.-elect, Bishop Michael W. Warfel

Laity, Chmn., Bishop David A. Zubik

Liturgy, Chmn., Bishop Donald W. Trautman

Marriage and Family Life, Chmn., Bishop Joseph E. Kurtz

Migration, Chmn., Bishop Gerald Barnes

Pastoral Practices, Chmn., Bishop Jerome E. Listecki

Priestly Formation, Chmn., Bishop Thomas J. Olmsted

Priestly Life and Ministry, Chmn., Archbishop Timothy M. Dolan; Chmn.-elect, Bishop Robert J. Carlson

Pro-Life Activities, Chmn., Cardinal William Keeler; Cardinal Justin Rigali

Protection of Young People, Chmn. Bishop Gregory M. Aymond

Relationship Between Eastern and Latin Catholic Churches, Chmn., Archbishop Stefan Soroka

Science and Human Values, Chmn., Bishop John C. Dunne

Vocations, Chmn., Bishop Blase Cupich

Woman in Society and in the Church, Chmn., Bishop Joseph A. Pepe

World Mission, Chmn., Bishop Daniel Walsh

For information on related organizations and individual dioceses, consult the Official Catholic Directory (published annually by P.J. Kenedy and Sons) and the USCCB website (www.usccb.org).

Periodicals

Catholic News Service, L'Osservatore Romano, The Living Light, Origins, Lay Ministry Update, Bishops Committee on the Liturgy Newsletter, Life Insight, SEIA Newsletter on the Eastern Churches and Ecumenism, Law Briefs, Catholic Trends

Christ Catholic Church

The church is a catholic communion established in 1968 to minister to the growing number of people who seek an experiential relationship with God and who desire to make a total commitment of their lives to God. The church is catholic in faith and tradition. Participating cathedrals, churches and missions are located in several states.

Headquarters

405 Kentling Rd., Highlandville, MO 65669 Tel. (417)443-3951

Media Contact, Archbishop, Most Rev. Karl Pruter

Email: bishopkarl@juno.com

Website: christcatholicchurch.freeyellow.com

Officers

Archbishop, Most Rev. Karl Pruter, P.O. Box 63, Highlandville, MO 65669 Tel. (417)823-9902

Periodicals

St. Willibrord Journal

Christ Community Church (Evangelical-Protestant)

This church was founded by the Rev. John Alexander Dowie on Feb. 22, 1896 at Chicago, Ill. In 1901 the church founded the city of Zion, IL and moved their headquarters there. Theologically, the church is rooted in evangelical orthodoxy. The Scriptures are accepted as the rule of faith and practice. Other doctrines call for belief in the necessity of repentance for sin and personal trust in Christ for salvation.

The Christ Community Church is a denominational member of The National Association of Evangelicals. It has work in six other nations in addition to the United States. Branch ministries are found in Tonalea, Arizona.

Headquarters

2500 Dowie Memorial Dr., Zion, IL 60099 Tel. (847)746-1411 Fax (847)746-1452

Officers

Senior Pastor, Ken Langley

Christadelphians

The Christadelphians are a body of people who believe the Bible to be the divinely inspired word of God, written by "Holy men who spoke as they were moved by the Holy Spirit" (2 Peter Ch. 1 vs. 21). They believe that the Old Testament presents God's plan to establish His Kingdom on earth in accord with the promises He made to Abraham and David; and that the New Testament declares how that plan works out in Jesus Christ, who died a sacrificial death to redeem sinners. They believe in the personal return of Jesus Christ as King, to establish "all that God spoke by the mouth of his holy prophets from of old" (Acts Ch.3 vs.21). They believe that at Christ's return many of the dead will be raised by the power of God to be judged. Those whom God deems worthy will be welcomed into eternal life in the Kingdom on earth. Christadelphians

81

believe in the mortality of man; in spiritual rebirth requiring belief and immersion in the name of Jesus; and in a godly walk in this life. They have no ordained clergy, and are organized in a loose confederation of 2500 autonomous congregations (ecclesias) in approximately 150 countries. They are conscientiously opposed to participation in war. They endeavor to be enthusiastic in work, loyal in marriage, generous in giving, dedicated in preaching, and cheerful in living.

The denomination was organized in 1844 by a medical doctor, John Thomas, who came to the United States from England in 1832, having survived a near shipwreck in a violent storm. This experience affected him profoundly, and he vowed to devote his life to a search for the truth of God and a future hope from the Bible.

Headquarters

Media Contact, Trustee, Norman D. Zilmer, Christadelphian Action Society, 904 Woodview Ct, Mahomet, IL 61853-3623 Tel. (217)590-4108 Fax (847)888-3334
Email: nzilmer@aol.com
Website: www.christadelphia.org

Leaders

(Co-Ministers) Norman Fadelle, 815 Chippewa Dr., Elgin, IL 60120; Norman D. Zilmer, 904 Woodview Ct, Mahomet, IL 61853-3623, Email:nzilmer@aol.com or NFADELLE@juno.com

Periodicals

Christadelphian Tidings (www.Tidings.org), *Christadelphian Advocate* (www.Christadelphia.org)

Christian Brethren (also known as Plymouth Brethren)

Christian Brethren churches are bound together by common beliefs and practices but not by central organization. They are committed to the inerrancy of Scripture, to Trinitarian doctrine, and to the evangelical message of salvation by faith apart from works or sacrament. Their most recognizable feature is the weekly observance of the Lord's Supper as the focus of a full length service of worship, not prearranged and not clergy-led.

Originating in England and Ireland in the late 1820s, the Brethren were influenced by the counsel of Anthony Norris Groves, an English dentist, and the teaching of John Nelson Darby, an Irish clergyman. They recovered aspects of church practice and simplicity that had been obscured in the course of the centuries, such as an unwillingness to establish denominational governing structures and a reluctance to accept sectarian names. The nickname Plymouth Brethren arose spontaneously when a large Plymouth congregation was evangelizing throughout the English countryside. In recent years the term Christian Brethren has replaced Plymouth Brethren for the open branch of the movement in Canada and the British Commonwealth and to some extent in the United States. Neither name has legal status, except where required by national governments. There are no central offices and no corporate property in the USA or Canada.

In the late 1840s the movement divided. The so-called open assemblies, led initially by George Mueller of orphanage fame, stressed evangelism and foreign missions. It has grown to be the larger of the two branches. The autonomy of local congregations permits variations in practice and generally avoids wide-ranging division.

The other branch focused more on doctrinal and ecclesiastical issues. From it came notable Bible teachers like Darby, William Kelly, C.H. Mackintosh (CHM), and F. W. Grant. Their books have had a wide influence, especially among premillennialists. These assemblies stress the interdependency of congregations. Local church decisions on doctrine and discipline are generally held to be binding on all assemblies. At times, when actions were debatable, division spread throughout the group. By 1900, there were seven or eight main groups. Since 1925, some divisions have been healed, reducing that number to three or four.

CORRESPONDENT

James A. Stahr, 327 W. Prairie Ave., Wheaton, Il 60187-3408 Tel. (630)665-3757

RELATED ORGANIZATIONS

Believers' Bookshelf, P.O. Box 261 Sunbury, PA 17801

Believers' Stewardship Services, 2250 Chaney Rd., Dubuque, IA 50201 Tel. (563)582-4818

ECS Ministries, 2250 Chaney Rd., Dubuque, IA 50201 Tel. (563)585-2070

Emmaus Bible College, 2570 Asbury Rd., Dubuque, IA 52001-3044 Tel. (563)588-8000

Christian Missions in Many Lands, P.O. Box 13, Spring Lake, NJ 07762-0013 Tel. (732)449-8880

Interest Ministries, 2060 Stonington Ave., Suite 101, Hoffman Estates, IL 60195 Tel. (847) 519-1495

Stewards Foundation, 14285 Midway Rd., Ste. 330, Addison, TX 75001-3622 Tel. (972)726-6550

Stewards Ministries, 18-3 E. Dundee Rd., Ste. 100, Barrington, IL 60010 Tel. (847)842-0227

Walterick Publishing Ministries, 6549 State Ave., Kansas City, KS 66102 Tel. (913)334-0100

Christian Church (Disciples of Christ) in the United States and Canada*

Born on the American frontier in the early 1800s as a movement to unify Christians, this body drew its major inspiration from Thomas and Alexander Campbell in western Pennsylvania and Barton W. Stone in Kentucky.

Developing separately, the "Disciples," under Alexander Campbell, and the "Christians," led by Stone, united in 1832 in Lexington, Ky.

The Christian Church (Disciples of Christ) is marked by informality, openness, individualism, and diversity. The Disciples claim no official doctrine or dogma. Membership is granted after a simple statement of belief in Jesus Christ and baptism by immersion—although most congregations accept transfers baptized by other forms in other denominations. The Lord's Supper—generally called Communion—is open to Christians of all persuasions. The practice is weekly Communion, although no church law insists upon it.

Thoroughly ecumenical, the Disciples helped organize the National and World Councils of Churches. The church is a member of the Churches Uniting in Christ. The Disciples and the United Church of Christ have declared themselves to be in "full communion" through the General Assembly and General Synod of the two churches. Official theological conversations have been going on since 1967 directly with the Roman Catholic Church.

Disciples have vigorously supported world and national programs of education, agricultural assistance, urban reconciliation, care of persons with retardation, family planning, and aid to victims of war and calamity. Operating ecumenically, Disciples' personnel or funds work in more than 100 countries outside North America.

Three manifestations or expressions of the church (general, regional and congregational) operate as equals, with strong but voluntary covenantal ties to one another. Entities in each manifestation manage their own finances, own their own property, and conduct their own programs. A General Assembly meets every two years and has voting representation from each congregation.

Headquarters

Disciples Center, 130 E. Washington St., P.O. Box 1986, Indianapolis, IN 46206-1986 Tel. (317)635-3100 Fax (317)635-3700

Media Contact, Communication Ministeries, Executive Director, Wanda Bryant Wills Email: cmiller@cm.disciples.org

Officers

Gen. Minister & Pres., Rev. Dr. Sharon E. Watkins, Tel. (317)635-3100 Fax (317)713-2417, Email: swatkins@ogmp.disciples.org

Mod., D. Newell Williams, Brite Divinity School, Texas Christian University, P.O. Box 298130, Fort Worth, Texas 76129, Tel. (817)257-7575, Email: n.williams@tcu.edu.

1st Vice-Mod., Ayanna Johnson, 2324 Orchard St, Blue Island, Illinois, Tel. (773)483-2115,

2nd Vice-Mod., Robert (Bob) Alvarez, Forest Park, Georgia, Tel. (770)614-0314, Email: bobalvarez@npointgroup.com.

GENERAL OFFICERS

Gen. Minister & Pres., Rev. Dr. Sharon E. Watkins, Tel. (317)635-3100 Fax (317)713-2417, Email: swatkins@ogmp.disciples.org

Assoc. Gen. Minister & Vice Pres., Todd A Adams, Tel. (317)635-3100 Fax (317)713-2417, Email: tadams@ogmp.disciples.org

Assoc. Gen Min. & Admin. Sec. Of the National Convocation, Timothy M. James, Email: tjames@ogmp.disciples.org

ADMINISTRATIVE UNITS

Board of Church Extension, dba Church Extension, Pres., James L. Powell, 130 E. Washington St., P.O. Box 7030, Indianapolis, IN 46207-7030 Tel. (317)635-6500 Fax (317)635-6534, Email: bce@churchextension.org

Christian Board of Publication (Chalice Press), Pres., Cyrus N. White, 1221 Locust St., Suite 1200, P.O. Box 179, St. Louis, MO 63166-0179 Tel. (314)231-8500 or (800)366-3383 Fax (314)231-8524, Email: customerservice@cbp21.com

Christian Church Foundation, Inc., Pres., Gary W. Kidwell, Tel. (317)635-3100 or (800)366-8016 Fax (317)635-1991, Email: jcullumb@ccf.disciples.org

Council on Christian Unity, Inc., Pres., Robert K. Welsh, Tel (317)713-2586 Fax (317)713-2588, Email: rozanne@ccu.disciples.org

Disciples of Christ Historical Society, Pres., Glen T. Carson, 1101 19th Ave. S., Nashville, TN 37212-2196 Tel. (615)327-1444 Fax (615)327-1445, Email: mail@dishistsoc.org

Higher Education and Leadership Ministries (HELM), Pres., Dennis L. Landon, 11477 Olde Cabin Rd., Ste. 310, St. Louis, MO 63141-7130 Tel. (314)991-3000 Fax (314)991-2957, Email: dhe@dhedisciples.org

Division of Homeland Ministries, dba Disciples Home Missions, Pres., Vacant. Tel. (317)635-3100 or (888)346-2631 Fax (317)635-4426, Email: homelandministries@dhm.disciples.org

Division of Overseas Ministries, Pres., David A. Vargas, Fax (317)635-4323, Email: dom@disciples.org

National Benevolent Association, Pres., Dennis Hagemann, 149 Weldon Parkway, Suite 115, Maryland Heights, MO 63043-3103 Tel. (314)993-9000 Fax (314)993-9018, Email: nba@nbacares.org

Pension Fund, Pres., James P. Hamlett, 130 E. Washington St., Indianapolis, IN 46204-3645 Tel. (317)634-4504 Fax (317)634-4071, Email: pfcc1@pension.disciples.org

REGIONAL UNITS OF THE CHURCH

Alabama-Northwest Florida, Regional Minister, John P. Mobley, 861 Highway 52, Helena, AL 35080 Tel. (205)425-5245 Fax (205)425-5246, Email: alnwfl@aol.com

Arizona, Regional Minister, Dennis L. Williams, 4423 N. 24th St., Ste 700, Phoenix, AZ 85016-

83

5544 Tel. (602)468-3815 Fax (602)468-3816, Email: region@arizonadisciples.com

California, Northern-Nevada, Regional Min. and Pres., Ben Bohren, 9260 Alcosta Blvd., C-18, San Ramon, CA 94583-4143 Tel. (925)556-9900 Fax (925)556-9904, Email: info@ccncn.org

Canada, Regional Minister, Catherine Hubbard, P.O. Box 25087, London, ON N6C 6A8 Tel. (519)472-9083, Email: ccic1@sympatico.ca

Capital Area, Regional Minister, Lari R. Grubbs, 11501 Georgia Ave., Ste. 400, Wheaton, MD 20902-1955 Tel (301)942-8266 Fax (301)942-8366, Email: lgrubbs@cccadisciples.org

Central Rocky Mountain Region, Exec. Regional Minister, Ronald L. Parker, 2950 Tennyson #300, Denver, CO 80212-3029 Tel. (303)561-1790 Fax (303)561-1795, Email: jrowe@crmrdoc.org

Florida, Regional Minister, William C. Morrison, Jr., 924 N. Magnolia Ave., Ste. 200, Orlando, FL 32803-3845 Tel. (407)843-4652 Fax (407)843-0272, Email: RegionalOffice@floridadisciples.org

Georgia, Regional Minister, Ray Miles, 2370 Vineville Ave., Macon, GA 31204-3163 Tel. (478)743-8649 or (800)755-0485 Fax (478)741-1508, Email: ccinga@bellsouth.net

Great River Region, Executive Regional Minister, Barbara E. Jones, 9302 Geyer Springs Rd, P.O.Box 192058, Little Rock, AR 72219-2058 Tel. (501)562-6053 & (888)241-5531 Fax (501)562-7089

Idaho, South, Regional Minister, Larry Crist, 6465 Sunrise Ave., Nampa, ID 83686-9461 Tel. (208)468-8976 Fax (208)468-8973, Email: ccsi1@mindspring.com

Illinois and Wisconsin, Regional Minister and Pres., Herbert L. Knudsen, 1011 N. Main St., Bloomington, IL 61701-1753 Tel. (309)828-6293 Fax (309)829-4612, Email: herb@cciwdiciples.org

Indiana, Regional Minister, Richard L. Spleth, 1100 W. 42nd St., Indianapolis, IN 46208-3375 Tel. (317)926-6051 Fax (317)931-2034, Email: cci@ccindiana.org

Kansas, Regional Minister/Pres., Paxton Jones, 2914 S.W. MacVicar Ave., Topeka, KS 66611-1787 Tel. (785)266-2914 Fax (785)266-0174, Email: ccks@ksmessenger.org

Kansas City, Greater, Regional Min./Pres., Paul J. Diehl, Jr., 5700 Broadmoor, Ste. 702, Mission, KS 66202-2405 Tel. (913)432-1414 Fax (913)432-3598, Email: KCDisciple@aol.com

Kentucky, General Minister, J. Gregory Alexander, 1125 Red Mile Rd., Lexington, KY 40504-2660 Tel. (859)233-1391 Fax (859)233-2079, Email: cck@ccinky.net

Michigan, Regional Minister, Jon Lacey, 2820 Covington Ct., Lansing, MI 48912-4830 Tel. (517)372-3220 Fax (517)372-2705, Email: ccmr@michigandisciples.org

Mid-America Region, Regional Minister, Danny Stewart, 3328 Bennett Ln., P.O. Box 104298 , Jefferson City, MO 65110-4298 Tel. (573)636-8149 Fax (573)636-2889, Email: ccma@socket.net

Montana, Regional Minister, Ruth A, Fletcher, 1019 Central Ave., Great Falls, MT 59401-3784 Tel. (406)452-7404 Fax (406)452-7404, Email: ccm@imt.net

Nebraska, Regional Ministers, Kenneth W. Moore, 1268 S. 20th St., Lincoln, NE 68502-1612 Tel. (402)476-0359 or (800)580-8851 Fax (402)476-0350, Email: ccnebraska@alltel

North Carolina, Regional Minister, John M. Richardson, 509 N.E. Box 1568, Wilson, NC 27894-1568 Tel. (252)291-4047 Fax (252)291-3338, Email: ccnc@ncdisciples.org

Northeastern Region, Co-Regional Ministers, Lonnie F. Oates, Rafael Rivera-Rosa, 475 Riverside Dr., Rm. 1950, New York, NY 10115-1999 Tel (212)870-2734 Fax (870)2735, Email: n.christian.church@worldnet.att.net

Northwest Region, Regional Minister and Pres., Rebecca Hale, 18000 72nd Ave, S, Suite 171, Kent, WA, 98032 Tel. (253)893-7202 Fax (425)251-4967, Email: nwrcc@disciplesnw.org

Ohio, Regional Pastor and Pres., William H. Edwards, 355 E. Campus View Blvd, Suite 110, Columbus, OH 43235 Tel. (614)433-0343 Fax (614)433-7285, Email: ccio@christianchurchinohio.org

Oklahoma, Regional Pastor, Thomas R. Jewell, 301 N.W. 36th St., Oklahoma City, OK 73118-8661 Tel. (405)528-3577 Fax (405)528-3584, Email: tjewell@okdisciples.org

Oregon, Co-Regional Ministers, Douglas Wirt & Cathy Myers-Wirt, 0245 S.W. Bancroft St., Ste. F, Portland, OR 97239-4267 Tel. (503)226-7648 Fax (503)226-0598, Email: odmail@oregondisciples.org

Pacific Southwest Region, Regional Minister-Pres., Don W. Shelton, 2401 N. Lake Ave., Altadena, CA 91001-2418 Tel. (626)296-0385 Fax (626)296-1280, Email: pswr@discipleswr

Pennsylvania, Regional Minister, W. Darwin Collins, 105 Water St., Suite #7, New Stanton, PA 15672 Tel. (724)925-1350 Fax (724)925-1358, Email: wdar@padisciples.org

South Carolina, Regional Minister, Sotello V. Long, 1293 Orange Grove Rd., Charleston, SC 29407-3947 Tel. (843)852-4537 Fax (843)744-5787, Email: rcccsc@aol.com

Southwest Region, Regional MinisterDani Loving Cartwright, 3209 S. University Dr., Fort Worth, TX 76109-2239 Tel. (817)926-4687 Fax (817)926-5121, Email: ccsw@ccsw.org

Tennessee, Regional Minister and Pres., Glen J. Stewart, 50 Vantage Way, Ste. 251, Nashville, TN 37228-1523 Tel. (615)251-3400 Fax (615)251-3415, Email: ccdctn@yahoo.com

Upper Midwest Region, Regional Minister and Pres., Richard L. Guentert, 3300 University Ave., P.O. Box 41217, Des Moines, IA 50311-0504 Tel. (515)255-3168 Fax (515)255-2625, Email: rg@uppermidwestcc.org

Virginia, Regional Minister, George Lee Parker, 1290 Enterprise Dr., Lynchburg, VA 24502 Tel. (434)846-3400 Fax (434)528-4919, Email: regoffice.ccinva@verizon.net

West Virginia, Regional Minister, William B. Allen, 1402 Washington Ave., P.O. Box 264, Parkersburg, WV 26102-0264 Tel. (304)428-1681 Fax (304)428-1684, Email: linda@ccwv.org

Periodicals
DiscipleWorld, Call To Unity

Christian Church of North America, General Council

Originally known as the Italian Christian Church, its first General Council was held in 1927 at Niagara Falls, N.Y. This body was incorporated in 1948 at Pittsburgh, Pa., and is described as Pentecostal but does not engage in the "the excesses tolerated or practiced among some churches using the same name."

The movement recognizes two ordinances-baptism and the Lord's Supper. Its moral code is conservative and its teaching is orthodox. Members are exhorted to pursue a life of personal holiness, setting an example to others. A conservative position is held in regard to marriage and divorce. The governmental form is, by and large, congregational. District and National officiaries, however, are referred to as Presbyteries led by Overseers.

The group functions in cooperative fellowship with the Italian Pentecostal Church of Canada and the Evangelical Christian Churches-Assemblies of God in Italy. It is an affiliate member of the Pentecostal Fellowship of North America and of the National Association of Evangelicals.

Headquarters
1294 Rutledge Rd., Transfer, PA 16154-2299 Tel. (724)962-3501 Fax (724)962-1766

Exec. Sec., Christine Marini; Asst., Candace Tarr
Email: cnna@nauticom.net
Website: www.ccna.org

Officers
Executive Bd., Gen. Overseer, Rev. Dennis G. Karaman, 1294 Rutledge Road, Transfer, PA 16154

Exec. Vice Pres., Rev. Joseph Shipley, 44-19 Francis Lewis Blvd., Bayside, NY 11361

Asst. Gen. Overseers, Rev. Joseph Shipley 44-19 Francis Lewis Blvd., Bayside, NY 11361; Rev. Trevor Cobarn, 3325 Dry Brook Rd., Falconer, NY 14733 ; Rev. Patrick Bossio, Sr., 667 Capitol, Lincoln Park, MI 48146; Rev. Thomas Geyser, 2 Cynthia Circle, Medway,

MA 02060, Rev. Douglas Bedgood, Sr., 442 Trinidad Ln., Teadkwood Village, Largo, FL 33770

DEPARTMENTS
Benevolence, Rev. Eugene De Marco, 136 Dana Dr., New Brighton PA 15066

Home Missions, Rev. Richard George, 3395 Waterside Dr., Akron, OH 44319

Faith, Order & Credentials, Rev. Rev. Joseph Shipley, 44-19 Francis Lewis Blvd., Bayside, NY 11361

Missions, Rev. Mark Charles, 703 Somcenter Rd., Mayfield Hts., OH 44143

Publications Relations, Rev. John Tedesco, 1188 Heron Rd., Cherry Hill, NJ 08003

Lay Ministries, Rev. Carmine Zottoli, 27D Shear Hill Rd., Mahopac, NY 10541

Education, Rev. Lucian Gandolfo, 3141 Highland Dr. Easton, PA. 18045

Periodicals
Vista

Christian Churches and Churches of Christ

The fellowship, whose churches were always strictly congregational in polity, has its origin in the American movement to "restore the New Testament church in doctrine, ordinances and life" initiated by Thomas and Alexander Campbell, Walter Scott and Barton W. Stone in the early 19th century.

Headquarters
Media Contact, No. American Christian Convention Dir., Rod Huron, 4210 Bridgetown Rd., Box 11326, Cincinnati, OH 45211 Tel. (513)598-6222 Fax (513)598-6471
Email: Jowston@cwv.edu
Website: www.cctoday.com; www.naccthecon nectingplace.org

CONVENTIONS
North American Christian Convention, Dir., Rod Huron, 4210 Bridgetown Rd., Box 11326, Cincinnati, OH 45211 Tel. (513)598-6222; NACC Mailing Address, Box 39456, Cincinnati, OH 45239

National Missionary Convention, Coord., Walter Birney, Box 11, Copeland, KS 67837 Tel. (316)668-5250

Eastern Christian Convention, Kenneth Meade, 5300 Norbeck Rd., Rockville, MD 20853 Tel. (301)460-3550

Periodicals
Christian Standard, Restoration Herald, Horizons, The Lookout

The Christian Congregation, Inc.

The Christian Congregation is a denominational evangelistic association that originated in 1787 and was active on the frontier in areas adjacent to the Ohio River. The church was an unincorporated

85

organization until 1887. At that time a group of ministers who desired closer cooperation formally constituted the church. The charter was revised in 1898 and again in 1970.

Governmental polity basically is congregational. Local units are semi-autonomous. Doctrinal positions, strongly biblical, are essentially universalist in the sense that ethical principles, which motivate us to creative activism, transcend national boundaries and racial barriers. A central tenet, John 13:34-35, translates to such respect for sanctity of life that abortions on demand, capital punishment and all warfare are vigorously opposed. All wars are considered unjust and obsolete as a means of resolving disputes.

Early leaders were John Chapman, John L. Puckett and Isaac V. Smith. Bishop O. J. Read was chief administrative and ecclesiastic officer for 40 years until 1961. Rev. Dr. Ora Wilbert Eads has been general Superintendent since 1961. Ministerial affiliation for independent clergymen is provided.

Headquarters

812 W. Hemlock St., LaFollette, TN 37766
Media Contact, Gen. Supt., Rev. Ora W. Eads, D.D., Tel. (423)562-5809
Email: Revalnas@aol.com
Website: netministries.org/see/churches.exe/ch10619

Officers

Gen. Supt., Rev. Ora W. Eads, D.D., 812 W. Hemlock St. LaFollette, TN 37766

Christian Methodist Episcopal Church*

The Christian Methodist Episcopal Church (CME) is a historically African-American denomination that was established in Jackson, Tennessee in 1870 when a group of former slaves, representing eight annual conferences of the Methodist Episcopal Church South organized the Colored Methodist Episcopal Church in America. In 1954 at its General Conference in Memphis, Tennessee it was overwhelmingly voted to change the term "Colored" to "Christian." On January 3, 1956 the official name became Christian Methodist Episcopal Church. Its boundaries reach from the continental United States, Alaska, Haiti, Jamaica, and the West African countries of Nigeria, Ghana, and Liberia. One of its most significant witnessing arenas has been the education of African Americans. Today the CME Church supports Paine College, August, GA; Lane College, Jackson, TN; Miles College, Birmingham, AL; Texas College, Tyler, TX; and the Phillips School of Theology in Atlanta, GA.

Headquarters

First Memphis Plaza, 4466 Elvis Presley Blvd., Memphis, TN 38116

Media Contact, Exec. Sec., Attorney Juanita Bryant, 3675 Runnymede Blvd., Cleveland Hts., OH 44121 Tel. (216)382-3559 Fax (216) 382-3516
Email: juanbr4law@aol.com
Website: www.c-m-e.org

Officers

Exec. Sec., Attorney Juanita Bryant, 3675 Runnymede Blvd., Cleveland Hts., OH 44121 Tel. (216)382-3559 Fax (216)382-3516, Email, juanbr4law@aol.com
Sec. Gen. Conf., Vacant

OTHER ORGANIZATIONS

Christian Education, Gen. Sec., Dr. Carmichael Crutchfield, 4466 Elvis Presley Blvd., Ste. 214, Box 193, Memphis, TN 38116-7100 Tel. (901)345-0580 Fax (901)345-4118

Lay Ministry, Gen. Sec., Dr. Victor Taylor, 9560 Drake Ave., Evenston, IL 60203, Tel. (800) 782-4335 x 6029 Fax (312)345-6056, Email: taylor617@comcast.net

Evangelism & Missions, Gen. Sec., Dr. Willie C. Champion, 102 Pearly Top Dr., Glen Heights, TX 75154 Tel. (214)372-9505, Email: champ_dr@sbcglobal.net

Finance, Sec., Dr. Joseph C. Neal, Jr., P.O. Box 75085, Los Angeles, CA 90075 Tel. (323)233-5050

Editor, The Christian Index, Dr. Kenneth E. Jones, P.O. Box 431, Fairfield, AL 35064 Tel. (205929-1640 Fax (205)791-1910, Email: Goodoc@aol.com

Publication Services, Gen. Sec., Rev. William George, 4466 Elvis Presley Blvd., Memphis, TN 38116 Tel. (901)345-0580 Fax (901)767-8514, Email: WEG38@aol.com

Personnel Services, Gen. Sec., Rev. Tyrone T. Davis, P.O.Box 74, Memphis, TN 38101-0074 Tel. (901)261-3228, Email: cmegbps@myexcel.com

Women's Missionary Council, Pres., Dr. Elnora P. Hamb, 11321 S. Aberdeen St., Chicago, IL 60643 Tel. (773)264-2273, Email: hamb@sbcglobal.net Ministry to Men, Gen. Sec., Mr. Leo Pinkett, 2850 Shoreland De. S.W., Atlanta, GA 30331, Email: lpinkettace@yahoo.com

BISHOPS

First District, Bishop William H. Graves, Sr., 4466 Elvis Presley Blvd., Ste. 222, Memphis, TN 38116 Tel. (901)345-0580

Second District, Bishop E. Lynn Brown, 7030 Reading Rd., Suite 244, Cincinnati, OH 45237 Tel. (513)772-8622

Third District, Bishop Paul A. G. Stewart, Sr., 5925 W. Florissant Ave., St. Louis, MO 63136 Tel. (314)381-3111

Fourth District, Bishop Thomas L. Brown Sr., P.O. Box 2793, Jackson, MS 39207 Tel. (601) 398-3926, Email: thomasl30087@bellsooth.net

Fifth District, Bishop Lawerence L. Reddick III, 310 18th St., N, Ste. 400D, Birmingham, AL 35203 Tel. (205)655-0346 Fax (205)251-4371

Sixth District, Bishop Othal H. Lakey, 1776 Peachtree Rd. NW, Suite 210, South Tower, Atlanta, GA 30309 Tel. (404)745-9689 Fax (404)745-0691

Seventh District, Bishop Thomas L. Hoyt, Jr., 6524 16th St. N.W., Washington, DC Tel: (318)820-9512 & (318)780-8467

Eighth District, Bishop Ronald M. Cunningham, 1616 E. Illinois, Dallas, TX 75216 Tel. (214) 372-9073

Ninth District, Bishop Henry M. Williamson, 3844 W. Slauson Ave., Ste. 1, Los Angeles, CA 90043 Tel. (213)294-3830, Email: hwillia 531@aol.com

Tenth District, Bishop Kenneth Wayne Carter, 2202 Emerald Oaks Ct., Arlington, TX 76017 Tel. (817)468-1397, Email: KWCarter@hot-mail.com

Retired, Bishop Nathaniel L. Linsey, Canterbury Subdivision, 190 Squire Lane, Fayettsville, GA 30214 Tel. (770)460-6897, Email: lin-seyn@bellsouth.net; Bishop Dotcy I. Isom, 4326 Richwood Place, Memphis, TN 36125, Tel. (901)753-8123; Bishop Marshall Gilmore, 683 Beacontree Court, Concord, NC 28027, Tel. (704)786-3226

Periodicals
The Christian Index, *The Missionary Messenger*

The Christian and Missionary Alliance

The Christian and Missionary Alliance was formed in 1897 by the merger of two organizations begun in 1887 by Dr. Albert B. Simpson, The Christian Alliance and the Evangelical Missionary Alliance. The Christian and Missionary Alliance is an evangelical church that stresses the sufficiency of Jesus as Savior, Sanctifier, Healer, and Coming King and has earned a worldwide reputation for its missionary accomplishments. The Canadian districts became autonomous in 1981 and formed The Christian and Missionary Alliance in Canada.

NATIONAL OFFICE
P.O. Box 35000, Colorado Springs, CO 80935-3500 Tel. (719)599-5999 Fax (719)593-8234

Media Contact, Peter Burgo, Assistant Vice President for Advancement
Email: info@cmalliance.org
Website: www.cmalliance.org

Officers
Pres., Rev. Gary M. Benedict D.D.
Corp. Vice Pres., Rev. John P. Stumbo
Corp. Sec., Rev. David L. Goodin
Vice Pres., for Advancement, Open
Vice Pres. for International Ministries, Rev. Robert L. Fetherlin, D. Min.
Vice Pres. for National Church Ministries, Open

Vice Pres. for Operations/Treasurer, Mr. Kenneth E. Baldes, MBA

BOARD OF DIRECTORS
Chpsn., Rev. Ronald J. Morrison
Vice Chpsn., Rev. Douglas L. Grogan

DISTRICTS
Cambodian, Rev. Nareth May, 1616 S. Palmetto Ave., Ontario, CA 91762 Tel. (909)988-9434

Central, Rev. Gordon F. Meier, D.Min., 1218 High St., Wadsworth, OH 44281 Tel. (330) 336-2911

Central Pacific, Rev. R. Douglas Swinburne, J. R., 715 Lincoln Ave., Woodland, CA 95695 Tel (530)662-2500

E. Pennsylvania, Rev. J. Wayne Spriggs, 1200 Spring Garden Dr., Middletown, PA 17057 Tel. (717)985-9240

Great Lakes,Rev. Jeffrey P. Brown, 2250 Huron Parkway, Ann Arbor, MI 48104 Tel (734)677-8555

Haitian, Rev. Emaneuelle Seide, 14 Glen Road, W. Hempstead, NY 11552 Tel. (516)594-1046

Haitian South, Rev. Joe Kong (Interim Director), P.O.Box 35000 Colorado Springs, CO 80935 Tel. (719)265-2052

Hmong, Rev. Timothy T. Vang, 12287 Pennsylvania St., Thornton, CO 80241 Tel. (303)252-1793

Korean, Rev. Hyung J. Moon, 550 Durie Avenue, #201, Closter, NJ 07640 Tel. (201)750-6750

Metropolitan, Rev. John F. Soper, P.O.Box 7060, 275 Sussex Ave., Ste. B, Newark, NJ 07107 Tel. (973)412-7025

MidAmerica, Rev. Randall S. Burg, 1301 S. 119th St., Omaha, NE 68144 Tel. (402)330-1888

Mid-Atlantic, Rev. Randall B. Corbin, D.Min., Jr., 292 Montevue Lane, Frederick, MD 21702 Tel. (301)620-9934

Midwest, Rev. M. Fred Polding, D. Miss., 260 Glen Ellyn Road, Bloomingdale, IL 60108 Tel. (630)893-1355

Native American, Rev. Craig S. Smith, 19019 N. 74th Dr., Glendale, AZ 85308 Tel 623-561-8134

New England, Rev. Richard E. Bush, D.Min., P.O. Box 288, South Easton, MA 02375 Tel. (508)238-3820

Northeastern, Rev. David J. Phillips, 6275 Pillmore Dr., Rome, NY 13440 Tel. (315)336-4720

Northwestern, Rev. Craig L. Strawser, 6425 CTYRD 30 #, 740 St. Bonifacius, MN 55375 Tel. (952)446-9318

Ohio Valley, Rev . P. David Klinsing, D.Min., 4050 Executive Park Dr., Ste.402, Cincinnati, OH 45241, Tel. (513)733-4833

Pacific NW, Rev. Kelvin J. Gardiner, P.O. Box 1030, Canby, OR 97013 Tel. (503)266-2238

Puerto Rico, Rev. Luis F. Felipa, P.O. Box 191794, San Juan, PR 00919, Tel. (787)281-0101

Rocky Mountain, Rev. Timothy P. Owen,

D.Min., 2545 St. Johns Ave., Billings, MT 59102 Tel. (406)656-4233

South Atlantic, Rev. L. Ferrell Towns, 10801 Johnston Rd., Ste. 125, Charlotte, NC 28226 Tel. (704)543-0470

South Pacific, Rev. Donald M. Brust, 4130 Adams St., Ste. A, Riverside, CA 92504 Tel. (909)351-0111

Southeastern, Rev. Mark T. O' Farrell, D.D., P.O. Box 720430, Orlando, FL 32872-0430 Tel. (407)823-9662

Southern, Rev. Fred G. King, 5998 Deerfoot Parkway, Trussville, AL 35173 Tel. (205)661-9585

Southwestern, Rev. Daniel R. Wetzel, 5600 E. Loop 820 South, Ste. 100, Fort Worth, TX 76119 Tel. (817)561-0879

Spanish Central, Rev. C. José Bruno, P.O.Box 5477 McAllen, TX 78504 Tel. (956)565-1600

Spanish Eastern, Rev. Marcelo Realpe, P.O.Box 865, Union City, NJ 07087 Tel. (201)866-7202

Vietnamese, Dr. Tai Anh Nguyen, Th.D., 2275 W. Lincoln Ave., Anaheim, CA 92801 Tel. (714)491-8007

W. Great Lakes, Rev. Gary E. Russell, W6107 Aerotech Dr., Appleton, WI 54914, Tel. (920)734-1123

W. Pennsylvania, Rev. Jeffrey A. Norris, P.O.Box 600, Punxsutawney, PA 15767, Tel. (814)938-6920

NATIONAL ETHNIC ASSOCIATIONS

African-American: President, Rev. Terrence L. Nichols, 120 Lancaster Way, Vallejo, CA 94591 Tel. (707)310-3926

Exec. Sec., Rev. Gus H. Brown, 688 Diagonal Rd., Akron, OH 44320 Tel. (330)376-4654

Chinese: President, Rev. Abraham H. Poon., DMin., 2360 McLaughlin Ave., San Jose, CA 95122-3560 Tel. (408)280-1021

Dega: President, Rev. Ha Giao Cilpam, 3119 Westerwood Dr., Charlotte, NC 28214 Tel. (704)393-7159

Filipino: President, Exec. Dir., Rev. Abednego Ferrer, 20143 Royal Ave., Hayward, CA 94541 Tel. (510)887-6261

Haitian: President, Rev. Emmanuel Seide, 14 Glen Rd., West Hempstead, NY 11552 Tel. (516)594-1046

ETHNIC/CULTURAL MINISTRIES

Arab & South Asian: Rev. Joseph S. Kong, P.O. Box 35000, Colorado Springs, CO 80935 Tel 719-599-5999 x. 2052

Alliance Jewish Ministries: Rev. Abraham Sandler, 9820 Woodfern Rd., Philadelphia, PA 19115 Tel. 215-676-5122

Periodicals

Alliance Life

Christian Reformed Church in North America

The Christian Reformed Church represents the historic faith of Protestantism. Founded in the United States in 1857 and active in Canada since 1905, it asserts its belief in the Bible as the inspired Word of God, and is creedally united in the Belgic Confession (1561), the Heidelberg Catechism (1563), and the Canons of Dort (1618–19).

Headquarters

2850 Kalamazoo Ave., SE, Grand Rapids, MI 49560 Tel. (616)224-0832 Fax (616)224-5895

Media Contact, Exec. Dir., Rev. Gerard Dykstra

Email: dykstraj@crcna.org

Website: www.crcna.org

Officers

Exec. Dir. of Ministries, Rev. Gerard Dykstra

Dir. of Canadian Ministries, Rev. Bruce Adema

Director of Finance and Administration, Mr. John Bolt

OTHER ORGANIZATIONS

The Back to God Hour, Dir. Dr. Robert C. Heerspink

Christian Reformed Home Missions, Dir., Rev. John A. Rozeboom

Christian Reformed World Missions, US, Dir., Dr. Gary Bekker

Christian Ref. World Missions, Canada, Dir., Albert Karsten

Christian Reformed World Relief, US, Dir., Andrew Ryskamp

Christian Reformed World Relief, Canada, Dir., Ms. Ida Kaastra Mutoigo

CRC Publications, Dir., Gary Mulder

Ministers' Pension Fund, Admn., Marjorie Csomor

Periodicals

The Banner

Christian Union

Organized in 1864 in Columbus, Ohio, the Christian Union stresses the oneness of the Church with Christ as its only head. The Bible is the only rule of faith and practice and good fruits the only condition of fellowship. Each local church governs itself.

Headquarters

6711 South Calhoun, Fort Wayne, IN 46807 Tel. (260)745-1942

Media Contact, Rev. Phil Harris, Pres.

Email: pharris316@juno.com

Website: www.christianunion.com

Officers

Pres., Rev. Phil Harris, 6711 South Calhoun, Fort Wayne, IN 46807 Tel. (260)745-1942

Vice Pres., Rev. Marion Hunerdosse, 10619 N. Marsh Ave., Kansas City, MO—64057 Tel. (816)781-5044

Sec., Joseph Cunningham, 1005 N. 5th St., Greenfield, OH 45123 Tel. (937)981-3476

Asst. Sec., Jim Eschenbrenner, 308 North Waugh Road., Hedrick, IA 52563 Tel. (641)653-4785

Treas., Rev. Neal Skiles, 80 Licking View Dr.,

Heath, OH 43056-1530 Tel.(740)522-4845
Fax 740-522-6076, Email: skiles@roadrunner.
com

Periodicals
The Christian Union Witness

Church of the Brethren*

Eight German Pietists/Anabaptists, including
their leader, Alexander Mack, founded the
Brethren movement in 1708 in Schwarzenau,
Germany. Begun in reaction to spiritual stagnation
in state churches, the Brethren formed their own
movement, modeled on the first-century church.
They practice church discipline, believer baptism,
anointing, and the love feast. They have no other
creed than the New Testament, hold to principles
of nonviolence, no force in religion, Christian service, and simplicity. They migrated to the colonies
beginning in 1710 and settled at Germantown,
Pennsylvania, moving westward and southward
over the next 200 years. Emphasis on religion in
daily life led to the formation of Brethren
Volunteer Service in 1948, which continues today.

Headquarters

Church of the Brethren General Offices, 1451
Dundee Ave., Elgin, IL 60120 Tel. (847)742-
5100 x 206 Fax (847)753-6103, Email: cob-
web@brethren.org

Brethren Service Center, 500 Main Street, P.O.
Box 188, New Windsor, MD 21776-0188 Tel.
(410)635-8710 Fax (410)635-8789, Email:
bsc_gb@brethren.org

Washington Office, 337 North Carolina Ave. SE,
Washington, DC 20003 Tel. (202)546-3202
Fax (202)544-5852, Email: washington_
office_gb@brethren.org

Media Contact, Cheryl Brumbaugh-Cayford,
Director of News Services, 1451 Dundee Ave.,
Elgin, IL 60120 (847)742-5100 x260 Fax 847-
742-1407, Email: cbrumbaugh-cayford_gb@
brethren.org

Email: cobweb@brethren.org; jclements_gb@
brethren.org

Website: www.brethren.org

OFFICERS

Moderator, James M. Beckwith, P.O. Box 237,
Annville, PA 17003 Tel. (717)867-2972,
Email: moderator@brethren.org

Moderator-elect, David K. Shumate, 330
Hershberger Rd., NW, Roanoke, VA 24012
Tel. (540)362-1816, Email: virlina@aol.com

Secretary, Fred W. Swartz, 102 W. Rainbow
Drive, Bridgewater, VA 22812 Tel. (540)828-
4871, Email: acsecretary@brethren.org

GENERAL BOARD STAFF

General Secretary, Stanley J. Noffsinger, 1451
Dundee Ave., Elgin, IL 60120-1694, Tel. 847-
742-5100 x201, snoffsinger_gb@brethren.org

Manager of Office Operations, Jon Kobel, 1451
Dundee Ave., Elgin, IL 60120-1694, Tel. 847-
742-5100 x202, jkobel_gb@brethren.org

Director, Human Resources, Karin Krog, 1451
Dundee Ave., Elgin, IL 60120-1694, Tel. 847-
742-5100 x258, kkrog_gb@brethren.org

LEADERSHIP TEAM

General Secretary, Stanley J. Noffsinger, 1451
Dundee Ave., Elgin, IL 60120-1694 Tel. (847)
742-5100 x 201, Email: snoffsinger_gb@
brethren.org

Executive Director, Centralized Resources and
Chief Financial Officer/Treasurer, Judy E.
Keyser, 1451 Dundee Ave., Elgin, IL 60120-
1694 Tel. (847)742-5100 x 270, Email:
jkeyser_gb@brethren.org

Executive Director and Publisher, Brethren
Press, Wendy McFadden, 1451 Dundee Ave.,
Elgin, IL 60120-1694 Tel. (847)742-5100 x
278, Email: wmcfadden_gb@brethren.org

Executive Director of Congregational Life
Ministries, position currently vacant

Executive Director of Global Mission
Partnerships, Mervin B. Keeney, 1451 Dundee
Ave., Elgin, IL 60120-1694 Tel. (847)742-
5100 x 226, Email: mission_gb@brethren.org

Executive Director, Brethren Service Center,
Roy Winter, P.O. Box 188, New Windsor, MD
21776-0188 Tel. (410)635-8748, Email: rwin-
ter_gb@brethren.org

Executive Director of Ministry, Mary Jo Flory-
Steury 1451 Dundee Ave., Elgin, IL 60120 Tel.
(847)742-5100 x 466, Email:
mjflorysteury_gb@brethren.org

Periodicals
Messenger

Church of Christ

Joseph Smith and five others organized the
Church of Christ on April 6, 1830 at Fayette,
New York. In 1864 this body was directed by
revelation through Granville Hedrick to return in
1867 to Independence, Missouri to the "consecrated land" dedicated by Joseph Smith. They
did so and purchased the temple lot dedicated in
1831.

Headquarters

Temple Lot, 200 S. River St., P.O. Box 472,
Independence, MO 64051 Tel. (816)833-3995

Media Contact, Gen. Church Rep., William A.
Sheldon, P.O. Box 472, Independence, MO
64051 Tel. (816)833-3995

Website: church-of-christ.com

Officers

Council of Apostles, Secy., Apostle Smith N.
Brickhouse, P.O. Box 472, Independence, MO
64051

Gen. Bus. Mgr., Bishop Alvin Harris, P.O. Box
472, Independence, MO 64051

Periodicals
Zion's Advocate

The Church of Christ (Holiness) U.S.A.

The Church of Christ (Holiness) U.S.A. has a Divine commission to propagate the gospel throughout the world, to seek the conversion of sinners, to reclaim backsliders, to encourage the sanctification of believers, to support divine healing, and to advance the truth for the return of our Lord and Savior Jesus Christ. This must be done through proper organization.

The fundamental principles of Christ's Church have remained the same. The laws founded upon these principles are to remain unchanged. The Church of Christ (Holiness) U.S.A. is representative in form of government; therefore, the final authority in defining the organizational responsibilities rests with the national convention. The bishops of the church are delegated special powers to act in behalf of or speak for the church. The pastors are ordained ministers, who under the call of God and His people, have divine oversight of local churches. However, the representative form of government gives ministry and laity equal authority in all deliberate bodies. With the leadership of the Holy Spirit, Respect, Loyalty and Love will greatly increase.

Headquarters

329 East Monument Street, P.O. Box 3622, Jackson, MS 39207 Tel. (601)353-0222 Fax (601)353-4002

Media Contact, Maurice D. Bingham, Ed. D., Senior Bishop Emeritus

Email: Everything@cochusa.com

Website: www.cochusa.com

BOARD OF BISHOPS

Senior Bishop Emeritus, Maurice D. Bingham, Ed. D., P.O.Box 6182, Jackson, MS 39308 Tel. (601)353-0222, Email: Pminis3659@aol.com

Eastern Diocese, Bishop Lindsay E. Jones, 1033 Winchester Way, Chesapeake, VA 23320 Tel. (757)547-1653, Email: Ljones5@aol.com

North Central Diocese, Bishop Bennett Wolfe, 14315 River Oak Court, Florissant, MO 63034 Tel. (314)741-4590, Email: Ned6@Hotmail.com

Northern Diocese, Bishop Emery Lindsay, 62 West 111th Place, Chicago, IL 60628 Tel. (773)821-0088, Email: Bpelind@aol.com

Pacific Northwest Diocese, Bishop Robert Winn, 1376 Oakwood Ave, Vallejo, CA 94591 Tel. (707)554-2493, Email: Awinner323@aol.com

South Central Diocese, Bishop Joseph Campbell, Jr., P.O. Box 3663, Jackson, MS 39207 Tel. (601)373-6223, Email: Bisjcsd@Bellsouth.net

Southeastern Diocese, Bishop Victor P. Smith, 3783 Treebark Trail, Decatur, GA 30034 Tel. (404)288-4885, Email: Victor@hotmail.com

Southwestern Diocese, President Bishop Vernon Kennebrew, 13900 Edgemond Drive, Little Rock, AR 72212, Email: Tel. (501)954-7676

Western Diocese, Bishop Robert Winn, 1376 Oakwood Ave, Vallejo, CA 94591 Tel. (707) 554-2493, Email: Awinner323@aol.com

Board Member, Bishop James K. Mitchell, 1580 Waite St., Gary, IN 46404 Tel. (219)944-0051, Email: Jasmitch9@aol.com

Periodicals

Truth

Church of Christ, Scientist

The Church of Christ, Scientist, was founded in 1879 by Mary Baker Eddy "to commemorate the word and works of our Master [Christ Jesus], which should reinstate primitive Christianity and its lost element of healing" (Church Manual, p. 17). Central to the Church's mission is making available worldwide Mrs. Eddy's definitive work on health and Bible-based Christian healing, Science and Health With Key to the Scriptures, as well as its publications, Internet sites, and broadcast programs, all of which respond to humanity's search for spiritual answers to today's pressing needs.

The Church also maintains an international speakers' bureau to introduce the public to Christian Science and Mrs. Eddy. Christian Science practitioners, living in hundreds of communities worldwide are available full-time to pray with anyone seeking comfort and healing. And Christian Science teachers hold yearly classes for those interested in a more specific understanding of how to practice the Christian Science system of healing.

The worldwide activities and business of the Church are transacted by a five-member Board of Directors in Boston. About 2000 congregations, each democratically organized and governed, are located in approximately 80 countries. The church has no clergy. Worship services are conducted by lay persons elected to serve as Readers. Each church maintains a Reading Room—a bookstore open to the community for spiritual inquiry and research; and a Sunday School where young people discuss the contemporary relevance of ideas from the Bible and Science and Health.

Headquarters

The First Church of Christ, Scientist, 175 Huntington Ave., A-13, Boston, MA 02115

Media Contact, Mgr., Committees on Publication, Phil Davis, Tel. (617)450-3300 Fax (617) 450-7397

Websites: www.spirituality.com and churchof christscientist.org

Officers

Bd. of Directors: J. Thomas Black; Walter D. Jones; M. Victor Westberg; Mary Metzner Trammell; Nathan Talbot

President, Marian English

Treas., Edward Odegaard

Clk., Nathan Talbot

First Reader, Lyle Young

Second Reader, Christiane Little

Christian Science College Organizations

Website: www.csoconnection.com

Periodicals

The Christian Science Monitor (www.csmonitor. com), *The Christian Science Journal*, *Christian Science Sentinel*, *The Herald of Christian Science* (13 languages), *Christian Science Quarterly Bible Lessons* (in 16 languages and English Braille).

Church Communities International

Church Communities International is a movement of Christian Church Communities originating in Germany in 1920. Driven to England by Nazi persecution in 1937, Church Community members migrated to Paraguay in 1942 with the help of the Mennonite Church. In 1954 the first Church Community in the United States was founded in Rifton New York, where it continues to flourish. Today, a dozen Church Communities are located in New York and Pennsylvania as well as others in Australia, England, Germany and Thailand. Within each Church Community, residents practice their faith in the manner and spirit of the first-century Christians and the Reformation of the early 1500's, sharing everything in common and caring for each other and their neighbors. Members are baptized as adults on confession of the Apostolic Creed, making a voluntary lifetime commitment to living out the teachings of Jesus.

Headquarters

2032 Route 213, Rifton, NY 12471 Tel. (845) 658-8351
Media Contact: Johann Huleatt, Tel. (845)658-7766
Email: johannh@rifton.com

Officers

Pedo Cavanna—Secretary Treasurer, 10 Hellbrook Lane, Ulster Park, NY 12487
The Bruderhof Foundation

Church of God (Anderson, Indiana)

The Church of God (Anderson, Indiana) began in 1881 when Daniel S. Warner and several associates felt constrained to forsake all denominational hierarchies as formal creeds, trusting solely in the Holy Spirit as their overseer and the Bible as their statement of belief.

These people saw themselves at the forefront of a movement to restore unity and holiness to the church, not to establish another denomination, but to promote primary allegiance to Jesus Christ so as to transcend denominational loyalties.

Deeply influenced by Wesleyan theology and Pietism, the Church of God has emphasized conversion, holiness and attention to the Bible. Worship services tend to be informal, accentuating expository preaching and robust singing. There is no formal membership. Persons are assumed to be members on the basis of witness to a conversion experience and evidence that supports such witness. The absence of formal membership is also consistent with the church's understanding of how Christian unity is to be achieved- that is, by preferring the label Christian before all others. The Church of God is congregational in its government. Each local congregation may call any recognized Church of God minister to be its pastor and may retain him or her as long as is mutually pleasing. Ministers are ordained and disciplined by state or provincial assemblies made up predominantly of ministers. National program agencies serve the church through coordinated ministries and resource materials. There are Church of God congregations in 89 foreign countries, most of which are resourced by one or more missionaries. There are slightly more Church of God adherents overseas than in North America.

Headquarters

General Director (President): Dr. Ronald V. Duncan, P.O. Box 2420,Anderson, IN 46018-2420, Tel. (765)642-0256 Fax (765)642-5652
Media Contact: David Farlow, Chief of Strategic Communications, Email: dfarlow@chog.org
Email: RDUNCAN@chog.org
Website: www.chog.org

Officers

General Director (President): Dr. Ronald V. Duncan, P.O. Box 2420, Anderson, IN 46018-2420, Tel. (765)642-0256 Fax (765)642-5652
Media Contact: David Farlow, Chief of Strategic Communications, Email: dfarlow@chog.org

OTHER CHURCH OF GOD ORGANIZATIONS

Board of Pensions, President, Jeffery A. Jenness, Box 2299, Anderson IN 46018
Warner Press, Inc., President, Eric King, Box 2499, Anderson IN 46018
Anderson University, President, James L. Edwards, 1100 E 5th St., Anderson IN 46012
Mid-America Christian University, President, John Fozard, 3500 SW 119th St., Oklahoma City OK 73170
Warner Pacific College, President, Jay A. Barber, Jr., 2219 SE 68th Ave, Portland OR 97215
Warner Southern College, President, Gregory V. Hall, 13895 Hwy 27, Lake Wales, FL 33859
Women of the Church of God, Executive Director, Arnetta Bailey, Box 2328, Anderson, IN 46018

Periodicals

Missions Magazine, *Pathways to God*, *Communion*, *People to People*, *YMI Update*, *One Voice*

The Church of God in Christ

The Church of God in Christ was founded in 1897 in Lexington, Mississippi by Bishop Charles Harrison Mason, a former Baptist minister, and organized as a Pentecostal Church during the early stages of the holiness movement and, more specifically, as an outgrowth of the Azusa Street Revival of Los Angeles, California, in 1906–1909.

Initial growth of the church was attributable to the organization of four departments between 1910–1916, the Women's Department, the Sunday School, Young People's Willing Workers and Home and Foreign Missions.

The Church is Trinitarian and teaches the infallibility of Holy Scripture, the need for regeneration and baptism of the Holy Ghost evidenced by speaking in tongues. It emphasizes holiness as God's standard for Christian conduct and recognizes as ordinances Holy Communion, Water Baptism and Feet Washing.

Its governmental structure is basically episcopal and consists of three branches. The General Board represents the Executive Branch, the General Assembly is the Legislative Branch, and the Judiciary Board represents the Judicial Branch.

Headquarters

Mason Temple Church of God in Christ, 938 Mason St., Memphis, TN 38126 Tel. (901)947-9300

Elder J.H. Lyles, Jr., General Secretary, Mailing Address, P.O. Box 320, Memphis, TN 38101

Email: EJOHNCOGIC@aol.com

Website: www.cogic.org

THE PRESIDIUM

Presiding Bishop, Bishop C.E. Blake, 938 Mason St., Memphis, TN 38126 Tel. (901)947-9340

1st Assistant, Bishop .N. Haynes, 1267 Whispering Oaks Dr., Desoto, TX 75115 Tel. (214)375-4105

2nd Assistant, Bishop P.A. Brooks, 30945 Wendbrook Ln., Beverly Hills, MI 48025 Tel. (313)835-5329

Secretary, Bishop W.W. Hamilton, 14570 Mountain Quail Rd., Salinas, CA 93908 Tel. (831)395-2774

Asst. Secretary, Bishop R.L.H. Winbush, 235 Diamond Dr., Lafayette, LA 70501 Tel. (318) 232-6958

Member, Bishop C.D. Owens, 406 Roswell St., Marietta, GA 30060 Tel. (770)590-8510

Member, Bishop L.R. Anderson, 1023 E. Brook Hollow Dr., Phoenix, AZ 85022 Tel. (602) 993-4906

Member, Bishop G.D. McKinney, 5825 Imperial Ave., San Diego, CA 92114 Tel. (619)262-2671

Member, Bishop S.L. Green, Jr., 41 St. Johns Dr., Hampton, VA 23666 Tel. (757)380-6118

Member, Bishop N.W. Wells, 717 Bridgeview Bay, Muskegon, MI 49441 Tel. (231)722-3219

Member, Bishop J.W. Macklin, 1027 W. Tennyson Road, Haywood, CA 94544 Tel. (510)783-9377

GENERAL OFFICERS

General Secretary, Elder A.Z. Hall, Jr., P.O. Box 320, Memphis, TN 38101 Tel. (901)947-9356

General Treasurer, Bishop S.L. Lowe, Tel. 938 Mason St., Memphis, TN 38126 Tel. (901) 947-9319

Financial Secretary, Bishop F.O. White, 312 Grand Ave., Freeport, NY 11520 Tel. (516)623-7513

ELECTED OFFICERS, DEPARTMENTAL HEADS AND AUXILLIARY LEADERS

Chairman – General Assembly: Bishop J.O. Patterson, Jr., 229 Danny Thomas, Memphis, TN 38126

Chairman – Judiciary Board: Bishop T.L. Westbrook, 1623 S. 11th St., Tacoma, WA 98405

Chairman – Board of Bishops: Bishop J. Sheard, 19511 Afton Rd., Detroit, MI 48203

Chairman – Board of Trustees: Bishop C.M. Ford, 4525 S. Wabash, Chicago, IL 60653 Tel. (773)538-4526

Chief of Staff: Bishop J.L. Maynard, 930 Mason St., Memphis, TN 38126 Tel. (901)947-9338

Chief Accountant: Minister A. Perpener, P.O. Box 320, Memphis, TN 38126 Tel. (901)947-9361

National Properties: Elder D.L.S. Wells, 938 Mason St., Memphis, TN 38126 Tel. (901) 947-9332

Chairman – Pastors/Elders: Elder D. Hutchins

Adjutant General: Bishop Matthew Williams, 1516 Dumont Dr., Valrico, FL 33594

President – Women's Dept.: Mother W.M. Rivers, P.O. Box 1052, Memphis, TN 38101

President – Missions Dept.: Bishop C.L. Moody, P.O. Box 320, Memphis, TN 38101 Tel. (901)947-9316

President – Evangelism: Bishop R. White, 4121 Thurman Ave., Conley, GA 30288 Tel. (404) 361-7020

President – Youth Dept.: Elder Michael Hill, 23746 Riverside Dr., Lathrup, MI 48076

President – Sunday School: Elder Alton Gatlin, 229 Diamond Dr., Lafayette, LA 70501

President – Music Dept.: Professor I. Stevenson

President – Men's Conference: Bishop D. Hines, 8605 W. Goodhope Rd., Milwaukee, WI 53224

President – Sunshine Band: Dr. R.L. Howard

President – Purity: Missionary T. Cotton

Executive Director – Fine Arts: Mrs. S.J. Powell

CEO – Publishing House: Dr. D.A. Hall, Sr., 930 Mason St., Memphis, TN 38126

Chairman – Board of Pub.: Bishop R.L.H. Winbush, 235 Diamond Dr., Lafayette, LA 70501

Manager – COGIC Bookstore: Mrs. G. Miller, 285 S. Main, Memphis, TN 38101 Tel. (901) 947-9304

EDUCATIONAL INSTITUTIONS

Charles Harrison Mason Theological Seminary, 671 Beckwith St. SW, Atlanta, GA 30314 Attn: Dean O.L. Haney

C.H. Mason System of Bible Colleges, 930 Mason St., Memphis, TN 38126 Attn: Dr. M.L. Johnson

All Saints Bible College, 930 Mason St., Memphis, TN 38126 Attn: Dr. P. Little

Saints Academy, C.H. Mason Highway, Lexington, MS Attn: Elder L. Weems

Periodicals

The Whole Truth Magazine, The Voice of Missions, The McBrayer Report

Church of God in Christ, International

The Church of God in Christ, International was organized in 1969 in Kansas City, Mo., by 14 bishops of the Church of God in Christ of Memphis, Tenn. The doctrine is the same, but the separation came because of disagreement over polity and governmental authority. The Church is Wesleyan in theology (two works of grace) but stresses the experience of full baptism of the Holy Ghost with the initial evidence of speaking with other tongues as the Spirit gives utterance.

Headquarters

170 Adelphi St., Brooklyn, NY 11205 Tel. (718) 625-9175

Media Contact, Natl. Sec., Rev. Sis. Sharon R. Dunn

Email: laity@cogic.org

Website: www.cogic.org/main

Officers

Presiding Bishop, Most Rev. Carl Williams, Jr.

Vice Presiding Bishop, Rt. Rev. J. C. White

Exec. Admn., Horace K. Williams, Word of God Center, Newark, NJ

Women's Dept., Natl. Supervisor, Evangelist Elvonia Williams

Youth Dept., Pres., Dr. Joyce Taylor, 137-17 135th Ave., S., Ozone Park, NY 11420

Music Dept., Pres., Isaiah Heyward

Bd. of Bishops, Chpsn., Bishop J. C. White, 360 Colorado Ave., Bridgeport, CT 06605

Church of God in Christ, Mennonite

The Church of God in Christ, Mennonite was organized by the evangelist-reformer John Holdeman in Ohio. The church unites with the faith of the Waldensians, Anabaptists and other such groups throughout history. Emphasis is placed on obedience to the teachings of the Bible, including the doctrine of the new birth and spiritual life, noninvolvement in government or the military, head-coverings for the women, beards for the men and separation from the world shown by simplicity in clothing, homes, possessions and lifestyle. The church has a worldwide membership of about 21,300, largely concentrated in the United States and Canada.

Headquarters

P.O. Box 313, 420 N. Wedel Ave., Moundridge, KS 67107 Tel. (620)345-2532 Fax (620)345-2582

Media Contact, Dale Koehn, P.O. Box 230, Moundridge, KS 67107 Tel. 620-345-2532 Fax 620-345-2582

Email: dalekoehn.gp@cogicm.org

Periodicals

Messenger of Truth

Church of God (Cleveland, Tennessee)

It is one of America's oldest Pentecostal churches founded in 1886 as an outgrowth of the holiness revival under the name Christian Union. In 1907 the church adopted the organizational name Church of God. It has its foundation upon the principles of Christ as revealed in the Bible. The Church of God is Christian, Protestant, foundational in its doctrine, evangelical in practice and distinctively Pentecostal. It maintains a centralized form of government and a commitment to world evangelization. The first church of Canada was established in 1919 in Scotland Farm, Manitoba. Paul H. Walker became the first overseer of Canada in 1931.

Headquarters

Intl. Offices, 2490 Keith St., NW, Cleveland, TN 37320 Tel. (423)472-3361 Fax (423)478-7066

Media Contact, Dir. of Communications, T. Scot Carter, P.O.Box 2430, Cleveland, TN 37320-2430; Tel. (423)478-7112 Fax (423)478-7066

Email: julianrobinson@churchofgod.org

Website: www.churchofgod.org

EXECUTIVES

Gen. Overseer, G. Dennis McGuire

Asst. Gen. Overseers, Raymond F. Culpepper; Orville Hagan; and Timothy M. Hill

Sec.-Gen., Paul L. Walker

Canada-Eastern, Rev. George S. Pears, P.O.Box 2036, Brampton, ON L6T 3TO Tel. (905)793-2213 Fax (905)793-9173

Canada-Western, Rev. Stephen P. Darnell, Box 54055, 2640 52 St. NE, Calgary, AB T1Y 6S6 Tel. (403)293-8817 Fax (403)293-3466

Canada-Quebec-Maritimes, Rev. Jaques Houle, 19 Orly, Granby, QC J2H 1Y4 Tel. (450)378-4442 Fax (450)378-8646

Canada-National, Rev. Ralph R. Glagau, P.O.Box 333, Stn B, Etobicoke, ON M9W 5L3 Tel. (416)741-9222 Fax (416)741-3717

DEPARTMENTS

Benefits Board—CEO, Arthur D. Rhodes

Business & Records—Exec. Dir., Julian B. Robinson

Care Ministries—Dir., Donnie W. Smith

Chaplains Commission—Dir., Robert D. Crick

Communications, Media Ministries—Dir., T. Scot Carter

Division of Education—Chancellor, Donald S. Aultman

93

Education—European Bible Seminary, Dir., Paul Schmidgall

Education—USA Hispanic Educational Ministries Dir., Rudy Giron

Education—International Bible College, Pres., James Dill

Education—Lee University, Pres., Charles Paul Conn

Education—Patten University, Pres., Gary Moncher

Education—Puerto Rico Bible School, Pres., Ildefonso Caraballo

Education—Theological Seminary, President, Steven J. Land

Evangelism & Home Missions—Dir., Wallace J. Sibley

Evangelism—Black Ministries, Dir., Jimmy Campbell

Evangelism—Multi-Cultural Min., Dir., Harvey L. Turner, Sr.

Evangelism—Hispanic Ministries, Dir., Fidenaio Burgueno

Evangelism—Native American Ministries, Dir., Douglas M. Cline

Family Ministries—Coordinator, John K. Vining

Lay Ministries—Dir., Leonard Albert

Legal Services—Dir., Dennis W. Watkins

Men/Women of Action—Dir., L. Hugh Carver

Ministerial Care—Dir., Bill Leonard

Ministerial Development—Dir., Donald S. Aultman

Ministry to Israel—Dir., J. Michael Utterback

Ministry to the Military—Dir., Robert A. Moore

Music Ministries—Dir., Delton L. Alford

Pentecostal Resource Center—Director, Donald D. Smeeton

Pentecostal Research Center—Dir., David G. Roebuck

Publications—Dir., Joseph A. Mirkovich

SpiritCare—Dir., Gene D. Rice

Stewardship—Dir., Kenneth R. Davis

Women's Ministries—Coordinator, Mary Ruth Stone

World Missions—Dir., Roland E. Vaughan

Youth & Christian Education—Dir., Mark S. Abbott

Romanian Ministries—Dir., Thomas A. George

Periodicals
Church of God Evangel, *Church of God Editorial Evangelica*, *Save Our World*, *Ministry Now Profiles*

Church of God by Faith, Inc.

Founded 1914, in Jacksonville Heights, Florida., by Elder John Bright, this church believes the word of God as interpreted by Jesus Christ to be the only hope of salvation and Jesus Christ the only mediator for people.

Headquarters
1315 Lane Ave. S., Suite 6, Jacksonville, FL 32205 Tel. (904)783-8500 Fax (904)783-9911
Media Contact, Ofc. Mgr., Sarah E. Lundy

Email: natl-hq@cogbf.org
Website: www.cogbf.org

Officers
Presiding Bishop, James E. McKnight, P.O. Box 121, Gainesville, FL 32601

Treas., Elder John Robinson, 300 Essex Dr., Ft. Pierce, FL 34946

Exec. Sec., David C. Rourk, 207 Chestnut Hill Drive, Rochester, NY. 14617

Ruling Elder, James E. McKnight, Jr., P.O. Box 101, Starke, FL 32091

The Church of God of the Firstborn

The Church of God of the Firstborn was founded by Pentecostal evangelist Adolph Gustav Etterman in 1936. Headquarters are located in Newton, KS, where annual summer conferences are held. In 2002, the denomination consisted of 26 congregations, located primarily in the south central United States and in Mexico. In recent years, the number of Caucasian churches has declined and Hispanic membership has surged. James Etterman, the son of the founder, became president of the denomination in 1986.

Headquarters
P.O. Box 1041, 720 S. Kansas Ave., Newton, KS 671114-1041
Media Contact, Pres., Rev. James Etterman

Officers
Pres., Rev. James Etterman

Periodicals
The True Messenger

Church of God General Conference (Oregon, IL and Morrow, GA)

This church is the outgrowth of several independent local groups of similar faith. Some were in existence as early as 1800, and others date their beginnings to the arrival of British immigrants around 1847. Many local churches carried the name Church of God of the Abrahamic Faith. State and district conferences of these groups were formed as an expression of mutual cooperation. A national organization was instituted at Philadelphia in 1888. Because of strong convictions on the questions of congregational rights and authority, however, it ceased to function until 1921, when the present General Conference was formed at Waterloo, Iowa.

The Bible is accepted as the supreme standard of faith. Adventist in viewpoint, the second (premillenial) coming of Christ is strongly emphasized. The church teaches that the kingdom of God will be literal, beginning in Jerusalem at the time of the return of Christ and extending to all nations. Emphasis is placed on the oneness of God and the Sonship of Christ, that Jesus did not pre-exist prior to his birth in Bethlehem and that the Holy Spirit is the power and influence of God. Membership is dependent on faith, repentance and baptism by immersion.

The work of the General Conference is carried on under the direction of the board of directors. With a congregational church government, the General Conference exists primarily as a means of mutual cooperation and for the development of yearly projects and enterprises.

The headquarters and Bible College were moved to Morrow, GA in 1991.

Headquarters

P.O. Box 100,000, Morrow, GA 30260 Tel. (404) 362-0052 Fax (404)362-9307
Media Contact, Tim Jones
Email: info@abc-coggc.org
Website: www.abc-coggc.org

Officers

Chief Administrative Officer, Mr. Tim Jones, Box 100,000, Morrow , GA 30260 Tel. (404)362-9307, Email: tjones@abc-coggc.org
Chpsn., Pastor Michael Hoffman, 740 W. Oregon Trail, Oregon, IL 61061 Tel. (815)732-6847, Email: hoffon@aol.com
Vice Chpsn., Pastor Dale Bliss, 2696 Wynterpointe Ct., Kokomo IN 46901 Tel. (765)455-9866, Email: dale_bliss@hotmail.com
Sec., Andrea Anders, 301 North Ellis St., Salisbury, NC 28144 Tel. (803)461-2150, Email: aanders@suggskelly.com
Treas. Mr. Joe James, 100 Buck Drive, Piedmont, SC 29673 Tel. (864)845-5808, Email: jjoecarol@aol.com

OTHER ORGANIZATIONS

Bus. Admn., Operations Manager, Mr. Gary Burnham, Box 100,000, Morrow, GA 30260 Tel. (404)362-0052 Fax (404)362-9307, Email: gburnham@abc-coggc.org
Atlanta Bible College, President, Mr. Tim Jones, Box 100,000, Morrow, GA 30260 Tel. (404) 362-9307, Email: tjones@abc- coggc.org

Periodicals

The Restitution Herald and Progress Journal, A Journal From the Radical Reformation, Church of God

Church of God, Mountain Assembly, Inc.

The church was formed in 1895 and organized in 1906 by J. H. Parks, S. N. Bryant, Tom D. Moses and William Douglas.

Headquarters

256 N. Florence Ave., P.O. Box 157, Jellico, TN 37762 Tel. (423)784-8260 Fax (423)784-3258
Media Contact, Gen. Sec.-Treas., Rev. James Kilgore
Email: cgmahdq@jellico.com
Website: www.cgmahdq.org

Officers

Gen. Overseer, Rev. Fred R. Cornelius
Asst. Gen. Overseer, World Missions Dir., Rev. Jay Walden
Gen. Sec.-Treas., Rev. James Kilgore
Youth Ministries & Camp Dir., Rev. Nick Hill

Periodicals

The Gospel Herald

Church of God of Prophecy

The Church of God of Prophecy is one of the churches that grew out of the work of A. J. Tomlinson in the first half of the twentieth century. Historically it shares a common heritage with the Church of God (Cleveland Tennessee) and is in the mainstream of the classical Pentecostal-Holiness tradition.

At the death of A.J. Tomlinson in 1943, M.A. Tomlinson was named General Overseer and served until his retirement in 1990. He emphasized unity and fellowship unlimited by racial, social, or political differences. The next General Overseer, Billy D. Murray, Sr., who served from 1990 until his retirement in 2000, emphasized a commitment to the promotion of Christian unity and world evangelization. In July 2000, Fred S. Fisher, Sr. Was duly selected to serve as the fourth General Overseer of the Church of God of Prophecy until his retirement in September 2006. In August 2006, Bishop Randall E. Howard, then Global Outreach Ministries Director, was selected as the fifth General Overseer of the Church.

From its beginnings, the Church has based its beliefs on "the whole Bible, rightly divided," and has accepted the Bible as God's Holy Word, inspired, inerrant and infallible. The church is firm in its commitment to orthodox Christian belief. The Church affirms that there is one God, eternally existing in three persons, Father, Son and Holy Spirit. It believes in the deity of Christ, His virgin birth, His sinless life, the physical miracles He performed, His atoning death on the cross, His bodily resurrection, His ascension to the right hand of the Father and his Second coming. The church professes that salvation results from grace alone through faith in Christ, that regeneration by the Holy Spirit is essential for the salvation of sinful men, and that sanctification by the blood of Christ makes possible personal holiness. It affirms the present ministry of the Holy Spirit by Whose indwelling believers are able to live godly lives and have power for service. The church believes in, and promotes, the ultimate unity of believers as prayed for by Christ in John 17. The church stresses the sanctity of human life and is committed to the sanctity of the marriage bond and the importance of strong, loving Christian families. Other official teachings include Holy Spirit baptism with tongues as initial evidence; manifestation of the spiritual gifts; divine healing; premillenial second-coming of Christ; total abstinence from the use of tobacco, alcohol and narcotics; water baptism by immersion; the Lord's supper and washing of the saints' feet; and a concern for moderation and holiness in all dimensions of lifestyle.

The Church is racially integrated on all levels, including top leadership. Women play a prominent role in church affairs, serving in pastoral roles and other leadership positions. The church presbytery has recently adopted plurality of leadership in the selection of a General Oversight Group. This group consists of eight bishops located around the world who, along with the General Overseer, are responsible for inspirational leadership and vision casting for the church body.

The Church has local congregations in all 50 states and more than 120 nations worldwide. Organizationally there is a strong emphasis on international missions, evangelism, youth and children's ministries, women's and men's ministries, stewardship, communications, publishing, leadership development and discipleship.

CHURCH OF GOD OF PROPHECY INTERNATIONAL OFFICES

P.O. Box 2910, Cleveland, TN 37320-2910
Email: betty@cogop.org
Website: www.cogop.org

Officers

Gen. Overseer, Bishop Randall E. Howard
General Presbyters, Sherman Allen, Sam Clements, David Browder, Clayton Endecott, Miguel Mojica, Felix Santiago, Brice Thompson
International Offices Ministries Directors Finance, Communications, and Publishing, Benjamin Feliz Global Outreach Ministries, David Bryan Leadership Development and Discipleship Ministries, Larry Duncan.

Periodicals

White Wing Messenger (ENG), *White Wing Messenger* (Spanish)

The Church of God (Seventh Day), Denver, Colorado

The Church of God (Seventh Day) began in southwestern Michigan in 1858, when a group of Sabbath-keepers led by Gilbert Cranmer refused to give endorsement to the visions and writings of Ellen G. White, a principal in the formation of the Seventh-Day Adventist Church. Another branch of Sabbath-keepers, which developed near Cedar Rapids, Iowa, in 1860, joined the Michigan church in 1863 to publish a paper called The Hope of Israel, the predecessor to the Bible Advocate, the church's present publication. As membership grew and spread into Missouri and Nebraska, it organized the General Conference of the Church of God in 1884. The words "Seventh Day" were added to its name in 1923. The headquarters of the church was in Stanberry, Missouri, from 1888 until 1950, when it moved to Denver.

The Church teaches salvation is a gift of God's grace, and is available solely by faith in Jesus Christ, the Savior; that saving faith is more than mental assent, it involves active trust and repentance from sin. Out of gratitude, Christians will give evidence of saving faith by a lifestyle that conforms to God's commandments, including the seventh-day Sabbath, which members observe as a tangible expression of their faith and rest in God as their Creator and Redeemer. The church believes in the imminent, personal, and visible return of Christ; that the dead are in an unconscious state awaiting to be resurrected, the wicked to be destroyed, and the righteous to be rewarded to eternal life in the presence of God on a restored earth. The church observes two ordinances, baptism by immersion and an annual Communion service accompanied by foot washing.

Headquarters

330 W. 152nd Ave., P.O. Box 33677, Denver, CO 80233 Tel. (303)452-7973 Fax (303)452-0657
Media Contact, Pres., Whaid Rose
Email: whaidrose@cog7.org
Website: www.cog7.org

MINISTRIES

Missions Ministries, Dir., William Hicks, Church Planting Dir., Mike Vlad; Home Missions Dir., Mike Vlad; Missions Abroad, Dir., William Hicks
Publications/Bible of Advocate Press, Dir., Eddie Villalba
Ministerial Training System, Chairman, Harvey Fischer
Young Adult Ministry, Dir., Kristy Lang
Youth Ministry, Dirs., Kurt & Kristi Lang
Women's Ministry, Dir., Mary Ling

Periodicals

The Bible Advocate (English & Spanish), *Pulse* (English & Spanish)

The Church of Illumination

The Church of Illumination was organized in 1908 for the express purpose of establishing congregations at large, offering a spiritual, esoteric, philosophic interpretation of the vital biblical teachings, thereby satisfying the inner spiritual needs of those seeking spiritual truth, yet permitting them to remain in, or return to, their former church membership.

Headquarters

Beverly Hall, 5966 Clymer Rd., Quakertown, PA 18951 Tel. (800)779-3796
Media Contact, Dir. General, Gerald E. Poesnecker, P.O. Box 220, Quakertown, PA 18951 Tel. (215)536-7048 Fax (215)536-7058
Email: bevhall@comcat.com
Website: www.soul.org

Officers

Dir.-General, Gerald E. Poesnecker, P.O. Box 220, Quakertown, PA 18951

The Church of Jesus Christ (Bickertonites)

This church was organized in 1862 at Green Oak, Pa., by William Bickerton, who obeyed the Restored Gospel under Sidney Rigdon's following in 1845.

Headquarters

Sixth & Lincoln Sts., Monongahela, PA 15063 Tel. (412)258-3066

Media Contact, Exec. Sec., John Manes, 2007 Cutter Dr., McKees Rocks, PA 15136 Tel. (412)771-4513

Officers

Pres., Dominic Thomas, 6010 Barrie, Dearborn, MI 48126

First Counselor, Paul Palmieri, 319 Pine Dr., Aliquippa, PA 15001 Tel. (412)378-4264

Second Counselor, Robert Watson, Star Rt. 5, Box 36, Gallup, NM 87301

Exec. Sec., John Manes, 2007 Cutter Dr., McKees Rocks, PA 15136 Tel. (412)771-4513

The Church of Jesus Christ of Latter-day Saints

This church was organized April 6, 1830, at Fayette, N.Y., by Joseph Smith. Members believe Joseph Smith was divinely directed to restore the gospel to the earth, and that through him the keys to the Aaronic and Melchizedek priesthoods and temple work also were restored. Members believe that both the Bible and the Book of Mormon (a record of the Lord's dealings with His people on the American continent 600 BC–421 AD) are scripture. Membership is over twelve million.

In addition to the First Presidency, the governing bodies of the church include the Quorum of the Twelve Apostles, the Presidency of the Seventy, the Quorums of the Seventy and the Presiding Bishopric.

Headquarters

47 East South Temple St., Salt Lake City, UT 84150 Tel. (801)240-1000 Fax (801)240-1167

Media Contact, Dir., Media Relations, Michael Otterson, Tel. (801)240-1111 Fax (801)240-1167

Website: www.lds.org

Officers

Pres., Gordon B. Hinckley

1st Counselor, Thomas S. Monson

2nd Counselor, Henry B. Eyring

Quorum of the Twelve Apostles, Pres., Boyd K. Packer; L. Tom Perry; Russell M. Nelson; Dallin H. Oaks; M. Russell Ballard; Joseph B. Wirthlin; Richard G. Scott; Robert D. Hales; Jeffrey R. Holland; Dieter F. Uchtdorf; David A. Bednar; Quentin L. Cook

AUXILIARY ORGANIZATIONS

Sunday Schools, Gen. Pres., A. Roger Merrill

Relief Society, Gen. Pres., Bonnie D. Parkin

Young Women, Gen. Pres., Susan W. Tanner

Young Men, Gen. Pres., Charles W. Dahlquist II

Primary, Gen. Pres., Cheryl C. Lant

Periodicals

The Ensign, Liahona, New Era, Friend Magazine

Church of the Living God (Motto, Christian Workers for Fellowship)

The Church of the Living God was founded by William Christian in April 1889 at Caine Creek, Arkansas. It was the first black church in America without Anglo-Saxon roots and not founded by white missionaries.

Chief Christian, as he is now referred, was born a slave in Mississippi on Nov. 10, 1856 and grew up uneducated. In 1875, he united with the Missionary Baptist Church and began to preach. In 1888, he left the Baptist Church and began what was known as Christian Friendship Work. Believing himself to have been inspired by the Spirit of God through divine revelation and close study of the Scriptures, he was led to the truth that the Bible refers to the church as The Church of the Living God (I Timothy. Ch.3 vs.15). In 1889, he established the Church of the Living God organization.

The organization is nondenominational, non-sectarian and Trinitarian and believers in the infallibility of the Scriptures. It emphasizes believer's baptism by immersion, the use of water and unleavened bread element in the Lord's Supper and the washing of feet that is required only when one unites with the church.

The local organizations are know as "Temple" rather than as "Churches" and are subject to the authority of the general assembly. The presiding officer is styled as "chief bishop." The ministry includes bishops, overseers, evangelists, pastors, missionaries and local preachers. The Executive Board is in charge of the operation of the entire organization, in the absence of the Annual Assembly. Synod, Annual, General Assembly meets quadrennial.

The Church of the Living God, now headquartered in Cincinnati, Ohio, has been in existence for more than 114 years. It is represented by approximately 10,000 members throughout 25 states within the U.S. The presiding officer, Chief Bishop W. E. Crumes, has led the organization for more than 30 years.

Headquarters

430 Forest Ave., Cincinnati, OH 45229 Tel. (513) 569-5660 Fax (513)569-5661

Media Contact: Chief Bishop, W. E. Crumes

EXECUTIVE BOARD

Chief Bishop, W. E. Crumes, 430 Forest Ave., Cincinnati, OH 45229

Vice-Chief Bishop, Robert D. Tyler, 3802 Bedford, Omaha, NE 68110

Exec. Sec., Bishop C. A. Lewis, 1360 N. Boston, Tulsa, OK 73111

Gen. Sec., Elder Raymond Powell, Sr., 2159 E. 95th St., Chicago, IL 60617

Gen. Treas., Elder Harry Hendricks, 11935 Cimarron Ave., Hawthorne, CA 90250

Bishop E. L. Bowie, 2037 N.E. 18th St., Oklahoma City, OK 73111

Bishop Leroy Smith, Jr., 1418 Faraday, Peoria, IL 61605

Bishop Jeff Ruffin, 302 E. Monte Way, Phoenix, AZ 85040

Bishop S. E. Shannon, 1034 S. King Hwy., St. Louis, MO 63110

Bishop, Elbert Jones, 4522 Melwood, Memphis, TN 38109

Bishop, Harold Edwards, P.O.Box 411489, Dallas, TX 75249

NATIONAL DEPARTMENTS

Convention Planning Committee
Young People's Progressive Union
Christian Education Dept.
Sunday School Dept.
Natl. Evangelist Bd.
Natl. Nurses Guild
Natl. Women's Work Dept.
Natl. Music Dept.
Natl. Usher Board
Natl. Sec. Office

Periodicals

The Gospel Truth

Church of the Lutheran Brethren of America

The Church of the Lutheran Brethren of America was organized in December 1900. Five independent Lutheran congregations met together in Milwaukee, Wisconsin, and adopted a constitution patterned very closely on that of the Lutheran Free Church of Norway.

The spiritual awakening in the Midwest during the 1890s crystallized into convictions that led to the formation of a new church body. Chief among the concerns were church membership practices, observance of Holy Communion, confirmation practices and local church government.

The Church of the Lutheran Brethren practices a simple order of worship with the sermon as the primary part of the worship service. It believes that personal profession of faith is the primary criterion for membership in the congregation. The Communion service is reserved for those who profess faith in Christ as savior. Each congregation is autonomous and the synod serves the congregations in advisory and cooperative capacities.

The synod supports a world mission program in Cameroon, Chad, Japan and Taiwan. Approximately 40 percent of the synodical budget is earmarked for world missions. A growing home mission ministry is planting new congregations in the United States and Canada. Affiliate organizations operate several retirement, nursing homes, conference and retreat centers.

Headquarters

1020 Alcott Ave., W., Box 655, Fergus Falls, MN 56538 Tel. (218)739-3336 Fax (218)739-5514
Media Contact, Pres., Rev. Joel Egge
Email: clba@clba.org
Website: www.clba.org

Officers

Pres., Rev. Joel Egge
Vice Pres., Rev. Richard Bridston
Sec., Rev. Richard Vettrus, 1020 Alcott Ave. W, Fergug Falls, MN 56537
Exec. Dir. of Finance, Bradley Martinson
Lutheran Brethren Seminay President, Dr. David Veum
World Missions, Exec. Dir., Rev. Matthew Rogness
North American Mission Church Services, Exec. Dir., Rev. Joel Nordtredt

Periodicals

Faith & Fellowship

Church of the Lutheran Confession

The Church of the Lutheran Confession held its constituting convention in Watertown, S.D., in August of 1960. The Church of the Lutheran Confession was begun by people and congregations who withdrew from church bodies that made up what was then known as the Synodical Conference over the issue of unionism. Following such passages as I Corinthians 1 vs.10 and Romans 16 vs.17-18, the Church of the Lutheran Confession holds the conviction that mutual agreement with the doctrines of Scripture is essential and necessary before exercise of church fellowship is appropriate.

Members of the Church of the Lutheran Confession uncompromisingly believe the Holy Scriptures to be divinely inspired and therefore inerrant. They subscribe to the historic Lutheran Confessions as found in the Book of Concord of 1580 because they are a correct exposition of Scripture.

The Church of the Lutheran Confession exists to proclaim, preserve and spread the saving truth of the gospel of Jesus Christ, so that the redeemed of God may learn to know Jesus Christ as their Lord and Savior and follow him through this life to the life to come.

Headquarters

501 Grover Rd., Eau Claire, WI 54701 Tel. (715)836-6622
Media Contact, Pres., Daniel Fleischer Tel.(361)241-5147
Email: JohnHLau@juno.com
Website: www.clclutheran.org

Officers

Pres., Rev. John Schierenbeck, 3015 Ave. K NW, Winter Haven, FL 33881
Mod., Prof. Ronald Roehl, 515 Ingram Dr. W., Eau Claire, WI 54701

Vice Pres., Rev. Mark Bernthal, 3232 West Point Rd., Middleton, WI 53562, Tel. (608)233-2244

Sec., Rev. James Albrecht, 102 Market St., P.O. Box 98 Okebena, MN 55432-2408

Treas., Dr. James Sydow, 500 Grover Rd., Eau Claire, WI 54701

Archivist, Prof. David Lau, 507 Ingram Dr., Eau Claire, WI 54701

Statistician, Dr. James Sydow, 500 Grover Rd., Eau Claire, WI 54701

Periodicals
The Lutheran Spokesman, Journal of Theology

Church of the Nazarene

The Church of the Nazarene resulted from the merger of three independent holiness groups. The Association of Pentecostal Churches in America, located principally in New York and New England, joined at Chicago in 1907 with a largely West Coast body called the Church of the Nazarene and formed the Pentecostal Church of the Nazarene. A southern group, the Holiness Church of Christ, united with the Pentecostal Church of the Nazarene at Pilot Point, Texas, in 1908. In 1919 the word "Pentecostal" was dropped from the name. Principal leaders in the organization were Phineas Bresee, William Howard Hoople, H. F. Reynolds and C. B. Jernigan. Dr. H. F. Reynolds organized the first Canadian congregation in 1902 at Oxford, Nova Scotia.

The Church of the Nazarene emphasizes entire sanctification or Christian Holiness. It stresses the importance of a devout and holy life and a positive witness through Christ-like character shaped by the Holy Spirit. Nazarenes express their faith through evangelism, compassionate ministries, and education. The church is connectional. Its polity combines episcopal, presbyterian, and congregational elements. Churches call pastors. Districts conduct annual assemblies and elect leaders. The quadrennial General Assembly, a delegated body, is international in scope and establishes doctrine and order, elects the general superintendents (currently six), and elects members to various church boards and agencies.

Internationally the church has 11 liberal arts colleges and universities, three graduate seminaries, 37 Bible colleges, three schools of nursing, an education college, and a junior college. The church maintains 788 missionaries in 144 world areas. World services include medical, educational and religious ministries. Books, periodicals and other Christian literature are published at the Nazarene Publishing House.

The church is a member of the Christian Holiness Partnership, National Association of Evangelicals and the World Methodist Council.

Headquarters
6401 The Paseo, Kansas City, MO 64131 Tel. (816)333-7000 Fax (816)822-9071

Media Contact, Gen. Sec./Headquarters Operations Officer (HOO), Dr. David P. Wilson, Tel. (816)333-7000 x 2366 Fax (816) 362-4983 or (816)822-9071, Email: dwilson @nazarene.org

Email: ssm@nazarene.org

Website: www.nazarene.org

Officers

Gen. Supts., Dr. James H. Diehl; Dr. Paul G. Cunningham; Dr.Jerry D. Porter; Dr. Nina Gunter; Dr. J.K. Warrick; Dr. Jesse C. Middendorf; 6401 The Paseo, Kansas City, MO 64131 Tel. (816)333-7000

Gen. Sec./Headquarters Operation Officer (HOO), Dr. David P. Wilson, Tel. (816)333-7000 Fax (816)822-9071, Email: dwilson@ nazarene.org

Gen. Treas./Headquarters Financial Officer (HFO), Dr. Marilyn McCool, Tel. (816)333-7000 Fax (816)361-6216, Email: mmccool@ nazarene.org

Sunday School and Discipleship Ministries International Director, Dr. Woodie Stevens, 6401 The Paseo, Kansas City, MO 64131, Tel. (816)333-7000 Fax (816)363-7092, Email: stevens@nazarene.org

USA/Canada Mission/Evangelism Director, Dr. Tom Nees, 6401 The Paseo, Kansas City, MO 64131 Tel. 816-333-7000 Fax 816-361-5202, Email: tnees@nazarene.org

Education Commissioner, Dr. Jerry Lambert, 6401 The Paseo, Kansas City, MO 64131 Tel. 816-333-7000 Fax 816-333-2891, Email: jlambert@nazarene.org

Nazarene Youth International Director., Rev. Gary Hartke, 6401 The Paseo, Kansas City, MO 64131 Tel. 816-333-7000 Fax 816-333-4315, Email: ghartke@nazarene.org

World Mission Director., Dr. Louie Bustle, 6401 The Paseo, Kansas City, MO 64131 Tel. 816-333-7000 Fax 816-363-8216, Email: lbustle@ nazarene.org

Periodicals
Holiness Today, Preacher's Magazine, Grow Magazine

The Church of God

The Church of God was established in about 28 A.D. by Jesus Christ on Mt. Kurn Hattin (Mark 3:13-15). It was endued with power on the Day of Pentecost, but was in operation prior to this point in time.

The true Church plunged into the Dark Ages on June 14th, 325 A.D. with the signing of the "Nicene Creed" and remained in darkness for 1578 years. From 325 A.D. to 1903, God was not asleep! He began revealing the truth to men once again: Martin Luther—justification by faith; John Wesley—sanctification; Dr. Albert Simpson —divine healing; (though some received the Holy Ghost prior to 1903, it is generally regarded the Pentecostal Movement began with a Holy

99

Ghost revival in California in 1906—Dr. Seymour).

On June 13,1903 The Church arose from darkness (as prophesied by Isaiah 60:1-5) in North Carolina. In 1923 a disruption caused a split in the Church, resulting in two groups both calling themselves the Church of God. In 1933 God gave the banner (Psalms 60:3, 4), the Church flag, to His Church; to those who feared Him too much to be led astray from the truth. (August 31, 2001 the Holy Ghost gave a new design for the banner of truth.)

On May 2nd, 1952 "of Prophecy" was added to the name Church of God. In 1990, the Church of God of Prophecy departed from theocratic government. Through the Holy Ghost, God called for a Solemn Assembly to be held July 23-25, 1993. On July 24th, the Holy Ghost gave direction to separate ourselves from the apostasy of the past three years, and to continue truly as The Church of God, clearly designating Robert J. Pruitt as the General Overseer. The Church of God thus returned to the true theocracy.

This constituted not a new organization, but the reorganization of The Church of God as the true theocracy of God, the exclusive Body of Christ:

1. Which was set in order by Christ and functioned in theocratic order until A.D. 325;
2. Which arose from the Dark Ages on June 13, 1903;
3. Which continued true to God in "faith and practice, government and discipline" following the 1923 disruption;
4. Which is doing likewise since the similar disruption in 1993.

Details of the future are, of course, unknown; but the prophecies of God are clear concerning His Church. The hour is late, but the brightness of the "Arise, Shine" lies just ahead. Without a doubt, perfection will be attained, for it has already been declared of the Church that Christ will "present it unto himself a glorious church, not having spot, or wrinkle, or any such thing; but that it should be holy and without blemish." (Ephesians 5:27; see also Revelations 19:6-9).

Headquarters

P.O. Box 450, Charleston, TN 37310 Tel. (423) 339-8264

Officers

General Overseer, Stephen Smith, 197 Tillie Road, Cleveland, TN

Field Secretary, Ray D. Dupre

Field Secretary, Robert F. Strong

Field Secretary, Donaldo Acosta

General Treasurer/ Assistant Editor of The Evening Light, Kevin D. Werkheiser

World Mission Coordinator/ Bible Training Institute Director, Herman D. Ard

Mission Representative (Africa, Asia & Europe), Robert J. Hawkins, Jr.

Assembly Band Movement Coordinator, Donald W. Branscum

Evangelism Coordinator, Lanny W. Carter

Church of Prophecy Marker Association Coordinator, Melvin Byers, Jr.

Sunday School Coordinator, Maudie E. Wood

Victory Leaders Band Coordinator, Sharon Griffin

Women's Missionary Band Coordinator, Betty Bishop

STATES

Alabama, James C. Anders

Alaska, Michael A. Grant

Arizona/Colorado/New Mexico/Texas (W), James R. Horne

Arkansas/Kansas/Missouri/Oklahoma/Texas (E), Dewayne Smith

Idaho (S)/California/Nevada/Utah, Serafin Pimentel

Idaho (N)/Montana (W)/Oregon/Washington, Ray D. Adams

Florida/Georgia, Melvin F. Kramer

Indiana/Illinois (S)/Kentucky/Ohio, Paul S. Jernigan

Louisiana/Mississippi, A. T. Dewberry

North Carolina, Melvin Byers, Jr.

South Carolina, Carl J. Neal

Pennsylvania/Delaware/Maryland/Massachusett, James T. Smith

Virginia/ West Virginia, Clive Jared

N. Dakota/S. Dakota/Minnesota/Montana (E)/ Nebraska/Wyoming, Delbert G. Bock

Tennessee, Ray D. Dupre

Wisconsin/Illinois (N)/Iowa/Michigan, E. Roger Ammons

Periodicals

The Evening Light

Church of Our Lord Jesus Christ of the Apostolic Faith, Inc.

This church body was founded by Bishop R.C. Lawson in Columbus, Ohio, and moved to New York City in 1919. It is founded upon the teachings of the apostles and prophets, Jesus Christ being its chief cornerstone.

Headquarters

2081 Adam Clayton Powell Jr. Blvd., New York, NY 10027 Tel. (212)866-1700

Media Contact, Exec. Sec., Bishop T. E. Woolfolk, P.O. Box 119, Oxford, NC 27565 Tel. (919)693-9449 Fax (919)693-6115

Email: tewmsw@earthlink.net

Website: www.apostolic-faith.org

Board of Apostles

Bishop William L. Bonner; Chief Apostle

Bishop Matthew A Norwood., Presiding Apostle

Bishop Robert L Sanders Sr., Vice-Presider

Bishop Gentle L. Groover;

Bishop Fred Rubin

Bishop James A. Maye

Bishop Henry A. Moultrie, II

Bishop Wesley M. Taylor

Bishop Samuel R. Peters, Sr.

100

Bishop Walter L. Jackson
Bishop Bradford Berry
Bishop Herbert Edwards
Bd. of Bishops, Chmn., Bishop James Darby
Bd. of Presbyters, Chairman, Elder Marcus McCoy
Exec. Sec., Bishop Thomas E. Woolfolk
Natl. Rec. Sec., Bishop Raymond J. Keith, Jr.
Natl. Fin. Sec., Bishop Clarence Groover
Natl. Corr. Sec., Bishop Darryl Forhand
Natl Treas., Elder Jonathan K. Jefferson

Periodicals

Contender for the Faith, Minute Book, and *The Beacon*

Church of the United Brethren in Christ, USA

The Church of the United Brethren in Christ had its beginning with Philip William Otterbein and Martin Boehm, who were leaders in the revival movement in Pennsylvania and Maryland from the late 1760s into the early 1800s.

On Sept. 25, 1800, they and others associated with them formed a society under the name of United Brethren in Christ. Subsequent conferences adopted a Confession of Faith in 1815 and a constitution in 1841. The Church of the United Brethren in Christ adheres to the original constitution as amended in 1957, 1961 and 1977.

Headquarters

302 Lake St., Huntington, IN 46750 Tel. (260)356-2312 Fax (260)356-4730 ext. 210
Media Contact, Communications Dir., Steve Dennie
Email: sdennie@ub.org
Website: www.ub.org

Officers

Bishop, Rev. Ron Ramsey
Finance Director, Marci Hammel
Director of Higher Education, Dr. G. Blair Dowden
Global Ministries Director, Rev. Gary Dilley
Director of Healthy Church Ministries, Rev. Patrick Jones
Communications Director, Mr. Steve Dennie

Churches of Christ

Churches of Christ are autonomous congregations whose members appeal to the Bible alone to determine matters of faith and practice. There are no central offices or officers. Publications and institutions related to the churches are either under local congregational control or are independent of any congregation. Churches of Christ shared a common fellowship in the 19th century with the Christian Churches/Churches of Christ and the Christian Church (Disciples of Christ). This fellowship ended in the decades following the American Civil War due to erosion of confidence in Scripture among many of those who formed denominational ties. This shift in belief embraced theistic evolution, doubted the complete truth of Scripture, and permitted unscriptual practices into the work and worship of the church. Chief among the changes in practice were using instrumental music in worship, permitting women to officiate in worship services, and conducting the work of the church through centralized agencies. Churches of Christ, following this division, remained strongly united in their belief in the inerrancy and sufficiency of Scripture. From this standpoint, they affirm faith in one God who subsists in three persons: Father, Son, and Holy Spirit; they teach that salvation is through the sacrificial death of Christ and is available to all who come to God through repentance and faith, initially expressed through confession of faith and baptism by immersion. Churches of Christ follow the New Testament pattern to direct every facet of the teaching and work of the church.

Headquarters

Media Contact, Ed., Gospel Advocate, Mr. Neil Anderson, 1006 Elm Hill Pike, Nashville, TN 37102 Tel. (800)251-8446 Fax (615)254-7411

Periodicals

Action, Christian Woman, Christian Bible Teacher, The Christian Chronicle, Firm Foundation, Gospel Advocate, Guardian of Truth, Restoration Quarterly, Think, 21st Century Christian, Rocky Mountain Christian, The Spiritual Sword, Word and Work

Churches of Christ in Christian Union

Organized in 1909 at Washington Court House, Ohio, as the Churches of Christ in Christian Union, this body believes in the new birth and the baptism of the Holy Spirit for believers. It is Wesleyan, with an evangelistic and missionary emphasis.

The Reformed Methodist Church merged with the Churches of Christ in Christian Union in 1952.

Headquarters

1426 Lancaster Pike, Box 10, Circleville, OH 43113 Tel. (740)474-8856 Fax (740)477-7766
Media Contact, Dir. of Comm., Rev. Ralph Hux

Officers

Gen. Supt., Dr. Tom Hermiz
Asst. Gen. Supt., Rev. Dan Harrison
Gen. Treas., Rev. Bruce Crabtree
Gen. Bd. of Trustees, Chpsn., Dr. Tom Hermiz; Vice-Chpsn., Rev. Dan Harrison
District Superintendents, West Central District, Rev. Ron Reese; South Central District, Rev. Don Spurgeon; Northeast District, Rev. Brad Dixon; West Indies District, David Chandler

Periodicals

The Evangelical Advocate

101

Churches of God, General Conference

The Churches of God, General Conference (CGGC) had its beginnings in Harrisburg, Pa., in 1825.

John Winebrenner, recognized founder of the Church of God movement, was an ordained minister of the German Reformed Church. His experience-centered form of Christianity, particularly the "new measures" he used to promote it, his close connection with the local Methodists, his "experience and conference meetings" in the church and his "social prayer meetings" in parishioners' homes resulted in differences of opinion and the establishment of new congregations. Extensive revivals, camp meetings and mission endeavors led to the organization of additional congregations across central Pennsylvania and westward through Ohio, Indiana, Illinois and Iowa.

In 1830 the first system of cooperation between local churches was initiated as an "eldership" in eastern Pennsylvania. The organization of other elderships followed. General Eldership was organized in 1845, and in 1974 the official name of the denomination was changed from General Eldership of the Churches of God in North America to its present name.

The Churches of God, General Conference, is composed of 7 conferences in the United States and 1 conference in Haiti. The polity of the church is presbyterial in form. The church has mission ministries in the southwest among native Americans and is extensively involved in church planting and whole life ministries in Bangladesh, Brazil, Haiti and India.

The General Conference convenes in business session triennially. An Administrative Council composed of 16 regional representatives is responsible for the administration and ministries of the church between sessions of the General Conference.

Headquarters

Legal Headquarters, United Church Center, Rm. 213, 900 S. Arlington Ave., Harrisburg, PA 17109 Tel. (717)652-0255

Administrative Offices, General Conf. Exec. Dir., Pastor Wayne W. Boyer, 700 E. Melrose Ave., P.O. Box 926, Findlay, OH 45839 Tel. (419)424-1961 Fax (419)424-3343, Email: director@cggc.org

Media Contact, Editor, Rachel L. Foreman, P.O. Box 926, Findlay, OH 45839 Tel. (419)424-1961 Fax (419)424-3343, Email: com munications@cggc.org

Email: director@cggc.org
Website: www.cggc.org

Officers

Pres., Pastor Earl E. Mills, 242 Audubon Ct., Chambersburg, PA 17201 Tel. (717)263-9523 Fax (717)263-6219, Email: pastormills@ earthlink.net

Sec., Pastor E. David Green, 700 E. Melrose Ave., P.O. Box 1132, Findlay, OH 45839 Tel. (419)423-7694 Fax (419)423-9092, Email: GLCdirector@cggc.org

Treas., Robert E. Stephenson, 700 E. Melrose Ave., P.O. Box 926, Findlay, OH 45839 Tel. (419)424-1961 Fax (419)424-3433, Email: treasurer@cggc.org

DEPARTMENTS

Cross-Cultural Ministries, Pastor Don Dennison
Pensions, Mr. James P. Thomas
Denominational Communications, Rachel L. Foreman
Church Development, Dr. Charles A. Hirschy
Youth & Family Ministries, Pastor J. Lance Finley
Children's Ministries, Miss. Charlene Bunch
CGWM—Churches of God Women's Ministries

Periodicals

The Church Advocate, The Gem, The Missionary Signal

Community of Christ

Community of Christ's mission is to proclaim Jesus Christ and promote communities of joy, hope, love, and peace. Founded on April 6, 1830, this Christian denomination is present in nearly 50 nations with approximately 250,000 members worldwide. The church's Temple, located in the international headquarters complex, is dedicated to peace, reconciliation, and healing of the Spirit. Priesthood includes both men and women.

Headquarters

International Headquarters, 1001 W. Walnut, Independence, MO 64050-3562 Tel. (816) 833-1000 Fax (816)521-3096

Media Contact, Kendra Friend, Email: kfriend @cofchrist.org or Jennifer Killpack, Email: jkillpack@cofchrist.org

Email: blindgren@CofChrist.org
Website: www.CofChrist.org

Officers

(Mailing address for all officers is 1001 W. Walnut, Independence, MO 64050, Tel. (816) 833-1000)

First Presidency

President, Stephen M. Veazey, Email: sveazey@ cofchrist.org
Counselor, Kenneth N. Robinson, Email: krobinson@cofchrist.org
Counselor, David D. Schaal, Email: dschaal@ cofchrist.org

Council of Twelve Apostles

President, James E. Slauter, Email: jslauter@cof christ.org

Presiding Bishopric

Presiding Bishop, Larry R. Norris, Email: lnorris@cofchrist.org
Counselor, R. Paul Davis, Email: pdavis@ cofchrist.org

Counselor, Stephen M. Jones, Email: sjones@cofchrist.org

Presiding Evangelist
Danny A. Belrose, Email: dbelrose@cofchrist.org

World Church Secretary
Bruce Lindgren, Email: blindgren@cofchrist.org
Public Relations, Fax (816)521-3043
Kendra Friend, Email: kfriend@cofchrist.org
Jennifer Killpack, Email: jkillpack@cofchrist.org

Periodicals
Herald

Congregational Holiness Church

This body was organized in 1921 and embraces the doctrine of Holiness and Pentecost. It carries on mission work in Mexico, Honduras, Costa Rica, Cuba, Brazil, Guatemala, India, Nicaragua, El Salvador, Venezuela, Panama, Chile, Argentina, Belize, Zimbabwe, Haiti, and Peru.

Headquarters
3888 Fayetteville Hwy., Griffin, GA 30223 Tel. (404)228-4833 Fax (404)228-1177
Media Contact, Gen. Supt., Bishop Ronald Wilson
Email: chchurch@bellsouth.net
Website: www.chchurch.com

EXECUTIVE BOARD
Gen. Supt., Bishop Ronald Smith
1st Asst. Gen. Supt., Rev. William L. Lewis
2nd Asst. Gen. Supt., Rev. Wayne Hicks
Gen. Sec., Rev. Leslee Bailey
Gen. Treas., Rev. Stephen Phillips
World Missions Supt., Rev. Billy Anderson

Periodicals
The Gospel Messenger

Conservative Baptist Association of America (CBAmerica)

The Conservative Baptist Association of America (now known as CBAmerica) was organized May 17, 1947 at Atlantic City, N.J. The Old and New Testaments are regarded as the divinely inspired Word of God and are therefore infallible and of supreme authority. Each local church is independent, autonomous and free from ecclesiastical or political authority.

CBAmerica provides wide-ranging support to its affiliate churches and individuals through nine regional associations. CBA offers personnel to assist churches in areas such as growth and health conflict resolution and financial analysis. The association supports its clergy with retirement planning, referrals for new places of ministry and spiritual counseling. The Conservative Baptist Women's Ministries assists women in the church to be effective in their personal growth and leadership.

Each June or July there is a National Conference giving members an opportunity for fellowship, inspiration and motivation.

Headquarters
1501 W. Mineral Ave., Suite B, Littleton, CO 80120-5612 Tel. (888)627-1995 or (720)283-3030 Fax (720)283-3333
Media Contact, Executive Director, Dr. Dennis L. Gorton
Email: cba@cbamerica.org
Website: www.cbamerica.org

OTHER ORGANIZATIONS
CBInternational, Exec. Dir., Dr. Hans Finzel, 1501 W. Mineral Ave., Littleton, CO 80120-5612
Mission to the Americas, Exec. Dir., Rev. Rick Miller, Box 828, Wheaton, IL 60189
Conservative Baptist Higher Ed. Council, Dr. Bert Downs, Western Seminary, 5511 S. E. Hawthorne Blvd., Portland, OR 97215

Periodicals
Front Line Turnings

Conservative Congregational Christian Conference

In the 1930s, evangelicals within the Congregational Christian Churches felt a definite need for fellowship and service. By 1945, this loose association crystallized into the Conservative Congregational Christian Fellowship, committed to maintaining a faithful, biblical witness.

In 1948 in Chicago, the Conservative Congregational Christian Conference was established to provide a continuing fellowship for evangelical churches and ministers on the national level. In recent years, many churches have joined the Conference from backgrounds other than Congregational. These churches include Community or Bible Churches and churches from the Evangelical and Reformed background that are truly congregational in polity and thoroughly evangelical in conviction. The CCCC welcomes all evangelical churches that are, in fact, congregational. The CCCC believes in the necessity of a regenerate membership, the authority of the Holy Scriptures, the Lordship of Jesus Christ, the autonomy of the local church and the universal fellowship of all Christians.

The Conservative Congregational Christian Conference is a member of the World Evangelical Congregational Fellowship (formed in 1986 in London, England) and the National Association of Evangelicals.

Headquarters
8941 Highway 5, Lake Elmo, MN 55042 Tel. (651)739-1474 Fax (651)739-0750
Media Contact, Conf. Min., Mrs. Diane Johnson
Email: CCCC4@juno.com
Website: www.ccccusa.com

Officers
Pres., Rev. Nicholas G. Granitsas, 68 Eustis Rd, Revere, MA 02151

Vice Pres., Rev. Dr. John Kimball, 3657 Carolina Rd., Suffolk, VA 23434

Conf. Min., Rev. Dr. Stephen A. Gammon, 7583 Currell Blvd. #108, St. Paul, MN 55125

Controller, Mr. Leslie Pierce, 5220 E 105th St S, Tulsa, OK 74137

Treas., Rev. Tay Kersey, 8450 Eastwood Rd., Moundsview, MN 55112

Sec., Rev. Peter Murdy, 4 Plympton St., Middleboro, MA 02346

Editor, Dr. Richard and Mrs. Shirley Leonard, P.O. Box 250, Kirkland, IL 60146

Historian, Rev. Alwyn York, 709 N. Cheyenne Ave., Hardin MT 59034

Periodicals
Foresee

Conservative Lutheran Association

The Conservative Lutheran Association (CLA) was originally named Lutheran's Alert National (LAN) when it was founded in 1965 by 10 conservative Lutheran pastors and layman meeting in Cedar Rapids, Iowa. Its purpose was to help preserve from erosion the basic doctrines of Christian theology, including the inerrancy of Holy Scripture. The group grew to a worldwide constituency, similarly concerned with maintaining the doctrinal integrity of the Bible and the Lutheran Confessions.

Headquarters
Trinity Lutheran Church, 4101 E. Nohl Ranch Rd., Anaheim, CA 92807 Tel. (714)637-8370
Media Contact, Pres., Rev. P. J. Moore
Email: PastorPJ@ix.netcom.com
Website: www.tlcanaheim.com/CLA

Officers
Pres., Rev. P. J. Moore, 4101 E. Nohl Ranch Rd., Anaheim, CA 92807 Tel. (714)637-8370

Vice Pres., Rev. Dr. R. H. Redal, 409 Tacoma Ave. N., Tacoma, WA 98403 Tel. (206)383-5528

Faith Seminary, Dean, Rev. Dr. Michael J. Adams, 3504 N. Pearl St., P.O. Box 7186, Tacoma, WA 98407 Tel. (888)777-7675 Fax (206)759-1790

Coptic Orthodox Church*

This body is part of the ancient Coptic orthodox Church of Alexandria, Egypt which is currently headed by His Holiness Pope Shenouda III, 116th Successor to St. Mark the Apostle. Egyptian immigrants have organized many parishes in the United States. Copts exist outside Egypt in Africa, Europe, Asia, Australia, Canada and the United States. The total world Coptic community is estimated at 27 million. The church is in full communion with the other members of The Oriental Orthodox Church Family, The Syrian Orthodox Church, Armenian Orthodox Church, Ethiopian Orthodox Church, the Indian Orthodox Church and the Eritrean Orthodox Church.

Headquarters
427 West Side Ave., Jersey City, NJ 07304
Email: Webmaster@coptic.org
Website: www.coptic.org

Officers
Bishop of Los Angeles, Bishop Serapion, 3803 3803 W. Mission Blvd., Pomona, CA 91766 Tel. (909)865-8378 Fax (909)865-8348, Email: bishopserapion@lacopts.org

Periodicals
Agape Magazine, El Keraza

Cumberland Presbyterian Church

The Cumberland Presbyterian Church was organized in Dickson County, Tennessee, on Feb. 4, 1810. It was an outgrowth of the Great Revival of 1800 on the Kentucky and Tennessee frontier. The founders were Finis Ewing, Samuel King and Samuel McAdow, ministers in the Presbyterian Church who rejected the doctrine of election and reprobation as taught in the Westminster Confession of Faith.

By 1813, the Cumberland Presbytery had grown to encompass three presbyteries, which constituted a synod. This synod met at the Beech Church in Sumner County, Tenn., and formulated a "Brief Statement" which set forth the points in which Cumberland Presbyterians dissented from the Westminster Confession. These points are:

1. That there are no eternal reprobates;
2. That Christ died not for some, but for all people;
3. That all those dying in infancy are saved through Christ and the sanctification of the Spirit;
4. That the Spirit of God operates on the world, or as coextensively as Christ has made atonement, in such a manner as to leave everyone inexcusable.

From its birth in 1810, the Cumberland Presbyterian Church grew to a membership of 200,000 at the turn of the century. In 1906 the church voted to merge with the then-Presbyterian Church. Those who dissented from the merger became the nucleus of the continuing Cumberland Presbyterian Church.

Headquarters
1978 Union Ave., Memphis, TN 38104 Tel. (901)276-4572 Fax (901)272-3913
Media Contact, Stated Clk., Rev. Robert D. Rush Fax (901)276-4578
Email: assembly@cumberland.org
Website: www.cumberland.org

Officers
Mod., The Rev. Frank Ward, Union Avenue, Memphis, TN 38104, Email: fdw@cumberland.org

Stated Clk., The Rev. Robert D. Rush, Tel.(901)276-4572 x 225 Fax (901)276-4578, Email: rdr@cumberland.org

INSTITUTIONS

Cumberland Presbyterian Children's Home, Exec. Dir., Mr. Randy Spencer, Drawer G, Denton, TX 76202 Tel. (940)382-5112 Fax (940)387-0821; Email: cpch@cpch.org

Cumberland Presbyterian Center, Tel.(901)276-4572 Fax (901)272-3913 or (901)276-4578

Memphis Theological Seminary, 168 E. Parkway S., Memphis, TN 38104 Tel. (901)458-8232 Fax (901)452-4051, Pres., Dr. Jay Earheart –Brown, Website: www.memphisseminary.edu

Bethel College, Pres., Dr. Robert Prosser, 325 Cherry St., McKenzie, TN 38201 Tel. (901)352-4004 Fax (901)352-4069, Email: rprosser@bethel-college.edu

Historical Foundation, Archivist, Susan K. Gore, 1978 Union Avenue, Memphis, TN 38104 Tel. (901)276-8602 Fax (901)272-3913, Email: skg@cumberland.org

BOARDS

Bd. of Christian Education, 1978 Union Ave., Memphis, TN 38104 Tel. (901)276-4572 x223 Fax (901)272-3913

Bd. of Missions, Exec. Dir., Rev. Michael Sharpe, 1978 Union Ave., Memphis, TN 38104 Tel. (901)276-9988 Fax (901)272-3913, Email: mgs@cumberland.org

Bd. of Stewardship, 1978 Union Ave., Memphis, TN 38104 Tel. (901)276-4572 x 207

Bd. Of the Cumberland Presbyterian, Editor, Mrs. Patricia White, P.O. Box 935, Antioch, TN 37011 Tel. (615)731-5556, Email: cpmag @comcast.net

Commission on the Ministry, 1978 Union Ave., Memphis, TN 38104 Tel. (901)276-4572 x235 Fax (901)272-3913, Exec. Dir., The Rev. Stephanie S. Brown

Periodicals

The Cumberland Presbyterian, The Missionary Messenger

Cumberland Presbyterian Church in America

This church, originally known as the Colored Cumberland Presbyterian Church, was formed in May 1874. In May 1869, at the General Assembly meeting in Murfreesboro, Tennessee, Moses Weir of the Black delegation sucessfully appealed for help in organizing a separate African church so that- Blacks could learn self-reliance and independence; they could have more financial assistance; they could minister more effectively among Blacks; and they could worship close to the altar, not in the balconies. He requested that the Cumberland Presbyterian Church organize Blacks into presbyteries and synods, develop schools to train black clergy, grant loans to assist Blacks to secure hymnbooks, Bibles and church buildings and establish a separate General Assembly.

In 1874 the first General Assembly of the Colored Cumberland Presbyterian Church met in Nashville. The moderator was Rev. P. Price and the stated clerk was Elder John Humphrey.

The denomination's General Assembly, the national governing body, is organized around its three program boards and agencies—Finance, Publication and Christian Education, and Missions and Evangelism. Other agencies of the General Assembly are under these three program boards.

The church has four synods (Alabama, Kentucky, Tennessee and Texas), 15 presbyteries and 153 congregations. The CPC extends as far north as Cleveland, Ohio, and Chicago, as far west as Marshalltown, Iowa, and Dallas, Tx., and as far south as Selma, Ala.

Headquarters

Media Contact, Stated Clk., Rev. Dr. Robert. Stanley Wood, 226 Church St., Huntsville, AL 35801 Tel. (205)536-7481 Fax (205)536-7482
Email: mleslie598@aol.com
Website: www.cumberland.org/cpca

Officers

Mod., Rev. Endia Scruggs, 1627 Carroll Rd., Harvest, AL 35749

Stated Clk., Rev. Dr. Rorbert. Stanley Wood, 226 Church St., Huntsville, AL 35801 Tel. (205) 536-7481

SYNODS

Alabama, Stated Clk., Arthur Hinton, 511 10th Ave. N.W., Aliceville, AL 35442

Kentucky, Stated Clk., Mary Martha Daniels, 8548 Rhodes Ave., Chicago, IL 60619

Tennessee, Stated Clk., Elder Clarence Norman, 145 Jones St., Huntington, TN 38334

Texas, Stated Clk., Arthur King, 2435 Kristen, Dallas, TX 75216

Disciples of Christ—please see Christian Church (Disciples of Christ) in the United States and Canada.

Elim Fellowship

The Elim Fellowship, a Pentecostal Body established in 1947, is an outgrowth of the Elim Missionary Assemblies formed in 1933.

It is an association of churches, ministers and missionaries seeking to serve the whole Body of Christ. It is of Pentecostal conviction and charismatic orientation, providing ministerial credentials and counsel and encouraging fellowship among local churches. Elim Fellowship sponsors leadership seminars at home and abroad and serves as a transdenominational agency sending long-term, short-term and tent-making missionaries to work with national movements.

Headquarters

1703 Dalton Rd., Lima, NY 14485 Tel. (585)582-2790 Fax (585)624-1229
Media Contact, Gen. Sec., Rev. Chris Ball
Email: executive@elimfellowship.org
Website: www.ElimFellowship.org

Officers

Pres., Rev. Dr. Ronald V. Burgio
Gen. Treas., Stephanie Zeller

Periodicals

Elim Herald

Episcopal Church*

The Episcopal Church entered the colonies with the earliest settlers at Jamestown, Va., in 1607 as the Church of England. After the American Revolution, it became autonomous in 1789 as The Protestant Episcopal Church in the United States of America. (The Episcopal Church became the official alternate name in 1967.) Samuel Seabury of Connecticut was elected the first bishop and consecrated in Aberdeen by bishops of the Scottish Episcopal Church in 1784.

In organizing as an independent body, the Episcopal Church created a bicameral legislature, the General Convention, modeled after the new U.S. Congress. It comprises a House of Bishops and a House of Deputies and meets every three years. A 38-member Executive Council, which meets three times a year, is the interim governing body. An elected presiding bishop serves as Primate and Chief Pastor.

After severe setbacks in the years immediately following the Revolution because of its association with the British Crown and the fact that a number of its clergy and members were Loyalists, the church soon established its own identity and sense of mission. It sent missionaries into the newly settled territories of the United States, establishing dioceses from coast to coast, and also undertook substantial missionary work in Africa, Latin America and the Far East. Today, the overseas dioceses are developing into independent provinces of the Anglican Communion, the worldwide fellowship of 38 churches in communion with the Church of England and the Archbishop of Canterbury.

The beliefs and practices of The Episcopal Church, like those of other Anglican churches, are both Catholic and Reformed, with bishops in the apostolic succession and the historic creeds of Christendom regarded as essential elements of faith and order, along with the primary authority of Holy Scripture and the two chief sacraments of Baptism and Eucharist.

EPISCOPAL CHURCH CENTER

815 Second Ave., New York, NY 10017 Tel. (212)716-6240 or (800)334-7626 Fax (212) 867-0395 or (212)490-3298
Media Contact, Dir. of News Service., Robert Williams, (212)922-5385
Email: cepting@episcopalchurch.org
Website: www.ecusa.anglican.org

Officers

Presiding Bishop & Primate, Most Rev. Katherine Jefferts-Schori
Chief Operating Officer, Linda Watt

Treas., Kurt Barnes
Canon to the Primate and Presiding Bishop, The Rev. Canon Charles Robertson
House of Deputies, Pres., Bonnie Anderson
Exec. Officer and Sec. of the General Convention, Sec. Of the House of Deputies, Sec. Of the Domestic and Foreign Missionary Society, and Sec. Of the Executive Council, The Rev. Gregory Straub

OFFICE OF THE PRESIDING BISHOP

Presiding Bishop, Most Rev. Katherine Jefferts Schori, Tel. (212)716-6276
Chief Operating Officer, Linda Watts, Tel. (212)922-5313
Canon to the Presiding Bishop, Rev. Canon Charles Robertson, Tel. (212)922-5282
Exec. Dir., Church Deployment Office, Vacant, Tel. (212)922-5251
Asst. Dir., Church Deployment Office, Pamela Ramsden, Tel. (212)716-6063
Coordinator for Ministry Development, The Rev. Dr. Melford E. Holland, Jr., Tel. (212)922-5246
Exec. Dir., Office of Pastoral Dev., Rt. Rev. Clayton Matthews, Tel (212)716-6163
Exec. Sec., General Board of Examining Chaplains, The Rev. Dr. Richard F. Tombaugh, Tel. (860)233-2271
Chaplaincies, Suffragan Bishop, Rt. Rev., George Packard, Tel. (212)716-6202
Convocation of American Churches in Europe, Bishop-in-Charge, Rt. Rev. Pierre Whalon, 011-33-1-472-01792
Deputy, Ecumenical and Interfaith Relations, The Rt. Rev. C. Christopher Epting, Tel. (212)716-6220

ADMINISTRATION AND FINANCE

Treasurer of the Domestic and Foreign Missionary Society and Chief Financial Officer, Kurt Barnes, Tel. (212)922-5296
Controller, Alpha Contech, Tel. (212)922-5366
Archivist, Mark Duffy, Tel. (512)472-6816
Director, Human Resources Management, John Colon, Tel. (212)716-6331

SERVICE, EDUCATION AND WITNESS

Director of Mission, The Very Rev. James Lemler, Tel. (212)922-5198
Dir., Anglican and Global Relations, Margaret Larom, Tel. (212)716-6224
Associate Editor, Episcopal Life, Nan Cobbey, Tel. (212)716-6103
Dir., Communication, Robert Williams, Tel. (212)922-5385
Dir., News Service, Robert Williams, Tel. (212)922-5385
Dir., Migration Ministries, Richard Parkins, Tel. (212)716-6252
Dir., Peace & Justice Ministries, The Rev. Canon Brian Grieves, Tel. (212)922-5207
Dir., Ministries with Young People, Thomas Chu, Tel. (212)922-5267

President, Episcopal Relief and Development, Robert Radtke , Tel. (212)716-6020

BISHOPS IN THE U.S.A.

(C)= Coadjutor; (S)= Suffragan; (A)= Assistant Address, Right Reverend

Presiding Bishop & Primate, Most Rev. Katherine Jefferts-Schori, 815 Second Ave, New York, NY 10017 Tel. (212)716-6276;

Pastoral Dev., The Rt. Rev. F. Clayton Matthews, 815 Second Ave, New York, NY 10017 Tel. (212)716-6163

Alabama, Henry N. Parsley, Jr., 521 N. 20th St., Birmingham, AL 35203 Tel. (205)715-2066

Alaska, Mark MacDonald, 1205 Denali Way, Fairbanks, AK 99701-4137 Tel.(907)452-3040

Albany, Daniel W. Herzog, 68 S. Swan St., Albany, NY 12210-2301 Tel. (518)465-4737

Arizona, Kirk Stevan Smith, 114 W.Roosevelt, Phoenix, AZ 85003-1406 Tel. (602)254-0976

Arkansas, Larry E. Maze, P.O. Box 164668, Little Rock, AR 72216 Tel. (501)372-2168

Atlanta, John Neil Alexander, 2744 Peachtree Rd. N.W., Atlanta, GA 30305 Tel. (404)365-1010

Bethlehem, Paul Marshall, 333 Wyandotte St., Bethlehem, PA 18015 Tel. (610)691-5655

California, Marc Handly Andrus, 1055 Taylor St., San Francisco, CA 94115 Tel. (415)673-5015

Central Ecuador, Wilfrido Ramos-Orench, Apartado Aereo 17-03-353-A, Quito, Ecuador, Ecuador

Central Florida, John W. Howe, 1017 E. Robinson St., Orlando, FL 32801 Tel. (407) 423-3567

Central Gulf Coast, Philip M. Duncan II, P.O. Box 13330, Pensacola, FL 32591-3330 Tel. (850)434-7337

Central New York, Gladstone B. Adams III, 310 Montgomery St., Ste. 200, Syracuse, NY 13202 Tel. (315)474-6596

Central Pennsylvania, Nathan D. Baxter, P.O. Box 11937, Harrisburg, PA 17108 Tel. (717) 236-5959

Chicago, William D. Persell, 65 E. Huron St., Chicago, IL 60611 Tel. (312)751-4200

Colombia, Francisco Duque, Cra. 6 No. 49-85, Bogota, Colombia Tel. 011-57-1-288-3167

Colorado, Robert J. O'Neill, 1300 Washington St., Denver, CO 80203 Tel. (303)837-1173

Connecticut, Andrew D. Smith, 1335 Asylum Ave., Hartford, CT 06105-2295 Tel. (860)233-4481

Dallas, James M. Stanton, 1630 Garrett Avenue., Dallas, TX 75206 Tel. (214)826-8310

Delaware, Wayne P. Wright, 2020 N. Tatnall St., Wilmington, DE 19802 Tel. (302)656-5441

Dominican Republic, Julio C. Holguin, DMG 13602, 7990 15th ST E, Sarasota, FL 34243

East Carolina, Clifton Daniel III, P.O. Box 1336, Kinston, NC 28503 Tel. (252)522-0885

East Tennessee, Charles vonRosenberg, 814 Episcopal School Way, Knoxville, TN 37932 Tel. (865)966-2110

Eastern Michigan, S. Todd Ousley, 924 N. Niagara St., Saginaw, MI 48602 Tel. (989)752-6020

Eastern Oregon, William O. Gregg, P.O. Box 1548, The Dalles, OR 97058 Tel. (541)298-4477

Easton, James J. Shand, P.O. Box 1027, Easton, MD 21601 Tel. (410)822-1919

Eau Claire, Keith B. Whitmore, 510 S. Farwell St., Eau Claire, WI 54701 Tel. (715)835-3331

El Camino Real, Assisting, Sylvestre Romero-Palma, 1092 Noche Buena ST, Seaside, CA 93955 Tel. (831)394-4465

Europe, American Ches in-Jurisdiction, Pierre W. Whalon, Bishop in-charge, The American Cathedral, 23 Avenue Georges V, 75008, Paris, France, Tel. 011-33-1-53-23-84-04

Florida, S. Johnson Howard, 325 Market St., Jacksonville, FL 32202, 904-356-1328

Fond du Lac, Russell E. Jacobus, P.O. Box 149, Fond du Lac, WI 54936-0149 Tel. (920)921-8866

Fort Worth, Jack L. Iker, 2900 Alemeda Street, Fort Worth, TX 76116 Tel. (817)244-2885

Georgia, Henry Louttit, Jr., 611 East Bay St., Savannah, GA 31401 Tel. (912)236-4279

Haiti, Jean Zache Duracin, c/o Lynx Air P.O. Box 407139, Ft Lauderdale, FL 33340 Tel. 011-509-257-1624

Hawaii, Richard S.O. Chang, 229 Queen Emma Square, Honolulu, HI 96813 Tel. (808)536-7776

Honduras, Lloyd Emmanuel Allen, IMC-SAP, Dept 215, P.O. Box 52-3900, Miami, FL 33152-3900 Tel. 011-504-556-6155

Idaho, Harry B. Bainbridge III, P.O. Box 936, Boise, ID 83701 Tel. (208)345-4440

Indianapolis, Catherine M. Waynick,1100 W. 42nd St., Indianapolis, IN 46208 Tel. (317)926-5454

Iowa, Alan Scarfe, 225 37th St., Des Moines, IA 50312-4305 Tel. (515)277-6165

Kansas, Dean E. Wolfe, 835 S.W. Polk St., Topeka, KS 66612-1688 Tel. (785)235-9255

Kentucky, Edwin F. Gulick Jr., 425 S. 2nd Street, Ste. 200, Louisville, KY 40202 Tel. (502)584-7148

Lexington, Stacy F. Sauls, P.O. Box 610, Lexington, KY 40586-0610 Tel. (606)252-6527

Long Island, Orris G. Walker, Jr., 36 Cathedral Ave., Garden City, NY 11530 Tel. (516)248-4800

Los Angeles, J. Jon Bruno; Chester Talton, (S), P.O. Box 512164, Los Angeles, CA 90051-0164 Tel. (213)482-2040

Louisiana, Charles E. Jenkins, III, 1623 7th St., New Orleans, LA 70115-4411 Tel. (504)895-6634

Maine, Chilton R. Knudsen, 143 State St., Portland, ME 04101-3799 Tel. (207)772-1953

Maryland, Robert W. Ihloff, 4 University Pkwy, Baltimore, MD 21218 Tel. (410)467-1399

Massachusetts, M. Thomas Shaw,III, SSJE, 138 Tremont St., Boston, MA 02111-1356 Tel. (617)482-5800

Michigan, Wendell N. Gibbs, Jr., 4800 Woodward Ave., Detroit, MI 48201 Tel. (313)832-4400

Milwaukee, Steven A. Miller, 804 E. Juneau Ave., Milwaukee, WI 53202 Tel. (414)272-3028

Minnesota, James L. Jelinek; 1730 Clifton Place, #201, Minneapolis, MN 55403 Tel. (612)871-5311

Mississippi, Duncan Montgomery Gray, III, P.O. Box 23107, Jackson, MS 39225-3107 Tel. (601)948-5954

Missouri, G. Wayne Smith, 1210 Locust St., St. Louis, MO 63103 Tel. (314)231-1220

Montana, C. Franklin Brookhart,, 515 North Park Ave., Helena, MT 59601 Tel. (406)442-2230

Navajoland Area Mission, Mark MacDonald, Assisting Bishop, P.O. Box 720, Farmington, NM 87499-0720 Tel. (505)327-7549

Nebraska, Joe G. Burnett, 109 N. 18th Street, Omaha, NE 68102 Tel. (402)341-5373

Nevada, Jerry Lamb, Assisting Bishop, 6135 S. Harrison Drive, Ste. 1, Las Vegas, NV 89120 Tel. (702)737-9190

New Hampshire, V. Gene Robinson, 63 Green St., Concord, NH 03301 Tel. (603)224-1914

New Jersey, George E. Councell, 808 W. State St., Trenton, NJ 08618-5326 Tel. (609)394-5281

New York, Mark Sisk, 1047 Amsterdam Ave., New York, NY 10025 Tel. (212)316-7400

Newark, Jack P. Croneberger; 31 Mulberry St., Newark, NJ 07102 Tel. (973)622-4306

North Carolina, Michael B. Curry, 200 W Morgan ST, Ste 300, Raleigh, NC 27601-1338 Tel. (919)787-6313

North Dakota, Michael Gene Smith, 3600 25 St. SW, Fargo, ND 58104-6861 Tel. (701)235-6688

Northern California, Barry Beisner, P.O. Box 161268, Sacramento, CA 95816 Tel. (916)442-6918

Northern Indiana, Edward S. Little III, 117 N. Lafayette Blvd., South Bend, IN 46601 Tel. (574)233-6489

Northern Michigan, James A. Kelsey, 131 E. Ridge St., Marquette, MI 49855 Tel. (906)228-7160

Northwest Texas, C. Wallis Ohl, Jr., 1802 Broadway, Lubbock, TX 79401-3016 Tel. (806)763-1370

Northwestern Pennsylvania, Robert D. Rowley, Jr., 145 W. 6th St., Erie, PA 16501 Tel. (814)456-4203

Ohio, Mark Hollingsworth, Jr., 2230 Euclid Ave., Cleveland, OH 44115 Tel. (216)771-4815

Oklahoma, Robert M. Moody, 924 N. Robinson, Oklahoma City, OK 73102-2499 Tel. (405)232-4820

Olympia, Vincent W. Warner, P.O. Box 12126, Seattle, WA 98102 Tel. (206)325-4200

Oregon, Johncy Itty, 11800 SW Military Lane, Portland, OR 97219-8436 Tel. (503)636-5613

Pennsylvania, Charles E. Bennison, Jr., 240 S. 4th St., Philadelphia, PA 19106 Tel. (215)627-6434

Pittsburgh, Robert W. Duncan, Jr., 535 Smithfield Street, Pittsburgh, PA 15222 Tel. (412)281-6131

Puerto Rico, David Alvarez, Centro Diocesano San Justo, P.O. Box 902, St Just Station, St Just, PR 00978 Tel. (787)761-9800

Quincy, Keith L. Ackerman, 3601 N. North St., Peoria, IL 61604-1599 Tel. (309)688-8221

Rhode Island, Geralyn Wolf, 275 N. Main St., Providence, RI 02903-1298 Tel. (401)274-4500

Rio Grande, Jeffrey Steenson, 4304 Carlisle Blvd NE, Albuquerque, NM 87107 Tel. (505)881-0636

Rochester, Jack M. McKelvey, 935 East Ave., Rochester, NY 14607 Tel. (585)473-2977

San Diego, James R. Mathes, 2728 6th Ave., San Diego, CA 92103 Tel. (619)291-5947

San Joaquin, John-David Schofield, 4159 East Dakota Ave., Fresno, CA 93726 Tel. (559)244-4828

South Carolina, Edward L. Salmon, Jr., P.O. Box 20127, Charleston, SC 29413-0127 Tel. (843)722-4075

South Dakota, Creighton L. Robertson, 500 S. Main Ave.., Sioux Falls, SD 57104-6814 Tel. (605)338-9751

Southeast Florida, Leopold Frade, 525 NE 15th St., Miami, FL 33132 Tel. (305)373-0881

Southern Ohio, Thomas Breidenthal, 412 Sycamore St., Cincinnati, OH 45202 Tel. (513)421-0311

Southern Virginia, John C. Buchannan, 600 Talbot Hall Rd., Norfolk, VA 23505 Tel. (757)423-8287

Southwest Florida, John B. Lipscomb, 7313 Merchant Court, Sarasota, FL 34240 Tel. (941)556-0315

Southwestern Virginia, F. Neff Powell, P.O. Box 2279, Roanoke, VA 24009 Tel. (540)342-6797

Spokane, James E. Waggoner, Jr., 245 E. 13th Ave., Spokane, WA 99202 Tel. (509)624-3191

Springfield, Peter H. Beckwith, 821 S. 2nd St., Springfield, IL 62704 Tel. (217)525-1876

Tennessee, Bertram N. Herlong, 50 Vantage Way, Suite 107, Nashville, TN 37228 Tel. (615)251-3322

Texas, Don A. Wimberly, 3203 W. Alabama St., Houston, TX 77098 Tel. (713)520-6444

Upper South Carolina, Dorsey F. Henderson, Jr., 1115 Marion Street, Columbia, SC 29201 Tel. (803)771-7800

Utah, Carolyn T. Irish, Box 3090, Salt Lake City, UT 84110-3090 Tel. (801)322-4131

Vermont, Thomas C. Ely, 5 Rock Point Road, Burlington, VT 05401 Tel. (802)863-3431

Virgin Islands, Ambrose Gumbs, P.O. Box 7488, Charlotte, Amalie, St Thomas, VI 00801

Virginia, Peter J. Lee, 110 W. Franklin St., Richmond, VA 23220 Tel. (804)643-8451

Washington, John Bryson Chane, Episc. Church House, Mt. St. Alban, Washington, DC 20016-5094 Tel. (202)537-6555

West Missouri, Barry R. Howe, P.O. Box 413227, Kansas City, MO 64141-3227 Tel. (816)471-6161

West Tennessee, Don E. Johnson, 692 Poplar Ave., Memphis, TN 38105 Tel. (901)526-0023

West Texas, Gary R. Lillibridge, P.O. Box 6885, San Antonio, TX 78209 Tel. (210)824-5387

West Virginia, W. Michie Klusmeyer, P.O. Box 5400, Charleston, WV 25361-0400 Tel. (304)344-3597

Western Kansas, James Marshall Adams, P.O. Box 2507, Salina, KS 67402-2507 Tel. (785)825-1626

Western Louisiana, D. Bruce MacPherson, P.O. Box 2031, Alexandria, LA 71309 Tel. (318) 442-1304

Western Massachusetts, Gordon P. Scruton, 37 Chestnut St., Springfield, MA 01103 Tel. (413)737-4786

Western Michigan, Robert Ronald Gepert, 2600 Vincent Ave., Portage, MI 49024 Tel. (269) 381-2710

Western New York, J. Michael Garrison, 1114 Delaware Ave., Buffalo, NY 14209 Tel. (716) 881-0660

Western North Carolina, G. Porter Taylor, 900-B Centre Park Dr., Asheville, NC 28805 Tel. (828)225-6656

Wyoming, Bruce Caldwell, 104 S. 4th St., Laramie, WY 82070 Tel. (307)742-6606

Periodicals

Episcopal Life

The Episcopal Orthodox Church

This body was incorporated in 1964 as a self-governing Orthodox Anglican church. The Church is committed to the Biblical world view contained in the Holy Scriptures, confessed in the three ancient creeds of the Catholic Church (the Apostles', Nicene, and Athanasian Creeds), experienced in the Sacraments, and practiced through the use of orthodox editions of the Book of Common Prayer. The Church is the United States member of the Orthodox Anglican Communion, the creation of which it authorized in 1967. The Orthodox Anglican Communion is a fellowship of churches around the world that adhere to orthodox theology. In 1971 the Church opened its own theological educational institution: clergy in the United States are trained at the denomination's school, St. Andrew's Theological college and Seminary.

Headquarters

464 County Home Road, Lexington, NC 27292 Tel. (336)236-9565 Fax (336)236-4822 Email: eoc@orthodoxanglican.net Website: orthodoxanglican.net

Officers

Presiding Bishop, The Most Rev. Scott McLaughlin, The Chancery Of The Archdiocese, 464 County Home Road, Lexington, NC 27292 Tel. (336)236-9565 Fax (336)236-4822, Email: abpmclaughlin@orthodox anglican.net

Periodicals

The Episcopal Orthodox Encounter

The Estonian Evangelical Lutheran Church

For information on the Estonian Evangelical Lutheran Church (EELC), please see the listing in Chapter 4, "Religious Bodies in Canada."

Headquarters

383 Jarvis St., Toronto, ON M5B 2C7 Email: konsistoorium@eelk.ee Website: www.eelk.ee

The Evangelical Church

The Evangelical Church was born June 4, 1968 in Portland, Oregon, when 46 congregations and about 80 ministers, under the leadership of V. A. Ballantyne and George Millen, met in an organizing session. Within two weeks a group of about 20 churches and 30 ministers from the Evangelical United Brethren and Methodist churches in Montana and North Dakota became a part of the new church. Richard Kienitz and Robert Strutz were the superintendents.

Under the leadership of Superintendent Robert Trosen, the former Holiness Methodist Church became a part of the Evangelical Church in 1969, bringing its membership and a flourishing mission field in Bolivia. The Wesleyan Covenant Church joined in 1977, with its missionary work in Mexico, in Brownsville, Texas and among the Navajos in New Mexico.

The Evangelical Church in Canada, where T. J. Jesske was superintendent, became an autonomous organization on June 5, 1970. In 1982, after years of discussions with the Evangelical Church of North America, a founding General Convention was held at Billings, Montana, where the two churches united. In 1993 the Canadian conference merged with the Canadian portion of the Missionary Church to form the Evangelical Missionary Church. The new group maintains close ties with their American counterparts. Currently there are nearly 150 U.S. congregations of the Evangelical Church. The headquarters is located in Minneapolis, Minnisota.

The following guide the life, program and devotion of this church—faithful, biblical and

109

sensible preaching and teaching of those truths proclaimed by scholars of the Wesleyan-Arminian viewpoint; an itinerant system which reckons with the rights of individuals and the desires of the congregation; local ownership of all church properties and assets.

The church is officially affiliated with the Christian Holiness Partnership, the National Association of Evangelicals, Wycliffe Bible Translators, World Gospel Mission and OMS International. The denomination has nearly 150 missionaries.

Headquarters
Denominational Office, 9421 West River Rd., Minneapolis, MN 55444 Tel. (763)421-2589 Fax (763)424-9230, Email: ecm@usfamily.net
Media Contact, Gen. Supt., Dr. William Vermillion
Email: jsditzel@juno.com
Website: quakertownecna.com/conferences

Officers
Gen. Supt., Dr. William Vermillion, 9421 West River Rd., Minneapolis, MN 55444
Denominational Secretary, Dr. Bruce Moyer, P.O. Box 29, University Park, IA 52595, Tel. 641-673-8391
Exectuive Director, Evangelical Church Mission, Rev. Duane Erickson, 9421 West River Rd., Minneapolis, MN 55444

Periodicals
HeartBeat, *The Evangelical Challenge*

The Evangelical Church Alliance
What is known today as the Evangelical Church Alliance began in 1887 under the name World's Faith Missionary Association. Years later, on March 28, 1928, a nonprofit organization was incorporated in the state of Missouri under the same name. In October, 1931, the name Fundamental Ministerial Association was chosen to reflect the organization's basis of unity.

On July 21, 1958, during the annual convention at Trinity Seminary and Bible College in Chicago, Illinois, a more comprehensive constitution was created and the name was changed to The Evangelical Church Alliance.

The ECA licenses and ordains ministers who are qualified providing them with credentials from a recognized ecclesiastical body; provides training courses through the Bible Extension Institute for those who have not had the opportunity to attend Seminary or Bible School; provides Associate Membership for churches and Christian organizations giving opportunity for fellowship and networking with other evangelical ministers and organizations who share the same goals and mission, while remaining autonomous; provides endorsement for military, prison, hospital & other institutional chaplains; provides Regional Conferences and an Annual International Conference where members can find fellowship, encouragement and training;

cooperates with churches in finding new pastors when they have openings.

ECA is an international, nonsectarian, Evangelical organization.

Headquarters
205 W. Broadway St., P.O. Box 9, Bradley, IL 60915 Tel. (815)937-0720 Fax (815)937-0001
Media Contact, Pres./CEO, Dr. Samuel Goebel
Email: info@ecainternational.org
Website: www.ecainternational.org

Officers
Pres./CEO, Dr. Samuel Goebel Chairman, Dr. George L. Miller First Vice-Chairman, Dr. Rene Moreno Vice Pres. Dr. Henry A. Roso

Periodicals
The Evangel

Evangelical Churches—please see Fellowship of Evangelical Churches.

The Evangelical Congregational Church
This denomination had its beginning in the movement known as the Evangelical Association, organized by Jacob Albright in 1796. A division which occurred in 1891 in the Evangelical Association resulted in the organization of the United Evangelical Church in 1894. An attempt to heal this division was made in 1922, but a portion of the United Evangelical Church was not satisfied with the plan of merger and remained apart, taking the above name in 1928. This denomination is Wesleyan-Arminian in doctrine, evangelistic in spirit and Methodist in church government, with congregational ownership of local church property.

Congregations are located from New Jersey to Illinois. A denominational center, two retirement villages and a seminary are located in Myerstown, Pennsylvania. Three summer youth camps and four camp meetings continue evangelistic outreach. A worldwide missions movement includes conferences in North East India, Liberia, Mexico, Costa Rica, and Japan. The denomination is a member of National Association of Evangelicals.

Headquarters
Evangelical Congregational Church Center, 100 W. Park Ave., Myerstown, PA 17067 Tel. (800)866-7581 Fax (717)866-7383
Media Contact, Bishop, Rev. Michael W. Sigman, Tel. (717)866-7581
Email: eccenter@eccenter.com
Website: www.eccenter.com/church

Officers
Presiding Bishop, Rev. Michael W. Sigman
1st Vice Chpsn., Rev. Gary Brown
Sec., Rev. Kirk Marks
Conference Attorney, David Roland, Esquire
Treas., Patricia Hartman, Annville, PA

E.C.C. Retirement Village, Exec. Dir., Steven J. Reiter Fax (717)866-6448

Evangelical School of Theology, Pres., Dr. Dennis Hollinger Fax (717)866-4667

OTHER ORGANIZATIONS

Evangelism & Discipleship Commission, Chpsn., Bishop Michael Sigman

Leadership Commission, Chpsn., Bishop Michael Sigman

Church Health Commission, Chpsn., Rev. Fred Moury

Church Planting Commission, Chpsn,, Rev. Keith Miller

Church Services Commission, Chpsn., Rev. Keith Miller

Global Ministries Commission, Chpsn., Rev. John Ragsdale

Bd. of Pensions, Pres., William Kautz, New Cumberland, PA; Controller, Douglas White, Myerstown, PA

Periodicals

Window on the World (Global Ministries Commission)

The Evangelical Covenant Church

The Evangelical Covenant Church has its roots in historic Christianity as it emerged during the Protestant Reformation, in the biblical instruction of the Lutheran State Church of Sweden and in the great spiritual awakenings of the 19th century.

The Covenant Church adheres to the affirmations of the Protestant Reformation regarding the Holy Scriptures, believing that the Old and the New Testament are the Word of God and the only perfect rule for faith, doctrine and conduct. It has traditionally valued the historic confessions of the Christian church, particularly the Apostles' Ethe Nicene Creed, while at the same time emphasizing the sovereignty of the Word over all creedal interpretations. It has especially cherished the pietistic restatement of the doctrine of justification by faith as basic to its dual task of evangelism and Christian nurture. It recognizes the New Testament emphasis upon personal faith in Jesus Christ as Savior and Lord, the reality of a fellowship of believers which acknowledges but transcends theological differences, and the belief in baptism and the Lord's Supper as divinely ordained sacraments of the church.

While the denomination has traditionally practiced the baptism of infants, in conformity with its principle of freedom it has also recognized the practice of believer baptism. The principle of personal freedom, so highly esteemed by the Covenant, is to be distinguished from the individualism that disregards the centrality of the Word of God and the mutual responsibilities and disciplines of the spiritual community.

Headquarters

5101 N. Francisco Ave., Chicago, IL 60625 Tel. (773)784-3000 Fax (773)784-4366

Media Contact, Donald L. Meyer, Email: don.meyer@covchurch.org

Email: Elliott.johnson@covchurch.org

Website: www.covchurch.org

Officers

Pres., Dr. Glenn R. Palmberg

Exec. Vice Pres., Rev. Donn Engebretson

Vice Pres. Finance, Dr. Dean A. Lundgren

ADMINISTRATIVE BOARDS

Executive Board, Rev. D. Darrell Griffes, Chair

Bd. of Women Ministries, Exec.. Minister, Rev. Ruth Y. Hill

Bd. Of Nominations, Advisory Member, (vacant)

Bd. of the Ordered Ministry, Exec. Minister, Rev. Dr. David Kersten

Bd. of Pensions & Benefits, Dir. of Pensions, Dean A. Lundgren

Bd. of Benevolence, Pres. of Covenant Ministries of Benevolence, David A. Dwight, 5145 N. California Ave., Chicago, IL 60625

North Park University, Pres., Dr. David l. Parkyn, 3225 W. Foster Ave., Chicago, IL 60625; North Park Theological Seminary, Pres. And Dean, Dr. John E. Phelan Jr.

SERVICE ORGANIZATIONS

National Covenant Properties, Pres., David W. Johnson, 5101 N. Francisco, Chicago, IL 60625 Tel. (773)784-3000

Covenant Trust Company, Pres., Charles A. Walles, 5215 Old Orchard Rd., Ste 725, Skokie, IL 60077 Tel. (847)583-3200, (800) 483-2177

REGIONAL CONFERENCES OF THE E.C.C.

Central Conference, Supt., Rev. Jerome O. Nelson, 3319 W. Foster Ave., Chicago, IL 60625 Tel. (773)267-3060

East Coast Conference, Supt., Rev. Howard K. Burgoyne, 52 Missionary Rd., Cromwell, CT 06416 Tel. (860)635-2691

Great Lakes Conference, Supt., Rev. Richard Lucco, 42219 Ann Arbor Road. E., Plymouth, MI 48170 Tel. (734)451-4670

Midwest Conference, Supt., Rev. Kenneth P. Carlson, 13304 W. Center Rd. #223, Omaha, NE 68144 Tel. (402)334-3060

North Pacific Conference, Supt., Rev. Mark A. Novak, 9311 SE 36th t., Ste 120, Mercer Island, WA 98040 Tel. (206)275-3903

Northwest Conference, Supt., Rev. James A. Fretheim, 3106 47th Avenue S., Minneapolis, MN 55406 Tel. (612)721-4893

Pacific Southwest Conference, Supt., Rev. Evelyn M. R. Johnson, 1333 Willow Pass Rd., Ste 212, Concord, CA 94502 Tel. (925)677-2140

Southeast Conference, Supt., Rev. Kurt A. Miericke, 1759 W. Broadway St., #7, Oviedo, FL 32765 Tel. (407)977-8009

Canada Conference, Supt., Rev.Jeffrey Anderson, PO BOX 34025 RPO, Fort

Richmond, Winnipeg, MB R3T, Tel.
(204)269-3437

Midsouth Conference, Supt., Rev. Garth T
Bolinder, 6119 E. 91st Street, Ste. 2000, Tulsa,
OK 74137 Tel. (918)481-9097

E.C.C. of Alaska, Field Dir., Rev. Rodney J.
Sawyer, P.O. Box 770749, Eagle River, AK
99577 Tel. (907)694-6348

The Paul Carlson Partnership (affiliated), Pres.,
Rev. Cartis D. Peterson Exec. Dir., Rev. James
V. Sundholm, 5101 N. Francisco Ave.,
Chicago, IL, 60625 Tel. (773)907-3302

Periodicals
*Covenant Companion, Covenant Quarterly,
Covenant Home Altar*

The Evangelical Free Church of America

In October 1884, 27 representatives from
Swedish churches met in Boone, Iowa, to establish the Swedish Evangelical Free Church. In the
fall of that same year, two Norwegian-Danish
groups began worship and fellowship (in Boston
and in Tacoma) and by 1912 had established the
Norwegian-Danish Evangelical Free Church
Association. These two denominations, representing 275 congregations, came together at a
merger conference in 1950.

The Evangelical Free Church of America is an
association of local, autonomous churches across
the United States and Canada, blended together
by common principles, policies and practices. A
12-point statement addresses the major doctrines
but also provides for differences of understanding on minor issues of faith and practice.

Overseas outreach includes 500 missionaries
serving in 31 countries.

Headquarters
901 East 78th St., Minneapolis, MN 55420-1300
Tel. (952)854-1300 Fax (952)853-8488
Media Contact, Exec. Dir. of International
Mission, Timothy Addington
Email: president@efca.org
Website: www.efca.org

Officers
Pres., Dr. William J. Hamel
Exec. Dir. International Mission, Timothy
Addington
Exec. Dir. National Ministries, Rev. Steven Hudson
C.F.O., John R. Torvik, CPA
Chair, Brian Cole, 2404 Park Dr., West Des
Moines, IA 60265
Sec., Rev. William Culbertson, 958 5th Ave. S.,
Bloomington, MN 55420
Moderator, Dr. Roland Peterson, 235 Craigbrook
Way NE, Fridley, MN 55432
Vice Moderator, Dr. Louis Diaz, 520 E.
Roosevelt Rd., Wheaton, IL 60187

Periodicals
EFCA Today

Evangelical Friends International— North American Region

The organization restructured from
Evangelical Friends Alliance in 1990 to become
internationalized for the benefit of its world-wide
contacts. The North America Region continues to
function within the United States as EFA formerly did. The organization represents one corporate
step of denominational unity, brought about as a
result of several movements of spiritual renewal
within the Society of Friends. These movements
are, (1) the general evangelical renewal within
Christianity, (2) the new scholarly recognition of
the evangelical nature of 17th-century Quakerism,
and (3) EFA, which was formed in 1965.

EFI-NA is conservative in theology and makes
use of local pastors. Sunday morning worship
includes singing, Scripture reading, a period of
open worship and a sermon by the pastor.

Headquarters
5350 Broadmoor Cir. NW, Canton, OH 44709
Tel.: (330)493-1660 Fax: (330)493-0852
Media Contact, Gen. Supt., Dr. John P. Williams,
Jr.
Email: efcer@aol.com
Website: www.evangelical-friends.org

YEARLY MEETINGS
Evangelical Friends Church, Eastern Region,
Wayne Ickes, 5350 Broadmoor Cir., N.W.,
Canton, OH 44709 Tel. (330)493-1660 Fax
(330)493-0852
Rocky Mountain YM, John Brawner, 3350 Reed
St., Wheatridge, CO 80033 Tel. (303)238-
5200 Fax (303)238-5200
Mid-America YM, Duane Hansen, 2018 Maple,
Wichita, KS 67213 Tel. (316)267-0391 Fax
(316)267-0681
Northwest YM, Mark Ankeny, 200 N. Meridian
St., Newberg, OR 97132 Tel. (503)538-9419
Fax. (503)538-9410
Alaska YM, Sam Williams, P.O. Box 687,
Kotzebue, AK 99752 Tel. (907)442-3906
Evangelical Friends Church Southwest, YM,
Linda Coop, P.O. Box 1607, Whittier, CA
90609-1607 Tel. (562)947-2883 Fax (562)
947-9385

Periodicals
The Friends Voice

Evangelical Lutheran Church in America*

The Evangelical Lutheran Church in America
(ELCA) was organized April 30-May 3, 1987,
in Columbus, Ohio, bringing together the 2.25
million-member American Lutheran Church,
the 2.85 million-member Lutheran Church in
America, and the 100,000-member Association
of Evangelical Lutheran Churches.

The ELCA is, through its predecessors, the oldest of the major U.S. Lutheran churches. In the
mid-17th century, a Dutch Lutheran congregation

was formed in New Amsterdam (now New York). Other early congregations were begun by German and Scandinavian immigrants to Delaware, Pennsylvania, New York and the Carolinas.

The first Lutheran association of congregations, the Pennsylvania Ministerium, was organized in 1748 under Henry Melchior Muhlenberg. Numerous Lutheran organizations were formed as immigration continued and the United States grew.

In 1960, The American Lutheran Church (ALC) was created through a merger of an earlier American Lutheran Church, formed in 1930, the Evangelical Lutheran Church, begun in 1917, and the United Evangelical Lutheran Church started in 1896. In 1963 the Lutheran Free Church, formed in 1897, merged with the ALC.

In 1962, the Lutheran Church in America (LCA) was formed by a merger of the United Lutheran Church in America, formed in 1918, with the Augustana Evangelical Lutheran Church, begun in 1860, the American Evangelical Lutheran Church, founded in 1872, and the Finnish Evangelical Lutheran Church or Suomi Synod, founded in 1891.

The Association of Evangelical Lutheran Churches arose in 1976 from a doctrinal split within the Lutheran Church-Missouri Synod.

The ELCA, through its predecessor church bodies, was a founding member of the Lutheran World Federation, the World Council of Churches, and the National Council of the Churches of Christ in the USA.

The church is divided into 65 geographical areas called synods. These 65 synods are grouped into nine regions for mission, joint programs and service.

Headquarters

8765 W. Higgins Rd., Chicago, IL 60631 Tel. (773)380-2700 Fax (773)380-1465

Media Contact, Dir. for News, John Brooks, Tel. (773)380-2958 Fax (773)380-2406

Email: info@elca.org

Website: www.elca.org

Officers

Presiding Bishop, Rev. Mark S. Hanson

Sec., Rev. Dr. Lowell G. Almen

Treas., Ms. Christina L. Jackson-Skelton

Vice Pres., Mr. Carlos E. Pena

Exec. for Admn., Rev. Charles S. Miller

Office of the Presiding Bishop, Exec. Asst to the Presiding Bishop for Federal Chaplaincies, Rev. Darrell D. Morton; Exec. Asst. to the Presiding Bishop, Ms. Myrna J. Sheie

PROGRAM UNITS

Vocation and Education, Exec. Dir., Rev. Stanley Nolson, Chpsn., Dr. Kathryn L. Johnson

Global Mission, Exec. Dir., Rev. Rafael Malpica Padilla, Bd. Chpsn., Rev. Virginia Anderson-Larson

Evangelical Outreach and Congregational Mission, Exec. Dir., Rev. Dr. Richard A. Magnus, Jr.; Chpsn., Mr. Francis R Ramos-Scharron

Church in Society, Exec. Dir., Rev. Rebecca S. Larson; Chpsn., Ms. Kristin Anderson-Ostrom

ELCA Publishing House, Exec. Dir., Ms. Beth A. Lewis; Bd. Chpsn.,MS. Annette Citzler

Women of the ELCA, Exec. Dir., Ms. Linda Post Bushkofsky; President., Ms. Carmen K. Richards

COMMISSIONS

Multicultural Ministries, Exec. Dir., Rev. Sherman Hicks; Chpsn., Mr. Aureo F. Andino

OTHER CHURCHWIDE UNITS

Conference of Bishops, Church Periodical, Editor, Mr. Daniel J. Lehmann; Shpsn. Rev. Karen Bockelman; Rev. E. Roy Riley

Development Services, Exec. Dir., Rev. Donald M. Hallberg, Stat. Ms. Tonia I. Lindquist

ELCA Bd. of Pensions, Exec. Dir., Mr. John G. Kapanke; Bd. Chpsn, Ms. Mary S. Ranum

SECTIONS

Communication Services, Dir., Ms. Kristi Bangert

Ecumenical and Inter-Religious Relations, Dir., Bishop Donald McCoid

Human Resources, Dir., Ms. Else B Thompson

Research & Evaluation, Dir., Dr. Kenneth W. Inskeep

Synodical Relations, Executive for Synodical Relations, Rev. Kathie Bender Schwich

Worship and Liturgical Resources, Dir., Rev. Michael L. Burk

SYNODICAL BISHOPS

REGION 1

Alaska, Rev. Michael F. Keys, 1847 W. Northern Lights Blvd., #2, Anchorage, AK 99517-3343 Tel. (907)272-8899 Fax(907)274-3141

Northwest Washington, Rev. Wm Chris Boerger, 5519 Pinney Ave. N, Seattle, WA 98103-5899 Tel. (206)783-9292 Fax(206)783-9833

Southwestern Washington, Rev. Robert D. Hofstad, 420 121st St., S., Tacoma, WA 98444-5218 Tel. (253)535-8300 Fax(253)535-8315

Eastern Washington-Idaho, Rev. Martin D. Wells, 314 South Spruce St., Ste. A, Spokane, WA 99204-1098 Tel. (509)838-9871 Fax (509) 838-0941

Oregon, Rev. Paul R. Swanson, 2800 N. Vancouver Ave., Ste. 101, Portland, OR 97227-1643 Tel. (503)413-4191 Fax(503)413-2407

Montana, Rev. Dr. Richard R. Omland, 2415 13th Ave. S., Great Falls, MT 59405-5199 Tel. (406)453-1461 Fax(406)761-4632

Regional Coord., Mr. Steven H. Lansing, Region 1, 766-B John St., Seattle, WA 98109-5186 Tel. (206)624-0093 Fax(206)626-0987

113

REGION 2

Sierra Pacific, Rev. David G. Mullen, 401 Roland Way, #215, Oakland, CA 94621-2011 Tel. (510)430-0500 Fax(510)430-8730

Southwest California, Rev. Dean W. Nelson, 1300 E. Colorado St., Glendale, CA 91205-1406 Tel. (818)507-9591 Fax (818)507-9627

Pacifica, Rev. Murray D. Finck, 23655 Via Del Rio, Ste. B, Yorba Linda, CA 92887-2738 Tel. (714)692-2791 Fax(714)692-9317

Grand Canyon, Rev. Stephen S. Talmage, Interchurch Center 4423 N. 24th St., Ste. 400, Phoenix, AZ 85016-5544 Tel. (602)957-3223 Fax(602)956-8104

Rocky Mountain, Rev. Allan C. Bjornberg, 455 Sherman St., Ste. 160, Denver, CO 80203 Tel. (303)777-6700 Fax(303)733-0750

Region 2, Ms. Margaret Schmitt Ajer, Region 2, 3755 Avocado Blvd., PMB 411, La Mesa, CA 91941 Tel (619)460-9312 Fax (619)460-9314

REGION 3

Western North Dakota, Rev. Duane C. Danielson, 1614 Capitol Way, P.O. Box 370, Bismarck, ND 58502-0370 Tel. (701)223-5312 Fax (701)223-1435

Eastern North Dakota, Rev. Richard J. Foss, 1703 32nd Ave., S., Fargo, ND 58103-5936 Tel. (701)232-3381 Fax(701)232-3180

South Dakota, Rev. Andrea F. DeGroot-Nesdahl, Augustana College, 29th & S. Summit, Sioux Falls, SD 57197-0001 Tel. (605)247-4011 Fax(605)274-4028

Northwestern Minnesota, Rev. Rolf P. Wangberg, Concordia College, 901 8th St. S., Moorhead, MN 56562-0001 Tel. (218)299-3019 Fax (218)299-3363

Northeastern Minnesota, Rev. E. Peter Strommen, 1105 E. Superior St., Upper Suite, Duluth, MN 55802-2085 Tel. (218)724-4424 Fax(218)724-4393

Southwestern Minnesota, Rev. Jon V. Anderson 175 E. Bridge St., P.O. Box 499, Redwood Falls, MN 56283-0499 Tel. (507)637-3904 Fax(507)637-2809

Minneapolis Area, Rev. Craig E. Johnson, 122 W. Franklin Ave., Ste. 600, Minneapolis, MN 55404-2474 Tel. (612)870-3610 Fax(612)870-0170

Saint Paul Area, Rev. Peter Rogness, 105 W. University Ave., St. Paul, MN 55103-2094 Tel. (651)224-4313 Fax(651)224-5646

Southeastern Minnesota, Rev. Harold L. Usgaard, Assisi Heights, 1001 14th St. NW, Ste. 300, Rochester, MN 55901-2511 Tel. (507)280-9457 Fax(507)280-8824

Regional Coord., Rev. Craig A. Boehlke, Region 3, Luther Seminary, 2481 Como Ave., St. Paul, MN 55108-1445 Tel. (651)649-0454 ext. 232 Fax(651)649-0468

REGION 4

Nebraska, Rev. David L. deFreese, 4980 S. 118th St., Ste. D, Omaha, NE 68137-2220 Tel. (402) 896-5311 Fax(402)896-5354

Central States, Rev. Dr. Gerald L. Mansholt, 3210 Michigan Ave., 4th Fl., Kansas City, MO 64109, Tel. (816)861-6584 Fax (816)861-4753

Arkansas-Oklahoma, Rev. Floyd M. Schoenhals, 693 S. 66th E. Ave., Ste. 310, Tulsa, OK 74133-1760 Tel. (918)492-4288 Fax(918)491-6275

Northern Texas-Northern Louisiana, Rev. Kevin S. Kanouse, 1230 Riverbend Dr., Ste. 105, P.O. Box 560587, Dallas, TX 75356-0587 Tel. (214)637-6865 Fax(214)637-4805

Southwestern Texas, Rev. Ray Tiemann, 1090 Oestreich Dr., Seguin, TX 78155, Tel. (830) 379-9900 Fax (830)379-9990

Texas-Louisiana Gulf Coast, Rev. Paul J. Blom, 12707 North Fwy, #580, Houston, TX 77060-1239 Tel. (281)873-5665 Fax(281)875-4716

Acting Regional Coord., Rev. Donald R. Just, 7016 Ameranth Ln, Austin, TX, 78723, Tel.512-585-4809 Fax (512)272-9699

REGION 5

Metropolitan Chicago, Rev. Paul R. Landahl, 1420 West Dickens Ave., Chicago, IL 60614-3004 Tel. (773)248-0021 Fax(773)248-8455

Northern Illinois, Rev. Gary M. Wollersheim, 103 W. State St., Rockford, IL 61101-1105 Tel. (815)964-9934 Fax(815)964-2295

Central-Southern Illinois, Rev. Warren D. Freiheit, 524 S. Fifth St., Springfield, IL 62701-1822 Tel. (217)753-7915 Fax(217)753-7976

Southeastern Iowa, Rev. Philip L. Hougen, 2635 Northgate Dr., P.O. Box 3167, Iowa City, IA 52244-3167 Tel. (319)338-1273 Fax (319) 351-8677

Western Iowa, Rev. Michael A. Last, 318 E. Fifth St., P.O. Box 577, Storm Lake, IA 50588-0577 Tel. (712)732-4968 Fax(712)732-6540

Northeastern Iowa, Rev. Steven L. Ullestad, 201-20th St. SW, P.O. Box 804, Waverly, IA 50677-0804 Tel. (319)352-1414 Fax(319)352-1416

Northern Great Lakes, Rev. Thomas A. Skrenes, 1029 N. Third St., Marquette, MI 49855-3588 Tel. (906)228-2300 Fax(906)228-2527

Northwest Synod of Wisconsin, Rev. Robert D. Berg, 12 W. Marshall St., P.O. Box 730, Rice Lake, WI 54868-0730 Tel. (715)234-3373 Fax(715)234-4183

East-Central Synod of Wisconsin, Rev. James A. Justman, 16 Tri-Park Way, Appleton, WI 54914-1658 Tel. (920)734-5381 Fax(920)734-5074

Greater Milwaukee, Rev. Paul W. Stumme-Diers, 1212 S. Layton Blvd., Milwaukee, WI 53215-1653 Tel. (414)671-1212 Fax (414)671-1756

South-Central Synod of Wisconsin, Rev. George G. Carlson, 2909 Landmark Pl., Ste. 202, Madison, WI 53713-4237 Tel. (608)270-0201 Fax (608)270-0202

114

La Crosse Area, Rev. April Culring Larson, 3462 Losey Blvd. S., La Crosse, WI 54601-7217 Tel. (608)788-5000 Fax (608)788-4916

Regional Coord., Rev. Carl R. Evenson, Region 5, 675 Deerwood Dr., Ste. 4., Neenah, WI 54956-1629 Tel. (920)720-9880 Fax (920)720-9881

REGION 6

Southeast Michigan, Rev. John H. Schreiber, 218 Fisher Bldg., 3011 W. Grand Ave., Detroit, MI 48202-3011 Tel. (313)875-1881 Fax (313) 875-1889

Northwest Lower Michigan, Rev. Gary L. Hansen, 801 S. Waverly Rd., Ste. 201, Lansing, MI 48917-4254 Tel. (517)321-5066 Fax (517)321-2612

Indiana-Kentucky, Rev. James R. Stuck, 911 E. 86th St., Ste. 200, Indianapolis, IN 46240-1840 Tel. (317)253-3522 Fax (317)254-5666

Northwestern Ohio, Rev. Marcus C. Lohrmann, 621 Bright Rd., Findlay, OH 45840-6987 Tel. (419)423-3664 Fax (419)423-8801

Northeastern Ohio, Rev. Lee M. Miller, Interim Bishop, 1890 Bailey Rd., Cuyahoga Falls, OH 44221-5259, Tel. 330-929-9022 Fax 330-929-9018

Southern Ohio, Rev. Dr. Callon W. Holloway, Jr., 300 S. 2nd St., Columbus, OH 43215-5001 Tel. (614)464-3532 Fax (614)464-3422

Regional Coord., Marilyn McCann Smith, Region 6, P.O. Box 91, 119 1/2 N. Main St. Bluffton, OH 45817 Tel. (419)369-4006 Fax (419)369-4007

REGION 7

New Jersey, Rev. E. Roy Riley, Jr., 1930 State Highway. 33, Hamilton Square, Trenton, NJ 08690-1799 Tel. (609)586-6800 Fax (609) 586-1597

New England, Rev. Margaret G. Payne, 20 Upland St., Worcester, MA 01607-1624 Tel. (508)791-1530 Fax (508)797-9295

Metropolitan New York, Rev. Stephen P. Bouman, Interchurch Center, 475 Riverside Dr., Ste.1620, New York, NY 10115 Tel. (212) 665-0732 Fax (212)665-8640

Upstate New York, Rev. Marie C. Jerge, 890 E. Brighton Ave., Syracuse, NY 13205, Tel. (315) 446-2502 Fax (315)446-4642

Northeastern Pennsylvania, Rev. Dr. David R. Strobel, 4865 Hamilton Blvd., Wescosville, PA 18106-9705 Tel. (610)395-6891 Fax (610) 398-7083

Southeastern Pennsylvania, Rev. Claire S. Burkat, 506 Haws Ave., Norristown, PA 19401-4543 Tel. (610)278-7342 Fax (610) 696-2782

Slovak Zion, Rev. Wilma S. Kucharek, 124 Barbero Dr., Torrington, CT 06790, P.O.Box 1003 (06790-1003), Tel. (860)482-6100 Fax (860)482-7463

Regional Coord., Rev. Peggy M. Wvertele Tel. (215)248-6319 Fax (215)248-7377

REGION 8

Northwestern Pennsylvania, Rev. Ralph E. Jones, 308 Seneca St., 5th Fl., Oil City, PA 16301, Tel. (814)677-5706 Fax (814)676-8591

Southwestern Pennsylvania, Rev. Donald J. McCoid, 9625 Perry Hwy., Pittsburgh, PA 15237-5590 Tel. (412)367-8222 Fax (412) 369-8840

Allegheny, Rev. Gregory R. Pile, 701 Quail Ave., Altoona, PA 16602-3010 Tel. (814)942-1042 Fax (814)941-9259

Lower Susquehanna, Rev. Carol S. Hendrix, 900 S. Arlington Ave., Ste. 208, Harrisburg, PA 17109-5031 Tel. (717)652-1852 Fax (717) 652-2504

Upper Susquehanna, Rev. Dr. A. Donald Main, Rt. 192 & Reitz Blvd., P.O. Box 36, Lewisburg, PA 17837-0036 Tel. (570)524-9778 Fax (570)524-9757

Delaware-Maryland, Rev. Dr. H. Gerard Knoche, 700 Light St., Baltimore, MD 21230-3850 Tel. (410)230-2860 Fax (410)230-2871

Metropolitan Washington, D.C., Rev. Theodore F. Schneider, 1030-15th St., NW, Ste 1010, Washington, DC 20005-1503 Tel. (202)408-8110 Fax (202)408-8114

West Virginia-Western Maryland, Rev. Ralph W. Dunkin, The Atrium, 503 Morgantown Avenue, Ste. 100, Fairmont, WV 26554-4374 Tel. (304)363-4030 Fax (304)366-9846

Regional Coord., Rev. Judith Cobb, Lutheran Theological Sem. at Gettysburg, 61 Seminary Ridge, Gettysburg, PA 17325-1795 Tel. (717) 338-3033 ext. 2133 Fax (717)334-3469

REGION 9

Virginia, Rev. James F. Mauney, Roanoke College, 221 College Ln., Bittle Hall, P.O. Drawer 70, Salem, VA 24153-0070 Tel. (540) 389-1000 Fax (540)389-5962

North Carolina, Rev. Leonard H. Bolick, 1988 Lutheran Synod Dr., Salisbury, NC 28144-4480 Tel. (704)633-4861 Fax (704)638-0508

South Carolina, Rev. David A. Donges, 1003 Richland St., P.O. Box 43, Columbia, SC 29202-0043 Tel. (803)765-0590 Fax (803)252-5558

Southeastern, Rev. Ronald B. Warren, 100 Edgewood Ave., NE, Ste. 1600, Atlanta, GA 30303 Tel. (404)589-1977 Fax (404)521-1980

Florida-Bahamas, Rev. Edward R. Benoway, 3838 W. Cypress St., Tampa, FL 33607-4897 Tel. (813)876-7660 Fax (813)870-0826

Caribbean, Rev. Margarita Martinez, PMB Num 359 Ste. 1, 425 CARR 693, Ste. 1, Dorado, PR 00646-4802 Tel. (787)273-8311 Fax (787) 796-3365

Regional Coord., Rev. Harvey L. Huntley Jr., Region 9, Lutheran Theological Southern Seminary, 4201 N. Main St., Columbia, SC 29203 Tel. (803)461-3263 Fax (803)461-3380

Periodicals

The Lutheran, Lutheran Partners, Lutheran Woman Today, Seeds for the Parish

Evangelical Lutheran Synod

The Evangelical Lutheran Synod had its beginning among the Norwegian settlers who brought with them their Lutheran heritage. The synod was organized in 1853. It was reorganized in 1918 by those who desired to adhere to the synod's principles not only in word but also in deed.

The synod owns and operates Bethany Lutheran College and Bethany Lutheran Theological Seminary. It has congregations in 20 states and maintains foreign missions in Peru, Chile, India, Korea, the Czech Republic, Latvia, and Ukraine. It operates a seminary in Lima, Peru and in Ternopil, Ukraine.

Headquarters

6 Browns Court, Mankato, MN 56001 Tel. (507)344-7356 Fax (507)344-7426
Media Contact, Pres., John A. Moldstad
Email: gorvick@blc.edu
Website: www.EvLuthSyn.org

Officers

Pres., Rev. John A. Moldstad, 6 Browns Ct., Mankato, MN 56001
Sec., Rev. Craig Ferkenstad, 37777 State Hwy 22, St. Peter, MN 56082
Vice Pres., Rev. Glenn Obengerger, 12309 Pacific Ave., Tacoma, WA 98444

OTHER ORGANIZATIONS

Lutheran Synod Book Co., Bethany Lutheran College, 700 Luther Dr., Mankato, MN 56001
Bethany Lutheran Theological Seminary, 6 Browns Court, Mankato, MN 56001

Periodicals

Lutheran Sentinel, Lutheran Synod Quarterly, Young Branches, Oak Leaves, Mission News

Evangelical Mennonite Church—please see Fellowship of Evangelical Churches.

Evangelical Methodist Church

The Evangelical Methodist Church was organized in 1946 at Memphis, Tenn., largely as a movement of people who opposed modern liberalism and wished for a return to the historic Wesleyan position. In 1960, it merged with the Evangel Church (formerly Evangelistic Tabernacles) and with the People's Methodist Church in 1962.

Headquarters

P.O. Box 17070, Indianapolis, IN 46217 Tel. (317)780-8017 Fax (317)780-8078
Media Contact, Gen. Conf. Sec.-Treas., Rev. James A. Coulston
Email: headquarters@emchurch.org
Website: www.emchurch.org

Officers

Gen. Supt., Dr. Edward W. Williamson
Gen. Conf. Sec.-Treas., Rev. James A. Coulston

Periodicals

The Connection

Evangelical Presbyterian Church

The Evangelical Presbyterian Church (EPC), established in March 1981, is a conservative denomination of 8 geographic presbyteries. From its inception with 12 churches, the EPC has grown to 182 churches with a membership of over 74,000.

Planted firmly within the historic Reformed tradition, evangelical in spirit, the EPC places high priority on church planting and development along with world missions. Eighty missionaries serve the church's mission.

Based on the truth of Scripture and adhering to the Westminster Confession of Faith plus its Book of Order, the denomination is committed to the "essentials of the faith." The historic motto "In essentials, unity; in nonessentials, liberty; in all things charity" catches the irenic spirit of the EPC, along with the Ephesians theme, "truth in love."

The Evangelical Presbyterian Church is a member of the World Alliance of Reformed Churches, National Association of Evangelicals, World Evangelical Fellowship and the Evangelical Council for Financial Accountability.

Headquarters

Office of the General Assembly, 17197 N. Laurel Park Dr., Suite 567, Livonia, MI 48152 Tel. (734)742-2020 Fax (734)742-2033
Media Contact, Stated Clerk, Dr. Jeffrey Jeremiah
Email: EPCHURCH@epc.org
Website: www.epc.org

Officers

Administration Committee, Chmn., Rev. William Meyer, 2020 Shangrila Dr. # 205, Clearwater, FL 33763
Board of Benefits, Chmn., Rev. Ron Horgan, c/o EPC, 17197 N. Laurel Park Dr. Suite 567, Livonia, MI 48152
Committee on Fraternal Relations, Chmn., Rev. Craig Vaniber, 4700 Victory Dr., Marshall, TX 75670
Committee on National Outreach, Chmn., Rev. Rodger Woodworth, New Hope EPC, 2710 Shadeland Ave., Pittsburgh, PA 15212
Committee on Presbytery Review, Chmn., Mr.Jay Curtis, 3018 Forest Club Drive, Plant City, FL 33566
Committee on World Outreach, Chmn., Dr. Bern Draper, 8103 Saguaro Ridge Road, Parker, CL 80138
Committee on Ministerial Vocation, Chmn., Mr. Jerry Kidd, 624 Reasor Dr., Virginia Beach, VA 23464
Comm. on Christian Educ. & Publ., Chmn., Mr. Dan Tidwell, 3310 Oyster Cove Dr., Missouri City, TX 77459
Committee on Women's Ministries, Chmn., Mrs.

116

Jeane Mobley, 100 Turtle Cay—Unit 6, Wilmington NC 28412

Committee on Theology, Chmn., Dr. Jeffrey Jeremiah, First Evangelical Presbyterian Church, 19800 108th Avenue SE, Renton, WA 98055

Committee on Student and Young Adult Ministries, Chmn., Rev. George Boomer, Knox Presbyterian Church, 25700 Crocker Blvd, Harrison Township, MI 48045

College Ministries Committee, Chmn., Rev. Rick Stauffer, Tabernacle EPC, 2432 S. Raccoon Rd., Youngstown, OH 44515

PRESBYTERIES

Central South, Stated Clk., Rev. Dennis Flach, New Covenant Evangelical Presbyterian Church, P.O. Box 842, Natchez, MS 39121

East, Stated Clk., Rev. Ron Meyer, Fourth Presbyterian Church, 5500 River Road, Bethesda, MD 20816

Florida, Stated Clk., Rev. Robert Garment, Hope EPC, 4680 Thomasville Rd., Tallahassee, FL 32309

Mid-America, Stated Clk., Mr. Dexter Kuhlman, 1926 Prospector Ridge, Ballwin, MO 63011

Mid-Atlantic, Stated Clk., Dr. Howard Shockley, P.O. Box 10, Moore, SC 29369

Midwest, Stated Clk., Mr. John C. Manon, P.O. Box 6047, Auburn, IN 46706-6047

Southeast, Stated Clk., Rev. Bill Sharp, 1222 Village Green Dr., Chattanooga, TN 39343

West, Stated Clk., Rev. Marc Huebl, Interim, 1250 S. Buckely Rd., Suite # 146, Aurora, CO 80017

Fellowship of Evangelical Bible Churches

Formerly known as Evangelical Mennonite Brethren, this body emanates from the Russian immigration of Mennonites into the United States, 1873-74. Established with the emphasis on true repentance, conversion and a committed life to Jesus as Savior and Lord, the conference was founded in 1889 under the leadership of Isaac Peters and Aaron Wall. The founding churches were located in Mountain Lake, Minnesota, and in Henderson and Jansen, Nebraska. The conference has since grown to a fellowship of 42 churches with approximately 5000 members in Canada, Paraguay and the United States.

Foreign missions have been a vital ingredient of the total ministry. Today one missionary is serving for every 45 members in the home churches. The fellowship does not develop and administer foreign mission fields of its own, but actively participates with existing evangelical "faith" mission agencies. The Fellowship has missionaries serving under approximately 40 different agencies around the world.

The church is holding fast to the inerrancy of Scripture, the deity of Christ and the need for spiritual regeneration of man from his sinful natural state by faith in the death, burial and resurrection of Jesus Christ as payment for sin. Members look forward to the imminent return of Jesus Christ and retain a sense of urgency to share the gospel with those who have never heard of God's redeeming love.

Headquarters

3339 N 109th Plz., Omaha, NE 68164 Tel. (402)965-3860 Fax (402)965-3871

Admn., Paul Boeker, 3339 N 109th Plz., Omaha, NE 68164 Tel. 402-965-3860 Fax 402-965-3871

Email: info@febcministries.org

Website: www.febcministries.org

Officers

Pres., Mr. Gerald Epp, P.O. Box 86, Waldheim, SK S0K 4R0 Tel. (306)945-2023, Email: president@febcministries.org

Vice President, Mr.Don Krehbiel, 1514 Park Wild Ave., Omaha, NE 68108, Email: vicepres@febcministries.org

Admn., Paul Boeker, 3339 N 109th Plz., Omaha, NE 68164 Tel. (402)965-3860 Fax (402)965-3871, Email: info@febcministries.org

Ministries Coordinator, Harvey Schultz, 3011 3rd Ave. East, P.O. Box 8, Waldheim, SK S0K 4R0, Tel. (306)945-2220 Fax (306)945-2088, Email: ministries@febcministries.org

Periodicals

Fellowship Focus

Fellowship of Evangelical Churches

The Evangelical Mennonite Church is an American denomination in the European free church tradition, tracing its heritage to the Reformation period of the 16th century. The Swiss Brethren of that time believed that salvation could come only by repentance for sins and faith in Jesus Christ; that baptism was only for believers; and that the church should be separate from controls of the state. Their enemies called them Anabaptists, since they insisted on rebaptizing believers who had been baptized as infants. As the Anabaptist movement spread to other countries, Menno Simons became its principal leader. In time his followers were called Mennonites.

In 1693 a Mennonite minister, Jacob Amman, insisted that the church should adopt a more conservative position on dress and style of living and should more rigidly enforce the "ban"—the church's method of disciplining disobedient members. Amman's insistence finally resulted in a division within the South German Mennonite groups; his followers became known as the Amish.

Migrations to America, involving both Mennonites and Amish, took place in the 1700s and 1800s, for both religious and economic reasons.

117

The Evangelical Mennonite Church was formed in 1866 out of a spiritual awakening among the Amish in Indiana. It was first known as the Egly Amish, after its founder Bishop Henry Egly. Bishop Egly emphasized regeneration, separation and nonconformity to the world. His willingness to rebaptize anyone who had been baptized without repentance created a split in his church, prompting him to gather a new congregation in 1866. The conference, which has met annually since 1895, united a number of other congregations of like mind. This group became The Defenseless Mennonite Church in 1898 and has been known as the Evangelical Mennonite Church since 1948. At the 2003 convention the delegates voted to change the name to Fellowship of Evangelical Churches.

Headquarters

Resource Center, 1420 Kerrway Ct., Fort Wayne, IN 46805 Tel. (260)423-3649 Fax (260)420-1905

Media Contact, Admn. Asst., Lynette Augsburger
Email: FECministries@aol.com
Website: www.fecministries.org

Officers

Pres., Mr. Ronald J. Habegger, 1535 Holliston Tr., Fort Wayne, IN 46825
Chpsn., Rev. Roger Andrews, 5622 Downing St., Portage, MI 49024
Vice-Chpsn., Rev. Steve Shaffer, 3115 W. Forsythe Rd., Peoria, IL 61614
Sec., Mark Wyse, 7183 SR 66, Archbold, OH 43502
Treas., Alan Rupp, 7304 Brackenwood Ct., Fort Wayne, IN 46825

Periodicals

FEConnections

Fellowship of Fundamental Bible Churches

The churches in this body represent the 1939 separation from the Methodist Protestant Church, when some 50 delegates and pastors (approximately one-third of the Eastern Conference) withdrew to protest the union of the Methodist Protestant Church with the Methodist Episcopal Church and the Methodist Episcopal Church South, and what they considered the liberal tendencies of those churches. These churches subsequently changed their name to the Bible Protestant Church. In 1985, this group again changed its name to the Fellowship of Fundamental Bible Churches to more accurately define their position.

As fundamentalists, this group strongly adheres to the historic fundamentals of the faith, including the doctrine of separation. This group accepts a literal view of the Bible and, consequently, accepts premillennial theology and a pre-tribulational rapture.

The churches are currently located in New Jersey, New York, Pennsylvania, Virginia, Michigan, and California. It is a fellowship of independent Bible and Baptist churches. Baptism, by immersion, and the Lord's Supper, as a memorial, are recognized as ordinances. There are currently 22 churches representing 1200 members. This constituent body is a member of the American Council of Christian Churches.

The Fellowship of Fundamental Bible Churches owns and operates Tri-State Bible Camp and Conference Center in Montague, New Jersey, oversees a mission board called Fundamental Bible Missions, and conducts a Bible Institute called Fundamental Bible Institute.

Headquarters

P.O. Box 206, Penns Grove, NJ 08069
Media Contact, Sec., Rev. Edmund G. Cotton, 80 Hudson St., Port Jervis, NY 12771 Tel. (845)856-7695
Email: FFBC-USA@juno.com
Website: www.churches-ffbc.org

Officers

Pres., Rev. Mark Franklin, 284 Whig Lane, Monroeville, NJ 08343 Tel. (609)881-0057
Vice Pres., Rev. Joe Roof, 17 Thoroughbred Lane, Albany, NY 12205 (518)459-2717
Sec., Rev.Ron Whitehead, 30 Elmwood Ave., Carneys Point, NJ 08069 (856)299-3307
Treas., Ken Thompson, 501 N. Main Street, Elmer, NJ 08318 (865)358-0515

Fellowship of Grace Brethren Churches

A division occurred in the Church of the Brethren in 1882 on the question of the legislative authority of the annual meeting. It resulted in the establishment of the Brethren Church under a legal charter requiring congregational government. This body divided in 1939 with the Grace Brethren establishing headquarters at Winona Lake, Ind., and the Brethren Church at Ashland, Ohio.

Headquarters

Media Contact, Fellowship Coord., Rev. Thomas Avey, P.O. Box 386, Winona Lake, IN 46590 Tel. (219)269-1269 Fax (219)269-4066
Email: fgbc@fgbc.org
Website: www.fgbc.org

Officers

Mod., Dr. Galen Wiley, 22713 Ellsworth Ave., Minerva, OH 44657
1st Mod.-Elect, Dr. James Custer, 2515 Carriage Rd., Powell, OH 43065
2nd Mod.-Elect, Dr. Ron Manahan, 2316 E. Kemo Ave., Warsaw, IN 46580Fellowship Coord., Rev. Thomas Avey, P.O. Box 386, Winona Lake, IN 46590 Tel. (219)269-1269 Fax (219)269-4066

118

Sec., Fellowship Coord., Rev. Thomas Avey, P.O. Box 386, Winona Lake, IN 46590

Treas., Thomas Staller, 2311 S. Cost-a-Plenty Drive, Warsaw, IN 46580

OTHER BOARDS

Grace Brethren International Missions, Exec. Dir., Rev. Tom Julien, P.O. Box 588, Winona Lake, IN 46590

Grace Brethren Home Missions, Exec. Dir., Larry Chamberlain, P.O. Box 587, Winona Lake, IN 46590

Grace College & Seminary, Pres., Ronald E. Manahan, 200 Seminary Dr., Winona Lake, IN 46590 Tel. (210)372-5100

Brethren Missionary Herald Co., Pub. & Gen. Mgr., James Bustram, P.O. Box 544, Winona Lake, IN 46590

CE National, Exec. Dir., Rev. Ed Lewis, P.O. Box 365, Winona Lake, IN 46590

Grace Brethren Navajo Ministries, Dir., Steve Galegor, Counselor, NM 87018

Grace Village Retirement Community, Admn., Jeff Carroll, P.O. Box 337, Winona Lake, IN 46590

Natl. Fellowship of Grace Brethren Ministries, Pres., Dr. Steve Taylor, 132 Summerall Ct., Aiken, SC 29801 Women's Missionary Council, Pres., Janet Minnix, 3314 Kenwick Tr., S.W., Roanoke, VA, 24015

Grace Brethren Men International, Pres., Morgan Burgess, 163 N. Franklin St., Delaware, OH 43015

Free Christian Zion Church of Christ

This church was organized in 1905 at Redemption, Ark., by a company of African-American ministers associated with various denominations. Its polity is in general accord with that of Methodist bodies.

Headquarters

1315 S. Hutchinson St., Nashville, AR 71852

Media Contact, Gen. Sec., Shirlie Cheatham

Officers

Chief Pastor, Willie Benson, Jr.

Free Methodist Church of North America

The Free Methodist Church was organized in 1860 in Western New York by ministers and laymen who had called the Methodist Episcopal Church to return to what they considered the original doctrines and lifestyle of Methodism. The issues included human freedom (anti-slavery), freedom and simplicity in worship, free seats so that the poor would not be discriminated against and freedom from secret oaths (societies) so the truth might be spoken freely at all times. The founders emphasized the teaching of the entire sanctification of life by means of grace through faith.

The denomination continues to be true to its founding principles. It communicates the gospel and its power to all people without discrimination through strong missionary, evangelistic and educational programs. Six colleges, a Bible college and numerous overseas schools train the youth of the church to serve in lay and ministerial roles.

Its members covenant to maintain simplicity in life, worship, daily devotion to Christ, responsible stewardship of time, talent and finance.

Headquarters

World Ministries Center, 770 N. High School Rd., Indianapolis, IN 46214 Tel. (317)244-3660 Fax (317)244-1247

Mailing Address, P.O. Box 535002, Indianapolis, IN 46253 Tel. (800)342-5531

Media Contact, Yearbook Ed., P.O. Box 535002, Indianapolis, IN 46253

Email: info@fmcna.org

Website: www.freemethodistchurch.org

Officers

Bishops, Bishop Roger W. Haskins, Jr.; Bishop Joseph F. James; Bishop David W. Kendall; Bishop David T. Roler; Bishop Mathew A. Thomas

General Conference Secretary, Mr John Ellis

Dir. of Administraion and Finance, Mr. Gary Kilgore

Free Methodist Communications, Gerald Coates

Free Methodist World Missions, Dr. Arthur Brown

Men's Ministries International, Director, Rev. Jeffrey Johnson

Women's Ministries International, President, LaWanda Bullock

Periodicals

Light and Life Magazine, *Free Methodist World Mission People*

Friends General Conference

Friends General Conference (FGC) is an association of fourteen yearly meetings open to all Friends meetings which wish to be actively associated with FGC's programs and services. Friends General Conference includes Baltimore, Canadian, Illinois, Lake Erie, New England, New York, Northern, Ohio Valley, Philadelphia, South Central and Southeastern Yearly Meetings; Alaska Friends Conference, Southern Appalachian Yearly Meeting and Association, and Piedmont Friends Fellowship; plus seven independently affiliated monthly meetings. Friends General Conference is primarily a service organization with the stated purpose of nurturing the spiritual life within its constituency of predominantly unprogrammed Friends. FGC offers services to all Friends, but has no authority over constituent meetings. A Central Committee, to which constituent Yearly Meetings name appointees (in proportion to membership), and its Executive Committee, are

119

responsible for the direction of FGC's programs and services which include a bookstore, conferences, and traveling ministries program. The 1995 Central Committee approved the following Minute of Purpose,

Friends General Conference is a Quaker organization in the unprogrammed tradition of the Religious Society of Friends which primarily serves affiliated yearly and monthly meetings. It is our experience that

- Faith is based on direct experience of God.
- Our lives witness this experience individually and corporately.
- By answering that of God in everyone, we build and sustain inclusive community.

Friends General Conference provides resources and opportunities that educate and invite members and attenders to experience, individually and corporately, God's living presence, and to discern and follow God's leadings. Friends General Conference reaches out to seekers and to other religious bodies inside and outside the Religious Society of Friends.

Headquarters

1216 Arch St., 2B, Philadelphia, PA 19107 Tel. (215)561-1700 Fax (215)561-0759 Email Friends@fgcquaker.org
Media Contact, Gen. Sec., Bruce Birchard
Email: friends@fgcquaker.org
Website: www.fgcquaker.org

Officers

Gen. Sec., Bruce Birchard, 1216 Arch St., 2B Philadelphia, PA 19107
Presiding Clerk, Marian Beane, 7125 Cardigan Ave, Charlotte, NC 28215
Treas., Byron Sandford, 515 E Capitol St. SE, Washington DC 20003-1142

YEARLY MEETINGS

Alaska Friends Conference, Clerk, Bill Schoder-Ehri, 480 Grubstake Ave., Homer, AK, 99603-7639 Tel. (907)479-5257, Email: lovenest@ptialaska.net
*Baltimore, Clerk, Lauri Perman; Staff, Robert H. Robinson, 17100 Quaker Ln., Sandy Spring, MD 20860 Tel. (301)774-7663, Email: rileyrobinson@bym-rsf.org
*Canadian, Clerk, Beverley Shepard; Staff, Kerry McAdam, 91A Fourth Ave., Ottawa, ON K1S 2L1 Tel. (613)235-8553, Email: cym-office@quaker.ca
Illinois, Clerk, Susanna Davison; Staff, Sharon Haworth, 608 W. Illinois St. Urbana, Il. 61801, Tel. (217)384-9591, Email: shaworth@sbc global. et
Lake Erie, Clerk, Shirley Bechil, 185 Pineviews Dr. Alma, MI 48801-2156 Tel. (989)463-4539, Email: bechill@alma.edu
*New England, Clerk, Christopher McCandless; Staff, Katharine Clark, 901 Pleasant St., Worcester, MA 01602-1908 Tel. (508)754-6760, Email: adminsec@neym.org

*New York, Clerk, Linda Chidsey; Staff, Helen Garay Toppins, 15 Rutherford Pl., New York, NY 10003 Tel. (212)673-5750, Email: office@ nyym.org
Northern, Clerk, Doug Kirk, 1602 Wicklowway Madison, WI 53711 Tel. (608)442-1642 Email: quirks@tds.net
Ohio Valley, Clerk, Virginia Wood; Staff, Krystin Schmidt, P.O. Box 1333, Richmond, IN 47374, Email: vwovym@donet.com
Philadelphia, Clerk, Thomas Swain, 1515 Cherry St., Philadelphia, PA 19102 Tel. (215)241-7210, Email: tswain@ccil.org
Piedmont Friends Fellowship, Clerk, Virginia Driscoll, 504 Willowbrookt Dr., Greensboro, NC 27403 Tel. (336)855-5233, Email: dachel-mama@yahoo.com
South Central, Clerk, John Coffin, 7106 Shamrock, Little Rock, AR 72205, Tel. (501)663-1439, Email: joticof@aol.com
*Southeastern, Clerk, Susan Taylor; Staff, Lyn Cope-Robinson P.O. Box 510975, Melbourne Beach, FL 32951 Tel. (321)724-1162, Email: admin@seym.org
Southern Appalachian, Clerk, Kristi Estes, Email: adminasst@sayma.org
*also affiliated with Friends United Meeting

Periodicals

Newsletter, FGConnections, Friends Journal

Friends International—please see Evangelical Friends International—North American Region.

Friends United Meeting*

Friends United Meeting was organized in 1902 (the name was changed in 1963 from the Five Years Meeting of Friends) as a confederation of North American yearly meetings to facilitate a united Quaker witness in missions, peace work Christian education and outreach.

Today Friends United Meeting is comprised of 26full-member and 3association member yearly meetings representing about half the Friends in the world. FUM's current work includes programs of mission and service, leadership development and outreach. FUM publishes Christian education curriculum, books of Quaker history and religious thought and a magazine, Quaker Life.

Headquarters

101 Quaker Hill Dr., Richmond, IN 47374-1980 Tel. (765)962-7573 Fax (765)966-1293
Media Contact, Interim General Secretary, Sylvia Graves
Email: info@fum.org
Website: www.fum.org

Officers

Presiding Clk., Brent McKinney
Treas., Don Garner
Interim Gen. Sec., Sylvia Graves

DEPARTMENTS

Quaker Hill Bookstore, Mgr., Paul Smith
Quaker Life, Ed., Trish Edwards-Konic
Friends United Press, Ed., Trish Edwards-Konic

YEARLY MEETINGS

Baltimore Yearly Meeting, 17100 Quaker Ln., Sandy Spring, MD 20860-1296 Tel. (301)774-7663 or (800)962-4766 Fax (301)774-7087 Lamar Matthew, clerk; Frank Massey, Gen. Sec.

Bware Yearly Meeting, P.O. Box 179, Suna, Kenya; Samuel Kaguni, Gen. Sect., Epainitus Adego, Gen Supt., Jonathan M. Sande, Presiding Clerk

Canadian Yearly Meeting, 91-A Fourth Ave., Ottawa ON K1S 2L1 Tel. & Fax (613)235-8553 Fax (613)235-1753; George McClure, Clerk

Central Yearly Meeting, P.O.Box 1510, Kakamega, Kenya, E. Africa, Evans Nyenzo, Gen. Supt.

Chavakali Yearly Meeting, P.O. Box 102, Chavakali, Kenya, East Africa; Andrew Mukulu, Gen. Sec., Wilson Andenya, Clerk

Cuba Yearly Meeting, Calle 20 #118 Esquina Paz, Reparto Vista, Alegre 80300, Hoguin, Cuba; Maria Renya Yi, President

East Africa Yearly Meeting of Friends, (Kaimosi) P.O. Box 35, Tiriki, Kenya, East Africa; Matthew Tsimbaki, Presiding Clerk, Ephraim Konsolo, Gen. Sec., Erastus Kesohole, Gen Supt.

East Africa Yearly Meeting of Friends (North), P.O. Box 544, Kitale, Kenya, East Africa; Geoffrey M. Wukwanja, Gen. Sec., Titus Adira, Gen. Supt., H. M Mukwanja. Presiding Clerk

VIHIGA Yearly Meeting of Friends, P.O. Box 160, Vihiga, Kenya, East Africa; Joseph Kisia, Presiding Clerk; Lam Kisanya Osodo, Gen. Sec., Gilbert Akenga Oyando, Gen. Supt.

Elgon East Yearly Meeting, P.O. Box 2322, Kitale, Kenya, East Africa; Maurice Simiyu, Gen. Supt, Philip Musungu, Gen. Sec., John Kitui, Presiding Clerk.

Elgon Religious Society of Friends, (West) P.O. Box 4, Lugulu Via Webuye, Kenya, East Africa, Tom Isiye, General Sec., John Ngoya, Gen. Supt., Charles Mbachi, Presiding Clerk

Evangelical Friends Church Uganda, P.O. Box 129, Mbale, Uganda, East Africa; Simon Tsapwe, Gen. Supt., Peter Kutosi, Gen. Sec.

Great Plains Yearly Meeting, 1262 Richland Rd., Lacon, IL 61540 Tel. (309)246-8397, Email: mesnerret@cconline.net, Neil Mesner, Clerk

Indiana Yearly Meeting, 4715 N. Wheeling Ave., Muncie, IN 47304-1222 Tel. (765)284-6900 Fax (765)284-8925, Email: iyminfo@iym.org; Susan Kirkpatrick, Clerk; Alan Weinacht, Gen. Supt.

Iowa Yearly Meeting, Box 657, Oskaloosa, IA 52577-0657 Tel. (641)673-9717 Fax (641) 673-9718, Email: wpdc9717@wmpenn.edu; Margaret Stoltzfus, Clerk, Ron Bryan, Gen. Superintendent

Jamaica Yearly Meeting, 4 Worthington Ave., Kingston 5, Jamaica WI Tel. (876)926-7371

Kakamega Yearly Meeting, P.O. Box 465, Kakamega, Kenya, East Africa; Jonathan Shisanya, Gen. Sec., Blastus Wawire, Presiding Clerk, Meschack Musindi, Gen. Supt.

Lugari Yearly Meeting, P.O. Box 483, Turbo, Kenya, East Africa; David A. Mulama, Gen. Sec., Joshuah Lilande Presiding Clerk, Japheth Vidolo, Gen. Supt.

Malava Yearly Meeting, P.O. Box 26, Malava, Kenya, East Africa; Andrew Namasaka Mulongo, Gen. Sec., Samson Marani, Presiding Clerk, Enoch Shinachi, Gen. Supt.

Nairobi Yearly Meeting, P.O. Box 8321, Nairobi, Kenya, East Africa; Benson Simiyu, Gen. Supt., Zablon Isaac Malenge, Gen. Sec., Nilson Shivachi, Vice President

New England Yearly Meeting, 901 Pleasant St., Worcester, MA 01602-1908 Tel. (508)754-6760, Email: neym@neym.org; Deana Chase, Clerk; Jonathan Vogel-Borne, Field Secretary

New York Yearly Meeting, 15 Rutherford Pl., New York, NY 10003 Tel. (212)673-5750, Email: office@nyym.org; Linda Chidsey, Clerk; Helen Garay Toppins, Admin. Sec.

North Carolina Yearly Meeting, 5506 W. Friendly Ave., Greensboro, NC 27410 Tel. (336)292-6957 Email: ncfriends@juno.com; Michael Fulp, Clerk; John Porter, Gen. Superintendent

Southeastern Yearly Meeting, P.O. Box 510795, Melbourne Beach, FL 32951-0795 Tel. (321) 724-1162, Lyn Cope-Robinson, Adm. Sec., Email: seym@bv.net

Tanzania Yearly Meeting, P.O. Box 151, Mugumu, Serengeti, Tanzania; Joseph Lavuna Oguma, Gen. Supt. & Clerk

Tuloi Yearly Meeting, P.O. Box 102, Kapsabet, Kenya, East Africa; Joseph Anyonge Mulama, Presiding clk., Solomon Mwanzi, Gen. Supt., Frederick Inyangu, Gen. Sec.

Uganda Yearly Meeting, P.O. Box 2384, Mbale, Uganda, East Africa; Francis Wamala, Gen. Supt., Andrew H.S. Kurima, Gen. Sec., Sylvester Khasufa, Clerk

Vokoli Yearly Meetings, P.O. Box 266, Wodanga, Kenya, East Africa; Javan Chondo, Gen. Sec., Hannington Mbato, Presiding Clerk, Thomas Kivuya, Gen Supt.

Western Yearly Meeting, P.O. Box 70, Plainfield, IN 46168; Tel (317)839-2789 and (317)839-2849 Fax (317)839-2616, Steve and Marlene Pediso, Co-Superintendents, Wayne Carter, Clerk

Wilmington Yearly Meeting, Pyle Center Box 1194, Wilmington, OH 45177 Tel. (937)382-2491 Fax (937)382-7077, Email: phackney@wilmington.edu, Gary Farlow, Clerk; Marvin Hall, Ex. Sec.

121

Quaker Life, Trish Edwards-Konic

Full Gospel Assemblies International

The Full Gospel Assemblies International was founded in 1962 under the leadership of Dr. Charles Elwood Strauser. The roots of Full Gospel Assemblies may be traced to 1947 with the beginning of the Full Gospel Church of Coatesville, Pennsylvania. As an Assemblies of God Pentecostal church, the Full Gospel Church of Coatesville was active in evangelization and educational ministries to the community. In service to the ministers and students of the Full Gospel Church ministries, the Full Gospel Trinity Ministerial Fellowship was formed in 1962, later changing its name to Full Gospel Assemblies International.

Retaining its original doctrine and faith, Full Gospel Assemblies is Trinitarian, believing that the Bible is God's infallible Word to mankind, baptism in the Holy Spirit according to Acts 2, divine healing is made possible by the sufferings of our Lord Jesus Christ, and in the imminent return of Christ for those who love him.

The body of Full Gospel Assemblies is an evangelical missionary fellowship sponsoring ministry at home and abroad, composed of self governing ministries and churches. Congregations, affiliate ministries and clerical body are located throughout the United States and over 15 countries of the world.

Headquarters

International Headquarters: 3018 Lincoln Hwy, Parkesburg, PA

Mailing Address, P.O. Box 1230, Coatesville, PA 19320 Tel. (610)857-2357 Fax (610)857-3109

Media Contact, Simeon Strauser

Officers

Gen. Supt., Dr. AnnaMae Strauser

Exec. Dir. of Ministry, J. Victor Fisk

Exec. Dir of Admn., Simeon Strauser

Exec. Dir. of Communications, Archie Neale

Exec. Sec., Betty Stewart

Exec. Trustee, Edward Popovich

National Ministers Council and Trustees

Chpsn. Simeon Strauser, Sadsburyville, PA

James Capets, Trafford, PA

Donald Schiemant, Marilla, NY

Michael Mathews, Eau Claire, WI

Bette Elgin, Zenia, CA

John Tortoriello, Fort Lauderdale, FL

Raymond Favicha, Spring Hill, FL

Carol Strauser, Parkesburg, PA

Periodicals

Full Gospel Ministries Outreach Report, *Denominational Code*

Full Gospel Fellowship of Churches and Ministers International

In the early 1960s a conviction grew in the hearts of many ministers that there should be closer fellowship between the people of God who believed in the apostolic ministry. At the same time, many independent churches were experiencing serious difficulties in receiving authority from the IRS to give governmentally accepted tax-exempt receipts for donations.

In September 1962 a group of ministers met in Dallas, Texas, to form a Fellowship to give expression to the essential unity of the Body of Christ under the leadership of the Holy Spirit— a unity that goes beyond individuals, churches or organizations. This was not a movement to build another denomination, but rather an effort to join ministers, churches and ministry organizations of like mind across denominational lines.

To provide opportunities for fellowship and to support the objectives and goals of local and national ministries- regional conventions and an annual international convention are held.

Headquarters

1000 N. Belt Line Rd., Irving, TX 75061 Tel. (214)492-1254

Media Contact & Convention Planner, Sec., Dr. Harry Schmidt, 400 E. Gregory, Mt. Prospect, IL 60056

Email: TheFellowship@fgfcmi.org

Website: www.fgfcmi.org

Officers

Pres., Dr. Don Arnold, P.O. Box 324, Gadsden, AL 35901

1st Vice Pres., Dr. Harry Schmidt, 400 E. Gregory, Mt. Prospect, IL 60056

Sec., Rev. Deloris Kendrick, 10201 Beacon Ave. S., Seattle, WA 98178

Treas., Rev. Gene Evans P.O. Box 813 Douglasville, GA 30133

CFO, Dr. S.K. Biffle, 1000 N. Belt Line Rd., Irving, TX 75061

Ofc. Sec., Mrs. Anita Sullivan & Voni Lassiter

Receptionist, Mrs. Nita Biffle

Vice Pres. at Large, Rev. Maurice Hart, P.O. Box 4316, Omaha, NE 68104; Rev. Don Westbrook, 3518 Rose of Sharon Rd., Durham, NC 27705

Chmn. of Evangelism, David Ellis

Chmn of Mission, Rev. David Robinson, 1121 Shuler St., Elgin. IL 60123

Chmn of Youth, Rev. Steven K. Biffle, 3833 Westerville Rd., Columbus, OH 43224

Past Pres., Dr. James Helton

REGIONAL VICE PRESIDENTS

Southeast, Rev. Steve Holder, 103 Hawkins Dr., Pikeville, NC 27863

South Central, Rev. Billy Gibson, 4249 Winding Brook Dr., Plano, TX 75093

Southwest, Dr. R.G. Dunbar, 121 N. 32nd Street, Colorado Springs, CO 80904

Northeast, Rev. David Ellis, 3636 Winchester Rd., Allertown, PA 18104

North Central, Rev. David Robinson, 1121 Shuler Street, Elgin, IL 60123

Northwest, Rev. Jon R. Engstrom, 19605 12th Ave. W, Lynnwood, WA 98036

Periodicals

Fellowship Tidings

Fundamental Methodist Church, Inc.

This group traces its origin through the Methodist Protestant Church. It withdrew from The Methodist Church and organized on August 27, 1942.

Headquarters

1034 N. Broadway, Springfield, MO 65802
Media Contact, Betty Nicholson, Rt. 2, Box 397, Ash Grove, MO 65604 Tel. (417)672-2268

Officers

Treas., and Sec., Betty Nicholson, Rt. 2, Box 397, Ash Grove, MO 65604 Tel. (417)672-2268

General Association of General Baptists

Similar in doctrine to those General Baptists organized in England in the 17th century, the first General Baptist churches were organized on the Midwest frontier following the Second Great Awakening. The first church was established by the Rev. Benoni Stinson in 1823 at Evansville, Ind.

Stinson's major theological emphasis was general atonement—Christ tasted death for every man. The group also allows for the possibility of apostasy. It practices open Communion and believer's baptism by immersion.

Called "liberal" Baptists because of their emphasis on the freedom of man, General Baptists organized a General Association in 1870 and invited other "liberal" Baptists (e.g., "Free Will" and Separate Baptists) to participate.

The policy-setting body is composed of delegates from local General Baptist churches and associations. Each local church is autonomous but belongs to an association. The group currently consists of more than 60 associations in 16 states, as well as associations in the Philippines, Guam, Saipan, Jamaica , Honduras, and India. Ministers and deacons are ordained by a presbytery.

The denomination operates Oakland City University in Oakland City, Indiana, and Nursing Homes in Illinois and Missouri.. General Baptists belong to the Baptist World Alliance, the North American Baptist Fellowship and the National Association of Evangelicals.

Headquarters

100 Stinson Dr., Poplar Bluff, MO 63901 Tel. (573)785-7746 Fax (573)785-0564
Media Contact, Exec. Dir., Dr. Ron Black

Officers

Mod., Rev. Clint Cook
Clk., Rev. James Schremp
Exec. Dir., Dr. Ron Black

OTHER ORGANIZATIONS

International Missions, Dir., Rev. Jack Eberhardt
National Missions, Dir., Dr. Stephen Gray
Women's Ministries, Dir., Barbara Wigger
Oakland City University, Dr. Ray Barber, Executive Vice-President, 138 North Lucretia St., Oakland City, IN 47660
Congregational Ministries, Dir., Dr. Franklin Dumond, 100 Stinson Dr., Poplar Bluff, MO 63901
Pastoral Ministries, Dir., Dr. John Sloan, 100 Stinson Dr., Poplar Bluff, MO 63901
Admin., Financial Services, Financial Officer, Linda McDonough, 100 Stinson Dr., Poplar Bluff, MO 63901
Stinson Press, Inc., Pres., Rev. Dale Bates, 400 Stinson Dr., Poplar Bluff, MO 63901
Nursing Home Board, CEO Rev. Jack Cole, Rt. #3, Box 650 , Campbell, MO 63933
Compassionate Care Adoption Agency, Dir., Rev. Darrell Hillouse, 26 Jones Road, Sebree, KY 42455
Stewardship/General Baptist Investment Fund Dir., Rev. Stephen Naff, 100 Stinson Dr., Poplar Bluff, MO 63901

General Association of Regular Baptist Churches

This association was founded in May, 1932, in Chicago by a group of churches which had withdrawn from the Northern Baptist Convention (now the American Baptist Churches in the U.S.A.) because of doctrinal differences. Its Confession of Faith, which it requires all churches to subscribe to, is essentially the old, historic New Hampshire Confession of Faith with a premillennial ending applied to the last article.

The churches of the General Association of Regular Baptist Churches voluntarily join together to accomplish four goals. (1) Champion Biblical truth—committed to communicating the whole counsel of God in its timeless relevance. (2) Impact the world for Christ—obeying the Lord's Great Commission to take the life-changing gospel to the entire world. (3) Perpetuate Its Baptist heritage—faithfully promoting its Scriptural legacy and identity. (4) Advancing GARBC churches—strengthening existing churches and planting new churches for the purposes of evangelism and edification.

Headquarters

1300 N. Meacham Rd., Schaumburg, IL 60173 Tel. (847)843-1600 Fax (847)843-3757
Media Contact, Natl. Rep., Dr. John Greening
Email: garbc@garbc.org
Website: www.garbc.org

Officers

Chpsn., Rev. Braaley Quick

123

Vice Chpsn., David Warren
Treas., Michael Nolan
Sec., John Hastag, III
Natl. Rep., Dr. John Greening

Periodicals

Baptist Bulletin, Synergy Newsletter, E-Info Newsletter

General Church of the New Jerusalem

The General Church of the New Jerusalem, also called the New Church, was founded in 1897. It is based on the teachings of the 18th Century scientist Emanuel Swedenborg, and stresses the oneness of God, who is the Lord Jesus Christ, a life of faith and love in service to others, in true married love, and in life after death.

Headquarters

1100 Cathedral Rd, P.O. Box 743, Bryn Athyn, PA 19009 Tel. (267)502-2682
Media Contact, Ed., Church Journal, Rev. Kurt H. Asplundh, Box 26, Bryn Athyn, PA 19009 Tel. (267)502-2682 Fax (267)502-4929
Email: svsimpso@newchurch.edu
Website: www.newchurch.org

Officers

Presiding Bishop, Rt. Rev. Thomas L. Kline
Sec., Susan V. Simpson
Treas., Dvid Frazier

Periodicals

New Church Life

General Conference of Mennonite Brethren Churches

A small group, requesting that closer attention be given to prayer, Bible study and a consistent lifestyle, withdrew from the larger Mennonite Church in the Ukraine in 1860. Anabaptist in origin, the group was influenced by Lutheran pietists and Baptist teachings and adopted a quasi-congregational form of church government. In 1874 and years following, small groups of these German-speaking Mennonites left Russia, settled in Kansas and then spread to the Midwest west of the Mississippi and into Canada. Some years later the movement spread to California and the West Coast. In 1960, the Krimmer Mennonite Brethren Conference merged with this body.

Today the General Conference of Mennonite Brethren Churches conducts services in many European languages as well as in Vietnamese, Mandarin and Hindi. It works with other denominations in missionary and development projects in 25 countries outside North America.

Headquarters

4812 E. Butler Ave., Fresno, CA 93727 Tel. (209)452-1713 Fax (209)452-1752
Media Contact, Exec. Sec., Marvin Hein

Officers

Mod., Ed Boschman, 12630 N. 103rd Ave., Suite 215, Sun City, AZ 85351
Asst. Mod., Herb Kopp, 200 McIvor Ave., Winnipeg, NB R20 028
Sec., Valerie Rempel
Exec. Sec., Marvin Hein

Periodicals

Christian Leader

Grace Gospel Fellowship

The Grace Gospel Fellowship was organized in 1944 by a group of pastors who held to a dispensational interpretation of Scripture. Most had ministries in the Midwest. Two prominent leaders were J. C. O'Hair of Chicago and Charles Baker of Milwaukee. Subsequent to 1945, a Bible Institute was founded (now Grace Bible College of Grand Rapids, Mich.), and a previously organized foreign mission (now Grace Ministries International of Grand Rapids) was affiliated with the group. Churches have now been established in most sections of the country.

The body has remained a fellowship, each church being autonomous in polity. All support for its college, mission and headquarters is on a contributory basis.

The binding force of the Fellowship has been the members' doctrinal position. They believe in the Deity and Saviorship of Jesus Christ and subscribe to the inerrant authority of Scripture. Their method of biblical interpretation is dispensational, with emphasis on the distinctive revelation to and the ministry of the apostle Paul.

Headquarters

Media Contact, Pres., Frosty Hansen, 2125 Martindale SW, P.O. Box 9432, Grand Rapids, MI 49509 Tel. (616)245-0100 Fax (616)241-2542
Email: ggfinc@aol.com
Website: www.ggfusa.org

Officers

Pres., Traynor ("Frosty") Hansen, Jr.

OTHER ORGANIZATIONS

Grace Bible College, Pres., Rev. Ken Kemper, 1011 Aldon St. SW, Grand Rapids, MI 49509
Grace Ministries Intl., Exec. Dir., Dr. Samuel Vinton, 2125 Martindale Ave. SW, Grand Rapids, MI 49509
Prison Mission Association, Gen. Dir., Donald Sommer, P.O. Box 1587, Port Orchard, WA 98366-0140
Grace Publications Inc., Exec. Dir., Wayne Schoonover, 2125 Martindale Ave. SW, Grand Rapids, MI 49509
Bible Doctrines to Live By, Exec. Dir., Lee Homoki, P.O. Box 2351, Grand Rapids, MI 49501

Periodicals

Truth

124

Greek Orthodox Archdiocese of America*

The Orthodox Church today, numbering over 250 million worldwide, is a communion of self-governing Churches, each administratively independent of the other, but united by a common faith and spirituality. Their underlying unity is based on identity of doctrines, sacramental life and worship, which distinguishes Orthodox Christianity. All recognize the spiritual preeminence of the Ecumenical Patriarch of Constantinople who is acknowledged as *primus inter pares*, first among equals. All share full communion with one another. The living tradition of the Church and the principles of concord and harmony are expressed through the common mind of the universal episcopate as the need arises. In all other matters, the internal life of each independent Church is administered by the bishops of that particular Church. Following the ancient principle of the one people of God in each place and the universal priesthood of all believers, the laity share equally in the responsibility for the preservation and propagation of the Christian faith and Church.

THE GREEK ORTHODOX ARCHDIOCESE OF AMERICA

Before the establishment of an Archdiocese in the Western Hemisphere there were numerous communities of Greek Orthodox Christians. The first Greek Orthodox community in the Americas was founded in New Orleans, LA by a small colony of Greek merchants. History also records that on June 26,1768 the first Greek colonists landed at St. Augustine,FL, the oldest city in America. The first permanent community was founded in New York City in 1892, today's Archdiocesan Cathedral of the Holy Trinity and the See of the Archbishop of America. The Greek Orthodox Archdiocese of North and South America was incorporated in 1921 and officially recognized by the State of New York in 1922.

The Greek Orthodox Archdiocese of America is composed of the Direct Archdiocesan District—New York and eight Metropolises: Chicago,Pittsburgh, Boston, Denver, Atlanta, Detroit, San Francisco and New Jersey. It is governed by the Archbishop and the Synod of Bishops. The Synod of Bishops is headed by the Archbishop and comprised of the Metropolitans who are in charge of a metropolis.It has all the authority and responsibility which the Church canons provide for a provincial synod.

Headquarters

8-10 E. 79th St., New York, NY 10021 Tel. (212)570-3500 Fax (212)570-3569
Media Contact, Nikki Stephanopoulos, Director, News and Information/Public Affairs Tel. (212)570-3530 Fax. (212)774-0215 Email, nikki@goarch.org
Email: archdiocese@goarch.org
Website: www.goarch.org

HOLY EPARCHIAL SYNOD OF BISHOPS

His Eminence Archbishop Demetrios, Primate of the Greek Orthodox Archdiocese of America, Exarch of the Atlantic and Pacific Oceans, Chairman of the Holy Synod of Bishops, Greek Orthodox Church in America, 8-10 East 79th Street, New York, NY 10021, Tel. (212) 570-3500 Fax (212)570-3592

METROPOLIS

His Eminence Metropolitan Iakovos of Chicago,Metropolis of Chicago,40 East Burton Place, Chicago, IL 60610, Tel. (312) 337-4130 Fax (312)337-9391
His Eminence Metropolitan Maximos of Pittsburgh,Metropolis of Pittsburgh, 5201 Ellsworth Avenue, Pittsburgh, PA 15232, Tel. (412)621-5529 Fax (412)621-1522
His Eminence Metropolitan Methodios of Boston,Metropolis of Boston, 162 Goddard Avenue, Brookline, MA 02146, Tel. (617)277-4742 Fax (617)739-9229
His Eminence Metropolitan Isaiah of Denver, Metropolis of Denver, 4610 East Alameda Avenue, Suite D1, Denver, CO 80222, Tel. (303)333-7794 Fax (303)333-7796
His Eminence Metropolitan Alexios of Atlanta, Metropolis of Atlanta, 2480 Clairmont Road NE, Atlanta, GA 30329, Tel. (404)634-9345 Fax (404)634-2471
His Eminence Metropolitan Nicholas of Detroit, Metropolis of Detroit, 19405 Renfrew Road, Detroit, MI 48221, Tel. (313)664-5433 Fax. (313)864-5543
His Eminence Metropolitan Gerasimos of San Francisco,Metropolis of San Francisco, 372 Santa Clara Avenue, San Francisco, CA 94127, Tel. (415)753-3075 Fax (415)753-1165
His Eminence Metropolitan Evangelos of New Jersey, Metropolis of New Jersey 629 Springfield Road, Kenilworth, NJ 07033, Tel. (908)686-0003 Fax (908)686-0046
Auxiliary Bishops: His Grace Bishop Dimitrios of Xanthos, His Grace Bishop Savas of Troas,His Grace Bishop Andonios of Phasiane, His Grace Bishop Demetrios of Mokissos.

CLERGY-LAITY CONGRESS

The Clergy-Laity Congress, the highest legislative body of the Archdiocese, is convened biennially and presided over by the Archbishop. It is concerned with all matters, other than doctrinal or canonical, affecting the life, growth and unity of the Church, the institutions, finances, administration, educational and philanthropic concerns and its increasing growing role in the life of the nations of the Western Hemisphere. The delegates are the pastors and elected lay representatives.

There are 560 parishes, 840 priests and approximately 1.5 million faithful in the Greek Orthodox Archdiocese of America

THE ARCHDIOCESAN COUNCIL

The Archdiocesan Council is the deliberative body of the Greek Orthodox Archdiocese which meets in the interim period between Clergy-Laity Congresses, held every two years.

Executive Committee, His Eminence Archbishop Demetrios Chairman

The Holy Synod of Bishops

Vice Chairman, Michael Jaharis; Nicholas Bouras, Treasurer; Catherine Bouffides-Walsh, Secretary; George Behrakis, Elini Huszagh, Peter Kikis, George Mathews, Anthony Stefanis, George Vourvoulias; Emanuel G. Demos, General Counsel to the Archdiocese.

INSTITUTIONS

Archdiocesan Cathedral of the Holy Trinity
The Rev. Frank Marangos, Dean, 319-337 East 74th Street, New York, NY 10021 Tel. (212)288-3215 Fax (212)288-5876 Website: www.thecathedral.goarch.org

Hellenic College/Holy Cross School of Theology, The Rev. Nicholas Triantafilou, President, 50 Goddard Avenue, Brookline, MA 02445 Tel. (617)731-3500 Fax (617)850-1460, Email: admission@hchc.edu

Saint Basil Academy, The Rev. Constantine L. Sitaras, Director, 79 Saint Basil Road Garrison, NY 10524, Tel. (845)424-3500 Fax (845)424-4172, Email: stbasil@bestweb.net, Website: www.stbasil.goarch.org

St. Michael's Home, His Grace Bishop Andonios of Phasiane,Director, 3 Lehman Terrace, Yonkers, NY 10705 Tel. (914)476-3374 Fax (914)476-1744, Email: Stmichaelshome@msn.com, Website: stmichael.goarch.org

ARCHDIOCESE OF NEW YORK

Office of the Archbishop, Alice Keurian; Director; Office of the Chancellor,His Grace Bishop Savas of Troas, Chancellor; Office of Administration, Jerry Dimitriou, Executive Director.

ARCHDIOCESAN DEPARTMENTS

Registry, Finance, Stewardship & LOGOS, Religious Education, Greek Education, Communications, Internet Ministries, Information Technologies, Youth and Young Adults, Camping Ministry, Ionian Village Ecumenical, Interfaith/Interchurch Marriages, Archives, Benefits

Related Organizations, auxiliaries

Ladies Philoptochos Society, Presbyters Council, Sisterhood of Presvyteres, Retired Clergy of America, National Forum of Greek Orthodox Musicians, Hellenic Cultural Center, Archons of the Ecumenical Patriarchate, Archbishop Iakovos Leadership 100 Endowment Fund, St. Photios National Shrine, International Orthodox Christian Charities (IOCC), Orthodox Christian Mission Center, Trinity Children & Family Services.

OTHER JURISDICTIONS OF THE ECU-MENICAL PATRIARCHATE IN THE USA

Albanian Orthodox Diocese in America; Belarusian Council of Orthodox Churches in North America; American Carpatho-Russian Orthodox Greek Catholic Diocese of the USA; Ukrainian Orthodox Church of the USA

Periodicals

THE ORTHODOX OBSERVER

The Holy Eastern Orthodox Catholic and Apostolic Church in North America, Inc.

Canonically established by the Russian Orthodox Synod of Bishops in North America on Feb. 2, 1927 this church was incorporated on Feb. 1, 1928 by Archbishop Aftimios Ofiesh, the first Archbishop-president. Archbishop Aftimios continued as head of this church until he reposed in July 1966. The name and logo are registered service marks of this church. We are a western rite Church but some of our clergy do celebrate the Eastern Liturgy.

The first Synod included Archbishop Aftimios and Bishops Sophronios and Zuk. Over the years many have claimed to be this Church, its successor, this Church under a different name or having our lines. These are members of the independent movement who claim to have lines of apostolic succession that are traced back to us but not recognized by this or nay canonical Church since they were not administered in accordance with the Rudder (Canons) of the Orthodox Church.

Headquarters

Monastery: St. Pachomius Monastery, P.O.Box 8122, Columbus, OH 43201 Tel. (614)297-8055

Primate, Metropolitan Victor
Email: tmetropolitan@theocacna.org
Website: www.theocacna.org

Officers

Archbishop Peter Mar Kepa—Archdiocese of the East

Metropolitan Victor—Archdiocese of the West

Bishop Christopher—Diocese of Houston, Tx.

Bishop Cassian—Diocese of Columbus, Oh.

Bishop Arthur—Diocese of Michigan

SYNOD ADVISORS

Archbishop James

Bishop Donald

Society: The Society of Clerks Secular of St. Basil, est. 1931

Holy Synod for the American Diaspora

The Christian Church was established by the Lord Jesus Christ and His Holy Apostles in Jerusalem in 33 A.D. From Jerusalem, the Church spread to other centers of the known world, including Constantinople (founded in 37

A.D.) and Kiev (45 A.D.), founded by St. Andrew the First-Called Holy Apostle. In 864, missionary of the Church of Constantinople further extended the Orthodox Christian Faith in present-day Russia. In 988, Rus' Prince Vladimir converted and declared Orthodoxy the State religion, while hundreds of thousands were baptized in the Dnieper River at Kiev. The resulting Russian Orthodox Church became the greatest safe-guard and body of Orthodox Christians in the world.

The history of Apostolic Orthodox Catholic Christianity began in 1794 when Russian Orthodox Church missionaries established the first Orthodox mission on North American soil at present-day Kodiak, Alaska. Their missionary efforts continued down the Pacific coast in 1824, then across the whole continent. Being the canonical founder of Orthodox Christianity in North America, the Russian Orthodox Church maintained and presided over all Orthodox missions, churches, and Christians throughout North America without question or challenge for over 100 years. However, the 1917 Bolshevik Revolution which resulted in severe persecution and imprisonment of the Russian Orthodox Mother Church also resulted in the unrestrained rise of old-country nationalism and great ethnic turbulence between Orthodox Catholic Christians and their churches in North America. They seperated and divided, often violently, along ethnic and nationalist lines with each creating their own old-world ethnic administrations. The once long-held unity and single Orthodox Church canonical administration in North America was destroyed.

The Holy Synod for the American Diaspora is canonically independent and indigenous to North America and comprised of bishops, clergy and faithful possessing unbroken Apostolic Succession since the time of Jesus Christ's appointment of His Twelve Holy Apostles to the present day through American Orthodoxy's Luminary and Defender, Russian Orthodox Prelate-Archbishop Aftimios Ofiesh of Blessed Memory.

The Holy Synod for the American Diaspora maintains unquestionable, canonical Apostolic Succession passed on to its bishops through its Russian Orthodox Mother Church by Archbishop Aftimios Ofiesh, his succeeding Bishops Sophronios Beshara and Christopher Contogeorge, their legal successors and through consecrating support of such memorable Orthodox leaders as Russian Patriarchal Exarch of North America Metropolitan Benjamin Fedchenkov and and Albanian Orthodox Church Metropolitan Theophan Noli. In 1945, the Apostolic Succession and Canonicity of these bishops "and their successors" were declared in binding agreement to be unquestionable, valid, authentic and independent by the Orthodox Church Ecumenical Patriarchate of Constantinople, and recognition was further-more attested to in 1951. English-speaking and non-ethnic restrictive, the Holy Synod for the American Diaspora's further validity is evidenced by its life, mind, discourse and teaching all being governed and directed in accordance with the Sacred Canons of the Most Ancient Holy Orthodox Catholic Church. The Holy Synod for the American Diaspora embraces the ideals and theology of Orthodoxy and freedom which Archbishop Aftimios Ofiesh stood for, taught and passed on by selfless devotion and love for Christ and His Church, and by his personal example.

Headquarters

Holy Synod for the American Diaspora, P.O. Box 346, Seward, NE 68434 Tel. (503)375-6175

Media Contact, Most Rev. Aftimios (L. Sinclair), Vice Presiding Archbishop, 4696 Horseshoe Court SE, Salem, OR 97301; Tel (575)375-6175

Email: synod@oldorthodox.org

Officers

Archbishop, Most Rev. Mar Melchizedek

The Secretary of the Synod, Most. Rev. Bishop Aftimios

Synod of Bishops, Most Rev. Bishop Spyridon, Most Rev. Bishop Valerian, Most Rev. Bishop Maximus

SEMINARY

St Elias School of Orthodox Theology, P.O. Box 346, Seward, NE 68434, Tel. (402)643-9365

Holy Ukrainian Autocephalic Orthodox Church in Exile

This church was organized in a parish in New York in 1951 by Ukrainian laymen and clergy who settled in the Western Hemisphere after World War II. In 1954 two bishops, immigrants from Europe, met with clergy and laymen and formally organized the religious body.

Headquarters

103 Evergreen St., W. Babylon, NY 11704

Officers

Admn., Rt. Rev. Serhij K. Pastukhiv

House of God, Which is the Church of the Living God, the Pillar and Ground of the Truth, Inc.

This body, founded by Mary L. Tate in 1919, is episcopally organized.

Headquarters

1301 N. 58th St., Philadelphia, PA 19131

Media Contact, Sec., Rose Canon, 515 S. 57th St., Philadelphia, PA 19143 Tel. (215)474-8913

Officers

Bishop, Raymond W. White, 6107 Cobbs Creek Pkwy., Philadelphia, PA 19143 Tel. (215)748-6338

127

Hungarian Reformed Church in America*

A Hungarian Reformed Church was organized in New York in 1904 in connection with the Reformed Church of Hungary. In 1922, the Church in Hungary transferred most of its congregations in the United States to the Reformed Church in the U.S. Some, however, preferred to continue as an autonomous, self-supporting American denomination, and these formed the Free Magyar Reformed Church in America. This group changed its name in 1958 to Hungarian Reformed Church in America.

This church is a member of the World Alliance of Reformed Churches, Presbyterian and Congregational, the World Council of Churches and the National Council of Churches USA.

Headquarters

Bishop's Office, 13 Grove St., Poughkeepsie, NY 12601 Tel. (914)454-5735

Officers

Bishop, Rt. Rev. Alexander Forro
Chief Lay-Curator, Prof. Stephen Szabo, 464 Forest Ave., Paramus, NJ 07652
Gen. Sec. (Clergy), Rt. Rev. Stefan M. Torok, 331 Kirkland Pl., Perth Amboy, NJ 08861 Tel. (908)442-7799
Gen Sec. (Lay), Zoltan Ambrus, 3358 Maple Dr., Melvindale, MI 48122
Eastern Classes, Dean (Senior of the Deans, Chair in Bishop's absence), Very Rev. Imre Bertalan, 10401 Grosvenor Pl., #1521, Rockville, MD 20852 Tel. (301)493-5036 Fax (301)571-5111; Lay-Curator, Balint Balogh, 519 N. Muhlenberg St., Allentown, PA 18104
New York Classes, Supervisor, Rt. Rev. Alexander Forro; Lay-Curator, Laszlo B. Vanyi, 229 E 82nd St., New York, NY 10028
Western Classes, Dean, V. Rev. Andor Demeter, 3921 W. Christy Dr., Phoenix, AZ 85029; Lay-Curator, Zolton Kun, 2604 Saybrook Dr., Pittsburgh, PA 15235

Periodicals

Magyar Egyhaz

Hutterian Brethren

Small groups of Hutterites derive their names from Jacob Hutter, a 16th-century Anabaptist who taught true discipleship after accepting Jesus as Saviour, advocated communal ownership of property and was burned as a heretic in Austria in 1536.

Many believers are of German descent and still use their native tongue at home and in church. Much of the denominational literature is produced in German and English. "Colonies" share property, practice non-resistance, dress plainly, do not participate in politics and operate their own schools. There are 428 colonies with 42,000 members in North America. Each congregation conducts its own youth work through Sunday school. Until age 15, children attend German and English school which is operated by each colony. All youth ages 15 to 20 attend Sunday school. They are baptized as adults upon confession of faith, around age 20.

Headquarters

Media Contact, Philip J. Gross, 3610 N. Wood Rd., Reardon, WA 99029 Tel. (509)299-5400 Fax (509)299-3099
Email: philsjg@juno.com

Officers

Smiedleut Chmn., No. 1, Jacob Waldner—Blumengard Colony, Box 13 Plum Coulee, MB R0G 1R0 Tel. (204)829-3527
Smiedleut Chmn., No. 2, Jacob Wipf, Spring Creek Colony, 36562 102 Street, Forbes, ND 58439 Tel. (701)358-8621
Dariusleut, Chmn., No. 1, Martin Walter, Springpoint Colony, Box 249, Pincher Creek, AB T0K 1W0 Tel. (403)553-4368
Lehrerleut, Chmn., Rev. John Wipf, Rosetown Colony, Box 1509, Rosetown, SK S0L 2V0 Tel. (306)882-3344

IFCA International, Inc.

This group of churches was organized in 1930 at Cicero, Illinois, by representatives of the American Council of Undenominational Churches and representatives of various independent churches. The founding churches and members had separated themselves from various denominational affiliations. Founders included J. Oliver Buswell of Wheaton College, Billy McCarrell of Cicero Bible Church and Moody Bible Institute, and M. R. DeHaan of Grand Rapids, MI and Radio Bible Class. Members have included J. Vernon McGee, Charles Ryrie, John Walvoord, and John MacArthur.

The IFCA provides a way for independent churches and ministers to unite in close fellowship and cooperation, in defense of the fundamental teachings of Scripture and in the proclamation of the gospel of God's grace.

Today it consists of 1000 associated churches and 1200 individual members (pastors, professors, missionaries, chaplains, and other Christian workers).

Headquarters

3520 Fairlanes, Grandville, MI 49418 Tel. (616)531-1840 Fax (616)531-1814
Mailing Address, P.O. Box 810, Grandville, MI 49468-0810
Media Contact, Exec. Dir., Rev. Les Lofquist
Email: office@ifca.org
Website: www.ifca.org

Officers

Exec. Dir., Rev. Les Lofquist
Pres., Dr. Roy Sprague, Lakewood, WA

Periodicals
The Voice

International Church of the Foursquare Gospel

Founded by Aimee Semple McPherson in 1927, the International Church of the Foursquare Gospel proclaims the message of Jesus Christ the Savior, Healer, Baptizer with the Holy Spirit and Soon-coming King. Headquartered in Los Angeles, this evangelistic missionary body of believers consists of nearly 1,900 churches in the United States and Canada. The International Church of the Foursquare Gospel is incorporated in the state of California and governed by a Board of Directors who direct its corporate affairs. A Foursquare Cabinet, consisting of the Corporate Officers, Board of Directors and District Supervisors of the various districts of the Foursquare Church in the United States and other elected or appointed members, serves in an advisory capacity to the President and the Board of Directors. Each local Foursquare Church is a subordinate unit of the International Church of the Foursquare Gospel. The pastor of the church is appointed by the Board of Directors and is responsible for the spiritual and physical welfare of the church. To assist and advise the pastor, a church council is elected by the local church members. Foursquare churches seek to build strong believers through Christian education, Christian day schools, youth camping and ministry, Foursquare Women International who support and encourage Foursquare mission-aries abroad, local radio and television ministries, the Foursquare World ADVANCE Magazine and over 550 Bible colleges worldwide. Worldwide missions remains the focus of the Foursquare Gospel Church with 38,217 churches and meeting places, 49,287 national pastors, leaders and 4,113,981 members with a combined constituency nearing 5 million in over 140 countries of the world. The Church is affiliated with the Pentecostal/Charismatic Churches of North America, the National Association of Evangelicals and the Pentecostal World Conference.

Headquarters
1910 W. Sunset Blvd., Ste. 200, P.O. Box 26902, Los Angeles, CA 90026-0176 Tel. (213)989-4234 Fax (213)989-4590
Media Contact, Editor, Dr. Ron Williams
Email: comm@foursquare.org
Website: www.foursquare.org

Officers
President: Dr. Jack W. Hayford
Vice President/General Supervisor: Rev. Glenn C. Burris Jr.
Vice President/Director of Global Operations and Missions: Rev. Michael Larkin
Vice President/Church Operations: Rev. James C. Scott Jr.
Vice President/Director of Urban and Multicultural Ministries: Rev. Arthur J. Gray II

Vice President/Corporate Secretary-Treasurer: Dr. Sterling Brackett
Chief Financial Officer: Rev. Jeffrey L. Bird
Vice President/Chief Information Technologies Officer: Rev. Dan Ussery
All of the above can be reached through the corporate address: International Church of the Foursquare Gospel, P.O. Box 26902, Los Angeles, CA 90026 Tel. (888)635-4234 Fax. 213-989-4590, Email: comm@foursquare.org, Website: www.foursquare.org

Periodicals
Foursquare World ADVANCE

International Council of Community Churches*

This body is a fellowship of locally autonomous, ecumenically minded, congrega-tionally governed, non-creedal Churches. The Council came into being in 1950 as the union of two former councils of community churches, one formed of black churches known as the Biennial Council of Community Churches in the United States and Elsewhere and the other of white churches known as the National Council of Community Churches.

Headquarters
21116 Washington Pky., Frankfort, IL 60423-3112 Tel. (815)464-5690 Fax (815)464-5692
Media Contact, Exec. Dir., Rev. Michael E. Livingston
Email: iccc60423@sbcglobal.net

Officers
Pres., Rev. Leroy McCreory
Vice Pres., Rev. Paul Drake
Vice Pres., Rev. Saundra Nelson
Sec., Rev. Dick Griffith
Treas., Nick Foraine

OTHER ORGANIZATIONS
Commission on Laity and Church Relations, J Philip Smith
Commission on Ecumenical and Inter-faith Relations, Rev. Herman Harmelink, III
Commission on Clergy Relations, Virginia Leopold
Commission on Faith, Justice & Mission, Rev. Dr. Richard Griffith
Women's Christian Fellowship, Pres., Loretta Watts
Samaritans (Men's Fellowship), Pres., Nicholas Brame
Young Adult Fellowship, Pres., Daniel Nelson
Youth Fellowship, Pres., Monique Whiting

Periodicals
The Christian Community, *The Inclusive Pulpit*, *Key Lay Notes*, *Clergy comminique*

International Fellowship of Bible Churches, Inc

Founded August, 1988 from three groups of ministers and churches of conservative Wesleyan

129

holiness tradition. Sponsor mission works in six countries on four continents. Locally autonomous congregations cooperate for missions, education, youth camps, religious gatherings, etc. Congregational goverment at Assembly level. International Assembly held biannually on even numbered years. Officers include General Superintendent and a 20-member Board comprised of 10 clergy and 10 non-clergy, elected by the International Assembly.

The International Fellowship of Bible Churches, Incorporated is an association of autonomous congregations and parachurch ministries joined together by common persuasions, purposes and principles.

International refers to our commitment to maintaining a consciousness of the global and universal nature of the Church of Jesus Christ, as well as our firm commitment to active service as part of that universal and international church. The Fellowship currently operates an international ministry in several locations across the globe.

Fellowship refers to our commitment to the autonomy of the local congregation while maintaining the belief that we really do need each other.

Bible refers to our commitment to the authority of Scripture as the final guide for all matters of faith and practice, both public and private.

Churches refers to our belief that ministry occurs most efficiently and effectively at the local church level, not at the denominational or organizational level.

Headquarters

3511 N. Geraldine Avenue, Oklahoma City, OK 73008 Tel. & Fax (405)948-9388
Media Contact, Gen. Superintendent, William Harrison Sillings
Email: williamsillins@ibfc.org
Website: www.ifbc.org

Officers

Gen. Superintendent, William Harrison Sillings, 3511 N. Geraldine Avenue, Oklahoma City, OK 73008 Tel. & Fax (405)948-9388, Email: williamsillins@ibfc.org

Secretary, Rev. Howard Russell, 16163 Galehouse Rd., Doylesville, OH 44230 Tel. (330)798-5248 Fax (330)658-1431, Email: hrussell@cbnews.org

Treasurer, Rev. Ronald Ruyle, 7512 S. Villa, Oklahoma City, OK 73159 Tel. (405)681-7475

Director of Missions, Rev. Robert Gilbert, 5334 Old Mission Rd., Chattanooga, TN 3741 Tel. (423)296-8612 Fax (423)499-0357, Email: rgilbert@precept.org

Director of Chaplains, Rev. Gary Hedges, P.O. Box 5555, Ft. Oglethorpe, GA 30742 Tel. (706)861-7733 Fax (706)861-7777, Email: gary@chswebsite.com

Pastoral Consultant, Rev. Don Hicks, 116 Rosewood Way, Parachute, CO 81635 Tel. (970)285-9609

The International Pentecostal Church of Christ

At a General Conference held at London, Ohio, Aug. 10, 1976, the International Pentecostal Assemblies and the Pentecostal Church of Christ consolidated into one body, taking the name International Pentecostal Church of Christ.

The International Pentecostal Assemblies was the successor of the Association of Pentecostal Assemblies and the International Pentecostal Missionary Union. The Pentecostal Church of Christ was founded by John Stroup of Flatwoods, Ketucky, on May 10, 1917 and was incorporated at Portsmouth, Ohio, in 1927. The International Pentecostal Church of Christ is an active member of the Pentecostal/Charismatic Churches of North America, as well as a member of the National Association of Evangelicals.

The priorities of the International Pentecostal Church of Christ are to be an agency of God for evangelizing the world, to be a corporate body in which people may worship God and to be a channel of God's purpose to build a body of saints being perfected in the image of His Son.

The Annual Conference is held each year during the first full week of August in London, Ohio.

Headquarters

2245 St. Rt. 42 SW, P.O. Box 439, London, OH 43140 Tel. (740)852-4722 Fax (740)852-0348
Media Contact, Gen. Overseer, Clyde M. Hughes
Email: hqipcc@aol.com
Website: members.aol.com/hqipcc

EXECUTIVE COMMITTEE

Gen. Overseer, Clyde M. Hughes, P.O. Box 439, London, OH 43140 Tel. (740)852-4722 Fax (740)852-0348

Asst. Gen. Overseer, B.G. Turner, RR5, Box 1286, Harpers Ferry, WV 25425 Tel. (304)535-221 Fax (304)535-1357

Gen. Sec., Asa Lowe, 513 Johnstown Rd., Chesapeake, VA 23322 Tel. (757)547-4329

Gen. Treas., Ervin Hargrave, P.O. Box 439, London, OH 43140 Tel. (740)852-4722 Fax (740)852-0348

Dir. of Global Missions, Dr. James B. Keiller, P.O. Box 18145, Atlanta, GA 30316 Tel. (404)627-2681 Fax (404)627-0702

DISTRICT OVERSEERS

Central District, Lindsey Hayes, 609 Lansing Rd., Akron, OH 44312, Tel. 330-784-3453

Mid-Eastern District, H. Gene Boyce, 705 W. Grubb St., Hertford, NC 27944 Tel. (252)426-5403

Mountain District, Terry Lykins, P.O. Box 131, Staffordsville, KY 41256 Tel. (606)297-3282

130

New River District, Calvin Weikel, RR. 2, Box 300, Ronceverte, WV 24970 Tel. (304)647-4301

North Central District, Edgar Kent, P.O. Box 275, Hartford, MI 49057 Tel. (616)621-3326

North Eastern District, Wayne Taylor, 806 8th St., Shenandoah, VA 22849 Tel (540)652-8090

South Eastern District, Frank Angie, 2507 Old Peachtree Rd., Duluth, GA 30097 Tel (770)476-5196

Tri-State District, Cline McCallister, 5210 Wilson St., Portsmouth, OH 45662 Tel. & Fax (740)776-6357

Portugese District, Pedro Messias, 34 Woodside Ave., Danbury, CT 06810 Tel. (203)790-9628

OTHER ORGANIZATIONS

Beulah Heights Bible College, Pres., Samuel R. Chand, P.O. Box 18145, Atlanta, GA 30316 Tel. (404)627-2681 Fax (404)627-0702

Women's Ministries, Gen. Pres., Janice Boyce, 121 W. Hunters Tr., Elizabeth City, NC 27909 Tel. & Fax (252)338-3003

Pentecostal Ambassadors, Dustin Hughes, National Youth Dir., P.O Box 439, London, OH 43140 Tel. (740)852-0448 Fax (740)852-0348

National Christian Education Dept., Dir., Dustin Hughes, P.O. Box 439, London, OH 43140 Tel. (740)852-0448 Fax (740)852-0348

Periodicals

The Bridegroom's Messenger, *The Pentecostal Leader*

International Pentecostal Holiness Church

This body grew out of the National Holiness Association movement of the nineteenth century, with roots in Methodism. Beginning in the South and Midwest, the church represents the merger of the Fire-Baptized Holiness Church founded by B. H. Irwin in Iowa in 1895; the Pentecostal Holiness Church founded by A. B. Crumpler in Goldsboro, North Carolina, in 1898; and the Tabernacle Pentecostal Church founded by N. J. Holmes in 1898.

All three bodies joined the ranks of the pentecostal movement as a result of the Azusa Street revival in Los Angeles in 1906 and a 1907 pentecostal revival in Dunn, N.C., conducted by G. B. Cashwell, who had visited Azusa Street. In 1911, the Fire-Baptized and Pentecostal Holiness bodies merged in Falcon, N.C., to form the present church; the Tabernacle Pentecostal Church was added in 1915 in Canon, Georgia.

The church stresses the new birth, the Wesleyan experience of sanctification, the pentecostal baptism in the Holy Spirit, evidenced by speaking in tongues, divine healing and the premillennial second coming of Christ.

Headquarters

P.O. Box 12609, Oklahoma City, OK 73157-2609 Tel. (405)787-7110 Fax (405)789-3957

Media Contact, Admn. Asst.
Email: jdl@iphc.org
Website: www.iphc.org

Officers

Gen. Supt., Bishop James D. Leggett, Email: jdl@iphc.org

Vice Chpsn. Executive Director of Evangelism USA, Dr. Ronald Carpenter, Sr.

Exec. Dir. Of World Missions Ministries, Dr. A.D.Beacham Jr.

Executive Director of Church Education Ministries, Rev. Talmadge Gardner

Executive Director of Stewardship Ministries/ General Secretary-Treasurer, Rev. Edward W. Wood

OTHER ORGANIZATIONS

The Publishing House (LifeSprings Resources), CEO, Greg Hearn, Franklin Springs, GA 30639

Women's Ministries, Exec. Dir., Mrs. Jewelle Stewart

Men's Ministries, Exec. Dir., Rev. Bill Terry, P.O. Box 12609, Oklahoma City, OK 73157

Periodicals

IPHC Experience

Jehovah's Witnesses

Modern-day Jehovah's Witnesses began in the early 1870s when Charles Taze Russell was the leader of a Bible study group in Allegheny City, Pennsylvania. In July 1879, the first issue of Zion's Watch Tower and Herald of Christ's Presence (now called The Watchtower which is published in more than 150 languages with a circulation of upwards of 27 million) appeared. In 1884 Zion's Watch Tower Tract Society was incorporated, later changed to Watch Tower Bible and Tract Society. Congregations spread into other states and countries, and followers witnessed from house to house.

By 1913, printed sermons were in four languages in 3,000 newspapers in the United States, Canada and Europe. Hundreds of millions of books, booklets and tracts were distributed. Publication of the magazine now known as Awake! Began in 1919. Today, it is published in more than 80 languages and has a circulation of upwards of 32,000,000. In 1931 the name Jehovah's Witnesses, based on Isaiah 43 vs.10-12, was adopted.

During the 1930s and 1940s , and as recently as 2002, Jehovah's Witnesses fought many court cases in the interest of preserving freedom of speech, press, assembly and worship. They have won a total of 48 cases before the United States Supreme Court. A missionary training school was established in 1943, and it has been a major factor in the international expansion of the Witnesses. There are now 6.6 million Witnesses in 235 lands.

131

Jehovah's Witnesses believe in one almighty God, Jehovah, who is the Creator of all things. They believe in Jesus Christ as God's Son, the first of His creations. While Jesus is now an immortal spirit in heaven, ruling as King of God's Kingdom, he is still subject to his heavenly Father, Jehovah God. Christ's human life was sacrificed as a ransom to open up for obedient mankind the opportunity of eternal life. With Christ in heaven, 144,000 individuals chosen from among mankind will rule in righteousness over an unnumbered great crowd who will survive the destruction of wickedness and receive salvation into an earth cleansed of evil. (Rev. Ch.7 vs.9, 10; Ch.14 vs.1-5). These, along with the resurrected dead, will transform the earth into a global earthly paradise and will have the prospect of living forever on it.

Headquarters
25 Columbia Heights, Brooklyn, NY 11201-2483 Tel. (718)560-5000
Media Contact, Office of Public Information, J. R. Brown
Editorial Contact, Writing Department, James N. Pellechia
Website: www.watchtower.org

Officers
Pres. Watch Tower Bible and Tract Society of Pennsylvania, Don Adams

Periodicals
Awake!, *The Watchtower*

Korean Presbyterian Church in America, General Assembly of the*

This body came into official existence in the United States in 1976 and is currently an ethnic church, using the Korean and English languages.

Headquarters
General Assembly of the Korean Presbyterian Church in America
17200 Clark Ave., Bellflower, CA 90706 Tel. (714)816-1100 Fax (714)816-1120

Officers
General Secretary, Rev. Jacob Se Jang, 5848 Pimlico Road, Baltimore, MD 21209 Tel. (410)542-6952
Moderator: Rev. Dr. Young Chin Huh, 12601 Leda Lane, Garden Grove, CA 92840 Tel. (714)537-2687

Latter-day Saints—please see The Church of Jesus Christ of Latter-day Saints.

The Latvian Evangelical Lutheran Church in America

This body was organized into a denomination on Aug. 22, 1975 after having existed as the Federation of Latvian Evangelical Lutheran Churches in America since 1955. This church is a regional constituent part of the Lutheran Church of Latvia Abroad, a member of the Lutheran World Federation and the World Council of Churches.

The Latvian Evangelical Lutheran Church in America works to foster religious life, traditions and customs in its congregations in harmony with the Holy Scriptures, the Apostles', Nicean and Athanasian Creeds, the unaltered Augsburg Confession, Martin Luther's Small and Large Catechisms and other documents of the Book of Concord.

The LELCA is ordered by its Synod (General Assembly), executive board, auditing committee and district conferences.

Headquarters
7225 Oak Highlands Dr., Kalamazoo, MI 49009 Tel. (269)375-0389, Email: kaugars@earthlink.net
Media Contact, Juris Pulins, 9531 Knoll Top Rd., Union, IL 60180 Tel. (815)923-5919
Email: pulins@earthlink.net

Officers
Pres., Dean Lauma Zusevics, Tel. (414)421-3934, Email: izunpz@wi.rr.com
Vice Pres., Rev. Anita Varsberga-Paza Email: macavp@yahoo.com
Sec.,Girts Kaugars, 7225 Oak Highlands Dr., Kalamazoo, MI 49009 Tel. (269)375-0389 Email: kaugars@earthlink.net
Treas., Vilmars Beinikis, 17 John Dr., Old Bethpage, NY 11804 Tel. (516)293-8432

Periodicals
Cela Biedrs, *Lelba Zinas*

Liberal Catholic Church (International)

Founded as a reorganization of the Dutch Old Catholic Church in 1915-16. In 1941 a controversy broke out in the Church regarding whether or not certain teachings of Theosophy (reincarnation, etc.) were to become official teachings of the Church. This was resolved by a court decision holding we (the non-Theosophist party) were the legal Liberal Catholic Church.

Headquarters
741 Cerro Gordo Avenue, San Diego, CA 92102, USA. Tel. & Fax (619)239-0637

Officers
The Most Rev. James P. Roberts, Jr., President and Regionary Bishop, 39 Claire Ave., New Rochelle, NY 10804 Tel. (914)636-7917, Email: Bppal32@aol.com
The Most Rev. Charles W. Finn, Vice-President and Presiding Bishop, 741 Cerro Gordo Ave., San Diego, CA 92102 Tel. & Fax (619)239-0637, Email: abpchas@msn.com
St. Alban Theological Seminary, P.O. Box 1125, Morongo Valley, CA 92256 Tel. (760)363-6260, Email: liberalcatholic@aol.com
St. Alban Press, 741 Cerro Gordo Avenue, San Diego, CA 92102 Tel. & Fax (858)689-8610, Email: info@stalbanpress.com

132

The Liberal Catholic Church— Province of the United States of America

The Liberal Catholic Church was founded Feb. 13, 1916 as a reorganization of the Old Catholic Church in Great Britain with the Rt. Rev. James I. Wedgwood as the first Presiding Bishop. The first ordination of a priest in the United States was Fr. Charles Hampton, later a Bishop. The first Regionary Bishop for the American Province was the Rt. Rev. Irving S. Cooper (1919-1935).

Headquarters

Pres., The Rt. Rev. William S.H. Downey, 1206 Ayers Ave., Ojai, CA 93023 Tel. (805)646-2573 Fax (805)646-2575

Media Contact, Regionary Bishop, The Rt. Rev. William S.H. Downey

Email: W.Downey@sbcglobal.net

Website: www.thelcc.org

Officers

Pres. & Regionary Bishop, The Rt. Rev. William S.H. Downey

Vice Pres., Rev. L. Marshall Heminway, P.O. Box 19957 Hampden Sta., Baltimore, MD 21211-0957

Sec. (Provincial), Rev. Lloyd Worley, 1232 24th Avenue Ct., Greeley, CO 80631 Tel. (303)356-3002

Provost, Rev. Lloyd Worley

Treas., Rev. Milton Shaw

BISHOPS

Regionary Bishop for the American Province, The Rt. Rev. William S.H. Downey

Aux. Bishops of the American Province, Rt. Rev. Dr. Robert S. McGinnis, Jr., 3612 N. Labarre Rd., Metaire, LA 70002; Rt. Rev. Joseph L. Tisch, P.O. Box 1117, Melbourne, FL 32901; Rt. Rev. Dr. Hein VanBeusekom, 12 Krotona Hill, Ojai, CA 93023; Rt. Rev. Ruben Cabigting, P.O. Box 270, Wheaton, IL 60189; The Rt. Rev. Lawrence Smith 9740 S. Avers Ave., Evergreen Park, IL.

Periodicals

Ubique

Lutheran Association, Conservative—please see Conservative Lutheran Association.

Lutheran Church—please see American Association of Lutheran Churches.

Lutheran Church in America—please see Evangelical Lutheran Church in America.

Lutheran Church of America—please see Apostolic Lutheran Church of America.

The Lutheran Church— Missouri Synod (LCMS)

The Lutheran Church-Missouri Synod, which was founded in 1847, has more than 6,000 congregations in the United States and works in 78 other countries. It has 2.5 million members and is the second-largest Lutheran denomination in North America.

Christian education is offered for all ages. The North American congregations operate the largest elementary and secondary school systems of any Protestant denomination in the nation, and 18,216 students are enrolled in 12 LCMS institutions of higher learning.

Traditional beliefs concerning the authority and interpretation of Scripture are important. The synod is known for mass-media outreach through "The Lutheran Hour" on radio, "This Is The Life" dramas on television, and the products of Concordia Publishing House, the third-largest Protestant publisher, whose Arch Books children's series has sold more than 60 million copies.

An extensive network of more than 1,000 volunteers in 60 work centers produces Braille, large-type, and audiocassette materials for the blind and visually impaired. Most of the eighty-five or so deaf congregations affiliated with U.S. Also, there are 30 centers in the U.S. sponsored by LCMS Blind Missions where Blind people are trained for christian outreach. Lutheran denominations are LCMS; and many denominations use the Bible lessons prepared for developmentally disabled persons.

The involvement of women is high, although they do not occupy clergy positions. Serving as teachers, deaconesses and social workers, women comprise approximately half of total professional workers.

The members' responsibility for congregational leadership is a distinctive characteristic of the synod. Power is vested in voters' assemblies, generally comprised of adults of voting age. Synod decision making is given to the delegates at triennial national and district conventions, where the franchise is equally divided between lay and pastoral representatives.

Headquarters

The Lutheran Church-Missouri Synod, International Center, 1333 S. Kirkwood Rd., St. Louis, MO 63122-7295

Media Contact, Manager, Publc Affairs & Media Relations, Ms. Vicki Biggs, Tel. (314)996-1236; Managing Editor, Reporter, Mr. Joe Isenhower, Tel. (314)996-1231 Fax (314)996-1126

Email: infocenter@lcms.org

Website: www.lcms.org

Officers

Pres., Dr. Gerald B. Kieschnick, St. Louis, MO Tel. (314)995-9000

1st Vice Pres., Dr. William R. Diekelman, St. Louis MO Tel. (314)995-9000

2nd Vice Pres., Dr. Paul L. Maier, Kalamazoo, MI

3rd Vice Pres., Dr. John C. Wohlrabe, Virginia Beach, VA

4th Vice Pres., Dr. Dean W. Nadasdy, Woodbury, MN

5th Vice Pres., Dr. David D. Buegler, Avon, OH
Sec., Dr. Raymond L. Hartwig, St. Louis, MO Tel. (314)995-9000
Treas., Dr. Thomas Kuchta, St. Louis, MO Tel. (314)995-9000
Chief Admn. Officer, Mr. Ronald Schultz, St. Louis, MO Tel. (314)995-9000
Legal Counselor, Mrs. Sherri Strand, Thompson Coburn, LLP, 1 US Bank Plaza, St. Louis, MO 63101 Tel. (314)552-6000

BOARD OF DIRECTORS

Rev. Edward Balfour, Cape Elizabeth, ME; Dr. Victor T. Belton, Decatur, GA; Mr. Walter Brantz, Cody, WY; Mr. Kermit Brashear, Omaha, NE; Dr. William Diekelman, St. Louis, MO; Dr. Betty Duda, Cocoa Beach, FL; Dr. Gloria Edwards, Portola Valley, CA; Dr. Raymond L. Hartwig, St. Louis, MO; Dr. Gerald B. Kieschnick, St. Louis, MO; Dr. Tom Kuchta, St. Louis, MO; Dr. Robert Kuhn, Oviedo, FL; Chaplain Donald Muchow, Buda, TX; Mr. David Piehler, Wausau, WI; Mr. Curtis Pohl, St. Michael, MN; Mr. Roy Schmidt, Bay City, MI; Dr. Kurt Senske, Austin, TX; Mr. Walter Tesch, Milwaukee, WI

BOARDS AND COMMISSIONS

Black Ministry, Exec. Dir., Dr. Phillip Campbell Communication Services, Exec. Dir., Mr. David Strand
District & Congregational Services, Exec. Dir., Rev. Jeffery Schubert
Ministerial Growth and Support, Exec. Dir., Rev. David Meunch Mission Services, Exec. Dir., Dr. Robert Roegner Pastoral Education, Exec. Dir., Rev. Glen Thomas
Theology & Church Relations, Exec. Dir., Dr. Samuel Nafzger
University Education, Exec. Dir., Dr. Kurt Kreuger
World Relief and Human Care, Exec. Dir., Rev. Matthew Harrison
Worship, Exec. Dir., Interim Exec. Dir., Rev. Jon Vieker

RELATED ORGANIZATIONS

Concordia Plan Services, Pres., Paul W. Middeke, St. Louis, MO Tel. (314)995-9000
LCMS Foundation, Pres., Rev. Thomas Ries, St. Louis, MO Tel. (314)995-9000
Lutheran Church Extension Fund, Pres., Merle Freitag, St. Louis, MO Tel. (314)995-9000
Concordia Publishing House, Pres., Bruce Kintz, 3558 S. Jefferson Ave., St. Louis, MO 63118-3968 Tel. (314)268-1000
Concordia Historical Institute, Dir., Dr. Martin Noland, 804 Seminary Place, St. Louis, MO 63105 Tel. (314)505-7900
Lutheran Hour Ministries, Exec. Dir., Greg E. Lewis, 660 Mason Ridge Ctr. Dr., St. Louis, MO, 63141-8557 Tel. (314)317-4100
Lutheran Women's Missionary League, Pres., Jan Wendorf, 3558 S. Jefferson Ave., St. Louis, MO 63118 Tel. (314)268-1530
KFUO Radio, Dir., Dennis Stortz, 85 Founders Lane, St. Louis, MO 63105 Tel. (314)725-3030

Periodicals

The Lutheran Witness (www.lcms.org/witness), *Reporter* (www.reporter.lcms.org)

Malankara Orthodox Syrian Church, Diocese of America*

Malankara (Indian) Orthodox Church is an ancient Church of India and it traces its origin to as far back as A. D. 52 when St. Thomas one of the Disciples of Jesus Christ came to India and established Christanity in the South Western parts of the sub-continent.

The St. Thomas Christians or the Syrian Christians exist at present in different churches and denominations. But a major section of the parent body of St. Thomas Christians which has maintained its independent nature consti-tute the Orthodox Church under the Catholicos of the East and Malankara Metropolitan, whose seat is at Devalokam, Kottayam, Kerala, India. The Church has dioceses and churches in most parts of India as well as in the United States, Canada, United Kingdom, Western Europe, Persian Gulf nations, South Africa, Malaysia, Singapore, Australia and New Zealand. The official title of the head of the Church is the "Catholicos of the East, Catholicos of the Apostolic throne of St. Thomas and the Malankara Metropolitan." The present Catholicos of the East and Malankara Metropolitan is H.H. Mar Baselios Mar Thoma Didymos I.

The Church, though modern in its vision and outlook, keeps the traditional Orthodox faith and liturgy. It accepts the first three Ecumenical Synods. The liturgy now in use is the translation of the liturgy adopted from the Antiochian Church in the 17th century. However, the liturgi-cal rites are uniquely Indian. Today the Church uses liturgy in Malayalam,Syriac, Hindi, and English.

The Indian Orthodox community inherited many aspects of Indian civilization and they are as any other member of any other community in India, in their customs, manners, and life style. The Church has a Theological Seminary at Kottayam, Kerala, which was established in AD 1815. Another seminary is situated in Nagpur, Maharashtra. The latter was established fairly recently in the later part of the 20th century.

Headquarters

Indian Orthodox Church Center, 80-34 Common-wealth Boulevard, Bellerose, NY 11426
Tel. (718)470-9844 Fax (718)470-9219
Media Contact, His Grace Mathews Mar Barnabas, Diocesan Metropolitan
Email: Malankara@malankara.org
Website: www.malankara.org/american

Officers

Diocesan Metropolitan: His Grace Mathews Mar Barnabas

Assistant Metropolitan: His Grace Zachariah Mar Nicholovos

Diocesan Sec., The Rev. Fr. John Thomas

Diocesan Council Member: The Very Rev. Dr. P. S. Samuel Cor Episcopos

Diocesan Center Manager: The Rev. Dr. P. C. Thomas

Periodicals

Diocesan Voice, Family and Youth Conference Souvenir

Mar Thoma Syrian Church of India*

According to tradition, the Mar Thoma Church was established as a result of the apostolic mission of St. Thomas, the apostle in 52 AD. Church history attests to the continuity of the community of faithful, throughout the long centuries in India. The liturgy and faith practices of the Church were based on the relationship between the Church in Kerala, India, which St. Thomas founded, with the East-Syrian and Persian Churches. This started in the 3rd century and continued up to the 16th century. In the 17th century, the Malabar Church of St. Thomas (as the Church in Kerala was known) renewed her relationship with the Orthodox Patriarchate of Antioch as part of the resistance to forced Latinization by the Portuguese. This process also led to the development of the Kerala Episcopacy, whereby the first Indian Bishop Mar Thoma I was consecrated in Kerala.

The Mar Thoma Church retains her Eastern Orthodoxy. She follows an Orthodox worship form and liturgy, believes in the catholicity of grace, is missionary and evangelistic in approach. She derives Episcopal succession from the Syrian Orthodox Church of Antioch and follows Eastern Reformed Theology. She is independent, autonomous, and indigenous, constitutionally combining democratic values and Episcopal authority. She has been in full communion with the Anglican Church since 1954.

The Mar Thoma Church has been dynamically involved in the socio-cultural settings of North America and Europe for the past 30 years. Fundamentally an immigrant Church, she has contextualized her ministry in her new life situation without compromising the rich ethos and tradition received from her motherland of Kerala, India. Currently, under the rubric of the Diocese, there are 51 parishes and 20 congregations. In order to cater to the ministerial needs of the Diocese, there are 48 clergy as well as functioning organizations for children, youth, women, and evangelistic work. The Diocese is presided over by the Diocesan Bishop, The Rt. Rev. Dr. Euyakim Mar Coorilos, Episcopa.

The history of the Mar Thoma Church in the North American and European continent represents the dreams and aspirations of the faithful members of the Church. Commencing as a small prayer group in Queens, New York, in 1972, the first approved parish was recognized in New York in 1976. The churches in North America and United Kingdom have become constituents of the newly formed "Diocese of North America and United Kingdom." The Headquarters has subsequently moved to its current location at 2320 South Merrick Avenue, Merrick, N.Y.

Headquarters

Sinai Mar Thoma Center, 2320 S. Merrick Avenue, Merrick, New York 11566 Tel. (516)377-3311 Fax (516)377-3322

Email: webmaster@marthomachurch.org

Website: www.marthomanae.org

Officers

Diocesan Bishop, The Rt. Rev. Dr. Euyakim Mar Coorilos

Diocesan Bishop's Sec., Rev. Joseph Oommen

Diocesan Treasurer, Dr. T. A. Mathew

Periodicals

Mar Thoma Messenger

Mennonite Brethren Churches—please see General Conference of Mennonite Brethren Churches

Mennonite Church of God in Christ—please see Church of God in Christ, Mennonite

Mennonite Church USA

Mennonite Church USA, with 109,000 members, is one of several denominations that traces their beginnings to the Protestant Reformation in the early 1500s. Mennonites hold common core beliefs with other Christian denominations, but they live out God's call in some ways that make them distinct. Mennonites believe in giving ultimate loyalty to God rather than to the nations in which they live. They believe that Jesus revealed a way for people to live peacefully and nonviolently, and they seek to be peacemakers in everyday life.

Mennonite church USA is committed to sharing its faith and passion for Jesus with others and is open to anyone who confesses Jesus Christ as Lord and Savior and wants to live as Jesus taught.

The vision statement of Mennonite Church USA reads, "God calls us to be followers of Jesus Christ and, by the power of the Holy Spirit, to grow as communities of grace, joy, and peace, so that God's healing and hope flow through us to the world."

Mennonite Church USA—its congregations, area conferences, Executive Board, ministry offices and churchwide agencies—focus on four priorities as it seeks to nurture missional congregations that join in God's activity in the world:

1. In our holistic witness we practice and proclaim the Gospel of Jesus Christ through a seamless web of evangelism, justice and peacebuilding.

2. We create a culture of call by calling, training anf nurturing new leaders.

3. We honor the dignity and value of all people, regardless of their race or ethnicity and denounce racist behavior.

4. We build global connections by fostering and developing partnerships with the broader body of Christ around the world. Mennonite Church USA lists as its strengths a high level of integrity recognized in both society and the religious community; high church attendance (90% of members attend church regularly); expanded global awareness through exposure to other world cultures; strong commitment to nonviolence and use of conflict resolution skills; above average giving to the work of the church; a natural communitarian impulse demonstrated by an emphasis on congregational relationships and mutual accountabilities; strong support of volunteer efforts, relief and service activities; and a holistic theology that holds word and deed together.

Headquarters

Great Plains Office: 722 Main St., P.O. Box 347, Newton, KS 67114 Tel. (316)283-5100 Fax (316)283-0454, toll free phone number for churchwide agencies (866)866-2872

Great Lakes Office: 500 S. Main St., P O Box 1245, Elkhart, IN 46515-1245 Tel. (574)294-7523 Fax (574)293-1892

Media contact, Laura Lee Williard, Communications Director, Tel. (316)283-5100 x 241, Email: lauraleew@mennoniteusa.org

Email: info@MennoniteUSA.org

Website: www.MennoniteChurchUSA.org

Officers

Moderator, Sharon Waltner, 28142 448th Avenue, Parker SD 57053 Tel. (605)648-3224, Email: sharonw@mennoniteusa.org

Moderator Elect, Edward Diller, 30 Thomas Pointe Dr., Ft. Thomas, KY 41075, Tel. (859)781-2796

Executive Director, James M. Schrag, 722 Main St., P.O. Box 347, Newton, KS 67114 Tel. (316) 283-5100, Email: jims@mennonite usa.org

Associate Executive Director, J. Ron Byler, 500 S. Main St., P.O.Box 1245, Elkhart, IN 46515 Tel. (574)523-3040, Email: ronb@mennonite usa.org

Mennonite Education Agency, Executive Director, Carlos Romero, 63846 County Road, 35 Ste. 1, Goshen, IN 46528-9621 Tel. (574)642-3164 Fax (574)642-4863, Email: carlosr@mennoniteeducation.org

Mennonite Mission Network, Executive Director, Stanley Green, 500 S Main Box 370, Elkhart, IN 46515-0370 Tel. (574)294-7523, Email: stanleyg@mennonitemission.net

Mennonite Mutual Aid, President, Howard Brenneman, P.O. Box 486, Goshen, IN 46527 Tel. (219)533-9511, Email: howard.brenneman @mma-online.org

Mennonite Publishing Network, Executive Director, Ron Rempel, 616 Walnut Ave., Scottdale, PA 15683 Tel. (724)887-8500, Email: rrempel@mph.org

Periodicals

The Mennonite, Leader, Rejoice!, Mennonite Historical Bulletin, Mennonite Quarterly Review, On the Line, Purpose, Story Friends

Methodist Church—please see The United Methodist Church

Methodist Church, Evangelical—please see Evangelical Methodist Church

Methodist Church, Fundamental—please see Fundamental Methodist Church, Inc.

The Missionary Church

The Missionary Church was formed in 1969 through a merger of the United Missionary Church (organized in 1883) and the Missionary Church Association (founded in 1898). It is evangelical and conservative with a strong emphasis on missionary work and church multiplication.

There are three levels of church government with local, district and general conferences. There are 11 church districts in the United States. The general conference meets every two years. The denomination operates one college [Bethel College, Mishawaka, IN] in the United States.

Headquarters

3811 Vanguard Dr., P.O. Box 9127, Ft. Wayne, IN 46899-9127 Tel. (260)747-2027 Fax (260) 747-5331

Media Contact, Pres., Rev. William Hossler

Email: ronphipps@mcusa.org

Website: www.mcusa.org

Officers

Pres., Rev. William Hossler

Vice Pres., Rev. Joel DeSelm

Sec., Rev. Dave Engbrecht

Treas., Darrel Schlabach

Director of U.S. Ministries, Rev. Robert Ransom

Director of World PartnersUSA, Rev. David Mann

Healthy Church Initiatives Coordinator, Dr. Dan Riemenschneider

Servant Leadership Coordinator, Rev. Greg Getz

Support Ministries Coordinator, Rev. Ron Phipps

Pastoral Leadership Institute Director, Rev. Greg Getz

Director of Development/Communications, Dr. Tom Murphy

Dir. of Ad. Services, Eric Smith

Director of Financial Services, Neil Rinehart

Coordinator of Church Multiplication, Rev. Jeff Getz

Coordinator of Ethnic Ministries, Rev. Jose Manuel Mendez
Missionary Men Liaison, Rev. Ron Phipps
Missionary Women Intl., Pres., Charlotte Beals
Missionary Church Investment Foundation, Mr. Eric Smith

Periodicals
Missionary Church Today

Moravian Church in America (Unitas Fratrum)*

In 1735 German Moravian missionaries of the pre-Reformation faith of Jan Hus came to Georgia, in 1740 to Pennsylvania, and in 1753 to North Carolina. They established the American Moravian Church, which is broadly evangelical, ecumenical, liturgical, "conferential" in form of government and has an episcopacy as a spiritual office. The Northern and Southern Provinces of the church operate on a semi-autonomous basis.

Headquarters
Denominational offices or headquarters are called the Provincial Elders' Conference.
See addresses for Northern and Southern Provinces.

NORTHERN PROVINCE HEADQUARTERS
1021 Center St., P.O. Box 1245, Bethlehem, PA 18016-1245 Tel. (610)867-7566 Fax (610) 866-9223
Media Contact, Ms. Deanna Hollenbach
Website: www.moravian.org (for Moravian Church, Northern and Southern Provinces)

PROVINCIAL ELDERS' CONFERENCE
Pres., Rev. David L. Wickmann, Email: dave@mcnp.org
Vice Pres./Sec. Rev. Gary Straughan, Email: gary@mcnp.org
Vice Pres. Rev. Lawrence Christianson, Email: christlr@aol.com
Other Members: Nancy Baldwin; Paul DeTilla; Glenn Hertzog; Stephen Gohdes; Carol Messina
Comptroller, Theresa E. Kunda, 1021 Center St., P.O. Box 1245, Bethlehem, PA 18016-1245, Email: theresa@mcnp.org

NORTHERN PROVINCE
1021 Center St., P.O. Box 1245, Bethlehem, PA 18016-1245 Tel. (610)867-7566 Fax (610) 866-9223
Northern Province Pres., Rev. David L. Wickmann, P.O. Box 1245, Bethlehem, PA 18016-1245, Email: dave@mcnp.org
Eastern District Pres., Rev. Gary Straughan P.O. Box 1245, Bethlehem, PA 18016-1245, Email: gary@mcnp.org
Western District Pres., Rev. Lawrence Christianson, P.O. Box 386, Sun Prairie, WI 53590, Email: christlr@aol.com
Canadian District Pres., Rev. Stephen Gohdes,

600 Arcadia Dr. SE, Calgary, AB T2J 0B8, Email: sgohdes@shaw.ca

SOUTHERN PROVINCE HEADQUARTERS
459 S. Church St., Winston-Salem, NC 27101 Winston-Salem, NC 27108 Tel. (336)725-5811 Fax (336)723-1029, Email: rsawyer@mcsp.org

PROVINCIAL ELDERS' CONFERENCE
Pres., Rt. Rev.Wayne Burkette
Vice President, Mrs. Betsy Bombick
Sec.—vacant
Treas.,—vacant
Other Members, Ms. Donna Hurt; Rev. Tom Shelton; Rev. Richard Sides
Asst. to Pres., Robert Hunter, Email: rhunter@mcsp.org
ALASKA PROVINCE
P.O. Box 545, 361 3rd Ave., Bethel, AK 99559

PROVINCIAL ELDERS' CONFERENCE
Pres., Rev.Peter Green
Vice Pres., Frank Matthew, Sr.
Sec., Moses Owen
Treas., Arthur Sharp
Dir. of Theological Education,—Ray Caldwell
Email: gloria@mcnp.org, wburkette@mcsp.org
Website: www.moravian.org

Periodicals
The Moravian

Mormons—please see The Church of Jesus Christ of Latter-day Saints

National Association of Congregational Christian Churches

This association was organized in 1955 in Detroit, Michigan, by delegates from Congregational Christian Churches committed to continuing the Congregational way of faith and order in church life. Participation by member churches is voluntary.

Headquarters
P.O. Box 288, Oak Creek, WI 53154 Tel. (414)764-1620 Fax (414)764-0319
Media Contact, Assoc. Exec. Sec., Rev. Dr. Donald P. Olsen, 8473 So. Howell Ave., Oak Creek, WI 53154 Tel. (414)764-1620 Fax (414)764-0319
Email: naccc@naccc.org
Website: www.naccc.org

Officers
Exec. Sec., Rev. Dr. Thomas M. Richard, 8473 South Howell Ave., Oak Creek, WI 53154
Assoc. Exec. Secs., Rev. Phil Jackson and Rev. Dr. Donald P. Olsen

Periodicals
The Congregationalist

National Association of Free Will Baptists

This evangelical group of Armenian Baptists was organized by Paul Palmer in 1727 at

Chowan, North Carolina. Another movement (teaching the same doctrines of free grace, free salvation and free will) was organized June 30, 1780, in New Durham, N.H., but there was no connection with the southern organization except for a fraternal relationship.

The northern line expanded more rapidly and extended into the West and Southwest. This body merged with the Northern Baptist Convention Oct. 5, 1911, but a remnant of churches reorganized into the Cooperative General Association of Free Will Baptists Dec. 28, 1916, at Pattonsburg, Mo.

Churches in the southern line were organized into various conferences from the beginning and finally united in one General Conference in 1921.

Representatives of the Cooperative General Association and the General Conference joined Nov. 5, 1935 to form the National Association of Free Will Baptists.

Headquarters

5233 Mt. View Rd., Antioch, TN 37013-2306 Tel. (615)731-6812 Fax (615)731-0771

Mailing Address, P.O. Box 5002, Antioch, TN 37011-5002

Media Contact, Exec. Sec., Keith Burden CMP

Email: webmaster@nafwb.org

Website: www.nafwb.org

Officers

Exec. Sec.,Keith Burden CMP

Mod., Tim York, 2204 Foster Ave., Nashville, TN 37010

DENOMINATIONAL AGENCIES

Free Will Baptist Foundation, Exec. Dir., David Brown

Free Will Baptist Bible College, Pres., Mathew Pinson

Foreign Missions Dept., Dir., Rev. James Forlines

Home Missions Dept., Dir., Rev. Larry Powell

Bd. of Retirement, Dir., Rev. D. Ray Lewis

Historical Commission, Chpsn., Dr. Darrell Holley, 3606 West End Avenue, Nashville, TN 37205

Comm. for Theological Integrity, Chpsn., Rev. Leroy Forlines, 3606 West End Avenue, Nashville, TN 37205

Music Commission, Chpsn., Chris Truett, 1936 Banks School Road, Kinston, NC 28504

Media Comm., Chpsn., Not Available

Randall House Publications, Dir., Rev. Ron Hunter

Women Nationally Active for Christ, Exec. Sec., Majorie Workman

Master's Men Dept., Dir., Kenneth Akers

Periodicals

ONE Magazine, Co-Laborer

National Baptist Convention of America, Inc.*

The National Baptist Convention of America, Inc., was organized in 1880. Its mission is articulated through its history, constitution, articles of incorporation and by-laws. The Convention (corporate churches) has a mission statement with fourteen (14) objectives including fostering unity throughout its membership and the world Christian community by proclaiming the gospel of Jesus Christ; validating and propagating the Baptist doctrine of faith and practice, and its distinctive principles throughout the world; and harnessing and encouraging the scholarly and Christian creative skills of its membership for Christian writing and publications.

Headquarters

Liaison Officer, Dr. Richard A. Rollins, 777 S. R.L. Thornton Fwy., Ste. 205, Dallas, TX 75203 Tel. (214)946-8913 Fax (214)946-9619

Email: president@nbcamerica.net; djones@nbcamerica.net

Website: www.nbcamerica.net

Officers

Pres., Rev. Stephen J. Thurston, President, 1327 Pierre Ave., Shreveport, LA 71103 Tel. (773)224-5570 Fax (773)224-8200

Gen. Rec. Sec., Dr. Clarence C. Pennywell, 2016 Russell Rd., Shreveport, LA 71107

Corres. Sec., Rev. E. E. Stafford, 6614 South Western Ave., Los Angeles, CA 90047

Mrs. Donna Jones, Administrative Assistant, Tel. (800)543-4019 x 10 Fax (318)222-7512, Email: djones@nbcamerica.net

Periodicals

The Lantern

National Baptist Convention, U.S.A., Inc.*

The National Baptist Convention, one of the oldest African American organization in the nation, traces it history back to 1895. It was formed as a cosolidation of the Baptist Foreign Mission Convention (1880), Consolidated American Baptist Convention (1896), and the National Baptist Educational Convention (1882). Rev. W. H. Alpine of Alabama was the first president of the Baptist Foreign Mission Board which later became the Baptist Foreign Mission Convention, USA.

The constitution of the convention 1895 states: "Whereas, It is the sense of the Colored Baptists of the United States of America, convened in the city of Atlanta, Georgia, September 28, 1895 in the several organizations as 'The Baptist Foreign Mission Convention of the United States of America,' hithero engaged in Mission work on the West Coast of Africa: and the 'National Baptist Convention' which has been engaged in mission work in the United States of America; and the 'National Baptist Educational Convention,' which has sought to look after the educational interest that the interest of the way of the Kingdom of God requires that the several bodies above named should, and do now, unite in one body. Therefore, we do now agree to and adopt the following constitution:

"This body shall become known and styled, The National Baptist Convention of the United States of America.

"The object of this convention shall be 'to do mission work in the United States of America, in Africa, and elsewhere and to foster the cause of education.' Dr. L. M. Luke was elected the first Corresponding Secretary of the Foreign Board. In October, 1896 Rev. L.G. Jordan, pastor of the Union Baptist Church of Philadelphia was selected successor of Luke" (The Epoch of Negro Baptists and The Foreign Mission Board, NBC, USA, Inc. Dr. Edward A. Freeman, The Central Seminary Press 1953.)

In September 1915 at the annual meeting of the convention the constitution was revised with the following changes:

"The particular business and object of this Convention shall be to promote a growth and propagamation of religion, morality, and intelligence among the races of mankind, by engaging in missionary work in the United States of America, and elsewhere, by fostering the cause of education and publishing and circulating literature, and in providing the necessary ways and means for carrying on such work."

Headquarters
1700 Baptist World Center Dr., Nashville, TN 37207 Tel. (615)228-6292 Fax (615)226-5935

Officers
Pres., Dr. William J. Shaw, 1700 Baptist World Center Dr., Nashville, TN 37207 Tel. (615)228-6292 Fax (615)226-5935
Gen. Sec., Dr. Harry Blake, Mt. Canaan Baptist Church, 1666 Alston St., Shreveport, LA 71101, Tel. (318)227-9993

Periodicals
Mission Herald

National Missionary Baptist Convention of America*
The National Missionary Baptist Convention of America was organized in 1988 as a separate entity from the National Baptist Convention of America, Inc., after a dispute over control of the convention's publishing efforts. The new organization intended to remain committed to the National Baptist Sunday Church School and Baptist Training Union Congress and the National Baptist Publishing Board.

The purpose of the National Missionary Baptist Convention of America is to serve as an agency of Christian education, church extension and missionary efforts. It seeks to maintain and safeguard full religious liberty and engage in social and economic development.

Headquarters
4269 S. Figueroa St., Los Angeles, CA 90037 Tel. (323)846-1950 Fax (323)846-1964

Media Contact, Dr. Melvin Von Wade, Sr.
Email: gensec@jiacom.net
Website: www.nmbca.com

Officers
Pres., Dr. C.C. Robertson, President, Dallas, Texas
Vice President-at-Large, Dr. Nehemiah Davis, Fort Worth, Texas
Vice Pres., Ecumenical Affairs, Dr. L.C. Firle Collins, MS
Vice Pres., Auxiliaries, Dr. Bernard Black, Phoenix, AZ
Vice Pres., Boards, Dr. A. Charles Bowie, Cleveland, OH
Vice Pres., Financial Affairs, Dr. Ray W. Williams, Oakland, CA
Pres., National Baptist Publishing Bd., Dr. T. B. Boyd, III, 6717 Centennial Blvd., Nashville, TN 37209
Gen. Sec., Dr. A. Wayne Johnson, 106 NE Ivy St., Portland, OR 97212 Tel. (503)281-4925 Fax (503)281-6520, Email: gensec@jiacom.net
Corres. Sec., Dr. Walter Houston, Houston, TX
Treas., Dr. William R. Lott, Chicago, IL
Rec. Sec., Dr. T.L. Brown, Dallas, TX

National Organization of the New Apostolic Church of North America
The New Apostolic Church of North America claims common origin with the Catholic Apostolic movement in England, which began with the calling of an apostle in 1832. The New Apostolic Church distinguished itself from the parent body in 1863 by recognizing a succession of Apostles.

Headquarters
3753 N. Troy St., Chicago, IL 60618
Media Contact, Sec. & Treas., Ellen E. Eckhardt, Tel. (773)539-3652 Fax (773)478-6691
Email: info@nak.org
Website: www.nak.org

Officers
Pres., Rev. Rev. Richard C. Freund, 404 Glen Cone Ave., Sea Cliff, NY 11579
Vice Pres., Rev. John W. Fendt, Jr., 2 Willets Ln., Plandome, NY 11030-1023
Vice Pres., Rev. Leonard R. Kolb, 5250 Robinhood Ln., Erle, PA 16509-2563
Treas. And Sec., Ellen E. Eckhardt, 6380 N. Indian Rd., Chicago, IL 60646

Periodicals
Our Family

National Primitive Baptist Convention, Inc.
Throughout the years of slavery and the Civil War, the Negro population of the South worshipped with the white population in their

various churches. At the time of emancipation, their white brethren helped them establish their own churches, granting them letters of fellowship, ordaining their deacons and ministers and helping them in other ways.

The doctrine and polity of this body are quite similar to that of white Primitive Baptists, yet there are local associations and a national convention, organized in 1907.

Each church is independent and receives and controls its own membership. This body was formerly known as Colored Primitive Baptists.

Headquarters
6433 Hidden Forest Dr., Charlotte, NC 28213
Tel. (704)596-1508
Media Contact, Elder T. W. Samuels

Officers
Natl. Convention, Pres., President – Elder Ernest Ferrell, Tallahassee, FL
Natl. Convention, Vice Pres., Elder Bernard Yates, Pensacola, FL
Natl. Convention, Secretary, Elder W. J. Williams, Tampa, Florida
Natl. Church School Training Union, Pres., Dr. Jonathan Yates, Mobile, AL
Natl. Ushers Congress, Pres., Dea.. Carl Batts, 21213 Garden View Dr., Maple Heights, OH 44137
Publishing Bd., Chpsn., Elder John R. Cox, Birmingham, AL
Women's Congress, Pres., Mother Ann Cartes, Dallas, TX
Natl. Laymen's Council, Pres., Dea. Densimore Robinson, Huntsville, AL
Natl. Youth Congress, Pres., Minister Jacques Mood, Concord, NC

National Spiritualist Association of Churches

This organization is made up of believers that Spiritualism is a science, philosophy and religion based upon the demonstrated facts of communication between this world and the next.

Headquarters
NSAC General Offices, Rev. Sharon L. Snowman, Secretary, P.O. Box 217, Lily Dale, NY 14752-0217
Media Contact, Rev. Lelia Cutler, 7310 Midfield St. #1, Norfolk, VA 23505-4126
Email: nsac@nsac.org
Website: www.nsac.org

Officers
Pres., Rev. Lelia Cutler, 7310 Midfield St. #1, Norfolk, VA 23505-4126
Vice Pres., Rev. Catherine Snell 23 Pleasant St. Windham, NH 03087
Sec., Rev. Sharon L. Snowman, P.O. Box 217, Lily Dale, NY 14752 Tel. (716)595-2000 Fax (716)595-2020
Treas., Peter Berg, 20916 Bellerive Dr., Pflugerville, TX 78660

OTHER ORGANIZATIONS
Department of Education, Rev. Barbara Starr, Director, 4245 Woodmont Road, Great Cacapon, WV 25422
Department of Lyceums, Rev. Arsenia Williams, Director, 10913 S. Parnell, Chicago, IL 60628
Department of Missionaries, Rev. E. Ann Otzelberger, Director, 4332 Woodlynne Lane, Orlando, FL 32812-7562
Department of Phenomenal Evidence, Revs. Brian and Lynn Kent, Directors 28-3rd Street 4308, Warren, RI 02885
Department of Public Relations, Mary Montgomery Clifford, Director, 2426 North Kimball Street, Chicago, IL 60647
Department of Publications, Joe Owen, Director, 5 Third St. Suite 724, San Francisco, CA 94103
NSAC Healing Center, Rev. Kathleen Rottino, President, 74 Scenic Dr., Lebanon, CT 06249
NSAC Minsterial Association, Rev. Barbara Star, NST, Pres., 4245 Woodmont Road, Great Cacapon, WV 25422
National Spiritualist Teachers Club, Rev. E. Ann Otzelberger, NST, Pres., 4332 Woodlynne Lane, Orlando, FL 32812
Spiritualist Healers League, Rev. E. Annotzelberger, NST President
Licentiate Ministers & Certified Mediums Society, Rev. Janet Tisdale, NST, Pres., 1616 N. Alta Mesa Drive #51, Mesa, AZ 85205
The Stow Memorial Foundation, Sec., Rev. Sharon L. Snowman, P.O. Box 217, Lily Dale, NY 14752 Tel. (716)595-2000 Fax (716)595-2020
Spiritualist Benevolent Society, Inc., P.O. Box 217, Lily Dale, NY 14752

Periodicals
The National Spiritualist, Spotlight

Netherlands Reformed Congregations

The Netherlands Reformed Congregations organized denominationally in 1907. In the Netherlands, the so-called Churches Under the Cross (established in 1839, after breaking away from the 1834 Secession congregations) and the so-called Ledeboerian churches (established in 1841 under the leadership of the Rev. Ledeboer, who seceded from the Reformed State Church), united in 1907 under the leadership of the then 25-year-old Rev. G. H. Kersten, to form the Netherlands Reformed Congregations. Many of the North American congregations left the Christian Reformed Church to join the Netherlands Reformed Congregations after the Kuyperian presupposed regeneration doctrine began making inroads.

All Netherlands Reformed Congregations, office-bearers and members subscribe to three Reformed Forms of Unity, The Belgic Confession of Faith (by DeBres), the Heidelberg

Catechism (by Ursinus and Olevianus) and the Canons of Dort. The Heidelberg Catechism is preached weekly, except on church feast days.

Headquarters

Media Contact, Rev. A.H.Verhoef, 1142 Lakeshore Rd. W, RR#3, St. Catherines, ON L2R 6P9 CANADA Tel. (905)935-4934

OTHER ORGANIZATIONS

Netherlands Reformed Book and Publishing, 1233 Leffingwell NE, Grand Rapids, MI 49505

Periodicals

The Banner of Truth, Paul (mission magazine), *Insight Into, Learning and Living*

New Church—please see General Church of the New Jerusalem

North American Baptist Conference

The North American Baptist Conference was begun by immigrants from Germany. The first church was organized by the Rev. Konrad Fleischmann in Philadelphia in 1843. In 1865 delegates of the churches met in Wilmot, Ontario, and organized the North American Baptist Conference. Today only a few churches still use the German language, mostly in a bilingual setting.

The Conference meets in general session once every three years for fellowship, inspiration and to conduct the business of the Conference through elected delegates from the local churches. The General Council, composed of representatives of the various Associations and Conference organizations and departments, meets annually to determine the annual budget and programs for the Conference and its departments and agencies. The General Council also makes recommendations to the Triennial Conference on policies, long-range plans and election of certain personnel, boards and committees.

Approximately 60 missionaries serve in Brazil, Cameroon, Japan, Mexico, Nigeria, Philippines, and Russia.

Eight homes for the aged are affiliated with the Conference and 11 camps are operated on the association level.

Headquarters

1 S. 210 Summit Ave., Oakbrook Terrace, IL 60181 Tel. (630)495-2000 Fax (630)495-3301
Media Contact, Marlene Minor, Senior Leader/Stewardship and Communications
Email: serve@nabconf.org
Website: www.nabconference.org

Officers

Exec. Dir., Rev. Ron Berg, 1 So 210 Summit Ave., Oakbrook Terrace, IL 60181 Tel. (630) 495-2000 Fax (630)475-3301, Email: RBerg @nabconf.org

OTHER ORGANIZATIONS

Church Extension Investors Fund, Dir., Les D. Collins

Periodicals

NABtoday

North American Old Roman Catholic Church (Archdiocese of New York)

This body is identical with the Roman Catholic Church in faith but differs from it in discipline and worship. The Mass is offered with the appropriate rite either in Latin or in the vernacular. All other sacraments are taken from the Roman Pontifical. This jurisdiction allows for married clergy.

PRIMATIAL HEADQUARTERS

60 ST. Felix St., Brooklyn, NY 11217-1206 Tel. (718)855-0600 Fax (718)522-1231
Media Contact, Primate, Most Rev. Albert J. Berube
Email: info@orccna.org
Website: www.orccna.org

Officers

Primate, The Most Rev. Albert J. Berube
Diocese of New York, Ordinary, Most Rev. Albert J. Berube
Diocese of Montreal & French Canada, Ordinary, Most Rev. Herve L. Quessy

The Old Catholic Orthodox Church

The Old Catholic Orthodox Church (formerly, the Apostolic Orthodox Old Catholic Church) was founded in Illinois in the year 1985, originally as a Spanish speaking community of faith. It has now grown to include English speaking and other international provinces. We subscribe to the Apostles', Nicene and Athanasian Creeds as matters of faith. Along with upholding all sacraments of the One, Holy, Catholic and Apostolic Church.

Headquarters

The Most Reverend Jorge Rodriguez-Villa, Apostolic Primate (Presiding Bishop)
P.O. Box 80193, Rancho Santa Margarita, CA 92688, Tel. (323)806-4045
Website: www.oldcatholicorthodoxchurch.org

Officers

The Most Reverend Jorge Rodriguez-Villa, Apostolic Primate (Presiding Bishop)
The Most Rev. William Anthony Harrison, Apostolic Vicar General

Old German Baptist Brethren Church

This group separated from the Church of the Brethren (formerly German Baptist Brethren) in 1881 in order to preserve and maintain historic Brethren Doctrine.

141

Vindicator Ofc. Ed., Steven L. Bayer, 6952 N. Montgomery County Line Rd., Englewood, OH 45322-9748 Tel. (937)884-7531

Periodicals
The Vindicator

Old Order Amish Church
The congregations of this Old Order Amish group have no annual conference. They worship in private homes. They adhere to the older forms of worship and attire. This body has bishops, ministers and deacons.

Headquarters
Der Neue Amerikanische Calendar, c-o Raber's Book Store, 2467 C R 600, Baltic, OH 43804, LeRoy Beachy, Beachy Amish Mennonite Church, 4324 SR 39, Millerburg, OH 44654, Tel./Fax (330)893-2883

Old Order (Wisler) Mennonite Church
This body arose from a separation of Mennonites dated 1872, under Jacob Wisler, in opposition to what were thought to be innovations.

The group is in the Eastern United States and Canada. Each state, or district, has its own organization and holds semi-annual conferences.

Headquarters
Media Contact, Amos B. Hoover, 376 N. Muddy Creek Rd., Denver, PA 17517 Tel. (717)484-4849 Fax (717)484-104

Periodicals
Home Messenger, *Exchange Messenger*

Open Bible Standard Churches
Open Bible Standard Churches originated from two revival movements, Bible Standard Conference, founded in Eugene, Oregon, under the leadership of Fred L. Hornshuh in 1919, and Open Bible Evangelistic Association, founded in Des Moines, Iowa, under the leadership of John R. Richey in 1932.

Similar in doctrine and government, the two groups amalgamated on July 26, 1935 as "Open Bible Standard Churches, Inc." with headquarters in Des Moines, Iowa.

The original group of 210 ministers has enlarged to incorporate over 2,500 ministers and 1,509 churches in 40 countries. The first missionary left for India in 1926. The church now ministers in Asia, Africa, South America, Europe, Canada, Mexico, Central America, and the Caribbean Islands.

Historical roots of the parent groups reach back to the outpouring of the Holy Spirit in 1906 at Azusa Street Mission in Los Angeles and to the full gospel movement in the Midwest. Both groups were organized under the impetus of pentecostal revival. Simple faith, freedom from fanaticism, emphasis on evangelism and missions and free fellowship with other groups were characteristics of the growing organizations.

The highest governing body of Open Bible Standard Churches meets biennially and is composed of all ministers and one voting delegate per 100 members from each church. A National Board of Directors, elected by the national and regional conferences, conducts the business of the organization. Official Bible College is Eugene Bible College in Oregon.

Open Bible Standard Churches is a charter member of the National Association of Evangelicals and of the Pentecostal/Charismatic Churches of North America. It is a member of the Pentecostal World Conference.

NATIONAL OFFICE
2020 Bell Ave., Des Moines, IA 50315 Tel. (515)288-6761 Fax (515)288-2510
Media Contact, Exec. Dir., Communications & Resources, Jeff Farmer, Tel. (515)288-6761 Fax (515)288-2510
Email: info@openbible.org
Website: www.openbible.org

Officers
Pres., Jeffrey E. Farmer, 2020 Bell Ave., Des Moines, Iowa 50315 Tel. (515)288-6761 Fax (515)288-2510, Email: jeff@openbible.org
Esq.,Sec.-Treas., Teresa A. Beyer, 2020 Bell Ave., Des Moines, Iowa 50315 Tel. (515)288-6761 Fax (515)288-2510, Email: tbeyer@openbible.org
Dir., of Intl. Min., Vince S. McCarty, 2020 Bell Ave., Des Moines, Iowa 50315 Tel. (515)288-6761 Fax (515)288-2510, Email: missions@openbible.org

Periodicals
Message of the Open Bible

The (Original) Church of God, Inc.
This body was organized in 1886 as the first church in the United States to take the name "The Church of God." In 1917 a difference of opinion led this particular group to include the word (Original) in its name. It is a holiness body and believes in the whole Bible, rightly divided, using the New Testament as its rule and government.

Headquarters
P.O. Box 592, Wytheville, VA 24382
Media Contact, Gen. Overseer, Rev. William Dale, Tel. (800)827-9234

Officers
Gen. Overseer, Rev. William Dale
Asst. Gen. Overseer, Rev. Alton Evans

The Orthodox Church in America*
The Orthodox Church of America entered Alaska in 1794 before its purchase by the United States in 1867. Its canonical status of indepen-

dence (autocephaly) was granted by its Mother Church, the Russian Orthodox Church, on April 10, 1970, and it is now known as The Orthodox Church in America.

Headquarters

P.O. Box 675, Syosset, NY 11791-0675 Tel. (516)922-0550 Fax (516)922-0954

Media Contact, Dir. of Communications, V. Rev. John Matusiak, 1 Wheaton Center, # 912, IL 60187 Tel. (630)668-3071 Fax (708)923-1706

Email: jjm@oca.org

Website: www.oca.org

HOLY SYNOD OF BISHOPS

RULING BISHOPS

Primate, Archbishop of Washington & New York, Metropolitan of All America & Canada, His Beatitude, Most Blessed Herman, P.O. Box 675, Syosset, NY 11791

Archbishop of Pittsburgh & Western PA, Most Rev. Kyrill, P.O. Box R, Wexford, PA 15090

Archbishop of Dallas, Archbishop Dmitri, 4112 Throckmorton, Dallas, TX 75219

Archbishop of Detroit, Rt. Rev. Nathaniel, P.O. Box 309, Grass Lake, MI 49240-0309

Archbishop of Chicago, Rt. Rev. Job, 927 N. LaSalle, Chicago, IL 60610

Bishop of San Francisco and Los Angeles, Rt. Rev. Tikhon, 649 North Robinson St., Los Angeles, CA 90026

Bishop of Ottawa and Canada, Rt. Rev. Seraphim, P.O. Box 179, Spencerville, ON K0E 1X0 Tel. (613)925-5226

Bishop of Sitka, Anchorage, and Alaska, Rt. Rev. Nikolai, 513 E. 24 Ave. Ste. #3, Anchorage, AK 99503

Bishop of Boston, Rt. Rev. Nikon, P.O.Box 149, Southbridge, MA 01550; Tel. (508)764-3222

Bishop of Philadelphia and Eastern PA, Rt. Rev. Tikhon, P.O.Box 130, South Canaan, PA 18459

AUXILIARY BISHOPS

Bishop of Dearborn Heights, Rt. Rev. Irineu, 23300 Davison Ave. West, Detriot, MI 48223

Bishop of Berkeley, Rt. Rev. Benjamin, 701 Park Place, Boulder City, NV 89005

Bishop of Mexico City, Rt. Rev. Alejo, Rio Consulado e Irapuato, Col. Penon de los banos, 15520 Mexico D.F.

RETIRED BISHOPS

Retired Metropolitan, Most Blessed Theodosius, 156 Rifgon Drive, Canonsburg, PA 15317

Retired Archbishop, Most Rev. Gregory, P.O.Box 94, Jackson, NJ 08527-0094

Retired Archbishop, Most Rev. Lazar, 37323 Hawkins Pickle Rd., Dewdney, BC, Canada V0M 1H0

Retired Bishop, Rt. Rev. Mark, 9511 Sun Pointe Dr., Boynton Beach, FL 33437

Retired Bishop, Rt. Rev. Varlaam, 37323 Hawkins Pickle Rd., Dewdney, BC, Canada V0M 1H0

OTHER ORGANIZATIONS

Alumni Association of St. Herman Seminary, 414 Mission Rd., Kodiak, AK 99615-9985

Alumni Association of St. Tikhon Seminary, South Canaan, PA 18459

Alumni Association of St. Vladimir Seminary, 575 Scarsdale Rd., Crestwood, NY 10707

Orthodox Peace Fellowship, P.O. Box 390838, Cambridge, MA 02139

Orthodox Theological Society of America, 50 Goddard Ave., Brookline, MA 02445

Association of Romanian Orthodox Ladies' Auxiliaries of America, P.O. Box 309, Grass Lake, MI 49240

Association of Romanian Canadian Orthodox Ladies' Auxiliaries, Box 4023, Regina, SK, Canada S4P 3R9

Fellowship of Orthodox Christians in America, 10 Downs Drive, Wilkes-Barre, PA 18705

Orthodox Brotherhood USA, P.O. Box 309, Grass Lake, MI 49240

Orthodox Brotherhood of Canada, Box 4023, Regina, SK, Canada S4P 3R9

American Romanian Orthodox Youth, P.O. Box 309, Grass Lake, MI 49240

Project Mexico, P.O. Box 120028, Chula Vista, CA 91912

Orthodox Christian Adoption Referral Service, P.O. Box 675, Syosset, NY 11791

Fellowship of Orthodox Stewards, P.O. Box 675, Syosset, NY 11791

Orthodox Christian Publications Center, 4653 Memphis Villas South, Brooklyn, OH 44144

The Orthodox Presbyterian Church

On June 11, 1936, certain ministers, elders and lay members of the Presbyterian Church in the U.S.A. withdrew from that body to form a new denomination. Under the leadership of the late Rev. J. Gresham Machen, noted conservative New Testament scholar, the new church determined to continue to uphold the Westminster Confession of Faith as traditionally understood by Presbyterians and to engage in proclamation of the gospel at home and abroad.

The church has grown modestly over the years and suffered early defections, most notably one in 1937 that resulted in the formation of the Bible Presbyterian Church under the leadership of Dr. Carl McIntire. It now has congregations throughout the states of the continental United States.

The denomination is a member of the North American Presbyterian and Reformed Council and the International Council of Reformed Churches.

Headquarters

607 N. Easton Rd., Bldg. E, Box P, Willlow Grove, PA 19090-0920 Tel. (215)830-0900 Fax (215)830-0350

Media Contact, Stated Clerk, Rev. Donald J. Duff

Email: duff.1@opc.org

Website: www.opc.org

Officers

Moderator of General Assembly, The Rev. Robert Y. Eckardt, 2041 Sierra Trail, Xenia, OH 45385 Tel. (937)374-0240, Email: eckadt.1@opc.org

Stated Clk., Rev. Donald J. Duff

Periodicals

New Horizons in the Orthodox Presbyterian Church

Patriarchal Parishes of the Russian Orthodox Church in the U.S.A.*

This group of parishes is under the direct jurisdiction of the Patriarch of Moscow and All Russia, His Holiness Aleksy II, in the person of a Vicar Bishop, His Grace Mercurius, Bishop of Zaraisk.

Headquarters

St. Nicholas Cathedral, 15 E. 97th St., New York, NY 10029 Tel. (212)831-6294 Fax (212)427-5003

Media Contact, Sec. to the Bishop, Hieromonk Joseph, Tel. (212)996-6638

Email: bmercurius@ruscon.com

Website: www.russianchurchusa.org

Officers

Secretary to the Bishop, Hieromonk Joseph

Secretary of the Representation, Rev. Alexander Abramov

Pentecostal Assemblies of the World, Inc.

This organization is an interracial Pentecostal holiness of the Apostolic Faith, believing in repentance, baptism in Jesus's name and being filled with the Holy Ghost, with the evidence of speaking in tongues. It originated in the early part of the century in the Middle West and has spread throughout the country.

Headquarters

3939 Meadows Dr., Indianapolis, IN 46205 Tel. (317)547-9541 Fax (317)543-0513

Media Contact, Admin., John E. Hampton, Fax (317)543-0512

Website: www.pawinc.org

Officers

Presiding Bishop, Horace E. Smith

Suff. Bishop, A. Glenn Brady, General Secretary, Youngstown, OH

Bishops, Arthus Brazier; George Brooks; Ramsey Butler; Morris Golder; Francis L. Smith, Francis L.; Brooker T. Jones; C. R. Lee; Robert McMurray; Philip L. Scott; William L. Smith; Samuel A. Layne; Freeman M. Thomas; James E. Tyson; Charles Davis; Willie Burrell; Harry Herman; Jeremiah Reed; Jeron Johnson; Clifton Jones; Robert Wauls; Ronald L. Young; Henry L. Johnson; Leodis Warren; Thomas J. Weeks; Eugene Redd; Thomas W. Weeks, Sr.; Willard Saunders; Davis L. Ellis; Earl Parchia; Vanuel C. Little; Norman Wagner; George Austin; Benjamin A. Pitt; Markose Thopil; John K. Cole; Peter Warkie; Norman Walters; Alphonso Scott; David Dawkins

Gen. Sec, Suffragan Bishop Edward Roberts

Assist. Gen Sec., Suffragan Bishop A. Glenn Brady

Gen. Treas., Suffragan Bishop Mark C. Tolbert

Asst. Treas., Suffragan Bishop Carl A. Turner

Pentecostal Church of God

Growing out of the pentecostal revival at the turn of the 20th century, the Pentecostal Church of God was organized in Chicago on Dec. 30, 1919, as the Pentecostal Assemblies of the U.S.A. The name was changed to Pentecostal Church of God in 1922; in 1934 it was changed again to The Pentecostal Church of God of America, Inc.; and finally the name became the Pentecostal Church of God (Incorporated.) in 1979.

The International Headquarters was moved from Chicago, Illinois to Ottumwa, Iowa, in 1927, then to Kansas City, Missoui, in 1933 and finally to Joplin, Missouri, in 1951.

The denomination is evangelical and pentecostal in doctrine and practice. Active membership in the National Association of Evangelicals and the Pentecostal/Charismatic Churches North America is maintained.

The church is Trinitarian in doctrine and teaches the absolute inerrancy of the Scripture from Genesis to Revelation. Among its cardinal beliefs are the doctrines of salvation, which includes regeneration; divine healing, as provided for in the atonement; the baptism in the Holy Ghost, with the initial physical evidence of speaking in tongues; and the premillennial second coming of Christ.

Headquarters

4901 Pennsylvania, P.O. Box 850, Joplin, MO 64802 Tel. (417)624-7050 Fax (417)624-7102

Media Contact, Gen. Sec., Wayman C. Ming Jr.

Email: generalsecretary@pcg.org

Website: www.pcg.org

Officers

Gen. Bishop., Dr. Charles G. Scott

Gen. Sec., Wayman C. Ming Jr.

OTHER GENERAL EXECUTIVES

Dir. of World Missions, Rev. Loyd L. Naten

Dir. of Indian Missions, Dr. C. Don Burke

Dir. of Youth Ministries, Rev. Joe Skiles, Jr.

Dir. of Home Missions, Rev. Harry O. "Pat" Wilson

ASSISTANT GENERAL SUPERINTENDENTS/BISHOPS

Northwestern Division, Rev. Donald Manning

Southwestern Division, Rev. Jan Lake

North Central Division, Rev. Joseph Skiles, Sr.

South Central Division, Rev. Leon A. McDowell

Northeastern Division, Rev. Thomas E. Branham
Southeastern Division, Rev. C.W. Goforth

OTHER DEPARTMENTAL OFFICERS
Bus. Mgr., None at the present time
Director of Women's Ministry, Mrs. Janice Scott

Periodicals
The Pentecostal Messenger

Pentecostal Fire-Baptized Holiness Church

Organized in 1918, this group consolidated with the Pentecostal Free Will Baptists in 1919. It maintains rigid discipline over members.

Headquarters
P.O. Box 261, La Grange, GA 30241-0261 Tel. (706)884-7742
Media Contact, Gen. Mod., Wallace B. Pittman, Jr.

Officers
Gen. Treas., Alan Sparkman, 1961 Norjon circle, Clio, SC 29525 Tel. (843)586-9095
Gen. Sec., Joel Powell, 16841 Springs Mill Rd. Lauringbury, NC 28352 Tel. (901)462-3379
Gen. Mod., Wallace B. Pittman, Jr.
Gen. Supt. Mission Bd., Jerry Powell, Rt. 1, Box 384, Chadourn, NC 28431

The Pentecostal Free Will Baptist Church, Inc.

The Cape Fear Conference of Free Will Baptists, organized in 1855, merged in 1959 with The Wilmington Conference and The New River Conference of Free Will Baptists and was renamed the Pentecostal Free Will Baptist Church, Inc. The doctrines include regeneration, sanctification, the Pentecostal baptism of the Holy Ghost, the Second Coming of Christ and divine healing.

Headquarters
P.O. Box 1568, Dunn, NC 28335 Tel. (910)892-4161 Fax (910)892-6876
Media Contact, Gen. Supt., Preston Heath
Email: pheath@intrstar.net
Website: www.pfwb.org

Officers
Gen. Supt., Rev. Preston Heath
Asst. Gen. Supt., Jim Wall
Gen. Sec., Mr. Stephen Garriss
Gen. Treas., Mr. Dewayne Weeks
Christian Ed. Dir., Rev. Randy Barker
World Witness Dir., Rev. Hobbs
Gen. Services Dir., Ms. Cathy Muzingo
Ministerial Council Dir., Rev. Ed Taturn
Ladies' Auxiliary Dir., Dollie Davis
Heritage Bible College, Pres., Dr. Dwarka Ramphal
Crusader Youth Camp, Dir., Rev. Randy Barker

OTHER ORGANIZATIONS
Heritage Bible College
Crusader Youth Camp

Blessings Bookstore, 1006 W. Cumberland St., Dunn, NC 28334 Tel. (910)892-2401

Periodicals
The Messenger

Philadelphia Yearly Meeting of the Religious Society of Friends*

PYM traces its roots to the yearly meeting of 1681 in Burlington, New Jersey. For more than three centuries, PYM has served Monthly Meetings and Quarterly Meetings throughout eastern Pennsylvania, southern New Jersey, eastern Maryland and Delaware. In general, the activities of PYM are organized under five Standing Committees- Standing Committee on Worship and Care; Standing Committee on Education; Standing Committee on Peace and Concerns; Standing Committee on Support and Outreach; Standing Committee on General Services.

Headquarters
Philadelphia Yearly Meeting, 1515 Cherry Street, Philadelphia, PA 19102-1479 Tel. (215)241-7000 Fax (215)241-7045
Website: www.pym.org

Officers
Presiding Clerk, Thomas Swain
Clerk of Interim Meeting, Arthur Larrabee
Interim Gen. Sec., Mark Myers
Clerk, Standing Committee on Worship and Care, Alison A. Anderson
Clerk, Standing Committee on Education, Deborah Lyons
Clerk, Standing Committee on Peace and Concerns, Patricia Finley
Clerk, Standing Committee on Support and Outreach, Susan White & Pamela Carter
Clerk, Standing Committee on General Services, Patricia Hunt

Periodicals
PYM News

Pillar of Fire

The Pillar of Fire was founded by Alma Bridwell White in Denver on Dec. 29, 1901 as the Pentecostal Union. In 1917, the name was changed to Pillar of Fire. Alma White was born in Kentucky in 1862 and taught school in Montana where she met her husband, Kent White, a Methodist minister, who was a University student in Denver.

Because of Alma White's evangelistic endeavors, she was frowned upon by her superiors, which eventually necessitated her withdrawing from Methodist Church supervision. She was ordained as Bishop and her work spread to many states, to England, and since her death to Liberia, West Africa, Malawi, East Africa, Yugoslavia, Spain, India and the Philippines.

145

The Pillar of Fire organization has a college and two seminaries stressing Biblical studies. It operates eight separate schools for young people. The church continues to keep in mind the founder's goals and purposes.

Headquarters

P.O. Box 9159, Zarephath, NJ 08890 Tel. (732) 356-0102

Western Headquarters, 1302 Sherman St., Denver, CO 80203 Tel. (303)427-5462

Media Contact, 1st Vice Pres., Robert B. Dallenbach, 3455 W. 83 Ave., Westminster, CO 80031 Tel. (303)427-5462 Fax (303)429-0910

Email: info@zarephath.edu

Website: www.gospelcom.net/pof

Officers

Pres. & Gen. Supt., Dr. Robert B. Dallenbach

1st Vice Pres. & Asst. Supt., Rev. Joseph Gross

2nd Vice Pres./Sec.-Treas., Lois R. Stewart

Trustees, Kenneth Cope; S. Rea Crawford; Lois Stewart; Dr. Donald J. Wolfram; Robert B. Dallenbach; Rob W. Cruver; Joseph Gross

Polish National Catholic Church of America*

After a number of attempts to resolve differences regarding the role of the laity in parish administration in the Roman Catholic Church in Scranton, Pennsylvania, this Church was organized in 1897. With the consecration to the episcopacy of the Most Rev. F. Hodur, this Church became a member of the Old Catholic Union of Utrecht in 1907.

Headquarters

Office of the Prime Bishop, 1006 Pittston Ave., Scranton, PA 18505 Tel. (570)346-9131

Media Contact, Prime Bishop, Most Rev. Robert M. Nemkovich, 1006 Pittston Ave., Scranton, PA 18505 Tel. (570)346-9131 Fax (570) 346-2188

Email: PNCCCenter@adelphia.net

Website: www.PNCC.org

Officers

Prime Bishop, Most Rev. Robert M. Nemkovich, 115 Lake Scranton Rd., Scranton, PA 18505

Central Diocese, Bishop, Rt. Rev. Anthiny Mikovsky, 529 E Locust St. Scranton, PA 18505

Eastern Diocese, Bishop, Rt. Rev. Thomas J. Gnat, 166 Pearl St., Manchester, NH 03104

Buffalo-Pittsburgh Diocese, Bishop, Rt. Rev. Thaddeus S. Peplowski, 5776 Broadway, Lancaster, NY 14086

Western Diocese, Rt. Rev. Jan Dawidziuk, 920 N. Northwest Hwy., Park Ridge, IL 60068

Canadian Diocese, Bishop, Rt. Rev. Sylvester Bigaj, 880 Barton Steet East, Hamilton, ON L8L3B7, Canada

Ecumenical Officer, Rev. Robert M. Nemkovich, Jr.

Savonarola Theological Seminary, 1031 Cedar Avenue, Scranton, PA 18505 Rector: Most Rev. Robert M. Nemkovich Vice Rector: Rev. Dr. Czeslaw Kuliczkowski

Periodicals

God's Field, Polka

Plymouth Brethren—please see Christian Brethren

Presbyterian Church—please see Evangelical Presbyterian Church

Presbyterian Church in America

The Presbyterian Church in America is an Evangelical, Reformed covenant community of churches in the United States and Canada committed to a common doctrinal standard (The Westminster Standards), mutual accountability (representative church government), and cooperative ministry. The PCA traces its historical roots to the First General Assembly of the Church of Scotland of 1560, the establishment of the Presbytery of Philadelphia, 1789, and the General Assembly of the Southern Presbyterian Church, Augusta in 1861. Organized in 1973 by conservative churches formerly associated with the Presbyterian Church in the United States, the Church was first known as the National Presbyterian Church but changed its name in 1974 to the Presbyterian Church in America. The PCA seeks to be "Faithful to the Scriptures, True to the Reformed Faith, and Obedient to the Great Commission." In 1982 the Reformed Presbyterian Church, Evangelical Synod joined the PCA bringing with it a rich tradition that had antecedents in colonial America.

The PCA holds to the ancient creeds of the Church such as the Apostles' Creed and the Nicene Creed and has a firm commitment to its doctrinal standards, The Westminster Confession of Faith, Larger and Shorter Catechisms, that have been significant in Presbyterianism since 1645, These doctrinal standards reflect the distinctives of the Reformed tradition, Calvinism, and Covenant Theology. Ministers, ruling elders, and deacons are required to subscribe to the Westminster Standards in good faith. Individuals are received by a Session as communing members of the Church upon their profession of faith in Jesus Christ as Lord and Saviour, their promise to live a Christian lifestyle, and their commitment to worship and service in the Church.

The PCA is a connectional Church, led by ruling elders (lay leaders) and teaching elders (ministers). The Session governs a local congregation; the Diaconate carries out mercy ministries. The Presbytery is responsible for regional matters and the General Assembly is responsible for national matters in the USA and Canada. Cooperative ministry is carried out through over sixty Presbyteries and ten General Assembly Ministries.

The educational institutions of the Church are Covenant College of Lookout Mountain, GA and Covenant Theological Seminary of St. Louis, MO. The PCA and the Orthodox Presbyterian Church participate in a joint publication venture, Great Commission Publications, for the publication of Christian Education materials.

In its ecumenical relations the PCA is a member of the North American Presbyterian and Reformed Council, the National Association of Evangelicals, and the World Reformed Fellowship.

The General Assembly approved a statement of purpose, "It is the purpose of the PCA to bring glory to God as a worshipping and serving community until the nations in which we live are filled with churches that make Jesus Christ and His word their chief joy, and the nations of the world, hearing the Word, are discipled in obedience to the Great Commission."

The Church has grown beyond its origin in the southeastern states to have congregations in forty-nine states in the USA and in several provinces of Canada. Growth is due to the PCA's ministry in evangelism, discipleship, church planting, church renewal, and campus ministry. Indicative of her concern for cross-cultural ministry, the PCA has the largest international missionary force in Presbyterian Church history.

Headquarters

1700 N. Brown Rd., Lawrenceville, GA 30043-8122, Tel. (678)825-1000
Email: ac@pcanet.org
Website: www.pcanet.org

Officers

Moderator: Ruling Elder E. J. Nusbaum, Village Seven Presbyterian Church, 4055 South Nonchalant Circle, Colorado Springs, CO 80917 Tel. (719)574-6700 Fax (719)574-3330, Email: e.j.nusbaum.b7ci@statefarm.com

Stated Clerk/Coordinator of Administration – Dr. L. Roy Taylor, 1700 N. Brown Rd., Suite 105, Lawrenceville, GA 30043-8122 Tel. (678)825-1100, Email: ac@pcanet.org

Christian Education & Publications Coordinator– Dr. Charles Dunahoo, 1700 N. Brown Rd., Suite 102, Lawrenceville, GA 30043-8122 Tel. (678)825-1100, Email: cep@pacnet.org

Mission to the World Coordinator, Dr. Paul D. Kooistra, 1600 N. Brown Rd., Lawrenceville, GA 30043-8141 Tel. (678)823-0004, Email: mtw@mtw.org

Mission to North America Coordinator, Dr. James C. Bland, 1700 N. Brown Rd., Suite 101, Lawrenceville, GA 30043-8122 Tel. (678)825-1200, Email: mna@pcanet.org

Reformed University Ministries Coordinator— Dr. Rod Mays, 1700 N. Brown Rd., Suite 104, Lawrenceville, GA 30043-8122 Tel. (678)825-1070, Email: rum@pcanet.org

PCA Foundation President, Mr. Randel Stair, 1700 N. Brown Rd., Suite 103, Lawrenceville, GA 30043-8122 Tel. (678)825-1040, Email: pcaf@pcanet.org

PCA Retirement and Benefits Inc., Pres., Mr. Gary D. Campbell, 1700 North Brown Road, Suite 106, Lawrenceville, GA 30043-8143 Tel. (678) 825-1260, Email: gcampbell@pcanet.org

Ridge Haven Conference Director—Rev. Morse Up De Graff, P.O. Box 969, Rosman, NC 28772 Tel. (828)862-3916 Fax (828)884-6988, Email: ridgehaven@citcom.net

Covenant College President—Dr. Niel Nielson, 14049 Scenic Highway, Lookout Mountain, GA 30750 Tel. (706)820-1560 Fax (706)820-2165, Email: webmaster@covenant.edu

Covenant Theological Seminary President—Dr. Bryan Chapell, 12330 Conway Rd., St. Louis, MO 63141 Tel. (314)434-4044 Fax (314)434-4819, Email: president@covenantseminary.edu

Periodicals

ByFaith, Equip, Covenant, Mission Report, The View

Presbyterian Church (U.S.A.)*

The Presbyterian Church (U.S.A.) was organized June 10, 1983, when the Presbyterian Church in the United States and the United Presbyterian Church in the United States of America united in Atlanta. The union healed a major division which began with the Civil War when Presbyterians in the South withdrew from the Presbyterian Church in the United States of America to form the Presbyterian Church in the Confederate States.

The United Presbyterian Church in the United States of America had been created by the 1958 union of the Presbyterian Church in the United States of America and the United Presbyterian Church of North America. Of those two uniting bodies, the Presbyterian Church in the U.S.A. dated from the first Presbytery organized in Philadelphia, about 1706. The United Presbyterian Church of North America was formed in 1858, when the Associate Reformed Presbyterian Church and the Associate Presbyterian Church united.

Strongly ecumenical in outlook, the Presbyterian Church (U.S.A.) is the result of at least 10 different denominational mergers over the last 250 years. A restructure, adopted by the General Assembly meeting in June 1993, has been implemented. The Presbyterian Church (U.S.A.) dedicated its new national offices in Louisville, Kentucky in 1988.

Headquarters

100 Witherspoon St., Louisville, KY 40202 Tel. (888)728-7228 Fax (502)569-5018

Media Contact, Assoc. Dir. for Communications, Barry Creech Tel. (502)569-5515 Fax (502)569-8073

Email: presytel@pcusa.org
Website: www.pcusa.org

147

Officers

Mod., Joan Gray, 100 Witherspoon St, Louisville KY 40202 Tel. (888)728-7228

Vice Mod., Robert Wilson, 100 Witherspoon St, Louisville KY 40202 Tel. (888)728-7228

Stated Clk., Clifton Kirkpatrick, 100 Witherspoon St, Louisville KY 40202 Tel. (888) 728-7228

THE OFFICE OF THE GENERAL ASSEMBLY

100 Witherspoon St, Louisville KY 40202-1396 Tel. (888)728-7228 x 5424 Fax (502)569-8005

Stated Clk., Rev. Clifton Kirkpatrick

Strategic Operations, Dir., Rev. Gradye Parsons

Middle Governing Body Relations, Coord., Rev. Jill Hudson

Dept. of the Stated Clerk, Dir., Loyda Aja

Dept. of Constitutional Services, Dir., Rev. Mark Tammen

Ecumenical & Agency Relations, Dir., Rev. Robina Winbush

Dept. of Communication, Development & Technology, Dir., Rev. Kerry Clements

Dept. of Hist., Philadelphia, 425 Lombard St., Philadelphia, PA 19147 Tel. (215)627-1852 Fax (215)627-0509; Dir., Frederick J. Heuser, Jr.; Deputy Dir., Margery Sly

GENERAL ASSEMBLY COUNCIL

Exec. Dir., Linda Valentine

Deputy Exec. Dir. for Mission, Rev. Tom Taylor

Deputy Exec. Dir. for Communication & Funds Development, Eld Karen Schmidt

Deputy Exec. Dir. for Shared Services & Chief Financial Officer, Eld Joey Bailey

Theology, Worship & Education, Dir., Rev Joseph Small

Evangelism & Church Growth, Dir., Rev Eric Hoey

Peace & Justice, Dir, Eld Sara Lisherness

Relief & Development, Int Dir., Eld Sara Lisherness

World Mission, Dir., Rev Hunter Farrell

Racial Ethnic & Women's Ministries/ Presbyterian Women, Dir., Rev Rhashell Hunter

BOARD OF PENSIONS

200 Market St., Philadelphia, PA 19103-3298, Tel. (800)773-7752 Fax (215)587-6215

Chpsn. of the Bd., Earldean V. S. Robbins

Pres., & CEO, Robert W. Maggs, Jr.

PRESBYTERIAN CHURCH (U.S.A.) FOUNDATION

200 E. Twelfth St., Jeffersonville, IN 47130, Tel. (812)288-8841 Fax (502)569-5980

Chpsn. of the Bd., James Henderson

Pres. & CEO, Robert E. Leech

PRESBYTERIAN CHURCH (U.S.A.) INVESTMENT & LOAN PROGRAM, INC.

Tel. (800)903-7457 Fax (502)569-8868

Chpsn. of the Board, Ben McAnally

Pres. & CEO, James L. Hudson

PRESBYTERIAN PUBLISHING CORPORATION

Chpsn. of the Bd., Robert Bohl

Pres. & CEO, Vacant

SYNOD EXECUTIVES

Alaska-Northwest, Rev. Joyce Emery Martin, Int., 217 6th Ave. N., Seattle, WA 98109 Tel. (206)448-6403

Boriquen in Puerto Rico, Rev. Edwin Quiles Rodriquez Int., Ave. Hostos Edificio 740, Cond. Medical Center Plaza, Ste. 216, Mayaguez, PR 00680 Tel. (787)832-8375

Covenant, Rev. Richard D. Brownlee and Rev. Marie T. Cross, 1911 Indian Wood Cir #B Tel. (419)754-4050

Lakes & Prairies, Rev. Philip Brown, 8012 Cedar Ave. S., Bloomington, MN 55425-1210 Tel. (612)854-0144

Lincoln Trails, Rev. Carol McDonald and Rev. David Crittenden, 1100 W. 42nd St., Indianapolis, IN 46208-3381 Tel. (317)923-3681

Living Waters, Rev. Terry Newland, 318 Seaboard Ln, Ste. 205, Franklin, TN 37067 Tel. (615)261-4008

Mid-America, Rev. John Williams, 6400 Glenwood, Ste. 111, Overland Park, KS 66202-4072 Tel. (913)384-3020

Mid-Atlantic, Rev. John Winings, P.O. Box 27026, Richmond, VA 23261-7026 Tel. (804)342-0016

Northeast, Rev. Clinton McCoy, Int., 5811 Heritage Landing Dr., East Syracuse, NY 13057-9360 Tel. (315)446-5990

Pacific, Rev. Robert Brinks, 8 Fourth St., Petaluma, CA 94952-3004 Tel. (707)765-1772

Rocky Mountains, Rev. Zane Buxton, 7061 S University Blvd #206., Centennial, CO 80211 Tel. (303)477-9070

South Atlantic, Rev. Reginald Parsons, 118 E. Monroe St., Ste. 3, Jacksonville, FL 32202 Tel. (904)356-6070

Southern California & Hawaii, Rev. Edith Gause, 1501 Wilshire Blvd., Los Angeles, CA 90017-2293 Tel. (213)483-3840

Southwest, Rev. Janet DeVries, 401 E. 4th St. #A, Tucson, AZ 85705 Tel. (520)791-9600

The Sun, Rev. Judy R. Fletcher, 6100 Colwell Blvd #200, Irving, TX 75039 Tel. (214)390-1894

The Trinity, Rev. Bruce G. Stevens and Thomas E. Robinson, 3040 Market St., Camp Hill, PA 17011-4599 Tel. (717)737-0421

Periodicals

American Presbyterians, Journal of Presbyterian History, Presbyterian News Service, Church & Society Magazine, Horizons, Presbyterians Today, Interpretation, Presbyterian Outlook

Primitive Advent Christian Church

This body split from the Advent Christian Church. All its churches are in West Virginia.

The Primitive Advent Christian Church believes that the Bible is the only rule of faith and practice and that Christian character is the only test of fellowship and communion. The church agrees with Christian fidelity and meekness; exercises mutual watch and care; counsels, admonishes, or reproves as duty may require and receives the same from each other as becomes the household of faith. Primitive Advent Christians do not believe in taking up arms.

The church believes that three ordinances are set forth by the Bible to be observed by the Christian church, (1) baptism by immersion; (2) the Lord's Supper, by partaking of unleavened bread and wine; (3) feet washing, to be observed by the saints' washing of one another's feet.

Headquarters

Media Contact, Sec.-Treas., Roger Wines, 1971 Grapevine Rd., Sissonville, WV 25320 Tel. (304)988-2668

Officers

Pres., Herbert Newhouse, 7632 Hughart Dr., Sissonville, WV 25320 Tel. (304)984-9277

Vice Pres., Roger Hammons, 273 Frame Rd., Elkview, WV 25071 Tel. (304)965-6247

Sec. & Treas., Roger Wines, 1971 Grapevine Rd., Sissonville, WV 25320 Tel. (304)988-2668

Primitive Baptists

This group of Baptists has churches in the United States, the Philippines, India and Africa. While they oppose centralization and modern mission boards, they believe in the circulation of the gospel. They preach salvation by grace alone.

Headquarters

P.O. Box 38, Thornton, AR 71766 Tel. (501)352-3694

Media Contact, Elder W. Hartsel Cayce

Officers

Elder W. Hartsel Cayce

Elder Lasserre Bradley, Jr., Box 17037, Cincinnati, OH 45217 Tel. (513)821-7289

Elder S. T. Tolley, P.O. Box 68, Atwood, TN 38220 Tel. (901)662-7417

Periodicals

Baptist Witness

Primitive Methodist Church in the U.S.A.

Hugh Bourne and William Clowes, local preachers in the Wesleyan Church in England, organized a daylong meeting at Mow Cop at Staffordshire on May 31, 1807, after Lorenzo Dow, an evangelist from America, told them of American camp meetings. Thousands attended and many were converted but the Methodist church, founded by the open-air preacher John Wesley, refused to accept the converts and reprimanded the preachers.

After waiting for two years for a favorable action by the Wesleyan Society, Bourne and Clowes established The Society of the Primitive Methodists. This was not a schism, Bourne said, for "we did not take one from them...it now appeared to be the will of God that we...should form classes and take upon us the care of churches in the fear of God." Primitive Methodist missionaries were sent to New York in 1829. An American conference was established in 1840.

Missionary efforts reach into Guatemala, Spain and other countries. The denomination joins in federation with the Evangelical Congregational Church, the United Brethren in Christ Church and the Southern Methodist Church and is a member of the National Association of Evangelicals.

The church believes the Bible is the only true rule of faith and practice, the inspired Word of God. It believes in one Triune God, the Deity of Jesus Christ, the Deity and personality of the Holy Spirit, the innocence of Adam and Eve, the Fall of the human race, the necessity of repentance, justification by faith of all who believe, regeneration witnessed by the Holy Spirit, sanctification by the Holy Spirit, the second coming of the Lord Jesus Christ, the resurrection of the dead and conscious future existence of all people and future judgments with eternal rewards and punishments.

Headquarters

Media Contact, Pres., Rev. Kerry Ritts, 723 Preston Ln., Hatboro, PA 19040 Tel. (215)675-2639/(215)672-1576

Email: pmconf@juno.com

Website: www.primitivemethodistchurch.org

Officers

Pres., Rev. Kerry R. Ritts, 723 Preston Ln., Hatboro, PA 19040-2321 Tel.(215)672-1576

Vice Pres., Rev. Reginald H. Thomas, 110 Pittston Blvd., Wilkes-Barre, PA. 18702-9620 Tel. (570)823-3425

Recording Secretary, Rev. John Stange, 55 Cherry St., Plymouth, PA 18651-2336 Tel. (570)779-1332

General. Secretary., Rev. David Allen, Jr., 1199 Lawrence St., Lowell, MA 01852-5526 Tel. (978)453-2052, Email: pahson@earthlink.net

Treas., Mr. Raymond C. Baldwin, 18409 Mill Run Ct., Leesburg, VA 20176-4583 Email: Rbaldwin32@aol.com

Progressive National Baptist Convention, Inc.*

This body held its organizational meeting in Cincinnati in November, 1961. Subsequent regional sessions were followed by the first annual session in Philadelphia in 1962.

Headquarters

601 50th Street, N.E., Washington, DC 20019 Tel. (202)396-0558 Fax (202)398-4998

Media Contact, Gen. Sec., Dr. Tyrone S. Pitts
Website: www.pnbc.org

CONVENTION OFFICERS
Dr. T. DeWitt Smith Jr., President
Dr. Carroll A. Baltimore Sr., 1st Vice President
Dr. James C. Perkins, 2nd Vice President
Dr. Tyrone S. Pitts, General Secretary

REGIONAL VICE PRESIDENTS
Dr. Frank Blackshear, Eastern Region
Rev David Peoples, Midwest Region
Dr. Wilbur Lewis, Southwest Region
Dr. Michael N. Harris, Southern Region
Dr. Francis Sarpong, International Region
Dr. Terry Streeter, Congress of Christian Education
Mrs. Brenda Tribett, Executive Director, Christian Education
Rev. James H. Hunter, Chairman, Mission Ministry
Dr. Earl Trent, Executive Director, Mission Ministry
Dr. Arabella Rich, President, Women's Department, 324 Reed St., Anderson SC 29624, Tel. (864)226-2108
Mr. Wilmer Jones, Laymen's Department
The Rev. Samuel Nixon, Seminarian Development
Mr. Clifton Caldwell, Young Adult Men
Ms. Denise Carter-McCormick, Young Adult Women
Mrs. Rita Johnson, Principal, Nannie Helen Burroughs School, Tel. (202)398-5266

Protestant Reformed Churches in America

The Protestant Reformed Churches (PRC) have their roots in the sixteenth century Reformation of Martin Luther and John Calvin, as it developed in the Dutch Reformed churches. The denomination originated as a result of a controversy in the Christian Reformed Church in 1924 involving the adoption of the "Three Points of Common Grace." Three ministers in the Christian Reformed Church, the Reverends Herman Hoeksema, George Ophoff, and Henry Danhof, and their consistories (Eastern Avenue, Hope, and Kalamazoo, respectively) rejected the doctrine. Eventually these men were deposed, and their consistories were either deposed or set outside the Christian Reformed Church. The denomination was formed in 1926 with three congregations. Today the denomination is comprised of some twenty-eight churches (more than 7,000 members) in the USA and Canada. The presbyterian form of church government as determined by the Church Order of Dordt is followed by the PRC. The doctrinal standards of the PRC are the Reformed confessions—the Heidelberg Catechism, Belgic Confession of Faith, and Canons of Dordrecht. The doctrine of the covenant is a cornerstone of their teaching. They maintain an unconditional, particular covenant of grace that God establishes with His elect.

Headquarters
16511 South Park Ave., South Holland, IL 60473 Tel. (708)333-1314
Media Contact, Stated Clerk, Don Doezema, 4949 Ivanrest Ave., Grandville, MI 49418 Tel. (616)531-1490
Email: doezema@prca.org
Website: www.prca.org

Officers
Stat. Clk., Don Doezema, 4949 Ivanrest Ave., Grandville, MI 49418 Tel. (616)531-1490 Fax (616)531-3033, Email: doezema@prca.org

Periodicals
The Standard Bearer

Quakers—please see Friends General Conference

Quakers, Philadelphia—please see Philadelphia Yearly meeting of the Religious Society of Friends

Quakers, Conservative—please see Religious Society of Friends (Conservative)

Quakers, International—please see Evangelical Friends International—North American Region

Quakers, Unaffiliated Meetings—please see Religious Society of Friends (Unaffiliated Meetings)

Reformed Catholic Church

The Reformed Catholic Church was founded in 1988, and incorporated in 1989, as an alternative to the structures and strictures of the Roman Catholic Church, yet without denying basic catholic beliefs of faith and love, spirituality and community, prayer and sacramentality. The Reformed Catholic Church is a federation of independent churches offering a progressive alternative in the Catholic tradition. It is a newly formed rite, as in the tradition of the Orthodox churches of the Catholic tradition and the Old Catholic Church of Utrecht. It remains a Catholic Church, and its priests are considered Catholic priests.

Headquarters
P.O. Box 2, Worthington, OH 43085-9998
Email: PresidingBishop@reformedcatholicchurch.org
Website: www.reformedcatholicchurch.org

Officers
Metropolitan Archbishop, Archbishop Phillip Zimmerman, DD RSJ, P.O. Box 2, Worthington, OH 43085-9998
Bishop David Frazee, DD RSJ, 1529 Runaway Bay, Suite 1 D Columbus, OH 43204 Bishop Patrick Batuyong, DD, 1712 Connally Drive, Atlanta, GA 30316 Bishop Peter Posthumus, DD OPJB, 255 Plymouth SE East Grand Rapids, MI 49506 Bishop Shane Price, DD,

825 N. 26th St. Bismark, ND 58501 Bishop Raelyn Scott, DD RCF, 2202 Greenwood, Weatherford, TX 76088

Reformed Church in America*

The Reformed Church in America was established in 1628 by the earliest settlers of New York. It is the oldest Protestant denomination with a continuous ministry in North America. Until 1867 it was known as the Reformed Protestant Dutch Church.

The first ordained minister, Domine Jonas Michaelius, arrived in New Amsterdam from The Netherlands in 1628. Throughout the colonial period, the Reformed Church lived under the authority of the Classis of Amsterdam. Its churches were clustered in New York and New Jersey. Under the leadership of Rev. John Livingston, it became a denomination independent of the authority of the Classis of Amsterdam in 1776. Its geographical base was broadened in the 19th century by the immigration of Reformed Dutch and German settlers in the midwestern United States. The Reformed Church now spans the United States and Canada.

The Reformed Church in America accepts as its standards of faith the Heidelberg Catechism, Belgic Confession and Canons of Dort. It has a rich heritage of world mission activity. It claims to be loyal to reformed tradition which emphasizes obedience to God in all aspects of life.

Although the Reformed Church in America has worked in close cooperation with other churches, it has never entered into merger with any other denomination. It is a member of the World Alliance of Reformed Churches, the World Council of Churches and the National Council of the Churches of Christ in the United States of America. In 1998 it also entered into a relationship of full communion with the Evangelical Lutheran Church in America, Presbyterian Church (U.S.A.), and the United Church of Christ by way of the Formula of Agreement.

Headquarters

475 Riverside Dr., New York, NY 10115 Tel. (212)870-3243 Fax (212)870-2499

Media Contact, Communication Officer, Paul Boice, 4500 60th St. SE, Grand Rapids, MI 49512 Tel. (616)698-7071 Fax (616)698-6606

Email: dmorris@rca.org

Website: www.rca.org

OFFICERS AND STAFF OF GENERAL SYNOD

President, The Rev. Bradley Lewis, 18th Floor, New York, NY 10115

General Snod Council; Moderator, The Rev. Steven VanderMolen 475 Riverside Drive., 18th Floor, NY, NY 10115

General Secretary, The Rev. Wesley Granberg-Michaelson, 475 Riverside Dr., 18th Floor, New York, NY 10115; 4500 69th St. SE, Grand Rapids, Michigan 49512

Operations and Support, Director, The Rev. Kenneth Bradsell, 475 Riverside Drive, 18th Floor, New York, NY 10115

Leadership/Revitalization, Director, The Rev. Kenneth Eriks

Church Multiplication/Discipleship, Director, The Rev. Richard Welscott

Finance Services, Treasurer, Ms. Susan Converse

Global Mission, Director, The Rev. Bruce Menning,

African-American Council, Executive Director, The Rev. Dr. Glen Missick

Council for Hispanic Ministries, Executive Secretary, The Rev. Brigido Cabrera

Native American Indian Ministries Council, Vacant

Council for Pacific/Asian-American Ministries, Executive Secretary, Ms. Ella Campbell

OTHER ORGANIZATIONS

Board of Benefits Services, Director, Mr. L. Wood Bedell, 475 Riverside Drive, 18th Floor, New York, NJ 10115; President, The Rev. Thomas Bos; Secretary, The Rev. Kenneth Bradsell

RCA Building and Extension Fund, Fund Executive, Mr. Paul Karssen, 612 8th St. SE, Orange City, IA 51014

Periodicals

Perspectives, The Church Herald

Reformed Church in the United States

Lacking pastors, early German Reformed immigrants to the American colonies were led in worship by "readers." One reader, schoolmaster John Philip Boehm, organized the first congregations near Philadelphia in 1725. A Swiss pastor, Michael Schlatter, was sent by the Dutch Reformed Church in 1746. Strong ties with the Netherlands existed until the formation of the Synod of the German Reformed Church in 1793.

The Eureka Classis, organized in North and South Dakota in 1910 and strongly influenced by the writings of H. Kohlbruegge, P. Geyser and J. Stark, refused to become part of the 1934 merger of the Reformed Church with the Evangelical Synod of North America, holding that it sacrificed the Reformed heritage. (The merged Evangelical and Reformed Church became part of the United Church of Christ in 1957.) Under the leadership of pastors W. Grossmann and W. J. Krieger, the Eureka Classis in 1942 incorporated as the continuing Reformed Church in the United States.

The growing Eureka Classis dissolved in 1986 to form a Synod with four regional classes. An heir to the Reformation theology of Zwingli and Calvin, the Heidelberg Catechism, the Belgic Confession and the Canons of Dort are used as the confessional standards of the church.

151

The Bible is strictly held to be the inerrant, infallible Word of God.

The RCUS supports Dordt College, Mid-America Reformed Seminary, New Geneva Theological Seminary, West Minster Theological Seminary in California, and Hope Haven. The RCUS is the official sponsor to the Reformed Confessing Church of Zaire.

Headquarters

Media Contact, Rev. Frank Walker Th.M., 6121 Pine Vista Way, Elk Grove City, CA 95758-4205 Tel. (661)827-9885

Email: TriWheeler@aol.com

Website: www.rcus.org

Officers

Pres., Rev. Vernon Pollema, 235 James Street, Shafter, CA 93263 Tel. (661)746-6907

Vice Pres., Rev. Robert Grossmann, Th.M., 1905 200th St., Garner, IA 50438 Tel. (515)923-3060

Stated Clk., Rev. Frank Walker Th.M., 5601 Spring Blossom St., Bakersfield, CA 93313-6025 Tel. (661)827-9885

Treas., Clayton Greiman, 2115 Hwy. 69, Garner, IA 50438 Tel. (515)923-2950

Reformed Episcopal Church

The Reformed Episcopal Church was founded December 2, 1873 in New York City by Bishop George D. Cummins, an assistant bishop in the Protestant Episcopal Church from 1866 until 1873. Cummins and other evangelical Episcopalians were concerned about the exclusiveness propagated by what they perceived to be an excessive ritualism then sweeping the church. Throughout the late 1860's evangelicals and ritualists clashed over ceremonies, vestments, open or closed communion, the Articles of Religion, interpretation of the meaning of the sacraments, and the understanding of Apostolic Succession.

In October, 1873, other bishops of the Episcopal Church publicly attacked Cummins in major newspapers for participating in an ecumenical communion service sponsored by the Evangelical Alliance. Cummins resigned from the Episcopal Church and drafted a call to organize a new Episcopal Church for the "purpose of restoring the old paths of their fathers." On December 2, 1873, a Declaration of Principles which expressed the evangelical understanding of the Articles of Religion was adopted. Dr. Charles Edward Cheney of Chicago was elected as bishop to serve with Bishop Cummins. The Second General Council, meeting in May 1874 in New York City, approved a Constitution and Canons and adopted the 1785 Proposed Book of Common Prayer for use in the new Church.

In recent years the Reformed Episcopal Church has revised the Prayer Book to conform to the 1662 and 1928 Books of Common Prayer. The Church still embraces the Thirty Nine Articles of Religion, and has approved the Chicago-Lambeth Quadrilateral of 1886-1888.

Since 1993, the Reformed Episcopal Church has been in official dialogue with the Episcopal Church U.S.A. with occasional meetings at the demoninational level.

There are presently five geographic diocese in the United States and Canada, as well as various missionary jurisdictions including India, Liberia, the West Indies, and others.

The Reformed Episcopal Church is a member of the National Association of Evangelicals.

Headquarters

826 2nd Ave, Blue Bell, PA 19422-1257 Tel. (215)483-1196 Fax (215)483-5235

Media Contact, Rt. Rev. Leonard Riches

Media Contact, Rt. Rev. Royal U. Grote, Jr., Church Growth Office, 211 Byrne Ave., Houston, TX 77009 Tel. (713)862-4929

Email: wycliffe@jps.net

Website: recus.org

Officers

Pres. & Presiding Bishop, Rt. Rev. Leonard W. Riches

Vice Pres., Rt. Rev. Royal U. Grote, Jr.

Sec., Rev. Walter Banek

Treas., Ven. Jon W. Abboud

OTHER ORGANIZATIONS

Bd. of Foreign Missions, Pres., Dr. Barbara J. West, 316 Hunters Rd., Swedesboro, NJ 08085 Tel. (609)467-1641

Bd. of Natl. Church Extension, Pres., Rt. Rev. Royal U. Grote, Jr., 211 Byrne Ave., Houston, TX 77009 Tel. (713)862-4929

Publication Society, Pres., Rt. Rev. Royal U. Grote; 211 Byrne Ave., Houston, TX 77009 Tel. (713)862-4929 , 7372 Henry Ave., Philadelphia, PA 19128 25-956-0655

The Reapers, Pres., Susan Higham, 472 Leedom St., Jenkintown, PA 19046

Committee on Women's Work, Pres., Joan Workowski, 1162 Beverly Rd., Rydal, PA 19046

Committee on Constitutions and Canons, Rev. Canon James T. Payne, P.O. Box 973, Missouri City TX 77495

BISHOPS

Leonard W. Riches, Sr., 85 Smithtown Rd., Pipersville, PA 18947 Tel. (215)483-1196 Fax (215)294-8009

Royal U. Grote, Jr., 211 Byrne Ave., Houston, TX 77009

James C. West, Sr., 408 Red Fox Run, Summerville, SC 29485

Robert H. Booth, 1611 Park Ave., #212, Quakertown, PA 18951

Gregory K. Hotchkiss, 318 E. Main St., Somerville, NJ 08876

George B. Fincke, 155 Woodstock Circle, Vacaville, CA 95687-3381

Daniel R. Morse, 11259 Wexford Dr., Eads, TN 38025

Michael Fedechko, Box 2532, New Liskeard, ON P0J 1P0

Charles W. Dorrington, 626 Blanshard St., Victoria, BC V8W 3G6

Ray R. Sutton, 17405 Muirfield Dr., Dallas TX 75287 Tel. (972)248-6505

Periodicals
Reformed Episcopalians

Reformed Mennonite Church

This is a small group of believers in Pennsylvania, Ohio, Michigan, Illinois, and Ontario, Canada who believe in non-resistance of evil, and non-conformity to the world and who practice separation from unfaithful worship. They believe that Christian unity is the effect of brotherly love and are of one mind and spirit. Their church was established in 1812 by John Herr who agreed with the teachings of Menno Simon as well as those of Jesus Christ.

Headquarters
Lancaster County only, Reformed Mennonite Church, 602 Strasburg Pike, Lancaster, PA 17602

Media Contact, Bishop, Glenn M. Gross, Tel. (717)697-4623

Email: beehlerg@quadro.net

Website: www.reformedmennonitechurch.org

Officers
Bishop Glenn M. Gross, 906 W. Grantham Rd., Mechanicsburg, PA 17055

Reformed Methodist Union Episcopal Church

The Reformed Methodist Union Episcopal church was formed after a group of ministers withdrew from the African Methodist Episcopal Church following a dispute over the election of ministerial delegates to the General Conference.

These ministers organized the Reformed Methodist Union church during a four-day meeting beginning on January 22, 1885 at Hills Chapel (now known as Mt. Hermon RMUE church), in Charleston, South Carolina. The Rev. William E. Johnson was elected president of the new church. Following the death of Rev. Johnson in 1896, it was decided that the church would conform to regular American Methodism (the Episcopacy). The first Bishop, Edward Russell Middleton, was elected, and "Episcopal" was added to the name of the church. Bishop Middleton was consecrated on Dec. 5, 1896, by Bishop P. F. Stephens of the Reformed Episcopal Church.

Headquarters
1136 Brody Ave., Charleston, SC 29407

Media Contact, Gen. Secretary, Brother Willie B. Oliver, P.O. Box 1995, Orangeburg, SC 29116 Tel. (803)536-3293

Officers
Bishop, Rt. Rev. Leroy Gethers, Tel. (803)766-3534

Asst. Bishop, Rt. Rev. Jerry M. DeVoe, Jr.

Gen. Sec., Brother Willie B. Oliver

Treas., Rev. Daniel Green

Sec. of Education, Rev. William Polite

Sec. of Books Concerns, Sister Ann Blanding

Sec. of Pension Fund, Rev. Joseph Powell

Sec. of Church Extension, Brother William Parker

Sec. of Sunday School Union, Sister Wine

Sec. of Mission, Rev. Warren Hatcher

Reformed Presbyterian Church of North America

Also known as the Church of the Covenanters, this church's origin dates back to the Reformation days of Scotland when the Covenanters signed their Covenants in resistance to the king and the Roman Church in the enforcement of state church practices. The Church in America has signed two Covenants in particular, those of 1871 and 1954. The Westminster Confession of Faith and the Larger and Shorter Catechism are among the subordinant standards of the denomination.

Headquarters
Media Contact, Stated Clk., James K. McFarland, 7408 Penn Ave., Pittsburgh, PA 15208 Tel. (412)731-1177 Fax (412)731-8861

Email: RPTrustees@aol.com

Website: www.reformedpresbyterian.org

Officers
Mod., The Rev. Dr. Jonathan Watt, 2907 Fifth Ave., Beaver Falls, PA 15010 Tel. (724)846-5430

Clk., J. Bruce Martin, 310 Main St., Ridgefield Park, NJ 07660 Tel. (201)440-5993

Asst. Clk., Raymond E. Morton, 411 N. Vine St., Sparta, IL 62286 Tel. (618)443-3419

Stated Clk., James K. McFarland, 7408 Penn Ave., Pittsburgh, PA 15208 Tel. (412)731-1177

Geneva College, 3200 College Ave, Beaver Falls, PA 15010 Tel. (724)846-5100 Pres., Kenneth A. Smith, Ph.D.

Reformed Presbyterian Theological Seminary, 7418 Penn Ave., Pittsburgh, 15208 Tel. (412)731-8690, Pres., The Rev. Jerry F. O'Neill, D.D.

Reformed Presbyterian Home, 2344 Perrysville Ave., Pittsburgh, PA 15214 Tel. (412)321-4139 Director, Margaret Hemphill

Crown and Covenant Publications, 7408 Penn Ave., Pittsburgh, PA 15208 Tel. (412)241-0436 Drew and Lynne Gordon Managing Editors.

Periodicals
The Witness, The Reformed Presbyterian Witness

153

Reformed Zion Union Apostolic Church

This group was organized in 1869 at Boydton, Va., by Elder James R. Howell of New York, a minister of the A.M.E. Zion Church, with doctrines of the Methodist Episcopal Church.

Headquarters

Rt. 1, Box 64D, Dundas, VA 23938 Tel. (804) 676-8509

Media Contact, Bishop G. W. Studivant

Officers

Exec. Brd., Chair, Rev. Hilman Wright, Tel. (804)447-3988

Sec., Joseph Russell, Tel. (804)634-4520

Religious Society of Friends (Conservative)

These Friends mark their present identity from separations occurring by regions at different times from 1845 to 1904. They hold to a minimum of organizational structure. Their meetings for worship, which are unprogrammed and based on silent, expectant waiting upon the Lord, demonstrate the belief that all individuals may commune directly with God and may share equally in vocal ministry.

They continue to stress the importance of the Living Christ and the experience of the Holy Spirit working with power in the lives of individuals who obey it.

YEARLY MEETINGS

North Carolina YM, Sidney Lee Kitchens, P.O.Box 4591, Greensboro, NC 27404 Tel. (252)587-2571

Iowa YM, Deborah Frisch, Clerk, 3400 King Dian Blvd, Des Moines, Iowa 50311

Ohio YM, Seth Hinshaw, Clerk, 61830 Sandy Ridge Road, Barnesville, OH 43713

Religious Society of Friends (Unaffiliated Meetings)

Though all groups of Friends acknowledge the same historical roots, 19th-century divisions in theology and experience led to some of the current organizational groupings. Many newer yearly meetings, have chosen not to identify with past divisions by affiliating in traditional ways with the larger organizations within the Society.

YEARLY MEETINGS

Central Yearly Meeting [Friends Evangel] (I), Supt., Jonathan Edwards, 5597 West County Rd., 700 N., Ridgeville, IN 47380, Tel. (765)857-2347 Fax (765)857-2347

Intermountain Yearly Meeting (I), Clerk, Rebecca Henderson, Website: www.imym.org

North Pacific Yearly Meeting (I), Email: npym-06 @npym.org

Pacific Yearly Meeting (I), Clerk, Jim Anderson, 25 Gideon Lane, Chico, CA 95973

Website: www.pacificyearlymeeting.org

Email: margaretf@fwccamericas.org

Website: www.centralyearlymeetingoffriends.org

Officers

Central Yearly Meeting
255 Members
Intermountain Yearly Meeting
1008 Members
North Pacific Yearly Meeting
921 Members
Pacific Yearly Meeting
1,527 Members

Periodicals

Friends Bulletin, Friends Evangel

Reorganized Church of Jesus Christ of Latter-day Saints—please see Community of Christ

The Romanian Orthodox Church in America

The Romanian Orthodox Church in America is an autonomous Archdiocese chartered under the name of "Romanian Orthodox Archdiocese in America." The diocese was founded in 1929 and approved by the Holy Synod of the Romanian Orthodox Church in Romania in 1934. The Holy Synod of the Romanian Orthodox Church granted ecclesiastical autonomy in American Diocese on July 12, 1950. The Diocese continues to hold dogmatic and canonical ties with the Holy Synod and the Romanian Orthodox Patriarchate of Romania.

In 1951, approximately 40 parishes with their clergy from the United States and Canada separated from this church. In 1960, they joined the Russian Orthodox Greek Catholic Metropolia, now called the Orthodox Church in America, which reordained for these parishes a bishop with the title "Bishop of Detroit and Michigan."

On June 11, 1973 the Holy Synod of the Romanian Orthodox church elevated the Bishop of Romanian Orthodox Missionary Episcopate in America to the rank of Archbishop.

Headquarters

P.O. Box 27, Skokie, IL 60076-0027 Tel. (847)674-3900 Fax (847)674-4110

Media Contact, Archdiocesan Secretary, V. Rev. Fr. Nicholas Apostola, 44 Midland St., Worcester, MA 01602-4217 Tel. (508)845-0088 Fax (508)845-8850, Email: Nicholas. Apostola@verizon.net

Email: ArchNicolae@aol.com

Website: www.romarch.org

Officers

Archbishop, His Eminence Dr. Nicolae Condrea, P.O. Box 27, Skokie, IL 60076-0027 Tel. (847)674-3900 Fax: (847)674-4110, Email: ArchNicolae@aol.com, Website: www.romarch. org

Vicar, V. Rev. Fr. Ioan Ionita, 17601 Wentworth Avenue, Lansing, IL 60438-2074 Tel. & Fax: (708)474-0340, Email: Tintari@aol.com

Inter-Church Relations, Dir., V. Rev. Fr. Nicholas Apostola, 44 Midland St., Worcester, MA 01602-4217 Tel. (508)845-0088 Fax (508) 845-8850, Email: Nicholas.Apostola@verizon.net

Periodicals

Credinta-The Faith

The Romanian Orthodox Episcopate of America

This body of Eastern Orthodox Christians of Romanian descent is part of the Orthodox Church in America. For complete description and listing of officers, please see Orthodox Church in America.

Headquarters

2535 Grey Tower Rd., Jackson, MI 49201 Tel. (517)522-4800, Web www.roea.org

Mailing Address, P.O. Box 309, Grass Lake, MI 49240-0309

Media Contact, Ed. -Sec., Rev. Archdeacon David Oancea, P.O.Box 185, Grass Lake, MI 49240-0185 Tel. (517)522-3656

Email: roeasolia@aol.com

Website: www.roea.org

Officers

Ruling Hierarch, Most Rev. Archbishop Nathaniel Popp

P.O. Box 309, Grass Lake, MI 49240-0309

Periodicals

Solia-The Herald, Good News-Buna Vestire (in Canada only)

Russian Orthodox Church—please see Patriar-chal Parishes of the Russian Orthodox Church in the U.S.A.

The Russian Orthodox Church Outside of Russia

This group was organized in 1920 to unite in one body of dioceses the missions and parishes of the Russian Orthodox Church outside of Russia. The governing body, set up in Constantinople, was sponsored by the Ecumenical Patriarchate. In November 1950, it came to the United States. The Russian Orthodox Church Outside of Russia emphasizes being true to the old traditions of the Russian Church. In May 2007, it re-established communion with the Moscow Patriarchate.

Headquarters

75 E. 93rd St., New York, NY 10128 Tel. (212)534-1601 Fax (212)426-1086

Media Contact, Dep. Sec., Nicholas A. Ohotin, Tel: (212)534-1610 x 37

Email: nohotin@synod.com

SYNOD OF BISHOPS

Pres., His Eminence Metropolitan Laurus

Vice Pres., His Eminence Archbishop Hilarion, Tel. (212)534-1601

Periodicals

Living Orthodoxy, Orthodox Family, Orthodox Russia, Pravoslavnaya Rus, Pravoslavnaya Zhisn, Orthodox America

The Salvation Army

The Salvation Army, founded in 1865 by William Booth (1829-1912) in London, England, and introduced into America in 1880, is an international religious and charitable movement organized and operated on a paramilitary pattern and is a branch of the Christian church. To carry out its purposes, The Salvation Army has established a widely diversified program of religious and social welfare services which are designed to meet the needs of children, youth and adults in all age groups.

Headquarters

615 Slaters Ln., Alexandria, VA 22313 Tel. (703)684-5500 Fax (703)684-5538

Media Contact, National Community Rel. & Dev. Secretary, Major George Hood, Tel. (703) 684-5526 Fax (703)684-5538

Email: george_hood@usn.salvationarmy.org

Website: www.salvationarmyusa.org

Officers

Natl. Commander, Commissioner Israel L. Gaither

Natl. Chief Sec., LT. Colonel David Jeffrey

Natl. Community Relations and Development Secretary, Dir., Major George Hood

TERRITORIAL ORGANIZATIONS

Central Territory, 10 W. Algonquin Rd., Des Plaines, IL 60016 Tel. (847)294-2000 Fax (847)294-2299; Territorial Commander, Commissioner Kenneth Baillie

Eastern Territory, 440 W. Nyack Rd., P.O. Box C-635, West Nyack, NY 10994 Tel. (914)620-7200 Fax (914)620-7766, Territorial Commander, Commissioner Lawrence Moretz

Southern Territory, 1424 Northeast Expressway, Atlanta, GA 30329 Tel. (404)728-1300 Fax (404)728-1331; Territorial Commander, Commissioner Maxwell Feener

Western Territory, 180 E. Ocean Blvd., Long Beach, CA Tel. (562)436-7000 Fax (562)491-8792, Territorial Commander, Commissioner Philip Swyers

Periodicals

The War Cry

The Schwenkfelder Church

The Schwenkfelders are the spiritual descendants of the Silesian nobleman Caspar Schwenkfeld von Ossig (1489-1561), a scholar, reformer, preacher and prolific writer who

155

endeavored to aid in the cause of the Protestant Reformation. A contemporary of Martin Luther, John Calvin, Ulrich Zwingli and Phillip Melanchthon, Schwenkfeld sought no following, formulated no creed and did not attempt to organize a church based on his beliefs. He labored for liberty of religious belief, for a fellowship of all believers and for one united Christian church.

He and his cobelievers supported a movement known as the Reformation by the Middle Way. Persecuted by state churches, ultimately 217 Schwenkfelders exiled from Silesia emigrated to Pennsylvania in six migrations, 1731–1734. The largest migration, about 180 landed at Philadelphia Sept. 22, 1734. In 1782, the Society of Schwenkfelders, the forerunner of the present Schwenkfelder Church, was formed. The church was incorporated in 1909.

The Schwenkfelder Church is a voluntary association of six Schwenkfelder Churches at Palm, Worcester, Lansdale, Norristown and two in Philadelphia, Pennsylvania.

They practice adult baptism, dedication and baptism of children, and observe the Lord's Supper regularly with open Communion. In theology, they are Christo-centric; in polity, congregational; in missions, world-minded; in ecclesiastical organization, ecumenical.

The ministry is recruited from graduates of accredited theological seminaries. The churches take leadership in ecumenical concerns through ministerial associations, community service and action groups, councils of Christian education and other agencies.

Headquarters
105 Seminary St., Pennsburg, PA 18073 Tel. (215)679-3103
Media Contact, David W. Luz
Email: info@schwenkfelder.com

Officers
Mod., David W. Luz, Pennsburg, PA
Sec., Linda Anders, Souderton, PA
Treas., Pat McGinnis, Central Schwenkfelder Church, Worcester, PA 19490

Periodicals
The Schwenkfeldian

Separate Baptists in Christ
The Separate Baptists in Christ are a group of Baptists found in Indiana, Ohio, Kentucky, Tennessee, Virginia, West Virginia, Florida and North Carolina dating back to an association formed in 1758 in North Carolina and Virginia.

Today this group consists of approximately 100 churches. They believe in the infallibility of the Bible, the divine ordinances of the Lord's Supper, feetwashing, baptism and that those who endureth to the end shall be saved.

The Separate Baptists are Arminian in doctrine, rejecting both the doctrines of predestination and eternal security of the believer.

At the 1991 General Association, an additional article of doctrine was adopted. "We believe that at Christ's return in the clouds of heaven all Christians will meet the Lord in the air, and time shall be no more," thus leaving no time for a literal one thousand year reign. Seven associations comprise the General Association of Separate Baptists.

Headquarters
Media Contact, Clk., Greg Erdman, 10102 N. Hickory Ln., Columbus, IN 47203 Tel. (812) 526-2540
Email: mail@separatebaptist.org
Website: www.separatebaptist.org

Officers
Mod., Rev. Jim Goff, 1020 Gagel Ave., Louisville, KY 40216
Asst. Mod., Rev. Jimmy Polston, 785 Kitchen Rd., Mooresville, IN 46158 Tel. (317)831-6745
Clk., Greg Erdman, 10102 N. Hickory Ln., Columbus, IN 47203 Tel. (812)526-2540
Asst. Clk., Rev. Mattew Cowan, 174 Oak Hill School Rd., Lot 30, Smiths Grove, KY 42171 Tel. (270)678-5599

Serbian Orthodox Church in the U.S.A. and Canada*
The Serbian Orthodox Church is an organic part of the Christian Orthodox Church. As a local church it received its autocephaly from Constantinople in 1219 A.D.

In 1921, a Serbian Orthodox Diocese in the United States of America and Canada was organized. In 1963, it was reorganized into three dioceses, and in 1983 a fourth diocese was created for the Canadian part of the church. The Serbian Orthodox Church in the USA and Canada received its administrative autonomy in 1928. However, it remains canonically an integral part of the Serbian Orthodox Patriarchate with its see in Belgrade. The Serbian Orthodox Church is in absolute doctrinal unity with all other local Orthodox Churches.

Headquarters
St. Sava Monastery, P.O. Box 519, Libertyville, IL 60048 Tel. (847)367-0698
Email: oea@oea.serbian-church.net
Website: oea.serbian-church.net

BISHOPS
Metropolitan of Midwestern America, Most Rev. Metropolitan Christopher
Bishop of Canada, Georgije, 5A Stockbridge Ave., Toronto, ON M8Z 4M6 Tel. (416)231-4009
Bishop of Eastern America, Rt. Rev. Bishop Mitrophan, 138 Carriage Hill Dr., Mars, PA 16046 Tel. (724)772-8866
Diocese of Western America, Bishop Maxim, 2541 Crestline Terr., Alhambra, CA 91803 Tel. (818)264-6825

OTHER ORGANIZATIONS

Brotherhood of Serbian Orth. Clergy in U.S.A. & Canada, Pres., V. Rev. Dennis Pavichevich
Federation of Circles of Serbian Sisters
Serbian Singing Federation

Periodicals

The Path of Orthodoxy

Seventh-day Adventist Church

The Seventh-day Adventist Church grew out of a worldwide religious revival in the mid-19th century. People of many religious persuasions believed Bible prophecies indicated that the second coming or advent of Christ was imminent.

When Christ did not come in the 1840s, a group of these disappointed Adventists in the United States continued their Bible studies and concluded they had misinterpreted prophetic events and that the second coming of Christ was still in the future. This same group of Adventists later accepted the teaching of the seventh-day Sabbath and became known as Seventh-day Adventists. The denomination organized formally in 1863.

The church was largely confined to North America until 1874, when its first missionary was sent to Europe. Today, over 61,818 congregations meet in 203 countries. Membership exceeds 15 million and increases between four and five percent each year.

In addition to a mission program, the church has the largest worldwide Protestant parochial school system with approximately 7,3001 schools with more than 1,436,000 students on elementary through college and university levels.

The Adventist Development and Relief Agency (ADRA) helps victims of war and natural disasters, and many local congregations have community service facilities to help those in need close to home.

The church also has a worldwide publishing ministry with 63 printing facilities producing magazines and other publications in over 350 languages and dialects. In the United States and Canada, the church sponsors a variety of radio and television programs, including Christian Lifestyle Magazine, It Is Written, Breath of Life, Ayer, Hoy, y Mañana, Voice of Prophecy, and La Voz de la Esperanza.

The North American Division of Seventh-day Adventist includes 58 Conferences which are grouped together into nine organized Union Conferences. The various Conferences work under the general direction of these Union Conferences.

Headquarters

12501 Old Columbia Pike, Silver Spring, MD 20904-6600 Tel. (301)680-6000
Media Contact, Dir., Communication, Rajmund Dabrowski
Email: kjones@gc.adventist.org
Website: www.adventist.org

WORLD-WIDE OFFICERS

Pres., Jan Paulsen
Sec., Matthew A. Bediako
Treas., Robert E. Lemon

WORLD-WIDE DEPARTMENTS

Adventist Chaplaincy Ministries, Dir., Martin W. Feldbush
Children's Ministries, Dir., Linda Koh
Education, Dir.,C. Garland Dulan
Communication, Dir., Rajmund Dabrowski
Family Ministries, Dir., Ronald M. Flowers
Health Ministries, Dir., Allan R. Handysides
Ministerial Assoc., Dir., James A. Cress
Public Affairs & Religious Liberty, Dir., John Graz
Publishing, Dir., Howard F Faigao
Sabbath School & Personal Ministries, Jonathan Kuntaraf
Stewardship, Dir., Erika Puni
Trust Services, Jeffrey K. Wilson
Women's Ministries, Heather-Dawn Small
Youth, Baraka G. Muganda

NORTH AMERICAN OFFICERS

Pres., Don C. Schneider
Vice Pres., Debra Brill; Gerald Kovalski; Alvin M. Kibble; R. Ernest Castillo
Sec., Roscoe J. Howard III
Treas., Thomas Evans
Assoc. Treas., Michael Park; Delbert L. Johnson; Kenneth W. Osborn, Mrshall Chase

NORTH AMERICAN ORGANIZATIONS

Atlantic Union Conf., P.O. Box 1189, South Lancaster, MA 01561-1189; Pres., Donald G. King
Canada, Seventh-day Adventist Church in Canada (see Ch. 4)
Columbia Union Conf., 5427 Twin Knolls Rd., Columbia, MD 21045; Pres., David Weigley
Lake Union Conf., P.O. Box C, Berrien Springs, MI 49103; Pres., Walter L. Wright
Mid-America Union Conf., P.O. Box 6128, Lincoln, NE 68506; Pres., Dennis N. Carlson
North Pacific Union Conf., Pres., Jere D. Patzer, 5709 N 20th St, Ridgefield, WA 98642-7742
Pacific Union Conf., P.O. Box 5005, Westlake Village, CA 91359; Pres., Thomas J. Mostert, Jr
Southern Union Conf., P.O. Box 849, Decatur, GA 30031; Pres., Gordon L. Retzer
Southwestern Union Conf., P.O. Box 4000, Burleson, TX 76097; Pres., Max A. Trevino

Periodicals

ADRA Works, The Adventist Chaplain, Adventist Review, ASI Magazine, Children's Friend, Christian Record, College and University Dialogue, Collegiate Quarterly, Cornerstone Youth Resource Magazine, Cornerstone Connections, Elder's Digest, Encounter, For God and Country, Geoscience Reports, Evangelist, Message, Ministry, Mission, Origins, Our Little Friend, Primary Treasure,

Publishing Mirror, *Shabbat Shalom*, *Shepherdess International Journal*, *Signs of the Times*, *Transmissions*, *Vibrant Life*, *Voice of Prophecy News*, *Winner*, *Women of Spirit*, *Young and Alive*, *Youth Ministry ACCENT*

Seventh Day Baptist General Conference, USA and Canada

Seventh Day Baptists emerged during the English Reformation, organizing their first churches in the mid-1600s. The first Seventh Day Baptists of record in America were Stephen and Ann Mumford, who emigrated from England in 1664. Beginning in 1665 several members of the First Baptist Church at Newport, R.I. began observing the seventh day Sabbath, or Saturday. In 1671, five members, together with the Mumfords, formed the first Seventh Day Baptist Church in America at Newport.

Beginning about 1700, other Seventh Day Baptist churches were established in New Jersey and Pennsylvania. From these three centers, the denomination grew and expanded westward. They founded the Seventh Day Baptist General Conference in 1802.

The organization of the denomination reflects an interest in home and foreign missions, publications and education. Women have been encouraged to participate. From the earliest years religious freedom has been championed for all and the separation of church and state, advocated.

Seventh Day Baptists are members of the Baptist World Alliance and Baptist Joint Committee. The Seventh Day Baptist World Federation has 17 member conferences on six continents.

Headquarters

Seventh Day Baptist Center, 3120 Kennedy Rd., P.O. Box 1678, Janesville, WI 53547-1678 Tel. (608)752-5055 Fax (608)752-7711
Media Contact, Ex. Dir., Robert Appel
Financial Dir., Morgan D. Shepard
Email: sdbgen@inwave.com
Website: www.seventhdaybaptist.org

OTHER ORGANIZATIONS

Seventh Day Baptist Missionary Society, Exec. Dir., Kirk Looper, 119 Main St., Westerly, RI 02891
Seventh Day Bapt. Bd. of Christian Ed., Exec. Dir., Rev. Andrew Camenga, Box 115, Alfred Station, NY 14803
Women's Soc. of the Gen. Conference, Pres., Mrs. Marjorie Jacob, P.O. Box 122, Pomona Park, FL 32181-0122
American Sabbath Tract & Comm. Council, Dir. of Communications, Rev. Kevin J. Butler, 3120 Kennedy Rd., P.O. Box 1678, Janesville, WI 53547
Seventh Day Baptist Historical Society, Historian, Nicholas Kersten, 3120 Kennedy Rd., P.O. Box 1678, Janesville, WI 53547

Seventh Day Baptist Center on Ministry, Dir. of Pastoral Services, Rev. Gordon Lawton, 3120 Kennedy Rd., P.O. Box 1678, Janesville, WI 53547

Periodicals

Sabbath Recorder

Southern Baptist Convention

The Southern Baptist Convention was organized on May 10, 1845, in Augusta, Georgia. Cooperating Baptist churches are located in all 50 states, the District of Columbia, Puerto Rico, American Samoa and the Virgin Islands. The members of the churches work together through 1,185 district associations and 41 state conventions or fellowships. The Southern Baptist Convention has an Executive Committee and 12 national agencies—four boards, six seminaries, one commission, and one auxiliary organization.

The purpose of the Southern Baptist Convention is "to provide a general organization for Baptists in the United States and its territories for the promotion of Christian missions at home and abroad and any other objects such as Christian education, benevolent enterprises, and social services which it may deem proper and advisable for the furtherance of the Kingdom of God". (Constitution, Article II)

The Convention exists in order to help the churches lead people to God through Jesus Christ.

From the beginning, there has been a mission desire to share the Gospel with the peoples of the world. The Cooperative Program is the basic channel of mission support. In addition, the Lottie Moon Christmas Offering for Foreign Missions and the Annie Armstrong Easter Offering for Home Missions support Southern Baptists' world mission programs.

In 2006, there were approximately 5,100 foreign missionaries serving in foreign countries and more than 5,300 home missionaries serving in North America.

Headquarters

901 Commerce St., Nashville, TN 37203 Tel. (615)244-2355
Media Contact, Vice Pres. for Convention Relations, Roger S. Oldham, Tel. (615)244-2355 Fax (615)782-8684
Email: bmerrell@sbc.net
Website: www.sbc.net

Officers

Pres., Frank Page, 200 West Main St., Taylors, SC 29687
Recording Sec., John Yeats, 1250 MacArthur Dr., Alexandria, LA 71303
Executive Committee, Pres., Morris H. Chapman; Vice Pres., Business & Finance, Clark Logan; Vice Pres., Convention News, Will Hall; Vice Pres., Convention Relations, Roger S. Oldham; Vice Pres., Convention Policy, Augie Boto; Vice Pres., Cooperative Program, Bob Rodgers

GENERAL BOARDS AND COMMISSION

International Mission Board, Pres., Jerry A. Rankin, 3806 Monument Ave, Richmond, VA 23230 Tel. (804)353-6655 x 1207

North American Mission Board, Pres., Geff Hammond, 4200 No. Point Pkwy., Alpharetta, GA 30022-4176 Tel. (770)410-6519

Pres., O. S. Hawkins, 2401 Cedar Springs Rd, Dallas, TX 75201 Tel. (214)720-4700

LifeWay Christian Resources, Pres., Thomas Rainer, One Lifeway Plaza, Nashville, TN 37234 Tel. (615)251-2605

Ethics and Religious Liberty Commission, Pres., Richard D. Land, 901 Commerce St., Suite 550, Nashville, TN 37203 Tel. (615)782-8404

STATE CONVENTIONS

Alabama, Rick Lance, 2001 E. South Blvd., Montgomery, AL 36116 Tel. (334)288-2460

Alaska, David N. Baldwin, 1750 O'Malley Rd., Anchorage, AK 99516 Tel. (907)344-9627

Arizona, Steve Bass, 2240 N. Hayden Rd., Ste. 100 Scottsdale, AZ 85257 Tel. (480)945-0880

Arkansas, Emil Turner, 525 West Capitol, Little Rock, AR 72203 Tel. (501)376-4791 x 5102

California, Fermin A. Whittaker, 678 E. Shaw Ave., Fresno, CA 93710 Tel. (559)229-9533 x 230

Colorado, Mark Edlund, 7393 So. Alton Way, Centennial, CO 80112 Tel. (303)771-2480

Dakota Baptist Comvention, Jim Hamilton, P.O.Box 2616, Bismarck, ND 58502 Tel. (701) 255-3765

District of Columbia, Rev. Jeffrey Haggray, 1628 16th St. NW, Washington, DC 20009 Tel. (202)265-1526

Florida, John Sullivan, 1230 Hendricks Ave., Jacksonville, FL 32207 Tel. (904)396-2351 x 8101

Georgia, J. Robert White, 6405 Sugarloaf Pkwy., Duluth, GA 30097 Tel. (770)455-0404

Hawaii, Veryl F. Henderson, 2042 Vancouver Dr., Honolulu, HI 96822 Tel. (808)946-9581 x 229

Illinois, Nate Adams, Exec. Dir, 3085 Stevenson Dr, Springfield, IL 62794 Tel. (217)786-2600

Indiana, Stephen P. Davis, 900 N. High School Rd., Indianapolis, IN 46214 Tel. (317)241-9317

Iowa, Jimmy L. Barrentine, Suite #27, 2400 86th St., Des Moines, IA 50322 Tel. (515)278-4369

Kansas-Nebraska, R. Rex Lindsay, 5410 SW. Seventh St., Topeka, KS 66606 Tel. (785)273-4880

Kentucky, Bill F. Mackey, 13420 Eastpoint Centre Dr., Louisville, KY 40223 Tel. (502) 489-3370

Louisiana, David E. Hankins, 1250 MacArthur Dr., Alexandria, LA 71303 Tel. (318)448-3402

Maryland-Delaware, David H. Lee, 10255 Old Columbia Rd., Columbia, MD 21046 Tel. (410)290-5290

Michigan, Michael R. Collins, 8420 Runyan Lake Rd., Fenton, MI 48430 Tel. (810)714-1907

Minnesota-Wisconsin, Leo Endel, Exec. Dir., 519 16th St. SE, Rochester, MN 55904 Tel. (507)282-3636

Mississippi, James R. Futral, 515 Mississippi St., Jackson, MS 39201 Tel. (601)968-3800

Missouri, David Tolliver, Exec. Dir., 400 E. High Street, Jefferson City, MO 65101 Tel. (573)635-7931 x 200

Montana, Joe Pickard, P.O. Box 99, Billings, MT 59103-0099 Tel. (406)252-7537

Nevada, Thane E. Barnes, Exec. Dir., 406 California Ave., Reno, NV 89509 Tel. (775) 786-0406

New England, James Wideman, 87 Lincoln St., Northborough, MA 01532 Tel. (508)393-6013 x 224

New Mexico, Joseph L. Bruce, 5325 Wyoming, NE, Albuquerque, NM 87109 Tel. (505)924-2300 x 11

New York, Terry M. Robertson, 6538 Baptist Way, East Syracuse, NY 13057 Tel. (315)433-1001

North Carolina, Milton Hollifield, 205 Convention Dr., Cary, NC 27511 Tel. (919) 467-5100 x 102

Northwest, Bill Crews, 3200 NE 109th Ave., Vancouver, WA 98682 Tel. (360)882-2100 x 121

Ohio, Exec. Dir., Jack P. Kwok, 1680 E. Broad, Columbus, OH 43203 Tel. (614)827-1777

Oklahoma, Anthony L. Jordan, 3800 N. May Ave., Oklahoma City, OK 73112 Tel. (405) 942-3800

Pennsylvania-South Jersey, David C. Waltz, 4620 Fritchey St., Harrisburg, PA 17109 Tel. (717)652-5856

South Carolina, James W. Austin, 190 Stoneridge Dr., Columbia, SC 29210 Tel. (803)765-0030 x 1200

Tennessee, James M. Porch, 5001 Maryland Way, Brentwood, TN 37027 Tel. (615)371-2090

Texas, (BGCT) Baptist General Convention of Texas, Charles R. Wade, 333 N. Washington, Dallas, TX 75246 Tel. (214)828-5301

Texas, (SBTC) Southern Baptists of Texas, James W. Richards, 4500 State Hwy. 360, Grapevine, TX 76051 Tel. (817)552-2500

Utah-Idaho, Tim Clark, 12401 South 450 East #G-1, Draper, UT 84020 Tel. (801)572-5350

Virginia, (BGAV) Baptist General Association of Virginia, John V. Upton Jr., 2828 Emerywood Pkwy, Richmond, VA 23226 Tel. (804)915-2430 x 223

Virginia, (SBCV) Southern Baptist Conservatives of Virginia, H. Doyle Chauncey, 4101 Cox Rd., Suite 100, Glen Allen, VA 23060 Tel. (804)270-1848

West Virginia, Terry L. Harper, Number One Missions Way, Scott Depot, WV 25560 Tel. (304)757-0944

Wyoming, Lynn Nikkel, 3925 Casper Mountain Rd., Casper, WY 82601 Tel. (307)472-4087

159

Periodicals
The Commission, SBC Life, On Mission

Southern Methodist Church

Organized in 1939, this body is composed of congregations desirous of continuing in true Biblical Methodism and preserving the fundamental doctrines and beliefs of the Methodist Episcopal Church, South. These congregations declined to be a party to the merger of the Methodist Episcopal Church, The Methodist Episcopal Church, South and the Methodist Protestant Church into The Methodist Church.

Headquarters

425 Broughton St., Orangeburg, SC 29115, Tel. (803)536-1378 Fax (803)535-3881
Media Contact, Pres., Rev. John T. Hucks, Jr.
Email: smchq@juno.com; smpresid@bellsouth.net

Officers

Pres., Rev. John T. Hucks, Jr.
Dir. Of Admin. & Finance, Rev. Cecil Clark, 425 Broughton St., Orangeburg, SC 29115
Director of Foreign Missions, Rev. Marvin Clark, 425 Broughton St., Orangeburg, SC 29115
Southern Methodist College Pres., Rev. Gary Briden, P.O. Box 1027, Orangeburg, SC 29116-1027

Periodicals

The Southern Methodist

Sovereign Grace Believers

The Sovereign Grace Believers are a contemporary movement which began its stirrings in the mid-1950s when some pastors in traditional Baptist churches returned to a Calvinist-theological perspective.

The first "Sovereign Grace" conference was held in Ashland, Kentucky, in 1954 and since then, conferences of this sort have been sponsored by various local churches on the West Coast, Southern and Northern states and Canada. This movement is a spontaneous phenomenon concerning reformation at the local church level. Consequently, there is no interest in establishing a Sovereign Grace Baptist "Convention" or "Denomination." Each local church is to administer the keys to the kingdom.

Most Sovereign Grace Believers formally or informally relate to the "First London" (1646), "Second London" (1689) or "Philadelphia" (1742) Confessions.

There is a wide variety of local church government in this movement. Many Calvinist Baptists have a plurality of elders in each assembly. Other Sovereign Grace Believers, however, prefer to function with one pastor and several deacons.

Membership procedures vary from church to church but all require a credible profession of faith in Christ, and proper baptism as a basis for membership.

Calvinistic Baptists financially support gospel efforts (missionaries, pastors of small churches at home and abroad, literature publication and distribution, radio programs, etc.) in various parts of the world.

Headquarters

Media Contact, Corres., Jon Zens, P.O. Box 548, St. Croix Falls, WI 54024 Tel. (651)465-6516 Fax (651)465-5101
Email: jon@searchingtogether.org
Website: www.searchingtogether.org

Periodicals

Searching Together, Sound of Grace

The Swedenborgian Church*

Founded in North America in 1792 as the Church of the New Jerusalem, the Swedenborgian Church was organized as a national body in 1817 and incorporated in Illinois in 1861. Its biblically-based theology is derived from the spiritual, or mystical, experiences and exhaustive biblical studies of the Swedish scientist and philosopher Emanuel Swedenborg (1688–1772).

The church centers its worship and teachings on the historical life and the risen and glorified present reality of the Lord Jesus Christ. It looks with an ecumenical vision toward the establishment of the kingdom of God in the form of a universal Church, active in the lives of all people of good will who desire and strive for freedom, peace and justice for all. It is a member of the NCCC and active in many local councils of churches.

With churches and groups throughout the United States and Canada, the denomination's central administrative offices and its seminary, "Swedenborg House of Studies" are located in Newton, Massachusetts and Berkeley, California. Affiliated churches are found in Africa, Asia, Australia, Canada, Europe, the United Kingdom, Japan, South Korea and South America. Many philosophers and writers have acknowledged their appreciation of Swedenborg's teachings.

Headquarters

11 Highland Ave., Newtonville, MA 02460 Tel. (617)969-4240 Fax (617)964-3258
Media Contact, Central Ofc. Mgr., Martha Bauer
Email: manager@swedenborg.org
Website: www.swedenborg.org

Officers

Pres., Rev. Christine Laitner, 10 Hannah Court, Midland, MI 48642
Vice Pres., James Erickson, 1340 Snelling Ave, N.,St. Paul, MN 55108
Rec. Sec., Susan Wood, 552 Fifth Court, Palm Beach Gardens, FL 33410-5105

Treas., Lawrence Conant, 290 Berlin St., Apt. 89, Clinton, MA 01510 Tel. (978)368-6269

Ofc. Mgr., Martha Bauer, Tel. (617)969-4240, Email: manager@swedenborg.org

Periodicals

The Messenger, Our Daily Bread

Syrian (Syriac) Orthodox Church of Antioch*

The Syrian Orthodox Church of Antioch traces its origin to the Patriarchate established in Antioch by St. Peter the Apostle. It is under the supreme ecclesiastical jurisdiction of His Holiness the Syrian Orthodox Patriarch of Antioch and All the East, now residing in Damascus, Syria. The Syrian Orthodox Church— composed of several archdioceses, numerous parishes, schools and seminaries—professes the faith of the first three Ecumenical Councils of Nicaea, Constantinople and Ephesus, and numbers faithful in the Middle East, India, the Americas, Europe, Australia and New Zealand.

The first Syrian Orthodox faithful came to North America during the late 1800s, and by 1907 the first Syrian Orthodox priest was ordained to tend to the community's spiritual needs. In 1949, His Eminence Archbishop Mor Athanasius Y. Samuel came to America and was appointed Patriarchal Vicar in 1952. The Archdiocese was officially established in 1957. In 1995, the Archdiocese of North America was divided into three separate Patriarchal Vicariates (Eastern United States, Western United States and Canada), each under a hierarch of the Church.

There are 28 official archdiocesan parishes in the United States, located in Arizona, California, District of Columbia, Florida, Georgia, Indiana, Illinois, Massachusetts, Michigan, New Jersey, New York, Oregon, Rhode Island and Texas. In Canada, there are six official parishes—three in the Province of Ontario and two in the Province of Quebec and one in the Province of Alberta.

Headquarters

Archdiocese of the Eastern U.S., 260 Elm Avenue, Teaneck, NJ 07666 Tel. (201)801-0660 Fax (201)801-0603

Archdiocese of the Western U.S., 417 E. Fairmount Rd., Burbank, CA 91501 Tel. (818) 953-7170 Fax (818)953-7203

Media Contact, Archdiocesan Gen. Sec., Very Rev. Chorepiscopus John Meno, 260 Elm Ave., Teaneck, NJ 07666 Tel. (201)907-0122 Fax (201)907-0551

Email: hasio@syrianorthodoxchurch.org

Website: www.syrianorthodoxchurch.org

Officers

Archdiocese for Eastern U.S., Archbishop, Mor Cyril Aphrem Karim

Archdiocese of Los Angeles and Environs, Archbishop, Mor Clemis Eugene Kaplan

Syro-Russian Orthodox Catholic Church

The Syro-Russian Orthodox Catholic Church was established in May of 1892 as the American Orthodox Catholic Archdiocese of America, and was canonized by His Holiness Ignatius Peter III, Patriarch of Antioch. It was this same Patriarch that issued the Bull for the consecration of its first Archbishop Metropolitan, Timotheos Vilathi, as he was later named by Patriarch Ignatius. The Syro-Russian Orthodox Catholic Church is an Eastern Rite jurisdiction but also has a few Western Rite parishes. It is the only true Byzantine Rite jurisdiction coming from Metropolitan Timotheos. The Synod of Bishops is referred to as the "Syro-Russian Synod of Bishops." This jurisdiction is the only canonical Byzantine Rite continuation of what Metropolitan Timotheos established in the United States. First parishes of this jurisdiction were established in Wisconsin among Belgians, Italians, Slavs, and other ethnic groups. After Archbishop Timotheos' consecration, parishes were later formed in Ohio, Indiana, Illinois, and New York, and some missionary work begun in Canada. Today parishes exist throughout the United States and several foreign countries.

After much disagreement with the Patriarchate concerning administration, especially in the appointing of bishops, and the Christology issue, i.e., Christ's two Natures, that surfaced at the Council of Chalcedon, Archbishop Timotheos separated from the Patriarchate. A Consistory was convened on January 1, 1910 concerning the future of the Archdiocese of America. The Bishops agreed upon and decided that, "Our reality as a branch, a part of the true Catholic and Orthodox Church of God, is not dependent upon the recognition of any ecclesiastical authority outside the Councils of our own American Ecclesiastical Consistory and National Synod of Bishops and Clergy." Archbishop Timotheos believed strongly in the truths of the Council of Chalcedon and all the Ecumenical Councils, and the right of the American Church to name its own bishops, and from then on the Church was known as Autocephalous and severed from the Patriarchate of Antioch. However, after this time several schisms occurred that gave way to some heretical and newly established "churches" that caused the Church to eventually be renamed "Syro-Russian Orthodox Catholic." In the 1970's, after the retirement for health reasons of Archbishop John, Archbishop Joseph of Blessed Memory became the newly enthroned Metropolitan Protohierarch of the Church. He possessed Apostolic Succession from both the Syrian and Russian Orthodox Churches later giving the Synod its the name of Syro-Russian Orthodox Catholic Church. In 1987, before the death of Metropolitan Joseph, a meeting was held at St. Paul's Monastery in LaPorte, Indiana and Very Right Reverend Archimandrite Stephen

(Thomas) was duly elected Metropolitan Hierarch. He was consecrated Bishop on October 18th, 1987, by Archbishop Joseph assisted by Archbishop George of Chicago (IL) and Bishop Norman of Central Indiana at St. Mary's Chapel, LaPorte, Indiana. In the following year Bishop Stephen was enthroned as Metropolitan Archbishop Protohierarch. Metropolitan Archbishop Stephen has caused the Church to grow throughout the world. In 1994–96, he endured many sufferings in Colorado as the result of some clergy who went astray and who took part in a conspiracy to ruin the name of the Archbishop for their own gain. These clergy were since deposed of their faculties and offices. Some without having completed seminary studies were swept up by an Old Catholic group in Canada and made instant priests and bishops, some who later went and created their own churches. Since that time, the Church has experienced peace, growth, and new viability.

There is one monastic order, The Monastic Community of Saint Basil, which is open to men and women that is currently headquartered in St Cloud Minnesota. The national headquarters at this time is located at St. Mary the Theotokos Cathedral in Duluth, Minnesota, with some of the chancery offices located at St Michael & All Angels Parish in St Cloud Minnesota. The Church has 2 monsateries and 4 convents: Our Lady of Sitka Monastery, Cleveland OH; St John Monastery, Rivas Nicaragua; St Mary Mother of God Convent, DR Congo in Africa; Holy Archangels Convent, DR Congo in Africa; St Anne Convent, Lagos Nigeria; and St Barbara Convent, London England.

Headquarters

St. Mary the Theotokos Cathedral, 5907 Grand Ave, Duluth, MN 55087 Tel. (218)590-8435 Fax (864)248-4715

Primate: Metropolitan Stephen

Coadjutor of Metropolia: Bishop Timothy of Duluth

Email: rbsocc@juno.com

Website: www.rbsocc.org

Officers

His Beatitude Metropolitan Archbishop Stephen, Primate, St. Mary Pro-Cathedral, 5907 Grand Avenue, Duluth, MN 55807 Tel. (218)590-8435, Email: rbsocc@juno.com

His Excellency Bishop Timothy, Vicar General, St. Nicholas Center, 1318 Baxter Avenue, Superior, WI 54880 Tel. (218)590-8435

V.R. Father Patrick Lemming, Archdiocesan Chaplain, St. James the Apostle House & Chapel, 304 Grace Avenue, Sevierville, TN 37862 Tel. (865)429-3641

His Grace Bishop Cyril, Monastic Abbot— Managua Nicaragua

His Grace Bishop Simeon, Chancery Official— Cleveland, OH

Father Stephen Lawrence DDS JCD, Metropolia Judicial Vicar—Carlsbad, CA

Father Steven M Johnson, Chancery Official, St Thomas House, 1719 South 7th Avenue, St Cloud, MN 56301

Father Demetrios E Wruck DC, Senior Advisor to Metropolitan—Maui, Hawaii

Father Padraig Kneafsey, Archdiocesan Advisor— County Mayo, Ireland

Synodal Council Advisors

VR Father Paul Jensen, Honorary—Texas

Dr Peter Smyth, Honorary—Ontario, Canada

Father Stephen Lawrence—California

Father Steven M Johnson—Minnesota

Dr Andrew Gill—Texas

Dr Audrey Daniel—South Carolina

Dr Bekki Medsker—South Carolina

Mr Hamptom Bumgarner—New Jersy

Dr Janet Maus—Maryland

Dr Sandra Dobiash—Colorado

Christ the Pantocrator Sovereign Order of Chivalry; Father Demetrios E Wruck DC, Protector of Chivalric Orders of the Metropolia

Commission on Religious Counseling and Healing; Dr Audrey Daniel, Interim President, Dr Peter Smyth (Canadian Liaison)

Monastic Community of St. Basil and Sisters of the Community of St. Basil; Bishop Cyril of Nicaragua, Mother Helena (Abbess, St. Mary Mother of God Convent, Democratic Republic of the Congo, Africa)

Periodicals

Orthodox Christian Herald, St Mark (Seminary & College) Newsletter

Triumph the Church and Kingdom of God in Christ Inc. (International)

This church was given through the wisdom and knowledge of God to the Late Apostle Elias Dempsey Smith on Oct. 20, 1897, in Issaquena County, Mississippi, while he was pastor of a Methodist church.

The Triumph Church, as this body is more commonly known, was founded in 1902. Its doors opened in 1904 and it was confirmed in Birmingham, Alabama, with 225 members in 1915. It was incorporated in Washington, D.C. in 1918 and currently operates in 31 states and overseas. The General Church is divided into 13 districts, including the Africa District.

Triumphant doctrine and philosophy are based on the principles of life, truth and knowledge; the understanding that God is in man and expressed through man; the belief in manifested wisdom and the hope for constant new revelations. Its concepts and methods of teaching the second coming of Christ are based on these and all other attributes of goodness.

Triumphians emphasize that God is the God of the living, not the God of the dead.

Headquarters

213 Farrington Ave. S.E., Atlanta, GA 30315

Media Contact, Bishop Zephaniah Swindle, 7114 Idlewild, Pittsburg, PA 15208 Tel. (412)731-2286

Officers

Chief Bishop, Bishop Zephaniah Swindle, Rt. 1, Box 1927, Shelbyville, TX 75973 Tel. (936)598-3082

Gen. Bd of Trustees, Chmn., Rev. Oprah Francis

Gen. Rec. Sec., Bishop R.D. Clarke

Gen. Treas., Bishop W.R. Matt Malcolm

True Orthodox Church of Greece (Synod of Metropolitan Cyprian), American Exarchate

The American Exarchate of the True (Old Calendar) Orthodox Church of Greece adheres to the tenets of the Eastern Orthodox Church, which considers itself the legitimate heir of the historical Apostolic Church.

When the Orthodox Church of Greece adopted the New, or Gregorian, Calendar in 1924, many felt that this breach with tradition compromised the Church's festal calendar, based on the Old, or Julian, Calendar, and its unity with world Orthodoxy. In 1935, three State Church Bishops returned to the Old Calendar and established a Synod in Resistance, the True Orthodox Church of Greece. When the last of these Bishops died, the Russian Orthodox Church Abroad consecrated a new Hierarchy for the Greek Old Calendarists and, in 1969, declared them a Sister Church.

In the face of persecution by the State Church, some Old Calendarists denied the validity of the Mother Church of Greece and formed two synods, now under the direction of Archbishop Chrysostomos of Athens and Archbishop Andreas of Athens. A moderate faction under Metropolitan Cyprian of Oropos and Fili does not maintain communion with the Mother Church of Greece, but recognizes its validity and seeks a restoration of unity by a return to the Julian Calendar and traditional ecclesiastical polity by the State Church. About 1.5 million Orthodox Greeks belong to the Old Calendar Church.

The first Old Calendarist communities in the United States were formed in the 1930s. The Exarchate under Metropolitan Cyprian was established in 1986. Placing emphasis on clergy education, youth programs, and recognition of the Old Calendarist minority in American Orthodoxy, the Exarchate has encouraged the establishment of monastic communities and missions. Cordial contacts with the New Calendarist and other Orthodox communities are encouraged. A center for theological training and Patristic studies has been established at the Exarchate headquarters in Etna, California.

In July 1994, the True Orthodox Church of Greece (Synod of Metropolitan Cyprian), the True Orthodox Church of Romania, the True Orthodox Church of Bulgaria, and the Russian Orthodox Church Abroad entered into liturgical union, forming a coalition of traditionalist Orthodox bodies several million strong.

Headquarters

St. Gregory Palamas Monastery, P.O. Box 398, Etna, CA 96027-0398 Tel. (530)467-3228 Fax (530)467-5828

Media Contact, Exarch in America, His Eminence, Archbishop Chrysostomos

Officers

Acting Synodal Exarch in America, His Grace Bishop Auxentios

Chancellor of the Exarchate, The Very Rev. Raphael Abraham, 3635 Cottage Grove Ave. S.E., Cedar Rapids, IA 52403-1612

Periodicals

Orthodox Tradition

Ukrainian Orthodox Church of the U.S.A.*

The Ukrainian Orthodox Church of the USA has its origin in the ancient lands of Rus-Ukraine (present day Ukraine). It was to the inhabitants of these lands that the Apostle Andrew first preached the Gospel. Christianization began early in the history of Rus-Ukraine by missionaries from the Orthodox Christian See of Constantinople. In 988 AD, the Saintly Prince Volodymyr, crowned a process of Christian Evangelization begun in the 4th century, by personally accepting Orthodox Christianity and inspiring his subjects to do the same. The baptism of Volodymyr, his household and the inhabitants of Kyiv, altered the face of Kyivan Rus-Ukraine and Slavic history for all time. Kyiv became the spiritual heart of Orthodox Christians in Rus-Ukraine. It was from this See that missionaries were sent into every corner of St. Volodymyr's realm. Through their efforts the Gospel was preached and new communities were established. The Mother Church of Kyiv and its See of Saint Sophia, modeled after Constantinople's See of the same name, gave birth to many Orthodox Christian centers and communities in the west, east and north of the Dnipro river, among them the Orthodox Christian See of Moscow, Russia (Rosia).

The Ukrainian Orthodox Church of USA ministers to the needs of the faithful whose ancestral roots are in Ukraine. The Church found haven in America in the early 1920s. Its first bishop, Metropolitan Ioan (John) Teodorovych, arrived from Ukraine in 1924 and shepherded the Church as Metropolitan until his death in 1971. His successor, Archbishop Mstyslav, arrived in the USA in 1950, and shepherded the Church as Metropolitan from 1971 until his death in 1993. It was Metropolitan

163

Mstyslav who, as a consequence of Ukraine's independence, was named Patriarch of Kyiv and All Ukraine, in 1990. Previous to 1996 there were two Ukrainian Orthodox jurisdictions in the USA. Formal unification of the Ukrainian Orthodox Church of the USA, shepherded by His Beatitude Metropolitan Constantine, and the Ukrainian Orthodox Church of America, shepherded by His Grace Bishop Vsevolod, was concluded in November 1996.

Headquarters

Saint Andrew the Firstcalled Apostle Ukrainian Orthodox Church Center, P.O. Box 495, South Bound Brook, NJ 08880 Tel. (732)356-0090 Fax (732)356-5556

Media Contact, His Eminence Antony, Archbishop of New York, Consistory President

Email: consistory@uocofusa.org

Website: www.uocofusa.org

Officers

Metropolitan, His Beatitude Constantine, 1803 Sidney Street, Pittsburgh, PA 15203

CENTRAL EPARCHY

Eparchial Bishop, Metropolitan Constantine

Eparchial See, St. Volodymyr Cathedral, 5913 State Rd., Parma, OH 44134 Tel. (440)885-1509

Eparchial Territory: Florida, Georgia, Ohio, Western Pennsylvania

EASTERN EPARCHY

Eparchial Bishop, Archbishop Antony.

Eparchial Seat, St. Volodymyr Cathedral, 160 West 82nd St. New York, NY 10024 Tel. (212)873-8550

Eparchial Territory: Connecticut, Deleware, Massachusetts, Maryland, New Jersey, New York, Pennsylvania and Rhode Island

WESTERN EPARCHY

Eparchial Bishop, Archbishop Vsevolod

Eparchial Seat, St. Volodymyr Cathedral, 2230-50 West Cortez St. Chicago, IL 60622 Tel. (312)278 2827

Eparchial Territory: Arizona, California, Colorado, Illinois, Indiana, Michigan, Minnesota, North Dakota, Nebraska, Oregon, Washington, Wisconsin, Ontario Province

COUNCIL OF BISHOPS OF THE UKRAINIAN ORTHODOX CHURCH OF THE USA

Metropolitan Constantine—Chair

Achbishop Antony—Secretary

Achbishop Vsevolod—Member

METROPOLITAN COUNCIL MEMBERS

Archimandrite Andriy—Vice-chairman

Protopresbyter William Diakiw

Protopresbyter Frank Estocin, JCB

Protopriest John Nakonachny

Protopriest Michael Kochis

Protopriest Eugene Meschisen

Protopriest Bazyl Zawierucha

Dr. Gayle Woloschak—English Language Secretary

Mr. Emil Skocypec

Dr. Paul Micevych

Dr. George Krywolap—Ukrainian Language Secretary

Dr. Anatol Lysyj

Mrs. Helen Greenleaf

Mr. Michael Kapeluck

Daria Pishko, Ukrainian Orthodox League President

Mrs. Nadia Mirchuk, United Ukrainian Orthodox Sisterhoods President

Mr. Michael Heretz, Saint Andrew Society, President

CONSISTORY

Consistory President, His Eminence Antony, Archbishop of New York, P.O. Box 495, South Bound Brook, NJ 08880, Tel. (732)356-0090 Fax (732)356-5556, Email, uocofusa@aol.com

Vice Pres., Protopresbyter Willam Diakiw

Sec., Protopriest Frank Estocin

Treas., Mr. Emil Skocypec

Member, Protopriest John Nakonachny

Member, Protopriest Bazyl Zawierucha

Member, Dr. George Krywolap

Deaneries: New England—Protopriest Roman Tarnavsky, Dean; New York/New York, Protopresbyter Taras Chubenko, Dean; Mid-Atlantic, Protopresbyter Frank Estocin, Dean; Pittsburgh, Protopresbyter George Hnatko, Dean; Penn-Ohio, V. Rev. Dennis Kristof, Dean; Upstate New York, V. Rev. Mykola Krywonos, Dean; Florida, Protopresbyter Michael Petlak, Dean; Chicago, V. Rev. Bohdan Kalyniuk, Dean; Minneapolis, V. Rev. Evhen Kumka, Dean; West Coast, Rev. Vasile Sauciur, Dean

Ecclesiastical Court: Rev. Stephen Masliuk, President, Rev. Vasile Sauciur, Rev. Myroslav Schirta, Mr. Michael Slavich, Mr. Wesley Dunn

Audit Commission: Ms. Hanja Cherniak, Chairman, V. Rev. Yurij Siwko, V. Rev. Timothy Tomson, Mr. Edward Zetick, Mrs. Mary Lee Leszczuk

Office of Youth and Young Adult Ministry: Natalie Kapeluck-Nixon, Director

Office of Missions and Christian Ministry: Rev. Deacon Dr. Ihor Mahlay, Director

Office of Family and Adult Ministry: Rev. Harry Linsinbigler, Director

Office of Religious Education: Rev. Harry Linsinbigler, Temporary Director

Office of Development: Dr. Stephen Sivulich, Director

Office of Financial Affairs: Eng. Emil Skocypec, Director

Office of External Affairs and Interchurch Relations: Protopresbyter Frank Estocin, Director

Office of Publications: Protopresbyter William Diakiw, Director
Office of Archival and Historical Information: Dr. George Krywolap
Office of Public Relations: Hieromonk Daniel, Director
All Saints Camp: Stephen Sheptak, Director
Historical and Educational Museum Complex: Natalia Honcharenko, Director
St. Sophia Seminary: V. Rev. Bazyl Zawierucha, Rector
St. Sophia Seminary—Ukrainian Orthodox Church Library: Larissa Bulya, Librarian
Jr. Ukrainian Orthodox League: Mark Meschisen, President
St. Andrew Cemetery: Anastasia Hrybowych, Director
St. Andrew Bookstore: Shirley Skocypec, Director

Periodicals
Ukrainian Orthodox Word, *Vira*

Unitarian Universalist Association of Congregations

The Unitarian Universalist Association (UUA), created in 1961 through a consolidation of the Universalist Church of America with the American Unitarian Association, combines two liberal religious traditions. The religion traces its roots back to Europe where in 1569, the Transylvanian king, John Sigismund (1540–1571), issued an edict of religious freedom. The religious philosophy led to the organization of the Universalists in this country in 1793, and the Unitarians (organized here in 1825).

Founders of Universalism believed in universal salvation of all humans by God, while founders of Unitrarianism believed in the unity of God (as opposed to the Trinity). Unitarian Universalism is a liberal, creedless religion with Judeo-Christian roots. It draws also from Eastern, humanist, and other religious traditions, and encourages its members to seek religious truth out of their own reflection and experience. The denomination teaches tolerance and respect for other religious viewpoints, and affirms the worth and dignity of every person.

The Unitarian Universalist Association consists of over 1,010 congregations in the United States and Canada, with over 220,000 members, and is served by more than 1,100 ministers. The Association is the fastest-growing liberal religion in North America, and this year completed its twenty-first consecutive year of growth, at an average annual rate of nearly 2 percent. Each member congregation within the UUA is governed independently. In North America, the Association is made up of 20 Districts (served by a District Executive who is a member of the UUA staff), with each congregation having district affiliation. The Association is governed by an elected Board of Trustees, chaired by an elected Moderator. An elected President, three vice presidents, and directors of five departments form the Executive Staff that administers the daily activities of the Association.

The General Assembly, held each June in a different UUA District, serves as the Association's annual business meeting. The UUA includes Departments of Ministry and Professional Leadership; Lifespan Faith Development; Congregational Services; Identity Based Ministries; District Services; Advocacy and Witness; Financial Development; and Communications. " The World", published bimonthly, is the denominational journal. Beacon Press, an internationally honored publishing house, is wholly owned by the Unitarian Universalist Association.

Headquarters
25 Beacon Street, Boston, MA 02108 Tel. (617) 742-2100 Fax (617)367-3237
Media Contact, John Hurley, Director of Information, Tel. (617)742-2100 x 131
Email: jhurley@uua.org
Website: www.uua.org

Officers
President, The Rev. William Sinkford
Moderator, Gini Courter
Executive Vice President, Kathleen C. Montgomery

Periodicals
UU World, *InterConnections*

The United Catholic Church, Inc.

In 1996, a group of Independent Catholic Bishops, meeting in Synod, asked then Bishop, Robert M. Bowman to draw up guidelines for "inclusivity." Under these guidelines a fellowship of independent Catholic churches and clergy was born under the leadership of now Archbishop Robert M. Bowman. This fellowship was Incorporated in the State of Florida as a not-for-profit corporation in August of 1996 for the purposes of educatiing and ordaining clergy, organizing dioceses, parishes and ministries, conducting religious services, entering into various affiliations with other Christian churches, and educating the public on religious, moral and social issues. In June 2006, Bishop Rose Tressel became Presiding Bishop.

Headquarters
Media Contact, Bishop Rose Tressel, Presiding Bishop, 51 Hilltop Rd., Bethany, CT 06524 Tel. (203)393-3260, Email: unitedcatholic@snet.net
Email: catholic@rmbowman.com
Website: www.united-catholic-church.org

Officers
Archbishop Robert M. Bowman, Primate, 5017 Bellflower Ct, Melbourne, FL 32940 Tel. (321) 752-5955, Email: catholic@rmbowman. com

Bishop Rose Tressel, Presiding Bishop, 51 Hilltop Rd., Bethany, CT 06524 Tel. (203)393-3260, Email: unitedcatholic@snet.net

Monsignor William Menter, Vicar General; member, Board of Directors, 271 Dickinson St NE, Palm Bay, FL 32907 Tel. (321)956-6792, Cell. (321)223-1179, Email: menterwm@earthlink.net Bishop Hollis Dodge, Vicar for Military Chaplaincy, 802 Donaghue St., Staunton, VA 4401 Tel. (540)448-4623, Email: Christchurchstaunton@msn.com Deacon Margaret E. Bowman, Director of Music and Liturgy, 5017 Bellflower Ct, Melbourne, FL 32940 Tel. (321)752-5955, Cell. (321)759-5726, Email: maggie@rmbowman.com

Bishop Bernardo Morales, Docesan Bishop, 6315 Bass Highway, P.O.Box 702192, St. Cloud, FL 34771 Tel. (407)498-0333, Email: bmorales3@cfl.rr.com

Bishop Hollis Dodge, Diocesan Bishop, 802 Donaghue St., Staunton, VA 24401, Tel. (540) 448-4623, Email: Christchurchstaunton@msn.com Bishop William Christen, Associate Church Bishop, 3060 W. Belle Ave, Queen Creek, AZ 85242, Cell. (480)857-4070, Email: frbill2002@yahoo.com

Periodicals

The United Catholic Quarterly

United Christian Church

The United Christian Church originated about 1864. There were some ministers and laymen in the United Brethren in Christ Church who disagreed with the position and practice of the church on infant baptism, voluntary bearing of arms and belonging to oath-bound secret combinations. This group developed into United Christian Church, organized at a conference held in Campbelltown, Pennsylvania, on May 9, 1877. The principal founders of the denomination were George Hoffman, John Stamn and Thomas Lesher. Before they were organized, they were called Hoffmanites.

The United Christian Church has district conferences, a yearly general conference, a general board of trustees, a mission board, a board of directors of the United Christian Church Home, a camp meeting board, a young peoples' board and local organized congregations.

It believes in the Holy Trinity and the inspired Holy Scriptures with the doctrines they teach. The church practices the ordinances of Baptism, Holy Communion and Foot Washing.

It welcomes all into its fold who are born again, believe in Jesus Christ as Savior and Lord and have received the Holy Spirit.

Headquarters

Media Contact, Presiding Elder, John W. Graybill, 35 Oakwood Dr. Palmyra, PA 17078 Tel. (717)838-4798, Email: graybilly@aol.com

Officers

Presiding Elder, Elder John W. Graybill

Conf. Sec., Mr. Lee Wenger, 1625 Thompson Ave., Annville, PA 17003

Conf. Moderator, Elder Gerald Brinser, 2360 Horseshoe Pike, Annville, PA 17003

OTHER ORGANIZATIONS

Mission Board, Pres., Elder John Graybill, 35 Oakwood Drive, Palmyra, PA 17078 Email: graybilly@aol.com; Sec., Elder David Heagy, 4129 Oak St., Lebanon, PA 17042; Treas., Mr. Robert Morgan, 1413 Harding Ave., Hershey, PA 17033

United Church of Christ*

The United Church of Christ was constituted on June 25, 1957 by representatives of the Congregational Christian Churches and of the Evangelical and Reformed Church, in Cleveland, Ohio.

The Preamble to the Constitution states, "The United Church of Christ acknowledges as its sole head, Jesus Christ . . . It acknowledges as kindred in Christ all who share in this confession. It looks to the Word of God in the Scriptures, and to the presence and power of the Holy Spirit . . . It claims . . . the faith of the historic Church expressed in the ancient creeds and reclaimed in the basic insights of the Protestant Reformers. It affirms the responsibility of the Church in each generation to make this faith its own in . . . worship, in honesty of thought and expression, and in purity of heart before God. . . . it recognizes two sacraments, Baptism and the Lord's Supper."

The creation of the United Church of Christ brought together four unique traditions:

(1) Groundwork for the Congregational Way was laid by Calvinist Puritans and Separatists during the late 16th-early 17th centuries, but achieved prominence among English Protestants during the civil war of the 1640s. Opposition to state control prompted followers to emigrate to the United States, where they helped colonize New England in the 17th century. Congregationalists have been self-consciously a denomination from the mid-19th century.

(2) The Christian Churches, an 18th-century American restorationist movement emphasized Christ as the only head of the church, the New Testament as their only rule of faith, and "Christian" as their sole name. This loosely organized denomination found in the Congregational Churches a like disposition. In 1931, the two bodies formally united as the Congregational Christian Churches.

(3) The German Reformed Church comprised an irenic aspect of the Protestant Reformation, as a second generation of Reformers drew on the insights of Zwingli, Luther and Calvin to formulate the Heidelberg Catechism of 1563. People of the German Reformed Church began immigrating to the New World early in the 18th century,

the heaviest concentration in Pennsylvania. Formal organization of the American denomination was completed in 1793. The church spread across the country. In the Mercersburg Movement, a strong emphasis on evangelical catholicity and Christian unity was developed.

(4) In 19th-century Germany, Enlightenment criticism and Pietist inwardness decreased longstanding conflicts between religious groups. In Prussia, a royal proclamation merged Lutheran and Reformed people into one United Evangelical Church (1817). Members of this new church way migrated to America. The Evangelicals settled in large numbers in Missouri and Illinois, emphasizing pietistic devotion and unionism; in 1840 they formed the German Evangelical Church Society in the West. After union with other Evangelical church associations, in 1877 it took the name of the German Evangelical Synod of North America.

On June 25, 1934, this Synod and the Reformed Church in the U.S. (formerly the German Reformed Church) united to form the Evangelical and Reformed Church. They blended the Reformed tradition's passion for the unity of the church and the Evangelical tradition's commitment to the liberty of conscience inherent in the gospel.

Headquarters

700 Prospect Avenue, Cleveland, OH 44115 Tel. (216)736-2100 Fax (216)736-2103 Toll-free 866-822-8224 (866-UCC-UCC4)

Media Contact, Rev. J. Bennett Guess, 700 Prospect Ave., Cleveland, OH 44115 Tel. (216)736-2177 Fax (216)736-2223

Email: kellys@ucc.org

Website: www.ucc.org

Officers

Gen. Minister and Pres., Rev. John H. Thomas

Assoc. Gen. Minister, Ms. Edith A. Guffey

Exec. Minister, Wider Church Ministries, Rev. Cally Rogers-Witte

Exec. Minister, Justice and Witness Ministries, Rev. M. Linda Jaramillo

Exec. Minister, Local Church Ministries, Rev. José A. Malayang

Chair, Executive Council, Rev. Sharom MacArthur

Vice Chair, Executive Council, Mr. Aaron Gould

Mod., General Synod, Mr. Merlyn Lawrence

Asst. Mod., General Synod, Rev. Elizabeth King

Asst. Mod., General Synod, Mr. Kevin Manz

ORGANIZATIONS

Office of General Ministries, National Office, 700 Prospect Avenue, Cleveland, Ohio 44115 Tel. (216)736-2100 Fax (216)736-2103, General Minister and President, Rev. John H. Thomas; Associate General Minister, Ms. Edith A. Guffey

Justice and Witness Ministries, National Offices (as above), Tel. (216)736-3700 Fax (216)736-

3703, Franklinton Center at Bricks, P.O. Box 220, Whitakers, NC 27891 Tel. (252)437-1723 Fax (252)437-1278, Washington Office, 100 Maryland Avenue North East, Suite 330, Washington, DC. 20002 Tel. (202)543-1517 Fax (202)543-5994, Executive Minister, Rev. M. Linda Jaramillo

Local Church Ministries, National Offices, Tel. (216)736-3800 Fax (216)736-3803 Executive Minister, Rev. José A. Malayang

Wider Church Ministries, National Offices (as above), Tel. (216)736-3200 Fax (216)736-3203

Disciples of Christ Division of Overseas Ministries, P.O. Box 1986, Indianapolis, IN 46206 Tel. (317)635-3100 Fax (317)635-4323, Executive Minister, Rev. Cally Rogers-Witte

Pension Boards, Main Office, 475 Riverside Drive, New York, NY 10115 Tel. (212)729-2700 Fax (212)729-2701; National Office, 475 Riverside Drive, New York, NY 10115 Tel. (216)736-2271 Fax (216)736-2274, Executive Vice President, Mr. Michael A. Downs

United Church Foundation, Inc., 475 Riverside Drive, New York, NY 10115 Tel. (212)729-2600 Fax (212)729-2601, President/ Chief Executive Officer , Mr. Donald G. Hart, Council for American Indian Ministry, 1200E. Highland Acres Rd., Bismarck, ND 58501 Tel. (701)255-2035, Executive Director, Vacant

Council for Health and Human Services Ministries, National Office (as above) Tel. (216)736-2250 Fax (216)736-2251, President and Chief Executive Officer, Rev. Bryan W. Sickbert

CONFERENCES

Western Region

California, Nevada, Northern, Rev. Mary Susan Gast, 21425 Birch Street, Hayward, CA 94541-2131

California, Southern, Rev. Daniel F. Romero and Rev. Jane E. Heckles, 2401 N. Lake Ave., Altadena, CA 91001

Central Pacific, Rev. Héctor E. López and Eugene Ross, 0245 SW Bancroft St. Ste. E, Portland, OR 97239

Hawaii, Rev. Charles Buck, 15 Craigside Pl., Honolulu, HI 96817

Montana-Northern Wyoming, Rev. Randall Hyvonen, 2016 Alderson Ave., Billings, MT 59102

Pacific Northwest, Rev. Mark Miller, 6218 Beacon Ave. So., Seattle, WA 98108

Rocky Mountain, Rev. Tom Rehling, 1140 W. 5th Ave., Denver, CO 80204

Southwest, Rev. Cally Rogers-Witte, 4423 N. 24th St., Ste. 600, Phoenix, AZ 85016

West Central Region

Iowa, Rev. Lark J. Hapke, 600 42nd St., Des Moines, IA 50312

Kansas-Oklahoma, Rev. David Hansen, 1245 Fabrique, Wichita, KS 67218

Minnesota, Rev. David McMahill, 122 W. Franklin Ave., Rm. 323, Minneapolis, MN 55404

Missouri, Mid-South, Rev. A. Gayle Engel, 461 E. Lockwood Ave., St. Louis, MO 63119

Nebraska, Rev. Roddy Dunkerson, 825 M St. #201, Lincoln, NE 68508

Northern Plains, Rev. Wade Schemmel, 1200 E. Highland Acres Rd., Bismarck, ND 58501

South Dakota, Rev. Gene E. Miller, 3500 S. Phillips Ave., #241, Sioux Falls, SD 57105-6864

Great Lakes Region

Illinois, Rev. Jane Fisler Hoffman, 1840 Westchester Blvd. #200, Westchester, IL 60154

Illinois South, Rev. Gene Kraus, Box 325, 1312 Broadway, Highland, IL 62249

Indiana-Kentucky, Rev. Stephen C. Gray, 1100 W. 42nd St. #350, Indianapolis, IN 46208

Michigan, Rev. Kent J. Ulery, P.O. Box 1006, 5945 Park Lake Rd., East Lansing, MI 48826

Ohio, Rev. Jack Seville, 6161 Busch Blvd.,#95, Columbus, OH 43229

Wisconsin, Rev. David Moyer, 4459 Gray Rd., Box 435, De Forest, WI 53532-0495

Southern Region

Florida, Rev. Jack Richards, 924 Magnolia Ave. #250, Orlando, FL 32803

South Central, Rev. Bill Royster, 6633 E. Hwy. 290, #200, Austin, TX 78723-1157

Southeast, Rev. Timothy C. Downs, 756 W. Peachtree St., NW, Atlanta, GA 30308

Southern, Rev. Steve Camp, 216 S. Antioch Ave., Box 215, Elon, NC 27244

Middle Atlantic Region

Central Atlantic, Rev. John R. Deckenback, 916 S. Rolling Rd., Baltimore, MD 21228

New York, Rev. Geoffrey A. Black, 5800 Heritage Landing Drive, Suite 2D, East Syracuse, NY 13057

Penn Central, Rev. Marja Coons-Torn, 900 S. Arlington Ave. #112, Harrisburg, PA 17109

Penn Northeast, Rev. Alan C. Miller, 431 Delaware Ave., Palmerton, PA 18071

Pennsylvania Southeast, Rev. F. Russell Mittman, 505 S. Second Ave., P.O. Box 26400, Collegeville, PA 19426-0400

Penn West, Rev. Alan McLarty, 320 South Maple Ave., Greensburg, PA 15601

Puerto Rico, Rev. Luis Rosario, Box 8609, Caguas, PR 00762

New England Region

Connecticut, Rev. Davida Foy Crabtree, 125 Sherman St., Hartford, CT 06105

Maine, Rev. David R. Gaewski, 28 Yarmouth Crossing Dr., P.O. Box 966, Yarmouth, ME 04096

Massachusetts, Rev. Jim Antal, 1 Badger Rd., Framingham, MA 01702

New Hampshire, Rev. Gary Schulte, 140 Sheep Davis Rd, Pembroke, NH 03275

Rhode Island, Rev. Charles Barnes, 56 Walcott St., Pawtucket, RI 02860

Vermont, Rev. Susan Henderson,INT, 36 N. Main St., Randolph, VT 05060

Nongeographic

Calvin Synod, Rev. Koloman K. Ludwig, 7319 Tapper Ave., Hammond, IN 46324

Periodicals

United Church News, Common Lot

United Holy Church of America, Inc.

The United Holy Church of America, Inc. is an outgrowth of the great revival that began with the outpouring of the Holy Ghost on the Day of Pentecost. The church is built upon the foundation of the Apostles and Prophets, Jesus Christ being the cornerstone.

During a revival of repentence, regeneration and holiness of heart and life that swept through the South and West, the United Holy Church was born. The founding fathers had no desire to establish a denomination but were pushed out of organized churches because of this experience of holiness and testimony of the Spirit-filled life.

On the first Sunday in May 1886, in Method, North Carolina, what is today known as the United Holy Church of America, Inc. was born. The church was incorporated on Sept. 25, 1918.

Baptism by immersion, the Lord's Supper and feet washing are observed. The premillennial teaching of the Second Coming of Christ, Divine healing, justification by faith, sanctification as a second work of grace and Spirit baptism are accepted.

Headquarters

5104 Dunstan Rd., Greensboro, NC 27405 Tel. (336)621-0669

Media Contact, Gen. Statistician, Ms. Jacquelyn B. McCain, 1210 N. Euclid Ave., Apt. A, St. Louis, MO 63113-2012 Tel. (314)367-8351 Fax (314)367-1835

Email: books@mohistory.org

GENERAL ADMINISTRATION

Gen. Pres., The Rt. Rev. Odell McCollum, 707 Woodmark Run, Gahanna, OH 43230 Tel. (614)475-4713 Fax (614)475-4713

Gen. Vice Pres., Bishop Elijah Williams, 901 Briarwood St., Reidsville, NC 27320 Tel. (919)349-7275

Gen. 2nd Vice Pres., The Rt. Rev. Kenneth O. Robinson, Sr., 33 Springbrook Road, Nanuet, NY 10954-4423 Tel. (914)425-8311 Fax (914) 352-2686

Gen. Rec. Sec., Rev. Mrs. Elsie Harris, 2304 Eighth Street, Portsmouth, VA 23704 Tel. (757)399-0926

Asst. Rec. Sec., Mrs. Cassandra Jones, 3869 JoAnn Drive, Cleveland, OH 44122, Tel. (216) 921-0097

Gen. Fin. Sec., Vera Perkins-Hughes, P.O. Box 6194, Cleveland, OH Tel. (216)851-7448

Asst. Fin. Sec., Bertha Williams, 4749 Shaw Dr., Wilmington, NC 28405 Tel. (919)395-4462

Gen. Corres. Sec., Ms. Gwendolyn Lane, 3069 Hudson Street, Columbus, OH 43219

Gen. Treas., Louis Bagley, 8779 Wales Dr., Cincinnati, OH 45249 Tel. (513)247-0588

GENERAL OFFICERS

Gen Pres. Missionary Dept., Rev. Ardelia M. Corbett, 519 Madera Dr., Youngstown, OH 44504 Tel. (216)744-3284

Gen. Evangelism & Extension Dept., Pres., Elder Clifford R. Pitts, 3563 North 14th St., Milwaukee, WI 53206 Tel. (414)244-1319

Gen. Bible Church School Dept., Superintendent, Robert L. Rollins, 1628 Avondale Ave., Toledo, OH 43607 Tel. (419)246-4046

Gen. Y.P.H.A., Pres., Elder James W. Brooks, Rt. 3 Box 105, Pittsboro, NC 27312 Tel. (919)542-5357

Gen. Ushers Department, Pres., Ms. Sherly M. Hughes, 1491 East 191st Street, #H-604, Euclid, OH 44117 Tel. (216)383-0038

Gen. Educ. Dept., Elder Roosevelt Alston, 168 Willow Creek Run, Henderson, NC 27636 Tel. (919)438-5854

Gen. Music Dept., Chair, Rosie Johnson, 2009 Forest Dale Dr., Silver Spring, MD 20932

Gen. Historian, Dr. Chester Gregory, Sr., 1302 Lincoln Woods Dr., Baltimore, MD 21228 Tel. (410)788-5144

Gen. Counsel, Mr. Joe L. Webster, Esquire, Attorney-At-Law, P.O. Box 2301, Chapel Hill, NC 27515-2301 Tel. (919)542-5150

UHCA Academy, Dir., Ms. Stephanie Davis, The United Holy Church of America, Inc., 5104 Dunstan Road, Greensboro, NC 27405 Tel. (336)621-0069

Gen. Statistician, Ms. Jacquelyn B. McCain, 1210 N. Euclid Ave., Apt. A, St. Louis, MO 63113-2012, Tel. (314)367-8351 Fax (314)367-1835

PRESIDENTS OF CONVOCATIONAL DISTRICTS

Barbados District; The Rt. Rev. Jestina Gentles, 5 West Ridge St., Britton's Hill, St. Michael, BH2 Barbados, West Indies, Tel. (246)427-7185

Bermuda Dist., The Rt. Rev. Calvin Armstrong, P.O. Box 234, Paget, Bermuda, Tel. (441)296-0828 or (441)292-8383

Central Western Dist., Bishop Bose Bradford, 6279 Natural Bridge, Pine Lawn, MO 63121 Tel. (314)355-1598

Ghana, West Africa Dist., The Rt. Rev. Robert Blount, 231 Arlington Av., Jersey City, NJ 07035 Tel. (201)433-5672

New England Dist., The Rt. Rev. Lowell Edney, 85 Woodhaven St., Mattapan, MA 02126 Tel. (617)296-5366

Northern Dist., The Rt. Rev. Kenneth O. Robinson, Sr., 33 Springbrook Rd., Nanuet, NY 10954 Tel. (914)425-8311

Northwestern Dist., The Rt. Rev. M. Daniel Borden, 8655 North Melody Lane, Macedonia, OH 44056 Tel. (330)468-0270

Pacific Coast Dist., The Rt. Rev. Irvin Evans, 235 Harvard Rd., Linden, NJ 07036 Tel. (908) 925-6138

Southeastern Dist., The Rt. Rev. James C. Bellamy, 1825 Rockland Dr., SE, Atlanta, GA 30316 Tel. (404)241-1821

Southern Dist.- Goldsboro, The Rt. Rev. Ralph E. Love, Sr., 200 Barrington Rd., Greenville, NC 27834 Tel. (252)353-0495

Southern Dist.- Henderson, The Rt. Rev. Jesse Jones, 608 Cecil Street, Durham, NC 27707 Tel. (919)682-8249

St. Lucia Dist., The Rt. Rev. Carlisle Collymore, P.O. Box 51, Castries, St. Lucia, West Indies Tel. (758)452-5835

Virginia Dist., The Rt. Rev. Albert Augson, 1406 Melton Ave., Richmond, VA 23223 Tel. (804) 222-0463

West Virginia Dist., The Rt. Rev. Alvester McConnell, Route 3, Box 263, Bluefield, WV 24701 Tel. (304)248-8046

Western North Carolina Dist., The Rt. Rev. Elijah Williams, 901 Briarwood St., Reidsville, NC 27320-7020 Tel. (336)349-7275

United House of Prayer

The United House of Prayer was founded and organized as a hierarchical church in the 1920s by the late Bishop C. M. Grace, who had built the first House of Prayer in 1919 in West Wareham, MA, with his own hands. The purpose of the organization is to establish, maintain and perpetuate the doctrine of Christianity and the Apostolic Faith throughout the world among all people; to erect and maintain houses of prayer and worship where all people may gather for prayer and to worship the almighty God in spirit and in truth, irrespective of denomination or creed, and to maintain the Apostolic faith of the Lord and Savior, Jesus Christ.

Headquarters

628 M St. NW, Washington, DC 20001 Tel. (202)289-9890 Fax (202)289-3690

Media Contact, Apostle S. Green

Email: apostlegreen@hotmail.com

Officers

CEO, Bishop S. C. Madison, 1665 N. Portal Dr. NW, Washington, DC 20012 Tel. (202)882-3956 Fax (202)829-4717

NATIONAL PROGRAM STAFF

The General Assembly, Presiding Officer, Bishop S. C. Madison, 1665 N. Portal Dr. NW, Washington, DC 20012 Tel. (202)882-3956 Fax (202)829-4717

General Council Ecclesiastical Court, Clerk, Apostle R. Price, 1665 N. Portal Dr. NW, Washington, DC 20012 Tel. (202)882-3956 Fax (202)829-4717

169

Nationwide Building Program, General Builder, Bishop S. C. Madison, 1665 N. Portal Dr. NW, Washington, DC 20012 Tel. (202)882-3956 Fax (202)829-4717

Special Projects, Dir., Apostle S. Green

Annual Truth & Facts Publication, Exec. Editor, Bishop S. C. Madison, 1665 N. Portal Dr. NW, Washington, DC 20012 Tel. (202)882-3956 Fax (202)829-4717

The United Methodist Church*

The United Methodist Church was formed April 23, 1968, in Dallas by the union of The Methodist Church and The Evangelical United Brethren Church. The two churches shared a common historical and spiritual heritage. The Methodist Church resulted in 1939 from the unification of three branches of Methodism—the Methodist Episcopal Church, the Methodist Episcopal Church, South, and the Methodist Protestant Church.

The Methodist movement began in eighteenth-century England under the preaching of John Wesley, but the Christmas Conference of 1784 in Baltimore is regarded as the date on which the organized Methodist Church was founded as an ecclesiastical organization. It was there that Francis Asbury was elected the first bishop in this country.

The Evangelical United Brethren Church was formed in 1946 with the merger of the Evangelical Church and the Church of the United Brethren in Christ, both of which had their beginnings in Pennsylvania in the evangelistic movement of the 18th and early 19th centuries. Philip William Otterbein and Jacob Albright were early leaders of this movement among the German-speaking settlers of the Middle Colonies.

Headquarters

Media Contact, Executive Director, Public Information, Diane Denton, Tel. (615)742-5406, Email: ddenton@umcomm.org

General Information, Director, InfoServ, Vicki Wallace, Tel. (800)251-8140 Fax (615) 742-5423

Email: infoserv@umcom.umc.org

Website: www.umc.org

Officers

General Conference, Sec., Rev. L. 'Gere' Fitzgerald Reist II, 2420 Nottingham Rd, Williamsport, PA 17701-4057

Council of Bishops, Pres., Bishop Peter D. Weaver, (276 Essex St., 5th Fl, 01840-1516), P.O. Box 249, Lawrence, MA 01842-0449 Tel. (978)682-7555 Fax (978)682-9555, Email: bishopsoffice@neumc.org; Sec., Bishop Ernest S. Lyght, United Methodist Center, 900 Washington St. E., Ste. 300, Charleston, WV 25301-1710 Tel. (304)344-8330 Fax (304) 344-8330, Email: WVareaumc@aol.com

JURISDICTIONAL BISHOPS

NORTH CENTRAL JURISDICTION

Chicago Episcopal Area, Bishop Hee-Soo Jung, 77 W. Washington St., Ste. 1820, Chicago, IL 60602-3181 Tel. (312)346-9766 x 102 Fax (312)214-9031, Email: hsjung@umcnic.org

Dakotas Episcopal Area, Bishop Deborah L. Kiesey, 3910 25th St. S., Fargo, ND 58104-6880 Tel. (701)232-2241 Fax (701)232-2615, Email: bishopdakumc@ideaone.net

Illinois Episcopal Area, Bishop Sharon Brown Christopher, (5900 S 2nd St., 62711), P.O. Box 19215, Springfield, IL 62794-9215 Tel. (217)529-3820 Fax (217)529-4190, Email: bishopsabc@aol.com

Indiana Episcopal Area, Bishop Michael J. Coyner, 1100 W. 42nd St., Ste. 210, Indianapolis, IN 46208-3382 Tel. (317)924-1321 Fax (317)924-1380, Email: Bishopcoyner @inareaumc.org

Iowa Episcopal Area, Bishop Gregory V. Palmer, 2301 Rittenhouse St, Des Moines, IA 50321-3101 Tel. (515)974-8902 Fax (515)974-8952, Email: bishop.palmer@iaumc.org

Michigan Episcopal Area, Bishop Jonathan D. Keaton (2164 University Park Dr., Ste. 250, Okemos, MI 48864), P.O. Box 25068, Lansing MI 48909-5068 Tel. (517)347-4030 Fax (517) 347-4003, Email: bishopsoffice@miareaumc. org

Minnesota Episcopal Area, Bishop Sally Dyck, 122 W. Franklin Ave., Ste. 200, Minneapolis, MN 55404-2472 Tel. (612)870-4007 Fax (612)870-3587, Email: bishop.dyck@mnumc. org

Ohio East Episcopal Area, Bishop John L. Hopkins (8800 Cleveland Ave. NW), P.O. Box 2800, North Canton, OH 44720-0800 Tel. (330)499-3972 x 112 Fax (330)497-4911, Email: bishop@eocumc.com

Ohio West Episcopal Area, Bishop Bruce R. Ough, 32 Wesley Blvd., Worthington, OH 43085-3585 Tel. (614)844-6200 x 215 Fax (614)781-2625, Email: Bishop@wocumc.org

Wisconsin Episcopal Area, Bishop Linda Lee, 750 Windsor St., Ste. 303, Sun Prairie, WI 53590-2149 Tel. (608)837-8526 Fax (608)837-0281, Email: bishoplee@wisconsin umc.org

NORTHEASTERN JURISDICTION

Albany Episcopal Area, Bishop Susan W. Hassinger, 215 Lancaster St., Albany, NY 12210-1131 Tel. (518)426-0386 Fax (518) 426-0347, Email: AlbEpisArea@verizon.net

Boston Episcopal Area, Bishop Peter D. Weaver (276 Essex St. 5th Fl., 01840), P.O. Box 249, Lawrence, MA 01842-0449 Tel. (978)682-7555 x 250 Fax (978)682-9555, Email: bishops office@neumc.org

Harrisburg Episcopal Area, Bishop Jane Allen Middleton, 303 Mulberry Dr., Ste. 100, Mechanicsburg, PA 17050-3141 Tel. (717)

766-7871 x 3100 Fax (717)766-3210, Email: bishop@cpcumc.org

New Jersey Episcopal Area, Bishop Sudarshana Devadhar, 1001 Wickapecko Dr., Ocean, NJ 07712-4733 Tel. (732)359-1010 Fax (732) 359-1019, Email: Bishop@gnjumc.org

New York Episcopal Area, Bishop Jeremiah J. Park, 20 Soundview Ave., White Plains, NY 10606-3302 Tel. (914)615-2221 Fax (914) 615-2246, Email: Bishop@nyac.com

New York West Episcopal Area, Bishop Violet L. Fisher, 1010 East Ave, Rochester, NY 14607-2220 Tel. (585)271-3400 Fax (585)271-3404, Email: nywaumc@frontiernet.net

Philadelphia Episcopal Area, Bishop Marcus Matthews (980 Madison Ave, Norristown, 19403), P.O. Box 820, Valley Forge, PA 19482-0820 Tel. (610)666-9090 x 233 Fax (610)666-9181, Email: marcus.matthews@epaumc.org

Pittsburgh Episcopal Area, Bishop Thomas J. Bickerton (1204 Freedom Rd.), P.O. Box 5002, Cranberry Township, PA 16066-1902 Tel. (724)776-1499/1599 Fax (724)776-1683, Email: bishopsoffice@wpaumc.org

Washington Episcopal Area (DC), Bishop John R. Schol, 100 Maryland Ave,. NE Ste. 510, Washington, DC 20002-5625 Tel. (202)546-3110 Fax (202)546-3186, Email: bishopchol@bwcumc.org

West Virginia Episcopal Area, Bishop Ernest S. Lyght, United Methodist Center, 900 Washington St. E., Ste. 300, Charleston, WV 25301-1710 Tel. (304)344-8330 Fax (304) 344-8330, Email: WVareaumc@aol.com

SOUTH CENTRAL JURISDICTION

Arkansas Episcopal Area, Bishop Charles N. Crutchfield, 2 Trudie Kibbe Reed Dr, Little Rock, AR 72202-3770 Tel. (501)324-8001 Fax (501)324-8021, Email: bishopcnc@arumc.org

Dallas Episcopal Area, Bishop Alfred L. Norris, P.O. Box 866186, Plano, TX 75086-6188 Tel. (972)526-5015 Fax (972)526-5014, Email: bishop@ntcumc.org

Fort Worth Episcopal Area, Bishop Ben R. Chamness, 464 Bailey Ave., Fort Worth, TX 76107-2153 Tel. (817)877-5222 Fax (817) 332-4609, Email: bishop@ctcumc.org

Houston Episcopal Area, Bishop Janice Riggle Huie, 5215 Main St., Houston, TX 77002-9792 Tel. (713)528-6881 Fax (713)529-7736, Email: bishop.huie@txcumc.org

Kansas Episcopal Area, Bishop Scott J. Jones 9440 E. Boston, Ste 160, Wichita, KS 67207-3600 Tel. (316)686-0600 Fax (316)684-0044, Email: kansasbishop@kswestumc.org

Louisiana Episcopal Area, Bishop William W. Hutchinson, 527 North Blvd., Baton Rouge, LA 70802-5700 Tel. (225)346-1646 x 212 Fax (225)387-3662, Email: lcumc@bellsouth.net

Missouri Episcopal Area, Bishop Robert C. Schnase, 3601 Amron Ct, Columbia, MO 65202-1918 Tel. (573)441-1770 Fax (573) 441-0765, Email: rschnase@moumethodist. org

Nebraska Episcopal Area, Bishop Ann Brookshire Sherer, 2641 N. 49th St., Lincoln, NE 68504-2802 Tel. (402)466-4955 Fax (402) 466-7931, Email: bishopsherer@umcneb.org

Northwest Texas-New Mexico Episcopal Area, Bishop D. Max Whitfield, 11816 Lomas Blvd NE, Albuquerque, NM 87112-5614 Tel. (505) 255-9361 Fax (505)255-8738, Email: whitmax @nmconfum.com

Oklahoma Episcopal Area, Bishop Robert E. Hayes, Jr. (1501 NW 24th St, 73106), P.O. Box 60467, Oklahoma City, OK 73146-0467 Tel. (405)530-2025 Fax (405)530-2040, Email: jhayes@okbishop.org

San Antonio Episcopal Area, Bishop Joel N. Martinez (16400 Huebner Rd, 78248), P.O. Box 781688, San Antonio, TX 78278-1688 Tel. (210)408-4500 Fax (210)408-4501, Email: bishop@umcswtx.org

SOUTHEASTERN JURISDICTION

Alabama-West Florida Episcopal Area, Bishop Larry M. Goodpaster, 100 Interstate Park Dr., P.O. Box 11108 Montgomery, AL 36111-0108 Tel. (334)277-1787 Fax (334)277-0109, Email: bishop.awf@knology.net

Birmingham Episcopal Area, Bishop William H. Willimon, 898 Arkadelphia Rd., Birmingham, AL 35204-5011 Tel. (205)226-7991 Fax (205) 226-7998, Email: wwillimon@northalabama umc.org

Charlotte Episcopal Area, Bishop J. Lawrence McCleskey (3400 Shamrock Dr., 28215), P.O. Box 18750, Charlotte, NC 28218-0750 Tel. (704)535-2260 Fax (704)535-9160, Email: bishop@wnccumc.org

Columbia Episcopal Area, Bishop Mary Virginia Taylor, 4908 Colonial Dr., Ste. 121, Columbia, SC 29203-6080 Tel. (803)786-9486 Fax (803)754-9327, Email: bishop@umcsc.org

Florida Episcopal Area, Bishop Timothy Whitaker (1122 E. McDonald St., 33801), Lakeland, FL 33801-5641 Tel. (863)688-4427 Fax (863)687-0568, Email: bishop@flumc.org

Holston Episcopal Area, Bishop James E. Swanson, Sr. P.O. Box 850, Alcoa, TN 37701-0850 Tel. (865)690-4080 Fax (865)690-7112, Email: bishop@holston.org

Louisville Episcopal Area, Bishop James R. King, Jr., 7400 Floydsburg Rd., Crestwood, KY 40014-8202 Tel. (502)425-4240 Fax (502)425-9232, Email: jking@kyumc.org

Mississippi Episcopal Area, Bishop Hope Morgan Ward (321 Mississippi St., 39201), P.O. Box 931, Jackson, MS 39205-0931 Tel. (601)948-4561 Fax (601)948-5981, Email: bishop@mississippi-umc.org

Nashville Episcopal Area, Bishop Richard J. Wills, Jr., 520 Commerce St., Ste. 201, Nashville, TN 37203-3714 Tel. (615)742-8834 Fax (615)742-3726, Email: bishop@ nasharea.org

171

North Georgia Episcopal Area, Bishop G. Lindsey Davis 4511 Jones Bridge Cir. NW, Norcross, GA 30092-1406 Tel.(678)533-1360 Fax (678)533-1361, Email: bishop@ngumc.org

Raleigh Episcopal Area, Bishop Alfred W. Gwinn, Jr. (1307 Glenwood Ave., Rm. 203), P.O. Box 10955, Raleigh, NC 27605-0955 Tel. (919)832-9560 x 243 Fax (919)-832-4721, Email: bishopgwinn@nccumc.org

Richmond Episcopal Area, Bishop Charlene Payne Kammerer (10330 Staples Mill Rd.), P.O. Box 1719, Glen Allen, VA 23060-0659 Tel. (804)521-1100 Fax (804)521-1171, Email: bishopk@vaumc.org

South Georgia Episcopal Area, Bishop B. Michael Watson 3370 Vineville Ave., Ste. 101, Macon, GA 31204-2331 Tel. (478)475-9286 Fax (478)475-9248, Email: bishopsga@aol.com

WESTERN JURISDICTION

Denver Episcopal Area, Bishop Warner H. Brown, Jr., 6110 Greenwood Plaza Blvd, Greenwood Village, CO 80111-4803 Tel. (303)733-0083 Fax (303)733-5047, Email: bishop@rmcumc.com

Los Angeles Episcopal Area, Bishop Mary Ann Swenson (110 S. Euclid Ave., 91101), P.O. Box 6006, Pasadena, CA 91102-6006 Tel. (626)568-7312 Fax (626)568-7377, Email: alpacbishop@earthlink.net

Phoenix Episcopal Area, Bishop Minerva G. Carcaño, 1550 E. Meadowbrook Ave., Phoenix, AZ 85014-4040 Tel. (602)266-6956 x 209 Fax (602)279-1355, Email: Bishopmc @desertsw.org

Portland Episcopal Area, Bishop Robert T. Hoshibata, 1505 SW 18th Ave., Portland, OR 97201-2599 Tel. (503)226-1530 Fax (503) 228-3189, Email: bishop@umoi.org

San Francisco Episcopal Area, Bishop Beverly J. Shamana (1276 Halyard Dr., 95691), P.O. Box 980250, West Sacramento, CA 95798-0250 Tel. (916)374-1510 Fax (916)372-9062, Email: bishop@calnevumc.org

Seattle Episcopal Area, Bishop Edward W. Paup, (816 S 216th St #2, 98198), P.O. Box 13650, Des Moines, WA 98198-1009 Tel. (206)870-6810 Fax (206)870-6811, Email: bishop@pnwumc.org

Periodicals

Mature Years, *El Intérprete*, *New World Outlook*, *Newscope*, *Interpreter*, *Methodist History*, *Christian Social Action*, *Pockets*, *Response*, *Social Questions Bulletin*, *United Methodist Reporter*, *Quarterly Review*, *Alive Now*, *Circuit Rider*, *El Aposento Alto*, *Weavings—A Journal of the Christian Spiritual Life*, *The Upper Room*

United Pentecostal Church International

The United Pentecostal Church International came into being through the merger of two one-ness Pentecostal organizations—the Pentecostal Church, Inc., and the Pentecostal Assemblies of Jesus Christ. The first of these was known as the Pentecostal Ministerial Alliance from its inception in 1925 until 1932. The second was formed in 1931 by a merger of the Apostolic Church of Jesus Christ with the Pentecostal Assemblies of the World.

The church contends that the Bible teaches that there is one God who manifested himself as the Father in creation, in the Son in redemption, and as the Holy Spirit in regeneration; that Jesus is the name of this absolute deity and that water baptism should be administered in his name, not in the titles Father, Son and Holy Ghost (Acts ch.2 vs.38, ch.8 vs.16, and ch.19 vs.6).

The Fundamental Doctrine of the United Pentecostal Church International, as stated in its Articles of Faith, is "the Bible standard of full salvation, which is repentance, baptism in water by immersion in the name of the Lord Jesus Christ for the remission of sins, and the baptism of the Holy Ghost with the initial sign of speaking with other tongues as the Spirit gives utterance."

Further doctrinal teachings concern a life of holiness and separation, the operation of the gifts of the Spirit within the church, the second coming of the Lord, and the church's obligation to take the gospel to the whole world.

Headquarters

8855 Dunn Rd., Hazelwood, MO 63042 Tel. (314)837-7300 Fax (314)837-4503

Media Contact, Gen. Sec.-Treas., Rev. Jerry Jones Email: rfuller@upci.org

Officers

Gen. Supt., Rev. Kenneth F. Haney

Asst. Gen. Supts., Rev. Paul. Mooney and Rev. Randy Keyes

Gen. Sec.-Treas., Rev. Jerry Jones

Dir. of Foreign Missions, Rev. Bruce Howell

Gen. Dir. of Home Missions, Rev. Carlton Coon

Editor-in-Chief, Rev. Robert H. Fuller

Gen. Sunday School Dir., Rev. Gary Erickson

Youth Pres., Rev. Todd Gaddy

OTHER ORGANIZATIONS

Pentecostal Publishing House, Mgr., Rev. Robert H. Fuller

Ladies Ministries, Pres., Gwyn Oakes

Stewardship Dept., Dir., Rev., Stephen Drury

Division of Education, Supt., Rev. Don Batchelor

Media Missions Asst. Dir., Rev. Morman R. Paslay II

Media Missions Announcer, Rev. J. Hugh Rose

Word Aflame Publications, Editor, Rev. Richard Davis

Public Relations, Contact Church Administration
Historical Society & Archives
Urshan Graduate School of Theology

Periodicals
The Pentecostal Herald, *World Harvest Today*,
The North American Challenge, *Conqueror*,
Reflections, *Forward*, *Apostolic Man*

The United Pentecostal Churches of Christ

In a time when the Church of Jesus Christ is
challenged to send the "Evening Light Message"
to the uppermost part of the Earth, a group of
men and women came together on May 29, 1992
at the Pentecostal Church of Christ in Cleveland,
Ohio to form what is now called The United
Pentecostal Churches of Christ.

Organized and established by Bishop Jesse
Delano Ellis, II, the United Pentecostal Churches
of Christ is about the business of preparing people to see the Lord of Glory. The traditional barriers of yesteryear must not keep saints or like
faith apart ever again and this fellowship of
Pentecostal, Apostolic Independent Churches
have discovered the truth of Our Lord's Prayer in
the seventeenth chapter of Saint John, "that they
may all be One."

The United Pentecostal Churches of Christ is a
fellowship of holiness assemblies which has
membership in the universal Body of Christ. As
such, we preserve the message of Christ's
redeeming love through His atonement and
declare holiness of life to be His requirement for
all men who would enter into the Kingdom of
God. We preach repentence from sin, baptism in
the Name of Jesus Christ, a personal indwelling
of the Holy Spirit, a daily walk with the Lord and
life after death. Coupled with the cardinal truths
of the Church are the age old customs of ceremony and celebration.

Headquarters
10515 Chester Ave., Cleveland, OH 44106 Tel.
(216)721-5935 Fax (216)721-6938
Contact Person, Public Relations., Rev.
Gwendolyn G. Saunder

REGIONAL OFFICE
493-5 Monroe St., Brooklyn, New York 11221
Tel. (718)574-4100 Fax (718)574-8504
Contact Person, Secretary General., Rev. Rodney
McNeil Johnson
Email: community@pcccleveland.com
Website: www.pcccleveland.com

Officers
Presiding Bishop and Prelate, J. Delano Ellis, II,
Cleveland, OH
Pastor for Business Administration, Sabrina J.
Ellis
Senior Assistant Pastor and Bishop Coadjutor,
Benjamin T. Douglass
General Secretary, Gwendolyn G. Saunders
Assistant Pastor of Worship, Yvonne Tufts Jeans

Periodicals
The Pentecostal Flame

United Zion Church

A branch of the Brethren in Christ which settled in Lancaster County, Pennsylvania, the
United Zion Church was organized under the
leadership of Matthias Brinser in 1855.

Headquarters
United Zion Retirement Community, 722
Furnace Hills Pk., Lititz, PA 17543
Media Contact, Bishop Charles Brown, 4041
Shanamantown Rd., Annville, PA 17003 Tel.
(717)867-1133
Website: www.unitedzionchurch.org

Officers
Gen. Conf. Mod., Bishop Charles Brown, 4041
Shanamantown Rd., Annville, PA 17003, Tel.
(717)867-1133
Asst. Mod., Rev. Paul H. Martin
Gen. Conf. Sec., Rev. Clyde Martin
Gen. Conf. Treas., Kenneth Kleinfelter, 919
Sycamore Lane, Lebanon, PA 17042

Unity of the Brethren

Czech and Moravian immigrants in Texas
(beginning about 1855) established congregations which grew into an Evangelical Union in
1903, and with the accession of other Brethren in
Texas, into the Evangelical Unity of the Czech-
Moravian Brethren in North America. In 1959, it
shortened the name to the original name used in
1457, the Unity of the Brethren (Unitas Fratrum,
or Jednota Bratrska).

Headquarters
4009 Hunter Creek, College Station, TX 77845
Media Contact, Sec. of Exec. Committee, Ginger
McKay, 148 N. Burnett, Baytown, TX 77520
Email: lkoslovsky@teleshare.net
Website: www.unityofthebrethren.org

Officers
President: Claren Kotrla, 1501 Echo Bluff Cove,
Austin Texas 78754 Tel. (512)491-7802,
Email: kotrla@flash.net
1st Vice President: Rev. Linda Chandler, 13108
N. Ridge Circle, Leander, TX 78641 Tel.
(512)267-4826, Email: L77c@aol.com
2nd Vice President: Pastor Joe Emerson, P.O.
Box 4615, Temple, TX 76505 Tel. (254)791-
0420, Email: pastorjde@juno.com
3rd Vice President: Rev. James Hejl, 309
Cherrywood Circle, Taylor, TX 76574 Tel.
(512)365-6890, Email: jhejl@austin.rr.com
Secretary: Kathy Harrison, P.O. Box 593, Little
River-Academy, Texas 76554 Tel. (254)721-
1815, Email: kathy@pearson-lawfirm.com
Financial Secretary: Dewyan Weise, 6006 FM
Hwy 765, San Angelo, TX 76905, Email:
DWeise@academicplanet.com
Treasurer: James Marek, 1304 T.H. Johnson
Drive, Taylor, Texas 76574 Tel. (512)352-6165,
Email: james@cnbt.com

OTHER ORGANIZATIONS

Bd. of Christian Educ., Dr., Donald Ketcham, 900 N. Harrison, West, TX 76691

Brethren Youth Fellowship, Pres., Jamie Brooke Bryan, 1231 Four Corners, West, TX 76691

Friends of the Hus Encampment, Jim Baletka, 727 San Benito, College Station, TX 77845

Christian Sisters Union, Pres., Janet Pomykal, P.O. Box 560, Brenham, TX 77834

Sunday School Union, Pres., Dorothy Kocian, 107 S. Barbara Dr., Waco, TX 76705

Youth Director, Kimberly Stewart, 1500 Lawnmont Dr., Apt. 208, Round Rock, TX 78664

Periodicals

Brethren Journal

Universal Fellowship of Metropolitan Community Churches

The Universal Fellowship of Metropolitan Community Churches was founded Oct. 6, 1968 by the Rev. Troy D. Perry in Los Angeles, with a particular but not exclusive outreach to the gay community. Since that time, the Fellowship has grown to include congregations throughout the world.

The group is Trinitarian and accepts the Bible as the divinely inspired Word of God. The Fellowship has two sacraments, baptism and holy communion, as well as a number of traditionally recognized rites such as ordination.

This Fellowship acknowledges "the Holy Scriptures interpreted by the Holy Spirit in conscience and faith, as its guide in faith, discipline, and government." The government of this Fellowship is vested in its General Council (consisting of Elders and District Coordinators), clergy and church delegates, who exert the right of control in all of its affairs, subject to the provisions of its Articles of Incorporation and By-Laws.

Headquarters

8704 Santa Monica Blvd. 2nd Floor, West Hollywood, CA 90069-4548 Tel. (310)360-8640 x 226 Fax (310)360-8680

Media Contact, Dir. of Communications, Jim Birkett

Email: CindiLove@MCCchurch.org

Website: www.mccchurch.org

Officers

Mod., Rev. Elder Troy D. Perry

Vice Mod., Rev. Elder Nancy L. Wilson

Treas., Rev. Elder Donald Eastman

Clk., Rev. Elder Darlene Garner

Elder Mel Johnson, PMB #63, 2261 Market St., San Francisco, CA 94114-1600

Rev. Elder Nori Rost, 214 S. Prospect St., Colorado Springs, CO 80903

Rev. Elder Hong Kia Tan, 72 Fleet Rd., Hampstead, London, NW3 2QT England

Deputy Chief Executive Officer, Jane Wagner, 8704 Santa Monica Blvd., 2nd Floor, West Holywood, CA 90069-4548

Dir., Communications, Jim Birkett, 8704 Santa Monica Blvd., 2nd Floor, West Hollywood, CA 90069-4548

OTHER COMMISSIONS & COMMITTEES

Min. of Global Outreach, Field Dir., Rev. Judy Dahl

Commission on the Laity, Chpsn., Stan Kimer

Clergy Credentials & Concerns, Admn., Rev. Justin Tanis

UFMCC AIDS Ministry, AIDS Liaison., Rev. Robert Griffin

Chief Financial Officer, Margaret Mahlman, 8704 Santa Monica Blvd., 2nd Floor, West Hollywood, CA 90069-4548

Periodicals

Keeping in Touch

Volunteers of America

Volunteers of America is a national, nonprofit, spiritually based organization that provides local human service programs and opportunities for individual and community involvement through 39 local affiliate offices and the National Services Housing and Health Care Division. Founded in 1896 by Christian social reformers Ballington and Maud Booth, Volunteers of America provides over 100 different types of programs and services in more than 400 communities nationwide. Programs include services for abused and neglected children, youth at risk, the elderly, people with disabilities, homeless individuals and families, and many others. Volunteers of America is one of the nation's largest providers of affordable housing for seniors and low income families and individuals. It also provides a national Prison After-Care program that engages local congregations of all denominations as mentors to newly released prisoners. It employs 14,000 individuals whose work is assisted by over 70,000 committed volunteers.

Headquarters

1660 Duke St., Alexandria, VA 22314-3427 Tel. (800)899-0089

Email: voa@voa.org

Website: www.voa.org

Officers

Chpsn., David Kikumoto

Pres., Charles W. Gould, 1660 Duke St., Alexandria, VA. 22314 Tel. (703)341-5000

Dir., of Ecclesiastical Services, Harry V. Quiett, 1660 Duke St., Alexandria, VA. 22314, Tel. (703)341-5054 Fax (703)341-7000, Email: hquiett@voa.org

39 local affiliate offices and one National Services Division. Information accesible through the national Website: www.voa.org

Periodicals
Spirit Magazine, *Gazette*

The Wesleyan Church

The Wesleyan Church was formed on June 26, 1968, through the union of the Wesleyan Methodist Church of America (1843) and the Pilgrim Holiness Church (1897). The headquarters was established at Marion, Ind., and relocated to Indianapolis in 1987,and relocated again in Fishers, Indiana in 2004.

The Wesleyan movement centers around the beliefs, based on Scripture, that the atonement in Christ provides for the regeneration of sinners and the entire sanctification of believers. John Wesley led a revival of these beliefs in the 18th century.

When a group of New England Methodist ministers led by Orange Scott began to crusade for the abolition of slavery, the bishops and others sought to silence them. This led to a series of withdrawals from the Methodist Episcopal Church. In 1843, the Wesleyan Methodist Connection of America was organized and led by Scott, Jotham Horton, LaRoy Sunderland, Luther Lee and Lucius C. Matlack.

During the holiness revival in the last half of the 19th century, holiness replaced social reform as the major tenet of the Connection. In 1947 the name was changed from Connection to Church and a central supervisory authority was set up.

The Pilgrim Holiness Church was one of many independent holiness churches which came into existence as a result of the holiness revival. Led by Martin Wells Knapp and Seth C. Rees, the International Holiness Union and Prayer League was inaugurated in 1897 in Cincinnati. Its purpose was to promote worldwide holiness evangelism and the Union had a strong missionary emphasis from the beginning. It developed into a church by 1913.

The Wesleyan Church is now spread across most of the United States and Canada and in over 80 other countries. The International Conference of The Wesleyan Church, originally named Wesleyan World Fellowship, was organized in 1972 to unite Wesleyan mission bodies developing into mature churches. The Wesleyan Church is a member of the Christian Holiness Partnership, the National Association of Evangelicals and the World Methodist Council.

Headquarters

P.O. Box 50434, Indianapolis, IN 46250 Tel. (317)774-7900

Media Contact, Gen. Sec., Dr. Ronald D. Kelly, Tel. (317)744-3922 Fax (317)744-3924 Email: kellyr@wesleyan.org, Mailing Address: P.O.Box 50434, Indianapolis, IN 46250Email: generalsecretary@wesleyan.org

Website: www.wesleyan.org

General Superintendents

Dr. Earle L. Wilson, Tel. (317)774-3932 Fax (317)774-3931, Email: wilsone@wesleyan. org

Dr. Thomas E. Armiger, Tel. (317)774-3933 Fax (317)774-3931, Email: armigert@wesleyan. org

Dr. Jerry G. Pence, Tel. (317)774-3934 Fax (317) 774-3931, Email: pencej@wesleyan.org

General Officers

Gen. Sec., Dr. Ronald D. Kelly, Tel. (317)774-3922 Fax (317)744-3924, Email: kellyr@wesleyan.org

Gen. Treas., Donald M. Frase, Tel. (317)774-3941 Fax (317)744-3948, Email: frased@wesleyan.org

Gen. Publisher, Mr. Donald D. Cady, Tel. (317) 774-3853 Fax (317)774-3860, Email: cadyd@wesleyan.org

Gen. Director of Communications, Dr. Norman G. Wilson, Tel. (317)774-7907 Fax (317)774-7913, Email: wilsonn@wesleyan.org

Gen. Dir. of Spiritual Formation, Dr. James A. Dunn, Tel. (317)744-3888 Fax (317)774-3880, Email: dunnj@jwesleyan.org

Gen. Dir. of Evangelism & Church Growth, Rev. Philip T. Stevenson, Tel. (317)744-3900 Fax (317)774-3899, Email: stevensonp@wesleyan. org

Gen. Dir. of Education & the Ministry, Rev. Kerry D. Kind, Tel. (317)774-3911 Fax (317) 774-3915, Email: kindk@wesleyan.org

Gen. Dir. of World Missions, Dr. Donald L. Bray, Tel. (317)774-7950 Fax (317)774-7948, Email: brayd@wesleyan.org

Auxiliaries/Subsidiary Agencies

Estate & Gift Planning, Gen. Dir., Rev. Larry J. Moore, Tel. (317)774-7338 Fax (317)774-7341, Email: moorej@wesleyan.org

Wesleyan Investment Foundation, Gen. Dir., Dr. Craig A. Dunn, Tel. (317)774-7300 Fax (317)774-7321, Email: wif@wesleyan.org

Wesleyan Pension Fund, Gen. Dir., Dr. Craig A. Dunn, Tel. (317)774-7300 Fax (317)774-7321, Email: dunnc@wesleyan.org

Wesleyan Women, Mrs. Martha Blackburn, Tel. (317)774-7974 Fax (317)774-7975, Email: blackburnm@wesleyan.org

Wesleyan Kids for Mission, Mrs. Peggy Ann Camp, Tel. (704)892-3744 Fax (317)570-5254, Email: camppeg@aol.com

Wesleyan Men, Dr. James A. Dunn, Tel. (317) 774-3888 Fax (317)774-3880, Email: dunnj@wesleyan.org

Address Service, Tel. (317)744-7900

Archives & Historical Library, Tel. (317)774-7996

Computer Information Services, Tel. (317)774-7922

Wesleyan Publishing House, Tel. (317)774-3954

Periodicals

Wesleyan Life, *Wesleyan World*

175

Wesleyan Holiness Association of Churches

This body was founded Aug. 4, 1959 near Muncie, Indiana by a group of ministers and laymen who were drawn together for the purpose of spreading and conserving sweet, radical, scriptural holiness. These men came from various church bodies. This group is Wesleyan in doctrine and standards.

Headquarters

1141 North US Hwy 27, Fountain City, IN 47341-9757 Tel. (765)584-3199

Media Contact, Gen. Sec.-Treas., Rev. Robert W. Wilson, RR3 Box 218, Selinsgrove, PA 17870

Officers

Gen. Supt., Rev. John Brewer

Asst. Gen. Supt., Rev. Armen O. Rhoads, 7812 Portland Ave., Tacoma, WA 98404

Gen. Sec.-Treas., Rev. Robert W. Wilson, RR3 Box 218, Selinsgrove, PA 17870 Tel. (570)539-9821

Gen. Youth Pres., Rev. Nathan Shockley, 504 W. Tyrell St., St. Louis, MI 48880 Tel. (517)681-2591

Periodicals

Eleventh Hour Messenger

Wisconsin Evangelical Lutheran Synod

Organized in 1850 at Milwaukee, Wisconsin, by three pastors sent to America by a German mission society, the Wisconsin Evangelical Lutheran Synod still reflects its origins, although it now has congregations in 50 states and three Canadian provinces. It supports missions in 26 countries.

The Wisconsin Synod federated with the Michigan and Minnesota Synods in 1892 in order to more effectively carry on education and mission enterprises. A merger of these three Synods followed in 1917 to give the Wisconsin Evangelical Lutheran Synod its present form.

Although at its organization in 1850 WELS turned away from conservative Lutheran theology, today it is ranked as one of the most conservative Lutheran bodies in the United States. WELS confesses that the Bible is the verbally inspired, infallible Word of God and subscribes without reservation to the confessional writings of the Lutheran Church. Its interchurch relations are determined by a firm commitment to the principle that unity of doctrine and practice are the prerequisites of pulpit and altar fellowship and ecclesiastical cooperation. It is a founding member of the Confessional Evangelical Lutheran Conference, a federation of 21 like-minded bodies worldwide.

Headquarters

2929 N. Mayfair Rd., Milwaukee, WI 53222 Tel. (414)256-3888 Fax (414)256-3899

MCG Director, Rev. J.D. Liggett

Email: webbin@sab.wels.net

Website: www.wels.net

Officers

Pres., Rev. Karl R. Gurgel, 2929 N Mayfair Rd., Milwaukee, WI 53222,

1st Vice Pres., Rev. Wayne D. Mueller, 2929 N Mayfair Rd., Milwaukee, WI 53222 Tel. (414)256-3888 Fax. (414)256-3899

2nd Vice Pres., Rev. Thomas F. Zarling, 6 Wiltshire C T E, Sterling, VA 20165

Sec., Rev. Robert Pasbrig, 876 Fairview Dr., Hartford, WI 53027

OTHER ORGANIZATIONS

Bd. for Ministerial Education, Admn., Rev. Peter Kruschel

Bd. for Parish Services, Admn., Rev. Bruce Becker

Bd. for Home Missions, Admn., Rev. Harold J. Hagedorn

Bd. for World Missions, Admn., Rev. Daniel Koelpin

Periodicals

Forward in Christ, Wisconsin Lutheran Quarterly, The Lutheran Educator, Lutheran Leader, Mission Connection

Religious Bodies in the United States Arranged by Families

The following list of religious bodies appearing in the Directory Section of the *Yearbook* shows the "families," or related clusters into which American religious bodies can be grouped. For example, there are many communions that can be grouped under the heading "Baptist" for historical and theological reasons. It should not be assumed, however, that all denominations under one family heading are necessarily consistent in belief or practice. The family clusters tend to represent historical factors more often than theological or practical ones. These family categories provide one of the major pitfalls when compiling church statistics because there is often a tendency to combine the statistics by "families" for analytical and comparative purposes. Such combined totals are deeply flawed, even though they are often used as variables for sociological analysis. The arrangement by families offered here is intended only as a general guide for conceptual organization when viewing the broad sweep of American religious culture.

Religious bodies that cannot be categorized under family headings appear alphabetically and are not indented in the following list.

Adventist Bodies

Advent Christian Church
Church of God General Conference (Oregon, IL and Morrow, GA)
Primitive Advent Christian Church
Seventh-day Adventist Church

American Evangelical Christian Churches
American Rescue Workers

Anglican Bodies

Episcopal Church
The Episcopal Orthodox Church
Reformed Episcopal Church

Apostolic Christian Church (Nazarene)
Apostolic Christian Churches of America
Apostolic Episcopal Church

Baptist Bodies

The Alliance of Baptists
The American Baptist Association
American Baptist Churches in the U.S.A.
Baptist Bible Fellowship International
Baptist General Conference
Baptist Missionary Association of America
Conservative Baptist Association of America
General Association of General Baptists
General Association of Regular Baptist Churches
National Association of Free Will Baptists
National Baptist Convention of America, Inc.
National Baptist Convention, U.S.A., Inc.
National Missionary Baptist Convention of America
National Primitive Baptist Convention, Inc.
North American Baptist Conference
Primitive Baptists
Progressive National Baptist Convention, Inc.
Separate Baptists in Christ
Seventh Day Baptist General Conference, USA and Canada
Southern Baptist Convention
Sovereign Grace Believers

Berean Fellowship of Churches

Brethren (German Baptists)

Brethren Church (Ashland, Ohio)
Church of the Brethren
Fellowship of Grace Brethren Churches
Old German Baptist Brethren Church

Brethren, River

Brethren in Christ Church
United Zion Church

The Catholic Church
Christ Community Church (Evangelical-Protestant)
Christadelphians
Christian Brethren (also known as Plymouth Brethren)
The Christian Congregation, Inc.
The Christian and Missionary Alliance
Christian Union
The Church of Christ (Holiness) U.S.A.
Church of Christ, Scientist
Church Communities International
The Church of Illumination
Church of the Living God
Church of the Nazarene

Churches of Christ—Christian Churches

Christian Church (Disciples of Christ) in the United States and Canada
Christian Churches and Churches of Christ
Churches of Christ

Churches of Christ in Christian Union

Churches of God

Church of God (Anderson, Indiana)
The Church of God (Seventh Day), Denver,
Colorado
Churches of God, General Conference

Churches of the New Jerusalem

General Church of the New Jerusalem
The Swedenborgian Church

Conservative Congregational Christian
Conference

Eastern Orthodox Churches

Albanian Orthodox Diocese of America
The American Carpatho-Russian Orthodox
Greek Catholic Church
The Antiochian Orthodox Christian
Archdiocese of North America
Apostolic Catholic Assyrian Church of the
East, North American Dioceses
Apostolic Orthodox Catholic Church of North
America
Greek Orthodox Archdiocese of America
The Holy Eastern Orthodox Catholic and
Apostolic Church in North America, Inc.
Holy Ukrainian Autocephalic Orthodox
Church in Exile
The Orthodox Church in America
Patriarchal Parishes of the Russian Orthodox
Church in the U.S.A.
The Romanian Orthodox Church in America
The Romanian Orthodox Episcopate of
America
The Russian Orthodox Church Outside of
Russia
Serbian Orthodox Church in the U.S.A. and
Canada
The Syro-Russian Orthodox Catholic Church
True Orthodox Church of Greece (Synod of
Metropolitan Cyprian), American
Exarchate
Ukrainian Orthodox Church of the U.S.A.

The Evangelical Church
The Evangelical Church Alliance
The Evangelical Congregational Church
The Evangelical Covenant Church
The Evangelical Free Church of America
Fellowship of Fundamental Bible Churches
Free Christian Zion Church of Christ

Friends

Evangelical Friends International—North
American Region
Friends General Conference
Friends United Meeting
Philadelphia Yearly Meeting of the Religious
Society of Friends
Religious Society of Friends (Conservative)
Religious Society of Friends (Unaffiliated
Meetings)

Grace Gospel Fellowship
IFCA International, Inc.
International Council of Community
Churches
Jehovah's Witnesses

Latter Day Saints (Mormons)

Church of Christ
The Church of Jesus Christ (Bickertonites)
The Church of Jesus Christ of Latter-day
Saints
Community of Christ

The Liberal Catholic Church—Province of
the United States of America

Lutheran Bodies

The American Association of Lutheran
Churches
Apostolic Lutheran Church of America
The Association of Free Lutheran
Congregations
The Association of Independent Evangelical
Lutheran Churches
Church of the Lutheran Brethren of America
Church of the Lutheran Confession
Conservative Lutheran Association
The Estonian Evangelical Lutheran Church
Evangelical Lutheran Church in America
Evangelical Lutheran Synod
The Latvian Evangelical Lutheran Church in
America
The Lutheran Church—Missouri Synod
Wisconsin Evangelical Lutheran Synod

Mennonite Bodies

Beachy Amish Mennonite Churches
Bible Fellowship Church
Church of God in Christ, Mennonite
Fellowship of Evangelical Bible Churches
Fellowship of Evangelical Churches
General Conference of Mennonite Brethren
Churches
Hutterian Brethren
Mennonite Church, USA
Old Order Amish Church
Old Order (Wisler) Mennonite Church
Reformed Mennonite Church

Methodist Bodies

African Methodist Episcopal Church
The African Methodist Episcopal Zion
Church
Allegheny Wesleyan Methodist Connection
(Original Allegheny Conference)
Bible Holiness Church
Christian Methodist Episcopal Church
Evangelical Methodist Church
Free Methodist Church of North America
Fundamental Methodist Church, Inc.
Primitive Methodist Church in the U.S.A.

Reformed Methodist Union Episcopal Church
Reformed Zion Union Apostolic Church
Southern Methodist Church
The United Methodist Church
The Wesleyan Church

The Missionary Church

Moravian Bodies

Moravian Church in America (Unitas Fratrum)
Unity of the Brethren

National Association of Congregational Christian Churches
National Organization of the New Apostolic Church of North America
National Spiritualist Association of Churches
North American Old Roman Catholic Church (Archdiocese of New York)

Old Catholic Churches

Apostolic Catholic Orthodox Church
Christ Catholic Church
Liberal Catholic Church (International)
The Old Catholic Orthodox Church (formerly the Apostolic Orthodox Old Catholic Church)
The United Catholic Church, Inc.

Oriental Orthodox Churches

Armenian Apostolic Church of America
Armenian Apostolic Church, Diocese of America
Coptic Orthodox Church
Malankara Orthodox Syrian Church, Diocese of America
Syrian (Syriac) Orthodox Church of Antioch

Pentecostal Bodies

Apostolic Faith Mission Church of God
Apostolic Faith Mission of Portland, Oregon
Assemblies of God
Assemblies of God International Fellowship (Independent/Not affiliated)
Association of Vineyard Churches
The Bible Church of Christ, Inc.
Bible Way Church of Our Lord Jesus Christ World Wide, Inc.
Calvary Chapel
Christian Church of North America, General Council
The Church of God
The Church of God In Christ
Church of God in Christ, International
Church of God (Cleveland, Tennessee)
The Church of God of the Firstborn
Church of God by Faith, Inc.
Church of God, Mountain Assembly, Inc.
Church of God of Prophecy
Church of Our Lord Jesus Christ of the Apostolic Faith, Inc.
Congregational Holiness Church
Elim Fellowship
Full Gospel Assemblies International

Full Gospel Fellowship of Churches and Ministers International
House of God, Which is the Church of the Living God, the Pillar and Ground of the Truth
International Church of the Foursquare Gospel
The International Pentecostal Church of Christ
International Pentecostal Holiness Church
Open Bible Standard Churches
The (Original) Church of God, Inc.
Pentecostal Assemblies of the World, Inc.
Pentecostal Church of God
Pentecostal Fire-Baptized Holiness Church
The Pentecostal Free Will Baptist Church, Inc.
United Holy Church of America, Inc.
United House of Prayer
United Pentecostal Church International
The United Pentecostal Churches of Christ

Pillar of Fire
Polish National Catholic Church of America

Reformed Bodies

Associate Reformed Presbyterian Church (General Synod)
Christian Reformed Church in North America
Cumberland Presbyterian Church
Cumberland Presbyterian Church in America
Evangelical Presbyterian Church
Hungarian Reformed Church in America
Korean Presbyterian Church in America, General Assembly of the
Netherlands Reformed Congregations
The Orthodox Presbyterian Church
Presbyterian Church in America
Presbyterian Church (U.S.A.)
Protestant Reformed Churches in America
Reformed Church in America
Reformed Church in the United States
Reformed Presbyterian Church of North America
United Church of Christ

Reformed Catholic Church
The Salvation Army
The Schwenkfelder Church

Thomist Churches

Mar Thoma Syrian Church of India

Triumph the Church and Kingdom of God in Christ Inc. (International)
Unitarian Universalist Association of Congregations

United Brethren Bodies

Church of the United Brethren in Christ
United Christian Church

Universal Fellowship of Metropolitan Community Churches
Volunteers of America
Wesleyan Holiness Association of Churches

179

4. Religious Bodies in Canada

A large number of Canadian religious bodies were organized by immigrants from Europe and elsewhere, and a smaller number sprang up originally on Canadian soil. In the case of Canada, moreover, many denominations that transcend the U.S.-Canada border have headquarters in the United States.

A final section in this directory lists churches according to denominational families. This can be a helpful tool in finding a particular church if you don't know the official name. Complete statistics for Canadian churches are found in the statistical section in chapter III: table 1 contains membership figures, and table 4 contains giving figures. Addresses for periodicals are found in directory11, "Religious Periodicals in Canada."

The Anglican Church of Canada

Anglicanism came to Canada with the early explorers such as Martin Frobisher and Henry Hudson. Continuous services began in Newfound- land about 1700 and in Nova Scotia in 1710. The first Bishop, Charles Inglis, was appointed to Nova Scotia in 1787 The Anglican Church of Canada includes a large number of the original inhabitants of Canada (Indians, Inuit and Metis) and has been a strong advocate of their rights.

The Anglican Church of Canada has enjoyed self-government for over a century since 1893 and is an autonomous member of the worldwide Anglican Communion. The Church also has a strong international role in development and disaster relief through the Primate's World Relief and Development Fund (PWRDF). The General Synod, which normally meets triennially (next meeting 2010), consists of the Archbishops, Bishops and elected clerical and lay representatives of the 30 dioceses. Each of the Ecclesiastical Provinces—Canada, Ontario, Rupert's Land and British Columbia—is organized under a Metropolitan and has its own Provincial Synod and Executive Council. Each diocese has its own Diocesan Synod.

Headquarters

Church House, 80 Hayden St., Toronto, ON M4Y 3G2 Tel. (416)924-9192 (Switchboard) 416 924-9199 (Voice mail) Fax (416)968-7983, Email: info@national.anglican.ca Web: www.anglican.ca

Media Contact, Mr. Vianney (Sam) Carriere

GENERAL SYNOD OFFICERS

Primate of the Anglican Church of Canada, The Most Rev. Fred J. Hiltz
Prolocutor, The Rev. Dr. Stephen Andrews
Gen. Sec., The Ven. Michael F. Pollesel
Treas., Gen. Synod, Mr. Peter Blachford

DEPARTMENTS AND DIVISIONS

Faith, Worship & Ministry, Dir., Rev. Canon Alyson Barnett-Cowan
Financial Management and Dev., Dir., Mr. Peter Blachford
Inform. Resources Dir., Mr. Vianney (Sam) Carriere
Partnerships, Dir., Dr. Eleanor Johnson
Pensions, Dir., Ms. Judith Robinson
Primate's World Relief and Dev. Fund, Dir., Ms. Cheryl Curtis

METROPOLITANS (ARCHBISHOPS)

British Columbia, The Most Rev. Terrence O. Buckle, Metropolitan, Box 31136, Whitehorse YT Y1A 5P7 Tel. (867)667-7746 Fax (867) 667-6125, Email: synodoffice@klondiker com

Ecclesiastical Province of, Canada, The Most Rev. A. Bruce Staver, 31 rue des Jardins, Quebec, QC G1R 4L6 Tel. (418)692-3858 Fax (418)692-3876, Email: synodoffice@quebec. anglican.ca

Ontario, The Most Rev. Caleb J. Lawrence, Box 841, Schumacher, ON P0N 1G0 Tel. (705) 360-1129 Fax (705)360-1120, Email: dmoose @domaa.ca

Rupert's Land, The Most Rev. John R. Clarke, Box 6868, Peace River, AB T8S 1S6 Tel. (780)624-2767 Fax (780)624-2365, Email: bpath@telusplanet.net

DIOCESAN BISHOPS

Algoma, The Rt. Rev. Ronald Ferris, Box 1168, Sault Ste. Marie, ON P6A 5N7 Tel. (705)256-5061 Fax (705)946-1860, Email: dioceseof algoma@on.aibn.com

Arctic, The Rt. Rev. Andrew P. Atagotaalnuk, 4910 51st St., Box 190, Yellowknife, NT X1A 2N2 Tel. (867)873-5432 Fax (867)873-8478, Email: diocese@arcticnet.org

Athabasca, The Most Rev. John R. Clarke, Box 6868, Peace River, AB T8S 1S6 Tel. (780)624-2767 Fax (780)624-2365, Email: bpath@ telusplanet.net

Brandon, Rt. Rev. James D. Njegovan, Box 21009 WEPO, Brandon, MB R7B 3W8 Tel. (204)727-7550 Fax (204)727-4135, Email: bishopbdn@mts.net

British Columbia, The Rt. Rev. A.J. Cowan, 900 Vancouver St., Victoria, BC V8V 3V7 Tel. (250)386-7781 Fax (250)386-4013, Email: synod@bc.anglican.ca

Caledonia, The Rt. Rev. William J. Anderson,

Box 278, Prince Rupert, BC V8J 3P6 Tel. (250)624-6013 Fax (250)624-4299, Email: synodofc@citytel.net

Calgary, The Rt. Rev. Derek B.E. Hoskin , #560, 1207 11th Ave., SW, Salgary, AB T3C 0M5 Tel. (403)243-3673 Fax (403)243-2182, Email: synod@calgary.anglican.ca

Central Interior, Anglican Parishes (APCI) The Rt. Rev. Gordon Light, Box 1979, 100 Mile House, BC V0K 2E0 Tel. (250)395-1222 Fax (250)395-1252, Email: apci-office@telus.net

Central Newfoundland, The Rt. Rev. F. David Torraville, 34 Fraser Rd., Gander, NF A1V 2E8 Tel. 709-256-2372 Fax 709-256-2396, Email: bishopcentral@nfld.net

Eastern Newfoundland and Labrador, The Rt. Rev. Cyrus C.J. Pitman , 19 King's Bridge Rd., St. John's, NF A1C 3K4 Tel. (709)576-6697 Fax (709)576-7122, Email: cpitman@anglicanenl.nf.net

Edmonton, -vacant, 10035—103 St., Edmonton, AB T5J 0X5 Tel. (780)439-7344 Fax (780)439-6549, Email: churched@edmonton.anglican.ca

Fredericton, The Rt. Rev. Claude E.W. Miller, 115 Church St., Fredericton, NB E3B 4C8 Tel. (506)459-1801 Fax (506)459-8475, Email: bishfton@nbnet.nb.ca

Huron, The Rt. Rev. Bruce H. W. Howe, 190 Queens Ave., London, ON N6A 6H7 Tel. (519)434-6893 Fax (519)673-4151, Email: bishops@huron.anglican.ca

Keewatin, Rt. David N. Ashdown, 915 Ottawa St., Keewatin, ON P0X 1C0 Tel. (807)547-3353 Fax (807)547-3356, Email: dioceseof keewatin@gokenora.com

Kootenay, The Rt. Rev. John E. Privett, 1876 Richter St., Kelowna, BC V1Y 2M9 Tel. (250)762-3306 Fax (250)762-4150, Email: diocese_of_kootenay@telus.net

Montreal, The Rt. Rev. Barry B. Clarke, 1444 Union Ave., Montreal, QC H3A 2B8 Tel. (514)843-6577 Fax (514)843-3221, Email: bishops.office@montreal.anglican.ca

Moosonee, The Most Rev. Caleb J. Lawrence, Box 841, Schumacher, ON P0N 1G0 Tel. (705)360-1129 Fax (705)360-1120, Email: dmoose@domaa.ca

New Westminster, The Rt. Rev. Michael C. Ingham, 580-401 W. Georgia St., Vancouver, BC V6B 5A1 Tel. (604)684-6306 Fax (604) 684-7017, Email: bishop@vancouver.anglican. ca

Niagara, The Rt. Rev. Michael A. Bird, 252 James St. N., Hamilton, ON L8R 2L3 Tel. (905)527-1278 Fax (905)527-1281, Email: bishop@niagara.anglican.ca

Nova Scotia and Prince Edward Is., -vacant-, 5732 College St., Halifax, NS B3H 1X3 Tel. (902)420-0717 Fax (902)425-0717, Email: office@nspeidiocese.ca

Ontario, The Rt. Rev. George L. R. Bruce, 90 Johnson St., Kingston, ON K7L 1X7 Tel. (613)544-4774 Fax (613)547-3745, Email: synod@ontario.anglican.ca

Ottawa, The Rt. Rev. John H. Chapman, 71 Bronson Ave., Ottawa, ON K1R 6G6 Tel. (613)232-7124 Fax (613)232-7088, Email: dayadmin@ottawa.anglican.ca

Qu'Appelle, The Rt. Rev. Gregory K. Kerr-Wilson, 1501 College Ave., Regina, SK S4P 1B8 Tel. (306)522-1608 Fax (306)352-6808, Email: quappelle@ca sasktel.net

Quebec, The Most Rev. A. Bruce Stavert, 31 rue des Jardins, Quebec, QC G1R 4L6 Tel. (418)692-3858 Fax (418)692-3876, Email: synodoffice@quebec.anglican.ca

Rupert's Land, The Rt. Rev. Donald D. Phillips, 935 Nesbitt Bay, Winnipeg, MB R3T 1W6 Tel. (204)922-4200 Fax (204)922-4219, Email: general@rupertsland.ca

Saskatchewan, The Rt. Rev. Anthony Burton, 1308 5th Ave. East, Prince Albert, SK S6V 2H7 Tel. (306)763-2455 Fax (306)764-5172, Email: synod@sasktel.net

Saskatoon, The Rt. Rev. Rodney Andrews, Box 1965, Saskatoon, SK S7K 3S5 Tel. (306)244-5651 Fax (306)933-4606, Email: anglican bishop@sasktel.net

Toronto, The Rt. Rev. Colin R. Johnson, 135 Adelaide St. East, Toronto, ON M5C 1L8 Tel. (416)363-6021 Fax (416)363-3683, Email: cjohnson@toronto.anglican.ca

Western Newfoundland, The Rt. Rev. Percy D. Coffin, 25 Main St., Corner Brook, NF A2H 1C2 Tel. (709)639-8712 Fax (709)639-1636, Email: dsownc@nf.aibn.com

Yukon, The Most Rev. Terry Buckle, Box 4247, Whitehorse, YT Y1A 3T3 Tel. (867)667-7746 Fax (867)667-6125, Email: synodoffice@klondiker.com

Periodicals

Anglican Journal (National Newspaper), *Ministry Matters*

The Antiochian Orthodox Christian Archdiocese of North America

The approximately 100,000 members of the Antiochian Orthodox community in Canada are under the jurisdiction of the Antiochian Orthodox Christian Archdiocese of North America with headquarters in Englewood, N.J. There are churches in Edmonton, Winnipeg, Halifax, London, Ottawa, Toronto, Windsor, Montreal, Saskatoon, Hamilton, Vancouver, Charlottestown, PEI, Calgary, and Mississauga.

Headquarters

Metropolitan Philip Saliba, 358 Mountain Rd., Englewood, NJ 07631 Tel. (201)871-1355 Fax (201)871-7954

Media Contact, Rev. Fr. Thomas Zain, 355 State Street, Brooklyn, NY 11217 Tel. (718)855-6225 Fax (718)855-3608

Email: abouna@aol.com

Web: www.antiochian.org

Periodicals

The Word, Again, Handmaiden

181

Apostolic Christian Church (Nazarene)

This church was formed in Canada as a result of immigration from various European countries. The body began as a movement originated by the Rev. S. H. Froehlich, a Swiss pastor, whose followers are still found in Switzerland and Central Europe.

Headquarters

Apostolic Christian Church Foundation, 1135 Sholey Rd., Richmond, VA 23231 Tel. (804) 222-1943

Media Contact, James Hodges

Officers

Exec. Dir., James Hodges

The Apostolic Church in Canada

The Apostolic Church in Canada is affiliated with the worldwide organization of the Apostolic Church with headquarters in Great Britain (www.apostolicworld.net). A product of the Welsh Revival (1904 to 1908), its Canadian beginnings originated in Nova Scotia in 1927. Today its main centers are in Nova Scotia, Ontario and Quebec. This church is evangelical, fundamental and Pentecostal, with special emphasis on the ministry gifts listed in Ephesians 4:11-12.

Headquarters

27 Castlefield Ave., Toronto, ON M4R 1G3

Media Contact, Pres., Rev. D. Karl Thomas, 220 Adelaide St. London, ON N6B-3H4, Tel. (519) 438-7036 Fax (705)742-2948,

Email: nlcrevival@goldon.net

Web: www.apostolic.ca

Officers

Pres., Rev. D. Karl Thomas, 220 Adelaide St., London, ON N6B 344, Tel. (519)438-7036 Fax (519)438-5800, Email: nlcrevival@goldon. net Natl. Sec., Rev. James Hackner, R.R. #1 Uxbridge, ON L9P-1R1 Tel. (905)852-3563

Periodicals

Canadian News Up-Date, *The News Magazine of the Apostolic Church in Canada*

Apostolic Church of Pentecost of Canada Inc.

The Apostolic Church of Pentecost, Incorporated, was founded in 1921 at Winnipeg, Manitoba, by Pastor Frank Small and is a network of ministers and churches providing fellowship, encouragement and accountability in the proclamation of the Gospel of Jesus Christ by the power of the Holy Spirit.

Headquarters

#119-2340 Pegasus Way NE, Calgary, AB T2E 8M5, Email: acop@acop.ca, Web: www.acop.ca

Media Contact, Moderator, Rev. Wes Mills, Tel. (403)273-5777 Fax (403)273-8102

Officers

President., Rev. Wes Mills

Mission Director, Rev. Brian Cooper

Periodicals

Fellowship Focus, *Apostolic Women's Ministry (AWM) Newsletter*

Armenian Evangelical Church

Founded in 1960 by immigrant Armenian evangelical families from the Middle East, this body is conservative doctrinally, with an evangelical, biblical emphasis. The polity of churches within the group differ with congregationalism being dominant, but there are presbyterian Armenian Evangelical churches as well. Most of the local churches have joined main-line denominations. All of the remaining Armenian Evangelical (congregational or presbyterian) local churches in the United States and Canada have joined with the Armenian Evangelical Union of North America.

Headquarters

Armenian Evangelical Church of Toronto, 2851 John St., P.O. Box 42015, Markham, ON L3R 5R0 Tel. (905)305-8144

Media Contact, Chief Editor, Rev. Yessayi Sarmazian

A.E.U.N.A. OFFICERS

Min. to the Union, Rev. Karl Avakian, 1789 E. Frederick Ave., Fresno, CA 93720

Mod., Rev. Bernard Geulsgeugian

Officers

Min., Rev. Yessayi Sarmazian

Periodicals

Armenian Evangelical Church

Armenian Holy Apostolic Church—Canadian Diocese

The Canadian branch of the ancient Church of Armenia founded in A.D. 301 by St. Gregory the Illuminator was established in Canada at St. Catharines, Ontario, in 1930. The diocesan organization is under the jurisdiction of the Holy See of Etchmiadzin, Armenia. The Diocese has churches in St. Catharines, Hamilton, Toronto, Ottawa, Vancouver, Mississauga, Montreal, Laval, Windsor, Halifax, Winnipeg, Edmonton and Calgary.

Headquarters

Diocesan Offices, Primate, Canadian Diocese, Archbishop Hovnan Derderian, 615 Stuart Ave., Outremont, QC H2V 3H2 Tel. (514)276-9479 Fax (514)276-9960, Email: adiocese@ aol.com, Web: www.canarmdiocese.org

Media Contact, Exec. Dir. Deacon Hagop Arslanian; Silva Mangassarian, Secretary

Officers

Sec., Silva Mangassarian

Webmaster, Albert Yeglikian

Associated Gospel Churches

The Associated Gospel Churches (AGC) traces its historical roots to the 1890s. To counteract the growth of liberal theology evident in many established denominations at this time, individuals and whole congregations seeking to uphold the final authority of the Scriptures in all matters of faith and conduct withdrew from those denominations and established churches with an evangelical ministry. These churches defended the belief that "all Scripture is given by inspiration of God" and also declared that the Holy Spirit gave the identical word of sacred writings of holy men of old, chosen by Him to be the channel of His revelation to man.

At first this growing group of independent churches was known as the Christian Workers' Churches of Canada, and by 1922 there was desire for forming an association for fellowship, counsel and cooperation. Several churches in southern Ontario banded together under the leadership of Dr. P. W. Philpott of Hamilton and Rev. H. E. Irwin, K. C. of Toronto.

When a new Dominion Charter was obtained on March 18, 1925, the name was changed to Associated Gospel Churches. Since that time the AGC has steadily grown, spreading across Canada by invitation to other independent churches of like faith and by actively beginning new churches.

Headquarters

1500 Kerns Rd., Burlington, ON L7P 3A7 Tel. (905)634-8184 Fax (905)634-6283

Email: admin@agcofcanada.com, Web: www. agcofcanada.com

Administrative Assistant, Donna Leung, 1500 Kerns Rd., Burlington, ON L7P 3A7 Tel. (905)634-8184 Fax (905)634-6283 Email: donna@agcofcanada.com

Officers

Pres., Rev. A.F. (Bud) Penner, 1500 Kerns Rd., Burlington, ON L7P 3A7 Tel. (905)634-8184 Fax (905)634-6283

Mod., Rev. David Collins, 1500 Kerns Rd, Burlington, L7P3A7 Tel. (905)634-8184 Fax (905)634-6283

Sec.-Treas., Mr. Charles Lyle, 1245 Stephenson Dr., Burlington, ON L7S 2L9 Tel. (905)633-8960

Periodicals

Insidedge

Association of Regular Baptist Churches (Canada)

The Association of Regular Baptist Churches was organized in 1957 by a group of churches for the purpose of mutual cooperation in missionary activities. The Association believes the Bible to be God's word, stands for historic Baptist principles, and opposes modern ecumenism.

Headquarters

17 Laverock St., Tottenham, ON L0G 1W0, Tel. 905-936-3786

Officers

Chmn., Rev. S. Kring, 67 Sovereen St., Delhi, ON N4B 1L7

Baptist Convention of Ontario and Quebec

The Baptist Convention of Ontario and Quebec is a family of 365 churches in Ontario and Quebec, united for mutual support and encouragement and united in missions in Canada and the world.

The Convention was formally organized in 1888. Its one educational institution—McMaster Divinity College was founded in 1887. The Convention works through the all-Canada missionary agency, Canadian Baptist Ministries. The churches also support the Sharing Way, the relief and development arm of Canadian Baptist Ministries.

Headquarters

195 The West Mall, Ste. 414, Etobicoke, ON M9C 5K1 Tel. (416)622-8600 Fax (416)622-2308, Web: www.Baptist.ca

Media Contact, Exec. Min., Dr. Ken Bellous.

Officers

Past Pres., Rev. John Torrance

President, Mr. Evan Whitehead

1st Vice Pres., Mrs. Marie Toompuu

2nd Vice Pres., Mr. Don Hallman

Treas.-Bus. Admn., Nancy Bell

Exec. Min., Dr. Ken Bellous

Periodicals

The Canadian Baptist

Baptist General Conference of Canada

The Baptist General Conference was founded in Canada by missionaries from the United States. Originally a Swedish body, BGC Canada now includes people of many nationalities and is conservative and evangelical in doctrine and practice.

Headquarters

#205 15824 131 Avenue Edmonton, AB T5V 1J4 Tel. (780)438-9127 Fax (780)435-2478

Media Contact, Exec. Dir., Jamey S. McDonald

Officers

Exec. Dir., Jamey S. McDonald , #205 15824 131 Avenue Edmonton, AB T5V 1J4 Tel. (780) 438-9127 Fax (780)435-2478

Exec. Dir., Gordon H. Sorensen, BGC Stewardship Foundation, #205 15824 131 Avenue Edmonton, AB T5V 1J4 Tel. (780) 438-9127 Fax (780)435-2478

DISTRICTS

Baptist Gen. Conf.- Central Canada, Exec. Min.,

Lorne Meisner, 877 Wilkes Avenue, Winnipeg, MB R3P 1B8 Tel. (204) 772-6742 Fax (204) 269-5505

Baptist General Conference in Alberta, Exec. Min., Cal Netterfield, 11525 23 Ave., Edmonton, AB T6J 4T3 Tel. (780) 438-9126 Fax (780) 438-5258

British Columbia Baptist Conference, Exec. Min., Walter W. Wieser, 7600 Glover Rd., Langley, BC V2Y 1Y1 Tel. (604) 888-2246 Fax (604) 888-0046

Baptist General Conf. in Saskatchewan, Exec. Min., Abe Funk

Baptist Union of Western Canada

Headquarters
302,902-11 Ave., SW, Calgary, AB T2R 0E7
Media Contact, Exec. Min., Dr. Gerald Fisher

Officers
Pres., Mr. Bill Mains, 4576 Rainer Crescent, Prince George, BC V2K 1X4

Exec. Minister, Dr. Gerald Fisher, 302, 902-11 Ave SW, Calgary, AB T2R 0E7

Alberta Area Minister, Rev. Ed Dyck, 302, 902-11 Ave SW, Calgary, AB T2R 0E7

BC Area Minister, Dr. Paul Pearce, 201, 20349-88th Ave., Langely, BC V1M 2K5

SK-MB Area Minister, Dr. Robert Krahn, 414 Cowley Place, Saskatoon, SK S7N 3X2

Carey Theological College, Principal, Dr. Brian Stelck, 5920 Iona Dr., Vancouver, BC V6T 1J6

Baptist Resources Centre, 302, 902-11 Ave SW, Calgary, AB T2R 0E7

The Bible Holiness Movement

The Bible Holiness Movement, organized in 1949 as an outgrowth of the city mission work of the late Pastor William James Elijah Wakefield, an early-day Salvation Army officer, has been headed since its inception by his son, Evangelist Wesley H. Wakefield, its Bishop-General.

It derives its emphasis on the original Methodist faith of salvation and scriptural holiness from the late Bishop R. C. Horner. It adheres to the common evangelical faith in the Bible, the Deity and the atonement of Christ. It stresses a personal experience of salvation for the repentant sinner, of being wholly sanctified for the believer and of the fullness of the Holy Spirit for effective witness.

Membership involves a life of Christian love and evangelistic and social activism. Members are required to totally abstain from liquor and tobacco. They may not attend popular amusements or join secret societies. Divorce and remarriage are forbidden. Similar to Wesley's Methodism, members are, under some circumstances, allowed to retain membership in other evangelical church fellowships. Interchurch affiliations are maintained with a number of Wesleyan-Arminian Holiness denominations.

Year-round evangelistic outreach is maintained through open-air meetings, visitation, literature and other media. Noninstitutional welfare work, including addiction counseling, is conducted among minorities. There is direct overseas famine relief, civil rights action, environment protection and antinuclearism. The movement sponsors a permanent committee on religious freedom and an active promotion of Christian racial equality.

The movement has a world outreach with branches in the United States, India, Nigeria, Philippines, Ghana, Liberia, Cameroon, Kenya, Zambia, South Korea, Mulawi, and Tanzania. It also ministers to 89 countries in 42 languages through literature, radio and audiocassettes.

Headquarters
Box 223, Postal Stn. A, Vancouver, BC V6C 2M3 Tel. (250) 492-3376

Media Contact, Bishop-General, Evangelist Wesley H. Wakefield, P.O. Box 223, Postal Station A, Vancouver, BC V6C 2M3 Tel. (250) 492-3376

Website: www.bible-holiness-movement.com

DIRECTORS
Bishop-General, Evangelist Wesley H. Wakefield, (Intl. Leader)

Evangelist M. J. Wakefield, Penticton, BC

Pastor Vincente & Mirasal Hernando, Phillipines

Pastor & Mrs. Daniel Stinnett, 1425 Mountain View W., Phoenix, AZ 85021 Pastor Monday S. Attai, Abak, Akwalbom, Nigeria, West Africa

Pastor Choe Chong Dee, Iksun City, S. Korea

Pastor T. Chandra, Sekhor Rao, India

Pastor and Mrs. Daniel Vandee, Ghana, W. Africa Pastor L.W. Hutchings, Protem, Vancouver, B.C., Canada

Pastor Victor Freeman Holmquist, Vancouver, B.C., Canada

Bro. Aaron Louis Birch, Vancouver, B.C., Evangelist, Mrs. Stephen Richards, Uyo, Akwa Ibom State, Nigeria, West Africa

Periodicals
Hallelujah!

Brethren in Christ Church, Canadian Conference

The Brethren in Christ, formerly known as Tunkers in Canada, arose out of a religious awakening in Lancaster County, Pennsylvania late in the 18th century. Representatives of the new denomination reached Ontario in 1788 and established the church in the southern part of the present province. Presently the conference has congregations in Ontario, Alberta, Quebec and Saskatchewan. In theology they have accents of the Pietist, Anabaptist, Wesleyan and Evangelical movements.

Headquarters
Brethren in Christ Church, Gen. Ofc., P.O. Box A, Grantham, PA 17027-0901 Tel. (717)697-2634 Fax (717)697-7714

184

Canadian Headquarters, Bishop's Ofc., 416 North Service Rd. E., Suite 1, Oakville, ON L6H 5R2 Tel. (905)339-2335
Media Contact, Mod., Dr. Warren L. Hoffman, Brethren in Christ Church Gen. Ofc.

Officers

Mod., Bishop Brian Bell, 416 North Service Road, Suite 1, Oakville, ON L6H 5R2 Tel. (905)339-2335 Fax (905)337-2120
Sec., Betty Albrecht, RR 2, Petersburg, ON N0B 2H0
Sec., Carole Phillips, 416 North Service Rd. E., Suite 1, Oakville, ON L6H 5R2

Periodicals

Evangelical Visitor, "Yes," *Shalom*

British Methodist Episcopal Church of Canada

The British Methodist Episcopal Church was organized in 1856 in Chatham, Ontario and incorporated in 1913. It has congregations across the Province of Ontario.

Headquarters

430 Grey Street, London, ON N6B 1H3
Media Contact, Gen. Sec., Rev. Jacqueline Collins, 47 Connolly St., Toronto, ON M6N 4Y5 Tel. (416)653-6339

Officers

Gen. Supt., Rt. Rev. Dr. Douglas Birse, R.R. #5, Thamesville, ON N0P 2K0 Tel. (519)692-3628
Asst. Gen. Supt., Maurice M. Hicks, 3 Boxdene Ave., Scarborough, ON M1V 3C9 Tel. (416) 298-5715
Gen. Sec., Rev. Jacqueline Collins, 47 Connolly St., Toronto, ON M6N 4Y5 Tel. (416)653-6339
Gen. Treas., Ms. Hazel Small, 7 Wood Fernway, North York, ON M2J 4P6 Tel. (416)491-0313

Periodicals

B.M.E. Church Newsletter

Canadian and American Reformed Churches

The Canadian and American Reformed Churches accept the Bible as the infallible Word of God, as summarized in The Belgic Confession of Faith (1561), The Heidelberg Cathechism (1563) and The Canons of Dort (1618-1619). The federation was founded in Canada in 1950 and in the United States in 1955.

Headquarters

Synod, 607 Dynes Rd., Burlington, ON L7N 2V4
Canadian Reformed Churches, Ebenezer Canadian Reformed Church, 607 Dynes Rd., Burlington, ON L7N 2V4
Theological College, Dr. N. H. Gootjes, 110 W. 27th St., Hamilton, ON L9C 5A1 Tel. (905)575-3688 Fax (905)575-0799
Media Contact, Rev. Dr. G. Nederveen, 3089 Woodward Ave., Burlington, ON L7N 2M3 Tel. (905)681-7055 Fax (905)681-7055

Periodicals

Reformed Perspective, A Magazine for the Christian Family; Evangel, The Good News of Jesus Christ, Clarion, The Canadian Reformed Magazine; Diakonia—A Magazine of Office-Bearers; Book of Praise; Koinonia, A periodical of the Ministers of the CanRC; Horizon (a quarterly magazine published by the League of CanRC Women Societies); *A Gift from Heaven, A Reformed Bible course.*

Canadian Baptist Ministries

The Canadian Baptist Ministries has four federated member bodies, (1) Baptist Convention of Ontario and Quebec, (2) Baptist Union of Western Canada, (3) the United Baptist Convention of the Atlantic Provinces, (4) Union d'Églises Baptistes Françaises au Canada (French Baptist Union). Its main purpose is to act as a coordinating agency for the four groups for mission in all five continents.

Headquarters

7185 Millcreek Dr., Mississauga, ON L5N 5R4 Tel. (905)821-3533 Fax (905)826-3441
Email: daver@cbmin.org, Web: www.cbmin.org
Media Contact, Communications, David Rogelstad

Officers

Pres., Doug Coomas
Gen. Sec., Rev. Gart Nelson, Email: NelsonG@cbmin.org

Canadian Conference of Mennonite Brethren Churches

The conference was incorporated November 22, 1945.

Headquarters

1310 Taylor Ave., Winnipeg, MB R3M 3Z6 Tel. (204)669-6575 Fax (204)654-1865 Toll Free: 888-669-6575, Web: www.mbconf.ca
Media Contact, Exec. Dir., Dave Wiebe

Periodicals

Mennonite Brethren Herald, Mennonitische Rundschau, IdeaBank, Le Lien, Expression, Chinese Herald, Mennonite Historian

Canadian Convention of Southern Baptists

The Canadian Convention of Southern Baptists was formed at the Annual Meeting, May 7-9, 1985, in Kelowna, British Columbia. It was formerly known as the Canadian Baptist Conference, founded in Kamloops, British Columbia, in 1959 by pastors of existing churches.

Headquarters

100 Convention Way, Cochrane, AB T4C 2G2, Tel. (403)932-5688 Fax (403)932-4937, Email: office@ccsb.ca
Media Contact, Exec. Dir.-Treas., Rev.Gerald Taillon

185

Officers

Exec. Dir.-Treas., Gerald Taillon, 17 Riverview Close, Cochrane, AB T4C 1K7

Pres., Robert Blackaby, 9920 Fairmount Drive SE, Calgary, AB T2J 0S4

Periodicals

The Baptist Horizon

Canadian District of the Moravian Church in America, Northern Province

The work in Canada is under the general oversight and rules of the Moravian Church, Northern Province, general offices for which are located in Bethlehem, Pennsylvania. For complete information, see directory 3, "Religious Bodies in the United States," in this *Yearbook.*

Headquarters

1021 Center St., P.O. Box 1245, Bethlehem, PA 18016-1245

Media Contact, Ms. Deanna Hollenbach

Officers

Pres.,Rev. Stephen Gohdes, 600 Acadia Dr. SE Calgary, AB T2J OB8, Email: sgohdes@shaw. ca

Periodicals

The Moravian

Canadian Evangelical Christian Churches

The Canadian Evangelical Christian Church is an international, full-gospel new apostolic denomination, emphasizing the New Testament apostolic paradigm pattern which recognizes the ministry gifts beyond the apostle, prophet, evangelist, pastor and teacher to spread the Gospel, according to Ephesians 4:11,12. The congregations are associated through full-gospel doctrine that is in combination with Calvinistic and Arminian beliefs. Each and every congregation is connected with CECC as congregational and ordination is supervised by National Office.

Headquarters

General Superintendent, Rev. David P. Lavigne, 410-125 Lincoln Rd., Waterloo, ON N2J 2N9 Tel. (519)880-9110 Toll free (888)981-8881, Email: cecc@rogers.com, Web: www.ceccon line.com

Officers

Gen. Supt., Rev. David P. Lavigne, 410-125 Lincoln Rd., Waterloo, ON N2J 2N9 Tel. (519) 725-5578, Toll free (888)981-8881, Email: cecc@rogers.com

Gen. Sec., Rev. Bill St. Pierre, Box 7, Oro, ON N3P 1B9 Tel. (888)297-5551

Canadian Yearly Meeting of the Religious Society of Friends

Canadian Yearly Meeting of the Religious Society of Friends was founded in Canada as an offshoot of the Quaker movement in Great Britain and colonial America. Genesee Yearly Meeting, founded 1834, Canada Yearly Meeting (Orthodox), founded in 1867, and Canada Yearly Meeting, founded in 1881, united in 1955 to form the Canadian Yearly Meeting. Canadian Yearly Meeting is affiliated with Friends United Meeting and Friends General Conference. It is also a member of Friends World Committee for Consultation.

Headquarters

91A Fourth Ave., Ottawa, ON K1S 2L1 Tel. (613) 235-8553 or Tel. (888)296-3222 Fax (613)235-1753, Email: cym-office@quaker.ca

Media Contact, Gen. Sec.-Treas.,

Officers

Clerk, Dale Dewar

Archivist, Jane Zavitz Bond

Archives, Arthur G. Dorland, Pickering College, 389 Bayview St., Newmarket, ON L3Y 4X2 Tel. (416)895-1700

Periodicals

The Canadian Friend, Quaker Concern

Christ Catholic Church International

Christ Catholic Church International now has churches and-or missions in 14 countries spread over four continents. They are located in the United States, Canada, Poland, Bahamas, Ukraine, Trinidad-Tobago, Colombia, Australia, Slovakia, Belarus, Kenya and the Phillipines. Some countries have active churches and missions; some just missions and-or prayer groups.

CCCI is an Orthodox-Catholic Communion tracing Apostolic Succession through the Old Catholic and Orthodox Catholic Churches.

The church ministers to a growing number of people seeking an experiential relationship with their Lord and Savior Jesus Christ in a Sacramental and Scripture based church.

Headquarters

4695 St. Lawrence Ave., Niagara Falls, ON L2G 1Y4, Email: dioceseofniagara@cogeco.net, Web: www3.sympatico.ca/dwmullan

Media Contact, The Rt. Rev. John W. Brown, 1504-75 Queen St., Hamilton, ON L8R 3J3 Tel. (905)527-9089 Fax (905)522-6240, Email: bishopjohn@primus.ca

PRESIDING ARCHBISHOP

The Most Rev. Donald Wm. Mullan, 6190 Barker St., Niagara Falls, ON L2G 1Y4 Tel. (905)354-2329 Fax (905)357-9934, Email: dmullan1@cogeco.net

ARCHBISHOPS

The Most Rev. Jose Ruben Garcia Matiz, Calle 52 Sur #24A-35-Bq. #1, Ap. 301, Santa Fe de Bogota, D.C., Colombia, South America, Tel. 57-71447 87, Email: jorugama@col1.telecom. com.co

The Rt. Rev. John Wm. Brown, 1504-75 Queen St., N. Hamilton, ON L8R 3J3 Tel. (905)522-6240, Email: bishopjohn@primus.ca

The Rt. Rev. Luis Fernando Hoyos Maldonado, A. A. 24378 Santa Fe de Bogota, D.C., Colombia, South America, Tel. 57-276-68-16, Email: jourgama@col1.telecom.com.co

The Rt. Rev. Jose Moises Moncada Quevedo, A.A. 24378 Santa Fe de Bogota, D.C., Colombia, South America, Tel. 57-276-68-16, Email: jourgama@col1.telecom.com.co

The Rt. Rev. Jerome Robben, Vicar General, P.O. Box 566, Chesterfield, MO 63006-0566 Tel. (314)205-8422, Email: abbajn17@aol.com

The Rt. Rev. Andrzej J. Sarwa, ul. Krucza 16 27-600 Sandomierz, Poland Tel. & Fax 084-(0-15) 833-21-41, Email: andrzej-san@poczta.wp.pl

The Rt. Rev. Robert Smith, 824 Royal Oak Dr., Orlando, FL 32809 Tel. (407)240-7833, Email: yshwa@webtv.net

The Rt. Rev. Ted Lorah Jr., 430 Wawassan Drive, P.O. Box 208, Honey Brook, PA 19344 Tel. (610)273-7209, Email: tlorah@temple.edu

The Rt. Rev. John Gilbert-Cougar, Box 7305, D. L. Atkinson Station, Pasadena, TX 77508-7305

Periodicals

St. Luke Magazine

Christian Brethren (also known as Plymouth Brethren)

The Christian Brethren are a loose grouping of autonomous local churches, often called "assemblies." They are firmly committed to the inerrancy of Scripture and to the evangelical doctrine of salvation by faith alone apart from works or sacrament. Characteristics are a weekly Breaking of Bread and freedom of ministry without a requirement of ordination. For their history, see directry 3, "Religious Bodies in the United States" in this *Yearbook.*

CORRESPONDENT

James A. Stahr, 327 W. Prairie Ave., Wheaton, IL 60187 Tel. (630)665-3757

RELATED ORGANIZATIONS

Christian Brethren Churches in Quebec, P.O. Box 1054, Sherbrooke, QC J1H 5L3 Tel. (819)820-1693 Fax (819)821-9287

Kawartha Lakes Bible College, Box 1101, Peterborough, ON K9J 7H4 Tel. (705)742-2437

Mount Carmel Bible School, 4725 106th Ave., Edmonton, AB T6A 1E7 Tel. (780)465-3015

MSC Canada, 509-3950 14th Ave., Markham, ON L3R 0A9 Tel. (905)947-0468 Fax (905)947-0352

Vision Ministries Canada, 145 Lincoln Road, Waterloo, ON N2J 2N8 Tel. (519)725-1212 Fax (519)725-9421

Periodicals

News of Quebec (819) 820-1693

Christian Church (Disciples of Christ) in Canada

Disciples have been in Canada since 1810, and were organized nationally in 1922. This church served the Canadian context as a region of the whole Christian Church (Disciples of Christ) in the United States and Canada.

Headquarters

Christian Church in Canada, P.O. Box 23030, 417 Wellington St., St. Thomas, ON N5R 6A3 Tel. (519)633-9083 Fax (519)637-6407, Email: ccic@netrover.com

Media Contact, Reg. Min., F. Thomas Rutherford

Officers

Mod., Peter Fountain, P.O. Box 344, Milton, NS B0T 1P0 Tel. (902)354-5988, Email: pj fountain@auracom.com

Reg. Min., F. Thomas Rutherford, P.O. Box 23030, 417 Wellington St., St. Thomas, ON N5R 6A3 Tel. (519)633-9083 Fax (519)637-6407, Email: ccic@netrover.com

Christian Churches / Churches of Christ

First congregation organized: Cross Roads Christian Church, Cross Roads, Prince Edward Island, Canada, 1810, by "Scotch Baptists" influenced by James and Robert Haldane of Edinburgh. Since the 1820s when the writings of Thomas and Alexander Campbell were widely circulated and reprinted in periodicals, these congregations have identified with the 19th-c. "Restoration Movement" (also known as, "Stone-Campbell Movement") which came to be known as "Disciples of Christ." In late 19th-c. Ontario, some congregations separated over the use of musical instruments into a group known as the a capella Churches of Christ. From the 1880s to the 1930s, Disciples of Christ migrating from Ontario and emigrating from the United States organized congregations in Manitoba, Saskatchewan, Alberta, and British Columbia. From about 1948, when the Disciples of Christ in Canada first moved toward and, then, declared a formal denominational structure in 1968, 65-70 congregations across Canada did not identify with this structure preferring to remain free, congregationally governed fellowships. While especially in western Canada these congregations cooperate and fellowship with congregations identified with the Disciples of Christ in Canada, a capella Churches of Christ, and people and congregations of several other traditions, they generally tend to identify with the interpretation of the Restoration or Stone-Campbell Movement as exemplified by U.S. Christian Churches and Churches of Christ in affinity with the North American Christian

Convention, an annual, non-delegated, preaching and teaching convention. (See *The Movement in Canada, Encyclopedia of the Stone-Campbell Movement*. Grand Rapids, Mich.: Eerdmans, 2004, pp. 151-163).

Headquarters

Media Contact: Russell E. Kuykendall, 25 Grenville Street, 1507, Toronto, ON M4Y 2X5 Tel. (416)895-1098, Email: kuykendall@canada.com

Other Institutions

All of the following are free-standing, para-church institutions. Mortgage financing for congregations and para-church institutions: Church of Christ Development Company, Edmonton, Alberta. Church-planting associations: Partners in Atlantic Canada Evangelism, Impact Ontario, and Alberta Church Planting Association. Degree-granting colleges: Maritime Christian College, Charlottetown, PEI, and Alberta Bible College, Calgary, AB. Cross-cultural missions: Church of Christ Mission Jamaica; Church of Christ Mission India; Global Missionary Ministries (Central Europe); Frontier Labourers for Christ Canada (Thailand, Laos, and Myanmar); Graceland Ministries (Poland); Terri Scruggs, Partners with Nationals; Wycliffe Bible Translators; Benevolent Social Services of India; and others. Christian camps: Canoe Cove (PEI), Ontario Christian Assembly, Camp Christian (Pine Lake, AB), Pine Ridge Christian (Grande Prairie, AB), and Double VM (Lumby, BC). Annual fellowship meetings: Maritime Christian Fellowship, Ontario Christian Missionary Conference, Western Canada Christian Convention (with Disciples of Christ and a capella Churches of Christ), and the North American Christian Convention.

Christian and Missionary Alliance in Canada

A Canadian movement, dedicated to the teaching of Jesus Christ the Saviour, Sanctifier, Healer and Coming King, commenced in Toronto in 1887 under the leadership of the Rev. John Salmon. Two years later, the movement united with The Christian Alliance of New York, founded by Rev. A. B. Simpson, becoming the Dominion Auxiliary of the Christian Alliance, Toronto, under the presidency of the Hon. William H. Howland. Its four founding branches were Toronto, Hamilton, Montreal, and Quebec. The movement focused on the deeper life and missions. In 1980, the Christian and Missionary Alliance in Canada became autonomous. Its General Assembly is held every two years.

NATIONAL OFFICE

30 Carrier Dr, Suite 100, Toronto, ON M9W 5T7 Tel. (416)674-7878 Fax (416)674-0808 Email: info@cmacan.org

Media Contact, Director of Communications, Barrie Doyle

Officers

Pres., Dr. Franklin Pyles, Email: pylesf@cmacan.org
Vice Pres.-Global Ministries, Dr. Ray Downey, Email: downeyr@cmacan.org
Vice Pres.-Fin., Paul D. Lorimer, Email: lorimerp@cmacan.org
Vice Pres.-Canadian Ministries, Rev. C. Stuart Lightbody, Email: lightbodys@cmacan.org
Vice Pres.-Advancement, Rev. David Freeman, Email: freemand@cmacan.org
Chairman of the Board, Dr. T. V. Thomas
Secretary of the Board, Connie Driedger

Periodicals

Alliance Life

Christian Reformed Church in North America

Canadian congregations of the Christian Reformed Church in North America have been formed since 1905. For detailed information about this denomination, please refer to the listing for the Christian Reformed Church in North America in directory 3, "Religious Bodies in the United States."

Headquarters

United States Office, 2850 Kalamazoo Ave., S.E., Grand Rapids, MI 49560 Tel. (616)224-0832 Fax (616) 224-5895
Canadian Office, 3475 Mainway, P.O. Box 5070 STN LCR 1, Burlington, ON L7R 3Y8 Tel. (905)336-2920 Fax (905)336-8344, Web: www.crcna.org
Media Contact, Exec. Dir., Dr. Peter Borgdorff, U.S. Office; Director of Communication, Mr. Henry Hess, Canadian Office

Officers

Executive Director: Rev. Gerard Dykstra
Director of Finance & Administration: Mr. John Bolt, U.S. Office
Director of Denominational Ministries: Rev. Gerard L. Dykstra

Periodicals

The Banner

Church of God (Anderson, Ind.)

This body is one of the largest of the groups which have taken the name "Church of God." Its headquarters are at Anderson, Indiana. It originated about 1880 and emphasizes Christian unity.

Headquarters

Western Canada Assembly, Chpsn., Hilda Nauenburg, 4717- 56th St., Camrose, AB T4V 2C4 Tel. (780)672-0772 Fax (780)672-6888
Eastern Canada Assembly, Chpsn., Jim Wiebe, 38 James St., Dundas, ON L9H 2J6

Email: admincoo@cable-lynx.net; baughman@ cable-lynx.net, Web: www.chog.ca

Media Contact for Western Canada, Executive Dir. Of Ministry Services, John D. Campbell, 4717 56th St., Camrose, AB T4V 2C4 Tel. (780)672-0772 Fax (780)672-6888

Periodicals
The Gospel Contact, The Messenger

Church of God in Christ (Mennonite)

The Church of God in Christ, Mennonite was organized by the evangelist-reformer John Holdeman in Ohio. The church unites with the faith of the Waldenses, Anabaptists and other such groups throughout history. Emphasis is placed on obedience to the teachings of the Bible, including the doctrine of the new birth and spiritual life, noninvolvement in government or the military, a head-covering for women, beards for men and separation from the world shown by simplicity in clothing, homes, possessions and lifestyle. The church has a worldwide membership of about 20,150, largely concentrated in the United States and Canada.

Headquarters
P.O. Box 313, 420 N. Wedel Ave., Moundridge, KS 67107 Tel. (620)345-2532 Fax (620)345-2582

Media Contact, Dale Koehn, P.O.Box 230, Moundridge, KS 67107 Tel. (620)345-2532 Fax (620)345-2582

Periodicals
Messenger of Truth

Church of God (Cleveland, Tenn.)

It is one of America's oldest Pentecostal churches founded in 1886 as an outgrowth of the holiness revival under the name Christian Union. In 1907 the church adopted the organizational name Church of God. It has its foundation upon the principles of Christ as revealed in the Bible. The Church of God is Christian, Protestant, foundational in its doctrine, evangelical in practice and distinctively Pentecostal. It maintains a centralized form of government and a commitment to world evangelization.

The first church in Canada was extablished in 1919 in Scotland Farm, Manitoba. Paul H. Walker became the first overseer of Canada in 1931.

Headquarters
Intl. Offices, 2490 Keith St., NW, Cleveland, TN 37320 Tel. (423)472-3361 Fax (423)478-7066

Media Contact, Dir. of Communications, Michael L. Baker, P.O. Box 2430, Cleveland, TN 37320-2430 Tel. (423)478-7112 Fax (423) 478-7066

EXECUTIVES
Gen. Overseer, G. Dennis McGuire

Asst. Gen. Overseers, Raymond F. Culpepper; Orville Hagan; and Paul L. Walker

Sec.-Gen., Timothy M. Hill

Canada-Eastern, Rev. Andrew Binda, P.O.Box 2036, Brampton, ON L6T 3TO, Tel. (905) 793-2213 Fax (905)793-9173

Canada-Western, Rev. Stephen P. Darnell, Box 54055, 2640 52 St. NE, Calgary, AB T1Y 6S6 Tel. (403)293-8817 Fax (403)293-3466

Canada-Quebec-Maritimes, Rev. Jaques Houle, 19 Orly, Granby, QC J2H 1Y4 Tel. (450)378-4442 Fax (450)378-8646

Canada-National, Rev. Ralph R. Glagau, P.O.Box 333, Stn B, Etobicoke, ON M9W 5L3 Tel. (416)741-9222 Fax (416)741-3717

DEPARTMENTS
Benefits Board—CEO, Arthur D. Rhodes

Business & Records—Exec. Dir., Julian B. Robinson

Care Ministries—Dir., John D. Nichols

Chaplains Commission—Dir., Robert D. Crick

Communications, Media Ministries—Dir., T. Scot Carter

Division of Education—Chancellor, R. Lamar Vest

Education—European Bible Seminary, Dir., Paul Schmidgall

Education—Hispanic Institute of Ministry, Dir., Jose D. Montanez

Education—International Bible College, Pres., Cheryl Busse

Education—Lee University, Pres., Charles Paul Conn

Education—Patten University, Pres., Gary Moncher

Education—Puerto Rico Bible School, Pres., Ildefonso Caraballo

Education—School of Ministry, Dir., Donald S. Aultman

Education—Theological Seminary, President, Steven J. Land

Evangelism & Home Missions—Dir., Larry J. Timmerman

Evangelism—Black Ministries, Dir., Asbury R. Sellers

Evangelism—Multi-Cultural Min., Dir., Wallace J. Sibley

Evangelism—Hispanic Ministries, Dir., Esdras Betancourt

Evangelism—Native American Ministries, Dir., Douglas M. Cline

Family Ministries—Coordinator, John K. Vining

Lay Ministries—Dir., Leonard Albert

Legal Services—Dir., Dennis W. Watkins

Men/Women of Action—Dir., L. Hugh Carver

Ministerial Care—Dir., Bill Leonard

Ministerial Development—Dir., Larry G. Hess

Ministry to Israel—Dir., J. Michael Utterback

Ministry to the Military—Dir., Robert A. Moore

Music Ministries—Dir., Delton L. Alford

Pentecostal Resource Center—Director, Donald D. Smeeton

Pentecostal Research Center—Dir., David G. Roebuck

Publications—Dir., M. Thomas Propes

SpiritCare—Dir., Gene D. Rice

Stewardship—Dir., Kenneth R. Davis

Women's Ministries—Coordinator, Mary Ruth Stone

World Missions—Dir., Roland E. Vaughan

Youth & Christian Education—Dir., Mark S. Abbott

Romanian Ministries—Dir., Thomas A. George

Periodicals

Church of God Evangel, *Editorial Evangelica*, *Save Our World*, *Ministry Now Profiles*, *Ministries Now Profiles*

The Church of God of Prophecy Canada East

The Church of God of Prophecy is one of the churches that grew out of the work of A. J. Tomlinson in the first half of the twentieth century. Historically it shares a common heritage with the Church of God (Cleveland Tennessee) and is in the mainstream of the classical Pentecostal-holiness tradition.

At the death of A.J. Tomlinson in 1943, M.A. Tomlinson was named General Overseer and served until his retirement in 1990. He emphasized unity and fellowship unlimited by racial, social, or political differences. The next General Overseer, Billy D. Murray, Sr., who served from 1990 until his retirement in 2000, emphasized a commitment to the promotion of Christian unity and world evangelization. In July 2000, Fred S. Fisher, Sr. Was duly selected to serve as the fourth General Overseer of the Church of God of Prophecy.

From its beginnings, the Church has based its beliefs on "the whole Bible, rightly divided," and has accepted the Bible as God's Holy Word, inspired, inerrant and infallible. The church is firm in its commitment to orthodox Christian belief. The Church affirms that there is one God, eternally existing in three persons, Father, Son and Holy Spirit. It believes in the deity of Christ, His virgin birth, His sinless life, the physical miracles He performed, His atoning death on the cross, His bodily resurrection, His ascension to the right hand of the Father and his Second coming. The church professes that salvation results from grace alone through faith in Christ, that regeneration by the Holy Spirit is essential for the salvation of sinful men, and that sanctification by the blood of Christ makes possible personal holiness. It affirms the present ministry of the Holy Spirit by Whose indwelling believers are able to live godly lives and have power for service. The church believes in, and promotes, the ultimate unity of believers as prayed for by Christ in John 17. The church stresses the sanctity of human life and is committed to the sanctity of the marriage bond and the importance of strong, loving Christian families.

Other official teachings include Holy Spirit baptism with tongues as initial evidence; manifestation of the spiritual gifts; divine healing; premillenial second-coming of Christ; total abstinence from the use of tobacco, alcohol and narcotics; water baptism by immersion; the Lord's supper and washing of the saints' feet; and a concern for moderation and holiness in all dimensions of lifestyle.

The Church is racially integrated on all levels, including top leadership. Women play a prominent role in church affairs, serving in pastoral roles and other leadership positions. The church presbytery has recently adopted plurality of leadership in the selection of a General Oversight Group. This group consists of eight bishops located around the world who, along with the General Overseer, are responsible for inspirational leadership and vision casting for the church body.

The Church has local congregations in all 50 states and more than 100 nations worldwide. Organizationally there is a strong emphasis on international missions, evangelism, youth and children's ministries, women's and men's ministries, stewardship, communications, publishing, leadership development and discipleship.

CHURCH OF GOD OF PROPHECY INTERNATIONAL OFFICES

P.O. Box 2910, Cleveland, TN 37320-2910

Media Contact, National Overseer, Levi Clarke, 5145 Tomken Rd, Mississauga, ON L4 W1P1 Tel. (905)625-1278 Fax (905)625-1316, Web: www.cogop.ca

Officers

Gen. Overseer, Bishop Randy E. Howard, Sr.; General Presbyters, Sherman Allen, Sam Clements, Daniel Corbett, Clayton Endecott, Miguel Mojica, José Reyes, Sr., Felix Santiago, Brice Thompson

International Offices Ministries Dirs., Finance, Communications, and Publishing, Perry Gillum; Global Outreach and Administrative Asst. to the General Presbyters, Randy Howard; Leadership Development and Discipleship Ministries, Larry Duncan.

Periodicals

White Wing Messenger (ENG), *Victory* (Youth Magazine/Sunday School Curriculum), *The Happy Harvester*, *White Wing Messenger* (Spanish).

The Church of Jesus Christ of Latter-day Saints in Canada

The Church has had a presence in Canada since the early 1830s. Joseph Smith and Brigham Young both came to Eastern Canada as missionaries. There are now 157,000 members in Canada in more than 400 congregations.

Leading the Church in Canada are the presidents of over 40 stakes (equivalent to a diocese). World headquarters is in Salt Lake City,

UT (See directory 3, "Religious Bodies of the United States," in this *Yearbook*).

Headquarters

50 East North Temple St., Salt Lake City, UT 84150
Media Contact, Public Affairs Dir., Bruce Smith, 1185 Eglinton Ave., Box 116, North York, ON M3C 3C6 Tel. (416)431-7891 Fax (416)438-2723

Church of the Lutheran Brethren

The Church of the Lutheran Brethren of America was organized in December 1900. Five independent Lutheran congregations met together in Milwaukee, Wisconsin, and adopted a constitution patterned very closely to that of the Lutheran Free Church of Norway.

The spiritual awakening in the Midwest during the 1890s crystallized into convictions that led to the formation of a new church body. Chief among the concerns were church membership practices, observance of Holy Communion, confirmation practices and local church government.

The Church of the Lutheran Brethren practices a simple order of worship with the sermon as the primary part of the worship service. It believes that personal profession of faith is the primary criterion for membership in the congregation. The Communion service is reserved for those who profess faith in Christ as savior. Each congregation is autonomous and the synod serves the congregations in advisory and cooperative capacities.

The synod supports a world mission program in Cameroon, Chad, Japan and Taiwan. Approximately 40 percent of the synodical budget is earmarked for world missions. A growing home mission ministry is planting new congregations in the United States and Canada. Affiliate organizations operate several retirement-nursing homes, conference and retreat centers.

Headquarters

1020 Alcott Ave., W., P.O. Box 655, Fergus Falls, MN 56538 Tel. (218)739-3336 Fax (218)739-5514, Email: rmo@clba.org, Web: www.clba.org
Media Contact, Rev. Brent Juliot

Officers

Pres., Rev. Arthur Berge, 72 Midridge Close SE, Calgary, AB T2X 1G1
Vice Pres., Rev. Luther Stenberg, P.O. Box 75, Hagen, SK S0J 1B0
Sec., Mr. Alvin Herman, 3105 Taylor Street E., Saskatoon, SK S7H 1H5
Treas., Edwin Rundbraaten, Box 739, Birch Hills, SK S0J 0G0
Youth Coord., Rev. Harold Rust, 2617 Preston Ave. S., Saskatoon, SK S7J 2G3

Periodicals

Faith and Fellowship

Church of the Nazarene in Canada

The first Church of the Nazarene in Canada was organized in November, 1902, by Dr. H. F. Reynolds. It was in Oxford, Nova Scotia. The Church of the Nazarene is Wesleyan Arminian in theology, representative in church government and warmly evangelistic.

Headquarters

20 Regan Rd., Unit 9, Brampton, ON L7A 1C3 Tel. (905)846-4220 Fax (905)846-1775
Email: national@nazarene.ca, Web: www.nazarene.ca
Media Contact, Gen. Sec., Dr. Jack Stone, 6401 The Paseo, Kansas City, MO 64131 Tel. (816)333-7000 Fax (816)822-9071

Officers

Natl. Dir., The Rev. Clare MacMillan, 20 Regan Rd. Unit 9, Brampton, ON L7A 1C3 Tel. (905)846-4220 Fax (905)846-1775, Email: cmacmillan@nazarene.ca
Exec. Asst., John T. Martin, 20 Regan Rd. Unit 9, Brampton, ON L7A 1C3 Tel. (905)846-4220 Fax (905)846-1775, Email: national@nazarene.ca

Churches of Christ in Canada

Churches of Christ are autonomous congregations, whose members appeal to the Bible alone to determine matters of faith and practice. There are no central offices or officers. Publications and institutions related to the churches are either under local congregational control or independent of any one congregation.

Churches of Christ shared a common fellowship in the 19th century with the Christian Churches-Churches of Christ and the Christian Church (Disciples of Christ). Fellowship was broken after the introduction of instrumental music in worship and centralization of church-wide activities through a missionary society. Churches of Christ began in Canada soon after 1800, largely in the middle-eastern provinces. The few pioneer congregations were greatly strengthened in the mid-1800s, growing in size and number.

Members of Churches of Christ believe in the inspiration of the Scriptures, the divinity of Jesus Christ, and immersion into Christ for the remission of sins. The New Testament pattern is followed in worship and church organization.

Headquarters

Media Contact, Man. Ed., Gospel Herald, Max Craddock, 5 Lankin Blvd., ON M4J 4W7 Tel. (416)461-7406 Fax (416)424-1850, Email: maxc@strathmorecofc.ca

Periodicals

Gospel Herald

Community of Christ

Founded April 6, 1830, by Joseph Smith, Jr., the church was reorganized under the leadership of the founder's son, Joseph Smith III, in 1860. The Church is established in nearly 50 countries including the United States and Canada, with nearly a quarter of a million members. A world conference is held every three years in Independence, Missouri. The current president is Stephen M. Veazey.

Headquarters
International Headquarters, 1001 W. Walnut, Independence, MO 64050 Tel. (816)833-1000 Fax (816)521-3043

Ontario Regional Ofc., 390 Speedvale Ave. E., Guelph, ON N1E 1N5

Media Contact, Media Relations, Kendra Friend

Officers
Canada East Mission Centre:
Ken Barrows, Mission Centre President, 390 Speedvale Ave E., Guelph, ON N1E 1N5 Tel. (519)822-4150, Email: ken@communityof christ.ca

Jim Poirier, Mission Centre Financial Officer, 390 Speedvale Ave. E., Guelph, ON N1E 1N5 Tel. (519)822-4150, Email: jim@communityof christ.ca

Canada West Mission Centre:
Darrell Belrose, Mission Centre President, 6415 Ranchview Drive NW, Calgary AB T3G 1B5 Tel. (877)411-2632, Email: darrell@community ofchrist.ca

Greg Goheen, Mission Centre Financial Officer, Email: greag@communityofchrist.ca

Periodicals
Herald

Congregational Christian Churches in Canada

This body originated in the early 18th century when devout Christians within several denominations in the northern and eastern United States, dissatisfied with sectarian controversy, broke away from their own denominations and took the simple title "Christians." First organized in 1821 at Keswick, Ontario, the Congregational Christian Churches in Canada was incorporated on Dec. 4, 1989, as a national organization. In doctrine the body is evangelical, being governed by the Bible as the final authority in faith and practice. It believes that Christian character must be expressed in daily living; it aims at the unity of all true believers in Christ that others may believe in Him and be saved. In church polity, the body is democratic and autonomous. It is also a member of The World Evangelical Congregational Fellowship.

Headquarters
241 Dunsdon St. Ste. 405, Brantford, ON N3R 7C3 Tel. (519)751-0606 Fax (519)751-0852

Media Contact, Rev.David Schrader, 241 Dunsdon St. Ste. 405, Brantford, ON N3R 7C3 Tel. (519)751-0606 Fax (519)751-0852

Officers
Pres., Rev. Jim Potter
Exec. Dir., Rev.David Schrader
Sec., Rev. Ron Holden

Convention of Atlantic Baptist Churches

The Convention of Atlantic Baptist Churches is the largest Baptist Convention in Canada. Through the Canadian Baptist Ministries, it is a member of the Baptist World Alliance.

In 1763 two Baptist churches were organized in Atlantic Canada, one in Sackville, New Brunswick and the other in Wolfville, Nova Scotia. Although both these churches experienced crises and lost continuity, they recovered and stand today as the beginning of organized Baptist work in Canada.

Nine Baptist churches met in Lower Granville, Nova Scotia in 1800 and formed the first Baptist Association in Canada. By 1846 the Maritime Baptist Convention was organized, consisting of 169 churches. Two streams of Baptist life merged in 1905 to form the United Baptist Convention. This is how the term "United Baptist" was derived. Today there are 554 churches within 21 associations across the Convention.

The Convention has two educational institutions, Atlantic Baptist University in Moncton, New Brunswick, a Christian Liberal Arts University, and Acadia Divinity College in Wolfville, Nova Scotia, a Graduate School of Theology. The Convention engages in world mission through Canadian Baptist Ministries, the all-Canada mission agency. In addition to an active program of home mission, evangelism, training, social action and stewardship, the Convention operates ten senior citizen complexes and a Christian bookstore.

Headquarters
1655 Manawagonish Rd., Saint John, NB E2M 3Y2 Tel. (506)635-1922 Fax (506)635-0366, Email: cabc@baptist.atlantic.ca, Web: www. baptist.atlantic.ca

Media Contact, Executive Minister, Dr. Harry G. Gardner

Officers
Pres. (2004-2005), Mr. George H. Powell, 3 Elton Place, St. John's, WL A1A 5B8 Tel. (709)722-5007

Vice Pres. (2004-2005), Dr. Ralph Richardson, 129 Athabaska Ave., Riverview, NB E1B 2T2 Tel. (506)863-8456

Exec. Min., Dr. Harry G. Gardner, 1655 Manawagonish Rd., Saint John, NB E2M 3Y2 Tel. (506)635-1922 Fax (506)635-0366, Email: harry.gardner@baptist-atlantic.ca

Dir. of Operations., Daryl MacKenzie, 1655 Manawagonish Rd., Saint John, NB E2M 3Y2 Tel. (506)635-1922 Fax (506)635-0366, Email: daryl.mackenzie@baptist-atlantic.ca

Dir. of Atlantic Baptist Mission, Dr. Malcolm

Beckett, 1655 Manawagonish Rd., Saint John, NB E2M 3Y2 Tel. (506)635-1922 Fax (506) 635-0366, Email: malcolm.beckett@baptist-atlantic.ca

Dir. of Youth and Family, Rev. Bruce Fawcett, 1655 Manawagonish Rd., Saint John, NB E2M 3Y2, Tel. (506)635-1922 Fax (506)635-0366, Email: bruce.fawcett@baptist-atlantic.ca

Dir. Of Development, Rev. Greg Jones, 1655 Manawagonish Rd., Saint John, NB E2M 3Y2 Tel. (506)635-1922 Fax (506)635-0366, Email: greg.jones@baptist-atlantic.ca

Part-time Dir. of Public Witness and Social Concern, Dr. Lois P. Mitchell c/o 1655 Manawagonish Rd., Saint John, NB E2M 3Y2 Tel. (506)635-1922 Fax (506)635-0366, Email: lois.mitchell@baptist-atlantic.ca

The Coptic Orthodox Church in Canada

The Coptic Orthodox Church in North America was begun in Canada in 1964 and was registered in the province of Ontario in 1965. The Coptic Orthodox Church has spread rapidly since then. The total number of local churches in both Canada and the USA exceeded one hundred twenty. Two dioceses, two monasteries with monks and novices, and two theological seminaries were established in the USA.

The Coptic Orthodox Church is the church of Alexandria founded in Egypt by St. Mark the Apostle in the first century A.D. She is a hierarchical church and the administrative governing body of each local church is an elected Board of Deacons approved by the Bishop. The current patriarch of the church is H. H. Pope Shenouda III, Pope of Alexandria and Patriach of the see of St. Mark. The Coptic Orthodox Church is a member of the Canadian Council of Churches.

Headquarters

St. Mark's Coptic Orthodox Church, 41 Glendinning Ave., Toronto, ON M1W 3E2 Tel. (416)494-4449 Fax (416)494-2631, Email: mail@coptorthodox.ca, Web: www.stmark.toronto.on.coptorthodox.ca

Media Contact, Fr. Ammonius Guirguis, Tel. (416)494-4449 Fax (416)494-2631, Email: frammonius@coptorthodox.ca

Disciples of Christ—please see Christian Church (Disciples of Christ) in Canada

Doukhobars—please see Union of Spiritual Communities in Christ

Elim Fellowship of Evangelical Churches and Ministers

The Elim Fellowship of Evangelical Churches and Ministers, a Pentecostal body, was established in 1984 as a sister organization of Elim Fellowship in the United States.

This is an association of churches, ministers and missionaries seeking to serve the whole body of Christ. It is Pentecostal and has a charismatic orientation.

Headquarters

379 Golf Road, RR#6, Brantford, ON N3T 5L8 Tel. (519)753-7266 Fax (519)753-5887 Email: elim@bfree.on.ca, Web: Bfree.ON.ca/comdir/churchs/elim

Ofc. Mgr., Larry Jones

Officers

Pres., Howard Ellis, 102 Ripley Crescent., Kitchener, ON N2N 1V4

Vice Pres., Rev. Errol Alchin, 1694 Autumn Crescent, Pickering, ON L1V 6X5

Sec./Treas., Larry Jones, 107 Hillside Ave., Paris ON K2G 4N1

COUNCIL OF ELDERS

Rev. Bud Crawford, Brampton, ON

Rev. Howard Ellis, Kitchener, ON

Rev. Bernard Evans, Lima, New York

Rev. Claude Favreau, Drummondville, Quebec

Rev. Aubrey Phillips, Blairsville, Georgia

The Estonian Evangelical Lutheran Church Abroad

The Estonian Evangelical Lutheran Church (EELC) was founded in 1917 in Estonia and reorganized in Sweden in 1944. The teachings of the EELC are based on the Old and New Testaments, explained through the Apostolic, Nicean and Athanasian confessions, the unaltered Confession of Augsburg and other teachings found in the Book of Concord.

Headquarters

383 Jarvis St., Toronto, ON M5B 2C7 Tel. (416) 925-5465 Fax (416)925-5688, Email: udo.petersoo@eelk.ee, Web: www.eelk.ee/~e.e.l.k./

Media Contact, Archbishop, Rev. Udo Petersoo

Officers

Archbishop, The Rev. Udo Petersoo

Gen. Sec., Mr. Ivar Nippak

Sec./Clerk, Mrs. Eerika Lage

Periodicals

Eesti Kirik

The Evangelical Covenant Church of Canada

A Canadian denomination organized in Canada at Winnipeg in 1904 which is affiliated with the Evangelical Covenant Church of America and with the International Federation of Free Evangelical Churches, which includes 31 federations in 26 countries.

This body believes in the one triune God as confessed in the Apostles' Creed, that salvation is received through faith in Christ as Saviour, that the Bible is the authoritative guide in all matters of faith and practice. Christian Baptism and the Lord's Supper are accepted as divinely ordained

193

sacraments of the church. As descendants of the 19th century northern European pietistic awakening, the group believes in the need of a personal experience of commitment to Christ, the development of a virtuous life and the urgency of spreading the gospel to the "ends of the world."

Four Core Values: To be a Missional Church; To be a Biblical Church; To be a Devotional Church; and to be a Connnectional Church.

Four Ministry Priorities: Leadership Development; Church Planting & Mission; Church Renewal/ Transition; and Christian Services.

Headquarters
P.O. Box 34025, RPO Fort Richmond, Winnipeg, MB R3T 5T5

Media Contact, Supt., Jeff Anderson

Officers

Pres./Supt., Rev. Jeff Anderson, PO 34025, RPO Fort Richmond, Winnipeg, MB R3T 5T5

Chpsn., Rod Johnson, Box 217, Norquay, SK S0A 2V0

Sec., Judy Nelson, Box 194, Norquay, SK S0A 2V0

Treas., Ingrid Wildman, Box 93, Norquay, SK S0A 2V0

Periodicals
The Covenant Messenger

Evangelical Free Church of Canada

The Evangelical Free Church of Canada traces its beginning back to 1917 when the church in Enchant, Alberta opened its doors. Today the denomination has 140 churches from the West Coast to Quebec. Approximately 80 missionaries are sponsored by the EFCC in 17 countries. The Evangelical Free Church is the founding denomination of Trinity Western University in Langley, British Columbia. Church membership is 8,441, average attendance is 18,455

Headquarters
Mailing Address, P.O. Box 850 LCD1, Langley, BC V3A 8S6 Tel. (604)888-8668 Fax (604) 888-3108, Email: efcc@twu.ca, Web: www. efcc.ca

Media Contact, Executive Assistant Maureen Wilson, P.O. Box 850 LCD1, Langley, BC V3A 8S6 Tel. (604)888-8668 Fax (604)888-3108

Officers
President, Dr. Ron Unruh, P.O.Box 850 LCD 1, Langley, BC, Canada V3A 8S6 Tel. (604)888-8668 Fax (604)888-3108, Email: efcc@twu.ca

Periodicals
The Pulse

Evangelical Lutheran Church in Canada

The Evangelical Lutheran Church in Canada was organized in 1985 through a merger of The Evangelical Lutheran Church of Canada (ELCC) and the Lutheran Church in America—Canada Section.

The merger is a result of an invitation issued in 1972 by the ELCC to the Lutheran Church in America—Canada Section and the Lutheran Church—Canada. Three-way merger discussions took place until 1978 when it was decided that only a two-way merger was possible. The ELCC was the Canada District of the ALC until autonomy in 1967.

The Lutheran Church in Canada traces its history back more than 200 years. Congregations were organized by German Lutherans in Halifax and Lunenburg County in Nova Scotia in 1749. German Lutherans, including many United Empire Loyalists, also settled in large numbers along the St. Lawrence and in Upper Canada. In the late 19th century, immigrants arrived from Scandinavia, Germany and central European countries, many via the United States. The Lutheran synods in the United States have provided the pastoral support and help for the Canadian church.

Headquarters
302-393 Portage Avenue, Winnipeg, MB R3B 3H6 Tel. (204)984-9150 Fax (204)984-9185

Media Contact, Bishop, Rev. Raymond L. Schultz

Other Institutions
Evangelical Lutheran Women Inc., ELCIC Group Services Inc.

Periodicals
Canada Lutheran, Esprit

Evangelical Mennonite Conference

The Evangelical Mennonite Conference is a modern church of historic Christian convictions, tracing its indebtedness to the Radical Reformation, which, in turn, is rooted in the Protestant Reformation of the 16th century. The Centre of faith, and of Scripture, is found in Jesus Christ as Saviour and Lord.

The church's name was chosen in 1959. Its original name, Kleine Gemeinde, which means "small church," reflected its origins as a renewal movement among Mennonites in southern Russia. Klaas Reimer, a minister, was concerned about a decline of spiritual life and discipline in the church, and inappropriate involvement in the Napoleanic War. About 1812, Reimer and others began separate worship services, and two years later were organized as a small group.

Facing increasing government pressure, particularly about military service, the group migrated to North America in 1874 to 1875. Fifty families settled in Manitoba and 36 in Nebraska. Ties between the groups weakened and eventually the U.S. group gave up its KG identity. The KG survived several schisms and migrations, dating from its years in Russia through the 1940s.

As an evangelical church, The Evangelical Mennonite Conference holds that Scripture has final authority in faith and practice, a belief in Christ's finished work, and that assurance of salvation is possible. As Mennonite, the denomination has a commitment to discipleship, baptism upon confession of faith, community, social concern, non-violence and the Great Commission. As a conference, it seeks to encourage local churches, to work together on evangelism and matters of social concern, and relates increasingly well to other denominations.

In the year 2006 its membership surpassed 7270, with many more people as treasured adherents and a wider circle of ministry influence. Membership is for people baptized on confession of faith (usually in adolescence or older). Children are considered safe in Christ until they reach an age where they are accountable for their own spiritual decision and opt out; they are considered part of the church, while full inclusion occurs upon personal choice.

The Conference has 60 churches from British Columbia to Ontario (37 in Manitoba) and roughly 149 mission workers in 25 countries. The cultural make-up of the Conference is increasingly diverse, though its Dutch-German background remains dominant nationally. Twelve churches have pastors or leaders who are of non-Dutch-German background.

Some churches have a multiple leadership pattern (ministers and deacons can be selected from within the congregation); others have new patterns. Most churches support their leading minister full time. Its church governance moved from a bishop system to greater local congregational autonomy. It currently functions as a conference of churches with national boards, a conference council, and a moderator.

Women can serve on most national boards, as conference council delegates, as missionaries, and within a wide range of local church activities; while they can be selected locally, they cannot currently serve as nationally recognized or commissioned ministers.

It is a supporting member of Mennonite Central Committee and the Evangelical Fellowship of Canada. About 80 percent of its national budget goes toward mission work in Canada and other countries.

Headquarters

440 Main St., Steinbach, MB R5G 1Z5 Tel. (204) 326-6401 Fax (204)326-1613 Email: emconf @mts.net

Media Contact, Conf. Pastor, David Thiessen

Officers

Conf. Mod., Ron Penner

General Sec., Tim Dyck

Conference Pastor, Bd. of Leadership and Outreach, David Thiessen

Bd. of Missions, Exec. Sec., Tim Dyck

Bd. of Missions, Foreign Sec., Ken Zacharias

Bd. of Church Ministries, Exec. Sec.-Editor, Terry M. Smith

Bd. Of Trustees, Exec. Sec. Tim Dyck

Canadian Church Planting Coordinator, Exec. Sec.—Ward Parkinson

Conference Youth Minister, Gerald Reimer

Periodicals

The Messenger

Evangelical Mennonite Mission Conference

This group was founded in 1936 as the Rudnerweider Mennonite Church in Southern Manitoba and organized as the Evangelical Mennonite Mission Conference in 1959. It was incorporated in 1962. The Annual Conference meeting is held in July.

Headquarters

Box 52059, Niakwa P.O., Winnipeg, MB R2M 5P9 Tel. (204)253-7929 Fax (204)256-7384, Email: emmc@mb.sympatico.ca

Media Contact, Lil Goertzen, Email: lil@ emmc.ca

Officers

Mod., David Penner, 906-300 Sherk St., Leamington, ON N8H 4N7

Vice-Mod., Carl Zacharias, R.R. 1, Box 205, Winkler, MB R6W 4A1

Sec., Darrell Dyck, R.R. 1, Box 186, Winkler, MB R6W 4A1

Dir. of Conference Ministries, Jack Heppner

Dir. of Missions, Rev. Leonard Sawatzky

Business Admin., Henry Thiessen

Other Organizations

The Gospel Message, Box 1622, Saskatoon, SK S7K 3R8 Tel. (306)242-5001 Fax (306)242-6115; 210-401-33rd St. W., Saskatoon, SK S7L 0V5 Tel. (306)242-5001;

Radio Pastor, Rev. Ed Martens

Periodicals

EMMC Recorder

The Evangelical Missionary Church of Canada

This denomination was formed in 1993 with the merger of The Evangelical Church of Canada and The Missionary Church of Canada. The Evangelical Missionary Church of Canada maintains fraternal relations with the worldwide body of the Missionary Church, Inc. and with the Evangelical Church of North America. The Evangelical Church of Canada was among those North American Evangelical United Brethern Conferences which did not join the EUB in merging with the Methodist Church in 1968. The Missionary Church of Canada is Anabaptist in heritage. Its practices and theology were shaped by the Holiness Revivals of the late 1800s. The Evangelical Missionary Church consists of 135 churches in two conferences in Canada.

195

Headquarters

4031 Brentwood Rd., NW, Calgary, AB T2L 1L1 Tel. (403)250-2759 Fax (403)291-4720

Media Contact, Exec. Dir., Missions and Administration, G. Keith Elliott

Email: info@emcc.ca

Officers

Pres. and Canada East District, Dist. Supt., Rev. Phil Delsaut, 130 Fergus Ave., Kitchener, ON N2A 2H2 Tel. (519)894-9800, Email: pdelsaut @emcced.ca

Canada West District, Acting Dist. Supt., Rev. Don Adolf, 4031 Brentwood Rd., NW, Calgary, AB T2L 1L1 Tel. (403)291-5525 Fax (403)291-4720, Email: don@emcwest.ca

The Fellowship of Evangelical Baptist Churches in Canada

The Fellowship is a family of 500 Evangelical Baptist Churches across Canada, holding worship services in 13 different languages.

Headquarters

P.O. Box 457, Guelph ON, Canada, N1H 6K9 Tel. (519)821-4830 Fax (519)821-9829

Periodicals

B.C. Fellowship Baptist, The Evangelical Baptist Magazine, Intercom

Foursquare Gospel Church of Canada

The Western Canada District was formed in 1964 with the Rev. Roy Hicks as supervisor. Prior to 1964 it had been a part of the Northwest District of the International Church of the Foursquare Gospel with headquarters in Los Angeles, California.

A Provincial Society, the Church of the Foursquare Gospel of Western Canada, was formed in 1976; a Federal corporation, the Foursquare Gospel Church of Canada, was incorporated in 1981 and a national church formed. The provincial society was closed in 1994.

Headquarters

#100 8459 160th St., Surrey, BC V3S 3T9, Email: fgcc@canada.com

Media Contact, Pres., Timothy J. Peterson, #100-8459 160th St., Surrey, BC V3S 3T9 Tel. (604)543-8414 Fax (604)543-8417

Officers

Pres., Timothy J. Peterson

Periodicals

VIP Communique

Free Methodist Church in Canada

The Free Methodist Church was founded in New York in 1860 and expanded in 1880. It is Methodist in doctrine, evangelical in ministry and emphasizes the teaching of holiness of life through faith in Jesus Christ.

The Free Methodist Church in Canada was incorporated in 1927 after the establishment of a Canadian Executive Board. In 1959 the Holiness Movement Church merged with the Free Methodist Church. Full autonomy for the Canadian church was realized in 1990 with the formation of a Canadian General Conference. Mississauga, Ontario, continues to be the location of the Canadian Headquarters.

The Free Methodist Church ministers in 70 countries through its World Ministries Center in Indianapolis, Indiana.

Headquarters

4315 Village Centre Ct., Mississauga, ON L4Z 1S2 Tel. (905)848-2600 Fax (905)848-2603, Email: ministrycentre@fmc-canada.org, Web: www.fmc-canada.org

Media Contact, Dan Sheffield

Officers

Bishop, Rev. Keith Elford

Dir. of Admn. Ser., Norman Bull

Dir. Of Global and Intercultural Ministries, Rev. Dan Sheffield

Supt., Personnel, Rev. Alan Retzman

Supt., Growth Ministries, in transition

Periodicals

Mosaic

Free Will Baptists

As revival fires burned throughout New England in the mid- and late 1700s, Benjamin Randall proclaimed his doctrine of Free Will to large crowds of seekers. In due time, a number of Randall's converts moved to Nova Scotia. One such believer was Asa McGray, who was to become instrumental in the establishment of several Free Baptist churches. Local congregations were organized in New Brunswick. After several years of numerical and geographic gains, disagreements surfaced over the question of music, Sunday school, church offerings, salaried clergy and other issues. Adherents of the more progressive element decided to form their own fellowship. Led by George Orser, they became known as Free Christian Baptists.

The new group faithfully adhered to the truths and doctrines which embodied the theological basis of Free Will Baptists. Largely through Archibald Hatfield, contact was made with Free Will Baptists in the United States in the 1960s. The association was officially welcomed into the Free Will Baptist family in July 1981, by the National Association.

Headquarters

5233 Mt. View Rd., Antioch, TN 37013-2306 Tel. (615)731-6812 Fax (615)731-0771

Media Contact, Mod., Dwayne Broad, RR 3, Bath, NB E0J 1E0 Tel. (506)278-3771

Officers

Mod., Dwayne Broad

Promotional Officer, Dwayne Broad

General Church of the New Jerusalem

The Church of the New Jerusalem, also called The New Church, is a Christian Church founded on the Bible and the Writings of Emanuel Swedenborg (1688–1772). These Writings were first brought to Ontario in 1835 by Christian Enslin.

Headquarters

c-o Olivet Church, 279 Burnhamthorpe Rd., Etobicoke, ON M9B 1Z6 Tel. (416)239-3054 Fax (416)239-4935, Email: olivetchurch @on.aibn.com, Web: www.newchurch.org
Media Contact, Exec. Vice Pres., Rev. Michael D. Gladish

Officers

Pres., Rt. Rev. T. Kline, Bryn Athyn, PA 19009
Exec. Vice Pres., Rev. Michael D. Gladish
Sec., Carolyn Bellinger, 110 Chapel Hill Dr., Kitchener, ON N2G 3W5

General Conference of the Canadian Assemblies of God

This body had its beginnings in Hamilton, Ontario, in 1912 when a few people of an Italian Presbyterian Church banded themselves together for prayer and received a Pentecostal experience of the baptism in the Holy Spirit. Since 1912, there has been a close association with the teachings and practices of the Pentecostal Assemblies of Canada.

The work spread to Toronto, then to Montreal, where it also flourished. In 1959, the church was incorporated in the province of Quebec. The early leaders of this body were the Rev. Luigi Ippolito and the Rev. Ferdinand Zaffuto. The churches carry on their ministry in both the English and Italian languages.

Headquarters

6724 Fabre St., Montreal, QC H2G 2Z6 Tel. (514)279-1100 Fax (514)279-1131
Media Contact, Gen. Sec., Rev. John DellaForesta, 12216 Pierre Baillargeon, Montreal, QC H1E 6R7 Tel. (514)494-6969 Fax (514)279-1131

Officers

Gen. Supt., Rev. David Mortelliti, 6724 Fabre St., Montreal, QC H2G 2Z6 Tel. (514)279-1100 Fax (514)279-1131
Gen. Sec., Rev. John DellaForesta, 12216 Pierre Baillargeon, Montreal, QC H1E 6R7 Tel. (514)494-6969
Gen. Treas., Rev. David Quackenbush, 686 Ossington, Toronto ON M6G 3T7 Tel. (416)532-3951 Fax (416)532-0267
Overseer, Rev. David DiStaulo, 5811 Maurice Duplessis, Montreal QC H1G 1Y2 Tel. (514)328-3131

Periodicals

Voce Evangelica-Evangel Voice

Greek Orthodox Metropolis of Toronto (Canada)

Greek Orthodox Christians in Canada are under the jurisdiction of the Ecumenical Patriarchate of Constantinople (Istanbul).

Headquarters

86 Overlea Blvd., Toronto, ON M4H 1C6 Tel. (416)429-5757 Fax (416)429-4588,
Email: greekomt@on.aibn.com
Media Contact, Orthodox Way Committee

Officers

Metropolitan Archbishop of the Metropolis of Toronto (Canada), His Eminence Metropolitan Archbishop Sotirios

Periodicals

Orthodox Way

Independent Assemblies of God International (Canada)

This fellowship of churches has been operating in Canada for over 58 years. It is a branch of the Pentecostal Church in Sweden. Each church within the fellowship is completely independent.

Headquarters

Media Contact, Gen. Sec., Gen. Sec., Rev. Paul McPhail, Box 653 Chatham, ON, N7M 5K8 Tel. (519)352-1743 Fax (519)3516070, Email: pmcphail@ciaccess.com

Officers

Gen. Sec., Rev. Paul McPhail, Box 653 Chatham, ON, N7M 5K8 Tel. (519)352-1743 Fax (519)3516070
Treas., Rev. David Ellyatt, 1795 Parkhurst Ave., London, ON N5V 2C4, Email: david.ellyatt @odyssey.on.ca

Periodicals

The Mantle (published in March, July & October),

Independent Holiness Church

The former Holiness Movement of Canada merged with the Free Methodist Church in 1958. Some churches remained independent of this merger and they formed the Independent Holiness Church in 1960, in Kingston, Ontario. The doctrines are Methodist and Wesleyan. The General Conference is every three years, next meeting in 2004.

Headquarters

Rev. R. E. Votary, 1564 John Quinn Rd., R.R.1, Greely, ON K4P 1J9 Tel. (613)821-2237
Media Contact, Gen. Sec., Dwayne Reaney, 5025 River Rd. RR #1, Manotick, ON K4M 1B2 Tel. (613)692-3237

Officers

Gen. Supt., Rev. R. E. Votary, 1564 John Quinn Rd., Greeley, ON K4P 1J9
Gen. Sec., Dwayne Reaney

197

Additional Officers: E. Brown, 104-610 Pesehudoff Cresc., Saskatoon, SK S7N 4H5; D. Wallace, 1456 John Quinn Rd., R#1, Greely, ON K4P 1J9

Periodicals
Gospel Tidings

Jehovah's Witnesses

For a description of Jehovah's Witnesses see directory 3, "Religious Bodies in the United States" in this *Yearbook*.

Headquarters
25 Columbia Heights, Brooklyn, NY 11201-2483 Tel. (718)560-5600 Fax (718)560-8850

Canadian Branch Office, Box 4100, Halton Hills, ON L7G 4Y4 Tel. (888)301-4259

Media Contact, Office of Public Information, J. Richard Brown

Media Contact, Office of Public Information in Canada, Mark Ruge Editorial Contact, Writing Department, James N. Pellechia

Latter-day Saints—please see The Church of Jesus Christ of Latter-day Saints in Canada

Lutheran Church—please see Evangelical Lutheran Church in Canada

Lutheran Church-Canada

Lutheran Church-Canada was established in 1959 at Edmonton, Alberta, as a federation of Canadian districts of the Lutheran Church-Missouri Synod; it was constituted in 1988 at Winnipeg, Manitoba, as an autonomous church.

The church confesses the Bible as both inspired and infallible, the only source and norm of doctrine and life and subscribes without reservation to the Lutheran Confessions as contained in the Book of Concord of 1580.

Headquarters
3074 Portage Ave., Winnipeg, MB R3K 0Y2 Tel. (204)895-3433 Fax (204)832-3018, Email: info@lutheranchurch.ca

Media Contact, Dir. of Comm., Ian Adnams, Email: communications@lutheranchurch.ca

Officers
Pres., The Rev. Dr. Ralph Mayan, 3074 Portage Ave., Winnipeg, MB R3K 0Y2 Tel. (204)895-3433 Fax (204)897-4319, Email: president@lutheranchurch.ca

Pres. Emeritus, Rev. Dr. Edwin Lehman, 686 Lee Ridge Road, Edmonton AB T6K 0P2 Tel. (780)462- 9608 Fax (780)468-2172, Email: edwinlehman@shaw.ca

Vice Pres., Rev. Daryl Solie, P.O.Box 500, Church Bridge, SK SOA OMD (2008) Tel. (306)896-2566 Fax (306)896-2617, Email: lutheran.trinity@sasktel.net

Vice Pres., Rev. Robert C. Krestrick, 78 John St., W. Waterloo, ON N2L 1B8 Tel. (519)745-5027 Fax (519)745-7165, Email: rekrestick

@sympatico.ca Vice Pres., Rev. Nolan D. Astley, 2925-57A Lloydminster, AB T9V 1W5 Tel. (780)875-9797 Fax (780)875-9799, Email: luthfrst@telusplanet.net

Treas.: Mr. Dwayne Cleave, 3074 Portage Avenue, Winnipeg, MB R3K 0Y2 Email: treasurer@lutheranchurch.ca Tel. (204)895-3433 Fax (204)897-4319

DISTRICT OFFICES
Alberta-British Columbia, Pres., Rev. D. Schiemann, 7100 Ada Blvd., Edmonton, AB T5B 4E4 Tel. (780)474-0063 Fax (780)477-9829, Email: info@lccabc.ca

Central, Pres., Rev. T. Prachar, 1927 Grant Dr., Regina, SK S4S 4V6 Tel. (306)586-4434 Fax (306)586-0656, Email: tprachar@access comm.ca

East, Pres., Rev. A. Maleske, 275 Lawrence Ave., Kitchener, ON N2M 1Y3 Tel. (519)578-6500 Fax (519)578-3369, Email: amaleske@lcceast district.ca

Periodicals
The Canadian Lutheran

Mennonite—please see also Canadian Conference of Mennonite Brethren Churches, Evangelical Mennonite Mission Conference or Reinland Mennonite Church

Mennonite Church Canada

Mennonite Church Canada (formerly Conference of Mennonites in Canada) was founded in 1903 by 15 praire congregations. In the late 1990's it merged with the Mennonite Church to become Mennonite Church Canada.

The first Mennonites came to Canada in 1786, moving from Pennsylvania in Conestoga wagons. Over the next 150 years, more arrived by ship from Europe, in at least four successive waves.

Its members hold to traditional Christian beliefs, believer's baptism and congregational polity. They emphasize practical Christianity, opposition to war, service to others and personal ethics.

Some people who have joined the Canadian Mennonite body in recent years have arrived from Asia, from Africa, or from Latin and South America. Native brothers and sisters, whose people were here long before the first conastoga wagons arrived, have added their voices to the mix.

Meanwhile, French-speaking and English-speaking Canadians from the wider community have enriched the Mennonite people. Together we are Christian believers moving into the future under the umbrella of the Mennonite Church Canada.

Mennonite Church Canada is affiliated with Mennonite Church USA whose offices are at Newton, Kansas and Elkhart, Indiana. (See, Mennonite Church USA description in directory 3, "Religious Bodies in the United States")

Headquarters

600 Shaftesbury Blvd., Winnipeg, MB R3P 0M4
Tel. (204)888-6781 Fax (204)831-5675
Media Contact, Dan Dyck
Email: ddyck@mennonitechurch.ca
Website: www.mennonitechurch.ca

Officers

Chpsn., Henry Krause
Gen. Sec., Robert J. Suderman

Periodicals

Canadian Mennonite, Der Bote, Intotemak

Moravian Church—please see Canadian District of the Moravian Church in America, Northern Province

Mormons—please see the Church of Jesus Christ of Latter-day Saints in Canada

North American Baptist Conference

Churches belonging to this conference emanated from German Baptist immigrants of more than a century ago. Although scattered across Canada and the U.S., they are bound together by a common heritage, a strong spiritual unity, a Bible-centered faith and a deep interest in missions.

Note, the details of general organization, officers, and periodicals of this body will be found in the North American Baptist Conference listing in directry 3, "Religious Bodies in the United States," in this *Yearbook*.

Headquarters

1 S. 210 Summit Ave., Oakbrook Terrace, IL 60181 Tel. (630)495-2000 Fax (630)495-3301
Media Contact, Marilyn Schaer

Officers

Exec. Dir., Dr. Philip Yntema

Periodicals

N.A.B. Today

The Old Catholic Church of Canada

The church was founded in 1948 in Hamilton, Ontario. The first bishop was the Rt. Rev. George Davis. The Old Catholic Church of Canada accepts all the doctrines of the Eastern Orthodox Churches and, therefore, not Papal Infallibility or the Immaculate Conception. The ritual is Western (Latin Rite) and is in the vernacular language. Celibacy is optional.

Headquarters

2185 Sheridan Park Drive, Apt. 105, Mississauga, ON L5K 1C7 Tel. (905)855-3643
Media Contact, Bishop, The Right Rev. Pat Davies, Vicar General

Officers

Vicar General and Auxiliary Bishop, The Rt. Rev. A.C. Keating, PhD., 5066 Forest Grove

Crest, Burlington, ON L7L GG6 Tel. (905) 681-9983

Old Order Amish Church

This is the most conservative branch of the Mennonite Church and direct descendants of Swiss Brethren (Anabaptists) who emerged from the Reformation in Switzerland in 1525. The Amish, followers of Bishop Jacob Ammann, became a distinct group in 1693. They began migrating to North America about 1737; all of them still reside in the United States or Canada. They first migrated to Ontario in 1823 directly from Bavaria, Germany and later from Pennsylvania and Alsace-Lorraine. Since 1953 more Amish have migrated to Ontario from Ohio, Indiana and Iowa.

As of 2007 there are 30 congregations in Ontario, each being autonomous. No membership figures are kept by this group, and there is no central headquarters. Each congregation is served by a bishop, two ministers and a deacon, all of whom are chosen from among the male members by lot for life.

Officers

Correspondent, Pathway Publishers, David Luthy, Rt. 4, Aylmer, ON N5H 2R3

Periodicals

Blackboard Bulletin, Herold der Wahreit, The Budget, The Diary, Die Botschaft, Family Life, Young Companion, Plain Interests.

Open Bible Faith Fellowship of Canada

This is an Evangelical, Full Gospel Fellowship of Churches and Ministries emphasizing evangelism, missions and the local church for success in the present harvest of souls. OBFF was chartered January 7, 1982.

Headquarters

Niagara Celebration Church, P.O. Box 31020, St. Catharines, ON L2N 7S5 Tel. (905)646-0970

Officers

President, David Youngren
Vice President, Lindsey Burt
Sec./Treasurer, George Woodward
Director, Jim Buslon
Director, Lindsey Burt
Director, Mike Welch
Director, Christer Ihreborg

Orthodox Church in America (Archdiocese of Canada)

The Archdiocese of Canada of the Orthodox Church in America was established in 1916. First organized by St. Tikhon, martyr Patriarch of Moscow, previously Archbishop of North America, it is part of the Russian Metropolia and its successor, the Orthodox Church in America.

The Archdiocesan Council meets twice yearly, the General Assembly of the Archdiocese takes place every three years. The Archdiocese is also known as "Orthodox Church in Canada."

Headquarters

P.O. Box 179, Spencerville, ON K0E 1XO Tel. (613)925-5226, Email: zoe@ripnet.com

Officers

Bishop of Ottawa & Canada, The Rt. Rev. Seraphim; Chancellor, V. Rev. Dennis Pihach, 15992-107A Ave, Edmonton, AB T5P 0Z2

Treas., Nikita Lopoukhine, P.O. Box 179, Spencervillt, ON K0E 1X0

Sec., Archpriest Cyprian Hutcheon, P.O. Box 179, Spencerville, ON K0E 1X0

ARCHDIOCESAN COUNCIL

Clergy Members, Rev. Lawrence Farley; Rev. R.S. Kennaugh; Rev. Larry Reinheimer; Igumen Irenee Rochon; Rev. John Jillions, Rev. Ovest Olekshy

Lay Members, David Grier, John Hadjinicolaou, Mother Sophia (Zion), David Rystephanuk, Rod Tkachuk, Sandra Ellis, Alexei Vassiouchkine

Ex Officio, Chancellor; Treas.; Sec.

Periodicals

Canadian Orthodox Messenger

Patriarchal Parishes of the Russian Orthodox Church in Canada

This is the diocese of Canada of the former Exarchate of North and South America of the Russian Orthodox Church. It was originally founded in 1897 by the Russian Orthodox Archdiocese in North America.

Headquarters

St. Barbara's Russian Orthodox Cathedral, 10105 96th St., Edmonton, AB T5H 2G3

Media Contact, Roman Lopushinsky, 11620 134 Ave., Edmonton, AB T5E 1K9, Tel./Fax (780) 455-6314

Officers

Admn., Bishop of Kashira, Most Rev. Iov, 10812-108 St., Edmonton, AB T5H 3A6 Tel. (780)420-9945

The Pentecostal Assemblies of Canada

This body is incorporated under the Dominion Charter of 1919 and is also recognized in the Province of Quebec as an ecclesiastical corporation. Its beginnings are to be found in the revivals at the turn of the century, and most of the first Canadian Pentecostal leaders came from a religious background rooted in the Holiness movements.

The original incorporation of 1919 was implemented among churches of eastern Canada only. In the same year, a conference was called in Moose Jaw, Saskatchewan, to which the late Rev. J. M. Welch, general superintendent of the then-organized Assemblies of God in the U.S., was invited. The churches of Manitoba and Saskatchewan were organized as the Western District Council of the Assemblies of God. They were joined later by Alberta and British Columbia. In 1921, a conference was held in Montreal, to which the general chairman of the Assemblies of God was invited. Eastern Canada also became a district of the Assemblies of God, joining Eastern and Western Canada as two districts in a single organizational union.

In 1920, at Kitchener, Ontario, eastern and western churches agreed to dissolve the Canadian District of the Assemblies of God and unite under the name The Pentecostal Assemblies of Canada.

Today the Pentecostal Assemblies of Canada operates throughout the nation and in about 30 countries around the world. Religious services are conducted in more than 25 different languages in the 1,100 local churches in Canada. Members and adherents number about 230,000. The number of local churches includes approximately 100 Native congregations.

Headquarters

2450 Milltower Court, Mississauga, ON L5N 5Z6 Tel. (905)542-7400 Fax (905)542-7313

Officers

Gen. Supt., Rev. William D. Morrow

Asst. Supt., for Ministerial Services, Rev. David E. Hazzard

Asst. Supt. for Financial Resources, Rev. David Ball

DISTRICT SUPERINTENDENTS

British Columbia, Rev. D.R. Wells, 20411 Douglas Crescent, Langley, BC V3S 4B6 Tel. (604)533-2232 Fax (604)533-5405

Alberta, Rev. Lorne D. McAlister, 10585-111 St., #101, Edmonton, AB T5H 3E8 Tel. (403)426-0084 Fax (403)420-1318

Saskatchewan, Rev. J. I. Guskjolen, 3488 Fairlight Dr., Saskatoon, SK S7M 3Z4 Tel. (306)683-4646 Fax (306)683-3699

Manitoba, Rev. R.W. Pierce, 187 Henlow Bay, Winnipeg, MB R3Y 1G4 Tel. (204)940-1000 Fax (204)940-1009

Western Ontario, Rev. D.A Shepherd, 3214 S. Service Rd., Burlington, ON L7N 3J2 Tel. (905)637-5566 Fax (905)637-7558

Eastern Ontario and Quebec, Rev. R. T. Hilsden, Box 337, Cobury, ON K9A 4K8 Tel. (905) 373-7374 Fax (905)373-1911

Quebec, Rev. G.C. Connors, 911, Boul Roland-Therrien, Longueuil, QC JAJ 4L3 Tel (4005) 442-2732 Fax (405) 442-3818

Maritime Provinces, Rev. Douglas Moore, Box 1184, Truro, NS B2N 5H1 Tel. (902)895-4212 Fax (902)897-0705

BRANCH CONFERENCES

Eastern Slavic, Rev. A. Muravski, 445 Stevenson Rd., Oshawa, ON L1J 5N8 Tel (905) 576-3584

Western Slavic, Rev. Michael Brandebura, 17-9420 172 St., Edmonton, T5T 6KI Tel (780) 743-2410 Fax (780) 473-2410

Finnish Conference, Rev. P. A. Korpela, 2592 Bayview Ave, North York, ON M2L1B3 Tel (416)733-0854 Fax (416)222-3356

Periodicals

Testimony (The official magazine of The Pentecostal Assemblies of Canada), *Enrich* (National Leadership magazine), *Contact* (magazine for those 50 years+), *HonorBound* (magazine for Men)

The Pentecostal Assemblies of Newfoundland

This body began in 1911 and held its first meetings at Bethesda Mission at St. John's. It was incorporated in 1925 as The Bethesda Pentecostal Assemblies of Newfoundland and changed its name in 1930 to The Pentecostal Assemblies of Newfoundland.

Headquarters

57 Thorburn Rd., Box 8895, Stn. "A", St. John's, NF A1B 3T2 Tel. (709)753-6314 Fax (709) 753-4945, Email: paon@paon.nf.ca

Media Contact, Gen. Sup't., H. Paul Foster, 57 Thorburn Rd., Box 8895, Stn. "A", St. John's, NF A1B 3T2

GENERAL EXECUTIVE OFFICERS

Gen. Sup't.: H. Paul Foster, 57 Thorburn Rd., Box 8895, Stn. "A", St. John's, NF A1B 3T2

Gen. Sec.-Treas.: Clarence Buckle, 57 Thorburn Rd., Box 8895, Stn. "A", St. John's, NF A1B 3T2

Ex. Dir. of Home Missions: Andrew R. Anstey, 57 Thorburn Rd., Box 8895, Stn. "A", St. John's, NF A1B 3T2

Ex. Dir. of Ch. Ministries: Robert H. Dewling, 57 Thorburn Rd., Box 8895, Stn. "A", St. John's, NF A1B 3T2

PROVINCIAL DIRECTORS

Sunday School & Children's Ministries: Kelly L. Brenton, 42 Franks Road, Conception Bay South, NL A1X 6W8

Women's Ministries: Catherine J. Snow, 14 Jeddores Lane, Deer Lake, NL A8A 1P4

Men's Ministries: Wilfred S. Buckle, 52 Premier Dr., Corner Brook, NL A2H 1S4

Youth Ministries: B. Dean Brenton, Box 21100, St. John's, NF A1B 3L5

Mature Adult Ministries: Barry D. Pelley, Box 1715, Lewisporte, NL A0G 3A0

Family Ministries: Sharmaine R. Reid, Box 2, Hant's Harbour, NL A0B 1Y0

AUXILIARY SERVICES

Chaplain of Institutions: Robert G. Parsons, 29 Caster's Drive, Mount Pearl, NL A1N 4X3

Pentecostal Senior Citizens Home Administrator: Beverley Bellefleur, Box 130, Clarke's Beach, NF A0A 1W0

Evergreen Manor, Summerford, NF A0G 4E0

Chaplain: Memorial University of Newfoundland, Gregory R. Dewling, Memorial University of Newfoundland, Box 102, St. John's, NF A1C 5S7

Emmanuel Convention Centre Administrator: Sterling E. Warr, P.O. Box 1409, Lewisporte, NL A0G 3A0

Managing Editor, Good Tidings: Burton K. Janes, 57 Thornburn Rd., Box 8895, Stn. "A", St. John's, NF A1B 3T2

Periodicals

Good Tidings

Plymouth Brethren—please see Christian Brethren

Presbyterian Church in America (Canadian Section)

Canadian congregations of the Reformed Presbyterian Church, Evangelical Synod, became a part of the Presbyterian Church in America when the RPCES joined PCA in June 1982. Some of the churches were in predecessor bodies of the RPCES, which was the product of a 1965 merger of the Reformed Presbyterian Church in North America, General Synod and the Evangelical Presbyterian Church. Others came into existence later as a part of the home missions work of RPCES. Congregations are located in seven provinces, and the PCA is continuing church extension work in Canada. The denomination is committed to world evangelization and to a continuation of historic Presbyterianism. Its officers are required to subscribe to the Reformed faith as set forth in the Westminster Confession of Faith and Catechisms.

Headquarters

Media Contact, Dr. Dominic Aquila, Editor Byfaithonline Newletter, New Geneva Seminary, 3622 East Galley Rd,, Colorado Springs, CO, 80909 Tel. (719)573-5395 Fax (719)573-5398, Email: daquila6@aol.com

Periodicals

Equip for Ministry, *Multiply*, *Network*, *byFaith*

Presbyterian Church in Canada

This is the nonconcurring portion of the Presbyterian Church in Canada that did not become a part of The United Church of Canada in 1925.

Headquarters

50 Wynford Dr., Toronto, ON M3C 1J7 Tel. (416)441-1111 Fax (416)441-2825

Web: www.presbyterian.ca

Media Contact, Principal Clk., Rev. Stephen Kendall or Associate Secretary for Resource Production & Communication, Mr. Keith Knight

Officers

Principal Clk., Rev. Stephen Kendall

Periodicals

Channels, The Presbyterian Message, Presbyterian Record, Glad Tidings, La Vie Chrétienne

Reformed Church in Canada

The Canadian region of the Reformed Church in America was organized under the General Synod of the Reformed Church in America. The RCA in Canada has 40 churches which includes three classes (lower assemblies). The Reformed churches in Canada are member congregations of the Reformed Church in America and the Regional Synod of Canada (one of eight RCA regional synods established by its General Synod) and three classes, Ontario, Canadian Prairies and British Columbia.

The first ordained minister, Domine Jonas Micahelius, arrive in New Amsterdam from The Netherlands in 1628. Throughout the colonial period, the Reformed Church lived under the authority of the Classis of Amsterdam. Its churches were clustered in New York and New Jersey. Under the leadership of Rev. John Livingston, it became a denomination independent of the authority of the Classis of Amsterdam in 1776. Its geographical base was broadened in the 19th century by the immigration of Reformed Dutch and German settlers in the midwestern United States. The Reformed Church now spans the United States and Canada. The Reformed Church in America accepts as its standards of faith the Heidelberg Catechism, Belgic Confession and Canons of Dort. It has a rich heritage of world mission activity. It claims to be loyal to Reformed tradition which emphasizes obedience to God in all aspects of life.

Although the Reformed Church in America has worked in close cooperation with other churches, it has never entered into merger with any other denomination. It is a member of the World Alliance of Reformed Churches, the World Council of Churches and the National Council of the Churches of Christ in the United States of America. In 1998 it also entered into a relationship of full communion with the Evangelical Lutheran Church in America, Presbyterian Church (U.S.A.), and the United Church of Christ by way of the Formula of Agreement.

Headquarters

475 Riverside Dr., 18th Floor, New York, NY 10115 Tel. (212)870-3243 Fax (212)870-2499, Web: www.rca.org

Media Contact, Communications Officer, Paul Boice, 4500 60th St., SE, Grand Rapids, MI 49512 Tel. (616)698-7071 Fax (616) 698-6606

OFFICERS AND STAFF OF GENERAL SYNOD

Regional Synod of Canada, Synod Executive, Mr. Fred Algera, 1985 Beke Rd. RR#4, Cambridge, ON N1R 5S5

President, The Rev. Bradley Lewis, 475 Riverside Dr., 18th Floor, New York, NY 10115

General Synod Council; Moderator, The Rev. Steven Vander Molen, 475 Riverside Dr., 18th Floor, New York, NY 10115

General Secretary, The Rev. Wesley Granberg-Michelson, 475 Riverside Dr., 18th Floor, New York, NY 10115; 4500 60th St. S.E., Grand Rapids, MI 49512

Operations and Support, Director & Assistant Secretary, The Rev. Kenneth Bradsell

Global Mission, Director, The Rev. Bruce Menning

Leadership/Revitalization, Director, The Rev. Kenneth Eriks

Church Multiplication/Discipleship, Director, The Rev. Richard Welscott

Finance Services, Treasurer, Ms. Susan Converse

The Reformed Episcopal Church of Canada

The Reformed Episcopal Church is a separate entity. It was established in Canada by an act of Parliament given royal assent on June 2, 1886. It maintains the founding principles of episcopacy (in historic succession from the apostles), Anglican liturgy and Reformed doctrine and evangelical zeal. In practice it continues to recognize the validity of certain nonepiscopal orders of evangelical ministry. The Church has reunited with the Reformed Episcopal Church and is now composed of two Dioceses in this body—the Diocese of Central and Eastern Canada and the Diocese of Western Canada and Alaska.

Headquarters

Box 2532, New Liskeard, ON P0J 1P0 Tel. (705) 647-4565 Fax (705)647-1340

Email: fed@nt.net, Web: www.recus.org

Media Contact, Pres., The Rt. Rev. Michael Fedechko, M. Div., D.D.

Officers

Pres., The Rt. Rev. Michael Fedechko, 320 Armstrong St., Temiskaming Shores, ON P0J 1P0

Vice Pres., Jeff Shanlin, Hamilton, ON

Sec., Sharlene Graham, New Liskeard, ON P0J 1P0

BISHOPS

Diocese of Central & Eastern Canada, The Rt. Rev. Michael Fedechko, 320 Armstrong St., Temiskaming Shores, ON P0J 1P0 Tel. (705)647-4565 Fax (705)647-1340

Diocese of Western Canada & Alaska, Rt. Rev. Charles W. Dorrington, 54 Blanchard St., Victoria, BC V8X 4R1 Tel. (604)744-5014 Fax (604)388-5891

Periodicals

The Messenger

Reinland Mennonite Church

This group was founded in 1958 when 10 ministers and approximately 600 members separated from the Sommerfelder Mennonite Church. In 1968, four ministers and about 200 members migrated to Bolivia. The church has work in five communities in Manitoba and one in Ontario

Headquarters

Bishop William H. Friesen, P.O. Box 96, Rosenfeld, MB R0G 1X0 Tel. (204)324-6339
Media Contact, Deacon, Henry Wiebe, Box 2587, Winkler, MB R6W 4C3 Tel. (204)325-8487

Reorganized Church of Jesus Christ of Latter-day Saints—please see Community of Christ

The Roman Catholic Church in Canada

The largest single body of Christians in Canada, the Roman Catholic Church is under the spiritual leadership of His Holiness the Pope. Catholicism in Canada dates back to 1534, when the first Mass was celebrated on the Gaspé Peninsula on July 7, by a priest accompanying Jacques Cartier. Catholicism had been implanted earlier by fishermen and sailors from Europe. Priests came to Acadia as early as 1604. Traces of a regular colony go back to 1608 when Champlain settled in Quebec City. The Récollets (1615), followed by the Jesuits (1625) and the Sulpicians (1657), began the missions among the native population. The first official Roman document relative to the Canadian missions dates from March 20, 1618. Bishop François de Montmorency-Laval, the first bishop, arrived in Quebec in 1659. The church developed in the East, but not until 1818 did systematic missionary work begin in western Canada.

In the latter 1700s, English-speaking Roman Catholics, mainly from Ireland and Scotland, began to arrive in Canada's Atlantic provinces. After 1815 Irish Catholics settled in large numbers in what is now Ontario. The Irish potato famine of 1847 greatly increased that population in all parts of eastern Canada.

By the 1850s the Catholic Church in both English- and French-speaking Canada had begun to erect new dioceses and found many religious communities. These communities did educational, medical and charitable work among their own people as well as among Canada's native peoples. By the 1890s large numbers of non-English and non-French-speaking Catholics had settled in Canada, especially in the Western provinces. In the 20th century the pastoral horizons have continued to expand to meet the needs of what has now become a very multicultural church.

The Canadian Conference of Catholic Bishops is the national association of the Latin and Eastern Catholic Bishops of Canada. Its main offices are in Ottawa, Ontario.

CANADIAN ORGANIZATION

Conférence des évêques catholiques du Canada-Canadian Conference of Catholic Bishops, 2500 Don Reid Drive, Ottawa, ON k1H 2J2, Tel. (613)241-9461 Fax (613)241-9048, Email: cecc@cccb.ca, Website: www.cccb.ca

Headquarters

Media Contact, M. Sylvain Salvas, Tel. (613) 241-7538 or (800)769-1147, Email: salvas@cecc.ca or cecc@cccb.ca

Officers

General Secretariat of the Canadian Conference of Catholic Bishops
General Secretary: Msgr. Mario Paquette, P.H.
Associate General Secretaries: M. Benoît Bariteau (French Sector); Mr. Bede Hubbard (English Sector)

EXECUTIVE COMMITTEE

Pres., Most Rev. Andre Gaumond; Vice Pres., Most Rev. V. James Weisgerber; Co-Treas., Most Rev. Pierre Morissette and Most Rev. V. James M. Wingle

EPISCOPAL COMMISSIONS—NATIONAL LEVEL

Social Affairs: Most Rev. Roger Ebacher
Canon Law: Most Rev. Robert Harris
Relations with Assoc. of Clergy, Consecrated Life & Laity: Most Rev. Fred Colli
Evangelization of Peoples: Most Rev. Vincent Cadieux, O.M.I.
Christian Unity, Religious Relations with the Jews, and Interfaith Dialogue: Most Rev. John Boissonneau
Theology: Most Rev. Luc Bouchard

EPISCOPAL COMMISSIONS—SECTOR LEVEL

Communications sociales: Most Rev. Louis Dicaire
Social Communication: Most Rev. J. Keron Fougere
Christian Education; Most Rev. Richard Smith
Liturgie: Most Rev. Dorylas Moreau
Liturgy: Most Rev. Gerald Wiesner, O.M.I.

OFFICES

Justice, Paix et Missions – Justice Peace and Missions, Mr. Benoit Bariteau
Dir. Communications: M. Sylvain Salvas
Dir. Droit canonique—inter-rites-Canon Law—Inter-rite: Msgr. Mario Paquette
P.H. Secr. Éditions-Publications, Dr. Vicki Bennett
Dir. Liturgie-Liturgy -: M. Gaëtan Baillargeon
Dir. (French Sector); Rev. Camille Jacques, O.S.M., Dir. (English Sector)
National Office of Religious Education: Ms. Joanne Chafe
Dir. Relations ecclésiales et doctrine – Ecclesial Relations and Doctrine: Mr. Beck Hubbard
Tribunal d'appel du Canada-The Canadian Appeal Tribunal: Msgr. Alan McCormack, P.H., Vicaire judiciaire-Judicial Vicar

REGIONAL EPISCOPAL ASSEMBLIES

Atlantic Episcopal Assembly-Assemblée des évêques de l'Atlantique: Pres., Most Rev. Raymond I Lahey; Vice Pres., Most Rev. Terrence Prendergast, S.J. and Most Francois Thibodeau, C.J.M.; Secretary-Treasurer, Fr. Léo Grégoire, I.V. Dei, Tel. (506)735-5578 Fax (506)735-4271

Assemblée des évêques Catholiques du Québec: Pres., Most Rev. Gilles Cazabon, O.M.I.; Vice Prés., Most Rev. Martin Veillette, O.M.I.; Secrétaire général, M. Pierre Gaudette, Tel. (514)274-4323 Fax (514)274-4383

Ontario Conference of Catholic Bishops-Conférence des évêques catholique de l'Ontario: Pres., Most Rev. Richard Smith, Vice Pres., Most Rev. Richard Grecco; Secretary-Treasurer, Mr. Alphonse Ainsworth, Tel. (416)923-1423 Fax (416)923-1509

Assembly of Western Catholic Bishops Assembliee ches e veques catholique de l'ouest Pres., Most Rev. Gerald Weisner, O.M.I.; Vice Pres., Most Rev. Raymond Roussin, S.M.; Sec.- Treasurer, Rt. Rev. Peter Novecosky, O.S.B. Tel. (306)682-1788 Fax (306)682-1766

MILITARY ORDINARIATE-ORDINARIAT MILITAIRE

Bishop, Most Rev. Donald J. Theriault, Military Ordinariate of Canada, Canadian Forces Support Unit (Ottawa), Uplands Site Building 469, Ottawa, ON K1A 0K2 Tel. (613)990-7824 Fax (613)991-1056

Canadian Religious Conference, Sec. Gen., Sr. Margaret Toner, SCIC. 4135, rue de Rouen, Montréal, Québec H1V 1G5 Tel. (514)259-0856 Fax (514)259-0857

Organisme catholique pour la vie et la famille/Catholic Organization for Life and Family, Co-directors, Ms. Michèle Boulva (French Sector) Tel. (613)241-9461 Fax (613)241-9048, Email: ocvfcolf@cccb.ca

Periodicals

Foi et Culture (Bulletin natl. de liturgie)

Romanian Orthodox Church in America (Canadian Parishes)

The first Romanian Orthodox immigrants in Canada called for Orthodox priests from their native country of Romania. Between 1902 and 1914, they organized the first Romanian parish communities and built Orthodox churches in different cities and farming regions of western Canada (Alberta, Saskatchewan, Manitoba) as well as in the eastern part (Ontario and Quebec).

In 1929, the Romanian Orthodox parishes from Canada joined with those of the United States in a Congress held in Detroit, Michigan, and asked the Holy Synod of the Romanian Orthodox Church of Romania to establish a Romanian Orthodox Missionary Episcopate in America. The first Bishop, Policarp (Morushca),

was elected and consecrated by the Holy Synod of the Romanian Orthodox Church and came to the United States in 1935. He established his headquarters in Detroit with jurisdiction over all the Romanian Orthodox parishes in the United States and Canada.

In 1950, the Romanian Orthodox Church in America (i.e. the Romanian Orthodox Missionary Episcopate in America) was granted administrative autonomy by the Holy Synod of the Romanian Orthodox Church of Romania, and only doctrinal and canonical ties remain with this latter body.

In 1974 the Holy Synod of the Romanian Orthodox Church of Romania recognized and approved the elevation of the Episcopate to the rank of the Romanian Orthodox Archdiocese in America and Canada and completed the administrative autonomy.

Headquarters

Romanian Orthodox Archdiocese in the Americas, 5410 N. Newland Ave., Chicago, IL 60656 USA

Officers

Archbishop, Most Rev. Nicolae Condrea,5410 N. Newland Ave., Chicago, IL 60656 Tel. (773) 774-1677 Fax (773)774-1805, Email: archnicolae@aol.com

Secretary, V. Rev. Fr. Nicholas Apostola, 44 Midland St. Worchester, MA 01602-4217, Tel. (508)845-0088 Fax (508)752-8180

Periodicals

Credinta-The Faith

The Romanian Orthodox Episcopate of America (Jackson, MI)

This body of Eastern Orthodox Christians of Romanian descent is part of the Orthodox Church in America. For complete description and listing of officers, please see Orthodox Church in America in directory 3, "Religious Bodies in the United States."

Headquarters

2535 Grey Tower Rd., Jackson, MI 49201 Tel. (517)522-4800, Mailing Address, P.O. Box 309, Grass Lake, MI 49240-0309, Email: chancery@roea.org, Web: www.roea.org

Media Contact, Ed.-Sec., Rev. Archdeacon David Oancea, P.O. Box 185, Grass Lake, MI 49240-0185 Tel. (517)522-3656

Officers

Ruling Hierarch, Most. Rev. Archbishop Nathaniel Popp

Dean of All Canada, Very Rev. Daniel Nenson, 2855 Helmsing St., Regina, SK S4V 0W7 Tel. (306)761-2379

Periodicals

Solia-The Herald, *Good News- Buna Vestire* (in Canada only)

CANADIAN RELIGIOUS BODIES

Russian Orthodox Church—please see the Patriarchal Parishes of the Russian Orthodox Church in Canada

The Salvation Army in Canada

The Salvation Army, an evangelical branch of the Christian Church, is an international movement founded in 1865 in London, England. The ministry of Salvationists, consisting of clergy (officers) and laity, comes from a commitment to Jesus Christ and is revealed in practical service, regardless of race, color, creed, sex or age.

The goals of The Salvation Army are to preach the gospel, disseminate Christian truths, instill Christian values, enrich family life and improve the quality of all life.

To attain these goals, The Salvation Army operates local congregations, provides counseling, supplies basic human needs and undertakes spiritual and moral rehabilitation of any needy people who come within its influence.

A quasi-military system of government was set up in 1878, by General William Booth, founder (1829–1912). Converts from England started Salvation Army work in London, Ontario, in 1882. Two years later, Canada was recognized as a Territorial Command, and since 1933 it has included Bermuda. An act to incorporate the Governing Council of The Salvation Army in Canada received royal assent on May 19, 1909.

Headquarters

2 Overlea Blvd., Toronto, ON M4H 1P4 Tel. (416)425-2111
Media Contact, Major Len Miller, Tel. (416)425-6153 Fax (416)425-6157
Email: len-miller@can.salvationarmy.org, Web: www.salvationarmy.ca

Officers

Territorial Commander, Commissioner Bill Luttrell
Territorial Pres., Women's Organizations, Commissioner Gwen Lutterell
Chief Sec., Col. Bob Redhead
Sec. for Personnel, Lt. Col. Wayne Pritchett
Bus. Adm. Sec., Lt. Col. Susan McMillan
Fin. Sec., Major Paul Goodyear
Program Sec., Lt. Col. David Luginbuhl
Public Rel., Major Len Millar
Property Sec., Major Neil Watt

Periodicals

The War Cry, *Faith & Friends*, *En Avant!*, *The Edge*, *Horizons*

Serbian Orthodox Church in the U.S.A. and Canada, Diocese of Canada

The Serbian Orthodox Church is an organic part of the Eastern Orthodox Church. As a local church it received its autocephaly from Constantinople in A.D. 1219. The Patriarchal seat of the church today is in Belgrade, Yugoslavia. In 1921, a Serbian Orthodox Diocese in the United States of America and Canada was organized. In 1963, it was reorganized into three dioceses, and in 1983 a fourth diocese was created for the Canadian part of the church. The Serbian Orthodox Church is in absolute doctrinal unity with all other local Orthodox Churches.

Headquarters

7470 McNiven Rd., RR 3, Campbellville, ON L0P 1B0 Tel. (905)878-0043 Fax (905)878-1909, Email: vladika@istocnik.com, Web: www. istocnik.com
Media Contact, Rt. Rev. Georgije

Officers

Serbian Orthodox Bishop of Canada, Rt. Rev. Georgije
Dean of Western Deanery, V. Rev. Mirko Malinovic, 924 12th Ave., Regina, SK S4N 0K7 Tel. (306)352-2917
Dean of Eastern Deanery, V. Rev. Zivorad Subotic, 351 Mellville Ave., Westmount, QC H3Z 2Y7 Tel. Fax (514)931-6664

Periodicals

Istocnik, Herald of the Serbian Orthodox Church-Canadian Diocese

Seventh-day Adventist Church in Canada

The Seventh-day Adventist Church in Canada is part of the worldwide Seventh-day Adventist Church with headquarters in Silver Spring, Maryland (See "Religious Bodies in the United States" section of this Yearbook for a fuller description.) The Seventh-day Adventist Church in Canada was organized in 1901 and reorganized in 1932.

Headquarters

1148 King Street East, Oshawa, ON L1H 1H8 Tel. (905)433-0011 Fax (905)433-0982
Media Contact, Nilton D. Amorim

Officers

Pres., Daniel R. Jackson
Sec., Nilton D. Amorim
Treas., John Ramsay

DEPARTMENTS

Asst. Treas., Joyce Jones
Education, Mike Lekic
Family Ministries, Celest Corkum, Ken Corkum
Sabbath School and Personal Ministries, Gary Hodder
Trust Services, Barry W. Bussey
ADRA Canada, Oliver Lofton-Brook

Periodicals

Canadian Adventist Messenger

Southern Baptists—please see Canadian Convention of Southern Baptists

205

Syriac Orthodox Church of Antioch

The Syriac Orthodox Church professes the faith of the first three ecumenical councils of Nicaea, Constantinople and Ephesus and numbers faithful in the Middle East, India, the Americas, Europe and Australia. It traces its origin to the Patriarchate established in Antioch by St. Peter the Apostle and is under the supreme ecclesiastical jurisdiction of His Holiness the Syrian Orthodox Patriarch of Antioch and All the East, now residing in Damascus, Syria.

The Archdiocese of the Syrian Orthodox Church in the U.S. and Canada was formally established in 1957. In 1995, the Archdiocese of North America was divided into three separate Patriarchal Vicariates, including one for Canada. The first Syrian Orthodox faithful came to Canada in the 1890s and formed the first Canadian parish in Sherbrooke, Quebec. Today five official parishes of the Archdiocese exist in Canada—two in Quebec and three in Ontario. There is also an official mission congregation in Calgary, Alberta and Ottawa, Ontario.

Headquarters

Archdiocese of Canada, The New Archdiocesan Centre, 4375 Henri-Bourassa Ouest, St.-Laurent, Quebec H4L 1A5 Tel. (514)334-6993 Fax (514)334-8233

Officers

Archbishop Mor Timotheos Aphrem Aboodi

Ukrainian Orthodox Church of Canada

Toward the end of the 19th century many Ukrainian immigrants settled in Canada. In 1918, a group of these pioneers established the Ukrainian Orthodox Church of Canada (UOCC), today the largest Ukrainian Orthodox Church beyond the borders of Ukraine. In 1990, the UOCC entered into a eucharistic union with the Ecumenical Patriarchate at Constantinople (Istanbul).

Headquarters

Ukrainian Orthodox Church of Canada, Office of the Consistory, 9 St. Johns Ave., Winnipeg, MB R2W 1G8 Tel. (204)586-3093 Fax (204) 582-5241, Email: consistory@uocc.ca, Web: www. uocc.ca

Media Contacts, Rev. Fr. Andrew Jarmus, 9st. John's Ave., Winnipeg, MB R2W 1G8 Tel. (204)586-3093 Fax (204)582-5241, Ms. M. Zurek, 9 St. Johns Ave., Winnipeg, MB R2W 1G8 Tel. (204)586-3093 Fax (204)582-5241

Officers

Primate, Most Rev. Metropolitan Wasyly Fedak, 9 St. Johns Ave., Winnipeg, MB R2W 1G8 Tel. (204)586-3093 Fax (204)582-5241

Chancellor, Rt. Rev. Fr. William Makarenko

Periodicals

Visnyk-The Herald-Le Messager (newspaper), *Ridna Nyva* (almanac-annual)

Union d'Eglises Baptistes Françaises au Canada

Baptist churches in French Canada first came into being through the labors of two missionaries from Switzerland, Rev. Louis Roussy and Mme. Henriette Feller, who arrived in Canada in 1835. The earliest church was organized in Grande Ligne (now St. Blaise), Quebec in 1838.

By 1900 there were 7 churches in the province of Quebec and 13 French-language Baptist churches in the New England states. The leadership was totally French Canadian.

By 1960, the process of Americanization had caused the disappearance of the French Baptist churches in the New England states. During the 1960s, Quebec as a society, began rapidly changing in all its facets, education, politics, social values and structures. Mission, evangelism and church growth once again flourished. In 1969, in response to the new conditions, the Grande Ligne Mission passed control of its work to the newly formed Union of French Baptist Churches in Canada, which then included 8 churches. By 2005 the French Canadian Baptist movement had grown to include 34 congregations present in three provinces: Quebec, New Brunswick, and Ontario.

The Union d'Églises Baptistes Françaises au Canada is a member body of the Canadian Baptist Ministries and thus is affiliated with the Baptist World Alliance.

Headquarters

2285 Avenue Papineau, Montreal, QC H2K 4J5 Tel. (514)526-6643 Fax (514)526-9269

Media Contact, Gen. Sec., Rev. Roland Grimard

Officers

Sec. Gen., Rev. Roland Grimard

Periodicals

www.UnionBaptiste.com (Internet)

Union of Spiritual Communities of Christ (Orthodox Doukhobors in Canada)

The Doukhobors are Canadians of Russian origin living primarily in the western provinces of Canada, but their beginnings in Russia are unknown. The name "Doukhobors," or "Spirit Wrestlers," was given them in derision by the Russian Orthodox clergy in Russia as far back as 1785. The Doukhobors were persecuted by the church for rejecting Orthodoxy, and following the counsel of their leader, Peter V. Verigin, earned the wrath of the Tsarist government by destroying all of their weapons and adopting pacifism in 1895. In 1899 the Tsarist government allowed 8,000 Doukhobors to leave Russia in response to an international uproar over their persecution by the church and state. They made their way to Canada with the assistance of Count Leo Tolstoy, who saw in these people the living embodiment of his philosophy, the Religious

206

Society of Friends, commonly known as Quakers and other people of good will. Originally settled in Saskatchewan, by 1911 the majority followed Verigin to Bristish Columbia because of government efforts to assismilate them.

The teaching of the Doukhobors is penetrated with the Gospel spirit of love. Worshiping God in the spirit, they affirm that the outward church and all that is performed in it and concerns it has no importance for them; the church is where two or three are gathered together, united in the name of Christ. They do not believe in icon worship or in intermediaries between themselves and God. Their spiritual teachings are founded on ancient tradition, which they call the "Book of Life," because it lives in their memory and hearts. In this book are psalms composed by their elders and leaders, partly formed out of the contents of the Bible partly out of their historical experience. These are committed to memory by each succeeding generation. Doukhobors observe complete pacifism and non-violence, are lacto-vegetarians, and attempt to maintain a communal lifestyle.

The majority of Canadian Doukhobors were reorganized in 1938 by Peter P. Verigin, son of P.V. Verigin, shortly before his death, into the Union of Spiritual Communities of Christ to distinguish themselves from a radical off shoot who call themselves Sons of Freedom, and whose embrace of nudity and depradations has been sensationalized by the media and has stigmatized all Doukhobors. Today the USCC is governed by Trustees elected from member communities and administered by an elected Executive Committee headed by Honourary Chairman, John J. Verigin, CM OBC. The USCC executes the will and protects the interests of its member communities and its members living beyond south central British Columbia where the USCC is headquartered. The USCC is the largest organization of Doukhobors and maintains relations with other Doukhobor groups across Canada, in the USA, the Russian Federation, the Ukraine, and Georgia. The USCC also cooperates with other non governmental organizations working non violently to promote peace and justice, and respect for human didgnity and ecological integrity.

Headquarters
USCC Central Office, Box 760, Grand Forks, BC V0H 1H0 Tel. (250)442-8252 Fax (250)442-3433

Media Contact, John J. Verigin, Sr.

Officers
Hon. Chmn. of the Exec. Comm., John J. Verigin, Sr.

Chpsn., Fred Bojey

Periodicals
ISKRA

United Brethren Church in Canada
Founded in 1767 in Lancaster County, Pennsylvania, missionaries came to Canada about 1850. The first class was held in Kitchener in 1855, and the first building was erected in Port Elgin in 1867.

The Church of the United Brethren in Christ had its beginning with Philip William Otterbein and Martin Boehm, who were leaders in the revivalistic movement in Pennsylvania and Maryland during the late 1760s.

Headquarters
302 Lake St., Huntington, IN 46750 Tel. (219) 356-2312 Fax (219)356-4730

GENERAL OFFICERS
Pres., Rev. Brian Magnus, 120 Fife Rd., Guelph, ON N1H 6Y2 Tel. (519)836-0180

Treas., Brian Winger, 2233 Hurontario St., Apt. 916, Mississauga, ON L5A 2E9 Tel. (905)275-8140

The United Church of Canada
The United Church of Canada was formed on June 10, 1925, through the union of the Methodist Church, Canada, the Congregational Union of Canada, the Council of Local Union Churches and 70 percent of the Presbyterian Church in Canada. The union culminated years of negotiation between the churches, all of which had integral associations with the development and history of the nation.

In fulfillment of its mandate to be a uniting as well as a United Church, the denomination has been enriched by other unions during its history. The Wesleyan Methodist Church of Bermuda joined in 1930. On January 1, 1968, the Canada Conference of the Evangelical United Brethren became part of The United Church of Canada. At various times, congregations of other Christian communions have also become congregations of the United Church.

The United Church of Canada is a full member of the World Methodist Council, the World Alliance of Reformed Churches (Presbyterian and Congregational), and the Canadian and World Councils of Churches. The United Church is the largest Protestant denomination in Canada.

NATIONAL OFFICES
General Council Office, 3250 Bloor St. W., Ste. 300, Toronto, ON M8X 2Y4 Tel. (416)231-5931 Fax (416)231-3103, Email: info@united-church.ca, Web: www.united-church.ca

Media Contact, Communications Officer, Mary Frances Denis

GENERAL COUNCIL
Mod., Rt. Rev. Peter B. Short

Gen. Sec., Rev. James H. Sinclair

GENERAL COUNCIL MINISTERS
Planning Processes, Janet McDonald Programs for Mission & Ministry, Rev. Bruce Gregersen

207

Racial Justice, Kim Uyeded-Kai

Regional Relations, Rev. Carol L. Hancock

Resources for Mission & Ministry, Ian S. Fraser

Archivist, Sharon Larade, 73 Queen's Park Cr. E., Toronto, ON M5C 1K7 Tel. (416)585-4563 Fax (416)585-4584, Email: uccvu.archives @utoronto.ca, Web: www.united-church.ca/ archives

ADMINISTRATIVE UNITS
(Executive Ministers)

Ethnic Ministries, Exec. Min., Rev. Richard C. Choe

Faith Formation and Education, Exec. Min., Rev. Steven Chambers

Financial Services, Exec. Officer, Ron Olsen

Financial Stewardship, Exec. Min., Rev. William Steadman

Information Technology Services, Exec. Officer, -vacant-

Justice, Global & Ecumenical Relations, Exec. Min., Omega C. Bula

Ministries in French, Exec. Min., Rev. Pierre Goldberger

Ministry & Employment Policies & Services, Exec. Min., Michael Burke

Resource Production and Distribution, Exec. Min., -vacant-

Support to Local Ministries, Exec. Min., Rev. Harry Oussoren

CONFERENCE EXECUTIVE SECRETARIES

Alberta and Northwest, Rev. Lynn I. Maki, 9911-48 Ave., NW, Edmonton, AB T6E 5V6 Tel. (780)435-3995 Fax (780)438-3317, Email: coffice@anwconf.com

All Native Circle, Speaker, Cheryl Jourdain, 367 Selkirk Ave., Winnipeg, MB R2W 2M3 Tel. (204)582-5518 Fax (204)582-6649, Email: allnative@mts.net

Bay of Quinte, Rev. Wendy Bulloch, P.O. Box 700, 67 Mill St., Frankford, ON K0K 2C0 Tel. (613)398-1051 Fax (613)398-8894, Email: bayq.conference@sympatico.ca

British Columbia, Rev. Douglas Goodwin, 4383 Rumble St., Burnaby, BC V5J 2A2 Tel. (604)431-0434 Fax (604)431-0439, Email: bcconf@bc.united-church.ca

Hamilton, Rev. Fred Monteith, Box 100, Carlisle, ON L0R 1H0 Tel. (905)659-3343 Fax (905)659-7766, Email: office@hamconf.org

London, W. Peter Scott, 747 Hyde Park Rd., Ste 116, London, ON N6H 3S3 Tel. (519)672-1930 Fax (519)439-2800, Email: lonconf @execulink.com

Manitoba and Northwestern Ontario, Rev. Bruce Faurschou, 170 Saint Mary's Rd., Winnipeg, MB R2H 1H9 Tel. (204)233-8911 Fax (204) 233-3289, Email: office@confmnwo.mb.ca

Manitou, Rev. Rev. William Kunder, 319 McKenzie Ave., North Bay, ON P1B 7E3 Tel. (705)474-3350 Fax (705)497-3597, Email: office@manitouconference.ca

Maritime, Rev. Catherine H. Gaw, 32 York St., Sackville, NB E4L 4R4 Tel. (506)536-1334 Fax (506)536-2900, Email: info@marconf.ca

Montreal and Ottawa, Rev. Rosemary Lambie, 225-50 Ave., Lachine, QC H8T 2T7 Tel. (514) 634-7015 Fax (514)634-2489, Email: lachine @istar.ca

Newfoundland and Labrador, Rev. William G. Bartlett, 320 Elizabeth Ave., St. John's, NL A1B 1T9 Tel. (709)754-0386 Fax (709)754-8336, Email: unitedchurch@nfld.net

Saskatchewan, Rev. G. Robert Campbell, 418 A. McDonald St., Regina, SK S4N 6E1 Tel. (306)721-3311 Fax (306)721-3171, Email: ucskco@sasktel.net

Toronto, Rev. David W. Allen, 65 Mayall Ave., Downsview, ON M3L 1E7 Tel. (416)241-2677 Fax (416)241-2689, Email: torontoconference @bellnet.ca

Periodicals

United Church Observer, Mandate, Aujourd'hui Credo

United Pentecostal Church in Canada

This body, which is affiliated with the United Pentecostal Church, International, with headquarters in Hazelwood, Missouri, accepts the Bible standard of full salvation, which is repentance, baptism by immersion in the name of the Lord Jesus Christ for the remission of sins and the baptism of the Holy Ghost, with the initial signs of speaking in tongues as the Spirit gives utterance. Other tenets of faith include the Oneness of God in Christ, holiness, divine healing and the second coming of Jesus Christ.

Headquarters

United Pentecostal Church Intl., 8855 Dunn Rd., Hazelwood, MO 63042 Tel. (314)837-7300 Fax (314)837-4503

Media Contact, Gen. Sec.-Treas., Rev. C. M. Becton

DISTRICT SUPERINTENDENTS

Atlantic, Rev. Harry Lewis, P.O. Box 1046, Perth Andover, NB E0J 1V0

British Columbia, Rev. Paul V. Reynolds, 13447-112th Ave., Surrey, BC V3R 2E7

Canadian Plains, Rev. Johnny King, 615 Northmount Dr., NW, Calgary, AB T2K 3J6

Central Canadian, Rev. Clifford Heaslip, 4215 Roblin Blvd., Winnipeg, MB R3R 0E8

Newfoundland, Jack Cunningham

Nova Scotia, Superintendent, Rev. John D. Mean, P.O. Box 2183, D.E.P.S., Dartmouth, NS B2W 3Y2

Ontario, Rev. Carl H. Stephenson, 63 Castlegrove Blvd., Don Mills, ON M3A 1L3

Universal Fellowship of Metropolitan Community Churches

The Universal Fellowship of Metropolitan Community Churches is a Christian church which directs a special ministry within, and on behalf of, the gay and lesbian community. Involvement, however, is not exclusively limited to gays and lesbians; U.F.M.C.C. tries to stress its openness to all people and does not call itself a "gay church."

Founded in 1968 in Los Angeles by the Rev. Troy Perry, the U.F.M.C.C. has over 300 member congregations worldwide. Congregations are in Vancouver, Edmonton, Windsor, London, Toronto, Ottawa (2), Guelph, Fredericton, Winnipeg, Halifax, Barrie and Belleville.

Theologically, the Metropolitan Community Churches stand within the mainstream of Christian doctrine, being "ecumenical" or "interdenominational" in stance (albeit a "denomination" in their own right).

The Metropolitan Community Churches are characterized by their belief that the love of God is a gift, freely offered to all people, regardless of sexual orientation and that no incompatibility exists between human sexuality and the Christian faith.

The Metropolitan Community Churches in Canada were founded in Toronto in 1973 by the Rev. Robert Wolfe.

Headquarters
Media Contact: The Rev.Cheryl Meyer, 135 Simpson Ave., Totonto, ON M4K 1A4

The Wesleyan Church of Canada
This group is the Canadian portion of The Wesleyan Church which consists of the Atlantic and Central Canada districts. The Central Canada District of the former Wesleyan Methodist Church of America was organized at Winchester, Ontario, in 1889 and the Atlantic District was founded in 1888 as the Alliance of the Reformed Baptist Church, which merged with the Wesleyan Methodist Church in July, 1966.

The Wesleyan Methodist Church and the Pilgrim Holiness Church merged in June, 1968, to become The Wesleyan Church. The doctrine is evangelical and Wesleyan Arminian and stresses holiness beliefs. For more details, consult the U.S. listing under The Wesleyan Church.

Headquarters
The Wesleyan Church Intl. Center, P.O. Box 50434, Indianapolis, IN 46250-0434

Media Contact, Dist. Supt., Central Canada, Rev. Donald E. Hodgins, 17 Saint paul St., Belleview, ON K8N 1A4 Tel. (613)966-7527 Fax (613)968-6190

DISTRICT SUPERINTENDENTS
Central Canada, Rev. Donald E. Hodgins, 17 Saint paul St., Belleview, ON K8N 1A4, Email: ccd@on.aibn.com

Atlantic, Rev. Dr. H. C. Wilson, 1600 Main st., Ste. 216, Moncton, NB E1E 1G5, Email: ncwilson@nbnet.nb.ca

Periodicals
Central Canada, The Clarion

Religious Bodies in Canada
Arranged by Families

The following list of religious bodies appearing in the Directory Section of the *Yearbook* shows the "families," or related clusters into which Canadian religious bodies can be grouped. For example, there are many communions that can be grouped under the heading "Baptist" for historical and theological reasons. It should not be assumed, however, that all denominations under one family heading are necessarily consistent in belief or practice. The family clusters tend to represent historical factors more often than theological or practical ones. These family categories provide one of the major pitfalls when compiling church statistics because there is often a tendency to combine the statistics by "families" for analytical and comparative purposes. Such combined totals are deeply flawed, even though they are often used as variables for sociological analysis. The arrangement by families offered here is intended only as a general guide for conceptual organization when viewing the broad sweep of Canadian religious culture.

Religious bodies that cannot be categorized under family headings appear alphabetically and are not indented in the following list.

The Anglican Church of Canada
Apostolic Christian Church (Nazarene)
Armenian Evangelical Church
Associated Gospel Churches

Baptist Bodies
Association of Regular Baptist Churches (Canada)
Baptist Convention of Ontario and Quebec
Baptist General Conference of Canada
Baptist Union of Western Canada
Canadian Baptist Ministries
Canadian Convention of Southern Baptists
Convention of Atlantic Baptist Churches
The Fellowship of Evangelical Baptist Churches in Canada
Free Will Baptists
North American Baptist Conference
Union d'Eglises Baptistes Françaises au Canada

Brethren in Christ Church, Canadian Conference
Canadian District of the Moravian Church in America, Northern Province
Canadian Evangelical Christian Churches
Canadian Yearly Meeting of the Religious Society of Friends
Christ Catholic Church International
Christian Brethren (also known as Plymouth Brethren)
Christian and Missionary Alliance in Canada
Church of God (Anderson, Ind.)
Church of the Nazarene in Canada

Churches of Christ—Christian Churches
Christian Church (Disciples of Christ) in Canada
Christian Churches / Churches of Christ
Churches of Christ in Canada

Congregational Christian Churches in Canada

Eastern Orthodox Churches
The Antiochian Orthodox Christian Archdiocese of North America
Greek Orthodox Metropolis of Toronto (Canada)
Orthodox Church in America (Canada Section)
Patriarchal Parishes of the Russian Orthodox Church in Canada
Romanian Orthodox Church in America (Canadian Parishes)
The Romanian Orthodox Episcopate of America (Jackson, MI)
Serbian Orthodox Church in the U.S.A. and Canada, Diocese of Canada
Ukrainian Orthodox Church of Canada

The Evangelical Covenant Church of Canada
Evangelical Free Church of Canada
The Evangelical Missionary Church of Canada
General Church of the New Jerusalem
Jehovah's Witnesses

Latter-day Saints (Mormons)
The Church of Jesus Christ of Latter-day Saints in Canada
Community of Christ

Lutheran Bodies
Church of the Lutheran Brethren
The Estonian Evangelical Lutheran Church
Evangelical Lutheran Church in Canada
Lutheran Church—Canada

Mennonite Bodies
Canadian Conference of Mennonite Brethren Churches
Church of God in Christ (Mennonite)

The Evangelical Mennonite Conference
Evangelical Mennonite Mission Conference
Mennonite Church Canada
Old Order Amish Church
Reinland Mennonite Church

Methodist Bodies
British Methodist Episcopal Church of Canada
Free Methodist Church in Canada
Independent Holiness Church
The Wesleyan Church of Canada

The Old Catholic Church of Canada
Open Bible Faith Fellowship of Canada

Oriental Orthodox Churches
Armenian Holy Apostolic Church—Canadian Diocese
The Coptic Orthodox Church in Canada
Syriac Orthodox Church of Antioch

Pentecostal Bodies
The Apostolic Church in Canada
Apostolic Church of Pentecost of Canada Inc.
The Bible Holiness Movement
Canadian Assemblies of God (formerly The Italian Pentecostal Church of Canada)
Church of God (Cleveland, Tenn.)
The Church of God of Prophecy in Canada
Elim Fellowship of Evangelical Churches and Ministers
Foursquare Gospel Church of Canada
Independent Assemblies of God International (Canada)
The Pentecostal Assemblies of Canada
Pentecostal Assemblies of Newfoundland
United Pentecostal Church in Canada

Reformed Bodies
Canadian and American Reformed Churches
Christian Reformed Church in North America
Presbyterian Church in America (Canadian Section)
Presbyterian Church in Canada
Reformed Church in Canada

The Reformed Episcopal Church of Canada
The Roman Catholic Church in Canada
The Salvation Army in Canada
Seventh-day Adventist Church in Canada
Union of Spiritual Communities of Christ (Orthodox Doukhobors in Canada)
United Brethren Church in Canada
The United Church of Canada
Universal Fellowship of Metropolitan Community Churches

211

5. Sources of Religion-Related Research
I. Directory of Selected Research Organizations

The editorial office of the *Yearbook of American & Canadian Churches* receives innumerable requests for data about churches, religious organizations, attendance patterns, and comparative religion concerns. Sometimes we are able to furnish the requested data, but more often we refer the inquirer to other research colleagues in the field. We are always interested in and aided by such requests, and we find ourselves informed by each question.

In response to such inquiries, the "Sources in Religion-Related Research" directory was initiated in the 1999 edition of the *Yearbook* In addition to asking each organization to provide a brief overall description, each was also asked to indicate any special research foci (i.e., denominational, congregational, interfaith, gender, etc.). Further, each organization is asked to identify the sociological, methodological, or theological approaches that serve to guide their research, and to describe any current or recent research projects. Lastly, we asked for a list of recurrent publications. Below the organizations' responses to these questions are reported as clearly and completely as possible. Contact information appears just beneath the title of each organization. In most cases, the organization's website provides very detailed information about current research projects.

Numerous other research centers in the area of American religious life, each with specific areas of concern, conduct timely and significant research. We hope that readers will find utility in this directory and we invite them to identify additional sources by email: yearbook@ncccusa.org or by Fax: (212) 870-2817.

American Academy of Religion (AAR)

AAR Executive Office
825 Houston Mill Rd., Ste. 300
Atlanta, GA 30329
Tel. (404)727-7920
Fax (404)727-7959
Email: aar@aarweb.org
Website: www.aarweb.org
President: Dr. Diana Eck
Exec. Dir.: Dr.John Fitzmier

The AAR is the major learned society and professional association for scholars whose object of study is religion. Its mission—in a world where religion plays so central a role in social, political and economic events, as well as in the lives of communities and individuals—is to meet a critical need for ongoing reflection upon and understanding of religious traditions, issues, questions and values. As a learned society and professional association of teachers and research scholars, the American Academy of Religion has over 8500 members who teach in some 1,500 colleges, universities, seminaries, and schools in North America and abroad. The Academy is dedicated to furthering knowledge of religion and religious institutions in all their forms and manifestations. This is accomplished through Academy-wide and regional conferences and meetings, publications, programs, and membership services. Within a context of free inquiry and critical examination, the Academy welcomes all disciplined reflection on religion—both from within and outside of communities of belief and practice—and seeks to enhance its broad public understanding.

The AAR's annual meeting, over 8,000 scholars gather to share research and collaborate on scholarly projects. The annual meeting sessions are grouped into over 70 program units, each representing an ongoing community of scholars who are collectively engaged in pursuing knowledge about a specific religious tradition or a specific aspect of religion. In addition, the AAR's ten regional organizations sponsor smaller annual meetings that are similar in structure to the Academy-wide meeting. All of the world's major religious traditions, as well as indigenous and historical religions, are explored in the work of AAR members.

Current or Recent Research
Currently, for example, the AAR offers Teaching Workshops for both junior and senior scholars. It is organizing efforts to gather data on the field to facilitate departmental planning and funding. A full explanation of the many current research projects is available on the AAR website, which is listed above.

Periodicals
The Journal of the American Academy of Religion is the scholarly periodical of the AAR. In addition, the AAR publishes a quarterly newsletter, *Religious Studies News, AAR Edition.*

Association of Religion Data Archives (ARDA)

Department of Sociology
The Pennsylvania State University
211 Oswald Tower
University Park, PA 16802-6207
Tel. (814)865-6258
Fax (814)863-7216
Email: arda@pop.psu.edu
Website: www.TheARDA.com
Director: Dr. Roger Finke

The ARDA allows you to interactively explore the highest quality data on American and international religion using online features for generating national profiles, maps, church membership overviews, denominational heritage trees, tables, charts, and other summary reports. Nearly 400 data files are available for online preview and most can be downloaded for additional review. The ARDA (www.TheARDA.com) is supported by the Lilly Endowment and the John Templeton Foundation and is housed in the Social Science Research Institute at the Pennsylvania State University. All services are provided free of charge.

Association of Theological Schools (ATS)

10 Summit Park Dr.
Pittsburgh, PA 15275-1103
Tel. (412)788-6505
Fax (412)788-6510
Email: ats@ats.edu
Website: www.ats.edu
Exec. Dir.: Daniel O. Aleshire
Dir. of Communications and Membership Services: Nancy Merrill

The mission of The Association of Theological Schools in the United States and Canada (ATS) is to promote the improvement and enhancement of theological schools to the benefit of communities of faith and the broader public. The Association seeks to fulfill this mission by engaging in four core areas of work, (1) accreditation, (2) leadership education for administrative officers and faculty, (3) development of theological education, which involves the study of critical issues in theological education, and (4) communications and data.

The Association is a membership organization of approximately 250 graduate schools of theology, including Protestant, Roman Catholic, and Orthodox schools, both freestanding seminaries and university-related divinity schools. A full list of members is available on the above website.

Targeted areas of the Association's work currently include Theological Schools and the Church, the Character and Assessment of Learning for Religious Vocation, Race and Ethnicity in Theological Education, Women in Leadership in Theological Education, and Technology and Educational Practices.

Current or Recent Research

The ATS project on Theological Schools and the Church has three goals that, together, will provide a perspective about theological schools' relationships with ecclesial bodies and prescriptions for strengthening them. The goals are (1) to cultivate a broad-based conversation about the institutional relationships between theological schools and church bodies, (2) to define the current patterns of relationship between seminaries and their respective communities of faith, and (3) to develop proposals for strengthening and renewing institutional relationships that benefit both the church and theological schools.

A project on Technology and Educational Practices is identifying best practices in the use of educational technology in theological education, conducting educational events that provide information about and skill development in the use of educational technology, and creating resources about education and technology for use by theological schools.

Periodicals

Fact Book on Theological Education is published annually and provides statistical data on the member institutions. The Association publishes a journal, *Theological Education*, bi-annually, a bi-monthly newsletter entitled Colloquy, and the formal institutional documents of the Association entitled *Bulletin, part 2* of which is the ATS membership list.

Auburn Theological Seminary

3041 Broadway
New York, NY 10027

SOURCES

213

Tel. (212)662-4315
Fax (212)663-5214
Email: cste@auburnsem.org; krh@auburnsem.org; slm@auburnsem.org
Website: www.auburnsem.org
President: Dr. Barbara G. Wheeler
Executive Vice-President: Rev. Katharine R. Henderson

Auburn Theological Seminary's mission is to strengthen religious leadership. It carries out its mission through programs of non-degree theological education for clergy and laity; through programs for Presbyterian students enrolled at its partner institution, Union Seminary in New York City; and by conducting research on theological education at its Center for the Study of Theological Education. Auburn was founded in 1818 in Auburn, New York; it is currently located on Union Seminary's campus.

Auburn Seminary is related by covenant agreement with Presbyterian Church (U.S.A.), but most of its programs are ecumenical, and many have a multi-faith focus. The Center for the Study of Theological Education includes rabbinical schools and Protestant and Roman Catholic seminaries and divinity schools in its studies.

Research is conducted using a variety of methods, including survey and ethnographic research, structured interview and documentary research, research reports on surveys and case studies. Reports of findings are frequently published with accompanying information on the history of the issue being studied and with theological commentaries written from a variety of perspectives.

Current or Recent Research

The Center is undertaking a systematic study of U.S. and Canadian MA's level graduates from across the religious spectrum in order to find out how graduates have used their theological training, how many are in ministry five and ten years after graduation, and how they look back and assess their seminary experience. A second study underway is on seminary institutional advancement. Through analysis of available data, site visits, surveys and interviews, the researchers will examine the techniques, costs, best practices and barriers to effective fundraising in theological schools.

Periodicals

Auburn Studies, an occasional bulletin in which the Center publishes its research results. Research reports are also available on Auburn's website (listed above).

The Barna Group, Ltd.

1957 Eastman Ave., Suite B
Ventura, CA 93003
Tel. (805)658-8885
Fax (805)658-7298
Email: barna@barna.org
Website: www.barna.org
President: George Barna
President: David Kinnaman

The Barna Group conducts primary research related to cultural change, people's lifestyles, values, attitudes, beliefs and religious practices.

Its vision is to provide current accurate and reliable information, in bite-sized pieces and at reasonable costs, to its clients to facilitate strategic decisions. Barna also produces many research-based books, reports, and ministry tools to help churches understand the national context of ministry. The organization works with churches from all Christian denominations.

It conducts projects based upon existing needs in the Church at-large, or for its clients specifically. Methodologically, The Barna Group uses both qualitative approaches (focus groups, depth interviews) and quantitative approaches (cross-sectional surveys, longitudinal studies, panel research).

Data collection methods include telephone surveys, mail surveys, in-person interviews, on-line surveys, self-administered surveys, focus groups.

Current or Recent Research

The Barna Group conducts more than 50 studies each year, covering a broad range of topics. Some of the recent non-proprietary studies completed are focused on understanding the state of the Church; the habits of highly effective churches; worship efficacy; the unchurched; strategies and techniques for developing lay leaders; understanding effective discipleship processes; pastoral profiles; beliefs, behaviors and core attitudes of ministry donors; Biblical knowledge, and many others.

Periodicals

The Barna Group offers a free bi-weekly report—*The Barna Update*—on current information related

214

to faith matters from its national non-proprietary research. This information is free to those who register for it at the website (listed above).

Center for Applied Research in the Apostolate (CARA)

Georgetown University
Washington, DC 20057
Tel. (202) 687-8080
Fax (202) 687-8083
Email: cara@georgetown.edu
Website: www.georgetown.edu/research/cara/index.html
Executive Director: Mary E. Bendyna, RSM, Ph.D.
Sr. Research Associate: Mary Gautier

CARA-the Center for Applied Research in the Apostolate is a not-for-profit research organization of the Roman Catholic Church. It operates on the premise that not only theological principles but also findings of the social sciences must be the basis for pastoral care.

CARA's mission since its founding in 1964 has been "To discover, promote, and apply modern techniques and scientific informational resources for practical use in a coordinated and effective approach to the Church's social and religious mission in the modern world, at home and overseas."

CARA performs a wide range of research studies and consulting services. Since its roots are Roman Catholic, many of its studies are done for dioceses, religious orders, parishes, and the United States Conference of Catholic Bishops. Interdenominational studies are also performed. Publishes The CARA Report, a research newsletter on Catholic Church related topics, four times a year and The Catholic Ministry Formation Directory, a guide and statistical compilation of enrollments for Catholic seminaries, diaconate formation programs, and lay ministry formation programs.

Periodicals
The Catholic Ministry Formation Directory

Center for the Study of Religion and American Culture

Indiana University
Purdue University at Indianapolis
425 University Blvd, Room 341
Indianapolis, IN 46202-5140
Tel. (317)274-8409
Fax (317)278-3354
Email: pgoff@iupui.edu
Website: www.iupui.edu/~raac
Director: Dr. Phillip Goff
Program Coordinator: Rebecca Vasko

The Center for the Study of Religion and American Culture is a research and public outreach institute devoted to the promotion of the understanding of the relation between religion and other features of American culture. Research methods are both inter-disciplinary and multi-disciplinary. Established in 1989, the Center is based in the School of Liberal Arts and Indiana University-Purdue University at Indianapolis. Center activities include national conferences and symposia, commissioned books, essays, bibliographies, and research projects, fellowships for younger scholars, data based communication about developments in the field of American religion, a newsletter devoted to the promotion of Center activities, and the semi-annual scholarly periodical, Religion and American Culture, A Journal of Interpretation.

Current or Recent Research
The Center is presently overseeing two intiatives. The "Young Scholars in American Religion Program" is a multi-year project to assist early-career scholars in developing their teaching skills and research agendas. The "Centers and Institutes Project," meanwhile, brings together those organizations dedicated to the academic study of religion in the U.S. in order to discuss common problems and solutions, as well as to identify areas for cooperative efforts. The work of these various centers and institutes will be highlighted in future issues of the "Newsletter from the Center for the Study of Religion and American Culture" and the Center's reception at the annual meeting of the American Academy of Religion.

We continue to explore other areas of potential research in the relation between religion and other aspects of American culture. As these projects materialize, they will be announced on this website and in the "Newsletter."

215

Periodicals

Religion and American Culture, A Journal of Interpretation. Center books include the series, *The Public Expressions of Religion in America.*

empty tomb, inc.

301 North Fourth Street
P.O. Box 2404
Champaign, IL 61825-2404
Tel. (217)356-9519
Fax (217)356-2344
Email: research@emptytomb.org
Website: www.emptytomb.org
CEO: John L. Ronsvalle
Exec.Vice-Pres.: Sylvia Ronsvalle

empty tomb, inc. is a Christian research and service organization. On a local level, it coordinates direct services to people in need in cooperation with area congregations. On a national level, it studies church member giving patterns of historically Christian churches, including Roman Catholic, mainline and evangelical Protestant, Anabaptist, Pentecostal, Orthodox, and fundamentalist communions. empty tomb publishes the annual State of Church Giving series. Also, empty tomb offers a mission funding incentive program, Mission Match, in an effort to help reverse the negative giving trends indicated by national data.

Current or Recent Research

Current research monitors and analyzes church member giving patterns, and is published in The State of Church Giving series produced by empty tomb, inc.

Periodicals

The State of Church Giving series is an annual publication. It considers denominational giving data, analysis of giving and membership trends, and other estimates of charitable giving. Each edition has featured a special focus chapter, which discusses giving issues relevant to church giving patterns. Past *State of Church Giving* special focus chapters are posted on the www.emptytomb.org website.

The Hartford Institute for Religion Research of Hartford Seminary

Hartford Seminary
77 Sherman Street
Hartford, CT 06105
Tel. (860)509-9543
Fax (860)509-9551
Email: hirr@hartsem.edu
Website: www.hirr.hartsem.edu
Director of Research: Dr. David A. Roozen
Administrative Assistant: Mary Jane Ross

The Hartford Institute for Religion Research of Hartford Seminary was established in 1981, formalizing a research program initiated by the Seminary in 1974. Until recently it was known as The Center for Social and Religious Research. The Institute's work is guided by a disciplined understanding of the interrelationship between (a) the inner life and resources of American religious institutions and (b) the possibilities and limits placed on those institutions by the social and cultural context into which God has called them.

Its twenty-one year record of rigorous, policy-relevant research, anticipation of emerging issues, commitment to the creative dissemination of learning, and strong connections to both theological education and the church has earned the Institute an international reputation as an important bridge between the scholarly community and the practice of ministry.

Current or Recent Research

Some of the titles of current projects at the Institute are, Organizing Religious Work for the 21st Century, Exploring Denominationalism; Cooperative Congregational Studies Project; Congregational Consulting Services; New England Religion Discussion Society (NERDS); Congregational Studies Team. Descriptions of these programs are available on the Institute's website, listed above.

Periodicals

Praxis is Hartford Seminary's magazine, which focuses on the activities and faculty of the Seminary.

Institute for Ecumenical & Cultural Research

14027 Fruit Farm Road
PO Box 2000
Collegeville, MN 56321-2000
Tel. (320)363-3366
Fax (320)363-3313
Email: iecr@iecr.org; mbanken@iecr.org
Website: www.iecr.org
Exec. Dir.: Dr. Don B. Ottenhoff
Administrative Assistant: Mary Beth Banken, OSB

The Institute for Ecumenical and Cultural Research brings together well-trained, creative, articulate men and women for careful thought and dialogue in a place of inquiry and prayer. The Resident scholars Program welcomes researchers and their families for either individual semesters or for an entire academic year. Resident scholars work on their own projects but meet once a week for seminars, and have other occasions for conversation. Each scholar presents a public lecture. Ecumenism happens at the Institute as people come to know one another in community. The Institute is an independent corporation, but shares in the Benedictine and academic life of Saint John's Abbey and University, and of nearby Saint Benedict's Monastery and the College of Saint Benedict. In the summer the Institute uses its facilities for invitational consultations on subjects considered by the Board of Directors to be of special ecumenical interest.

In the Resident Scholars Program, the subjects of research are determined by the interests of the applicants who are invited to come by the Admissions Committee. While most of the work tends to be in traditional theological areas, we encourage people in all fields to consider applying, both because ecumenism is of concern across the spectrum of disciplines, and because the term "cultural" in our title extends our reach beyond theology and religious studies. In particular cases, work done here may have a denominational, congregational, or interfaith focus, but the Institute does not prescribe or delimit, in any narrow way, what is appropriate.

Current or Recent Research

Recent summer consultations have had the following titles, "Ecumenical Formation: The Heart of the Matter"; "Igniting Biblical Imagination." Among subjects dealt with in earlier years are "Prayer in the Ecumenical Movement"; "Virtues for an Ecumenical Heart"; "The Price of Disunity"; "Living Faithfully in North America Today"; "Orthodoxy at Home in North America"; "transmitting Tradition to Children and Young People"; "The Nature of Christian Hope"; "Women and the Church"; "Jewish and Christian Relatedness to Scripture"; "Confessing Christian Faith in a Pluralistic Society."

Periodicals

Ecumenical People, Programs, Papers is an bi-annual newsletter containing brief sketches of resident scholars, reports on Institute programs, and, in nearly every issue, *An Occasional Paper* on a subject of ecumenical interest. The newsletter is free.

Institute for the Study of American Evangelicals (ISAE)

Wheaton College
Wheaton, IL 60187
Tel. (630)752-5437
Fax (630)752-5516
Email: isae@wheaton.edu
Website: www.wheaton.edu/isae
Director: Dr. Edith Blumhofer
Reserch and Resource Assistant: Katria Delac

Founded in 1982, the Institute for the Study of American Evangelicals is a center for research and functions as a program of Wheaton College. The purpose of the ISAE is to encourage and support research on evangelical Christianity in the United States and Canada. The institute seeks to help evangelicals develop a mature understanding of their own heritage and to inform others about evangelicals' historical significance and contemporary role. For the most part, the ISAE focuses on historical research, with occasional sociological or economic researchers participating in the projects.

Current or Recent Research

One recently completed project entitled "Hymnody in American Protestantism" was a research project focusing on the history of hymnology in American religious life. We have published two books from this project: "Singing the Lord's Song in a Strange Land" by University of Alabama Press and

"Wonderful Words of Life: Hymns in American Protestant History and Theology" published by William B. Eerdmans.

Two new projects include "Confessional Traditions and American Christianity," a grant from the Lilly Endowment, Inc., and "The Changing Face of American Evangelicalism," a grant from the Henry Luce Foundation.

Periodicals

Evangelical Studies Bulletin (ESB) is designed to aid both the scholar and the layman in his or her education and research of evangelicalism. Issued quarterly, the bulletin contains articles, book reviews, notices, a calendar of events, and bibliographic information on the latest dissertations, articles and books related to the study of evangelicals.

Institute for the Study of American Religion

P.O. Box 90709
Santa Barbara, CA 93190-0709
Tel. (805)967-7721
Email: jgordon@linkline.com
Website: www.americanreligion.org
Director: Dr. J. Gordon Melton
Associate Director: Dr. James Beverley

The Institute for the Study of American Religion was founded in 1968 in Evanston, Illinois as a religious studies research facility with a particular focus upon the smaller religions of the United States. Those groups that it has concentrated upon have been known under a variety of labels including sect, cult, minority religion, alternative religion, non-conventional religion, spiritual movement, and new religious movement. In the 1970'2 the Institute extended its attention to Canada and in the 1990s developed an even more global focus. In 1985, the institute moved to its present location in Santa Barbara, California.

Over the years the institute built a large collection of both primary and secondary materials on the religious groups and movements it studied. In 1985 this collection of more than 40,000 volumes and thousands of periodicals and archival materials was deposited with the Davidson Library at the University of California in Santa Barbara. The reference material exists today as the American Religions Collection and is open to scholars and the interested public. The institute continues to support the collection with donations of additional materials.

Current or Recent Research

Today the institute has two main foci. It monitors all of the religious denominations, organizations, and movements functioning in North America and regularly publishes reports drawing from that activity in a series of reference books. The most important of these reference books is the *Encyclopedia of American Religions* (Detroit, Gale Group, 7th edition, 2002).

Among the most called for information is factual data on the many new and more controversial religious movements, which are popularly labeled as "cults." The institute's second focus developed out of its more recent refocusing on the international scene, provoked by the international life of most of the religious groups which it has studied in previous decades.

J.M. Dawson Institute of Church-State Studies at Baylor University

P.O. Box 97308
Waco, TX 76798-7308
Tel. (254)710-1510
Fax (254)710-1571
Email: derek_davis@baylor.edu
Website: www.baylor.edu/~Church_State
Director: Dr. Derek Davis
Administrative Assistant: Wanda Gilbert

Baylor University established the J.M. Dawson Institute of Church-State Studies in 1957, so named in honor of an outstanding alumnus, an ardent advocate of religious liberty, and a distinguished author of publications on church and state. The Institute is the oldest and most well-established facility of its kind located in a university setting. It is exclusively devoted to research in the broad field of church and state and the advancement of religious liberty around the world.

From its inception in 1957, the stated purpose of the Institute has been to stimulate academic interest and encourage research and publication in the broad area of church-state relations. In carrying out its statement of purpose, the Institute has sought to honor a threefold commitment, to be interfaith, interdisciplinary, and international.

218

Current or Recent Research

Some current research includes, Government persecution of minority religions in Europe; original intent of Founding Fathers regarding religion and public life; Christian Right views on political activism; conservative versus moderate Baptist views on church-state relations; role of civil religion in America; international treaties and religious liberty.

Periodicals

Journal of Church and State is the only scholarly journal expressly devoted to church-state relations.

The Louisville Institute

1044 Alta Vista Road
Louisville, KY 40205-1798
Tel. (502) 992-9341
Fax (502) 894-2286
Email: jlewis@louisville-institute.org
Website: www.louisville-institute.org
Exec. Dir.: Dr. James W. Lewis
Exec. Dir.: Dr. James W. Lewis

The Louisville Institute is a Lilly Endowment program for the study of American religion based at the Louisville Presbyterian Seminary. As a program of Lilly Endowment, the Louisville Institute builds upon the Endowment's long-standing support of both leadership education and scholarly research on American religion. The distinctive mission of the Louisville Institute is to enrich the religious life of American Christians and to encourage the revitalization of their institutions by bringing together those who lead religious institutions with those who study them, so that the work of each might stimulate and inform the other. The Louisville Institute seeks to fulfill its mission through a coordinated strategy of grantmaking and convening within a programmatic focus on three issues. The first, Christian faith and life, concerns the character and role of the theology and spirituality that are effectively at work in the lives of American Christians. The second, religious institutions, asks how America's religious institutions might respond most constructively in the midst of the bewildering institutional reconfiguration occurring in American society.

The third, pastoral leadership, explores various strategies for improving the quality of religious leadership in North America. The several grant programs of the Louisville Institute offer financial support to a broad range of projects that seek to address both the mission of the Louisville Institute to bring pastors and academics together and the Institute's focus on Christian faith and life, religious institutions, and pastoral leadership. Although many of these grants support research projects, an increasing number of them support other types of projects that contribute to the work of the Louisville Institute.

Current or Recent Research

Please see the Louisville Institute website (listed above) for lists of recent grants made by the Louisville Institute.

Periodicals

Intersections

The Pluralism Project

Harvard University
1531 Cambridge St.
Cambridge, MA 02139
Tel. (617)496-2481
Fax (617)496-2428
Email: staff@pluralism.org
Website: www.pluralsm.org
Director: Dr. Diana L. Eck
Assistant Manager: Kathryn Lohre

The Pluralism Project was developed by Dr. Diana L. Eck at Harvard University to study and document the growing religious diversity of the United States, with a special view to its new immigrant religious communities. The religious landscape of the U.S. has radically changed in the past forty years; in light of these changes, how Americans of all faiths begin to engage with one another in shaping a positive pluralism is one of the most important questions American society faces in the years ahead. In addressing these phenomena, the Project has four goals: 1) To document and

219

better understand the changing contours of American religious demography, focusing especially on those cities and towns where the new plurality has been most evident and discerning the ways in which this plurality is both visible and invisible in American public life. 2) To study the religious communities themselves ¬ their temples, mosques, gurudwaras and retreat centers, their informal networks and emerging institutions, their forms of adaptation and religious education in the American context, their encounter with the other religious traditions of our common society, and their encounter with civic institutions. 3) To explore the ramifications and implications of America's new plurality through case studies of particular cities and towns, looking at the response of Christian and Jewish communities to their new neighbors; the development of interfaith councils and networks; the new theological and pastoral questions that emerge from the pluralistic context; and the recasting of traditional church-state issues in a wider context. 4) To discern, in light of this work, the emerging meanings of religious "pluralism," both for religious communities and for public institutions, and to consider the real challenges and opportunities of a public commitment to pluralism in the light of the new religious contours of America.

The Pluralism Project has the most comprehensive archive anywhere of the print materials of America's new immigrant religious communities, including newsletters, serial publications, anniversary programs, handbooks, prayer books, calendars, and educational materials donated directly by centers. The Project files also include numerous research papers, profiles of centers, and information on events, all available at www.pluralism.org.

The Pluralism Project On-Line Directory maintains an extensive directory of religious centers in the United States. At present, this directory exists in a searchable database, with listings of over six thousand centers across the U.S.

Current or Recent Research

The Pluralism Project produced a CD-ROM, "On Common Ground — World Religions in America," to present some of the wide range of work that had emerged from three years of research. Numerous affiliate research reports from a wide network of university professors and students are available on their website. Religious Diversity News summarizes news stories on pressing issues in the United States including most minority faiths, with a companion International News; both of these resources are available online in searchable databases, with archives back to 1997. In 2005 the Pluralism Project released, "Acting on Faith: Women's New Religious Activism," available on VHS and DVD. "World Religions in Boston: A Guide to Communities and Resources," is an online resource that profiles many of the diverse religions centers in the Boston area. Current research includes The Interfaith Initiative, The City Hall Initiative, The Women's Initiative, and The International Initiative. One can subscribe to their monthly e-newsletter online.

II. Directory of Selected Faith Communities in America

Compiling a directory of faith communities is an arduous but rewarding task in religiously plural America. In part, this is true because the very self-understanding and definition of community varies so greatly from tradition to tradition. In order to present a reasonably parallel and well-balanced listing of organizations for each faith, care must be taken not to impose categories or terms from one's own universe of understanding upon other contexts. The very terms, "church," "membership," "denomination," and "hierarchy", which are essential constructs of certain Christian universes of understanding, are rendered meaningless when applied to other faith groups.

Further, it is important to remember that many religious communities lack a centralized organization that speaks for the whole. Often, this lack of centralization reflects the existence of several distinct forms or branches of the religion. In some instances, different ethnic groups immigrating to the U.S., bring with them a distinctive form of their religion, which is particular to their culture of origin. In other cases, plural forms of a faith exist resulting from theological, political, or economic differences. Still other faith groups may be more tightly organized, but the religious center that provides guidance in matters of faith and, perhaps, even organizational discipline may not be in the United States. Hence, the organizations before us are not necessarily religious hierarchical organizations, but are often groups assembled for other purposes that are associated with a particular faith group, or subdivision of that faith group. Caution is advised in regarding these entries as one might regard a "church headquarters."

The compilation of any directory relies upon the existence of some common organizational structure within all the entities listed. Yet, when compiling a directory of faith groups, it cannot be assumed such organizational parallels exist. Oblique ways must be found to adequately represent individual faith groups. The many religious communities in the United States are associated with myriad organizations of all different types. Some of these are primarily places of worship; others are organizations seeking to represent either the religious community as a whole or some particular constituency within it. Others are community centers; some are educational groups; some are organizations particularly for women or youths; and some are political action groups. Still others are peace organizations or relief organizations. That said, a directory of this sort cannot include an exhaustive list of organizations for each faith group nationwide. The omission of any particular organization or branch of any of the major faith groups listed does not reflect a deliberate attempt to homogenize the rich pluralities that exist within faith groups. Instead, the listings that follow are intended to provide the interested reader with a few initial contacts within each religious community, in alphabetical order within the tradition.

Despite the above cautions, this directory provides a rich resource for readers and researchers who wish to learn more about other faith groups. The agencies listed here consist of organizations of importance within the communities they represent, and serve as excellent introductory points of contact with those communities.

In some cases, these religious communities are in a state of flux; the Internet is an excellent way to keep contact with changing religious organizations. There is a plethora of information available about nearly all religious traditions online, but sites vary widely in their accuracy and reliability. Nearly any Internet search engine will provide extensive links to information about specific religious traditions.

For directory information about national interfaith organizations in the United States, please see Directory 1, "U.S. Cooperative Organizations." For directory information on local interfaith organizations, please see Directory 7, "U.S. Regional and Local Ecumenical Bodies."

BAHÁ'Í FAITH

The Bahá'í Faith arose in 19th-century Persia, and refers to followers of Mirza Hussein Ali Nuri, whom they call Baha'ullah (Arabic for *Glory of God*). In 1863, Bahá'u'lláh proclaimed himself to be the Manifestation of God for the present age. His coming had been heralded in 1844 by Mirza Ali Muhammad, also known as the Báb (*the Door*) whom Bahá'ís consider a Manifestation of God as well. Shortly afterward there was a severe persecution. The Báb was executed in 1850; Bahá'u'lláh died in exile, under house arrest in Acre, Palestine, in 1892. Bahá'ís believe in Progressive Revelation. Thus, as the manifestation of God for the present age, Bahá'u'lláh is considered to be the most recent in a lineage of messengers which includes Abraham, Krishna, the Buddha, Zarathustra, Jesus, and Muhammad. The oneness of God, the oneness of religion, and the oneness of humanity (with stress on racial and gender equality) are key principles of the Bahá'í Faith. Bahá'u'lláh's son Abd-al-Baha organized the religion's sacred texts, and established its system of representative governance through consensus, collaboration, and consultation. This includes the Universal House of Justice (the supreme administrative body, which meets in Haifa, Israel), National Spiritual Assemblies, and Local Spiritual Assemblies.

The Baha'i National Center of the U.S.A.
and, **The National Spiritual Assembly of the Bahà'ìs of the United States**

1233 Central Street
Evanston, IL 60201
Tel. (847)733-3559/3400 Fax (847)733-3578
Website: www.bahai.org

> The home of the National Spiritual Assembly of the Bahá'ís of the United States the center is an official source of information about the Bahá'í Faith, resources on many issues (such as peace, justice, economic development, racial unity, and education), and networking with Bahá'í spiritual assemblies throughout the world, of which there are more than 1700 in the U.S.A.

BUDDHISM

Buddhism is a Western term for the many and varied expressions of practices based on the teachings of Siddhartha Gautama, who lived in northern India c. 563-483 B.C.E.. Called the Buddha (the Enlightened One) by his followers, Siddhartha proposed a Middle Way between self-indulgence and extreme Hindu asceticism. Central to Buddhist teaching are the Four Noble Truths: that life inevitably involves suffering; that the origin of suffering is desire; that suffering can be eradicated by extinguishing desire; and that the way to accomplish this is to follow the Noble Eightfold Path of morality, concentration, and wisdom. Buddhists "take refuge" in the Triple Gem: the Buddha, the dhamma (his teachings), and the sangha (the community). Buddhism has two major branches. Theravada (Way of the Elders) which defines the sangha primarily as the community of ascetics. Mahayana (Great Vehicle) defines the sangha as all Buddhists, and includes the many schools Pure Land, Zen (Ch'an), and Tibetan Buddhism. Vajrayana (Diamond Vehicle) is a rigorous form of Mahayana associated frequently (but not exclusively) with Tibetan practice. Distinctive Western eclectic forms have emerged in recent decades. While there is much variation, Buddhist practice is characterized by meditation, chanting, and emphasis on compassion. Although most practice-groups and temples function autonomously and some are affiliated with a particular teacher or movement, there are continuing local or regional attempts to bridge philosophical differences.

American Buddhist Association

4524 N. Richmond Street
Chicago, IL 60625
Tel: (773)583-5794
Contact person: Richard Brandon (Zenyo)
Email: brightdawn_1@juno.org
Website: www.awakenedone.org

> Founded in 1955 for the study and propagation of Buddhism and to encourage the understanding and application of Buddhist principles in the general American public, this organization's roots are in Japanese Buddhism (Jodo Shinshu and Zen), but is now independent and nonsectarian. It publishes books, pamphlets, and audio-visual materials, sponsors seminars, and acts as a resource center.

American Buddhist Congress

3835 E. Thousand Oaks Blvd., Ste. 450
Westlake Village, CA 91362
Tel. (877)7BUDDHA, (877)728-3342
Email: BuddhistCongress@adelphia.net
Website: www.americanbuddhistcongress.org

> Founded in 1987 to bring together individuals and organizations of various Buddhist traditions, denominations, and ethnic backgrounds, this organization is dedicated to developing an "American" Buddhism which, while paying respect and acknowledging its debt to Buddhist traditions of other cultures, seeks to synthesize American values and traditions with the basic Buddhism of the tripitaka (scripture) without the linguistic and cultural aspects which are not understood or confusing to most Americans.

Buddhist Churches of America

1710 Octavia St.
San Francisco, CA 94109
Tel. (415)776-5600
Fax (415)771-6293
Email: bcahq@pacbell.net
Website: buddhistchurchesofamerica.org

Founded in 1899, this is a national headquarters and resource center for temples in the Japanese Shin (Pure Land) tradition. It also serves as a regional center of the World Fellowship of Buddhists

Buddhist Council of the Midwest

1812 Washington Street
Evanston, IL 60202
Tel. (847)869-5806
Fax (847)869-5806
Website: www.buddhistcouncilmidwest.org

Incorporated as a non-profit religious organization in 1987, the Buddhist Council of the Midwest includes 95 Buddhist groups in Chicago and the Midwest area. Its purpose is to foster the learning and practice of Buddhism; to represent the Midwest Buddhist community in matters affecting its membership; and to pool resources and coordinate efforts by its membership to create an atmosphere of fellowship and cooperation.

Buddhist Council of the Northwest

1530 184th Ave NE
Bellevue, WA 98008
Tel: (425)442-0986
Fax: (425)643-2490
Email: info@buddhistcouncilnw.org
Website: www.buddhistcouncilnw.org

Founded in 2002, the Buddhist Council of the Northwest is a non-profit organization formed to pool resources and coordinate efforts by its membership. It serves as a consultant to and advocate for Buddhist temples, study groups, and individuals on matters of cultural, legal, and government concern related to the preservation and promotion of the Buddha Dhamma (teaching) in the Pacific Northwest, with special focus on the Asian-American Buddhist temples and communities, and realizing and respecting the diversity of Buddhist traditions within the Pacific Northwest. It initiates and supports religious, cultural or social welfare project which will help to disseminate the spirit of the Buddha Dhamma, and works ecumenically with over religious groups.

The Buddhist Peace Fellowship

P.O. Box 3470
Berkeley, CA 94703
Tel. (510)655-6169
Fax (510)655-1369
Website: www.bpf.org

Founded in 1978, the Buddhist Peace Fellowship's purpose is to serve as a catalyst for socially engaged Buddhism, striving for peace where there is conflict, promoting communication and cooperation among Buddhist sanghas, and seeking to alleviate suffering wherever possible. BPF's programs, publications, and practice groups link Buddhist teachings of wisdom and compassion with progressive social change.

Insight Meditation Society

1230 Pleasant St.
Barre, MA 01005
Tel: (978)355-4378
Email: RC@dharma.org
Website: www.dharma.org

Dedicated to Vipassana (insight meditation), a practice associated with Theravada Buddhism, this is a loosely associated network of groups, including major centers in New York, Washington DC, Seattle, San Francisco, Los Angeles, and Boston, and smaller centers and practice groups in many other cities and towns.

New York Buddhist Council

c/o Staten Island Buddhist Vihara
115 John Street
Staten Island, NY 10302
Tel: (718)556-2051
Website: www.newyorkbuddhistcouncil.com

223

An umbrella organization bringing together the leaders of New York City's Buddhist organizations across traditions and ethnicities.

Soka Gakkai International-USA

National Headquarters
606 Wilshire Blvd.
Santa Monica, CA 90401
Tel: (310)260-8900
Fax: (310)260-8917
Website: www.sgi-usa.org

An American Buddhist association that promotes world peace and individual happiness based on the teachings of the Nichiren school of Mahayana Buddhism. Its members reflect a cross section of our diverse American society, representing a broad range of ethnic and social backgrounds.

Texas Buddhist Council

6007 Spindle Dr.
Houston, TX 77086
Tel. (281)445-5773

A regional coordinating body and advocacy agency for Buddhists of all traditions, it seeks to unify Buddhist practitioners across Texas by increasing communication between temples, study groups, and individuals from various schools and by providing opportunities for mutually beneficial interaction. It also strives to bring Buddhist teachings into the Texas mainstream through education and opportunities for social service.

Unified Buddhist Church, Inc.

c/o Green Mountain Dharma Center
Ayers Lane, P.O. Box 182
Hartland-Four-Corners, Vermont 05049, USA
Tel: (802)436-1103
Fax: (802)436-1101
Email: MF-Office@plumvillage.org
Website: www.plumvillage.org

This organization of Thich Nhat Hanh and his Sangha (network of practitioners and practice-groups) in the United States of America is also known as the Community of Mindful Living.

Won Buddhism of America Headquarters

143-42 Cherry Avenue
Flushing, NY 11355
Tel: (718)762-4103
Email: info@wonbuddhism.info

Won Buddhism is a Korean reform movement with many non-Korean adherents and an abiding commitment to promoting interreligious understanding. While this is the seat of the U.S. branch of the Won movement, English-speakers may find it easier to contact the Manhattan temple, 431 East 57th Street, New York, NY 10022, Tel: (212)750-2773

HINDUISM

Hinduism is a western term for *Sanatana Dharma* (Eternal Law), the various streams of practice, ancient texts, and theological traditions associated with the Indian subcontinent. Hindus worship Brahman (Ultimate Reality) which is both the formless Absolute and the divine-as-personal. Hindus fall into schools of devotion to particular forms of the ultimate-as-personal: *Vaishnavites* (devotees of Vishnu, known also through his *avatars* [manifestations] such as Rama and Krishna), *Shaivites* (devotees of Shiva), and devotees of the Parashakti, the Divine Feminine (embodied variously as Durga, Parvati, Kali, and more). Other deities may be regarded as subordinate to, or as personifications of various functions of, the ultimate-as-personal. In the U.S.A., an ecumenical Hindu theology which sees all deities as pointers to the one Brahman, and emphasizes the non-duality of all things is also prevalent. Hindus agree for the most part on notions of *karma* and reincarnation, but fall into various philosophical schools of thought regarding the nature of the divine-human relationship. Yoga can take the form of intellectual or physical discipline, selfless service, or devotional practices. Most Hindus acknowledge the authority of the Vedas, but some pay more attention to the Bhaghavad-Gita, the Yoga Sutras of Patanjali, or the writings of the founding guru of their movement. Most North American *mandirs* (temples) are autonomous, but some are affiliated with a national or international movement.

224

American Hindus Against Defamation

8914 Rotherdam Ave.
San Diego, CA 92129
Tel. (858)484-4564
Email: ajay@hindunet.org
Website: www.hindunet.org/ahad
Director, Mr. Ajay Shah

An organization devoted to defending Hindus from stereotyping and discriminatory or defamatory acts or speech.

Bochasanwasi Shri Akshar Purushottam Swaminarayan Sanstha (B.A.P.S.)

BAPS Swaminarayan Sanstha
81 Suttons Lane
Piscattaway, NJ 08854-5723
Tel. (732)777-1414
Fax (732)777-1616
Website: www.swaminarayan.org

B.A.P.S. is a reform movement within the Vaishnava Visishtadvaita tradition. This North American headquarters serves about 50 temples in U.S. & Canada.

Council of Hindu Temples of North America

Sri Siva Vishnu Temple
6905 Cipriano Road
Lanham, MD 20706
Tel. (301)552-3335
Email: info@councilofhindutemples.org
Website: www.councilofhindutemples.org
President: Dr. Siva Subramanian

The council is an independent association of autonomous temples and Hindu religious organizations which promotes the establishment of Hindu temples, encourages interfaith dialogue, and aids in instruction in Indian languages and culture.

The International Society for Krishna Consciousness (ISKCON)

26 Second Avenue, 10003
(mail: P. O. Box 2509)
New York, NY 10009
Tel. (212)253-6182
Email: Krishna.nyc@gmail.com

A modern expression of Vaishnavite belief and practice established by A. C. Bhaktivedanta Swami (called Prabhubapa by devotees), ISKCON is one of many Indian spiritual movements planted in North America during the 20th century. The Second Avenue temple, which dates from 1966, was the movement's first in the U.S.

Vedanta Society of New York

34 West 71st Street
New York, NY 10023
Tel. (212)877-9197, (212)873-7439
Email: Vedantasoc@aol.com
Website: www.vedanta-newyork.org

Founded in 1894, Vedanta Society of New York is the first Vedanta Center in the West, and has been joined by many other such centers. The various centers of the Vedanta Society are affiliates of the worldwide network of the Ramakrishna Order, headquartered in Belur Math, India. Adherents follow the teachings and example of Sri Ramakrishna (1836-1886), his wife and spiritual companion Holy Mother Sri Sarada Devi (1853-1920), and Ramakrishna's chief disciple Swami Vivekananda.

ISLAM

Islam dates to 7th-century Arabia and the Prophet Muhammad's receipt of the Qur'an. The word islam means submission, and is related linguistically to *salaam*, the Arabic word for peace. A Muslim is one who practices Islam by following the Qur'an and the Prophet's *sunna* (example). Muslims consider the Qur'an (in its original Arabic) to be God's speech. They place great emphasis on *tawhid*

225

(God's absolute oneness and its implications). They use the Arabic word Allah for God, stressing that it refers to God as worshiped by Jews and Christians as well. Muslims are to maintain Five Pillars of practice. The first of these is *iman*, the profession of faith called the *shahadah*, which states "There is no God but God, and Muhammad is his prophet." The second, *salah* is the ritual prayer, done five times a day, facing Mecca. Third, is *zakah*, the returning of a portion of one's wealth to the community annually. Fourth, is swam, the fasting from dawn to dusk during the holy month of Ramadan. Fifth, is *Hajj*, the pilgrimage to Mecca once in one's lifetime (health and means permitting). Early in its history, Islam split into two branches, Sunni and Shi'ah (and several subgroups of the latter) which differ on some matters of belief and practice, and notions of transmission of authority.

The Islamic Society of North America (ISNA)

P.O. Box 38
Plainfield, IN 46168
Tel. (317)839-8157
Fax (317)839-1840
Website: www.isna.com
Sec. Gen., Dr. Munner Fareed

> The Islamic Society of North America grew out of the Muslim Students Association and is one of the oldest national Muslim organizations in the United States. It has a varied program primarily serving the Muslim community, but also seeks to promote relations between Muslims and non-Muslims. It has a speakers' bureau, film loans, library assistance program, and several other services. It has also has a number of publications. Its annual convention during Labor Day weekend usually in Chicago attracts over 35,000 participants.

Council for American-Islamic Relations (CAIR)

453 New Jersey Ave. SE
Washington DC 20003-4034
Tel. (202)488-8787
Fax (202)488-0833
Email: info@cair.com
Website: www.cair.com

> CAIR's mission is to enhance understanding of Islam, encourage dialogue, protect civil liberties, empower American Muslims and build coalitions that promote justice and mutual understanding.

Islamic Circle of North America (ICNA)

166-26 89th Avenue
Jamaica, NY 11432
Tel. (718)658-1199
Fax (718)658-1255
Website: www.icna.org

> A non-ethnic, non-sectarian grassroots organization with a varied program of education and support for Muslims. Its subsidiary, ICNA Relief, provides humanitarian aid wherever it is needed.

The Mosque Cares (Ministry of Imam W. Deen Mohammed)

P.O. Box 1061
Calumet City, IL 60409
Tel. (708)798-6750
Fax (708)798-6827
Email: WdMinistry@aol.com
Website: www.themosquecares.com

> Also known as the American Society of Muslims, this is the headquarters of the community in association with the leadership of W. D. Mohammed.

Muslim American Society

P.O. Box 1896
Falls Church, VA 22041
Tel. (703)998-6525
Fax (703)998-6526
Email for General Information: mas@masnet.org
Email for Inquiries by non-Muslims: sg@masnet.org
Website: www.masnet.org

Founded in 1992, this is a charitable, religious, social, cultural, and educational, not-for-profit organization. It is a pioneering Islamic organization, an Islamic revival, and reform movement that uplifts the individual, family, and society. This organization is not to be confused with the ministry of W. D. Mohammad, which once used this name.

Muslim Peace Fellowship

PO Box 271
Nyack, New York 10960 USA
Tel. (845)358-4601
Fax (845)358-4924
Email: mpf@mpfweb.org
Website: www.mpfweb.org

The Muslim Peace Fellowship (Ansar as-Salam) is a network of peace and justice-oriented Muslims of all backgrounds who are dedicated to making the beauty of Islam evident in the world.

Muslim Public Affairs Council (MPAC)

3010 Wilshire Blvd. Ste. 217
Los Angeles, CA 90010
Tel. (213)383-3443
Fax (213)383-9674
Email: mpac-contact@mpac.org
Website: www.mpac.org
Exec. Dir. Salam Al-Marayati

MPAC seeks to establish a vibrant Maerican Msulim community that will enrich American society through promoting the Islamic values of mercy, justice, peace, human dignity, freedom and equality for all.

JAINISM

Jainism is an ancient Indian religion based on the notion that, periodically, humanity is blessed with a series of twenty-four *tirthankaras* (crossing-makers)—great spiritual leaders who attain infinite knowledge; revive a way of life that is based on the principles of non-harming, non-attachment, and openmindedness, and directed by right knowledge, right faith, and right conduct; establish an order of renunciates; and assist in the liberation of countless other human beings from the cycle of reincarnation. Vardhamana (599–527 B.C.E.), a contemporary of the Buddha, was the twenty-fourth and last tirthankara for the current eon, and is known as Mahavira (Great Hero). His sermons provide the core of Jain scriptures, the Agam Sutras, but Jainism's two main branches differ over the exact contents. Jainism stresses asceticism. Digambara (sky-clad) monks renounce all clothing; Svetambara (white-clad) monks and nuns wear simple, white robes. Both branches may use *murtis* (images) of *tirthankaras* in devotional practice, but Digambara *murtis* will be plainer. The doctrine of *ahimsa* (non-harming) leads to strict vegetarianism, avoidance of animal products of any kind, and avoidance of interpersonal conflicts. Mahatma Gandhi was influenced greatly by Jain teachings.

JAINA: Federation of Jain Associations in North America

P.O. Box 700
Getzville, NY 14068
Tel. (716)636-5342
Email: jainahq@jaina.org
Website: www.jaina.org

An umbrella organization linking local U.S. and Canadian Jain associations. It seeks to promote Jain principles and better understanding of Jainism. It also engages in humanitarian work.

Siddhachalam International Mahavira Jain Mission

65 Mud Pond Road
Blairstown, NJ 07825
Tel. (908)362-9793
Fax (908)362-9649
Email: info@siddhachalam.org
Website: www.siddhachalam.org

Founded by Acharya Shri Shushil Kumarji in 1983, this resident community for monks, nuns, laymen, and laywomen is described as the first Jain pilgrimage site outside India. It promotes ahimsa for world peace, vegetarianism, and nonviolence to animals; and is headquarters for the International Jain Mission, the World Fellowship of Religions, and the World Jain Congress.

JUDAISM

Judaism is one of the world's oldest religions, encompassing a rich and complex tradition that has evolved over centuries and has given rise to, or influenced, other major world traditions. Numerous expressions of Judaism have always coexisted with one another, as they do today. The central concern shared by all is to live in relation to God and to follow God's will. Jews understand themselves to be in covenant with God, who is the one transcendent God, Creator of the Universe. God revealed the Torah to the people of Israel as his way of life. History brought the Jewish people into contact with many cultures and civilizations, contacts that continuously transformed the nature of their worship, the understanding of God's law, and even their conceptualization of peoplehood. At the time of the second Diaspora, or great migration of Jews throughout the Middle East, North Africa, and Europe at the beginning of the common era, was the rise of the Rabbinical Tradition, with its emphasis on the study of scripture. Today's Judaism has grown out of these roots. In the 19th century, Reform Judaism arose in Europe and the United States as one Jewish response to modernity. Conservative Judaism and Reconstructionism are branches of Jewish practice that first developed in America. Orthodox Judaism also has a number of modern forms.

ALEPH Administrative Office

7000 Lincoln Drive #B2
Philadelphia, PA 19119-3046
Email: aleph-info@aleph.org
Website: www.aleph.org
CEO, Ms. Susan Saxe
> A core institution of the Jewish Renewal movement dedicated to the Jewish people's sacred purpose of partnership with the Divine in the inseparable tasks of healing the world and healing our hearts.

The American Jewish Committee

P.O. Box 705
New York, NY 10150
Tel. (212)751-4000
Fax (212)891-1492
Email: pr@ajc.org
Website: www.ajc.org
Exec. Dir., David A. Harris
> Founded in 1906, The AJC protects the rights and freedoms of Jews world-wide; combats bigotry and anti-Semitism and promotes democracy and human rights for all. It is an independent community-relations organization, with strong interest in interreligious relations and public-policy advocacy. The AJC publishes the *American Jewish Yearbook*, and *Commentary magazine*.

The Anti-Defamation League of B'nai B'rith

823 United Nations Plaza
New York, NY 10017
Tel. (212)885-7707
Fax (212)867-9406
Website: www.adl.org
National Dir., Abraham H. Foxman
> Since 1913, the Anti-Defamation League has been involved in combating and documenting anti-Semitism. It also works to secure fair treatment for all citizens through law, education and community relations.

Jewish Council for Public Affairs

443 Park Ave. S., 11th Floor
New York, NY 10016
Tel. (212)684-6950
Fax (212)686-1353
Email: contactus@thejcpa.org
Website: www.jewishpublicaffairs.org
> This national coordinating body for the field of Jewish community relations comprises 13 national and 122 local Jewish communal agencies. Through the Council's work, and in its col-

laboration with other religious groups, its constituent agencies work on public policy issues, both international and domestic.

Jewish Reconstructionist Federation

Beit Devora, 101 Greenwood Avenue
Jenkintown, PA 19046
Tel. (215)885-5601
Fax:(215)885-5603
Email: info@jrf.org
Website: www.jrf.org

Fosters the establishment and ongoing life of Reconstructionist congregations and fellowship groups. Publishes *The Reconstructionist* and other materials. Rabbis who relate to this branch of Judaism are often members of the Reconstructionist Rabbinical Association.

Religious Action Center of Reform Judaism

2027 Massachusetts Ave. NW
At Kivie Kaplan Way
Washington, DC 20036
Tel. (202)387-2800
Fax (202)667-9070
Website: www.rac.org
Exec. Dir., Rabbi David Saperstein

The Religious Action Center pursues social justice and religious liberty by mobilizing the American Jewish community and serving as its advocate in the capitol of the United States.

The Union of Orthodox Jewish Congregations of America

11 Broadway
New York, NY 10004-1003
Tel. (212)563-4000
Fax (212)564-9058
Website: www.ou.org
Exec. Vice-Pres., Rabbi Tzvi Hersh Weinreb

The national central body of Orthodox synagogues since 1898, providing kashrut supervision, women's and youth organizations, and a variety of educational, religious and public policy programs and activities. Publishers of *Jewish Action* magazine and other materials. The Rabbinical Council of America is the related organization for Orthodox Rabbis.

Union of Reform Judaism

633 Third Ave.
New York, NY 10017
Tel. (212)650-4000
Website: www.urj.org
Pres., Rabbi Eric H. Yoffie

The central congregational body of Reform Judaism, founded in 1873. It serves approx. 875 affiliated temples and its members through religious, educational, cultural and administrative programs. Women's Men's and Youth organizations. Reform Judaism is one of its publications. The Central Conference of American Rabbis is the affiliated rabbinical body.

The United Synagogue of Conservative Judaism

155 Fifth Ave.
New York, NY 10010-6802
Tel. (212)533-7800
Fax (212)353-9439
Website: www.uscj.org
Exec. Vice-Pres., Rabbi Jerome M. Epstein

The International organization of 800 congregations, founded in 1913. Provides religious, educational, youth, community and administrative programming. Publishes *United Synagogue Review* and other materials. The Rabbinical Assembly is the association of Conservative Rabbis.

NATIVE AMERICAN TRADITIONAL SPIRITUALITY

Native American spirituality is difficult to define or categorize because it varies so greatly across the continent. Further, it is deeply entwined with elements of nature which are associated with different geographical regions. For example, while Plains Indians possess a spiritual relationship with the buffalo, Indigenous Peoples from the Northwest share a similar relationship with salmon. Hence, the character of Native American spirituality is dependent, to some extent, on the surrounding geography and its incumbent ecosystems. Despite this great variety, there are some similarities which allow us to consider the many Native American forms of spirituality together: Contrary to popular belief, Native American peoples are monotheistic; they do not worship the sun or buffalo or salmon, but rather understand that these elements of nature are gifts from the "Great Mystery," and are parts of it. Today, while still working toward religious freedom in the United States, Native Americans are also struggling to protect sacred sites, which they consider to be comparable to "churches." But since these sites are actually part of the land, not man-made structures, many are constantly under attack for the natural resources they contain. Such exploitation of these resources is an offense to the Native American sense of spirituality, which views resources like timber, oil, and gold, as gifts from the Great Mystery. The struggle to protect and respect these sacred sites is a universal and essential part of Native American spirituality.

National Congress of American Indians (NCAI)

1301 Connecticut Ave. NW, Ste. 200
Washington, DC 20036
Tel. (202)466-7767
Fax (202)466-7797
Email: ncia@ncia.org
Website: www.ncai.org
Exec. Dir., Jacqueline Johnson

The National Congress of American Indians (NCAI), founded in 1944, is the oldest, largest and most representative national Indian organization serving the needs of a broad membership of American Indian and Alaska Native governments. NCAI stresses the need for unity and cooperation among tribal governments and people for the security and protection of treaty and sovereign rights. As the preeminent national Indian organization, NCAI is organized as a representative congress aiming for consensus on national priority issues.

The NCAI website contains links for a directory of Indian nations in the continental U.S. and Alaska as well as a directory of tribal governments. There are also links to other Native American websites.

Native American Rights Fund (NARF)

1506 Broadway
Boulder, CO 80302
Tel. (303)447-8760
Fax (303)433-7776
Email: pereira@narf.org
Website: www.narf.org
Exec. Dir., John Echohawk

The Native American Rights Fund is the non-profit legal organization devoted to defending and promoting the legal rights of the Indian people. NARF attorneys, most of whom are Native Americans, defend tribes who otherwise cannot bear the financial burden of obtaining justice in the courts of the United States. The NARF mission statement outlines five areas of concentration: 1) Preservation of tribal existence; 2) Protection of tribal natural resources; 3) Promotion of human rights; 4) Accountability of government; 5) Development of Indian law.

SIKHISM

Sikhism was founded by Guru Nanak during the 15th and 16th centuries C.E. in the state of Punjab in northwestern India. Nanak was greatly influenced by the teachings of Kabir, a Muslim who became deeply inspired by Hindu philosophies. Kabir's poems called for a synthesis between Islam and Hinduism. In the footsteps of Kabir's wisdom, Nanak drew upon elements of Bhakti Hinduism and Sufi Islam: He stressed the existence of a universal, single God, who transcends religious distinctions. Union with God is accomplished through meditation and surrender to the divine will. Nanak also called for the belief in reincarnation, karma, and also the cyclical destruction and recreation of the universe. However, he rejected the caste system, the devotion to divine incarnations, priesthood, idol worship, all of which were elements of the Hindu tradition. Nanak was the first of ten *gurus*, or teachers.

230

The fourth guru, built the Golden Temple in Amritsar, the Sikh religious center. The fifth guru compiled the *Adi Granth*, a sort of hymn-book of spiritual authority. All male sikhs are initiated into the religious brotherhood called the *Khalsa*. Members of this order vow never to cut their beard or hair, to wear special pants, to wear an iron bangle as an amulet against evil, to carry a steel dagger, and a comb.

Sikh American Heritage Organization (SAHO)

P.O. Box 63
Wayne, IL 60184-0063
Tel. (630)377-5893
Fax (630)377-5893
Email: SikhAmerican@aol.com
 Promotes and fosters fellowship with the American mainstream and minority communities while maintaining Sikh values, heritage, and identity; participates in Asian American events, interfaith programs, community affairs, social services, and other civic activities.

Sikh American Legal Defense and Education Fund (SALDEF)

1413 K Street
5th Floor
Washington, DC 20005
Tel. (202)393-2700
Fax (202)318-4433
Website: www.saldef.org
 Formerly Sikh Mediawatch and Research Task Force (SMART), SALDEF is a national civil rights and educational organization which provides legal assistance, educational outreach, legislative advocacy, and media relations

Sikh Coalition

40 Exchange Place, Suite 728
New York, N.Y. 10005
Email: info@sikhcoalition.org
Website: www.sikhcoalition.org
 Founded in response to bias attacks following the September 11, 2001, Sikh Coalition defends civil rights and liberties, educates the broader community about Sikhs and diversity, promotes local community empowerment, and fosters civic engagement amongst Sikh Americans.

Sikh Foundation

580 College Avenue
Palo Alto, CA 94306
Tel. (650)494-7454
Fax (650)494-3316
Email: info@sikhfoundation.org
Website: www.sikhfoundation.org
 Founded in 1967 to promote the heritage and future of Sikhism, the Sikh Foundation's sponsors academic courses, conferences and chairs of Sikh studies at leading universities in the West; promotes Sikh art exhibitions and the establishing permanent Sikh art galleries at major museums worldwide; and works to provide the community with highest quality of educational products on Sikhism.

Sikh Research Institute

P.O. Box 690504
San Antonio, TX 78269-0504
Tel. (210)582-3371
Email: info@sikhri-org
Website: www.sikhri.org
 The goals of this organization are leadership enhancement, community revival, and facilitation of connections between various Sikh organizations. It is active in interfaith work, and education of Americans about Sikhism.

World Sikh Council – America Region

P.O. Box 3635,
Columbus, Ohio 43210

Tel. (614)210-0591
Fax (419)535-6794
Email: contact@worldsikhcouncil.org
Website: www.worldsikhcouncil.org
Secretary General, Dr. Manmohan Singh

A national unit of the World Sikh Council, WSC-AR is a representative and elected body of Sikh Gurudwaras and institutions in the U.S. Its members include 31 Gurudwaras (Sikh places of worship) and 6 other Sikh institutions across the nation. Its mission is to promote Sikh interests at the national and international level focusing on issues of advocacy, education, and well-being of humankind

ZOROASTRIANISM

The western name for "The Good Religion" based on the teachings of the Prophet Zarathustra, who lived sometime between 1200 and 550 B.C.E., in what is now Iran. Zoroastrians from India are often called Parsis (Parsees). Zoroastrians worship Ahura Mazda (Wise Lord): the one God, the uncreated, immanent and transcendent source of all that is good, true, and beautiful, for whom the only appropriate symbol is fire. Zoroastrians fall into two streams: traditionalists, for whom all ancient Zoroastrian texts are scripture; and progressives, for whom only the Gathas (the oldest texts) have authority. The two streams differ sharply in beliefs and practices. There are also informal denominations according to which of several Zoroastrian calendars one prefers.

Federation of Zoroastrian Associations of North America (FEZANA)

1932 New Bedford Drive
Sun City Centers, FL 33573
Tel. (408)264-4395
Website: www.fezana.org
President, Dr. Rustom Kevala

A coordinating organization for Zoroastrian Associations of North America.

6. United States Regional and Local Ecumenical Bodies

One of the many ways Christians and Christian churches relate to one another locally and regionally is through ecumenical bodies. The membership in these ecumenical organizations is diverse. Historically, councils of churches were formed primarily by Protestants, but many local and regional organizations now include Orthodox and Roman Catholics. Many are made up of congregations or judicatory units of churches. Some have a membership base of individuals. Others foster cooperation between ministerial groups, community ministries, coalitions, or church agencies. While "council of churches" is a term still commonly used to describe this form of cooperation, other terms such as "conference of churches," "ecumenical councils," "churches united," "metropolitan ministries," are coming into use. Ecumenical organizations that are national in scope are listed in directory 1, "United States Cooperative Organizations."

An increasing number of ecumenical bodies have been exploring ways to strengthen the interreligious aspect of life in the context of religious pluralism in the U.S. today. Some organizations in this listing are fully interfaith agencies primarily through the inclusion of Jewish congregations in their membership. Other organizations nurture partnerships with a broader base of religious groups in their communities, especially in the areas of public policy and interreligious dialogue.

This list does not include all local and regional ecumenical and interfaith organizations in existence today. The terms regional and local are relative, making identification somewhat ambiguous. Regional councils may cover sections of large states or cross-state borders. Local councils may be made up of several counties, towns, or clusters of congregations. State councils or state-level ecumenical contacts exist in 45 of the 50 states. These state-level or multi-state organizations are marked with an asterisk (*). The organizations are listed alphabetically by state.

ALABAMA

Greater Birmingham Ministries
2304 12th Ave. N, Birmingham, AL 35234-3111
Tel. (205)326-6821 Fax (205)252-8458
Email: robert@gbm.org
Website: www.gbm.org
Media Contact, Robert Montgomery
Exec. Dir., Scott Douglas
Economic Justice, Co-Chpsn., Helen Holdefer, Betty Likis
Direct Services, Chpsn., Patty Warren
Faith in Community, Chpsn., Patricia Ross
Finance & Fund-Raising, Chpsn., Richard Ambrose
Pres., Tom Forsee
Treas., Helen Tibbs Wilson
Major Activities: Direct Service Ministries (Food, Utilities, Rent and Nutrition Education, Shelter); Alabama Arise (Statewide legislative network focusing on low income issues); Economic Justice Issues (Low Income Housing and Advocacy, Health Care, Community Development, Jobs Creation, Public Transportation); Faith in Community Ministries (Interchurch Forum, Interpreting and Organizing, Bible Study)

Interfaith Mission Service
701 Andrew Jackson Way NE, Huntsville, AL 35801-3504 Tel. (256)536-2401 Fax (256) 536-2284
Email: ims@hiwaay.net
Exec. Dir., Susan J. Smith
Pres., Richard C. Titus

Major Activities: Foodline & Food Pantry; Local FEMA Committee; Ministry Development; Clergy Luncheon; Workshops; Response to Community Needs; Information and Referral; Interfaith Understanding; Christian Unity; Homeless Needs; School Readiness Screenings

ALASKA

Alaska Christian Conference
Episcopal Diocese of Alaska, 1205 Denali Way, Fairbanks, AK 99701-4178 Tel. (907)452-3040
Email: mmcdonald@gci.net
Media Contact, Rt. Rev. Mark MacDonald
Pres., The Rt. Rev. Mark MacDonald
Vice Pres., The Rev. David I. Blanchett, 1100 Pullman Drive, Wasilla, AK 99654 Tel. (907) 352-2517
Treas., Carolyn M. Winters, 2133 Bridgewater Drive, Fairbanks, AK 99709-4101 Tel. (907) 456-8555
Major Activities: Legislative & Social Concerns; Resources and Continuing Education; New Ecumenical Ministries; Communication; Alcoholism (Education & Prevention); Family Violence (Education & Prevention); Native Issues; Ecumenical-Theological Dialogue; HIV-AIDS Education and Ministry; Criminal Justice

ARIZONA

Arizona Ecumenical Council*
4423 N. 24th St., Ste. 750, Phoenix, AZ 85016
Tel. (602)468-3818 Fax (602)468-3311

Email: aec@aecunity.net
Website: www.aecunity.net
Media Contact, Exec. Dir., Rev. Jan Olav Flaaten, Tel. (602)468-3818 Fax (602)468-3311, Cell (602)670-1594, Email: jflaaten@ aecunity.net
Exec. Dir., The Rev. Jan Olav Flaaten
Pres., Bishop Michael Neils
Major Activities: Facilitating collaboration among the 20 judicatories for Theological Dialogue, Services of Prayer, Public Policy and Social Justice, Church Leadership School (called Survival School), Local Ecumenism (encouraging and being a resource for local ecumenical groupings), Earth Care Commission (presents annual "Caring for Creation" conference), Arizonans for the Protection of Exploited Children and Adults (APECA), Disaster Relief, Non-Violence Education for Youth, Souper-Bowl

ARKANSAS
Arkansas Interfaith Conference*
P.O. Box 151, Scott, AR 72142 Tel. (501)961-2626
Email: aicark@aol.com
Media Contact, Conf. Exec., Mimi Dortch
Conf. Exec., Mimi Dortch
Pres., Rev. Steve Copley. 6701 JFK Blvd., N. Little Rock, AR. 72116 (Methodist)
Sec., Imam John Hasan. P.O.Box 1607, Little Rock, AR 72203. (Muslim)
Treas., Jim Davis, Box 7239, Little Rock, AR 72217 (Catholic)
Major Activities: Institutional Ministry; Interfaith Executives' Advisory Council; Interfaith Relations; Church Women United; Our House-Shelter; Legislative Liaison; Ecumenical Choir Camp; Tornado Disaster Relief; Camp for Jonesboro School Children Massacre; Welfare Reform Work; Med Center Chaplaincy; Peace Service

CALIFORNIA
California Council of Churches-California Church Impact*
2715 K Street, Suite D, Sacramento, CA 95816
Tel. (916)488-7300 Fax (916)488-7310
Email: cccinfo@calchurches.org
Website: www.calchurches.org
Media Contact, Exec. Dir., The Rev. Rick Schlosser, Email: rick@calchurches.org
Exec. Dir., The Rev. Rick Schlosser
Major Activities: Monitoring State Legislation; California IMPACT Network; Legislative Principles; Food Policy Advocacy; Family Welfare Issues; Health; Church-State Issues; Violence Prevention; Child Care Program-Capacity Coordinator to Increase Quality Child Care within California for the Working Poor; Building Bridges of Understanding: An Interfaith Response to Septerber 11.

The Council of Churches of Santa Clara County
1710 Moorpark Avenue, San Jose, CA 95128 Tel. (408)297-2660 Fax (408)297-2661
Email: councilofchurches@sbcglobal.net
Website: www.councilofchurches-scc.org
Media Contact, Co-executive Directors: Rev. Margo Tenold, Rev. Diana Gibson
Co-executive Directors: Rev. Margo Tenold, Rev. Diana Gibson
Major Activities: Social Education-Action; Ecumenical and Interfaith Witness; Affordable Housing; Environmental Ministry; Family-Children; Convalescent Hospital Ministries; Gay Ministry; Strengthening Congregations for Ministry

The Ecumenical Council of Pasadena Area Churches
P.O. Box 41125, 444 E. Washington Blvd., Pasadena, CA 91114-8125 Tel. (626)797-2402 Fax (626)797-735
Email: ecpac@prodigy.net
Exec. Dir., Rev. Frank B. Clark
Major Activities: Christian Education; Community Worship; Community Concerns; Christian Unity; Ethnic Ministries; Hunger; Peace; Food, Clothing Assistance for the Poor; Emergency Shelter

Ecumenical Council of San Diego County
1880 Third Ave., #13, San Diego, CA 92101 Tel.
Email: nrankin@ecsd.org
Website: www.ecsd.org
Exec. Dir. (interim), Nancy Rankin
Pres. Jane Barry
Treas., Rev. Robert Ard
Major Activities: Interfaith Shelter Network-Rational Shelter and El Nido Transitional Living Program; Emerging Issues; Faith Order & Witness; Worship & Celebration; Ecumenical Tribute Dinner; Advent Prayer Breakfast; Seminars and Workshops; Called to Dance Assn.; Children's Sabbath Workshops and events; Edgemoor Chaplaincy; Stand for Children events; Continuing Education for clergy and laypersons;Inter-Religious Council; Sacred Spaces church tour

Fresno Metro Ministry
1055 N. Van Ness, Ste. H, Fresno, CA 93728 Tel. (559)485-1416 Fax (559)485-9109
Email: metromin@fresnometmin.org
Website: www.fresnometmin.org
Media Contact, Exec. Dir., Rev. Walter P. Parry
Exec. Dir., Rev. Walter P. Parry
Pres., Tony Gonzalez
Major Activities: Hunger Relief & Nutrition Advocacy; Cultural Diversity and Anti-Racism; Health Care Advocacy; Environmental Health

234

and Quality; Access and Public Health; Public Education Concerns; Children's Needs; Air Quality; Ecumenical & Interfaith Celebrations & Cooperation; Youth Needs; Community Network Building; Human Services Facilitation; Anti-Poverty Efforts; Low-Income and Immigrant Leadership Development related to public policies

Interfaith Council of Contra Costa County

1543 Sunnyvale Ave., Walnut Creek, CA 94596 Tel. (925)933-6030 Fax (925)952-4554

Chaplains, The Rev. Charles Tinsley; The Rev. Duane Woida; The Rev. Harold Wright; Laurie Maxwell

Pres., Rev. Steve Harms

Treas., Robert Bender

Major Activities: Institutional Chaplaincies, Community Education, Interfaith Cooperation; Social Justice

Interfaith Service Bureau

2212 K. St., Sacramento, CA 95816-4923 Tel. (916)456-3815 Fax (916)456-3816

Email: isbdexter@aol.com

Media Contact, Exec. Dir., Dexter McNamara

Executive Dir., Dexter McNamara

Pres., Richard Montgomery

Vice Pres., Lloyd Hanson

Major Activities: Religious and Racial Cooperation and Understanding; Welfare Reform Concerns; Refugee Resettlement & Support; Religious Cable Television; Violence Prevention; Graffiti Abatement

Marin Interfaith Council

1510 5th Avenue, San Rafael, CA 94901-1807 Tel. (415)456-9657 Fax (415)456-6959

Email: admin@marinifc.org

Website: marininterfaithcouncil.org

Media Contact, Exec. Dir., Rev. Carol Hovis

Exec. Dir., Rev. Carol Hovis

Major Activities: Interfaith Dialogue; Education; Advocacy; Convening; Interfaith Worship Services & Commemorations

Northern California Interreligious Conference

534 22nd St., Oakland, CA 94612 Tel. (510)433-0822 Fax (510)433-0813

Email: NCIC@igc.org

Website: ncic.home.igc.org

Media Contact, Pres., Rev. Phil Lawson

Exec. Dir., Catherine Coleman

Pres., Rev. Phil Lawson

Vice Pres., Esther Ho

Sec., Robert Forsberg

Major Activities: Peace with Justice Commission; Interreligious Relationships Commission; Public Policy Advocacy; Welfare Reform, Founding member of California Council of Churches and of California

Interfaith Power and Light; Soul of Justice, a spiritual and leadership concepts interactive performance troupe of teens and young adults; death penalty moratorium; video produced for sale for congregations-organizations to study legal, theological and social implications of marriage and same gender marriage, widening our circle of religious groups participating; a cooperating circle of URL.

Pomona Inland Valley Council of Churches

1753 N. Park Ave., Pomona, CA 91768 Tel. (909)622-3806 Fax (909)622-0484

Media Contact, Dir. of Dev., Mary Kashmar

Pres., The Rev. Henry Rush

Acting Exec. Dir., The Rev. La Quetta Bush-Simmons

Sec., Ken Coates

Treas., Anne Ashford

Major Activities: Advocacy and Education for Social Justice; Ecumenical Celebrations; Hunger Advocacy; Emergency Food and Shelter Assistance; Farmer's Market; Affordable Housing; Transitional Housing

San Fernando Valley Interfaith Council

10824 Topanga Canyon Blvd., No. 7, Chatsworth, CA 91311 Tel. (818)718-6460 Fax (818)718-0734

Email: info@vic-LA.org

Website: www.vic-LA.org

Media Contact, Comm. Coord., Eileen Killoren, ext. 3002

Pres., Barry Smedberg; Ext. 3011

Chair, Board of Dir., Earl Fagin, Esq.

Major Activities: Seniors Multi-Purpose Centers; Nutrition & Services; Meals to Homebound; Meals on Wheels; Interfaith Reporter; Interfaith Relations; Social Adult Day Care; Hunger-Homelessness; Volunteer Care-Givers; Clergy Gatherings; Food Pantries and Outreach; Social Concerns; Aging; Hunger; Human Relations; Immigration Services; Self-Sufficiency Program for Section 8 Families

South Coast Interfaith Council

759 Linden Ave., Long Beach, CA 90813 Tel. (562)983-1665 Fax (562)983-8812

Email: scic@charterinternet.com

Website: www.SCInterfaith.org

Media Contact, Exec. Dir., Rev. Ginny Wagener

STAFF

Exec. Dir., Rev. Ginny Wagener

President, John Ishuaradas Abdallah

Farmers' Markets, Rev. Dale Whitney

Centro Shalom, Amelia Nieto

Good Samaritan Counseling Center, Dr. William Scar

Major Activities: Farmers' Markets; CROP Hunger Walks; Church Athletic Leagues;

235

Community Action; Easter Sunrise Worships; Interreligious Dialogue; Justice Advocacy; Martin Luther King, Jr. Celebration; Violence Prevention; Long Beach Interfaith Clergy; Publishing Area Religious Directories, Crop Hunger, Walks, Counseling services

Southern California Ecumenical Council

195 So. Hill Ave., Pasadena, CA 91106 Tel. (626) 578-6371 Fax (626)578-6358
Email: scec1@scec1.net
Website: www.scec1.net
Media Contact, Exec. Dir., Rev. Albert G. Cohen
Exec. Dir., The Rev. Albert G. Cohen
Pres., The Rev. Dr. Paul Lance
Treas., The Rev. Larry Hixon
Sec., Ms. Lucy Guernsey
Vice Pres. The Rev. Dr. Gwynne Guibord
Second Vice Pres., Carol Kostura
Members at Large, The Rev. Frank Brougker, Rev. Sara Armstrong, Fr. Alexei Smith
Faith and Order Chair, The Rev. Dr. Rod Parrott
Past Pres., Fr. Arshag Khatchadorian
Major Activities: Consultation with the regional religious sector concerning the well being and spiritual vitality of this most diverse and challenging area

Westside Interfaith Council

P.O. Box 1402, Santa Monica, CA 90406 Tel. (310)394-1518 Fax (310)576-1895
Media Contact, Rev. Janet A. Bregar
Exec. Dir., Rev. Janet A. Bregar
Major Activities: Meals on Wheels; Community Religious Services; Convalescent Hospital Chaplaincy; Homeless Partnership; Hunger & Shelter Coalition

COLORADO

Colorado Council of Churches*

3690 Cherry Creek S. Dr., Denver, CO 80209 Tel. (303)825-4910 Fax (303)744-8605
Email: jrryan7@qwest.net
Website: www.coloradocouncilofchurches.org
Media Contact, Council Exec., Rev. Dr. Jim R. Ryan
Pres., Rev. Janet Schlenker
Staff Assoc, Dori Wilson
Major Activities: Addressing issues of Christian Unity, Justice, and Environment

Interfaith Council of Boulder

3700 Baseline Rd., Boulder, CO 80303 Tel. (303)494-8094
Media Contact, Pres., Stan Grotegut, 810 Kalma Ave., Boulder, CO 80304 Tel. (303)443-2291
Pres., Stan Grotegut
Major Activities: Interfaith Dialogue and Programs; Thanksgiving Worship Services; Food for the Hungry; Share-A-Gift; Monthly Newsletter

CONNECTICUT

Association of Religious Communities

325 Main St., Danbury, CT 06810 Tel. (203)792-9450 Fax (203)792-9452
Email: arc325@aol.com
Media Contact, Exec. Dir., Rev. Phyllis J. Leopold
Exec. Dir., Rev. Phyllis J. Leopold
Pres., The Rev. Mark Lingle
Major Activities: Refugee Resettlement; Family Counseling; Family Violence Prevention; Affordable Housing, Inter-Faith Dialogue, Racial Justice

The Capitol Region Conference of Churches

60 Lorrain St., Hartford, CT 06105 Tel. (860) 236-1295 Fax (860)236-8071
Email: crcc@conferenceofchurches.org
Website: www.conferenceofchurches.org
Media Contact, Exec. Dir., Rev. Shelley Copeland
Exec. Dir., The Rev. Shelley Copeland
Pastoral Care & Training, Dir., The Rev. Kathleen Davis
Aging Project, Dir., Barbara Malcolm
Community Organizer, Joseph Wasserman
Broadcast Ministry Consultant, Ivor T. Hugh
Pres., Mr. David O. White
Major Activities: Organizing for Peace and Justice; Aging; Legislative Action; Cooperative Broadcast Ministry; Ecumenical Cooperation; Interfaith Reconciliation; Chaplaincies; Low-Income Senior Empower-ment; Anti-Racism Education

Center City Churches

40 Pratt Street,, Ste. 210, Hartford, CT 06103-1601 Tel. (860)728-3201 Fax (860)549-8550
Email: info@centercitychurches.org
Website: www.centercitychurches.org
Media Contact, Exec. Dir., Paul C. Christie
Exec. Dir., Paul C. Christie
Pres., Jeannette L. Brown
Treas., Rusty Spears
Major Activities: Senior Services; Family Resource Center; Food Pantry; Assistance & Advocacy; After School Tutoring and Arts Enrichment; Summer Day Camp; Housing for persons with AIDS; Community Soup Kitchen

Christian Community Action

168 Davenport Ave., New Haven, CT 06519 Tel. (203)777-7848 Fax (203)777-7848
Email: cca@ccahelping.org
Website: www.ccahelping.org
Media Contact, Exec. Dir., The Rev. Bonita Grubbs
Exec. Dir., The Rev. Bonita Grubbs
Major Activities: Emergency Food Program; Used Furniture & Clothing; Security and Fuel;

Emergency Housing for Families; Advocacy; Transitional Housing for Families

Christian Conference of Connecticut*

60 Lorraine St., Hartford, CT 06105 Tel. (860) 236-4281 Fax (860)236-9977
Email: ssidorak@aol.com
Website: www.christconn.org
Media Contact, Exec. Dir., Rev. Dr. Stephen J. Sidorak, Jr.
Exec. Dir., The Rev. Dr. Stephen J. Sidorak, Jr.
Pres., The Rt. Rev. Andrew D. Smith
Vice Pres., The Rev. Dr. Robert C. Dvorak
Sec., The Rev. Samuel N. Slie
Treas., Mr. Minot B. Nettleton
Major Activities: Communications; Institutional Ministries; Connecticut Ecumenical Small Church Project; Ecumenical Forum; Faith & Order; Social Concerns; Public Policy; Peace and Justice Convocation; Restorative Justice & Death Penalty; Interreligious Dialogue ; Anti—Nuclear Activities; Problem Gambling; Jewish-Christian Dialogue

Council of Churches of Greater Bridgeport, Inc.

180 Fairfield Ave., Bridgeport, CT 06604 Tel. (203)334-1121 Fax (203)367-8113
Email: ccgb@ccgb.org
Website: www.ccgb.org
Media Contact, Exec. Dir., Rev. Dr. Brian R. Schofield-Bodt
Exec. Dir., Rev. Dr. Brian R. Schofield-Bodt
Pres. Bonnie McWain
Vice Pres., Rev. Hopeton Scott
Sec., Valerie Peterkin
Treas., Roger Perry
Major Activities: Youth in Crisis; Youth In Crisis Hotline, Responses & Safe Places; Host Home Shelter Care; Criminal Justice Services for Ex-offenders; Jail Ministry; Hunger Outreach and Networking; Ecumenical & Inter-Religious Relations, Prayer and Celebration; Covenantal Ministries; Homework Help; Summer Programs; Race Relations-Bridge Building

Council of Churches and Synagogues of Southwestern Connecticut

461 Glenbrook Rd, Stamford, CT 06901 Tel. (203)348-2800 Fax (203)358-0627
Email: council@flvax.ferg.lib.ct.us
Website: www.interfaithcouncil.org
Media Contact, Comm. Ofc., Lois Alcosser
Exec. Dir., Jack Penfield, Interim Director
Major Activities: Partnership Against Hunger; The Food Bank of Lower Fairfield County; Friendly Visitors and Friendly Shoppers; Senior Neighborhood Support Services; Christmas in April; Interfaith Programming; Prison Visitation; Friendship House; Help a Neighbor; Operation Fuel; Teaching Place

Greater Waterbury Interfaith Ministries, Inc.

16 Church St, Waterbury, CT 06702 Tel. (203) 756-7831 Fax (203)419-0024
Media Contact, Exec. Dir., Carroll E. Brown
Exec. Dir., Carroll E. Brown
Pres., The Rev. Dr. James G. Bradley
Major Activities: Emergency Food Program; Emergency Fuel Program; Soup Kitchen; Ecumenical Worship; Christmas Toy Sale; Annual Hunger Walk

Manchester Area Conference of Churches

P.O. Box 3804, Manchester, CT 06045-3804 Tel. (860)647-8003
Media Contact, Exec. Dir., Denise Cabana
Exec. Dir., Denise Cabana
Dir. of Community Ministries, Joseph Piescik
Dept.of Ministry Development, Dir., Karen Bergin
Pres., Rev. Charles Ericson
Vice Pres., Theresa Ghabrial
Sec., Jean Richert
Treas., Clive Perrin
Major Activities: Provision of Basic Needs (Food, Fuel, Clothing, Furniture); Emergency Aid Assistance; Emergency Shelter; Soup Kitchen; Reentry Assistance to Sex-Offenders; Pastoral Care in Local Institutions; Interfaith Day Camp; Advocacy for the Poor; Ecumenical Education and Worship

New Britain Area Conference of Churches (NEWBRACC)

830 Corbin Ave., New Britain, CT 06052 Tel. (860)229-3751 Fax (860)223-3445
Media Contact, Acting Exec. Dir., Rev. Teresa A. Hughes
Acting Exec. Dir., The Rev. Teresa A. Hughes
Pastoral Care-Chaplaincy, The Rev. Ron Smith; The Rev. Will Baumgartner
Pres., The Rev. Charles Tillet
Treas., Dierdre Elloian
Major Activities: Worship; Social Concerns; Emergency Food Bank Support; Communications-Mass Media; Hospital; Elderly Programming; Homelessness and Hunger Programs; Telephone Ministry

DELAWARE

The Christian Council of Delaware and Maryland's Eastern Shore*

2020 N. Tatnall Street, Wilmington, DE 19802 Tel. (302)-656-5441
Website: www.DeMdSynod.org
Media Contact, Pres., Bishop Wayne P. Wright, Diocese of Delaware, 2020 N. Tatnall Street, Wilmington, DE 19802
Pres., Bishop Wayne P. Wright, Diocese of Delaware, 2020 N. Tatnall Street, Wilmington, DE 19802

237

Major Activities: Exploring Common Theological, Ecclesiastical and Community Concerns; Racism; Prisons

DISTRICT OF COLUMBIA

The Council of Churches of Greater Washington

5 Thomas Circle N.W., Washington, DC 20005 Tel. (202)722-9240 Fax (202)722-9240
Media Contact, Exec. Dir., The Rev. Rodger Hall Reed, Sr.
Pres., The Rev. Lewis Anthony
Exec. Dir., The Rev. Rodger Hall Reed, Sr.
Program Officer, Daniel M. Thompson
Major Activities: Promotion of Christian Unity-Ecumenical Prayer & Worship; Coordination of Community Ministries; Summer Youth Employment; Summer Camping-Inner City Youth; Supports wide variety of social justice concerns

InterFaith Conference of Metropolitan Washington

1426 Ninth St., NW, Washington, DC 20001-3344 Tel. (202)234-6300 Fax (202)234-6303
Email: ifc@ifcmw.org
Website: www.ifcmw.org
Media Contact, Exec. Dir., Rev. Dr. Clark Lobenstine
Exec. Dir., Rev. Dr. Clark Lobenstine
Admn. Sec., Judy Bond
Pres., Mrs. Carole Miller
1st Vice Pres., Siva Subramanian, M.D.
Chpsn., Rev. Dr. Robert Maddo
Sec., Mrs. Iris Lav
Treas., Sheikh Bassam Estwani
Major Activities: Helps end hunger, homelessness, and racism. Strengthens families and youth and deepens understanding by bringing together 10 world religions to build a just, compassionate community in metropolitan Washington D.C.

FLORIDA

Christian Service Center for Central Florida, Inc.

808 W. Central Blvd., Orlando, FL 32805-1809 Tel. (407)425-2523 Fax (407)425-9513
Website: www.christianservicecenter.org
Media Contact, Exec. Dir., Robert F. Stuart
Exec. Dir., Robert F. Stuart
Family Emergency Services, Dir.,Rev. Haggeo Gautier
Fresh Start, Dir., Rev. Haggeo Gautier
Dir. of Mktg.,
Pres., Dr. Bryan Fulwider
Treas., Peter Reinert
Sec., Terry Bitner
Major Activities: Provision of Basic Needs (food, clothing, shelter); Emergency Assistance; Noon-time Meals; Collection and Distribution of Used Clothing; Shelter & Training for Homeless; Children After-School and Summer Programs

Florida Council of Churches*

5025 Southampton Circle, Tampa, FL 33647 Tel. (813)910-1532 Fax (813)435-3239
Email: rmeyer@floridachurches.org
Website: www.floridachurches.org
Media Contact, Exec. Dir., Rev. Russell L. Meyer
Exec. Dir., The Rev. Russell L. Meyer
Major Activities: Justice and Peace; Disaster Response; Legislation & Public Policy; Local Ecumenism; Farmworker Ministry; Cherishing the Creation (Environmental Stewardship)

GEORGIA

Georgia Christian Council*

P.O. Box 7193 (2370 Vineville Ave.), Macon, GA 31209-7193 Tel. (478)743-2085 Fax (478) 743-2085
Email: GAChristiancouncil@alltel.net
Media Contact, Exec. Dir., Rev. Leland C. Collins
Exec. Dir., Rev. Leland C. Collins
Pres., Bishop B. Michael Watson, 3370 Vineville, Ave., Suite 101, Macon, GA 31204
Sec., Dr. Willis Moore, 5312 W. Mountain St., Suite 200, Stone Mountain, GA 30083-2073
Major Activities: Local Ecumenical Support and Resourcing; Legislation; Rural Development; Racial Justice; Networking for Migrant Coalition; Aging Coalition; GA To GA With Love; Medical Care; Prison Chaplaincy; Training for Church Development; Souper Bowl; Disaster Relief; Clustering; Development of Local Ecumenism; Prison Ministry; Hunger Advocacy; Family Advocacy; Developing Discipleship

The Regional Council of Churches of Atlanta

2195 Defoor Hills Rd., Suite L, Atlanta, GA 30318 Tel. (404)389-0590 Fax (404)389-0594
Email: info@rccatl.org
Website: www.rccatl.org
Pres., Dr. Robert Franklin
Vice Pres., Mr. Steve Brown
Vice Pres., Dr. R. Alan Culpepper
Vice Pres., Rev. Tim McDonald
Sec., Dr. C.P. Huang
Treas., Ms. Dorothy James
Exec. Dir., Roy Craft
Assoc. Dir., Ethel Ware Carter
Major Activities: Forums of ecumenical interests; promotional collaboration and communication across denominational lines; and across geographical areas of Atlanta, interfaith work, coalition building.

IDAHO

The Regional Council for Christian Ministry, Inc.
237 N. Water, Idaho Falls, ID 83403 Tel. (208) 524-9935
Email: rccm@onewest.net
Exec. Sec., Daniel Sene
Major Activities: Island Park Ministry; Community Food Bank; Community Observances; F.I.S.H.

ILLINOIS

Churches United of the Quad City Area
630 9th St., Rock Island, IL 61201 Tel. (309)786-6494 Fax (309)786-5916
Email: mjones@churchesunited.net
Website: www.churchesunited.net
Media Contact, Exec. Dir., Rev. Ronald Quay
Exec. Dir., Ronald Quay
Program Manager, Anne E. Wachal
Shelter Manager, Kit Miller
Financial Manager, Melanie Jones
Major Activities: Jail Ministry; Hunger Projects; Minority Enablement; Criminal Justice; Radio-TV; Peace; Local Church Development; Living Wage; Women's Shelter

Community Renewal Society
332 South Michigan Ave. Suite 500, Chicago, IL 60604 Tel. (312)673-3835 Fax (312)427-6130
Email: bborst@crs-ucc.org
Website: www.crs-ucc.org
Media Contact, Exec. Dir., Dr. Calvin S. Morris

Contact Ministries of Springfield
1100 E. Adams, Springfield, IL 62703 Tel. (217) 753-3939 Fax (217)753-8643
Email: rtarrcm@springnetl.com
Media Contact, Exec. Dir., Rita Tarr
Exec. Dir., Rita Tarr
Major Activities: Information; Referral and Advocacy; Ecumenical Coordination; Low Income Housing Referral; Food Pantry Coordination; Prescription & Travel Emergency; Low Income Budget Counseling; 24 hours on call; Emergency Shelter On-site Women with Children

Evanston Ecumenical Action Council
P.O. Box 1414, Evanston, IL 60204 Tel. (847) 475-1150 Fax (847)475-2526
Website: members.aol.com/eeachome/eeac.html
Media Contact, Comm. Chpsn., Ken Wylie
Dir. Hospitality Cntr. for the Homeless, Sue Murphy
Co-Pres., The Rev. Ted Miller; The Rev. Hardist Lane
Treas., Caroline Frowe
Major Activities: Interchurch Communication and Education; Peace and Justice Ministries; Coordinated Social Action; Soup Kitchens; Multi-Purpose Hospitality Center for the Homeless; Worship and Renewal, Racial Reconciliation, Youthwork

Greater Chicago Broadcast Ministries
112 E. Chestnut St., Chicago, IL 60611-2014 Tel. (312)988-9001 Fax (312)988-9004
Email: gcbm@ameritech.net
Website: gcbm.org
Media Contact, Exec. Dir., Lydia Talbot
Pres., Bd. of Dir., Rev. Phil Blackwell
Exec. Dir., Lydia Talbot
Major Activities: Television, Inter-faith-Ecumenical Development; Social-Justice Concerns

The Hyde Park & Kenwood Interfaith Council
5745 S. Blackstone Ave., Chicago, IL 60637 Tel. (773)752-1911 Fax (773)752-2676
Media Contact, Exec. Dir., Lesley M. Radius
Exec. Dir., Lesley M. Radius
Pres., The Rev. David Grainger
Sec., Barbara Krell
Major Activities: Interfaith Work; Hunger Projects; Community Development

Illinois Conference of Churches*
522 East Monroe, Ste. 208, Springfield, IL 62701 Tel. (217)522-7099 Fax (217)522-7105
Email: adminstaff@ilconfchurches.org
Website: ilconfchurches.org
Media Contact, Admin. Asst., Ms. Andrea Wilson, Email: awilson@ilconfchurhces.org
Exec. Dir., Rev. David A. Anderson
Pres., Rev. Donald E. Mason
Major Activities: Ecumenical Education and Dialogue, Public Policy Education and Advocacy.

Oak Park-River Forest Community of Congregations
P.O. Box 3365, Oak Park, IL 60303-3365 Tel. (708)386-8802 Fax (708)386-1399
Website: http://lgrossman.comcomcong.htm
Media Contact, The Rev. Marguerite Rourke
Pres., The Rev. Marguerite Rourke
Treas., The Rev. Dwight Bailey
Major Activities: Community Affairs; Ecumenical-Interfaith Affairs; Youth Education; FOOD PANTRY; Senior Citizens Worship Services; Interfaith Thanksgiving Services; Good Friday Services; Literacy Training; CROP-CWS Hunger Walkathon; Work with Homeless Through PADS (Public Action to Deliver Shelter; Diversity Education; Walk-in Ministry

Peoria Friendship House of Christian Service
800 N.E. Madison Ave., Peoria, IL 61603 Tel. (309)671-5200 Fax (309)671-5206

239

Media Contact, Exec. Dir., Beverly Isom

Pres. of Bd., David Dadds

Major Activities: Children's After-School; Teen Programs; Recreational Leagues; Senior Citizens Activities; Emergency Food-Clothing Distribution; Emergency Payments for Prescriptions, Rent, Utilities; Community Outreach; Economic Development; Neighborhood Empowerment; GED Classes; Family Literacy; Mother's Group; Welfare to Work Programs

INDIANA

The Associated Churches of Fort Wayne & Allen County, Inc.

602 E. Wayne St., Fort Wayne, IN 46802 Tel. (260)422-3528 Fax (260)422-6721

Email: Vernchurch@aol.com

Website: www.associatedchurches.org

Media Contact, Exec. Dir., Rev. Vernon R. Graham

Exec. Dir., Rev. Vernon R. Graham

Administrative Assistant, Elaine Williamson

Foodbank- Director, Ellen Graham; John Kaiser; Isaac Nickleson;Gordon Matoon

Dir. Of Prog. Development & Mission Outreach, Ellen Graham

Dir. Of Weekday Religious Education, Kathy Rolf

Pres., Charles Hutton, 10211 Greenmoor Drive, New Haven, Indiana 46774

Treas., The Rev. Alycia Smith, 3223 Hobson Rd., Ft. Wayne, IN 46805

Major Activities: Weekday Religious Ed.; Church Clusters; Overcoming Racism; A Baby's Closet;; Hunger Walk; Campus Ministry; Feeding the Babies; Food Bank System; Peace & Justice Commission; Welfare Reform; Endowment Development; Child Care Advocacy; Advocates Inc.; Ecumenical Dialogue; Children Feeding Children; Vincent House (Homeless); A Learning Journey (Literacy); Reaching Out in Love; The Jail Ministry; The Samaritan Counseling Center; Habitat for Humanity.

Christian Ministries of Delaware County

401 E. Main St., Muncie, IN 47305 Tel. (317) 288-0601 Fax (317)282-4522

Email: christianministries@netzero.net

Website: www.christianministries.ws

Media Contact, Exec. Dir., Marie Evans

Exec. Dir., Marie Evans

Pres., Dr. J. B. Black, Jr.

Treas., Joan McKee

Major Activities: Baby Care Program; Youth Ministry at Detention Center; Community Church Festivals; Food Pantry; Emergency Assistance; CROP Walk; Social Justice; Family Life Education; Homeless Shelter (sleeping room only); Clothing and household items available free; workshops for low income clients; homeless apartments available- short stays only at no cost; provide programs and workshops for pastors and churches in community; work with schools sponsoring programs.

Church Community Services

629 S. 3rd Street, Elkhart, IN 46516-3241 Tel. (574)295-3673 Fax (574)295-5593

Email: ccs6293rd@aol.com

Website: www.soupofsuccess.com

Exec. Director, Dean Preheim-Bartel

Major Activities: Financial Assistance for Emergencies; Food Pantry; Information and Referral; Clothing Referral; Rent Assistance; Utility Assistance; Medication Vouchers; Transportation Vouchers; Job and Life Skills Training Program for Women

The Church Federation of Greater Indianapolis, Inc.

1100 W. 42nd St., Ste. 345, Indianapolis, IN 46208 Tel. (317)926-5371 Fax (317)926-5373

Email: churches@churchfederationindy.org

Website: www.churchfederationindy.org

Media Contact, Comm. Consultant, Julie Foster

Exec. Dir., Rev. Dr. Angelique Walker-Smith

Pres., Father John Beitans

Treas., Hugh Moore

Major Activities: "Preserving Christian Diversity & Impacting Our Society-Through Unity in Christ": Organizing, Energizing, Mobilizing Since 1912 (John 17: 20-23), Benevolence Ministry-C.R.O.P. (Church World Service; Celebration of Hope Partnership (Racial Reconciliation); Clergy ID Badge Program; Faith and Fathers; Family Congregation and Mentoring Program(FCMP); Hispanic-Latino Forum; Faith and Education Initiative; Church and Neighborhood Partnership; Greater Indianapolis Prayer Network to Stop the Violence-Ecumenical Project for Reconciliation and Healing; TV Broadcasts; Caring Churches Network; Indianapolis Prayer Breakfast (Partnership)

Evansville Area Community of Churches, Inc.

713 N. 2nd Ave., Evansville, IN 47710 Tel. (812) 425-3524 Fax (812)425-3525

Email: eacc@evansville.net

Media Contact, EACC Administrator and Weekday Dir., Janet Battram

Pres., The Rev. G. Philip Hoy

V. Pres., Evelyn Cave

Sec., The Rev. C. E. Erickson

Treas., Paul Farmer

Major Activities: Food Pantry System; Jail Ministry; Weekday Christian Ed.; Ecumenical and Community Service & Activities

Indiana Partners for Christian Unity and Mission

P.O. Box 88790, Indianapolis, IN 46208-0790
Tel. (800)746-2310 Fax (315)292-5990
Email: dfrischemouri@comcast.net
Website: www.ipcum.org
Media Contact, The Rev. Dennis Frische-Mouri, Ministry Coordinator
Executive Dir., The Rev. Dennis Frische-Mouri
Pres., The Rev. Janet Wanner
Treas., Mrs. Marilyn Moffett
Major Activities: Initiating dialogue on issues of social concern by organizing conferences on the death penalty, racism, welfare reform and violence; facilitating communication through an electronic newsletter and web site; promoting the National Day of Prayer and the Week of Prayer for Christian Unity; and advancing Churches Uniting in Christ.

Interfaith Community Council, Inc.

702 E. Market St., New Albany, IN 47150 Tel. (812)948-9248 Fax (812)948-9249
Email: icc@digicove.com
Website: www.interfaithinc.org
Media Contact, Exec. Dir., Houston Thompson
Exec. Dir., Houston Thompson
Programs - Emergency Assistance
RSVP, Dir., Ceil Sperzel
Major Activities: Emergency Assistance; Retired Senior Volunteer Program; New Clothing and Toy Drives; Emergency Food Distribution; Homeless Prevention; Kids' Café; Youth Development Services

Kentuckiana Interfaith Community (see listing under Kentucky)

Lafayette Urban Ministry

525 N. 4th St., Lafayette, IN 47901 Tel. (317) 423-2691 Fax (317)423-2693
Media Contact, Exec. Dir., Joseph Micon
Exec. Dir., Joseph Micon
Advocate Coord., Rebecca Smith
Public Policy Coord., Harry Brown
Pres., John Wilson
Major Activities: Social Justice Ministries with and among the Poor

United Religious Community of St. Joseph County

2015 Western Ave., Suite 336, South Bend, IN 46629 Tel. (574)282-2397 Fax (574)282-8014
Email: urc@urcsjc.org
Website: www.urcsjc.org
Media Contact, Exec. Dir., Carol Thon
Exec. Dir., Carol Thon
Pres.,Tom Callahan
Refugee Program Director, Carol McDonnell
Victim Impact Panel Director, Marchell Wesaw
Advocacy Centers Director, Marchell Wesaw

Major Activities: Religious Understanding; Interfaith-Ecumenical Education; Interfaith Newsletter "Torch"; CROP Walk; On-site Prayer Ministry; Peacemaker Awards; Hunger Education; Housing and Homelessness Issues; Clergy Education and Support; Refugee Resettlement; Victim Assistance; Advocacy for the Needy; Family Justice Center (Partner addressing chaplaincy), Housing Project for Grandparents raising Grandchildren

Wellspring Interfaith Social Services, Inc. (previously West Central Neighborhood Ministry, Inc.)

1316 Broadway, Fort Wayne, IN 46802-3304 Tel. (219)422-6618 Fax (219)422-9319
Email: fzirille@wellspringinterfaith.org
Media Contact, Exec. Dir., Francis M. Zirille
Exec. Dir., Francis M. Zirille
Ofc. Mgr., J. R. Stopperich
Neighborhood Services Dir., Carol Salge
Senior Citizens Dir., Gayle Mann
Youth Director, Lois Ehinger
Major Activities: After-school Programs; Teen Drop-In Center; Summer Day Camp; Summer Overnight Camp; Information and Referral Services; Food Pantry; Nutrition Program for Senior Citizens; Senior Citizens Activities; Tutoring; Developmental Services for Families & Senior Citizens; Parent Club

IOWA

Churches United, Inc.

1035 3rd Ave., Suite 202, Cedar Rapids, IA 52403-2463 Tel. (319)366-7163 Fax (319)366-7163
Email: churchesunited@yahoo.com
Website: www.churchesunitedcr.org
Media Contact, Exec. Dir., Darci Morin
Exec. Dir., Darci Morin
Pres., Rev. David Loy
Treas., Ellen Bruckner
Major Activities: Communication-resource center for member churches; Community Information and Referral; Ecumenical City-wide Celebrations; Restorative Justice programs

Des Moines Area Religious Council

3816 36th St., Ste. 202, Des Moines, IA 50310 Tel. (515)277-6969 Fax (515)274-8389
Email: info@dmreligious.org
Website: dmreligious.org
Media Contact, Exec. Dir., Forrest Harms
Exec. Dir., Forrest Harms
Pres., James Swanstrom
Pres. Elect, Faith Ferre
Treas., Leonara Waller
Major Activities: Education; Social Initiatives Advocacy; Mission; Emergency Food Pantry; Ministry to Widowed; Child Care Assistance, Compassion in Action, Cross-cultural

241

Ecumenical Ministries of Iowa (EMI)*

P.O. Box 41487, Des Moines, IA 50311 Tel. (515) 274-2278 Fax (515)274-2278
Email: emofiowa@aol.com
Website: www.iowachurches.org
Media Contact, Comm. Coord., Mary Swalla Holmes
Exec. Dir., Rev. Sarai Schnucker Beck
Major Activities: Facilitating the denominations' cooperative agenda of resourcing local expression of the church; Assess needs & develop responses through Justice and Unity Commissions

Iowa Religious Media Services*

3816 36th Street, Suite 100, Des Moines, IA 50310-4710 Tel. (515)277-2920 Fax (515) 277-0842
Email: questions@irms.org
Website: www.irms.org
Media Contact, Exec. Dir., Sharon E. Strohmaier
Exec. Dir., Sharon E. Strohmaier
Major Activities: Media Library for Churches in 7 Denominations in the Midwest; Provide Video Production Services for Churches, Non-profit & Educational organizations; will rent media to churches in the continental U.S. (details on the website)

KANSAS

Cross-Lines Cooperative Council

736 Shawnee Ave., Kansas City, KS 66105 Tel. (913)281-3388 Fax (913)281-2344
Email: theresa@cross-lines.org
Website: www.cross-lines.org
Media Contact, Dir. of Dev., Theresa Swartwood
Exec. Dir., Rick Caplan
Dir. of Programs, Lora McDonald
Major Activities: Emergency Assistance; Family Support Advocacy; Thrift Store; Workcamp Experiences; School Supplies; Christmas Store; Hunger Relief

Inter-Faith Ministries-Wichita

829 N. Market, Wichita, KS 67214-3519 Tel. (316) 264-9303 Fax (316)264-2233
Email: smuyskens@ifmnet.org
Website: www.ifmnet.org
Media Contact, Exec. Dir., Sam Muyskens
Exec. Dir., Rev. Sam Muyskens
Adm. Asst.- Kathy Freed
ASAP Haiti, Dir. Bonnie Chadick
Homeless and Housing Services, Dir., Sandy Swank
Special Projects, Dir., Ashley Davis
Development, Dir., Karen Dobbin
Campaign to End Childhood Hunger, Karole Bradford
Community Ministry/Restorative Justice/Family Group Conferencing/Racial Justice
Coord., Jeannine Little

Faith in Action, Coord., Richard Hanley
GoZones! Dir., Johanna Wilson
Major Activities: Communications; Urban Education; Inter-religious Understanding; Community Needs and Issues; Theology and Worship; Hunger; Family Life; Multi-Cultural Concerns

Kansas Ecumenical Ministries*

5833 SW 29th St., Topeka, KS 66614-2499 Tel. (785)272-9531
Email: kemstaff@ecunet.org
Media Contact, Exec. Dir., Rev. Linda Kemp
Pres., Rev. Nancy Gammil
Vice Pres., Marvin Zehr
Sec., Rev. Lee Lever
Exec. Dir., Rev. Linda Kemp
Pres., Rev. Nancy Gammi
Vice Pres., Marvin Zehr
Sec., Rev. Lee Lever
Major Activities: State Council of Churches; Legislative Activities; Program Facilitation and Coordination; Education; Mother-to-Mother Program; Rural Concerns; Hate group monitoring; Children & Families; Faith and Order

KENTUCKY

Eastern Area Community Ministries

P.O. Box 43049, Louisville, KY 40253-0049 Tel. (502)244-6141 Fax (502)254-5141
Email: easternacm@cs.com
Media Contact, Acting Exec. Dir., Sharon Eckler
Acting Exec. Dir., Sharon Eckler
Board Pres., Rev. Elwood Sturtevant
Board Sec., Mary Stephens
Board Treas., Homer Lacy, Jr.
Youth and Family Services,Rachael Elrod
Older Adult Services, Associate Program Dir., Joni Snyder
Neighborhood Visitor Program, Acting Prog. Dir., Jane Parker
Major Activities: Emergency Assistance; Clothes Closet; Meals on Wheels; Community Worship Services; Good Start for Kids; Juvenile Court Diversion; Community Development; Transient Fund; Ministerial Association; Juvenile Court Diversion

Fern Creek-Highview United Ministries

7502 Tangelo Dr., Louisvlle, KY 40228 Tel. (502)239-7407 Fax (502)239-7454
Email: FernCreek.Ministries@crnky.org
Media Contact, Exec. Dir., Kay Sanders, 7502 Tangelo Dr., Louisville, KY 40228 Tel. (502)239-7407
Exec. Dir., Kay Sanders
Pres., David Pooler
Major Activities: Ecumenically supported social service agency providing services to the com-

242

munity, including Emergency Financial Assistance, Food-Clothing, Health Aid Equipment Loans, Information-Referral, Advocacy, Checks; Holiday Programs, Life Skills Training; Mentoring; Case Management; Adult Day-Care Program

Hazard-Perry County Community Ministries, Inc.

P.O. Box 1506, Hazard, KY 41702-1506 Tel. (606)436-0051 Fax (606)436-0071
Media Contact, Gerry Feamster-Roll
Exec. Dir., Gerry Feamster-Roll
Chpsn., Sarah Hughes
V. Chpsn., Susan Duff
Sec., Virginia Campbell
Treas., Margaret Adams
Major Activities: Food Pantry-Crisis Aid Program; Day Care; Summer Day Camp; After-school Program; Christmas Tree; Family Support Center; Adult Day Care; Transitional Housing

Highlands Community Ministries

1140 Cherokee Rd., Louisville, KY 40204 Tel. (502)451-3695 Fax (502)451-3609
Email: hcmexecu@hotmail.com
Website: www.hcmlou.org
Media Contact, Exec. Dir., Stan Esterle
Exec. Dir., Stan Esterle
Major Activities: Welfare Assistance; Children Day Care; Adult DayHealth Care; Social Services for Elderly; Housing for Elderly and Handicapped; Ecumenical Programs; Interfaith Programs; Community Classes; Activities for Children; Neighborhood and Business organization

Kentuckiana Interfaith Community

PO BOX 7128, Louisville, KY 40257 Tel. (502) 587-6265 Fax (502)451-9827
Email: churchoffice@salemucc.com
Website: www.neighborhoodlink.com/org/kic
Media Contact, Exec. Dir., Rev. Douglas Fowler
Pres., Ron Gaddie
Vice Pres., Laura Metzger
Treas., Charles Hawkins
Major Activities: Christian-Jewish, Islamic, Bahai Ministries in KY, Southern IN; Consensus Advocacy; Interfaith Dialogue; Community Hunger Walk; Racial Justice Forums; Network for Neighborhood-based Ministries; Hunger & Racial Justice Commission; Faith Channel-Cable TV Station, Horizon News Paper; Police-Comm. Relations Task Force; Ecumenical Strategic Planning; Networking with Seminaries & Religious-Affiliated Institutions

Kentucky Council of Churches*

1500 Leestown Rd., Suite 108, Lexington, KY 40511 Tel. (859)269-7715 Fax (859)269-1240
Email: kcc@kycouncilofchurches.org

Website: www.kycouncilofchurches.org
Media Contact, Exec. Dir., Nancy Jo Kemper
Exec. Dir., The Rev. Dr. Nancy Jo Kemper
Pres., The Rev. Ron Gaddie
Kentucky Interchurch Disaster Recovery Program Coodinator., Mr. Harper Davis
Director Associate for Local Ecumenism, The Rev. W. Chris Benham Skidmore
Major Activities: Christian Unity; Public Policy; Justice; Disaster Response; Peace Issues; Anti-Racism; Health Care Issues; Local Ecumenism; Rural Land-Farm Issues; Gambling; Capital Punishment

Ministries United South Central Louisville (M.U.S.C.L., Inc.)

1207 Hart Avenue, Louisville, KY 42013 Tel. (502)363-9087 Fax (502)363-9087
Media Contact, Exec. Dir., Rev. Antonio (Tony) Aja, M.Div., Tel. (502)363-2383, Email Tony_Aja@pcusa.org
Ex. Dir., Rev. Antonio (Tony) Aja, M.Div.
Airport Relocation Ombudsman, Rev. Phillip Garrett, M.Div. Tel. (502)361-2706; E-mail, philombud@aol.com
Senior Adults Programs, Dir., Mrs. Jeannine Blakeman, BSSW
Emergency Assistance, Dir., Mr. Michael Hundley
Low-Income Coord., Ms. Wanda Irvio
Youth Services, Dir., The Rev. Bill Sanders, M.Div.
Volunteers Coord., Mrs. Carol Stemmle

Northern Kentucky Interfaith Commission, Inc.

901 York St., PO Box 72296, Newport, KY 41072-0296 Tel. (859)581-2237 Fax (859)261-6041
Website: www.nkyinterfaith.com
Media Contact, Exec. Dir., Rev. James A. Bishop
Pres., Mr. Paul Whalen
Sec., Ms.Cordelia Koplow
Treas., Mr. John Wilgus
Admin. Asst., Pat McDermott
Major Activities: Understanding Faiths; Meeting Spiritual and Human Needs; Enabling Churches to Greater Ministry

Paducah Cooperative Ministry

1359 S. 6th St., Paducah, KY 42003 Tel. (270) 442-6795 Fax (270)442-6812
Email: pcministry@hotmail.com
Media Contact, Dir., Heidi Suhrheinrich
Dir., Heidi Suhrheinrich
Chpsn., Rev. Larry mcBride
Vice-Chpsn., Tommy Tucker
Major Activities: Programs for Hungry, Elderly, Poor, Homeless, Handicapped, Undereducated

St. Matthews Area Ministries

201 Biltmore Rd., Louisville, KY 40207 Tel. (502)893-0205 Fax (502)893-0206

243

Media Contact, Exec. Dir., Dan G. Lane
Exec. Dir., Dan G. Lane
Child Care, Dir., Janet Hennessey
Dir. Assoc., Eileen Bartlett
Major Activities: Child Care; Emergency Assistance; Youth Services; Interchurch Worship and Education; Housing Development; Counseling; Information & Referral; Mentor Program; Developmentally Disabled

South East Associated Ministries (SEAM)

6500 Six Mile Ln., Ste.A, Louisville, KY 40218 Tel. (502)499-9350
Media Contact, Mary Beth Helton
Exec. Dir., Mary Beth Helton
Life Skills Center, Dir., Robert Davis
Youth Services, Dir., Bill Jewel
Pres., David Ehresman
Treas., Bill Trusty
Major Activities: Emergency Food, Clothing and Financial Assistance; Life Skills Center (Programs of Prevention and Case Management and Self-Sufficiency Through Education, Empowerment, Support Groups, etc.); Bloodmobile; Ecumenical Education and Worship; Juvenile Court Diversion; TEEN Court; Teen Crime & the Community

South Louisville Community Ministries

Peterson Social Services Center,4803 Southside Dr., Louisville, KY 40214 Tel. (502)367-6445 Fax (502)361-4668
Email: slcm@slcm.org
Website: www.slcm.org
Media Contact, Exec. Dir., J. Michael Jupin
Bd. Chair., Ray Whitener
Bd. Vice-Chair., Jim Woodward
Bd. Treas., Greg Greenwood
Exec. Dir., Rev. J. Michael Jupin
Major Activities: Food, Clothing & Financial Assistance; Home Delivered Meals; Ecumenical Worship; Affordable Housing; Adult Day Care; Truancy Prevention; Dare to Care Kids Café

LOUISIANA

Greater Baton Rouge Federation of Churches and Synagogues

3112 Convention St., Baton Rouge, LA 70806 Tel. (225)267-5600 Fax (225)267-5100
Website: gbrfed.org
Media Contact, Exec. Dir., Rev. Jeff Day
Exec. Dir., Rev. Jeff Day
Admn. Asst., Ashley Griffin
Pres., Rev. Amy Mercer
Pres.-Elect, Joyce Robinson
Treas., Melvin Davis
Major Activities: Combating Hunger; Interfaith Relations; Interfaith Concert; Race Relations; Interfaith Caregivers (Faith in Action)

Greater New Orleans Federation of Churches

4640 S. Carrollton Ave, Suite 2B, New Orleans, LA 70119-6077 Tel. (504)488-8788 Fax (504)488-8823
Exec. Dir., The Rev. J. Richard Randels
Major Activities: Information and Referral; Food Distribution(FEMA); Forward Together TV Program; Sponsors seminars for pastors (e.g. church growth, clergy taxes,etc.); Police Chaplaincy; Fire Chaplaincy

Louisiana Interchurch Conference*

527 North Boulevard, Fourth Floor, Baton Rouge, LA 70802 Tel. (225)924-0213 Fax (225)927-7860
Email: lainterchurch@aol.com
Website: www.lainterchurch.org
Media Contact, Exec. Dir., Rev. C. Dana Krutz
Exec. Dir., Rev. C. Dana Krutz
Pres., Bishop C. Garnett Henning
Major Activities: Ministries to Aging; Prison Reform; Liaison with State Agencies; Ecumenical Dialogue; Institutional Chaplains; Racism; Environmental; Public Policy Advocacy

MAINE

Maine Council of Churches*

19 Pleasant Ave., Portland, ME 04103 Tel. (207)772-1918 Fax (207)772-2947
Email: info@mainecouncilofchurches.org
Website: www.mainecouncilofchurches.org
Media Contact, Exec Dir., Jill Saxby, Email: jsaxby@mainecouncilofchurches.org
Exec. Dir., Jill Saxby
Assoc. Dir., Douglas Cruger
Admin. Asst., Sandra Buzzell
Pres., Br. Francis Blouin
Treas., Rev. Richard Swan
Major Activities: Criminal Justice Reform/Restorative Justice; Economic Justice; Environmental Justice; Peace Issues; Civil Rights

MARYLAND

Central Maryland Ecumenical Council*

Cathedral House, 4 E. University Pkwy., Baltimore, MD 21218 Tel. (410)467-6194 Fax (410)554-6387
Email: cmecoffice@aol.com
Media Contact, Exec. Dir., Mr. Tim Hanavan
Pres., The Rev. Iris Farabee-Lewis
Major Activities: Interchurch Communications and Collaboration; Information Systems; Ecumenical Relations; Urban Mission and Advocacy; Staff for Judicatory Leadership Council; Commission on Dialogue; Commission on Church & Society; Commission

on Admin. & Dev.; Ecumenical Choral Concerts; Ecumenical Worship Services

The Christian Council of Delaware and Maryland's Eastern Shore (see listing under Delaware)

Community Ministries of Rockville

114 West Montgomery Ave., Rockville, MD 20850 Tel. (301)762-8682 Fax (301)762-2939
Email: asaenz@cmrocks.org
Media Contact, Managing Dir., Agnes Saenz
Exec. Dir. & Comm. Min., Mansfield M. Kaseman
Managing Dir., Agnes Aaenz
Major Activities: Shelter Care; Emergency Assistance; Elderly Home Care; Affordable Housing; Political Advocacy; Community Education; Education to Recent Immigrants

Community Ministry of Montgomery County

114 West Montgomery Ave., Rockville, MD 20850 Tel. (301)762-8682 Fax (301)762-2939
Media Contact, Exec. Dir., Rebecca Wagner
Exec. Dir., Rebecca Wagner
Major Activities: Interfaith Clothing Center; Emergency Assistance Coalition; The Advocacy Function; Information and Referral Services; Friends in Action; The Thanksgiving Hunger Drive; Thanksgiving in February; Community Based Shelter

MASSACHUSETTS

Attleboro Area Council of Churches, Inc.

7 North Main St., Ste. 200, Attleboro, MA 02703 Tel. (508)222-2933 Fax (508)222-2008
Email: aacc@naisp.net
Media Contact, Pres., Bd. of Dir., Rev. Ruth Shaver
Exec. Adm., Kathleen Trowbridge
Staff Asst., Food `n Friends Program Dir., Dorothy Embree
Hosp. Chplns., Rev. Dr. William B. Udall, Rev. Lynn MacLagan
Pres., Rev. Ruth Shaver, Minister of Christian Ed. And Family Life, Second Congregational Ch., 50 Pk. St., Attleboro, MA 02703
Treas., Mr. Richard Shaw, 70 Stanson Dr., N. Attleboro, MA 02760
Major Activities: Hospital Chaplaincy; personal Growth-Skill Workshops; Ecumenical Worship; Interfaith Worship; Media Resource Center; Referral Center; Communications-Publications; Community Social Action; Food'n Friends Kitchens; Nursing Home Volunteer Visitation Program; Clergy Fellowship-Learning Events

The Cape Cod Council of Churches, Inc.

P.O. Box 758, Hyannis, MA 02601 Tel. (508) 775-5073

Email: cccounchur@capecod.net
Media Contact, Exec. Dir., Diane Casey-Lee
Exec. Dir., Diane Casey-Lee
Chaplain, Rev. Sandra Junier
Chaplain, Rehabilitation Hospital of the Cape and Islands, Rev. Stanley Knull
Hand of Hope Outreach Center, P.O. Box 125, Dennisport, MA 02639 Tel. (508)394-6361
Major Activities: Social Concerns; Religious Education; Emergency Distribution of Food, Clothing, Furniture; Referral and Information; Church World Service; Interfaith Relations; Media Presence; Hospital & Jail Chaplaincy; Arts & Religion

Cooperative Metropolitan Ministries

474 Centre St., Newton, MA 02158 Tel. (617) 244-3650 Fax (617)630-9172
Email: coopmet@aol.com
Website: www.coopment.org
Media Contact, Exec. Dir., Claire Kashuck
Exec. Dir., Claire Kashuck
Bd. Pres., Robert Stephens
Treas., Ricardo Neal
Clk., The Rev. John Odams
Major Activities: Low Income; Suburban-Urban Bridges; Racial and Economic Justice

Council of Churches of Greater Springfield

39 Oakland St., Springfield, MA 01108 Tel. (413) 733-2149 Fax (413)733-9817
Media Contact, Asst. to Dir., Andrea Skeene
Exec. Dir., Rev. Dr. David F. Hunter
Community Min., Dir. Don A. Washington
Pres., The Rev. Dr. David Hunter
Treas., John Pearson, Esq
Major Activities: Advocacy; Emergency Fuel Fund; Peace and Justice Division; Community Ministry; Hospital and Jail Chaplaincies; Pastoral Service; Crisis Counseling; Christian Social Relations; Relief Collections; Ecumenical and Interfaith Relations; Church-Community Projects and Community Dialogues; Publication, "Knowing My Neighbor-Religious Beliefs and Traditions at Times of Death"

Greater Lawrence Council of Churches

95 E. Haverhill Street, Lawrence, MA 01841 Tel. (978)686-4012 Fax (978)689-2006
Email: davidedwards@conversent.net
Website: greater-lawrence-churches.org
Media Contact, Exec. Dir., David Edwards
Exec. Dir., David Edwards
Pres., Jane Barlow
Vice Pres., Rev. Dr. Richard Haley
Admn. Asst., Barbara Payson
Major Activities: Ecumenical Worship; Radio Ministry; Hospital and Nursing Home

245

Chaplaincy; Afterschool Children's Program; Vacation Bible School, Interfaith care givers of Greater Lawrence

Inter-Church Council of Greater New Bedford

412 County St., New Bedford, MA 02740-5096 Tel. (508)993-6242 Fax (508)991-3158
Email: administration@inter-churchcouncil.org
Website: www.inter-churchcouncil.org
Media Contact, Min., Rev. Edward R. Dufresne, Ph.D.
Exec. Min., Rev. Edward R. Dufresne, Ph.D.
Pres., The Rev. David Lima
Treas., George Mock
Major Activities: Counseling; Spiritual Direction; Chaplaincy; Housing for Elderly and Disabled; Urban Affairs; Community Spiritual Leadership; Parish Nurse Ministry; Accounting and Spiritual Care for the Developmentally Challenged; Ecumenical and Interfaith Ministries; Advocacy for the Homeless; Support for Urban Schhol District; Opposition to Expanded Gambling

Massachusetts Commission on Christian Unity

82 Luce St, Lowell, MA 01852 Tel. (978)453-5423 Fax (978)453-5423
Email: kgordonwhite@msn.com
Media Contact, Exec. Dir., The Rev. K. Gordon White
Exec. Sec., Rev. K. Gordon White
Pres., Rev. Fr. Edward O'Flaherty, Ecumenical Officer, Roman Catholic Archdiocese of Boston
Major Activities: Faith and Order Dialogue with Church Judicatories; Guidelines & Pastoral Directives for Inter-Church Marriages; Guidelines for Celebrating Baptism in an Ecumenical Context

Massachusetts Council of Churches*

14 Beacon St., Suite 416, Boston, MA 02108 Tel. (617)523-2771 Fax (617)523-1486
Email: www.council@masscouncilofchurches. org
Website: www.masscouncilofchurches.org
Media Contact, Dir., Rev. Jack Johnson
Exec. Dir., The Rev. Jack Johnson
Adjunct Assoc. Dir., The Rev. Dr. Carol Flett
Pres., The Rev. John Stendahl
Vice Pres., Fr. John Maheras
Sec., The Rev. Sara Irwin
Treas., The Rev. Kenneth G. Y. Grant
Major Activities: Christian Unity; Education and Evangelism; Social Justice & Individual Rights; Ecumenical Worship; Services and Resources for Individuals and Churches

Worcester County Ecumenical Council

128 Providence Street, Worcester, MA 01604-5432 Tel. (508)757-8385 Fax (508)795-7704

Email: wcec@verizon.net
Media Contact, Exec. Dir., Rev. Allyson D. Platt
The Rev. Allyson D. Platt, Email: wcec.Allyson @verizon.net
Pres.,Mrs. Fran Langille
Major Activities: Ecumenical worship and dialogue networking congregations together in partnerships of mission, education and spiritual renewal. Clusters of Churches; Ecumenical Worship and Dialogue; Interfaith Activities; Resource Connection for Churches; Group Purchasing Consortium

MICHIGAN

Bay Area Ecumenical Forum

103 E. Midland St., Bay City, MI 48706 Tel. (517)686-1360
Media Contact, Rev. Karen Banaszak
Major Activities: Ecumenical Worship; Community Issues; Christian Unity; Education; CROP Walk

Berrien County Association of Churches

275 Pipestone, Benton Harbor, MI 49022 Tel. (616)926-0030 Fax (616)926-2159*51
Website: berrienchurches.org
Media Contact, Sec., Mary Ann Hinz
Pres., Rev. George Lawton
Dir., Street Ministry, The Rev. Yvonne Hester
Major Activities: Street Ministry; CROP Walk; Community Issues; Fellowship; Christian Unity; Hospital Chaplaincy Program; Publish Annual County Church Directory and Monthly Newsletter; Resource Guide for Helping Needy; Distribution of Worship Opportunity—Brochure for Tourists

Grand Rapids Area Center for Ecumenism (GRACE)

207 East Fulton, Grand Rapids, MI 49503-3210 Tel. (616)774-2042 Fax (616)774-2883
Email: dbaak@graceoffice.org
Website: www.graceoffice.org
Media Contact, Rev. David P. Baak
Leadership Team: Rev. David P. Baak; Lisa H. Mitchell; Rev. David G. May
Major Activities: AIDS Care Network; Volunteer Transportation; Hunger Walk ; Education; Christian Unity Worship (Ecumenical Lecture, Christian Unity Worship Events, Interfaith Dialogue Conference); (Affiliate, FISH for My People-transportation); Racial Justice Institute; West Michigan Call to Renewal (Response to Poverty Advocacy); Publications (Grace In~Site); Faith In Motion (Mass Transit and Land Use); Restorative Justice Coalition

Greater Flint Council of Churches

310 E. Third St., Suite 600, Flint, MI 48502 Tel. (810)238-3691 Fax (810)238-4463

Email: gfcc1929@aol.com
Media Contact, Coord., Mrs. Constance D. Neely
Barbara Spaulding Westcott, Publicity Chairperson
President, Overseer Bernadel L. Jefferson
Major Activities: Christian Education; Christian Unity; Christian Missions; Nursing Home Visitor; Church in Society; American Bible Society Materials; Interfaith Dialogue; Church Teacher Exchange Sunday; Directory of Area Faiths and Clergy; Thanksgiving & Easter Sunrise Services; CROP Walks

The Jackson County Interfaith Council

425 Oakwood, P.O. Box 156, Clarklake, MI 49234-0156 Tel. (517)529-9721
Media Contact, Exec. Dir., -vacant-
Exec. Dir., - vacant-
Major Activities: Chaplaincy at Institutions and Senior Citizens Residences; Martin L. King, Jr. Day Celebrations; Ecumenical Council Representation; Radio and TV Programs; Food Pantry; Interreligious Events; Clergy Directory

The Metropolitan Christian Council: Detroit-Windsor

28 W. Adams, Suite 320, Detroit, MI 48226 Tel. (313)962-0340 Fax (313)962-9044
Email: councilweb@aol.com
Website: users.aol.com/councilweb
Media Contact, Rev. Richard Singleton
Exec. Dir., Rev. Richard Singleton
Meals for Shut-ins, Prog. Dir., John Simpson; Admin. Asst., Mrs. Elaine Kisner
Web Calendar Supervisor, Mr. Gerald Morgan
Major Activities: Theological and Social Concerns; Ecumenical Worship; Educational Services; Electronic Media; Print Media; Meals for Shut-Ins; Summer Feeding Program

Muskegon County Cooperating Churches

1095 Third St., Suite 10, Muskegon, MI 49441-1976 Tel. (231)727-6000 Fax (231)727-0841
Media Contact, Prog. Coord., Delphine Hogston
Co-Presidents, Judy Clark-Ochs and Rev. Donna Smith-Snyder
Major Activities: Local Faith Community Information Source, Racial Reconciliation, Dialogue, & Healing; Multiracial Family Support; Responsible Fathers Empowerment; Ecumenical Worship; Faith News TV Ministry; CROP Walk Against Hunger; Jewish-Christian Dialogue; Environmental Issues, Social Justice Issues, Pastoral Support, Homeless Sheltering, Second Harvest Gleaners Food Trucks

SUBSIDIARY ORGANIZATION
Muskegon Responsible Fathers' Initiative
Tel. 231-725-7268, Fax 231-728-4558
Media Contact: Christopher Sandford, Program Coordinator
Major Activities: Responsible Fathers Empowerment; Providing education, job skills & support for fathers to connect and support their children financially, emotionally, & spiritually; Fatherhood skills for incarcerated fathers; Teen Pregnancy Prevention, Prisoner Re-Entry.

Community Uniting for Peace
Media Contact: Delphine Hogston, Secretary
Major Activities: Advocacy to remove the effects of Racism; Community Civil Rights Health Assessment Survey; Responsible Consumer Spending Initiative

Interfaith Hospitality Network in Muskegon
Media Contact: Delphine Hogston
Major Activities: Helping congregations shelter homeless families

Community Connects Choir
Media Contact: Darlene Collett
Major Activities: Winter Holiday Concert. Intentionally interracial, intergenerational, ecumenical singing blending gospel and traditional music. Supports other diverse music opportunities for the community.

In the City for Good—Muskegon
Media Contact: Kryssis Bjork
Major Activities: Bringing together residents, churches, schools, and businesses for hands-on activities to promote cultural diversity and community good. Back-to-school fairs including health screenings, summer work projects, and quarterly gatherings. Interfaith worship events and education. Focus is on urban areas of Muskegon County.

Mall Area Religious Council (MARC)

Mall of America, 7200 York Avenue South, #416, Edina, MN 55435-4406 Tel. (952)831-0447
Email: jchell@manrol.com
Website: www.meaningstore.org
Media Contact, Rev. John Chell, Executive Director

MINNESOTA

Arrowhead Interfaith Council*

102 W. 2nd St., Duluth, MN 55802 Tel. (218)722-7166
Email: president@arrowheadinterfaith.org
Website: www.arrowheadinterfaith.org
Media Contact, Pres., Doug Bowen-Bailey
Pres., Doug Bowen-Bailey
Sec., Sister Lois Eckes
Treas., David Carlson

247

Major Activities: InterFaith Dialogue; Joint Religious Legislative Coalition; Corrections Chaplaincy; Human Justice and Community Concerns; Community Seminars; Children's Concerns

Community Emergency Assistance Program (CEAP)

6840 78th Ave N, Brooklyn Park, MN 55445 Tel. (763)566-9600 Fax (763)566-9604
Email: smklein@isd.net
Website: www.ceap.homestead.com
Media Contact, Exec. Dir., Stephen Klein
Exec. Dir., Stephen Klein
Major Activities: Provision of Basic Needs (Food, Clothing); Emergency Financial Assistance for Shelter; Home Delivered Meals; Chore Services and Homemaking Assistance; Family Loan Program; Volunteer Services

Greater Minneapolis Council of Churches

1001 E. Lake St., P.O. Box 7509, Minneapolis, MN 55407-0509 Tel. (612)721-8687 Fax (612)722-8669
Email: info@gmcc.org
Website: www.gmcc.org
Media Contact, Dir. of Communications, Darcy Hanzlik
President and CEO, The Rev. Dr. Gary B. Reierson E-mail: reierson@gmcc.org
Chair, Kent Eklund
Treas., Mervin Winston
Division Indian Work, Senior Vice President & Exec. Dir., Noya Woodrich
Advancement Vice President., G. James Olsen
Finance & Administration, Vice President and CFO, Peter Lee
Program Development, Exec. Dir., Bruce Bjork
Minnesota FoodShare, Dir., Barbara Thell
Handyworks, Dir., Megan Nolan-Elliasen
Correctional Chaplains, Rev. Dr. Susan Allers Hatlie; Rev. Thomas Van Leer; Rev. Paula Nordhem; Rev. Cheryl Powers Williams
Div. of Indian Work, Dir., Youth Leadership Development Program, Louise Matson
Div. Of Indian Work Adult Services, Dir., Suzanne Tibbetts Young
Div. Of Indian Work Horizons Unlimited, Food Shelf Mgr., Jay Bad Hear Bull
Div. Of Indian Work Strenthening Family Circles, Dir., Carol Ladd;
Div. Of Indian Work Healing Spirit Program, Dir., Kirk Crowshoe;
Div. Of Indian Work American Indian Community Wellness Project, Proj. Mgr., Cheryl Secola
Urban Immersion Service Retreats,. Dir., Gennae Falconer
Metro Paint-A-Thon, Dir., Deidre Pope
Discover Parent Groups, Coord Sandra Vaughn-Kelley

Community Justice Project, Co-Dirs., Brian Herron, Hillary Freeman
Center for Families, Exec. Dir., Sara Nelson, Paul Meyer
Project Preserve, Cord., La Donna White
Church and Community Initiatives/Compassion Capital Fund, Coord., Bridget Ryan
Major Activities: Indian Work (Emergency Assistance, Youth Leadership, self-sufficiency, teen Indian parents, Healing Spirit Program (Foster Care), supportive housing, American Indian Community Wellness Project, and Family Violence Program); Minnesota FoodShare; Metro Paint-A-Thon; Correctional Chaplaincy Program; HandyWorks; Social Justice Advocacy; Supportive Housing; Urban Immersion Service Retreats; Welfare Reform; Economic Self-Sufficiency; Discover Parent Groups; Church and Community Initiatives/ Compassion Capital Fund; Immigrant and Refugee Services; Community Health Promotion; Correctional Aftercare; Restora-tive Justice, Born to Learn

The Joint Religious Legislative Coalition

122 W. Franklin Ave., Ste 315, Minneapolis, MN 55404 Tel. (612)870-3670 Fax (612)870-3671
Email: info@jrlc.org
Website: www.jrlc.org
Media Contact, Exec. Dir., Brian A. Rusche
Exec. Dir., Brian A. Rusche
Research Dir., Dr. James Casebolt
Network Organizer, Jody McCardle
Major Activities: Lobbying at State Legislature; Researching Social Justice Issues and Preparing Position Statements; Organizing Grassroots Citizen's Lobby, Social Justice Advocacy.

Metropolitan Interfaith Council on Affordable Housing (MICAH)

122 W. Franklin Ave., #310, Minneapolis, MN 55404 Tel. (612)871-8980 Fax (612)813-4501
Email: info@micah.org
Website: www.micah.org
Media Contact, Exec. Dir., Joy Sorensen Navarre
Ex. Dir., Joy Sorensen Navarre
Assoc. Dir., José Trejo
Congregational Organizer, Jodi Nelson, Jean Pearson, The Rev. John Buzza, The Rev. John Buzza
Sec., Sue Watlov Phillips
Pres., The Rev. Paul Robinson
Vice Pres., Nancy L. Anderson
Treas., Joseph Holmberg
Past Pres. Kristine Reynolds
Major Activities: The Metropolitan Interfaith Council on Affordable Housing, MICAH, seeks to live out the prophetic vision that calls us "to do justice, to love mercy and to walk humbly with God." (Micah 6:8). We envision

248

a metropolitan area where everyone without exception has a safe, decent and affordable home. MICAH will realize this vision through organizing congregations of faith and community partners to change the political climate and public policies so that all communities preserve and build affordable housing. MICAH's faith-based organizing creates power that produces results. During the past five years MICAH:

Mobilized congregations to build community support for 1,348 affordable homes for families with very low incomes.

Prevented the demolition and gentrification of 1,919 structurally sound apartments. Half of the tenants were people of color or people with disabilities.

Earned HUD's 1999 National Best Practices Award and the Headwaters Fund Social Justice Award in 2001.

Minnesota Council of Churches*

122 W. Franklin Ave., Rm. 100, Minneapolis, MN 55404 Tel. (612)870-3600 Fax (612)870-3622
Email: mcc@mnchurches.org
Website: www.mnchurches.org
Media Contact, Exec. Dir., Rev. Peg Chemberlin, Email: chemberlinp@mnchurches.org

Officers and Staff

Exec. Dir., Rev. Peg Chemberlin, Email: hemberlinp@mn.churches.org
Director of Programs, Rev. Christopher Morton, Email: mortonc@mnchurches.org
Unity & Relationships, Organizer,
Refugee Services, Dir., Joel Luedtke, Email: luedtkej@mnchurches.org
Indian Ministry, Field Organizer,
Communications, Dir., Christopher Dart, Email: dartc@mnchurches.org
Finance & Facilities, Dir., Douglas Swanson, Email: swansond@mnchurches.org
Tri-Council Coordinating Commission, Co-Dirs., James Addington, Carmen Valenzuela
Joint Religious Legislative Coalition, Research Dir. & Admn. Asst., James Casebolt
Joint Religious Legislative Coalition, Exec., Brian A. Rusche
Pres. Bishop James Jelinek
Major Activities: Minnesota Church Center; Rural Life-Ag Crisis; Racial Reconciliation; Indian Ministry; Legislative Advocacy; Refugee Services; Service to Newly Legalized-Undocumented persons; Unity & Relationships, Sexual Exploitation within the Religious Community; Jewish-Christian Relations; Muslim-Christian Relations; Tri-Council Coordinating Commission (Minnesota Churches Anti-Racism Initiative); Hindu-Christian Relations; Peace Works; Minnesota Foodshare

Saint. Paul Area Council of Churches

1671 Summit Ave, St. Paul, MN 55105 Tel. (651)646-8805 Fax (651)646-6866
Email: info@spacc.org
Website: www.spacc.org
Media Contact, Mary Kane
Exec. Dir., The Rev. Grant Abbott
Dir. of Development, Kristi Anderson
Congregations in Community, Julie Quello
Congregations in Community Organizer, Lee Erickson
Congregations in Community Organizer, Inspired to Serve, Megan Paul-Cook
Project Spirit, Dir., Darcel Hill
Project Home, Dir., Sara Liegl
Dept. of Indian Work, Dir., Sheila WhiteEagle
Pres. of the Board, Art Sidner
Treas., Mr. Ezekiel Jackson
Sec., Stella Lundquist
Major Activities: Education and Advocacy Regarding Children and Poverty; Assistance to Churches Developing Children's Parenting Care Services; Ecumenical Encounters and Activities; Indian Ministries; Leadership in Forming Cooperative Ministries for Children and Youth; After School Tutoring; Interfaith Youth Service project engaging young people in effective service-learning that increases interfaith cooperation, contributes to healthy development, and enriches community life; Assistance to Congregations; Training Programs in Anti-racism; Shelters for homeless

Tri-Council Coordinating Commission

122 W. Franklin, Rm. 100, Minneapolis, MN 55404 Tel. (612)871-0229 Fax (612)870-3622
Email: naja@gmcc.org
Website: www.gmcc.org/tcc.html
Media Contact, Co.-Dir., R. James Addington, Assoc. Rev. Carmen Valenzuela
Exec. Cmte.: The Rev. Peg Chemberlin, The Rev. Gary Reierson and The Rev. Thomas Duke
Major Activities: Anti-Racism training and organizational consultation; Institutional anti-racism team development and coaching; training and coaching of anti-racism trainers and organizers (in cooperation with corss roads ministry)

MISSISSIPPI

Mississippi Religious Leadership Conference*

P.O. Box 68123, Jackson, MS 39286-8123 Tel. (601)924-7430 Fax (601)924-7430
Email: mrlc@netdoor.com
Media Contact, Exec. Dir., Rev. Paul Griffin Jones, II, Th.D., PhD.
Exec. Dir.,The Rev. Paul Griffin Jones, II, Th.D., PhD.
Chair, Bishop Duncan Gray, III
Treas., The Rev. Jim White

249

Major Activities: Cooperation among Religious Leaders; Lay-Clergy Retreats; Social Concerns Seminars; Disaster Task Force; Advocacy for Disadvantaged

MISSOURI

Council of Churches of the Ozarks
P.O. Box 3947, Springfield, MO 65808-3947 Tel. (417)862-3586 Fax (417)862-2129
Email: ccozarks@ccozarks.org
Website: www.ccozarks.org
Media Contact, Comm. Dir., Susan Jackson
Exec. Dir., Dr. David W. Hockensmith, Jr.
Chief Operating Officer, Julie Guillebeau
Major Activities: Ministerial Alliance; Child Care Food Program-FDA Food Program; Child Care Resource & Referral; Connections Handyman Service; Crosslines-Food and Clothing Pantry; Daybreak Adult Day Care Center; Long-Term Care Ombudsman Programs; Ozarks Food Harvest; Retired and Senior Volunteer Program; Sigma House-Treatment Center for Alcohol and Drug Abuse; Therapeutic Riding of the Ozarks

Ecumenical Ministries
829 Jefferson St., Fulton, MO 65251 Tel. (573) 642-6065 Fax (573)592-0247
Email: emfulton@coin.org
Website: www.callaway.county.missouri.org/em
Media Contact, Admin. Asst., Karen Luebbert
Chair, Bd. Of Dir.; Rev. Raymond Dunlap
Major Activities: Kingdom Respite Care and Hospice; CROP Hunger Walk; Little Brother and Sister; Unity Service; Senior Center Bible Study; County Jail Ministry; Fulton High School Baccalaureate Service, HAVEN House; Missouri Youth Treatment Center Ministry, Parish Nurses of Callaway

Interfaith Community Services
200 Cherokee St., P.O. Box 4038, St. Joseph, MO 64504-0038 Tel. (816)238-4511 Fax (816)238-3274
Email: DaveB@PonyExpress.net
Website: www.inter-serv.org
Media Contact, Exec. Dir., David G. Berger
Exec. Dir., David G. Berger
Major Activities: Child Development; Neighborhood Family Services; Group Home for Girls; Retired Senior Volunteer Program; Nutrition Program; Mobile Meals; Southside Youth Program; Church and Community; Housing Development; Homemaker Services to Elderly; Emergency Food, Rent, Utilities; AIDS Assistance; Family Respite; Family and Individual Casework

Interfaith Partnership of Metropolitan St. Louis
4144 Lindell Blvd Ste 221, St Louis, MO 63108 Tel. (314)531-4784 Fax (314)531-4785

Email: okimbrough@interfaithpartnership.org
Website: http://www.interfaithpartnership.org/
Media Contact, R. Irene Randall, Program Manager, Membership & Events
Cabinet Chair, The Rev. Anthony Witherspoon
President, Ghazala Hayat, M.D.
Executive Director, Orvin Kimbrough
Major Activities: Speaking out with a concerted faith voice on public issues
Celebrating our diversity encouraging respect for our faith traditions through interfaith dialogue, music events, dinner programs, and public forums.
Projects that promote bridge building across racial, religious, and cultural divides, and health promotion through congregational health initiatives.
Projects responding to hunger, natural disasters, environmental restoration, improving impoverished neighborhood

MONTANA

Montana Association of Churches*
25 South Ewing, Ste 408, Helena, MT 59601 Tel. (406)449-6010 Fax (406)449-6657
Email: montanachurches@earthlink.net
Website: www.montana-churches.org
Media Contact, Exec Dir.: The Rev. Dr. Brady J. Vardemann
Exec Dir.: The Rev. Dr. Brady J. Vardemann
Pres., Fr. Jay Peterson, Box 1399, Great Falls, MT 59403
President Elect: Dr. Walter Gulick, 2018 12th Street West, Billings, MT 59102
Treas., The Rev. Barbara Archer, 2210 Pryor Lane, Billings, MT 59102
Sec., The Rev. Kama Morton, PO Box 115, Choteau, MT 59422
Major Activities: Christian Unity; Lay Ministries Institute; Junior Citizen Camp; Montana Christian Advocates Network; Renewing the Public Church; Partnership For Rural Life; Health Ministries.

NEBRASKA

Interchurch Ministries of Nebraska*
215 Centennial Mall S., Suite 300, Lincoln, NE 68508-1888 Tel. (402)476-3391 Fax (402) 202-2005
Email: im50427@alltel.net
Website: www.interchurchministries.org
Media Contact, Exec., Mrs. Marilyn P. Mecham
Pres., Rev. Roddy Dunkerson
Treas., Ms. Susan Gillies
Exec., Mrs. Marilyn Mecham
Adm. Asst., Sharon K. Kalcik
Domestic Violence Program Coordinator, Patricia L. Brown
Disaster Response Program: Caroline Walles, Harry Walles

250

Major Activities: Planning and Development; Indian Ministry; Rural Church Strategy; United Ministries in Higher Education; Disaster Response; Rural Response Hotline; Health Ministry; Community Organizing Initiative Planning; Peace with Justice; Angel Connection; Domestic Violence Program; Social Ministries; Nurturing & Enhancing the Spiritual Tapestry

Lincoln Interfaith Council
140 S. 27th St., Ste. B, Lincoln, NE 68510-1301 Tel. (402)474-3017 Fax (402)475-3262
Email: mail@lincolninterfaith.org
Website: www.lincolninterfaith.org
Media Contact, Doug Boyd
Interim Coordinator, Kim Beyer Nelson
Pres., Sue Howe
Vice Pres., Gene Crump
Sec., Stephanie Dohner
Treas.,Terri Lee
Major Activities: MLK, Jr. Observance; Week of Prayer Christian Unity; Festival of Faith & Culture; Holocaust Memorial Observance; Citizens Against Racism & Discrimination; Community organization; Multi-Faith & Multi-Cultural Training; New Clergy Orientation; Directory of Clergy, Congregations & Religious Resources; Multi-Faith Planning Calendar Publication

NEW HAMPSHIRE
New Hampshire Council of Churches*
140 Sheep Davis Road, Ste. 1, Pembroke, NH 03275 Tel. (603)224-1352 Fax (603)224-9161
Email: churches@nhchurches.org
Website: www.nhchurches.org
Media Contact, Exec. Dir., David Lamarre-Vincent, PO Box 1087, Concord, NH 03302-1087 Tel. (603)224-1352 Fax (603)224-9161, Email: david@nhchurches.org
Pres., The Rev. David Yasenka, Triumphant Cross ELCA, 171 Zion's Hill Rd, Salem, NH 03079
Treas., Mr. Alvah Chisholm
Major Activities: Statewide Ecumenical Work For Christian Unity, Interfaith Understanding, and Social Justice

NEW JERSEY
Bergen County Council of Churches
58 James Street, Bergenfield, NJ 07621 Tel. (201)384-7505 Fax (201)384-2585
Email: bergenccc@hotmail.com
Website: www.bergenccc.org
Media Contact, Pres., Rev. Dr. Stephen T. Giordano, Clinton Avenue Reformed Church, Clinton Ave. & James St., Bergenfield, NJ 07621 Tel. (201)384-2454 Fax (201)384-2585
Exec. Sec., Anne Annunziato

Major Activities: Ecumenical and Religious Institute; Brotherhood-Sisterhood Breakfast; Center for Food Action; Homeless Aid; Operation Santa Claus; Aging Services; Boy & Girl Scouts; Easter Dawn Services; Music; Youth; Ecumenical Representation; Support of Chaplains in Jails & Hospitals; Faith & Values Online project www.njfaithandvalues.org; Welfare into Workplace

Ecclesia
700 West State St., Trenton, NJ 08618 Tel. (609) 394-9229
Media Contact, Sec., Mrs. Tina Swan
Pres., Rev. Joseph P. Ravenell
Campus Chaplains- Rev. Nancy Schulter; Rev. Robert Wittin, Rev. Richard Kocses
Major Activities: Racial Justice; Children & Youth Ministries; Advocacy; CROP Walk; Ecumenical Worship; Hospital Chaplaincy; Church Women United; Campus Chaplaincy; Congregational Empowerment; Prison Chaplaincy; Substance Abuse Ministry Training

Metropolitan Ecumenical Ministry
525 Orange St., Newark, NJ 07107 Tel. (973)485-8100 Fax (973)485-1165
Media Contact, Consultant, Rev. M. L. Emory
Exec. Dir., C. Stephen Jones
Major Activities: Community Advocacy (education, housing, environment); Church Mission Assistance; Community and Clergy Leadership Development; Economic Development; Affordable Housing

Metropolitan Ecumenical Ministry Community Development Corp.
525 Orange St., Newark, NJ 07107 Tel. (973)481-3100 Fax (201)481-7883
Email: memcdc@juno.com
Exec. Dir., Jacqueline Jones
Major Activities: Housing Development; Neighborhood Revitalization; Commercial-Small Business Development; Economic Development; Community Development; Credit Union; Home Ownership Counseling; Credit Repair; Mortgage Approval; Technical Assitance To Congregations

New Jersey Council of Churches*
176 W. State St., Trenton, NJ 08608 Tel. (609) 396-9546 Fax (609)396-7646
Media Contact, Public Policy Dir., Joan Diefenbach, Esq.
Pres., Rev. Jack Johnson
Sec., Beverly McNally
Treas., Marge Christie
Major Activities: Racial Justice; Children's Issues; Theological Unity; Ethics Public Forums; Advocacy; Economic Justice

251

Faith Community Assistance Center

PO Box 15517, Santa Fe, NM 87592 Tel. (505)438-4782 Fax (505)473-5637
Media Contact, Barbara A. Robinson
Major Activities: Faith Community Assistance Center; providing emergency assistance to the poor; Interfaith Dialogues-Celebrations-Visitations; Peace Projects; Understanding Hispanic Heritage; Newsletter

New Mexico Conference of Churches*

720 Vassar Dr NE, Albuquerque, NM 87106-2724 Tel. (505)255-1509 Fax (505)256-0071
Email: nmcc@nmchurches.org
Website: www.nmchurches.org
Media Contact, Exec. Dir.., Rev. Barbara E Dua
Pres., Mr. Jim Gleason
Treas., Robert Sandoval
Exec. Dir., Rev. Dr. Barbara E. Dua
Major Activities: Affordable Housing; Social Justice Coalitions; Spiritual Life & Ministries

NEW YORK

Brooklyn Council of Churches

125 Ft. Greene Place, Brooklyn, NY 11217 Tel. (718)625-5851 Fax (718)522-1231
Media Contact, Dir., Charles Henze
Program Dir., Charles Henze (Deacon)
Pres., The Rev. James H. Eggleston
Treas., The Rev. Charles H. Straut , Jr.
Major Activities: Education Workshops; Food Pantries; Hospital and Nursing Home Chaplaincy; Church Women United; Legislative Concerns; Directory of Churches; Ecumenical Dialogue

Broome County Council of Churches, Inc.

William H. Stanton Center, 3 Otseningo St., Binghamton, NY 13903 Tel. (607)724-9130 Fax (607)724-9148
Email: mfrick@broomecouncil.ort
Website: www.broomecouncil.net
Media Contact, Rev. Dr. Murray Frick
Exec. Dir., Rev. Dr. Murray Frick
Exec. Asst., Brigitte Stella
Hospital Chaplains, Betty Pomeroy; Rev. David Rockwell
Jail Chaplain, Rev. Cris Mogenson
Aging Ministry Coord., Linda McColgin
CHOW Prog. Coord., Wendy Primavera
Pres., Dr. Thomas Kelly
Treas., Rey Hull
Caregiver Program Coord., Joanne Kays
Community and Donor Relations, Dir., Dr. Murray Frick
Major Activities: Hospital and Jail Chaplains; Youth and Aging Ministries; Broome Bounty (Food Rescue Program); Emergency Hunger & Advocacy Program; Faith & Family Values; Ecumenical Worship and Fellowship; Media; Community Affairs; Peace with Justice; Day by Day Marriage Prep Program; Interfaith Coalition; Interfaith Volunteer Caregiver Program

Capital Area Council of Churches, Inc.

646 State St., Albany, NY 12203-1217 Tel. (518) 462-5450 Fax (518)462-5450
Email: capareacc@aol.com
Website: www.capareacc.org
Media Contact, Admin. Director, Kitt Jackson
Exec. Dir., Rev. John U. Miller
Admn. Dir., Kitt Jackson
Pres., Rev. Joan Lipscomb
Treas., William Hedberg
Major Activities: CROP Walk; Jail and Nursing Home Ministries; Martin Luther King Memorial Service and Scholarship Fund; Emergency Shelter for the Homeless; Campus Ministry; Ecumenical Dialogue; Forums on Social Concerns; Peace and Justice Education; Inter-Faith Programs; Legislative Concerns; Comm. Thanksgiving Day and Good Friday Services; Annual Ecumenical Musical Celebration

Capital Region Ecumenical Organization (CREO)

812 N. Church St., Schenectady, NY 12305 Tel. (518)382-7505 Fax (518)382-7505
Email: mishamarvel@juno.com
Media Contact, Coord., Misha Marvel
Rev. Donna Elia, President (PCUSA)
Rev. John U. Miller, Vice President (UCC)
Rev. Dr. Charles Lindhdm, Treasurer (ELCA)
Ms. Kitt Jackson, Secretary (RCA)
Misha Marvel, Coord.,
Major Activities: Promote Cooperation-Coordination Among Member Judicatories and Ecumenical Organizations in the Capital Region in Urban Ministries, Social Action

Chautauqua County Rural Ministry

127 Central Ave., P.O. Box 362, Dunkirk, NY 14048 Tel. (716)366-1787 Fax (716)366-1787
Email: ccrm@netsync.net
Website: www.ccrm.netsync.net
Exec. Dir., Kathleen Peterson
Major Activities: Chautauqua County Food Bank; Collection-Distribution of Furniture, Clothing, & Appliances; Homeless Services; Advocacy for the Poor; Soup Kitchen; Emergency Food Pantry; Thrift Store

Concerned Ecumenical Ministry to the Upper West Side

286 Lafayette Ave., Buffalo, NY 14213 Tel. (716)882-2442 Fax (716)882-2477

Email: information@cembuffalo.org
Website: www.cembuffalo.org
Media Contact, Exec. Dir., The Rev. Catherine Rieley-Goddard
Pres., Mr. Peter Hogan
Major Activities: Community Center Serving Youth, Families, Seniors and the Hungry

Cortland County Council of Churches, Inc.

7 Calvert St., Cortland, NY 13045 Tel. (607)753-1002
Media Contact, Office Mgr., Joy Niswender
Exec. Dir., The Rev. Donald M. Wilcox
Major Activities: College Campus Ministry; Hospital Chaplaincy; Nursing Home Ministry; Newspaper Column; Interfaith Relationships; Hunger Relief; CWS; Crop Walk; Leadership Education; Community Issues; Mental Health Chaplaincy; Grief Support; Jail Ministry

Council of Churches of Chemung County, Inc.

330 W. Church St., Elmira, NY 14901 Tel. (607)734-2294
Email: ecumenic2000@yahoo.com
Media Contact, Exec. Dir., Joan Geldmacher, Tel. (607)734-7622
Exec. Dir., Joan Geldmacher
Pres., Rev. Ann Taylor, 115 Dewitt, Elmira, NY 14901
Major Activities: CWS Collection; CROP Walk; UNICEF; Institutional Chaplaincies; Radio, Easter Dawn Service; Communications Network; Produce & Distribute Complete Church Directories; Representation on Community Boards and Agencies; Ecumenical Services; Interfaith Coalition; Taskforce on Children & Families; Compeer; Interfaith Hospitality Center

Council of Churches of the City of New York

475 Riverside Dr., Rm. 727, New York, NY 10115 Tel. (212)870-1020 Fax (212)870-1025
Email: jimmylim@cccny.net
Media Contact, Exec. Dir., Rev. Jimmy S. Lim
Exec. Dir., Rev. Jimmy S. Lim
Pres., The Rev. Calvin O. Butts
1st Vice Pres., Rev. A.R. Bernard
2nd Vice Pres., Mr. G. Morris Gurley, Esq.
3rd Vice Pres., The Venerable Michael Kendall
Sec., The Rev. N. J. L'Heureux
Treas., The Rev. Jon Norton
Major Activities: Radio & TV; Pastoral Care; Christ for the World Chapel, Kennedy International Airport; Coordination and Strategic Planning; Interfaith Coordinator, Religious Conferences; Interfaith Commission of Religious Leaders; Referral & Advocacy; Youth Development; Directory of Churches and Database Available

Dutchess County Interfaith Council, Inc.

9 Vassar St., Poughkeepsie, NY 12601 Tel. (845) 471-7333 Fax (845)471-5253
Email: dic@bestweb.net
Website: www.dutchessinterfaithcouncil.org
Media Contact, Exec. Dir., The Rev. Philip Carr-Harris
Exec. Dir., The Rev. Philip Carr-Harris
Pres., Rabbi Paul Golumb
Treas., Amy Harding King
Major Activities: CROP Hunger Walk; Interfaith Music Festival; Public Worship Events; Interfaith Story Circles; Oil Purchase Group; Tour Of Houses Of Worship; Weekly Radio Program; Racial Unity Work; Poverty Forums

Genesee County Churches United, Inc.

P.O. Box 547, Batavia, NY 14021 Tel. (716)343-6763
Media Contact, Pres.,Captain Leonard Boynton, Salvation Army, 529 East Main St., Batavia, NY 14020 Tel. (716)343-6284
Pres., James Woodruff
Exec. Sec., Cheryl Talone
Chaplain, The Rev. Peter Miller
Major Activities: Jail Ministry; Food Pantries; Serve Needy Families; Radio Ministry; Pulpit Exchange; Community Thanksgiving; Ecumenical Services at County Fair

Genesee-Orleans Ministry of Concern

Arnold Gregory Memorial Complex, Suite 271
243 South Main St., Albion, NY 14411 Tel. (585)589-9210 Fax (585)589-9617
Email: gomoc1@rochester.rr.com
Media Contact, Exec. Dir., Malika Hill
Exec. Dir., Malika Hill
Pres., John W. Cebula, Esq.
Vice Pres., Rev. Joseph Fifagrowicz
Sec., Jane Balbick
Treas., Mary Grace Demarse
Major Activities: Advocacy Services for the Disadvantaged, Homeless, Ill, Incarcerated and Victims of Family Violence; Emergency Food, Shelter, Utilities, Medicines, just Friends (a mentoring program for children), Parenting Program, Furniture Program.

Greater Rochester Community of Churches

2 Riverside St., Rochester, NY 14613-1222 Tel. (585)254-2570 Fax (585)254-6551
Email: grcc1@frontiernet.net
Website: www.grcc.org
Media Contact, Administrator., Elder Marie E. Gibson
Pres., Rev. Richard N. Myers
Vice Pres. for Program and Discipleship, Sue Murray
Vice Pres. for Organization, Elder Jack Wheeler

253

Vice Pres. for Social Justice Ministry, Deacon Marvin Mich
Secretary, Sister Patricia Switzer
Treasurer, Kenneth Anderson
Interfaith Liaison, Rev. Gordon V. Webster
Officer-at-Large, Rev. Roy Hedman
Major Activities: Ecumenical Worship; Christian Unity; Interfaith Health Care Coalition; Interfaith Dialogue; Annual Faith in Action Celebration; Rochester's Religious Community Directory; Religious Information-Resources; Justice Issues; Children's Emergency Fund

InterReligious Council of Central New York

3049 E. Genesee St., Syracuse, NY 13224 Tel. (315)449-3552 Fax (315)449-3103
Email: mbowles@irccny.org
Website: www.irccny.org
Media Contact, Dir. of Dev., Renée McCaffrey
Executive Dir., Dr. James B. Wiggins
Pres., The Rev. Dr. Thomas V. Wolfe
Bus. Mgr., Laura J. Haley
Director for Resource Development, Renée McCaffrey
Spiritual Care Program Director, The Rev. Tanya Atwood-Adams
Center for New Americans, Dir. Hope Wallis
Senior Companion Prog., Dir., Karen O'Hara
Long Term Ombudsman Prog., Dir., Linda Kashdin
Covenant Housing Prog., Dir., Kimberlee Dupcak
Community Wide Dialogue on Racism, Race Relations and Racial Healing, Beth Broadway
InterReligious Council News, Ed., Renée McCaffrey
Major Activities: Pastoral Ministries; Community Ministries; Interrreligious and Ecumenical Relations; Diversity Education; Worship; Community Advocacy and Planning

The Long Island Council of Churches

1644 Denton Green, Hempstead, NY 11550 Tel. (516)565-0290 Fax (516)565-0291
Email: licchemp@aol.com
Website: www.ncccusa.org/ecmin/licc
Media Contact, Rev. Thomas W. Goodhue
Exec. Dir., Rev. Thomas W. Goodhue
Pastoral Care, Dir., Rev. Richard Lehman
Community Resources Dir., Alric Kennedy, Tel. (516)565-0390 ext. 204
Nassau County Ofc., Social Services Sec., Yolanda Murray
Suffolk County Ofc., Food Program & Family Support, Carolyn Gumbs, Tel: (631)727-2210
Major Activities: Pastoral Care in Jails; Emergency Food; Family Support & Advocacy; Advocacy for Peace & Justice; Church World Service; Multifaith Education; Clergy-Laity Training; Newsletter; Church Directory; AIDS Interfaith of Long Island

Network of Religious Communities

1272 Delaware Ave., Buffalo, NY 14209-2496 Tel. (716)882-4793 Fax (716)882-3797
Email: nrc@religiousnet.org
Website: ReligiousNet.org
Media Contact, Co-Exec. Dir., Rev. Dr. G. Stanford Bratton
Co-Exec. Dir. & COO, The Rev. Dr. G. Stanford Bratton
Co-Exec. Dir., The Rev. Francis X. Mazur (Ecumenical Officer, Diocese of Buffalo-Roman Catholic)
Co-Presidents, Marlene Clickman (Judaism); Rev. Frances Manly (Unitarian Universalist Church of WNY)
Immediate Past President, Imam Fajri Ansari (Masjid Nu"Man)
Vice Pres. For Program, Deacon James Anderson, National Baptist
Vice Pres. For Administration, Dr. ViJay Chakravarthy (Hindu Cultural Society)
Secretary, Rev. Mary Masters (Unitarian Church of Practical Christitanity)
Treasurer, Ms Eula Hooker, Christian Methodist Episcopal
Chpsn., Interreligious Concerns, Rabbi Charles Shalman (Buffalo Board of Rabbis) and Dr. Othman Shibly (Islamic Society of the Niagara Frontier)
Chpsn., Personnel, The Rev. James Croglio (Diocese of Buffalo- Roman Catholic)
Chpsn., Membership, The Rev. Jeff Carter (Pentecostal)
Chpsn., Christian Concerns, The Rev. Robert Grimm (United Church of Christ)
Chpsn., Riefler Enablement Fund, Rev. Charles Bang (Evangelical Lutheran Church in America)
Chpsn., Public Issues, The Rev. Merle Showers (United Methodist Church)
Chpsn., Religious Leaders Forum, The Rev. Paul Litwin (Chancelor, Diocese of Buffalo - Roman Catholic)
Chpsn., Church Women United, Ms. Norma Roscover (Presbytery WNY)

STAFF
(OTHER THAN EXECUTIVE DIRECTORS)
Financial/office administrator, Ms. Bonnie Jehle
Church Women United Coordinator, Ms. Sally Giordano
Food For All, Coordinator, Ms. Kelly Kowalski
Medicaid Coordinator, Mr. Bruce Davidson
Major Activities: Regionwide Interreligious Conversation, Hunger Advocacy, Food Distribution, Roll Call Against Racism, Buffalo Coalition for Common Ground, Ecumenical and Interreligious Relations and Celebrations, Radio-TV Broadcast and Production, Church Women United, Lay-Religious Leaders Education, Community Development, Chaplaincy, Yom Hashoah Commemoration Service, Aids Memorial

Service, Police-Community Relations, CROP Walks, Interfaith Thanksgiving Service. Spirituality and Health Initiative. Community-wide interreligious education. U.S.-Canadian Border Policy and enforcement issues.

New York State Council of Churches, Inc.*

18 Computer Dr. West, Suite 107, Albany, NY 12205 Tel. (518)436-9319 Fax (518)427-6705
Email: nyscoc@nycap.rr.com
Website: www.nyscoc.org
Media Contact, Ms. Mary Lu Bowen, Email: marylubowen@aol.com
Executive Dir., Ms. Mary Lu Bowen
Pres., The Rev. Geoffrey A. Black
Vice Pres., The Rev. Clint McCoy
Vice Pres., Bishop Marie C. Jerge
Corp. Sec., The Rev. Dr. Jon Norton
Treas., The Rev. Dr. John Hiemstra
Convener of Collegium, -vacant-
Coordinator of Chaplaincy Services, Ms. Damaris McGuire
Public Policy Consultant, The Rev. Daniel Hahn
Communications Consultant, The Rev. Daniel Hahn
Admin. Asst., Sylvenia F. Cochran
Major Activities: State Chaplaincy; Public Policy Advocacy in the following areas, Anti-Racism; Campaign Reform; Criminal Justice System Reform; Disability; Ecomomic-Social Justice; Environmental; Health care; Homelessness-Shelter; Hunger-Food; Immigrant Issues; Public Education; Rural Issues; Substance Abuse; Violence; Women's Issues; Peace

The Niagara Council of Churches Inc.
St. Paul UMC, 723 Seventh St., Niagara Falls, NY 14301 Tel. (716)285-7505
Media Contact, Pres., Nessie S. Bloomquist, 7120 Laur Rd., Niagara Falls, NY 14304 Tel. (716)297-0698 Fax (716)298-1193
Exec. Dir., Ruby Babb
Pres., Nessie S. Bloomquist
Treas., Shirley Bathurst
Trustees Chpsn., The Rev. Vincent Mattoni, 834 19th St., Niagara Falls, NY 14304
Major Activities: Ecumenical Worship; Bible Study; Christian Ed. & Social Concerns; Church Women United; Evangelism & Mission; Institutional Min. Youth Activities; Hymn Festival; Week of Prayer for Christian Unity; CWS Projects; Audio-Visual Library; UNICEF; Food Pantries and Kitchens; Community Missions, Inc.; Political Refugees; Eco-Justice Task Force; Migrant-Rural Ministries; Interfaith Coalition on Energy

Queens Federation of Churches

86-17 105th St., Richmond Hill, NY 11418-1597 Tel. (718)847-6764 Fax (718)847-7392
Email: qfc@queenschurches.org
Website: www.queenschurches.org

Media Contact, The Rev. N. J. L'Heureux, Jr.
Exec. Dir., The Rev. N. J. L'Heureux, Jr.
York College Chaplain, The Rev. Dr. Henrietta Fullard
Pres., Shirley K. Ford, Rev Lois B. Stewart
Treas., Annie Lee Phillips
Major Activities: Queens Interfaith Hunger Network—Emergency Food Service; York College Campus Ministry; Scouting & Youth Ministry; Christian Education Workshops; Planning and Strategy; Church Women United; Community Consultations; Seminars for Church Leaders; Online Directory of Congregations; Christian Relations (Prot-RC); Chaplaincies; Public Policy Issues; N.Y.S. Interfaith Commission on Landmarking of Religious Property; "The Nexus of Queens" (online, weekly newspaper)

Rural Migrant Ministry

P.O. Box 4757, Poughkeepsie, NY 12602 Tel. (845)485-8627 Fax (845)485-1963
Email: rmmhope3@aol.com
Website: ruralmigrantministry.org
Media Contact, Exec. Dir., Rev. Richard Witt
Exec. Dir., The Rev. Richard Witt
Pres., Melinda Trotti
Major Activities: Serving the Rural Poor and Migrants Through a Ministry of Advocacy & Empowerment; Youth Program; Latino Committee; Organization and Advocacy with and for Rural Poor and Migrant Farm Workers

Schenectady Inner City Ministry

930 Albany St., Schenectady, NY 12307-1514 Tel. (518)374-2683 Fax (518)382-1871
Email: INFORMATION@SICM.US
Website: www.Timesunion.com/community/sicm
Media Contact, Patricia Rush
Urban Agent, Rev. Phillip N. Grigsby
Business Manager, Barbara Bieniek
Emergency Food, Gail Van Vallenburgh
Pres., Helga Sutroeter
Damien Center, Ujuana Anderson
Jobs, Etc, Annalene Antonio
Summer Food, Crystal Hameliml
Housing Task Force, Rev. Phil Grigsby
Major Activities: Food Security; Advocacy; Housing; Neighborhood and Economic Issues; Ecumenical Worship and Fellowship; Community Research; Education in Congregations on Faith Responses to Social Concerns; Legislative Advocacy; CROP Walk; HIV-AIDS Ministry; Job Training and Placement Center; Summer Lunch for Youth; Study Circles Initiative on Embracing Diversity; Community Crisis Nework; Housing Services and Advocacy; Youth Initiative; After-School Program; Committee for Social Justice; Theological Center; Computer for Kids

255

Southeast Ecumenical Ministry

25 Westminster Rd., Rochester, NY 14607 Tel. (585)271-5350 Fax (585)271-8526
Email: sem@frontiernet.net
Media Contact, Laurie Jenkins
Dir., Laurie Jenkins
Pres., Ronald K. Fox
Major Activities: Transportation of Elderly & Disabled; Emergency Food Cupboard for Case Managers to access for their clients; Supplemental Nutrition Program for seniors;Community Health and Pharmacy Partnership (CHAPP).

Staten Island Council of Churches

2187 Victory Blvd., Staten Island, NY 10314 Tel. (718)761-6782
Email: sicoc@verizon.net
Media Contact, Pres., Rev. Virginia Kaada, 2187 Victory Blvd., Staten Island, NY 10314 Tel. (718)761-6782
Pres., The Rev. Virginia Kaada
Exec. Sec., Rebekah A. Ellis
Major Activities: Congregational Support & Outreach; Education & Pastoral Care; Ecumenical & Interfaith Witness; Social Witness

Troy Area United Ministries

392 Second St., Troy, NY 12180 Tel. (518)274-5920 Fax (518)271-1909
Email: info@TAUM.org
Website: www.taum.org
Media Contact, Exec. Dir., Rev. Donna Elia
Pres., Laura M. Rogers
Chaplain, R.P.I. And Russel Sage, Rev. Beth Illingworth
Damien Center, Dir., Glenn Read
Furniture Program, Dir., Michael Barrett
Major Activities: College Ministry; Nursing Home Ministry; CROP Walk; Homeless and Housing Concerns; Weekend Meals Program at Homeless Shelter; Community Worship Celebrations; Racial Relations; Furniture Program; Damien Center of Troy Hospitality for persons with HIV-AIDS; Computer Ministries; Youth Ministry

Wainwright House

260 Stuyvesant Ave., Rye, NY 10580 Tel. (914) 967-6080 Fax (914)967-6114
Email: frandavies@wainwright.org
Website: www.wainwright.org
Media Contact, Exec. Dir., Fran Davies
Exec. Dir., Fran Davies
Pres., Robert Laughlin
Vice Pres., Michael Standen
Major Activities: Educational Programs, Retreat and Conference Center; Intellectual, Psychological, Physical and Spiritual Growth; Healing and Health

NORTH CAROLINA

Asheville-Buncombe Community Christian Ministry (ABCCM)

30 Cumberland Ave., Asheville, NC 28801 Tel. (828)259-5300 Fax (828)259-5923
Email: srogers@abccm.org
Website: www.abccm.org
Media Contact, Exec. Dir., Rev. Scott Rogers, Fax (828)259-5323
Exec. Dir., The Rev. Scott Rogers
Pres., Stephen Williamson
Major Activities: Crisis Ministry; Jail-Prison Ministry; Shelter Ministry; Medical Ministry

Greensboro Urban Ministry

305 West Lee St., Greensboro, NC 27406 Tel. (910)271-5959 Fax (910)271-5920
Email: Guministry@aol.com
Website: www.greensboro.com/gum
Media Contact, Exec. Dir., Rev. Mike Aiken
Exec. Dir., The Rev. Mike Aiken
Major Activities: Emergency Financial Assistance; Emergency Housing; Hunger Relief; Inter-Faith and Inter-Racial Understanding; Justice Ministry; Chaplaincy with the Poor

North Carolina Council of Churches*

Methodist Bldg., 1307 Glenwood Ave., Suite 156, Raleigh, NC 27605-3256 Tel. (919)828-6501 Fax (919)828-9697
Email: nccofc@nccouncilofchurches.org
Website: www.nccouncilofchurches.org
Media Contact, Comm. Assoc., Aleta Payne
Exec. Dir., The Rev. J. George Reed, Email: GReed@nccouncilofchurches.org
Program Associate, Steve Smith
Program Associate, Denise Long
Program Associate, Barbara Zelter
Communications Associate, Aleta Payne
Health Program Associate, Dr. Gordon DeFriese
Pres., The Rev. Michael Cogsdale, 806 College Ave., Lenoir, NC 28645
Treas., Dr. James W. Ferree, 168 Brook Landing Drive Winston-Salem, NC 27106
Climate Connection Associate, Alice Boyd
Program Associates, Jason Jenkins, Rollin Russell
Major Activities: Health Care Justice; Christian Unity; Legislative Program; Farmworker Ministry; Rural
Crisis; Racial and Ethnic Justice; Climate Change; Public Education; Economic Justice; Peace

NORTH DAKOTA

North Dakota Conference of Churches*

9195 70th Avenue, SE, Ashley, ND 58413-9600 Tel. (701)647-2063
Email: ndconchu@drtel.net

Website: www.ndconference.org
Media Contact, Exec. Sec., Renee Gopal
Pres., Dr. Wade Schemmel
Vice Pres. I, Grace Wisthoff
Treas., The Rev. Michael Hicken
Secretary, Bishop Duane Danielson
Major Activities: Rural Life Ministry; Faith and Order; North Dakota 101; Victims & Offenders Ministry; Rural Life Convocation; Restorative Justice

OHIO

Akron Area Association of Churches

800 East Market Street, Akron, OH 44305-2424 Tel. (330)535-3112 Fax (330)374-5041
Email: akronchurches@earthlink.net
Website: www.triple-ac.org
Media Contact, Exec. Dir., Chloe Ann Kriska
Bd. of Trustees, Pres., Rev. Dr. J. Wayman Butts
Vice Pres., The Rev. Mark Frey
Sec., Dale Kline
Treas., Ms. Sherrie Petrochuk
Major Activities: Messiah Sing; Interfaith Council; Newsletters; Resource Center; Community Worship; Training of Local Church Leadership; Radio Programs; Clergy and Lay Fellowship Luncheons; Neighborhood Development; Community Outreach; Church Interracial Partnerships; Pastor Peer Group Program; Advocacy, Social Justice

Alliance of Churches

470 E. Broadway, Alliance, OH 44601 Tel. (330)821-6648
Media Contact, Dir., Lisa A. Oyster
Dir., Lisa A. Oyster
Pres., Rev. Bud Hoffman
Treas., Betty Rush
Major Activities: Christian Education; Community Relations & Service; Ecumenical Worship; Community Ministry; Peacemaking; Medical Transportation for Anyone Needing It; Emergency Financial Assistance

Churchpeople for Change and Reconciliation

Box 488, Lima, OH 45802-0488 Tel. (419)224-2086 Fax (419)224-2086
Media Contact, Exec. Dir., The Rev. Darwin Ralston
Exec. Dir., The Rev. Darwin Ralston
Major Activities: Developing Agencies for Minorities, Poor, Alienated and Despairing; especially Our Daily Bread Soup Kitchen

Council of Christian Communions of Greater Cincinnati

7030 Reading Road
Suite 642, Cincinnati, OH 45237 Tel. (513)-351-6789 Fax 513-458-2252
Email: joellengrady@zoomtown.com

Website: www.cccgc.org
Media Contact, Exec. Dir., Joellen W. Grady
Exec. Dir., Joellen W. Grady
Justice Chaplaincy, Assoc. Dir., Rev. Jack Marsh
Educ., Assoc., Lillie D. Bibb
Pres., Rev. Damon Lynch III
Major Activities: Christian Unity & Interfaith Cooperation; Justice Chaplaincies; Police-Clergy Team; Adult and Juvenile Jail Chaplains; Religious Education

Greater Dayton Christian Connections

601 W. Riverview Ave., Dayton, OH 45406 Tel. (937)227-9485 Fax (937)227-9407
Email: gdcc@Christianconnections.org
Website: www.christianconnections.org
Media Contact, Exec. Dir., Rev. Darryl Fairchild
Exec. Dir., Rev. Darryl Fairchild
Major Activities: Ecumenical and Interfaith Dialogue; Peace Making; Environmental Justice; Racial Reconciliation; Pastoral Leadership Resources; Ministry Recruitment and Placement; Communication

Mahoning Valley Association of Churches

30 W. Front St., Youngstown, OH 44503 Tel. (330)744-8946 Fax (330)774-0018
Email: mvac@onecom.com
Media Contact, Exec. Dir., Elsie L. Dursi
Exec. Dir., Elsie L. Dursi
Pres., Rev. Joyce Lawson
Treas., Carol Williams
Major Activities: Communications; Christian Education; Ecumenism; Social Action; Advocacy

Metropolitan Area Church Council

760 E. Broad St., Columbus, OH 43205 Tel. (614)461-7103 Fax (614)280-0352
Email: church_council@yahoo.com
Media Contact, Exec. Dir., Alvin Hadley
President: The Rev. Melvin Richardson
Vice Pres.: The Rev. Ken Coy
Secretary: Ms. Margaret Stansbery
Treasurer: Mr. Brian Shaffer
Exec. Dir.:Alvin Hadley
Major Activities: Newspaper; Published nine times annually; Annual Living Faiths Awards; Quarterly Racial unity Services; Clergy Hospital Indentification Badges; Community Computer Center; Social Concerns relating to human needs in our community; Older Adult ministries; Collaborations to facilitate unity among religious denominations.

Metropolitan Area Religious Coalition of Cincinnati

617 Vine St., Suite 1035, Cincinnati, OH 45202-2423 Tel. (513)721-4843 Fax (513)721-4891
Email: marcc@fuse.net

257

Media Contact, Dir., Rev. Duane Holm
Pres., Mr. William K. Woods
Dir., Rev. Duane Holm
Major Activities: Local social policy decisions chosen annually. 2005, Affordable Housing & Youth & Violence

Ohio Council of Churches*

6230 Busch Blvd., Ste 430, Columbus, OH 43229-1879 Tel. (614)885-9590 Fax (614)885-6097
Email: mail@ohcouncilchs.org
Website: www.ohcouncilchs.org
Exec. Dir., The Rev. Rebecca J. Tollefson
Public Policy, Dir., Tom Smith
Major Activities: Economic & Social Justice; Ecumenical Relations; Health Care Reform; Theological Dialogue; Racial Relations; Education-Funding; Childcare-Children Issues; Poverty-Welfare; Environment, Gambling, Global Warming

Pike County Outreach Council

107-9 West Second Street, Waverly, OH 45690
Tel. (740)941-4348
Email: bridgehaven@intelliwave.com
Website: http://www.pcoutreach.org/
Dir., Judy Dixon
Major Activities: Emergency Service Program; Self Help Groups; Homeless Shelter, Food Pantry

Toledo Ecumenical Area Ministries

444 Floyd St., Toledo, OH 43620 Tel. (419)242-7401 Fax (419)242-7404
Media Contact, Admin., Nancy Lee Atkins
Metro-Toledo Churches United, Admn., Nancy Lee Atkins
Toledo Metropolitan Mission, Exec. Dir., Nancy Lee Atkins
Major Activities: Ecumenical Relations; Interfaith Relations; Food Program; Housing Program; Social Action—Public Education; Health Care; Urban Ministry; Employment; Welfare Rights; Housing; Mental Retardation; Voter Registration-Education; Substance Abuse Treatment; Youth Leadership; Children At-risk; Elimination of Discrimination

Tuscarawas County Council for Church and Community

1458 5th St. NW, New Philadelphia, OH 44663
Tel. (330)343-6012 Fax (330)343-9845
Email: mooredj3@adelphia.net
Media Contact, Donna J. Moore
Exec. Dir., Donna J. Moore
Pres., Lillian Devlin 1767 Hillandale Rd. NE, New Philadelphia, OH 44663
Treas., James Barnhouse, 120 N. Broadway, New Philadelphia, OH 44663
Major Activities: Human Services; Legislative Concerns; Home Improvements; Character Counts; Abstinence Education; Youth Boosters; Emergency Assistance

West Side Ecumenical Ministry

5209 Detroit Ave, Cleveland, OH 44102 Tel. (216)651-2037 Fax (216)651-4145
Email: Eotero@wsem.org
Website: www.wsem.org
Media Contact, Dir. of Marketing and Public Relations, Kami L. Marquardt
Pres., & CEO, Judith Peters
Chief Operation Officer, Adam Roth
Major Activities: WSEM is dedicated to serving urban low-income families by providing programs that encourage self-sufficiency. Three food pantries and outreach centers, a job-training program, early childhood, preschool, and schol-age child care, crisis intervention, counseling, youth services, a theatre education program and a senior nutrition program are among the services available. WSEM serves more than 56,000 children, families, and individuals annually with a staffing of more than 300 employees and 3,200 volunteers.

OKLAHOMA

Oklahoma Conference of Churches*

301 Northwest 36th St., Oklahoma City, OK 73118 Tel. (405)525-2928 Fax (405)525-2636
Email: okchurches@okchurches.org
Website: www.okchurches.org
Media Contact, Deborah Canary-Marshall
Exec. Dir., The Rev. Joanne Kurklin, Email: joanne.kurklin@okchurches.org
Pres., Rev. George Young
Major Activities: Christian Unity Issues; Community Building Among Members; Rural Community Care; Children's Advocacy; Day at the Legislature; Impact; Criminal Justice; Hunger & Poverty; Legislative Advocacy; Aging; Women's Issues; Interfaith Coalition and Activities

Tulsa Metropolitan Ministry

221 S. Nogales, Tulsa, OK 74127 Tel. (918)582-3147 Fax (918)582-3159
Email: tummtulsa@aol.com
Website: www.TUMM.org
Media Contact, Exec. Dir., The Rev. James W. Mishler
Exec. Dir., The Rev. James W. Mishler
Pres., The Rev. Mazlin Lasanhar
Treas., Virginia Katz
Major Activities: Religious Understanding; Legislative Issues; Christian Unity; Criminal and Justice Issues; Committee against Racism; Disability Awareness; Directory of Metropolitan Religious Community; Airport Interfaith Chapel; Native American Issues.

OREGON

Ecumenical Ministries of Oregon*

0245 S.W. Bancroft St., Ste. B, Portland, OR 97239 Tel. (503)221-1054 Fax (503)223-7007

Email: emo@emoregon.org
Website: www.emoregon.org
Media Contact, Bob Baker, Dir. Of Development & Communications
Exec. Dir., David A. Leslie, Email: dleslie@emoregon.org
Finance and Administrative Services, Dir., Gary B. Logsdon
Development & Communications, Bob Baker
Sponsors Organized to Assist Refugees, Vesna Vila
Russian Oregon Social Services, Yelena Sergeva
Portland International Community School, Skip Adams
Public Policy Dir., Phillip Kennedy-Wong
Interfaith Network for Earth Concerns, Jenny Holmes
Parent Mentor Program, Patti Clothier
HIV Day Center, Lowen Berman
Shared Housing, Barbara Stone
Oregon Recovery Homes, Mike Morgester
Northeast Emergency Food Program, John Elizade
President, The Rev. Mark Knutson
Major Activities: Ecumenical Ministries of Oregon is a statewide association of seventeen christian denominations including Protestant, Roman Catholic and Orthodox bodies working together to improve the lives of Oregonians through theological education and dialogue, public policy advocacy, environmental ministry and community ministry programs.

PENNSYLVANIA

Allegheny Valley Association of Churches

1913 Freeport Rd., Natrona Heights, PA 15065 Tel. (724)226-0606 Fax (724)226-3197
Email: avac@avaoc.org
Website: www.avaoc.org
Media Contact, Exec. Dir., Karen Snair
Exec. Dir., Karen Snair
Pres., The Rev. Dr. W. James Legge, 232 Tarentum-Culmerville Rd., Tarentum, PA 15084
Treas., Libby Grimm, 312 Butternut Ln., Tarentum, PA 15084
Major Activities: Ecumenical Services; Dial-a-Devotion; Walk for Hunger; Food Bank; Emergency Aid; Cross-on-the-Hill; AVAC Hospitality Network for Homeless Families; Senior Citizen Housing-Pine Ridge Heights Senior Complex, AVAC Chaplaincy Program; Summer Camp for Children, Case Management, Faith-in-Action

Christian Associates of Southwest Pennsylvania

204 37th St., Suite 201, Pittsburgh, PA 15201 Tel. (412)688-9070 Fax (412)688-9091
Email: info@casp.org
Website: www.casp.org

Media Contact, Dir. of Television Ministry, Monica Kao
Exec., Dir., Rev. Dr. Donald B. Green
Chair of Council, Bishop Robert W. Duncan
Pres., Board of Delegates, Rev. Deane Lavender
Executive Administrative Asst., Tracy Ritchie
Director of Television Ministry, Monica Kao
Television Studio Director, Frank Cindrich
Director of Jail Chaplaincy Services, Chaplian Lynn Yeso
Protestant Chaplain- Shuman Youth Detention Center, Rev. Floyd Palmer
Protestant Chaplains, Rev. Dallas Brown and Rev. Shawn Drummond
Catholic Chaplain, Fr. Malcolm McDonald
Jail Administrative Assistant, Karen Mack
Major Activities: Jail Chaplaincy; Youth-Incarceration Chaplaincies; Theological Dialogue-Religious Education; Religious Leadership Forum; Christian Associates Television (CATV); The Call...Newsletter; Media Ministries Internet ministry; Indigent Burial program; Interfaith Dialogue

Christian Churches United of the Tri-County Area

413 South 19th St.
P.O. Box 60750, Harrisburg, PA 17106-0750 Tel. (717)230-9550 Fax (717)230-9554
Email: ccuhbg@aol.com
Website: christianchurchesunited.com
Media Contact, Exec. Dir., Jacqueline P. Rucker
Exec. Dir., Jacqueline P. Rucker
Pres., John Carroll
Treas., Henry Greenawald
Vice Pres., Rev. Paul Baranek
Sec., Patricia Greenawald
HELP & LaCasa Ministries, John Scarpato, Program Director, P.O. Box 60750, Harrisburg, PA 17106-0750 Tel. (717)238-2851 Fax (717)238-1916
Major Activities: Volunteer Ministries to Prisons; HELP (Housing, Rent, Food, Medication, Transportation, Home Heating, Clothing); La Casa de Amistad (The House of Friendship) Social Services; AIDS Outreach; Prison Chaplaincy;

Christians United in Beaver County

1098 Third St., Beaver, PA 15009 Tel. (724)774-1446 Fax (724)774-1446
Email: cubc@access995.com
Media Contact, Exec. Sec., Lois L. Smith
Exec. Sec., Lois L. Smith
Chaplains—The Rev. Dennis Ugoletti; The Rev. Anthony Massey; The Rev. Arthur Peters; John Pusateri, Rev. Bertha Lay
Pres., Mrs. Delores Tisdale, 1021-5th Street, New Brighton, PA. 15066
Treas., Mr. Richard Puryear, 2 McCabe Street, Sewickley, PA. 15143

259

Major Activities: Christian Education; Evangelism; Social Action; Church Women United; United Church Men; Ecumenism; Hospital, Detention Home and Jail Ministry, Behavioral Health Clinic.

East End Cooperative Ministry

250 N. Highland Ave., Pittsburgh, PA 15206 Tel. (412)361-5549 Fax (412)361-0151
Email: eecm@eecm.org
Website: www.eecm.org
Media Contact, Exec. Dir., Myrna Zelenitz
Exec. Dir., Myrna Zelenitz
Ass. Dir., Rev. Darnell Leonard
Major Activities: Food Pantry; Soup Kitchen; Men's Emergency Shelter; Drop-In Shelter for Homeless; Meals on Wheels; Information and Referral; Programs for Children and Youth; Bridge Housing Program for Men and PennFree Housing for Women in Recovery

Ecumenical Conference of Greater Altoona

PO Box 771, Altoona, PA 16693 Tel. (814)942-0512 Fax (814)942-0512
Email: ecumenaltoona@charter.net
Media Contact, Exec. Dir., Susanna M. Tomlinson
Exec. Dir., Susanna M. Tomlinson
Major Activities: Religious Education; Workshops; Ecumenical Activities; Religious Christmas Parade; Campus Ministry; Community Concerns; Peace Forum; Religious Education for Mentally Challenged, and Interfaith Committee

Greater Bethlehem Area Council of Churches

1021 Center St., P.O. Box 1245, Bethlehem, PA 18016-1245 Tel. (610)867-8671 Fax (610) 866-9223
Email: gbacc@enter.net
Exec. Dir.,The Rev. Patricia Dwyer MacMillan
Pres., William L. Cauller
Treas., Mr. David G. Boltz, 1831 Levering Place, Bethlem, PA. 18017
Major Activities: World-local hunger projects; Ecumenical Worship-Cooperation; Prison Ministry Programs; Support for Homeless and Welfare to Work Programs; Emergency Food Pantry; Support for Hospice and Share Care Programs; Regional Grave Bank; Support Summer Youth Camps and Church Sports League

Hanover Area Council of Churches

136 Carlisle St., Hanover, PA 17331-2406 Tel. (717)633-6353 Fax (717)633-1992
Email: opsmanhacc@netrax.net
Website: www.hanoverareacouncilofchurches.org
Operations Manager, Carol Hinkle
Major Activities: Meals on Wheels, Provide a Lunch Program, Fresh Air Program, Clothing

Bank, Hospital Chaplaincy Services; Congregational & Interfaith Relations, Public Ecumenical Programs and Services, State Park Chaplaincy Services & Children's Program; Compeer; Faith at Work; CROP Walk; Stolte Scholarship Fund; Community Needs; Cold Weather Shelter; AA

Inter-Church Ministries of Erie County

2216 Peach St., Erie, PA 16502 Tel. (814)454-2411
Email: icm@icmeriecounty.com
Website: www.icmeriecounty.com
Pres., The Rev. Dr. Andrew Harvey
Treas., Mary C. Stewart
Major Activities: Local Ecumenism; Social Ministry; Continuing Education; North West Pennsylvania Conference of Bishops and Judicatory Execs.; Theological Dialogue; Coats for Kids; Voucher Program for Emergency Assistance; Worship; Advocacy

Lancaster County Council of Churches

344 N. Marshall St., Lancaster, PA 17602 Tel. (717)291-2261 Fax (717)291-6403
Email: office@lccouncilofchurches.org
Website: www.lccouncilofchurches.org
Media Contact, Interim Exec. Dir., Kenneth Trauger
Pres.: Steve Mentzer
Service Ministry Interim Director: Doug Hopwood
Major Activities: Social Ministries

Lebanon County Christian Ministries

250 S. 7th St., P.O. Box 654, Lebanon, PA 17042 Tel. (717)274-2601
Email: lccm@lmf
Media Contact, Exec. Dir., Lillian Morales
Exec. Dir., Lillian Morales
Noon Meals Coord., Wenda Dinatale
Major Activities: H.O.P.E. (Helping Our People in Emergencies); Food & Clothing Bank; Free Meal Program; Commodity Distribution Program; Ecumenical Events

Lehigh County Conference of Churches

534 Chew St., Allentown, PA 18102 Tel. (610) 433-6421 Fax (610)439-8039
Email: lccc@lcconfchurch.org
Website: www.lcconfchurch.org
Media Contact, Dir. of Dev., Ira Faro
Exec. Dir., The Rev. Dr. Christine L. Nelson
Pres., Ms. Joanne Gantz-Jalowiecki
1st Vice Pres.,The Rev. Thomas Thomas
Sec., Mrs. Eunice Schermerhorn
Treas., Mr. Nelson Rabenold
Major Activities: Social Concerns and Action; Clergy Dialogues; Daybreak Drop-In-Center

for Mental Health Adults; Soup Kitchen; Housing Advocacy Program; Pathways (Referral to Social Services); Street Ministry via Linkage; Homelessness Prevention; Pharmaceutical Assistance; Campbell Christian-Unity lecture; Clothing Distribution; Aspires Mentoring Program; Ecumenical & Interfaith Services; Homeless Supportive Services; CROPWalk

Lewisburg Council of Churches

5. S. Asper Place, Lewisburg, PA 17837 Tel. (570)524-2834
Media Contact, Guy Temple
139 Iron Cave Lane
Lewisburg, PA 17837
(570)-524-4877
President, Mrs. Gail Pepper, First Baptist Church, 51 S. 3rd St, Lewisburg, PA 17837; Tel. (570)524-7438
Treasurer, Mrs. Jan Temple, 139 Iron Cave Lane, Lewisburg, PA 17837; Tel. (570)524-4877
Major Activities: Supplementary and Emergency Food Pantries; Clothing Bank; CROP Walk; Week of Prayer for Christian Unity; Soup & Scripture Lenten Series; 3-hour Good Friday Service; Human Services Directory; Transient-Homeless Aid

Metropolitan Christian Council of Philadelphia

1501 Cherry St., Philadelphia, PA 19102-1429 Tel. (215)563-7854 Fax (215)563-6849
Email: geiger@mccp.org
Website: www.mccp.org
Media Contact, Assoc. Communications, Nancy L. Nolde
Exec. Dir., Rev. C. Edward Geiger
Assoc. Communications, Nancy L. Nolde
Office Mgr., Joan G. Shipman
Pres., Rev. Steven B. Laurence
First Vice Pres., Rev. G. Daniel Jones
Treas., A. Louis Denton, Esq.
Major Activities: Congregational Clusters; Public Policy Advocacy; Communication; Theological Dialogue (Christian & Interfaith); Women's Issues

North Hills Youth Ministry Counseling Center

802 McKnight Park Dr., Pittsburgh, PA 15237 Tel. (412)366-1300
Email: NHYM@nhymcc.org
Website: www.nhymcc.org
Media Contact, Exec. Dir., Rev. Ronald B. Barnes
Exec. Dir., Ronald B. Barnes
Major Activities: Elementary, Junior and Senior High School Individual and Family Counseling; Elementary Age Youth Early Intervention Counseling; Educational Programming for Churches and Schools;

Youth Advocacy; Parent Education; Marital Counseling; Tutoring for Elementary, Junior and Senior High Students; Healthy Communities-Healthy Youth Training and workshops based on Search Institutes (out of Mineapolis, MN); 40 Assets

Northside Common Ministries

P.O. Box 99861, Pittsburgh, PA 15233 Tel. (412)323-1163 Fax (412)323-1749
Email: NCM@city-net.com
Media Contact, Exec. Dir., Janet E. Holtz
Exec. Dir., Janet E. Holtz
Major Activities: Pleasant Valley Shelter for Homeless Men; Advocacy around Hunger, Housing, Poverty, and Racial Issues; Community Food Pantry and Service Center; Supportive Housing

Northwest Interfaith Movement

6757 Greene St., Philadelphia, PA 19119 Tel. (215)843-5600 Fax (215)843-2755
Email: jejohnson@nim-phila.org
Website: www.nim-phila.org
Media Contact, Exec. Dir., Rabbi George M. Stern
Exec. Dir., Rabbi George M. Stern
Chpsn., Judy Weinstein
Long Term Care Program, Dir., Donald Carlin
Neighborhood Child Care Resource Prog., Dir., Leslie S. Eslinger
Major Activities: Resources amd Technical Assistance for Child Care Programs; Conflict Mediation and Support for Nursing and Boarding Home Residents

Pennsylvania Conference on Interchurch Cooperation*

P.O. Box 2835, 223 North St., Harrisburg, PA 17105 Tel. (717)238-9613 Fax (717)238-1473
Email: staff@pacatholic.org
Website: www.pacatholic.org/ecumenism
Media Contact, Carolyn Astfalk
Co-Staff, Dr. Robert J. O'Hara, Jr., Rev. Gary Harke
Co-Chpsns., Bishop Joseph Martino; Bishop Donald Main.
Major Activities: Theological Consultation; Social Concerns; Public Policy; Conferences and Seminars

The Pennsylvania Council of Churches*

900 S. Arlington Ave., Ste. 100, Harrisburg, PA 17109-5089 Tel. (717)545-4761 Fax (717) 545-4765
Email: pcc@pachurches.org
Website: www.pachurches.org
Media Contact, Exec. Dir.,The Rev. Gary L. Harke, Email: g.harke@pachurches.org
Exec. Dir., The Rev. Gary L. Harke
Dir. of Public Advocacy, The Rev. Sandra L. Strauss

261

Dir. Of Finance & Facilities, Janet A. Gulick
Coord. for Leisure Ministries, Dr. Paul L. Herring
Pres., Rev. Bishop A. Donald Main
Vice Pres., Ms. Barbara Adams-Smelter
Sec., The Rev. Dr. Warren M. Eshbach
Treas., Ms. Zedna M. Haverstock
Major Activities: Inter-church dialogue; trade association activities; faith and order; seasonal farmworker ministry; trucker-traveler ministry; public policy advocacy and education; leisure ministry; conferences and continuing education events; disaster response

Project of Easton, Inc.
330 Ferry St., Easton, PA 18042 Tel. (215)258-4361
Pres., Dr. John H. Updegrove
Vice Pres. Public Relations, Rev. Charles E. Staples
Vice Pres. Operations, Don Follett
Sec., Rosemary Reese
Treas., Steve Barsony
Exec. Dir., Maryellen Shuman
Major Activities: Food Bank; Adult Literacy Program; English as a Second Language; Children's Programs; Parents as Student Support; CROP Walk; Interfaith Council; Family Literacy; Emergency Assistance; Even Start Family Literacy

Reading Berks Conference of Churches
519 Elm St., P.O.Box 957, Reading, PA 19603 Tel. (610)375-6108 Fax (610)375-6205
Email: rdgbrkscc@comcast.net
Website: www.readingberksconferenceofchurches.com
Media Contact, Exec. Dir., Rev. Calvin Kurtz
Admin Asst., Donna Boyajcan
Exec. Dir., Rev. Calvin Kurtz
Pres., John Roland
Treas., William Maslo
Major Activities: Institutional Ministry; Social Action; CROP Walk for Hunger; Emergency Assistance; Prison Chaplaincy; Hospital Chaplaincy; Interchurch-Intercultural Services; Children & Youth Ministry; Healthy Family & Marriage Initiatives; Lazarus Project

South Hills Interfaith Ministries
1900 Sleepy Hollow Rd., South Park, PA 15129 Tel. (412)854-9120 Fax (412)854-9123
Website: www.shimcenters.org
Media Contact, Exec. Dir., Jerry Ellis
Prog. Dir., Director of Youth Programs, Sarah Henkel
Psychological Services, Don Zandier
Family Assistance Coordinator, Harry Dietz
Business Mgr., Amy Puglisi
Volunteer Coordinator, Barbara Houston
Major Activities: Basic Human Needs; Community Organization and Development;

Inter-Faith Cooperation; Personal Growth; At-Risk Youth Development; Women in Transition; Elderly Support; After School Homework Club; Early Childhood Program (Pre-School); Interfaith Educational Programs & Observances

United Churches of Lycoming County
202 E. Third St., Williamsport, PA 17701 Tel. (570)322-1110 Fax (570)326-4572
Email: uclc@sunlink.net
Website: www.uclc.org
Media Contact, Exec. Dir., Rev. Gwen Nelson Bernstine
Exec. Dir., Rev. Gwen Nelson Bernstine
Ofc. Sec., Linda Winter
Pres., Rev. Glenn McCreary, 526 South Main Street, Muncy PA17756
Treas., Mrs. Madeline Bird, 407 South Market Street, Muncy PA17756
Shepherd of the Streets, Rev. J. Morris Smith, 669 Center Street., Williamsport, PA 17701
Ecumenism, Dir., Rev. Leo McKernan, 800 Mulberry Street, Montoursville PA 17754
Educ. Ministries, Dir., Rev. Ted Corcelius, 148 South Main Street, Hughesville PA 17737
Institutional Ministry, Dir., Rev. Dr. James Behrens, 1971 Lycoming Creek Rd., Williamsport, PA 17701
Radio-TV, Dir., Rev. Judy Stanley, 102 East Third St., Williamsport, PA 17701
Prison Ministry, Dir., Mrs. Evadna Cline, 3336 West Fourth St., Williamsport, PA 17701
Christian Social Concerns, Dir., Rev. Dr. J. Jeffrey Zetto, 369 Broad St., Montoursville, PA 17754
Major Activities: Ecumenism; Educational Ministries; Church Women United; Church World Service and CROP; Prison Ministry; Radio-TV; Nursing Homes; Fuel Bank; Food Pantry;
Family Life; Shepherd of the Streets Urban Ministry; Peace Concerns; Housing Initiative; Interfaith Dialogue, Youth Ministry, Campus Ministry

Wilkinsburg Community Ministry
710 Mulberry St., Pittsburgh, PA 15221 Tel. (412) 241-8072 Fax (412)241-8315
Email: wcm15221@juno.com
Website: trfn.clpgh.org/wcm
Media Contact, Dir., Rev. Vivian Lovingood
Acting Dir., Elizabeth Mulvaney, MSW, LSW
Pres. Of Bd., Glenna Wilson, MSW, LSW
Major Activities: Hunger Ministry;Summer Reading Camp; Teen-Moms Infant Care; Meals on Wheels; Church Camp Scholarships; Utility Assistance; Clothing-Furniture Assistance; Case Management for Elderly Homebound Persons and Families, Soup Kitchen

Wyoming Valley Council of Churches

70 Lockhart St., Wilkes-Barre, PA 18702 Tel. (570)825-8543
Media Contact, Exec. Dir., Beth Titus
Exec. Dir., Beth Titus
Ofc. Sec., Sandra Karrott
Pres., Very Rev. Joseph Martin
Treas., Rev. Dr. Robert Zanicky
Major Activities: Nursing Home Chaplaincy; Hospital Referral Service; CROP Hunger Walk; Pastoral Care Ministries; Clergy Retreats and Seminars; Meals on Wheels Fuel Service; Citizen's Voice articles

York County Council of Churches

P.O. Box 1865, York, PA 17405-1865 Tel. (717) 854-9504 Fax (717)843-5295
Email: ycccoffice@yccchurches.org
Website: www.yc, churches.org
Media Contact, Ryan Sttler, Chariman of P.R. Comm.
Pres., Mrs. Jody Appell
Vice Pres., Rev. William Snyder
Exec. Dir., in hiring process
Major Activities: Educational Development; Spiritual Growth and Renewal; Worship and Witness; Congregational Resourcing; Outreach and Mission

RHODE ISLAND

The Rhode Island State Council of Churches*

225 Chapman Street, Ste. 303, Providence, RI 02905 Tel. (401)461-5558 Fax (401)461-5233
Email: pmacnie@councilofchurchesri.org
Website: www.councilof churchesri.org
Media Contact, Exec. Minister, Dr. Donald C. Anderson, Email: danderson@councilof churchesri.org
Exec. Min., Dr. Donald C. Anderson
Admn. Asst., Peggy Macnie
Pres., Marie Bouvier-Newman
Treas., George Weavill
Major Activities: Urban Ministries; Institutional Chaplaincy; Advocacy-Justice & Service, Legislative Liaison; Faith & Order; Community Network; Campus Ministries; Prison Ministry

SOUTH CAROLINA

South Carolina Christian Action Council, Inc.*

P.O. Drawer 3248, Columbia, SC 29230 Tel. (803)786-7116 Fax (803)786-7116
Email: sccouncil@sccouncil.net
Website: www.sccouncil.net
Media Contact, Exec. Minister, Rev. Brenda Kneece, Email: bkneece@sccouncil.net
Exec. Minister, The Rev. Brenda Kneece

Pres., Debbie Dantzler, Attorney
Pres. Elect, The Rev. Dr. Joseph Darby, AME Pastor
Secretary, The Rev. Terry Brooks, CBF
Treasurer, Mr. John Harmon, ELCA
Major Activities: Advocacy and Ecumenism; Continuing Education; Interfaith Dialogue; Citizenship and Public Affairs; Publications; Race Relations; Child Advocacy; Faith and Health; Environmental Stewardship

United Ministries

606 Pendleton St., Greenville, SC 29601 Tel. (864)232-6463 Fax (864)370-3518
Email: info@united-ministries.org
Website: www.united-ministries.org
Media Contact, Exec. Dir., Rev. Beth Templeton
Exec. Dir., The Rev. Beth Templeton
Pres., Nancy Orders Smith
Vice Pres., Anne Ellefson
Sec., Becky Bouton
Treas., Lan Nix
Major Activities: Assistance with rent, utilities, prescriptions, food, heat; Place of Hope (A day shelter for people who are homeless); Assistance with getting and keeping jobs; A GED program for adults; Case Management as part of all activities, College assistance with books and scholarships.

SOUTH DAKOTA

Association of Christian Churches of South Dakota*

100 S. Spring Ave., Suite 106, Sioux Falls, SD 57104-3626 Tel. (605)334-1980
Email: office@accsd.org
Website: www.accsd.org
Media Contact, Gary Nesdahl, 100 S. Spring Ave., Sioux Falls, SD 57104 Tel. (605)334-1980
Pres., Bd. Of Directors, Dr. Gail Arnold
Major Activities: Ecumenical Forums; Continuing Education for Clergy; Legislative Information;
Resourcing Local Ecumenism; Native American Issues; Ecumenical Fields
Ministries; Rural Economic Development; Children at Risk

Metropolitan Inter Faith Association (MIFA)

P.O. Box 3130, Memphis, TN 38173-0130 Tel. (901)527-0208 Fax (901)527-3202
Media Contact, Dir., Media Relations, Caroline Vonicessler
Exec. Dir., Margaret Craddock
Major Activities: Emergency Services (Rent, Utility, Food, Clothing Assistance); Home-Delivered Meals and Senior Support Services; Youth Services; Homeless Programs

263

Tennessee Association of Churches*

4612 Billingsgate Rd., Antioch, TN 37103 Tel. (615)367-4347
Exec. Dir., The Rev. Bill Middleton
Pres., Rev. Steve Mosley
Treas., Paul Milliken
Major Activities: Faith and Order; Christian Unity; Social Concern Ministries; Governmental Concerns; Governor's Prayer Breakfast

Volunteer Ministry Center

103 South Gay St., Knoxville, TN 37902 Tel. (423)524-3926 Fax (423)524-7065
Media Contact, Exec. Dir., Angelia Moon
Exec. Dir., Angelia Moon
Pres., David Leech
Vice Pres., John Moxham
Treas., Doug Thompson
Major Activities: Homeless Program; Food Line; Crisis Referral Program; Subsidized Apartment Program; Counselling Program; Parenting Education for Single Parents

TEXAS

Austin Area Interreligious Ministries

701 Tillery St., Ste. 8, Austin, TX 78705 Tel. (512)386-9145 Fax (512)385-1430
Email: aaim@ammaustin.org
Website: www.ammaustin.org
Media Contact, Exec. Dir., Susan Wills, LPC
Exec. Dir., Susan Wills
Pres., Rev. Mel Waxler
Treas., Anita Maxwell
Major Activities: Youth at Risk Mentoring; Housing Rehabilitation; Broadcast Ministry; Interfaith Dialogues; Family Issues; Homeless Issues; Hunger Issues; Racial Reconciliation, ESL

Border Association for Refugees from Central America (BARCA), Inc.

P.O. Box 1725, Edinburg, TX 78540 Tel. (956) 631-7447 Fax (956)687-9266
Email: barcainc@aol.com
Media Contact, Exec. Dir., Ninfa Ochoa-Krueger
Exec. Dir, Ninfa Ochoa-Krueger
Outreach Services, Dir., Juanita Ledesma
Major Activities: Food, Shelter, Clothing to Newly Arrived Indigent Immigrants & Refugees; Medical and Other Emergency Aid; Special Services to Children; Speakers on Refugee and Immigrant Concerns for Church Groups; Orientation, Advocacy and Legal Services for Immigrants and Refugees

Corpus Christi Metro Ministries

1919 Leopard St., P.O. Box 4899, Corpus Christi, TX 78469-4899 Tel. (361)887-0151 Fax (361)887-7900
Email: edseeger@ccmetrominstries.com

Website: www.ccmetroministries.com
Media Contact, Exec. Dir., The Reverend Robert G. Trache
Exec. Dir., The Reverend Robert G. Trache, Email; btrache@ccmetroministries.com
Admn. Dir., Ginger Flewelling-Leeds
Volunteer Dir., Ann Cox
Fin. Coord., Sue McCown
Loaves & Fishes Dir., Ray Gomez
Emergency Services Mgr., Ann Cox
Employment Dir., Larry Curtis
Health and Human Services, Dir., Ann Cox
Major Activities: Clothing Distribution, Employment Assistance, Healthcare, Homelessness/ Shelter, and Hunger/Food Programs.

East Dallas Cooperative Parish

P.O. Box 720305, Dallas, TX 75372-0305 Tel. (214)823-9149 Fax (214)823-2015
Email: edcp@swbell.net
Media Contact, Exec. Dir., Nancy Jellinek
Pres., Debbie Thorpe
Major Activities: Emergency Food, Clothing, Job Bank; Medical Clinic; Legal Clinic, Tutorial Education; Home Companion Service; Pre-School Education; Hispanic Ministry; Activity Center for Low Income Older Adults; Pastoral Counseling; English Language Ministry, Pre-GED program

Greater Dallas Community of Churches

624 N. Good-Latimer #100, Dallas, TX 75204-5818 Tel. (214)824-8680 Fax (214)824-8726
Email: gdcc@churchcommunity.org
Media Contact, Exec. Dir., Rev. Elzie Odom
Exec. Dir., Rev. Elzie Odom
AmeriCorps-Building Blocks Dir., Venita Allen-Kent
Development Vice Pres., Charlotte Coyle
Pres.,Richard Selby
Treas., John Rutzler
Major Activities: Interdenominational, Interfaith and Interracial Understanding and Joint Work; AmeriCorps-Building Blocks (Direct Service to Develop Inner City Children, Youth & Families); Summer Food & Reading; Hunger; Peacemaking; Public Policy; Social Justice; Faith & Life; Children's Health Outreach; Child Advocacy; Dismantaling Racism

Interfaith Ministries for Greater Houston

3217 Montrose Blvd., Houston, TX 77006 Tel. (713)522-3955 Fax (713)520-4663
Media Contact, Exec. Dir., Betty P. Taylor
Exec. Dir., Betty P. Taylor
Pres., Charles R. Erickson
Development, Dir., Sharon Ervine
Assoc. Exec. Dir., Larry Norton
Treas., Fort D. Flowers, Jr.
Sec., Darlene Alexander

Major Activities: Community Concerns, Hunger; Older Adults; Families; Youth; Child Abuse; Refugee Services; Congregational Relations and Development; Social Service Programs, Refugee Services; Hunger Coalition; Youth Victim Witness; Family Connection; Meals on Wheels; Senior Health; RSVP; Foster Grandparents

North Dallas Shared Ministries

2530 Glenda Ln., #500, Dallas, TX 75229 Tel. (214)620-8696 Fax (214)620-0433
Media Contact, Exec. Dir., J. Dwayne Martin
Exec. Dir., J. Dwayne Martin
Pres., -vacant-
Major Activities: Emergency Assistance; Job Counseling; ESL

Northside Inter-Church Agency (NICA)

1600 Circle Park Blvd., Fort Worth, TX 76106-8943 Tel. (817)626-1102 Fax (817)626-9043
Email: nicaagency@sbcglobal.net
Website: www.nicaagency.org
Media Contact, Exec. Dir., Connie Nahoolewa
Exec. Dir., Connie Nahoolewa
Major Activities: Food; Clothing; Counseling; Information and Referral; Furniture and Household Items; Nutrition Education; Employment Services; Thanksgiving Basket Program; "Last Resort" Christmas Program; Community Networking; Ecumenical Worship Services; Volunteer Training; Newsletter; Senior Home Repairs; School Clothing Program; Advocacy; GED Preparation; Literacy; Computer Training; English as a Second Language

San Antonio Community of Churches

1101 W. Woodlawn, San Antonio, TX 78201 Tel. (210)733-9159 Fax (210)733-5780
Email: SACC@juno.com
Media Contact, Exec. Dir., Dr. Kenneth Thompson
Exec. Dir., Dr. Kenneth Thompson
Pres., Rev. Thomas Robinson
Major Activities: Christian Education; Missions; Infant Formula and Medical Prescriptions for Children of Indigent Families; Continuing Education For Clergy and Laity; Media Resource Center; Social Issues; Aging Concerns; Youth Concerns; Family Concerns; Sponsor annual CROP Walk for Hunger; Peace and Anti-Violence Initiatives

San Antonio Urban Ministries

535 Bandera Rd., San Antonio, TX 78228
Media Contact, Sue Kelly
Exec. Dir., Sue Kelly
Pres., Rev. Leslie Ellison
Major Activities: Homes for Discharged Mental Patients; After School Care for Latch Key Children; Christian Based Community Ministry

Southeast Area Churches (SEARCH)

P.O. Box 51256, Fort Worth, TX 76105 Tel. (817)531-2211
Exec. Dir., Dorothy Anderson-Develrow
Major Activities: Emergency Assistance; Advocacy; Information and Referral; Community Worship; School Supplies; Direct Aid to Low Income and Elderly

Tarrant Area Community of Churches

P.O. Box 11471, Fort Worth, TX 76110-0471 Tel. (817)534-1790 Fax (817)534-1995
Email: revkm@flash.net
Pres., Regina Taylor
Treas., Don Hoak
Exec. Dir., Dr. Kenneth W. McIntosh
Major Activities: Eldercare Program; Children's Sabbath Sponsorship; Week of Prayer for Christian Unity; CROP Walk for Hunger Relief; Community Issues Forums; Family Pathfinders

Texas Conference of Churches*

1033 La Posada, Ste. 125, Austin, TX 78752 Tel. (512)451-0991 Fax (512)451-5348
Email: tcc@txconfchurches.org
Website: www.txconfchurches.org
Media Contact, Comm. and Web Services, Caryn Wontor
Exec. Dir., Vacant
Dir. Of Business Administration, Caryn Wontor
Pres., Rev. Dr. T. Randall Smith
Major Activities: Faith & Order; Related Ecumenism; Christian-Jewish Relations; Church and Society Issues

United Board of Missions

1701 Bluebonnet Ave., P.O. Box 3856, Port Arthur, TX 77643-3856 Tel. (409)982-9412 Fax (409)985-3668
Media Contact, Admin. Asst., Carolyn Schwarr
Exec. Dir., Clark Moore
Pres., Glenda McCoy
Major Activities: Emergency Assistance (Food and Clothing, Rent and Utility, Medical, Dental, Transportation); Share a Toy at Christmas; Counseling; Back to School Clothing Assistance; Information and Referral; Hearing Aid Bank; Meals on Wheels; Super Pantry; Energy Conservation Programs; Job Bank Assistance to Local Residents Only

VERMONT

Vermont Ecumenical Council and Bible Society*

P.O. Box 728, Richmond, VT 05477 Tel. (802)434 -7307 Fax (802) 434-7306

265

Email: info@vecbs.org
Website: www.vecbs.org
Media Contact, Admin. Asst., Betsy Wackernagel
Exec. Officer, Dr. Linda Marek Howe
Pres., The Rev. Robert Lowenthal
Vice Pres., The Rev. Robert Atlas
Treas., Mr. Christopher McCandless
Major Activities: Christian Unity; Bible Distribution; Social Justice; Committee on Faith and Order; Committee on Peace, Justice and the Integrity of Creation; Committee on Prayer and Worship

VIRGINIA

Virginia Council of Churches, Inc.*

1214 W. Graham Rd., Richmond, VA 23220-1409 Tel. (804)321-3300 Fax (804)329-5066
Email: Barton@vcc-net.org
Website: www.vcc-net.org
Media Contact, Gen. Min., Rev. Jonathan Barton
President, The Rev. Tom Joyce
Vice President, The Rev. Jim Parke
Treasurer, The Rev. David Shumate
Secretary, Ms. Betty Altic
Gen. Min., The Rev. Jonathan Barton
Migrant Head Start, Dir., The Rev. Victor Gomez
Refugee Resettlement, Dir., The Rev. Richard D. Cline
Weekday Rel. Educ., Coord., Ms. Joanne Shirley
Campus Ministry Forum, Coord., The Rev. Steve Darr
Major Activities: Faith and Order; Network Building & Coordination; Ecumenical Communications; Justice and Legislative Concerns; Educational Development; Rural Concerns; Refugee Resettlement; Migrant Ministries and Migrant Head Start; Disaster Coordination; Infant Mortality Prevention

WASHINGTON

Associated Ministries of Tacoma-Pierce County

1224 South I St., Tacoma, WA 98405-5021 Tel. (253)383-3056 Fax (253)383-2672
Email: info@associatedministries.org
Website: www. associatedministries.org
Media Contact, Exec. Dir., Rev. David T. Alger
Dir. Of Communications, Judy Jones
Pres., Rev. Arne Bergland
Vice Pres., Danna Clancy
Sec., Connie Robey
Treas., Jeff Cunningham
Exec. Dir., Rev. David T. Alger
Deputy Dir., Diane Powers
Dir. of Mental Health Chaplaincy, Terry Mattock
Dir. of Project Interdependence, Valorie Crout
Dir. of Paint Tacoma-Pierce Beautiful, Sallie Shawl
Dir. Of Development, Stephanie Paige Barnett
Dir. of Hilltop Action Coalition, Jeanie Peterson
Director of Communication and Education, Judy Jones

Program Manager of Pierce County Asset Building Coalition, Barbara Gorzinski
Major Activities: County-wide Hunger Walk; Hunger Awareness; Economic Justice; Religious Education; Social Service Program Advocacy; Communication and Networking of Churches; Housing; Paint Tacoma-Pierce Beautiful; Mental Health Chaplaincy; Theological Dialogue; Welfare to Work Mentoring; Hilltop Action Coalition; Compeer; Homelessness; Youth Ministry; Ecumenical Formation; Interfaith Roundtable, Domestic Violence Chaplain, Asset Building Coalition; Family Emergency Fund

Church Council of Greater Seattle

4 Nickerson Street, Seattle, WA 98109-1699 Tel. (206)525-1213 Fax (206)525-1218
Email: info@thechurchcouncil.org
Website: www.thechurchcouncil.org
Media Contact, Exec. Dir.,The Rev. Dr. Sanford Brown
Executive Dir., The Rev. Dr. Sanford Brown
Emergency Feeding Prog., Dir., Arthur Lee
Friend to Friend, Dir., Marilyn Soderquist
Youth Chaplaincy Program, Dir., Chaplain Rev. Benny Wright
The Sharehouse, Dir., Michal Nortness
The Homelessness Project, Dir., Nancy Dorman
Mission for Music & Healing, Dir., Susan Gallaher & Esther "Little Dove" John
Sound Youth-AmeriCorps, Dir., Cat Koehn
Academy of Religious Broadcasting, Dir., Rev. J. Graley Taylor
Board Chair,Verlene Jones
Board Treas., The Rev. Jeb Parr
Board Secretary, Susan Segall
Editor, The Source, Tricia Schug
Seattle Youth Garden Works, Dir.,Conner Sharpe
SW King County Mental Health Ministry, Dir., The Rev. Stephen Jones
JOY Initiative, Prog. Dir., Rick Jump
St. Petersburg- Seattle Sister Churches Program Chair, Nigel Taber-Hamilton
Asia Pacific Task Force, Contact Person, Akio Yanagihara
Self-Managed Housing Programs, Dir., Misti Uptain
Cuba Friendshipment Committee, Chair, Monica Zapeda
Palestinian Concerns Task Force, Chair, Constance Trowbridge
Interfaith Network of Concern for the People of Iraq, Chair, The Rev. Rich Gamble & Andrew Fung
Major Activities: Children; Youth & Families; Hunger Relief; Global Peace and Justice; Housing and Homelessness; Pastoral Care; Services for the Aging; Public Witness; Interfaith and Ecumenical Relations; Publisher of the The Source, monthly ecumenical newspaper

266

FaithTrust Institute

2400 N. 45th St, Suite 10, Seattle, WA 98103 Tel. (206)634-1903 Fax (206)634-0115
Email: info@faithtrustinstitute.org
Website: www.faithtrustinstitute.org
Media Contact, Ko-Eun Kim
Executive Director, Rev. Kathryn J. Johnson, kjohnson@faithtrustinstitute.org
Founder & Senior Analyst, Rev. Dr. Marie M. Fortune, mfortune@faithtrustinstitute.org
Director of Training & Education, Rev. Thelma Burgonio-Watson, burgonio@faithtrustinstitute.org
Director of the Jewish Program, Rabbi Cindy Enger, cenger@faithtrustinstitute.org
Clearinghouse Coordinator, Dinah Hall, dhall@faithtrustinstitute.org
Finance Director, Marion J. Ward
Major Activities: Training - Domestic Violence, Healthy teen relationships, Child Abuse, Sexual Abuse by Clergy and Religious Leaders, Sexual Violence Consultation - Expertise to develop policies to address and prevent sexual abuse by clergy, guidance on integrating issues of sexual and domestic violence into religious education
Educational Materials—multicultural and multifaith educational materials, extensive resource catalog includes videos, books and curricula

The Interfaith Association of Snohomish County

2301 Hoyt, P.O. Box 12824, Everett, WA 98206 Tel. (206)252-6672
Email: admin@.tiasccom
Website: www.tiasc.com
Media Contact, Exec. Dir., Janet Pope
Exec. Dir., Janet Pope
Pres., William Comfort
Major Activities: Housing and Shelter; Economic Justice; Hunger; Interfaith Worship and Collaboration

Interfaith Council

1620 N. Monroe, Spokane, WA 99205 Tel. (509) 329-1410 Fax (509)329-1409
Email: info@interfaithnw.org
Website: www.interfaithnw.org
Media Contact, Dir., Kateri Caron
Director: Kateri Caron
Board President: Stephen Rorie
Vice President: Elliot Fabric
Sec., Rev. Dr. Richard Erhardt
Major Activities: Camp PEACE; Multi-Cultural Human Relations; High School Youth Camp; Eastern Washington Legislative Conference; CROP Walk; Interfaith Thanksgiving Worship; Easter Sunrise Service; Dir. Of Churches & Community Agencies; Circle of Caring (for Women in Domestic Violence); Guatemala Dialogues

Interfaith Works

P.O. Box 1221, Olympia, WA 98507 Tel. (360) 357-7224
Email: InterfaithWorks@comcast.net
Website: www.interfaith-works.org
Media Contact, Exec. Dir., Kathy Erlandson
Exec. Dir., Kathy Erlandson
Pres., Jim Fulton
Treas., Paddy Mackin
Major Activities: Interfaith Relations; Social and Health Concerns; Community Action; Social Justice

Northwest Harvest-E. M. M.

P.O. Box 12272, Seattle, WA 98102 Tel. (206) 625-0755 Fax (206)625-7518
Email: nharvest@blarg.net
Website: www. northwestharvest.org
Media Contact, Comm. Affairs Dir., Ellen Hansen
Exec. Dir., Ruth M. Velozo
Chpsn., Patricia Barcott
Major Activities: Northwest Harvest (Statewide Hunger Response); Cherry Street Food Bank (Community Hunger Response); Northwest Infants Corner (Special Nutritional Products for Infants and Babies)

Washington Association of Churches*

419 Occidental Ave. S., Ste. 201, Seattle, WA 98104-2886 Tel. (206)625-9790 Fax (206) 625-9791
Email: wac@thewac.org
Website: www.thewac.org
Media Contact, Mr. Darel Grothaus, Interim
Exec. Min., Mr. Darel Grothaus, Interim
Director for Operations, Bette Schneider, Email: schneider@thewac.org
Major Activities: Faith and Order; Ecumenical Dialogue; Justice Advocacy; Confronting Poverty; Hunger Action; Legislation; Denominational Ecumenical Coordination; Theological Formation; Leadership Development; Immigrant Rights Advocacy; Racial Justice Advocacy; International Solidarity; Environmental Justice Advocacy; Tax Justice Advocacy; Congregation Public Policy Organizing

WEST VIRGINIA

Greater Fairmont Council of Churches

P.O. Box 108, Fairmont, WV 26554 Tel. (304) 367-0962
Media Contact, Pres., Rev. Jeremiah Jasper
President, Rev. Jeremiah Jasper
Major Activities: Community Ecumenical Services; Youth and Adult Sports Leagues; CROP Walk Sponsor; Weekly Radio Broadcasts

West Virginia Council of Churches*

2207 Washington St. E., Charleston, WV 25311-2218 Tel. (304)344-3141 Fax (304)342-1506
Email: wvcc@wvcc.org
Website: www.wvcc.org
Media Contact, Exec. Dir., The Rev. Dennis D. Sparks, Email: dsparks@wvcc.org
Office Manager, Bob Rosier, Email: bob@wvcc.org
Pres., Bishop Ralph Dunkin (ELCA)
1st Vice Pres., The Rt. Rev. W. Michie Klusmeyer (ECUSA)
2nd Vice Pres., Ms. Ernestine Casson (AME)
Sec., Rev. Dr. William B. Allen (DOC)
Treas., The Very Rev. Frederick P. Annie (RC)
Major Activities: Disaster Response; Faith and Order; Family Concerns; Inter-Faith Relations; Peace and Justice; Government Concerns; Support Services Network

WISCONSIN

Christian Youth Council

1715-52nd St., Kenosha, WI 53140 Tel. (262) 654-6200 x120 Fax (414)652-4461
Media Contact, Exec. Dir., Steven L. Nelson
Exec. Dir., Steven L. Nelson
Sports Dir., Jerry Tappen
Outreach Dir., Linda Osborne
Accountant, Debbie Cutts
Class Director, Jill Cox
Pres. & Chmn. of Board, Lon Knoedler
Gang Prevention Dir., Sam Sauceda
Major Activities: Leisure Time Ministry; Institutional Ministries; Ecumenical Committee; Social Concerns; Outreach Sports(with a Christian Philosophy)

Interfaith Conference of Greater Milwaukee

1442 N. Farwell Ave., Ste. 200, Milwaukee, WI 53202 Tel. (414)276-9050 Fax (414)276-8442
Email: IFCGM@aol.com
Media Contact, Exec. Dir., Marcus White
Chpsn., Rev. Velma Smith
First Vice-Chair, Archbishop Rembert G. Weakland
Second Vice-Chair, Rev. Charles Graves
Sec., Paula Simon
Treas., The Rev. Mary Ann Neevel
Exec. Dir., Marcus White
Consultant in Communications, Rev. Robert P. Seater
Major Activities: Economic Issues; Racism; CROP Walk; Public Policy; Suburban and Urban Partnerships; TV Programming; Peace and International Issues Committee; Annual Membership Luncheon; Religion Diversity; Restorative Justice

Madison-area Urban Ministry

2300 S. Park St., Madison, WI 53713 Tel. (608) 256-0906 Fax (608)256-4387

Email: mum@emum.org
Website: www.emun.org
Media Contact, Office Mgr., Jackie Austin
Exec. Dir., Mary K. Baum
Program Mgr., - vacant
Major Activities: Community Projects; Dialogue-Forums

Wisconsin Council of Churches*

750 Windsor St. Ste. 301, Sun Prairie, WI 53590-2149 Tel. (608)837-3108 Fax (608)837-3038
Email: wcoc@wichurches.org
Website: www.wichurches.org
Exec. Dir., Exec. Dir., Scott D. Anderson, Email: sanderson@wichurches.org
Public Policy Coordinator, Dr. Peter Bakker
Coordinator for Local Ecumenism, The Rev. Kenneth Pennings
Pres., The Rt. Rev. Russell E. Jacobus
Treas., Dr. Robert Bock
Accountant, Rick Fluechtling
Coordinator for Program Support Services, Mr. Christopher Marceil
Major Activities: Social Witness; Migrant Ministry; Peace and Justice; Faith and Order; Anti-Hunger Campaign; American Indian Ministries Council; Park Ministry; Wisconsin Housing Partnership; Nonviolence, Affordable Housing; Economic Justice; Corporate Responsibility

WYOMING

Wyoming Association of Churches*

1131 13th St., Suite 210, Cody, WY 82414 Tel. (307)635-4251 Fax (307)637-4737
Email: wychurches@wyoming.com
Website: www.wyomingassociationofchurches.org
Media Contact, The Rev. Warren Murphy
Exec. Dir., Rev. Warren Murphy
Chair, The Rev. Tim Trippel
Treasurer, Don Kesselheim
Office Manager, Pam Noesner
Major Activities: Alternatives to Violence; Beyond Tolerance; Malicious Harrasment; Domestic Violence; Empowering the Poor and Oppressed; Peace and Justice; Public Health Issues; Welfare Reform; Anti-Death Penalty, Community Networking Facilitation

Index of Select Programs for U.S. Regional and Local Ecumenical Bodies

For many years the *Yearbook of American & Canadian Churches* has published the previous chapter, The Directory of U.S. Regional and Local Ecumenical Bodies. Each entry of that directory contains a brief description of the diverse programs offered by each agency. However, researchers, pastors, service organizations and theological seminaries often inquire about specific programs and which agencies carry out such programs. In response we have created this chapter, which indexes the various regional and local ecumenical agencies by twenty-five different program areas. These program areas are the twenty-five that have been the most frequent subjects of inquiry in our office. We have collected this program information directly from these organizations by means of a simple response form. There is an enormous diversity of ministries and missions conducted by these diverse organizations. Most organizations pursue several kinds of programs at once. However, some of these may focus their efforts most especially on only one of their programs; their other programs may be less well developed than their specialty. Consequently, the extent to which any of these ministries is a priority for any particular organization cannot be inferred from this list. For detailed information about the nature and extent of any particular ministry, the reader is urged to contact the organization directly using the directory of "U.S. Regional and Local Ecumenical Bodies," which is found in the pages just prior to this index.

AIDS/HIV Programs

Arizona Ecumenical Council—Phoenix, AZ

Center City Churches—Hartford, CT

Christian Churches United of the Tri-County Area—Harrisburg, PA

The Council of Churches of Santa Clara County—San Jose, CA

East Dallas Cooperative Parish—Dallas, TX

Ecumenical Ministries of Oregon—Portland, OR

Grand Rapids Area Center for Ecumenism (GRACE)—Grand Rapids, MI

Greater Baton Rouge Federation of Churches and Synagogues—Baton Rouge, LA

Greater Chicago Broadcast Ministries—Chicago, IL

Interfaith Community Services—St. Joseph, MO

Lehigh County Conference of Churches—Allentown, PA

Metropolitan Ecumenical Ministry—Newark, NJ

Network of Religious Communities—Buffalo, NY

The Regional Council of Churches of Atlanta—Atlanta, GA

Schenectady Inner City Ministry—Schenectady, NY

South Carolina Christian Action Council, Inc.—Columbia, SC

Southeast Ecumenical Ministry—Rochester, NY

Troy Area United Ministries—Troy, NY

Tulsa Metropolitan Ministry—Tulsa, OK

Wyoming Valley Council of Churches—Wilkes-Barre, PA

York County Council of Churches—York, PA

Anti-Gambling Programs

The Associated Churches of Fort Wayne & Allen County, Inc.—Fort Wayne, IN

Associated Ministries of Tacoma-Pierce County—Tacoma, WA

Ecumenical Ministries of Iowa (EMI)—Des Moines, IA

Genesee County Churches United, Inc.—Batavia, NY

Greater Chicago Broadcast Ministries—Chicago, IL

Greater Lawrence Council of Churches—Lawrence, MA

The Joint Religious Legislative Coalition—Minneapolis, MN

Kentuckiana Interfaith Community—Louisville, KY

Kentucky Council of Churches—Lexington, KY

Lehigh County Conference of Churches—Allentown, PA

Mahoning Valley Association of Churches—Youngstown, OH

Massachusetts Council of Churches—Boston, MA

Mississippi Religious Leadership Conference—Jackson, MS

Montana Association of Churches—Helena, MT

Network of Religious Communities—Buffalo, NY

New Mexico Conference of Churches—Albuquerque, NM

The Pennsylvania Council of Churches—Harrisburg, PA

The Rhode Island State Council of Churches—Providence, RI

South Carolina Christian Action Council, Inc.—Columbia, SC

Texas Conference of Churches—Austin, TX

United Churches of Lycoming County—Williamsport, PA

Washington Association of Churches—Seattle, WA

West Virginia Council of Churches—Charleston, WV

Wisconsin Council of Churches—Sun Prairie, WI

Worcester County Ecumenical Council—Worcester, MA

Anti-Racism Programs

Akron Area Association of Churches—Akron, OH

Arizona Ecumenical Council—Phoenix, AZ

The Associated Churches of Fort Wayne & Allen County, Inc.—Fort Wayne, IN

Associated Ministries of Tacoma-Pierce County—Tacoma, WA

Association of Religious Communities—Danbury, CT

Austin Area Interreligious Ministries—Austin, TX

Broome County Council of Churches, Inc.—Binghamton, NY

The Cape Cod Council of Churches, Inc.—Hyannis, MA

Capital Region Ecumenical Organization (CREO)—Schenectady, NY

The Capitol Region Conference of Churches—Hartford, CT

Christian Ministries of Delaware County—Muncie, IN

The Church Federation of Greater Indianapolis, Inc.—Indianapolis, IN

Colorado Council of Churches—Denver, CO

Community Emergency Assistance Program (CEAP)—Brooklyn Park, MN

Cooperative Metropolitan Ministries—Newton, MA

Council of Churches of the City of New York—New York, NY

Council of Churches of Greater Bridgeport, Inc. —Bridgeport, CT

The Council of Churches of Santa Clara County—San Jose, CA

Council of Churches and Synagogues of South-western Connecticut—Stamford, CT

Dutchess County Interfaith Council, Inc.—Poughkeepsie, NY

East Dallas Cooperative Parish—Dallas, TX

Ecclesia—Trenton, NJ

Ecumenical Conference of Greater Altoona—Altoona, PA

Ecumenical Ministries of Oregon—Portland, OR

Evanston Ecumenical Action Council—Evanston, IL

Faith Community Assistance Center—Santa Fe, NM

FaithTrust Institute—Seattle, WA

Fresno Metro Ministry—Fresno, CA

Georgia Christian Council—Macon, GA

Grand Rapids Area Center for Ecumenism (GRACE)—Grand Rapids, MI

Greater Baton Rouge Federation of Churches and Synagogues—Baton Rouge, LA

Greater Birmingham Ministries—Birmingham, AL

Greater Chicago Broadcast Ministries—Chicago, IL

Greater Dallas Community of Churches—Dallas, TX

Greater Dayton Christian Connections—Dayton, OH

Greater Rochester Community of Churches—Rochester, NY

Greensboro Urban Ministry—Greensboro, NC

Illinois Conference of Churches—Springfield, IL

Indiana Partners for Christian Unity and Mission—Indianapolis, IN

Inter-Church Council of Greater New Bedford—New Bedford, MA

Interfaith Conference of Greater Milwaukee—Milwaukee, WI

InterFaith Conference of Metropolitan Washington—Washington, DC

Interfaith Council—Spokane, WA

Interfaith Council of Contra Costa County—Walnut Creek, CA

Inter-Faith Ministries-Wichita—Wichita, KS

Interfaith Mission Service—Huntsville, AL

Interfaith Service Bureau—Sacramento, CA

InterReligious Council of Central New York—Syracuse, NY

The Joint Religious Legislative Coalition—Minneapolis, MN

Kansas Ecumenical Ministries—Topeka, KS

Kentuckiana Interfaith Community—Louisville, KY

Kentucky Council of Churches—Lexington, KY

Lincoln Interfaith Council—Lincoln, NE

The Long Island Council of Churches—Hempstead, NY

Louisiana Interchurch Conference—Baton Rouge, LA

Madison-area Urban Ministry—Madison, WI

Mahoning Valley Association of Churches—Youngstown, OH

Massachusetts Council of Churches—Boston, MA

The Metropolitan Christian Council: Detroit-Windsor—Detroit, MI

Metropolitan Christian Council of Philadelphia—Philadelphia, PA

Metropolitan Ecumenical Ministry—Newark, NJ

Metropolitan Interfaith Council on Affordable Housing (MICAH)—Minneapolis, MN

Minnesota Council of Churches—Minneapolis, MN

Mississippi Religious Leadership Conference—Jackson, MS

Montana Association of Churches—Helena, MT

270

Muskegon County Cooperating Churches—Muskegon, MI

Network of Religious Communities—Buffalo, NY

New Britain Area Conference of Churches (NEWBRACC)—New Britain, CT

New Hampshire Council of Churches—Pembroke, NH

New Mexico Conference of Churches—Albuquerque, NM

North Carolina Council of Churches—Raleigh, NC

Northern California Interreligious Conference—Oakland, CA

Northside Common Ministries—Pittsburgh, PA

The Pennsylvania Council of Churches—Harrisburg, PA

The Regional Council of Churches of Atlanta—Atlanta, GA

The Rhode Island State Council of Churches—Providence, RI

Saint. Paul Area Council of Churches—St. Paul, MN

South Carolina Christian Action Council, Inc.—Columbia, SC

South Hills Interfaith Ministries—South Park, PA

Tarrant Area Community of Churches—Fort Worth, TX

Texas Conference of Churches—Austin, TX

Tri-Council Coordinating Commission—Minneapolis, MN

Troy Area United Ministries—Troy, NY

Tulsa Metropolitan Ministry—Tulsa, OK

United Churches of Lycoming County—Williamsport, PA

Virginia Council of Churches, Inc.—Richmond, VA

Wainwright House—Rye, NY

Washington Association of Churches—Seattle, WA

West Virginia Council of Churches—Charleston, WV

Wisconsin Council of Churches—Sun Prairie, WI

Wyoming Association of Churches—Cody, WY

Christian Education Programs

Akron Area Association of Churches—Akron, OH

Arizona Ecumenical Council—Phoenix, AZ

Arkansas Interfaith Conference—Scott, AR

The Associated Churches of Fort Wayne & Allen County, Inc.—Fort Wayne, IN

Associated Ministries of Tacoma-Pierce County—Tacoma, WA

Attleboro Area Council of Churches, Inc.—Attleboro, MA

Berrien County Association of Churches—Benton Harbor, MI

Border Association for Refugees from Central America (BARCA), Inc.—Edinburg, TX

Brooklyn Council of Churches—Brooklyn, NY

The Cape Cod Council of Churches, Inc.—Hyannis, MA

Christian Ministries of Delaware County—Muncie, IN

Christians United in Beaver County—Beaver, PA

Council of Christian Communions of Greater Cincinnati—Cincinnati, OH

The Council of Churches of Santa Clara County—San Jose, CA

Council of Churches and Synagogues of Southwestern Connecticut—Stamford, CT

East Dallas Cooperative Parish—Dallas, TX

Ecclesia—Trenton, NJ

Ecumenical Conference of Greater Altoona—Altoona, PA

Ecumenical Ministries of Oregon—Portland, OR

Evansville Area Community of Churches, Inc.—Evansville, IN

FaithTrust Institute—Seattle, WA

Georgia Christian Council—Macon, GA

Grand Rapids Area Center for Ecumenism (GRACE)—Grand Rapids, MI

Greater Bethlehem Area Council of Churches—Bethlehem, PA

Greater Chicago Broadcast Ministries—Chicago, IL

Greater Dayton Christian Connections—Dayton, OH

Greater Fairmont Council of Churches—Fairmont, WV

Greater Flint Council of Churches—Flint, MI

Greater Lawrence Council of Churches—Lawrence, MA

Greater New Orleans Federation of Churches—New Orleans, LA

Greensboro Urban Ministry—Greensboro, NC

Inter-Church Council of Greater New Bedford—New Bedford, MA

InterReligious Council of Central New York—Syracuse, NY

Iowa Religious Media Services—Des Moines, IA

Massachusetts Council of Churches—Boston, MA

The Metropolitan Christian Council: Detroit-Windsor—Detroit, MI

Metropolitan Christian Council of Philadelphia—Philadelphia, PA

Metropolitan Ecumenical Ministry—Newark, NJ

Montana Association of Churches—Helena, MT

New Britain Area Conference of Churches (NEWBRACC)—New Britain, CT

New Hampshire Council of Churches—Pembroke, NH

New Mexico Conference of Churches—Albuquerque, NM

Northern Kentucky Interfaith Commission, Inc.—Newport, KY

271

Oklahoma Conference of Churches—Oklahoma City, OK

Peoria Friendship House of Christian Service—Peoria, IL

Reading Berks Conference of Churches—Reading, PA

The Regional Council of Churches of Atlanta—Atlanta, GA

San Antonio Community of Churches—San Antonio, TX

Schenectady Inner City Ministry—Schenectady, NY

South Carolina Christian Action Council, Inc.—Columbia, SC

Staten Island Council of Churches—Staten Island, NY

Tarrant Area Community of Churches—Fort Worth, TX

Texas Conference of Churches—Austin, TX

Troy Area United Ministries—Troy, NY

Wainwright House—Rye, NY

Wyoming Association of Churches—Cody, WY

Wyoming Valley Council of Churches—Wilkes-Barre, PA

Clothing Distribution Programs

Asheville-Buncombe Community Christian Ministry (ABCCM)—Asheville, NC

Associated Ministries of Tacoma-Pierce County—Tacoma, WA

Attleboro Area Council of Churches, Inc.—Attleboro, MA

The Cape Cod Council of Churches, Inc.—Hyannis, MA

Chautauqua County Rural Ministry—Dunkirk, NY

Christian Ministries of Delaware County—Muncie, IN

Christian Service Center for Central Florida, Inc.—Orlando, FL

Community Emergency Assistance Program (CEAP)—Brooklyn Park, MN

Community Ministry of Montgomery County—Rockville, MD

Contact Ministries of Springfield—Springfield, IL

Cooperative Metropolitan Ministries—Newton, MA

Corpus Christi Metro Ministries—Corpus Christi, TX

Council of Churches of the Ozarks—Springfield, MO

Cross-Lines Cooperative Council—Kansas City, KS

East Dallas Cooperative Parish—Dallas, TX

Eastern Area Community Ministries—Louisville, KY

The Ecumenical Council of Pasadena Area Churches—Pasadena, CA

Evanston Ecumenical Action Council—Evanston, IL

Fern Creek-Highview United Ministries—Louisvlle, KY

Greater Birmingham Ministries—Birmingham, AL

Greater Fairmont Council of Churches—Fairmont, WV

Greater Lawrence Council of Churches—Lawrence, MA

Greater Minneapolis Council of Churches—Minneapolis, MN

Greensboro Urban Ministry—Greensboro, NC

Hanover Area Council of Churches—Hanover, PA

Highlands Community Ministries—Louisville, KY

Inter-Church Ministries of Erie County—Erie, PA

Interfaith Community Services—St. Joseph, MO

Lancaster County Council of Churches—Lancaster, PA

Lebanon County Christian Ministries—Lebanon, PA

Lehigh County Conference of Churches—Allentown, PA

Lewisburg Council of Churches—Lewisburg, PA

Madison-area Urban Ministry—Madison, WI

Metropolitan Ecumenical Ministry—Newark, NJ

New Mexico Conference of Churches—Albuquerque, NM

Northside Inter-Church Agency (NICA)—Fort Worth, TX

Peoria Friendship House of Christian Service—Peoria, IL

Reading Berks Conference of Churches—Reading, PA

Saint. Paul Area Council of Churches—St. Paul, MN

South East Associated Ministries (SEAM)—Louisville, KY

South Hills Interfaith Ministries—South Park, PA

Tuscarawas County Council for Church and Community—New Philadelphia, OH

West Side Ecumenical Ministry—Cleveland, OH

Wilkinsburg Community Ministry—Pittsburgh, PA

CROP Walks

Akron Area Association of Churches—Akron, OH

Asheville-Buncombe Community Christian Ministry (ABCCM)—Asheville, NC

Associated Ministries of Tacoma-Pierce County—Tacoma, WA

Attleboro Area Council of Churches, Inc.—Attleboro, MA

Austin Area Interreligious Ministries—Austin, TX

Berrien County Association of Churches—Benton Harbor, MI

Broome County Council of Churches, Inc.—Binghamton, NY

Capital Area Council of Churches, Inc.—Albany, NY

Chautauqua County Rural Ministry—Dunkirk, NY

Christian Churches United of the Tri-County Area—Harrisburg, PA

Christian Ministries of Delaware County—Muncie, IN

Christian Service Center for Central Florida, Inc.—Orlando, FL

Church Community Services—Elkhart, IN

Churches United, Inc.—Cedar Rapids, IA

Churches United of the Quad City Area—Rock Island, IL

Community Emergency Assistance Program (CEAP)—Brooklyn Park, MN

Council of Churches of Chemung County, Inc.—Elmira, NY

Council of Churches of Greater Bridgeport, Inc.—Bridgeport, CT

Council of Churches of Greater Springfield—Springfield, MA

The Council of Churches of Santa Clara County—San Jose, CA

Dutchess County Interfaith Council, Inc.—Poughkeepsie, NY

East Dallas Cooperative Parish—Dallas, TX

East End Cooperative Ministry—Pittsburgh, PA

Ecclesia—Trenton, NJ

The Ecumenical Council of Pasadena Area Churches—Pasadena, CA

Ecumenical Ministries—Fulton, MO

Evanston Ecumenical Action Council—Evanston, IL

Evansville Area Community of Churches, Inc.—Evansville, IN

Greater Bethlehem Area Council of Churches—Bethlehem, PA

Greater Dayton Christian Connections—Dayton, OH

Greater Fairmont Council of Churches—Fairmont, WV

Greater Flint Council of Churches—Flint, MI

Greater Waterbury Interfaith Ministries, Inc.—Waterbury, CT

Greensboro Urban Ministry—Greensboro, NC

Hanover Area Council of Churches—Hanover, PA

Inter-Church Ministries of Erie County—Erie, PA

Interfaith Conference of Greater Milwaukee—Milwaukee, WI

Interfaith Council—Spokane, WA

Inter-Faith Ministries-Wichita—Wichita, KS

Interfaith Works—Olympia, WA

Lancaster County Council of Churches—Lancaster, PA

Lebanon County Christian Ministries—Lebanon, PA

Lehigh County Conference of Churches—Allentown, PA

Lewisburg Council of Churches—Lewisburg, PA

The Long Island Council of Churches—Hempstead, NY

Mahoning Valley Association of Churches—Youngstown, OH

The Metropolitan Christian Council: Detroit-Windsor—Detroit, MI

Metropolitan Ecumenical Ministry—Newark, NJ

Muskegon County Cooperating Churches—Muskegon, MI

Network of Religious Communities—Buffalo, NY

New Mexico Conference of Churches—Albuquerque, NM

Northside Inter-Church Agency (NICA)—Fort Worth, TX

Oak Park-River Forest Community of Congregations—Oak Park, IL

Peoria Friendship House of Christian Service—Peoria, IL

Pike County Outreach Council—Waverly, OH

Reading Berks Conference of Churches—Reading, PA

Saint. Paul Area Council of Churches—St. Paul, MN

San Antonio Community of Churches—San Antonio, TX

San Fernando Valley Interfaith Council—Chatsworth, CA

Schenectady Inner City Ministry—Schenectady, NY

South Coast Interfaith Council—Long Beach, CA

Staten Island Council of Churches—Staten Island, NY

Tarrant Area Community of Churches—Fort Worth, TX

Troy Area United Ministries—Troy, NY

Tuscarawas County Council for Church and Community—New Philadelphia, OH

United Churches of Lycoming County—Williamsport, PA

United Religious Community of St. Joseph County—South Bend, IN

Wilkinsburg Community Ministry—Pittsburgh, PA

Worcester County Ecumenical Council—Worcester, MA

Wyoming Valley Council of Churches—Wilkes-Barre, PA

York County Council of Churches—York, PA

273

Domestic Violence

Arizona Ecumenical Council—Phoenix, AZ
Asheville-Buncombe Community Christian Ministry (ABCCM)—Asheville, NC
Associated Ministries of Tacoma-Pierce County—Tacoma, WA
Association of Religious Communities—Danbury, CT
Chautauqua County Rural Ministry—Dunkirk, NY
Churches United of the Quad City Area—Rock Island, IL
Colorado Council of Churches—Denver, CO
Contact Ministries of Springfield—Springfield, IL
The Council of Churches of Santa Clara County—San Jose, CA
Dutchess County Interfaith Council, Inc.—Poughkeepsie, NY
The Ecumenical Council of Pasadena Area Churches—Pasadena, CA
Ecumenical Council of San Diego County—San Diego, CA
Ecumenical Ministries of Oregon—Portland, OR
FaithTrust Institute—Seattle, WA
Genesee-Orleans Ministry of Concern—Albion, NY
Greater Chicago Broadcast Ministries—Chicago, IL
Greater Minneapolis Council of Churches—Minneapolis, MN
Indiana Partners for Christian Unity and Mission—Indianapolis, IN
Inter-Church Council of Greater New Bedford—New Bedford, MA
Interchurch Ministries of Nebraska—Lincoln, NE
Interfaith Council—Spokane, WA
Interfaith Service Bureau—Sacramento, CA
The Long Island Council of Churches—Hempstead, NY
The Metropolitan Christian Council: Detroit-Windsor—Detroit, MI
Metropolitan Ecumenical Ministry—Newark, NJ
Mississippi Religious Leadership Conference—Jackson, MS
Network of Religious Communities—Buffalo, NY
New Hampshire Council of Churches—Pembroke, NH
New Mexico Conference of Churches—Albuquerque, NM
North Hills Youth Ministry Counseling Center—Pittsburgh, PA
Peoria Friendship House of Christian Service—Peoria, IL
The Rhode Island State Council of Churches—Providence, RI
Saint. Paul Area Council of Churches—St. Paul, MN
San Antonio Community of Churches—San Antonio, TX

Southeast Ecumenical Ministry—Rochester, NY
Troy Area United Ministries—Troy, NY
Tulsa Metropolitan Ministry—Tulsa, OK
United Religious Community of St. Joseph County—South Bend, IN
Vermont Ecumenical Council and Bible Society—Richmond, VT
West Side Ecumenical Ministry—Cleveland, OH
Wyoming Association of Churches—Cody, WY

Economic/Social Justice Programs

Arizona Ecumenical Council—Phoenix, AZ
Arkansas Interfaith Conference—Scott, AR
Asheville-Buncombe Community Christian Ministry (ABCCM)—Asheville, NC
The Associated Churches of Fort Wayne & Allen County, Inc.—Fort Wayne, IN
Associated Ministries of Tacoma-Pierce County—Tacoma, WA
Association of Christian Churches of South Dakota—Sioux Falls, SD
Austin Area Interreligious Ministries—Austin, TX
Brooklyn Council of Churches—Brooklyn, NY
Broome County Council of Churches, Inc.—Binghamton, NY
California Council of Churches-California Church Impact—Sacramento, CA
The Cape Cod Council of Churches, Inc.—Hyannis, MA
Capital Area Council of Churches, Inc.—Albany, NY
Capital Region Ecumenical Organization (CREO)—Schenectady, NY
The Capitol Region Conference of Churches—Hartford, CT
Chautauqua County Rural Ministry—Dunkirk, NY
Christian Associates of Southwest Pennsylvania—Pittsburgh, PA
Christian Churches United of the Tri-County Area—Harrisburg, PA
Christian Ministries of Delaware County—Muncie, IN
Christian Service Center for Central Florida, Inc.—Orlando, FL
Church Council of Greater Seattle—Seattle, WA
The Church Federation of Greater Indianapolis, Inc.—Indianapolis, IN
Churches United, Inc.—Cedar Rapids, IA
Colorado Council of Churches—Denver, CO
Community Emergency Assistance Program (CEAP)—Brooklyn Park, MN
Community Ministry of Montgomery County—Rockville, MD
Community Renewal Society—Chicago, IL
Contact Ministries of Springfield—Springfield, IL
Cooperative Metropolitan Ministries—Newton, MA

Council of Churches of the City of New York —New York, NY

Council of Churches of Greater Bridgeport, Inc.—Bridgeport, CT

Council of Churches of Greater Springfield—Springfield, MA

The Council of Churches of Santa Clara County—San Jose, CA

Eastern Area Community Ministries—Louisville, KY

Ecclesia—Trenton, NJ

Ecumenical Conference of Greater Altoona—Altoona, PA

The Ecumenical Council of Pasadena Area Churches—Pasadena, CA

Ecumenical Ministries of Oregon—Portland, OR

Evanston Ecumenical Action Council—Evanston, IL

Faith Community Assistance Center—Santa Fe, NM

Florida Council of Churches—Tampa, FL

Fresno Metro Ministry—Fresno, CA

Grand Rapids Area Center for Ecumenism (GRACE)—Grand Rapids, MI

Greater Birmingham Ministries—Birmingham, AL

Greater Chicago Broadcast Ministries—Chicago, IL

Greater Dallas Community of Churches—Dallas, TX

Greater Dayton Christian Connections—Dayton, OH

Greater Minneapolis Council of Churches—Minneapolis, MN

Greater Rochester Community of Churches—Rochester, NY

Highlands Community Ministries—Louisville, KY

Illinois Conference of Churches—Springfield, IL

Inter-Church Council of Greater New Bedford—New Bedford, MA

Inter-Church Ministries of Erie County—Erie, PA

Interchurch Ministries of Nebraska—Lincoln, NE

Interfaith Community Council, Inc.—New Albany, IN

Interfaith Conference of Greater Milwaukee—Milwaukee, WI

InterFaith Conference of Metropolitan Washington—Washington, DC

Interfaith Council—Spokane, WA

Interfaith Council of Contra Costa County—Walnut Creek, CA

Inter-Faith Ministries-Wichita—Wichita, KS

Interfaith Mission Service—Huntsville, AL

Interfaith Service Bureau—Sacramento, CA

InterReligious Council of Central New York—Syracuse, NY

The Joint Religious Legislative Coalition—Minneapolis, MN

Kansas Ecumenical Ministries—Topeka, KS

Kentuckiana Interfaith Community—Louisville, KY

Kentucky Council of Churches—Lexington, KY

Lancaster County Council of Churches—Lancaster, PA

Lehigh County Conference of Churches—Allentown, PA

Lincoln Interfaith Council—Lincoln, NE

Louisiana Interchurch Conference—Baton Rouge, LA

Madison-area Urban Ministry—Madison, WI

Mahoning Valley Association of Churches—Youngstown, OH

Maine Council of Churches—Portland, ME

Marin Interfaith Council—San Rafael, CA

Massachusetts Council of Churches—Boston, MA

The Metropolitan Christian Council: Detroit-Windsor—Detroit, MI

Metropolitan Christian Council of Philadelphia—Philadelphia, PA

Metropolitan Ecumenical Ministry—Newark, NJ

Metropolitan Inter Faith Association (MIFA) —Memphis, TN

Metropolitan Interfaith Council on Affordable Housing (MICAH)—Minneapolis, MN

Minnesota Council of Churches—Minneapolis, MN

Mississippi Religious Leadership Conference —Jackson, MS

Montana Association of Churches—Helena, MT

Muskegon County Cooperating Churches—Muskegon, MI

New Britain Area Conference of Churches (NEWBRACC)—New Britain, CT

New Hampshire Council of Churches—Pembroke, NH

New Mexico Conference of Churches—Albuquerque, NM

North Carolina Council of Churches—Raleigh, NC

North Dakota Conference of Churches—Ashley, ND

Northern California Interreligious Conference —Oakland, CA

Northside Inter-Church Agency (NICA)—Fort Worth, TX

Northwest Interfaith Movement—Philadelphia, PA

Oak Park-River Forest Community of Congregations—Oak Park, IL

Oklahoma Conference of Churches—Oklahoma City, OK

Pennsylvania Conference on Interchurch Cooperation—Harrisburg, PA

The Pennsylvania Council of Churches—Harrisburg, PA

Peoria Friendship House of Christian Service—Peoria, IL

Queens Federation of Churches—Richmond Hill, NY

275

The Regional Council of Churches of Atlanta —Atlanta, GA

The Rhode Island State Council of Churches—Providence, RI

Rural Migrant Ministry—Poughkeepsie, NY

Saint. Paul Area Council of Churches—St. Paul, MN

San Antonio Community of Churches—San Antonio, TX

San Fernando Valley Interfaith Council—Chatsworth, CA

Schenectady Inner City Ministry—Schenectady, NY

South Carolina Christian Action Council, Inc.—Columbia, SC

South East Associated Ministries (SEAM)—Louisville, KY

South Louisville Community Ministries—Louisville, KY

Southern California Ecumenical Council—Pasadena, CA

Tarrant Area Community of Churches—Fort Worth, TX

Texas Conference of Churches—Austin, TX

Troy Area United Ministries—Troy, NY

Tulsa Metropolitan Ministry—Tulsa, OK

United Churches of Lycoming County—Williamsport, PA

United Religious Community of St. Joseph County—South Bend, IN

Vermont Ecumenical Council and Bible Society—Richmond, VT

Virginia Council of Churches, Inc.—Richmond, VA

Wainwright House—Rye, NY

Washington Association of Churches—Seattle, WA

West Virginia Council of Churches—Charleston, WV

Wilkinsburg Community Ministry—Pittsburgh, PA

Wisconsin Council of Churches—Sun Prairie, WI

Wyoming Association of Churches—Cody, WY

Employment Assistance Programs

Asheville-Buncombe Community Christian Ministry (ABCCM)—Asheville, NC

The Associated Churches of Fort Wayne & Allen County, Inc.—Fort Wayne, IN

Chautauqua County Rural Ministry—Dunkirk, NY

Christian Community Action—New Haven, CT

Community Emergency Assistance Program (CEAP)—Brooklyn Park, MN

Contact Ministries of Springfield—Springfield, IL

Corpus Christi Metro Ministries—Corpus Christi, TX

Council of Churches of Greater Bridgeport, Inc.—Bridgeport, CT

East Dallas Cooperative Parish—Dallas, TX

East End Cooperative Ministry—Pittsburgh, PA

Eastern Area Community Ministries—Louisville, KY

Evanston Ecumenical Action Council—Evanston, IL

Fern Creek-Highview United Ministries—Louisvlle, KY

Genesee-Orleans Ministry of Concern—Albion, NY

Greater Chicago Broadcast Ministries—Chicago, IL

Greater Dallas Community of Churches—Dallas, TX

Greater Minneapolis Council of Churches—Minneapolis, MN

Greensboro Urban Ministry—Greensboro, NC

Kentuckiana Interfaith Community—Louisville, KY

Lehigh County Conference of Churches—Allentown, PA

Madison-area Urban Ministry—Madison, WI

Metropolitan Ecumenical Ministry—Newark, NJ

Muskegon County Cooperating Churches—Muskegon, MI

Network of Religious Communities—Buffalo, NY

Northside Inter-Church Agency (NICA)—Fort Worth, TX

Peoria Friendship House of Christian Service—Peoria, IL

Schenectady Inner City Ministry—Schenectady, NY

South East Associated Ministries (SEAM)—Louisville, KY

Southeast Ecumenical Ministry—Rochester, NY

United Ministries—Greenville, SC

Virginia Council of Churches, Inc.—Richmond, VA

West Side Ecumenical Ministry—Cleveland, OH

Environmental Programs

Akron Area Association of Churches—Akron, OH

Arizona Ecumenical Council—Phoenix, AZ

California Council of Churches-California Church Impact—Sacramento, CA

The Capitol Region Conference of Churches—Hartford, CT

Christian Associates of Southwest Pennsylvania—Pittsburgh, PA

Colorado Council of Churches—Denver, CO

The Council of Churches of Santa Clara County—San Jose, CA

Ecumenical Ministries of Iowa (EMI)—Des Moines, IA

Ecumenical Ministries of Oregon—Portland, OR

Florida Council of Churches—Tampa, FL

Fresno Metro Ministry—Fresno, CA

Georgia Christian Council—Macon, GA

Greater Chicago Broadcast Ministries—Chicago, IL

Greater Dayton Christian Connections—Dayton, OH

Inter-Church Council of Greater New Bedford—New Bedford, MA

Interfaith Conference of Greater Milwaukee—Milwaukee, WI

InterFaith Conference of Metropolitan Washington—Washington, DC

Interfaith Mission Service—Huntsville, AL

Kentucky Council of Churches—Lexington, KY

Louisiana Interchurch Conference—Baton Rouge, LA

Maine Council of Churches—Portland, ME

Marin Interfaith Council—San Rafael, CA

Massachusetts Council of Churches—Boston, MA

The Metropolitan Christian Council: Detroit-Windsor—Detroit, MI

Metropolitan Christian Council of Philadelphia—Philadelphia, PA

Metropolitan Ecumenical Ministry—Newark, NJ

Mississippi Religious Leadership Conference—Jackson, MS

Montana Association of Churches—Helena, MT

Muskegon County Cooperating Churches—Muskegon, MI

Network of Religious Communities—Buffalo, NY

New Hampshire Council of Churches—Pembroke, NH

New Mexico Conference of Churches—Albuquerque, NM

North Carolina Council of Churches—Raleigh, NC

Northern California Interreligious Conference—Oakland, CA

Oklahoma Conference of Churches—Oklahoma City, OK

The Pennsylvania Council of Churches—Harrisburg, PA

The Regional Council of Churches of Atlanta—Atlanta, GA

South Carolina Christian Action Council, Inc.—Columbia, SC

South Coast Interfaith Council—Long Beach, CA

Southern California Ecumenical Council—Pasadena, CA

United Churches of Lycoming County—Williamsport, PA

Vermont Ecumenical Council and Bible Society—Richmond, VT

Washington Association of Churches—Seattle, WA

West Virginia Council of Churches—Charleston, WV

Faith and Order Programs

Akron Area Association of Churches—Akron, OH

Arizona Ecumenical Council—Phoenix, AZ

Associated Ministries of Tacoma-Pierce County—Tacoma, WA

Association of Christian Churches of South Dakota—Sioux Falls, SD

The Cape Cod Council of Churches, Inc.—Hyannis, MA

Capital Area Council of Churches, Inc.—Albany, NY

Capital Region Ecumenical Organization (CREO)—Schenectady, NY

Christian Associates of Southwest Pennsylvania—Pittsburgh, PA

Church Council of Greater Seattle—Seattle, WA

The Church Federation of Greater Indianapolis, Inc.—Indianapolis, IN

Churches United, Inc.—Cedar Rapids, IA

Churches United of the Quad City Area—Rock Island, IL

Colorado Council of Churches—Denver, CO

Council of Churches of the City of New York—New York, NY

Council of Churches of Greater Bridgeport, Inc.—Bridgeport, CT

Council of Churches of Greater Springfield—Springfield, MA

The Council of Churches of Santa Clara County—San Jose, CA

Council of Churches and Synagogues of Southwestern Connecticut—Stamford, CT

East Dallas Cooperative Parish—Dallas, TX

Ecclesia—Trenton, NJ

Ecumenical Council of San Diego County—San Diego, CA

Ecumenical Ministries of Iowa (EMI)—Des Moines, IA

Ecumenical Ministries of Oregon—Portland, OR

Evansville Area Community of Churches, Inc.—Evansville, IN

Florida Council of Churches—Tampa, FL

Georgia Christian Council—Macon, GA

Greater Chicago Broadcast Ministries—Chicago, IL

Greater Dallas Community of Churches—Dallas, TX

Greater Dayton Christian Connections—Dayton, OH

Greater Lawrence Council of Churches—Lawrence, MA

Greater New Orleans Federation of Churches—New Orleans, LA

Greater Waterbury Interfaith Ministries, Inc.—Waterbury, CT

Illinois Conference of Churches—Springfield, IL

Inter-Church Council of Greater New Bedford—New Bedford, MA

Interchurch Ministries of Nebraska—Lincoln, NE

InterFaith Conference of Metropolitan Washington—Washington, DC

277

Interfaith Council of Contra Costa County—Walnut Creek, CA

InterReligious Council of Central New York—Syracuse, NY

Kansas Ecumenical Ministries—Topeka, KS

Kentuckiana Interfaith Community—Louisville, KY

Kentucky Council of Churches—Lexington, KY

Lehigh County Conference of Churches—Allentown, PA

Louisiana Interchurch Conference—Baton Rouge, LA

Mahoning Valley Association of Churches—Youngstown, OH

The Metropolitan Christian Council: Detroit-Windsor—Detroit, MI

Metropolitan Christian Council of Philadelphia—Philadelphia, PA

Metropolitan Ecumenical Ministry—Newark, NJ

Minnesota Council of Churches—Minneapolis, MN

Montana Association of Churches—Helena, MT

Network of Religious Communities—Buffalo, NY

New Britain Area Conference of Churches (NEWBRACC)—New Britain, CT

New Hampshire Council of Churches—Pembroke, NH

New Mexico Conference of Churches—Albuquerque, NM

North Carolina Council of Churches—Raleigh, NC

North Dakota Conference of Churches—Ashley, ND

Northern California Interreligious Conference—Oakland, CA

Northern Kentucky Interfaith Commission, Inc.—Newport, KY

Ohio Council of Churches—Columbus, OH

Oklahoma Conference of Churches—Oklahoma City, OK

The Pennsylvania Council of Churches—Harrisburg, PA

Queens Federation of Churches—Richmond Hill, NY

The Rhode Island State Council of Churches—Providence, RI

Schenectady Inner City Ministry—Schenectady, NY

South Carolina Christian Action Council, Inc.—Columbia, SC

Southern California Ecumenical Council—Pasadena, CA

Texas Conference of Churches—Austin, TX

Troy Area United Ministries—Troy, NY

Tulsa Metropolitan Ministry—Tulsa, OK

United Religious Community of St. Joseph County—South Bend, IN

Vermont Ecumenical Council and Bible Society—Richmond, VT

Virginia Council of Churches, Inc.—Richmond, VA

Wainwright House—Rye, NY

Washington Association of Churches—Seattle, WA

West Virginia Council of Churches—Charleston, WV

Wisconsin Council of Churches—Sun Prairie, WI

Wyoming Valley Council of Churches—Wilkes-Barre, PA

Health Care Issues

Asheville-Buncombe Community Christian Ministry (ABCCM)—Asheville, NC

California Council of Churches-California Church Impact—Sacramento, CA

Churchpeople for Change and Reconciliation—Lima, OH

Community Ministries of Rockville—Rockville, MD

Community Renewal Society—Chicago, IL

Corpus Christi Metro Ministries—Corpus Christi, TX

Council of Churches of the City of New York—New York, NY

The Council of Churches of Santa Clara County—San Jose, CA

East Dallas Cooperative Parish—Dallas, TX

Eastern Area Community Ministries—Louisville, KY

Ecumenical Ministries of Iowa (EMI)—Des Moines, IA

Fresno Metro Ministry—Fresno, CA

Greater Baton Rouge Federation of Churches and Synagogues—Baton Rouge, LA

Greater Chicago Broadcast Ministries—Chicago, IL

Greater Rochester Community of Churches—Rochester, NY

Greensboro Urban Ministry—Greensboro, NC

Highlands Community Ministries—Louisville, KY

Inter-Church Council of Greater New Bedford—New Bedford, MA

Interfaith Conference of Greater Milwaukee—Milwaukee, WI

Lehigh County Conference of Churches—Allentown, PA

Louisiana Interchurch Conference—Baton Rouge, LA

Madison-area Urban Ministry—Madison, WI

Marin Interfaith Council—San Rafael, CA

The Metropolitan Christian Council: Detroit-Windsor—Detroit, MI

Metropolitan Ecumenical Ministry—Newark, NJ

Metropolitan Ecumenical Ministry Community Development Corp.—Newark, NJ

Mississippi Religious Leadership Conference—Jackson, MS

Montana Association of Churches—Helena, MT

278

Network of Religious Communities—Buffalo, NY

New Hampshire Council of Churches—Pembroke, NH

New Mexico Conference of Churches—Albuquerque, NM

North Carolina Council of Churches—Raleigh, NC

Oklahoma Conference of Churches—Oklahoma City, OK

The Pennsylvania Council of Churches—Harrisburg, PA

Peoria Friendship House of Christian Service—Peoria, IL

Pike County Outreach Council—Waverly, OH

The Regional Council of Churches of Atlanta—Atlanta, GA

Schenectady Inner City Ministry—Schenectady, NY

Southeast Ecumenical Ministry—Rochester, NY

Tarrant Area Community of Churches—Fort Worth, TX

Tuscarawas County Council for Church and Community—New Philadelphia, OH

United Religious Community of St. Joseph County—South Bend, IN

Washington Association of Churches—Seattle, WA

West Virginia Council of Churches—Charleston, WV

Homelessness/Shelter Programs

Allegheny Valley Association of Churches—Natrona Heights, PA

Arkansas Interfaith Conference—Scott, AR

Asheville-Buncombe Community Christian Ministry (ABCCM)—Asheville, NC

The Associated Churches of Fort Wayne & Allen County, Inc.—Fort Wayne, IN

Associated Ministries of Tacoma-Pierce County—Tacoma, WA

Attleboro Area Council of Churches, Inc.—Attleboro, MA

Austin Area Interreligious Ministries—Austin, TX

The Cape Cod Council of Churches, Inc.—Hyannis, MA

Capital Area Council of Churches, Inc.—Albany, NY

The Capitol Region Conference of Churches—Hartford, CT

Center City Churches—Hartford, CT

Chautauqua County Rural Ministry—Dunkirk, NY

Christian Churches United of the Tri-County Area—Harrisburg, PA

Christian Community Action—New Haven, CT

Christian Ministries of Delaware County—Muncie, IN

Christian Service Center for Central Florida, Inc.—Orlando, FL

Church Council of Greater Seattle—Seattle, WA

Churches United, Inc.—Cedar Rapids, IA

Churches United of the Quad City Area—Rock Island, IL

Colorado Council of Churches—Denver, CO

Community Emergency Assistance Program (CEAP)—Brooklyn Park, MN

Community Ministries of Rockville—Rockville, MD

Community Ministry of Montgomery County—Rockville, MD

Community Renewal Society—Chicago, IL

Contact Ministries of Springfield—Springfield, IL

Cooperative Metropolitan Ministries—Newton, MA

Corpus Christi Metro Ministries—Corpus Christi, TX

Council of Churches of the City of New York—New York, NY

Council of Churches of Greater Bridgeport, Inc.—Bridgeport, CT

Council of Churches of Greater Springfield—Springfield, MA

The Council of Churches of Santa Clara County—San Jose, CA

East End Cooperative Ministry—Pittsburgh, PA

The Ecumenical Council of Pasadena Area Churches—Pasadena, CA

Ecumenical Council of San Diego County—San Diego, CA

Ecumenical Ministries—Fulton, MO

Ecumenical Ministries of Oregon—Portland, OR

Evanston Ecumenical Action Council—Evanston, IL

Faith Community Assistance Center—Santa Fe, NM

Genesee-Orleans Ministry of Concern—Albion, NY

Grand Rapids Area Center for Ecumenism (GRACE)—Grand Rapids, MI

Greater Bethlehem Area Council of Churches—Bethlehem, PA

Greater Chicago Broadcast Ministries—Chicago, IL

Greater Minneapolis Council of Churches—Minneapolis, MN

Greensboro Urban Ministry—Greensboro, NC

Hanover Area Council of Churches—Hanover, PA

Highlands Community Ministries—Louisville, KY

Inter-Church Ministries of Erie County—Erie, PA

Interfaith Community Council, Inc.—New Albany, IN

Interfaith Community Services—St. Joseph, MO

Interfaith Conference of Greater Milwaukee—Milwaukee, WI

279

InterFaith Conference of Metropolitan Washington—Washington, DC
Inter-Faith Ministries-Wichita—Wichita, KS
Interfaith Mission Service—Huntsville, AL
Interfaith Works—Olympia, WA
InterReligious Council of Central New York—Syracuse, NY
Lehigh County Conference of Churches—Allentown, PA
Lewisburg Council of Churches—Lewisburg, PA
The Long Island Council of Churches—Hempstead, NY
Madison-area Urban Ministry—Madison, WI
Maine Council of Churches—Portland, ME
Marin Interfaith Council—San Rafael, CA
Metropolitan Ecumenical Ministry—Newark, NJ
Metropolitan Inter Faith Association (MIFA)—Memphis, TN
Metropolitan Interfaith Council on Affordable Housing (MICAH)—Minneapolis, MN
Mississippi Religious Leadership Conference—Jackson, MS
Montana Association of Churches—Helena, MT
Muskegon County Cooperating Churches—Muskegon, MI
New Britain Area Conference of Churches (NEWBRACC)—New Britain, CT
New Hampshire Council of Churches—Pembroke, NH
New Mexico Conference of Churches—Albuquerque, NM
North Carolina Council of Churches—Raleigh, NC
Northside Common Ministries—Pittsburgh, PA
Northside Inter-Church Agency (NICA)—Fort Worth, TX
Paducah Cooperative Ministry—Paducah, KY
Peoria Friendship House of Christian Service—Peoria, IL
Pike County Outreach Council—Waverly, OH
Reading Berks Conference of Churches—Reading, PA
The Regional Council of Churches of Atlanta—Atlanta, GA
The Rhode Island State Council of Churches—Providence, RI
Saint. Paul Area Council of Churches—St. Paul, MN
San Antonio Community of Churches—San Antonio, TX
Schenectady Inner City Ministry—Schenectady, NY
South Louisville Community Ministries—Louisville, KY
Tarrant Area Community of Churches—Fort Worth, TX
Troy Area United Ministries—Troy, NY
Tulsa Metropolitan Ministry—Tulsa, OK
Tuscarawas County Council for Church and Community—New Philadelphia, OH

United Ministries—Greenville, SC
United Religious Community of St. Joseph County—South Bend, IN
Wyoming Valley Council of Churches—Wilkes-Barre, PA

Hunger/Food Program

Allegheny Valley Association of Churches—Natrona Heights, PA
Arkansas Interfaith Conference—Scott, AR
Asheville-Buncombe Community Christian Ministry (ABCCM)—Asheville, NC
The Associated Churches of Fort Wayne & Allen County, Inc.—Fort Wayne, IN
Associated Ministries of Tacoma-Pierce County—Tacoma, WA
Attleboro Area Council of Churches, Inc.—Attleboro, MA
Austin Area Interreligious Ministries—Austin, TX
Brooklyn Council of Churches—Brooklyn, NY
Broome County Council of Churches, Inc.—Binghamton, NY
California Council of Churches-California Church Impact—Sacramento, CA
The Cape Cod Council of Churches, Inc.—Hyannis, MA
Capital Area Council of Churches, Inc.—Albany, NY
Center City Churches—Hartford, CT
Chautauqua County Rural Ministry—Dunkirk, NY
Christian Churches United of the Tri-County Area—Harrisburg, PA
Christian Community Action—New Haven, CT
Christian Ministries of Delaware County—Muncie, IN
Christian Service Center for Central Florida, Inc.—Orlando, FL
Church Community Services—Elkhart, IN
Church Council of Greater Seattle—Seattle, WA
The Church Federation of Greater Indianapolis, Inc.—Indianapolis, IN
Churches United of the Quad City Area—Rock Island, IL
Community Emergency Assistance Program (CEAP)—Brooklyn Park, MN
Community Ministry of Montgomery County—Rockville, MD
Concerned Ecumenical Ministry to the Upper West Side—Buffalo, NY
Contact Ministries of Springfield—Springfield, IL
Corpus Christi Metro Ministries—Corpus Christi, TX
Council of Churches of the City of New York—New York, NY
Council of Churches of Greater Bridgeport, Inc.—Bridgeport, CT
Council of Churches of the Ozarks—Springfield, MO

280

The Council of Churches of Santa Clara County—San Jose, CA

Council of Churches and Synagogues of Southwestern Connecticut—Stamford, CT

Cross-Lines Cooperative Council—Kansas City, KS

Des Moines Area Religious Council—Des Moines, IA

Dutchess County Interfaith Council, Inc.—Poughkeepsie, NY

East Dallas Cooperative Parish—Dallas, TX

East End Cooperative Ministry—Pittsburgh, PA

Eastern Area Community Ministries—Louisville, KY

Ecclesia—Trenton, NJ

The Ecumenical Council of Pasadena Area Churches—Pasadena, CA

Ecumenical Ministries of Oregon—Portland, OR

Evanston Ecumenical Action Council—Evanston, IL

Evansville Area Community of Churches, Inc.—Evansville, IN

Faith Community Assistance Center—Santa Fe, NM

Fern Creek-Highview United Ministries—Louisvlle, KY

Fresno Metro Ministry—Fresno, CA

Genesee County Churches United, Inc.—Batavia, NY

Genesee-Orleans Ministry of Concern—Albion, NY

Grand Rapids Area Center for Ecumenism (GRACE)—Grand Rapids, MI

Greater Baton Rouge Federation of Churches and Synagogues—Baton Rouge, LA

Greater Bethlehem Area Council of Churches—Bethlehem, PA

Greater Birmingham Ministries—Birmingham, AL

Greater Chicago Broadcast Ministries—Chicago, IL

Greater Dallas Community of Churches—Dallas, TX

Greater Minneapolis Council of Churches—Minneapolis, MN

Greater New Orleans Federation of Churches—New Orleans, LA

Greater Waterbury Interfaith Ministries, Inc.—Waterbury, CT

Greensboro Urban Ministry—Greensboro, NC

Hanover Area Council of Churches—Hanover, PA

Highlands Community Ministries—Louisville, KY

Inter-Church Ministries of Erie County—Erie, PA

Interfaith Community Council, Inc.—New Albany, IN

Interfaith Community Services—St. Joseph, MO

InterFaith Conference of Metropolitan Washington—Washington, DC

Inter-Faith Ministries-Wichita—Wichita, KS

Interfaith Mission Service—Huntsville, AL

InterReligious Council of Central New York—Syracuse, NY

Kentuckiana Interfaith Community—Louisville, KY

Lancaster County Council of Churches—Lancaster, PA

Lebanon County Christian Ministries—Lebanon, PA

Lehigh County Conference of Churches—Allentown, PA

Lewisburg Council of Churches—Lewisburg, PA

The Long Island Council of Churches—Hempstead, NY

Madison-area Urban Ministry—Madison, WI

The Metropolitan Christian Council: Detroit-Windsor—Detroit, MI

Metropolitan Ecumenical Ministry—Newark, NJ

Minnesota Council of Churches—Minneapolis, MN

Mississippi Religious Leadership Conference—Jackson, MS

Montana Association of Churches—Helena, MT

Muskegon County Cooperating Churches—Muskegon, MI

Network of Religious Communities—Buffalo, NY

New Britain Area Conference of Churches (NEWBRACC)—New Britain, CT

New Hampshire Council of Churches—Pembroke, NH

New Mexico Conference of Churches—Albuquerque, NM

Northside Common Ministries—Pittsburgh, PA

Northside Inter-Church Agency (NICA)—Fort Worth, TX

Northwest Harvest-E. M. M.—Seattle, WA

Oak Park-River Forest Community of Congregations—Oak Park, IL

Paducah Cooperative Ministry—Paducah, KY

Peoria Friendship House of Christian Service—Peoria, IL

Pike County Outreach Council—Waverly, OH

Queens Federation of Churches—Richmond Hill, NY

Reading Berks Conference of Churches—Reading, PA

The Regional Council for Christian Ministry, Inc.—Idaho Falls, ID

The Regional Council of Churches of Atlanta—Atlanta, GA

The Rhode Island State Council of Churches—Providence, RI

Saint. Paul Area Council of Churches—St. Paul, MN

San Antonio Community of Churches—San Antonio, TX

San Fernando Valley Interfaith Council—Chatsworth, CA

Schenectady Inner City Ministry—Schenectady, NY

South East Associated Ministries (SEAM)—Louisville, KY

South Hills Interfaith Ministries—South Park, PA

South Louisville Community Ministries—Louisville, KY

Southeast Ecumenical Ministry—Rochester, NY

Staten Island Council of Churches—Staten Island, NY

Tulsa Metropolitan Ministry—Tulsa, OK

Tuscarawas County Council for Church and Community—New Philadelphia, OH

United Churches of Lycoming County—Williamsport, PA

United Ministries—Greenville, SC

United Religious Community of St. Joseph County—South Bend, IN

Washington Association of Churches—Seattle, WA

Wellspring Interfaith Social Services, Inc. (previously West Central Neighborhood Ministry, Inc.)—Fort Wayne, IN

West Side Ecumenical Ministry—Cleveland, OH

Wilkinsburg Community Ministry—Pittsburgh, PA

Wyoming Valley Council of Churches—Wilkes-Barre, PA

York County Council of Churches—York, PA

Immigration Issues

Arkansas Interfaith Conference—Scott, AR

Association of Religious Communities—Danbury, CT

Austin Area Interreligious Ministries—Austin, TX

Chautauqua County Rural Ministry—Dunkirk, NY

Community Emergency Assistance Program (CEAP)—Brooklyn Park, MN

Community Ministries of Rockville—Rockville, MD

Council of Churches of the City of New York—New York, NY

Council of Churches of Greater Bridgeport, Inc.—Bridgeport, CT

East Dallas Cooperative Parish—Dallas, TX

Eastern Area Community Ministries—Louisville, KY

The Ecumenical Council of Pasadena Area Churches—Pasadena, CA

Ecumenical Ministries of Oregon—Portland, OR

Florida Council of Churches—Tampa, FL

Fresno Metro Ministry—Fresno, CA

Greater Minneapolis Council of Churches—Minneapolis, MN

Interfaith Community Services—St. Joseph, MO

InterReligious Council of Central New York—Syracuse, NY

Marin Interfaith Council—San Rafael, CA

Minnesota Council of Churches—Minneapolis, MN

Mississippi Religious Leadership Conference—Jackson, MS

Network of Religious Communities—Buffalo, NY

New York State Council of Churches, Inc.—Albany, NY

Northside Inter-Church Agency (NICA)—Fort Worth, TX

Ohio Council of Churches—Columbus, OH

Peoria Friendship House of Christian Service—Peoria, IL

Reading Berks Conference of Churches—Reading, PA

The Regional Council of Churches of Atlanta—Atlanta, GA

The Rhode Island State Council of Churches—Providence, RI

San Antonio Community of Churches—San Antonio, TX

San Fernando Valley Interfaith Council—Chatsworth, CA

South Coast Interfaith Council—Long Beach, CA

Tulsa Metropolitan Ministry—Tulsa, OK

United Religious Community of St. Joseph County—South Bend, IN

Virginia Council of Churches, Inc.—Richmond, VA

Washington Association of Churches—Seattle, WA

Interfaith Dialogue/Relationships

Akron Area Association of Churches—Akron, OH

Arizona Ecumenical Council—Phoenix, AZ

Arkansas Interfaith Conference—Scott, AR

The Associated Churches of Fort Wayne & Allen County, Inc.—Fort Wayne, IN

Associated Ministries of Tacoma-Pierce County—Tacoma, WA

Association of Religious Communities—Danbury, CT

Attleboro Area Council of Churches, Inc.—Attleboro, MA

Austin Area Interreligious Ministries—Austin, TX

Brooklyn Council of Churches—Brooklyn, NY

Broome County Council of Churches, Inc.—Binghamton, NY

California Council of Churches-California Church Impact—Sacramento, CA

The Cape Cod Council of Churches, Inc.—Hyannis, MA

Capital Area Council of Churches, Inc.—Albany, NY

The Capitol Region Conference of Churches—Hartford, CT

Christian Associates of Southwest Pennsylvania
—Pittsburgh, PA

Christian Churches United of the Tri-County
Area—Harrisburg, PA

Christian Ministries of Delaware County—
Muncie, IN

Churches United, Inc.—Cedar Rapids, IA

Churches United of the Quad City Area—
Rock Island, IL

Colorado Council of Churches—Denver, CO

Community Emergency Assistance Program
(CEAP)—Brooklyn Park, MN

Community Ministries of Rockville—
Rockville, MD

Community Ministry of Montgomery County
—Rockville, MD

Community Renewal Society—Chicago, IL

Cooperative Metropolitan Ministries—
Newton, MA

Council of Churches of Chemung County,
Inc.—Elmira, NY

Council of Churches of the City of New
York—New York, NY

Council of Churches of Greater Bridgeport,
Inc.—Bridgeport, CT

Council of Churches of Greater Springfield—
Springfield, MA

The Council of Churches of Santa Clara
County—San Jose, CA

Council of Churches and Synagogues of
Southwestern Connecticut—Stamford, CT

Des Moines Area Religious Council—Des
Moines, IA

Dutchess County Interfaith Council, Inc.—
Poughkeepsie, NY

East Dallas Cooperative Parish—Dallas, TX

Eastern Area Community Ministries—
Louisville, KY

Ecclesia—Trenton, NJ

Ecumenical Conference of Greater Altoona—
Altoona, PA

The Ecumenical Council of Pasadena Area
Churches—Pasadena, CA

Ecumenical Council of San Diego County—
San Diego, CA

Ecumenical Ministries of Iowa (EMI)—Des
Moines, IA

Ecumenical Ministries of Oregon—Portland,
OR

Evanston Ecumenical Action Council—
Evanston, IL

Faith Community Assistance Center—Santa
Fe, NM

FaithTrust Institute—Seattle, WA

Florida Council of Churches—Tampa, FL

Fresno Metro Ministry—Fresno, CA

Georgia Christian Council—Macon, GA

Grand Rapids Area Center for Ecumenism
(GRACE)—Grand Rapids, MI

Greater Baton Rouge Federation of Churches
and Synagogues—Baton Rouge, LA

Greater Bethlehem Area Council of Churches
—Bethlehem, PA

Greater Birmingham Ministries—Birmingham,
AL

Greater Chicago Broadcast Ministries—
Chicago, IL

Greater Dallas Community of Churches—
Dallas, TX

Greater Dayton Christian Connections—
Dayton, OH

Greater Flint Council of Churches—Flint, MI

Greater Lawrence Council of Churches—
Lawrence, MA

Greater New Orleans Federation of Churches
—New Orleans, LA

Greater Rochester Community of Churches—
Rochester, NY

Greater Waterbury Interfaith Ministries, Inc.
—Waterbury, CT

Greensboro Urban Ministry—Greensboro, NC

Highlands Community Ministries—
Louisville, KY

Inter-Church Council of Greater New
Bedford—New Bedford, MA

Inter-Church Ministries of Erie County—Erie,
PA

Interchurch Ministries of Nebraska—Lincoln,
NE

Interfaith Community Services—St. Joseph,
MO

Interfaith Conference of Greater Milwaukee—
Milwaukee, WI

InterFaith Conference of Metropolitan
Washington—Washington, DC

Interfaith Council—Spokane, WA

Interfaith Council of Contra Costa County—
Walnut Creek, CA

Inter-Faith Ministries-Wichita—Wichita, KS

Interfaith Mission Service—Huntsville, AL

Interfaith Service Bureau—Sacramento, CA

Interfaith Works—Olympia, WA

InterReligious Council of Central New York—
Syracuse, NY

The Joint Religious Legislative Coalition—
Minneapolis, MN

Kentuckiana Interfaith Community—Louisville,
KY

Lancaster County Council of Churches—
Lancaster, PA

Lehigh County Conference of Churches—
Allentown, PA

Lewisburg Council of Churches—Lewisburg,
PA

Lincoln Interfaith Council—Lincoln, NE

The Long Island Council of Churches—
Hempstead, NY

Louisiana Interchurch Conference—Baton
Rouge, LA

Madison-area Urban Ministry—Madison, WI

Mahoning Valley Association of Churches—
Youngstown, OH

Maine Council of Churches—Portland, ME

Marin Interfaith Council—San Rafael, CA

Massachusetts Council of Churches—Boston,
MA

The Metropolitan Christian Council: Detroit-Windsor—Detroit, MI

Metropolitan Christian Council of Philadelphia—Philadelphia, PA

Metropolitan Ecumenical Ministry—Newark, NJ

Metropolitan Interfaith Council on Affordable Housing (MICAH)—Minneapolis, MN

Minnesota Council of Churches—Minneapolis, MN

Mississippi Religious Leadership Conference—Jackson, MS

Montana Association of Churches—Helena, MT

Muskegon County Cooperating Churches—Muskegon, MI

Network of Religious Communities—Buffalo, NY

New Britain Area Conference of Churches (NEWBRACC)—New Britain, CT

New Hampshire Council of Churches—Pembroke, NH

New Mexico Conference of Churches—Albuquerque, NM

North Dakota Conference of Churches—Ashley, ND

Northern California Interreligious Conference—Oakland, CA

Northern Kentucky Interfaith Commission, Inc.—Newport, KY

Northwest Interfaith Movement—Philadelphia, PA

Oak Park-River Forest Community of Congregations—Oak Park, IL

Oklahoma Conference of Churches—Oklahoma City, OK

Paducah Cooperative Ministry—Paducah, KY

Pennsylvania Conference on Interchurch Cooperation—Harrisburg, PA

The Pennsylvania Council of Churches—Harrisburg, PA

Peoria Friendship House of Christian Service—Peoria, IL

Reading Berks Conference of Churches—Reading, PA

The Regional Council of Churches of Atlanta—Atlanta, GA

The Rhode Island State Council of Churches—Providence, RI

Saint. Paul Area Council of Churches—St. Paul, MN

San Antonio Community of Churches—San Antonio, TX

San Fernando Valley Interfaith Council—Chatsworth, CA

South Carolina Christian Action Council, Inc.—Columbia, SC

South Coast Interfaith Council—Long Beach, CA

South Hills Interfaith Ministries—South Park, PA

Staten Island Council of Churches—Staten Island, NY

Texas Conference of Churches—Austin, TX

Troy Area United Ministries—Troy, NY

Tulsa Metropolitan Ministry—Tulsa, OK

Tuscarawas County Council for Church and Community—New Philadelphia, OH

United Churches of Lycoming County—Williamsport, PA

United Religious Community of St. Joseph County—South Bend, IN

Vermont Ecumenical Council and Bible Society—Richmond, VT

Virginia Council of Churches, Inc.—Richmond, VA

Wainwright House—Rye, NY

Washington Association of Churches—Seattle, WA

West Side Ecumenical Ministry—Cleveland, OH

West Virginia Council of Churches—Charleston, WV

Wisconsin Council of Churches—Sun Prairie, WI

Worcester County Ecumenical Council—Worcester, MA

Wyoming Association of Churches—Cody, WY

Wyoming Valley Council of Churches—Wilkes-Barre, PA

Peace Advocacy

Arkansas Interfaith Conference—Scott, AR

The Associated Churches of Fort Wayne & Allen County, Inc.—Fort Wayne, IN

Associated Ministries of Tacoma-Pierce County—Tacoma, WA

Association of Christian Churches of South Dakota—Sioux Falls, SD

Capital Area Council of Churches, Inc.—Albany, NY

Church Council of Greater Seattle—Seattle, WA

The Church Federation of Greater Indianapolis, Inc.—Indianapolis, IN

Churches United of the Quad City Area—Rock Island, IL

Community Renewal Society—Chicago, IL

Council of Churches of the City of New York—New York, NY

Council of Churches of Greater Springfield—Springfield, MA

The Council of Churches of Santa Clara County—San Jose, CA

Ecumenical Conference of Greater Altoona—Altoona, PA

Ecumenical Ministries of Iowa (EMI)—Des Moines, IA

Ecumenical Ministries of Oregon—Portland, OR

Greater Chicago Broadcast Ministries—Chicago, IL

Greater Dallas Community of Churches—Dallas, TX

Greater Rochester Community of Churches—Rochester, NY

Interchurch Ministries of Nebraska—Lincoln, NE

Interfaith Works—Olympia, WA
Kentuckiana Interfaith Community—Louisville, KY
Lancaster County Council of Churches—Lancaster, PA
Lincoln Interfaith Council—Lincoln, NE
Madison-area Urban Ministry—Madison, WI
Massachusetts Council of Churches—Boston, MA
Minnesota Council of Churches—Minneapolis, MN
Montana Association of Churches—Helena, MT
Network of Religious Communities—Buffalo, NY
New Mexico Conference of Churches—Albuquerque, NM
North Carolina Council of Churches—Raleigh, NC
Ohio Council of Churches—Columbus, OH
Oklahoma Conference of Churches—Oklahoma City, OK
The Pennsylvania Council of Churches—Harrisburg, PA
The Regional Council of Churches of Atlanta—Atlanta, GA
The Rhode Island State Council of Churches—Providence, RI
San Fernando Valley Interfaith Council—Chatsworth, CA
South Carolina Christian Action Council, Inc.—Columbia, SC
Southern California Ecumenical Council—Pasadena, CA
Staten Island Council of Churches—Staten Island, NY
Texas Conference of Churches—Austin, TX
Tulsa Metropolitan Ministry—Tulsa, OK
United Religious Community of St. Joseph County—South Bend, IN
Vermont Ecumenical Council and Bible Society—Richmond, VT
Washington Association of Churches—Seattle, WA
West Virginia Council of Churches—Charleston, WV
Worcester County Ecumenical Council—Worcester, MA

Prison Chaplaincy

Akron Area Association of Churches—Akron, OH
Asheville-Buncombe Community Christian Ministry (ABCCM)—Asheville, NC
Berrien County Association of Churches—Benton Harbor, MI
Broome County Council of Churches, Inc.—Binghamton, NY
The Cape Cod Council of Churches, Inc.—Hyannis, MA
Capital Area Council of Churches, Inc.—Albany, NY
Christian Associates of Southwest Pennsylvania—Pittsburgh, PA

Christian Churches United of the Tri-County Area—Harrisburg, PA
Christians United in Beaver County—Beaver, PA
Church Council of Greater Seattle—Seattle, WA
The Church Federation of Greater Indianapolis, Inc.—Indianapolis, IN
Churches United of the Quad City Area—Rock Island, IL
Churchpeople for Change and Reconciliation—Lima, OH
Community Renewal Society—Chicago, IL
Council of Christian Communions of Greater Cincinnati—Cincinnati, OH
Council of Churches of the City of New York—New York, NY
Council of Churches of Greater Bridgeport, Inc.—Bridgeport, CT
Council of Churches of Greater Springfield—Springfield, MA
The Council of Churches of Santa Clara County—San Jose, CA
Ecclesia—Trenton, NJ
Ecumenical Ministries—Fulton, MO
Evansville Area Community of Churches, Inc.—Evansville, IN
Genesee County Churches United, Inc.—Batavia, NY
Greater Bethlehem Area Council of Churche—Bethlehem, PA
Greater Chicago Broadcast Ministries—Chicago, IL
Greater Minneapolis Council of Churches—Minneapolis, MN
Inter-Church Ministries of Erie County—Erie, PA
Interfaith Council of Contra Costa County—Walnut Creek, CA
InterReligious Council of Central New York—Syracuse, NY
The Long Island Council of Churches—Hempstead, NY
Louisiana Interchurch Conference—Baton Rouge, LA
Maine Council of Churches—Portland, ME
Montana Association of Churches—Helena, MT
New Hampshire Council of Churches—Pembroke, NH
New Mexico Conference of Churches—Albuquerque, NM
Reading Berks Conference of Churches—Reading, PA
The Rhode Island State Council of Churches—Providence, RI
San Antonio Community of Churches—San Antonio, TX
United Churches of Lycoming County—Williamsport, PA
United Religious Community of St. Joseph County—South Bend, IN
West Virginia Council of Churches—Charleston, WV

285

Wyoming Association of Churches—Cody, WY

York County Council of Churches—York, PA

Programs with/for Persons with Disabilities

Associated Ministries of Tacoma-Pierce County—Tacoma, WA

Christian Ministries of Delaware County—Muncie, IN

Ecumenical Ministries of Oregon—Portland, OR

Greater Chicago Broadcast Ministries—Chicago, IL

Greater Minneapolis Council of Churches—Minneapolis, MN

Inter-Church Council of Greater New Bedford—New Bedford, MA

Inter-Faith Ministries-Wichita—Wichita, KS

InterReligious Council of Central New York—Syracuse, NY

Lehigh County Conference of Churches—Allentown, PA

Massachusetts Council of Churches—Boston, MA

Metropolitan Ecumenical Ministry—Newark, NJ

New Hampshire Council of Churches—Pembroke, NH

Reading Berks Conference of Churches—Reading, PA

The Rhode Island State Council of Churches—Providence, RI

Southeast Ecumenical Ministry—Rochester, NY

Tulsa Metropolitan Ministry—Tulsa, OK

Public Education

Akron Area Association of Churches—Akron, OH

Arizona Ecumenical Council—Phoenix, AZ

The Associated Churches of Fort Wayne & Allen County, Inc.—Fort Wayne, IN

Associated Ministries of Tacoma-Pierce County—Tacoma, WA

Austin Area Interreligious Ministries—Austin, TX

California Council of Churches-California Church Impact—Sacramento, CA

Center City Churches—Hartford, CT

Christian Ministries of Delaware County—Muncie, IN

The Church Federation of Greater Indianapolis, Inc.—Indianapolis, IN

Colorado Council of Churches—Denver, CO

Community Emergency Assistance Program (CEAP)—Brooklyn Park, MN

Community Ministries of Rockville—Rockville, MD

Community Ministry of Montgomery County—Rockville, MD

Community Renewal Society—Chicago, IL

Concerned Ecumenical Ministry to the Upper West Side—Buffalo, NY

Contact Ministries of Springfield—Springfield, IL

Council of Churches of the City of New York—New York, NY

Council of Churches of Greater Springfield—Springfield, MA

Evanston Ecumenical Action Council—Evanston, IL

Fresno Metro Ministry—Fresno, CA

Greater Baton Rouge Federation of Churches and Synagogues—Baton Rouge, LA

Greater Bethlehem Area Council of Churches—Bethlehem, PA

Greater Birmingham Ministries—Birmingham, AL

Greater Chicago Broadcast Ministries—Chicago, IL

Greater Fairmont Council of Churches—Fairmont, WV

Greater Minneapolis Council of Churches—Minneapolis, MN

Greater Rochester Community of Churches—Rochester, NY

Greater Waterbury Interfaith Ministries, Inc.—Waterbury, CT

Inter-Church Council of Greater New Bedford—New Bedford, MA

Interfaith Conference of Greater Milwaukee—Milwaukee, WI

InterFaith Conference of Metropolitan Washington—Washington, DC

Interfaith Council—Spokane, WA

The Joint Religious Legislative Coalition—Minneapolis, MN

Lehigh County Conference of Churches—Allentown, PA

Louisiana Interchurch Conference—Baton Rouge, LA

Madison-area Urban Ministry—Madison, WI

Maine Council of Churches—Portland, ME

Metropolitan Christian Council of Philadelphia—Philadelphia, PA

Metropolitan Ecumenical Ministry—Newark, NJ

Metropolitan Inter Faith Association (MIFA)—Memphis, TN

Metropolitan Interfaith Council on Affordable Housing (MICAH)—Minneapolis, MN

Mississippi Religious Leadership Conference—Jackson, MS

Network of Religious Communities—Buffalo, NY

New Hampshire Council of Churches—Pembroke, NH

New Mexico Conference of Churches—Albuquerque, NM

North Carolina Council of Churches—Raleigh, NC

Oak Park-River Forest Community of Congregations—Oak Park, IL

Oklahoma Conference of Churches—Oklahoma City, OK

The Pennsylvania Council of Churches—Harrisburg, PA

Peoria Friendship House of Christian Service
—Peoria, IL
San Antonio Community of Churches—San
Antonio, TX
South Carolina Christian Action Council, Inc.
—Columbia, SC
Tarrant Area Community of Churches—Fort
Worth, TX
Tulsa Metropolitan Ministry—Tulsa, OK
Tuscarawas County Council for Church and
Community—New Philadelphia, OH
United Religious Community of St. Joseph
County—South Bend, IN
Washington Association of Churches—Seattle,
WA
West Virginia Council of Churches—Charleston,
WV
Wisconsin Council of Churches—Sun Prairie,
WI

Refugee Assistance Programs

Association of Religious Communities—
Danbury, CT
Austin Area Interreligious Ministries—Austin,
TX
The Capitol Region Conference of Churches
—Hartford, CT
Community Emergency Assistance Program
(CEAP)—Brooklyn Park, MN
Ecumenical Ministries of Oregon—Portland,
OR
Fresno Metro Ministry—Fresno, CA
Greater Chicago Broadcast Ministries—
Chicago, IL
Greater Minneapolis Council of Churches—
Minneapolis, MN
Interfaith Service Bureau—Sacramento, CA
InterReligious Council of Central New York—
Syracuse, NY
Kentuckiana Interfaith Community—Louisville,
KY
Metropolitan Ecumenical Ministry—Newark,
NJ
Minnesota Council of Churches—Minneapolis,
MN
Network of Religious Communities—Buffalo,
NY
The Regional Council of Churches of Atlanta
—Atlanta, GA
United Religious Community of St. Joseph
County—South Bend, IN
Virginia Council of Churches, Inc.—Richmond,
VA

Rural Issues

Alaska Christian Conference—Fairbanks, AK
Association of Christian Churches of South
Dakota—Sioux Falls, SD
Berrien County Association of Churches—
Benton Harbor, MI
Chautauqua County Rural Ministry—Dunkirk,
NY
Christian Associates of Southwest Pennsylvania
—Pittsburgh, PA

Ecumenical Ministries of Iowa (EMI)—Des
Moines, IA
Ecumenical Ministries of Oregon—Portland,
OR
Fresno Metro Ministry—Fresno, CA
Georgia Christian Council—Macon, GA
Interchurch Ministries of Nebraska—Lincoln,
NE
Interfaith Conference of Greater Milwaukee—
Milwaukee, WI
Kansas Ecumenical Ministries—Topeka, KS
Kentucky Council of Churches—Lexington,
KY
Louisiana Interchurch Conference—Baton
Rouge, LA
Minnesota Council of Churches—Minneapolis,
MN
Mississippi Religious Leadership Conference
—Jackson, MS
Montana Association of Churches—Helena,
MT
North Carolina Council of Churches—
Raleigh, NC
North Dakota Conference of Churches—
Ashley, ND
Oklahoma Conference of Churches—Oklahoma
City, OK
Pike County Outreach Council—Waverly, OH
Reading Berks Conference of Churches—
Reading, PA
United Churches of Lycoming County—
Williamsport, PA
United Religious Community of St. Joseph
County—South Bend, IN
Virginia Council of Churches, Inc.—Richmond,
VA
West Virginia Council of Churches—Charleston,
WV

Senior Citizen Programs

Allegheny Valley Association of Churches—
Natrona Heights, PA
Associated Ministries of Tacoma-Pierce
County—Tacoma, WA
Attleboro Area Council of Churches, Inc.—
Attleboro, MA
The Capitol Region Conference of Churches
—Hartford, CT
Center City Churches—Hartford, CT
Christian Ministries of Delaware County—
Muncie, IN
Church Council of Greater Seattle—Seattle,
WA
Community Emergency Assistance Program
(CEAP)—Brooklyn Park, MN
Community Ministries of Rockville—Rockville,
MD
Community Renewal Society—Chicago, IL
Concerned Ecumenical Ministry to the Upper
West Side—Buffalo, NY
Council of Churches of Greater Springfield—
Springfield, MA
Council of Churches of the Ozarks—
Springfield, MO

287

Council of Churches and Synagogues of Southwestern Connecticut—Stamford, CT

Cross-Lines Cooperative Council—Kansas City, KS

East Dallas Cooperative Parish—Dallas, TX

East End Cooperative Ministry—Pittsburgh, PA

Eastern Area Community Ministries—Louisville, KY

Ecumenical Ministries—Fulton, MO

Ecumenical Ministries of Oregon—Portland, OR

Fern Creek-Highview United Ministries—Louisvlle, KY

Florida Council of Churches—Tampa, FL

Georgia Christian Council—Macon, GA

Greater Baton Rouge Federation of Churches and Synagogues—Baton Rouge, LA

Greater Chicago Broadcast Ministries—Chicago, IL

Greater Lawrence Council of Churches—Lawrence, MA

Greater Minneapolis Council of Churches—Minneapolis, MN

Highlands Community Ministries—Louisville, KY

Inter-Church Council of Greater New Bedford—New Bedford, MA

Interfaith Community Council, Inc.—New Albany, IN

Interfaith Community Services—St. Joseph, MO

Interfaith Council of Contra Costa County—Walnut Creek, CA

Inter-Faith Ministries-Wichita—Wichita, KS

InterReligious Council of Central New York—Syracuse, NY

The Long Island Council of Churches—Hempstead, NY

Louisiana Interchurch Conference—Baton Rouge, LA

Metropolitan Ecumenical Ministry—Newark, NJ

Metropolitan Inter Faith Association (MIFA)—Memphis, TN

Mississippi Religious Leadership Conference—Jackson, MS

Montana Association of Churches—Helena, MT

New Hampshire Council of Churches—Pembroke, NH

New Mexico Conference of Churches—Albuquerque, NM

Northside Inter-Church Agency (NICA)—Fort Worth, TX

Northwest Interfaith Movement—Philadelphia, PA

Oklahoma Conference of Churches—Oklahoma City, OK

Paducah Cooperative Ministry—Paducah, KY

Peoria Friendship House of Christian Service—Peoria, IL

San Antonio Community of Churches—San Antonio, TX

San Fernando Valley Interfaith Council—Chatsworth, CA

Schenectady Inner City Ministry—Schenectady, NY

South Hills Interfaith Ministries—South Park, PA

South Louisville Community Ministries—Louisville, KY

Southeast Ecumenical Ministry—Rochester, NY

Tarrant Area Community of Churches—Fort Worth, TX

Troy Area United Ministries—Troy, NY

Tulsa Metropolitan Ministry—Tulsa, OK

Tuscarawas County Council for Church and Community—New Philadelphia, OH

United Churches of Lycoming County—Williamsport, PA

United Religious Community of St. Joseph County—South Bend, IN

Wainwright House—Rye, NY

Wellspring Interfaith Social Services, Inc.—Fort Wayne, IN

West Side Ecumenical Ministry—Cleveland, OH

Wilkinsburg Community Ministry—Pittsburgh, PA

Substance Abuse Programs

Community Ministries of Rockville—Rockville, MD

Corpus Christi Metro Ministries—Corpus Christi, TX

Council of Churches of Greater Bridgeport, Inc.—Bridgeport, CT

Council of Churches of the Ozarks—Springfield, MO

East End Cooperative Ministry—Pittsburgh, PA

Ecumenical Ministries of Iowa (EMI)—Des Moines, IA

Ecumenical Ministries of Oregon—Portland, OR

Evanston Ecumenical Action Council—Evanston, IL

Greater Chicago Broadcast Ministries—Chicago, IL

Greensboro Urban Ministry—Greensboro, NC

Hanover Area Council of Churches—Hanover, PA

The Metropolitan Christian Council: Detroit-Windsor—Detroit, MI

Metropolitan Ecumenical Ministry—Newark, NJ

Metropolitan Ecumenical Ministry Community Development Corp.—Newark, NJ

Mississippi Religious Leadership Conference—Jackson, MS

Montana Association of Churches—Helena, MT

Muskegon County Cooperating Churches—Muskegon, MI

New Hampshire Council of Churches—Pembroke, NH

North Hills Youth Ministry Counseling Center—Pittsburgh, PA

Pike County Outreach Council—Waverly, OH

San Antonio Community of Churches—San Antonio, TX

Southeast Ecumenical Ministry—Rochester, NY

United Religious Community of St. Joseph County—South Bend, IN

Vermont Ecumenical Council and Bible Society—Richmond, VT

West Side Ecumenical Ministry—Cleveland, OH

Theology and Worship Programs

Akron Area Association of Churches—Akron, OH

Allegheny Valley Association of Churches—Natrona Heights, PA

Arizona Ecumenical Council—Phoenix, AZ

Arkansas Interfaith Conference—Scott, AR

The Associated Churches of Fort Wayne & Allen County, Inc.—Fort Wayne, IN

Associated Ministries of Tacoma-Pierce County—Tacoma, WA

Association of Christian Churches of South Dakota—Sioux Falls, SD

Attleboro Area Council of Churches, Inc.—Attleboro, MA

Border Association for Refugees from Central America (BARCA), Inc.—Edinburg, TX

Brooklyn Council of Churches—Brooklyn, NY

Broome County Council of Churches, Inc.—Binghamton, NY

The Cape Cod Council of Churches, Inc.—Hyannis, MA

Capital Area Council of Churches, Inc.—Albany, NY

Christian Associates of Southwest Pennsylvania—Pittsburgh, PA

Christian Churches United of the Tri-County Area—Harrisburg, PA

Christians United in Beaver County—Beaver, PA

Church Council of Greater Seattle—Seattle, WA

The Church Federation of Greater Indianapolis, Inc.—Indianapolis, IN

Churches United of the Quad City Area—Rock Island, IL

Colorado Council of Churches—Denver, CO

Council of Churches of the City of New York—New York, NY

The Council of Churches of Santa Clara County—San Jose, CA

Council of Churches and Synagogues of Southwestern Connecticut—Stamford, CT

Dutchess County Interfaith Council, Inc.—Poughkeepsie, NY

East Dallas Cooperative Parish—Dallas, TX

The Ecumenical Council of Pasadena Area Churches—Pasadena, CA

Ecumenical Ministries—Fulton, MO

Ecumenical Ministries of Iowa (EMI)—Des Moines, IA

Ecumenical Ministries of Oregon—Portland, OR

FaithTrust Institute—Seattle, WA

Florida Council of Churches—Tampa, FL

Georgia Christian Council—Macon, GA

Grand Rapids Area Center for Ecumenism (GRACE)—Grand Rapids, MI

Greater Bethlehem Area Council of Churches—Bethlehem, PA

Greater Chicago Broadcast Ministries—Chicago, IL

Greater Dallas Community of Churches—Dallas, TX

Greater Dayton Christian Connections—Dayton, OH

Greater Fairmont Council of Churches—Fairmont, WV

Greater Lawrence Council of Churches—Lawrence, MA

Greater New Orleans Federation of Churches—New Orleans, LA

Greater Rochester Community of Churches—Rochester, NY

Greensboro Urban Ministry—Greensboro, NC

Illinois Conference of Churches—Springfield, IL

Inter-Church Council of Greater New Bedford—New Bedford, MA

Inter-Church Ministries of Erie County—Erie, PA

Interchurch Ministries of Nebraska—Lincoln, NE

Interfaith Council—Spokane, WA

Interfaith Mission Service—Huntsville, AL

InterReligious Council of Central New York—Syracuse, NY

Kentuckiana Interfaith Community—Louisville, KY

Lehigh County Conference of Churches—Allentown, PA

The Long Island Council of Churches—Hempstead, NY

Mahoning Valley Association of Churches—Youngstown, OH

Marin Interfaith Council—San Rafael, CA

The Metropolitan Christian Council: Detroit-Windsor—Detroit, MI

Metropolitan Christian Council of Philadelphia—Philadelphia, PA

Metropolitan Ecumenical Ministry—Newark, NJ

Montana Association of Churches—Helena, MT

Muskegon County Cooperating Churches—Muskegon, MI

New Britain Area Conference of Churches (NEWBRACC)—New Britain, CT

New Hampshire Council of Churches—Pembroke, NH

New Mexico Conference of Churches—Albuquerque, NM

289

North Carolina Council of Churches—Raleigh, NC

Northern Kentucky Interfaith Commission, Inc.—Newport, KY

Oak Park-River Forest Community of Congregations—Oak Park, IL

Oklahoma Conference of Churches—Oklahoma City, OK

The Pennsylvania Council of Churches—Harrisburg, PA

Reading Berks Conference of Churches—Reading, PA

The Regional Council for Christian Ministry, Inc.—Idaho Falls, ID

The Regional Council of Churches of Atlanta—Atlanta, GA

The Rhode Island State Council of Churches—Providence, RI

San Antonio Community of Churches—San Antonio, TX

Schenectady Inner City Ministry—Schenectady, NY

South Carolina Christian Action Council, Inc.—Columbia, SC

South East Associated Ministries (SEAM)—Louisville, KY

Tarrant Area Community of Churches—Fort Worth, TX

Texas Conference of Churches—Austin, TX

Troy Area United Ministries—Troy, NY

Tulsa Metropolitan Ministry—Tulsa, OK

United Religious Community of St. Joseph County—South Bend, IN

Vermont Ecumenical Council and Bible Society—Richmond, VT

Virginia Council of Churches, Inc.—Richmond, VA

Wainwright House—Rye, NY

Washington Association of Churches—Seattle, WA

West Virginia Council of Churches—Charleston, WV

Worcester County Ecumenical Council—Worcester, MA

Wyoming Association of Churches—Cody, WY

York County Council of Churches—York, PA

Women

Associated Ministries of Tacoma-Pierce County—Tacoma, WA

California Council of Churches-California Church Impact—Sacramento, CA

Chautauqua County Rural Ministry—Dunkirk, NY

Christian Ministries of Delaware County—Muncie, IN

Church Community Services—Elkhart, IN

Community Ministries of Rockville—Rockville, MD

Council of Churches of the City of New York—New York, NY

The Council of Churches of Santa Clara County—San Jose, CA

East Dallas Cooperative Parish—Dallas, TX

Ecumenical Ministries of Oregon—Portland, OR

FaithTrust Institute—Seattle, WA

Fresno Metro Ministry—Fresno, CA

Genesee-Orleans Ministry of Concern—Albion, NY

Georgia Christian Council—Macon, GA

Greater Birmingham Ministries—Birmingham, AL

Greater Chicago Broadcast Ministries—Chicago, IL

Greater Dallas Community of Churches—Dallas, TX

Inter-Church Council of Greater New Bedford—New Bedford, MA

Interfaith Community Services—St. Joseph, MO

Interfaith Council—Spokane, WA

Madison-area Urban Ministry—Madison, WI

The Metropolitan Christian Council: Detroit-Windsor—Detroit, MI

Metropolitan Christian Council of Philadelphia—Philadelphia, PA

Metropolitan Ecumenical Ministry—Newark, NJ

Mississippi Religious Leadership Conference—Jackson, MS

Montana Association of Churches—Helena, MT

Network of Religious Communities—Buffalo, NY

New Mexico Conference of Churches—Albuquerque, NM

Oklahoma Conference of Churches—Oklahoma City, OK

The Pennsylvania Council of Churches—Harrisburg, PA

Peoria Friendship House of Christian Service—Peoria, IL

The Regional Council of Churches of Atlanta—Atlanta, GA

San Antonio Community of Churches—San Antonio, TX

South Hills Interfaith Ministries—South Park, PA

Tulsa Metropolitan Ministry—Tulsa, OK

Wainwright House—Rye, NY

West Side Ecumenical Ministry—Cleveland, OH

Youth

Arizona Ecumenical Council—Phoenix, AZ

Associated Ministries of Tacoma-Pierce County—Tacoma, WA

Austin Area Interreligious Ministries—Austin, TX

The Cape Cod Council of Churches, Inc.—Hyannis, MA

Center City Churches—Hartford, CT

Christian Ministries of Delaware County—Muncie, IN

The Church Federation of Greater Indianapolis, Inc.—Indianapolis, IN

Churches United of the Quad City Area—Rock Island, IL

Concerned Ecumenical Ministry to the Upper West Side—Buffalo, NY

Cooperative Metropolitan Ministries—Newton, MA

Council of Churches of the City of New York—New York, NY

Council of Churches of Greater Bridgeport, Inc.—Bridgeport, CT

The Council of Churches of Santa Clara County—San Jose, CA

Dutchess County Interfaith Council, Inc.—Poughkeepsie, NY

East Dallas Cooperative Parish—Dallas, TX

East End Cooperative Ministry—Pittsburgh, PA

Eastern Area Community Ministries—Louisville, KY

Ecclesia—Trenton, NJ

Ecumenical Ministries—Fulton, MO

Evanston Ecumenical Action Council—Evanston, IL

Genesee-Orleans Ministry of Concern—Albion, NY

Greater Bethlehem Area Council of Churches—Bethlehem, PA

Greater Chicago Broadcast Ministries—Chicago, IL

Greater Dallas Community of Churches—Dallas, TX

Greater Fairmont Council of Churches—Fairmont, WV

Greater Minneapolis Council of Churches—Minneapolis, MN

Highlands Community Ministries—Louisville, KY

Inter-Church Council of Greater New Bedford—New Bedford, MA

Interfaith Community Council, Inc.—New Albany, IN

Interfaith Community Services—St. Joseph, MO

Interfaith Conference of Greater Milwaukee—Milwaukee, WI

InterFaith Conference of Metropolitan Washington—Washington, DC

Interfaith Council—Spokane, WA

Inter-Faith Ministries-Wichita—Wichita, KS

Lehigh County Conference of Churches—Allentown, PA

Marin Interfaith Council—San Rafael, CA

The Metropolitan Christian Council: Detroit-Windsor—Detroit, MI

Metropolitan Ecumenical Ministry—Newark, NJ

Metropolitan Ecumenical Ministry Community Development Corp.—Newark, NJ

Metropolitan Inter Faith Association (MIFA)—Memphis, TN

Montana Association of Churches—Helena, MT

New Mexico Conference of Churches—Albuquerque, NM

Northern California Interreligious Conference—Oakland, CA

Peoria Friendship House of Christian Service—Peoria, IL

Queens Federation of Churches—Richmond Hill, NY

Reading Berks Conference of Churches—Reading, PA

The Regional Council of Churches of Atlanta—Atlanta, GA

Rural Migrant Ministry—Poughkeepsie, NY

Saint. Paul Area Council of Churches—St. Paul, MN

San Antonio Community of Churches—San Antonio, TX

Schenectady Inner City Ministry—Schenectady, NY

South East Associated Ministries (SEAM)—Louisville, KY

South Hills Interfaith Ministries—South Park, PA

South Louisville Community Ministries—Louisville, KY

Southeast Ecumenical Ministry—Rochester, NY

Staten Island Council of Churches—Staten Island, NY

Troy Area United Ministries—Troy, NY

Tuscarawas County Council for Church and Community—New Philadelphia, OH

United Churches of Lycoming County—Williamsport, PA

Vermont Ecumenical Council and Bible Society—Richmond, VT

Wainwright House—Rye, NY

Wellspring Interfaith Social Services, Inc. (previously West Central Neighborhood Ministry, Inc.)—Fort Wayne, IN

West Side Ecumenical Ministry—Cleveland, OH

291

7. Canadian Regional and Local Ecumenical Bodies

Most of the organizations listed below are councils of churches in which churches participate officially, whether at the parish or judicatory level. They operate at the city, metropolitan area, or county level. Parish clusters within urban areas are not included.

Canadian local ecumenical bodies operate without paid staff, with the exception of a few which have part-time staff. In most cases, the name and address of the president or chairperson is listed. As these offices change from year to year, some of the information may be out of date by the time the *Yearbook of American and Canadian Churches* is published.

CANADIAN ECUMENICAL BODIES

ALBERTA

Calgary Inter-Faith Community Action Association
2405 Macleod Trail SW, Calgary, AB T2G 2P3 Tel. (403)262-5171
Media Contact: J. McGrath
Email: jmcgrath@shawcable.com
Website: www.calgary-interfaith.ab.ca

Calgary Council of Churches
120 17th Ave., Calgary, AB T2S 2T2 Tel. (403) 218-5521
Media Contact: Anna Tremblay, Ecumenical & Inter-religious Affairs

BRITISH COLUMBIA

Greater Victoria Council of Churches
St. Alban's Church, 1468 Ryan St. at Balmont, Victoria, BC V8R 2X1
Media Contact: Rev. Edwin Taylor

Multifaith Action Society of British Columbia
5 - 305 41st Ave. W, Vancouver, BC V5Y 2S5 Tel. (604)321-1302 Fax (604)321-1370
Media Contact: Nancy A. Chiavario
Email: admin@multifaithaction.org
Website: www.multifaithaction.org

Vancouver Council of Churches
700 Kingsway, Vancouver, BC V5V 3C1 Tel. (604)420-0761
Media Contact: Murray Moerman

MANITOBA

Association of Christian Churches in Manitoba
150 de la Cathedrale Ave., Winnipeg, MB R2H 0H6 Tel. (204)237-9851

NEW BRUNSWICK

Atlantic Ecumenical Council of Churches
170 Daniel Ave., Saint John, NB E2K 4S7 Tel. (506)538-2491
Media Contact: Rev. Rufus Onyewuchi

First Miramichi Inter-Church Council
Doaktown, NB E0C 1G0
Media Contact: Ellen Robinson

Moncton Area Council of Churches
135 Mount Royal Blvd., Moncton, NB E1E 2V5 Tel. (506)382-7725
Media Contact: Rev. Donald Routledge

NEWFOUNDLAND

St. John's Area Council of Churches
31 Hazelwood Cres., St. John's, NF A1E 6B3 Tel. (709)579-0536
Media Contact: Rev. Canon Ralph Billard

NOVA SCOTIA

Atlantic Ecumenical Council of Churches
Box 637, 90 Victoria St., Amherst, NS B4H 4B4
Media Contact: Rev. John E. Boyd

Bridgewater Inter-Church Council
30 Parkdale Ave., Bridgewater, NS B4V 1L8
Media Contact: Wilson Jones

Cornwallis District Inter-Church Council
Centreville, RR 2, Kings County, NS B0T 1J0
Media Contact: Mr. Tom Regan

Industrial Cape Breton Council of Churches
24 Huron Ave., Sydney Mines, NS B1S 1V2
Media Contact: Rev. Karen Ralph

Kentville Council of Churches
325-325 Main St., Kentville, NS B4N 1C5
Media Contact: Rev. Canon S.J.P. Davies

Lunenburg Queens BA Association
66 Hillside Dr., RR 4, Bridgewater, NS B4V 2W3 Tel. 902-543-3328
Media Contact: Mrs. Nilda Chute
Email: n-chute@ns.sympatico.ca

Mahone Bay Interchurch Council
RR 1, Blockhouse, NS B0J 1E0
Media Contact: Patricia Joudrey

Queens County Association of Churches
Box 537, Liverpool, NS B0T 1K6
Media Contact: Mr. Donald Burns

Pictou Council of Churches
P.O. Box 70, Pictou, NS B0K 1H0
Media Contact: Rev. D.J. Murphy

ONTARIO

Burlington Inter-Church Council
425 Breckenwood, Burlington, ON L7L 2J6
Media Contact: Mr. Fred Townsend

Christian Leadership Council of Downtown Toronto
40 Homewood Ave. #509, Toronto, ON M4Y 2K2
Media Contact: Ken Bhagan

Ecumenical Committee
76 Eastern Ave., Sault Ste. Marie, ON P6A 4R2
Media Contact: Rev. William B. Kidd

Glengarry-Prescott-Russell Christian Council
St. Eugene's, Prescott, ON K0B 1P0
Media Contact: Rev. G. Labrosse

The Greater Toronto Council of Christian Churches
1155 Yonge St., Toronto, ON M4T 1W2 Tel. (416)934 - 3400 ext. 344
Media Contact: Father Damian MacPherson

Hamilton & District Christian Churches Association
86 Homewood Ave., Hamilton, ON L8P 2M4 Tel. (905)387-2135 Fax (905)387-5858
Media Contact: Rev. John Allsop
Email: allsopjs@hotmail.com

Ignace Council of Churches
Box 5, 205 Pine St., Ignace, ON P0T 1H0

Inter Church Council of Burlington
P.O. Box 62120, Burlington Mall R.P.O., Burlington, ON L7R 4K2 Tel. (905)333-0515
Media Contact: Rev. Moe Anderson
Website: www.iccb.ca

Kitchener-Waterloo Council of Churches
53 Allen St. E., Waterloo, ON N2J 1J3
Media Contact: Rev. Clarence Hauser, CR

London Inter-City Faith Team
United Church, 711 Colbourne St., London, ON N6A 3Z4
Media Contact: David Carouthers

Massey Inter-Church Council
Box 238, Massey, ON P0P 1P0 Tel. (705)865-2202
Media Contact: Rev. Brian Sonnenburg

Ottowa Christian Council of the Capital Area
1247 Kilborn Ave., Ottawa, ON K1H 6K9

St. Catharines & District Clergy Fellowship
663 Vince St., St. Catharines, ON L2M 3V8
Media Contact: Rev. Victor Munro

Spadina-Bloor Interchurch Council
Bathurst St. United Church, 427 Bloor St. W., Toronto, ON M5S 1X7
Media Contact: Rev. Frances Combes

Stratford & District Council of Churches
202 Erie St., Stratford, ON N5A 2M8
Media Contact: Rev. Ted Heinze

Thorold Inter-Faith Council
1 Dunn St., St. Catharines, ON L2T 1P3

Thunder Bay Council of Churches
1800 Moodie St. E., Thunder Bay, ON P7E 4Z2
Media Contact: Rev. Richard Darling

PRINCE EDWARD ISLAND

Atlantic Ecumenical Council
Immaculate Conception Church, St. Louis, PEI C0B 1Z0 Tel. (902)963-2202 or (902)882-2610
Media Contact: Rev. Arthur J. Pendergast

Summerside Christian Council
P.O. Box 1551, Summerside, PEI C1N 4K4
Media Contact: Ms. A. Kathleen Miller

QUEBEC

Action des Chrétiens pour l'Abolition de la Torture
15 rue de Castelnau Ouest, Montréal, QC H2R 2W3 Tel. (514)890-6169
Media Contact: Raoul Lincourt

AGAPÉ Deux-Montagnes
1002 chemin d'Oka, Deux-Montagnes, QC J7R 1L7 Tel. (450)473-9877
Media Contact: Donald Tremblay

Canadian Centre for Ecumenism
2065 Sherbrooke St. West, Montreal, QC H3H 1G6 Tel. (514) 937-9176

Media Contact: Dr. Stuart Brown, Director
Email: ccocce@oecumenisme.ca

Centre Emmaüs
Centre de spiritualité des Églisesd'Orient, 3774 chemin Queen-Mary, 3e étage, Montréal, QC H3V 1A6 Tel. (514)276-2144
Website: www.centre-emmaus.qc.ca

Christian-Jewish Dialogue of Montreal
c/oTemple Emanu-El-Beth Sholom, 4100 Sherbrooke St. West, Westmount, QC H3Z 1A5 Tel. (514)937-3575 or (514)937-3708
Media Contact: Rev. Ihor Kutash

Québécois du Dialogue musulman-chrétien
1640 rueSt. Hubert, Montréal, QC H2L 3Z2 Tel. (514)849-1167 Fax (514)284-2034
Media Contact: RP Bernard Tremblay
Email: bernard@bcube.com

Direction Chrétienne
1450 rue City Councillors, bureau 520, Montréal, QC H3A 2E6 Tel. (514)878-3035 Fax (514) 878-8048
Media Contact: Rev. Glenn Smith
Email: info@direction.ca
Website: www.direction.ca

Hemmingford Ecumenical Committee
Box 300, Hemmingford, QC J0L 1H0
Media Contact: Catherine Priest

Interfaith Council of Montréal
2065 Sherbrooke West, Montréal, QC H3H 1G6 Tel. (514) 937-9176 Fax (514) 937-4986
Media Contact: Mandit Singh, President
Email: ccocce@oecumenisme.ca
Website: www.oecumenisme.ca

Montreal Association for the Blind Foundation
7000 Sherbrooke St. W., Montréal, QC H4B 1R3 Tel. (514)489-8201 Fax (514)489-3477
Media Contact: Rev. Dr. John A. Simms
Email: info@mab.ca
Website: www.mab.ca

Radio Ville-Marie
Radio religieuse, 505 avenue de Mont-Cassin, Montréal, QC H3L 1W7 Tel. (514)382-3913 or (877)668-6601 Fax (514)858-0965
Media Contact: Friends
Email: cira@radiovm.com
Website: www.radiovm.com

Réseau Oecuménique Justice et Paix
114 Secc. D., Montréal, QC H3K 3B9 Tel. (514)937-2683 Fax (514)937-2683

Media Contact: Jean-Luc Djigo
Email: info@justicepaix.org
Website: www.justicepaix.org

Réseau Oecuménique du Québec (Quebec Ecumenical Network)
le Centre canadien d'oecuménisme en assure le secretariat, 2065 rue Sherbrooke ouest, Montréal, QC H3H 1G6 Tel. (514)937-9176 Fax (514)937-9176
Media Contact: Friends
Email: ccocce@oecumenisme.ca
Website: www.oecumenisme.ca

The St. Bruno Ecumenical Group
Holy Trinity Anglican Church, 140 Beaumont St. East, St. Bruno, QC J3V 5L9 Tel. (450)653-4531

UNITAS
Centre oecuménique de meditation chrétienne et de spiritualité, 1950 rue St. Antoine Ouest, Montréal, QC H3J 1A5 Tel. (514)485-0009
Media Contact: Friends
Email: info@unitasmeditation.ca
Website: www.unitasmeditation.ca

SASKATCHEWAN

Humboldt Clergy Council
Box 1989, Humboldt, SK S0K 2A0
Media Contact: Fr. Leo Hinz, OSB

Melville Association of Churches
Box 878, Melville, SK S0A 2P0
Media Contact: Catherine Gaw

Prairie Centre for Ecumenism
600 45th Street W., Saskatoon, SK S7L 5W9 Tel. (306)653-1633 Fax (306)653-1821
Media Contact: Rev. Dr. Jan Bigland-Pritchard, Director
Email: pce@ecumenism.net
Website: www.ecumenism.net

Regina Council of Churches
2660 Albert St, Regina, SK S4P 2V9 Tel. (306)545-3375
Media Contact: Joan Galvin

294

8. Theological Seminaries and Bible Colleges in the United States

The following list includes theological seminaries, Bible colleges, and departments in colleges and universities in which ministerial training is given. Many denominations have additional programs.

Inclusion in or exclusion from this list implies no judgment about the quality or accreditation of any institution. Those schools that are members of the Association of Theological Schools are marked with this symbol (†). Those schools that are accredited by the Transnational Association of Christian Colleges and Schools are marked with this symbol (‡). Additional information about enrollment in ATS member schools can be found in the "Trends in Seminary Enrollment" section of chapter III. Information about TRACS and ATS can be found in the "United States Cooperative Organizations" section of chapter II.

Each of the listings include when available: the institution name, denominational sponsor, location, the president or dean of the institution, telephone and fax numbers and email and website addresses.

Abilene Christian University Graduate School of Theology† (Churches of Christ), Jack R. Reese, Dean, College of Biblical Studies, ACU Box 29422 1850 N. Judge Ely Boulevard, CBS Room 297, Abilene, TX 79699-9422 Tel. (325) 674-3700 Fax (325) 674-6180
Email: thompson@bible.acu.edu
Website: www.acu.edu/GST

Alaska Bible College (Nondenominational), Gary G. Willford, Interim President, P.O. Box 289, Glennallen, AK 99588 Tel. (907)822-3201 Fax (907)822-5027
Email: info@akbible.edu
Website: www.akbible.edu

Alliance Theological Seminary† (The Christian and Missionary Alliance), Michael G. Scales, President, 350 N. Highland Ave., Nyack, NY 10960-1416 Tel. (845)353-2020 Fax (845) 727-3002
Website: www.alliance.edu

American Baptist College (National Baptist Convention USA, Inc.), Forrest E. Harris, Sr., President, 1800 Baptist World Center Dr., Nashville, TN 37207 Tel. (615)256-1463 Fax (615)226-7855
Email: jwright@abcnash.edu
Website: www.abcnash.edu

American Baptist Seminary of the West† (American Baptist Churches in the USA), Keith A. Russell, President, 2606 Dwight Way, Berkeley, CA 94704-3029 Tel. (510)841-1905 Fax (510)841-2446
Email: krussell@absw.edu
Website: www.absw.edu

Anderson University School of Theology† (Church of God, Anderson, IN), James L. Edwards, President, 1100 East Fifth Street, Anderson, IN 46012-3495 Tel. (765)641-4032 Fax (765)641-3851
Website: www.anderson.edu/academics/sot

Andover Newton Theological School† (American Baptist Churches in the USA; United Church of Christ), Nick Carter, President, 210 Herrick Rd., Newton Centre, MA 02459 Tel. (617) 964-1100 Fax (617)558-9785
Email: admissions@ants.edu
Website: www.ants.edu

Apex School of Theology (Interdenominational), Joseph E. Perkins, President, 5104 Revere Road, Durham, NC 27713 Tel. (919)572-1625 Fax (919)572-1762
Email: info@apexsot.edu
Website: www.apexsot.edu

Appalachian Bible College (Nondenominational), Daniel L. Anderson, President, P.O. Box ABC, Bradley, WV 25818 Tel. (304)877-6428 Fax (304)877-5082
Email: abc@abc.edu
Website: www.abc.edu

Aquinas Institute of Theology† (Catholic Church), The Rev. Charles E. Bouchard, O.P., President, 3642 Lindell Blvd., St. Louis, MO 63108-3396 Tel. (314)977-3882 Fax (314) 977-7225
Email: aquinas@slu.edu
Website: www.ai.edu

Arlington Baptist College (Baptist), David Bryant, President, 3001 W. Division, Arlington, TX 76012-3425 Tel. (817)461-8741 Fax (817)274-1138

Asbury Theological Seminary† (Inter/Multidenominational), Jeffrey E Greenway, President, 204 N. Lexington Ave., Wilmore, KY 40390-1199 Tel. (859)858-3581
Website: www.asburyseminary.edu

Ashland Theological Seminary† (Brethren Church, Ashland, Ohio), John C. Shultz, President, 910 Center St., Ashland, OH 44805 Tel. (419)289-5161 Fax (419)289-5969
Email: ffinks@ashland.edu
Website: www.ashland.edu/seminary

295

Assemblies of God Theological Seminary† (Assemblies of God), Byron D. Klaus, President, 1435 North Glenstone Avenue, Springfield, MO 65802-2131 Tel. (417)268-1000 Fax (417)268-1001
Email: agts@agseminary.edu
Website: www.agts.edu

Associated Mennonite Biblical Seminary† (Mennonite Church; General Conference Mennonite Church), J. Nelson Kraybill, President, 3003 Benham Ave., Elkhart, IN 46517-1999 Tel. (574)295-3726 Fax (574) 295-0092
Email: nkraybill@ambs.edu
Website: www.ambs.edu

Athenaeum of Ohio† (The Catholic Church), Edward P. Smith, President and Rector, 6616 Beechmont Ave., Cincinnati, OH 45230-2091 Tel. (513)231-2223 Fax (513)231-3254
Email: atheathenaeum.edu
Website: www.athenaeum.edu

Atlanta Christian College (Christian Churches and Churches of Christ), R. Edwin Groover, President, 2605 Ben Hill Rd., East Point, GA 30344 Tel. (404)761-8861 Fax (404)669-2024
Email: admissions@acc.edu
Website: www.acc.edu

Austin Presbyterian Theological Seminary† (Presbyterian Church [USA]), Theodore J. Wardlaw, President, 100 E. 27th St., Austin, TX 78705-5797 Tel. (512)472-6736 Fax (512) 479-0738
Website: www.austinseminary.edu

Bakke Graduate University of Ministry‡ (Non-Denominational), Brad Smith, President, 1013 Eighth Ave, Seattle, WA 98104 Tel. (206) 264-9100 Fax (206)624-8828
Email: bgu@bgu.edu
Website: www.bgu.edu

Bangor Theological Seminary† (United Church of Christ), William C. Imes, President, Two College Circle, PO Box 411, Bangor, ME 04402-0411 Tel. (207)942-6781 Fax (207)942-4914
Email: mhuddy@bts.edu
Website: www.bts.edu

Baptist Bible College (Baptist Bible Fellowship International), Leland Kennedy, President, 628 E. Kearney, Springfield, MO 65803 Tel. (417)268-6060 Fax (417)268-6694

Baptist Bible College and Seminary (Baptist), Jim Jeffery, President, 538 Venard Rd., Clarks Summit, PA 18411 Tel. (570)586-2400 Fax (570)586-1753
Email: bbc@bbc.edu
Website: www.bbc.edu

Baptist Missionary Association Theological Seminary† (Baptist Missionary Association of America), Charley Holmes, President, 1530 E. Pine St., Jacksonville, TX 75766 Tel. (903)586-2501 Fax (903)586-0378
Email: bmatsem@bmats.edu
Website: www.bmats.edu

Baptist Theological Seminary at Richmond† (Cooperative Baptist Fellowship), Thomas H. Graves, President, 3400 Brook Rd., Richmond, VA 23227 Tel. (804)355-8135 Fax (804)355-8182
Email: tgraves@btsr.edu
Website: www.btsr.edu

Barclay College (Interdenominational), Maurice G. Chandler, President, 607 N Kingman, Haviland, KS 67059 Tel. (620)862-5252 Fax (620)862-5403
Email: carju@barclaycollege.edu
Website: www.barclaycollege.edu

Barry University Department of Theology and Philosophy† Mark E. Wedig, Chair of the Department of Theology and Philosophy, 11300 Northeast Second Avenue, Miami Shores, FL 33161-6695 Tel. (305)899-3469 Fax (305)899-3385
Email: theology@mail.barry.edu
Website: www.barry.edu/TheologyPhilosophy/default

Bay Ridge Christian College (Church of God, Anderson, IN), Verda Beach, President, P.O. Box 726, Kendleton, TX 77451 Tel. (979)532-3982 Fax (979)532-4352
Email: brcccampus@wcnet.net
Website: brcconline.org

Beacon College & Graduate School‡ (Non-Denominational), John Durden, Dean, 6003 Veterans Parkway, Columbus, GA 31909 Tel. (706)323-5364 Fax (706)323-3236
Email: beacon@beacon.edu
Website: www.beacon.edu

Beeson Divinity School of Samford University† (Inter/Multidenominational), Timothy George, Dean, 800 Lakeshore Dr., Birmingham, AL 35229-2252 Tel. (205)726-2991 Fax (205)726-2260
Email: JTPrince@samford.edu
Website: www.beesondivinity.com

Berkeley Divinity School† (Episcopal Church), Joseph H. Britton, Dean, 409 Prospect Street, New Haven, CT 06511 Tel. (203)432-9285 Fax (203)432-9353
Email: joseph.britton@yale.edu
Website: www.yale.edu/berkeleydivinity

Bethany Lutheran Theological Seminary (Evangelical Lutheran Synod), G. R. Schmeling, President, 6 Browns Court,

Mankato, MN 56001 Tel. (507)344-7354 Fax (507)344-7426
Email: gschmeli@blc.edu
Website: www.blts.edu

Bethany Theological Seminary† (Church of the Brethren), Ruthann K. Johansen, President, 615 National Rd. W., Richmond, IN 47374 Tel. (765)983-1800 Fax (765)983-1840
Email: snydesu@bethanyseminary.edu
Website: www.bethanyseminary.edu

Bethel Seminary† (Baptist General Conference), George K. Brushaber, President, 3949 Bethel Dr., St. Paul, MN 55112 Tel. (651)638-6180 Fax (651)638-6002
Email: c-pfingsten@bethel.edu
Website: www.bethel.edu

Bethel Seminary of the East† (Conservative Baptist Association of America—Baptist General Conference), Douglas W. Fombelle, Dean and Executive Officer, 1605 N. Limekiln Pike, Dresher, PA 19025 Tel. (215)641-4801 Fax (215)641-4804
Email: d-fombelle@bethel.edu
Website: www.seminary.bethel.edu

Bethel Seminary San Diego† (General Bapist Conference), George Brushaber, President, 6116 Arosa Street, San Diego, CA 92115-3902 Tel. (619)582-8188 Fax (619)583-9114
Email: bsem-admit@bethel.edu
Website: seminary.bethel.edu/sandiego

Beulah Heights Bible College‡ (The International Pentecostal Church of Christ), Benson M. Karanja, Ed. D., President, 892 Berne St. SE, Atlanta, GA 30316 Tel. (404)627-2681 Fax (404)627-0702
Email: Benson.Karanja@beulah.org
Website: www.beulah.org

Bexley Hall Seminary† (Episcopal Church), John R. Kevern, President and Dean, 583 Sheridan Avenue, Columbus, OH 43209-2325 Tel. (614)231-3095 Fax (614)231-3236
Email: bexleyhall@bexley.edu
Website: www.bexley.edu

Bible Church of Christ Theological Institute (Nondenominational), Roy Bryant, Sr., President, 1358 Morris Ave., Bronx, NY 10456-1402 Tel. (718)588-2284 Fax (718)992-5597
Website: www.thebiblechurchofchrist.org

Biblical Theological Seminary† (Inter/Multidenominational), David G. Dunbar, President, 200 N. Main St., Hatfield, PA 19440 Tel. (215)368-5000 Fax (215)368-2301
Email: president@biblical.edu
Website: www.biblical.edu

Blessed John XXIII National Seminary† (Catholic Church), Francis D. Kelly, Rector, 558 South Avenue, Weston, MA 02493-2699 Tel. (781)899-5500 Fax (781)899-9057
Email: seminary@blessedjohnxxiii.edu
Website: www.blessedjohnxxiii.edu

Boise Bible College (Christian Churches and Churches of Christ), Charles A. Crane, President, 8695 Marigold St., Boise, ID 83714 Tel. (208)376-7731 Fax (208)376-7743
Email: boisebible@boisebible.edu
Website: www.boisebible.edu

Boston Baptist College‡ (Baptist), Rev. David Melton, President, 950 Metropolitan Avenue, Boston, MA 02136 Tel. (617)364-3510 Fax (617)364-0723
Email: admin@boston.edu/gsnavely@boston.edu
Website: www.boston.edu

Boston College Institute of Religious Education and Pastoral Ministry and Department of Theology (Catholic Church), Thomas H. Groome, Director, 31 Lawrence Ave., Chestnut Hill, MA 02467-3931 Tel. (617)552-8440 Fax (617)552-0811
Website: www.bc.edu/irepm

Boston University School of Theology† (The United Methodist Church), Ray L. Hart, Dean, 745 Commonwealth Ave., Boston, MA 02215 Tel. (617)353-3050 Fax (617)353-3061
Website: www.bu.edu/STH

Brite Divinity School, Texas Christian University† (Christian Church-Disciples of Christ), Newell Williams, President, TCU Box 298130, Ft. Worth, TX 76129-0002 Tel. (817)257-7575 Fax (817)257-7305
Email: l.s.anderson@tcu.edu
Website: www.brite.tcu.edu

Byzantine Catholic Seminary of SS. Cyril and Methodius† (Byzantine Catholic Archeparchy of Pittsburgh), John G. Petro, Rector, 3605 Perrysville Ave., Pittsburgh, PA 15214 Tel. (412)321-8383 Fax (412)321-9936
Website: www.archeparchy.org/page/seminary

California Christian College‡ (Free Will Baptist), Wendell Walley, President, 4881 E. University Avenue, Fresno, CA 93703 Tel. (559)251-4215 Fax (559)251-4231
Email: cccregistrar@sbcglobal.net
Website: www.calchristiancollege.org

Calvary Bible College and Calvary Theological Seminary (Independent Fundamental Churches of America, International), Elwood H. Chipchase, D.Min., D.D., President, 15800 Calvary Rd., Kansas City, MO 64147-1341 Tel. (800)326-3960 Fax (816)331-4474

297

Email: president@calvary.edu
Website: www.calvary.edu

Calvin Theological Seminary† (Christian Reformed Church in North America), The Rev. Cornelius Plantinga, Jr., President, 3233 Burton St. S.E., Grand Rapids, MI 49546-4387 Tel. (616)957-6036; (616)957-6044 Fax (616) 957-8621
Email: sempres@calvinseminary.edu
Website: www.calvinseminary.edu

Campbell University Divinity School† (Baptist State Convention of North Carolina), Michael G. Cogdill, Dean, 116 T. T. Lanier Street, PO Drawer 4050, Buies Creek, NC 27506 Tel. (910)893-1830 Fax (910)893-1835
Email: cogdill@campbell.edu
Website: www.campbell.edu/divinity

Candler School of Theology of Emory University† (The United Methodist Church), Jan Love, Dean, 500 Kilgo Circle N.E., Emory Univ., Atlanta, GA 30322 Tel. (404)727-6324 Fax (404)727-3182
Email: candler@emory.edu
Website: www.emory.edu/candler

Capital Bible Seminary† (Nondenominational), Larry A. Mercer, President, 6511 Princess Garden Parkway, Lanham, MD 20706 Tel. (301)552-1400 Fax (301)614-1024
Email: bfox@bible.edu
Website: www.bible.edu

Carolina Evangelical Divinity School† (Religious Society of Friends), Frank P. Scurry, President, P.O. Box 5831, High Point, NC 27265 Tel. (336)882-3370 Fax (336)882-3370
Email: fscurry@ceds.edu
Website: www.ceds.edu

Catholic Theological Union at Chicago† (Catholic Church), Donald Senior, C.P., President, 5401 S. Cornell Ave., Chicago, IL 60615-5664 Tel. (773)371-5400 Fax (773) 324-8490
Email: donald@ctu.edu
Website: www.ctu.edu

Catholic University of America† (Catholic Church), Kevin W. Irwin, Dean, 620 Michigan Avenue NE, Washington, DC 20064 Tel. (202)319-5683 Fax (202)319-4967
Email: cua-deansrs@cua.edu
Website: www.religiousstudies.cua.edu

Central Baptist College (Baptist Missionary Association of Arkansas), Terry Kimbrow, President, 1501 College Ave., Conway, AR 72032 Tel. (501)329-6872 Fax (501)329-2941
Email: TKimbrow@cbc.edu
Website: www.cbc.edu

Central Baptist Theological Seminary† (Baptist), The Rev. Molly T. Marshall, President, 6601 Monticello Road, Shawnee, KS 66226-3513 Tel. (913)667-5700/5721 Fax (913)371-8110
Email: rsandbothe@cbts.edu
Website: www.cbts.edu

Central Baptist Theological Seminary in Indiana (National Baptist Convention USA, Inc.), Robert Lee, President-Dean, 1535 A. J. Brown Ave. N., Indianapolis, IN 46202 Tel. (317)636-6622
Email: henriettabrown@webtv.net

Central Bible College (Assemblies of God), Gary A. Denbo, President, 3000 N. Grant Ave., Springfield, MO 65803 Tel. (417)833-2551 Fax (417)833-5141
Email: info@cbcag.edu
Website: www.cbcag.edu

Central Christian College of the Bible (Christian Churches and Churches of Christ), Ronald L. Oakes, President, 911 E. Urbandale Dr., Moberly, MO 65270-1997 Tel. (660)263-3900 Fax (660)263-3936
Email: develop@cccb.edu
Website: www.cccb.edu

Central Indian Bible College (Assemblies of God), M George Kallappa, President, P.O. Box 550, Mobridge, SD 57601 Tel. (605)845-7801 Fax (605)845-7744

Chapman School of Religious Studies of Oakland City University† (General Association of General Baptists), James W. Murray, Chancellor and President, 143 Lucretia Street, Oakland City, IN 47660 Tel. (812)749-4781 Fax (812)749-1233
Email: ocuexec@oak.edu, ebenson@oak.edu
Website: www.oak.edu

Chicago Theological Seminary† (United Church of Christ), Susan Brooks Thistlethwaite, President, 5757 South University Ave., Chicago, IL 60637-1507 Tel. (773)752-5757 Fax (773)752-5925
Email: sthistle@ctschicago.edu, lredmond@ctschicago.edu
Website: www.ctschicago.edu

Christ the King Seminary† (Catholic Church), Rev. Richard W. Siepka, President and Rector, 711 Knox Rd., P.O. Box 607, East Aurora, NY 14052-0607 Tel. (716)652-8900 Fax (716) 652-8903
Email: rsiepka@cks.edu
Website: www.cks.edu

Christ the Savior Seminary (The American Carpatho-Russian Orthodox Greek Catholic Church), Nicholas Smisko, President, 225

Chandler Ave., Johnstown, PA 15906 Tel. (814)539-0116 Fax (814)536-4699
Email: csseminary@atlanticbb.net
Website: www.acrod.org/seminary

Christian Life College‡ (Non-Denominational), Harry Schmidt, President, 400 E. Gregory Street, Mount Prospect, IL 60056 Tel. (847)259-1840 Fax (847)259-3888
Email: admissions@christianlifecollege.edu
Website: www.christianlifecollege.edu

Christian Theological Seminary† (Christian Church [Disciples of Christ]), Edward L. Wheeler, President, 1000 W. 42nd St., Indianapolis, IN 46208-3301 Tel. (317)924-1331 Fax (317)923-1961
Email: wheeler@cts.edu
Website: www.cts.edu

Christian Witness Theological Seminary† (Nondenominational), Rev. David A. Cheung, President, 1040 Oak Grove Rd., Concord, CA 94518 Tel. (925)676-5002 Fax (925)676-5220
Email: admin@cwts.edu
Website: cwts.edu

Church Divinity School of the Pacific† (Episcopal Church), Donn F. Morgan, President, 2451 Ridge Rd., Berkeley, CA 94709-1217 Tel. (510)204-0700 Fax (510)644-0712
Email: jparkin@cdsp.edu
Website: www.cdsp.edu

Church of God Theological Seminary† (Church of God, Cleveland, TN), Steven J. Land, President, P.O. Box 3330, Cleveland, TN 37320-3330 Tel. (423)478-1131 Fax (423)478-7711
Email: tgilbert@cogts.edu
Website: www.cogts.edu

Cincinnati Christian University† (Christian Churches and Churches of Christ), David M. Faust, President, 2700 Glenway Ave., Cincinnati, OH 45204-3200 Tel. (513)244-8120, (513)244-8100, (800)949-4228 Fax (513)244-8434
Email: judy.pratt@ccuniversity.edu/linda.palmer ccuniversity.edu
Website: www.CCuniversity.edu

Circleville Bible College (Churches of Christ in Christian Union), John Conley, President, P.O. Box 458, Circleville, OH 43113 Tel. (740)474-8896 Fax (740)477-7755
Email: stolbert@biblecollege.edu
Website: www.biblecollege.edu

Claremont School of Theology† (The United Methodist Church), Jerry D. Campbell, President, 1325 N. College Ave., Claremont, CA 91711-3199 Tel. (909)447-2500 Fax (909)626-7062
Email: admission@cst.edu
Website: www.cst.edu

Clear Creek Baptist Bible College (Southern Baptist Convention), President Bill Whittaker, President, 300 Clear Creek Rd., Pineville, KY 40977 Tel. (606)337-3196 Fax (606)337-2372
Email: ccbbc@ccbbc.edu
Website: www.ccbbc.edu

Clinton Junior College‡ (African Methodist Episcopal Zion Church), Elaine Johnson Copeland, President, 1029 Crawford Road,, Rock Hill, SC 29730 Tel. (803)327-7402 Fax (803)327-3261
Email: ecopeland@clintonjrcollege.org
Website: www.clintonjrcollege.org

Colegio Biblico Pentecostal de Puerto Rico (Church of God, Cleveland, TN), Ildefonso Caraballo, President, P.O. Box 901, Saint Just, PR 00978 Tel. (787)761-0640 Fax (787)748-9228
Email: ildefonso@cbp.edu
Website: www.cbp.edu

Colgate Rochester Crozer Divinity School† (American Baptist Churches in the USA), Eugene C. Bay, President, 1100 S. Goodman St., Rochester, NY 14620 Tel. (585)271-1320 Fax (585)271-8013
Email: thalbrooks@crcds.edu
Website: www.crcds.edu

Colorado Christian University (Nondenominational), Larry R. Donnithorne, President, 180 S. Garrison St., Lakewood, CO 80226 Tel. (303)202-0100 Fax (303)274-7560
Email: dlong@ccu.edu
Website: www.ccu.edu

Columbia International University Seminary & School of Missions† (Multidenominational), William H. Jones, President, PO Box 3122, Columbia, SC 29230-3122 Tel. (803)754-4100 Fax (803) 786-4209
Email: publicrelations@ciu.edu
Website: www.ciu.edu

Columbia Theological Seminary† (Presby-ter-ian Church [USA]), Laura S. Mendenhall, President, 701 Columbia Dr., P.O. Box 520, Decatur, GA 30031 Tel. (404) 378-8821 Fax (404)377-9696
Email: MendenhallL@CTSnet.edu
Website: www.CTSnet.edu

Concordia Seminary† (The Lutheran Church-Missouri Synod), Dale A. Meyer, President, 801 Seminary Place, St. Louis, MO 63105 Tel. (314)505-7010 Fax (314)505-7002

299

Email: bartelta@csl.edu
Website: www.csl.edu

Concordia Theological Seminary† (The Lutheran Church-Missouri Synod), Dean O. Wenthe, President, 6600 N. Clinton St., Ft. Wayne, IN 46825- 4996 Tel. (260)452-2100 Fax (260)452-2121
Email: wenthedo@mail.ctsfw.edu
Website: www.ctsfw.edu

Covenant Theological Seminary† (Presbyterian Church in America), Bryan Chapell, President, 12330 Conway Rd., St. Louis, MO 63141-8697 Tel. (314)434-4044 Fax(314) 434-4819
Email: kathy.woodward@covenantseminary.edu
Website: www.covenantseminary.edu

Cranmer Seminary (The Episcopal Orthodox Church; The Anglican Rite Synod in the Americas; The Orthodox Anglican Communion), The Most Rev. Scott E. McLaughlin, President, 901 English Rd., High Point, NC 27262 Tel. (336) 885-6032 Fax (336)885-6021
Email: seminaryinfo@orthodoxanglican.net
Website: orthodoxanglican.net; divinityschool. org

Criswell Center for Biblical Studies (Southern Baptist Convention), President, 4010 Gaston Ave., Dallas, TX 75246 Tel. (214)821-5433 Fax (214)818-1320
Email: jjohnson@criswell.edu
Website: www.criswell.edu

Crossroads College (Christian Churches and Churches of Christ—Non-denominational), Michael Benson, Interim President, 920 Mayowood Rd. S.W., Rochester, MN 55902 Tel. (507)288-4563 Fax (507)288-9046
Email: academic@crossroadscollege.edu
Website: www.crossroadscollege.edu

Crown College (The Christian and Missionary Alliance), Timothy D. Savaloja, Interim President, 8700 College View Dr., St. Bonifacius, MN 55375-9001 Tel. (952)446-4100 Fax (952)446-4149
Email: crown@crown.edu
Website: www.crown.edu

Cummins Theological Seminary (Reformed Episcopal Church), James C. West, President, 705 S. Main St., Summerville, SC 29483 Tel. (843)873-3451 Fax (843)875-6200
Email: jcw121@aol.com, canon_moock@ prodigy. net
Website: www.recus.org

Dallas Christian College (Christian Churches and Churches of Christ), Dustin "Dusty" Rubeck, President, 2700 Christian Pkwy, Dallas, TX 75234 Tel. (972)241-3371 Fax

(972)241-8021
Email: dcc@dallas.edu
Website: www.dallas.edu

Dallas Theological Seminary† (Inter/Multi-denominational), Mark L. Bailey, President, 3909 Swiss Ave., Dallas, TX 75204 Tel. (214)824-3094 Fax (214)841-3625
Email: kgrassmick@dts.edu
Website: www.dts.edu

Davis College (Practical Bible College) (Independent Baptist), George Miller, President, 400 Riverside Drive, Johnson City, NY 13790 Tel. (607)729-1581 Fax (607)729-2962
Website: www.davisny.edu

Denver Seminary† (Nondenominational), Craig Williford, Ph.D., President, 6399 S. Santa Fe Drive, Littleton, CO 80120 Tel. (303)761-2482 Fax (303)761-8060
Email: info@denverseminary.edu
Website: www.denverseminary.edu

The Disciples Divinity House of the University of Chicago (Christian Church [Disciples of Christ]), Kristine A. Culp, Dean, 1156 E. 57th St., Chicago, IL 60637-1536 Tel. (773) 643-4411 Fax (773)643-4413
Email: ddh.uchicago.admin@attglobal.net
Website: ddh.uchicago.edu

Dominican House of Studies† (Catholic Church), Dwight Reginald Whitt, O.P., President, 487 Michigan Ave. N.E., Washington, DC 20017-1585 Tel. (202)529-5300 Fax (202)636-1700
Email: assistant@dhs.edu
Website: www.dhs.edu

Dominican School of Philosophy and Theology† (Catholic Church), Michael Sweeney, President, 2401 Ridge Rd., Berkeley, CA 94709 Tel. (510)849-2030 Fax (510) 849-1372
Email: msweeney@dspt.edu
Website: www.dspt.edu

Dominican Study Center of the Caribbean† (Catholic Church), Fr. Félix Struik, O.P., Regent of the Center, Apartado Postal 1968, Bayamon, PR 00960-1968 Tel. (787) 787-1826 Fax (787)798-2712
Email: fstruik@cedocpr.org
Website: www.cedocpr.org

Drew University Theological School† (The United Methodist Church), Maxine C. Beach, Vice President and Dean, 36 Madison Ave., Madison, NJ 07940-4010 Tel. (973)408-3258 Fax (973)408-3534
Email: miannuzzi@drew.edu
Website: www.drew.edu/theo

300

Duke University Divinity School† (The United Methodist Church), L. Gregory Jones, Dean, Box 90968, Durham, NC 27708-0968 Tel. (888)462-3853 Fax (919)660-3535
Email: admissions@div.duke.edu
Website: www.divinity.duke.edu

Earlham School of Religion† (Interdenominational-Friends), Jay Wade Marshall, Dean, 228 College Ave., Richmond, IN 47374 Tel. (800) 432-1377 Fax (765)983-1688
Email: esr@earlham.edu
Website: www.esr.earlham.edu

Eastern Mennonite Seminary of Eastern Mennonite University† (Mennonite Church), Ervin Stutzman, Dean, 1200 Park Road, Harrisonburg, VA 22802 Tel. (540)432-4260 Fax (540)432-4598
Email: swartlej@emu.edu
Website: www.emu.edu/seminary

Ecumenical Theological Seminary† (Inter/Multidenominational), Marsha Foster Boyd, President, 2930 Woodward Ave., Detroit, MI 48201 Tel. (313)831-5200 Fax (313)831-1353
Website: www.etseminary.edu

Eden Theological Seminary† (United Church of Christ), David M. Greenhaw, President, 475 E. Lockwood Ave., St. Louis, MO 63119-3192 Tel. (314)961-3627 Fax (314)918-2626
Email: dgreenhaw@eden.edu
Website: www.eden.edu

Emmanuel School of Religion† (Christian Churches and Churches of Christ), C. Robert Wetzel, President, One Walker Dr., Johnson City, TN 37601-9438 Tel. (423)926-1186 Fax (423)926-6198
Email: wetzelr@esr.edu
Website: www.esr.edu

Emmaus Bible College (Christian Brethren [also known as Plymouth Brethren]), Kenneth Alan Daughters, President, 2570 Asbury Rd., Dubuque, IA 52001 Tel. (563)588-8000 Fax (563)588-1216
Email: info@emmaus.edu
Website: www.emmaus.edu

Episcopal Divinity School† (Episcopal Church), The Rt. Rev. Steven Charleston, President and Dean, 99 Brattle St., Cambridge, MA 02138-3494 Tel. (617)868-3450 Fax (617)864-5385
Email: scharleston@episdivschool.org
Website: www.episdivschool.edu

Episcopal Theological Seminary of the Southwest† (Episcopal Church), Titus L. Presler, Dean and President, P.O. Box 2247, Austin, TX 78768-2247 Tel. (512)472-4133 Fax (512)472-3098

Email: salexander@etss.edu
Website: www.etss.edu

Erskine Theological Seminary† (Associate Reformed Presbyterian Church, General Synod), Dr. Randall T. Ruble, President, PO Box 668, Due West, SC 29639 Tel. (864)379-8833 Fax (864)379-2171
Email: ruble@erskine.edu
Website: www.erskineseminary.org

Eugene Bible College (Open Bible Standard Churches, Inc.), David Cole, President, 2155 Bailey Hill Rd., Eugene, OR 97405 Tel. (541) 485-1780 Fax (541)343-5801
Email: davidc@ebc.edu
Website: www.ebc.edu

Evangelical Theological Seminary† (The Evangelical Congregational Church), Dennis P. Hollinger, President, 121 S. College St., Myerstown, PA 17067 Tel. (717)866-5775 Fax (717)866-4667
Email: dhollinger@evangelical.edu
Website: www.evangelical.edu

Evangelical Seminary of Puerto Rico† (Inter/Multidenominational), Sergio Ojeda-Carcamo, President, Ponce de Leon Avenue 776, San Juan, PR 00925 Tel. (787)763-6700 Fax (787)751-0847
Website: www.seminarioevangelicopr.org

Faith Baptist Bible College and Theological Seminary (General Association of Regular Baptist Churches), Richard W. Houg, President, 1900 N.W. 4th St., Ankeny, IA 50021-2152 Tel. (515)964-0601 Fax (515) 964-1638
Website: www.faith.edu

Faith Evangelical Lutheran Seminary‡ (Conservative Lutheran Association), R. H. Redal, President, 3504 N. Pearl St., Tacoma, WA 98407 Tel. (253)752-2020/(888)777-7675 Fax (206)759-1790
Email: fsinfo@faithseminary.edu
Website: www.faithseminary.edu

Florida Center for Theological Studies† (Inter/Multidenominational), Patrick H. O'Neill, President, 111 NE First St., Eighth Floor, Miami, FL 33132 Tel. (305)379-3777 Fax (305)379-1006
Website: www.fcfts.org

Florida Christian College (Christian Churches and Churches of Christ), A. Wayne Lowen, President, 1011 Bill Beck Blvd., Kissimmee, FL 34744 Tel. (407)847-8966 Fax (407)847-3925
Email: fcc@fcc.edu
Website: www.fcc.edu

301

Franciscan School of Theology† (Catholic Church), Mario DiCicco, President, 1712 Euclid Ave., Berkeley, CA 94709 Tel. (510) 848-5232 Fax (510)549-9466
Email: mdicicco@fst.edu
Website: www.fst.edu

Free Will Baptist Bible College (National Association of Free Will Baptists), J. Matthew Pinson, President, 3606 West End Ave., Nashville, TN 37205 Tel. (615)383-1340 Fax (615)269-6028
Email: president@fwbbc.edu
Website: www.fwbcc.edu

Fuller Theological Seminary† (Multidenominational), Richard J. Mouw, President, 135 N. Oakland Ave., Pasadena, CA 91182 Tel. (626) 584-5200 Fax (626)795-8767
Email: lguernse@fuller.edu
Website: www.fuller.edu

Garrett-Evangelical Theological Seminary† (The United Methodist Church), Philip A. Amerson, President, 2121 Sheridan Rd., Evanston, IL 60201-3298 Tel. (847)866-3900 Fax (847)866-3957
Email: seminary@garrett.edu
Website: www.garrett.edu

The General Theological Seminary† (Episcopal Church), Ward B. Ewing, Dean and President, 175 Ninth Ave., New York, NY 10011-4977 Tel. (212)243-5150 Fax (212) 647-0294
Email: ewing@gts.edu
Website: www.gts.edu

George Fox Evangelical Seminary† (Inter/Multidenominational), Jules Glanzer, Dean, 12753 SW 68th Ave., Portland, OR 97223 Tel. (503)554-6150 Fax (503)554-6155
Email: seminary@georgefox.edu
Website: www.seminary.georgefox.edu

George Mercer Jr. Memorial School of Theology (Episcopal Church), The Rev. Canon Denis C. Brunelle, Director, 65 Fourth St., Garden City, NY 11530 Tel. (516) 248-4800 Fax (516)248-4883
Email: merceroffice@dioceseli.org
Website: www.mercerschool.org

George W. Truett Theological Seminary of Baylor University† (Baptist General Convention of Texas), David Garland, Dean, PO Box 97126, Waco, TX 76798-7126 Tel. (254)710-3755 Fax (254)710-3753
Email: Nancy_Floyd@Baylor.edu
Website: www.truettseminary.net

God's Bible School and College (Nondenominational), Michael Avery, President, 1810 Young St., Cincinnati, OH 45202 Tel. (513) 721-7944 Fax (513)721-3971
Email: president@gbs.edu
Website: www.gbs.edu

Golden Gate Baptist Theological Seminary† (Southern Baptist Convention), Jeff Iorg, President, 201 Seminary Dr., Mill Valley, CA 94941-3197 Tel. (415)380-1300 Fax (415) 380-1302
Email: seminary@ggbts.edu
Website: www.ggbts.edu

Gonzaga University Department of Religious Studies† (Catholic Church), Pat McCormick, Dept. Head, Spokane, WA 99258-0001 Tel. (509)328-6782 Fax (509)323-5718
Email: McCormick@Gonzaga.edu
Website: www.gonzaga.edu

Gordon-Conwell Theological Seminary† (Inter/Multidenominational), James Emery White, President, 130 Essex St., South Hamilton, MA 01982 Tel. (978)468-7111 Fax (978) 468-6691
Email: info@gcts.edu
Website: www.gordonconwell.edu

Grace Bible College (Grace Gospel Fellowship), Kenneth B. Kemper, President, P.O. Box 910, Grand Rapids, MI 49509 Tel. (616)538-2330 Fax (616)538-0599
Email: info@gbcol.edu
Website: www.gbcol.edu

Grace Theological Seminary† (Fellowship of Grace Brethren Churches), Ronald E. Manahan, President, 200 Seminary Dr., Winona Lake, IN 46590-1294 Tel. (574)372-5100 Fax (574) 372-5139
Email: rmanahan@grace.edu
Website: www.grace.edu

Grace University (Interdenominational), Dr. James Eckman, President, 1311 South 9th St., Omaha, NE 68108 Tel. (402)449-2809 Fax (402)341-9587
Email: jofast@graceu.edu
Website: www.graceuniversity.edu

Graduate Theological Foundation (Interdenominational/ Interfaith), John Morgan, President, 218 West Washington Street, The Tower Building, Suite 300, South Bend, IN 46601 Tel. (800) 423-5983, (574) 287-3642 Fax (574)287-7520
Email: gtfed@sbcglobal.net
Website: www.gtfeducation.org

Graduate Theological Union† (Inter-denominational), James A. Donahue, President, 2400 Ridge Rd., Berkeley, CA 94709-1212 Tel. (510)649-2400 Fax (510)649-1417

Email: president@gtu.edu
Website: www.gtu.edu

Grand Rapids Theological Seminary of Cornerstone University† (Non-Denominational), Douglas L. Fagerstrom, 1001 East Beltline NE, Grand Rapids, MI 49525-5897 Tel. (616) 222-1422 Fax (616)222-1502
Website: www.grts.cornerstone.edu

Great Lakes Christian College (Christian Churches and Churches of Christ), Larry Carter, President, 6211 W. Willow Hwy., Lansing, MI 48917 Tel. (517)321-0242 Fax (517)321-5902
Email: lcarter@glcc.edu
Website: www.glcc.edu

Greenville College (Free Methodist Church of North America), Robert E. Smith, President, 315 E. College Ave., P.O. Box 159, Greenville, IL 62246 Tel. (618)664-2800 Fax (618)664-1748
Email: rsmith@Greenville.edu
Website: www.greenville.edu

Haggard School of Theology at Azusa Pacific University† (Interdenominational), David W. Wright, President, 901 E. Alosta, P.O. Box 7000, Azusa, CA 91702-7000 Tel. (845)969-3434 Fax (845)969-7180
Website: www.apu.edu/theology

Harding University Graduate School of Religion† (Churches of Christ), Evertt W. Huffard, Executive Director, 1000 Cherry Rd., Memphis, TN 38117-5499 Tel. (901)761-1352 Fax (901)761-1358
Email: dean@hugsr.edu
Website: www.hugsr.edu

Hartford Seminary† (Interdenominational), Heidi Hadsell, President, 77 Sherman St., Hartford, CT 06105-2260 Tel. (860)509-9500 Fax (860)509-9509
Email: info@hartsem.edu
Website: www.hartsem.edu

Harvard University Divinity School† (Inter/Multidenominational), William A. Graham, Dean, 45 Francis Ave., Cambridge, MA 02138 Tel. (617)495-4513 Fax (617)496-8026
Email: suzanne_rom@harvard.edu
Website: www.hds.harvard.edu

Hebrew Union College-Jewish Institute of Religion (Jewish), Rabbi David Ellenson, President, 3077 University Ave., Los Angeles, CA 90007 Tel. (213)749-3424 Fax (213)747-6128
Email: presoff@huc.edu
Website: www.huc.edu

Hebrew Union College - Jewish Institute of Religion, NY (Reform Judaism), Rabbi David Ellenson, Ph.D., President, 1 W. 4th St., New York, NY 10012 Tel. (212)674-5300 Fax (212) 533-0129
Email: presoff@huc.edu/jrosensaft@huc.edu
Website: www.huc.edu

Heritage Bible College‡ (Pentecostal Free Will Baptist), Elvin R. Butts, President, 1747 Bud Hawkins Road, PO Box 1628, Dunn, NC 28335 Tel. (910)892-3178 Fax (910)892-1809
Email: generalinfo@heritagebiblecollege.org
Website: www.heritagebiblecollege.org

Hillsdale Free Will Baptist College‡ (Free Will Baptist), Carl Cheshier, President, PO Box 7208, Moore, OK 73153-1208 Tel. (405)912-9000 Fax (405)912-9050
Email: hillsdale@hc.edu
Website: www.hc.edu

Hobe Sound Bible College (Nondenominational), P. Daniel Stetler, President, P.O. Box 1065, Hobe Sound, FL 33475 Tel. (407)546-5534 Fax (407)545-1421

Holy Cross Greek Orthodox School of Theology† (Greek Orthodox Archdiocese of America), Rev. Nicholas C. Triantafilou, President, 50 Goddard Ave., Brookline, MA 02445-7495 Tel. (617)731-3500 Fax (617) 850-1460
Email: admissions@hchc.edu/jbakas@hchc.edu
Website: www.hchc.edu

Holy Trinity Orthodox Seminary (The Russian Orthodox Church Outside of Russia), Archbishop Laurus Skurla, President, P.O. Box 36, Jordanville, NY 13361 Tel. (315)858-0945 Fax (315)858-0945
Email: info@hts.edu
Website: www.hts.edu

Hood Theological Seminary† (African Methodist Episcopal Zion Church), Albert J.D. Aymer, President, 1810 Lutheran Synod Drive, Salisbury, NC 28144 Tel. (704)636-7611 Fax (704)636-7699
Email: pwells@hoodseminary.edu
Website: www.hoodseminary.edu

Hope International University (Christian Churches and Churches of Christ), Dr. John Derry, President, 2500 E. Nutwood Ave., Fullerton, CA 92831-3104 Tel. (714)879-3901 Fax (714)681-7451
Email: slcarter@hiu.edu
Website: www.hiu.edu

Houston Graduate School of Theology† (Friends), Keith A. Jenkins, President, 2501

303

Central Parkway, Suite A-19, Houston, TX 77092 Tel. (713)942-9505 Fax (713)942-9506 Email: hgst@hgst.edu Website: www.hgst.edu

Howard University School of Divinity† (Nondenominational), Bertram Melbourne, Interim Dean, 1400 Shepherd St. N.E., Washington, DC 20017 Tel. (202)806-0500 Fax (202)806-0711 Website: www.howard.edu/schooldivinity

Huntington University, Graduate School of Christian Ministries (Church of the United Brethren in Christ), G. Blair Dowden, President, 2303 College Ave., Huntington, IN 46750 Tel. (260)359-4039 Fax (260)359-4126 Email: gscm@huntington.edu Website: www.huntington.edu/gscm

Iliff School of Theology† (The United Methodist Church), David Trickett, President, 2201 S. University Blvd., Denver, CO 80210-4798 Tel. (303)744-1287 Fax (303)777-3387 Email: dgtrickett@iliff.edu Website: www.iliff.edu

Immaculate Conception Seminary Seton Hall University† (Catholic Church), Rev. Msgr. Robert F. Coleman, J. C. D., Rector and Dean, 400 S. Orange Ave., South Orange, NJ 07079 Tel. (973)761-9575 Fax (973)761-9577 Email: theology@shu.edu Website: www.theology.shu.edu

Indiana Wesleyan University (The Wesleyan Church), James Barnes, President, 4201 S. Washington, Marion, IN 46953-4974 Tel. (765)674-6901 Fax (765)677-2465 Email: james.barnes@indwes.edu Website: www.indwes.edu

Institute for Creation Research Graduate School‡ (Non-Denominational), John Morris, President, 10946 Woodside Avenue North, Santee, CA 92071 Tel. (619)448-0900 Fax (619)448-3469 Email: kcumming@icr.edu; jkriege@icr.org Website: www.icr.org

Inter-American Adventist Theological Seminary† (Seventh-day Adventist), Jaime Castrejon, President and Dean, PO Box 830518, Miami, FL 33283 Tel. (305)403-4700 Fax (305)403-4600 Email: Jaime@interamerica.org Website: www.interamerica.org

Interdenominational Theological Center† (Interdenominational), Michael A. Battle, President, 700 Martin Luther King, Jr. Dr. S.W., Atlanta, GA 30314-4143 Tel. (404)527-7702 Fax (404)527-7770

Email: info@itc.edu Website: www.itc.edu

International Baptist College†‡ (Baptist), Pastor David Brock, President, 2150 East Southern Avenue, Tempe, AZ 85282-7504 Tel. (480)838-7070 Fax (480)505-3299 Email: info@ibconline.edu Website: www.tri-citybaptist.org

International College & Graduate School‡ (Non-Denominational), Dr. Rick Stinton, President, 20 Dowsett Avenue, Honolulu, HI 96817 Tel. (808)595-4247 Fax (808)595-4779 Email: icgs@hawaii.rr.com Website: www.icgshawaii.org

International Theological Seminary† (Non-denominational), Joseph Tong, President, 3215-3225 N. Tyler Ave., El Monte, CA 91731 Tel. (626)448-0023 Fax (626)350-6343 Website: www.itsla.edu

James and Carolyn McAfee School of Theology of Mercer University† (Cooperative Baptist Fellowship), R. Alan Culpepper, Dean of the School of Theology, 3001 Mercer University Drive, Atlanta, GA 30341-4115 Tel. (678)547-6470 Fax (678)547-6478 Email: culpepper_ra@mercer.edu Website: theology.mercer.edu

Jesuit School of Theology at Berkeley† (Catholic Church), Joseph P. Daoust, President, 1735 LeRoy Ave., Berkeley, CA 94709-1193 Tel. (510)549-5000 Fax (510)841-8536 Email: cdodson@jstb.edu Website: www.jstb.edu

Jewish Theological Seminary of America (Jewish), Ismar Schorsch, President, 3080 Broadway, New York, NY 10027-4649 Tel. (212)678-8000 Fax (212)678-8947 Email: webmaster@jtsa.edu Website: www.jtsa.edu

The John Leland Center for Theological Studies† (Baptist), K. Randel Everett, President, 1301 N. Hartford St., Arlington, VA 22201 Tel. (703)812-4757 Fax (703)812-4764 Website: www.johnlelandcenter.edu

John Wesley College (Interdenominational), Brian C. Donley, President, 2314 N. Centennial St., High Point, NC 27265 Tel. (336)889-2262 Fax (336)889-2261 Email: admissions@johnwesley.edu Website: www.johnwesley.edu

Johnson Bible College (Christian Churches and Churches of Christ), Gary E. Weedman,

President, 7900 Johnson Dr., Knoxville, TN 37998 Tel. (865)573-4517 Fax (865)251-2336
Email: tnice@jbc.edu
Website: www.jbc.edu

Kansas City College and Bible School (Church of God [Holiness]), Gayle Woods, President, 7401 Metcalf Ave., Overland Park, KS 66204 Tel. (913)722-0272 Fax (913)722-2135

Kenrick-Glennon Seminary† (Catholic Church), Ted L. Wojcicki, President-Rector, 5200 Glennon Dr., St. Louis, MO 63119-4399 Tel. (314)792-6100 Fax (314)792-6500
Website: www.kenrick.edu

Kentucky Christian University (Christian Churches and Churches of Christ), Keith P. Keeran, Ph.D., President, 100 Academic Parkway, Grayson, KY 41143 Tel. (606)474-3000 Fax (606)474-3155
Email: TLW@kcu.edu
Website: www.kcu.edu

Kentucky Mountain Bible College (Interdenominational), Philip Speas, President, Box 10, Vancleve, KY 41385 Tel. (606)666-5000 Fax (606)666-7744

King's College and Seminary‡ (Non-Denominational), Paul G. Chappell, Chief Academic Officer, 14800 Sherman Way, Van Nuys, CA 91405 Tel. (818)779-8040 Fax (818)779-8241
Email: admissions@kingsseminary.edu
Website: www.kingsseminary.edu, www.kings college.edu

Knox Theological Seminary† (Presbyterian Church in America), R. Fowler White, Administrator and Dean of the Faculty, 5554 North Federal Highway, Fort Lauderdale, FL 33308 Tel. (954)771-0376 Fax (954)351-3343
Email: knox@crpc.org
Website: www.knoxseminary.org

Kuyper College (Interdenominational), Nicholas V. Kroeze, President, 3333 East Beltline N.E., Grand Rapids, MI 49525-9749 Tel. (616)222-3000 Fax (616)988-3608
Email: jheyboer@kuyper.edu
Website: www.kuyper.edu

La Sierra University School of Religion† (Seventh-day Adventist Church), Lawrence T. Geraty, President, 4500 Riverwalk Parkway, Riverside, CA 92515-8247 Tel. (951)785-2000 Fax (951)785-2901
Email: pr@lasierra.edu
Website: www.lasierra.edu

Lancaster Bible College (Nondenominational), Peter W. Teague, President, PO Box 83403, Lancaster, PA 17601 Tel. (717)560-8278 Fax (717)560-8260
Email: president@lbc.edu
Website: www.lbc.edu

Lancaster Theological Seminary† (United Church of Christ), Rev. Riess W. Potterveld, President, 555 W. James St., Lancaster, PA 17603-2897 Tel. (717)393-0654 Fax (717)393-4254
Email: seminary@lancasterseminary.edu
Website: www.lancasterseminary.edu

Lexington Theological Seminary† (Christian Church [Disciples of Christ]), R. Robert Cueni, President, 631 S. Limestone St., Lexington, KY 40508 Tel. (859)252-0361 Fax (859)281-6042
Website: www.lextheo.edu

Liberty Theological Seminary and Graduate School (Independent Baptist), Ergun Caner, Dean, 1971 University Blvd., Lynchburg, VA 24502-2269 Tel. (434)592-4140 Fax (434) 522-0415
Email: ecaner@liberty.edu
Website: www.liberty.edu/Academics/Religion/ Seminary

Liberty University‡ (Baptist), John Borek, President, 1971 University Boulevard, Lynchburg, VA 24502 Tel. (434)582-2000 Fax (434)582-2304
Email: admissions@liberty.edu
Website: www.liberty.edu

Life Pacific College (International Church of the Foursquare Gospel), Dan R. Stewart, President, 1100 Covina Blvd., San Dimas, CA 91773 Tel. (909)599-5433 Fax (909)599-6690
Email: info@lifepacific.edu
Website: www.lifepacific.edu

Lincoln Christian Seminary† (Christian Churches and Churches of Christ), Keith H. Ray, President, 100 Campus View Dr., Lincoln, IL 62656 Tel. (217)732-3168 x 2354 Fax (217)732-5718
Email: ttanner@lccs.edu
Website: www.lccs.edu

Lipscomb University College of Bible and Ministry† (Churches of Christ), Terry Briley, Dean, 3901 Granny White Pike, Nashville, TN 37204-3951 Tel. (615)279-6051 Fax (615) 279-6052
Website: www.lipscomb.edu

Logos Evangelical Seminary† (Evangelical Formosan Church), Felix Liu, President, 9358 Telstar Ave., El Monte, CA 91731 Tel. (626)571-5110 Fax (626)571-5119

Email: logos@les.edu
Website: www.logos-seminary.edu

Logsdon Seminary of Hardin-Simmons University† (Baptist General Convention of Texas), Thomas Brisco, Dean, P.O. Box 16235, Abilene, TX 79698-6235 Tel. (325) 670-1287 Fax (325)670-1406
Website: www.hsutx.edu/academics/logsdon

Louisville Presbyterian Theological Seminary† (Presbyterian Church [USA]), Dean K. Thompson, President, 1044 Alta Vista Rd., Louisville, KY 40205 Tel. (502)895-3411 Fax (502)895-1096
Email: dthompson@lpts.edu
Website: www.lpts.edu

Loyola Marymount University Department of Theological Studies† (Catholic Church), Jeffrey S. Siker, Chair, One LMU Drive, Los Angeles, CA 90045-2659 Tel. (310)338-7670 Fax (310)338-1947
Email: jsiker@lmu.edu
Website: bellarmine.lmu.edu/theology

Loyola University Chicago Institute of Pastoral Studies† (Catholic Church), Robert A. Ludwig, Director, 820 N. Michigan Ave., Chicago, IL 60611 Tel. (312)915-7400 Fax (312)915-7410
Email: rludwig@luc.edu
Website: www.luc.edu/depts/ips

Luther Rice Bible College & Seminary‡ (Baptist), James Flanagan, President, 3038 Evans Mill Road, Lithonia, GA 30038 Tel. (770)484-1204 Fax (770)484-1155
Email: lrs@lrs.edu
Website: www.lrs.edu

Luther Seminary† (Evangelical Lutheran Church in America), Richard H. Bliese, President, 2481 Como Ave., St. Paul, MN 55108 Tel. (651)641-3456 Fax (651)641-3425
Email: admissions@luthersem.edu
Website: www.luthersem.edu

Lutheran Bible Institute in California (Intersynodical Lutheran), Samuel Giesy, Acting President, 5321 University Dr., Ste. G, Irvine, CA 92612-2942 Tel. (949)262-9222, (800)261-5242 Fax (949)262-0283
Email: info@lbic.org
Website: www.lbic.org

Lutheran Brethren Seminary (Church of the Lutheran Brethren of America), Joel T. Nordtvedt, President, 815 W. Vernon, Fergus Falls, MN 56537 Tel. (218)739-3375 Fax (218)739-1259
Email: lbs@clba.org
Website: www.lbs.edu

Lutheran School of Theology at Chicago† (Evangelical Lutheran Church in America), James Kenneth Echols, President, 1100 E. 55th St., Chicago, IL 60615-5199 Tel. (773) 256-0700 Fax (773)256-0782
Email: jechols@lstc.edu
Website: www.lstc.edu

Lutheran Theological Seminary at Gettysburg† (Evangelical Lutheran Church in America), The Rev. Michael L. Cooper-White, President, 61 Seminary Ridge, Gettysburg, PA 17325-1795 Tel. (717)334-6286 Fax (717)334-3469
Email: ctroyer@ltsg.edu
Website: www.ltsg.edu

Lutheran Theological Seminary at Philadelphia† (Evangelical Lutheran Church in America), Philip D.W. Krey, President, 7301 Germantown Ave., Philadelphia, PA 19119 Tel. (215)248-4616 Fax (215)248-4577
Email: mtairy@ltsp.edu
Website: www.ltsp.edu

Lutheran Theological Southern Seminary† (Evangelical Lutheran Church in America), Marcus J. Miller, President, 4201 North Main St., Columbia, SC 29203 Tel. (803)786-5150 Fax (803)786-6499
Email: Mmiller@ltss.edu
Website: www.ltss.edu

M. Christopher White School of Divinity of Gardner-Webb University† (Baptist State Convention of North Carolina), Robert W. Canoy, Dean, 110 N. Main Street, Noel Hall, Boiling Springs, NC 28017 Tel. (704)406-4400 Fax (704)406-3935
Email: rcanoy@gardner-webb.edu
Website: www.divinity.gardner-webb.edu

Magnolia Bible College (Churches of Christ), Garvis Semore, President, P.O. Box 1109, Kosciusko, MS 39090 Tel. (662)289-2896 Fax (662)289-1850
Email: gsemore@magnolia.edu
Website: www.magnolia.edu

Manhattan Christian College (Christian Churches and Churches of Christ), Jolene Rupe, Secretary, Institutional Advancement, 1415 Anderson Ave., Manhattan, KS 66502 Tel. (785)539-3571 Fax (785)539-0832
Email: jrupe@mccks.edu
Website: www.mccks.edu

Maple Springs Baptist Bible College and Seminary‡ (Non-Denominational), Larry W. Jordan, President, 4130 Belt Road, Capital Heights, MD 20743 Tel. (301)736-3631 Fax (301)735-6507
Email: larry.jordan@msbbcs.edu
Website: www.msbbcs.edu

Mars Hill Graduate School†‡ (Non-Denominational), Dan Allander, President, 2525 - 220th Street, Bothell, WA 98021 Tel. (425) 415-0505 Fax (425)806-5599
Email: info@mhgs.edu
Website: www.mhgs.net

McCormick Theological Seminary† (Presbyterian Church [USA]), Cynthia M. Campbell, President, 5460 S. University Ave., Chicago, IL 60615-5108 Tel. (773)947-6300 Fax (773) 288-2612
Email: ccampbell@mccormick.edu
Website: www.mccormick.edu

Meadville Lombard Theological School† (Unitarian Universalist), Lee Barker, President, 5701 S. Woodlawn Ave., Chicago, IL 60637 Tel. (773)256-3000 Fax (773)753-1323
Email: LBarker@meadville.edu
Website: www.meadville.edu

Memphis Theological Seminary† (Cumberland Presbyterian Church), Daniel J. Earheart-Brown, President, 168 E. Parkway S at Union, Memphis, TN 38104-4395 Tel. (901)458-8232 Fax (901)452-4051
Email: jebrown@memphisseminary.edu
Website: www.memphisseminary.edu

Mennonite Brethren Biblical Seminary† (General Conference of Mennonite Brethren Churches), Jim Holm, President, 4824 E. Butler Ave. (at Chestnut Ave.), Fresno, CA 93727-5097 Tel. (559)251-8628 Fax (559)251-7212
Email: fresno@mbseminary.edu
Website: www.mbseminary.edu

Messenger College‡ (Pentecostal Church of God), Tiffany Stump, Dir. of Admissions, 300 E. 50th Street, Joplin, MO 64804 Tel. (417) 624-7070 Fax (417)624-5070
Email: info@messengercollege.edu
Website: www.messengercollege.edu

Methodist Theological School in Ohio† (The United Methodist Church), Jay Rundell, President, 3081 Columbus Pike, P.O. Box 8004, Delaware, OH 43015-8004 Tel. (740) 363-1146 Fax (740)362-3135
Email: ndewire@mtso.edu, pres@mtso.edu
Website: www.mtso.edu

Michigan Theological Seminary†‡ (Non-Denominational), Bruce W. Fong, President, 41550 E. Ann Arbor Trail, Plymouth, MI 48170-4308 Tel. (734)207-9581 Fax (734)207-9582
Email: admissions@mts.edu
Website: www.mts.edu

Mid-America Christian University (The Church of God, Anderson, IN), John D. Fozard, President, 3500 S.W. 119th St., Oklahoma City, OK 73170 Tel. (405)691-3800 Fax (405)692-3165
Email: info@macu.edu
Website: www.macu.edu

Mid-America Reformed Seminary†‡ (Inter/Multidenominational), Cornelius P. Venema, President, 229 Seminary Drive, Dyer, IN 46311 Tel. (219)864-2400 Fax (219)864-2410
Email: info@midamerica.edu
Website: www.midamerica.edu

Midwest University (Korean language)‡ (Interdenominational), James Song, President, 851 Parr Road, Wentzville, MO 63385 Tel. (636)327-4645 Fax (636)327-4715
Email: inf@midwest.edu
Website: www.midwest.edu

Midwestern Baptist Theological Seminary† (Southern Baptist Convention), R. Philip Roberts, President, 5001 N. Oak Trafficway, Kansas City, MO 64118 Tel. (816)414-3700 Fax (816)414-3799
Email: president@mbts.edu
Website: www.mbts.edu

Moody Bible Institute (Interdenominational), Michael J. Easley, President, 820 N. La Salle Blvd., Chicago, IL 60610 Tel. (312)329-4000 Fax (312)329-4109
Email: pr@moody.edu
Website: www.moody.edu

Moravian Theological Seminary† (Moravian Church in America-Unitas Fratrum), Christopher M. Thomforde, President, 1200 Main St., Bethlehem, PA 18018 Tel. (610)861-1516 Fax (610)861-1569
Email: seminary@moravian.edu
Website: www.moravianseminary.edu

Moreau Seminary (Congregation of Holy Cross) (Catholic Church), Rev. Wilson Miscamble, C.S.C., President, Moreau Seminary
University of Notre Dame, Notre Dame, IN 46556 Tel. (574)631-7735 Fax (574)631-9233
Website: www.nd.edu/‡mdiv

Morehouse School of Religion (Interdenominational Baptist), William T. Perkins, President, 645 Beckwith St. S.W., Atlanta, GA 30314 Tel. (404)527-7777 Fax (404)681-1005

Mount Angel Seminary† (Catholic Church), Very Rev. Fr. Richard Paperini, President Rector, St. Benedict, OR 97373 Tel. (503)845-3951 Fax (503)845-3126
Email: tswanson@mtangel.edu
Website: www.mtangel.edu

Mt. St. Mary's Seminary† (Catholic Church), Steven P. Rohlfs, Rector, 16300 Old

Emmitsburg Rd., Emmitsburg, MD 21727-7797 Tel. (301)447-5295 Fax (301)447-5636
Email: rhoades@msmary.edu
Website: www.msmary.edu

Mt. St. Mary's Seminary of the West (Catholic Church), Gerald R. Haemmerle, President, 6616 Beechmont Ave., Cincinnati, OH 45230 Tel. (513)231-2223 Fax (513)231-3254
Email: jhaemmer@mtsm.org
Website: mtsm.org

Multnomah Biblical Seminary† (Multnomah Biblical Seminary), Daniel R. Lockwood, President, 8435 N.E. Glisan St., Portland, OR 97220 Tel. (503)255-0332 Fax (503)251-6701
Email: dlockwood@multnomah.edu
Website: www.multnomah.edu

Mundelein Seminary of the Univ. of St. Mary-of-the-Lake† (The Catholic Church), Dennis J. Lyle, Rector-President, 1000 E. Maple, Mundelein, IL 60060-1174 Tel. (847)566-6401 Fax (847)566-7330
Email: dgiovannetti@usml.edu
Website: www.usml.edu

Nashotah House (Theological Seminary)† (Episcopal Church), Robert S. Munday, President and Dean, 2777 Mission Rd., Nashotah, WI 53058-9793 Tel. (262)646-6500 Fax (262)646-6504
Email: smills@nashotah.edu
Website: www.nashotah.edu

Nazarene Bible College (Church of the Nazarene), Hiram Sanders, President, 1111 Academy Park Loop, Colorado Springs, CO 80910-3704 Tel. (719)884-5000 Fax (719) 884-5199
Email: info@nbc.edu
Website: www.nbc.edu

Nazarene Theological Seminary† (Church of the Nazarene), Ron Benefiel, President, 1700 E. Meyer Blvd., Kansas City, MO 64131-1246 Tel. (816)333-6254 Fax (816)333-6271
Email: lneely@nts.edu
Website: www.nts.edu

Nebraska Christian College (Christian Churches and Churches of Christ), Richard D. Milliken, President, 1800 Syracuse Ave., Norfolk, NE 68701-2458 Tel. (402)379-5000 Fax (402) 391-5100
Email: info@nechristian.edu
Website: www.nechristian.edu

New Brunswick Theological Seminary† (Reformed Church in America), Gregg A. Mast, President, 17 Seminary Pl., New Brunswick, NJ 08901-1196 Tel. (732)247-5241 Fax (732)249-5412

Email: egm@nbts.edu
Website: www.nbts.edu

New Orleans Baptist Theological Seminary† (Southern Baptist Convention), Charles S. Kelley, President, 3939 Gentilly Blvd., New Orleans, LA 70126 Tel. (504)282-4455 Fax (504)816-8023
Email: nobts@nobts.edu
Website: www.nobts.edu

New York Theological Seminary† (Inter/Multi-denominational), Dale T. Irvin, President, 475 Riverside Drive, Ste. 500, New York, NY 10115 Tel. (212)870-1250 Fax (212)870-1236
Email: drhgaston@nyts.edu
Website: www.nyts.edu

North Central Bible College (Assemblies of God), Gordon L. Anderson, President, 910 Elliot Ave. S., Minneapolis, MN 55404 Tel. (612)332-3491 Fax (612)343-4778
Email: info@ncbc.edu
Website: www.ncbc.edu

North Park Theological Seminary† (The Evangelical Covenant Church), John E. Phelan Jr., President and Dean, 3225 W. Foster Ave., Chicago, IL 60625 Tel. (773)244-6214 Fax (773)244-6244
Email: jphelan@northpark.edu
Website: www.northpark.edu

Northeastern Seminary at Roberts Wesleyan College† (Nondenominational), John A. Martin, President, 2265 Westside Dr., Rochester, NY 14624-1977 Tel. (585)594-6800 Fax (585)594-6801
Website: www.nes.edu

Northern Baptist Theological Seminary† (American Baptist Churches in the USA), John Kirn, Interim President, 660 E. Butterfield Rd., Lombard, IL 60148-5698 Tel. (630)620-2100 Fax (630)620-2194
Email: cwmoore@northern.seminary.edu
Website: www.seminary.edu

Northwest Baptist Seminary‡ (Baptist), Mark Wagner, President, 4301 N. Stevens, Tacoma,, WA 98407 Tel. (253)759-6104 Fax (253)759-3299
Email: nbs@nbs.edu
Website: www.nbs.edu

Northwest College (Assemblies of God), Don H. Argue, President, 5520 108th Ave. N.E., P.O. Box 579, Kirkland, WA 98083-0579 Tel. (425)822-8266 Fax (425)827-0148
Email: receptionist@NorthwestU.edu
Website: www.nwcollege.edu

Notre Dame Seminary† (Catholic Church), Patrick J. Williams, M. Div., M.S., President

and Rector, 2901 S. Carrollton Ave., New Orleans, LA 70118-4391 Tel. (504)866-7426 Fax (504)866-3119
Email: pjwilliams@nds.edu
Website: www.nds.edu

Oak Hills Christian College (Interdenominational), Steven Hostetter, Provost, 1600 Oak Hills Rd. S.W., Bemidji, MN 56601 Tel. (218)751-8670 Fax (218)751-8825
Email: dclausen@oakhills.edu
Website: www.oakhills.edu

Oblate School of Theology† (Catholic Church), Ronald Rolheiser, President, 285 Oblate Dr., San Antonio, TX 78216-6693 Tel. (210)341-1366 Fax (210)341-4519
Email: oblate@connecti.com
Website: www.ost.edu

Oral Roberts University School of Theology† (Inter/Multidenominational), Thomson K. Mathew, Dean, 7777 S. Lewis Ave., Tulsa, OK 74171 Tel. (918)495-7016 Fax (918)495-6259
Email: jcope@oru.edu
Website: www.oru.edu

Ozark Christian College (Christian Churches and Churches of Christ), Matt Proctor, President, 1111 N. Main St., Joplin, MO 64801 Tel. (417)624-2518 Fax (417)624-0090
Email: pres@occ.edu
Website: www.occ.edu

Pacific Islands Bible College‡, The Rev. David L. Owen, President, PO Box 22619, GMF, GU 96921 Tel. (671) 734-1812 Fax (671) 734-1813
Email: GuamCampus@pibc.edu; Chuuk Campus @pibcedu
Website: www.pibc.edu

Pacific Lutheran Theological Seminary† (Evangelical Lutheran Church in America), Phyllis Anderson, President, 2770 Marin Ave., Berkeley, CA 94708-1530 Tel. (510)524-5264 Fax (510)524-2408
Email: president@plts.edu
Website: www.plts.edu

Pacific School of Religion† (Inter/Multi-denominational), William McKinney, President, 1798 Scenic Ave., Berkeley, CA 94709 Tel. (510)848-0528 Fax (510)845-8948
Email: wmckinney@psr.edu
Website: www.psr.edu

Palmer Theological Seminary† (American Baptist Churches in the USA), Wallace C. Smith, President, 6 Lancaster Ave., Wynnewood, PA 19096 Tel. (610)896-5000 Fax (610)649-3834
Email: sempres@eastern.edu
Website: www.ebts.edu

Payne Theological Seminary† (African Methodist Episcopal Church), Leah Gaskin Fitchue, President, P.O. Box 474, 230 Wilberforce-Clifton Rd., Wilberforce, OH 45384-0474 Tel. (937)376-2946 Fax (937) 376-3330
Email: LFitchue@payne.edu
Website: www.payne.edu

Pepperdine University (Churches of Christ), Randall Chesnutt, Chair of Religion Division, Religion Division, Malibu, CA 90263-4352 Tel. (310)506-4352 Fax (310) 317-7271
Email: randall.chesnutt@pepperdine.edu
Website: pepperdine.edu/religion

Perkins School of Theology (Southern Methodist University)† (The United Methodist Church), William B. Lawrence, Dean, PO Box 750133, Dallas, TX 75275-0133 Tel. (214) 768-2293 Fax (214)768-4245
Email: jpangiar@smu.edu
Website: www.smu.edu/perkins

Philadelphia Biblical University (Nondenominational), W. Sherrill Babb, President, 200 Manor Ave., Langhorne, PA 19047-2990 Tel. (215)752-5800 Fax (215)702-4341
Email: president@pbu.edu
Website: www.pbu.edu

Phillips Theological Seminary† (Christian Church-Disciples of Christ), William Tabbernee, President, 901 North Mingo Road, Tulsa, OK 74116 Tel. (918)610-8303 Fax (918)610-8404
Email: Myrna.Jones@ptstulsa.edu
Website: www.ptstulsa.edu

Phoenix Seminary† (Nondenominational), Darryl DelHousaye, President, 4222 E. Thomas Road,, Phoenix, AZ 85018 Tel. (480) 443-1020 Fax (480)443-1120
Email: ddelhousaye@phoenixseminary.edu
Website: www.phoenixseminary.edu

Piedmont Baptist College‡ (Baptist-Independent), Charles W. Petitt, President, 716 Franklin St., Winston-Salem, NC 27101 Tel. (336)725-8344 Fax (336)725-5522
Email: admissions@pbc.edu
Website: www.pbc.edu

Pittsburgh Theological Seminary† (Presbyterian Church [USA]), William J. Carl III, President, 616 N. Highland Ave., Pittsburgh, PA 15206 Tel. (412)362-5610 Fax (412)363-3260
Email: calian@pts.edu
Website: www.pts.edu

Pontifical College Josephinum† (Catholic Church), Msgr. Paul J. Langsfeld, Rector and President, 7625 N. High St., Columbus, OH 43235 Tel. (614)885-5585 Fax (614)885-2307
Email: plangsfeld@pcj.edu
Website: www.pcj.edu

309

Pope John XXIII National Seminary (Catholic Church), Francis D. Kelly, President, 558 South Ave., Weston, MA 02193 Tel. (617)899-5500 Fax (617)899-9057
Email: seminary@blessedjohnxxiii.edu
Website: www.blessedjohnxxiii.edu

Princeton Theological Seminary† (Presbyterian Church [USA]), Iain R. Torrance, President, P.O. Box 821, Princeton, NJ 08542-0803 Tel. (609)921-8300 Fax (609)924-2973
Email: comm-pub@ptsem.edu
Website: www.ptsem.edu

Protestant Episcopal Theological Seminary in Virginia† (Episcopal Church), Martha J. Horne, Dean and President, 3737 Seminary Rd., Alexandria, VA 22304 Tel. (703)370-6600 Fax (703)370-6234
Email: mhorne@vts.edu
Website: www.vts.edu

Puget Sound Christian College (Christian Churches and Churches of Christ), Randy J. Bridges, President, P.O. Box 13108, Everett, WA 98206-3108 Tel. (425)257-3090 Fax (425)258-1488
Email: president@pscc.edu
Website: www.pscc.edu

Rabbi Isaac Elchanan Theological Seminary (Jewish), Norman Lamm, President, 2540 Amsterdam Ave., New York, NY 10033 Tel. (212)960-5344 Fax (212)960-0061
Email: amlevin@ymail.yu.edu
Website: www.yu.edu/riets

Reconstructionist Rabbinical College (Jewish), Dan Ehrenkrantz, President, 1299 Church Rd, Wyncote, PA 19095 Tel. (215)576-0800 Fax (215)576-6143
Email: admissions@rrc.edu
Website: www.rrc.edu

Reformed Episcopal Seminary† (Reformed Episcopal Church), Wayne A. Headman, President, 826 Second Ave., Blue Bell, PA 19422-1257 Tel. (610)292-9852 Fax (610)292-9853
Email: reseminary.edu
Website: www.reseminary.edu

Reformed Presbyterian Theological Seminary† (Reformed Presbyterian Church of North America), Jerry F. O'Neill, President, 7418 Penn Ave., Pittsburgh, PA 15208-2594 Tel. (412)731-8690 Fax (412)731-4834
Email: info@rpts.edu
Website: www.rpts.edu

Reformed Theological Seminary† (Inter/Multidenominational), Robert C. Cannada, Jr., President, 5422 Clinton Blvd., Jackson, MS 39209-3099 Tel. (601)923-1600 Fax (601)923-1654
Email: rts.orlando@rts.edu
Website: www.rts.edu

Regent University School of Divinity†† (Nondenominational/Evangelical), Michael Palmer, Dean, 1000 Regent University Dr, Virginia Beach, VA 23464-9870 Tel. Fax (757)226-4597
Email: vinssyn@regent.edu
Website: www.regent.edu/acad/schdiv

Roanoke Bible College (Christian Churches and Churches of Christ), D. Clay Perkins, Ph.D., President, 715 N. Poindexter St, Elizabeth City, NC 27909-4054 Tel. (252)334-2070 Fax (252)334-2071
Email: wag@roanokebible.edu
Website: www.roanokebible.edu

Sacred Heart Major Seminary† (Catholic Church), Very Rev. Steven Boguslawski, OP, President, 2701 Chicago Blvd., Detroit, MI 48206 Tel. (313)883-8501 Fax (313)868-6440
Email: Information@shms.edu
Website: www.shmsonline.org

Sacred Heart School of Theology† (Catholic Church), Very Rev. Thomas Knoebel, Acting President-Rector, P.O. Box 429, Hales Corners, WI 53130-0429 Tel. (414)425-8300 Fax (414)529-6999
Email: rector@shst.edu
Website: www.shst.edu

St. Bernard's School of Theology and Ministry† (Catholic Church), Patricia A. Schoelles, President, 120 French Road, Rochester, NY 14618 Tel. (585)271-3657 Fax (585)271-2045
Email: pschoelles@sbi.edu
Website: www.stbernards.edu

St. Charles Borromeo Seminary† (Catholic Church), Rev. Msgr. Joseph G. Prior, President and Rector, 100 East Wynnewood Rd., Wynnewood, PA 19096-3001 Tel. (610)667-3394 Fax (610)667-0452
Email: developmentscs@adphila.org
Website: www.scs.edu

St. Francis Seminary† (Catholic Church), Very Rev.Donald J. Hying, Rector, 3257 S. Lake Dr., St. Francis, WI 53235 Tel. (414)747-6404 Fax (414)747-6442
Email: mwitczak@sfs.edu
Website: www.sfs.edu

St. John Vianney Theological Seminary† (Catholic Church), Michael Glenn, Rector, 1300 S. Steele St., Denver, CO 80210-2599 Tel. (303)282-3427 Fax (303)282-3453

St. John's Seminary† (Catholic Church), John Farren, Rector and President, 127 Lake St., Brighton, MA 02135 Tel. (617)254-2610 Fax (617)787-2336
Email: Reverend_John_L_Sullivan@rcab.org
Website: www.sjs.edu

St. John's Seminary† (Catholic Church), Monsignor Helmut Hefner, Rector and President, 5012 Seminary Rd., Camarillo, CA 93012-2598 Tel. (805)482-2755 Fax (805) 482-0637
Email: helmut@stjohnsem.edu
Website: www.stjohnsem.edu

St. John's University, School of Theology— Seminary† (Catholic Church), William J. Cahoy, Dean, Box 7288, Collegeville, MN 56321-7288 Tel. (320)363-2622 Fax (320) 363-3145
Email: bduffy@csbsju.edu
Website: www.csbsju.edu/sot

St. Joseph's Seminary† (Catholic Church), Peter G. Finn, President, 201 Seminary Ave., Yonkers, NY 10704 Tel. (914)968-6200 Fax (914)968-7912
Email: sjsirs@aol.com
Website: www.ny-archdiocese.org/pastoral/seminary.cfm

St. Louis Christian College (Christian Churches and Churches of Christ), Guthrie Veech, President, 1360 Grandview Dr., Florissant, MO 63033 Tel. (314)837-6777 Fax (314)837-8291
Email: agall@slcconline.edu
Website: www.slcconline.edu

St. Mary Seminary and Graduate School of Theology† (Catholic Church), Thomas W. Tifft, President, 28700 Euclid Ave., Wickliffe, OH 44092-2585 Tel. (440)943-7600 Fax (440)943-7577
Website: www.stmarysem.edu

St. Mary's Seminary† (Catholic Church), Very Rev. Brendan Cahill, Rector, 9845 Memorial Dr., Houston, TX 77024-3498 Tel. (713)686-4345 Fax (713)681-7550
Email: cahillb@stthom.edu
Website: www.diocese-gal-hou.org/education_stmarysseminary

St. Mary's Seminary and University† (Catholic Church), Robert F. Leavitt, President and Rector, 5400 Roland Ave., Baltimore, MD 21210 Tel. (410)864-4000 Fax (410)864-4278
Email: rleavitt@stmarys.edu
Website: www.stmarys.edu

Saint Meinrad School of Theology† (Catholic Church), Mark O'Keefe, President, 200 Hill Drive, St. Meinrad, IN 47577 Tel. (812)357-6611 Fax (812)357-6964
Email: theology@saintmeinrad.edu
Website: www.saintmeinrad.edu

St. Patrick's Seminary and University† (Catholic Church), Gerald L. Brown, President and Rector, 320 Middlefield Rd., Menlo Park, CA 94025 Tel. (650)325-5621 Fax (650)322-0997
Website: www.stpatricksseminary.org

Saint Paul School of Theology† (The United Methodist Church), Myron F. McCoy, President, 5123 Truman Rd., Kansas City, MO 64127-2499 Tel. (816)483-9600 Fax (816) 483-9605
Email: spst@spst.edu
Website: www.spst.edu

St. Paul Seminary School of Divinity of the University of St. Thomas† (Catholic Church), The Rev. Aloysius R. Callaghan, Rector and Vice-President, 2260 Summit Ave., St. Paul, MN 55105 Tel. (651)962-5050 Fax (651)962-5790
Email: jlubel@stthomas.edu
Website: www.stthomas.edu/spssod

St. Petersburg Theological Seminary‡ (Inter/Multidenominational), Myron P. Miller, President, 10830 Navajo Dr., St. Petersburg, FL 33708 Tel. (727)399-0276 Fax (727)399-1324
Email: sptseminary@tampabay.rr.com
Website: www.sptseminary.edu

St. Tikhon's Orthodox Theological Seminary† (The Orthodox Church in America), Metropolitan Herman (Swaiko), President and Very Rev. Michael G. Dahulich, Dean and Bishop Tikhon (Mollard), Rector, President, Box 130, St. Tikhon's Rd., South Canaan, PA 18459-0130 Tel. (570)937-4411 Fax (570) 937-3100
Email: info@stots.edu (General Information)
fr.michael@stots.edu (Dean's Office)
admissions@stots.edu (Admissions)
acadean@stots.edu (Academic Dean)
Website: www.stots.edu

St. Vincent de Paul Regional Seminary† (Catholic Church), Msgr. Keith R. Brennan, Rector and President, 10701 South Military Trail, Boynton Beach, FL 33436-4899 Tel. (561)732-4424 Fax (561)737-2205
Email: Kbrennan@svdp.edu
Website: www.svdp.edu

St. Vincent Seminary† (Catholic Church), Very Rev. Kurt Belsole, O.S.B., Rector, 300 Fraser Purchase Rd., Latrobe, PA 15650-2690 Tel. (724)537-4592 Fax (724)532-5052
Email: kurt.belsole@email.stvincent.edu
Website: benedictine.stvincent.edu/seminary

St. Vladimir's Orthodox Theological Seminary† (The Orthodox Church in America), John Behr, Dean, 575 Scarsdale Rd., Crestwood, NY 10707-1699 Tel. (914)961-8313 Fax (914) 961-4507
Email: info@svots.edu
Website: www.svots.edu

SS. Cyril and Methodius Seminary† (Catholic Church), Very Rev. Charles G Kosanke, Rector, 3535 Indian Trail, Orchard Lake, MI 48324-1623 Tel. (248)683-0310 Fax (248)738-6735
Email: info@sscms.edu
Website: www.sscms.edu

Samuel DeWitt Proctor School of Theology of Virginia Union University† (American Baptist Churches in the USA, National Baptist Convention, Progressive National Baptist Convention), John W. Kinney, Dean, 1500 North Lombardy Street, Richmond, VA 23330 Tel. (804)257-5715 Fax (804)342-3911
Email: JWKinney@vuu.edu
Website: www.vuu.edu

San Diego Christian College (Southern Baptist), 2100 Greenfield Drive, El Cajon, CA 92019 Tel. (619)441-2200 Fax (619)440-0209
Email: chcadm@christianheritage.edu
Website: www.christianheritage.edu

San Francisco Theological Seminary† (Presbyterian Church [USA]), Rev. Philip W. Butin, President, 105 Seminary Rd., San Anselmo, CA 94960 Tel. (415)451-2800 Fax (415)451-2811
Email: sftsinfo@sfts.edu
Website: www.sfts.edu

Savonarola Theological Seminary (Polish National Catholic Church of America), Most Rev. Robert M. Nemkovich, Prime Bishop, Rector, 1031 Cedar Ave., Scranton, PA 18505 Tel. (570)343-0100
Email: pncccenter@adelphia.net

Seabury-Western Theological Seminary† (Episcopal Church), The Very Rev. Gary Hall, Dean and President, 2122 Sheridan Rd., Evanston, IL 60201-2976 Tel. (847)328-9300 Fax (847)328-9624
Email: seabury@seabury.edu
Website: www.seabury.edu

Seattle University School of Theology and Ministry† (Catholic Church and 10 Mainline Protestant Denominations and Associations), Mark S Markuly, Dean, 901 12th Avenue, PO Box 222000, Seattle, WA 98122-1090 Tel. (206) 296-5330 Fax (206)296-5329
Email: sueh@seattleu.edu
Website: www.seattleu.edu/theomin

Seminario Evangelico de Puerto Rico (Inter-denominational), Samuel Pagán, President, 776 Ponce de León Ave., San Juan, PR 00925 Tel. (787)763-6700 Fax (787)751-0847
Email: drspagan@icepr.com, jvaldes@tld.net
Website: netministries.org/see/charmin/CM01399

Seminary of the Immaculate Conception† (Catholic Church), Msgr. Francis J. Schneider, J.C.D., Rector/President, 440 West Neck Rd., Huntington, NY 11743 Tel. (631)423-0483 Fax (631)423-2346
Email: eluckstone@icseminary.edu
Website: www.icseminary.edu

Seventh-day Adventist Theological Seminary of Andrews University† (Seventh-Day Adventist Church), Dennis Fortin, Dean, Andrews University, Berrien Springs, MI 49104-1500 Tel. (269)471-3537 Fax (269)471-6202
Email: seminary@andrews.edu
Website: www.andrews.edu/sem

Seventh Day Baptist School of Ministry (Seventh Day Baptist General Conference USA and Canada Ltd.), Gordon P. Lawton, Dean of School of Ministry, 3120 Kennedy Rd., P.O. Box 1678, Janesville, WI 53547 Tel. (608)752-5055 Fax (608)752-7711
Email: Com@sdbministry.org,
Website: sdbministry.org

Sewanee: The University of the South School of Theology† (Episcopal Church), The Very Rev. William S. Stafford, Dean, 335 Tennessee Ave., Sewanee, TN 37383-0001 Tel. (800)722-1974 Fax (931)598-1412
Email: theology@sewanee.edu
Website: www.theology.sewanee.edu

Shasta Bible College and Graduate School‡ (Baptist), David Nicholas, President, 2951 Goodwater Avenue, Redding, CA 96002 Tel. (530)221-4275 Fax (530)221-6929
Email: sbcadm@shasta.edu
Website: www.shasta.edu

Shaw University Divinity School† (General Baptist State Convention, N.C.; American Baptist Churches), James T. Roberson, Jr., Dean, PO Box 2090, Raleigh, NC 27602 Tel. (919)546-8569 Fax (919)546-8571
Email: JTRob@ShawU.edu
Website: www.shawuniversity.edu

Simpson College (The Christian and Missionary Alliance), James M. Grant, President, 2211 College View Dr., Redding, CA 96003 Tel. (916)224-5600 Fax (916)224-5608
Email: rerickson@simpsonuniversity.edu
Website: www.simpsonuniversity.edu

Sioux Falls Seminary† (North American Baptist Conference), G. Michael Hagan, President, 1525 S. Grange Ave., Sioux Falls, SD 57105-1526 Tel. (605)336-6588 Fax (605)335-9090
Email: shandas@sfseminary.edu
Website: www.sfseminary.edu

Southeastern Baptist College (Baptist Missionary Association of America), Medrick Savell, Interim President, 4229 Highway 15N, Laurel, MS 39440 Tel. (601)426-6346 Fax (601)426-6347
Email: info@southeasternbaptist.edu
Website: www.southeasternbaptist.edu

Southeastern Baptist Theological Seminary† (Southern Baptist Convention), Daniel L. Akin, President, PO Box 1889, Wake Forest, NC 27588-1889 Tel. (919)556-3101 Fax (919)556-8550
Email: president@sebts.edu
Website: www.sebts.edu

Southeastern Bible College (Interdenominational), Don Hawkins, President, 2545 Valleyvale Rd., Birmingham, AL 35244 Tel. (205)408-7073 or (205)970-9200 Fax (205) 970-9207
Email: President@sebc.edu
Website: www.sebc.edu

Southeastern University (Assemblies of God), Mark Rutland, President, 1000 Longfellow Blvd., Lakeland, FL 33801 Tel. (863)667-5000 Fax (863)667-5200
Email: info@seuniversity.edu
Website: www.seuniversity.edu

Southern Baptist Theological Seminary† (Southern Baptist Convention), R. Albert Mohler, Jr., President, 2825 Lexington Rd., Louisville, KY 40280- Tel. (502)897-4011 Fax (502)899-1770
Email: communications@sbts.edu
Website: www.sbts.edu

Southern California Seminary (Southern Baptist Convention), Gary F. Coombs, President, 2075 East Madison Avenue, El Cajon, CA 92019 Tel. (619)442-9841 or (619)590-2128 Fax (619)442-4510
Email: eherrelko@socalsem.edu
Website: www.socalsem.edu

Southern Evangelical Seminary†‡ (Inter-denominational), Dr. Norman Geisler, President, 3000 Tilley Morris Road, Matthews, NC 28104 Tel. (704)847-5600 Fax (704)845-1747
Email: ses@ses.edu
Website: www.ses.edu

Southern Methodist College‡ (Southern Methodist Church), The Rev. Gary Briden,

President, 541 Broughton Street PO Box 1027, Orangeburg, SC 29116-1027 Tel. (803)534-7826 Fax (803)534-7827
Email: smcinfo@smcollege.edu
Website: www.smcollege.edu

Southern Wesleyan University (The Wesleyan Church), President David J. Spittal, President, 907 Wesleyan Dr., P.O. Box 1020, Central, SC 29630-1020 Tel. (864)644-5000 Fax (864) 644-5900
Email: dspittal@swu.edu
Website: www.swu.edu

Southwestern Assemblies of God University (Assemblies of God), Kermit S. Bridges, President, 1200 Sycamore St., Waxahachie, TX 75165 Tel. (972)937-4010 Fax (972)923-0488
Email: president@sagu.edu
Website: www.sagu.edu

Southwestern Baptist Theological Seminary† (Southern Baptist Convention), Paige Patterson, President, 2001 W. Seminary Dr., Fort Worth, TX 76115 Tel. (817)923-1921 Fax (817)923-0610
Email: ppatterson@swbts.edu
Website: www.swbts.edu

Southwestern College (Conservative Baptist Association of America), Brent D. Garrison, President, 2625 E. Cactus Rd., Phoenix, AZ 85032 Tel. (602)992-6101 Fax (602)404-2159
Email: swc@swcaz.edu
Website: www.southwesterncollege.edu

Starr King School for the Ministry† (Unitarian Universalist Association), Rebecca Parker, President, 2441 LeConte Ave., Berkeley, CA 94709 Tel. (510)845-6232 Fax (510)845-6273
Email: rparker@sksm.edu; starrking@sksm.edu
Website: www.sksm.edu

Swedenborgian House of Studies at the Pacific School of Religion (The Swedenborgian Church), James F. Lawrence, Dean, 1798 Scenic Ave., Berkeley, CA 94709 Tel. (510)849-8228 Fax (510)849-8296
Email: jlawrence@shs.psr.edu
Website: www.shs.psr.edu

Talbot School of Theology of Biola University† (Inter/Multidenominational), Barry H. Corey, President, 13800 Biola Ave., La Mirada, CA 90639-0001 Tel. (562)903-4816 Fax (562)903-4759
Email: talbot.receptionist@biola.edu
Website: www.talbot.edu

Temple Baptist Seminary‡ (Interdenominational), Barkev Trachian, President, 1815 Union Ave., Chattanooga, TN 37404 Tel. (423)493-4221 Fax (423)493-4471

313

Email: tbsinfo@templebaptistseminary.edu
Website: www.templebaptistseminary.edu

Tennessee Temple University‡ President, 1815 Union Avenue, Chattanooga, TN 37404 Tel. (423)493-4202 Fax (423)493-4114
Email: ttuinfo@tntemple.edu
Website: www.tntemple.edu

Theological School of the Protestant Reformed Churches (Protestant Reformed Churches in America), David J. Engelsma, President, 4949 Ivanrest Ave., Grandville, MI 49418 Tel. (616)531-1490 Fax (616)531-3033
Email: doezema@prca.org
Website: www.prca.org/seminary

Toccoa Falls College (The Christian and Missionary Alliance), W. Wayne Gardner, President, P.O. Box 800777, Toccoa Falls, GA 30598 Tel. (706)886-6831 Fax (706)282-6005
Email: president@tfc.edu
Website: www.tfc.edu

Trevecca Nazarene University (Church of the Nazarene), Millard Reed, President, 333 Murfreesboro Rd., Nashville, TN 37210-2877 Tel. (615)248-1200 Fax (615)248-7728
Email: mlanden@trevecca.edu
Website: www.trevecca.edu

Trinity Baptist College‡ (Baptist), Tom Messer, Pastor, 800 Hammond Boulevard, Jacksonville, FL 32221 Tel. (904)596-2400 Fax (904)596-2531
Email: trinity@tbc.edu
Website: www.tbc.edu

Trinity Bible College (Assemblies of God), Dennis D. Niles, President, 50 S. 6th Ave., Ellendale, ND 58436 Tel. (701)349-3621, (800)523-1603 Fax (701)349-5443
Email: president@trinitybiblecollege.edu
Website: www.trinitybiblecollege.edu

Trinity College of Florida (Nondenominational), Mark T. O'Farrell, President, 2430 Welbilt Blvd., New Port Richey, FL 34655-4401 Tel. (727)376-6911 Fax (727)376-0781
Email: admissions@trinitycollege.edu
Website: www.trinitycollege.edu

Trinity Episcopal School for Ministry† (Episcopal Church), The Very Rev. Dr. Paul F.M. Zahl, Dean and President, 311 Eleventh St., Ambridge, PA 15003 Tel. (724)266-3838 Fax (724)266-4617
Email: tesm@tesm.edu
Website: www.tesm.edu

Trinity Evangelical Divinity School of Trinity International University† (Evangelical Free Church of America), Jeanette Hsieh, Interim President, 2065 Half Day Rd., Deerfield, IL 60015 Tel. (847)45-8800 Fax (847)317-8141
Email: gwaybrig@tiu.edu
Website: www.tiu.edu/divinity

Trinity Lutheran College (Interdenominational-Lutheran), John M. Stamm, President, 4221 - 228th Ave., S.E., Issaquah, WA 98029-9299 Tel. (425)392-0400 Fax (425)392-0404
Email: info@tlc.edu, sconner@tlc.edu
Website: www.tlc.edu

Trinity Lutheran Seminary† (Evangelical Lutheran Church in America), Mark R. Ramseth, President, 2199 East Main Street, Columbus, OH 43209-2334 Tel. (614)235-4136 Fax (614)238-0263
Email: mramseth@TrinityLutheranSeminary.edu
Website: www.TrinityLutheranSeminary.edu

Turner School Of Theology of Regions University† (Churches of Christ), Rex A. Turner, Jr., President, 1200 Taylor Rd., Montgomery, AL 36117-3553 Tel. (334)387-3877 Fax (334)387-3878
Email: rexturner@regionsuniversity.edu
Website: www.regionsuniversity.edu

Union Theological Seminary† (Inter/Multidenominational), Joseph C. Hough, Jr., President, 3041 Broadway at 121st Street, New York, NY 10027-0003 Tel. (212)662-7100 Fax (212)280-1440
Email: cbaker@uts.columbia.edu
Website: www.utsnyc.edu

Union Theological Seminary and Presbyterian School of Christian Education (Union-PSCE)† (Presbyterian Church [USA]), Brian K. Blount, President, 3401 Brook Rd., Richmond, VA 23227 Tel. (800)229-2990 Fax (804)355-3919
Email: gbirch@union-psce.edu
Website: www.union-psce.edu

United Theological Seminary† (The United Methodist Church), Rev. G. Edwin Zeiders, President and Chief Exec. Officer, 4501 Denlinger Rd, Dayton, OH 45426 Tel. (937)278-5817 Fax (937)278-1218
Email: utscom@united.edu
Website: www.united.edu

United Theological Seminary of the Twin Cities† (United Church of Christ), Kita McVay, President, 3000 Fifth St. N.W., New Brighton, MN 55112 Tel. (651)633-4311 Fax (651)633-4315
Email: general@unitedseminary-mn.org
Website: www.unitedseminary-mn.org

University of Chicago Divinity School† (Interdenominational), Richard A. Rosengarten,

314

Dean, 1025 E. 58th St., Chicago, IL 60637 Tel. (773)702-8221 Fax (773)702-6048
Email: raroseng@midway.uchicago.edu
Website: www.uchicago.edu/divinity

University of Dubuque Theological Seminary† (Presbyterian Church [USA]), Jeffrey Bullock, President, 2000 University Ave., Dubuque, IA 52001-5099 Tel. (563)589-3122 Fax (563) 589-3110
Email: udtsadms@dbq.edu
Website: www.UDTSeminary.net

University of Notre Dame Department of Theology† (Catholic Church), John C. Cavadini, Department Chair, 130 Malloy Hall, Notre Dame, IN 46556-5639 Tel. (574)631-6662 Fax (574)631-4291
Email: Cavadini.1@nd.edu
Website: www.nd.edu/‡theo

University of St. Mary of the Lake Mundelein Seminary† (Catholic Church), Dennis J. Lyle, Rector and President, 1000 E. Maple Avenue, Mundelein, IL 60060 Tel. (847)566-6401 Fax (847)566-7330
Email: LZubert@usml.edu
Website: www.usml.edu

University of St. Thomas School of Theology at St. Mary's Seminary† (Catholic Church), Sandra Magie, Dean, 9845 Memorial Dr., Houston, TX 77024 Tel. (713)686-4345 Fax (713)683-8673
Email: sms@stthom.edu
Website: www.stthom.edu/stmary

Urshan Graduate School of Theology† (United Pentecostal Church International), David Bernard, President, 704 Howdershell Road, Florissant, MO 63031 Tel. (314)921-9290 Fax (314) 921-9203
Email: info@ugst.org
Website: www.ugst.org

Valley Forge Christian College (Assemblies of God), Don Meyer, President, 1401 Charlestown Rd., Phoenixville, PA 19460 Tel. (610)935-0450 Fax (610)935-9353
Email: admissions@vfcc.edu
Website: www.vfcc.edu

Vanderbilt University Divinity School† (Inter/Multidenominational), James Hudnut-Beumler, Dean, 411 21st Av. So., Nashville, TN 37240 Tel. (615)322-2776 Fax (615)343-9957
Email: james.hudnut-beumler@vanderbilt.edu
Website: divinity.lib.vanderbilt.edu/vds/vds-home

Vennard College (Interdenominational), Bruce Moyer, President, Box 29, University Park, IA 52595 Tel. (641)673-8391 Fax (641) 673-8365

Email: bruce.moyer@vennard.edu
Website: www.vennard.edu

Virginia Union University (School of Theology) (American Baptist Churches in the USA, National Baptist Convention, USA, Inc., Progressive National Baptist Convention, Inc., Lott Carey), John W. Kinney, Dean, 1500 N. Lombardy St., Richmond, VA 23220 Tel. (804)257-5715 Fax (804)342-3911
Email: JWKinney@vuu.edu
Website: www.vuu.edu/theology

Wake Forest University Divinity School† (Inter/Multidenominational), Bill J. Leonard, Dean, P.O. Box 7719, Winston-Salem, NC 27109-7719 Tel. (336)758-5121 Fax (336) 758-4316
Website: www.wfu.edu

Walla Walla College (School of Theology) (Seventh-day Adventist Church), Jon Dybdahl, President, 204 S. College Ave., College Place, WA 99324-1198 Tel. (509)527-2194 Fax (509)527-2253
Email: dybdjo@wwc.edu
Website: www.wwc.edu

Wartburg Theological Seminary† (Evangelical Lutheran Church in America), Duane H. Larson, President, 333 Wartburg Pl., P.O. Box 5004, Dubuque, IA 52004-5004 Tel. (563)589-0200 Fax (563)589-0333
Email: mailbox@wartburgseminary.edu
Website: www.wartburgseminary.edu

Washington Baptist College and Seminary† (Baptist), Jacob S. Shin, President, 4300 Evergreen Lane, Annandale, VA 22003 Tel. (703)333-5904 Fax (703)333-5906
Website: www.wbcs.edu

Washington Theological Consortium (Non-denominational), The Rev. John W. Crossin, O.S.F.S., Executive Director, 487 Michigan Ave. N.E., Washington, DC 20017 Tel. (202) 832-2675 Fax (202)526-0818
Email: wtc@washtheocon.org
Website: www.washtheocon.org

Washington Theological Union† (Catholic Church), Louis Iasiello, President, 6896 Laurel St. N.W., Washington, DC 20012-2016 Tel. (202)726-8800 Fax (202)726-1716
Email: welch@wtu.edu
Website: www.wtu.edu

Wesley Biblical Seminary† (Interdenominational), Ronald E. Smith, President, PO Box 9938, Jackson, MS 39286-0938 Tel. (601)366-8880 Fax (601)366-8832
Email: rsmith@wbs.edu
Website: www.wbs.edu

315

Wesley Theological Seminary† (The United Methodist Church), David F. McAllister-Wilson, President, 4500 Massachusetts Ave. N.W., Washington, DC 20016-5690 Tel. (800)885-8600 or (800)882-4987 Fax (202) 885-8605
Email: caldridge@wesleysem.edu
Website: www.Wesleysem.edu

Western Seminary† (Conservative Baptist Association of America), Bert E. Downs, President, 5511 S.E. Hawthorne Blvd., Portland, OR 97215 Tel. (877)517-1800 or (503)517-1800 Fax (503)517-1801
Email: admiss@westernseminary.edu
Website: westernseminary.edu

Western Theological Seminary† (Reformed Church in America), Dennis N. Voskuil, President, 101 E. 13th St., Holland, MI 49423 Tel. (616)392-8555 Fax (616)392-7717
Email: dennis@westernsem.edu
Website: www.westernsem.edu

Westminster Theological Seminary† (various Reformed), Peter A. Lillback, President, Chestnut Hill, P.O. Box 27009, Philadelphia, PA 19118 Tel. (215)887-5511 Fax (215)887-5404
Email: admissions@wts.edu
Website: www.wts.edu

Westminster Seminary California† (Non-denominational), W. Robert Godfrey, President, 1725 Bear Valley Pkwy, Escondido, CA 92027-4128 Tel. (760)480-8474 Fax (760)480-0252
Email: info@wscal.edu
Website: www.wscal.edu

Weston Jesuit School of Theology† (Catholic Church), Robert Manning, President, 3 Phillips Place, Cambridge, MA 02138-3495 Tel. (617)492-1960 Fax (617)492-5833
Email: Admissionsinfo@wjst.edu
Website: www.wjst.edu

William Jessup University (Christian Churches and Churches of Christ), Bryce L. Jessup, D.D., President, 333 Sunset Blvd., Rocklin, CA 95765 Tel. (916)577-2210 Fax (916)577-2213
Email: bjessup@jessup.edu
Website: www.jessup.edu

William Tyndale College (Interdenominational), Robert E. Hagerty, President, 35700 W. Twelve Mile Rd., Farmington Hills, MI 48331 Tel. (248)553-7200 Fax (248)553-5963
Website: www.williamtyndale.edu

Williamson Christian College‡ (Non-Denominational), Ken Oosting, President, 200 Seaboard Lane, Franklin, TN 37067 Tel. (615)771-7821 Fax (615)771-7810
Email: info@williamsoncc.edu
Website: www.williamsoncc.edu

Winebrenner Theological Seminary† (Churches of God, General Conference), David E. Draper, President, 950 N. Main Street, Findlay, OH 45840 Tel. (419)434 4200 Fax (419)434 4267
Email: wts@winebrenner.edu
Website: www.winebrenner.edu

Wisconsin Lutheran Seminary (Wisconsin Evangelical Lutheran Synod), Paul O. Wendland, President, 11831 N. Seminary Dr., 65W, Mequon, WI 53092-1597 Tel. (262)242-8100 Fax (262)242-8110
Email: president@wls.wels.net
Website: www.wls.wels.net

Word of Life Bible Institute‡ (Non-Denominational), Joe Jordan, Chancellor, PO Box 129, 4200 Glendale Road, Pottersville, NY 12860 Tel. (518)494-4723 Fax (518)494-7474
Email: admissions@wol.org
Website: www.wol.org

Yale University Divinity School† (Inter/Multidenominational), Harold W. Attridge, Dean, 409 Prospect Sreet, New Haven, CT 06511-2167 Tel. (203)432-5303 Fax (203) 432-5356
Email: divinity.admissions@yale.edu
Website: www.yale.edu/divinity

9. Theological Seminaries and Bible Colleges in Canada

The following list includes theological seminaries and departments in colleges and universities in which ministerial training is provided. Many denominations have additional programs. The list has been developed from direct correspondence with the institutions. Inclusion in or exclusion from this list implies no judgment about the quality or accreditation of any institution. Those schools that are members of the Association of Theological Schools are marked with this symbol (†). Each of the listings include: the institution name, denominational sponsor when appropriate, location, the president or dean, telephone and fax numbers when known and email and website addresses when available.

Acadia Divinity College† (Convention of the Atlantic Baptist Church), Lee M. McDonald, Principal and Dean of the Faculty of Theology, 31 Horton Street, Wolfville, NS B4P 2R6 Tel. (866)875-8975 (902)585-2210 Fax (902)585-2233
Email: adcinfo@acadiau.ca
Website: adc.acadiau.ca

Alberta Bible College (Christian Churches and Churches of Christ in Canada), Ronald A. Fraser, President, 635 Northmount Dr. NW, Calgary, AB T2K 3J6 Tel. (877)542-9492 (403)282-2994 Fax (403)282-3084
Email: generalinquiries@abc-ca.org
Website: www.abc-ca.org

Ambrose University College (Church of the Nazarene Canada), Riley Coulter, President, 610, 833 4th Ave. SW, Calgary, AB T2P 3T5 Tel. (403)571-2550 Fax (403)571-2556
Email: wcampbell@auc-nuc.ca
Website: www.auc-nuc.ca

Arthur Turner Training School (The Anglican Church of Canada), Principal, Box 378, Pangnirtung, NU X0A 0R0 Tel. (867)873-5432 Fax (867)473-8375
Email: diocese@arcticnet.org

Associated Canadian Theological Schools of Trinity Western University† (Baptist General Conference of Canada, Evangelical Free Church of Canada, The Fellowship of Evangelical Baptist Churches in Canada, Christian and Missionary Alliance, Canadian Conference of Mennonite Brethren Churches), Dr. Phil Zylla, Principal, 7600 Glover Rd., Langley, BC V2Y 1Y1 Tel. (888)468-6898 (604)513-2044 Fax (604)513-2045
Email: acts@twu.ca
Website: www.acts.twu.ca

Atlantic School of Theology† (Interdenominational), The Rev. Canon Eric Beresford, President, 660 Francklyn St., Halifax, NS B3H 3B5 Tel. (902)423-6801 Fax (902)492-4048
Website: www.astheology.ns.ca

Bethany Bible College-Canada (The Wesleyan Church), David S. Medders, President, 26 Western St., Sussex, NB E4E 1E6 Tel. (506)432-4400 Fax (506)432-4425
Email: meddersd@bethany-ca.edu
Website: www.bethany-ca.edu

Bethany College (Canadian Conference of Mennonite Brethren Churches [Saskatchewan and Alberta Conferences]), Rick Schellenberg, President, Box 160, Hepburn, SK S0K 1Z0 Tel. (306)947-2175 Fax (306)947-4229
Email: info@bethany.sk.ca
Website: www.bethany.sk.ca

Briercrest Seminary† (Interdenominational), Dwayne Uglem, President, 510 College Dr., Caronport, SK S0H 0S0 Tel. (800)667-5199 Fax (306)756-5500
Email: admissions@briercrest.ca
Website: www.briercrest.ca

Canadian Bible College & Canadian Theological Seminary of Alliance University College† (Christian and Missionary Alliance in Canada), George Durance, President, 833-4th Avenue SW #630, Calgary, AB T2P 3T5 Tel. (403)410-2000 Fax (403)571-2556, Pres Email: gdurance@auc-nuc.ca
Email: Info: Info@aun-nuc.ca
Website: www.auc-nuc.ca

Canadian Lutheran Bible Institute (Lutheran), Pastor Harold Rust, President, 4837 52A St., Camrose, AB T4V 1W5 Tel. (780)672-4454 Fax (780)672-4455
Email: clbi@clbi.edu
Website: www.clbi.edu

Canadian Mennonite University (Mennonite Brethren Churches, Mennonite Church Canada), Gerald Gerbrandt, President, 500 Shaftesbury Blvd, Winnipeg, MB R3P 2N2 Tel. (204)487-3300 Fax (204)487-3858
Email: reception@cmu.ca
Website: www.cmu.ca

Canadian Southern Baptist Seminary† (Canadian Convention of Southern Baptists),

G. Richard Blackaby, President, 200 Seminary View, Cochrane, AB T4C 2G1 Tel. (877)922-2727 (403)932-6622 Fax (403)932-7049 Email: csbs@compuserve.com Website: www.csbs.edu

Carey Theological College† (Baptist Union of Western Canada), Brian F. Stelck, President, 5920 Iona Drive, Vancouver, BC V6T 1J6 Tel. (604)224-4308 Fax (604)224-5014 Website: www.careytheologicalcollege.ca

Central Pentecostal College, University of Saskatchewan (The Pentecostal Assemblies of Canada), D. Munk, Academic Dean, 1303 Jackson Ave., Saskatoon, SK S7H 2M9 Tel. (306)374-6655 Fax (306)373-6968 Email: admissions@cpc-paoc.edu Website: www.cpc-paoc.edu

Centre for Christian Studies (The Anglican Church of Canada, The United Church of Canada), Caryn Douglas, Principal, 60 Maryland, Winnipeg, MB R3G 1K7 Tel. (204)783-4490 Fax (204)786-3012 Email: info@ccsonline.ca Website: www.ccsonline.ca

College Biblique Québec (The Pentecostal Assemblies of Canada), William Raccah, President, 740 Lebourgneuf, Ste. 100, Ancienne Lorette, QC G2J 1E2 Tel. (418)622-7552 Fax (418)622-1470 Email: mlecompte@ibq-canada.org Website: http://www.ibq-canada.org/

Collège Dominicain de Philosophie et de Théologie (The Roman Catholic Church in Canada), Gabor Csepregi, President, 96 Avenue Empress, Ottawa, ON K1R 7G3 Tel. (613)233-5696 Fax (613)233-6064 Email: service.accueil@collegedominicain.ca Website: www.collegedominicain.ca

College of Emmanuel and St. Chad (The Anglican Church of Canada), Walter Deller, Principal, 114 Seminary Crescent, Saskatoon, SK S7N 0X3 Tel. (306)975-3753 Fax (306)934-2683 Email: emmanuel.stchad@usask.ca Website: www.usask.ca/stu/emmanuel

Columbia Bible College (BC Conference of Mennonite Brethren Churches & Mennonite Church in BC), Dr. Ron Penner, President, 2940 Clearbrook Rd., Abbotsford, BC V2T 2Z8 Tel. (604)853-3358 Fax (604)853-3063 Email: info@columbiabc.edu Website: www.columbiabc.edu

Concordia Lutheran Seminary† (Lutheran Church-Canada), Edward G. Kettner, President, 7040 Ada Blvd., Edmonton, AB T5B 4E3 Tel. (780)474-1468 Fax (780)479-3067

Email: info@concordiasem.ab.ca Website: www.concordiasem.ab.ca

Concordia Lutheran Theological Seminary† (Lutheran Church-Canada), Harald Tomesch, President, 470 Glenridge Ave., St. Catharines, ON L2T 4C3 Tel. (905)688-2362 Fax (905) 688-9744 Email: concordia@brocku.ca Website: www.brocku.ca/concordiaseminary

Covenant Bible College (The Evangelical Covenant Church of Canada), President, 630 Westchester Road, Strathmore, AB T1P 1H8 Tel. (403)934-6200 Fax (403)934-6220 Email: office@covenantbiblecollege.ab.ca, cbc @covbibcolorado.edu Website: www.covenantbiblecollege.ab.ca

Ecole de Theologie Evangelique de Montreal (Canadian Conference of Mennonite Brethren Churches), Eric Wingender, President, 1775, boul Édouard-Laurin, Ville Saint-Laurent, QC H4L 2B9 Tel. (514)331-0878 Fax (514)331-0879 Email: iblinstitute@proxyma.net

Emmanuel Bible College (The Evangelical Missionary Church of Canada), Thomas E. Dow, President, 100 Fergus Ave., Kitchener, ON N2A 2H2 Tel. (519)894-8900 Fax (519) 894-5331 Email: dmin@ebcollege.on.ca Website: www.ebcollege.on.ca

Emmanuel College of Victoria University† (The United Church of Canada), The Rev. Peter Wyatt, Principal, 75 Queens Park Crescent East, Toronto, ON M5S 1K7 Tel. (416)585-4539 Fax (416)585-4516 Email: ec.office@utoronto.ca Website: vicu.utoronto.ca

Faculté De Théologie Évangélique (Interdenominational), Amar Djaballah, President, 2285 Avenue Papineau, Montréal, QC H2K 4J5 Tel. (514)526-2003 Fax (514)526-6887 Email: reg@fteacadia.ca Website: www.fteacadia.ca

Faith Alive Bible College (Nondenominational), David Pierce, President, 637 University Dr., Saskatoon, SK S7N 0H8 Tel. (306)652-2230 Fax (306)665-1125 Email: faithalive@dlcwest.com

Full Gospel Bible Institute (Apostolic Church of Pentecost of Canada Inc.), Rev. Lauren E. Miller, President, Box 579, Eston, SK S0L 1A0 Tel. (306)962-3621 Fax (306)962-3810 Email: fgbi@fgbi.sk.ca Website: fgbi.sk.ca

Gardner College, A Centre for Christian Studies (Church of God (Anderson, Ind.)), John Alan Howard, President, 4707 56th St., Camrose, AB T4V 2C4 Tel. (780)672-0171 Fax (780)672-2465
Email: gardnercollege@gardnercollege.org
Website: www.gardnercollege.org

Grand Seminaire de Montréal† (The Roman Catholic Church in Canada), Monsg. Lionel Gendron.p.s.s., President, 2065 Sherbrooke Ouest, Montréal, QC H3H 1G6 Tel. (514)935-1169 Fax (514)935-5497
Email Information Generale: info@gsdm.qc.ca or Bibliotheque: biblio@gsdm.qc.ca
Website: www.gsdm.qc.ca

Great Lakes Bible College (Churches of Christ in Canada), J. Arthur Ford, President, 470 Glenelm Crescent, Waterloo, ON N2L 5C8 Tel. (519)884-4310 Fax (519)884-4412
Email: learn@glbc.on.ca
Website: www.glbc.on.ca

Heritage Theological Seminary† Marvin R. Brubacher, President, 175 Holiday Inn Dr., Cambridge, ON N3C 3T2 Tel. (519)651-2869 or (800)465-1961 Fax (519)651-2870
Email: recruitment@heritage-theo.edu
Website: www.DiscoverHeritage.ca

Huron University College Faculty of Theology† (The Anglican Church of Canada), Ramona Lumpkin, Principal, 1349 Western Rd., London, ON N6G 1H3 Tel. (519)438-7224 Fax (519)438-9981
Email: huron@uwo.ca
Website: www.huronuc.on.ca

Institut Biblique Beree (The Pentecostal Assemblies of Canada), André L. Gagnon, President, 1711 Est Boul. Henri-Bourassa, Montréal, QC H2C 1J5 Tel. (514)385-4238 Fax (514)385-4238
Email: mlecompte@ibq-canada.org
Website: http://www.ibq-canada.org

Institute for Christian Studies (Nondenominational), Harry Fernhout, President, 229 College St., Suite 200, Toronto, ON M5T 1R4 Tel. (416)979-2331 or (888)326-5347 Fax (416)979-2332
Email: email@icscanada.edu
Website: www.icscanada.edu

International Bible College (Church of God (Cleveland, Tenn.)), Cheryl Busse, President, 401 Trinity La., Moose Jaw, SK S6H 0E3 Tel. (306)692-4041 Fax (306)692-7968
Email: ibc@cofg.net
Website: www.ibc.cofg.net

Key-Way-Tin Bible Institute (Nondenominational), Jon Siebert, Administrator, Site 633 Comp 8 RR1, Lac La Biche, AB T0A 2C1 Tel. (780)623-4565 Fax (780)623-1788
Email: kbi@telus.net
Website: www.keywaytinbibleinstitute.org

Knox College† (The Presbyterian Church in Canada), J. Dorcas Gordon, Principal, 59 St. George St., Toronto, ON M5S 2E6 Tel. (416)978-4500 Fax (416)971-2133
Email: knox.college@utoronto.ca
Website: www.utoronto.ca/knox

Living Faith Bible College (Fellowship of Christian Assemblies (Canada)), Rev. David R. Wills, President, Box 100, Caroline, AB T0M 0M0 Tel. (403)722-2225, (800)838-2975 Fax (403)722-2459
Email: office@lfbc.net
Website: www.lfbc.net

Lutheran Theological Seminary† (Evangelical Lutheran Church in Canada), Kevin A. Ogilvie, President, 114 Seminary Crescent, Saskatoon, SK S7N 0X3 Tel. (306)966-7850 Fax (306)966-7852
Email: lutheran.seminary@usask.ca
Website: www.usask.ca/stu/luther

Maritime Christian College (Christian Churches and Churches of Christ), Fred C. Osborne, President, 503 University Ave., Charlottetown, PE C1A 7Z4 Tel. (902)628-8887 Fax (902)892-3959
Email: registrar@maritimechristiancollege.pe.ca
Website: www.maritimechristiancollege.pe.ca

Master's College and Seminary (The Pentecostal Assemblies of Canada), Rev. David Hazzard, President, 3080 Yonge St., Box 70, Suite 3040, Toronto, ON M4N 3N1 Tel. (416)482-2224 Fax (416)482-7004
Email: info@mcs.edu
Website: www.mcs.edu

McGill University Faculty of Religious Studies† (Interdenominational), B. Barry Levy, Dean, 3520 University St., Montréal, QC H3A 2A7 Tel. (514)398-4125 Fax (514) 398-6665
Website: www.mcgill.ca/religiousstudies

McMaster Divinity College† (Baptist Convention of Ontario and Quebec (BCOQ)), Stanley E. Porter, Principal/Dean, 1280 Main St. West, Hamilton, ON L8S 4K1 Tel. (905)525-9140 x24401 Fax (905)577-4782
Email: divinity@mcmaster.ca
Website: www.macdiv.ca

Millar College of the Bible (Interdenominational), A. Brian Atmore, President, Box 25, Pambrun, SK S0N 1W0 Tel. (306)582-2033 Fax (306)582-2027

319

Montreal Diocesan Theological College (The Anglican Church of Canada), Bishop of Montreal, President, 3473 University St., Montreal, QC H3A 2A8 Tel. (514)849-3004 Fax (514)849-4113
Email: diocoll@netrover.com
Website: www.montreal.anglican.org/mdtc

Montreal School of Theology† (Inter/ Multidenominational), Philip Joudrey, Administrative Officer, 3473 University St., Montréal, QC H3A 2A8 Tel. (514)849-8511 Fax (514)849-4113
Email: pjoudrey@utc.ca
Website: www.mst-etm.ca

Mount Carmel Bible School (Transdenominational), Wayne Tomalty, President, 4725 106 Ave., Edmonton, AB T6A 1E7 Tel. (780)465-3015 Toll-free 1(800) 561-6443 Fax (780)466-2485
Email: mail@mountcarmel.net
Website: www.mountcarmel.net

National Native Bible College (Elim Fellowship of Evangelical Churches and Ministers), Michael Hart, College Director, Box 478, Deseronto, ON K0K 1X0 Tel. (613) 396-2311 Fax

Newman Theological College† (The Catholic Church in Canada), Rev. John (Jack) Gallagher, President, 15611 St. Albert Trail, Edmonton, AB T6V 1H3 Tel. (780)447-2993 Fax (780)447-2685
Email: patricia.hauck@newman.edu
Website: www.newman.edu

Nipawin Bible Institute (Interdenominational), Mr. Wes Fehr, Acting President, Box 1986, Nipawin, SK S0E 1E0 Tel. (306)862-5095 Fax (306)862-3651
Email: info@nipawin.org
Website: www.nipawin.org

Northwest Baptist Theological College and Seminary† (The Fellowship of Evangelical Baptist Churches of Canada), Larry Perkins, President, 7600 Glover Rd., Langley, BC V2Y 1Y1 Tel. (604)888-7592 Fax (604) 513-8511
Email: nbs@twu.ca
Website: www.nbseminary.com

Ontario Christian Seminary (Christian Churches and Churches of Christ in Canada), James R. Cormode, President, 260 High Park Ave., Toronto, ON M6P 3J9 Tel. (416)769-7115 Fax (416)769-7047

Pacific Life Bible College (Foursquare), Rob Buzza, President, 15100 66 A Ave., Surrey, BC V3S 2A6 Tel. (604)597-9082 Fax (604)597-9090

Email: paclife@pacificlife.edu
Website: www.pacificlife.edu

Parole de Vie Bethel/Word of Life Bethel (Nondenominational), Mark Strout, Director, 1175, ch. Woodward, Lennoxville, QC J1M 2A2 Tel. (819)823-8435 Fax (819)823-2468
Email: quebec@pdvb.org
Website: www.pdvb.org

Peace River Bible Institute (Interdenominational), Wladie Neufeld, President, Box 99, Sexsmith, AB T0H 3C0 Tel. (780)568-3962 Fax (780)568-4431
Email: prbi@prbi.edu
Website: www.prbi.edu

Prairie Graduate School (Interdenominational), Dr. Charlotte Kinvig Bates, Co-President, 330 6th Ave., Three Hills, AB T0M 2N0 Tel. (403)443-5511 Fax (403)443-5540
Email: prairie@prairie.edu
Website: www.pbi.ab.ca

The Presbyterian College, Montreal† (Presbyterian Church in Canada), John Vissers, Principal, 3495 University St., Montreal, QC H3A 2A8 Tel. (514)288-5256 Fax (514)288-8072
Email: info@presbyteriancollege.ca
Website: www.presbyteriancollege.ca

Providence College and Theological Seminary† (Inter/Multidenominational), August H. Konkel, President, General Delivery, Otterburne, MB R0A 1G0 Tel. (204)433-7488 Fax (204)433-7158
Email: info@prov.ca
Website: www.prov.ca

Queens College Faculty of Theology† (The Anglican Church of Canada), John Mellis, President, 210 Prince Phillip Dr. Suite 3000, St. Johns, NF A1B 3R6 Tel. (709)753-0116 Fax (709)753-1214
Email: queens@mun.ca
Website: www.mun.ca/queens

Queen's Theological College† (The United Church of Canada), M. Jean Stairs, Principal, Room 212 Theological Hall, Kingston, ON K7L 3N6 Tel. (613)533-2110 Fax (613)533-6879
Email: theology@queensu.ca
Website: www.queensu.ca/theology

Reformed Episcopal Theological College (The Reformed Episcopal Church of Canada), Rt. Rev. Michael Fedechko, President, PO Box 2532, Hwy 11 North, New Liskeard, ON P0J 1P0 Tel. (705)647-4565 Fax (705)647-4565
Email: fed@nt.net
Website: www.retcc.com

Reformed Episcopal Theological College (Reformed Episcopal Church of Canada), Rt. Rev. Michael Fedechko, President, 320 Armstrong St., Box 2532, New Liskeard, ON P0J 1P0 Tel. (705)647-4565 Fax (705)647-4565
Email: fed@nt.net
Website: www.retcc.com

Regent College† (Interdenominational), Rod Wilson, President, 5800 University Blvd., Vancouver, BC V6T 2E4 Tel. (800)663-8664 or (604)224-3245 Fax (604)224-3097
Email: administration@regent-college.edu
Website: www.regent-college.edu

Regis College† (The Roman Catholic Church in Canada), Joseph G. Schner, S.J, President, 15 St. Mary St., Toronto, ON M4Y 2R5 Tel. (416)922-5474 Fax (416)922-2898
Email: regis.registrar@utoronto.ca
Website: www.regiscollege.ca

Rocky Mountain College, Centre for Biblical Studies (The Evangelical Missionary Church of Canada), Gordon Dirks, President, 4039 Brentwood Rd. NW, Calgary, AB T2L 1L1 Tel. (403)284-5100 Fax (403)220-9567
Email: admissions@rockymountaincollege.ca
Website: www.rockymountaincollege.ca

St. Andrew's College† (The United Church of Canada), Laura Balas, Actin Interim President, 1121 College Dr., Saskatoon, SK S7N 0W3 Tel. (306)966-8970, (877)644-8970 Fax (306)966-8981
Email: laura.balas@usask.ca
Website: www.standrews.ca

St. Augustine's Seminary of Toronto† (The Roman Catholic Church in Canada), Rev. Msgr. A. Robert Nusca, President and Rector, 2661 Kingston Rd., Toronto, ON M1M 1M3 Tel. (416)261-7207 Fax (416)261-2529
Email: info@staugustines.on.ca
Website: www.staugustines.on.ca

St. John's College, Univ. of Manitoba, Faculty of Theology (The Anglican Church of Canada), Janet A. Hoskins, Warden & Vice Chancellor, 92 Dysart Rd., Winnipeg, MB R3T 2M5 Tel. (204)474-8531 Fax (204)474-7610
Email: stjohns_college@umanitoba.ca
Website: www.umanitoba.ca/colleges/st_johns

Saint Paul University, Faculty of Theology (The Roman Catholic Church), Normand Bonneau, Dean, 223 Main St., Ottawa, ON K1S 1C4 Tel. (613)236-1393 x. 2246 Fax (613)751-4016
Email: fquesnel@ustpaul.uottawa.ca
Website: www.ustpaul.ca

St. Peter's Seminary† (The Roman Catholic Church in Canada), William T. McGrattan, Rector, 1040 Waterloo St. North, London, ON N6A 3Y1 Tel. (519)432-1824 Fax (519)432-0964
Website: www.stpetersseminary.ca

St. Stephen's College (The United Church of Canada), Tom Faulkner, President, 8810 112th St., Edmonton, AB T6G 2J6 Tel. (800) 661-4956 Fax (780)433-8875
Email: westema@ualberta.ca
Website: www.ststephenscollege.ca

Salvation Army College for Officer Training (The Salvation Army in Canada), Wayne N. Pritchett, Principal, 2130 Bayview Ave., North York, ON M4N 3K6 Tel. (416)481-6131 Fax (416)481-6810; (416)481-2895 (Library)
Email: sandra_rice@can.salvationarmy.org; ray_harris@can.salvationarmy.org

The Salvation Army William and Catherine Booth College (The Salvation Army in Canada), Jonathan S. Raymond, President, 447 Webb Pl., Winnipeg, MB R3B 2P2 Tel. (204)947-6701 Fax (204)942-3856
Email: wcbc@boothcollege.ca
Website: www.boothcollege.ca

Steinbach Bible College (Mennonite), Abe Bergen, President, 50 PTH 12 N, Steinbach, MB R5G 1T4 Tel. (204)326-6451 Fax (204)326-6908
Email: info@sbcollege.ca
Website: www.sbcollege.ca

Summit Pacific College (The Pentecostal Assemblies of Canada), David Demchuk, President, Box 1700, Abbotsford, BC V2S 7E7 Tel. (604)853-7491 Fax (604)853-8951
Email: pr@summitpacific.ca
Website: www.summitpacific.ca

Taylor College of Mission and Evangelism (Church Army Canada), Rev. Kim Salo, Principal, 105 Mountain View Drive, Saint John, NB E2J 5B5 Tel. (866)693-8975 Fax (506)657-8217
Email: info@taylorcollege.ca
Website: www.taylorcollege.com or www.churcharmy.com/taylor

Taylor University College and Seminary† (North American Baptist Conference), Marvin L. Dewey, President, 11525-23 Ave., Edmonton, AB T6J 4T3 Tel. (780)431-5200 Fax (780)436-9416
Email: marvin.dewey@taylor-edu.ca
Website: www.taylor-edu.ca

Theological College of the Canadian Reformed Churches (Canadian and American Reformed

Churches), N. H. Gootjes, President, 110 West 27th St., Hamilton, ON L9C 5A1 Tel. (905)575-3688 Fax (905)575-0799
Email: theocollege@seminary.canrc.org
Website: www.canrc.org/college

Toronto Baptist Seminary and Bible College (Baptist), Glendon G. Thompson, President, 130 Gerrard St., E., Toronto, ON M5A 3T4 Tel. (416)925-3263 Fax (416)925-8305
Email: inquiry@tbs.edu
Website: www.tbs.edu

Toronto School of Theology † (Inter/Multi-denominational), Alan Hayes, Director, 47 Queens Park Crescent E., Toronto, ON M5S 2C3 Tel. (416)978-4039 Fax (416)978-7821
Email: alan.hayes@utoronto.ca
Website: www.tst.edu

Trinity College Faculty of Divinity† (The Anglican Church of Canada), David Neelands, Dean, 6 Hoskin Ave., Toronto, ON M5S 1H8 Tel. (416)978-2146 Fax (416)978-4949
Email: divinity@trinity.utoronto.ca
Website: www.trinity.utoronto.ca/divinity

Tyndale University College & Seminary† (Trans-denominational), Dr. Brian C. Stiller, President, 25 Ballyconnor Ct., Toronto, ON M2M 4B3 Tel. (416)226-6380 Fax (416)226-9464
Email: info@tyndale.ca
Website: www.tyndale.ca

United Theological College/Le Séminaire Uni (The United Church of Canada), Rev. Philip Joudrey, President, 3521 rue Université, Montréal, QC H3A 2A9 Tel. (514)849-2042 Fax (514)849-8634
Email: admin@utc.ca
Website: www.utc.ca

Université Laval, Faculté de Théologie et de Sciences Religieuses (The Roman Catholic Church in Canada), Marcel Viau, Doyen, Cité Universitaire, Quebec, QC G1K 7P4 Tel. (418)656-3576 Fax (418)656-3273
Email: ftsr@ftsr.ulaval.ca
Website: www.ftsr.ulaval.ca

Université de Montréal, Faculté de théologie (The Roman Catholic Church in Canada), Jean-Marc Charron, President, C. P. 6128 Succ. Centre Ville, Montréal, QC H3C 3J7 Tel. (514)343-7160 Fax (514)343-5738
Email: theologie@ere.umontreal.ca
Website: www.theo.umontreal.ca

Université de Sherbrooke, Faculté de the-ologié, d'éthique et de philosophie (The Roman Catholic Church in Canada), Jean-François Malherbe, President, 1111, rue Saint-

Charles Ouest, Tourquest - Bureau 310, Longueuil, QC J4K 5G4 Tel. (450)670-7157 Fax (450)670-1959
Email: jf.malherbe@sympatico.ca
Website: www.usherb.ca/longueuil

University of St. Michael's College Faculty of Theology† (Roman Catholic Church), Anne T. Anderson, CSJ, Dean, 81 St. Mary St., Toronto, ON M5S 1J4 Tel. (416)926-7265 Fax (416)926-7294
Website: www.utoronto.ca/stmikes

The University of Winnipeg Faculty of Theology† (Multi-denominational and the United Church of Canada), Gordon E. Mac-Dermid, Dean, 515 Portage Ave., Winnipeg, MB R3B 2E9 Tel. (204)786-9390 Fax (204)772-2584
Email: theology@uwinnipeg.ca
Website: www.uwinnipeg.ca/academic/theology

Vancouver School of Theology† (Inter/Multi-denominational), Rev. Wendy Fletcher, Principal, 6000 Iona Dr., Vancouver, BC V6T 1L4 Tel. 1-(866)822-9031 Fax (604)822-9212
Email: vstinfo@vst.edu
Website: www.vst.edu

Vanguard College (The Pentecostal Assemblies of Canada), Stephen Hertzog, President, 12140 103 St., Edmonton, AB T5G 2J9 Tel. (780)452-0808 Fax (780)452-5803
Email: info@vanguardcollege.com
Website: www.vanguardcollege.com

Waterloo Lutheran Seminary† (Evangelical Lutheran Church in Canada), Richard C. Crossman, President, 75 University Ave. W., Waterloo, ON N2L 3C5 Tel. (519)884-1970 Fax (519)725-2434
Email: seminary@wlu.ca
Website: www.wlu.ca/~wwwsem/index.shtml

Western Christian College (Churches of Christ in Canada), John McMillan, President, 100-4400 4th Ave., Regina, SK S4T 0H8 Tel. (306)545-1515 Fax (306)352-2198
Email: president@westernchristian.ca
Website: www.westernchristian.ca

Wycliffe College† (The Anglican Church of Canada), Rev. George R. Sumner, Jr., President, 5 Hoskin Ave., Toronto, ON M5S 1H7 Tel. (416)946-3535 Fax (416)946-3545
Email: wycliffe.college@utoronto.ca
Website: www.utoronto.ca/wycliffe

10. Religious Periodicals in the United States

This directory lists publications primarily of the organizations listed in directory 3, "Religious Bodies in the United States." Some independent publications are also listed. The list does not include all publications prepared by religious bodies, and not all the publications listed here are necessarily the official publication of a particular church. Regional publications and newsletters are not included. A more extensive list of religious periodicals published in the United States can be found in Gale Directory of Publications and Broadcast Media, (Gale, P.O. Box 9187, Farmington Hills, MI 48333-9187).

Each entry in this directory contains: the title of the periodical, frequency of publication, religious affiliation, editor's name, address, telephone and fax number and email and website addresses when available. The frequency of publication, which appears in parenthesis after the name of the publication, is represented by a "W." for weekly; "M." for monthly; "Q." for quarterly; "I." for Internet.

21st Century Christian, (M.) Churches of Christ, M. Norvel Young and Prentice A. Meador, Jr., Box 40304, Nashville, TN 37204 Tel. (800)331-5991 Fax (615)385-5915 Email: eric@nafwb.org

Action, (6-Y.) Churches of Christ, John D. Reese, P.O. Box 2169, Cedar Park, TX 78630-2169 Tel. (512)345-8191 Fax (512)401-8265 Email: wbsinfo@wbschool.org Website: www.wbschool.org

Adra Today, (Q.) Seventh-day Adventist Church, Beth Schaefer, 12501 Old Columbia Pike, Silver Spring, MD 20904-6600 Tel. (301)680-6355 Fax (301)680-6370 Email: 74617.2105@compuserve.com Website: www.adra.org

The Adult Quarterly, (Q.) Associate Reformed Presbyterian Church (General Synod), The Rev. William B. Evans, PhD, P.O. Box 275, Due West, SC 29639 Tel. (864)379-8896 Email: wbevans@erskine.edu

Advent Christian News, (M.) Advent Christian Church, Rev. Keith D. Wheaton, P.O. Box 23152, Charlotte, NC 28227 Tel. (704)545-6161 Fax (704)573-0712 Email: Acpub@Adventchristian.org

The Adventist Chaplain, (Q.) Seventh-day Adventist Church, Deena Bartel-Wagner—Editor, Martin W. Feldbush—Executive Editor, Adventist Chaplaincy Ministries, General Conference of Seventh-day Adventists, 12501 Old Columbia Pike, Silver Spring, MD 20904-6600 Tel. (301)680-6780 Fax (301)680-6783 Email: acm@gc.adventist.org Website: www.adventistchaplains.org

Adventist Review, (3 times per month) Seventh-day Adventist Church, W. G. Johnsson, 12501 Old Columbia Pike, Silver Spring, MD 20904-6600 Tel. (301)680-6560 Fax (301)680-6638 Email: letters@adventistreview.org Website: www.adventistreview.org

Adventist World, (M) Seventh-day Adventist Church, William G. Johnson, 12501 Old Columbia Pike, Silver Spring, MD 20904-6600 Tel. (301)680-6560 Fax (301)680-6638

Again Magazine, (Q.) The Antiochian Orthodox Christian Archdiocese of North America, R. Thomas Zell, P.O. Box 76, Ben Lomond, CA 95005-0076 Tel. (831)336-5118 Fax (831)336-8882 Email: marketing@conciliarpress.com Website: www.conciliarpress.com

Agape Magazine, (bi-M.) Coptic Orthodox Church, Bishop Serapion, P.O.Box 4960, Diamond Bar, CA 91765 Tel. (909)865-8378 Fax (909)865-8348 Email: agape@lacopts.org Website: lacopts.org

Alive Now, (bi-M.) The United Methodist Church, JoyAnn Miller (Interim), P.O. Box 340004, Nashville, TN 37203-0004 Tel. (615)340-7218 Email: alivenow@upperroom.org Website: www.alivenow.org

The Allegheny Wesleyan Methodist, (M.) The Allegheny Wesleyan Methodist Connection (Original Allegheny Conference), William Cope, P.O. Box 357, Salem, OH 44460 Tel. (330)337-9376 Fax (330)337-9700 Email: awmc@juno.com

Alliance Life, (M.) The Christian and Missionary Alliance, Mark Failing, P.O. Box 35000, Colorado Springs, CO 80935 Tel. (719)599-5999 Fax (719)599-8234

Email: alife@cmalliance.org
Website: www.alliancelife.org

The A.M.E. Christian Recorder, (bi-W.)
African Methodist Episcopal Church, Dr.
Calvin H. Sydnor, III, 500 Eighth Ave. South,
Nashville, TN 37203-4181

American Baptist Quarterly, (Q.) American
Baptist Churches in the USA, Dr. Robert E.
Johnson, P.O. Box 851, Valley Forge, PA
19482-0851 Tel. (610)768-2269 Fax (610)
768-2266
Email: dbvanbro@abc-usa.org
Website: www.cbts.edu/rejohnsonweb/AB
Quarterly

American Baptists In Mission, (Q.) American
Baptist Churches in the USA, Richard W.
Schramm, P.O. Box 851, Valley Forge, PA
19482-0851 Tel. (610)768-2077 Fax (610)
768-2320
Email: richard.schramm@abc-usa.org
Website: www.abc-usa.org

American Bible Society Record, (Q) Non-
denominational, Liz Smith, 1865 Broadway,
New York, NY 10023-7505 Tel. (212)408-
1367 Fax (212)582-7245
Email: absrecord@americanbible.org
Website: www.americanbible.org

The Anchor of Faith, (M.) The Anglican
Orthodox Church, The Most Rev. Jerry L.
Ogles, Anglican Orthodox Church, P.O. Box
128, Statesville, NC 28687-0128 Tel.
(704)873-8365 Fax (704)873-5359
Email: aocusa@energyunited.net
Website: www.anglicanorthodoxchurch.org

Annual Catholic Directory, The, (Y.) The
Catholic Church, Michelle Laque Johnson,
222 N. 17th St., Philadelphia, PA 19103 Tel.
(215)587-3660 Fax (215)587-3979

El Aposento Alto, (bi-M.) The United Methodist
Church, Carmen Gaud, P.O. Box 340004,
Nashville, TN 37203-0004 Tel. (615)340-
7253 Fax (615)340-7267
Email: ElAposentoAlto@upperroom.org
Website: www.upperroom.org

The Armenian Church, (2-Y.) Diocese of the
Armenian Church of America, Arpie
McQueen, 630 Second Avenue, New York,
NY 10016 Tel. (212)686-0710 Fax (212)779-
3558
Email: tac@armeniandiocese.org
Website: www.armenianchurch.org

Around the Fellowship, (M.) Universal Fellow-
ship of Metropolitan Community Churches,
Director of Communications: James N.
Birkitt, Jr., 8704 Santa Monica Blvd, 2nd Fl.,

West Hollywood, CA 90069-4548 Tel.
(310)360-8640 Fax (310)360-8680
Email: info@mccchurch.org
Website: www.mccchurch.org

The Associate Reformed Presbyterian, (M.)
Associate Reformed Presbyterian Church
(General Synod), Mrs. Sabrina M. Cooper,
One Cleveland St., Greenville, SC 29601 Tel.
(864)232-8297 Fax (864)271-3729
Email: arpmaged@arpsynod.org
Website: www.arpmagazine.org

Attack, A Magazine for Christian Men, (Q.)
National Association of Free Will Baptists,
James E. Vallance, P.O. Box 5002, Antioch,
TN 37011-5002 Tel. (615)731-4950 Fax (615)
731-0771

Awake!, (M.) Jehovah's Witnesses, Watch Tower
Society, 25 Columbia Heights, Brooklyn, NY
11201-2483 Tel. (718)560-5000
Website: www.watchtower.org

The Banner, (M.) Christian Reformed Church in
North America, Robert DeMoor, 2850 Kala-
mazoo Ave., S.E., Grand Rapids, MI 49560
Tel. (616)224-0732 Fax (616)224-0834
Email: editorial@thebanner.org
Website: www.thebanner.org

The Banner of Truth, (M.) Netherlands
Reformed Congregations, J. den Hoed, 1113
Bridgeview Dr., Lynden, WA 98264 Tel.
(360)354-4203 Fax (360)354-7565

The Baptist Bible Tribune, (M.) Baptist Bible
Fellowship International, Mike Randall, P.O.
Box 309, Springfield, MO 65801-0309 Tel.
(417)831-3996 Fax (417)831-1470
Email: editors@tribune.org
Website: www.tribune.org

Baptist Bulletin, (M.) General Association of
Regular Baptist Churches, Sr Editor: Norman
A. Olson, 1300 N. Meacham Rd., Schaumburg,
IL 60173-4806 Tel. (847)843-1600 Fax (847)
843-3757
Email: baptistbulletin@garbc.org
Website: www.garbc.org

Baptist History And Heritage Society, (3-Y.)
Baptist, Pamela R. Durso, PO Box 728,
Brentwood, TN 37021-0728 Tel. (615)371-
7937 Fax (615)371-7939
Email: pdurso@tnbaptist.org
Website: www.baptisthistory.org

Baptist Peacemaker, (Q.) Baptist, Katie Cook,
4800 Wedgewood Dr., Charlotte, NC 28210
Tel. (704)521-6051 Fax (704)521-6053
Email: bpfna@bpfna.org
Website: www.bpfna.org

The **Baptist Preacher**, (bi-M.) Baptist Bible Fellowship International, Mike Randall, P.O. Box 309 HSJ, Springfield, MO 65801 Tel. (417)831-3996 Fax (417)831-1470
Email: editors@tribune.org
Website: www.tribune.org

The **Baptist Preacher's Journal**, (Q.) Baptist Bible Fellowship International, Keith Bassham, P.O.Box 309, Springfield, MO 65801 Tel. (417) 831-3996 Fax (417)831-1470
Email: editor@tribune.org
Website: tribune.org

Baptist Witness, (M.) Primitive Baptists, Lasserre Bradley, Jr., Box 17037, Cincinnati, OH 45217 Tel. (513)821-7289 Fax (513)821-7303
Email: bbh45217@aol.com
Website: www.BaptistBibleHour.org

BGC World, (8-Y.) Baptist General Conference, Bob Putman, 2002 S. Arlington Heights Rd., Arlington Heights, IL 60005 Tel. (847)228-0200 Fax (847)228-5376
Email: bgcworld@bgcworld.org
Website: www.bgcworld.org

The **Bible Advocate**, (8-Y.) The Church of God (Seventh Day), Denver, CO, Calvin Burrell, PO Box 33677, Denver, CO 80233 Tel. (303) 452-7973 Fax (303)452-0657
Email: bibleadvocate@cog7.org
Website: www.cog7.org/BA

The **Brethren Evangelist**, (4-6-Y.) The Brethren Church, 524 College Ave., Ashland, OH 44805 Tel. (419)289-1708 Fax (419)281-0450
Email: brethren@brethrenchurch.org
Website: www.brethrenchurch.org

Brethren Journal, (10-Y.) Unity of the Brethren, Rev. Milton Maly, 6703 FM 2502, Brenham, TX 77833-9803 Tel. (409)830-8762
Website: www.unityofthebrethren.org

Brethren Life and Thought, (Q.) Church of the Brethren, Carol Gardner, Managing Editor, Bethany Seminary, 615 National Road West, Richmond, IN 47374-4019 Tel. (765)983-1811 Fax (765)983-1840
Email: gardnca@bethanyseminary.edu
Website: www.bethanyseminary.edu/?page=blt

The **Bridegroom's Messenger**, (bi-M.) The International Pentecostal Church of Christ, Janice Boyce, 121 W. Hunters Trail, Elizabeth City, NC 27909 Tel. (919)338-3003 Fax (919)338-3003

The **Burning Bush**, (Q.) The Metropolitan Church Association, Inc. (Wesleyan), Rev. Gary Bowell, The Metropolitan Church Assoc., 2425 West Ramsey Ave, Milwaukee, WI 53221-4907 Tel. (414)282-8539

Email: metrochurch assn@wi.rr.com
Website: www.TheMCA.net

Call to Unity: Resourcing the Church for Ecumenical Ministry, (bi-M.) Christian Church (Disciples of Christ), Robert K. Welsh, P.O. Box 1986, Indianapolis, IN 46206-1986 Tel. (317)713-2586 Fax (317)713-2588
Email: rwelsh@ccu.disciples.org
Website: www.disciples.org/ccu

Calvary Messenger, (M.) Beachy Amish Mennonite Churches, Paul L. Miller, 7809 Soul Herren Road, Partridge, KS 67566 Tel. (620)567-2286 Fax (620)567-2286
Email: paullmiller@mindspring.com

Caring, (Q.) Assemblies of God, Owen Wilkie, Gospel Publishing House, 1445 N. Boonville Ave., Springfield, MO 65802 Tel. (417)862-2781 Fax (417)862-0503
Email: benevolences@ag.org
Website: www.benevolences.ag.org

Cathedral Age, (Q.) Interdenominational, Craig W. Stapert, Washington National Cathedral, 3101 Wisconsin Ave., NW, Washington, DC 20016-5098 Tel. (202)537-5681 Fax (202)364-6600
Email: cathedral_age@cathedral.org
Website: www.cathedralage.org

Catholic Chronicle, (M) The Catholic Church, Angela Kessler, P.O. Box 985, Toledo, OH 43697-0985 Tel. (419)244-6711 x 133 Fax (419) 244-0468
Email: ccnews@toledodiocese.org
Website: www.catholicchronicle.org

Catholic Digest, (M.) The Catholic Church, Dan Connors, P.O. Box 6015, New London, CT 06320 Tel. (800)321-0411 Fax (860)536-5600
Email: dconnors@catholicdigest.com
Website: www.CatholicDigest.org

Catholic Herald (Milwaukee), (W.) The Catholic Church, Brian T. Olszewski, 3501 S. Lake Dr., St. Francis, WI 53235-0913 Tel. (414)769-3500 Fax (414)769-3468
Email: chnonline@archmil.org
Website: www.chnonline.org

Catholic Light, (Every Three Weeks) The Catholic Church, William R. Genello, 300 Wyoming Ave., Scranton, PA 18503 Tel. (570)207-2229 Fax (570)207-2271
Email: william-genello@dioceseofscranton.org
Website: www.dioceseofscranton.org

The **Catholic Peace Voice**, (bi-M.) The Catholic Church, Dave Robinson, 532 W. 8th Street, Erie, PA 16502 Tel. (814)453-4955 Fax (814) 452-4784

Email: info@paxchristiusa.org
Website: www.paxchristiusa.org

The Catholic Review, (W.) The Catholic Church, Daniel L. Medinger—Associate Publisher, P.O. Box 777, Baltimore, MD 21203 Tel. (443)524-3150 Fax (443)524-3155 Email: mail@catholicreview.org Website: www.catholicreview.org

Catholic Standard and Times, (W.) The Catholic Church, Michelle Laque Johnson, 222 N. 17th St., Philadelphia, PA 19103 Tel. (215)587-3660 Fax (215)587-3979 Email: standard@adphila.org Website: www.cst-phl.com

Catholic Trends, (bi-W.) The Catholic Church, David E. Gibson, 3211 Fourth St. NE, Washington, DC 20017-1100 Tel. (202)541-3250 Fax (202)541-3255 Email: cns@catholicnews.com Website: www.catholicnews.com

The Catholic Worker, (7-Y.) The Catholic Church, Joanne Kennedy, Tanya Thevialt & Matt Vogel, Managing Editors, 36 E. First St., New York, NY 10003 Tel. (212)777-9617

Cela Biedrs, (bi-M.) The Latvian Evangelical Lutheran Church in America, Vieturs Bamban, 7630 S.W. 26th Ave., Portland, OR 97219 Tel. (503)781-6724 Email: celabiedrs@yahoo.com

Celebration: An Ecumenical Worship Resource, (M.) Interdenominational, Patrick Marrin, 115 East Armor Blvd., Kansas City, MO 64111 Tel. (816)531-0538 Fax (816)968-2291 Email: patmarrin@aol.com Website: www.ncrpub.com

The Challenge, (Q.) The Bible Church of Christ, Inc., A.M. Jones, 1358 Morris Ave., Bronx, NY 10456 Tel. (718)588-2284 Fax (718)992-5597 Website: www.thebiblechurchofchrist.org

Charisma, (M.) Nondenominational, J. Lee Grady, 600 Rinehart Rd., Lake Mary, FL 32746 Tel. (407)333-0600 Fax (407)333-7133 Email: grady@strang.com Website: www.charismamag.com

The Children's Friend, (Braille), (Q.) Seventh-day Adventist Church, Gaylena Gibson, P.O. Box 6097, Lincoln, NE 68506 Tel. (402)488-0981 Fax (402)488-7582 Email: editorial@christianrecord.org Website: www.ChristianRecord.org

Christadelphian Advocate, (M.) Christadelphians, James I. Millay, 27 Delphian Road, Springfield, VT 05156-9335 Tel. (802)885-2316 Fax (802)885-2319 Email: jimillay@vermontel.net Website: www.christadelphian-advocate.org

Christadelphian Tidings, (M.) Christadelphians, Donald H. Styles, 42076 Hartford Dr., Canton, MI 48187 Tel. (313)844-2426 Fax (313)844-8304

The Christian Baptist, (Q.) Primitive Baptists, Elder S. T. Tolley, P.O. Box 68, Atwood, TN 38220 Tel. (901)662-7417 Email: cbl@aeneas.net

Christian Bible Teacher, (Q) Churches of Christ, Bob Connel, P.O. Box 7385, Ft. Worth, TX 76111 Tel. (817)838-2644 Fax (817)838-2644

The Christian Century, (bi-W) Nondenominational, John Buchanan, 104 South Michigan Ave. Suite 700, Chicago, IL 60603 Tel. (312)263-7510 Fax (312)263-7540 Email: main@christiancentury.org Website: www.christiancentury.org

The Christian Chronicle, (M.) Churches of Christ, Lynn McMillon, Box 11000, Oklahoma City, OK 73136-1100 Tel. (405)425-5070 Fax (405)425-5076 Website: www.christianchronicle.org

The Christian Community, (8-Y.) International Council of Community Churches, Rev. Michael E. Livingston, 21116 Washington Pkwy., Frankfort, IL 60423 Tel. (815)464-5690 Fax (815)464-5692 Email: ICCC60423@sbcglobal.net Website: icccusa.com

The Christian Contender, (M.) Mennonite Church, James Boll, Box 3, Highway 172, Crockett, KY 41413 Tel. (606)522-4348 Fax (606)522-4896

The Christian Index, (M.) Christian Methodist Episcopal Church, Dr. Kenneth E. Jones, P.O. Box 431, Fairfield, AL 35064 Tel. (205)929-1410 Fax (205)744-0010 Email: goodoc@aol.com Website: www.c-m-e.org

Christian Journal, (Q) Churches of Christ, J.E. Snelson, P.O. Box 7385, Ft. Worth, TX 76111 Tel. (817)838-2644

Christian Leader, (M.) U.S. Conference of Mennonite Brethren Churches, Connie Faber, Box 220, Hillsboro, KS 67063 Tel. (316)947-5543 Fax (316)947-3266 Email: chleader@southwind.net

Christian Monthly, (M.) Apostolic Lutheran Church of America, Linda Mattson, P.O. Box 220, Yamhill, OR 97148 Tel. (360)687-6493 Fax (503)662-5909
Email: christianm@apostolic-lutheran.org
Website: www.Apostolic-Lutheran.org

Christian Record, (Braille), (Q.) Seventh-day Adventist Church, Gaylena Gibson, P.O. Box 6097, Lincoln, NE 68506 Tel. (402)488-0981 Fax (402)488-7582
Email: editorial@christianrecord.org
Website: www.ChristianRecord.org

Christian Record Talking Magazine (Audio), (Q) Seventh-day Adventist Church, Bert Williams, PO Box 6097, Lincoln, NE 68506 Tel. 402-488-0981
Email: Bert.Williams@christianrecord.org
Website: http://www.christianrecord.org/services/recorded_magazines/christianrecord.php

The Christian Science Journal, (M.) Church of Christ, Scientist, Mary M. Trammell, Editor in Chief; William G. Dawley, Editor, One Norway St., Boston, MA 02115-3195 Tel. (617)450-2000 Fax (617)450-2930
Email: trammellm@csps.com or dawleyw @csps.com
Website: www.csjournal.com

The Christian Science Monitor, (D. & W.) Church of Christ, Scientist, David T. Cook, One Norway St., Boston, MA 02115 Tel. (617) 450-2000 Fax (617)450-7575
Website: www.csmonitor.com

Christian Science Quarterly Weekly Bible Lessons, (M. & Q.) Church of Christ, Scientist, Carol Humphry, Circulation Marketing Manager, One Norway St., C-40, Boston, MA 02115 Tel. (617)450-2000 Fax (617)450-2930
Email: service@csps.com
Website: www.BibleLesson.com

Christian Science Sentinel, (W.) Church of Christ, Scientist, Mary M. Trammell, Editor in Chief; William G. Dawley, Editor, One Norway St., Boston, MA 02115-3195 Tel. (617)450-2000 Fax (617)450-2930
Email: sentinel@csps.com/trammellm@csps. com (the Editor)
Website: www.cssentinel.com

Christian Social Action, (bi-M.) The United Methodist Church, vacant, 100 Maryland Ave. NE, Washington, DC 20002 Tel. (202)488-5621 Fax (202)488-1617
Website: www.umc-gbcs.org

Christian Standard, (W.) Christian Churches and Churches of Christ, Mark A. Taylor, 8121 Hamilton Ave., Cincinnati, OH 45231 Tel.

(513)931-4050 Fax (513)931-0950
Email: christianstd@standardpub.com
Website: www.christianstandard.com

The Christian Union Witness, (M. (except Jy-Ag)) Christian Union, Joseph Cunningham, P.O. Box 361, Greenfield, OH 45123 Tel. (937)981-2760 Fax (937)981-2760
Email: ohiocu@bright.net
Website: christianunionbright.net

Christian Woman, (bi-M.) Churches of Christ, Sandra Humphrey, Box 150, Nashville, TN 37202 Tel. (615)254-8781 Fax (615)254-7411

The Church Advocate, (Q.) Churches of God, General Conference, Rachel L. Foreman, P.O. Box 926, 700 E. Melrose Ave., Findlay, OH 45839 Tel. (419)424-1961 Fax (419)424-3433
Email: communications@cggc.org
Website: www.cggc.org

Church of God Evangel, (M.) Church of God (Cleveland, Tenn.), James E. Cossey, P.O. Box 2250, Cleveland, TN 37320 Tel. (423)478-7592 Fax (423)478-7616
Email: editor@pathwaypress.org
Website: www.pathwaypress.org

The Church Herald, (11-Y.) Reformed Church in America, Christina Van Eyl, 4500 60th St., SE, Grand Rapids, MI 49512 Tel. (616)698-7071 Fax (616)698-6606
Email: herald@rca.org
Website: www.rca.org/herald

The Church Herald, (11-Y.) Reformed Church in America, Christina Van Eyl, 4500 60th St. SE, Grand Rapids, MI 49512 Tel. (616)698-7071
Email: herald@rca.org
Website: herald.rca.org

Church History: Studies in Christianity and Culture, (Q.) Scholarly, John Corrigan, Amanda Porterfield, Florida State Univesity Dept of Religion, M05 Dodd Hall, Tallahassee, FL 32306-1520 Tel. (850)644-9038 Fax (850) 644-7225
Email: church-history@admin.fsu.edu
Website: www.churchhistory.org/church history. html

The Church Messenger, (bi-W.) The American Carpatho-Russian Orthodox Greek Catholic Church, V. Rev. Michael Rosco, 145 Broad St., Perth Amboy, NJ 08861 Tel. (732)826-4442
Email: mrosco2@excite.com
Website: www.acrod.org/news/messenger1. html

Church School Herald, (Q.) African Methodist Episcopal Zion Church, Ms. Mary A. Love,

P.O. Box 26769, Charlotte, NC 28221-6769 Tel. (704)599-4630 x 324 Fax (704)688-2548 Email: MaLove@amezhqtr.org

Church & Society Magazine, (bi-M.) Presbyterian Church (U.S.A.), Rev. Dr. Bobbi Wells Hargleroad, 100 Witherspoon St., Louisville, KY 40202-1396 Tel. (502)569-5810 Fax (502)569-8116 Email: c-s@ctr.pcusa.org Website: www.pcusa.org/churchsociety

Churchwoman, (Q.) Interdenominational, Annie Llamoso-Songco, 475 Riverside Dr., Suite 500, New York, NY 10115 Tel. (212)870-3339 Fax (212)870-2338 Email: allamoso@churchwomen.org Website: www.churchwomen.org

Circuit Rider, (bi-M.) The United Methodist Church, Jill S. Reddig, 201 Eighth Ave. S, Nashville, TN 37203 Tel. (615)749-6538 Fax (615)749-6061 Email: jreddig@umpublishing.org Website: www.circuitrider.com

Clarion Herald, (bi-W.) The Catholic Church, Peter P. Finney, Jr., P. O. Box 53247, 1000 Howard Ave. Suite 400, New Orleans, LA 70153 Tel. (504)596-3035 Fax (504)596-3020 Email: clarionherald@clarionherald.org Website: www.clarionherald.org

Clergy Comminique, (2-Y.) International Council of Community Churches, Virginia Leopold, 21116 Washington Pky., Frankfort, IL 60423-3112 Tel. (815)464-5690 Fax (815) 464-5692 Email: iccc60423@aol.com Website: icccusa.com

The Clergy Journal, (9-Y.) Nondenominational, Sharon L. Firle, Managing Editor & Clyde J. Steckel, Executive Editor, 6160 Carmen Avenue E, Inver Grove Heights, MN 55076-4422 Tel. (800)328-0200 Fax (651)457-4617 Email: editor@logostaff.com Website: www.logosproductions.com

Club Connection, (Q.) Assemblies of God, Debby Seler, 1445 Boonville Ave., Springfield, MO 65802-1894 Tel. (417)862-2781 Fax (417) 862-0503 Email: clubconnection@ag.org Website: www.missionettes.ag.org

CoLaborer, (bi-M.) National Association of Free Will Baptists, Sarah Fletcher, Women Nationally Active for Christ, P.O. Box 5002, Antioch, TN 37011-5002 Tel. (615)731-6812 Fax (615)731-0771 Email: wnac@nafwb.org

College and University Dialogue, (3-Y.) Seventh-day Adventist Church, John M. Fowler, 12501 Old Columbia Pike, Silver Spring, MD 20904-6600 Tel. Fax (301)622-9627 Website: dialogue.adventist.org

Collegiate Quarterly, (Q.) Seventh-day Adventist Church, Gary B. Swanson, 12501 Old Columbia Pike, Silver Spring, MD 20904 Tel. (301)680-6160 Fax (301)680-6155

Columbia, (M.) The Catholic Church, Tim S. Hickey, One Columbus Plaza, New Haven, CT 06510 Tel. (203)752-4398 Fax (203)752-4109 Email: info@kofc.org Website: www.kofc.org

The Commission, (2-Y.) International Mission Board, Southern Baptist Convention, Michael Chute, Box 6767, Richmond, VA 23230-0767 Tel. (804)219-1373 Fax (804)219-1410 Email: commission@imb.org Website: www.tconline.org

Common Lot, (Q.) United Church of Christ, Martha J. Hunter, 700 Prospect Ave., Cleveland, OH 44115 Tel. (216)736-2150 Fax (216)736-2156

Commonwealth, (bi-W.) The Catholic Church, Paul Baumann, 475 Riverside Drive, Rm 405, New York, NY 10115 Tel. (212)662-4200 Fax (212)662-4183 Email: editors@commonwealmagazine.org Website: www.commonwealmagazine.org

Communion, (bi-M.) Church of God (Anderson, Indiana), Arthur Kelly, P.O. Box 2420, 1201 E. 5th Street, Anderson, IN 46018-2420 Tel. (765)642-0256 Fax (765)652-5652 Email: AKelly@chog.org Website: chog.org/news/communion.asp

The Congregationalist, (5-Y.) National Association Congregational Christian Churches, Rev. James E. Eaton, 87 Broadway, Norwich, CT 06360 Tel. (860)889-1363 Fax (860)887-5715Email: jeaton@unitedcongregational.org Website: www.congregationalist.org

Connections, (M.) The Alliance of Baptists, Sue Harper Poss, 1328 16th St. N.W.,, Washington, DC 20036 Tel. (202)745-7609 Fax (202)745-0023 Email: editor@allianceofbaptists.org Website: www.allianceofbaptists.org

Conqueror, (bi-M.) United Pentecostal Church International, Shay Mann, 8855 Dunn Rd., Hazelwood, MO 63042 Tel. (314)837-7300 Fax (314)837-4503 Email: smann@upci.org Website: www.pentecostalyouth.org

Context, (M.) Nondenominational, Martin Marty, 205 W. Monroe St., Chicago, IL 60606-5013 Tel. (312)236-7782 Fax (312)236-8207 Email: editors@uscatholic.org Website: www.contextonline.org

Covenant, (Q.) Presbyterian Church in America, Jackie Fogas, Covenant Theological Seminary, 12330 Conway Road, St. Louis, MO 63141 Tel. (314)434-4044 Fax (314)434-4819 Email: covenantmagazine@covenantseminary. edu Website: www.convenantseminary.edu

Cornerstone Connections, (Q.) Seventh-day Adventist Church, Gary B. Swanson, 12501 Old Columbia Pike, Silver Spring, MD 20904 Tel. (301)680-6160 Fax (301)680-6155

The Covenant Companion, (M.) Evangelical Covenant Church, Donald L. Meyer, Editor; Jane K. Swanson-Nystrom, Managing Editor, 5101 N. Francisco Ave., Chicago, IL 60625 Tel. (773)906-3328 Fax (773)784-4366 Email: communication@covchurch.org Website: www.covchurch.org/cov/ companion

Covenant Home Altar, (Q.) Evangelical Covenant Church, Jane K. Swanson-Nystrom, 5101 N. Francisco Ave., Chicago, IL 60625 Tel. (773)784-3000 Fax (773)784-4366 Email: communication@covchurch.org

Covenant Quarterly, (Q.) Evangelical Covenant Church, Paul E. Koptak, 3225 W. Foster Ave., Chicago, IL 60625-4895 Tel. (773)244-6242 Email: info@covenantbookstore.com

The Covenanter Witness, (11-Y.) Reformed Presbyterian Church of North America, Drew Gordon and Lynne Gordon, 7408 Penn Ave., Pittsburgh, PA 15208 Tel. (412)241-0436 Fax (412)731-8861 Email: info@psalms4u.com Website: www.psalms4u.com

Credinta—The Faith, (Q.) The Romanian Orthodox Church in America, V. Rev. Archim. Dr. Vasile Vasilac, 45-03 48th Ave., Woodside, Queens, NY 11377 Tel. (313)893-8390

The Cumberland Presbyterian, (11-Y.) Cumberland Presbyterian Church, Patricia P. White, Cumberland Presbyterian Church, 1978 Union Ave., Memphis, TN 38104 Tel. (615)731-5556 Email: cpmag@comcast.net Website: www.cumberland.org/cpmag/

Currents in Theology and Mission, (bi-M.) Evangelical Lutheran Church in America, Ralph W. Klein, 1100 E. 55th St., Chicago, IL 60615 Tel. (773)256-0751 Fax (773)256-0782 Email: currents@lstc.edu Website:www.lstc.edu/pub_peo/pub/currents. html

Cutting Edge, (Q.) Association of Vineyard Churches, Jeff Bailey, 2495 Howard St., Evanston, IL 60202 Tel. (847)328-4544 Fax (847)328-5153 Email: cuttingedge@vineyardusa.org Website: www.vineyardusa.org/publications/ newsletters/cutting_edge

Decision, (11-Y.) Nondenominational, Bob Paulson, 1 Billy Graham Parkway, Charlotte, NC 28201-0001 Tel. (704)401-2432 Fax (704) 401-3009 Email: decision@bgea.org Website: www.decisionmag.org

DisciplesWorld, (10-Y.) Christian Church (Disciples of Christ) in the United States and Canada, Verity A. Jones, 6325 N. Guilford Ave Suite 213, Indianapolis, IN 46220 Tel. (317) 375-8846 Fax (317)375-8849 Email: info@disciplesworld.com Website: www.disciplesworld.com

EcuLink, (Several Per Year) Interdenominational, Philip E.Jenks, 475 Riverside Drive, 8th Floor, New York, NY 10115-0050 Tel. (212)870-2227 Fax (212)870-2030 Email: pjenks@councilofchurches.org Website: www.councilofchurches.org

Ecumenical Trends, (M.) The Catholic Church, Rev. James Loughran, SA, Graymoor Ecumenical & Interreligious Institute, PO Box 300, Garrison, NY 10524-0300 Tel. (845)424-3671 x 3323 Fax (845)424-2163 Email: jlgeii@aol.com Website: www.geii.org

Eleventh Hour Messenger, (bi-M.) Wesleyan Holiness Association of Churches, John Brewer, 11411 N US Hwy 27, Fountain City, IN 47341-9757 Tel. (317)584-3199

Encounter (Audio), (Q) Seventh-day Adventist Church, Bert Williams, PO Box 6097, Lincoln, NE 68506 Tel. 402-488-0981 Email: Bert.Williams@christianrecord.org Website: www.christianrecord.org/services/ recorded_magazines/christianrecord.php

Enrichment: A Journal for Pentecostal Ministry, (Q.) Assemblies of God, Gary Allen; Rick Knoth, Managing Editor, 1445 N. Boonville Ave., Springfield, MO 65802 Tel. (417)862-2781 Fax (417)862-0416 Email: rKnoth@ag.org Website: www.enrichmentjournal.ag.org

The Ensign, (M.) The Church of Jesus Christ of Latter-day Saints, Don L. Searle, Managing Editor, 50 E North Temple Street, 24th Fl, Salt Lake City, UT 84150 Tel. (801)240-2950 Fax (801)240-2270
Email: ensign@ldschurch.org
Website: www.magazines.lds.org

Episcopal Life, (M.) The Episcopal Church, Jerrold Hames, 815 Second Ave., New York, NY 10017-4503 Tel. (800)334-7626 Fax (212) 949-8059
Email: jhames@episcopalchurch.org
Website: www.episcopal-life.org

Equip, (bi-M.) Presbyterian Church in America, Dr. Charles Dunahoo, 1700 N. Brown Road Ste. 102, Lawrenceville, GA 30043 Tel. (678)825-1100 Fax (678)825.1101
Email: cep@pcanet.org
Website: www.pcanet.org

The Evangel, (bi-M.) American Association of Lutheran Churches, The, Rev. Charles D. Eidum, 801 W. 106th St, Suite 203, Minneapolis, MN 55420-5603 Tel. (952)884-7784 Fax (952) 884-7894
Email: aa2taalc@aol.com
Website: www.taalc.com

The Evangel, (Q.) The Evangelical Church Alliance, Dr. Henry A. (Hank) Roso, 205 W. Broadway, PO Box 9, Bradley, IL 60915 Tel. (815)937-0720 Fax (815)937-0001
Email: info@ecainternatinal.org
Website: www.ecainternational.org

The Evangelical Advocate, (Bi-M.) Churches of Christ in Christian Union, Ralph Hux, P.O. Box 30, Circleville, OH 43113 Tel. (740)474-8856 Fax (740)477-7766
Email: doc@cccuhg.org
Website: www.cccuhq.org

Evangelical Beacon, (bi-M.) The Evangelical Free Church of America, Ms. Carol Madison, 901 East 78th St., Minneapolis, MN 55420-1300 Tel. (877)293-5653 Fax (952)853-8488
Email: beacon@efca.org
Website: www.efca.org

Evangelical Challenge, (Q.) The Evangelical Church, Shirley Roehl, 9421 West River Road, Minneapolis, MN 55444 Tel. (763)424-2589 Fax (763)424-9230
Email: ecdenom@usfamily.net
Website: www.theevangelicalchurch.org

The Evangelist, (W.) The Roman Catholic Church, James Breig, 40 N. Main Ave., Albany, NY 12203 Tel. (518)453-6688 Fax (518)453-8448
Email: james.breig@rcda.org
Website: www.evangelist.org

Explorations, (Q.) Nondenominational, Irvin J. Borowsky, 321 Chestnut Street, 4th Floor, Philadelphia, PA 19106-2779 Tel. (215)925-2800 Fax (215)925-3800
Email: aii@interfaith-scholars.org

Extension, (M.) The Catholic Church, Bradley Collins, Editor, 150 S. Wacker Drive, 20th Floor, Chicago, IL 60606 Tel. (312)236-7240 Fax (312)236-5276
Email: magazine@catholic-extension.org
Website: www.catholic-extension.org

Faith & Fellowship, (M.) Church of the Lutheran Brethren of America, Bruce Stumbo, P.O. Box 655, Fergus Falls, MN 56538 Tel. (218)736-7357 Fax (218)736-2200
Email: ffpress@clba.org
Website: www.faithandfellowship.org

Faith-Life, (bi-M.) Lutheran, Pastor Marcus Albrecht, 2107 N. Alexander St., Appleton, WI 54911 Tel. (920)733-1839 Fax (920)733-4834
Email: malbrecht@milwpc.com

FEConnections, (Q) Fellowship of Evangelical Churches, Ron Habegger, 1420 Kerrway Ct., Fort Wayne, IN 46805 Tel. (260)423-3649 Fax (260)420-1905
Email: FECministries@aol.com
Website: www.fecministries.org

Fellowship, (bi-M.) Interfaith, Ethan Vesely-Flad, Box 271, Nyack, NY 10960-0271 Tel. (845)358-4601 Fax (845)358-4924
Email: fellowship@forusa.org
Website: www.forusa.org

Fellowship Focus, (bi-M.) Fellowship of Evangelical Bible Churches, Sharon K. Berg, 3339 N 109th Plz, Omaha, NE 68164-2908 Tel. (402)965-3860 Fax (402)965-3871
Email: fellowshipfocus@febcministries.org
Website: www.febcministries.org

Fellowship News, (M.) Bible Fellowship Church, Carol Snyder, 3000 Fellowship Drive, Whitehall, PA 18052-3343 Tel. (877) 795-1212 Fax (215)536-2120
Email: ccsnyder@supernet.com
Website: www.bfc.org

Fellowship Tidings, (Q.) Full Gospel Fellowship of Churches and Ministers International, Cynthia Mattox, 1000 N. Beltline Road, Irving, TX 75061 Tel. (214)492-1254 Fax (214)492-1736
Email: FGFCMI@aol.com
Website: www.fgfcmi.org

FGConnections, (3-Y.) Friends General Conference, Barbara Hirshkowitz, 1216 Arch Street 2B, Philadelphia, PA 19107 Tel. (215)

561-1700 Fax (215)561-0759
Email: connections@fgcquaker.org
Website: www.fgcquaker.org/connect

Firm Foundation, (M.) Churches of Christ, H. A. Dobbs, P.O. Box 690192, Houston, TX 77269-0192 Tel. (713)469-3102 Fax (713) 469-7115
Email: had@worldnet.att.net

First Things: A Monthly Journal of Religion & Public Life, (10-Y.) Interdenominational, Richard J. Neuhaus, 156 Fifth Ave., Ste. 400, New York, NY 10010 Tel. (212)627-1985 Fax (212)627-2184
Email: ft@firstthings.com
Website: www.firstthings.com

The Flaming Sword, (M.) Bible Holiness Church, Susan Davolt, 10th St. & College Ave., Independence, KS 67301 Tel. (316)331-2580 Fax (316)331-2580

For God and Country, (Q.) Seventh-Day Adventist Church, Deena Bartel-Wagner—Editor; Gary R. Councell—Executive Editor, Adventist Chaplaincy Ministries
General Conference of Seventh-day Adventists, 12501 Old Columbia Pike, Silver Spring, MD 20904-6600

Foresee, (bi-M.) Conservative Congregational Christian Conference, Richard & Shirley Leonard, 8941 Highway 5, Lake Elmo, Lake Elmo, MN 55042 Tel. (651)739-1474 Fax (651)739-0750
Email: dmjohnson@ccccusa.com
Website: www.ccccusa.com

Forum Letter, (M.) Independent, Intra-Lutheran (companion publication to the quarterly, Lutheran Forum), Pastor Russell E. Saltzman, Ruskin Heights Lutheran Church, 10801 Ruskin Way, Kansas City, MO 64134 Tel. (816)761-6815 Fax (816)761-6523
Email: rhlcpastor@sbcglobal.net
Website: www.alpb.org

Forward, (Q.) United Pentecostal Church International, Rev. J. L. Hall, 8855 Dunn Rd., Hazelwood, MO 63042 Tel. (314)837-7300 Fax (314)837-4503

Forward in Christ, (M.) Wisconsin Evangelical Lutheran Synod, Rev. John A. Braun, 2929 N. Mayfair Rd., Milwaukee, WI 53222 Tel. (414) 256-3210 Fax (414)256-3862
Email: fic@sab.wels.net
Website: www.wels.net

Foursquare World Advance, (Q. w/ a bonus issue) International Church of the Foursquare Gospel, Dr. Ron Williams, PO Box 26902,

1910 W. Sunset Blvd., Ste 400, Los Angeles, CA 90026-0176 Tel. (213)989-4230 Fax (213) 989-4544
Email: comm@foursquare.org
Website: www.advancemagazine.org

Free Will Baptist Gem, (M.) National Association of Free Will Baptists, Gary Fry, P.O. Box 991/ 100 E. Commercial Street, Lebanon, MO 65530 Tel. (417)532-9131 Fax (417)588-7911
Email: gwfry@webound.com

Friend Magazine, (M.) The Church of Jesus Christ of Latter-day Saints, Vivian Paulsen, 50 E South Temple Street, 24th Fl, Salt Lake City, UT 84150 Tel. (801)240-2210 Fax (801)240-2270

Friends Bulletin, (10-Y.) Religious Society of Friends, Anthony Manousos, 3223 Danaha St., Torrance, CA 90505 Tel. (310)-325-3581
Email: friendsbul@aol.com
Website: www.westernquaker.net

Friends Journal, (M.) Religious Society of Friends, Susan Corson-Finnerty—Publisher & Exec. Editor, 1216 Arch St., 2A, Philadelphia, PA 19107-2835 Tel. (215)563-8629 Fax (215) 568-1377
Email: info@friendsjournal.org
Website: www.friendsjournal.org

The Friends Voice, (3-Y.) Evangelical Friends International—North America Region, Dr. Becky Towne, Sr. Editor
Dr. Kathy Roblyer, Assoc. Editor, 2748 E. Pikes Peak Ave, Colorado Springs, CO 80909 Tel. (719)632-5721 (800)351-2973
Email: thevoice@evangelicalfriends.org
Website: evangelicalfriends.org

Front Line, (3 times per year) Conservative Baptist Association of America, Al Russell, P.O. Box 58, Long Prairie, MN 56347 Tel. (320)732-8072 Fax (509)356-7112
Email: chaplruss@earthlink.net
Website: www.cbchaplains.net

Full Gospel Ministries Outreach Report, (Q.) Full Gospel Assemblies International, Simeon Strauser, P.O. Box 1230, Coatsville, PA 19320 Tel. (610)857-2357 Fax (610)857-3109

The Gem, (W.) Churches of God, General Conference, Rachel Foreman, P.O. Box 926, Findlay, OH 45839 Tel. (419)424-1961 Fax (419)424-3433
Email: communications@cggc.org
Website: www.cggc.org

God's Field, (bi-W. except Dec.) Polish National Catholic Church of America and Canada, Rev. Anthony Mikovsky (English) and Rt. Rev.

Casimir Grotnik (Polish), 1006 Pittston Ave., Scranton, PA 18505-4109 Tel. (570)346-9131 Fax (570)346-2188
Email: GodsField@adelphia.net
Website: www.pncc.org

Good News-Buna Vestire, (Q.) The Romanian Orthodox Episcopate of America, The Romanian Orthodox Deanery of Canada, 2855 Helmsing St., Regina, SK S4V 0W7 Tel. (306) 761-2379 Fax (306)525-9650
Email: danielnenson@sasktel.net

Gospel Advocate, (M.) Churches of Christ, Neil W. Anderson, 1006 Elm Hill Pike, Nashville, TN 37202 Tel. (615)254-8781 Fax (615)254-7411
Email: info@gospeladvocate.com
Website: www.gospeladvocate.com

The Gospel Herald, (M.) Church of God, Mountain Assembly, Inc., Scott Isham, P.O. Box 157, Jellico, TN 37762 Tel. (423)784-8260 Fax (423)784-3258
Email: cgmahdq@jellico.com
Website: www.cgmahdq.org

The Gospel Light, (2-Y.) The Bible Church of Christ, Inc., Carole Crenshaw, 1358 Morris Ave., Bronx, NY 10456 Tel. (718)588-2284 Fax (718)992-5597
Website: www.thebiblechurchofchrist.org

The Gospel Messenger, (M.) Congregational Holiness Church, Inc., Rev. Danny K. Jones, Congregational Holiness Church, 3888 Fayetteville Highway, Griffin, GA 30223 Tel. (770-228-4833 Fax (770-228-1177
Email: messenger@CHChurch.com
Website: www.CHChurch.com

The Gospel Truth, (bi-M.) Church of the Living God, C.W.F.F., W.E. Crumes, 430 Forest Avenue, Cincinnati, OH 45229 Tel. (513)569-5660 Fax (513)569-5661
Email: cwff430@aol.com

Grow Magazine, (Q.) Church of the Nazarene, Jim Dorsey, 6401 The Paseo, Kansas City, MO 64131 Tel. (816)333-7000 ext. 2828 Fax (816) 523-1872
Email: jdorsey@nazarene.org
Website: www.growmagazine.org

Guide, (W.) Seventh-day Adventist Church, Randy Fishell, 55 W. Oak Ridge Dr., Hagerstown, MD 21740 Tel. (301)393-4037 Fax (301)393-4055
Email: guide@rhpa.org
Website: www.guidemagazine.org

The Handmaiden, (Q.) The Antiochian Orthodox Christian Archdiocese of North America, Virginia Nieuwsma, P.O. Box 76,

Ben Lomond, CA 95005-0076 Tel. (831)336-5118 Fax (831)336-8882
Email: czell@conciliarpress.com
Website: www.conciliarpress.com

The Happy Harvester, (M.) Church of God of Prophecy, Diane Pace, P.O. Box 2910, Cleveland, TN 37320-2910 Tel. (423)559-5435 Fax (423)559-5444
Email: JoDiPace@wingnet.net

Herald, (M.) Community of Christ, Editorial Board, 1001 W. Walnut, Independence, MO 64050 Tel. (816)833-1000 Fax (816)521-3043
Email: Herald@cofchrist.org
Website: www.heraldhouse.org or www.cof christ.org

The Herald of Christian Science, (M. & Q.) Church of Christ, Scientist, Mary M. Trammell, Editor-in-Chief, The Christian Science Publishing Society, One Norway St., Boston, MA 02115-3195 Tel. (617)450-2000 Fax (617)450-2930
Email: trammellm@csps.com or herald@csps. com
Website: www.csherald.com

Heritage, (Annual) Assemblies of God, Darrin Rodgers, 1445 Boonville Ave., Springfield, MO 65802 Tel. (417)862-1447 Ext. 4400 Fax (417)862-6203
Email: drodgers@ag.org
Website: www.agheritage.org

High Adventure, (Q.) Assemblies of God, John M. Hicks, Gospel Publishing House, 1445 N. Boonville Ave., Springfield, MO 65802-1894 Tel. (417)862-2781 Fax (417)831-8230
Email: rangers@ag.org
Website: www.royalrangers.ag.org

Higher Way, (Q.) Apostolic Faith Mission of Portland, Oregon, Darrel D. Lee, 6615 S.E. 52nd Ave., Portland, OR 97206 Tel. (503)777-1741 Fax (503)777-1743
Email: kbarrett@apostolicfaith.org
Website: www.apostolicfaith.org

Holiness Today, (bi-M.) Church of the Nazarene, David J. Felter, 6401 The Paseo, Kansas City, MO 64131 Tel. (816)333-7000 Fax (816)333-1748
Email: HolinessToday@nazarene.org
Website: www.holinesstoday.com

Homiletic and Pastoral Review, (M.) The Roman Catholic Church, Kenneth Baker, 50 S Franklin Tpk, PO Box 297, Ramsey, NJ 07446 Tel. (201)236-9336

Horizons, (M.) Christian Churches and Churches of Christ, Leah Ellison Bradley,

Susan Jackson Dowd, 100 Witherspoon St, Louisville, KY 40202-1396 Tel. (505)569-5368 Fax (502)569-8085
Email: msa@missionservices.org
Website: www.missionservices.org

Horizons, (7-Y.) Presbyterian Church (U.S.A.), Leah Ellison Bradley, Susan Jackson Dowd, Presbyterian Women, 100 Witherspoon St., Louisville, KY 40202-1396 Tel. (502)569-5368 Fax (502)569-8085
Email: lbradley@ctr.pcusa.org
Website: www.pcusa.org/horizons

Ignite Your Faith, (9-Y.) Nondenominational, Christopher Lutes, 465 Gunderson Dr., Carol Stream, IL 60188 Tel. (630)260-6200 Fax (630)480-2004
Email: iyf@igniteyourfaith.com
Website: www.igniteyourfaith.com

The Inclusive Pulpit, (Y.) International Council of Community Churches, Larry and Carolyn Dipboye, 21116 Washington Pky., Frankfort, IL 60423-3112 Tel. (815)464-5690 Fax (815) 464-5692
Email: iccc60423@aol.com
Website: icccusa.com

Insight Into, (bi-M.) Netherlands Reformed Congregations, Mr. Schipper, 4732 E. C Avenue, Kalamazoo, MI 49004 Tel. (269)349-9448

InterLit, (Q.) Nondenominational magazine on Christian publishing worldwide, Kim A. Pettit, 4050 Lee Vance View Drive, Colorado Springs, CO 80918 Tel. (719)536-0100 Fax (719)536-3266
Email: ccmintl@ccmi.org
Website: www.ccmi.org

International Bulletin of Missionary Research, (Q.) Nondenominational, Jonathan J. Bonk, Overseas Ministries Study Center, 490 Prospect St., New Haven, CT 06511-2196 Tel. (203)624-6672 Fax (203)865-2857
Email: ibmr@OMSC.org
Website: www.OMSC.org, www.DACB.org

Interpretation: A Journal of Bible and Theology, (Q.) Ecumenical, Co-Editors, James Brashler and Sam Balentine, 3401 Brook Rd., Richmond, VA 23227 Tel. (804) 278-4296 Fax (804)278-4208
Email: email@interpretation.org
Website: www.interpretation.org

el Intérprete, (bi-M.) The United Methodist Church, Amanda M. Bachus, Director/Editor, Spanish Resources, United Methodist Communications
P.O. Box 320, Nashville, TN 37202-0320 Tel.

(615)742-5113 Fax (615)742-5460
Email: abachus@umcom.org
Website: www.interpretermagazine.org, www.noticias.umc.org

El Interprete (Spanish), (Internet) United Methodist Church, Amanda Bachus, UM Communi-cations, PO Box 320, Nashville, TN 37202-0320 Tel. (615)742.5113 Fax (615)742-5469
Email: abachus@umcom.org
Website: www.elinterprete.org/

Interpreter, (6-Y.) United Methodist Church, Kathy Noble, United Methodist Communications, P.O. Box 320, Nashville, TN 37202-0320 Tel. (615)742-5441 Fax (615)742-5469
Email: knoble@umcom.org
Website: www.interpretermagazine.org

IPHC Experience, (bi-M.) International Pentecostal Holiness Church, Shirley Spencer, P.O. Box 12609, Oklahoma City, OK 73157 Tel. (405)787-7110 Fax (405)789-3957
Website: www.iphc.org/wms

John Three Sixteen, (Q.) Bible Holiness Church, Mary Cunningham, 10th St. & College Ave., Independence, KS 67301 Tel. (316)331-2580 Fax (316)331-2580

Journal of Adventist Education, (5-Y.) Seventh-day Adventist Church, Beverly J. Robinson-Rumble, 12501 Old Columbia Pike, Silver Spring, MD 20904-6600 Tel. (301)680-5075/ (301)680-5069 Fax (301)622-9627
Email: rumbleb@gc.adventist.org, goffc@gc.adventist.org
Website: www.education.gc.adventist.org/jae

Journal of the American Academy of Religion, (Q.) Nondenominational, Charles T. Mathewes, Department of Religous Studies
University of Virginia, PO Box 400126, Charlottesville, VA 22904-4126
Email: jaar@virginia.edu
Website: www.aarweb.org

Journal of Christian Education, (Q.) African Methodist Episcopal Church, Kenneth H. Hill, 500 Eighth Ave., S., Nashville, TN 37203 Tel. (615)242-1420 Fax (615)726-1866
Email: cedoffice@ameced.com
Website: www.ameced.com

Journal of Ecumenical Studies, (Q.) Inter-denominational/Interfaith, Leonard Swidler, Temple Univ. (022-38), 1114 West Berks St.-Anderson #511, Philadelphia, PA 19122-6090 Tel. (215)204-7714 Fax (215)204-4569
Email: nkrody@temple.edu
Website: ecumene.org/jes

The Journal of Pastoral Care & Counseling, (Q.) Nondenominational, Orlo Strunk, Jr., 1068 Harbor Dr., SW, Calabash, NC 28467 Tel. (910)579-5084 Fax (910)579-5084
Email: jpcp@jpcp.org
Website: www.jpcp.org

Journal of Presbyterian History, (bi-Annual) Presbyterian Church (U.S.A.), James H. Moorhead; Frederick J. Heuser, Jr., 425 Lombard St., Philadelphia, PA 19147 Tel. (215)627-1852 Fax (215)627-0509
Email: jph@history.pcusa.org
Website: www.history.pcusa.org

Journal From the Radical Reformation, (Bi-A) Church of God General Conference (Morrow, GA), Kent Ross and Anthony Buzzard, Sr. Editors, Box 100,000, Morrow, GA 30260-7000 Tel. (404)362-0052 Fax (404) 362-9307
Email: info@abc-coggc.org
Website: www.abc-coggc.org

Journal of Theology, (Q.) Church of the Lutheran Confession, Prof. Steve Sippert, Immanuel Lutheran College, 501 Grover Rd., Eau Claire, WI 54701-7199 Tel. (715)832-9936 Fax (715)836-6634
Email: ilcgreekprof@yahoo.com
Website: www.clcpub/clc/clc.html

The Joyful Noiseletter, (10-Y.) Interdenominational, Cal Samra, P.O. Box 895, Portage, MI 49081-0895 Tel. (616)324-0990 Fax (616) 324-3984
Email: joyfulnz@aol.com
Website: www.joyfulnoiseletter.com

Judaism, (Q.) Jewish (Sponsored by the American Jewish Conference), Rabbi Shammai Engelmayer, 15 E. 84th St., New York, NY 10028 Tel. (212)879-4500 Fax (212) 249-3672
Email: judaism@ajcongress.org
Website: www.ucsc.edu/judaism/judaism.html

Key Lay Notes, (2-Y.) International Council of Community Churches, Phil Smith, 21116 Washington Pky., Frankfort, IL 60423-3112 Tel. (815)464-5690 Fax (815)464-5692
Email: iccc60423@aol.com
Website: icccusa.com

The Lantern, (bi-M.) National Baptist Convention of America, Inc., Robert Jeffrey, 1320 Pierre Avenue, Shreveport, LA 71103 Tel. (318)221-3701 Fax (318)222-7512

Leadership: A Practical Journal for Church Leaders, (Q.) Nondenominational, Marshall Shelley, 465 Gundersen Dr., Carol Stream, IL 60188 Tel. (630)260-6200 Fax (630) 260-0114

Email: LJeditor@leadershipjournal.net
Website: www.Leadershipjournal.net

Learning and Living, (Q.) Netherlands Reformed Congregations, David Engelsma, 1000 Ball, Northeast, Grandrapids, MI 49505 Tel. (616)458-4367 Fax (616)458-8532
Email: engelsma@plymouthchristian.put.k12.mi.us

Liberty, (bi-M.) Seventh-day Adventist Church, Clifford R. Goldstein, 12501 Old Columbia Pike, Silver Spring, MD 20904 Tel. (301)680-6691 Fax (301)680-6695

Lifeglow, Large Print, (6-Y) Seventh-day Adventist Church, Gaylena Gibson, Christian Record Services, Inc., P.O. Box 6097, Lincoln, NE 68506 Tel. (402)488-0981 Fax (402)488-7582
Email: editorial@christianrecord.org
Website: www.christianrecord.org

Light and Life Magazine, (bi-M.) Free Methodist Church, Douglas M. Newton, P.O. Box 535002, Indianapolis, IN 46253-5002 Tel. (317)244-3660
Email: llmeditor@fmcna.org
Website: www.freemethodistchurch.org

Liguorian, (10-Y.) The Catholic Church, William J. Parker, C.SS.R., 1 Liguori Dr., Liguori, MO 63057 Tel. (636)464-2500 Fax (636)464-8449
Email: liguorianeditor@liguori.org
Website: www.liguorian.org

Listen, (Sep-May) Seventh-day Adventist Church, Céleste Walker, 55 W. Oak Ridge Dr., Hagerstown, MD 21740 Tel. (301)393-4082 Fax (301)393-4055
Email: listen@healthconnection.org
Website: www.listenmagazine.org

Living Orthodoxy, (bi-M.) The Russian Orthodox Church Outside of Russia, Fr. Gregory Williams, 1180 Orthodox Way, Liberty, TN 37095 Tel. (615)536-5239 Fax (615)536-5945
Email: info@sjkp.org
Website: www.sjkp.org

The Long Island Catholic, (W.) The Roman Catholic Church, Elizabeth O'Connor, P. O. Box 9000, 200 W Centennial Ave Suite 201, Roosevelt, NY 11575 Tel. (516)594-1000 Fax (516)594-1092
Website: www.licatholic.org

The Lookout, (W.) Christian Churches and Churches of Christ, Shawn McMullen, 8121 Hamilton Ave., Cincinnati, OH 45231 Tel. (513)931-4050 Fax (513)931-0950
Email: lookout@standardpub.com
Website: www.lookoutmag.com

Lumicon Digital Productions, (Internet) Independent, Protestant, Rev. Dr. Tom Boomershine, UMR Communications, P.O. Box 660275, Dallas, TX 75266-0275 Tel. (214)630-6495 Fax (214)630-0079 Email: tboom@umr.org Website: www.lumicon.org

The Lutheran, (M.) Evangelical Lutheran Church in America, Daniel J. Lehmann, 8765 W. Higgins Rd., Chicago, IL 60631-4183 Tel. (773)380-2540 Fax (773)380-2751 Email: lutheran@elca.org Website: www.thelutheran.org

The Lutheran Ambassador, (16-Y.) The Association of Free Lutheran Congregations, Craig Johnson, 575 34th Street, Astoria, OR 97103 Tel. (541)687-8643 Fax (541)683-8496 Email: cjohnson@efn.org

The Lutheran Educator, (Q.) Wisconsin Evangelical Lutheran Synod, Prof. Jack N. Minch, Martin Luther College, 1995 Luther Ct., New Ulm, MN 56073 Tel. (507)354-8221 Fax (507)354-8225 Email: lutheraneducator@mlc-wels.edu

Lutheran Forum, (Q.) Interdenominational Lutheran, Ronald B. Bagnall, 207 Hillcrest Ave., Trenton, NJ 08618 Tel. (856)696-0417

The Lutheran Layman, (bi-M.) The Lutheran Church—Missouri Synod, Gerald Perschbacher, 660 Mason Ridge Center Dr, St. Louis, MO 63141-8557 Tel. (314)317-4100 Fax (314) 317-4295

Lutheran Partners, (bi-M.) Evangelical Lutheran Church in America, William A. Decker, 8765 W. Higgins Rd., Chicago, IL 60631-4101 Tel. (773)380-2884 Fax (773) 380-2829 Email: lutheran.partners@elca.org Website: www.elca.org/lutheranpartners

Lutheran Sentinel, (M.) Evangelical Lutheran Synod, Theodore Gullixson, 5530 Englewood Dr., Madison, WI 53705 Tel. (641)585-1683 Fax (641)585-1683 Email: Theodore Gullixson

Lutheran Spokesman, (M.) Church of the Lutheran Confession, Rev. Paul Fleischer, 1741 E. 22nd St., Cheyenne, WY 82001 Tel. (307)638-8006 Email: paulgf@qwest.net Website: www.lutheranspokeman.org

Lutheran Synod Quarterly, (Q.) Evangelical Lutheran Synod, G.R. Schmeling, Bethany Lutheran Theological Semi, 6 Browns Ct., Mankato, MN 56001 Tel. (507)344-7855 Fax

(507)344-7426 Email: elsynod@blc.edu Website: www.blts.edu

The Lutheran Witness, (M.) The Lutheran Church—Missouri Synod, Don Folkemer, 1333 S. Kirkwood Road, St. Louis, MO 63122-7295 Tel. (314)965-9000 Fax (314) 966-1126 Email: lutheran.witness@lcms.org Website: www.lcms.org/witness

Lutheran Woman Today, (10-Y.) Evangelical Lutheran Church in America, Kate Sprutta Elliott, Women of the ELCA, 8765 W. Higgins Rd., Chicago, IL 60631-4101 Tel. (773)380-2730 Fax (773)380-2419 Email: lwt@elca.org Website: www.elca.org/wo/lwthome.html

Lyceum Spotlight, (10-Y.) National Spiritualist Association of Churches, Rev. Cosie Allen, 1418 Hall St., Grand Rapids, MI 49506 Tel. (616)241-2761 Fax (616)241-4703 Email: cosie@dnx.net Website: www.nsac.org/spotlight

Magyar Egyhaz—Magyar Church, (Q.) Hungarian Reformed Church in America, Stephen Szabo, 464 Forest Ave., Paramus, NJ 07652 Tel. (201)262-2338 Fax (845)359-5771

Mar Thoma Messenger, (Q.) Mar Thoma Syrian Church of India, Eapen Daniel, 2320 S. Merrick Ave, Merrick, NY 11566 Tel. (516) 377-3311 Fax (516)377-3322 Email: marthoma@aol.com

Maranatha, (Q.) Advent Christian Church, John Roller, P.O. Box 23152, Charlotte, NC 28227 Tel. (704)545-6161 Fax (704)573-0712 Email: jroller@acgc.us Website: www.acgc.us

Marriage Partnership, (Q.) Nondenominational, Ginger Kolbaba—Managing Editor, 465 Gundersen Dr., Carol Stream, IL 60188 Tel. (630)260-6200 Fax (630)260-0114 Email: mp@marriagepartnership.com Website: www.marriagepartnership.com

Mature Years, (Q.) The United Methodist Church, Marvin W. Cropsey, 201 Eighth Ave. S, Nashville, TN 37202 Tel. (615)749-6292 Fax (615)749-6512 Email: matureyears@umpublishing.org

The Mennonite, (24-Y.) Mennonite Church USA, Everett J. Thomas, 1700 S. Main St., Goshen, IN 46526 Tel. (574)535-6051 Fax (574)535-6050 Email: editor@themennonite.org Website: www.themennonite.org

335

Mennonite Historical Bulletin, (Q.) Mennonite Church USA, Susan Fisher Miller, 1700 South Main St., Goshen, IN 46526 Tel. (574)535-7477 Fax (574)535-7756
Email: archives@goshen.edu
Website: www.MennoniteUSA.org/history

Mennonite Quarterly Review, (Q.) Mennonite Church, John D. Roth, 1700 S. Main St., Goshen, IN 46526 Tel. (574)535-7433 Fax (574)535-7438
Email: MQR@goshen.edu
Website: www.goshen.edu/mgr

Message, (bi-M.) Seventh-day Adventist Church, Dr. Ron C. Smith, Review and Herald Publishing Association, 55 West Oak Ridge Dr., Hagerstown, MD 21740 Tel. (301)393-4099 Fax 301-393-4103
Email: pharris@rhpa.org or ronsmith@rhpa.org
Website: www.messagemagazine.org

Message of the Open Bible, (bi-M.) Open Bible Standard Churches, Inc., Andrea Johnson, 2020 Bell Ave., Des Moines, IA 50315-1096 Tel. (515)288-6761 Fax (515)288-2510
Email: message@openbible.org
Website: www.openbible.org

Messenger, (11-Y.) Church of the Brethren, Walt Wiltschek, 1451 Dundee Ave., Elgin, IL 60120 Tel. (847)742-5100 Fax (847)742-1407
Email: messenger@brethren.org

The Messenger, (M.) The Swedenborgian Church, Patte LeVan, Central Office, 11 Higland Ave, Newton Ville, Julian, MA 02460 Tel. (760)765-2915
Email: messengerpwl@ixpres.com
Website: www.swedenborg.org

The Messenger, (M.) Pentecostal Free Will Baptist Church, Inc., Patte Levan, P.O. Box 1568, Dunn, NC 28335 Tel. (910)892-4161 Fax (910)892-6876
Email: messengerpwl@ixpres.com

Messenger of Truth, (bi-W.) Church of God in Christ (Mennonite), Gladwin Koehn, P.O. Box 230, Moundridge, KS 67107 Tel. (620)345-2532 Fax (620)345-2582
Email: gospelpublishers@cogicm.org

Methodist History, (Q.) The United Methodist Church, Charles Yrigoyen, Jr., P.O. Box 127, Madison, NJ 07940 Tel. (973)408-3189 Fax (973)408-3909
Email: cyrigoyen@gcah.org
Website: www.gcah.org

Ministry, (M.) Seventh-day Adventist Church, Nikolaus Satelmajer, 12501 Old Columbia Pike, Silver Spring, MD 20904 Tel. (301)680-6510 Fax (301)680-6502
Email: ministrymagazine@gc.adventist.org

Mission, Adult, and Youth Children's Editions, (Q.) Seventh-day Adventist Church, Charlotte Ishkanian, 12501 Old Columbia Pike, Silver Spring, MD 20904 Tel. (301)680-6167 Fax (301)680-6155

Mission Connection, (Q.) Wisconsin Evangelical Lutheran Synod, Rev. Gary Baumler, 2929 N. Mayfair Rd., Milwaukee, WI 53222 Tel. (414)256-3210 Fax (414)256-3862
Email: mc@sab.wels.net

Mission Herald, (Q) National Baptist Convention, U.S.A., Inc., Dr. Bruce N. Alick, 701 S. 19th Street, Philadelphia, PA 19146 Tel. (215)735-9853 Fax (215)735-1721

Missionary Church Today, (Q) Missionary Church, Rev. Thomas Murphy, PO Box 9127, Ft. Wayne, IN 46899 Tel. (260)747-2027 Fax (260)747-5331
Email: tommurphy@mcusa.org
Website: www.mcusa.org

The Missionary Messenger, (bi-M.) Christian Methodist Episcopal Church, Doris F. Boyd, 213 Viking Dr., W., Cordova, TN 38018 Tel. (901)757-1103 Fax (901)751-2104
Email: doris.boyd@williams.com

The Missionary Messenger, (bi-M.) Cumberland Presbyterian Church, Michael G. Sharpe, 1978 Union Ave., Memphis, TN 38104 Tel. (901)276-9988 Fax (901)276-4578
Email: messenger@cumberland.org
Website: ww.cumberland.org/bom/Communication_and_Publication_Unit/Missionary Messenger

Missionary Seer, (bi-M.) African Methodist Episcopal Zion Church, Rev. Kermit J. DeGraffenreidt, 475 Riverside Dr., Rm. 1935, New York, NY 10115 Tel. (212)870-2952 Fax (212)870-2808
Email: domkd5@aol.com

The Missionary Signal, (bi-M.) Churches of God, General Conference, Rachel Foreman, P.O. Box 926, Findlay, OH 45839 Tel. (419) 424-1961 Fax (419)424-3433
Email: communications@cggc.org
Website: www.cggc.org

Missions Ministry, (Q.) Progressive National Baptist Convention, Inc., Justus Y. Reeves, 601 50th St. NE, Washington, DC 20019 Tel. (202)396-0558 Fax (202)398-4998
Email: justusreeves@aol.com
Website: www.PNBC.org

The Moravian, (10-Y.) Moravian Church in North America (Unitas Fratrum), Deanna L. Hollenbach—Dir. Of Communication, Interprovincial Bd. Of Communication, 1021 Center St., P.O. Box 1245, Bethlehem, PA 18016 Tel. (610)867-0593/800-732-0591 Fax (610)866-9223
Email: pubs@mcnp.org
Website: www.moravian.org

The Mother Church, (bi-M.) Western Diocese of the Armenian Church of North America, Archpriest Fr. Sipan Mekhsian, 3325 N. Glenoaks Blvd., Burbank, CA 91504 Tel. (818)558-7474 Fax (818)558-6333
Email: mgizlechyan@armenianchurchwd.com
Website: www.armenianchurchwd.com

Multiply, (Q.) Presbyterian Church in America, Fred Marsh, Mission to North America, 1700 North Brown Road, Ste. 101, Lawrenceville, GA 30044 Tel. (678)825-1200 Fax (678)825-1201
Email: mna@pcanet.org
Website: www.pca-mna.org

NABtoday for you, (Q.) North American Baptist Conference, Lucinda Armas, 1 So 210 Summit Ave., Oakbrook Terrace, IL 60181 Tel. (630) 495-2000 Fax (630)495-3301
Email: serve@nabconference.org
Website: www.nabconference.org

NAE Leadership Alert, (bi-M.) Interdenominational, Rev. Richard Cizik, 701 G St SW, WASHINGTON, DC 20024 Tel. (202)789-1011 Fax 202-842-0392
Email: rcizike@nae.net

NAE Washington Insight, (M.) Interdenominational, Rev. Richard Cizik, 718 Capitol Square Place, SW, Washington, DC 20024 Tel. (202)789-1011
Email: rcizik@aol.com
Website: www.nae.net

National Catholic Reporter, (44-Y.) The Catholic Church, Tom Roberts, P.O. Box 419281, Kansas City, MO 64141 Tel. (816) 531-0538 Fax (816)968-2280
Email: editor@natcath.org
Website: www.NCRonline.org

The National Spiritualist Summit, (M.) National Spiritualist Association of Churches, Rev. Sandra Pfortmiller, 3521 W. Topeka Dr., Glendale, AZ 85308-2325 Tel. (623)581-6686 Fax (623)581-5544
Website: www.nsac.org

Network, (Q.) Presbyterian Church in America, Susan Fikse, 1600 North Brown Road, Lawrenceville, GA 30047 Tel. (678)823-0004 Fax (678)823-0027
Website: www.pca.org

New Church Life, (M.) General Church of the New Jerusalem, Rev. Donald L. Rose, Box 277, Bryn Athyn, PA 19009 Tel. (215)947-6225 ext. 209 Fax (215)938-1871
Email: DonR@BACS-GC.org
Website: www.newchurch.org

New Horizons in the Orthodox Presbyterian Church, (11-Y.) The Orthodox Presbyterian Church, Danny E. Olinger, 607 N. Easton Rd., Bldg. E, P.O. Box P, Willow Grove, PA 19090-0920 Tel. (215)830-0900 Fax (215)830-0350
Email: olinger.1@opc.org
Website: www.opc.org

New Oxford Review, (11-Y.) The Catholic Church, Dale Vree, 1069 Kains Ave., Berkeley, CA 94706 Tel. (510)526-5374 Fax (510)526-3492
Website: www.newoxfordreview.org

New World Outlook, (bi-M.) Mission Magazine of The United Methodist Church, Christie R. House, 475 Riverside Dr., Rm. 1476, New York, NY 10115 Tel. (212)870-3765 Fax (212) 870-3654
Email: NWO@gbgm-umc.org
Website: gbgm-umc.org/now

Newscope, (W.) The United Methodist Church, Andrew J. Schleicher, P.O. Box 801, Nashville, TN 37202 Tel. (615)749-6320 Fax (615)749-6512
Email: umnewscope@umpublishing.org
Website: www.umph.org

Newsline, (Internet; Bi-W.) Church of the Brethren, Cheryl Brumbaugh-Cayford, 1451 Dundee Ave., Elgin, IL 60120-1694 Tel. (847) 742-5100 (800) 323-8039 Fax (847)742-6103
Email: cbrumbaugh-cayford_gb@brethren.org
Website: http://www.brethren.org/genbd/news line/index.htm

The North American Catholic, (M.) North American Old Roman Catholic Church, Theodore J. Remalt, 4154 W. Berteau Ave, Chicago, IL 60641 Tel. (312)685-0461 Fax (312)485-0461
Email: chapelhall@aol.com

The North American Challenge, (M.) Home Missions Division of The United Pentecostal Church International, Joseph Fiorino, 8855 Dunn Rd., Hazelwood, MO 63042-2299 Tel. (314)837-7300 Fax (314)837-5632

NRB Magazine, (9-Y.) Nondenominational, Valerie Fraedrich, National Religious Broadcasters, 9510 Technology Drive, Manassas, VA 20110 Tel. (703)330-7000 Fax (703)330-6996

Email: vfraedrich@nrb.org
Website: www.nrb.org

On Course, (bi-M.) Assemblies of God, Kristi Arnold and Amber Weigand-Buckley (Interim co-editors), 1445 N. Boonville Ave., Springfield, MO 65802-1894 Tel. (417)862-2781 Fax (417)862-1693
Email: oncourse@ag.org
Website: oncourse.ag.org

On the Line, (M.) Mennonite Church, Mary C. Meyer, 616 Walnut Ave., Scottdale, PA 15683 Tel. (724)887-8500 Fax (724)887-3111
Email: info@mph.org
Website: www.mph.org/otl

On Mission, (Q.) Southern Baptist Convention, Carol Pipes, 4200 North Point Pkwy., Alphretta, GA 30202-4174 Tel. (770)410-6394 Fax (770)410-6105
Website: www.onmission.com

ONE Magazine, (bi-M) National Association of Free Will Baptists, Eric Thomsen, PO Box 5002, Antioch, TN 37011-5002 Tel. 615-731-6812 Fax 615-731-0771
Email: eric@nafwb.org
Website: http://www.onemag.org/plymouth_rock.htm

OnSite, (Q.) United Pentecostal Church International, Bryan Abernathy, 8855 Dunn Rd., Hazelwood, MO 63042 Tel. (314)837-7300 Fax (314)837-2387
Email: fmmail@upci.org
Website: www.foreignmissions.com

Orthodox America, (8-Y.) The Russian Orthodox Church Outside of Russia, Mary Mansur, P.O. Box 383, Richfield Springs, NY 13439-0383 Tel. (315)858-1518
Email: info@orthodoxamerica.org
Website: www.orthodoxamerica.org

The Orthodox Church, (M.) The Orthodox Church in America, Very Rev. John Matusiak, Managing Editor—Very Rev. Leonid Kishkovsky, Editor, Editorial Office, One Wheaton Center #912, Wheaton, IL 60187 Tel. (630)668-3071 Fax (630)668-5712
Email: tocmed@hotmail.com
Website: www.oca.org

Orthodox Family, (Q.) The Russian Orthodox Church Outside of Russia, George Johnson and Deborah Johnson, P.O. Box 45, Beltsville, MD 20705 Tel. Fax (301)890-3552
Email: llew@cais.com
Website: www.roca.org/orthodox

Orthodox Life, (bi-M.) The Russian Orthodox Church Outside of Russia, Fr. Luke, Holy Trinity Monastery, P.O Box 36, Jordanville, NY 13361-0036 Tel. (315)858-0940 Fax (315)858-0505
Email: orthlife@telenet.net

The Orthodox Observer, (M.) Greek Orthodox Archdiocese of America, Stavros H. Papagermanos, 8 E. 79th St., New York, NY 10021 Tel. (212)570-3555 Fax (212)774-0239
Email: observer@goarch.org
Website: www.observer.goarch.org

Orthodox Russia (English translation of Pravoslavnaya Rus), (24-Y.) The Russian Orthodox Church Outside of Russia, Archbishop Laurus, Holy Trinity Monastery, P.O. Box 36, Jordanville, NY 13361-0036 Tel. (315)858-0940 Fax (315)858-0505
Email: orthrus@telenet.net

Our Daily Bread, (M.) The Swedenborgian Church, Lee Woofenden, P.O. Box 396, Bridgewater, MA 02324 Tel. (508)946-1767 Fax (508)946-1757
Email: odb@swedenborg.org
Website: www.swedenborg.org/odb/index.cfm

Our Little Friend, (W.) Seventh-day Adventist Church, Aileen Andres Sox, P.O. Box 5353, Nampa, ID 83653-5353 Tel. (208)465-2500 Fax (208)465-2531
Email: ailsox@pacificpress.com
Website: www.pacificpress.com

Our Sunday Visitor, (W.) The Catholic Church, Gerald Korson, 200 Noll Plaza, Huntington, IN 46750 Tel. (219)356-8400
Email: oursunvis@osv.com
Website: www.osv.com

Outreach, (6 per year) Armenian Apostolic Church of America, Iris Papazian, 138 E. 39th St., New York, NY 10016 Tel. (212)689-7810 Fax (212)689-7168
Email: info@armenianprelacy.org
Website: www.armenianprelacy.org

The Path of Orthodoxy (Serbian), (M.) Serbian Orthodox Church in the U.S.A. and Canada, V. Rev. Nedeljko Lunich, 300 Striker Ave., Joliet, IL 60436 Tel. (815)741-1023 Fax (815)741-1883
Email: nedlunich300@comcast.net

Paul, (Q.) Netherlands Reformed Congregations, J. Spans, 47 Main Street E., Norwich, ON N0J 1P0 Tel. (519)863-3306 Fax (519)863-2793

Today's Pentecostal Evangel, (W.) Assemblies of God, Hal Donaldson, Gospel Publishing House, 1445 N. Boonville Ave., Springfield, MO 65802-1894 Tel. (417)862-2781 Fax (417)862-0416

Email: tpe@ag.org
Website: www.tpe.ag.org

The Pentecostal Herald, (M.) United Pentecostal Church International, Rev. J. L. Hall, 8855 Dunn Rd., Hazelwood, MO 63042 Tel. (314)837-7300 Fax (314)837-4503

Pentecostal Leader, (bi-M.) The International Pentecostal Church of Christ, Clyde M. Hughes, P.O. Box 439, London, OH 43140 Tel. (740)852-4722 Fax (740)852-0348
Email: hqipcc@aol.com
Website: www.ipcc.org

The Pentecostal Messenger, (M.) Pentecostal Church of God (Joplin, MO), John Mallinak, P.O. Box 850, Joplin, MO 64802 Tel. (417) 624-7050 Fax (417)624-7102
Email: johnm@pcg.org
Website: www.pcg.org

Perspectives, (10-Y.) Reformed Church in America, James Bratt, David E. Timmer, Scott Hoezee (co-editors), PO Box 1196, Holland, MI 49422-1196 Tel. (616)392-8555 ext. 131 Fax (616)392-7717
Email: perspectives_@rca.org
Website: www.perspectivesjournal.org

Perspectives on Science and Christian Faith, (Q.) Nondenominational, Roman J. Miller, 4956 Singers Glen Rd., Harrisonburg, VA 22802 Tel. (540)432-4412 Fax (540)432-4488
Email: millerrj@rica.net
Website: www.asa3.org

The Pilot-America's Oldest Catholic Newspaper, (W.-49 per year) The Catholic Archdiocese of Boston, Antonio Enrique, 2121 Commonwealth Ave., Brighton, MA 02135 Tel. (617)746-5889 Fax (617)783-2684
Email: editorial@bostonpilot.org
Website: www.rcab.org

Pockets, (11-Y.) The United Methodist Church, Lynn W. Gilliam, P.O. Box 340004, Nashville, TN 37203-0004 Tel. (615)340-7333 Fax (615) 340-7267
Email: pockets@upperroom.org
Website: www.pockets.org

Polka, (Q.) Polish National Catholic Church of America, Cecelia Lallo, 1127 Frieda St., Dickson City, PA 18519-1304 Tel. (570)489-4364 Fax (570)346-2188

Pravoslavnaya Rus (Russian), (24-Y.) The Russian Orthodox Church Outside of Russia, Archbishop Laurus, Holy Trinity Monastery, P.O. Box 36, Jordanville, NY 13361-0036 Tel. (315)858-0940 Fax (315)858-0505
Email: orthrus@telenet.net

Pravoslavnaya Zhisn (Monthly Supplement to Pravoslavnaya Rus), (M.) The Russian Orthodox Church Outside of Russia, Archbishop Laurus, Holy Trinity Monastery, P.O. Box 36, Jordanville, NY 13361-0036 Tel. (315) 858-0940 Fax (315)858-0505
Email: Orthrus@telenet.net

Preacher's Magazine, (3 time per year) Church of the Nazarene, Jeren Rowell and David Busic, 6401 Paseo Blvd, Kansas City, MO 64131-1213
Website: www.nph.com/nphweb/html/pmol/index.htm

Presbyterian News Service "The News", (bi-M.) Presbyterian Church (U.S.A.), Jerry L. VanMarter, 100 Witherspoon St., Rm. 5418, Louisville, KY 40202 Tel. (502)569-5493 Fax (502)569-8073
Email: JVanMart@ctr.pcusa.org
Website: www.pcusa.org/pcnews

Presbyterian Outlook, (43-Y.) Presbyterian Church (U.S.A.), Rev. Jack Haberer, 2112 W. Labaurnum Ave., Suite 109, Richmond, VA 23227 Tel. (800)446-6008 Fax (804)353-6369
Email: jhaberer@pres-outlook.com
Website: www.pres-outlook.com

Presbyterians Today, (10-Y.) Presbyterian Church (U.S.A.), Eva Stimson, 100 Witherspoon St., Louisville, KY 40202-1396 Tel. (502)569-5637 Fax (502)569-8632
Email: today@pcusa.org
Website: www.pcusa.org/today

Primary Source, (Q.) American Baptist Historical Society, Deborah Van Broekhoven, P.O. Box 851, Valley Forge, PA 19482-0851 Tel. Fax (610)768-2266
Email: dbvanbro@abc-usa.org
Website: www.abc-usa.org/abhs

Primary Treasure, (W.) Seventh-day Adventist Church, Aileen Andres Sox, P.O. Box 5353, Nampa, ID 83653-5353 Tel. (208)465-2500 Fax (208)465-2531
Email: ailsox@pacificpress.com
Website: www.pacificpress.com

Priority, (M.) Missionary Church, Dr. Thomas Murphy, P.O. Box 9127, Ft. Wayne, IN 46899 Tel. (260)747-2027 Fax (260)747-5331
Email: mcdenomusa@aol.com
Website: mcusa.org

Pulse, (M.) The Church of God (Seventh Day), Denver, CO, Jamie Stroupe, P.O. Box 33677, 330 W. 152nd Ave., Denver, CO 80233 Tel. (303)452-7973 Fax (303)452-0657
Email: offices@cog7.org
Website: cog7.org

Purpose, (M.) Mennonite Church Canada and Mennonite Church USA, James E. Horsch, 616 Walnut Ave., Scottdale, PA 15683 Tel. (724)887-8500 Fax (724)887-3111
Email: horsch@mph.org
Website: www.mph.org

PYM News, (5-Y.) Philadelphia Yearly Meeting of the Religious Society of Friends, Allen R. Reeder, 1515 Cherry St., Philadelphia, PA 19102-1479 Tel. (215)241-7000 Fax (215) 241-7045
Email: news@pym.org
Website: www.pym.org

Quaker Life, (6-Y.) Friends United Meeting, Patricia Edwards-Konic, 101 Quaker Hill Dr., Richmond, IN 47374-1980 Tel. (765)962-7573 Fax (765)966-1293
Email: QuakerLife@fum.org
Website: www.fum.org

Quarterly Review, A.M.E. Zion, (Q.) African Methodist Episcopal Zion Church, Rev. James D. Armstrong, P.O. Box 33247, Charlotte, NC 28233 Tel. (704)599-4630 Fax (704)688-2544
Email: jaarmstrong@amezhqtr.org

Reflections, (bi-M.) United Pentecostal Church International, Melissa Anderson, 8855 Dunn Rd, Hazelwood, MO 63042 Tel. (918)371-2659 Fax (918)371-6320
Email: manderson@tums.org
Website: www.upci.org/ladies

Reformed Worship, (Q.) Christian Reformed Chuch in North America, Rev. Joyce Borger, 2850 Kalamazoo Ave. SE, Grand Rapids, MI 49560-0001 Tel. (800)777-7270 Fax (616) 224-0834
Email: info@reformedworship.org
Website: www.reformedworship.org

Rejoice!, (Q.) Mennonite Church, Byron Rempel-Burkholder, 600 Shaftesbury Blvd., Winnipeg, MB R3P 0M4 Tel. (204)888-6781 Fax (204) 831-5675
Email: byronrb@mph.org
Website: www.mph.org/rejoice

Report From The Capital, (10-Y.) Baptist Joint Committee, Jeff Huett, 200 Maryland Ave. NE, Washington, DC 20002-5797 Tel. (202) 544-4226 Fax (202)544-2094
Email: jhuett@bjconline.org
Website: www.bjconline.org

Reporter, (M.) The Lutheran Church—Missouri Synod, Joe Isenhower Jr., Managing Editor, 1333 S. Kirkwood Rd., St. Louis, MO 63122-7295 Tel. (314)996-9000 Fax (314)966-1126
Email: vicki.biggs@lcms.org
Website: vicki.biggs@lcms.org

Reporter Interactive, (D.) Independent, Protestant, Cynthia B. Astle, UMR Communications, P.O. Box 660275, Dallas, TX 75266-0275 Tel. (214)630-6495 Fax (214) 630-0079
Email: news@umr.org
Website: www.lumicon.org

The Rescue Herald, (3-Y.) American Rescue Workers, Deborah La Valla, 24 Carriage House, Enfield, CT 06082 Tel. (860)741-0727
Email: deb@arwus.com
Website: www.arwus.com

Response, (M.) The United Methodist Church, Dana Jones, 475 Riverside Dr., Room 1356, New York, NY 10115 Tel. (212)870-3755 Fax (212)870-3940

The Restitution Herald and Church of God Progress Journal, (bi-M.) Church of God General Conference (Oregon, Ill. & Morrow GA), Tim Jones, Box 100,000, Morrow, GA 30260 Tel. (504)362-0052 Fax (404)362-9307
Email: info@abc-coggc.org
Website: www.abc-coggc.org

Restoration Herald, (M.) Christian Churches and Churches of Christ, H. Lee Mason, 7133 Central Parks Blvd., Mason, OH 45040 Tel. (513)229-8000 Fax (513)229-8003
Email: thecra@aol.com
Website: www.thecra.org

Restoration Quarterly, (Q.) Churches of Christ, James W. Thompson, Box 28227, Abilene, TX 79699-8227 Tel. (915)674-3781 Fax (915) 674-3776
Email: rq@bible.acu.edu
Website: www.rq.acu.edu

Review for Religious, (Q.) The Catholic Church, David L. Fleming, S.J., 3601 Lindell Blvd., St. Louis, MO 63108 Tel. (314)663-4160 Fax (314)633-4611
Email: review@slu.edu
Website: www.reviewforreligious.org

Review of Religious Research, (Q.) Non-denominational, Patricia Wittberg, Sociology Department, Indiana University Purdue University, Indianapolis, IN 46202 Tel. (317) 274-4478 Fax (317)278-3654
Email: pwittber@iupui.edu
Website: rra.hartsem.edu

Road to Emmaus, (Q.) Orthodox Christian, Nun Nectaria, 1516 N. Delaware, Indianapolis, IN 46202 Tel. (317)631-1344 Fax (317)637-1897
Email: csb@indy.net
Website: www.roadtoemmaus.net

Rocky Mountain Christian, (M.) Churches of Christ, Ron L. Carter, P.O. Box 803, Eastlake,

CO 80614-0803. Tel. (719)598-4197 Fax (719)528-1549
Email: rmcnews@pcisys.net

Sabbath Recorder, (M.) Seventh Day Baptist General Conference, USA and Canada, Rev. Kevin J. Butler, 3120 Kennedy Rd., P.O. Box 1678, Janesville, WI 53547 Tel. (608)752-5055 Fax (608)752-7711
Email: sdbmedia@charter.net
Website: www.seventhdaybaptist.org

Sabbath School Leadership, (M.) Seventh-day Adventist Church, Faith Crumbly, Review and Herald Publishing Assoc., 55 W. Oak Ridge Dr., Hagerstown, MD 21740 Tel. (301)393-4090 Fax (301)393-4055
Email: sabbathschoolleadership@rhpa.org
Website: www.rhpa.org

Saint Anthony Messenger, (M.) The Catholic Church, Fr. Pat McCloskey, O.F.M., St. Anthony Messenger Editorial, Dept., 28 W. Liberty St., Cincinnati, OH 45202 Tel. (513) 241-5615 Fax (513)241-0399
Email: StAnthony@AmericanCatholic.org
Website: www.AmericanCatholic.org

Saint Willibrord Journal, (Q.) Christ Catholic Church, The Rev. Monsignor Charles E. Harrison, P.O. Box 271751, Houston, TX 77277-1751 Tel. (713)515-8206 Fax (713)622-5311
Website: www.christcatholic.org

Saints Herald, (M.) Community of Christ, Linda Booth, The Herald Publishing House, P.O. Box 390, Independence, MO 64051-0390 Tel. (816)521-3015 Fax (816)521-3066
Email: Herald@CofChrist.org
Website: www.heraldhouse.org

SBC Life, (10-Y.) Southern Baptist Convention, John Revell
Executive Editor: Kenyn Cureton, VP for Convention Relations, 901 Commerce St., Nashville, TN 37203 Tel. (615)244-2355 Fax (615)782-8684
Email: jrevell@sbc.net
Website: sbc.net

The Schwenkfeldian, (3-Y.) The Schwenkfelder Church, Gerald Heebner, 105 Seminary Street, Pennsburg, PA 18073 Tel. (215)679-3103 Fax (215)679-8175
Email: info@schwenfelder.com
Website: www.schwenkfelder.com

Searching Together, (Q.) Sovereign Grace Believers, Jon Zens, Box 548, St. Croix Falls, WI 54024 Tel. (651)465-6516 Fax (651)465-5101
Email: jzens@searchingtogether.org
Website: www.searchingtogether.org

The Secret Place, (Q.) American Baptist Churches USA, Kathleen Hayes, Senior Editor, P.O. Box 851, Valley Forge, PA 19482-0851 Tel. (610)768-2434 Fax (610)768-2441
Email: thesecretplace@abc-usa.org
Website: www.judsonpress.com

Seeds for the Parish, (bi-M.) Evangelical Lutheran Church in America, Janice Rizzo, 8765 W. Higgins Rd., Chicago, IL 60631 Tel. (773)380-2949 Fax (773)380-2406
Email: Janice.Rizzo@elca.org
Website: www.elca.org/seeds

Shalom!, (Q.) Brethren in Christ Church, Harriet Bicksler, P.O. Box A, Grantham, PA 17027 Tel. (717)697-2634
Email: bickhouse@aol.com
Website: bic-church.org/shalom

Shiloh's Messenger of Wisdom, (M.) Israelite House of David, William Robertson, P.O. Box 1067, Benton Harbor, MI 49023

The Shofar, () Apostolic Catholic Church, Myra Calahan, 7813 N. Nebraska Ave., Tampa, FL 33604 Tel. (813)238-6060
Email: Bishop-Chuck@apostoliccatholicchurch.com
Website: www.ApostolicCatholicChurch.com

Signs of the Times, (M.) Seventh-day Adventist Church, Marvin Moore, P.O. Box 5353, Nampa, ID 83653-5353 Tel. (208)465-2577 Fax (208)465-2531
Website: www.signstimes.com

The Silver Lining, (M.) Apostolic Christian Churches of America, Bruce Leman, R.R. 2, Box 50, Roanoke, IL 61561-9625 Tel. (309)923-7777 Fax (309)923-7359

Social Questions Bulletin, (bi-M.) The United Methodist Church, Rev. Kathryn J. Johnson, 212 East Capitol St., NE, Washington, DC 20003 Tel. (202)546-8806 Fax (202)546-6811
Email: mfsa@mfsaweb.org
Website: www.mfsaweb.org

Sojourners, (Monthly) Ecumenical, Jim Wallis, 3333 14th Street NW, Suite 200, Washington, DC 20010 Tel. (202)328-8842 Fax (202)328-8757
Email: sojourners@sojo.net
Website: www.sojo.net

Solia Calendar, (Y.) The Romanian Orthodox Episcopate of America, The Department of Publications of the Romanian Orthodox Episcopate of America, P.O. Box 185, Grass Lake, MI 49240-0185 Tel. (517)522-4800 Fax (517)522-5907
Email: solia@roea.org
Website: roea.org

Solia-The Herald, (M.) The Romanian Orthodox Episcopate of America, Rev. Archdeacon David Oancea, P.O. Box 185, Grass Lake, MI 49240-0185 Tel. (517)522-3656 Fax (517)522-5907
Email: solia@roea.org
Website: www.roea.org

Sound of Grace, (Q.) Sovereign Grace Believers, 5317 Wye Creek Dr, Frederick, MD 21703-6938

The Southern Methodist, (bi-M.) Southern Methodist Church, Thomas M. Owens, Sr., P.O. Box 39, Orangeburg, SC 29116-0039 Tel. (803)534-9853 Fax (803)535-3881
Email: foundry@bellsouth.net

Spirit, (Q.) Volunteers of America, Arthur Smith and Denis N. Baker, 1809 Carrollton Ave, New Orleans, LA 70118-2829 Tel. (504)897-1731

The Spiritual Sword, (Q.) Churches of Christ, Alan E. Highers, 1511 Getwell Rd., Memphis, TN 38111 Tel. (901)743-0464 Fax (901)743-2197
Email: getwellcc@aol.com
Website: www.getwellchurchofchrist.org

The Standard Bearer, (21-Y.) Protestant Reformed Churches in America, Russell J. Dykstra, 4949 Ivanrest Ave. SW, Grandville, MI 49418 Tel. (616)531-1490 Fax (616)531-3033
Email: dykstra@prca.org
Website: www.rfpa.org/sb.asp

The Star of Zion, (bi-W.) African Methodist Episcopal Zion Church, Mr. Mike Lisby, P.O. Box 26770, Charlotte, NC 28221-6770 Tel. (704)599-4630 x 318 Fax (704)688-2546
Email: service@starofzion.org
Website: www.starofzion.org

The Student (Braille & Cassette), (M.) Seventh-day Adventist Church, Bert Williams, P.O. Box 6097, Lincoln, NE 68506-0097 Tel. (402) 488-0981 Fax (402)488-7582
Email: info@christianrecord.org
Website: www.ChristianRecord.org

Sunday, (Q.) Interdenominational, Timothy A. Norton, 2930 Flowers Rd., S., Atlanta, GA 30341-5532 Tel. (770)936-5376 Fax (770) 936-5385
Email: tnorton@ldausa.org
Website: www.sundayonline.org

The Tablet, (W.) The Catholic Church, Ed Wilkinson, 310 Prospect Park West, Brooklyn, NY 11215 Tel. (718)965-7333 Fax (718)965-7337

Email: TheTablet@aol.com
Website: http://www.dioceseofbrooklyn.org/tablet/contact/index.html

Theology Digest, (Q.) The Catholic Church, Bernhard Asen, Rosemary Jermann (co-editors), 3800 Lindell Blvd., St. Louis, MO 63108 Tel. (314)977-3410 Fax (314)977-3704
Email: thdigest@slu.edu

Theology Today, (Q.) Nondenominational, James F. Kay, Reviews Editor: Gordon S. Mikoski, P.O. Box 821, Princeton, NJ 08542-0803 Tel. (609)497-7714 Fax (609)497-1826
Email: theology.today@ptsem.edu

These Days, (Q.) Interdenominational, Vince Patton, 100 Witherspoon St., Louisville, KY 40202-1396 Tel. (502)569-5080 Fax (502) 569-5113
Website: www.ppcpub.com

The Three-Fold Vision, (M.) Apostolic Faith Mission Church of God, Alice Walker, 156 Walker Street, Munford, AL 36268 Tel. (256) 358-9763
Email: alicemtwalker@aol.com

Timbrel: The Publication for Mennonite Women The, (bi-M.) Mennonite Church Canada and USA, Laurie Oswald Robinson, 420 SE Richland Ave., Corvallis, Newton, OR 97333 Tel. (316) 283-5100
Email: timbrel@mennonitewomenUSA.org
Website: www.mennonitewomenusa.org

Today's Christian, (bi-M.) Nondenominational, Ed Gilbreath, 465 Gundersen Dr., Carol Stream, IL 60188 Tel. (630)260-6200 Fax (630)480-2004
Email: tceditor@todays-christian.com
Website: www.todays-christian.com

Today's Christian Woman, (bi-M.) Nondenominational, Jane Johnson Struck, 465 Gundersen Dr., Carol Stream, IL 60188 Tel. (630)260-6200 Fax (630)260-0114
Email: TCWedit@christianitytoday.com
Website: www.todayschristianwoman.com

Today's Pentecostal Evangel, Missions World Edition, (M.) Assemblies of God, Hal Donaldson, Editor in Chief, Gospel Publishing House, 1445 N. Boonville Ave., Springfield, MO 65802 Tel. (417)862-2781 Fax (417)862-0416
Email: pe@ag.org
Website: www.pe.ag.org

Tomorrow Magazine, (Q.) American Baptist Churches in the USA, Sara E. Hopkins, 475 Riverside Dr., Room 1700, New York, NY 10115-0049 Tel. (800)986-6222 Fax (800) 986-6782

The Tover of St. Cassian, (Bi-monthly) Apostolic Episcopal Church, Rev. Stacy C. Douglas MA, MTh, Society of St. Cassian; c/o S.C. Douglas, P.O.Box 5016, Athens, GA 30604 Tel. (917) 373-4036
Email: apostolic.episcopal@gmail.com
Website: www.apostolic-episcopal.org

Truth, (Q.) Grace Gospel Fellowship, Phil Cereghino, 2125 Martindale SW, Grand Rapids, MI 49509 Tel. (616)247-1999 Fax (616)241-2542
Email: ggfinc@aol.com
Website: www.ggfusa.org

Truth Magazine, (bi-W.) Churches of Christ, Mike Willis, Box 9670, Bowling Green, KY 42102 Tel. (800)428-0121
Website: www.truthmagazine.com

Ubique, (Q.) The Liberal Catholic Church—Province of the United States, Mrs. Erin S.W. Satterlee, 2033 22nd Ave. #302, Greeley, CO 80631
Email: ubiquetlcc@fastmail.fm
Website: www.TheLCC.org

Ukrainian Orthodox Herald, () Ukrainian Orthodox Church of America (Ecumenical Patriarchate), Rev. Dr. Anthony Ugolnik, P.O. Box 774, Allentown, PA 18105

Ukrainian Orthodox Word, (Monthly) Ukrainian Orthodox Church of the USA, Heiromonk Daniel (Zelinskyy), PO Box 495, South Bound Brook, NJ 08880 Tel. (732) 356-0090 Fax (732)356-5556
Email: FatherVZ@aol.com
Website: www.uocofusa.org

UMR Communications, Inc., (W., Bi-W.) Independent, Protestant, Robin Russell, P.O. Box 660275, Dallas, TX 75266-0275 Tel. (214)630-6495 Fax (214)630-0079
Email: rrussell@umr.org
Website: www.umr.org, www.reporterinteractive. org, www.lumicon.org

United Church News, (10-Y.) United Church of Christ, W. Evan Golder, 700 Prospect Ave., Cleveland, OH 44115 Tel. (216)736-2218 Fax (216)736-2223
Email: goldere@ucc.org
Website: www.ucc.org

The United Methodist Reporter, (W.) Independent, Protestant, Cynthia B. Astle, UMR Communications, P.O. Box 660275, Dallas, TX 75266-0275 Tel. (214)630-6495 Fax (214)630-0079
Email: news@umr.org
Website: www.umr.org

United Methodists in Service (Korean), (Every 2 months) United Methodist Church (Korean),

Keihwan Ryoo, UMCom, PO Box 320, Nashville, TN 37202-0320 Tel. (615)742-5400 Fax (615)742-5469
Email: kumc@umcom.org
Website: www.koreanumc.org

UOL Bulletin (Ukrainian Orthodox League Bulletin), (7 times per year) Ukrainian Orthodox Church of the USA, Dr. Stephen Sivulich, 206 Christopher Circle, Pittsburgh, PA 15205 Tel. (412)276-1140
Email: ssivulich1@juno.com
Website: www.uocofusa.org

The Upper Room, (bi-M.) The United Methodist Church, Steven D. Bryant, P. O. Box 340004, Nashville, TN 37203-0004 Tel. (877)899-2780 Fax (615)340-7289
Email: sbryant@upperroom.org
Website: www.upperroom.org

U.S. Catholic, (M.) The Catholic Church, Rev. John Molyneux, 205 W. Monroe St., Chicago, IL 60606 Tel. (312)236-7782 Fax (312)236-8207
Email: editors@uscatholic.org
Website: www.uscatholic.org

UU World, (Q) Unitarian Universalist Association of Congregations, Christopher L. Walton, Executive Editor, 25 Beacon St., Boston, MA 02108-2803 Tel. (617)948-6518 Fax (617)742-7025
Email: world@uua.org
Website: www.uuworld.org

Vibrant Life, (bi-M.) Seventh-day Adventist Church, Charles Mills, 55 W. Oak Ridge Dr., Hagerstown, MD 21740 Tel. (301)393-4019 Fax (301)393-4055
Email: vibrantlife@rhpa.org
Website: www.vibrantlife.com

Victory (Youth Sunday School/Bible Study Curriculum), (Q.) Church of God of Prophecy, David Bryan, P.O. Box 2910, Cleveland, TN 37320-2910 Tel. (423)559-5321 Fax (423) 559-5461
Email: david@cogop.org
Website: www.cogop.org

The Vindicator, (M.) Old German Baptist Brethren Church, Steven L. Bayer, 6952 N. Montgomery Co. Line Rd., Englewood, OH 45322-9748 Tel. (937)884-7531 Fax (937) 884-7531

Vira/Faith, (Q.) Ukrainian Orthodox Church of the U.S.A., Hieromonk Daniel (Zelinskyy), P.O. Box 495, South Bound Brook, NJ 08880 Tel. (732)356-0090 Fax (732)356-5556
Email: virafaith@aol.com
Website: www.uocofusa.org

Vista, (Q.) Christian Church of North America, General Council, Wallace Smith, 1294 Rutledge Rd., Transfer, PA 16154 Tel. (412)962-3501 Fax (412)962-1766 Email: ccnahq@adelphia.net Website: www.ccna.org

Vital Signs, (bi-M.) Conservative Baptist Association of America (CBAmerica), Rev. Stanley Rieb, 3686 Stagecoach Rd Unit F, Longmot, CO 80504 Tel. (720)283-3030 Email: info@CBAmerica.org Website: www.CBAmerica.org

The Voice, (Q.) The Bible Church of Christ, Inc., Montrose Bushrod, 1358 Morris Ave., Bronx, NY 10456 Tel. (718)588-2284 Fax (718)992-5597 Website: www.thebiblechurchofchrist.org

The Voice, (bi-M.) IFCA International, Inc., Les Lofquist, P.O. Box 810, Grandville, MI 49468-0810 Tel. (616)531-1840 Fax (616)531-1814 Email: Voice@ifca.org

Voice of Mission, (Q.) African Methodist Episcopal Church, Dr. John W.P. Collier, 1587 Savannah Highway, Ste. A, Charleston, SC 29407 Tel. (843)852-2645 Fax (843)852-2648 Email: gwmame@bellsouth.net Website: amegobalmissions.com

The War Cry, (bi-M.) The Salvation Army, Ed Forster, Editor in Chief; Jeff McDonald, Managing Editor, 615 Slaters Lane, Alexandria, VA 22314 Tel. (703)684-5500 Fax (703)684-5539 Email: war_cry@usn.salvationarmy.org

Watchtower, (bi-W.) Jehovah's Witnesses, Watch Tower Society, 25 Columbia Heights, Brooklyn, NY 11201-2483 Tel. (718)560-5000 Fax (718)560-8850 Website: www.watchtower.org

Weavings: A Journal of the Christian Spiritual Life, (bi-M.) The United Methodist Church, John S. Mogabgab, 1908 Grand Avenue, Nashville, TN 37212 Tel. (615)340-7254 Fax (615)340-7267 Email: weavings@upperroom.org Website: www.upperroom.org/weavings

Wesleyan Life, (Q.) The Wesleyan Church, Norman G. Wilson, P.O. Box 50434, Indianapolis, IN 46250-0434 Tel. (317)774-7909 Fax (317)774-7913 Email: wilsonn@wesleyan.org Website: www.wesleyan.org

Wesleyan World, (Q.) The Wesleyan Church, P.O. Box 50434, Indianapolis, IN 46250 Tel. (317)774-7950 Fax (317)774-7958

Email: ghpm@wesleyan.org Website: www.praygivego.com

The White Wing Messenger, (bi-W.) Church of God of Prophecy, Virginia E. Chatham, P.O. Box 2970, Cleveland, TN 37320-2970 Tel. (423)559-5129/24 Fax (423)559-5128 Website: www.cogop.org

Window on the World, (4-Y.) The Evangelical Congregational Church, Patricia Strain, 100 W. Park Ave, Myerstown, PA 17067 Tel. (717)866-7584 Fax (717)866-7383 Email: ecglobalministries@eccenter.com Website: www.eccenter.com

Wineskins, (bi-M.) Churches of Christ, Mike Cope and Rubel Shelly, Box 41028, Nashville, TN 37024-1028 Tel. (615)373-5004 Fax (615)373-5006 Email: wineskinsmagazine@msn.com Website: www.wineskins.org

Winner, (9-Y.) Nondenominational, Jan Schleifer, The Health Connection, P.O. Box 859, Hagerstown, MD 21741 Tel. (301)393-4082 Fax (301)393-4055 Email: jschleifer@rhpa.org Website: www.winnermagazine.org

Wisconsin Lutheran Quarterly, (Q.) Wisconsin Evangelical Lutheran Synod, John F. Brug, 11831 N. Seminary Dr., Mequon, WI 53092 Tel. (262)242-8139 Fax (262)242-8110 Email: brugj@wls.wels.net Website: www.wls.wels.net

With: The Magazine for Radical Christian Youth, (bi-M.) Mennonite Church USA, Carol Duerksen, P.O. Box 347, 722 Main Street, Newton, KS 67114 Tel. (620)367-8432 Fax (620)367-8218 Email: carold@mennoniteusa.org Website: withonline.org

The Witness, (10-Y.) Nondenominational, Julie A. Wortman, 7000 Michigan Ave., Detroit, MI 48210 Tel. (313)841-1967 Fax (313)841-1956 Email: office@thewitness.org Website: www.thewitness.org

Woman to Woman, (M.) General Association of General Baptists, Barbara Wigger, 100 Stinson Dr., Poplar Bluff, MO 63901 Tel. (573)785-7746 Fax (573)785-0564 Email: wmofc@generalbaptist.com Website: www.generalbaptist.com

The Woman's Pulpit, (Q.) Nondenominational, LaVonne Althouse, 14 St. Mark Avenue, Lititz, PA 17543 Tel. (717)626-0463 Email: revla32@.dejazzd.com Website: www.womenministers.org

344

11. Religious Periodicals in Canada

The religious periodicals below constitute a basic core of important journals and periodicals circulated in Canada. The list does not include all publications prepared by religious bodies, and not all the publications listed here are necessarily the official publication of a particular church. Each entry gives: the title of the periodical, frequency of publication, religious affiliation, editor's name, address, telephone and fax number and email and website addresses when available. The frequency of publication, which appears in parenthesis after the name of the publication, is represented by a "W." for weekly; "M." for monthly; "Q." for quarterly.

Again, (Q.) The Antiochian Orthodox Christian Archdiocese of North America, R. Thomas Zell, Conciliar Press, P.O. Box 76, Ben Lomond, CA 95005-0076 Tel. (800)967-7377 Fax (831)336-8882
Email: tzell@conciliarpress.com
Website: www.conciliarpress.com

The Anglican, (10-Y.) The Anglican Church of Canada, Stuart Mann, 135 Adelaide St. E., Toronto, ON M5C 1L8 Tel. (416)363-6021 Fax (416)363-7678
Email: smann@toronto.anglican.ca
Website: www.toronto.anglican.ca

Anglican Journal, (10-Y.) The Anglican Church of Canada, Leanne Larmondin, 80 Hayden St., Toronto, ON M4Y 3G2 Tel. (416)924-9199 x 306 Fax (416)921-4452
Email: editor@national.anglican.ca
Website: www.anglicanjournal.com

Armenian Evangelical Church Newsletter, (Bimonthly) Armenian Evangelical Church, Rev. Samuel Albarian, 2600 14th Avenue, Markham, ON L3R 3X1 Tel. (905)305-8144 Fax (905)305-8125
Email: aectoronto@yahoo.com

Aujourd'hui Credo, (10-Y.) The United Church of Canada, David Fines, 1332 Victoria, Longueuil, QC J4V 1L8 Tel. (450)446-7733 Fax (450)466-2664
Email: davidfines@egliseunce.org
Website: www.united-church/credo

The Baptist Horizon, (M.) Canadian Convention of Southern Baptists, Nancy McGough, 100 Convention Way, Cochrane, AB T4C 2G2 Tel. (403)932-5688 Fax (403)932-4937
Email: office@ccsb.ca

B.C. Fellowship Baptist, (Q.) The Fellowship of Evangelical Baptist Churches in BC and Yukon, David Horita, #201-26620-56th Ave, Langley, BC V4W 3X5 Tel. (604)607-1192 Fax (604)607-1193
Email: fellowship@shaw.ca
Website: www.bcfellowship.ca

Blackboard Bulletin, (10-Y.) Old Order Amish Church, Old Order Amish Church, Rt. 4, Aylmer, ON N5H 2R3

Die Botschaft, (W.) Old Order Amish Church, James Weaver, Brookshire Publishing, Inc., 200 Hazel St., Lancaster, PA 17603 Tel. (717)392-1321 Fax (717)392-2078

The Budget, (W.) Old Order Amish Church, Fannie Erb-Miller, P.O. Box 249, Sugarcreek, OH 44681 Tel. (330)852-4634 Fax (330)852-4421
Email: budgetnews@aol.com

Cahiers de Spiritualite Ignatienne, (3/year) The Roman Catholic Church in Canada, Gaetane Guillemette, Gaetane Guillemette, 2370 Rue Nicolas-Pinel, Ste-Foy, QC G1V 4L6 Tel. (418)653-6353 Fax (418)653-1208
Email: cahiersi@centremanrese.org
Website: www.centremanrese.org

Canada Lutheran, (8-Y.) Evangelical Lutheran Church in Canada, Ida Reichardt Backman, Interim Editor; Trina Gallop, Manager of Communications; Kristen Guy, Graphic Designer, 302-393 Portage Avenue, Winnipeg, MB R3B 3H6 Tel. (204)984-9150 Toll Free. (888)786-6707 Fax (204)984-9185
Email: canaluth@elcic.ca
Website: www.elcic.ca/clweb

Canada Update, (Q.) The Church of God of Prophecy in Canada, Editor, 5145 Tomkin Road, Mississaugh, ON L4W 1P1 Tel. (905) 625-1278 Fax (905)843-3990

Canadian Adventist Messenger, (12-Y.) Seventh-day Adventist Church in Canada, Carolyn Willis, 1148 King St. E., Oshawa, ON L1H 1H8 Tel. (905)433-0011 Fax (905)433-0982
Email: cwillis@sdacc.org
Website: www.sdacc.org

The Canadian Baptist, (10-Y.) Baptist Convention of Ontario and Quebec, Larry Matthews, 195 The West Mall, Ste.414, Etobicoke, ON M9C 5K1 Tel. (416)622-8600 Fax (416)622-0780
Email: thecb@baptist.ca

The Canadian Friend, (bi-M.) Canadian Yearly Meeting of the Religious Society of Friends, Anne Marie Zilliacus, 218 Third Ave., Ottawa, ON K1S 2K3 Tel. (613)567-8628 Fax (613)567-1078
Email: zilli@cyberus.ca

The Canadian Lutheran, (9-Y.) Lutheran Church—Canada, Ida Backman, Interim Editor, 3074 Portage Ave., Winnipeg, MB R3K 0Y2 Tel. (204)895-3433 x 24 Fax (204) 897-4319
Website: www.lutheranchurch.ca

Canadian Mennonite, (bi-W.) Mennonite Church Canada, Tim Miller Dyck, Suite C5, 490 Dutton Dr., Waterloo, ON N2L 6H7 Tel. (519)884-3810 Fax (519)884-3331
Email: editor@canadianmennonite.org
Website: www.canadianmennonite.org

Canadian Orthodox Messenger, (Q.) Orthodox Church in America (Canada Section), Nun Sophia (Zion), P.O. Box 179, Spencerville, ON K0E 1X0 Tel. (613)925-0645 Fax (613) 925-1521
Email: sophia@ripnet.com

The Catalyst, (6-Y.) Nondenominational, Murray MacAdam, Citizens for Public Justice, 229 College St. #311, Toronto, ON M5T 1R4 Tel. (416)979-2443 Fax (416)979-2458
Email: cpj@cpj.ca
Website: www.cpj.ca

The Catholic Register, (W.) The Roman Catholic Church in Canada, Joseph Sinasac, 1155 Yonge St., Ste. 401, Toronto, ON M4Y 1W2 Tel. (416)934-3410 Fax (416)934-3409
Email: editor@catholicregister.org
Website: www.catholicregister.org

The Catholic Times (Montreal), (10-Y.) The Roman Catholic Church in Canada, Eric Durocher, 2005 St. Marc St., Montreal, QC H3H 2G8 Tel. (514)937-2301 Fax (514)937-3051

Channels, (3-Y.) Presbyterian Church in Canada, Calvin Brown, Managing Editor, Dal Schindell, Renewal Fellowship, 3819 Bloor St W, Etobicoke, ON M9B 1K7 Tel. (416)233-6581 Fax (416)233-1743
Email: cbbrown@rogers.com
Website: www.presbycan.ca/rfpc

Chinese Herald, (bi-M.) Canadian Conference of Mennonite Brethren Churches, Joseph Kwan, 8143 Burnlake Drive, Burnaby, BC V5A 3R6 Tel. (604)421-4100 Fax (604)421-4100
Email: chineseherald@mbconf.ca

Church of God Beacon, (Q.) Church of God (Cleveland, Tenn.), Andrew Binda, P.O. Box 2036, Brampton Commercial Service Center, Brampton, ON L6T 3T0 Tel. (905)793-2213 Fax (905)793-9173
Email: afinda@cogontario.com

Clarion—The Canadian Reformed Magazine, (bi-W.) Canadian and American Reformed Churches, J. Visscher, One Beghin Ave., Winnipeg, MB R2J 3X5 Tel. (204)663-9000 Fax (204)663-9202
Email: clarion@premier.mb.ca
Website: premier.mb.ca/clarion.html

CLBI-Cross Roads, (6-Y.) Lutheran, Dean J. Rostand, 4837-52A St., Camrose, AB T4V 1W5 Tel. (780)672-4454 Fax (780)672-4455
Email: communications@clbi.edu
Website: www.clbi.edu

The Communicator, (3-Y.) The Roman Catholic Church in Canada, Editor, Box 2400, London, ON N6A 4G3 Tel. (519)439-7514 Fax (519)439-0207
Email: info@arccc.ca
Website: arccc.ca/news.htm

Connexions, (4-Y.) Interdenominational, Ulli Diemer, 489 College St., Ste. 305, Toronto, ON M6G 1A5 Tel. (416)964-1511
Website: www.connexions.org

The Covenant Messenger, (Q) The Evangelical Covenant Church of Canada, Doug Wildman, Box 93, Norquay, SK S0A 2V0 Tel. (204)269-3437 Fax (204)269-3584
Email: messengr@escape.ca
Website: www.canadacovenantchurch.org

Crux, (Q.) Nondenominational, Donald Lewis, Regent College, 5800 University Blvd., Vancouver, BC V6T 2E4 Tel. (604)224-3245 Fax (604)224-3097
Email: crux@regent.college.edu
Website: www.cruxonline.net

Diakonia-A Magazine of Office-Bearers, (4-Y.) Canadian and American Reformed Churches, J. Visscher, Brookside Publishing, 3911 Mt. Lehman Rd., Abbotsford, BC V4X 2M9 Tel. (604)856-4127 Fax (604)856-6724

The Diary, (M.) Old Order Amish Church, Don Carpenter, P.O. Box 98, Gordonville, PA 17529 Tel. (717)529-3938 Fax (717)529-3292

Ecumenism-Oecumenisme, (Q.) Interdenominational, Dr. Stuart E. Brown, 2065 Sherbrooke St. W, Montreal, QC H3H 1G6 Tel. (514)937-9176 Fax (514)937-4986
Email: ccocce@oecumenisme.ca
Website: www.oecumenisme.ca

346

The Edge (Christian Youth Magazine), (10-Y.) The Salvation Army in Canada, John McAlister, 2 Overlea Blvd., Toronto, ON M4H 1P4 Tel. (416)422-6116 Fax (416)422-6120
Email: edge@can.salvationarmy.org
Website: www.salvationarmy.ca

Eesti Kirik, (Q.) The Estonian Evangelical Lutheran Church Abroad, Rev. U. Petersoo, 383 Jarvis St., Toronto, ON M5B 2C7 Tel. (416)925-5465 Fax (416)925-5688

EMMC Recorder, (M.) Evangelical Mennonite Mission Conference, Lil Goertzen, Box 52059 Niakwa P.O., Winnipeg, MB R2M 5P9 Tel. (204)253-7929 Fax (204)256-7384
Email: info@emmc.ca
Website: www.emmc.ca

En Avant! (11-Y.) The Salvation Army in Canada, Marie-Michele Roy, 1655 Rue Richardson, Montreal, PQ H3K 3J7 Tel. (514)288-2848 x 2236 Fax (514)288-4657
Email: foivie@can.salvationarmy.org
Website: www.Salvationarmy.org

Esprit, (Q.) Evangelical Lutheran Church in Canada (Evangelical Lutheran Women), Catehrine Pate, 302-393 Portage Avenue, Winnipeg, MB R3B 3H6 Tel. (204)984-9160 Fax (204)984-9162
Email: esprit@elcic.ca
Website: www.elw.ca

Evangel-The Good News of Jesus Christ, (4-Y.) Canadian and American Reformed Churches, D. Moes, 21804 52nd Ave., Langley, BC V2Y 1L3 Tel. (604)576-2124 Fax (604)576-2101
Email: canrc@uniserve.com or jvisscher@telus.ca

Evangel Voice-Voce Evangelica, (Q.) Canadian Assemblies of God, Rev. Daniel Costanza, 140 Woodbridge Ave., Suite 400, Woodbridge, ON L4L 4K9 Tel. (905)850-1578 Fax (905)850-1578
Email: bethel@idirect.com
Website: www.the-ipcc.org

The Evangelical Baptist, (4-Y.) The Fellowship of Evangelical Baptist Churches in Canada, Dr. John Kaiser, P O Box 457, Guelph, ON N1H 6K9 Tel. (519)821-4830 Fax (519)821-9829
Email: president@fellowship.ca
Website: www.fellowship.ca

Faith & Friends, (M.) The Salvation Army in Canada, Geoff Moulton, 2 Overlea Blvd., Toronto, ON M4H 1P4 Tel. (416)422-6110 Fax (416)422-6120
Website: www.faithandfriends.sallynet.org

Faith Today, (bi-M.) The Evangelical Fellowship of Canada (a cooperative organization of more than 40 Protestant denominations), Gail Reid, M.I.P. Box 3745, Markham, ON L3R 0Y4 Tel. (905)479-5885 Fax (905) 479-4742
Email: ft@efc-canada.com
Website: www.faithtoday.ca

Family Life, (11-Y.) Old Order Amish Church, Joseph Stoll and David Luthy, Old Order Amish Church, Rt. 4, Aylmer, ON N5H 2R3

Family Life Network Newsline, (3-Y.) Canadian Conference of Mennonite Brethren Churches, Dorothy Siebert, 225 Riverton Ave., Winnipeg, MB R2L 0N1 Tel. (204)667-9576 Fax (204)669-6079
Email: info@fln.ca
Website: www.fln.ca

Fellowship Magazine, (4-Y.) The United Church of Canada, Rev. Diane Walker, Box 237, Barrie, ON L4M 4T2 Tel. (705)737-0114 or (800)678-2607 Fax (705)737-1086
Email: felmag@csolve.net
Website: www.fellowshipmagazine.org

Foi & Vie, (12-Y.) The Salvation Army in Canada, Marie-Michele Roy, 1655 Rue Richardson, Montreal, PQ H3K 3J7 Tel. (514)288-2848 x 2236 Fax (514)288-4657
Email: Edouard_Hoyer@can.salvationarmy.org
Website: www.SalvationArmy.ca

Glad Tidings, (6-Y.) Presbyterian Church in Canada, Holly Wilson, Women's Missionary Society, 50 Wynford Dr., Toronto, ON M3C 1J7 Tel. (800)619-7301/(416)441-1111 Fax (416)441-2825
Email: hwilson@presbyterian.ca
Website: www.presbyterian.ca/wms

Good Tidings, (10-Y.) The Pentecostal Assemblies of Newfoundland and Labrador, H. Paul Foster, 57 Thorburn Rd., P.O. Box 8895, Sta. A, St. John's, NL A1B 3T2 Tel. (709)753-6314 Fax (709)753-4945
Email: paon@paon.nf.ca

The Gospel Contact, (4-Y.) Church of God (Anderson, Ind.), Editorial Committee, 4717 56th St., Camrose, AB T4V 2C4 Tel. (780) 672-0772 Fax (780)672-6888
Email: wcdncog@cable-lynx.net
Website: www.chog.ca

Gospel Herald, (M.) Churches of Christ in Canada, Wayne Turner and Max E. Craddock, 4904 King St., Beamsville, ON L0R 1B6 Tel. (905)563-7503 Fax (905)563-7503
Email: editorial@gospelherald.org
Website: www.gospelherald.org

The Gospel Standard, (M.) Nondenominational, Perry F. Rockwood, Box 1660, Halifax, NS B3J 3A1 Tel. (902)423-5540 Fax (902)423-0820

Gospel Tidings, (M.) Independent Holiness Church, Marilyn E. Votary, 1564 John Quinn Rd., Greely, ON K4P 1J9 Tel. (613)821-2237 Fax (613)821-4663
Email: marilynv@hotmail.com
Website: www.holiness.ca

The Grape Vine, (12-Y.) Reformed Episcopal Church in Canada, Ingrid Andreller, 626 Blanshard Street, Victoria, BC V8W 3G6 Tel. (250)383-8915 Fax (250)383-8916
Email: office@churchofourlord.org
Website: www.churchofourlord.org

Hallelujah!, (bi-M.) The Bible Holiness Movement, Wesley H. Wakefield, Box 223, Postal Stn. A, Vancouver, BC V6C 2M3 Tel. (250)492-3376

Herold der Wahrheit, (M.) Old Order Amish Church, Cephas Kauffman, 1827 110th St., Kalona, IA 52247

Horizons, (bi-M.) The Salvation Army in Canada, 2 Overlea Blvd., Toronto, ON M4H 1P4 Tel. (416)425-6118 Fax (416)422-6120

Insight*Insound*In Touch, (6-Y. (Insight); 6-Y. (In Sound); 4-Y. (In Touch)) Interdenominational, Insight (large print newspaper); In Sound (audio magazine); In Touch (braille newspaper), Rebekah Chevalier, Graham Down, John Milton Society for the Blind in Canada, 40 St. Clair Ave. E., Ste. 202, Toronto, ON M4T 1M9 Tel. (416)960-3953 Fax (416)960-3570
Email: admin@jmsblind.ca
Website: www.jmsblind.ca

Intercom, (Q.) The Fellowship of Evangelical Baptist Churches in Canada, Terry D. Cuthbert, 679 Southgate Dr., Suite 100, Guelph, ON N1G 4S2 Tel. (519)821-4830 Fax (519)821-9829
Email: president@fellowship.ca
Website: www.fellowship.ca

ISKRA, (20-Y.) Union of Spiritual Communities of Christ (Orthodox Doukhobors in Canada), Dmitri E. (Jim) Popoff, Box 760, Grand Forks, BC V0H 1H0 Tel. (604)442-8252 Fax (604)442-3433
Email: iskra@sunshinecable.com

Istocnik, (4-Y.) Serbian Orthodox Church in the U.S.A. and Canada, Diocese of Canada, Very Rev. VasilijeTomic, 7470 McNiven Rd., RR 3, Campbellville, ON L0P 1B0 Tel. (905)878-0043 Fax (905)878-1909

Email: vladika@istocnik.com
Website: www.istocnik.com

Leader, (Q.) Mennonite Church USA and Mennonite Church Canada, Sr Editor: Richard A. Kaufman, Editor: Byron Rempel-Burkholder, 600 Shaftesbury Blvd., Winnipeg, MB R3P 0M4 Tel. (204)885-2565 x 179 Fax (204)831-2454
Email: byronrb@mph.org
Website: www.leaderonline.org

Leader: Equipping the Missional Congregation, (Q.) Mennonite Church, Byron Rempel-Burkholder, Faith & Life Resources/Mennonite Publishing Network, 600 Shaftesbury Blvd, Winnipeg, Manitoba R3P 0M4 Tel. (204)888-6781 x 179 Fax (204)831-5675
Email: byronrb@mph.org

Le Lien, (11-Y.) Canadian Conference of Mennonite Brethren Churches, Annie Brosseau, 1775 Edouard-Laurin, St. Laurent, QC H4L 2B9 Tel. (514)331-0878 Fax (514)331-0879
Email: LeLien@total.net
Website: www.mbconf.ca/comm/lelien

Liturgie, Foi et Culture (Bulletin Natl. de Liturgie), (4-Y.) The Roman Catholic Church in Canada, Service des Editions de la CECC, Office national de liturgie, 3530 rue Adam, Montreal, QC H1W 1Y8 Tel. (514)522-4930 Fax (514)522-1557
Email: onl.cecc@ccb.ca
Website: www.cccb.ca

Mandate, (4-Y.) The United Church of Canada, Rebekah Chevalier, 3250 Bloor St W., Ste. 300, Etobicoke Toronto, ON M8X 2Y4 Tel. (416)231-5931 Fax (416)231-3103
Email: rchevali@united-church.ca
Website: www.united-church.ca/mandate

The Mantle, (M.) Independent Assemblies of God International (Canada), Philip Rassmussen, P.O. Box 2130, Laguna Hills, CA 92654-9901 Tel. (514)522-4930 Fax (514)522-1557

Mennonite Brethren Herald, (3-W.) Canadian Conference of Mennonite Brethren Churches, Laura Kalmar, 1310 Taylor Ave., Winnipeg, MB R3M 3Z6 Tel. (204)654-5760 Fax (204)654-1865
Email: mbherald@mbconf.ca
Website: www.mbherald.com

Mennonite Historian, (Q.) Canadian Conference of Mennonite Brethren Churches, Mennonite Church Canada, Abe Dueck and Alf Redekopp, Ctr. for Menn. Brethren Studies, 169 Riverton Ave., Winnipeg, MB

R2L 2E5 Tel. (204)669-6575 Fax (204)654-1865
Email: adueck@mbconf.ca
Website: mbconf.ca/mbstudies

Die Mennonitische Post, (bi-M.) Mennonite Central Committee Canada, Kennert Giesbrecht, 383 Main St., Steinbach, MB R5G 1S1 Tel. (204)326-6790 Fax (204)326-6302
Email: mennpost@mts.net

Mennonitische Rundschau, (M.) Canadian Conference of Mennonite Brethren Churches, Brigitte Penner; Marianne Dulder, 3-169 Riverton Ave., Winnipeg, MB R2L 2E5 Tel. (204)669-6575 Fax (204)654-1865
Email: MR@mbconf.ca
Website: www.mbconf.ca

The Messenger, (Q.) The Reformed Episcopal Church of Canada, Rt. Rev. Michael Fedechko, 320 Armstrong St., New Liskeard, ON P0J 1P0 Tel. (705)647-4565 Fax (705) 647-4565
Email: fed@nt.net
Website: www.forministry.com/REC-Canada

The Messenger, (22-Y.) The Evangelical Mennonite Conference, Terry Smith, Editor; Becky Buhler, Assistant Editor, 440 Main Street, Steinbach, MB R5G 1Z5 Tel. (204) 326-6401 Fax (204)326-1613
Email: emcterry@mts.net/emcmessenger@mts.net
Website: www.emconf.ca/Messenger

The Messenger, (bi-M.) Church of God (in Eastern Canada), Rosemary Krashel, 20625 Winston Churchill Blvd., Alton, ON L0N 1A0 Tel. (514)938-9994
Email: rosemarykrushel@sympatico.ca

MinistryMatters, (3-Y.) The Anglican Church of Canada, Vianney (Sam) Carriere, 80 Hayden St., Toronto, ON M4Y 3G2 Tel. (905)833-6200 Fax (905)833-2116
Email: matters@national.anglican.ca
Website: www.ministrymatters.ca

Missions Today, (bi-M.) Roman Catholic, Patricia McKinnon, Society for the Propagation of the Faith, 3329 Danforth Ave., Scarborough, ON M1L 4T3 Tel. (416)699-7077 or 800-897-8865 Fax (416)699-9019
Email: missions@eda.net
Website: www.eda.net/~missions

Mosaic, (Q.) Canadian Baptist Ministries, Jennifer Lau, 7185 Millcreek Dr., Mississauga, ON L5N 5R4 Tel. (905)821-3533 Fax (905) 826-3441
Email: mosaic@cbmin.org
Website: www.cbmin.org

The New Freeman, (W.) The Roman Catholic Church in Canada, Margie Traftan, One Bayard Dr., Saint John, NB E2L 3L5 Tel. (506)653-6806 Fax (506)653-6818
Email: tnf@nbnet.nb.ca

News of Québec, (3-Y.) Christian Brethren (also known as Plymouth Brethren), Richard E. Strout, P.O. Box 1054, Sherbrooke, QC J1H 5L3 Tel. (819)820-1693 Fax (819)821-9287

Orthodox Way, (M.) Greek Orthodox Metropolis of Toronto (Canada), Orthodox Way Committee, 86 Overlea Blvd., 4th Floor, Toronto, ON M4H 1C6 Tel. (416)429-5757 Fax (416)429-4588
Email: greekomt@on.aibn.com
Website: www.gocanada.org

Passport, (3-Y.) Interdenominational, Mike Benallick, Briercrest Family of Schools, 510 College Dr., Caronport, SK S0H 0S0 Tel. (306)756-3200 Fax (306)756-3366
Email: passport@briercrest.ca
Website: www.briercrest.ca

Pourastan, (bi-M.) Armenian Holy Apostolic Church—St. Gregory the Illuminator Armenian Cathedral of Montreal, Editor, 615 Stuart Ave., Outremont, QC H2V 3H2 Tel. (514)279-3066 Fax (514)279-8008
Email: sourpkrikor@qc.aibn.com
Website: www.sourpkrikor.org

Prairie Messenger, (W.) The Roman Catholic Church in Canada, Peter Novecosky, O.S.B., Box 190, 11 College Drive, Muenster, SK S0K 2Y0 Tel. (306)682-1772 Fax (306)682-5285
Email: pm.editor@stpeters.sk.ca
Website: www.stpeters.sk.ca/prairie_messenger

The Presbyterian Message, (10-Y.) Presbyterian Church in Canada, Janice Carter, 563 Tweedie Brook Rd, Kouchibouguac, NB E4X 1M2 Tel. (506)876-4379
Email: mjcarter@nb.sympatico.ca

Presbyterian Record, (11-Y.) The Presbyterian Church in Canada, Rev. David Harris, 50 Wynford Dr., Toronto, ON M3C 1J7 Tel. (416) 441-1111 Fax (416)441-2825
Email: pcrecord@presbyterian.ca
Website: www.presbyterian.ca/record

Presence, (8-Y.) The Roman Catholic Church in Canada, Jean-Claude Breton, Presence Magazine Inc., 2715 chemin de la Cote Ste-Catherine, Montreal, QC H3T 1B6 Tel. (514)739-9797 Fax (514)739-1664
Email: presence@presencemag.qc.ca

The Pulse, (4-Y.) Evangelical Free Church of Canada, Dr. Ron Unruh, Editor-in-Chief;

Tracy Morris, Managing Editor, Box 850, LCDI, Langley, BC V3A 8S6 Tel. (604)888-8668 Fax (604)888-3108
Email: efcc@twu.ca
Website: www.efcc.ca

Quaker Concern, (3-Y.) Canadian Yearly Meeting of the Religious Society of Friends, Jane Orion Smith, 60 Lowther Ave., Toronto, ON M5R 1C7 Tel. (416)920-5213 Fax (416) 920-5214
Email: cfsc-office@quaker.ca
Website: www.cfsc.quaker.ca

Reformed Perspective- A Magazine for the Christian Family, (M.) Canadian and American Reformed Churches and United Reformed Churches in North America, Jon Dykstra, 3573 McKinley Dr., Abbotsford, BC V2S 8M7 Tel. (604)755-7717
Email: editor@reformedperspective.ca
Website: www.reformedperspective.ca

Relations, (8-Y.) The Roman Catholic Church in Canada, Jean-Marc Biron, 25 Jarry Ouest, Montreal, QC H2P 1S6 Tel. (514)387-2541 Fax (514)387-0206
Email: relations@cjf.qc.ca
Website: www.cjf.qc.ca

RESCUE, (bi-M.) Association of Gospel Rescue Missions, Philip Rydman, 1045 Swift, N. Kansas City, MO 64116 Tel. (816)471-8020 Fax (816)471-3718
Email: pwydman@agrm.org
Website: www.agrm.org

Revival News, (Q.) Interdenominational, John McGregor, Canadian Revival Fellowship, Box 584, Regina, SK S4P 3A3 Tel. (306)522-3685 Fax (306)522-3686
Email: crfellowship@accesscomm.ca
Website: www.revivalfellowship.com

Rupert's Land News, (10-Y.) The Anglican Church of Canada, Irvin J. Kroeker, Anglican Centre, 935 Nesbitt Bay, Winnipeg, MB R3T 1W6 Tel. (204)992-4205 Fax (204)992-4219
Email: rlnews@rupertsland.ca

St. Luke Magazine, (M.) Christ Catholic Church International, Donald W. Mullan, 4695 St. Lawrence Ave, Niagara Falls, ON L2E 6S8 Tel. (905)354-2329 Fax (905)354-9934
Email: dmullan1@cogeco.ca

Salvationist, (M.) The Salvation Army in Canada and Bermuda, Major Kenneth Smith, Associate Editor, 2 Overlea Blvd., Toronto, ON M4H 1P4 Tel. (416)425-2111 Fax (416) 422-6120
Email: kenneth_smith@can.salvationarmy.org
Website: salvationist/CAN/Sarmy

Scarboro Missions, (7-Y.) The Roman Catholic Church in Canada, Cathy Van Loon, 2685 Kingston Rd., Scarborough, ON M1M 1M4 Tel. (416)261-7135 or (800)260-4815 Fax (416)261-0820
Email: editor@scarboromissions.ca
Website: www.scarboromissions.ca

The Shantyman, (6-Y.) Nondenominational, Ken Godevenos, Editor in Chief: Phil Hood, Managing Editor, 1885 Clements Rd., Unite 226, Pickering, ON L1W 3V4 Tel. (905)686-2030 Fax (905)427-0334
Email: shanty@pathcom.com
Website: www.shantymen.org

Sister Triangle, (Q.) Churches of Christ, Marilyn Muller, P.O. 948, Dauphin, MB R7N 3J5 Tel. (204)638-9812 Fax (204)638-6231
Email: dmmuller@mb.sympatico.ca

SR-Studies in Religion-Sciences religieuses, (Q.) Nondenominational, Dr. Aaron Hughes, Dept. of Religion & Culture, University of CalgarAy, 2500 University Avenue NW, Calgary, AB T2N 1N4 Tel. (403)220-7063
Email: hugesa@ucalgaray.ca
Website: http://www.wlupress.wlu.ca

Testimony, (M.) The Pentecostal Assemblies of Canada, Steve Kennedy, 2450 Milltower Ct., Mississauga, ON L5N 5Z6 Tel. (905)542-7400 Fax (905)542-7313
Email: testimony@PAOC.org

Topic, (10-Y.) The Anglican Church of Canada, Neale Adams, 580-401 W. Georgia St., Vancouver, BC V6B 5A1 Tel. (604)684-6306 x 223 Fax (604)684-7017
Email: nadams@vancouver.anglican.ca
Website: www.vancouver.anglican.ca

United Church Observer, (M.) The United Church of Canada, Muriel Duncan, 478 Huron St., Toronto, ON M5R 2R3 Tel. (416)960-8500 Fax (416)960-8477
Email: general@ucobserver.org
Website: www.ucobserver.org

La Vie Chretienne (French), (M.) Presbyterian Church in Canada, Jean Porret, PO Box 272, Suzz. Rosemont, Montreal, QC H1X 3B8 Tel. (514)737-4168

La Vie des Communautes religieuses, (5-Y.) The Roman Catholic Church in Canada, Religious Communities (Consortium), 251 St-Jean-Baptiste, Nicolet, QC J3T 1X9 Tel. (819)293-8736 Fax (819)293-2419
Email: viecr@sogetel.net

Vie Liturgique, (6-Y.) The Roman Catholic Church in Canada, Jean Grou, 4475, rue

Frontenac, Montreal, QC H2H 2S2 Tel. (800) 668-2547 Fax (514)278-3030
Email: vieliturgique@ustpaul.ca
Website: www.novalis.ca

VIP Communique, () Foursquare Gospel Church of Canada, Timothy Peterson, 8459-160th St., Ste. 100, Surrey, BC V3S 3T9 Tel. (604)543-8414 Fax (604)543-8417
Email: foursquare@foursquare.ca
Website: www.foursquare.ca

Visnyk-The Herald, (2-M.) Ukrainian Orthodox Church of Canada, Rt. Rev. Fr. William Makarenko, 9 St. John's Ave., Winnipeg, MB R2W 1G8 Tel. (204)586-3093 Fax (204)582-5241
Email: visnky@uocc.ca
Website: www.uocc.ca

Word Alive, (Q.) Nondenominational, Dwayne Janke and Dave Crough, Wycliffe Bible Translators of Canada Inc., 4316 10 St. NE, Calgary, AB T2E 6K3 Tel. (403)250-5411 Fax (403)250-2623
Email: editors_wam@wycliffe.ca
Website: www.wycliffe.ca

Young Companion, (11-Y.) Old Order Amish Church, Joseph Stoll and Christian Stoll, Old Order Amish Church, Rt. 4, Aylmer, ON N5H 2R3

12. Church Archives and Historical Records Collections

American and Canadian history is interwoven with the social and cultural experience of religious life and thought. Most repositories of primary research materials in North America will include some documentation on religion and church communities. This directory is not intended to replace standard bibliographic guides to those resources. The intent is to give a new researcher entry to major archival holdings of religious collections and to programs of national scope. In the interest of space, no attempt has been made to list the specific contents of the archives or to include the numerous specialized research libraries of North America. The repositories listed herein are able to re-direct inquirers to significant regional and local church archives, and specialized collections such as those of religious orders, educational and charitable organizations, and personal papers.

Repositories marked with an asterisk (*) are designated by their denomination as the official archives. The reference departments at these archives will assist researchers in locating primary material of geographic or subject focus.

UNITED STATES

Adventist

Aurora University, Aurora University, Charles B. Phillips Library, 347 S. Gladstone, Aurora, IL 60506, Volunteer Curator: Susan L. Palmer, Tel. (630)844-5445 Fax (630)844-3848, Email: jenks@aurora.edu,

Adventual archival materials on the Millerite/Early Adventist movement (1830-1860); also denominational archives relating to Advent Christian Church, Life and Advent Union, and to a lesser extent, Evangelical Adventists and Age-to-Come Adventists.

Ellen G. White Estate Branch Office, Loma Linda University Library, Department of Archives and Special Collections, Loma Linda, CA 92350, Interim Chairman/Director: Michael Campbell, Tel. (909)558-4942 Fax (909)558-0381, Email: whiteestate@llu.edu, Website: www.llu.edu/llu/library/heritage
Photographs, sound and video recordings, personal papers, and library pertaining to the Seventh-day Adventist Church.

*General Conference of Seventh-day Adventists: Archives and Statistics, 12501 Old Columbia Pike, Silver Spring, MD 20904-6600, Director: Bert Haloviak, Tel. (301)680-5020 Fax (301)680-5038, Email: haloviakb@gc. adventist.org, Website: ast.gc.adventist.org
Repository of the records created at the world administrative center of the Seventh-day Adventist Church and includes the period from the 1860s to the present.

Center for Adventist Research, James White Library, Andrews University, Berrien Springs, MI 49104-1440, Director: Dr. Merlin D. Burt, Tel. (269)471-3209 Fax (269)471-2646, Email: car@andrews.edu, Website: www. andrews.edu/library/car

Assemblies of God

*Flower Pentecostal Heritage Center, 1445 Boonville Ave., Springfield, MO 65802, Director: Darrin Rodgers, Tel. (417)862-1447 x 4400 Fax (417)862-6203, Email: archives @ag.org, Website: www.ifphc.org
Official repository for materials related to the Assemblies of God, as well as materials related to the broader Pentecostal and charismatic movements.

Baptist

*Seventh-day Baptist Historical Society, 3120 Kennedy Rd., P.O. Box 1678, Janesville, WI 53547-1678, Historian-Librarian: Nicholas J. Kersten, Tel. (608)752-5055 Fax (608)752-7711, Email: sdbhist@seventhdaybaptist.org, Website: www.sdbhistory.org
Serves as a depository for records of Seventh-day Baptists, Sabbath and Sabbath-keeping Baptists since the mid-seventeenth century.

*Southern Baptists Historical Library & Archives, 901 Commerce St., Suite 400, Nashville, TN 37203-3630, Director and Archivist: Bill Sumners, Tel. (615)244-0344 Fax (615)782-4821, Email: bill@sbhla.org, Website: www.sbhla.org
Central depository of the Southern Baptist Convention. Materials include official records of denominational agencies; personal papers of denominational leaders; records of related Baptist organizations; and annual proceedings of national and regional bodies.

Primitive Baptist Library of Carthage, Illinois, 416 Main St., Carthage, IL 62321, Director of Library: Elder Robert Webb, Tel. (217)357-3723 Fax (217)357-3723, Email: bwebb9@ juno.com, Website: www.carthage.lib.il.us/ community/churches/primbap/pbl.html
Collects the records of congregations and associations.

American Baptist Historical Society, 3001 Mercer University Dr., Atlanta, GA 30341, Executive Director: Dr. Deborah Bingham Van Broekhoven, Tel. (678)547-6680 Fax (678) 547-6682, Website: www.baptisthistory.us

Manuscript holdings include collections of Baptist ministers, missionaries, and scholars, and records of Baptist churches, associations, and national and international bodies.

*American Baptist Archives Center, P.O. Box 851, Valley Forge, PA 19482-0851, Archivist: Betty Layton, Tel. (610)768-2374, Fax (610) 768-2266, Website: www.abc-usa.org/abhs

Repository for the non-current records of the national boards and administrative organizations of American Baptist churches in the USA. Collections include mission files, publications, correspondence, official minutes and annual reports.

Baptist and United Church of Christ

Andover Newton Theological School, Andover Newton Theological School, Franklin Trask Library, 169 Herrick Rd., Newton Centre, MA 02459, Associate Director for Special Collections: Diana Yount, Tel. (617)964-1100 x 252 Fax (617)965-9756, Email: dyount@ants.edu, Website: www.ants.edu/ftlibrary

The collections document Baptist, Congregational and United Church history, including personal papers relating to national denominational work and foreign missions, with emphasis on New England Church history.

Brethren in Christ

*Brethren in Christ Historical Library and Archives, One College Avenue, P.O. Box 3002, Grantham, PA 17027, Director: Glen A. Pierce, Tel. (717)691-6048 Fax (717)691-6042, Email: archives@messiah.edu, Website:

Records of general church boards and agencies, regional conferences, congregations and organizations; also includes library, manuscripts, and oral history collection.

Church of the Brethren

*Brethren Historical Library and Archives, 1451 Dundee Ave., Elgin, IL 60120, Librarian/Archivist: Kenneth M. Shaffer, Jr., Tel. (847)742-5100 x 294, Fax (847)742-6103, Email: kshaffer_gb@brethren.org, Website: www.brethren.org/genbd/bhla

Archival materials dating from 1800-present relating to the cultural, socio-economic, theological, genealogical, and institutional history of the Church of the Brethren.

Churches of Christ

Center for Restoration Studies, Abilene Christian University, 760 Library Court, P.O. Box 29208, Abilene, TX 79699, Archivist: Erma

Jean Loveland, Tel. (915)674-2538 Fax (915) 674-2202, Email: lovelande@acu.edu, Website: www.bible.acu.edu/crs

Archival materials connected with the Stone-Campbell Movement. The chief focus is on the Church of Christ in the twentieth century.

Emmanuel School of Religion Library, One Walker Drive, Johnson City, TN 37601-9438, Director: Thomas E. Stokes, Tel. (423)461-1541 Fax (423) 926-6198, Email: library@esr.edu, Website: library.esr.edu

Materials related to the Stone-Campbell/Restoration Movement tradition. Collection includes items from the Christian Church and Churches of Christ, the a cappella Churches of Christ, and the Christian Church (Disciples of Christ).

Churches of God General Conference

*Winebrenner Theological Seminary Library, Winebrenner Theological Seminary, 950 N. Main St., Findlay, OH 45840, Director of Library Services: Margaret Hirschy, Tel. (419)434-4260 Fax (419)434-4267, Email: library@winebrenner.edu, Website: www.winebrenner.edu/Library

Archival materials of the Churches of God, General Conference including local conference journals.

Disciples of Christ

Christian Theological Seminary Library, Christian Theological Seminary Library, 1000 W. 42nd St., P.O. Box 88267, Indianapolis, IN 46208, Archives Manager: Don Haymes, Tel. (317)931-2368 Fax (317)931-2363, Email: don.haymes@cts.edu, Website: www.cts.edu/Library

Archival materials dealing with the Disciples of Christ and related movements.

*Disciples of Christ Historical Society, 1101 19th Ave. S, Nashville, TN 37212, Director of Library and Archives: Sara Harwell, Tel. (615) 327-1444 Fax (615)327-1445, Email: harwellsj @dishistsoc.org, Website: www.dishistsoc.org

Collects documents of the Stone-Campbell Movement.

Episcopal

*Archives of the Episcopal Church, P.O. Box 2247, Austin, TX 78768-2247, Canonical Archivist and Director: Mark J. Duffy, Tel. (512)472-6816 Fax (512) 480-0437, Email: research@episcopalarchives.org, Website: www.episcopalarchives.org

Repository for the official records of the national Church, its corporate bodies and affiliated agencies, personal papers, and some diocesan archives. Contact the Archives for reference to diocesan and parochial church records.

Evangelical and Reformed

*Evangelical and Reformed Historical Society, Lancaster Theological Seminary, 555 W. James St., Lancaster, PA 17603, Archivist: Richard R. Berg, Tel. (717)290-8704 Fax (717)393-4254, Email: erhs@lancasterseminary. edu, Website: www.erhs.info

Manuscripts and transcriptions of early German Reformed Church (U.S.) 1725-1863; Reformed Church in the United States 1863-1934, and Evangelical and Reformed Church 1934-1957 records of coetus, synods, and classes, pastoral records, and personal papers.

Evangelical Congregational Church

*Archives of the Evangelical Congregational Church, Evangelical School of Theology, Rostad Library, 121 S. College St., Myerstown, PA 17067, Archivist: Terry M. Heisey, Tel. (717)866-5775 Fax (717)866-4667, Email: theisey@evangelical.edu, Website: www. evangelical. edu

Repository of records of the administrative units of the denomination, affiliated organizations, and closed churches. Also collected are records of local congregations and materials related to the United Evangelical Church and the Evangelical Association.

Friends

*Historical Library of Swarthmore, Swarthmore College, 500 College Ave., Swarthmore, PA 19081-1399, Curator: Christopher Densmore, Tel. (610)328-8499 Fax (610)690-5728, Email: friends@swarthmore.edu, Website: www.swarthmore.edu/library/friends

Official depository for the records of the Philadelphia, Baltimore, and New York Yearly Meetings. Comprehensive collection of originals and copies of other Quaker meeting archives.

Special Collections-Quaker Collection, Haverford College, 370 Lancaster Ave., Haverford, PA 19041-1392, Quaker Bibliographer: Emma Jones Lapsansky, Tel. (610)896-1161 Fax (610)896-1102, Email: elapsans@haverford.edu, Website: www.haverford.edu/library/special

Repository for material relating to the Society of Friends (Quakers), especially to the segment known from 1827 to the mid-20th century as "Orthodox" in the Delaware Valley.

Interdenominational

American Bible Society Library and Archives, 1865 Broadway, New York, NY 10023-9980, Archivist: Kristin Miller, Tel. (212)408-1429 Fax (212)408-8724, Email: kmiller@american bible.org, Website: www.american bible.org

Core of collections includes founders' documents, minutes, and correspondence related to the worldwide mission of the ABS.

Billy Graham Center Archives, Wheaton College, Wheaton, IL 60187-5593, Director of Archives: Paul Erickson, Tel. (630)752-5910 Fax (630)752-5916, Email: bgcarc@wheaton. edu, Website: www.wheaton. edu/bgc/archives/ archhp1.html

Graduate Theological Union Archives, 2400 Ridge Road, Berkeley, CA 94709, Archivist: Lucinda Glenn, Tel. (510)649-2507 Fax (510) 649-2508, Email: lglenn@gtu.edu, Website: library.gtu.edu/archives

Holy Spirit Research Center, Oral Roberts University, LRC 5E 02, 7777 S. Lewis Ave., Tulsa, OK 74171, Director: Mark E. Roberts, Tel. (918)495-6391 Fax (918)495-6662, Email: mroberts@oru.edu, Website: www.oru. edu/university/library/holyspirit

Pentecostal and Charismatic records with an emphasis on divine healing.

National Council of Churches of Christ in the USA Records, Presbyterian Historical Society, Presbyterian Church (USA), 425 Lombard St., Philadelphia, PA 19147-1516, Manager: Margery N. Sly, Tel. (215)627-1852 Fax (215) 627-0509, Email: refdesk@history. pcusa.org, Website: www.history.pcusa.org

Schomburg Center for Research in Black Culture, 515 Malcolm X Blvd., New York, NY 10037, Manuscripts, Archives, and Rare Books Division, Curator: Diana Lachatanere, Tel. (212)491-2200 Fax (212)491-6067, Email: scmarbref@nypl.org, Website: www. schomburgcenter.org

Union Theological Seminary, Union Theological Seminary, Burke Library, 3041 Broadway, New York, NY 10027, Archivist and Head of Special Collections: Michael Boddy, Tel. (212)280-1501 Fax (212)280-1456, Email: mboddy@uts.columbia.edu, Website: www. columbia.edu/cu/lweb/indiv/burke

The largest theological library in the western hemisphere with extensive rare and antique holdings.

University of Chicago, University of Chicago, Regenstein Library, 1100 E 57th St., Chicago, IL 60537-1502, Bibliographer for Religion and Philosophy: Beth Bidlack, Tel. (773)702-8442, Email: bbidlack@uchicago.edu, Website: www.lib.uchicago.edu/e/su/rel

Yale Divinity School Library, 409 Prospect St., New Haven, CT 06511, Special Collections Librarian/Curator of the Day Missions Collection: Martha Smalley, Tel. (203)432-5290 Fax (203)432-3906, Email: divinity. library@yale.edu, Website: www.library.yale. edu/div

Jewish

American Jewish Historical Society (NY Location), Center for Jewish History, 15 W.

16th St., New York, NY 10011, Director of Research: Michael Feldberg, Tel. (212)294-6160 Fax (212)294-6161, Email: info@ajhs.org, Website: www.ajhs.org

Archival repositories of the Jewish people in America, including significant religious contributions to American life.

American Jewish Historical Society (MA Location), Friedman Memorial Library, 160 Herrick Rd., Newton Centre, MA 02459, Director of Research: Michael Feldberg, Tel. (617)559-8880 Fax (617)559-8881, Email: info@ajhs.org, Website: www.ajhs.org

Archival repositories of the Jewish people in America, including significant religious contributions to American life.

Jacob Rader Marcus Center of the American Jewish Archives, Hebrew Union College, 3101 Clifton Ave., Cincinnati, OH 45220, Senior Archivist: Kevin Proffitt, Tel. (513) 221-1875 Fax (513) 221-7812, Email: aja@huc.edu, Website: www.huc.edu/aja

Materials documenting the Jewish experience in the Western Hemisphere with emphasis on the Reform movement. Included in the collection are congregational and organizational records, personal papers of rabbis and secular leaders, and genealogical materials.

Latter-day Saints

*Archives, Church of Jesus Christ of Latter-day Saints, 50 E. North Temple, Salt Lake City, UT 84150-3800, Director: Steven R. Sorensen, Tel. (801)240-2273 Fax (801) 240-6134

Repository of official records of church departments, missions, congregations, and associated organizations. Includes personal papers of church leaders and members.

Family History Library, 35 North West Temple, Salt Lake City, UT 84150-3400 Tel. (801)240-2331 Fax (801)240-5551, Email: fhl@ldschurch.org, Website:

Primarily microfilmed vital, church, probate, land, census, and military records including local church registers.

Lutheran

Lutheran History Center of the West, 1712 Greentree Dr., Concord, CA , Editor: Duane A. Peterson, Tel. (925)825-2109, Email: duanep@astound.net

*Archives of the Evangelical Lutheran Church in America, 321 Bonnie Lane, Elk Grove Village, IL 60007, Chief Archivist for Management, Reference Services, and Technology: Joel Thoreson, Tel. (847)690-9410 Fax (847)690-9502, Email: archives@elca.org, Website: www.elca.org/archives

Official repository for the churchwide offices of the ELCA and its predecessors. For further information on synod and regional archives,

contact the Chicago archives or check the ELCA World Wide Web site. For ELCA college and seminary archives, contact those institutions directly, or consult the ELCA Archives.

*Concordia Historical Institute, Concordia Seminary, 804 Seminary Place, St. Louis, MO 63105, Director: Martin R. Noland, Tel. (314)505-7900 Fax (314)505-7901, Email: chi@chi.lcms.org, Website: chi.lcms.org

Official repository of The Lutheran Church-Missouri Synod. Collects synodical and congregational records, personal papers and records of Lutheran agencies.

Mennonite

*Mennonite Church USA Archives-Goshen, 1700 South Main, Goshen, IN 46526, Director: Rich Preheim, Tel. (574)535-7477 Fax (574)535-7756, Email: archives@MennoniteUSA.org, Website: www.MennoniteUSA.org/History

Repository of the official organizational records of the Mennonite Church and personal papers of leaders and members.

Center for Mennonite Brethren Studies, 1717 S. Chestnut, Fresno, CA 93702, Archivist: Kevin Enns-Rempel, Tel. (559)453-2225 Fax (559) 453-2124, Email: kennsrem@fresno.edu, Website: fresno.edu/dept/library/cmbs

Official repository for the General Conference of Mennonite Brethren Churches.

*Mennonite Church USA Archives-North Newton, Bethel College, 300 E. 27th St., North Newton, KS 67117-0531, Archivist: John Thiesen, Tel. (316)284-5304 Fax (316) 284-5843, Email: mla@bethelks.edu, Website: www.bethelks.edu/services/mla

An official repository for the General Conference Mennonite Church and several other organizations related to the General Conference.

Methodist

B. L. Fisher Library, Asbury Theological Seminary, 204 N. Lexington Ave., Wilmore, KY 40390, Archivist and Special Collections Librarian: Grace Yoder, Tel. (859)858-2352 Fax (859)858-2350, Email: grace_yoder@asburyseminary.edu, Website: www.asburyseminary.edu

Documents the Holiness Movement and evangelical currents in the United Methodist Church. Holdings include records of related associations, camp meetings, personal papers, and periodicals.

*Heritage Hall at Livingstone College, 701 W. Monroe St., Salisbury, NC 28144, Director: Phyllis H. Galloway, Tel. (704)216-6094 Fax (704)216-6280, Email: pgallow@livingstone.edu, Website: www.livingstone.edu/heritage_hall.htm

Records of the African Methodist Episcopal Zion Church.

*Office of the Historiographer of the African Methodist Episcopal Church, P.O. Box 301, Williamstown, MA 02167, Historiographer: Dennis C. Dickerson, Tel. (413)597-2484 Fax (413)597-3673, Email: dennis.c.dickerson@williams.edu, Website:

General and annual conference minutes; reports of various departments such as missions and publications; and congregational histories and other local materials. The materials are housed in the office of the historiographer and other designated locations.

*General Commission on Archives and History, The United Methodist Church, P.O. Box 127, Madison, NJ 07940, Archivist/Records Administrator: L. Dale Patterson, Tel. (973) 408-3189 Fax (973)408-3909, Email: research@gcah.org, Website: www.gcah.org

Collects administrative and episcopal records, and personal papers of missionaries and leaders. Holds limited genealogical information on ordained ministers. Will direct researchers to local and regional collections of congregational records and information on United Methodism and its predecessors.

Center for Evangelical United Brethren Heritage, United Theological Seminary, 1810 Harvard Blvd., Dayton, OH 45406-4599, Interim Director: Sarah D. Brooks Blair, Tel. (937) 278-5817 x 2218 Fax (937)275-5701, Email: sblair@united.edu, Website: www.united.edu/eubcenter

Documents predecessor and cognate church bodies of the United Methodist Church including the Evangelical Association, United Brethren in Christ, United Evangelical, Evangelical, Evangelical United Brethren, Evangelical Congregational, and Evangelical of North America.

Moravian

Moravian Archives-Southern Province, 457 S. Church St., Winston-Salem, NC 27101, Archivist: C. Daniel Crews, Tel. (336)722-1742 Fax (336)725-4514, Email: moravianarchives@mcsp.org, Website: www.moravianarchives.org

Repository of the records of the Moravian Church, Southern Province, its congregations, and its members.

Moravian Archives-Northern Province, 41 W. Locust St., Bethlehem, PA 18018-2757, Archivist: Dr. Paul Peucker, Tel. (610)866-3255 Fax (610)866-9210, Email: info@moravianchurcharchives.org, Website: www.moravianchurcharchives.org

Records of the Northern Province of the Moravian Church in America, including affiliated provinces in the Eastern West Indies, Nicaragua, Honduras, Labrador, and Alaska.

Nazarene

*Nazarene Archives, Church of the Nazarene, 6401 The Paseo, Kansas City, MO 64131, Archives Manager: Stan Ingersol, Tel. (816)333-7000 x 2437 Fax (816)361-4983, Email: singersol@nazarene.org, Website: http://www.nazarene.org/ministries/administration/archives/display.aspx

Focus is on general and district materials, including those of leaders, agencies, and study commissions. The Archives also collects materials on congregations, church colleges and seminaries world-wide, and social ministries.

Pentecostal

David du Plessis Archives, Fuller Theological Seminary, 135 North Oakland Ave., Pasadena, CA 81182, Archivist: Roger Robins, Tel. (626)584-5311 Fax (626)584-5644, Email: archive@fuller.edu, Website: www.fuller.edu/archive

Collects material related to the Pentecostal and Charismatic movements; also includes material related to Charles Fuller and the Old Fashioned Revival Hour broadcast, Fuller Theological Seminary, and neo-evangelicalism.

*Hal Bernard Dixon Jr. Pentecostal Research Center, 260 11th St. NE, Cleveland, TN 37311, Director: David G. Roebuck, Tel. (423)614-8576 Fax (423)614-8555, Email: dixon_research@leeuniversity.edu, Website: faculty.leeu.edu/~drc

Official repository of the Church of God (Cleveland, TN); also collects other Pentecostal and Charismatic materials.

*International Pentecostal Holiness Church Archives and Research Center, P.O. Box 12609, Oklahoma City, OK 73157, Director: Dr. Harold D. Hunter, Tel. (405)787-7110 x 3132 Fax (405)789-3957, Email: archives@iphc.org, Website: www.pctii.org/arc/ archives.html

Official repository for records, publications and other media produced by the international headquarters, conferences, and influential leaders. Some of the most important publications are available on cds and dvds.

Center for the Study of Oneness Pentecostalism, 700 Howdershell Road, Florissant, MO 63031, Curator: Robin Jonston, Tel. (314)837-7304 x 432 Fax (314)838-8858, Email: Rjohnston@upci.org, Website: www.upci.org

Collects a variety of Pentecostal archives, primarily the United Pentecostal (Oneness) Branch.

Polish National Catholic

*Polish National Catholic Church Commission on History and Archives, 1031 Cedar Ave., Scranton, PA 18505, Chair: Joseph Wieczerzak, Tel. (717)343-0100

Documents pertaining to the Church's national office, parishes, Prime Bishop, leaders, and organizations.

Presbyterian

*Presbyterian Historical Society Headquarters, 425 Lombard St., Philadelphia, PA 19147-1516, Deputy Director: Margery N. Sly, Tel. (215)627-1852 Fax (215)627-0509, Email: refdesk@history.pcusa.org, Website: www.history.pcusa.org

Collects the official records of the Church's national offices and agencies, synods, presbyteries, and some congregations. The Society also houses records of the Church's predecessor denominations, personal papers of prominent Presbyterians, and records of ecumenical organizations. In addition, the Southern Regional Office in Montreat, NC holds local and regional records for the fourteen southern states.

*Presbyterian Church in America Historical Center, 12330 Conway Rd., St. Louis, MO 63141, Director: Wayne Sparkman, Tel. (314)469-9077 Fax (314)469-9077, Email: wsparkman@pcanet.org, Website: www.pcahistory.org

Center serves as the official archive of the Presbyterian Church in America. The Center also holds the records of five other Presbytrerian denominations and the manuscript collections of over one hundred individuals connected with these church bodies.

*Presbyterian Historical Society Southern Regional Office, P.O. Box 849, Montreat, NC 28757, Acting Deputy Director: Bill Bynum, Tel. (828)669-7061 Fax (828)669-5369, Email: refdesk@history.pcusa.org, Website: www.history.pcusa.org

Collects the official records of the Church's national offices and agencies, synods, presbyteries, and some congregations. The Society also houses records of the Church's predecessor denominations, personal papers of prominent Presbyterians, and records of ecumenical organizations. In addition, the Southern Regional Office in Montreat, NC holds local and regional records for the fourteen southern states.

*Historical Foundation of the Cumberland Presbyterian Church and the Cumberland Presbyterian Church in America, 1978 Union Ave., Memphis, TN 38104, Director and Archivist: Susan Knight Gore, Tel. (901)276-8602 Fax (901)272-3913, Email: archives@cumberland.org, Website: www.cumberland.org/hfcpc

Princeton Theological Seminary Libraries, Library Place and Mercer Street, P.O. Box 111, Princeton, NJ 08542-0803, Curator of Special Collections: Clifford Anderson, Tel. (609)497-7953 Fax (609)497-1826, Email: special.collections@ptsem.edu, Website: libweb.ptsem.edu/collections

The strengths of the collection are its documentation of the history of the Seminary; American Presbyterianism; English and American Puritanism; Presbyterian missions; hymnology; works by and about Reformed theologians Karl Barth and Abraham Kuyper; and the history of Presbyterians in Korea.

Reformed

*Heritage Hall, Calvin College, 1855 Knollcrest Circle SE, Grand Rapids, MI 49546, Curator of Archives: Richard H. Harms, Tel. (616)957-6313, (616)526-6313 Fax (616)957-6470, Email: crcarchives@calvin.edu, Website: www.calvin.edu/hh

Repository of the official records of the Christian Reformed Church in North America, including classes, congregations, and denominational agencies and committees.

*Reformed Church Archives, 21 Seminary Place, New Brunswick, NJ 08901-1159, Archivist: Russell Gasero, Tel. (732)246-1779 Fax (732) 249-5412, Email: rgasero@rca.org, Website: www.rca.org/aboutus/archives

Official repository for denominational records including congregations, classes, synods, missions, and national offices.

Roman Catholic

American Catholic History Research Center and University Archives, Catholic University of America, 101 Life Cycle Institute, Washington, DC 20064, Archivist: Timothy Meagher, Tel. (202)319-5065 Fax (202) 319-6554, Email: meagher@cua.edu, Website: libraries.cua.edu/achrcua

Department of Special Collections and Archives, Marquette University, P.O. Box 3141, Milwaukee, WI 53233-3141, Department Head and Archivist: Matt Blessing, Tel. (414) 288-7256 Fax (414)288-6709, Email: matt.blessing@marquette.edu, Website: www.marquette.edu/library/collections/archives

Collection strengths are in the areas of Catholic social action, American missions and missionaries, and other work with Native Americans and African Americans.

United States Catholic Historical Society, 201 Seminary Ave., Yonkers, NY 10704 Tel. (914)337-8381 Fax (914)337-6379, Email: Website: www.uschs.com

University of Notre Dame Archives, 607 Hesburgh Library, Notre Dame, IN 46556, Archivist and Curator of Manuscripts: William Kevin Cawley, Tel. (574)631-6448 Fax (574)631-7980, Email: archives@nd.edu, Website: archives.nd.edu

CHURCH ARCHIVES

357

Papers of bishops and prominent Catholics and records of Catholic organizations. Includes parish histories, but few parish records.

Salvation Army

*Salvation Army Archives and Research Center, 615 Slaters Lane, Alexandria, VA 22313, Archivist: Susan Mitchem, Tel. (703)684-5500, Fax (703)299-5552, Email: archives@usa.salvationarmy.org, Website: www.salvation army.org

Holds the documents of Salvation Army history, personalities, and events in the United States from 1880.

Swedenborgian

*Swedenborg Library, Bryn Athyn College of the New Church, 2875 College Drive, P.O. Box 740, Bryn Athyn, PA 19009-0740, Director: Carroll C. Odhner, Tel. (267)502-2547 Fax (267)502-2637, Email: carroll.odhner@brynathyn.edu, Website: www.brynathyn.edu/Library

Unitarian Universalist

*Andover-Harvard Theological Library, Andover-Harvard Theological Library, Harvard Divinity School, 45 Francis Ave., Cambridge, MA 02138, Curator: Frances O'Donnell, Tel. (617)496-5153 Fax (617)496-4111, Email: frances_odonnell@harvard.edu, Website: www.hds.harvard.edu/library

Institutional archives of the Unitarian Universalist Association including the Unitarian Universalist Service Committee; also houses records of many congregations; personal papers of ministers and other individuals.

Meadville-Lombard Theological School Library, Meadville/Lombard Theological School Library, 5701 S. Woodlawn Ave., Chicago, IL 60637, Director: Neil W. Gerdes, Tel. (773)256-3000 x 225 Fax (773)256-3008, Email: ngerdes@meadville.edu, Website: www.meadville.edu/library.html

Repository for materials relating to Unitarian Universalism in particular and liberal religion in general. Includes personal papers of several noted UU ministers, and church records from many UU churches in the Midwestern USA.

United Church of Christ

Elon University Library, Elon University Library, 2550 Campus Box, Elon, NC 27244, Archivist/Technical Services Librarian: Connie L. Keller, Tel. (336)278-6599 Fax (336)278-6639, Email: keller@elon.edu, Website: www.elon.edu/library

Collection of membership records and other archival material on the predecessor churches of the UCC: Christian Church and the Southern Conference of the Christian Church; also maintains records of churches that no longer exist.

*United Church of Christ Archives, 700 Prospect Ave, Cleveland, OH 44115, Archivist & Records Manager: Bridgette A. Kelly, Tel. (216)736-2106, Email: KellyB@ucc.org, Website: www.ucc.org/about-us/archives

Records created in the national setting of the Church since its founding in 1957, including the General Synod, Executive Council, officers, instrumentalities, and bodies created by and/or related to the General Synod.

Congregational Library, Congregational Library, 14 Beacon St., Boston, MA 02108, Archivist: Jessica Steytler, Tel. (617)523-0470 Fax (617)523-0491, Email: jsteytler@14beacon.org, Website: www.congregationallibrary.org

Documentation on the Congregational, Congregational Christian, Christian, and United Church of Christ throughout the world, including local church records, associations, charitable organizations, and papers of clergy, missionaries and others.

Archives of the Evangelical Synod, Eden Theological Seminary, Luhr Library, 475 E. Lockwood Ave., St. Louis, MO 63119-3192, Sr. Research Consultant: Lowell Zuck, Tel. (314)252-3140, Email: lzuck@eden.edu, Website: www.eden.edu/Archives/edenarch.html

Archival records include organization records, personal papers and immigration records.

CANADA

Anglican

*General Synod Archives, 80 Hayden St., Toronto, ON M4Y 3G2, Archivist: Nancy Hurn, Tel. (416)924-9199 x 279 Fax (416)968-7983, Email: nhurn@national.anglican.ca, Website: www.anglican.ca

Collects the permanent records of the General Synod, its committees, and its employees. The Archives has a national scope, and provides referral services on local Church records.

Baptist

*Atlantic Baptist Historical Collection of the Acadia University Archives, Vaughan Memorial Library, P.O. Box 4, Wolfville, NS B4P 2R6, Archives and Special Collections Services Assistant: Winnie Bodden, Tel. (902)585-1011 Fax (902)585-1748, Email: archives@acadiau.ca, Website: library.acadiau.ca/archives

Records of associations and churches of the United Baptist Convention of the Atlantic Provinces; also personal papers of pastors and missionaries.

Canadian Baptist Archives, McMaster Divinity College, 1280 Main St. W, Hamilton, ON L8S 4K1, Director: Dr. Gordon Heath, Tel. (905)525-9140 x 23511 Fax (905)577-4782, Email: gheath@mcmaster.ca, Website: divinitymcmaster.ca/academics/resources/baptistArchives

Friends

Canadian Yearly Meeting Archives, Pickering College, 16945 Bayview Ave., New Market, ON L3Y 4X2, Yearly Meeting Archivist: Jane Zavitz-Bond, Tel. (905)895-1700 x 247 Fax (905)895-9076, Email: cym-archivist@quaker.ca, Website: www.quaker.ca/archives.html

Holds the extant records for Quakers in Canada beginning with Adolphus in 1798 to the present, including the records of the Canadian Friends Service Committee.

Interdenominational

Canadian Council of Churches Archives, National Archives of Canada, 395 Wellington, Ottawa, ON, K1A 0N3, Tel. (613)992-3884 Fax (613)995-6274, Email: reference@archives.ca, Website: www.archives.ca

Genealogical assistance: (613) 996-7458

Library and Archives Canada, 395 Wellington, Ottawa, ON, K1A 0N4, Director: Ian E. Wilson, Tel. (613)996-5155, (866)578-7777 Fax (613)995-6274, Email: reference@lac-bac.gc.ca, Website: www.collectionscanada.ca

Records of interdenominational and ecumenical organizations, missionary societies, denominational churches, parish registers, and papers of prominent clergy.

Jewish

Canadian Jewish Congress Charities Committee National Archives, 1590 Avenue Docteur Penfield, Montreal, QC, H3G 1C5, Director of Archives: Janice Rosen, Tel. (514)931-7531 x 2 Fax (514)931-0548, Email: archives@cjccc.ca, Website: www.cjccc.ca/national_archives

Collects documentation on all aspects of social, political, and cultural history of the Jewish presence in Quebec and Canada.

Lutheran

*Archives of the Evangelical Lutheran Church in Canada, 302-393 Portage Ave., Winnipeg, MB, R3B 3H6, National Secretary/Archivist: Robert H. Granke, Tel. (204)984-9150 Fax (204)984-9185, Email: rhgranke@elcic.ca, Website: www.elcic.ca

Official repository for the ELCIC and its predecessor bodies, the Evangelical Lutheran Church of Canada and the Evangelical Lutheran Church of America-Canada Section.

Lutheran Historical Institute, 7100 Ada Blvd., Edmonton, AB T5B 4E4, Archivist: Karen Baron, Tel. (780)474-8156 Fax (780)477-9829, Email: abclcc@connect.ab.ca, Website: www.lccarchives.ca

Mennonite

*Centre for Mennonite Brethren Studies, 169 Riverton Ave., Winnipeg, MB R2L 2E5, Archivist: Conrad Stoesz, Tel. (204)669-6575, Fax (204)654-1865, Email: cstoesz@mbconf.ca, Website: www.mbconf.ca/mbstudies

Institutional records of the boards and agencies of the Mennonite Brethren Church in Canada with some holdings pertaining to other parts of North America; also personal papers of leaders.

*Mennonite Heritage Centre, Mennonite Church Canada, 600 Shaftesbury Blvd., Winnipeg, MB R3P 0M4, Director: Alf Redekopp, Tel. (204)888-6781 Fax (204)831-5675, Email: aredekopp@mennonitechurch.ca, Website: www.mennonitechurch.ca/programs/archives

Institutional records and personal papers of leaders within the Mennonite Community. Holdings include the records of the Conference and related agencies

Pentecostal

*Pentecostal Assemblies of Canada, 2450 Milltower Court, Mississauga, ON L5N 5Z6, Director of Archives: Marilyn Stroud, Tel. (905)542-7400 x 5282 Fax (905)542-1624, Email: mstroud@paoc.org, Website: www.paoc.org/administration/archives.html

Repository of archival records created by the Pentecostal Assemblies of Canada.

Presbyterian

*Presbyterian Church in Canada Archives and Records, 50 Wynford Dr., Toronto, ON M3C 1J7, Archivist/Records Administrator: Kim M. Arnold, Tel. (416)441-1111 x 310 Fax (416) 441-2825, Email: karnold@presbyterian.ca, Website: www.presbyterian.ca/archives

Records of the Presbyterian Church in Canada, its officials, ministers, congregations and organizations.

Roman Catholic

Research Centre for the Religious History of Canada, St. Paul University, 223 Main St., Ottawa, ON K1S 1C4, Director: Pierre Hurtubise, Tel. (613)236-1393 x 2270 Fax (613)782-3001, Email: crh-rc-rhc@ustpaul.uottowa.ca, Website: www.ustpaul.ca

Holds 900 linear feet of documents, mainly records on deposit from other institutions; and also guides to many Canadian Catholic archives.

359

Salvation Army

George Scott Railton Heritage Centre, 2130 Bayview Ave., North York, ON M4N 3K6, Director: Ira Barrow, Tel. (416)481-4441 Fax (416)481-6096, Email: Ira.Barrow@sally net.org

Records include publications; also financial, personnel, social welfare, and immigration records.

United Church of Canada

*United Church of Canada Central Archives, Victoria University, 73 Queens Park Crescent E., Toronto, ON M5S 1K7, Chief Archivist: Sharon Larade, Tel. (416)585-4563 Fax (416) 585-4584, Email: info@unitedchurcharchives. ca, Website: http://unitedchurcharchives.ca

III

STATISTICAL SECTION

Guide to Statistical Tables

Since questions regarding religious affiliation are no longer a part of the United States Census, the *Yearbook of American & Canadian Churches* is as near an "official" record of denominational statistics as is available.

Because these data represent the most complete annual compilation of church statistics, there is a temptation to expect more than is reasonable. These tables provide the answers to very simple and straightforward questions. Officials in church bodies were asked: "How many members does your organization have?" "How many clergy?" and "How much money does your organization spend?" Each respondent interprets the questions according to the policies of the organization.

Caution should, therefore, be exercised when comparing statistics across denominational lines, comparing statistics from one year to another and adding together statistics from different denominations.

Some particular methodological issues and therefore cautions in interpretation include the following considerations:

1. Definitions of membership, clergy, and other important characteristics differ from religious body to religious body. In this section, *Full* or *Confirmed Membership* refers to those with full communicant status. *Inclusive Membership* refers to those who are full communicants or confirmed members plus other members baptized, non-confirmed or non-communicant. Each church determines the age at which a young person is considered a member. Churches also vary in their approaches to statistics. For some, very careful counts are made of members. Other groups only make estimates.

2. Each year the data are collected with the same questions. While most denominations have consistent reporting practices from one year to the next, any change in practices is not noted in the tables. Church mergers and splits can also influence the statistics when they are compared over a number of years. Churches have different reporting schedules and some do not report on a regular basis.

3. The two problems listed above make adding figures from different denominations problematic. However, an additional complication is that individuals who attend two different churches may be included more than once. For example, a person who attends the Church of God in Christ Wednesday evening and an AME service on Sunday morning will likely be included in both counts.

4. Churches were asked to report figures for the full year ending December 31, 2006. Churches actually collect statistics according to their own ecclesial calendars. Data collected consistently from year to year accurately reflect trends over time, irrespective of when customarily collected. Caution should, therefore, be exercised when comparing statistics across denominational lines, comparing statistics from one year to another and adding together statistics from different denominations.

Table 1. Membership Statistics in Canada

Religious Body	Year Reporting	Number of Churches Reporting	Full Communicant or Confirmed Members	Inclusive Membership	Number of Pastors Serving Parishes	Total Number of Clergy	Number of Sunday or Sabbath Schools	Total Enrollment
The Anglican Church of Canada	2001	2,884	641,845	641,845	1,930	3,591	1,633	54,345
The Antiochian Orthodox Christian Archdiocese of North America	2003	16	105,000	150,000	30	31	16	1,300
Apostolic Christian Church (Nazarene)	1985	14		830	49	49		
The Apostolic Church in Canada	2002	20	1,450	1,740	22	28	17	687
Apostolic Church of Pentecost of Canada, Inc.	2006	144	26,000	26,000	306	383		
Armenian Holy Apostolic Church - Canadian Diocese	2002	9	85,000	85,000	10	49	5	400
Associated Gospel Churches	2005	137	10,758	10,758	130	263		
Association of Regular Baptist Churches (Canada)	1994	12			8	11		
Baptist Convention of Ontario and Quebec	2004	363	43,513	57,852	309	621		
Baptist General Conference of Canada	1999	103	7,500	14,000	150	240		
Baptist Union of Western Canada	2000	155	20,427	20,427	279	530		
The Bible Holiness Movement	2004	26	521	1,146	14	16	25	
Brethren in Christ Church, Canadian Conference	2003		3,287	3,287	81	81		

Table 1. Membership Statistics in Canada (*continued*)

Religious Body	Year Reporting	Number of Churches	Full Communicant or Confirmed Reporting	Inclusive Membership Members	Number of Pastors Serving	Total Number of Clergy Parishes	Number of Sunday or Sabbath Schools	Total Enrollment
Canadian and American Reformed Churches	2006	53	9,406	16,365	50	75		
Canadian Baptist Ministries	1996	1,133	129,055	129,055				
Canadian Conference of Mennonite Brethren Churches	2003	246	36,028	36,028				
Canadian Convention of Southern Baptists	2005	245	11,578	11,578	250	250	124	4,907
Canadian District of the Moravian Church in America, Northern Province	2006	9	972	1,290	9	12	7	289
Canadian Evangelical Christian Churches	2004	25	600	2,000	53	100	40	4,000
Canadian Yearly Meeting of the Religious Society of Friends	2005	24	1,175	1,232			24	101
Christian Brethren (also known as Plymouth Brethren)	2006	580		47,000		250	500	
Christian Church (Disciples of Christ) in Canada	2002	25	1,599	2,631	24	32	23	390
Christian Churches/Churches of Christ	2004	65	5,500	9,500	75	105	60	3,300
Christian and Missionary Alliance in Canada	2005	428	44,852	131,031	1,037	1,381	353	37,681

Table 1. Membership Statistics in Canada (continued)

Religious Body	Year Reporting	Number of Churches Reporting	Full Communicant or Confirmed Members	Inclusive Membership	Number of Pastors Serving Parishes	Total Number of Clergy	Number of Sunday or Sabbath Schools	Total Enrollment
Christian Reformed Church in North America	2006	249	46,400	72,900	226	375		
Church of God (Anderson, Ind.)	2002	48	3,711	3,711	41	88	37	1,794
Church of God (Cleveland, Tenn.)	2006	142	14,217	14,217	124	344	123	4,718
Church of God in Christ (Mennonite)	2006	52	4,767	4,767	187	196	52	
Church of God of Prophecy Canada East	2006	26	4,217	4,217	45	93	20	1,769
The Church of Jesus Christ of Latter-day Saints in Canada	2006	479	162,006	175,383	1,437	1,617	479	124,757
Church of the Lutheran Brethren	2004	8	425	676	10	13	7	336
Church of the Nazarene in Canada	2005	165	12,873	12,874	126	245	133	18,374
Churches of Christ in Canada	2005	149	6,857	6,857	122	122		
Community of Christ	2006	67	8,140	8,140	973	973		
Congregational Christian Churches in Canada		95		7,500	174	235		
Convention of Atlantic Baptist Churches	2003	539	62,766	62,766	282	619	314	
The Coptic Orthodox Church in Canada	2006	24	55,000	55,000	33	33		
The Estonian Evangelical Lutheran Church Abroad	2004	11	4,996	4,996	7	10	4	55

Table 1. Membership Statistics in Canada *(continued)*

Religious Body	Year Reporting	Number of Churches Reporting	Full Communicant or Confirmed Members	Inclusive Membership	Number of Pastors Serving Parishes	Total Number of Clergy	Number of Sunday or Sabbath Schools	Total Enrollment
The Evangelical Covenant Church of Canada	2002	21	1,384	1,384	6	25		1,763
Evangelical Free Church of Canada	2004	140	8,441	8,441	199	199		
Evangelical Lutheran Church in Canada	2006	623	174,555	174,555	485	866	447	17,926
The Evangelical Mennonite Conference	2006	60	7,250	7,250			55	
Evangelical Mennonite Mission Conference	1997	44	4,633	4,633	75	201		
The Evangelical Missionary Church of Canada	2003	130	10,390	10,390	218	309		
The Fellowship of Evangelical Baptist Churches in Canada	2004	499	71,073		318	348		
Foursquare Gospel Church of Canada	2004	55	3,031	3,031	117	141		860
Free Methodist Church in Canada	2003	149	7,603	7,603	123	223		5,955
Free Will Baptists	1998	10	347		3	4	8	
General Church of the New Jerusalem	2005	3	281	791	5	5	2	57
Greek Orthodox Metropolis of Toronto (Canada)	2004	76	350,000	350,000	62	73	76	

Table 1. Membership Statistics in Canada (*continued*)

Religious Body	Year Reporting	Number of Churches Reporting	Full Communicant or Confirmed Members	Inclusive Membership	Number of Pastors Serving Parishes	Total Number of Clergy	Number of Sunday or Sabbath Schools	Total Enrollment
Independent Holiness Church	1994	5		150	4	10	4	118
Jehovah's Witnesses	2003	1,325	110,221	110,221				
Lutheran Church—Canada	2005	329	54,955	75,616	233	369	1,381	6,183
Mennonite Church—Canada	2005	225	34,124	34,124				
North American Baptist Conference	2006	131	16,184	16,184	122	191	131	
The Old Catholic Church of Canada	2000	4	30	100	4	5		
Open Bible Faith Fellowship of Canada	2003	75	2,500	9,000	164	256	77	3,900
Orthodox Church in America (Archdiocese of Canada)	2004	68	2,000	10,000	59	73	20	450
Patriarchal Parishes of the Russian Orthodox Church in Canada	2005	24	1,200	1,200	5	6	4	108
The Pentecostal Assemblies of Canada	2006	1,108	62,062	234,040	2,130	2,130	552	23,777
The Pentecostal Assemblies of Newfoundland	2004	128	8,864	26,432	212	308	95	5,770
Presbyterian Church in America (Canadian Section)	2006	18	862	1,292				463
Presbyterian Church in Canada	2006	952	120,458	189,499		1,308	952	21,961

Table 1. Membership Statistics in Canada (continued)

Religious Body	Year Reporting	Number of Churches Reporting	Full Communicant or Confirmed Members	Inclusive Membership	Number of Pastors Serving Parishes	Total Number of Clergy	Number of Sunday or Sabbath Schools	Total Enrollment
Reformed Church in Canada	2004	40	3,753	5,642	38	67		
The Reformed Episcopal Church of Canada	2004	11	780	900	10	14	3	35
Reinland Mennonite Church	1995	6	877	1,816	10	13	5	347
The Roman Catholic Church in Canada	2003	5,391	12,987,637	12,987,637		8,641		
The Romanian Orthodox Church in America (Canadian Parishes)	2006	22	3,300	7,300	23	26	19	322
The Romanian Orthodox Episcopate of America (Jackson, MI)	2005	25	1,294	2,067	21	3	12	
The Salvation Army in Canada	2005	356	21,645	75,732	567	1,923		
Serbian Orthodox Church in the U.S.A. and Canada, Diocese of Canada	2004	23	8,500	230,000	26	31	14	2,068
Seventh-day Adventist Church in Canada	2006	337	557,324	57,324	203	333	415	27,317
Syriac Orthodox Church of Antioch	1995	5	2,500	2,500	3	4		
Ukranian Orthodox Church of Canada	1988	258		120,000	75	91		
Union d'Églises Baptistes Françaises au Canada	2004	34	1,868	1,868	29	40	62	629

Table 1. Membership Statistics in Canada (*continued*)

Religious Body	Year Reporting	Number of Churches Reporting	Full Communicant or Confirmed Members	Inclusive Membership	Number of Pastors Serving Parishes	Total Number of Clergy	Number of Sunday or Sabbath Schools	Total Enrollment
United Brethren Church in Canada	1992	9	835	835	5	12	9	447
The United Church of Canada	2004	3,527	593,600	1,441,000	1,902	4,129	2,686	51,960
Universal Fellowship of Metropolitan Community Churches	1992	12	50	1,500	8	9	1	36
The Wesleyan Church of Canada	2002	89	5,977	6,481	131	201	80	5,306
TOTALS		**25,117**	**16,314,829**	**18,053,137**	**16,198**	**35,648**	**11,106**	**436,961**

Table 2. Membership Statistics in the United States

Religious Body	Year Reporting	Number of Churches Reporting	Full Communicant or Confirmed Members	Inclusive Membership	Number of Pastors Serving Parishes	Total Number of Clergy	Number of Sunday or Sabbath Schools	Total Enrollment
Advent Christian Church	2006	293	25,617	25,617	233	494	235	12,656
African Methodist Episcopal Church*	1999	4,174	1,857,186	2,500,000	7,741	14,428	6,128	303,199
African Methodist Episcopal Zion Church*	2006	3,310	1,217,508	1,443,405	3,707	4,277	2,740	75,003
Albanian Orthodox Diocese of America	2004	2	2,407	2,407	3	3	2	60
The Allegheny Wesleyan Methodist Connection (Originall Allegheny Conference)	2006	103	1471	1,578	68	164	100	4,540
The Alliance of Baptists*	2006	127	65,000	65,000	320	465		
The American Association of Lutheran Churches	2006	73	12,400	26,537	55	187	88	3,920
The American Baptist Association	2000	1,760	275,000	275,000	1,740	1,760		
American Baptist Churches in the U.S.A.*	2006	5,659	1,371,278	1,371,278	3,438	6,947	78	89,942
The American Carpatho-Russian Orthodox Greek Catholic Church	2006	78	14,372	14,372	72	102	78	
American Evangelical Christian Churches	2006	192	16,000	17,400	192	224	192	
American Rescue Workers	2006	6	3,500	3,500	20	29	6	318
The Antiochian Orthodox Christian Archdiocese of North America	2006	252	425,000	425,000	450	517	252	21,700
Apostolic Catholic Church	2006	6	2,560	3,370	18	24	8	876
Apostolic Catholic Orthodox Church	2006	10	1,500	8,500	12	24	4	

Table 2. Membership Statistics in the United States *(continued)*

Religious Body	Year Reporting	Number of Churches Reporting	Full Communicant or Confirmed Members	Inclusive Membership	Number of Pastors Serving Parishes	Total Number of Clergy	Number of Sunday or Sabbath Schools	Total Enrollment
Apostolic Christian Church (Nazarene)	1993	57	3,629	3,629	201	201	53	1,548
Apostolic Christian Churches of America	2006	87	12,840	12,840	325	424	83	6,113
Apostolic Episcopal Church	2006	200	6,200	12,000	250	255		800
Apostolic Faith Mission Church of God	2005	18	8,100	10,730	48	98	18	3,905
Apostolic Faith Mission of Portland, Oregon	1994	54	4,500	4,500	60	85	54	
Apostolic Orthodox Catholic Church of North America	2005	25	15,900	15,900	40	49		
Armenian Apostolic Church of America	2006	38	360,000	360,000	27	46	24	1,705
Armenian Apostolic Church, Diocese of America*	1991	72	414,000	414,000	49	70		
Assemblies of God	2006	12,311	1,627,932	2,836,174	19,643	33,622	11,330	1,425,401
Associate Reformed Presbyterian Church (General Synod)	2004	256	35,211	41,019	229	401	208	16,374
The Association of Free Lutheran Congregations	2006	267	32,163	43,360	139	234	223	12,258
The Association of Independent Evangelical Lutheran Churches	2006	25	5,150	7,150	25	35	15	215
Association of Vineyard Churches	2004	600	140,000	140,000	700	1,205		54,000
Baptist Bible Fellowship International	1997	4,500	1,200,000	1,200,000				
Baptist General Conference	2002	902	145,148	145,148				65,735
Baptist Missionary Association of America	2006	1,254	225,723	225,723	1,300	1,500	1,250	68,072
Beachy Amish Mennonite Churches	2006	207	11,487	11,487	559	594	207	

Table 2. Membership Statistics in the United States (*continued*)

Religious Body	Year Reporting	Number of Churches Reporting	Full Communicant or Confirmed Members	Inclusive Membership	Number of Pastors Serving Parishes	Total Number of Clergy	Number of Sunday or Sabbath Schools	Total Enrollment
Berean Fellowship of Churches	2005	56	12,000	12,000				
The Bible Church of Christ, Inc.	1993	6	4,150	6,850	11	52	6	
Bible Fellowship Church	2005	61	7,470	7,470	61	130	52	5,526
Brethren in Christ Church	2001	232	20,739	20,739	151	295		12,404
Brethren Church (Ashland, Ohio)	2006	119	10,387	10,387	89	202	105	
The Catholic Church	2006	19,044	67,515,016	67,515,016	28,462	42,307	1	4,620,059
Christ Catholic Church	2005	6	1,797	2,887	7	7	1	23
Christ Community Church (Evangelical-Protestant)	2005	3	1,149	1,819	3	7	1	265
Christian Brethren (also known as Plymouth Brethren)	2006	1,150		86,000		600	1,000	
Christian Church (Disciples of Christ) in the United States and Canada*	2006	3,774	451,126	698,686	4,056	6,983	3,119	175,486
Christian Church of North America, General Council	2003	90	363	363	100	162	90	
Christian Churches and Churches of Christ	1988	5,579	1,071,616	1,071,616	5,525			
The Christian Congregation, Inc.	2004	1,496	122,181	122,181	1,574	1,575	1,347	41,891
Christian Methodist Episcopal Church*	2006	3,500	850,000	850,000	3,106	3,548	2,500	69,368
The Christian and Missionary Alliance	2006	2,010	189,969	417,008	2,429	3,014		
Christian Reformed Church in North America	2006	776	140,700	196,900	699	1,358		

Table 2. Membership Statistics in the United States (continued)

Religious Body	Year Reporting	Number of Churches Reporting	Full Communicant or Confirmed Members	Inclusive Membership	Number of Pastors Serving Parishes	Total Number of Clergy	Number of Sunday or Sabbath Schools	Total Enrollment
Christian Union	2005		5,129	6,034				2,407
Church of the Brethren*	2006	1,064	127,526	127,526	778	1,843	664	31,837
The Church of Christ (Holiness) U.S.A.	2003	154	10,460	10,460	192	214	148	7,489
Church Communities International	2006	13	819	1,515	26	36		
Church of God (Anderson, Indiana)	2006	2,215	249,845	249,845	5,098	5,974	2,215	119,318
The Church of God in Christ	1991	15,300	5,499,875	5,499,875	28,988	33,593		
Church of God in Christ, Mennonite	2006	138	13,938	13,938	499	529	138	
Church of God (Cleveland, Tennessee)	2006	6,569	1,032,550	1,032,550	5,796	16,452	5,888	339,559
Church of God by Faith, Inc.	2004	149	35,000	35,000	152	235		
Church of God, Mountain Assembly, Inc.	2005	120	7,200	7,200	140		120	11,040
Church of God of Prophecy	2006	1,871	84,762	84,762	2,905	4,509	1,871	59,000
The Church of God (Seventh Day), Denver, Colorado	2001	200	9,000	11,000	90	130	200	
The Church of Illumination	2000	4	1,200	1,200		16	1	216
The Church of Jesus Christ (Bickertonites)	2006	76	2,600	2,600	195	308		
The Church of Jesus Christ of Latter-day Saints	2006	13,010	5,168,359	5,779,316	39	43,617	13,010	4,426,536
Church of the Living God (Motto, Christian Workers for Fellowship)	2006	170	42,000	42,000	105	214	65	

Table 2. Membership Statistics in the United States (continued)

Religious Body	Year Reporting	Number of Churches Reporting	Full Communicant or Confirmed Members	Inclusive Membership	Number of Pastors Serving Parishes	Total Number of Clergy	Number of Sunday or Sabbath Schools	Total Enrollment
Church of the Lutheran Brethren of America	2006	110	8,907	14,427	140	222	108	10,608
Church of the Lutheran Confession	2006	87	6,365	8,390	64	90	67	943
Church of the Nazarene	2006	4,814	633,154	640,027	5,518	9,226	4,672	834,819
Church of the United Brethren in Christ	2004	215	23,000	23,000	160	210		
Churches of Christ	2006	13,000	1,250,000	1,250,000			10,500	
Churches of Christ in Christian Union	2005	231	10,645	10,645	153	341		12,948
Churches of God, General Conference	2006	324	33,208	33,208	243	399	324	13,585
Community of Christ	2005	1,236	180,339	180,339		20,420		
Congregational Holiness Church	2005	225	25,000	25,000	225	225		
Conservative Baptist Association of America (CBAmerica)	2006	12,000	200,000	200,000	1,800	2,200		
Conservative Congregational Christian Conference	2005	275	42,838	42,838	300	566	241	12,798
Conservative Lutheran Association	2002	3	852	1,267	8	29	3	120
Coptic Orthodox Church*	2000	100	250,000	300,000	140	145	100	5,500
Cumberland Presbyterian Church	2006	748	81,034	81,034	642	872	650	30,265
Cumberland Presbyterian Church in America	1996	152	15,142	15,142	141	156	152	9,465
Episcopal Church*	2006	7,095	1,796,017	2,154,572	5,534	15,051	6,184	266,080

373

Table 2. Membership Statistics in the United States *(continued)*

Religious Body	Year Reporting	Number of Churches Reporting	Full Communicant or Confirmed Members	Inclusive Membership	Number of Pastors Serving Parishes	Total Number of Clergy	Number of Sunday or Sabbath Schools	Total Enrollment
The Estonian Evangelical Lutheran Church	2001	21	3,508	3,508	10	12		
The Evangelical Church	2000	133	12,475	12,475	164	255	125	8,000
The Evangelical Church Alliance	2006		293,375	293,375	2,347	2,347		
The Evangelical Congregational Church	2003	146	20,743	20,743	169	252		
The Evangelical Covenant Church	2006	783	114,283	114,283	1,486	1,833		106,022
The Evangelical Free Church of America	2003	1,420	130,000	350,000	2,025	2,733		
Evangelical Friends International— North American Region	2006	283	27,431	39,569				
Evangelical Lutheran Church in America	2006	10,470	3,580,402	4,774,203	8,870	17,655	7,663	702,859
Evangelical Lutheran Synod	2006	138	16,319	20,559	108	168	118	2,631
Evangelical Methodist Church	2005	108	7,348	7,348	101	202	102	4,920
Evangelical Presbyterian Church	2005	182	65,924	73,019	295	498	155	32,840
Fellowship of Evangelical Bible Churches	2006	19	2,220	2,220	17	47	19	1,069
Fellowship of Evangelical Churches	2006	42	14,078	14,078	100	172	42	4,674
Fellowship of Fundamental Bible Churches	2004	22	821	1,208	33	48	19	872
Fellowship of Grace Brethren Churches	1997	260	30,371	30,371		564		

Table 2. Membership Statistics in the United States (*continued*)

Religious Body	Year Reporting	Number of Churches Reporting	Full Communicant or Confirmed Members	Inclusive Membership	Number of Pastors Serving Parishes	Total Number of Clergy	Number of Sunday or Sabbath Schools	Total Enrollment
Free Methodist Church of North America	2006	991	65,802	74,059		1,888		36,420
Friends General Conference	2002	832	32,000	32,000			400	
Friends United Meeting*	2005	427	37,595	42,680	306	355	273	
Full Gospel Assemblies International	2002	41	3,075	3,075	224		41	
Full Gospel Fellowship of Churches and Ministers International	2006	902	412,000	414,100	2,248	2,887		
Fundamental Methodist Church, Inc.	1993	12	682	787	17	22	12	454
General Association of General Baptists	2005	604	60,559	60,559	1,012	1,012	604	10,686
General Association of Regular Baptist Churches	2005	1,383	132,900	132,900				
General Church of the New Jerusalem	2006	37	3,519	6,760	34	71		
General Conference of Mennonite Brethren Churches	1996	368	50,915	82,130	590			34,668
Grace Gospel Fellowship	1992	128	60,000	60,000	160	196	128	
Greek Orthodox Archdiocese of America*	2006	560	1,500,000	1,500,000	553	840	550	
The Holy Eastern Orthodox Catholic and Apostolic Church in North America, Inc.	2001	17	4,138	4,138	9		17	
Hungarian Reformed Church in America*	2001	27	6,000	6,000	27	30		
Hutterian Brethren	2000	444	36,800	43,000	600	600		

Table 2. Membership Statistics in the United States *(continued)*

Religious Body	Year Reporting	Number of Churches Reporting	Full Communicant or Confirmed Members	Inclusive Membership	Number of Pastors Serving Parishes	Total Number of Clergy	Number of Sunday or Sabbath Schools	Total Enrollment
IFCA International, Inc.	1998	659	61,655	61,655			659	57,768
International Church of the Foursquare Gospel	2006	1,875	255,773	353,995	6,738	8,486	1,450	61,000
International Council of Community Churches*	2006	157	73,174	73,174	513	591		
International Fellowship of Bible Churches	2004	37	677	1,354	54	115	30	
The International Pentecostal Church of Christ	2003	67	2,004	4,961	51	157	48	1,918
International Pentecostal Holiness Church	2006	1,965	248,398	308,510	2,858	4,151		
Jehovah's Witnesses	2006	12,487	1,069,530	1,069,530				
Korean Presbyterian Church in America, General Assembly of the*	2003	302	38,500	55,000	465	583	16	17,760
The Latvian Evangelical Lutheran Church in America	2005	60	10,800	12,100	40	63		
Liberal Catholic Church (International)	2005	11	1,200	6,500	22	26	3	
The Liberal Catholic Church—Province of the United States of America	2006	21	5,800	5,800	41	44		
The Lutheran Church—Missouri Synod (LCMS)	2006	6,155	1,856,783	2,417,997	5,197	8,601	5,183	425,499
Malankara Orthodox Syrian Church, Diocese of America	2006	80	30,000	30,000	100	120	77	3,780

Table 2. Membership Statistics in the United States *(continued)*

Religious Body	Year Reporting	Number of Churches Reporting	Full Communicant or Confirmed Members	Inclusive Membership	Number of Pastors Serving Parishes	Total Number of Clergy	Number of Sunday or Sabbath Schools	Total Enrollment
Mar Thoma Syrian Church of India*	2005	74	25,000	40,000	46	46	60	4,500
Mennonite Church USA	2006	935	109,174	109,174	1,076	1,984		
The Missionary Church	2005	426	35,528	35,528	699	1,055		25,500
Moravian Church in America (Unitas Fratrum)*	2006	89	17,955	22,489	82	171	85	4,921
National Association of Congregational Christian Churches	2001	432	65,392	65,392	507	650		
National Association of Free Will Baptists	2005	2,399	187,193	187,193		3,901		108,949
National Baptist Convention of America, Inc.*	2000	9,000	3,500,000	3,500,000			9,000	
National Baptist Convention, U.S.A., Inc.*	2004	9,000	5,000,000	5,000,000			9,000	
National Missionary Baptist Convention of America*	1992		2,500,000	2,500,000				
National Organization of the New Apostolic Church of North America	2005	388	38,060	38,060	1,741	1,741	335	3,788
National Primitive Baptist Convention, Inc.	2002	1,565	600,000	600,000				
Netherlands Reformed Congregations	2003	27	4,523	9,524	9	10		
North American Baptist Conference	2006	272	47,150	47,150	296	418	272	

Table 2. Membership Statistics in the United States (continued)

Religious Body	Year Reporting	Number of Churches Reporting	Full Communicant or Confirmed Members	Inclusive Membership	Number of Pastors Serving Parishes	Total Number of Clergy	Number of Sunday or Sabbath Schools	Total Enrollment
North American Old Roman Catholic Church (Archdiocese of New York)	2005	6	575	590		7	3	16
The Old Catholic Orthodox Church		11	11,000	11,470	29	29		
Old German Baptist Brethren Church	2006	56	6,377	6,377	273	273		
Old Order Amish Church	2001	898	80,820	80,820	3,592	3,617	55	
Old Order (Wisler) Mennonite Church	2004	47	7,100	7,100	135	135		
Open Bible Standard Churches	2006	330	40,000	40,000	410	1,043		
The Orthodox Church in America	2004	737	970,000	1,064,000	824	905	517	
The Orthodox Presbyterian Church	2006	255	20,850	28,486	462	462		23,390
Patriarchal Parishes of the Russian Orthodox Church in the U.S.A.*	2006	31	7,000	17,000	37	63		
Pentecostal Assemblies of the World, Inc.	2006	1,750	1,500,000	1,500,000	4,500	4,500		
Pentecostal Church of God	2006	1,170	40,000	117,000		2,870	1,000	
Pentecostal Fire-Baptized Holiness Church	1996	27	223	223		28	25	400
Philadelphia Yearly Meeting of the Religious Society of Friends*	2006	104	11,681	11,681			80	2,500
Polish National Catholic Church of America*	2004	126	60,000	60,000	112	137		

Table 2. Membership Statistics in the United States (continued)

Religious Body	Year Reporting	Number of Churches Reporting	Full Communicant or Confirmed Members	Inclusive Membership	Number of Pastors Serving Parishes	Total Number of Clergy	Number of Sunday or Sabbath Schools	Total Enrollment
Presbyterian Church in America	2006	1,621	266,166	334,151	3,430	3,430		113,380
Presbyterian Church (U.S.A.)*	2006	11,903	2,267,118	3,025,740	9,115	21,360	8,547	1,063,827
Primitive Advent Christian Church	1993	10	345	345	11	11	10	292
Primitive Methodist Church in the U.S.A.	2006	72	3,833	3,984	55	93	61	2,252
Progressive National Baptist Convention, Inc.*	1995	2,000	2,500,000	2,500,000				
Protestant Reformed Churches in America	2006	27	4,298	7,457	26	41	23	
Reformed Catholic Church	2006	100	57,000	57,000	187	227	6	412
Reformed Church in America*	2006	891	163,160	265,217	837	1,968		
Reformed Church in the United States	2002	48	3,258	4,369	42	50	48	951
Reformed Episcopal Church	2003	142	8,631	11,281	185	211		
Reformed Mennonite Church	2006	8	152	164	22	22		
Reformed Presbyterian Church of North America	2004	80	4,542	6,347	77	147		
Religious Society of Friends (Conservative)	2004	1,200	104,000	104,000				
The Romanian Orthodox Episcopate of America	2006	64	7,135	10,635	116	138		

Table 2. Membership Statistics in the United States (*continued*)

Religious Body	Year Reporting	Number of Churches Reporting	Full Communicant or Confirmed Members	Inclusive Membership	Number of Pastors Serving Parishes	Total Number of Clergy	Number of Sunday or Sabbath Schools	Total Enrollment
The Russian Orthodox Church Outside of Russia	2006	190	480,000	480,000	210	258	32	2,120
The Salvation Army	2006	1,275	101,131	524,185	2,550	5,486	1,311	99,910
The Schwenkfelder Church	2005	6	2,500	2,500	9	11	6	700
Separate Baptists in Christ	1992	100	8,000	8,000	95	140	100	
Serbian Orthodox Church in the U.S.A. and Canada*	2005	68	67,000	67,000	60	82		
Seventh-day Adventist Church	2006	4,820	980,551	980,551	2,656	5,046	4,927	530,200
Seventh Day Baptist General Conference, USA and Canada	2006	96	5,200	6,200	60	80		
Southern Baptist Convention	2006	44,223	16,306,246	16,306,246	101,777	119,917	40,754	8,116,662
Southern Methodist Church	2006	101	6,000	6,000	109	158	105	3,774
Sovereign Grace Believers	2002	350	4,000	4,000	450	450	350	
The Swedenborgian Church*	2004	40	1,270	1,660	21	60		
Syrian (Syriac) Orthodox Church of Antioch*	2005	31	32,500	32,500	28	31	22	1,585
Syro-Russian Orthodox Catholic Church	2006	180	26,000	26,200	195	212	40	1,425
True Orthodox Church of Greece (Synod of Metropolitan Cyprian), American Exarchate	1999	9	1,095	1,095	18	19		
Ukrainian Orthodox Church of the U.S.A.*	2006	118	30,000	50,000	99	114	67	640

Table 2. Membership Statistics in the United States *(continued)*

Religious Body	Year Reporting	Number of Churches Reporting	Full Communicant or Confirmed Members	Inclusive Membership	Number of Pastors Serving Parishes	Total Number of Clergy	Number of Sunday or Sabbath Schools	Total Enrollment
Unitarian Universalist Association of Congregations	2002	1,010	214,738	214,738	1,267	171	1,010	1,819
The United Catholic Church, Inc.	2005	36	2,160	2,640	50	57		
United Christian Church	2006	9	280	280	9	15	7	577
United Church of Christ*	2006	5,452	1,218,541	1,218,541	4,076	10,268	4,616	220,766
The United Methodist Church*	2005	34,397	7,995,456	7,995,456	24,613	45,158	53,060	5,181,053
The United Pentecostal Church Inernational	2006	4,358		646,304	9,224	9,224		
The United Pentecostal Churches of Christ	2000	62	7,059	7,059	466	483	62	2,289
United Zion Church	2006	12	615	615	14	23	11	600
Unity of the Brethren	1998	27	2,548	3,218	25	39	24	1,442
Universal Fellowship of Metropolitan Community Churches	1998	300	44,000	44,000	324	372		
The Wesleyan Church	2005	1,626	116,151	128,385	2,182	3,341	1,626	441,495
Wisconsin Evangelical Lutheran Synod	2006	1,276	311,977	395,947	1,285	1,857	1,161	36,650
Totals		**340,657**	**155,404,043**	**163,774,246**	**365,935**	**598,323**	**235,742**	**30,800,520**

* National Council of Churches USA member communions.

Table 3. Membership Statistics
for the National Council of Churches USA

Religious Body	Year Reporting	Number of Churches Reporting	Inclusive Membership	Number of Pastors Serving Parishes
African Methodist Episcopal Church	1999	4,174	2,500,000	7,741
The African Methodist Episcopal Zion Church	2006	3,310	1,443,405	3,707
The Alliance of Baptists	2005	117	65,000	274
American Baptist Churches in the U.S.A.	2006	5,659	1,371,278	3,438
Armenian Apostolic Church, Diocese of America	1991	72	414,000	49
Christian Church (Disciples of Christ) in the United States and Canada	2006	3,774	698,686	4,056
Christian Methodist Episcopal Church	2006	3,500	850,000	3,106
Church of the Brethren	2006	1,064	127,526	778
Coptic Orthodox Church	2000	100	300,000	140
Episcopal Church	2006	7,095	2,154,572	5,534
Evangelical Lutheran Church in America	2006	10,470	4,774,203	8,870
Friends United Meeting	2005	427	42,680	306
Greek Orthodox Archdiocese of America	2006	560	1,500,000	553
Hungarian Reformed Church in America	2001	27	6,000	27
International Council of Community Churches	2006	157	73,174	513
Korean Presbyterian Church in America, General Assembly of the	2003	302	55,000	465
Malankara Orthodox Syrian Church, Diocese of America	2006	80	30,000	100
Mar Thoma Syrian Church of India	2005	74	40,000	46

Table 3. Membership Statistics
for the National Council of Churches USA *(continued)*

Religious Body	Year Reporting	Number of Churches Reporting	Inclusive Membership	Number of Pastors Serving Parishes
Moravian Church in America (Unitas Fratrum)	2006	89	22,489	82
National Baptist Convention of America, Inc.	2000		3,500,000	
National Baptist Convention, U.S.A., Inc.	2004	9,000	5,000,000	
National Missionary Baptist Convention of America	1992		2,500,000	
The Orthodox Church in America	2004	737	1,064,000	824
Patriarchal Parishes of the Russian Orthodox Church in the U.S.A.	2006	31	17,000	37
Philadelphia Yearly Meeting of the Religious Society of Friends	2006	104	11,681	
Polish National Catholic Church of America	2004	126	60,000	112
Presbyterian Church (U.S.A.)	2006	11,903	3,025,740	9,115
Progressive National Baptist Convention, Inc.	1995	2,000	2,500,000	
Reformed Church in America	2006	891	265,217	837
Serbian Orthodox Church in the U.S.A. and Canada	2005	68	67,000	60
The Swedenborgian Church	2006	40	1,660	29
Syrian (Syriac) Orthodox Church of Antioch	2005	31	32,500	28
Ukrainian Orthodox Church of the U.S.A.	2006	118	50,000	99
United Church of Christ	2006	5,452	1,218,541	4,076
The United Methodist Church	2005	34,397	7,995,456	24,613
TOTALS		**105,949**	**43,776,808**	**79,615**

Table 4. Selected Statistics of Church

Religious Body	Year	Full or Confirmed Members	Inclusive Members	TOTAL CONTRIBUTIONS		
				Total Contributions	Per Capita Full or Confirmed Members	Per Capita Inclusive Members
The Apostolic Church in Canada	2002	1,450	1,740	$1,705,737	$1,176.37	$980.31
Armenian Holy Apostolic Church—Canadian Diocese	2000	85,000	85,000	$855,000	$10.06	$10.06
Baptist Convention of Ontario and Quebec	2004	43,513	57,852	$42,120,960	$968.01	$728.08
Baptist Union of Western Canada	1999	20,427	20,427	$5,107,654	$250.04	$250.04
The Bible Holiness Movement	2004	521	1,146	$274,493	$526.86	$239.52
Canadian District of the Moravian Church in America, Northern Province	2006	972	1,290	$1,580,059	$1,625.58	$1,224.85
Canadian Evangelical Christian Churches	2004	600	2,000	$56,000	$93.33	$28.00
Christian Church (Disciples of Christ) in Canada	2002	1,599	2,631	$1,449,009	$906.20	$550.74
Christian and Missionary Alliance in Canada	2005	44,852	131,031	$136,297,640	$3,038.83	$1,040.19
Church of the Lutheran Brethren	2004	425	676	$755,605	$1,777.89	$1,117.76
Church of the Nazarene in Canada	2005	12,873	12,874	$14,359,388	$1,115.47	$1,115.38
Convention of the Atlantic Baptist Churches	2003	62,766	62,766	$36,457,660	$580.85	$580.85
Evangelical Lutheran Church in Canada	2002	174,555	174,555	$61,270,705	$351.01	$351.01
Foursquare Gospel Church of Canada	1996	3,031	3,031	$4,376,923	$1,444.05	$1,444.05
The Latvian Evangelical Lutheran Church in America	1995	4,162	4,647	$1,201,332	$288.64	$258.52
North American Baptist Conference	2006	16,184	16,184	$34,886,910	$2,155.64	$2,155.64
The Pentecostal Assemblies of Canada	2006	62,062	234,040	$266,084,058	$4,287.39	$1,136.92
The Pentecostal Assemblies of Newfoundland	2004	8,864	26,432	$5,624,770	$634.56	$212.80
Presbyterian Church in America (Canadian Section)	2006	862	1,292	$1,853,228	$2,149.92	$1,434.39
Reformed Church in Canada	2005	3,753	5,642	$4,909,664	$1,308.20	$870.20
The Reformed Episcopal Church of Canada	2004	780	900	$222,600	$285.38	$247.33
Seventh-day Adventist Church in Canada	2006	57,324	57,324	$83,128,445	$1,450.15	$1,450.15
Union d'Eglises Baptistes Françaises au Canada	2004	1,868	1,868	$888,230	$475.50	$475.50
The United Church of Canada	2004	593,600	1,441,000	$345,976,000	$582.84	$240.09
Totals		**1,202,043**	**2,346,348**	**$1,051,442,070**	**$874.71**	**$448.12**

Finances—Canadian Churches

CONGREGATIONAL FINANCES			BENEVOLENCES			
Total Congregational Contributions	Per Capita Full or Confirmed Members	Per Capita Inclusive Members	Total Benevolences	Per Capita Full or Confirmed Members	Per Capita Inclusive Members	Benevolences as a Percentage of Total Giving
$1,506,104	$1,038.69	$865.58	$199,633	$137.68	$114.73	12%
$430,000	$5.06	$5.06	$425,000	$5.00	$5.00	50%
$35,540,033	$816.77	$614.33	$6,580,927	$151.24	$113.75	16%
$562,511	$27.54	$27.54	$4,545,143	$222.51	$222.51	89%
$55,715	$106.94	$48.62	$219,078	$420.49	$191.17	80%
$1,456,715	$1,498.68	$1,129.24	$123,344	$126.90	$95.62	8%
$40,000	$66.67	$20.00	$16,000	$26.67	$8.00	29%
$1,230,384	$769.47	$467.65	$218,625	$136.73	$83.10	15%
$114,235,867	$2,546.95	$871.82	$22,061,773	$491.88	$168.37	16%
$605,137	$1,423.85	$895.17	$150,468	$354.04	$222.59	20%
$11,596,250	$900.82	$900.75	$2,763,138	$214.65	$214.63	19%
$36,457,660	$580.85	$580.85	$2,962,889	$47.21	$47.21	8%
$52,343,354	$299.87	$299.87	$7,518,028	$43.07	$43.07	12%
$4,248,451	$1,401.67	$1,401.67	$128,472	$42.39	$42.39	3%
$1,014,766	$243.82	$218.37	$186,566	$44.83	$40.15	16%
$28,670,810	$1,771.55	$1,771.55	$6,216,100	$384.09	$384.09	18%
$235,718,154	$3,798.11	$1,007.17	$31,365,904	$505.40	$134.02	12%
$3,948,770	$445.48	$149.39	$1,676,000	$189.08	$63.41	30%
$1,631,344	$1,892.51	$1,262.65	$221,884	$257.41	$171.74	12%
$3,703,250	$986.74	$656.37	$1,206,414	$321.45	$213.83	25%
$96,500	$123.72	$107.22	$5,500	$7.05	$6.11	2%
$27,828,604	$485.46	$485.46	$55,299,841	$964.69	$964.69	67%
$430.230	$230.32	$230.32	$458,000	$245.18	$245.18	52%
$301,259,400	$507.51	$209.06	$44,716,600	$75.33	$31.03	13%
$864,610,009	**$719.28**	**$368.49**	**$189,265,327**	**$157.45**	**$80.66**	**18%**

NOTE: Rounding may cause some totals to appear inaccurate.

385

Table 5. Selected Statistics of Church

Religious Body	Year	Full or Confirmed Members	Inclusive Members	TOTAL CONTRIBUTIONS		
				Total Contributions	Per Capita Full or Confirmed Members	Per Capita Inclusive Members
Albanian Orthodox Diocese of America	2004	2,407	2,407	$98,700	$41.01	$41.01
The Allegheny Wesleyan Methodist Connection (Original Allegheny Conference)	2006	1,471	1,578	$4,891,827	$3,325.51	$3,100.02
American Baptist Churches in the U.S.A.	2006	1,371,278	1,371,278	$312,485,103	$227.88	$227.88
The Antiochian Orthodox Christian Archdiocese of North America	2006	425,000	425,000	$6,791,000	$15.97	$15.97
Apostolic Catholic Church	2006	2,560	3,370	$192,728	$75.28	$57.19
Apostolic Faith Mission Church of God	2005	8,100	10,730	$1,206,839	$148.99	$112.47
Associate Reformed Presbyterian Church (General Synod)	2004	35,211	41,019	$44,640,298	$1,267.79	$1,088.28
Association of Independent Evangelical Lutheran Churches	2006	5,150	7,150	$15,000	$2.91	$2.10
Baptist Missionary Association of America	2006	225,723	225,723	$70,355,623	$311.69	$311.69
Berean Fellowship of Churches	2000	12,000	12,000	$10,309,605	$859.13	$859.13
Bible Fellowship Church	2005	7,470	7,470	$15,884,384	$2,126.42	$2,126.42
Brethren in Christ Church	2001	20,739	20,739	$36,431,223	$1,756.65	$1,756.65
Brethren Church (Ashland, Ohio)	2006	10,387	10,387	$1,395,344	$134.34	$134.34
Christian Church (Disciples of Christ) in the United States and Canada*	2006	451,126	698,686	$540,297,290	$1,197.66	$773.30
The Christian and Missionary Alliance	2006	189,969	417,008	$416,596,063	$2,086.69	$975.99
Christian Union	2005	5,129	6,034	$3,210,544	$625.96	$532.08
Church of the Brethren*	2006	127,526	127,526	$92,834,308	$727.96	$727.96
The Church of Christ (Holiness) U.S.A.	2003	10,460	10,460	$9,740,580	$931.22	$931.22
Church of the Lutheran Brethren of America	2006	8,907	14,427	$20,565,904	$2,308.96	$1,425.51
Church of the Lutheran Confession	2003	6,365	8,390	$5,855,961	$920.03	$697.97
Church of the Nazarene	2006	633,154	640,027	$792,831,191	$1,252.19	$1,238.75
Churches of God, General Conference	2006	33,208	33,208	$33,061,351	$92.19	$92.19
Community of Christ	2002	180,339	180,339	$42,535,613	$235.86	$235.86
Conservative Congregational Christian Conference	2005	42,838	42,838	$59,346,227	$1,385.36	$1,385.36
Cumberland Presbyterian Church	2006	81,034	81,034	$54,727,911	$675.37	$675.37

Note: Rounding off precise figures may cause some totals to appear inaccurate.

Finances—United States Churches

CONGREGATIONAL FINANCES			BENEVOLENCES			
Total Congregation Contributions	Per Capita Full or Confirmed Members	Per Capita Inclusive Members	Total Benevolences	Per Capita Full or Confirmed Members	Per Capita Inclusive Members	Benevolences as a Percentage
$90,000	$37.39	$37.39	$8,700	$3.61	$3.61	9%
$3,767,239	$2,561.01	$2,387.35	$1,124,588	$764.51	$712.67	23%
$261,159,450	$190.45	$190.45	$51,325,563	$37.43	$37.43	16%
$2,842,000	$6.69	$6.69	$3,949,000	$9.29	$9.29	58%
$175,260	$68.46	$52.01	$17,468	$6.82	$5.18	9%
$540,839	$66.77	$50.40	$666,000	$82.22	$62.07	55%
$36,752,134	$1,043.77	$895.98	$7,888,164	$224.03	$192.31	18%
$3,000	$0.58	$0.42	$12,000	$2.33	$1.68	80%
54,336,146	$245.15	$245.15	$16,019,477	$70.97	$70.97	23%
9,277,940	$773.16	$773.16	$1,031,665	$85.97	$85.97	10%
$12,268,254	$1,642.34	$1,642.34	$3,616,130	$484.09	$484.09	23%
$29,566,287	1,425.64	$1,425.64	$6,864,936	$331.02	$331.02	19%
$450,303	$43.35	$43.35	$945,041	$90.98	$90.98	68%
$490,900,321	$1,088.17	$702.61	$49,396,969	$109.50	$70.70	9%
$371,844,616	$1,849.89	$865.24	$47,597,978	$236.80	$110.75	11%
$2,299,850	$448.40	$381.15	$910,694	$177.56	$150.93	28%
$72,676,903	$569.90	$569.90	$20,157,405	$158.07	$158.07	22%
$9,178,816	$877.52	$877.52	$561,764	$53.71	$53.71	6%
18,576,152	$2,085.57	$1,287.60	$1,989,752	$223.39	$137.92	10%
$4,999,122	$785.41	$595.84	$856,839	$134.62	$102.13	15%
$655,937,953	$1,035.98	$1,024.86	$136,893,238	$216.21	$213.89	17%
$27,504,509	$828.25	$28.25	$5,556,842	$167.33	$167.33	17%
$18,217,887	$101.02	$101.02	$24,317,726	$134.84	$134.84	57%
$50,845,153	$1,186.92	$1,186.92	$8,501,074	$198.45	$198.45	14%
$46,396,330	$572.55	$572.55	$8,331,581	$102.82	$102.82	15%

Table 5. Selected Statistics of Church

Religious Body	Year	Full or Confirmed Members	Inclusive Members	TOTAL CONTRIBUTIONS		
				Total Contributions	Per Capita Full or Confirmed Members	Per Capita Inclusive Members
Cumberland Presbyterian Church in America	1996	15,142	15,142	$40,408,524	$2,668.64	$2,668.64
Episcopal Church*	2006	1,796,017	2,154,572	$2,185,698,918	$1,216.97	$1,014.45
The Evangelical Church	2000	12,475	12,475	$15,632,985	$1,253.15	$1,253.15
The Evangelical Congregational Church	2003	20,743	20,743	$19,628,647	$946.28	$946.28
The Evangelical Covenant Church	2006	114,283	114,283	$291,847,011	$2,553.72	$2,553.72
Evangelical Lutheran Church in America*	2006	3,580,402	4,774,203	$2,493,456,042	$696.42	$522.28
Evangelical Lutheran Synod	2006	16,319	20,559	$16,412,280	$1,005.72	$798.30
Fellowship of Evangelical Bible Churches	2006	2,220	2,220	$2,711,528	$1,221.41	$1,221.41
Fellowship of Evangelical Churches	2006	14,078	14,078	$21,771,519	$1,546.49	$1,546.49
Free Methodist Church of North America	2006	65,802	74,059	$158,820,542	$2,413.61	$2,144.51
General Conference of Mennonite Brethren Churches	1996	50,915	82,130	$65,851,481	$1,293.36	$801.80
The Holy Eastern Orthodox Catholic and Apostolic Church in North America, Inc.	2001	4,138	4,138	$14,673	$3.55	$3.55
International Church of the Foursquare Gospel	2003	255,773	353,995	$533,993,579	$2,087.76	$1,508.48
The International Pentecostal Church of Christ	2002	2,004	4,961	$3,551,761	$1,772.34	$715.94
The International Pentecostal Holiness Church	2006	248,398	308,510	$14,928,490	$60.10	$48.39
The Latvian Evangelical Lutheran Church in America	2004	10,800	12,100	$3,934,000	$364.26	$325.12
The Lutheran Church Missouri Synod (LCMS)	2006	1,856,783	$2,417,997	$1,355,458,558	$693.24	$531.29
Mar Thoma Syrian Church of India*	2004	25,000	40,000	$2,880,000	$115.20	$72.00
The Missionary Church	2005	35,528	35,528	$99,923,246	$2,812.52	$2,812.52
Moravian Church in America (Northern Province)	2006	17,955	22,489	$17,780,604	$990.29	$790.64
National Association of Free Will Baptists	2005	187,193	187,193	$134,086,807	$716.30	$716.30
North American Baptist Conference	2006	47,150	47,150	$72,279,470	$1,532.97	$1,532.97
The Orthodox Presbyterian Church	2006	20,850	28,486	$45,883,300	$2,200.64	$1,610.73
Presbyterian Church in America	2006	266,166	334,151	$650,091,428	$2,442.43	$1,945.50
Presbyterian Church (U.S.A.)*	2006	2,267,118	3,025,740	$2,854,719,850	$1,259.18	$943.48

388

CONGREGATIONAL FINANCES			BENEVOLENCES			
Total Congregation Contributions	Per Capita Full or Confirmed Members	Per Capita Inclusive Members	Total Benevolences	Per Capita Full or Confirmed Members	Per Capita Inclusive Members	Benevolences as a Percentage
$34,921,064	$2,306.24	$2,306.24	$5,487,460	$362.40	$362.40	14%
$1,871,718,992	$1,042.15	$868.72	$313,979,926	$174.82	$145.73	14%
$12,784,502	$1,024.81	$1,024.81	$2,848,483	$228.34	$228.34	18%
$17,648,320	$850.81	$850.81	$1,980,327	$95.47	$95.47	10%
$266,614,225	$2,332.93	$2,332.93	$25,232,786	$220.79	$220.79	9%
$2,243,047,177	$626.48	$469.83	$250,408,865	$69.94	$52.45	10%
$15,105,802	$925.66	$734.75	$1,306,478	$80.06	$63.55	8%
$2,232,204	$1,005.50	$1,005.50	$479,324	$215.91	$215.91	18%
$19,909,167	$1,414.20	$1,414.20	$1,862,352	$132.29	$132.29	9%
$142,861,676	$2,171.08	$1,929.03	$15,958,866	$242.53	$215.49	10%
$50,832,814	$998.39	$618.93	$15,018,667	$294.98	$182.86	23%
			$14,673	$3.55	$3.55	100%
$490,130,528	$1,916.27	$1,384.57	$43,863,051	$171.49	$123.91	8%
$2,648,634	$1,321.67	$533.89	$903,127	$450.66	$182.05	25%
$5,310,313	$21.38	$17.21	$9,618,177	$38.72	$31.18	64%
$3,473,000	$321.57	$287.02	$461,000	$42.69	$38.10	12%
$1,176,649,592	$629.00	$482.06	$120,169,146	$64.24	$49.23	9%
$2,405,000	$96.20	$60.13	$475,000	$19.00	$11.88	16%
$85,825,026	$2,415.70	$2,415.70	$14,098,220	$396.82	$396.82	14%
$16,729,653	$931.75	$743.90	$1,051,451	$58.56	$46.75	6%
$109,442,716	$584.65	$584.65	$24,644,091	$131.65	$131.65	18%
$62,175,197	$1,318.67	$1,318.67	$10,104,273	$214.30	$214.30	14%
$38,642,300	$1,853.35	$1,356.54	$7,241,000	$347.29	$254.20	16%
$532,611,674	$2,001.05	$1,593.93	$117,479,754	$441.38	$351.58	18%
$2,459,679,132	$1,084.94	$812.92	$395,040,718	$174.25	$130.56	14%

389

Table 5. Selected Statistics of Church

Religious Body	Year	Full or Confirmed Members	Inclusive Members	TOTAL CONTRIBUTIONS		
				Total Contributions	Per Capita Full or Confirmed Members	Per Capita Inclusive Members
Primitive Methodist Church in the U.S.A.	2006	3,833	3,984	$5,080,485	$1,325.46	$1,275.22
Reformed Church in America*	2006	163,160	265,217	$328,793,517	$2,015.16	$1,239.72
Reformed Church in the United States	2002	3,258	4,369	$6,241,428	$1,915.72	$1,428.57
Reformed Presbyterian Church of North America	2004	4,542	6,347	$7,129,652	$1,569.72	$1,123.31
The Schwenkfelder Church	2005	2,500	2,500	$1,910,514	$764.21	$764.21
Seventh-day Adventist Church	2006	980,551	980,551	$1,290,321,473	$1,315.91	$1,315.91
Southern Baptist Convention	2006	16,306,246	16,306,246	$11,372,608,393	$697.44	$697.44
Syro-Russian Orthodox Catholic Church	2006	26,000	26,200	$62,600	$2.41	$2.39
Unitarian Universalist Association of Congregations	2002	214,738	214,738	$152,722,868	$711.21	$711.21
United Church of Christ*	2006	1,218,541	1,218,541	$916,827,644	$752.40	$752.40
The United Methodist Church*	2005	7,995,456	7,995,456	$5,861,722,397	$733.13	$733.13
Unity of the Brethren	1998	2,548	3,218	$165,184	$64.83	$51.33
Universal Fellowship of Metropolitan Community Churches	1998	44,000	44,000	$1,570,860	$35.70	$35.70
The Wesleyan Church	2005	116,151	128,385	$280,214,570	$2,412.50	$2,182.61
Wisconsin Evangelical Lutheran Synod	2006	311,977	395,947	$315,677,440	$1,011.86	$797.27
TOTALS		42,224,304	46,101,429	$34,219,114,885	$810.41	$742.26

* National Council of Churches USA member communions
NOTE: Rounding may cause some totals to appear inaccurate.

Summary Statistics

Nation	Number Reporting	Full or Confirmed Members	Inclusive Members	Total Contributions	Per Capita Full or Confirmed Members	Per Capita Inclusive Members
Canada	24	1,202,043	2,346,348	$1,051,442,070	$874.71	$448.12
United States	65	42,224,304	46,101,429	$34,219,114,885	$810.41	$742.26

Finances—United States Churches (*continued*)

CONGREGATIONAL FINANCES			BENEVOLENCES			
Total Congregation Contributions	Per Capita Full or Confirmed Members	Per Capita Inclusive Members	Total Benevolences	Per Capita Full or Confirmed Members	Per Capita Inclusive Members	Benevolences as a Percentage
$4,434,026	$1,156.80	$1,112.96	$646,459	$168.66	$162.26	13%
$286,075,445	$1,753.34	$1,078.65	$42,718,072	$261.82	$161.07	13%
$5,309,445	$1,629.66	$1,215.25	$931,983	$286.06	$213.32	15%
$6,447,987	$1,419.64	$1,015.91	$681,665	$150.08	$107.40	10%
$1,682,568	$673.03	$673.03	$227,946	$91.18	$91.18	12%
$426,686,109	$435.15	$435.15	$863,635,364	$880.77	$880.77	67%
$10,086,992,362	$618.60	$618.60	$1,285,616,031	$78.84	$78.84	11%
$39,000	$1.50	$1.49	$23,600	$0.91	$0.90	38%
$152,722,868	$711.21	$711.21				
$843,215,750	$691.99	$691.99	$73,611,894	$60.41	$60.41	8%
$4,621,323,160	$577.99	$577.99	$1,240,399,237	$155.14	$155.14	21%
$51,465	$20.20	$15.99	$113,719	$44.63	$35.34	69%
$1,415,000	$32.16	$32.16	$155,860	$3.54	$3.54	10%
$241,309,396	$2,077.55	$1,879.58	$38,905,174	$334.95	$303.04	14%
$252,038,499	$807.88	$636.55	$63,638,941	$203.99	$160.73	20%
$28,773,748,252	**$681.45**	**$624.14**	**$5,389,573,754**	**$127.64**	**$116.91**	**16%**

# of Church Finances

Total Congregational Contributions	Per Capita Full or Confirmed Members	Per Capita Inclusive Members	Total Belevolences	Per Capita Full or Confirmed Members	Per Capita Inclusive Members	Benevolences as a Percentage of Total Contributions
$864,610,009	$719.28	$368.49	$189,265,327	$157.45	$80.66	18%
$28,773,748,252	$681.45	$624.14	$5,389,573,754	$127.64	$116.91	16%

Trends in Seminary Enrollment

Data Provided by The Association of Theological Schools (ATS) in the United States and Canada

Table 1: ATS total student enrollment figures include the number of individuals enrolled in degree programs as well as persons enrolled in non-degree programs of study. Growth in total enrollment is a function of both increased enrollment in the seminaries and the increased number of member schools in the Association. From fall 2005 to fall 2006, the total head count enrollment reported by ATS member schools decreased by 239 students, a decrease of 0.2%. In the same period, the full-time equivalent (FTE) enrollment decreased by 2.6%.

Table 1 Number of Member Schools from 1996 to 2006

Year	Number of Schools	Total Enrollment	Canada		United States		By Membership	
			Head Count	FTE	Head Count	FTE	Accredited	Non-Accredited
1996	233	65,637	5,568	3,304	60,069	40,111	60,527	5,110
1997	229	65,361	5,544	3,225	59,817	40,022	61,498	3,863
1998	237	68,875	5,847	3,683	63,028	40,994	64,412	4,463
1999	237	70,432	6,010	3,224	64,422	41,528	65,674	4,758
2000	243	72,728	5,868	3,251	68,860	44,627	69,850	2,878
2001	243	73,925	6,254	3,342	67,671	45,094	70,942	2,983
2002	244	76,530	6,643	3,512	69,887	44,557	73,615	2,895
2003	243	78,709	6,925	3,653	71,784	46,559	75,660	3,017
2004	251	80,773	7,036	3,597	73,737	48,093	77,513	2,627
2005	251	81,302	6.950	3,523	74,352	48,398	79,083	2,050
2006	253	81,063	6,395	3,205	74,668	47,377	79,618	1,445

Table 2: ATS computes enrollment both by the total number of individual students (Head Count) and the equivalent of full-time students (FTE). Full-time equivalency indicates the number of students who would be enrolled if all students were attending on a full-time basis. Decreasing full-time equivalent enrollment as a percentage of head count enrollment indicates an increasing number of part-time students.

Table 2 Head Count and FTE for all Member Schools 1996 to 2006

Year	Head Count	% Change	FTE	% Change	FTE % of Head Count
1996	65,637	1.79	43,415	0.73	66.1%
1997	65,361	-0.42	43,248	-0.38	66.2%
1998	68,875	5.38	44,678	3.31	64.9%
1999	70,432	2.17	44,845	0.68	63.7%
2000	72,728	3.26	47,876	6.76	65.8%
2001	73,925	1.65	48,435	1.17	65.5%
2002	76,550	3.50	48,130	-0.76	62.8%
2003	78,709	2.8	50,206	4.3	63.8%
2004	80,773	2.6	51,690	2.9	64.1%
2005	81,302	0.7	51,922	0.4	63.9%
2006	81,063	-0.2	50,582	-2.6	62.4%

Table 3: ATS member schools offer a variety of degree programs, Table 3 displays enrollment by categories of degree programs. The Master of Divinity (MDiv) degree is the normative degree to prepare persons for ordained ministry and for pastoral and religious leadership responsibilities in congregations. Over the past five years, from fall 2002 to fall 2006, the MDiv experienced a 7.6% increase in the *number* of students enrolled. Of those students enrolled in full degree programs in fall 2006 (eliminating the category "Other"), 49% of students were enrolled in the Master of Divinity degree, 16% in Basic Ministerial Leadership (Non-MDiv), 14% in General Theological Studies, 13% in Advanced Ministerial Leadership, and 8% in Advanced Theological Research.

Table 3 Head Count Enrollment by Degree Categories 1996 to 2006

Year	Basic Ministerial Leadership (M.Div.)	Basic Ministerial Leadership (Non-M.Div.)	General Theological Studies	Advanced Ministerial Leadership	Advanced Theological Research	Other
1996	28,035	7,474	7,157	8,315	5,499	8,157
1997	28,283	7,463	7,048	8,195	5,391	8,981
1998	29,263	8,066	7,602	8,641	5,712	9,591
1999	29,842	8,361	7,862	8,743	5,396	10,228
2000	30,427	9,098	8,436	8,758	5,692	10,317
2001	31,128	8,652	8,503	8,790	5,756	11,096
2002	32,005	9,493	8,626	9,209	5,653	11,544
2003	33,287	10,343	8,708	9,213	5,804	11,354
2004	34,096	10,417	9,257	9,435	5.541	11,394
2005	34,505	11,018	9,831	9,330	5,790	10,828
2006	34,442	11,057	9,811	9,366	5,876	10,511

Table 4: In fall 2006, women constituted 34.4% of the total enrollment in all ATS schools and 30.6% of the enrollment in the MDiv degree program. When ATS first began gathering enrollment data by gender in 1972, women represented 10% of the total enrollment and 5% of the MDiv enrollment.

Table 4 Women Student Head Count Enrollment 1996 to 2006

Year	Head Count	% Change	FTE % of Head Count
1996	21,523	3.50	32.76%
1997	21,652	0.60	33.10%
1998	23,176	7.04	33.65%
1999	24,057	3.73	34.16%
2000	25,391	5.55	34.91%
2001	25,999	2.39	35.17%
2002	27,328	5.06	35.70%
2003	27,920	2.2	35.50%
2004	28,875	3.4	36.03%
2005	29,257	1.3	35.98%
2006	27,921	-4.57	34.44%

393

Tables 5, 6, 7: Enrollment of North American racial/ethnic students in ATS schools has grown from 6% of total head count enrollment in 1977 to 22% in 2006. African American were 10.3% of the total enrollment in fall 2006; Hispanic students, 3.8%, and Pacific/Asian American students, 6.6%.

Table 5 African American Student Head Count Enrollment 1996 to 2006

Year	Number of Students	% Annual Increase	% of Total Enrollment
1996	5,550	-2.60	8.45%
1997	5,802	4.54	8.87%
1998	6,328	9.07	9.19%
1999	6,854	8.31	9.42%
2000	7,161	4.48	9.85%
2001	7,462	4.20	10.09%
2002	8,192	9.78	10.71%
2003	8,144	-0.6	10.30%
2004	8,393	3.06	10.47%
2005	8,946	6.59	12.10%
2006	8,344	-6.73	10.29%

Table 6 Hispanic Student Head Count Enrollment 1996 to 2006

Year	Number of Students	% Annual Increase	% of Total Enrollment
1996	1,785	-1.76	2.72%
1997	1,915	7.28	2.93%
1998	2,175	13.58	3.16%
1999	2,256	3.72	3.10%
2000	2,685	19.02	3.69%
2001	2,756	2.64	3.72%
2002	2,449	-11.14	3.20%
2003	2,863	16.9	3.60%
2004	2,842	-0.73	3.54%
2005	2,899	2.00	3.90%
2006	3,104	7.07	3.83%

Table 7 Pacific/Asian American Student Head Count Enrollment 1996 to 2006

Year	Number of Students	% Annual Increase	% of Total Enrollment
1996	4,492	5.82	6.84%
1997	4,545	1.18	6.95%
1998	4,992	8.95	7.25%
1999	4,932	-1.20	6.78%
2000	5,003	1.44	6.88%
2001	5,021	0.36	6.79%
2002	5,005	-0.32	6.54%
2003	5,499	9.90	7.00%
2004	5,226	-4.96	6.52%
2005	5,189	-7.08	7.00%
2006	5,370	3.49	6.62%

394

IV

A CALENDAR FOR CHURCH USE

2008–2011

This Calendar presents the major days of religious observances for Christians, Jews, Bahá'ís, and Muslims; and, within the Christian community, major dates observed by Catholic, Eastern and Oriental Orthodox, Episcopal, and Lutheran churches. Within each of these traditions many other observances, such as saints' days exist, but only those generally regarded as the most important are listed. Dates of interest to many Protestant communions are also included.

In the Orthodox dates, immovable observances are listed in accordance with the Gregorian calendar. Movable dates (those depending on the date of Easter) will often differ from Western observance, since the date of Easter (*Pascha*) in the Orthodox communions does not always correlate with the date for Easter of the Western churches. For Orthodox churches that use the old Julian calendar, observances are held thirteen days later than listed here.

Jewish and Muslim holidays begin after sunset the day previous to the date listed in this Calendar. For Jews and Muslims, who follow differing lunar calendars, the dates of major observances are translated into Gregorian dates. Since the actual beginning of a new month in the Islamic calendar is determined by the appearance of the new moon, the corresponding dates given here on the Gregorian calendar may vary by geographic location and practice. Following the lunar calendar, Muslim dates fall roughly eleven days earlier each year on the Gregorian calendar. Practice concerning transliteration of the titles of holidays varies widely as well.

(Note: This listing reflects the first full day of holidays extending over two or more days. "C" stands for Catholic, "O" for Orthodox, "E" for Episcopal, "L" for Lutheran, "ECU" for Ecumenical, "M" for Muslim).

Religious Event	2008	2009	2010	2011
New Year's Day (RC-Solemnity of Mary; O-Circumcision of Jesus Christ; E-Feast of Holy Name; L-Naming of Jesus) (*RC, O, E, L*)	Jan 1	Jan 1	Jan 1	Jan 1
Armenian Christmas (*O*)	Jan 6	Jan 6	Jan 6	Jan 6
Epiphany (*RC, O, E, L*)	Jan 6	Jan 6	Jan 6	Jan 6
Epiphany Sunday (*RC*)	Jan 6	Jan 4	Jan 3	Jan 2
Muharram Begins (First Day of the Month of Muharram; Muslim New Year) (*Muslim*)	Jan 10	Dec 18	Dec 7	Nov 26
First Sunday After Epiphany (Feast of the Baptism of Our Lord) (*Christian*)	Jan 13	Jan 11	Jan 10	Jan 9
Feast Day of St. John the Baptist (*Armenian O*)	Jan 13	Jan 13	Jan 13	Jan 13
Week of Prayer for Christian Unity (*ECU*)	Jan 18	Jan 18	Jan 18	Jan 18
Ashura' (Martyrdom of Imam Hussein) (*Muslim (Shi'a)*)	Jan 19	Jan 7	Dec 16	Dec 5
Theophany (*Oriental O*)	Jan 19	Jan 19	Jan 19	Jan 19
Ecumenical Sunday (*ECU*)	Jan 20	Jan 18	Jan 17	Jan 16
Week of Prayer for Christian Unity, Canada (*ECU*)	Jan 21	Jan 19	Jan 18	Jan 17
Tu B'Shevat (*Jewish*)	Jan 22	Feb 09	Jan 30	Jan 20
Presentation of Jesus in the Temple (Candlemas; Purification of the Virgin Mary; O-The Meeting of Our Lord and Savior Jesus Christ) (*Christian*)	Feb 2	Feb 2	Feb 2	Feb 2
Ash Wednesday (*Western Churches*)	Feb 6	Feb 25	Feb 17	Mar 9
Brotherhood Week (*Interfaith*)	Feb 17	Feb 15	Feb 21	Feb 20
Bahá'í Fasting Season begins (19 days) (*Bahá'í*)	Mar 2	Mar 2	Mar 2	Mar 2

395

Religious Event	2008	2009	2010	2011
World Day of Prayer (*ECU*)	Mar 7	Mar 6	Mar 5	Mar 4
Great Lent (First Day of Lent) (*O*)	Mar 9	Mar 1	Feb 21	Mar 13
Holy Week (Western Churches) (*Western Churches*)	Mar 16	Apr 05	Mar 28	Apr 7
Joseph, Husband of Mary *(RC, E, L)*	Mar 19	Mar 19	Mar 19	Mar 19
Holy Thursday (Western Churches) (*Western churches*)	Mar 20	Apr 9	Apr 1	Apr 21
Mawlid al-Nabi (Anniversary of the Prophet Muhammed's Birthday) (*Muslim*)	Mar 20	Mar 9	Feb 26	Feb 15
Feast of Naw-Ruz (Bahá'í New Year) (*Bahá'í*)	Mar 21	Mar 21	Mar 21	Mar 21
Purim (*Jewish*)	Mar 21	Mar 10	Feb 28	Mar 20
Good Friday (Friday of the Passion of Our Lord) (Western Churches) (*Western Churches*)	Mar 21	Apr 10	Apr 2	Apr 22
Easter (Western Churches) (*Western Churches*)	Mar 23	Apr 12	Apr 4	Apr 24
The Annunciation (*Christian*)	Mar 25	Mar 25	Mar 25	Mar 25
Passover (Pesach) (8 days) (*Jewish*)	Apr 20	Apr 9	Mar 30	Apr 19
Palm Sunday (O) (*O*)	Apr 20	Apr 12	Mar 28	Apr 17
Holy Week (O) (*O*)	Apr 20	Apr 12	Mar 28	Apr 17
Feast of Ridvan (Declaration of Bahá'u'llah) (12 days) (*Bahá'í*)	Apr 21	Apr 21	Apr 21	Apr 21
Holy Thursday (O) (*O*)	Apr 24	Apr 16	Apr 01	Apr 21
Holy Friday (Good Friday; Burial of Jesus Christ) (*O*)	Apr 25	Apr 17	Apr 2	Apr 22
Pascha (Orthodox Easter) (*O*)	Apr 27	Apr 19	Apr 4	Apr 24
Ascension Thursday (Western Churches) (*Western Churches*)	May 1	May 21	May 13	Jun 2
National Day of Prayer (*ECU*)	May 2	May 7	May 6	May 5
Yom Hashoah (*Jewish*)	May 2	Apr 21	Apr 11	May 1
May Friendship Day (*ECU*)	May 3	May 8	May 7	May 6
Yom Haatzma'ut (*Jewish*)	May 10	Apr 29	Apr 19	May 9
Pentecost (Whitsunday) (*Western Churches*)	May 11	May 31	May 23	Jun 12
Rural Life Sunday (*ECU*)	May 12	May 10	May 9	May 8
Holy Trinity (*RC, E, L*)	May 18	Jun 7	May 30	Jun 19
Lag B'Omer (*Jewish*)	May 23	May 12	May 2	May 22
Declaration of the Bab (*Bahá'í*)	May 23	May 23	May 23	May 23
Corpus Christi (*RC*)	May 25	Jun 14	Jun 6	Jun 26
Ascension of Baha'u'll ah (*Bahá'í*)	May 29	May 29	May 29	May 29
Sacred Heart of Jesus (*RC*)	May 30	Jun 19	Jun 11	Jul 1
Visitation of the Blessed Virgin Mary (*RC, E, L*)	May 31	May 31	May 31	May 31
Ascension Day (O) (*O*)	Jun 5	May 28	May 13	Jun 2
Martyrdom of the Bab (*Bahá'í*)	Jun 9	Jun 9	Jun 9	Jun 9
Shavuout (Pentacost) (2 days) (*Jewish*)	Jun 9	May 29	May 19	Jun 8
Pentecost (O) (*O*)	Jun 15	Jun 7	May 23	Jun 12
Nativity of St. John the Baptist (*RC, E, L*)	Jun 24	Jun 24	Jun 24	Jun 24
Saint Peter and Saint Paul, Apostles of Christ (*O*)	Jun 29	Jun 29	Jun 29	Jun 29
Feast Day of the Twelve Apostles of Christ (*O*)	Jun 30	Jun 30	Jun 30	Jun 30
Laylat al-Miraj (Ascension of the Prophet (*Muslim*)	Jul 31	July 20	July 9	Jun 29
'Id al-Fitr (Festival of the End of Ramadan; First day of the month of Shawwal) (*Muslim*)	Aug 1	Sep 20	Sep 10	Aug 30
Transfiguration of the Lord (*RC, O, E*)	Aug 6	Aug 6	Aug 6	Aug 6
Tish'a B'Av (*Jewish*)	Aug 10	Jul 30	Jul 20	Aug 9
Assumption of the Blessed Virgin Mary (E-Feast of the Blessed Virgin Mary; O-Falling Asleep (Domition) of the Blessed Virgin) (*RC, O, E*)	Aug 15	Aug 15	Aug 15	Aug 15
Laylat-ul-Bara'h (Night of Forgiveness) (*Muslim*)	Aug 16	Aug 6	July 27	Jul 16
Ramadan Begins (First day of the month of Ramadan) (*Muslim*)	Sep 1	Aug 22	Aug 11	Aug 1
The Birth of the Blessed Virgin (*RC, O*)	Sep 8	Sep 8	Sep 8	Sep 8
Holy Cross Day (RC-Triumph of the Cross; O-Adoration of the Holy Cross) (*Christian*)	Sep 14	Sep 14	Sep 14	Sep 14

Religious Event	2008	2009	2010	2011
Laylat al-Qadr (Night of Destiny, Revelation of the Holy Qur'an) (*Muslim*)	Sep 27	Sep 17	Sep 6	Aug 27
Michaelmas (St. Michael and All Angels) (*Christian*)	Sep 29	Sep 29	Sep 29	Sep 29
Rosh Hashanah (New Year) (2 days) (*Jewish*)	Sep 30	Sep 19	Sep 9	Sep 29
World Communion Sunday (*ECU*)	Oct 5	Oct 4	Oct 3	Oct 2
Yom Kippur (Day of Atonement) (*Jewish*)	Oct 9	Sep 28	Sep 18	Oct 8
Laity Sunday (*ECU*)	Oct 12	Oct 11	Oct 10	Oct 9
Thanksgiving Day (Canada) (*National*)	Oct 13	Oct 12	Oct 11	Oct 10
Sukkot (Tabernacles) (7 days) (*Jewish*)	Oct 14	Oct 9	Sep 23	Oct 13
Birth of the Bab (*Bahá'í*)	Oct 20	Oct 20	Oct 20	Oct 20
Shmini Atzeret (Solemn Assembly) (*Jewish*)	Oct 21	Oct 10	Sep 30	Oct 20
Shimchat Torah (Rejoicing of the Law) (*Jewish*)	Oct 22	Oct 11	Oct 1	Oct 21
Reformation Sunday (*L*)	Oct 26	Oct 25	Oct 31	Oct 30
Reformation Day (*L*)	Oct 31	Oct 31	Oct 31	Oct 31
All Saints Day (*RC, E, L*)	Nov 1	Nov 1	Nov 1	Nov 1
World Community Day (*ECU*)	Nov 6	Nov 5	Nov 4	Nov 3
Birth of Bahá'u'lláh (*Baha'i*)	Nov 12	Nov 12	Nov 12	Nov 12
Presentation of the Blessed Virgin Mary in the Temple (Presentation of the Theotokos) (*O*)	Nov 21	Nov 21	Nov 21	Nov 21
Last Sunday After Pentecost (L-Feast of Christ the King) (*RC, L*)	Nov 23	Nov 22	Nov 21	Nov 20
Thanksgiving Sunday (U.S.) (*Christian*)	Nov 23	Nov 22	Nov 21	Nov 20
National Bible Week (*ECU*)	Nov 23	Nov 15	Nov 21	Nov 20
Bible Sunday (*ECU*)	Nov 23	Nov 15	Nov 21	Nov 20
The Day of the Covenant (*Bahá'í*)	Nov 26	Nov 26	Nov 26	Nov 26
Thanksgiving Day (U.S.) (*National*)	Nov 27	Nov 26	Nov 25	Nov 24
Ascension of 'Abdu'l-Baha (*Bahá'í*)	Nov 28	Nov 28	Nov 28	Nov 28
Feast Day of St. Andrew the Apostle (*RC, O, E, L*)	Nov 30	Nov 30	Nov 30	Nov 30
First Sunday of Advent (Advent Sunday) (*Christian*)	Nov 30	Nov 29	Nov 28	Nov 27
Waqf al Arafah (Eve of 'Id al-Adha) (*Muslim*)	Dec 7	Nov 26	Nov 15	Nov 5
'Id al-Adha (Festival of Sacrifice at time of Pilgrimage to Mecca) (*Muslim*)	Dec 8	Nov 27	Nov 16	Nov 6
Immaculate Conception of the Blessed Virgin May (*RC*)	Dec 8	Dec 8	Dec 8	Dec 8
Fourth Sunday of Advent (Christmas Sunday) (*Christian*)	Dec 21	Dec 20	Dec 19	Dec 18
Hanukkah (Chanukah, Festival of Lights) (8 days) (*Jewish*)	Dec 22	Dec 11	Dec 1	Dec 20
Christmas (*Christian, Except Armenian*)	Dec 25	Dec 25	Dec 25	Dec 25

CALENDAR

397

V

INDEXES
Organizations

AAR (American Academy of Religion) 212
ABCCM (Asheville-Buncombe
    Community Christian Ministry) 256
ACAT (Action des Chrétiens pour
    l'Abolition de la Torture) 293
Action des Chrétiens pour
    l'Abolition de la Torture (ACAT)..............293
ADRIS (Association for the Development of
    Religious Information Services).................25
Advent Christian Church 58, 369
African Methodist Episcopal
    Church 58, 369, 382
African Methodist Episcopal Zion
    Church, The 369, 382
AGAPÉ Deux-Montagnes 293
Akron Area Association of Churches 257
Alaska Christian Conference 233
Alban Institute, Inc., The 21
Albanian Orthodox Archdiocese in
    America 62
Albanian Orthodox Diocese of
    America 62, 369
Alcohol and Drug Concerns, Inc................... 50
ALEPH Administrative Office.................... 228
Allegheny Conference, The. See Allegheny
    Wesleyan Methodist Connection (Original
    Allegheny Conference)
Allegheny Valley Association of
    Churches 259
Allegheny Wesleyan Methodist
    Connection (Original Allegheny
    Conference) 62, 369
Alliance for Christian Media, The 21
Alliance of Baptists, The 62, 369, 382
Alliance of Churches 257
AMERC (Appalachian Ministries
    Educational Resource Center).................... 23
American Academy of Religion (AAR) 212
American Association of Lutheran
    Churches, The...................................... 63, 369
American Baptist Association, The 63, 369
American Baptist Churches
    in the U.S.A..............................64, 369, 382
American Bible Society 21
American Buddhist Association 222
American Buddhist Congress 222
American Carpatho-Russian Orthodox
    Greek Catholic Church, The.................... 369
American Council of Christian Churches...... 22

American Evangelical Christian
    Churches 369
American Friends Service Committee.......... 22
American Hindus Against Defamation 225
American Jewish Committee 228
American Orthodox Catholic Church. See
    Apostolic Orthodox Catholic Church of
    North America
American Rescue Workers.................... 66, 369
American Theological Library
    Association, The 23
American Tract Society 23
American Waldensian Society, The 23
Amish. See Old Order Amish Church
Anglican Church of Canada, The 180, 362
Anglican Orthodox Church, The. See
    Episcopal Orthodox Church, The
Anti-Defamation League of B'nai
    B'rith, The 228
Antiochian Orthodox Christian
    Archdiocese of North
    America, The 66, 181, 362, 369
Apostolic Catholic Assyrian Church
    of the East, North American Dioceses 67
Apostolic Catholic Church 67, 369
Apostolic Catholic Orthodox Church 68, 369
Apostolic Christian Church
    (Nazarene) 69, 182, 362, 370
Apostolic Christian Churches
    of America 370
Apostolic Church in Canada, The 182, 362
Apostolic Church of Pentecost
    of Canada, Inc. 182, 362
Apostolic Episcopal Church 370
Apostolic Faith Mission Church
    of God... 70, 370
Apostolic Faith Mission of Portland,
    Oregon 70, 370
Apostolic Lutheran Church of America......... 71
Apostolic Orthodox Catholic Church
    of North America..................................... 370
Appalachian Ministries Educational
    Resource Center (AMERC) 23
ARDA (Association of Religion
    Data Archives)... 213
Arizona Ecumenical Council 233
Arkansas Interfaith Conference 234
Armenian Apostolic Church,
    Diocese of America 71, 370, 382

INDEX

Armenian Apostolic Church of
America 71, 370
Armenian Evangelical Church.................... 182
Armenian Holy Apostolic Church—
Canadian Diocese 182
Arrowhead Interfaith Council...................... 247
Asheville-Buncombe Community Christian
Ministry (ABCCM) 256
Assemblies of God.................................. 72, 370
Assemblies of God International Fellowship
(Independent/Not Affiliated) 73
Associate Reformed Presbyterian Church
(General Synod) 73, 370
Associated Church Press, The 24
Associated Churches of Fort Wayne
& Allen County, Inc., The 240
Associated Gospel Churches 362
Associated Gospel Churches, The 24
Associated Ministries of Tacoma-
Pierce County 266
Association for the Development of
Religious Information Services
(ADRIS) 25
Association of Catholic Diocesan
Archivists.. 25
Association of Christian Churches in
Manitoba... 292
Association of Christian Churches of
South Dakota 263
Association of Free Lutheran
Congregations, The 74, 370
Association of Gospel Rescue Missions........ 25
Association of Independent Evangelical
Lutheran Churches 74, 370
Association of Regular Baptist
Churches (Canada) 183, 362
Association of Religion Data
Archives (ARDA).................................... 213
Association of Religious Communities 236
Association of Statisticians of American
Religious Bodies.. 25
Association of Theological Schools
(ATS) 26, 213
Association of Theological Schools in
the United States and Canada, The 26, 213
Association of Vineyard Churches 75, 370
Atlantic Ecumenical Council 293
Atlantic Ecumenical Council of
Churches 292
ATS (Association of Theological
Schools) 26, 213
Attleboro Area Council of Churches,
Inc... 245
Auburn Theological Seminary 213
Austin Area Interreligious Ministries 264

Baha'i National Center of the U.S.A.,
The.. 222
B.A.P.S. (Bochasanwasi Shri Akshar
Purushottam Swaminarayan
Sanstha) 225
Baptist Bible Fellowship
International.. 75, 370

Baptist Convention of Ontario
and Quebec....................................... 183, 362
Baptist General Conference 76, 370
Baptist General Conference
of Canada... 183, 362
Baptist Missionary Association
of America.. 76, 370
Baptist Union of Western Canada 184, 362
BARCA (Border Association for
Refugees from Central America, Inc.) 264
Barna Group, Ltd., The 214
Bay Area Ecumenical Forum 246
Beachy Amish Mennonite Churches 77, 370
Berean Fellowship of Churches............. 77, 371
Bergen County Council of Churches........... 251
Berrien County Association of
Churches, 246
Bible Church of Christ, Inc., The 77, 371
Bible Fellowship Church 78, 371
Bible Holiness Church.................................. 78
Bible Holiness Movement, The 184, 362
Bible Way Church of Our Lord
Jesus Christ World Wide, Inc. 79
Blanton-Peale Institute.................................. 26
Bochasanwasi Shri Akshar Purushottam
Swaminarayan Sanstha (B.A.P.S.) 225
Border Association for Refugees from
Central America (BARCA), Inc. 264
Bread for the World 26
Brethren Church (Ashland, Ohio) 79, 371
Brethren in Christ Church 79, 371
Brethren in Christ Church, Canadian
Conference.. 184, 362
Bridgewater Inter-Church Council 292
British Methodist Episcopal Church
of Canada... 185
Brooklyn Council of Churches 252
Broome County Council of Churches,
Inc... 252
Buddhist Churches of America................... 222
Buddhist Council of the Midwest............... 223
Buddhist Council of the Northwest 223
Buddhist Peace Fellowship, The................. 223
Burlington Inter-Church Council 293

CAIR (Council for American-Islamic
Relations).. 226
Calgary Council of Churches 292
Calgary Inter-Faith Community Action
Association 292
California Council of Churches—
California Church Impact........................ 234
Calvary Chapel 79
Campus Crusade for Christ International 26
Canadian and American Reformed
Churches 185, 363
Canadian Baptist Ministries................. 185, 363
Canadian Bible Society................................. 50
Canadian Centre for Ecumenism........... 50, 293
Canadian Conference of Mennonite
Brethren Churches 185, 363
Canadian Convention of Southern
Baptists 185

Canadian Council of Churches, The.............. 51
Canadian District of the Moravian Church
    in America, Northern Province 186, 363
Canadian Evangelical Christian
    Churches 186, 363
Canadian Evangelical Theological
    Association 51
Canadian Society of Biblical Studies-Société
    Canadienne des Etudes Bibliques 52
Canadian Tract Society 52
Canadian Yearly Meeting of the
    Religious Society of Friends 186, 363
Cape Cod Council of Churches, Inc.,
    The 245
Capital Area Council of Churches, Inc........ 252
Capital Region Conference of
    Churches, The 236
Capital Region Ecumenical Organization
    (CREO) 252
CARA (Center for Applied Research
    in the Apostolate) 215
Catholic Church in Canada, The. See Roman
    Catholic Church in Canada, The
Catholic Church, The 80, 371
CB America (Conservative Baptist
    Association of America).................. 103, 373
CCTE, EF (Churches' Council on
    Theological Education in Canada,
    An Ecumenical Foundation)...................... 52
CCW (Center on Conscience & War)............ 27
CEAP (Community Emergency Assistance
    Program) 248
Center City Churches 236
Center for Applied Research in the
    Apostolate (CARA) 215
Center for Parish Development 27
Center for the Study of Religion and
    American Culture 215
Center on Conscience & War (CCW)............ 27
Central Maryland Ecumenical Council 244
Centre Emmaüs 294
Chaplaincy of Full Gospel Churches 27
Chautauqua County Rural Ministry............. 252
Christ Catholic Church 81, 371
Christ Catholic Church International........... 186
Christ Community Church (Evangelical-
    Protestant)... 81, 371
Christadelphians 81
Christian and Missionary Alliance in
    Canada 188, 363
Christian and Missionary Alliance,
    The 87, 371
Christian Associates of Southwest
    Pennsylvania... 259
Christian Brethren (also known as
    Plymouth Brethren) 82, 187, 363, 371
Christian Church (Disciples of Christ)
    in Canada.. 187, 363
Christian Church (Disciples of Christ)
    in the United States
    and Canada 82, 371, 382
Christian Church of North America,
    General Council................................. 85, 371

Christian Churches United of the
    Tri-County Area.. 259
Christian Churches/Churches
    of Christ............................. 85, 187, 363, 371
Christian Community Action 236
Christian Conference of Connecticut 237
Christian Congregation, Inc., The 85, 371
Christian Council of Delaware and
    Maryland's Eastern Shore, The 237
Christian Council on Persons with
    Disabilities 28
Christian Endeavor International 28
Christian Leadership Council of
    Downtown Toronto................................... 293
Christian Management Association 28
Christian Methodist Episcopal
    Church 86, 371, 382
Christian Ministries of Delaware
    County 240
Christian Ministry in the National
    Parks, A 28
Christian Reformed Church
    in North America................ 88, 188, 364, 371
Christian Service Center for
    Central Florida, Inc. 238
Christian Union 372
Christian Youth Council.............................. 268
Christian-Jewish Dialogue of Montreal....... 294
Christians United in Beaver County 259
Church Army in Canada, The 52
Church Communities International 91, 372
Church Community Services 240
Church Council of Greater Seattle.............. 266
Church Federation of Greater
    Indianapolis, Inc., The 240
Church Growth Center—Home of Church
    Doctor Ministries.. 29
Church of Christ 89, 373
Church of Christ in Christian Union 373
Church of Christ, Scientist.......................... 90
Church of Christ (Holiness)
    U.S.A., The 90, 372
Church of God (Anderson,
    Indiana) 91, 188, 364, 372
Church of God (Cleveland,
    Tennessee) 93, 189, 364, 372
Church of God by Faith, Inc.................. 94, 372
Church of God General Conference
    (Oregon, IL and Morrow, GA) 94, 373
Church of God in Christ, International.......... 93
Church of God in Christ, Mennonite..... 93, 189
Church of God in Christ, The 91, 372
(Original) Church of God, Inc., The 142
Church of God, Mountain Assembly,
    Inc... 95, 372
Church of God of Prophecy.................. 95, 372
Church of God of Prophecy Canada
    East, The 190, 364
Church of God of the Firstborn, The 94
Church of God, The 99
Church of God, The (Seventh Day),
    Denver, Colorado 96, 372
Church of Illumination, The 96, 372

401

Church of Jesus Christ of Latter-day
Saints in Canada, The........................ 190, 364
Church of Jesus Christ of Latter-day
Saints, The 97, 372
Church of Jesus Christ, The
(Bickertonites) 97
Church of Our Lord Jesus Christ of the
Apostolic Faith, Inc. 100
Church of the Brethren 89, 372, 382
Church of the Living God (Motto,
Christian Workers for Fellowship) 97, 372
Church of the Lutheran Brethren......... 191, 364
Church of the Lutheran Brethren
of America 98, 373
Church of the Lutheran Confession....... 98, 373
Church of the Nazarene 99, 373
Church of the Nazarene in Canada...... 191, 364
Church of the United Brethren in
Christ, USA 101, 373
Church Women United in the U.S.A. 29
Churches' Council on Theological
Education in Canada, An Ecumenical
Foundation (CCTE, EF) 52
Churches of Christ 101
Churches of Christ in Canada.............. 191, 364
Churches of Christ in Christian
Union 101, 373
Churches of God, General Conference........ 102
Churches United, Inc. 241
Churches United of the Quad City Area...... 239
Churches Uniting in Christ 29
Churchpeople for Change and
Reconciliation... 257
CLA (Conservative Lutheran
Association) 104
Colorado Council of Churches 236
Community Emergency Assistance
Program (CEAP) 248
Community Ministries of Rockville 245
Community Ministry of Montgomery
County 245
Community of Christ 102, 191, 364, 373
Community Renewal Society 239
Concerned Ecumenical Ministry
to the Upper West Side 252
Congregational Christian Churches
in Canada 192, 364
Congregational Holiness Church......... 103, 373
Conservative Baptist Association
of America (CB America) 103, 373
Conservative Congregational
Christian Conference 103, 373
Conservative Lutheran Association
(CLA) 104, 373
Consultation on Church Union 29
Contact Ministries of Springfield 239
Convention of Atlantic Baptist
Churches 192, 364
Cooperative Metropolitan Ministries........... 245
Coptic Orthodox Church 104, 373, 382
Coptic Orthodox Church in
Canada, The..................................... 193, 364
Cornwallis District Inter-Church Council ... 292

Corpus Christi Metro Ministries................. 264
Cortland County Council of
Churches, Inc.. 253
Council for American-Islamic
Relations (CAIR)..................................... 226
Council of Christian Communions
of Greater Cincinnati 257
Council of Churches and Synagogues of
Southwestern Connecticut 237
Council of Churches of Chemung
County, Inc. 253
Council of Churches of Greater
Bridgeport, Inc... 237
Council of Churches of Greater
Springfield 245
Council of Churches of Greater
Washington, The 238
Council of Churches of Santa
Clara County, The.................................... 234
Council of Churches of the
City of New York 253
Council of Churches of the Ozarks 250
Council of Hindu Temples
of North America...................................... 225
CREO (Capital Region Ecumenical
Organization).. 252
Cross-Lines Cooperative Council............... 242
Cumberland Presbyterian Church........ 104, 373
Cumberland Presbyterian Church
in America 105, 373

Des Moines Area Religious Council 241
Direction Chrétienne................................... 294
Disciples of Christ. See Christian Church
(Disciples of Christ) in Canada; Christian
Church (Disciples of Christ) in the United
States and Canada
Doukhobars. See Union of Spiritual
Communities of Christ (Orthodox
Doukhobors in Canada)
Dutchess County Interfaith Council, Inc..... 253

East Dallas Cooperative Parish................... 264
East End Cooperative Ministry................... 260
Eastern Area Community Ministries 242
Ecclesia 251
Ecumenical Committee 293
Ecumenical Conference of
Greater Altoona 260
Ecumenical Council of Pasadena Area
Churches, The.. 234
Ecumenical Council of
San Diego County 234
Ecumenical Ministries 250
Ecumenical Ministries of Iowa (EMI)......... 242
Ecumenical Ministries of Oregon............... 258
Elim Fellowship 105
Elim Fellowship of Evangelical
Churches and Ministers 193
EMI (Ecumenical Ministries of Iowa)......... 242
empty tomb, inc. 216
Episcopal Church........................ 106, 373, 382
Episcopal Orthodox Church, The 109, 193

Estonian Evangelical Lutheran
Church Abroad, The 364
Estonian Evangelical Lutheran
Church, The 109, 374
Evangelical Church Alliance,
The 110, 374
Evangelical Church, The 109, 374
Evangelical Churches. See Fellowship of
Evangelical Churches
Evangelical Congregational Church,
The 110, 374
Evangelical Council for Financial
Accountability 30
Evangelical Covenant Church of
Canada, The 193, 365
Evangelical Covenant Church, The 111, 374
Evangelical Fellowship of Canada 53
Evangelical Free Church of
America, The 112, 374
Evangelical Free Church of Canada 194, 365
Evangelical Friends International-
North American Region.................... 112, 374
Evangelical Lutheran Church
in America 112, 374, 382
Evangelical Lutheran Church
in Canada 194, 365
Evangelical Lutheran Synod 116, 374
Evangelical Mennonite Church.
See Fellowship of Evangelical Churches
Evangelical Mennonite Conference,
The 194, 365
Evangelical Mennonite Mission
Conference 195, 365
Evangelical Methodist Church............. 116, 374
Evangelical Missionary Church
of Canada, The 195, 365
Evangelical Presbyterian Church 116, 374
Evangelical Press Association 30
Evanston Ecumenical Action Council 239
Evansville Area Community
of Churches, Inc. 240

Faith Community Assistance Center 252
FaithTrust Institute 267
Federation of Christian Ministries 31
Federation of Jain Associations
in North America (JAINA)....................... 227
Federation of Zoroastrian Associations
of North America (FEZANA) 232
Fellowship of Evangelical Baptist
Churches in Canada, The 196, 365
Fellowship of Evangelical Bible
Churches 117, 374
Fellowship of Evangelical Churches ... 117, 374
Fellowship of Fundamental Bible
Churches 118, 374
Fellowship of Grace Brethren
Churches 118, 374
Fern Creek-Highview United Ministries 242
FEZANA (Federation of Zorastrian
Associations of North America)............... 232
First Miramichi Inter-Church Council 292
Florida Council of Churches....................... 238

Foundation for a Conference on Faith
and Order in North America...................... 31
Foursquare Gospel Church of
Canada 196, 365
Free Christian Zion Church of Christ 119
Free Methodist Church in Canada 196, 365
Free Methodist Church of North
America 119, 375
Free Will Baptists 196, 365
Fresno Metro Ministry 234
Friends General Conference 119, 375
Friends International. See Evangelical
Friends International-North American
Region
Friends United Meeting 120, 375, 382
Friends World Committee for Consultation
(Section of the Americas)......................... 32
Full Gospel Assemblies
International..................................... 122, 375
Full Gospel Fellowship of Churches
and Ministers International 122, 375
Fund for Theological Education,
Inc., The.. 32
Fundamental Methodist Church,
Inc.. 123, 375

GEII (Graymoor Ecumenical &
Interreligious Institute) 32
General Association of General
Baptists 123, 375
General Association of Regular
Baptist Churches...................................... 123
General Church of the New
Jerusalem 124, 365, 375
General Conference of Mennonite
Brethren Churches 124, 375
General Conference of the Canadian
Assemblies of God 197
Genesee County Churches United, Inc 253
Genesee-Orleans Ministry of Concern 253
Georgia Christian Council 238
Glengarry-Prescott-Russell Christian
Council 293
Glenmary Research Center 32
GRACE (Grand Rapids Area Center for
Ecumenism) 246
Grace Gospel Fellowship.................... 124, 375
Grand Rapids Area Center for
Ecumenism (GRACE) 246
Graymoor Ecumenical & Interreligious
Institute (GEII) 32
Greater Baton Rouge Federation of
Churches and Synagogues....................... 244
Greater Bethlehem Area Council of
Churches 260
Greater Birmingham Ministries 233
Greater Chicago Broadcast Ministries........ 239
Greater Dallas Community of
Churches 264
Greater Dayton Christian Connections 257
Greater Fairmont Council of
Churches 246, 267
Greater Flint Council of Churches 246

INDEX

403

Greater Lawrence Council of Churches 245
Greater Minneapolis Council of
  Churches 248
Greater New Orleans Federation of
  Churches 244
Greater Rochester Community of
  Churches 253
Greater Toronto Council of Christian
  Churches, The 293
Greater Victoria Council of Churches 292
Greater Waterbury Interfaith Ministries,
  Inc. 237
Greek Orthodox Archdiocese of
  America 125, 375, 382
Greek Orthodox Metropolis of Toronto
  (Canada) 365
Greensboro Urban Ministry 256

Hamilton & District Christian Churches
  Association 293
Hanover Area Council of Churches 260
Hartford Institute for Religion Research
  of Hartford Seminary, The 216
Hazard-Perry County Community
  Ministries, Inc. 243
Hemmingford Ecumenical Committee 294
Highlands Community Ministries 243
Holy Eastern Orthodox Catholic and
  Apostolic Church in North
  America, Inc., The 126, 375
Holy Synod for the American Diaspora 126
Holy Ukrainian Autocephalic Orthodox
  Church in Exile 127
House of God, Which is the Church of the
  Living God, the Pillar and Ground of
  the Truth, Inc. 127
Humboldt Clergy Council 294
Hungarian Reformed Church in
  America 128, 375, 382
Hutterian Brethren 128, 375
Hyde Park & Kenwood Interfaith
  Council, The 239

ICNA (Islamic Circle of North
  America) 226
IFCA International, Inc. 128, 376
IFCO (Interreligious Foundation for
  Community Organization) 35
Ignace Council of Churches 293
Illinois Conference of Churches 239
Independent Assemblies of God
  International (Canada) 197
Independent Holiness Church 197, 366
Indiana Partners for Christian Unity
  and Mission 241
Industrial Cape Breton Council of
  Churches 292
Insight Meditation Society 223
Institute for Ecumenical and Cultural
  Research 217
Institute for the Study of American
  Evangelicals (ISAE) 217

Institute for the Study of American
  Religion 218
Inter Church Council of Burlington 293
Interchurch Communications 53
Inter-Church Council of Greater
  New Bedford 246
InterChurch Ministries of Erie County 260
Interchurch Ministries of Nebraska 250
Interfaith Association of Snohomish
  County, The 267
Interfaith Community Council, Inc. 241
Interfaith Community Services 250
Interfaith Conference of Greater
  Milwaukee 268
InterFaith Conference of Metropolitan
  Washington 238
Interfaith Council 267
Interfaith Council of Boulder 236
Interfaith Council of Contra Costa
  County 235
Interfaith Council of Montréal 294
Interfaith Impact for Justice and Peace 33
Interfaith Ministries for Greater
  Houston 264
Inter-Faith Ministries—Wichita 242
Interfaith Mission Service 233
Interfaith Partnership of Metropolitan
  St. Louis 250
Interfaith Service Bureau 235
Interfaith Worker Justice 34
Interfaith Works 267
International Church of the Foursquare
  Gospel 129, 376
International Council of Community
  Churches 129, 376, 382
International Fellowship of Bible
  Churches 129, 376
International Pentecostal Church
  of Christ, The 130, 376
International Pentecostal Holiness
  Church 131, 376
International Society for Krishna
  Consciousness (ISKCON), The 225
InterReligious Council of Central
  New York 254
Interreligious Foundation for Community
  Organization (IFCO) 35
Inter-Varsity Christian Fellowship
  of Canada 53
InterVarsity Christian Fellowship
  of the U.S.A 33
Iowa Religious Media Services 242
ISAE (Institute for the Study of American
  Evangelicals) 217
ISKCON (The International Society
  for Krishna Consciousness) 225
Islamic Circle of North America
  (ICNA) 226
Islamic Society of North America
  (ISNA), The 226
ISNA (The Islamic Society of North
  America) 226

Jackson County Interfaith Council, The 247
JAINA (Federation of Jain Associations
   in North America) 227
JAINA: Federation of Jain Associations
   in North America 227
Jehovah's Witnesses 131, 198, 366, 376
Jewish Council for Public Affairs 228
Jewish Reconstructionist Federation 229
J.M. Dawson Institute of Church-State
   Studies at Baylor University 218
John Howard Society of Ontario 54
Joint Religious Legislative Coalition,
   The 248

Kairos Institute, Inc., The 35
Kansas Ecumenical Ministries 242
Kentuckiana Interfaith Community 243
Kentucky Council of Churches 243
Kentville Council of Churches 292
Kitchener-Waterloo Council of
   Churches 293
Korean Presbyterian Church in America,
   General Assembly of the 132, 376, 382

Lafayette Urban Ministry 241
Lancaster County Council of Churches 260
Latter-day Saints. See Church of Jesus
   Christ of Latter-day Saints in Canada,
   The; Church of Jesus Christ of Latter-day
   Saints, The
Latvian Evangelical Lutheran Church
   in America, The 132, 376
LCMS (Lutheran Church—Missouri
   Synod, The) 133, 376
Lebanon County Christian Ministries 260
Lehigh County Conference of Churches 260
Lewisburg Council of Churches 261
Liberal Catholic Church
   (International) 132, 376
Liberal Catholic Church—
   Province of the United States
   of America 133, 376
Lincoln Interfaith Council 251
Liturgical Conference, The 35
Lombard Mennonite Peace Center 35
London Inter-City Faith Team 293
Long Island Council of Churches, The 254
Lord's Day Alliance of the United
   States, The 36
Louisiana Interchurch Conference 244
Louisville Institute, The 219
Lunenburg Queens BA Association 292
Lutheran Association, Conservative. See
   Conservative Lutheran Association
Lutheran Church. See American Association
   of Lutheran Churches, The; Evangelical
   Lutheran Church in Canada
Lutheran Church of America. See Apostolic
   Lutheran Church of America; Evangelical
   Lutheran Church in America
Lutheran Church, The—Missouri Synod
   (LCMS) 133, 376
Lutheran Church—Canada 198, 366

Lutheran Council in Canada 54
Lutheran Synod. See Evangelical
   Lutheran Synod
Lutheran World Relief 36

Madison-area Urban Ministry 268
Mahone Bay Interchurch Council 293
Mahoning Valley Association of
   Churches 257
Maine Council of Churches 244
Malankara Orthodox Syrian Church,
   Diocese of America 134, 376, 382
Mall Area Religious Council (MARC) 247
Manchester Area Conference of
   Churches 237
Mar Thoma Syrian Church of
   India 135, 377, 382
MARC (Mall Area Religious Council) 247
Marin Interfaith Council 235
Massachusetts Commission on Christian
   Unity 246
Massachusetts Council of Churches 246
Massey Inter-Church Council 293
MCCC (Mennonite Central Committee
   Canada) 54
Melville Association of Churches 294
Mennonite. See Canadian Conference of
   Mennonite Brethren Churches; Reinland
   Mennonite Church
Mennonite Brethren Churches. See General
   Conference of Mennonite Brethren Churches
Mennonite Central Committee Canada
   (MCCC) 54
Mennonite Central Committee, The 36
Mennonite Church 135
Mennonite Church of God in Christ.
   See Church of God in Christ, Mennonite
Mennonite Church USA 377
Mennonite Church—Canada 198, 366
Methodist Church. See United Methodist
   Church, The
Methodist Church, Evangelical. See
   Evangelical Methodist Church
Methodist Church, Fundamental. See
   Fundamental Methodist Church, Inc.
Metropolitan Area Church Council 257
Metropolitan Area Religious Coalition
   of Cincinnati 257
Metropolitan Christian Council: Detroit-
   Windsor, The 247
Metropolitan Christian Council of
   Philadelphia 261
Metropolitan Ecumenical Ministry 251
Metropolitan Ecumenical Ministry
   Community Development Corp. 251
Metropolitan Inter Faith Association
   (MIFA) 263
Metropolitan Interfaith Council on
   Affordable Housing (MICAH) 248
MICAH (Metropolitan Interfaith Council
   on Affordable Housing) 248
MIFA (Metropolitan Inter Faith
   Association) 263

INDEX

Ministries United South Central Louisville (M.U.S.C.L., Inc.) 243
Minnesota Council of Churches 249
Missionary Church, The 136, 377
Mississippi Religious Leadership Conference 249
Moncton Area Council of Churches 292
Montana Association of Churches 250
Montreal Association for the Blind Foundation 294
Moravian Church. *See* Canadian District of the Moravian Church in America, Northern Province; Moravian Church in America
Moravian Church in America (Unitas Fratrum) 137, 377, 383
Mormons. *See* Church of Jesus Christ of Latter-day Saints in Canada, The; Church of Jesus Christ of Latter-day Saints, The
Mosque Cares (Ministry of Imam W. Deen Mohammed), The 226
MPAC (Muslim Public Affairs Council) 227
Multifaith Action Society of British Columbia 292
M.U.S.C.L., Inc. *See* Ministries United South Central Louisville
Muskegon County Cooperating Churches 247
Muslim American Society 226
Muslim Peace Fellowship 227
Muslim Public Affairs Council (MPAC) 227

NARF (Native American Rights Fund) 230
National Association of Congregational Christian Churches 137, 377
National Association of Ecumenical and Interreligious Staff 36
National Association of Evangelicals, The 37
National Association of Free Will Baptists 137, 377
National Baptist Convention of America, Inc. 138, 377, 383
National Baptist Convention, U.S.A., Inc 38, 377, 383
National Bible Association 37
National Conference for Community and Justice, The 37
National Conference on Ministry to the Armed Forces 38
National Congress of American Indians (NCAI) 230
National Council of the Churches of Christ in the U.S.A. 38
National Institute of Business and Industrial Chaplains 39
National Interfaith Cable Coalition, Inc. (NICC) 40
National Interfaith Coalition on Aging 40
National Missionary Baptist Convention of America 139, 377, 383

National Organization of the New Apostolic Church of North America 139, 377
National Primitive Baptist Convention, Inc. 139, 377
National Religious Broadcasters 40
National Spiritual Assembly of the Bahà'ìs of the United States 222
National Spiritualist Association of Churches 140
National Woman's Christian Temperance Union 41
Native American Rights Fund (NARF) 230
NCAI (National Congress of American Indians) 230
Netherlands Reformed Congregations 140, 377
Network of Religious Communities 254
New Britain Area Conference of Churches (NEWBRACC) 237
New Church. *See* General Church of the New Jerusalem
New Hampshire Council of Churches 251
New Jersey Council of Churches 251
New Mexico Conference of Churches 252
New York Buddhist Council 223
New York State Council of Churches, Inc. 255
NEWBRACC. *See* New Britain Area Conference of Churches
Niagara Council of Churches Inc., The 255
NICA (Northside Inter-Church Agency) 265
NICC (National Interfaith Cable Coalition, Inc.) 40
NISBCO. *See* CCW (Center on Conscience & War)
North American Baptist Conference 141, 199, 366, 377
North American Baptist Fellowship 41
North American Old Roman Catholic Church (Archdiocese of New York) 141, 378
North Carolina Council of Churches 256
North Dakota Conference of Churches 256
North Dallas Shared Ministries 265
North Hills Youth Ministry Counseling Center 261
Northern California Interreligious Conference 235
Northern Kentucky Interfaith Commission, Inc. 243
Northside Common Ministries 261
Northside Inter-Church Agency (NICA) 265
Northwest Harvest—E.M.M. 267
Northwest Interfaith Movement 261

Oak Park-River Forest Community of Congregations 239
Ohio Council of Churches 258
Oikocredit-Ecumenical Development Cooperative Society 41

406

Oklahoma Conference of Churches............. 258
Old Catholic Church of Canada,
  The.. 199, 366
Old Catholic Orthodox Church,
  The.. 141, 378
Old German Baptist Brethren
  Church.. 141, 378
Old Order Amish Church 142, 199, 378
Old Order (Wisler) Mennonite
  Church.. 142, 378
Open Bible Faith Fellowship of
  Canada....................................... 142, 199, 366
Open Bible Standard Churches................... 378
Orthodox Church in America
  (Archdiocese of Canada)................. 199, 366
Orthodox Church in America,
  The... 142, 378, 383
Orthodox Presbyterian Church,
  The.. 143, 378
Ottawa Christian Council of the
  Capital Area.. 293

Paducah Cooperative Ministry 243
Parish Resource Center, Inc.......................... 41
Patriarchal Parishes of the Russian
  Orthodox Church in Canada............. 200, 366
Patriarchal Parishes of the Russian
  Orthodox Church in the
  U.S.A...................................... 144, 378, 383
Pennsylvania Conference on Interchurch
  Cooperation 261
Pennsylvania Council of Churches,
  The.. 261
Pentecostal Assemblies of Canada,
  The.. 200, 366
Pentecostal Assemblies of
  Newfoundland, The 201, 366
Pentecostal Assemblies of the
  World, Inc.. 144, 378
Pentecostal Church of God 144, 378
Pentecostal Fire-Baptized Holiness
  Church 145, 378
Pentecostal Free Will Baptist
  Church, Inc., The 145
Pentecostal-Charismatic Churches of
  North America 42
Peoria Friendship House of Christian
  Service 239
Philadelphia Yearly Meeting of the Religious
  Society of Friends 145, 378, 383
Pictou Council of Churches 293
Pike Country Outreach Council.................. 258
Pillar of Fire 145
Pluralism Project, The................................ 219
Plymouth Brethren. See Christian
  Brethren (also known as Plymouth Brethren)
Polish National Catholic Church
  of America.............................. 146, 378, 383
Pomona Inland Valley Council
  of Churches... 235
Prairie Centre for Ecumenism 294
Presbyterian Church. See Evangelical
  Presbyterian Church

Presbyterian Church (U.S.A.)...... 147, 379, 383
Presbyterian Church in America.......... 146, 379
Presbyterian Church in America
  (Canadian Section) 201, 366
Presbyterian Church in Canada 201, 366
Primitive Advent Christian
  Church 148, 379
Primitive Baptists....................................... 149
Primitive Methodist Church
  in the U.S.A.................................... 149, 379
Progressive National Baptist
  Convention, Inc. 149, 379, 383
Project Equality, Inc..................................... 42
Project of Easton, Inc.................................. 262
Project Ploughshares.................................... 54
Protestant Reformed Churches
  in America 150, 379

Quakers. See Friends General Conference
Quakers, Conservative. See Religious
  Society of Friends (Conservative)
Quakers, International. See Evangelical Friends
  International-North American Region
Quakers, Philadelphia. See Philadelphia Yearly
  Meeting of the Religious Society of Friends
Quakers, Unaffiliated Meetings. See Religious
  Society of Friends (Unaffiliated Meetings)
Quebec Ecumenical Network (Réseau
  Oecuménique du Québec) 294
Québécois du Dialogue
  musulmanchrétien..................................... 294
Queens County Association of
  Churches... 293
Queens Federation of Churches.................. 255

Radio Ville-Marie 294
Reading Berks Conference of
  Churches 262
Reformed Catholic Church 150, 379
Reformed Church in America...... 151, 379, 383
Reformed Church in Canada 202, 367
Reformed Church in the United
  States 151, 379
Reformed Episcopal Church............... 152, 379
Reformed Episcopal Church of
  Canada, The..................................... 202, 367
Reformed Mennonite Church 153, 379
Reformed Methodist Union Episcopal
  Church 153
Reformed Presbyterian Church of North
  America 153, 379
Reformed Zion Union Apostolic
  Church 154
Regina Council of Churches....................... 294
Regional Council for Christian
  Ministry, Inc., The 239
Regional Council of Churches of
  Atlanta, The 238
Reinland Mennonite Church............... 203, 367
Religion Communicators Council,
  Inc., The.. 43, 367
Religion In American Life, Inc.................... 43
Religion News Service 43

407

Religion Newswriters Association and
Foundation 44
Religions for Peace-USA, Inc. 44
Religious Action Center of Reform
Judaism 229
Religious Conference Management
Association, Inc. 44
Religious Society of Friends
(Conservative) 154, 379
Religious Society of Friends (Unaffiliated
Meetings) 154
Religious Television Associates 55
Reorganized Church of Jesus Christ of Latter-
day Saints. *See* Community of Christ
Réseau Oecuménique du Québec (Quebec
Ecumenical Network) 294
Réseau Oecuménique Justice et Paix 294
Rhode Island State Council of
Churches, The 263
Roman Catholic Church in
Canada, The 203, 367
Romanian Orthodox Church in America
(Canadian Parishes) 204, 367
Romanian Orthodox Church in
America, The 154
Romanian Orthodox Episcopate of
America, The 155, 379
Romanian Orthodox Episcopate of
America, The (Jackson, MI) 204, 367
Rural Migrant Ministry 255
Russian Orthodox Church. *See* Patriarchal
Parishes of the Russian Orthodox Church
in Canada
Russian Orthodox Church Outside
of Russia, The 155, 380

SAHO (Sikh American Heritage
Organization) 231
Saint Paul Area Council of Churches 249
SALDEF (Sikh American Legal Defense
and Education Fund) 231
Salvation Army in Canada, The 205, 367
Salvation Army, The 380
San Antonio Community of Churches 265
San Antonio Urban Ministries 265
San Fernando Valley Interfaith Council 235
Schenectady Inner City Ministry 255
Schwenkfelder Church, The 155, 380
Scripture Union 55
SCUPE (Seminary Consortium for Urban
Pastoral Education, The) 45
SEAM. *See* South East Associated Ministries
SEAM (South East Associated
Ministries) 244
SEARCH (Southeast Area Churches) 265
Seminary Consortium for Urban Pastoral
Education, The (SCUPE) 45
Separate Baptists in Christ 156, 380
Serbian Orthodox Church in the
U.S.A and Canada 156, 205, 380, 383
Serbian Orthodox Church in the U.S.A
and Canada (Diocese of Canada) 367

Seventh Day Baptist General Conference,
USA and Canada 158, 380
Seventh-day Adventist Church 157, 380
Seventh-day Adventist Church in
Canada 205, 367
Siddhachalam International Mahavira
Jain Mission 227
Sikh American Heritage Organization
(SAHO) 231
Sikh American Legal Defense and
Education Fund (SALDEF) 231
Sikh Coalition 231
Sikh Foundation 231
Sikh Research Institute 231
Soka Gakkai International—USA 224
South Carolina Christian Action
Council, Inc. 263
South Coast Interfaith Council 235
South East Associated Ministries
(SEAM) 244
South Hills Interfaith Ministries 262
South Louisville Community
Ministries 244
Southeast Area Churches (SEARCH) 265
Southeast Ecumenical Ministry 256
Southern Baptist Convention 158, 380
Southern Baptists. *See* Canadian
Convention of Southern Baptists
Southern California Ecumenical
Council 236
Southern Methodist Church 160, 380
Sovereign Grace Believers 160, 380
Spadina-Bloor Interchurch Council 293
St. Bruno Ecumenical Group, The 294
St. Catharines & District Clergy
Fellowship 293
St. John's Area Council of Churches 292
St. Matthews Area Ministries 243
St. Paul Area Council of Churches 249
Staten Island Council of Churches 256
Stratford & District Council of
Churches 293
Student Christian Movement of Canada 55
Summerside Christian Council 293
Swedenborgian Church, The 160, 380, 383
Syriac Orthodox Church of
Antioch 206, 367
Syrian (Syriac) Orthodox Church
of Antioch 161, 367, 380, 383
Syro-Russian Orthodox Catholic
Church 161, 380

Tarrant Area Community of Churches 265
Tennessee Association of Churches 264
Texas Buddhist Council 224
Texas Conference of Churches 265
Thorold Inter-Faith Council 293
Thunder Bay Council of Churches 293
Toledo Ecumenical Area Ministries 258
Transnational Association of
Christian Colleges and Schools 45
Tri-Council Coordinating Commission 249

Triumph the Church and Kingdom of God
in Christ Inc. (International) 162
Troy Area United Ministries 256
True Orthodox Church of Greece (Synod
of Metropolitan Cyprian), American
Exarchate 163, 380
Tulsa Metropolitan Ministry 258
Tuscarawas County Council for Church
and Community 258

Ukrainian Orthodox Church of
Canada 206, 367
Ukrainian Orthodox Church of
the U.S.A. 163, 380, 383
Unified Buddhist Church, Inc. 224
Union d'Eglises Baptistes Françaises
au Canada 206, 367
Union of Orthodox Jewish Congregations
of America, The 229
Union of Reform Judaism 229
Union of Spiritual Communities of Christ
(Orthodox Doukhobors in Canada) 206
Unitarian Universalist Association
of Congregations 165, 381
UNITAS 294
United Board of Missions 265
United Brethren Church in
Canada 207, 368
United Catholic Church, Inc.,
The 165, 381
United Christian Church 166, 381
United Church of Canada, The 368
United Church of Christ 166, 381, 383
United Churches of Lycoming
County 262
United Holy Church of America, Inc. 168
United House of Prayer 169
United Methodist Church,
The 170, 381, 383
United Ministries 263
United Ministries in Higher Education.......... 45
United Pentecostal Church in Canada 208
United Pentecostal Church
International 172, 381
United Pentecostal Churches of
Christ, The 173, 381
United Religions Initiative 45
United Religious Community of St.
Joseph County 241
United States Conference for the
World Council of Churches 46
United States, The 22
United Synagogue of Conservative
Judaism, The 229
United Zion Church 173, 381
Unity of the Brethren 173, 381
Universal Fellowship of Metropolitan
Community Churches 174, 208, 368, 381

Vancouver Council of Churches 292
Vedanta Society of New York 225
Vellore Christian Medical College
Board (USA), Inc. 47

Vermont Ecumenical Council and
Bible Society 265
Virginia Council of Churches, Inc. 266
Volunteer Ministry Center 264
Volunteers of America 174

Wainwright House 256
Washington Association of Churches 267
Wellspring Interfaith Social
Services, Inc. 241
Wesleyan Church of Canada, The 209, 368
Wesleyan Church, The 175, 381
Wesleyan Holiness Association of
Churches 176
West Central Neighborhood Ministry. See
Wellspring Interfaith Social Services, Inc.
West Side Ecumenical Ministry 258
West Virginia Council of Churches 268
Westside Interfaith Council 236
Wilkinsburg Community Ministry 262
Wisconsin Council of Churches 268
Wisconsin Evangelical Lutheran
Synod 176, 381
Women's Inter-Church Council of
Canada 55
Won Buddhism of American
Headquarters 224
Worcester County Ecumenical Council 246
World Council of Churches, United
States Office 46
World Day of Prayer International
Committee 47
World Methodist Council-North American
Section 47
World Sikh Council—American
Region 231
World Vision 48
World Vision Canada 56
Wyoming Association of Churches 268
Wyoming Valley Council of Churches 263

YMCA of the USA 48
York County Council of Churches 263
Young Men's Christian Association
in Canada 56
Young Women's Christian Association
of Canada 56
Youth for Christ—Canada 56
Youth for Christ–USA 48
YWCA of the U.S.A 48

Individuals

Abbott, Grant 249
Abbott, Mark S. 94, 190
Abboud, Jon W. 152
Abdallah, John
   Ishuaradas......................235
Abernathy, Bryan...............338
Aboodi, Timotheos
   Aphrem..........................206
Abraham, Raphael 163
Abramov, Alexander.........144
Ackerman, Keith L. 108
Acosta, Donaldo 100
Acuña, Adolfo....................75
Adams, Don 132
Adams, Dorothy 62
Adams, Gladstone
   B., III..............................107
Adams, James Marshall.....109
Adams, Margaret 243
Adams, Michael J. 104
Adams, Nate 159
Adams, Neale 350
Adams, Ray D. 100
Adams, Skip 259
Adams, Todd A. 83
Adams-Smelter,
   Barbara 262
Addington, James 249
Addington, Timothy..........112
Adego, Epainitus 121
Adema, Bruce 88
Adira, Titus 121
Adnams, Ian 198
Adolf, Don 196
Aftimios (Archbishop).......126
Aiken, David A., Sr. 61
Aiken, Mike 256
Ainsworth, Alphonse 204
Aja, Antonio (Tony)..........243
Aja, Loyda 148
Ajer, Margaret Schmitt 114
Akers, Kenneth 138
Akin, Daniel L....................313
Alagiah, Sabapath 46
Albarian, Samuel 345
Albert, Leonard 94, 189
Albrecht, Betty 185
Albrecht, James 99
Albrecht, Marcus 330
Alchin, Errol 193
Alcosser, Lois 237
Aldred, Ray........................53
Alejo (Bishop) 143
Aleshire, Daniel O. 213
Alexander, Darlene 264
Alexander, J. Gregory.........84

Alexander, John Neil 107
Alexios (Metropolitan) 125
Alford, Delton L. 94, 189
Alger, David T. 266
Algera, Fred 202
Alick, Bruce N...................336
Allander, Dan....................307
Allbee, Judy G. 64
Allen, Cosie 335
Allen, David, Jr..................149
Allen, David W. 208
Allen, John........................26
Allen, Lloyd
   Emmanuel 107
Allen, Sherman 96, 190
Allen, William B. 84, 268
Allen-Kent, Venita 264
Allinson, Pat 56
Allsop, John 293
Almen, Lowell G. 113
Alston, Roosevelt 169
Alston, Wallace M., Jr. 31
Alterbarmakian, Varouj 72
Althouse, LaVonne 344
Altic, Betty 266
Alvarez, David...................108
Ambrose, Richard.............233
Ambrus, Zoltan 128
Amjad-Ali, Charles............34
Ammerman, E. H. Jim........27
Ammons, E. Roger 100
Amorim, Nilton D. 205
Anders, Andrea 95
Anders, James C. 100
Anders, Linda 156
Anderson, Alison A. 145
Anderson, Anne T. 322
Anderson, Billy.................103
Anderson, Bonnie 106
Anderson, Byron.................35
Anderson, Clifford............357
Anderson, Daniel L. 295
Anderson, David A. 239
Anderson, Donald C. 263
Anderson, James................254
Anderson, Jeff...................194
Anderson, Jeffrey 111
Anderson, Jim 154
Anderson, Jon V................114
Anderson, Kenneth 78, 254
Anderson, Kristi 249
Anderson, L. R. 92
Anderson, Leith 37
Anderson, Melissa 340
Anderson, Moe 293
Anderson, Nancy L............248

Anderson, Neil..........101, 332
Anderson, Phyllis 309
Anderson, Scott D. 268
Anderson, Ujuana 255
Anderson, Vinton................31
Anderson, William J. 180
Anderson-Develrow,
   Dorothy 265
Anderson-Larson,
   Virginia 113
Andino, Aureo F. 113
Andonios (Bishop)............126
Andreller, Ingrid 348
Andres, Oseas.....................66
Andrews, Rodney 181
Andrews, Roger 118
Andrews, Ruth 53
Andrews, Stephen 180
Andrus, Marc Handly 107
Angeline, Peter 54
Angie, Frank 131
Ankeny, Mark 112
Annie, Frederick P. 268
Annotzelberger, E. 140
Annunziato, Anne 251
Ansari, Fajri 254
Anstey, Andrew R.............201
Antal, Jim 168
Anthony, Lewis.................238
Antonio, Annalene 255
Antony (Archbishop).........164
Apostola,
   Nicholas 154, 155, 204
Appel, Robert 158
Appell, Jody 263
Aquila, Dominic 201
Archer, Barbara.................250
Ard, Herman D. 100
Ard, Robert 234
Ardis, Randy 22
Argue, Don H 308
Armas, Lucinda. 337
Armiger, Thomas E. 175
Armstrong, Calvin 169
Armstrong, George 46
Armstrong, James D 60, 340
Armstrong, Ken 76
Armstrong, Sara 236
Arnold, Don 122
Arnold, Gail 263
Arnold, Kim M 359
Arnold, Kristi 338
Arslanian, Hagop 182
Arthur (Bishop) 126
Ascough, Richard 52
Asen, Bernhard 342

INDEX

411

Ashdown, David N. 181
Ashford, Anne...................235
Ashmen, John 25
Asplundh, Kurt H. 124
Astfalk, Carolyn 261
Astin, Claude S., Jr. 66
Astle, Cynthia B. 340, 343
Astley, Nolan D. 198
Atagotaalnuk,
    Andrew P. 180
Atkins, Nancy Lee 258
Atlas, Robert......................266
Atmore, A. Brian 319
Attai, Monday S. 184
Atteberry, Philip 76
Attridge, Harold W 316
Atwood-Adams, Tanya 254
Augsburger, Lynette...........118
Augson, Albert...................169
Aultman,
    Donald S. 93, 94, 189
Austin, George...................144
Austin, Jackie 268
Austin, James W. 159
Auxentios (Bishop)............163
Avakian, Karl....................182
Avera, Alan 74
Avery, Michael..................302
Avey, Thomas 118, 119
Aykazian, Vicken 38
Ayloush, Hussam 34
Aymer, Albert J. D............303
Aymond, Gregory M...........81

Baak, David P. 246
Babb, Ruby 255
Babb, W. Sherrill 309
Bachus, Amanda 333
Backman, Ida............345, 346
Bad Hear Bull, Jay 248
Bagley, Louis 169
Bagnall, Ronald B. 335
Bahruth, Dick 28
Bailey, Arnetta 91
Bailey, Dwight 239
Bailey, Jeff 329
Bailey, Joey......................148
Bailey, Leslee 103
Bailey, Mark L...................300
Baillargeon, Gaëtan 203
Baillie, Kenneth 155
Bainbridge, Harry
    B., III 107
Baird, Bob..........................76
Baker, Bob 259
Baker, David 61
Baker, Denis N. 342
Baker, Kenneth 332
Baker, Marsha....................24
Baker, Michael L. 189
Bakker, Peter.....................268
Balanian, Nayira 71

Balas, Laura 321
Balbick, Jane.....................253
Baldes, Kenneth E. 87
Baldwin, David N.............159
Baldwin, Nancy 137
Baldwin, Raymond C. 149
Balentine, Sam..................333
Baletka, Jim 174
Balfour, Edward................134
Balke, Fred 63
Ball, Chris.........................105
Ball, David........................200
Ballard, M. Russell 97
Balogh, Balint...................128
Baltimore, Carroll A..........150
Bamban, Vieturs 326
Banaszak, Karen 246
Bancroft, Timothy..............40
Banek, Walter 152
Bang, Charles 254
Bangert, Kristi 113
Banken, Mary Beth...........217
Bankord, Mark A................28
Baranek, Paul....................259
Baranowski, Bernice..........51
Barber, Jay A. 91
Barber, Ray 123
Barbour, Johnny, Jr. 59
Barcott, Patricia 267
Barfoot, Gillian 56
Bariteau, Benoît 203
Barker, Lee 307
Barker, Randy 145
Barlow, Jane 245
Barna, George 214
Barnabas, Mathews
    Mar 134, 135
Barnes, Charles.................168
Barnes, Gerald 81
Barnes, James 304
Barnes, Kurt 106
Barnes, Ronald B..............261
Barnes, Thane 159
Barnett, Paige 266
Barnett-Cowan, Alyson 180
Barnhouse, James 258
Barrentine, Jimmy L..........159
Barrett, Michael 256
Barrow, Ira 360
Barrows, Ken 192
Barry, Jane 234
Barsamian, Khajag 43, 72
Barsony, Steve 262
Bartell-Wagner,
    Deena 323, 331
Bartlett, Eileen 244
Bartlett, William G. 208
Barton, Jonathan 266
Bass, Deborah 39
Bass, Steve........................159
Bassham, Keith 325
Batchelor, Don 172
Bates, Charlotte Kinvig 320

Bates, Dale........................123
Bathurst, Shirley 255
Battle, George
    Edward, Jr.......................59
Battle, Michael A...............304
Battler, Jack 54
Battram, Janet 240
Batts, Carl 140
Batuyong, Patrick 150
Bauer, Martha 160, 161
Baugham, Billy 24
Baugham, Eva.....................24
Baum, Mary K...................268
Baumann, Paul...................328
Baumgartner, Will.............237
Baumler, Gary...................336
Bawai, Mar 67
Baxter, Nathan D. 107
Bay, Eugene C 299
Bayer, Steven L. 142, 343
Bayiha, Suzie, II 47
Beach, Maxine C. 300
Beach, Verda.....................296
Beacham, A. D., Jr.............131
Beachy, Ivan 77
Beals, Charlotte 137
Beane, Marian...................120
Beard, C. Ronald 73
Beaupe, Richard 54
Bechil, Shirley 120
Beck, Sarai Schnucker.......242
Becker, Bruce 176
Becker, Susan 29
Beckett, Malcolm 192
Beckmann, David 26
Beckwith, James M. 89
Beckwith, Peter H..............108
Becton, C. M. 208
Bedell, L. Wood 151
Bedgood, Douglas 84
Bediako, Matthew A..........157
Bednar, David A. 97
Behr, John 312
Behr, Ken 30
Behrakis, George 126
Behrens, James 262
Beinikis, Vilmars 132
Beisher, Barry 108
Beitans, John.....................240
Beizer, Lance 68
Bekker, Gary 88
Bell, Brian.........................185
Bell, Nancy 183
Bellamy, James C. 169
Bellefleur, Beverley 201
Bellinger, Carolyn.............197
Bellinger, Gale 68
Bellous, Ken 183
Belous, Ken 41
Belrose, Danny A. 103
Belrose, Darrell.................192
Belsole, Kurt 311
Belton, Victor T. 134

Benallick, Mike 349
Bender, Robert 235
Bendyna, Mary E. 215
Benedict, Gary M. 87
Benefiel, Ron 308
Bennett, Robertson H. 43
Bennett, Vicki 203
Bennison, Charles
E., Jr...............................108
Benoway, Edward R. 115
Benson, Michael 300
Benson, Willie, Jr..............119
Beresford, Eric..................317
Berg, Peter 140
Berg, Richard R. 354
Berg, Robert D..................114
Berg, Ron 141
Berg, Sharon K. 330
Berge, Arthur 191
Bergen, Abe 321
Berger, David G................250
Berghes, DeLandes.............68
Bergin, Karen....................237
Bergland, Arne 266
Berlamino, Cheryl 22
Berman, Lowen 259
Bernard, A. R....................253
Bernard, David 315
Bernstine, Gwen
Nelson 262
Bernthal, Mark..................99
Berry, Bradford 101
Bertalan, Imre 128
Berube, Albert J. 141
Betancourt, Esdras 189
Betzer, Dan 73
Bevens, Stephen B..............27
Beverley, James 218
Beyer, Teresa A.................142
Bhagan, Ken 293
Bibb, Lillie D....................257
Bickerton, Thomas J..........171
Bicksler, Harriet................341
Bidlack, Beth 354
Bieniek, Barbara 255
Biffle, Nita 122
Biffle, S. K........................122
Biffle, Steven K. 122
Bigaj, Sylvester.................146
Biggs, Vicki 133
Bigland-Pritchard, Jan 294
Billard, Ralph 292
Binda, Andrew...........189, 346
Bingham, Maurice D..........90
Birch, Aaron Louis 184
Birchard, Bruce.................120
Bird, Jeffrey L. 129
Bird, Madeline 262
Bird, Michael A. 181
Birkett, Jim 174
Birkitt, James N., Jr. 324
Birney, Walter 84
Biron, Jean-Marc 350

Birse, Douglas 185
Bishop, Betty 100
Bishop, Cecil 60
Bishop, James A. 243
Bitner, Terry 238
Bjork, Bruce 248
Bjork, Kryssis 247
Bjornberg, Allan C.............114
Blachford, Peter 180
Black, Bernard 139
Black, Geoffrey A......168, 255
Black, J. B., Jr...................240
Black, J. Thomas 90
Black, Ron 123
Blackaby, Robert 186
Blackburn, Martha 175
Blackburn, Richard G.........35
Blackshear, Frank 150
Blackwell, George L...........61
Blackwell, Phil 239
Blair, Sarah D. Brooks.......356
Blake, C. E..........................92
Blake, Harry 139
Blakeman, Jeannine 243
Blanchett, David I..............233
Bland, James C. 147
Blanding, Ann 153
Blessing, Matt....................357
Blevins, Jordan 39
Bliese, Richard H 306
Bliss, Dale 95
Blodgett, Barbara................24
Bloem, Maurice 39
Blom, Paul J......................114
Bloom, Peter 52
Bloomquist, Nessie S. 255
Blouin, Francis 244
Blount, Brian K. 314
Blount, Robert 169
Blowers, David 62
Blumhofer, Edith 217
Bobo, Kim 35
Bock, Delbert G................100
Bock, Robert 268
Bockelman, Karen 113
Bodden, Winnie 358
Boddy, Michael..................354
Boehlke, Craig A. 114
Boeker, Paul 117
Boerger, Wm. Chris 113
Boguslawski, Steven..........310
Bohl, Robert 148
Bohren, Ben 84
Boice, Paul.................151, 202
Boissoneau, John 203
Bojey, Fred 206
Bolick, Leonard H..............115
Bolinder, Garth T. 112
Boll, James 326
Bolt, John....................88, 187
Boltz, David G...................260
Bombick, Betsy 137
Bond, Judy 238

Bonk, Jonathan J...............333
Bonneau, Normand 321
Bonner, Harrison.................30
Bonner, William L. 100
Boomer, George 117
Boomershine, Tom.............335
Boone, Martha Moody 29
Boonstra, John 34
Booth, Linda L 341
Booth, Robert H 152
Borden, M. Daniel 169
Borden, Paul D 65
Borek, John 305
Borgdorff, Peter 187
Borger, Joyce 340
Borowsky, Irvin J...............330
Bos, Thomas 151
Bossio, Patrick, Sr. 84
Boto, Augie 158
Bott, Richard......................40
Bottorff, Dan......................35
Bouchard, Charles E 295
Bouffides-Walsh,
Catherine 126
Boulva, Michèle 204
Bouman, Stephen P. 115
Bouras, Nicholas................126
Bouton, Becky 263
Bouvier-Newman,
Marie 263
Bowell, Gary......................325
Bowen, Mary Lu................255
Bowen-Bailey, Doug 247
Bowie, A. Charles..............139
Bowie, E. L..........................98
Bowman, Margaret E.........166
Bowman, Robert M............165
Boyajcan, Donna 262
Boyce, H. Gene 130
Boyce, Janice............131, 325
Boyd, Alice 256
Boyd, Doris F 336
Boyd, Douglas 251
Boyd, John E. 292
Boyd, Marsha Foster 301
Boyd, T. B. , III 139
Boyer, Wayne W. 102
Boyles, Lemuel 38
Boynton, Leonard 253
Brackett, Sterling 129
Bradford, Bose...................169
Bradford, Karole 242
Bradley, James G. 237
Bradley, Lasserre,
Jr. 149, 325
Bradley, Leah
Ellison 332, 333
Bradsell, Kenneth 151, 202
Brady, A. Glenn 144
Brandebura, Michael 201
Brandon, Richard
(Zenyo) 222
Brandt, Michael 74

Branham, Craig....................77
Branham, Thomas E. 145
Branscum, Donald W.........100
Brantz, Walter 134
Brashear, Kermit................134
Brashler, James 333
Bratt, James 339
Bratton, G. Stanford 254
Braun, John A. 331
Bravo-Guzman, Pedro 75
Brawner, John 112
Bray, Donald L. 175
Bray, Imam Mahdi...............34
Brazier, Arthus 144
Bregar, Janet A. 236
Breidenthal, Thomas..........108
Breig, James 330
Brennan, Keith 311
Brennan, Peter P. 70, 75
Brenneman, Howard..........136
Brenton, B. Dean 201
Brenton, Kelly L. 201
Breton, Jean-Claude 349
Breuggemann, Mary
    Miller..............................21
Brewer, John 176, 329
Brice, James T.......................74
Brickhouse, Smith N. 89
Briden, Gary 160, 313
Bridges, James K. 72, 73
Bridges, Kermit S 313
Bridges, Randy J................310
Bridston, Richard................98
Briggs, Robert L. 22
Briley, Terry 305
Brill, Debra 157
Brinks, Robert....................148
Brinser, Gerald...................166
Brisco, Thomas 306
Britton, Joseph H...............296
Broad, Dwayne 196
Broadway, Beth 254
Brock, David......................304
Brodeur, Adèle 51
Brookhart, C. Franklin........108
Brooks, George 144
Brooks, James W. 169
Brooks, John 113
Brooks, P. A. 92
Brooks, Terry 263
Brooks, Thomas 70
Brosseau, Annie 348
Brougker, Frank 236
Browder, David....................96
Brower, E. Alex 61
Brown, Arthur 119
Brown, Carroll E. 237
Brown, Charles 173
Brown, Cynthia Vasil...........62
Brown, Dallas 259
Brown, David 138
Brown, Don J.......................77
Brown, Donice.....................70

Brown, E............................198
Brown, E. Lynn 86
Brown, Elizabeth 79
Brown, Gary 110
Brown, Gerald L 311
Brown, Gus H.......................88
Brown, Harry 241
Brown, J. R. 132
Brown, J. Richard 198
Brown, James R....................66
Brown, Jeannett L...............236
Brown, Jeffrey P. 87
Brown, John W. 186, 187
Brown, Patricia L. 250
Brown, Philip.....................148
Brown, Sanford...................266
Brown, Stephanie S. 105
Brown, Steve 238
Brown, Stuart 51, 294, 346
Brown, T. L.........................139
Brown, Thomas L. ......Sr., 86
Brown, W. Wayne 64
Brown, Warner H., Jr.........172
Brown, Warren M. 59
Brownlee, Richard D...........148
Brubacher, Marvin R. 319
Bruce, George L. R............181
Bruce, Joseph L. 159
Bruckner, Ellen 241
Bruehl, J. Roger 27
Brug, John F 344
Brumbaugh-Cayford,
    Cheryl.................89, 337
Brunelle, Denis C. 302
Bruno, C. José 88
Bruno, J. Jon 107
Brushaber,
    George K. 76, 297
Brust, Donald M. 88
Bryan, David......................343
Bryan, Jamie Brooke 174
Bryan, Ron 121
Bryant, Darue 78
Bryant, David 295
Bryant, John Richard 59
Bryant, Juanita.....................86
Bryant, Roy, Sr. 77, 78, 297
Bryant, S. N. 95
Bryant, Sissieretta 78
Buchanan, John...................326
Buchannan, John C............108
Buck, Charles 167
Buckle, Clarence.................201
Buckle, Terry 181
Buckle, Wilfred S. 201
Buegler, David D...............134
Bueno, John 72, 73
Buhler, Becky 349
Bula, Omega C. 208
Bull, Norman 196
Bulloch, Wendy 208
Bullock, Jeffrey 315
Bullock, LaWanda 119

Bullock, Marcia 44
Bullock, Warren 72
Bulya, Larissa 165
Bumgarner, Hampton 162
Bunch, Charlene 102
Burden, Keith 138
Burg, Randall S. 87
Burgess, Morgan 119
Burgio, Ronald V. 106
Burgonio-Watson,
    Thelma...........................267
Burgoyne, Howard K........111
Burgueno, Fidenaio 94
Burk, Michael L.................113
Burkat, Claire S. 115
Burke, C. Don....................144
Burke, Michael 208
Burkette, Wayne 137
Burkhardt, Patricia..............29
Burleigh, Elizabeth F...........68
Burnett, Joe G....................108
Burney, Artie.......................78
Burnham, Gary 95
Burns, Donald....................293
Burns, Patricia 52
Burns, Robert J. 52
Burrell, Calvin 325
Burrell, Willie 144
Burris, Glenn C., Jr............129
Burt, Lindsey 199
Burt, Merlin D. 352
Burton, Anthony 181
Busby, Dan 30
Bush, Richard E...................87
Bushkofsky, Linda
    Post 113
Bushrod, Montrose 344
Bush-Simmons, La
    Quetta 235
Busic, David 339
Buslon, Jim 199
Busse, Cheryl...........189, 319
Bussey, Barry W. 205
Bustle, Louie.......................99
Bustram, James 119
Butimore, David............Sr., 63
Butin, Philip W 312
Butler, Kevin J...........158, 341
Butler, Ramsey 144
Butts, Calvin O. 253
Butts, Elvin R. 303
Butts, J. Wayman 257
Buxton, Zane 148
Buzza, John 248, 320
Buzzard, Anthony, Sr.........334
Buzzell, Sandra..................244
Byers, Melvin, Jr. 100
Byler, J. Ron 136
Bynum, Bill ....

Cabana, Denise 237
Cabigting, Ruben 133

Cabrera, Brigido 151
Cackler-Veazey,
   Cathleen D......................42
Cadieux, Vincent 203
Cady, Donald D. 175
Cahill, Brendan 311
Calahan, Myra 341
Caldwell, Bruce 109
Caldwell, Clifton 150
Caldwell, Ray 137
Caliandro, Arthur 26
Callaghan, Aloysius R. 311
Callahan, Tom...................241
Calvin, Elizabeth 47
Camenga, Andrew 158
Camp, Peggy Ann 175
Camp, Richard P., Jr. 28
Camp, Steve......................168
Campbell, Cynthia M. 307
Campbell, Ella 151
Campbell, Frederick F. 81
Campbell, G. Robert..........208
Campbell, Gary D..............147
Campbell, Jerry D..............299
Campbell, Jimmy................94
Campbell, John D...............189
Campbell, Joseph................90
Campbell, Michael 352
Campbell, Scott 53
Canary-Marshall,
   Deborah 258
Cannada, Robert C., Jr...310
Cannaday, Antoinette 78
Cannon, Edward 78
Cano-Landivar,
   Jeannette 75
Canoy, Robert W...............306
Capets, James 122
Caplan, Rick 242
Caraballo,
   Ildefonso 94, 189, 299
Carl, William J., III...........309
Carlin, Donald 261
Carlsen, William A. 64
Carlson, David 247
Carlson, Dennis N. 157
Carlson, George G. 114
Carlson, Kenneth P............111
Carlson, Robert J. 81
Carmi, Laila 47
Carmichael, Cassandra 39
Caron, Kateri 267
Carouthers, David 293
Carpenter, Don..................346
Carpenter, Ron 42
Carpenter, Ronald, Sr.........131
Carr, Clarence 59
Carr-Harris, Philip 253
Carrico, David L. 65
Carriere, Vianney
   (Sam).....................180, 349
Carroll, Jeff 119
Carroll, John 259

Carroo, Winton 39
Carson, John L....................74
Carson, Kathy 45
Carter, Alison 47
Carter, Ethel Ware 238
Carter, Janice 349
Carter, Jeff 254
Carter, Kenneth Wayne........87
Carter, Lanny W.................100
Carter, Larry 303
Carter, Nick.......................295
Carter, Pamela...................145
Carter, Ron L......................340
Carter, T. Scott.............93, 189
Carter, Wayne 121
Carter-McCormick,
   Denise..............................150
Cartes, Ann 140
Cartwright, Dani
   Loving 84
Carver, L. Hugh...........94, 189
Casal, Jose Luis 38
Casebolt, James 248, 249
Casey, Daniel E. 48
Casey-Lee, Diane 245
Cassian (Bishop)...............126
Casson, Ernestine 268
Castillo, R. Ernest.............157
Castrejon, Jaime 304
Cauller, William L. 260
Cavadini, John C. 315
Cavalero, Robert.................37
Cavanaugh, Donald 22
Cavanna, Pedro 91
Cave, Evelyn.....................240
Cawley, William Kevin 357
Cayce, W. Hartsel 149
Cazabon, Gilles..................204
Cebula, John W.................253
Cereghino, Phil 343
Chadden, Shane 55
Chadick, Bonnie 242
Chafe, Joanne 203
Chakravarthy, ViJay...........254
Chamberlain, Larry...........119
Chambers, Steven 208
Chamness, Ben R. 171
Champion, Willie C.............86
Chand, Samuel R................131
Chandler, David 101
Chandler, Linda 173
Chandler, Maurice G. 296
Chandra, T. 184
Chane, John Bryson...........109
Chang, Richard S. O..........107
Change, Lamont 45
Channan, James 46
Chapell, Bryan 147, 300
Chapman, Clare J. 38
Chapman, John H. 181
Chapman, Morris H...........158
Chappell, Paul G................305
Chappelle, Richard 59, 61

Charles, Mark 84
Charleston, Steven 301
Charron, Jean-Marc 322
Chase, Deana 121
Chase, Marshall 157
Chatham, Virginia E. 344
Chauncey, H. Doyle...........159
Chavez, Silvia 24
Chavez-Thompson,
   Linda 34
Cheatham, Shirlie 119
Chell, John 247
Chemberlin, Peg 38, 249
Cherniak, HanjA 164
Cheshier, Carl 303
Chesnutt, Randall 308, 309
Chetti, Samuel S 64
Cheung, David A 299
Chevalier, Rebekah...........348
Chiavario, Nancy A. 292
Chidsey, Linda...........120, 121
Chipchase, Elwood H. 297
Chisholm, Alvah 251
Choe, Richard C. 208
Chondo, Javan 121
Chow, Rita 40
Christen, William...............166
Christianson, Lawrence 137
Christie, Marge 251
Christie, Paul C..................236
Christopher
   (Bishop)..................126, 156
Christopher, Sharon
   Brown 170
Chrysostomos
   (Archbishop) 163
Chu, Thomas......................106
Chubenko, Taras 164
Chute, Michael 328
Chute, Nilda......................292
Ciceva-Aleksic, Marija.......47
Cilpam, Ha Giao 88
Cindrich, Frank 259
Cinson, Victor 35
Citronnelli, Eddie 78
Citzler, Annette 113
Cizik, Rich 37
Cizik, Richard 337
Clancy, Danna 266
Clark, Cecil 160
Clark, Charles 65
Clark, Frank B. 234
Clark, Katharine 120
Clark, Kathryn (Penny)
   Vennard 35
Clark, Marvin 160
Clark, Neal..........................63
Clark, R. D........................163
Clark, Tim 159
Clarke, Barry B..................181
Clarke, John R. 180
Clarke, Levi 190
Clark-Ochs, Judy 247

INDEX

415

Clay, Douglas E. 72
Cleave, Dwayne................198
Clement, Marilyn........34, 35
Clements, Kerry................148
Clements, Larry 64
Clements, Philip J...............37
Clements, Sam..........96, 190
Clickman, Marlene 254
Clifford, Mary
   Montgomery..................140
Cline, Douglas M. 94, 189
Cline, Evadna 262
Clothier, Patti....................259
Cloud, Randy 64
Cloud, Sanford, Jr...............38
Coates, Gerald 119
Coates, Ken.......................235
Coats, John W.....................66
Cobarn, Trevor....................84
Cobb, Judith......................115
Cobbey, Nan 106
Cochran, Sylvenia F..........255
Coen, Joseph W. 25
Coffin, John 120
Coffin, Percy D.................181
Cogdill, Michael G. 298
Cogsdale, Michael 256
Cohen, Albert G.................236
Colas, Ralph 22
Cole, David 301
Cole, Jack 123
Cole, John K......................144
Coleman, Catherine 235
Coleman, Robert F............304
Coles, Robert N 66
Collett, Darlene.................247
Colli, Fred 203
Collier, John W. P. 344
Colligan, John 22
Collins, Arnold 48
Collins, Bradley 330
Collins, David....................183
Collins, Jacqueline.............185
Collins, Leland C................238
Collins, Les D....................141
Collins, Michael R.............159
Collins, W. Darwin 84
Collymore, Carlisle............169
Colon, John 106
Combes, Frances................293
Comfort, William...............267
Compton, Gordon 28
Conant, Lawrence...............161
Condrea, Nicolae 154, 204
Conley, John 299
Conn, Charles
   Paul........................94, 189
Connel, Bob 326
Connors, Dan 325
Connors, G. C....................200
Constantine
   (Metropolitan) 164
Converse, Susan 151, 202

Cook, Clint 123
Cook, David T. 327
Cook, Katie........................324
Cook, Quentin L. 97
Coombs, Gary F.................313
Coon, Carlton 172
Coons-Torn, Marja.............168
Coop, Linda 112
Cooper, Brian.....................182
Cooper, Sabrina 74
Cooper, Sabrina M.............324
Cooper-White,
   Michael L 306
Coorilos, Euyakim Mar 135
Cope, Kenneth 146
Cope, Mike 344
Cope, William.............62, 323
Copeland, Elaine
   Johnson..........................299
Copeland, Shelley 236
Cope-Robinson,
   Lyn 120, 121
Copley, Steve.....................234
Corbett, Ardelia M.............169
Corbett, Daniel 190
Corbin, Randall B...............87
Corcelius, Ted 262
Corey, Barry H...................313
Corkum, Ken 205
Cormode, James R.............320
Cornelius, Fred R. 95
Corrigan, John 327
Corson-Finnerty,
   Susan. 331
Cossey, James E.................327
Costanza, Daniel................347
Cotton, Edmund G.............118
Cotton, T. 92
Coulston, James A. 116
Coulter, Riley....................317
Councell, Gary R.......108, 331
Courter, Gini 165
Cousin, Philip Robert 59
Cowan, A. J. 180
Cowan, Mattew..................156
Cox, Ann...........................264
Cox, Brian...........................53
Cox, Jill.............................268
Cox, John R. 140
Coy, Ken 257
Coyle, Charlotte.................264
Coyner, Michael J..............170
Crabtree, Bruce...................101
Crabtree, Charles T..............42
Crabtree, Davida Foy 168
Craddock, Margaret 263
Craddock, Max 191
Craddock, Max E...............347
Craft, Betty Jo.....................36
Craft, Roger L......................27
Craft, Roy 238
Crane, Charles A................297
Craven, Paul J......................36

Crawford, Bud 193
Crawford, S. Rea 146
Creech, Barry 43, 147
Crenshaw, Carole..............332
Crenshaw, Ray 78
Cress, James A...................157
Crews, Bill 159
Crews, C. Daniel 356
Crick, Robert D. 93, 189
Crist, Larry 84
Crittenden, David 148
Crocker, Richard..................35
Crockett, Joseph 22
Croft, Donna 52
Croglio, James 254
Croneberger, Jack P. 108
Crook, Eleanor Butt............26
Cropsey, Marvin W...........335
Cross, Marie T. 148
Cross, Roger 49
Crossin, John W.................315
Crossman,
   Richard C 53, 322
Crough, Dave....................351
Crough, Janke 351
Crouse, Capin 28
Crout, Valorie....................266
Crowshoe, Kirk..................248
Cruger, Douglas 244
Crum, John 70
Crumbly, Faith 341
Crumes, W. E...............97, 332
Crump Gene.......................251
Crutchfield, Carmichael 86
Crutchfield, Charles N.......171
Cruver, Rob W. 146
Cruz, John...........................22
Csepregi, Gabor 318
Csomor, Marjorie................88
Cueni, R. Robert 305
Culbertson, William 112
Culp, Kristine A................300
Culpepper, R.
   Alan 238, 304
Culpepper,
   Raymond F. 93, 189
Cunningham, Jack 208
Cunningham, Jeff...............266
Cunningham, Johnny 70
Cunningham,
   Joseph.....................88, 327
Cunningham, Mary............333
Cunningham, Paul G. 99
Cunningham, Ronald 30
Cunningham,
   Ronald M.......................87
Cupich, Blase 81
Cureton, Kenyn.................341
Curry, Michael B. 108
Curtis, Jay 116
Curtis, Larry 264
Cushman-Wood, Darren 34
Custer, James 118

Cuthbert, Richard 65
Cuthbert, Terry D..............348
Cutler, Lelia 140
Cutts, Debbie 268
Cyril (Bishop)...................162

Da Valle, Liliana 64
Dabrowski, Rajmund 157
Dadds, David 240
Dadourian, Haig 72
Dahl, Judy 174
Dahlquist, Charles W. II 97
Dahulich, Michael G..........311
Dale, Diana C 40, 68
Dale, William.....................142
Dallenbach, Robert B. 146
D'Angelo, Mary Rose 52
Daniel, Audrey...................162
Daniel, Clifton, III 107
Daniel, Eapen 335
Daniel, Hieromonk 165
Daniels, David
    Rwhynica, Jr.....................59
Daniels, Henrietta 61
Daniels, Mary Martha........105
Danielson, Duane.......114, 257
Dantzler, Debbie 263
Daoust, Joseph P................304
Darby, James......................101
Darden, Samuel 70
Darling, Richard 293
Darnell, Stephen P. 93, 189
Darr, Steve 266
Dart, Christopher 249
Daughters, Kenneth
    Alan 301
Davidson, Brian 74
Davidson, Bruce 254
Davies, Fran 256
Davies, Pat 199
Davies, S. J. P. 292
Davies, Susan E...................31
Davis, Ashley.....................242
Davis, Bessie 70
Davis, Charles....................144
Davis, Derek 218
Davis, Dollie 145
Davis, Earl 38
Davis, G. Lindsey 172
Davis, Harper.....................243
Davis, James Levert 59
Davis, Jim 234
Davis, Kathleen 236
Davis, Kenneth R. 94, 190
Davis, Melvin 244
Davis, Nehemiah 139
Davis, Phil 90
Davis, R. Paul 102
Davis, Richard 172
Davis, Robert 244
Davis, Sarah Frances 59
Davis, Stephanie 169

Davis, Stephen P. 159
Davis, Tyrone T. 86
Davolt, Philip 79
Davolt, Susan.....................331
Dawkins, David 144
Dawley, William G. 327
Day, Jeff.............................244
de Leon, Daniel 42
De Marco, Eugene 84
De Witt, Samuel 26
Dean, Amy Jacks 63
Deckenback, John R. 168
Decker, William A. 335
Dee, Choe Chong 184
deFreese, David L..............114
DeFriese, Gordon 256
DeGraffenreidt,
    Kermit 61, 336
DeGroot-Nesdahl,
    Andrea F. 114
Delac, Katria 217
DelHousaye, Darryl 309
DellaForesta, John 197
Deller, Walter 318
Delsaut, Phil 196
Demarse, Mary Grace........253
Demchuck, David 321
Demeter, Andor..................128
Demetrios
    (Archbishop) 31, 126
DeMoor, Robert..................324
Demos, Emanuel G.............126
Demson, Sandra...................51
den Hoed, J. 324
Denbo, Gary A...................298
Denis, Mary Frances..........206
Dennie, Steve 101
Dennison, Don 102
Densmore, Christopher 354
Denton, A. Louis. 261
Denton, Diane 170
Derderian, Hovnan 72, 182
DeRose, Robert....................34
Derr, Donna 39
Derrenbacker, Robert A 52
Derry, John 303
DeSelm, Joel 136
Desgagne, Jean 50
DeTilla, Paul 137
Devadhar, Sudarshana 171
DeVeaux, William................34
DeVeaux, William
    Philips 59
DeVoe, Jerry M., Jr............153
DeVries, Janet....................148
DeWall, Clem 31
Dewar, Dale 186
Dewberry, A. T...................100
Dewey, Marvin L................321
DeWitt, Jesse 35
Dewling, Gregory R. 201
Dewling, Robert H. 201
DeYoung, Terry 24

Diakiw, William.........164, 165
Diaz, Louis..........................112
Diaz-Montanez, Cristino 64
Dicaire, Louis 203
DiCicco, Mario 302
Dickerson, Dennis 22
Dickerson,
    Dennis C..................59, 356
Diefenbach, Joan 251
Diehl, James H. 99
Diehl, Paul J., Jr...................84
Diekelman, W
    illiam 133, 134
Diemer, Ulli 346
Dietz, Harry 262
Dill, James 94
Diller, Edward....................136
Dilley, Gary 101
Dimitrios (Bishop).............125
Dimitriou, Jerry 126
Dinatale, Wenda.................260
Dipboye, Carolyn 333
Dipboye, Larry 333
Dirks, Gordon 321
DiStaulo, David 197
Dixon, Brad 101
Dixon, Judy.......................258
Djaballah, Amar.................318
Djigo, Jean-Luc 294
Dobbin, Karen 242
Dobbs, H. A.......................331
Dobiash, Sandra.................162
Dobush, Christine 75
Dodds, Ed 25
Dodge, Hollis.....................166
Doezema, Don 150
Dohner, Stephanie..............251
Dolan, Timothy M. 81
Donahue, James A. 302
Donald (Bishop) 126
Donaldson, Hal 338, 342
Donges, David A................115
Donley, Brian C.................304
Donnithorne, Larry R 299
Dorland, Arthur G...............186
Dorman, Nancy..................266
Dorrington, Charles W.......153
Dorsey, Daniel 32
Dorsey, Jim 332
Dortch, Mimi 234
Douglas, Caryn 318
Douglas, S. C......................70
Douglas, Scott....................233
Douglas, Stacey C. 343
Douglas, William 95
Douglass, Benjamin T. 173
Douglass, Steve 27
Dow, Thomas E. 318
Dowd, Susan Jackson 333
Dowden, G. Blair 101, 304
Down, Graham 348
Downey, Ray 187
Downey, William S. H.......133

417

INDEX

Downs, Bert 103, 316
Downs, Michael A. 167
Downs, Timothy C. 168
Doyle, Barrie 187
Drake, Paul 129
Draper, Bern......................116
Draper, David E.................316
Dresselhaus, Richard 73
Drews, Julie 29
Driedger, Connie...............187
Driscoll, Virginia 120
Drummond, Shawn 259
Drury, Stephen 172
Dua, Barbara E. 252
Duda, Betty.......................134
Dudley, Cheryl....................39
Dueck, Abe 348
Duerksen, Carol 344
Duff, Donald J. 143, 144
Duff, Susan 243
Duffy, Mark 106, 353
Dufresne, Edward R. 246
Dugas, Jacqueline 53
Duggins, Dominic...............32
Duke, Thomas....................249
Dulan, C. Garland.............157
Dumond, Franklin.............123
Dunahoo, Charles 147, 330
Dunbar, David G................297
Dunbar, R. G....................122
Duncan, Donald B. 259
Duncan, Larry.............96, 190
Duncan, Muriel.................350
Duncan, Philip M. 107
Duncan, Robert W. 108, 259
Duncan, Ronald V..............91
Dunham, Rosetta J..............61
Dunkerson, Roddy 168, 250
Dunkin, Ralph...........115, 268
Dunlap, Raymond.............250
Dunn, Craig A...................175
Dunn, James A...................175
Dunn, John C. 81
Dunn, Sharon R. 93
Dunn, Wesley....................164
Dunston, Ann......................78
Dupcak, Kimberlee 254
Dupre, Ray D....................100
Duque, Francisco 107
Duracin, Jean Zache 107
Durakis, Thomas.................22
Durance, George 317
Durden, John.....................296
Durocher, Eric...................346
Dursi, Elsie L....................257
Durso, Pamela R................324
Dvorak, Robert C. 237
Dwight, David A................111
Dybdahl, Jon 315
Dyck, Dan.........................199
Dyck, Darrell 195
Dyck, Ed 184
Dyck, Sally 170

Dyck, Tim 195
Dyck, Tom Miller 346
Dykstra, Gerard 88, 187
Dykstra, Jon 350
Dykstra, Russell J. 342

Eads, Ora W.........................86
Earheart-Brown,
    Daniel J 307
Earheart-Brown, Jay 105
Easley, Michael J. 307
Eastman, Donald................174
Eaton, James E. 328
Ebacher, Roger 203
Eberhardt, Jack 123
Echohawk, John 230
Echols, James Kenneth 306
Eck, Diana 212, 219
Eckardt, Robert Y. 144
Eckes, Lois 247
Eckhardt, Ellen E...............139
Eckler, Sharon....................242
Eckman, James 302
Eckstrom, Kevin 44
Edlund, Mark 159
Edney, Lowell 169
Edwards, David 245
Edwards, Gloria.................134
Edwards, Gregory 40
Edwards, Harold 98
Edwards, Herbert 101
Edwards, James L........91, 295
Edwards, Jonathan 154
Edwards, William H. 84
Edwards-Konic,
    Patricia 121, 340
Egge, Joel 98
Eggleston, James H. 252
Egnew, Bruce E. 80
Ehinger, Lois 241
Ehrenkrantz, Dan 310
Ehresman, David 244
Eidson, E. Larry...................36
Eidum, Charles D. 330
Ekemam, Samuel
    Chuka, Sr. 59
Ekeroth, George E. 73
Ekeroth, M. J. 73
Eklund, Kent 248
Elam, Betty 40
Eldred, Timothy 28
Elgin, Bette 122
Elia, Donna 252
Eliason, Leland V................26
Elizade, John.....................259
Ellefson, Anne 263
Ellenson, David 303
Elliott, G. Keith 196
Elliott, Kate Sprutta 335
Ellis, David 122, 123
Ellis, Davis L.....................144
Ellis, Howard 193

Ellis, J. Delano II...............173
Ellis, Jerry.........................262
Ellis, Rebekah A. 256
Ellis, Sabrina.....................173
Ellis, Sandra......................200
Ellis, Wayne........................70
Ellison, Leslie 265
Elloian, Dierdre 237
Ellyatt, David....................197
Elmore, Don 76
Elrod, Rachael 242
Ely, Thomas C. 108
Embree, Dorothy 245
Emerson, Joe.....................173
Emory, M. L. 251
Endecott, Clayton 96, 190
Endel, Leo.........................159
Engbrecht, Dave 136
Engebretson, Donn............111
Engel, A. Gayle 168
Engelmayer, Shammai 334
Engelsma, David 314, 334
Enger, Cindy 267
English, Marian 90
Engstrom, Jon R. 123
Enns-Rempel, Kevin..........355
Enrique, Antonio...............339
Episcopos, P. S. Samuel
    Cor 135
Epp, Gerald 117
Epps, Barbara J....................61
Epstein, Jerome M............229
Erb-Miller, Fannie 345
Erdman, Greg 156
Erhardt, Richard 267
Erickson, C. E....................240
Erickson, Charles R. 264
Erickson, Duane................110
Erickson, Gary 172
Erickson, James 160
Erickson, Lee 249
Erickson, Paul 354
Ericson, Charles................237
Eriks, Kenneth 151
Erlandson, Kathy 267
Ervine, Sharon 264
Eschenbrenner, Jim............88
Eshbach, Warren M. 262
Eslinger, Leslie S..............261
Essey, Basil 67
Esterle, Stan 243
Estes, Kristi.......................120
Estocin, Frank 164
Estwani, Sheikh
    Bassam 238
Etterman, James................94
Evangelos
    (Metropolitan) 125
Evans, Alton 142
Evans, Bernard J...............193
Evans, Gene 122
Evans, Irvin......................169
Evans, Marie 240

418

Evans, Thomas...................157
Evans, William B.........73, 323
Evenson, Carl R................115
Everett, K. Randel.............304
Ewing, Ward B.................302
Eyring, Henry B. 97

Faber, Connie....................326
Fabric, Elliot.....................267
Fadelle, Norman 82
Fagerstrom, Douglas L......303
Fagin, Earl 235
Fahey, Brian.......................25
Faigao, Howard F. 157
Failing, Mark 323
Fairchild, Darryl 257
Falconer, Gennae 248
Farabee-Lewis, Iris 244
Fareed, Munner..................226
Faris, Robert 52, 53
Farley, Lawrence 200
Farlow, David 91
Farlow, Gary 121
Farmer, Jeff 42, 142
Farmer, Paul......................240
Faro, Ira 260
Farrell, Hunter 148
Farren, John 311
Fast, Rick 54
Faulkner, Tom 321
Faurschou, Bruce 208
Faust, David M 299
Favicha, Raymond 122
Favreau, Claude 193
Fawcett, Bruce..................193
Feamster-Roll, Gerry 243
Fecher, Roger J. 31
Fedak, Wasyly...................206
Fedechko, Michael 153,
      202, 320, 321, 349
Feener, Maxwell 155
Fehr, Wes 320
Feldberg, Michael 355
Feldbush,
   Martin W. 157, 323
Feldman, James 27
Felipa, Luis F. 87
Felter, David J....................332
Fendt, John W., Jr. 139
Ferkenstad, Craig..............116
Ferlino, Jack 23
Fernhout, Harry 319
Ferre, Faith 241
Ferree, James W................256
Ferrell, Ernest 140
Ferrer, Abednego 88
Ferris, Ronald 180
Fetherlin, Robert L. 87
Field, Ronald 40
Fifagrowicz, Joseph 253
Fikse, Susan 337
Finch, Dody 45

Finck, Murray D. 114
Fincke, George B...............152
Fines, David 345
Finke, Roger 213
Finley, J. Lance.................102
Finley, Patricia 145
Finn, Charles W.................132
Finn, Peter G.....................311
Finney, Peter P., Jr. 328
Finzel, Hans 103
Fiorino, Joseph 337
Firle, L. C. 139
Firle, Sharon L...................328
Fischer, Harvey...................96
Fishell, Randy 332
Fisher, Gerald 184
Fisher, Violet L. 171
Fisk, J. Victor....................122
Fitchue, Leah Gaskin.........309
Fitzgerald, Russell G. 45
Fitzmier, John 212
Flaaten, Jan Olav 234
Flach, Dennis 117
Flanagan, James................306
Fleischer, Daniel 98
Fleischer, Paul...................335
Fleming, David L 340
Flesher, Chuck 24
Fletcher, Alfred 64
Fletcher, James 23
Fletcher, Judy R.................148
Fletcher, Ruth A..................84
Fletcher, Sarah 328
Fletcher, Wendy 322
Flett, Carol 246
Flewelling-Leeds,
   Ginger..........................264
Florkey, Marcia L. 47
Flory-Steury, Mary Jo..........89
Flowers, Fort D., Jr............264
Flowers, George F...............59
Flowers, Ronald M............157
Fluechtling, Rick 268
Fluit, Charlie 56
Fluker, Sharon Watson.........32
Fogas, Jackie.....................329
Folkemer, Don 335
Follett, Don 262
Fombelle, Douglas W. 297
Fong, Bruce W...................307
Foraine, Nick 129
Ford, C. Barney 33
Ford, C. M. 92
Ford, J. Arthur 319
Ford, Lowell 66
Foreman, Rachel.......102, 327,
             331, 336,
Forhand, Darryl 101
Forlines, James 138
Forlines, Leroy 138
Forro, Alexander................128
Forsberg, Robert 235
Forsee, Tom 233

Fortin, Dennis 312
Fortin, Marilyn 47
Fortune, Marie M 267
Foss, Richard J...................114
Foster, H. Paul 201, 347
Fougere, J. Keron 203
Fountain, Peter...................187
Fowler, John M...................328
Fox, Ronald K. 256
Foxman, Abraham H. 228
Fozard, John D 307
Frade, Leopold...................108
Fraedrich, Valerie..............337
Francis, Maureen 38
Francis, Oprah 163
Franklin, Mark 118
Franklin, Robert M......31, 238
Frase, Donald M................175
Fraser, Ian S......................208
Fraser, Margaret..................32
Fraser, Ronald A 317
Frazee, David.....................150
Frazier, David 124
Freed, Kathy 242
Freelander, Daniel................40
Freeman, David 187
Freeman, George 48
Freeman, Hillary 248
Freeman, Linda Danby 45
Freiheit, Warren D. 114
Freitag, Merle 134
Frenchak, David 45
Fretheim, James A. 111
Freund, Richard C. 139
Frew, Don 46
Frey, Mark 257
Frick, Murray.....................252
Friend,
   Kendra............102, 103, 192
Friesen, William H. 203
Frisch, Deborah 154
Frisch Korn, Frank T. 64
Frische-Mouri, Dennis.......241
Frowe, Caroline 239
Fry, Gary 331
Fryling, Robert A................33
Fugh, Clement W.................59
Fulenwider, Douglas...........72
Fullard, Henriettaa 255
Fuller, John 40
Fuller, Paula 33
Fuller, Robert H.................172
Fullwood, James 66
Fulp, Michael.....................121
Fulton, Jim 267
Fulwider, Bryan 238
Fung, Andrew 266
Funk, Abe 53, 184
Futral, James R..................159

Gaddie, Ron 243
Gaddy, Todd......................172

Gaewski, David R..............168
Gage, J. Marshall................37
Gagnon, André L..............319
Gaither, Israel L................155
Galegor, Steve...................119
Gallagher, John (Jack)......320
Gallaher, Susan.................266
Gallop, Trina....................345
Galloway, Phyllis H..........355
Galvin, Joan.....................294
Gamble, Rich.....................266
Gammi, Nancy..................242
Gammon, Stephen A..........104
Gandolfo, Lucian................84
Gangler, Dan......................43
Gantz-Jalowiecki,
    Joanne..........................260
Garbidakis, Nicholas..........22
Gardiner, Kelvin J...............87
Gardner, Carol..................325
Gardner, Harry G..............192
Gardner, Joan.....................38
Gardner, Talmadge...........131
Gardner, W. Wayne...........314
Garis, Mark........................79
Garland, David..................302
Garment, Robert...............117
Garner, Darlene.................174
Garner, Don......................120
Garrett, Phillip..................243
Garrison, Brent D..............313
Garrison, J. Michael..........109
Garrison, L. Alton...............72
Garriss, Stephen................145
Gasero, Russell.................357
Gast, Mary Susan..............167
Gaston, H. Neely................74
Gatlin, Alton.......................92
Gaud, Carmen...................324
Gaudette, Pierre................204
Gaumond, André................203
Gause, Edith......................148
Gautier, Haggeo................238
Gautier, Mary..............26, 215
Gaw, Catherine..........208, 294
Geernaert, Donna................31
Geiger, C. Edward.............261
Geisler, Norman.................313
Geldmacher, Joan..............253
Gendron, Lionel.................319
Genello, William R............325
Gentle, Stanley...................79
Gentles, Jestina.................169
George, Francis...................80
George, J. Don....................73
George, Richard..................84
George, Thomas A......94, 190
George, Timothy................296
George, William..................86
Georgije (Bishop)..............205
Gepert, Robert Ronald.......109
Gerasimos
    (Metropolitan)...............125

Geraty, Lawrence T...........305
Gerbrandt, Gerald..............317
Gerdes, Neil W..................358
Gethers, Leroy..................153
Getz, Greg........................136
Getz, Jeff..........................136
Geulsgugian, Bernard........182
Geyser, Thomas..................84
Ghabrial, Theresa..............237
Ghougassian, Vazken..........71
Giacoletto, Kenneth P.........65
Gibbs, Charles P..................46
Gibbs, Wendell N., Jr.........108
Gibson, Billy.....................122
Gibson, David E. 326
Gibson, Diana....................234
Gibson, Gaylena...............326,
                               327, 334
Gibson, J. Daniel.................51
Gibson, Marie E. 253
Giesbrecht, Kennert...........349
Giesy, Samuel....................306
Gilbert, Jack........................32
Gilbert, Robert..................130
Gilbert, Wanda..................218
Gilbert-Cougar, John.........187
Gilbertson, Leon C..............54
Gilbreath, Ed.....................342
Gill, Andrew......................162
Gilliam, Lynn W................339
Gillians, Larry.....................50
Gillies, Susan..............64, 250
Gillming, Keith....................76
Gillum, Perry.....................190
Gilmore, Marshall................87
Gingerich, Elmer.................77
Gingerich, Melvin................77
Giordano, Sally..................254
Giordano, Stephen T..........251
Giron, Rudy........................94
Gist, Richard.......................41
Gladish, Michael D............197
Glagau, Ralph R. 93, 189
Glanzer, Jules....................302
Gleason, Jim......................252
Glenn, Lucinda..................354
Glenn, Michael..................310
Gnat, Thomas J.................146
Goatley, David
    Emmanuel......................41
Godevenos, Ken................350
Godfrey, W. Robert............316
Goebel, Samuel.................110
Goertzen, Lil............195, 347
Goff, Jim...........................156
Goff, Phillip......................215
Goforth, C. W....................145
Gohdes, Stephen........137, 186
Goheen, Greg....................192
Goldberger, Pierre.............208
Golder, Morris...................144
Golder, W. Evan................343
Goldstein, Clifford R. 334

Golumb, Paul....................253
Gomez, Ray......................264
Gomez, Victor...................266
Gonzalez, Gerado................46
Gonzalez, Tony.................234
Goodhue, Thomas W. 254
Goodin, David L...................87
Goodpaster, Larry M. 171
Goodwin, Douglas.............208
Goodyear, Paul..................205
Gootjes, N. H.............185, 322
Gopal, Renee.....................257
Gordon, Drew............153, 329
Gordon, J. Dorcas.......53, 319
Gordon, Lynne...........153, 329
Gore, Ralph J......................74
Gore, Susan K...................105
Gore, Susan Knight...........357
Gorton, Dennis L...............103
Gorzinski, Barbara............266
Gould, Aaron.....................167
Govier, Gordon...................33
Grady, J. Lee.....................326
Grady, Joellen W...............257
Graham, Ellen...................240
Graham, Sharlene..............202
Graham, Vernon R.............240
Graham, William A............303
Grainger, David.................239
Granberg-Michaelson,
    Wesley...................151, 202
Granitsas, Nicholas G........103
Granke, Robert H..............359
Grant, James M. 312, 313
Grant, Kenneth G. Y. 246
Grant, Michael A. 100
Grant, Sumner M................65
Graves, Charles.................268
Graves, Sylvia...................120
Graves, Thomas H..............296
Graves, William H., Sr. 86
Gray, Art............................42
Gray, Arthur J., II.............129
Gray, Duncan, III..............249
Gray, Duncan
    Montgomery, III............108
Gray, Joan.........................148
Gray, Stephen...................123
Gray, Stephen C................168
Graybill, John W................166
Graz, John........................157
Grecco, Richard................204
Greco, John........................22
Green, Alice B. 65
Green, Daniel....................153
Green, Donald B.................259
Green, E. David.................102
Green, Peter......................137
Green, S. 169, 170
Green, S. L., Jr...................92
Green, Samuel
    Lawrence, Sr...................59
Green, Stanley...................136

420

Greenawald, Henry 259
Greenfield, Larry L 64
Greenhaw, David M 301
Greening, John 123, 124
Greenleaf, Helen 164
Greenway, Jeffrey E 295
Greenwood, Greg 244
Gregg, William O. 107
Grégoire, Léo 204
Gregory, Chester, Sr 169
Greiman, Clayton 152
Grein, Richard F. 31
Grier, David 200
Grieves, Brian 106
Griffes, Darrell D 111
Griffin, Arlee, Jr. 64
Griffin, Ashley 244
Griffin, Robert 174
Griffin, Sharon 100
Griffith, Craig 22
Griffith, Dick 129
Griffith, Richard 129
Grigsby, Phillip N 255
Grimard, Roland 206
Grimm, Libby 259
Grimm, Robert 254
Grogan, Douglas L. 87
Groome, Thomas H. 297
Groover, Clarence 101
Groover, Gentle L 100
Groover, R. Edwin 296
Gross, Glenn M. 153
Gross, Joseph 146
Gross, Philip J 128
Grossman, Randall A 78
Grossman, Robert 152
Grote, Royal U., Jr 152
Grotegut, Stan 236
Grothaus, Darel 267
Grotnick, Casimir 332
Grou, Jean 350
Grubbs, Bonita 236
Grubbs, Lari R. 84
Guengerich, Larry 36
Guentert, Richard L. 84
Guernsey, Lucy 236
Guess, J. Bennett 167
Guffey, Edith A 167
Guibord, Gwynne 236
Guido, Sam 69, 70
Guidry, Carolyn Tyler 59
Guillebeau, Julie 250
Guillemette, Gaetane 345
Guirguis, Ammonius 193
Guiriguis, Lucy Ishak 47
Guiterrez, Rosalia 46
Gulasekharam, Nesa 50
Gulick, Edwin F., Jr. 107
Gulick, Walter 250
Gullixson, Theodore 335
Gumbs, Ambrose 109
Gumbs, Carolyn 254
Gunter, Nina 99

Guretzki, David 52
Gurgel, Karl R. 176
Gurley, Morris 253
Guskjolen, J. I 200
Guy, Kristen 345
Gwinn, Alfred W., Jr. 172

Haas, Steve 48
Habegger, Ron 330
Habegger, Ronald J 118
Haberer, Jack 339
Hackett, Jean 47
Hackner, D. Karl 181
Hackner, James 182
Hadjinicolaou, John 200
Hadley, Alvin 257
Hadsell, Heidi 303
Haemmerle, Gerald R 308
Hagan, Orville 93, 189
Hagedorn, Harold J 176
Hagemann, Dennis 83
Hagerty, Robert E 316
Haggray, Jeffrey 64, 159
Hagopian, Garo 71
Hahn, Daniel 255
Hai, Iftekhar 46
Hale, Rebecca 84
Hales, Robert D. 97
Haley, Laura J 254
Haley, Richard 245
Hall, A. Z., Jr. 92
Hall, Beverly 96
Hall, Dinah 267
Hall, Gary 312
Hall, Gregory V 91
Hall, J. L. 331, 339
Hall, Will 158
Hallberg, Donald M. 113
Hallman, Don 183
Haloviak, Bert 352
Hamb, Elnora P 86
Hambin, Lloyd 64
Hamel, William J. 112
Hamelink, Crystal 255
Hames, Jerrold 330
Hamilton, Jim 159
Hamilton, Karen 51
Hamilton, W. W. 92
Hamlett, James P 83
Hammel, Marci 101
Hammock, Cheryl 45
Hammond, Geff 159
Hammons, Roger 149
Hampton, John E. 144
Hanavan, Tim 244
Hancock, Carol L. 208
Handysides, Allan R. 157
Haney, Kenneth F. 172
Haney, O. L 92
Hankins, David E. 159
Hanley, Richard 242
Hanse, Brian W 36

Hansen, David 168
Hansen, Duane 112
Hansen, Ellen 267
Hansen, Gary L 115
Hansen, Traynor
 "Frosty," Jr 124
Hanson, Lloyd 235
Hanson, Mark S. 113
Hanus, Jerome G. 81
Hapke, Lark J. 167
Hardesty, Jane 75
Harding King, Amy 253
Hardy, Ralph, Jr. 40
Hargleroad, Bobbi
 Wells 327
Hargrave, Ervin 130
Harke, Gary 261
Harkins, Derrick 41
Harmon, John 263
Harms, Richard H 357
Harms, Steve 235
Harns, Forrest 241
Harper, Terry L. 159
Harris, Alvin 89
Harris, David 349
Harris, David A 228
Harris, Elsie 168
Harris, Forrest E. 295
Harris, Jerome V 59
Harris, Michael 150
Harris, Nanci 50
Harris, Phil 88
Harris, Robert 203
Harris, Ron L. 40
Harrison, Charles E. 341
Harrison, Dan 101
Harrison, David P. 42
Harrison, Kathy 173
Harrison, Matthew 134
Harrison, William
 Anthony 141
Hart, Maurice 122
Hart, Michael 320
Hart, Ray L. 297
Hartke, Gary 99
Hartman, Patricia 110
Hartwig, Raymond L. 134
Harvey, Andrew 260
Harvey, Carole
 (Kate) H 65
Harvey, Jane Hull 33
Harwell, Sara 353
Hasan, John 234
Haskins, Roger W., Jr. 119
Hassinger, Susan W. 170
Hastag, John, III 124
Hastey, Stan 63
Hatcher, Warren 153
Hatlie, Susan Allers 248
Hauser, Clarence 293
Haverstock, Zedna M 262
Hawkins, Charles 243
Hawkins, Don 313

421

Hawkins, Jimmie 39
Hawkins, O. S...................159
Hawkins, Robert J., Jr........100
Haworth, Sharon 120
Hayat, Ghazala 250
Hayes, Kathleen................341
Hayes, Lindsey 130
Hayes, Robert E., Jr..........171
Hayford, Jack....................129
Haymes, Don 353
Haynes, J. N.......................92
Hays, Franklin 63
Hazuda, Ronald A...............65
Hazzard,
    David E. 200, 319
Headman, Wayne A. 310
Heagy, David 166
Hearn, Greg 131
Heaslip, Clifford 208
Heath, Gordon 359
Heath, Preston...................145
Heckles, Jane E.................167
Heckman, Bud 44
Hedberg, William...............252
Hedges, Gary 130
Hedman, Roy 254
Heebner, Gerald................341
Heerspink, Robert C. 88
Hefner, Helmut 311
Heidkamp, Mary 34
Hein, Marvin......................124
Heinze, Ted 293
Heisey, Terry M. 354
Hejl, James 173
Heleine, Berton G..............66
Helton, James 122
Helton, Mary Beth 244
Heminway, L. Marshall 133
Hemphill, Margaret 153
Henderson, Dorsey
    F., Jr. 108
Henderson, James 148
Henderson,
    Katharine R. 214
Henderson, Rebecca 154
Henderson, Susan 168
Henderson, Veryl F. 159
Hendricks, Harry 98
Hendrickson, Mary Lynn.....24
Hendrix, Carol S. 115
Henkel, Sarah 262
Hennessy, Janet..................244
Henning, C. Garnett 59, 244
Henze, Charles...................252
Heppner, Jack 195
Herbrandson, DeWayne 28
Heretz, Michael 164
Herlong, Bertram N...........108
Herman (Metropolitan)......143
Herman, Alvin 191
Herman, Harry 144
Hermiz, Tom 101
Hernando, Mirasal 184

Hernando, Vincente 184
Heron, Claire 56
Herrling, Karen...................34
Herron, Brian 248
Hertzog, Glenn 137
Hertzog, Stephen 322
Herzog, Daniel W. 107
Hess, Henry 187
Hess, Larry G. 189
Hessel, Karen Mcclean.......34
Hester, Yvonne..................246
Heuser, Frederick
    J., Jr. 148, 334
Heyward, Isaiah 93
Hicken, Michael 257
Hickey, Tim S. 328
Hicks, John M....................332
Hicks, Maurice M..............185
Hicks, Sherman.................113
Hicks, Wayne 103
Hicks, William 96
Hiemstra, John E. 255
Higgens, Stan.....................28
Higgs, Grady L. 77
Higham, Susan...................152
Highers, Alan E. 342
Hilarion (Archbishop) 155
Hill, Alec.............................33
Hill, Darcel 249
Hill, Kenneth H. 333
Hill, Malika........................253
Hill, Michael.......................92
Hill, Nick.............................95
Hill, R. Eugene 66
Hill, Ruth Y. 111
Hill, Timothy M...........93, 189
Hilliard, William
    Alexander 60
Hillouse, Darrell 123
Hilsden, R. T......................200
Hiltz, Fred J. 180
Hinckley, Gordon B............97
Hines, D...............................92
Hinkle, Carol 260
Hinshaw, Seth 154
Hinton, Arthur....................105
Hinz, Leo 294
Hinz, Mary Ann 246
Hirschy, Charles A............102
Hirschy, Margaret 353
Hirshkowitz, Barbara........330
Hixon, Larry 236
Hnatko, George.................164
Ho, Esther.........................235
Hoak, Don.........................265
Hobbs (Reverend).............145
Hockensmith, David
    W., Jr. 250
Hodder, Gary 205
Hodges, James 69, 182
Hodgins, Donald E. 209
Hodgson, Robert................22
Hoey, Eric 148

Hoezee, Scott 339
Hoffman, Bud 257
Hoffman, Jane Fisler 168
Hoffman, Michael...............95
Hoffman, Warren L......79, 185
Hofstad, Robert D.............113
Hogan, Ed 74
Hogan, Peter 253
Hogston, Delphine 247
Hoke, Terry 79
Holbrook, Mark G. 28
Holdefer, Helen.................233
Holden, Ron......................192
Holder, Steve 122
Holguin, Julio C. 107
Holland, Grace....................79
Holland, Jeffrey R. 97
Holland, Melford
    E., Jr................................106
Hollenbach,
    Deanna 137, 186, 337
Holley, Darrell 138
Hollifield, Milton...............159
Hollinger, Dennis 111
Hollinger, Dennis P 301
Hollingsworth,
    Mark, Jr. 108
Holloway, Callon
    W., Jr...............................115
Holm, Duane.....................258
Holm, Jim 307
Holmberg, Joseph 248
Holmes, Charley 77, 296
Holmes, Jenny 259
Holmes, Mary Swalla 242
Holmes, Roy A 60
Holmquist, Victor
    Freeman...........................184
Holmstrom, Virginia 65
Holt, Jeanette 63
Holtz, Janet E 261
Homoki, Lee 124
Honcharenko, Natalia 165
Hood, George....................155
Hood, Phil.........................350
Hooker, Eula 254
Hoover, Amos B. 142
Hope, Monica 78
Hopkins, Jim 63
Hopkins, John L. 170
Hopkins, Sara E.................342
Hopyan, Takvor 72
Horgan, Ron......................116
Horita, David 345
Horne, James R. 100, 308
Horne, Martha J.................310
Horsch, James E. 340
Hoshibata, Robert T...........172
Hoskin, Derek B. E. 181
Hoskins, Janet A 321
Hossler, William 136
Hostetter, Steven...............309
Hotchkiss, Gregory K........152

INDEX

Houg, Richard W. 301
Hougen, Philip L. 114
Hough, Joseph C., Jr........314
Houle, Jaques..............93, 189
House, Alvin 65
House, Christie R 337
Houseal, Rich 26
Houser, Charles.................22
Houston, Barbara..............262
Houston, Walter 139
Hovis, Carol....................235
Hovsepian, Vatche 72
Howard, John Alan 319
Howard, R. L. 92
Howard, Randall E. 96
Howard, Randy...........42, 190
Howard, Roscoe J., III.......157
Howard, S. Johnson 107
Howe, Barry R...................109
Howe, Bruce H. W.............181
Howe, John W...................107
Howe, Linda Marek..........266
Howell, Bruce...................172
Howell, James R...............154
Hoy, G. Philip 240
Hoyt, Thomas L., Jr. 87
Hrybowych, Anastasia 165
Hsieh, Jeannette................314
Huang, C. P.....................238
Hubbard, Beck 203
Hubbard, Bede 203
Hubbard, Catherine............84
Hucks, John T., Jr. 160
Hudgens, Bobby L..............77
Hudnut-Beumler,
    James 315
Hudson, James L. 148
Hudson, Jill 148
Hudson, Matt 77
Hudson, Steven 112
Huebl, Marc 117
Huett, Jeff 340
Huffard, Everett W 303
Hugh, Ivor T. 236
Hughes, Aaron 350
Hughes,
    Clyde 42, 130, 339
Hughes, Dustin 131
Hughes, Sarah 243
Hughes, Sherly M.............169
Hughes, Teresa A..............237
Huh, Young Chin 132
Hukill, Jim 28
Huleatt, Johann 91
Hull, Rey..........................252
Hulst, Mary........................64
Hultquist, Timothy A...........43
Humphrey, Sandra 327
Humphry, Carol 327
Hundley, Michael 243
Hunerdosse, Marion 88
Hunn, Ken..........................79
Hunneus, Antonio 75

Hunt, Janet E. 26
Hunt, Patricia....................145
Hunt, Raymon 38, 61
Hunter, David 245
Hunter, Harold D. 356
Hunter, James H. 150
Hunter, Kent R.....................29
Hunter, Louis, Sr.................60
Hunter, Martha J. 328
Hunter, Rhashell 148
Hunter, Robert 137
Hunter, Ron.......................138
Hunter, Stewart 53
Huntley, Harvey L., Jr........115
Hurley, John 165
Hurn, Nancy 358
Huron, Rod 84
Hurt, Donna 137
Hurtubise, Pierre 359
Huszagh, Elini 126
Hutcheon, Cyprian 200
Hutchings, L. W.................184
Hutchins, D........................92
Hutchinson,
    William W. 171
Hutton, Charles 240
Hux, Ralph.................101, 330
Hying, Donald J................310
Hyvonen, Randall 167

Iakovos (Metropolitan)......125
Iasiello, Louis 315
Ickes, Wayne 112
Ihloff, Robert W.................108
Ihreborg, Christer..............199
Iker, Jack L. 107
Ilia (Bishop).......................62
Illingworth, Beth...............256
Imbens, Annie 46
Imes, William C.................296
Ingersol, Stan 356
Ingham, Michael C. 181
Ingram, Daryl B...................59
Ingram, Gregory Gerald
    McKinley.........................59
Ingram, Reginald 39
Inskeep, Kenneth W...........113
Inyangu, Frederick.............121
Ionita, Ioan 155
Iorg, Jeff............................302
Irish, Carolyn T.................108
Irvin, Dale T 308
Irvio, Wanda 243
Irwin, John 55
Irwin, Kevin 298
Irwin, Paul G. 22
Irwin, Sara 246
Isaiah (Metropolitan).........125
Isenhower, Joe 133, 340
Isham, Scott 332
Ishkanian, Charlotte..........336
Isiye, Tom 121

Isom, Beverly 240
Isom, Dotcy I......................87
Itty, Johncy 38, 39, 108
Jackson, Bernice
    Powell..............................47
Jackson, Daniel R.............205
Jackson, Elmira 61
Jackson, Ezekiel 249
Jackson, Kitt 252
Jackson, Mary 78
Jackson, Phil 137
Jackson, Susan 250
Jackson, Thomas M. 44
Jackson, Walter L. 101
Jackson-Skelton,
    Christina L.......................113
Jacob, Marjorie 158
Jacobs, Samuel G. 81
Jacobus, Russell
    E. 107, 268
Jacques, Camille 203
Jaharis, Michael 126
James (Archbishop) 126
James, Dorothy 238
James, Joe 95
James, Joseph F.................119
James, Timothy M. 83
Janes, Burton K. 201
Jang, Jacob Se...................132
Jaramillo, M. Linda 167
Jared, Clive 100
Jarmus, Andrew 206
Jarrett, Nathaniel, Jr............60
Jasper, Jeremiah 267
Jeans, Yvonne Tufts 173
Jefferson, Bernadel L.........247
Jefferson, Jonathan K. 101
Jefferts-Schori,
    Katherine 106, 107
Jeffery, Jim.......................296
Jeffrey, David...................155
Jeffrey, Robert 334
Jehle, Bonnie 254
Jelinek, James 249
Jelinek, James L. 108
Jellinek, Nancy 264
Jemerson, Robert 38
Jenkins, Charles E., III 107
Jenkins, Jason 256
Jenkins, Keith A 303
Jenkins, Laurie..................256
Jenks, Philip 38, 39, 329
Jenness, Jeffery A...............91
Jennings, Charles 66
Jensen, Paul 162
Jenson, Robert W................31
Jeremiah, Jeffrey 116, 117
Jerge, Marie C. 115, 255
Jermann, Rosemary 342
Jernigan, Paul S. 100
Jesson, Nicholas 52
Jessup, Bryce L.................316
Jewel, Bill 244

423

Jewell, Thomas R. 84
Jillions, John 200
Johanson, Ruthann K........297
John, Esther
  "Little Dove" 266
Johns, Cheryl Bridges.......31
Johns, Jackie 24
Johnson, A. Wayne 139
Johnson, Andrea 336
Johnson, Ayanna 83
Johnson, Ben......................71
Johnson, Colin R. 181
Johnson, Craig E........114, 335
Johnson, Dale 25
Johnson, David W. 111
Johnson, Deborah 338
Johnson, Delbert L. 157
Johnson, Diane 103
Johnson, Don E..................109
Johnson, Eleanor...............180
Johnson, Evelyn M. R.......111
Johnson, George 338
Johnson, Henry L. 144
Johnson, Holly 26
Johnson, Jack 246, 251
Johnson, Jacqueline 230
Johnson, Jeffrey 119
Johnson, Jeron 144
Johnson, Joseph 60
Johnson,
  Kathryn J 267, 341
Johnson, Kathryn L............113
Johnson, M. L. 93
Johnson, Mel.....................174
Johnson, Michelle
  Laque...................324, 326
Johnson, Nelson.................34
Johnson, Paul 76
Johnson, Rita 150
Johnson, Robert E.............324
Johnson, Rod 194
Johnson, Rodney
  McNeil...........................173
Johnson, Rosie 169
Johnson, Steven M. 162
Johnson, Thomas R. 26
Johnson, Thomas S.............43
Johnson, Todd 35
Johnson, W.
  Robert, III...................59, 60
Johnsson, W. G. 323
Jones, A. M..................78, 326
Jones, Abraham..................78
Jones, Barbara E. 84
Jones, Brooker T. 144
Jones, C. Stephen..............251
Jones, Cassandra...............168
Jones, Clifton 144
Jones, Dana.......................340
Jones, Daniel.....................261
Jones, Danny.....................332
Jones, Donna......................138
Jones, Elbert 98

Jones, Greg 193
Jones, Jacqueline 251
Jones, Jerry 172
Jones, Jesse 169
Jones, Joyce 205
Jones, Judy.......................266
Jones, Juliette.....................40
Jones, Kenneth E. 326
Jones, L. Gregory 301
Jones, Larry 193
Jones, Lindsay E.................90
Jones, Melanie 239
Jones, Patrick 101
Jones, Paul Griffin, II 249
Jones, Paxton 84
Jones, Perry.......................25
Jones, Ralph E. 115
Jones, Scott J. 171
Jones, Stephen 103, 266
Jones, Terrence J................61
Jones, Tim...................95, 340
Jones, Verity A...................329
Jones, Verlene 266
Jones, Walter D....................90
Jones, William H. 299
Jones, Wilmer 150
Jones, Wilson 292
Jonston, Robin 356
Jordan, Anthony L. 159
Jordan, Joe 316
Jordan, Larry W. 306
Joseph, Emmanuel 67
Joseph, Hieromonk 144
Joseph, Thomas 67
Joudrey, Patricia 293, 322
Joudrey, Philip 320
Jourdain, Cheryl 208
Joyce, Tom........................266
Judge, Beverly 40
Julien, Tom........................119
Juliot, Brent 191
Jump, Rick 266
Jung, Hee-Soo....................170
Junier, Sandra 245
Jupin, J. Michael................244
Just, Donald R. 114
Justman, James A...............114
Juuti, Richard C. 71

Kaada, Virginia 256
Kaguni, Samuel 121
Kaiser, John 240, 347
Kalcik, Sharon K. 250
Kallappa, M. George 298
Kalmanek, Edward 31
Kalmanek, Judy 31
Kalmar, Laura 348
Kalyniuk, Bohdan..............164
Kammerer, Charlene
  Payne 172
Kane, Mary 249
Kanouse, Kevin S. 114

Kao, Monica 259
Kapanke, John G................113
Kapeluck, Michael.............164
Kapeluck-Nixon,
  Natalie 164
Kaplan, Clemis Eugene 161
Karaman, Dennis G. 84
Karanja, Benson M.............297
Karim, Cyril Aphrem........161
Karrott, Sandra 263
Karssen, Paul 151
Karsten, Albert....................88
Kaseman, Mansfield M. 245
Kashdin, Linda 254
Kashmar, Mary 235
Kashuck, Claire 245
Kasimer, Sol 56
Katz, Virginia....................258
Kauffman, Cephas 348
Kaufman, Richard A..........348
Kaugers, Girts...................132
Kautz, William 111
Kawimbe, Paul Jones
  Mulenga.........................59
Kay, James R. 342
Kays, Joanne.....................252
Kazanjian, Shant................71
Keating, A. C. 199
Keaton, Jonathan D. 170
Keeler, William........31, 43, 81
Keener, Lamar 30
Keeney, Mervin B...............89
Keeran, Keith P 305
Keiller, James B................130
Keith, Raymond J., Jr. 101
Keller, Connie L 358
Kelley, Charles 308
Kelly, Arthur 328
Kelly, Bridgette..................358
Kelly, Francis D........297, 310
Kelly, Ronald D. 175
Kelly, Sue 265
Kelly, Thomas....................252
Kelsey, James A.................108
Kemp, Linda 242
Kemp, Roger.......................40
Kemper, Ken.............124, 302
Kemper, Nancy Jo 243
Kendall, David W. 119
Kendall, Michael 253
Kendall, Stephen...............201
Kendrick, Deloris 122
Kennebrew, Vernon 90
Kennedy, Alric 254
Kennedy, Joanne 326
Kennedy, Johnny 70
Kennedy, Leland................296
Kennedy, Steve 350
Kennedy-Wong,
  Phillip 259
Kent, Allen..........................65
Kent, Brian 140
Kent, Edgar.......................131

INDEX

Kent, Lynn 140
Kepa, Peter Mar.................126
Kerr-Wilson,
   Gregory K. 181
Kersey, Tay 104
Kersten, David 111, 352
Kersten, Nicholas 158
Kesohole, Erastus 121
Kesselheim, Don...............268
Kessler, Angela 325
Ketcham, Donald 174
Ketli, Vahe 72
Kettner, Edward G............318
Keurian, Alice...................126
Kevala, Rustom 232
Kevern, John R. 297
Keys, Michael 113
Keyser, Judy E. 89
Khamis, Aprim 67
Khasufa, Sylvester............121
Khatchadorian, Arshag 236
Khory, George 46
Khouri, Antoun 67
Kibble, Alvin M.................157
Kicanas, Gerald F. 81
Kidd, Jerry 116
Kidd, William B 293
Kidwell, Gary W.................83
Kieschnick,
   Gerald B. 133, 134
Kiesey, Deborah L. 170
Kikis, Peter 126
Kikumoto, David 174
Kiley, Clete 34
Kilgore, Gary 95, 119
Kilgore, James 95
Killam, Gillis 53
Killoren, Eileen..................235
Killpack, Jennifer 102, 103
Kim, Ko-Eun 267
Kim, Nam Soo 73
Kimball, John 104
Kimbrough, Orvin 250
Kimbrow, Terry.................298
Kimer, Stan 174
Kind, Kerry D....................175
King, Arthur......................105
King, Donald G. 157
King, Eileen 47
King, Elizabeth 167
King, Eric 91
King, Fred G.......................88
King, James R., Jr..............171
King, Johnny.....................208
King, Stephen 22
Kinnaman, David...............214
Kinnamon, Michael 38
Kinney,
   John W.............26, 312, 315
Kintz, Bruce......................134
Kirchhoff, Bernard.............39
Kireopoulos, Tony 38
Kirk, Doug 120

Kirk, Jennifer 46
Kirkland, Theodore
   Larry 59
Kirkpatrick, Clifton 148
Kirkpatrick, Susan 121
Kirn, John 308
Kishkovsky, Leonid 44
Kisia, Joseph 121
Kisner, Elaine 247
Kitchens, Sidney Lee.........154
Kitui, John 121
Kivuya, Thomas.................121
Klaassen, Martin 45
Klaus, Byron D.................296
Klein, Ralph W. 329
Klein, Stephen 248
Kleinfelter, Kenneth 173
Kline, Dale........................257
Kline, T..............................197
Kline, Thomas L. 124
Klinsing, P. David................87
Klusmeyer, W.
   Michie 109, 268
Klutz, C. H...........................67
Kneafsey, Padraig 162
Kneece, Brenda.................263
Knight, Keith 201
Knoche, H. Gerard.............115
Knoebel, Thomas...............310
Knoedler, Lon 268
Knoth, Rick.......................329
Knowles, Louis L. 47
Knudsen, Chilton R. 107
Knudsen, Herbert L. 84
Knull, Stanley 245
Knutson, Mark 259
Kobel, Jon 89
Kochis, Michael................164
Kocian, Dorothy 174
Kocses, Richard 251
Koehn, Cat 266
Koehn, Dale 93, 189
Koehn, Gladwin.................336
Koelpin, Daniel..................176
Koepke, Donald R. 40
Koh, Linda 157
Kohler, Ann.........................29
Kokesch, William 54
Kolb, Leonard R. 139
Kolbaba, Ginger 335
Kolowski, Donald..............33
Kolsti, Carol 29
Kong, Joe 87
Kong, Joseph S. 88
Konkel, August H 320
Kooistra, Paul D. 147
Koplow, Cordelia..............243
Kopp, Herb 124
Koptak, Paul E...................329
Korgen, Jeffry 34
Korpela, P. A.....................201
Korson, Gerald 338
Kosanke, Charles G 312

Kostura, Carol...................236
Kotrla, Claren 173
Kovalski, Gerald................157
Kowalski, Kelly 254
Krahn, Robert 184
Kramer, Melvin F...............100
Krashel, Rosemary 349
Kraus, Gene 168
Krause, Henry 199
Kraybill, J. Nelson.............296
Krehbiel, Don 117
Krell, Barbara 239
Krestrick, Robert C...........198
Kreuger, Kurt 134
Krey, Philip DW 306
Kring, S.............................183
Kriska, Chloe Ann 257
Kristof, Dennis 164
Kroeker, Irvin J.................350
Kroeze, Nicholas V 305
Krog, Karin 89
Krueger, Delton 27
Kruschel, Peter 176
Krutz, C. Dana............30, 244
Krywolap, George 164, 165
Krywonos, Mykola 164
Kucharek, Wilma S...........115
Kuchta, Thomas 134
Kuhlman, Dexter 117
Kuhn, Robert 134
Kuliczowski, Czeslan 146
Kumka, Evhen 164
Kun, Zolton......................128
Kunda, Theresa E. 137
Kunder, William 208
Kunselman, James 62
Kuntaraf, Jonathan............157
Kurima, Andrew H. S........121
Kurklin, Joanne.................258
Kurtz, Calvin 262
Kurtz, Joseph E..................81
Kuruvila, Alexander 47
Kutash, Ihor 294
Kutosi, Peter 121
Kvam, Roger A...................36
Kwan, Joseph 346
Kwok, Jack P. 159
Kwok, Meggy 50

La Valla, Deborah 340
Labrosse, G.......................293
Lacey, Jon 84
Lacey, Paul 23
Lachatanere, Diana 354
Lacy, Homer, Jr.................242
Ladd, Carol 248
Ladefaged, Jenny 29
Lage, Eerika......................193
Lahey, Raymond...............204
Laitner, Christine 160
Lake, Jan 144
Lakey, Othal H...................87

Lallo, Cecelia...................339
Lamarre-Vincent,
  David............................251
Lamb, Jerry......................108
Lambert, Jerry....................99
Lambie, Rosemary.............208
Lamm, Norman.................310
Lance, Paul.......................236
Lance, Rick.......................159
Land, Richard D. 159
Land, Steven J. 94, 189, 299
Landahl, Paul R. 114
Landon, Dennis...................45
Landon, Dennis L. 83
Lane, Dan G. 244
Lane, Gwendolyn 169
Lanes, T. A.........................73
Lang, Kristy.......................96
Lang, Kurt..........................96
Langille, Fran 246
Langley, Ken.......................81
Langsfeld, Paul J. 309
Lansing, Steven H..............113
Lant, Cheryl C. 97
Lapsansky, Emma
  Jones.............................354
Larade, Sharon...........208, 360
Larkin, Michael 129
Larmondin, Leanne............345
Larom, Margaret................106
Larrabee, Arthur 145
Larson, April Culring.........115
Larson, Duane H................315
Larson, Rebecca S. 113
Larson, Ronald 76
Lasanhar, Mazlin 258
Lassiter, Voni 122
Lau, David..........................99
Lau, Jennifer.....................349
Laughlin, Robert................256
Laurence, Steven B............261
Laurus (Archbishop)..........339
Lav, Iris............................238
Lavender, Deane................259
Lavigne, David P. 186
Lawrence, Caleb J. 180, 181
Lawrence, James F.............313
Lawrence, Merlyn..............167
Lawrence, Stephen 162
Lawrence, William B........309
Lawson, Jim........................35
Lawson, Joyce 257
Lawson, Phil.....................235
Lawton, George 246
Lawton, Gordon.........158, 312
Lay, Bertha 259
Layne, Samuel A. 144
Leavitt, Robert F...............311
Ledesma, Juanita 264
Lee, Arthur........................266
Lee, C. R...........................144
Lee, Darrel D...............71, 332
Lee, David H. 159

Lee, Jinwol 46
Lee, Linda.........................170
Lee, Peter..........................248
Lee, Peter J. 109
Lee, Robert 298
Lee, Terri 251
Leech, David......................264
Leech, Robert E. 148
Leflore, David......................23
Legge, W. James 259
Leggett, James D. 131
Lehman, Edwin..................198
Lehman, Richard 254
Lehmann, Daniel J.....113, 335
Leigh, Charles......................68
Lekic, Mike.......................205
Leman, Bruce 341
Lemler, James 106
Lemming, Patrick 162
Lemon, Robert E. 157
Leng, Janet..........................37
Lennick, Robert B. 43
Leonard, Bill........94, 189, 315
Leonard, Darnell................260
Leonard, Richard 104, 331
Leonard, Shirley 104, 331
Leopold, Phyllis J. 236
Leopold, Virginia.......129, 328
Leslie, David A...................259
Leszczuk, Mary Lee 164
Leung, Donna 183
LeVan, Patte......................336
Lever, Lee 242
Levy, B. Barry 319
Lew, Khristina 48
Lewis, Beth A. 113
Lewis, Bradley...........151, 202
Lewis, C. A..........................97
Lewis, D. Ray 138
Lewis, Donald....................346
Lewis, Ed 119
Lewis, Greg E....................134
Lewis, Harry 208
Lewis, James W. 219
Lewis, Richard Allen..........59
Lewis, Robert L............40, 68
Lewis, Wilbur 150
Lewis, William L. 103
L'Heureux, N.
  J., Jr.........................253, 255
Liebling, Mordechai 34
Liegl, Sara.........................249
Liggett, J. D. 176
Light, Gordon 181
Lightbody, C. Stuart 187
Likis, Betty 233
Lilande, Joshuah 121
Lillback, Peter A 316
Lillibridge, Gary R. 109
Lim, Jimmy.......................253
Lima, David 246
Lincourt, Raoul 293
Lindgren, Bruce 103

Lindhal, Kay 46
Lindham, Charles 252
Lindner, Eileen W...............38
Lindquist, Tonia I..............113
Lindsay, Emery 90
Lindsay, R. Rex 159
Ling, Mary..........................96
Lingle, Mark 236
Linsey, Nathaniel L. 87
LInsinbigler, Harry 164
Liolin, Arthur E. 62
Lipps, Robert T. 28
Lipscomb, Joan.................252
Lipscomb, John B..............108
Lisby, Michael 60, 342
Lisherness, Sara................148
Listecki, Jerome E. 81
Little, P...............................93
Little, Vanuel C..................144
Litwin, Paul 254
Liu, Felix 305
Livingston,
  Michael E........38, 129, 326
Llamoso-Songco, Annie 328
Llewellyn, Jim O. 21
Lloyd, Roy...........................22
Lobenstine, Clark 37, 238
Lockard, Christopher..........34
Lockwood, Daniel R...........308
Lofquist, Les..............128, 344
Lofton-Brook, Oliver.........205
Logan, Clark 158
Logsdon, Gary B. 259
Lohre, Kathryn 219
Lohrmann, Marcus C........115
London, Denise...................22
Long, Denise.....................256
Long, Sotello V....................84
Looper, Kirk 158
López, Héctor 167
Lopoukhine, Nikita 200
Lopushinsky, Roman 200
Lorah, Ted, Jr. 187
Lorentzen, Paul...................75
Lori, William E....................81
Lorimer, Paul D. 187
Lott, William R..................139
Lotz, Linda 34
Loughran, James..........33, 329
Louttit, Henry, Jr...............107
Love, Jan...........................298
Love, Mary A. 61, 327
Love, Ralph E., Sr. 169
Love-Jones, Vivian..............29
Loveland, Erma Jean 353
Lovett, Sidney.....................42
Lovingood, Vivian 262
Lowe, Asa 130
Lowe, S. L. 92
Lowen, A. Wayne 301
Lowenthal, Robert 266
Lowery, Joseph Echols 35
Loy, David 241

Lucco, Richard 111
Lucero, Karina 22
Ludwig, Koloman K. 168
Ludwig, Robert A 306
Luebbert, Karen 250
Luedtke, Joel.....................249
Luginbill, Betty..................29
Luginbuhl, David........53, 205
Luguin, Manuel 65
Luke (Father).....................338
Lumpkin, Ramona 319
Lundgren, Dean A.............111
Lundgren, Jim....................33
Lundin, Jack 46
Lundquist, Stella...............249
Lundy, Sarah E. 94
Lunich, Nedeljko 338
Lutes, Christopher 333
Luthy, David 199, 347
Luttrell, Bill 205
Luz, David W.....................156
Luzano, Christine 40
Lyght, Ernest S 170, 171
Lykins, Terry 130
Lyle, Charles....................183
Lyle, Dennis J 308, 315
Lyles, J. H., Jr....................92
Lynch, Damon, III 257
Lyons, Arthur 45
Lyons, Deborah.................145
Lyons, Marsha 28
Lysyj, Anatol...........................

MacAdam, Murray 346
MacArthur, Sharon 167
MacDermid, Gordon E 322
MacDonald,
    Mark. 107, 108, 233
MacDonald, Tim................238
MacDonald, Timothy...........33
Mack, Karen 259
Mack, Paget 70
MacKenzie, Daryl............192
MacKenzie, Margaret 56
Mackey, Bill F. 159
Mackin, Eileen...................31
Mackin, Paddy 267
Macklin, J. W.....................92
Macklin, Jerry...................42
Mackoul, Anne Glynn 47
MacLagan, Lynn................245
MacMillan, Clare..............191
MacMillan, Patricia
    Dwyer............................260
Macnie, Peggy 263
MacPherson, D. Bruce.......109
MacPherson, Damian 293
Maddo, Robert 238
Madison, Carol 330
Madison, S. C. 169, 170
Maggs, Robert W., Jr. 148
Magie, Sandra...................315

Magnus, Brian 206
Magnus, Paul 53
Magnus, Richard
    A., Jr. 113
Mahe, Sally 46
Maher, Philip 56
Maheras, John...................246
Mahlay, Ihor 164
Mahlman, Margaret 174
Maier, Paul L. 133
Main, A. Donald 115
Main, Donald.............261, 262
Makarenko, William 351
Maki, Lynn I. 208
Malayang, José A 167
Malcolm, Barbara 236
Malcolm, W. R. Matt........163
Maldonado, Luis Fernando
    Hoyos 187
Malenge, Zablon Isaac 121
Maleske, A. 198
Malherbe, Jean-
    François 322
Malinovic, Mirko..............205
Mallinak, John 339
Malloy, David 80
Maly, Milton 325
Manahan, Ron...................118
Manahan,
    Ronald E.................119, 302
Manes, John 97
Mangassarian, Silva...........182
Manis, H. Lee 22
Manly, Frances 254
Mann, David 136
Mann, Gayle 241
Mann, Stuart 345
Manning, Donald 144
Manning, Robert...............316
Mannoia, Kevin W.............31
Manon, John C...................117
Mansholt, Gerald L...........114
Mansur, Mary 338
Mantha, Ray 56
Manz, John R....................81
Manz, Kevin 167
Mapson, Charlrean B.........61
Maracle, John E..................73
Marangos, Frank 126
Marani, Samson 121
Al Marayati, Salam...........227
Marceil, Christopher.........268
Mardirossian, Moushegh 71
Mardoian, Jack 71
Marek, James 173
Marini, Christine................84
Marks, Kirk 110
Markuly, Mark S...............312
Markus, Carol O. 48
Marquardt, Kami L...........258
Marrin, Patrick...................326
Marsh, Fred.......................337

Marsh, Jack 257
Marshall, Jay Wade...........301
Marshall, Molly T..............298
Marshall, Paul.............53, 107
Martens, Ed.......................195
Martensen, Jean 27
Martin, Clyde....................173
Martin, J. Bruce 153
Martin, J. Dwayne 265
Martin, John A...................308
Martin, John T. 191
Martin, Joseph 263
Martin, Joyce Emery 148
Martin, Marty 329
Martin, Paul E....................66
Martin, Paul H...................173
Martinez, Joel N. 171
Martinez, Margarita 115
Martino, Joseph 261
Martinson, Bradley 98
Marvel, Misha...................252
Marx, Robert......................34
Masliuk, Stephen 164
Maslo, William 262
Mason, Debra 44
Mason, Donald E...............239
Mason, Frederick A............31
Mason, H. Lee 340
Mason, Larry D. 64
Massey, Anthony 259
Massey, Frank 121
Massey, Stephen K 66
Mast, Gregg A. 308
Masters, Mary 254
Mathai, Anish 47
Mathes, James R...............108
Mathew, T. A....................135
Mathew, Thomson K. 309
Mathewes, Charles T. 333
Mathews, George..............126
Mathews, Michael 122
Mathies, Ronald J. R. 36
Matiz, Jose Ruben
    Garcia 186
Matoon, Gordon 240
Matson, Louise 248
Matthew, Frank, Sr. 137
Matthew, Lamar 121
Matthews, Daniel Paul 40
Matthews, F.
    Clayton 106, 107
Matthews, Larry 345
Matthews, Marcus 171
Matthews, Mary..................61
Matthews, Victoria..............31
Mattock, Terry 266
Mattoni, Vincent 255
Mattox, Cynthia.................330
Mattson, Linda...................327
Maturan, Zenaida................47
Matusiak, John...........143, 338
Mauney, James F................115
Maus, Janet 162

INDEX

427

Maxim (Bishop)................156
Maximos (Metropolitan) ...125
Maxwell, Anita 264
Maxwell, Laurie 235
May, David G. 246
May, Nareth 87
May, Thomas R. 37
Mayan, Ralph 54
Maye, James A. 100
Maynard, J. L....................92
Mays, Rod........................147
Maze, Larry E...................107
Mazur, Francis X. 254
Mbachi, Charles................121
Mbato, Hannington............121
McAdam, Kerry................120
McAlister, John.................347
McAlister, Lorne D...........200
McAllister-Wilson,
    David F.......................316
McAnally, Ben..................148
McBride, Larry 243
McCaffrey, Renée
    Roeder 254
McCain, Jacquelyn B.168, 169
McCallister, Cline.............131
McCandless,
    Christopher............120, 266
McCann, Jeff 45
McCardle, Jody.................248
McCarty, Vince S..............142
McClain, Gene....................65
McClesky, J. Lawrence......171
McCloskey, Pat.................341
McCloud, E. Earl................59
McCloud, E. Earle, Jr. 30
McClure, George 121
McCoid,
    Donald 31, 113, 115
McColgin, Linda................252
McCombs, Jerry L..............61
McConnell, Alvester.........169
McCool, Marilyn 99
McCormack, Alan.............203
McCormick, Pat................302
McCown, Sue 264
McCoy, Clinton 148, 255
McCoy, Glenda.................265
McCoy, James E 60
McCoy, Marcus 101
McCoy, Myron F 311
McCray, Trinette V. 65
McCreary, Glenn 262
McCreory, Leroy 129
McCullough, John L...........39
McDermott, Pat 243
McDonald, Carol 148
McDonald, Jamey S. 183
McDonald, Jeff 344
McDonald, Lee M. 317
McDonald, Lora 242
McDonald, Malcom...........259
McDonnell, Carol 241

McDonough, Linda............123
McDowell, Leon A. 144
McFadden, Wendy..............89
McFarland, James K..........153
McFarlane, Dorothy 61
McGibbon, Carol Ann 45
McGinnis, Pat 156
McGinnis, Robert
    S., Jr................................133
McGlynn, Sheilagh..............55
McGough, Nancy 345
McGrath, J. 292
McGrattan, William T 321
McGregor, John 350
McGuire, Damaris 255
McGuire, G.
    Dennis 93, 189
McHugh, Matthew 26
McIntosh, Kenneth W 265
McJunkin, James E., Jr.......64
McKain, George E., II 61
McKay, Ginger 173
McKee, Joan 240
McKelvey, Jack M.............108
McKenzie, Vashti
    Murphy 59
McKernan, Leo 262
McKinney, Brent 120
McKinney, G. D. 92
McKinney, William 309
McKinnon, Patricia...........349
McKnight, James E. 94
McKnight, John 22
McLarty, Alan 168
McLaughlin, Roy L. 77
McLaughlin, Scott 109
McLaughlin, Scott E..........300
McMahill, David 168
McManus, Robert J. 81
McMillan, John.................322
McMillan, Susan...............205
McMillon, Lynn 326
McMullen, Shawn 334
McMurray, Robert 144
McNair, David C. 36
McNally, Beverly 251
McNamara, Dexter 235
McNamara, Mary 26
McNeil, J. E.......................27
McNish, Mary Ellen 23
McPhail, Paul 197
McQueen, Arpie 324
McSwain, Laurin M. 21
McVay, John K 314
McWain, Bonnie 237
Meade, Kenneth..................84
Meador, Prentice A., Jr......323
Meagher, Timothy 357
Mean, John D. 208
Mecham, Marilyn P. 250
Medders, David S 317
Medenwald, Greg 77
Medinger, Daniel L............326

Medley, A. Roy 64
Medsker, Bekki.................162
Meier, Gordon F..................87
Meisner, Lorne..................184
Mekhsian, Sipan 337
Melbourne, Bertram 304
Melchizedek (Mar) 127
Mellis, John 320
Melton, David...........218, 297
Mendenhall, Laura S. 299
Mendez, Jose Manuel 137
Mendoza, Salvador 42
Mengel, Gail 29
Menning, Bruce 151, 202
Meno, John 161
Menter, William 166
Mentzer, Steve 260
Mercer, Amy 244
Mercer, Larry....................298
Merrill, A. Roger 97
Merrill, John 66
Merrill, Nancy 26
Meschisen, Eugene 164
Meschisen, Mark 165
Mesiti, Martha 43
Mesner, Neil 121
Messer, Tom......................314
Messiah, Wilfred
    Jacobus 59
Messina, Carol 137
Methodios
    (Metropolitan) 125
Metzger, Laura 243
Meunch, David 134
Meyer, Cheryl 209
Meyer, Dale A...................299
Meyer, Donald L........111, 329
Meyer, Mary C. 338
Meyer, Paul 248
Meyer, Ron 117
Meyer, Russell L................238
Meyer, William 116
Mgonja, Assah E.................47
Micevych, Paul..................164
Mich, Marvin 254
Micon, Joseph 241
Middleton, Bill 264
Middleton, Jane Allen.......170
Miericke, Kurt A...............111
Mikovsky,
    Anthony..................146, 331
Miles, Ray..........................84
Millar, Len 205
Millay, James I..................326
Miller, Alan C. 168
Miller, Carol 238
Miller, Charles S................113
Miller, Claude E. W..........181
Miller, David 27, 61
Miller, G. 92
Miller, Gene E...................168
Miller, George...........110, 300
Miller, John U...................252

428

Miller, Joy Ann 323
Miller, Kathleen 293
Miller, Keith 111
Miller, Kit 239
Miller, Kristin 354
Miller, Lauren E 318
Miller, Lee M....................115
Miller, Len 205
Miller, Marcus J................306
Miller, Mark 167
Miller, Myron P 311
Miller, Paul L..............77, 325
Miller, Peter 253
Miller, Rick 103
Miller, Roman J. 339
Miller, Steven A................108
Miller, Susan Fisher..........336
Miller, Ted 239
Milliken, Paul 264
Milliken, Richard D..........308
Mills, Charles 343
Mills, Earl E. 102
Mills, Wes 182
Miloro, Frank P 65
Milsap, Cynthia 45
Minch, Jack N...................335
Ming, Wayman C., Jr.........144
Minnix, Janet 119
Minor, Marlene 141
Miranda, Jesse 73
Mirchuk, Nadia.................164
Mirek, Art 66
Mirkovich, Joseph A...........94
Miscamble, Wilson 307
Mishler, James W...............258
Missick, Glen 151
Mitchell, Christine 52
Mitchell, Lisa H..........37, 246
Mitchell, Lois P.................193
Mitchem, Susan 358
Mitrophan (Bishop) 156
Mittman, F. Russell............168
Mobley, Jeane 117
Mobley, John P. 83
Mock, George 246
Moerman, Murray.............292
Moes, D. 347
Moffett, Marilyn 241
Mogabgab, John S. 344
Mogenson, Cris.................252
Mohler, R. Albert, Jr. 313
Mojica, Miguel 96, 190
Moldstad, John A..............116
Molyneux, John 343
Moncher, Gary............94, 189
Monroe, Bill 76
Monroe, Kenneth 60
Monson, Thomas S.............97
Montanez, Jose D 189
Monteith, Fred 208
Montgomery, Charles 61
Montgomery,
    Kathleen C.....................165

Montgomery, Richard 235
Montgomery, Robert..........233
Mood, Jacques 140
Moody, C. L........................92
Moody, Robert M. 108
Moon, Angelia 264
Moon, Hyung J. 87
Mooney, Paul 172
Moore, Clark......................265
Moore, Donna J. 258
Moore, Douglas 200
Moore, Hugh 240
Moore, Kenneth W. 84
Moore, Larry J. 175
Moore, Marvin...................341
Moore, P. J.........................104
Moore, Robert A.........94, 189
Moore, Willis 238
Moorhead, James H............334
Moorjani-Vaswani,
    Shakuntala 46
Morales, Bernardo 166
Morales, Lillian 260
Moreau, Dorylas 203
Moreno, Rene 110
Moretz, Lawrence 155
Morgan, Donn F..................299
Morgan, Gerald.................247
Morgan, John 302
Morgan, Robert..................166
Morgester, Mike 259
Morin, Darci 241
Morissette, Pierre 203
Morris, Calvin S. 239
Morris, John......................304
Morris, Tracy.....................350
Morrison, Ronald J. 87
Morrison, William
    C., Jr. 84
Morrow, William 42
Morrow, William D. 200
Morse, Daniel R. 152
Mortelliti, David 197
Morton, Cristopher 249
Morton, Darrell D. 113
Morton, Kama....................250
Morton, Karon 33
Morton, Raymond E. 153
Mosaad, Mohamed 46
Moses, Tom 95
Mosley, Steve 264
Mostert, Thomas J., Jr. 157
Moulton, Geoff 347
Moultrie, Henry A., II........100
Moury, Fred 111
Mouw, Richard J..........31, 302
Mowatt, Ann 56
Moxham, John 264
Moyer, Bruce 110, 315
Moyer, David 168
Mphahlele, Louis 75
Muchow, Donald 134
Mueller, Craig 35

Mueller, Wayne D..............176
Mufarrij, Alexander 67
Muganda, Baraka G...........157
Mukulu, Andrew................121
Mulama, David A. 121
Mulama, Joseph
    Anyonge 121
Mulder, Gary.......................88
Mullan, Donald W. 186, 350
Mullen, David G................114
Muller, Marilyn.................350
Mulongo, Andrew
    Namasaka 121
Mulvaney, Elizabeth 262
Munday, Robert S 308
Munk, D.............................318
Munro, Victor 293
Muravski, A. 200
Murdoch, John 38
Murdy, Peter 104
Murphy, D. J. 293
Murphy, Thomas........336, 339
Murphy, Tom 136
Murphy, Warren 268
Murray, Edward J. 40
Murray, George W. 298
Murray, Harold 55
Murray, Michele 52
Murray, Sue 253
Murray, Yolanda 254
Musindi, Meschack...........121
Musoke-Lubega,
    Benjamin 39
Mussa, Joan 48
Musungu, Philip 121
Mutoigo, Ida Kaastra 88
Mutti, Albert F. 30
Muyskens, Samuel.......37, 242
Muzingo, Cathy 145
Mwanzi, Solomon..............121
Myers, Jerry 66
Myers, John J......................81
Myers, Mark 145
Myers, Richard N. 253
Myers-Wirt, Cathy 84

Nadasdy, Dean W...............133
Naff, Stephen 123
Nafzger, Samuel 134
Nahoolewa, Connie 265
Naik, Deepak 46
Nakonachny, John.............164
Namasaka, Andrew............121
Namwembe, Despina..........46
Nance, Cynthia 34
Naten, Loyd L....................144
Nauenburg, Hilda...............187
Navarre, Joy Sorensen 248
Neal, Carl J. 100
Neal, Joseph C., Jr. 86
Neal, Ricardo 245
Neale, Archie 122

INDEX

429

Nectaria (Nun) 340
Nederveen, G. 185
Neelands, David 322
Neely, Constance D. 247
Nees, Tom 99
Neevel, Mary Ann 268
Neff, David 30
Neils, Michael....................234
Nelson, Beter T. 70
Nelson, Christine L............260
Nelson, Daniel 129
Nelson, Dean W. 114
Nelson, Elden K. 74
Nelson, Gart.......................185
Nelson, J. Herbert 34
Nelson, Jerome O...............111
Nelson, Jodi 248
Nelson, Judy 194
Nelson, Kim Beyer 251
Nelson, Russell M. 97
Nelson, Sara......................248
Nelson, Saundra.................129
Nelson, Steven L. 268
Nemkovich,
    Robert M 146, 312
Nenson, Daniel 204
Nesdahl, Gary 263
Nesmith, Virginia.................39
Netterfield, Cal 184
Nettleton, Minot B.............237
Neufeld, John......................52
Neufeld, Wladie 320
Neuhaus, Richard J............331
Newcomer, Audrey 25
Newhouse, Herbert 149
Newland, Terry 148
Newport, Leroy 78, 79
Newton, Alan 64
Newton, Douglas M 334
N'goma, Joyce 46
Ngoya, John 121
Nguyen, Tai Anh..................88
Nicholas
    (Metropolitan) 125
Nicholas, David 312
Nicholovos, Zachariah
    Mar 135
Nichols, John D. 189
Nichols, Terrence L..............88
Nicholson, Betty 123
Nickleson, Isaac.................240
Nicodemus, Eugene J. 36
Nicoll, Niel 48
Niederauer, George H.........81
Nielsen, Nancy 46
Nielson, E. Kenneth............33
Nielson, Niel 147
Nieto, Amelia.....................235
Nieuwsma, Virginia 332
Nikkel, Lynn 159
Niles, Dennis D. 314
Nippak, Ivar 193
Niswender, Joy 253

Nix, Lan 263
Nixon, Samuel 150
Njegovan, James D............180
Noble, Kathy......................333
Noesner, Pam 268
Noffsinger, Stanley J. 38, 89
Nolan, Michael 124
Noland, Martin 134, 355
Nolan-Elliason, Megan......248
Nolde, Nancy L. 261
Noli, Fan Stylian.................62
Nolla, Ormara 47
Nolson, Stanley.................113
Nordhem, Paula 248
Nordtredt, Joel 98, 306
Norlin, Dennis A.................23
Norman, Clarence 105
Norris, Alfred L. 171
Norris, Jeffrey A. 88
Norris, Larry R...................102
Norris, Richard Franklin.....59
Nortness, Michal................266
Norton, Jon 253, 255
Norton, Larry 264
Norton, Timothy A. 36, 342
Norwood, Matthew A........100
Novak, Mark A...................111
Novecosky, Peter 204, 349
Nunes, John A......................36
Nunn, Harry, Sr...................73
Nusbaum, E. J....................147
Nusca, A. Robert 321
Nyenzo, Evans ....

Oakes, Gwyn 172
Oakes, Ronald L 298
Oaks, Dallin H. 97
Oancea,
    David 155, 204, 342
Oates, Lonnie F...................84
Obengerger, Glenn 116
Ochoa-Krueger, Ninfa 264
O'Connor, Elizabeth 334
Odams, John 245
Odegaard, Edward 90
Odhner, Carroll C 358
Odom, Elzie 264
O'Donnell, Frances............358
O'Farrell, Mark T. 88, 314
O'Flaherty, Edward 246
Ogilvie, Kevin A................319
Ogles, Jerry L. 324
Oguma, Joseph Lavuna 121
O'Hara, John......................26
O'Hara, Karen 254
O'Hara, Robert J. 261
Ohl, C. Wallis, Jr...............108
Ohotin, Nicholas A............155
Ojeda-Carcamo, Sergio 301
O'Keefe, Mark 311
Oldham, Roger S. 158
Olekshy, Ovest...................200

Olinger, Danny E...............337
Oliver, Lon D......................24
Oliver, Willie B...................153
Olmsted, Thomas J. 81
Olsen, Donald P. 137
Olsen, G. James 248
Olsen, Rob 29
Olsen, Ron 208
Olson, Norman A...............324
Olszewski, Brian T. 325
Olubalang, Alan A. 66
Omland, Richard R. 113
O'Neill, Jerry F..........153, 310
O'Neill, Patrick H..............301
O'Neill, Robert J. 107
Onyewuchi, Rufus 292
Oommen, Joseph 135
Oosting, Ken 316
Orians, Thomas...................33
Osborn, Kenneth W. 157
Osborne, Brenda 66
Osborne, Fred C 319
Osborne, Linda 268
Osodo, Lam Kisanya 121
Ottenhoff, Don B. 217
Otterson, Michael 97
Otzelberger, E. Ann 140
Oubre, Sinclair....................34
Ough, Bruce R....................170
Ousley, S. Todd..................107
Oussoren, Harry 208
Owen, David L 309
Owen, Dean 48
Owen, Joe 140
Owen, John 63
Owen, Moses 137
Owen, Timothy P. 87
Owens, C. D. 92
Owens, Thomas M., Sr. 342
Oyando, Gilbert
    Akenga 121
Oyster, Lisa A. 257

Paarlberg, John 41
Pace, Diane 332
Packard, George.................106
Packer, Boyd K....................97
Padilla, Rafael Malpica......113
Paez, Leticia 48
Pagán, Samuel 312
Pagano, Nicholas 22
Palmberg, Glenn R............111
Palmer, Floyd 259
Palmer, Gregory V. 170
Palmer, John M...................72
Palmer, Michael 310
Palmer, Robert M 68
Palmer, Susan L. 352
Palmieri, Paul 97
Papagermanos,
    Stavros H........................338
Papazian, Iris 338

Paperini, Richard 307
Pappas, Anthony 64
Paprocki, Thomas................25
Paquette, Mario................203
Parchia, Earl 144
Parish, Donny 77
Park, Jeremiah J.................171
Park, Michael....................157
Parke, Jim 266
Parker, George Lee 84
Parker, Jane 242
Parker, Rebecca 313
Parker, Ronald L................84
Parker, William 153
Parker, William J. 334
Parkin, Bonnie D. 97
Parkins, Richard 106
Parkinson, Ward................195
Parks, J. H.........................95
Parkyn, David I..................111
Parr, Jeb 266
Parrish, Walter L. ....II, 65
Parrott, Rod......................236
Parry, Walter P. 234
Parshall, Janet 40
Parsley, Henry N., Jr.........107
Parson, Robert G. 201
Parsons, Gradye 148
Parsons, Reginald 148
Pasbrig, Robert 176
Paslay, Mormon R............172
Pastukhiv, Serhij K...........127
Pate, Catherine..................347
Patterson, J. O., Jr..............92
Patterson, L. Dale 356
Patterson, Paige 313
Patterson, Tom....................74
Pattillo, Wesley M. 39
Patton, Marcia....................64
Patton, Vince....................342
Patzer, Jere D....................157
Paul-Cook, Megan 249
Paulsen, Jan 157
Paulsen, Vivian 331
Paulson, Bob.....................329
Paup, Edward W. 172
Pavichevich, Dennis 157
Payne, Aleta 256
Payne, James T. 152
Payne, Margaret G............115
Pearce, Paul 184
Pears, George S. 93
Pearson, Jean 248
Pearson, John..............24, 28
Pediso, Marlene 121
Pediso, Steve.....................121
Pelavin, Mark 34
Pell, Archie 52
Pellechia,
    James N. 132, 198
Pelles, Rosalyn 34
Pelley, Barry D. 201
Pena, Carlos F. 113

Pence, Jerry G....................175
Pendergast, Arthur J...........293
Penfield, Jack....................237
Penner, A. F. (Bud) 183
Penner, Brigitte 349
Penner, David 195
Penner, Rick........................53
Penner, Ron 195, 318
Pennings, Kenneth 268
Pennywell, Clarence C. 138
Penrose, Christina B. 62
Peoples, David 150
Pepe, Joseph A....................81
Peper, Mike.........................76
Peplowski, Thaddeus S......146
Pepper, Donald R................36
Pepper, Gail 261
Perkins, D. Clay................310
Perkins, James C...............150
Perkins, Joseph 295
Perkins, Larry 320
Perkins, Loveleen "Dee" 61
Perkins, William T.............307
Perkins-Hughes, Vera 169
Perman, Lauri 120
Perpener, A. 92
Perrin, Clive......................237
Perry, Joseph N....................80
Perry, L. Tom 97
Perry, Roger 237
Perry, Troy D.....................174
Perschbacher, Gerald 335
Persell, William D. 107
Persson, Bertil.....................70
Peterkin, Valerie................237
Peters, Arthur 259
Peters, Donald 36, 54
Peters, Judith.....................258
Peters, Marshall 64
Peters, Samuel R., Sr. 100
Peterson, Brian 30
Peterson, Curtis D.............112
Peterson, David....................38
Peterson, Duane A. 355
Peterson, Jay.....................250
Peterson, Jeanie 266
Peterson, Kathleen 252
Peterson, Rohn....................65
Peterson, Roland 112
Peterson, Timothy 351
Peterson, Timothy J. 196
Peterson, Wendy 53
Petersoo, Udo 193, 347
Petitt, Charles W 309
Petlak, Michael 164
Petrie, Lou 76
Petro, John G.....................297
Petrochuk, Sherrie 257
Petroff, Valerie....................50
Pettit, Kim A.....................333
Peucker, Paul 356
Pfortmiller, Sandra.............337
Phelan, John E., Jr......111, 308

Phillips, Annie Lee 255
Phillips, Aubrey 193
Phillips, Carole 185
Phillips, David J. 87
Phillips, Donald D. 181
Phillips, Stephen 103
Phillips, Sue Watlov..........248
Phipps, Ron 136, 137
Pickard, Joe.......................159
Piehler, David 134
Pierce, David 318
Pierce, Garland 38
Pierce, Glen A...................353
Pierce, Leslie 104
Pierce, R. W......................200
Pierre, Louis Marcel 75
Piescik, Joseph..................237
Pihach, Dennis 200
Piita, Vaieli Fuiono 47
Pile, Gregory R..................115
Pimentel, Serafin 100
Pinkett, Leo........................86
Pinson, J. Matthew 302
Pinson, Mathew 138
Pipes, Carol......................338
Pishko, Daria 164
Pitman, Cyrus C. J............181
Pitt, Benjamin A................144
Pittman, Wallace B., Jr. 145
Pitts, Clifford R. 169
Pitts, Tyrone S. 47, 150
Plantinga, Cornelius, Jr.....298
Platt, Allyson D..................246
Poandl, Robert 32
Poe, James 24
Poesnecker, Gerald E..........96
Pohl, Curtis 134
Pohl, Faye 41
Poirier, Jim.......................192
Poist, William 62
Poitier, Annette 47
Polding, M. Fred..................87
Polite, William 153
Pollema, Vernon................152
Pollesel, Michael F. 180
Polston, Jimmy 156
Pomeroy, Betty 252
Pomykal, Janet..................174
Poole, Philip 43
Pooler, David 242
Poon, Abraham H. 88
Pope, Deidre 248
Pope, Janet 267
Pope, Kenneth.....................66
Popoff, Dmitri E. (Jim)......348
Popovich, Edward..............122
Popp, Nathaniel 155, 204
Porch, James M. 159
Porter, Jerry D.....................99
Porter, John 121
Porter, Stanley E................319
Porterfield, Amanda...........327
Poss, Sue Harper................328

INDEX

431

Posterski, Don......................56
Posthumus, Peter 150
Potter, Jim..........................192
Potterveld, Riess W...........305
Powell, Christopher............78
Powell, F. Neff..................108
Powell, George H. 192
Powell, James L....................83
Powell, Jerry 145
Powell, Joel........................145
Powell, Joseph 153
Powell, Raymond, Sr. 98
Powell, S. J. 92
Powers, Diane.............38, 266
Prachar, T. 198
Preheim, Rich 355
Preheim-Bartel, Dean 240
Prendergast, Terrence 204
Presler, Titus L..................301
Price, Donald R. 63
Price, Ellen W....................43
Price, R. 169
Price, Shane 150
Priest, Catherine 294
Primavera, Wendy.............252
Priniski, Mary 34
Prior, Joseph G. 310
Pritchett, Wayne.........205, 321
Privett, John E....................181
Probus, Lawrence 48
Proctor, Matt 309
Proffitt, Kevin 355
Propes, M. Thomas.............190
Prosser, Robert...................105
Provance, Terry...................41
Pruter, Karl 81
Pue, Carson 53
Puglisi, Amy 262
Pugsley, John W..................37
Pulins, Juris.......................132
Pullen, Kristy Arneson 63
Puni, Erika 157
Puryear, Richard 259
Pusateri, John.....................259
Putman, Bob 325
Pyles, Franklin ....

Quackenbush, David..........197
Quay, Ronald 239
Quello, Julie......................249
Quessy, Herve L. 141
Quevedo, Jose Moises
    Moncada........................187
Quick, Braaley 123
Quiett, Harry V. 174
Quinn, John 197, 348
Quinn, Thomas 31
Quirog, Bonifacio 46

Rabenold, Nelson 260
Raccah, William 318

Radius, Lesley M...............239
Radtke, Robert 107
Ragsdale, John 111
Rainer, Thomas 159
Raines, James Ray 77
Ralph, Karen 292
Ralston, Darwin 257
Ramos, David 22
Ramos-Orench,
    Wilfrido 107
Ramos-Scharron,
    Francis R. 113
Ramphal, Dwarka 145
Ramsay, John 205
Ramsden, Pamela 106
Ramseth, Mark R..............314
Ramsey, Ron 101
Randall, Mike 324, 325
Randall, R. Irene...............250
Randels, J. Richard 244
Rankin, Jerry A..................159
Rankin, Nancy 234
Ransom, Robert 136
Ranum, Mary S................113
Rasell, Edith 34
Rassmussen, Philip 348
Rathbun, Peter 22
Ratliff, James 64
Ravenell, Joseph P. 251
Ray, Keith H 305
Raymond, Jonathan S 321
Read, Glenn 256
Read, James 53
Realpe, Marcelo..................88
Reaney, Dwayne 197
Rebeck, Victoria A..............24
Redal, R. H. 104, 301
Redd, Eugene....................144
Reddick, Lawrence
    L., III 87
Reddig, Jill S. 328
Reddin, George 77
Redekopp, Alf...........348, 359
Redhead, Bob 205
Reed, J. George.................256
Reed, Jeremiah 144
Reed, Michael B...........69, 70
Reed, Millard 314
Reed, Rodger Hall, Sr........238
Reeder, Allen R.................340
Reese, Jack R....................295
Reese, John D. 323
Reese, Ron 101
Reese, Rosemary 262
Reeves, Justus Y. 336
Reeves, Steve......................63
Regan, Tom.......................292
Regier, Rob 53
Regnier, Julie 48
Rehling, Tom 167
Reichter, Arlo R..................65
Reid, Gail..........................347
Reid, Joyce A......................61

Reid, Sharmaine R.............201
Reid-MacNevin, Susan........54
Reierson, Gary B. 248, 249
Reimer, Gerald..................195
Reinert, Peter 238
Reinheimer, Larry.............200
Reist, L. "Gere"
    Fitzgerald, II 170
Reiter, Steven J. 111
Reithmaier, Jan 31
Reithmaier, Paul 31
Remalt, Theodore J............337
Rempel, Ron 136
Rempel, Valerie 124
Rempel-Burkholder,
    Byron...................340, 348
Rendall, Joanne 39
Renick, Nancy 45
Retzer, Gordon L. 157
Retzman, Alan 196
Revell, John 341
Revis, Charles.....................64
Reyes, Emilio 22
Reyes, José, Sr..................190
Reynolds, Kristine 248
Reynolds, Paul V. 208
Rhéaume, Serge 50
Rhoads, Armen O. 176
Rhoden, H. Robert..............72
Rhodes, Arthur D........93, 189
Rhodes, Schuyler 35
Rice, Gene D. 94, 190
Rich, Arabella 150
Richard, Thomas M. 137
Richards, Carmen K. 113
Richards, Jack 168
Richards, Mrs. Stephen 184
Richardson, Adam
    Jefferson, Jr. 59
Richardson, John M............84
Richardson, Melvin 257
Richardson, Ralph 53, 192
Richardson, Wendell...........75
Richert, Jean 237
Riches, Leonard 152
Riddick, Jessie M. 61
Ridings, Dean 30
Rieb, Stanley.....................344
Rieley-Goddard,
    Catherine 253
Riemenschneider, Dan.......136
Ries, Thomas 134
Rigali, Justin 81
Riggs, Jennifer 39
Riley, Adele M....................61
Riley, E. Roy.............113, 115
Riley, Meg 34
Rinehart, Neil 136
Rist, Boyd C. 45
Ritchie, Tracy 259
Ritts, Kerry R. 149
Rivera-Rosa, Rafael............84
Rizzo, Janice.....................341

Robben, Jerome 187
Robbins, Earldean V. S......148
Roberson, James T., Jr. 312
Roberson, Joseph 39
Roberts, Edward 144
Roberts, James P., Jr. 132
Roberts, Mark E. 354
Roberts, R. Philip 307
Roberts, Sharon 22
Roberts, Tom 337
Robertson, C. C. 139
Robertson, Charles 106
Robertson, Cory................46
Robertson,
    Creighton L. 108
Robertson, Terry M. 159
Robertson, William 341
Robey, Connie 266
Robins, Roger 356
Robinson, Barbara A. 252
Robinson, Dave 325
Robinson, David 122, 123
Robinson, Densimore 140
Robinson, Ellen 292
Robinson, John 94
Robinson, Joyce.................244
Robinson, Judith 180
Robinson, Julian B. 93, 189
Robinson, Kenneth N. 102
Robinson, Kenneth
    O., Sr. 168, 169
Robinson, Laurie
    Oswald........................342
Robinson, Paul..................248
Robinson, Robert H..........120
Robinson, Thomas 265
Robinson, Thomas E. 148
Robinson, Tommy...............78
Robinson, V. Gene 108
Robinson-Rumble,
    Beverly J. 333
Roblyer, Kathy..................331
Rochon, Igumen Irenee 200
Rockwell, David 252
Rockwood, Perry F............348
Rodgers, Bob 158
Rodgers, Darrin 332, 352
Rodriguez, Edwin
    Quiles 148
Rodriguez, Placido 81
Rodriguez-Villa, Jorge 141
Roebuck,
    David G...........94, 190, 356
Roegner, Robert................134
Roehl, Ronald 98
Roehl, Shirley 330
Rogelstad, David 185
Rogers, Huie 79
Rogers, Laura M................256
Rogers, Scott....................256
Rogers-Witte, Cally 167
Rogness, Matthew 98
Rogness, Peter 114

Rohlfs, Steven P................307
Roland, David 110, 119
Roland, John 262
Rolf, Kathy 240
Rolheiser, Ronald 309
Roller, John 335
Rollins, Richard A. 138
Rollins, Robert L. 169
Romero, Carlos 136
Romero, Daniel F..............167
Romero-Palma,
    Sylvestre 107
Ronsvalle, John L. 216
Ronsvalle, Sylvia 216
Roof, Joe 118
Roozen, David A. 216
Rorie, Stephen 267
Rosario, Luis....................168
Rosco, Michael 328
Roscover, Norma 254
Rose, Donald L..................337
Rose, J. Hugh....................172
Rose, Jonathan 46
Rose, Whaid......................96
Rosen, Janice....................359
Rosengarten, Richard A.....314
Rosier, Bob 268
Roso, Henry A.
    (Hank)....................110, 330
Ross, Eugene 167
Ross, Kent........................334
Ross, Mary Jane 216
Ross, Nan 21
Ross, Patricia 233
Rost, Nori 174
Rostan, June......................23
Rostand, Dean J. 346
Roth, Adam 258
Roth, John D.....................336
Rottenberg, John 27
Rottino, Kathleen..............140
Rourk, David C...................94
Rourke, Marguerite...........239
Rouse, Michael 34
Roussin, Raymond.............204
Routledge, Donald 292
Rowell, Jeren 339
Rowley, Robert D., Jr. 108
Roy, Marie-Michèle 347
Royster, Bill 168
Royster, Carl 26
Rozeboom, John A. 88
Rubeck, Dustin
    "Dusty".........................300
Rubin, Fred 100
Ruble, Randall T. 301
Rucker, Jaqueline P.........259
Ruffin, Jeff 98
Ruge, Mark 198
Rundbraaten, Edwin 191
Rundell, Jay 307
Rupe, Jolene 306
Rupp, Alan 118

Rusch, Willam G. 31
Rusche, Brian A.........248, 249
Rush, Betty 257
Rush, Henry 235
Rush, Patricia 255
Rush, Robert D. 104
Russell, Al........................331
Russell, Dorothy 41
Russell, Gary E..................88
Russell, Howard 130
Russell, Keith A................295
Russell, Robin...................343
Russell, Rollin 256
Rust, Harold...............191, 317
Ruth, Gary 22
Rutherford, F. Thomas.......187
Rutland, Mark 313
Rutzler, John 264
Ruyle, Ronald 130
Ryan, Bridget 248
Rydman, Philip 25, 350
Ryoo, Keihwan 343
Ryskamp, Andrew..............88
Rystephanuk, David..........200
Ryzy, Emigidiusz H............70

Saenz, Agnes....................245
Sage, Russell.....................256
Salge, Carol 241
Saliba, Philip 66, 67, 181
Salmon, Edward L., Jr. 108
Salo, Kim 321
Saltzman, Russell E...........331
Salvas, M. Sylvain.............203
Samra, Cal 334
Samuel, Lloyd U. 69, 70
Samuels, T. W...................140
Sanchagrin, Kenneth M. 32
Sande, Jonathan M. 121
Sanders, Bill 243
Sanders, Chris 34
Sanders, Hiram 308
Sanders, Kay 242
Sanders, Robert L...............100
Sandford, Byron 120
Sandford, Christopher........247
Sandler, Abraham 88
Sandoval, Robert 252
Santiago, Felix 96, 190
Saperstein, David...............229
Sapp, W. David 36
Sarmazian, Yessayi 182
Sarpong, Francis 150
Sartain, J. Peter 81
Sarwa, Andrzej J................187
Satelmajer, Nikolaus 336
Satterfield, Ray 62
Satterlee, Erin S. W. 343
Sauceda, Sam....................268
Sauciur, Vasile 164
Sauls, Stacy F....................107
Saunder, Gwendolyn G......173

Saunders, Willard 144
Savaloja, Timothy D.........300
Savas (Bishop)..................126
Savell, Medrick...............313
Sawatzky, Leonard............195
Sawyer, Luke 28
Sawyer, Rodney J. 112
Saxby, J.............................244
Saxe, Susan......................228
Scales, Michael G.............295
Scar, William 235
Scarfe, Alan 107
Scarpato, John...................259
Schaal, David D.................102
Schaal, Wendell J................36
Schaefer, Beth...................323
Schaer, Marilyn.................199
Schaper, Michael 79
Schellenberg, Rick............317
Schemmel, Wade 168, 257
Schermerhorn, Eunice 260
Schiemant, Donald 122
Schierenbeck, John 98
Schindell, Dal 346
Schipper (Mr.)...................333
Schirta, Myroslav 164
Schlabach, Darrel 136
Schlatter, William R. 69
Schleicher, Andrew J. 337
Schleifer, Jan.....................344
Schlemmer, Douglas...........65
Schlenker, Janet 236
Schlosser, Rick 234
Schmeling, G. R. 296, 335
Schmidgall, Paul.........94, 189
Schmidt,
  Harry 122, 298, 299
Schmidt, Karen 148
Schmidt, Krystin...............120
Schmidt, Roy 134
Schnase, Robert C. 171
Schneider, Bette................267
Schneider, Don C..............157
Schneider, Francis J..........312
Schneider, Richard.............51
Schneider, Theodore F. 115
Schner, Joseph G. 321
Schnurr, Dennis M..............80
Schoder-Ehri, Bill 120
Schoelles, Patricia A..........310
Schoenhals, Floyd M. 114
Schofield, John-David 108
Schofield-Bodt, Brian........237
Schol, John R....................171
Schoonover, Wayne 124
Schori, Katharine
  Jefferts 106
Schorsch, Ismar 304
Schrader, David 192
Schrag, James M................136
Schramm, Richard W........324
Schreiber, John H..............115
Schremp, James 123

Schrock, Simon..................77
Schrock, Wayne 77
Schrodt, Paul......................23
Schubert, Jeffrey 134
Schueddig, Louis C. 21
Schug, Tricia 266
Schulte, Gary 168
Schulte, Raymond...............27
Schulter, Nancy.................251
Schultz, Harvey 117
Schultz, John C..................295
Schultz, Raymond................54
Schultz, Raymond L...........194
Schultz, Ronald..................134
Schultz, Stephen R. 76
Schwarr, Carolyn 265
Schwartz, Beth....................40
Schwich, Kathie
  Bender 113
Scott, Alphonso.................144
Scott, Charles G.................144
Scott, Hopeton 237
Scott, James C., Jr.............129
Scott, Janice 145
Scott, Philip L....................144
Scott, Richard G. 97
Scott, W. Peter 208
Scruggs, Endia 105
Scruton, Gordon P.............109
Scudder-Youth, Edwina......47
Scurry, Frank P..................298
Searle, Don L.....................330
Seater, Robert P.................268
Secola, Cheryl...................248
Segall, Susan.....................266
Seide, Emmanuel..........87, 88
Selby, Richard....................264
Seler, Debby 328
Sellers, Asbury R...............189
Semel, Rita 46
Semore, Garvis 306
Sene, Daniel 239
Senior, Donald 26, 298
Senske, Kurt 134
Seppala, Ivan M...................71
Serapion (Bishop) 323
Seres, Ted...........................50
Sergeva, Yelena.................259
Serratelli, Arthur J. 81
Sessions, Jim.......................34
Sewell, Don 41
Shada, Doug 77
Shaffer, Kenneth M., Jr.......353
Shaffer, Margaret 257
Shaffer, Steve 118
Shah, Ajay.........................225
Shahidi, Munirah 46
Shalman, Charles 254
Shamana, Beverly J............172
Shand, James J..................107
Shanlin, Jeff 202
Shannon, S. E. 98
Sharp, Arthur 137

Sharp, Bill 117
Sharp, Donald 45
Sharp, Stephen 22
Sharpe, Conner 266
Sharpe, Michael........105, 336
Shaver, Ruth 245
Shaw, Barbara L...................61
Shaw, M. Thomas, III 108
Shaw, Milton.....................133
Shaw, Richard 245
Shaw, William J.................139
Shawl, Sallie 266
Shea, William B...................36
Sheard, J. 92
Sheehan, Michael J.............80
Sheffield, Dan 196
Sheie, Myrna J. 113
Sheldon, William A. 89
Shellabarger, Thomas 34
Shelley, Marshall 334
Shellhammer, Destiny.........26
Shelly, Rubel.....................344
Shelton, Don W....................84
Shelton, Tom 137
Shepard, Beverley 120
Shepard, Morgan D. 158
Shepherd, D. A. 200
Sheptak, Stephen 165
Shequel, Sleiman 67
Sherer, Ann Brookshire 171
Sherry, Brian 22
Sherry, Paul 34
Sheveland, Gerald...............76
Shibly, Othman 254
Shields, Janis 23
Shields, Richard...................63
Shiemann, D. 198
Shin, Jacob S......................315
Shinachi, Enoch 121
Shipley, Joseph 84
Shipman, Joan G................261
Shirley, Joanne...................266
Shisanya, Jonathan 121
Shivachi, Nilson 121
Shlensky, Evely Laser 34
Shockley, Howard..............117
Shockley, Nathan 176
Short, Peter B. 206
Showers, Merle 254
Shuman, Maryellen.............262
Shumate, David 89, 266
Sibley, Wallace J..........94, 189
Sickbert, Bryan W..............167
Sides, Richard....................137
Sidner, Art.........................249
Sidorak, Stephen J., Jr. 237
Siebert, Dorothy 347
Siebert, John 55
Siebert, Jon 319
Siepka, Richard W. 298
Sigman, Michael 111
Sigman, Michael W. 110
Signer, Ray 46

Siker, Jeffrey S. 306
Sillings, William
Harrison..........................130
Silvey, James L....................77
Simeon (Bishop)...............162
Simiyu, Benson................121
Simiyu, Maurice 121
Simmons, Blanche.............29
Simms, John A..................294
Simon, Paula.....................268
Simpson, John...................247
Simpson, Susan V. 124
Sinasac, Joseph 346
Sinclair, James H. 206
Sinclair, L. (Aftimios) 127
Singh, Mandit 294
Singh, Manmohan..............232
Singh, Mohinder 46
Singleton, Richard 247
Sinkford, William 165
Sippert, Steve....................334
Sisk, Mark.........................108
Sitaras, Constantine L........126
Sivulich, Stephen 164, 343
Siwko, Yurij......................164
Skeene, Andrea 245
Skidmore, W. Chris 243
Skiles, Joe, Jr. 144
Skiles, Joseph, Sr. 144
Skiles, Neal 88
Sklba, Richard J...................81
Skocypec, Emil 164
Skocypec, Shirley 165
Skrenes, Thomas A............114
Skurla, Laurus...................303
Skylstad, William S. 80
Slauter, James E.................102
Slie, Samuel N. 237
Sloan, John 123
Sly, Margery 148, 354, 357
Small, Hazel.....................185
Small, Heather-Dawn 157
Small, Joseph 148
Smalley, Martha................354
Smedberg, Barry 235
Smeeton, Donald D. 94, 189
Smiley, Wayne 70
Smisko, Nicholas 65, 298
Smit, Pauline.......................47
Smith, Alexei 236
Smith, Alycia 240
Smith, Andrew D. 107, 237
Smith, Autholene 78
Smith, Brad.......................296
Smith, Bruce 191
Smith, Craig S. 87
Smith, Dewayne 100
Smith, Diana E. 26
Smith, Donnie W. 93
Smith, Edward P. 296
Smith, Eric 136, 137
Smith, Francis L. 144
Smith, G. Wayne...............108

Smith, Glenn...............53, 294
Smith, Guy H., III...............74
Smith, Horace E. 144
Smith, J. Morris 262
Smith, J. Philip 129
Smith, James T..................100
Smith, Jane Orion 350
Smith, Kenneth 350
Smith, Kenneth A. 153
Smith, Kirk Stevan 107
Smith, Lawrence 133
Smith, Leroy, Jr. 98
Smith, Liz 324
Smith, Lois L.....................259
Smith, Marilyn McCann 115
Smith, Marvin 78
Smith, Michael Gene 108
Smith, Nancy Orders 263
Smith, Paul 121
Smith, Phil 334
Smith, R. Bruce 52
Smith, Rebecca 241
Smith, Richard 203, 204
Smith, Robert....................187
Smith, Robert E. 303
Smith, Ron 237
Smith, Ron C. 336
Smith, Ronald 103
Smith, Ronald E. 315
Smith, Stephen 100
Smith, Steve......................256
Smith, Susan J. 233
Smith, T. DeWitt, Jr. 150
Smith, T. Randall 265
Smith, Terry 195, 349
Smith, Tom 258
Smith, Velma 268
Smith, Victor P....................90
Smith, Wallace 344
Smith, Wallace C. 309
Smith, William L. 144
Smith, Zollie 72, 73
Smith-Snyder, Donna 247
Smock, Robert W................78
Smyth, Peter 162
Snair, Karen 259
Snell, Catherine 140
Snelson, J. E. 326
Snow, Catherine J. 201
Snowman, Sharon L. 140
Snyder, Carol 330
Snyder, Joni 242
Snyder, William 263
Sobel, Ronald B..................43
Soderquist, Marilyn 266
Solie, Daryl.......................198
Sommers, Donald 43, 124
Song, James 307
Sonnenburg, Brian 293
Soper, John F. 87
Sophia (Zion)
(Nun) 200, 346
Sorensen, Gordon H. 183

Sorensen, Steven R...........355
Soroka, Stefan.....................81
Sotirios (Archbishop) 197
Soto, Jaime 81
Sox, Aileen Andres 338, 339
Spans, J.............................338
Sparkman, Alan 145
Sparkman, Wayne.............357
Sparks, Dennis D. 268
Sparks, William 54
Spataro,
Francis C. 69, 70, 75
Spears, Rusty 236
Speas, Philip 305
Speer, James 77
Spencer, Archie...................52
Spencer, Randy 105
Spencer, Shirley 333
Sperzel, Ceil 241
Spittal, David J. 313
Spitzer, Lee 64
Spleth, Richard L................84
Sprague, Roy 128
Spriggs, J. Wayne 87
Spurgeon, Don 101
St John, Clarence W. 72
St. Pierre, Bill 186
Stafford, E. E. 138
Stafford, Willian S..............312
Stahr, James A. 82, 187
Stair, Randel 147
Stairs, M. Jean 320
Staller, Thomas 119
Stallings, James O. 64
Stamm, John M..................314
Standen, Michael 256
Stanford, Alan 41
Stange, John......................149
Stanley, Heidi 50
Stanley, Judy 262
Stansbery, Margaret 257
Stanton, James M. 107
Stapert, Craig W. 325
Staples, Charles E..............262
Star, Barbara 140
Starnes, Darryl B.................61
Starr, Barbara 140
Stauch, Karimah 46
Stauffer, Rick 117
Staver, A. Bruce.........180, 181
Steadman, William 208
Stearns, Richard..................48
Steckel, Clyde J. 328
Steele, Charles 34
Steenson, Jeffrey...............108
Stefanis, Anthony 126
Steib, J. Terry.....................81
Steinbacher, Wil..................32
Steinwand, Randy L. 57
Stelck, Brian 184, 318
Stella, Brigitte...................252
Stemmle, Carol 243
Stenberg, Luther 191

Stendahl, John..................246
Stenson, Jane 40
Stephanopoulos, Nikki 125
Stephen (Metropolitan)......162
Stephens, Mary 242
Stephens, Robert................245
Stephenson, Carl H...........208
Stephenson, Robert E. 102
Stern, George M. 261
Stetler, P. Daniel 303
Stevens, Bruce G. 148
Stevens, Woodie 99
Stevenson, I. 92
Stevenson, Philip T............175
Stewart, Betty 122
Stewart, Dan R. 305
Stewart, Danny 84
Stewart, Glen J. 84
Stewart, Jewelle 131
Stewart, Kimberly...............174
Stewart, Lois......145, 146, 255
Stewart, Mary C. 260
Stewart, Paul A. G., Sr........86
Stewart, Richard 22
Steytler, Jessica.................358
Stief, Ron 34
Stiller, Brian.................53, 322
Stimson, Eva......................339
Stinesspring, James.............65
Stinnett, Daniel 184
Stinnett, J. Dwight 64
Stinton, Rick 304
Stith, Rhandi M. 61
Stoesz, Conrad 359
Stokes, Thomas E 353
Stokes-Buckle, Jim 47
Stoll, Christian 351
Stoll, Joseph.................347, 351
Stolov, Yehuda 46
Stoltzfus, Margaret 121
Stone, Barbara 259
Stone, Jack 191
Stone, Mary Ruth 94, 190
Stopperich, J. R. 241
Stortz, Dennis 134
Strain, Patricia 344
Strand, David 134
Strand, Jim 24
Strand, Sherri 134
Straub, Gregory 106
Straughan, Gary 137
Strauser, AnnaMae.............122
Strauser, Carol 122
Strauser, Simeon 122, 331
Strauss, Sandra L. 261
Straut, Charles H., Jr..........252
Strawser, Craig L. 87
Streeter, Terry 150
Strickland, Marshall H. 60
Strobel, David R. 115
Strohmaier, Sharon E........242
Strommen, E. Peter...........114
Strong, Robert F................100

Stroud, Marilyn..................359
Stroupe, Jamie 339
Strout, Mark.......................320
Strout, Richard E. 349
Struchen, Shirley
  Whipple 39, 43
Struck, Jane Johnson 342
Struik, Félix 300
Strunk, Orlo, Jr. 334
Sttler, Ryan 263
Stuart, Robert F.................238
Stuck, James R....................115
Studivant, G. W. 154
Stuehrenberg, Paul F...........23
Stumbo, Bruce 330
Stumbo, John P. 87
Stumme-Diers, Paul W. 114
Stump, Tiffany 307
Sturtevant, Elwood 242
Stutzman, Erwin 301
Styles, Donald H.................326
Subotic, Zivorad 205
Subramanian, Siva.....225, 238
Suderman, Derek 52
Suderman, Robert J. 199
Suhrheinrich, Heidi...........243
Sullivan, Anita 122
Sullivan, Bernard 61
Sullivan, John 159
Sullivan, Veronica...............33
Sumner, George R., Jr........322
Sumners, Bill 352
Sumter, Tyrone 78
Sundholm, James V............112
Sure, Heng 46
Sutroeter, Helga 255
Sutton, Edgar N. 64
Sutton, Ray R. 153
Svennungsen, Ann 32
Swain, Lawrence 64
Swain, Thomas 120, 145
Swan, Richard....................244
Swan, Tina 251
Swank, Sandy 242
Swanson, Douglas 249
Swanson, Gary B.......328, 329
Swanson, James E., Sr.......171
Swanson, Paul R. 113
Swanson-Nystrom,
  Jane K...........................329
Swantstrom, James 241
Swartwood, Theresa 242
Swartz, Fred W. 89
Swatkowski, Ray 76
Sweeney, Michael 300
Swenson, Kristin.................46
Swenson, Mary Ann 172
Swidler, Leonard................333
Swinburne, R. Douglas........87
Swindle, Zephaniah 163
Swing, William 46
Switzer, Patricia 254
Swyers, Philip....................155

Sydnor, Calvin
  H., III......................59, 324
Sydow, James 99
Szabo, Stephen 128, 335
Szo, Robert 55

Tabbernee, William............309
Taber-Hamilton, Nigel.......266
Taillon, Gerald 185, 186
Talbot, Lydia 239
Talbot, Nathan 90
Talcott, Sarah 46
Talmage, Stephen S. 114
Talone, Cheryl 253
Talton, Chester...................107
Tammen, Mark...................148
Tan, Hong Kia 174
Tandon, Atul 48
Tanis, Justin 174
Tanner, Susan W. 97
Tappen, Jerry 268
Tarnavsky, Roman 164
Tarr, Candace 84
Tarr, Rita 239
Tate, Mary L. 127
Taturn, Ed 145
Taylor, Ann 253
Taylor, Betty P. 264
Taylor, Don 51
Taylor, Edwin 292
Taylor, G. Porter 109
Taylor, Graley 266
Taylor, J. Glen 52
Taylor, James 51
Taylor, Joyce........................93
Taylor, L. Roy.....................147
Taylor, Mark A. 327
Taylor, Mary Virginia 171
Taylor, Regina.....................265
Taylor, Steve 119
Taylor, Susan 120
Taylor, Tom........................148
Taylor, Victor 86
Taylor, Wayne 131
Taylor, Wesley M.................100
Teague, Peter W..................305
Tebbe, Jim............................33
Tedesco, John......................84
Temple, Jan 261
Templeton, Beth..................263
Templeton, John M., Jr. 37
Tenold, Margo 234
Terry, Bill............................131
Tesch, Walter 134
Thell, Barbara 248
Theriault, Donald J. 204
Thevialt, Tanya 326
Thibodeau, Francois 204
Thiesen, John 355
Thiessen, David 195
Thiessen, Henry 195
Thistlethwaite, Susan

Brooks 298
Thomann, David A. 78
Thomas, D. Karl 182
Thomas, Dominic 97
Thomas, Everett...............335
Thomas, Freeman M.........144
Thomas, Glen 134
Thomas, James P...............102
Thomas, John....................135
Thomas, John H.................167
Thomas, Mathew A...........119
Thomas, P. C.....................135
Thomas, Reginald H.........149
Thomas, Ronald P., Jr. 58
Thomas, T. V.....................187
Thomas, Tenny 38
Thomas, Thomas 260
Thomason, Jeanette 30
Thomford,
   Christopher M. 307
Thompson, Brice 96, 190
Thompson, Daniel M........238
Thompson, Dean K...........306
Thompson, Doug 264
Thompson, Else B. 113
Thompson, Glendon G 322
Thompson, Houston 241
Thompson, James W 340
Thompson, Ken 118
Thompson, Kenneth 265
Thompson, Leonard............64
Thompson, Richard
   Keith 60
Thomsen, Eric...................338
Thon, Carol 241
Thopil, Markose 144
Thoreson, Joel...................355
Thorne, Leo S 64
Thornton, Bobby C............77
Thorpe, Debbie 264
Thurston, Stephen J. 138
Thurton, Winston 53
Tidwell, Dan 116
Tiemann, Ray....................114
Tiemeyer, Ann 39
Tifft, Thomas W.................311
Tillet, Charles 237
Timmer, David E. 339
Timmerman, Larry J..........189
Timothy (Bishop) 162
Tinsley, Charles 235
Tisch, Joseph L. 133
Tisdale, Delores 259
Tisdale, Janet 140
Titus, Beth 263
Titus, Richard C.................233
Tizzard, Brian 56
Tkachuk, Rod 200
Tolbert, Mark C. 144
Tolbert, Rosa......................70
Tolbert, T. C., Jr. 70
Tolbert, T. C., Sr. 70
Tolborh, Moses 78

Tollefson, Rebecca J.........258
Tolley, S. T.................149, 326
Tolliver, David 159
Tom, Phil 34
Tomalty, Wayne 320
Tombaugh, Richard F. 106
Tomesch, Harald 318
Tomlinson, Susanna M 260
Tomson, Timothy...............164
Toner, Margaret 204
Tong, Joseph 304
Toompuu, Marie 183
Tooze, George.....................65
Toppins, Helen
   Garay 120, 121
Torok, Stefan M.................128
Torrance, Iain R.................310
Torrance, John 183
Torraville, F. David............181
Tortoriello, John.................122
Torvik, John R....................112
Towne, Becky 331
Towns, L. Ferrell 88
Townsend, Fred 293
Toycen, Dave 56
Tracey, Yvonne A.................61
Trache, Robert G. 264
Trachian, Barkev 313
Traedwell, David 25
Traftan, Margie 349
Trammell,
   Mary M. 90, 327, 332
Trauger, Kenneth 260
Trautman, Donald W. 81
Treanor, John J....................25
Trejo, José 248
Tremblay, Anna..................292
Tremblay, Bernard 294
Tremblay, Donald 293
Trent, Earl 150
Tressel, Rose..............165, 166
Trevino, Max A. 157
Trevino, Yoland 46
Triantafilou,
   Nicholas 126, 303
Tribett, Brenda..................150
Trickett, David 304
Trine, Melinda 22
Tripp, Linda 56
Tripple, Tim 268
Trotter, LaTonya 46
Trotti, Melinda..................255
Troutman, Frank, Jr. 21
Trowbridge, Constance......266
Trowbridge, Kathleen 245
Truett, Chris 138
Trulson, Reid 65
Truss, James........................70
Trusty, Bill 244
Tsapwe, Simon...................121
Tse, James N........................30
Tsimbaki, Matthew 121
Tucker, Neville 61

Tucker, Tommy 243
Tunnicliffe, Geoff 53
Turnage, Juleen..............72, 73
Turner, B. G......................130
Turner, Carl A....................144
Turner, Emil 159
Turner, Harvey L. 94
Turner, Rex A., Jr...............314
Turner, Wayne...................347
Tweet, Margaret.................29
Tyler, Robert D. 97
Tyndall, Margaret 48
Tyrrell, Wilfred L.................33
Tyson, James E. 144

Uchtdorf, Dieter F...............97
Udall, William B...............245
Uglem, Dwayne 317
Ugoletti, Dennis................259
Ulery, Kent J.....................168
Ullestad, Steven L.............114
Ulmer, Greg 29
Unruh, Ron 349
Up De Graff, Morse...........147
Updegrove, John H 262
Uptain, Misti 266
Upton, John V., Jr. 159
Usgaard, Harold L. 114
Ussery, Dan.......................129
Utterback, J.
   Michael....................94, 189
Uyeded-Kai, Kim 208

Valentine, Linda................148
Valentine, Pamela 61
Valenzuela, Carmen 249
Vallance, James E. 324
Van Broekhoven,
   Deborah..................65, 339
Van Campen, Frank 77
Van Eyl, Christina.............327
van Laar, Erwin 50
Van Leer, Thomas.............248
Van Loon, Cathy 350
Van Marter, Jerry 24
Van Ostran, Steve 64
Van Spriell, Lawrence 64
Van Vallenburgh, Gail.......255
VanBeusekom, Hein 133
vanDalen, P. Frank.............74
Vandee (Mrs.) 184
Vandee, Daniel..................184
Vander Molen, Steven 202
VanderMolen, Steven 151
Vandervelde, George 31
Vang, Timothy T. 87
Vaniber, Craig 116
VanMarter, Jerry L.............339
Vansen, Beatrice 27
VanWyngaarden, Bill..........45
Vanyi, Laszlo B. 128

Vardemann, Brady J. 250
Vargas, David A..................83
Varlaam, (Rev.) 143
Varley, Peter......................50
Varsberga-Paza, Anita.......132
Vasilac, Vasile 329
VasilijeTomic (Rev.) 348
Vasko, Rebecca..................215
Vassiouchkine, Alexei........200
Vaughan,
    Roland E..................94, 190
Vaughn-Kelly, Sandra 248
Veazey, Stephen M. 102
Veech, Guthrie 311
Veeraswamy, B. 78
Veillette, Martin 204
Veitenhans, Michael 48
Veliko, Lydia......................30
Velozo, Ruth M..................267
Venema, Cornelius P 307
Verhoef, A. H....................141
Verigin, John J., Sr.............206
Vermillion, William 110
Vesely-Flad, Ethan.............330
Vest, R. Lamar.......22, 42, 189
Veum, David 98
Viau, Marcel 322
Vickery, David 74
Victor (Metropolitan)........126
Vieker, Jon 134
Vila, Vesna 259
Villafane, Eldin 31
Villalba, Eddie 96
Vining, John K.........94, 189
Vinton, Samuel 124
Visscher, J. 346
Vissers, John 320
Vlad, Mike 96
Vodden, Lori 25
Vogel, Matt 326
Vogel-Borne, Jonathan.......121
von Rosenberg,
    Charles..........................107
Von Wade, Melvin, Sr........139
Vonicessler, Caroline 263
Voskuil, Betty 39
Voskuil, Dennis N..............316
Votary, Marilyn E 348
Votary, R. E......................197
Vree, Dale 337
Vreeland, Richard L. 47

Wachal, Anne E. 239
Wackernagel, Betsy 266
Wade, Charles R. 159
Wade, Cheryl 38
Wade, James 59
Wagener, Ginny 235
Waggoner, Berten A............75
Waggoner, James
    E., Jr...............................108
Waghray, Rajyashri.............39

Wagner, Gary 28
Wagner, Jane 174
Wagner, Mark 308
Wagner, Norman 144
Wagner, Rebecca 245
Wakefield,
    Wesley H. 184, 348
Walden, Jay..........................95
Waldner, Jacob 128
Walker, Alice 342
Walker, Céleste 334
Walker, Dawn L..................61
Walker, Diane 347
Walker, Frank 152
Walker, Gail 35
Walker, George
    W. C...........................59, 60
Walker, Jewett L 61
Walker, Leonara.................241
Walker, Orris G., Jr............107
Walker, Paul L...........93, 189
Walker, Riley H. 64
Walker-Smith,
    Angelique 240
Wall, Jim 145
Wallace, Peter M. 21
Wallace, Vicki...................170
Walle, Ann 39
Walles, Caroline................250
Walles, Charles A..............111
Walles, Harry 250
Walley, Wendel 297
Wallis, Hope 254
Wallis, Jim 341
Walsh, Daniel......................81
Walsh, Gary 53
Walsh, Robert 50, 52
Walter, Bob 46
Walter, Martin 128
Walters, Norman 144
Waltner, Sharon 136
Walton, Christopher...........343
Waltz, David C. 159
Wamala, Francis 121
Wang, Karen 38
Wangberg, Rolf P. 114
Wanner, Janet....................241
Ward, Frank 104
Ward, George 48
Ward, Hope Morgan 171
Ward, Marion J. 267
Ward, Michael, Sr...............65
Ward, Sarah F. 41
Wardlaw, Theodore J. 296
Warfel, Michael W..............81
Warkie, Peter 144
Warner, Vincent W.............108
Warr, Sterling E. 201
Warren, Cindy.....................29
Warren, David....................124
Warren, Leodis..................144
Warren, Patty 233
Warren, Ronald B. 115

Wasielewski,
    Charles, Sr. 65
Wasserman, Joseph 236
Watkins, David 76
Watkins, David J.................78
Watkins, Dennis W. 94, 189
Watkins, Sharon R. 83
Watson, B. Michael ...172, 238
Watson, Robert 97
Watt, Jonathan 153
Watt, Linda 106
Watt, Neil..........................205
Watts, Loretta....................129
Wauls, Robert 144
Wawire, Blastus 121
Waxler, Mel 264
Waynick, Catherine M.......107
Weakland, Rembert G. 268
Weaver, David 39
Weaver, James 345
Weaver, Peter D. 170
Weavill, George 263
Webb, Robert 352
Webb, Suzanne 30
Webber, Robert D. 42
Webster, Gordon V.............254
Webster, Joe L. 169
Webster, Robert Vaughn 59
Wedig, Mark E...................296
Weedman, Gary E..............304
Weeks, Dewayne 145
Weeks, Thomas J. 144
Weeks, Thomas W., Sr.......144
Weems, L............................93
Weigand-Buckley,
    Amber.............................338
Weigley, David 157
Weikel, Calvin 131
Weiler, Jean-Jacques 49
Weinacht, Alan...................121
Weinreb, Tzvi Hersh 229
Weinstein, Judy..................261
Weise, Dewyan 173
Weisgerber, James 203
Weisner, Gerald 204
Welch, Mike.......................199
Welch, Shirley 60
Wells, D. L. S. 92
Wells, D. R. 200
Wells, Martin D. 113
Wells, N. W........................92
Welscott, Richard 151, 202
Welsh, Robert K. 83, 325
Welty, Marcel A..................38
Wendland, Paul O 316
Wendorf, Jan 134
Wendorf, Mark...................34
Wenger, Lee 166
Wenthe, Dean O................300
Werkheiser, Kevin D. 100
Werner, Paul 37
Wert, Rita 41
West, Barbara J..................152

INDEX

West, James C., Sr. 152, 300
West, Jonathan 23
West, Suzy 28
Westberg, M. Victor............90
Westbrook, T. L. 92
Westcott, Barbara
Spaulding.......................247
Wetzel, C. Robert 301
Wetzel, Daniel R................88
Whalen, Paul.....................243
Whalon, Pierre...................106
Whalon, Pierre W...............107
Wheaton, Keith D..............323
Wheeler, Barbara G. 214
Wheeler, Edward L...........299
Wheeler, Jack...................253
Whitaker, Timothy 171
White, Barbara....................37
White, Cyrus N...................83
White, David O................236
White, Douglas 111
White, F. O. 92
White, J. C. 93
White, J. Robert...............159
White, James Emery 302
White, Jim..........................249
White, K. Gordon 246
White, La Donna 248
White, Marcus 37, 268
White, Patricia 105
White, Patricia P. 329
White, R.............................92
White, R. Fowler 305
White, Raymond W. 127
White, Reid R., Jr. 61
White, Susan 145
White, Terry 30
WhiteEagle Sheila 249
Whitehead, Evan...............183
Whitehead, Ron 118
Whiten, Bennie, Jr. 35
Whitener, Ray 244
Whitfield, D. Max 171
Whiting, D. Douglas...........42
Whiting, Monique.............129
Whitmore, Keith B. 107
Whitney, Dale 235
Whitt, Dwight
Reginald 300
Whittaker, Bill 299
Whittaker, Fermin A 159
Wickmann, David L. 137
Wideman, James 159
Widger, Janet 77
Wiebe, Dave 185
Wiebe, Henry 203
Wiebe, Jim 187
Wiebe, Virgil......................77
Wieczerzak, Joseph............356
Wiens, Hart 50
Wieser, Walter W. 184
Wiesner, Gerald 203
Wigger, Barbara........123, 344

Wiggins, James B. 254
Wiginton, Melissa................32
Wilcox, Donald M. 253
Wildey, William 39
Wildman, Doug.................346
Wildman, Ingrid................194
Wiley, Galen 118
Wilgus, John 243
Wilkie, Owen 325
Wilkinson, Ed 342
Willemsma, Tena 24
Willford, Gary G...............295
Williams, Arsenia 140
Williams,
Bert.................327, 329, 342
Williams, Bertha.........41, 169
Williams, Carl, Jr. 93
Williams, Carol................257
Williams, Cheryl
Powers 248
Williams, Connie B. 61
Williams, Dennis L.............83
Williams,
Elijah 42, 168, 169
Williams, Elvonia................93
Williams, Gloria G. 61
Williams, Gregory 334
Williams, Horace K. 93
Williams, John 148
Williams, John P., Jr...........112
Williams, Matthew 92
Williams, Michael A...........64
Williams, Newell 83, 297
Williams, Patrick J............308
Williams, Preston
Warren, II 59
Williams, Ray 139
Williams, Richard 39
Williams, Robert...............106
Williams, Ron 129, 331
Williams, Sam...................112
Williams, W. J. 140
Williamson, Edward W.....116
Williamson, Elaine 240
Williamson, Henry M.........87
Williamson, Jack................38
Williamson, Portia
Turner 31
Williamson, Stephen.........256
Williard, Laura Lee...........136
Willimon, William H. 171
Willis, Carolyn..................345
Willis, Mike 343
Wills, David R. 319
Wills, Richard J., Jr............171
Wills, Susan 264
Wills, Wanda Bryant...........83
Wilson, Andrea 239
Wilson, David P. 99
Wilson, Dori 236
Wilson, Earle L.................175
Wilson, Glenna 262
Wilson, H. C. 209

Wilson, Harry O. "Pat"......144
Wilson, Helen Tibbs 233
Wilson, Holly....................347
Wilson, Ian E....................359
Wilson, Jeffrey K..............157
Wilson, Johanna................242
Wilson, John 241
Wilson, Maureen...............194
Wilson, Nancy L...............174
Wilson,
Norman G..............175, 344
Wilson, Robert..................148
Wilson, Robert W. 176
Wilson, Rod 321
Wilson, Ronald 30, 103
Wiltschek, Walt.................336
Wimberly, Don A...............108
Winbush, R. L. H...............92
Winbush, Robina 148
Wind, James P.....................21
Wine (Sister).....................153
Wines, Roger 149
Wingender, Eric 318
Winger, Brian....................206
Winger, Darrell S................79
Wingle, James M................203
Winings, John 148
Winn, Robert......................90
Winston, Mervin 248
Winter, Linda 262
Winter, Roy........................89
Winters, Carolyn M. 233
Wipf, Jacob 128
Wipf, John.........................128
Wirt, Douglas......................84
Wirthlin, Joseph B. 97
Wissel, Saney.....................32
Wisthoff, Grace.................257
Witherspoon, Anthony 250
Witt, Richard.....................255
Wittberg, Patricia 340
Wittin, Robert 251
Woelbern, James 27
Wohlrabe, John C. 133
Woida, Duane 235
Wojcicki, Ted L. 305
Wolf, Geralyn 108
Wolf, Patricia 39
Wolf, Peter 65
Wolfe, Bennet 90
Wolfe, Dean E. 107
Wolfe, Thomas V. 254
Wolfram, Donald J.............146
Wollersheim, Gary M. 114
Woloschak, Gayle 164
Womack, Anne....................23
Wong, Suk-Ling..................47
Wontor, Caryn...................265
Wood, Bertice Y..................30
Wood, Edward W..............131
Wood, George O. 72
Wood, Maudie E................100
Wood, Robert Stanley........105

INDEX

439

Wood, Susan 160
Wood, Virginia 120
Woodrich, Noya 248
Woodring,
    DeWayne S 44, 45
Woodruff, James 253
Woods, Gayle....................305
Woods, William K. 258
Woodward, George 199
Woodward, Jim 244
Woodworth, Rodger...........116
Woofenden, Lee 338
Woolfolk, T. E. 100, 101
Workman, Marjorie 138
Workowski, Joan 152
Worley, Lloyd 133
Worthington, Melvin 44
Wortman, Julie A. 344
Wray, J. T. 73
Wright, Abraham 30
Wright, Benny....................266
Wright, David 303
Wright, Frank......................40
Wright, Harold 235
Wright, Walter L. 157
Wright, Wayne P. 107, 237
Wright-Riggins,
    Aidsand F 65
Wruck, Demetrios E. 162
Wukwanja, Geoffrey M. 121
Wvertele, Peggy M. 115
Wyatt, Addie 35
Wyatt, Peter 318
Wylie, Ken 239
Wynick, Karmen 22
Wyse, Mark 118

Zabel, Nancy.......................41
Zacharias, Carl 195
Zacharias, Ken 195
Zahl, Paul F. M. 314
Zain, Thomas 67, 181
Zakian, Chris 72
Zander, Vera.......................29
Zandier, Don 262
Zangmeister, Pat 29
Zanicky, Robert 263
Zapeda, Monica 266
Zarling, Thomas F.............176
Zavalo, Gabino 34
Zavitz-Bond, Jane......186, 359
Zawierucha, Bazyl.....164, 165
Zehlaoui, Joseph 67
Zehr, Marvin 242
Zeiders, G. Edwin 314
Zelenitz, Myrna 260
Zelinsky, Daniel................343
Zell, R. Thomas 323, 345
Zeller, Stephanie 106
Zelter, Barbara 256
Zens, Jon 160, 341
Zetick, Edward 164
Zetto, J. Jeffrey 262
Ziemer, Dale 27
Zilliacus, Anne Marie 346
Zilmer, Norman D. 82
Zimmerman, Phillip...........150
Zirille, Francis M...............241
Zottoli, Carmine 84
Zubik, Davd A. 81
Zuck, Lowell......................358
Zusevics, Lauma................132
Zylla, Phil 317

Yaldezian, John 72
Yanagihara, Akio 266
Yasenka, David 251
Yates, Bernard....................140
Yates, Jonathan 140
Yeats, John 158
Yeglikian, Albert................182
Yeso, Lynn 259
Yessa, John 22
Yi, Maria Renya 121
Yntema, Philip 199
Yoder, Grace 355
Yoffie, Eric H. 229
York, Alwyn......................104
Young, George 258
Young, Lyle.........................90
Young, M. Norvel 323
Young, McKinley 59
Young, Ronald L................144
Young, Suzanne
    Tibbetts 248
Youngren, David...............199
Yount, Diana 352
Yrigoyen, Charles, Jr. 336

Notes

Notes

Notes

Notes

Notes

Notes

Notes

Notes